WHAT DO
I READ
NEXT?

Multicultural
Literature

WHAT DO I READ NEXT?

Multicultural Literature

RAFAELA G. CASTRO

EDITH MAUREEN FISHER, PH.D.

TERRY HONG

DAVID WILLIAMS, PH.D.

GALE Detroit   New York   Toronto   London

Gale Research Staff

Coordinating Editor: Shelly Dickey
Contributing Editors: Beverly Baer, Victoria A. Coughlin, Paula Cutcher-Jackson, Kathleen Dallas, Lydia Fink, Nancy Franklin, William Harmer, Arlene M. Johnson, Debra Kirby, Prindle LaBarge, Rebecca Mansour, Sharon McGilvray, Charlie Montney, Dana Shonta, Kelly Sprague
Managing Editor: Ann V. Evory

Production Director: Mary Beth Trimper
External Production Assistant: Shanna P. Heilveil
Product Design Manager: Cynthia Baldwin
Senior Art Director: Mary Krzewinski
Cover Design: Mary Krzewinski
Cover Illustration: "Ensemble" by Synthia Saint James

Manager, Data Entry Services: Eleanor Allison
Data Entry Coordinator: Gwendolyn Tucker
Data Entry Associate: Maleka Imrana

Manager, Technical Support Services: Theresa Rocklin
Programmer/Analyst: Joshua E. Cohen

Library of Congress Cataloging-in-Publication Data
What do I read next? : multicultural literature : African American, Asian American, Latino, Native American / Rafaela Castro ... [et al.].
   p.   cm.
   Includes indexes.
   ISBN 0-7876-0814-9 (alk. paper)
   1. American literature--Minority authors--Bibliography. 2. American literature--Afro-American authors--Bibliography.
3. American literature--Asian American authors--Bibliography. 4. American literature--Hispanic American authors--Bibliography.
5. American literature--Indian authors--Bibliography. 6. Multiculturalism in literature--Bibliography. 7. Ethnic groups
in literature--Bibliography. 8. Minorities in literature--Bibliography. 9. Books and reading--United States. I. Castro,
Rafaela, 1943-
Z1229.E87W49 1997
[PS153.M56]]
016.8108'0920693--dc21   97-204
                                          CIP

While every effort has been made to ensure the reliability of the information presented in this publication, Gale Research does not guarantee the accuracy of the data contained herein. Gale accepts no payment for listing; and inclusion in the publication of any organization, agency, institution, publication, service, or individual does not imply endorsement of the editors or publisher. Errors brought to the attention of the publisher and verified to the satisfaction of the publisher will be corrected in future editions.

This book is printed on acid-free paper that meets the minimum requirements of American National Standard for Information Sciences—Permanence Paper for Printed Library Materials, ANSI Z39.48-1984.

10 9 8 7 6 5 4 3 2 1

Printed in the United States of America

Contents

Introduction

Recent years have witnessed a significant rise in diverse American ethnic groups finding their own voice and telling their own stories. Until recently it was difficult to find children's books with Asian American characters or personal narratives by Native Americans outside the dominant European culture. One now finds these ethnic based literatures flourishing and attracting a larger, more encompassing audience without ethnic boundaries. *What Do I Read Next? Multicultural Literature* aims to help the reader as well as librarians and booksellers by pointing the way to recommended fiction, drama and anthologies in the distinct areas of Asian American, African American, Latino and Native American literature.

Designed as a tool to assist in the exploration of multicultural fiction, *What Do I Read Next? Multicultural Literature* guides the reader to both current and classic recommendations in four cultural groups: Asian American, African American, Latino and Native American literature. All have large numbers of readers who are eager to identify new authors or titles for further reading. *What Do I Read Next? Multicultural Literature* allows readers quick and easy access to specific data on recent or classic titles in these genres. Plus, each entry provides alternate reading selections, thus coming to the rescue of librarians and booksellers, who are often unfamiliar with a given culture's literature, yet must answer the question frequently posed by their patrons and customers "What do I read next?"

Highlights

Compiled by experts in each area—see page xi for their qualifications.

- Overview essay describes the history and current state of the literature.

- "Other books you might like," included in each entry, leads to the exploration of new authors or titles recommended by the experts.

- Nine indexes help locate specific titles or offer suggestions for reading in favorite time periods or geographic locations or about characters in specific professions.

- All authors and titles listed in entries under "Other books you might like" are indexed, allowing easy access to thousands of books recommended for further reading.

Details on 1,400 Titles...

This volume of *What Do I Read Next? Multicultural Literature* contains more than 1,350 entries. These titles are divided into sections for Asian American, African American, Latino and Native

American literature. Experts on the writing in each field compile the entries. Experts also present a history for their areas at the beginning of each section. The entries are listed alphabetically by author, so that an author's entries appear together.

Readers will find the following information:

Author or editor's name and illustrator. Co-authors and co-editors are also listed where applicable.

Book title

Date and place of publication; name of publisher.

Author Ethnicity when that information is known.

Reviews

Awards

Major characters: Names and brief descriptions of up to three characters featured in the title.

Time period: Tells when the story takes place.

Locale: Tells where the story takes place.

Summary: A brief (usually two- or three-sentence) plot summary.

About this book: A brief blurb that puts the book into context or provides further details about the book's history or significance.

Other books by the author: Lists other works the author has done.

Other books you might like: Titles by other authors written on a similar theme or in a similar style. These titles further the reader's exploration of the literature. The titles mentioned in this rubric range from contemporary books to classics, all sharing one or several components similar to the main title.

Indexes Answer Readers' Questions

The nine indexes in *What Do I Read Next? Multicultural Literature,* used separately or in conjunction with each other, create many pathways to the featured titles, answering general questions or

locating specific titles. For example:

"Do you know of any Native American stories set in South Dakota?"

The GEOGRAPHIC INDEX lists titles by their locale. This can help readers pinpoint an area in which they may have a particular interest, such as their hometown, another country, or even Cyberspace.

"Do you know of any African American stories set during the Civil Rights Era?"

The TIME PERIOD INDEX is a chronological listing of the time settings in which the main entry titles take place.

"Do you have any Latino novels with angels in them?"

The CHARACTER DESCRIPTION INDEX identifies the major characters by occupation (e.g. Accountant, Editor, Librarian) or persona (e.g. Historical Figure, Noblewoman).

"What books feature a character named Jose Antonio Rafa?"

The CHARACTER NAME INDEX lists the major characters named in the entries. This can help readers who remember some information about a book, but not an author or title.

"What has Louise Erdrich written recently?"

The AUTHOR INDEX contains the names of all authors featured in the entries and those listed under "Other books you might like."

"What books are like *The Joy Luck Club?"*

The TITLE INDEX includes all main entry titles and all titles recommended under "Other books by the author" and "Other books you might like" in one alphabetical listing. Thus a reader can find a specific title, new or old, then go to that entry to find out what new titles are similar.

"What are some recent books illustrated by John Steptoe?"

The ILLUSTRATOR INDEX contains the names of all illustrators featured in the entries.

"Do you know of any books about World War II and the Japanese?"

The SUBJECT INDEX lists books by what they are about. Topics include such things as fiction genres (e.g. Fantasy, Ghost Stories, Mystery and Detective Stories) and life and relationships (e.g. Family Life, Friendship), as well as historical events.

"What books are good for young adults?"

The AGE LEVEL INDEX lists titles appropriate for adult, young adult or child readers. Titles for chldren's and young adult books are listed by grade levels for which they are best suited. The wide variety of age ranges allows the user to select titles for all reading levels.

The indexes can also be used together to narrow down or broaden choices. A reader interested in African American stories set in New York during the 20th century would consult the TIME PERIOD INDEX and GEOGRAPHIC INDEX to see which titles appear in both. With the AUTHOR and TITLE indexes, which include all books listed under "Other books by the author" and "Other books you might like," it is easy to compile an extensive list of recommended reading, beginning with a recently published title or a classic

from the past.

Suggestions Are Welcome

The editors welcome any comments and suggestions for enhancing and improving *What Do I Read Next? Multicultural Literature*. Please address correspondence to:

Editors

What Do I Read Next? Multicultural Literature

Gale Research

835 Penobscot Bldg.

645 Griswold Street

Detroit, MI 48226-4094

Phone: 313-961-2242

Toll-free: 800-347-4253

Fax: 313-961-6083

About the Authors

Edith Maureen Fisher, Ph.D

An expert in the areas of diversity, race relations, human resources/relations and organizational development, Edith Maureen Fisher, Ph.D., is well qualified to author the African American section of *What Do I Read Next? Multicultural Literature*. Actively involved in regional, national and international organizations that deal with multiculturalism, she has held the national office of the President of the Black Caucus of the American Library Association and has been recognized for her leadership with a President's Award.

A contributor to *Multicultural Review*, she has also written several publications, including the article "Identification of Multiethnic Resources," in *Developing Collections for California's Emerging Majority: A Manual for Ethnic Collection Development*, edited by Katherine T.A. Scarborough (San Francisco: Bay Area Library and Information Systems, 1990).

Dr. Fisher was assisted in writing entries for *What Do I Read Next? Multicultural Literature* by Diana R. Card, a versatile executive manager who is the recipient of several Exceptional Performance Awards in the finance industry. Dr. Fisher and Ms. Card, partners for 17 years, have complemented each other well while blending their diverse cultural heritages, including African, Anglo, Cherokee, Chocktaw, French Creole, Danish, German and Welsh. Together they enjoy traveling, reading and attending church services.

Rafaela G. Castro

Cultural identity and survival. Immigration. Struggles for homelands and a voice in the U.S. These are recurring themes in Latino literature and Rafaela G. Castro's choice of entries for *What Do I Read Next? Multicultural Literature*, brings them to light for the reader. Her selection reflects, as well, the diversity of cultures represented by this body of literature. Debunking the notion that the publication of Latino literature in the U.S. is a recent phenomenon, she reviews its 150-year-old history, with its link to a rich literary heritage dating back to the 16th century.

A librarian, Castro is deeply involved with diversity through her experiences at several facilities, including librarian at the U.S. Department of Education. She has been a liason to academic ethnic studies programs, has taught in the Chicano Studies department at the University of California, Berkeley and has lectured on Chicano studies at various univiersities. She has also been involved in the Peace Corp in Brazil, is a member of the steering committee of the Chicana/Latina

Research Center, University of California, Davis and has written several articles for the *San Francisco Examiner*. Living in California with her daughters, Castro is currently working on two literary projects being published in 1997 and 1998. She has a B.A. in English Literature, a M.L.S. and an M.A. in Folklore.

Devotion to the understanding of Latino literature, its survival and excellence, as well as her own life experiences, amply qualify Ms. Castro to author the Latino section of *What Do I Read Next? Multicultural Literature*.

Terry Hong

In her essay, Terry Hong cautions the reader against ascribing narrow terms to the Asian American Literature piece of the "American ethnic pie". She regards the growing body of literature in this section as "diverse". This is accurate. Ms. Hong brings to *What Do I Read Next? Multicultural* a wide range of authors and stories. Begging the adjective, "diversity" clearly describes Terry Hong as well. She currently works for *A. Magazine: Inside Asian America*, as contributing editor and theatre columnist. On a special book project for Metro East Publications, publisher of *A.Magazine*, Hong co-authors *Eastern Standard Time: From Astro Boy to Zen Buddhism*, focusing on Asian influences on American popular culture. Her book credits extend to contributions for *Notable Asian Americans* and *The Asian American Almanac*, both Gale publications. She also evaluates play submissions for the Joseph Papp Public Theater and plays a prominent role in the Asian American Arts Alliance. Add to her writing credits, freelancing for other Asian American magazines, copywriting, advertising, marketing, interviews, film and theater reviews.

Diversity permeates other areas of her life as well. She holds two Masters Degrees, one in Comparative Literature and one in East Asian Languages and Literatures and attended university both in the U.S. and abroad. Proficient in five languages, she travels world-wide, claims five countries as previous residences, and in 10 years of marriage, 13 addresses in

the same amount of time. Ever energetic, she brags about traveling to Egypt and Israel, while seven months pregnant, and living to tell about it. Terry, her husband Gregor, and their daughter now reside in Connecticut and call it home. But that isn't all. She admits she is a theatre and film fanatic, active and interested in more than three sports and a part-time potter and knitter. Terry Hong reflects the diversity she brings to the Asian American segment of *What Do I Read Next? Multicultural Literature*, bringing to the task her absorption in the literature, her interest and rootedness in Asian American culture, an accomplished writing history, and her remarkable energy and enthusiasm.

David Williams, Ph.D.

Words possess power. Words affect change. Songs and stories, both, entertain and educate. Educator, writer, songwriter and performer, David Williams understands the power of words. A Ph.D. in creative writing with a secondary emphasis on Native American Literature, his allegiance to the power of words amply qualifies him to select Native American works that respect the cultural perspective, selections without "European bias". Words flesh out "Native Americans as human beings, like human beings everywhere, complex people with infinite facets to their personalities and their cultures" states Williams. His experiences with story and song illustrate his long kinship with words. Presently, he is in the English department at Northern Illinois University as visiting assistant professor. William's writing credits include numerous published short stories and poems, with awards and grants punctuating his literary career.

Most recently, in 1994, he received the Notable Award Winner from the National Council of Social Studies for his book *Grandma Essie's Covered Wagon*. His travels encompass the Midwest, where he has taught creative writing and music to students from elementary to high school. Playing the guitar and mandolin, he writes and performs his own songs for audiences in both the U.S. and Canada and has done so for over 20 years. Receiving rave reviews, his CD, *Route 66*, features 15 original art songs about people and places along this Midwestern highway. *Oh, The Animals*, fourteen orinignal songs for children, received the 1991 Notable Award in Children's Music from the ALA. Respecting word and story, David William's choice of literature for the Native American section brings us the voice of a people, the story of a people, in their own words.

WHAT DO
I READ
NEXT?

Multicultural
Literature

African American Literature

As a reader seeking the voices of contemporary American writers of African ancestry in adult, young adult, and children's fiction, you have likely experienced the frustration associated with identifying these authors among the volumes of published titles. Fiction in library collections and bookstores is arranged by an author's name on separate shelves and often lacks access by an author's identity. Specialized bibliographies and lists of fiction which do identify African American writers often focus primarily on authors from the historical heydays of the Harlem Renaissance or the Civil Rights eras. Some fiction guides often also include non-African American writers if their characters are African Americans. Other specialized guides to the literature of African American writers often include only a few, if any, fiction titles. Reviews of contemporary fiction titles often do not indicate if an author is African American, nor with rare exception can these authors often be found on popular best seller lists. Few among the contemporary African American authors achieve the celebrity status of becoming household names. Seldom do they become known as prestigious literary award winners and rarely are their fiction titles made into motion pictures. Thus contemporary African American fiction writers are often lost to you, their invaluable reader.

The focus of this section of this first multicultural volume of *What Do I Read Next?* is to highlight these contemporary African American writers of adult, young adult, and children's fiction. Nearly 500 fiction titles are represented by over 200 authors. The majority of the writers have produced at least one title in the 1990s. Their earlier titles included extend no further

back than the 1970s. And over 50 authors have published in multiple categories of adult, young adult, or children's fiction. Collectively these contemporary writers are contributors and literary heirs to a legacy of remarkable accomplishments inherited from pioneering writers of the past.

Editing this essay, a snapshot of some of the significant people and events from the past, on the eve of the February **Black History Month - 1997** I am excited to be sharing these contemporary African American writers and their works with you. My partner and co-writer of the contemporary author's entries Diana R. Card and I consider ourselves enriched by the voices of these writers and hope you find as much pleasure in reading them as we have.

A Historical Legacy

The voices of American fiction writers of African ancestry have a rich legacy spanning the history of the continent. The first known novel published in the United States by an African American writer is *Our Nig; Or, Sketches From the Life Of a Free Black, In a Two Story White House, North, Showing That Slavery's Shadows Fall Even There* (Boston: Rand and Avery, 1859; reprint New York: Vintage Books, 1983) by Harriet E. Adams Wilson (1827-1863), the foremother of the African American novel. Her landmark autobiographical novel delves into the theme of white racism in the North as experienced by a free

1

Black indentured servant during antebellum days. An inventive social commentary, it is credited with bringing to the forefront for the first time in American fiction the complex intertwined relationship of the issues of race and class. Written primarily in the third person, it differs from other earlier 18th and 19th century personal narratives which were written in the first person, such as what is generally credited as the first prose from an African American *A Narrative Of the Uncommon Sufferings and Surprizing Deliverance of Briton Hammon, A Negro Man-Servant To General Winslow of Marshfield In New England: Who Returned To Boston, After Having Been Absent Almost Thirteen Years, Written By Himself* (Boston: Green and Russell, 1760; reprint Fairfield, WA: Ye Galleon, 1994) or what has been credited as the first personal narrative produced by a Black woman in the United States *The History of Mary Prince, a West Indian Slave, Related By Herself, With a Supplement By the Editor, To Which Is Added the Narrative of Asa Asa, a Captured African* (London: F. Westley and A. H. Davis, 1831; reprint New York: Pandora, 1987).

Published abroad, the plantation novel *Clotel; Or, The President's Daughter: A Narrative of Slave Life in the United States* (London: Partridge and Oakley, 1853; reprint New York: Citadel Press, 1969) was written by the first known African American novelist William Wells Brown (1814-1884), the forefather of the African American novel. Containing what is said to be one of the most compelling and ironic descriptions of a slave sale, and describing the mask of contentment slaves had to wear, following its London publication the melodramatic novel later appeared in revised and retitled versions in the United States as *Miralda: Or the Beautiful Quadroon* (New York: Weekly Anglo-American, serialized 1860-1861; o.p.), *Clotelle; a Tale of Southern States* (Boston: James Redpath, 1864; o.p.), and *Clotelle; Or, the Colored Heroine, a Tale of the Southern States* (Boston: Lee and Shepard, 1867; reprint North Stratford, NH: Ayer, 1977). Among its several themes, this novel of President Thomas Jefferson's crime of miscegenation is credited with exposing the hypocrisy of a Christianity that perverts its teachings to its own end, and with examining the corrupting influence of slavery on the family.

The literary accomplishments of pioneers William Wells Brown and Harriet E. Adams Wilson, and indeed all African American writers of the period, were remarkable achievements given the reality that prior to their legal emancipation at the close of the Civil War (1861-1865) the majority of their people were captives held in bondage and by law, custom, and practice it was forbidden to teach them to read and write English. And even after learning those skills they faced many more formidable hurdles in developing their craft. Following the Civil War the population of African American novelists and their works continued to grow. The final decade of the 19th century into the first decade of the 20th century (1890-1910) was dominated by African American women writers, who collectively are credited with publishing more works of fiction in those two decades than had been produced by African American men in the previous half-century. Several of their often neglected and little-known pioneering works have been resurrected into the pages of the landmark 30-volume collection *The Schomburg Library Of Nineteenth-Century Black Women Writers* (New York: Oxford University Press, 1988) by General Editor Henry Louis Gates Jr. Among them, and long thought to be the first novel by an African American woman, is *Iola Leroy; Or Shadows Uplifted* (Philadelphia: Garrigues Brothers, 1892; reprinted New York: AMS Press, 1971) by Frances Ellen Watkins Harper (1825-1911), who is credited with publishing in 1859 what may be the first African American short story. A resourceful contingent of distinguished voices in early pioneering African American fiction, some of whom may still remain as yet undiscovered, established a solid foundation in American literature to be nurtured and further enhanced by their heirs in the 20th century.

20th Century Fiction

During the decades of the 20th century the voices of African American fiction writers increased in American literature. Writers from the formative years continued to contribute to the body of work while new writers emerged, exploring new territory and bringing forth new characters and directions.

1900-1920s

The first two decades of the 20th century in African American fiction might well be characterized as a journey toward a new awakening. From the valuable groundwork of early writers of the 1900s, among them contemporaries Pauline Elizabeth Hopkins (1859-1930) who authored the historical romance novel *Contending Forces: A Romance Illustrative of Negro Life North and*

South (Boston: The Colored Cooperative Publishing Company, 1900; reprint Carbondale: Southern Illinois University Press, 1978), and such serialized novels as her *Hagar's Daughter* (Boston: The Colored American, 1901-1902), *Winoma: A Tale Of Negro Life In the South and Southwest* (Boston: The Colored American, serialized 1902) and *Of One Blood; Or the Hidden Self* (Boston: The Colored American, serialized 1902-1903) all of which have been reissued as *The Magazine Novels of Pauline Hopkins* (The Schomburg Library of Nineteenth-Century Black Women Writers, New York: Oxford University Press, 1988), and Charles Waddell Chesnutt (1858-1932), a writer credited for his treatment of racially mixed characters, who wrote the novels *The House Behind the Cedars* (Boston: Houghton Mifflin, 1900; reprint Ridgewood, NJ: Gregg Press, 1968), *The Marrow of Tradition* (Boston: Houghton Mifflin, 1901; reprint New York: Arno Press, 1969), and *The Colonel's Dream* (New York: Doubleday, Page, 1905; reprint North Stratford, NH: Ayer, 1977); by the 1920s an explosive transformation occurred in African American literature— the acclaimed "Harlem Renaissance." Among noted luminaries during this period are Nella Larsen (1891-1964) known for her skilled portrayal of African American female and feminist concerns, her exploration of intraracial and class conflicts within the African American community, and as the first African American to win a creative writing award from the Guggenheim Foundation, she wrote the novels *Quicksand* (New York: Knopf, 1928; reprint Westport, CT: Greenwood Press, 1974), and *Passing* (New York, Knopf, 1929; reprint New York; Ayer Press, 1989). and Rudolph Fisher (1897-1934) credited with initiating the African American detective novel and authored the novels *The Walls of Jericho* (New York: Knopf, 1928; reprint Ann Arbor: University of Michigan Press, 1994) and *The Conjure-Man Dies: A Mystery Tale of Dark Harlem* (New York: Covici-Friede, 1932; reprint Ann Arbor: University of Michigan Press, 1992). Eclipsed by the social and economic conditions of the "Great Depression" the renaissance period ended in the early days of the 1930s.

1930-1940s

The decades from the 1930s through the 1940s evolved into what some have characterized as a somewhat quieter time in the development of African American fiction. The first full-length satire on American racism appeared during this period, the debut novel *Black No More; Being an Account of the Strange and Wonderful Workings of Science in the Land of the Free* (New York: Macaulay, 1931; reprint Boston: North Eastern University Press, 1989) of George S. Schuyler (1895-1977). It is also during this period that several well read authors emerge, among them Zora Neale Hurston (1891-1960) the most prolific and accomplished female writer of her day, whose debut novel is *Jonah's Gourd Vine* (Philadelphia: Lipponcott, 1934; reprint New York: HarperPerennial, 1990). The novel *Native Son* (New York: Harper, 1941; reprint New York: Harper and Row, 1979) by Richard Wright (1908-1960), a dominant voice in the fiction of the period, sold a record 200,000 copies in less than three weeks. Chester Himes (1909-1984), one of the most prolific writers of his day and acclaimed for his satire and detective novels, produced his debut novel *If He Hollers Let Him Go* (Garden City, NY: Doubleday, Doran, 1945; reprint New York: Thunder's Mouth Press, 1986). His final unfinished novel from the 1980s *Plan B* (1993) was published posthumously and appears among those in this publication's contemporary author entries. Deemed the "artistic success of the year" the debut novel *The Street* (Boston: Houghton-Mifflin, 1946; reprint Boston: Houghton Mifflin, 1991) of Ann Petry (1908-), credited with looking at the effects of poverty in an urban environment on the psyche of African American females, sold an impressive 1.5 million copies. Another commercially successful writer of this period who was to author over 30 novels selling more than 50 million copies, Frank Yerby (1916-1991) produced his debut swashbuckling costume novel *The Foxes of Harrow* (New York: Dial Press, 1946; reprint New York: Dial, 1986) which also later became a successful motion picture in the 1950s. In the first two years of its publication the debut novel *Knock on Any Door* (New York: Appleton-Century, 1947; reprint Dekalb: North Illinois University Press, 1989) by Willard Motley (1909-1965), one of the first novels to deal with the problem of juvenile delinquency, sold 350,000 copies and was released as a motion picture in 1949. Among the first writers exploring the African American urban life-style was the prolific short story author of the Harlem Renaissance era Dorothy West (1907-) who in 1948 published her debut novel *The Living Is Easy* (Boston: Houghton Mifflin, 1948; reprint New York: Feminist Press, 1995), and whose next novel, *The Wedding* (1994), is among this publication's contemporary author entries.

It is notable in the evolution of the genre of children's literature that during the 1930s the author characterized by some as the "contemporary father of

African American children's literature," Arna W. Bontemps (1902-1973), produced his debut children's fiction *Popo and Fifina: Children of Haiti* (New York: Macmillan, 1932; reprint New York: Oxford University Press, 1993) in collaboration with poet Langston Hughes (1902-1967). Remaining in print for more than 20 years and recently reissued, it was translated into several languages. A decade before the premiere periodical for African American children *Brownie's Book* (New York: DuBois and Dill, 1920-1921, o.p.) had been published, highlighting fiction and other literatures. Expanding the tradition it began, Carter G. Woodson (1875-1950) founded the Associated Publishers, the Association For the Study of Negro Life and History, and established Negro History Week during the 1930s, all of which had an impact on the development of African American children's literature. By the late 1940s, early 1950s, children's literature had evolved as a separate publishing market, and in the mid-1960s, early 1970s, several new voices were emerging in African American children's fiction. They and their descendants continued contributing to an evolving legacy into the next decades of the 1980s and 1990s. A growing population of African American writers has now evolved, many of whom write for multiple audiences, and appear among this publication's author entries.

1950-1960s

Those decades of the 1950s and 1960s witnessed profound changes in the social and political worlds of the United States, and brought forth a redirection toward a new aesthetic in the literature with new voices in African American fiction. The beginnings of the Civil Rights movement sparked, and in conjunction with the subsequent activist Black Power movement, a Black Arts movement evolved. This period has been said to be a "coming-of-age" for the literature of modern African Americans, a second literary renaissance.

The author who dominated the 1950s winning the National Book Award for his only novel is Ralph Ellison (1914-1994) *Invisible Man* (New York: Random House, 1952; reprint New York: Random House, 1995). It is also during this period that critically acclaimed writer James Baldwin (1924-1987) emerged with his debut novel *Go Tell It on the Mountain* (New York: Knopf, 1953; reprint New York: Random House, 1995). Decades later he published his only children's fiction *Little Man, Little Man: A Story of Childhood* (New York: Dial, 1977; o.p.), and his sixth and final novel was *Just Above My Head* (New York: Dial, 1979; reprint New York: Dell, 1980). Emerging among a groundswell of fiction writers contributing to the 1960s are poet Margaret Walker (1915-) with her prize-winning humanistic, historical debut novel *Jubilee* (Boston: Houghton Mifflin, 1966; reprint New York: Bantam, 1984), chronicling the trials and tribulations of her great-grandmother in a panoramic novel addressing issues of race and class in the South before, during, and after the Civil War era; and award winning writer Hal Bennett (1930-) with his satirical debut novel *A Wilderness of Vines* (Garden City, NY: Doubleday, 1966; o.p.), exploring the light-skinned/dark-skinned color hierarchies among African Americans.

Many writers who emerged during these two decades continued to publish into the 1980s and 90s and therefore appear among this publication's contemporary author entries. The debut novels produced by these authors during this period are: John Oliver Killens (1916-1987) *Youngblood* (New York: Dial Press, 1954; reprint Athens: University of Georgia, 1982); Paule Marshall (1929-) *Brown Girls, Brownstones* (New York: Random House, 1959, reprint New York: Feminist Press, 1981); John A. Williams (1925-) *The Angry Ones* (New York: Ace, 1960; reprint New York: W.W. Norton, 1996); Samuel R. Delany (1942-) *The Jewels Of Aptor* (New York: Ace, 1962; o.p.); Gordon Parks (1912-) *The Learning Tree* (New York: Harper and Row, 1963; reprint New York: Fawcett, 1987); Ernest J. Gaines (1933-) *Catherine Carmier* (New York: Atheneum, 1964; reprint New York: Random House, 1993); Kristin Hunter (1931-) *God Bless the Child* (New York: Scribners, 1964; reprint Washington, D.C.: Howard University Press, 1987); Ishmael Reed (1938-) *The Free-lance Pallbearers* (Garden City, NY: Doubleday, 1967; reprint New York: Avon, 1985) ; John E. Wideman (1941-) *A Glance Away* (New York: Harcourt, Brace and World, 1967; reprint New York: Holt, Henry and Co., 1985); Virginia Hamilton (1936-) *Zeely* (New York: Macmillan, 1967; reprint New York: Simon and Schuster, 1993) young readers; Nathan Heard (1936-) *Howard Street* (New York: Dial, 1968; reprint Los Angeles: Amok Books, 1992); Melvin Van Pebbles (1932-) *A Bear for the F.B.I.* (Seattle: Trident Press, 1968; o.p.); Cecil Brown (1943-) *The Life and Loves Of Mr. Jiveass Nigger* (New York: Farrar, Straus and Giroux, 1969; reprint Hopewell, NJ: Ecco Press, 1991); Clarence Major (1936-) *All-Night Visitors* (New York: Olympia Press, 1969; reprint New York: University Place Book Shop, 1973); Walter M. Myers (1937-) *Where Does the Day Go?* (New York: Parent's

Magazine Press, 1969; o.p.) children's fiction, author later publishes as Walter Dean Myers; and Mildred Pitts Walter (1922-) *Lillie Of Watts, a Birthday Discovery* (1969; o.p.) young readers. Joining with their historical predecessors and other contemporaries they contributed their voices to a continuum in building the legacy of African American fiction.

1970-1980s

With new interest sparked in the voices of African American writers, for a time in the decades of the 1970s and 80s they were published as never before. Many pioneering historical writers were revived and in print once again, joined by a growing population of new voices contributing to the legacy. A national feminist movement during this period also gave rise to increasing voices among women writers. The prestigious Coretta Scott King Award for African American authors and illustrators was inaugurated and subsequently became an official award unit of the American Library Association (Chicago), Social Responsibilities Round Table, Coretta Scott King Task Force.

In general a greater emphasis was made during these decades on "self-reflection" and interactions within the African American community. For the first time known in African American fiction the topic of interracial lesbian relationships was explored in the debut novel *Loving Her* (1974) by Ann Allen Shockley (1927-) and subsequently a lesbian relationship between African Americans was first explored by author Alice Walker (1944-) in the Pulitzer Prize winning novel *Color Purple* (1982) which was made into a motion picture. The debut novel *Women Of Brewster Place* (1982) by Gloria Naylor (1950-), also including an African American lesbian relationship, received the American Book Award and was subsequently produced for television. Joining fellow author Samuel R. Delany, the first African American woman to gain popularity and critical acclaim in the science fiction genre, Octavia Butler (1947-) emerges with her debut novel *Patternmaster* (1976). The following year with over 3 million copies sold of her third novel *Song Of Solomon* (1977) Toni Morrison (1931-) becomes only the second African American author to be chosen, since Richard Wright's novel *Native Son* (1940), for a Book-of-the-Month Club Selection and subsequently wins the National Book Critics' Circle Fiction Award. Her fourth novel *Tar Baby* (1981) becomes a commercial success, appearing on the New York Times Best Seller List and her next novel *Beloved* (1987) receives the Pulitzer Prize. All of these titles are included among this

publication's contemporary author entries. In 1993 author Morrison becomes the first African American to receive the Nobel Prize in Literature.

Many writers who emerged during these two decades continued publishing into the 1990s, and therefore appear among this publication's contemporary author entries. The debut novels produced by these authors during this period are: Lucille Clifton (1936-) *Some Of the Days Of Everett Anderson* (1970) children's fiction; Louise Meriwether (1923-) *Daddy Was a Number Runner* (1970) young readers; Toni Morrison (1931-) *The Bluest Eye* (1970); Alice Walker (1944-) *The Third Life Of Grange Copeland* (1970); Al Young (1939-) *Snakes* (1970); June Jordan (1936-) *His Own Where* (1971) young adults; Albert Murray (1916-) *Train Whistle Guitar* (1971) young adults; Cyrus Colter (1910-) *The Rivers Of Eros* (1972); Eloise Greenfield (1946-) *Good News* (1972) children's fiction; Alice Childress (1920-1994) *A Hero Ain't Nothin' But a Sandwich* (1973) young adults; Alexis De Veaux (1948-) *Na-ni* (1973) young readers; Leon Forrest (1937-) *There Is a Tree More Ancient Than Eden* (1973); Ray Prather (dates unknown) *Anthony and Sabrina* (1973) children's fiction; Charles Johnson (1948-) *Faith and the Good Thing* (1974); Ann Allen Shockley (1927-) *Loving Her* (1974); Mildred Taylor (1943-) *Song Of the Trees* (1975) young readers; Nikki Grimes (1950-) *Growin'* (1977) young readers; Wesley Brown (1945-) *Tragic Magic* (1978); Valerie Flournoy (1952-) *The Best Time Of Day* (1978) children's fiction; Barbara Chase-Riboud (1936-) *Sally Hemings* (1979); Toni Cade Bambara (1939-) *Salt Eaters* (1980); Joyce Hansen (1942-) *The Gift Giver* (1980) young readers; Eleanora Tate (1948-) *Just An Overnight Guest* (1980) young readers; Ntozake Shange (1948-) *Sassafrass, Cypress and Indigo* (1982); Joyce Carol Thomas (1938-) *Marked by Fire* (1982) young adults; Percival Everett (1956-) *Suder* (1983); Nettie Jones (1941-) *Fish Tales* (1983); Linda Brown Bragg (1939-) *Rainbow Roun' Mah Shoulder* (1984) author later publishes as Linda Beatrice Brown; Julius Lester (1939-) *Do Lord Remember Me* (1984); Pat Cummings (1950-) *Jimmie Lee Did It* (1985) children's fiction; Larry Duplechan, (1956-) *Eight Days a Week* (1985); Arthur Flowers (dates unknown) *De Mojo Blues* (1985); Marita Golden (1950-) *A Woman's Place* (1986); Xam Wilson Cartier (1949-) *Be-Bop, Re-Bop* (1987); Terry McMillan (1951-) *Mama* (1987); Trey Ellis, (1962-) *Platitudes* (1988); Gar Anthony Haywood (1954-) *Fear of the Dark* (1988); Elizabeth Fitzgerald Howard (1927-) *The Train To LuLu's* (1988) children's fiction; Rita Williams-Garcia (dates unknown) *Blue Tights* (1988) young adultss; Johnniece Marshall Wilson (1944-) *Oh, Brother* (1988) young readers; Tina McElroy Ansa (1949-) *Baby of the Family* (1989) young adults; Anita Bunkley (dates unknown) *Emily, The Yellow Rose* (1989); Steven Corbin (1953-) *No Easy Place to Be* (1989); Melvin Dixon (1950-1992) *Trouble the Water* (1989); Angela Johnson (1961-) *Tell Me a Story, Mama* (1989) children's fiction; and Sharon Dennis Wyeth (dates unknown) *Boys Wanted* (1989) young readers. In addition, included among this publication's contemporary author entries is a selection from among other authors of this period who have as yet not published in the 1990s.

1990s

As the 1990s unfold, new voices continue to contribute to the legacy of African American fiction. The debut novel of those "first time" writers included among this publication's contemporary author entries are: Reginald McKnight *I Get On The Bus* (1990); Walter Mosley *Devil In a Blue Dress* (1990); Cherry Muhanji *Her* (1990); Elaine Perry *Another Present Era* (1990); Benita Porter *Colorstruck* (1990); Nikki Baker *In the Game* (1991); J. California Cooper *Family* (1991); Frederick Leroy Davison *Black Thoroughbred: The Only Success Formula for Colored People* (1991); Louis Edwards *Ten Seconds* (1991); Jewelle Gomez *Gilda Stories* (1991); E. Lynn Harris *Invisible Life* (1991); Carolivia Herron *Thereafter Johnnie* (1991); Marsha Hunt *Joy* (1991); Yvette Moore *Freedom Songs* (1991); Vickie J. Oliver *Kayln's Life Adventures: Not Even in a Book!* (1991) young readers; Connie Porter *All-Bright Court* (1991); Eleanor Bland *Dead Time* (1992); Bebe Moore Campbell *Your Blues Ain't Like Mine* (1992); Eugenia Collier *Spread My Wings* (1992); Ricardo Cortez Cruz *Straight Outta Compton* (1992) young adults; Ossie Davis *Just Like Martin* (1992) young adults; Thulani Davis *1959* (1992) young adults; Rita Dove *Through the Ivory Gate* (1992); Darius James *Negrophobia: An Urban Parable* (1992); Yolanda Joe *Falling Leaves of Ivy* (1992); Canaan Parker *The Color of Trees* (1992) young adults; Darryl Pinckney *High Cotton* (1992); Brent Wade *The Company Man* (1992); Dennis Williams *Crossover* (1992); Albert French *Billy* (1993); Nelson George *Urban Romance* (1993); Angela Johnson *Toning the Sweep* (1993) young adults; Jewell Parker Rhodes *Voodoo Dreams: A Novel of Marie Laveau* (1993); Brenda Lane Richardson *Chesapeake Song* (1993); Jan S. Gilchrist *Indigo and Midnight Gold* (1993) children's fiction; Dori Sanders *Her Own Place* (1993); Ray Shell *Iced* (1993); Barbara Summers *The Price You Pay* (1993); Connie Briscoe *Sisters and Lovers* (1994); Maxine Clair *Rattlebone* (1994); Alexs

D. Pate *Losing Absalom* (1994); Sharon Draper *Tears of a Tiger* (1994) young adults; Tananarive Due *The Between* (1994); Helen Elaine Lee *The Serpent's Gift* (1994); Bonnie Greer *Hanging By Her Teeth* (1994); James Hardy *B-Boy Blues* (1994); Brian Pinkney *Max Found Two Sticks* (1994) children's fiction; Linda Raymond *Rocking the Babies* (1994); Duane Smith *The Nubian* (1994); Jervey Tervalon *Understand This* (1994) young adults; Lorene Cary *The Price of a Child* (1995); Christopher P. Curtis *The Watsons Go To Birmingham* (1995) young readers; David Haynes *Somebody Else's Mama* (1995); John R. Keene Jr. *Annotations* (1995); Devorah Major *An Open Weave* (1995); Nichelle Nichols *Saturn's Child* (1995); Andrea Davis Pinkney *Hold Fast to Dreams* (1995); Darieck Scott *Traitor to the Race* (1995); A.J. Verdelle *The Good Negress* (1995) young adults; Paul Beatty *White Boy Shuffle* (1996) young adults; Venise Berry *So Good* (1996); Eric Jerome Dickey *Sister, Sister* (1996); Gary Hardwick *Cold Medina* (1996); Hugh Holton *Presumed Dead* (1994); Florence Ladd *Sarah's Psalm* (1996); Diane McKinney-Whetstone *Tumbling* (1996); and Sapphire *Push* (1996) young adults.

There has also been an explosion of African American writers during this period in the paperback romance genre. Often quickly out-of-print and not found in library collections, none of these titles appear among this publication's contemporary author entries. For readers interested in this genre the following is a list by publisher of a selection of authors with one of their titles: From Pinnacle/Arabesque (New York)— Rochelle Alers *Careless Whispers* (1988); Donna Hill *Rooms of the Heart* (1990); Margie Walker *A Sweet Refrain* (1992); Angela Benson *Bands of Gold* (1994); Monique Gilmore *No Ordinary Love* (1994); Layle Guiston *Sweet Promise* (1994); Felicia Mason *For the Love of You* (1994); Francis Ray *Forever Yours* (1994); Eboni Snoe *Beguiled* (1994); Amanda Wheeler *Arms of the Magnolia* (1994); Neffertiti Austin *Eternity* (1995); Francine Craft *Devoted* (1995); Adrienne Ellis Reeves *Change of Heart* (1995); Lynn Emery *Night Magic* (1995); Bette Ford *Forever After* (1995); Gwynne Forster *Sealed With a Kiss* (1995); Carla Fredd *Fire and Ice* (1995); Roberta Gayle *Sunshine and Shadows* (1995); Shirley Hailstock *Whispers of Love* (1995); Brenda Jackson *Tonight and Forever* (1995); Amberlina Wicker *Made in Heaven* (1995); Maria Corley *Choices* (1996); Anna Larence *After Hours* (1996); Shelby Lewis *Delicious* (1996); Janice Sims *Affair Of the Heart* (1996); from Avon (New York)—Beverly Jenkins *Vivid* (1995); from Harlequin (New York)—Sandra Kitt *Rites of Spring* (1984); and from Odyssey (Miami)—Mildred

Riley *Yamilla: Proud Truth* (1989). The majority of these writers have multiple titles, and like their contemporaries in other genres are contributing to the solid legacy of African American fiction. Writers of short stories, and anthologies of African American fiction contribute to this legacy and should not be forgotten for consideration. Many of the writers in this publication have produced short stories and been anthologized.

Conclusion

Voices of American authors of African ancestry in adult, young adult, and children's fiction have a rich legacy. This essay provides a snapshot of some of the historical pioneers and events in that legacy. As you, the reader, explore these authors' contributions to this legacy, you will discover a wide range of contemporary multitalented writers.

As a new millennium emerges on the horizon this ever-growing population of African American writers of fiction will evolve to continue encouraging and supporting the voices of yesterday while embracing the new voices of tomorrow. There will be shifts and changes in direction, new themes will be explored while others are expanded, publishing trends will ebb and flow, and overall you, the reader, can anticipate exciting discoveries. So grab a book, pull up a chair, get comfortable, and ENJOY!

African American Titles

1

TINA MCELROY ANSA, African American

Baby of the Family
(New York: Harcourt Brace Jovanovich, 1989)

Subject(s): Coming of Age; Ghosts; Gifted Children
Age range(s): Grades 9-Adult
Major character(s): Lena McPherson, Teenager, African American; Bloom, Nurse; Miss Lizzie, Aged Person, Grandmother
Time period(s): 1950s
Locale(s): Mulberry, Georgia

Summary: Lena is learning to live with special powers making her different. When Lena was born in a small town with a thin veil (caul) over her face, Nurse Bloom performed a special ritual for her. Since then she has had visions, heard voices, and been visited by ghosts and the spirit of her grandmother, Miss Lizzie.

About this book: This is author's debut novel.

Where it's reviewed:
New York Times Book Review, November 26, 1989, page 6
Publishers Weekly, September 8, 1989, page 56
School Library Journal, June 1990, page 144

Other books by the same author:
Ugly Ways, 1993

Other books you might like:
Maxine Clair, *Rattlebone*, 1994
 Events in the life of a young girl coming of age in a small town of the 1950s.
Thulani Davis, *1959*, 1992
 Coming of age, a 12-year-old girl recounts events that changed her life and others around her during the historic civil rights movement.
Ntozake Shange, *Betsey Brown*, 1985
 Exploits of a young girl coming of age in an era of school integration, the worries of her family and the discoveries she makes at her new school.

Charlotte Sherman, *One Dark Body*, 1993
 Incidents in the life of a young girl abandoned at birth dealing with the return of her mother and her friend's entry into manhood.
A.J. Verdelle, *The Good Negress*, 1995
 A young country girl who moved to the city wants more from life than cooking, cleaning, and washing, and is encouraged to reach higher by her teacher.

2

TINA MCELROY ANSA, African American

The Hand I Fan With
(New York: Doubleday, 1996)

Subject(s): Ghosts; Interpersonal Relations; Small Town Life
Age range(s): Adult
Major character(s): Lena McPherson, Businesswoman, Wealthy, African American; Herman, Spirit
Time period(s): 1990s (1995)
Locale(s): Mulberry, Georgia

Summary: Everyone in town depends on Lena McPherson. A successful businesswoman, she remembers birthdays, sends little gifts to those in need, is active in the church and helps people out when they need money. It seems she is everywhere, and people begin to think she belongs to them. But Lena's success in business and constant activity cannot fill the hole in her life—she wants companionship and love. Lena and a friend perform a supernatural ritual to conjure up a man. A man appears, all right, a ghost named Herman, who has been dead 100 years. But for Lena he is all man, loving her as she never dreamed possible and changing her life forever.

Other books by the same author:
Ugly Ways, 1993
Baby of the Family, 1989 (debut novel, young adult)

Other books you might like:
Xam Wilson Cartier, *Muse-Echo Blues*, 1991
 A young woman suffering from an acute case of composer's block, finds inspiration from a fantasy soul sister and the jazz of the 1940s.

Tananarive Due, *The Between*, 1995
A man endures nightmares and a wavering sense of reality as he desperately tries to protect his family from the psychotic who stalks them.

Terry McMillan, *How Stella Got Her Groove Back*, 1996
A successful investment analyst takes a spur-of-the-moment vacation in Jamaica and meets a man half her age who changes her whole world.

Toni Morrison, *Beloved*, 1987
A mother escapes slavery but kills her baby to keep her former owner from stealing her, and is then haunted and consumed by the baby's ghost.

Gloria Naylor, *Bailey's Cafe*, 1992
A mythical way-station for lost souls, Bailey's cafe has a back door that opens on dimensions unknown.

3

TINA MCELROY ANSA, African American

Ugly Ways
(New York: Harcourt Brace, 1993)

Subject(s): Family Relations; Mothers and Daughters; Sisters
Age range(s): Adult
Major character(s): Betty Jean Lovejoy, Businesswoman, Sister (oldest), African American; Emily Mae Lovejoy, Divorced Person, Sister (middle), African American; Annie Ruth Lovejoy, Sister (youngest), Television Personality, African American
Time period(s): 1990s
Locale(s): Mulberry, Georgia

Summary: As three sisters prepare for their mother's funeral, they reflect on their upbringing in a small town where their mother's strange ways made their family different. While their mother's ghost watches over them they reveal how their lives evolved. Betty is single and now owns her own local business, Emily has divorced, and single Annie has become famous and is now pregnant.

Where it's reviewed:
Booklist, July 1993, page 1942
New York Times Book Review, October 10, 1993, page 20
Publishers Weekly, May 24, 1993, page 67

Other books by the same author:
Baby of the Family, 1989 (debut novel)

Other books you might like:
Connie Briscoe, *Sisters and Lovers*, 1994
Contemporary story about the lives and struggles of three sisters and the men they become involved with.

Steven Corbin, *No Easy Place to Be*, 1989
Explores the relationships among three sisters in urban New York during the 1920s Harlem Renaissance era.

Marsha Hunt, *Joy*, 1991
A childless woman befriends a neighbor girl who sings with her sisters and grows up to become a star. Her untimely death reveals shocking secrets.

4

DORIS JEAN AUSTIN, African American

After the Garden
(New York: New American Library, 1987)

Subject(s): Death; Family Relations; Grandparents
Age range(s): Adult
Major character(s): Rosalie Tompkins, Grandmother, Religious, African American; Elzina Tompkins, Granddaughter, Mother, African American; Jesse James, Husband, Father, African American
Time period(s): 20th century (1939-1961)
Locale(s): Jersey City, New Jersey

Summary: Her strict grandmother is displeased when Elzina falls in love and marries Jesse James. Nevertheless, the young couple lives with the ailing old woman, Jesse uncomfortable under her disapproval and Elzina strangely reluctant to leave. After their son is born and Jesse is imprisoned for a crime he may not have committed, Elzina continues to care for her grandmother until her death. After Jesse returns home, the family has a hard time adjusting to his return, and he goes regularly to all-night parties at his mother's home to get away. Jesse's accidental death sends Elzina beyond the edge of reality, and it is an image of Jesse that may help her survive.

About this book: Debut novel

Where it's reviewed:
Essence, October 1987, page 28
Kirkus Reviews, May 15, 1987, page 739
Library Journal, July 1987, page 91
New York Times Book Review, August 16, 1987, page 20
Publishers Weekly, April 22, 1988, page 80

Other books you might like:
Linda Brown Bragg, *Rainbow Roun' Mah Shoulder*, 1984
Episodes spanning forty years in the life of a woman who was called to heal and help other people.

Helen Elaine Lee, *The Serpent's Gift*, 1994
Children and grandchildren of two intertwined families endure hardship and triumph as they help each other remember a history beyond their knowing.

Terri McMillan, *Mama*, 1987
A proud and feisty mother does her best to provide for her five children through three marriages and uncertain times.

Cherry Muhanji, *Her*, 1990
A young light-skinned woman falls into "the life" of 1950s Detroit and finds a strength in herself and the women around her necessary to her survival.

Gloria Naylor, *Women of Brewster Place*, 1982
The story of seven women who come to live on the dead-end street of Brewster Place and what brings them together in their own redemption.

5

NIKKI BAKER, African American

In the Game
(Tallahassee: Naiad Press, 1991)

Story type: Amateur Detective; Lesbian/Contemporary

Series: Virginia Kelley
Subject(s): Murder; Mystery and Detective Stories; Friendship
Age range(s): Adult
Major character(s): Virginia ''Ginny'' Kelly, Detective—Amateur, Businesswoman (securities analyst), Lesbian; Beverly ''Bev'' Johnson, Businesswoman (business personnel), Lesbian, African American; Kelsey Beckett, Businesswoman (accounts executive), Lesbian, Caucasian
Time period(s): 1990s (1991)
Locale(s): Chicago, Illinois

Summary: Ginny, a ''hopeless mystery buff'', tries to put the pieces together when her best friend Bev's lover, Kelsey, is found murdered. During the process she uncovers a missing suspect, an embezzlement scheme, and a related suicide and ends up fearing for her own life as she single-handedly flushes out the killer.

About this book: Debut novel.

Where it's reviewed:
Booklist, November 15, 1991, page 604
Lambda Book Report, November 1991, page 28
Publishers Weekly, October 18, 1991, page 58

Other books by the same author:
Long Goodbyes, 1993 (Virginia Kelley series)
Lavender House Murder, 1992 (Virginia Kelley series)

Other books you might like:
Eleanor Taylor Bland, *Dead Time*, 1992
    A debut novel in a detective mystery series with a female heroine.
Gar Anthony Haywood, *Going Nowhere Fast*, 1994
    A debut novel of the life of a wife and her retired police detective husband as amateur detectives in a mystery series.
Penny Mickelbury, *Keeping Secrets*, 1994
    A debut novel in a murder mystery series with lesbian characters.
Barbara Neely, *Blanche on the Lam*, 1992
    A debut novel in a contemporary murder mystery series with an amateur detective as the heroine.
Valerie Wilson Wesley, *When Death Comes Stealing*, 1994
    A debut novel in a murder mystery series featuring an ex-policewoman who has become a private detective.

6

NIKKI BAKER, African American

Lavender House Murder

(Tallahassee: Naiad Press, 1992)

Story type: Adult; Lesbian/Contemporary
Series: Virginia Kelley
Subject(s): Murder; Mystery and Detective Stories; Interpersonal Relations
Age range(s): Adult
Major character(s): Virginia ''Ginny'' Kelly, Detective—Amateur, Businesswoman (securities analyst), Lesbian; Naomi Wolf, Lawyer, Lesbian, Caucasian; Joan DiMaio, Activist, Journalist, Caucasian
Time period(s): 1990s (1992)
Locale(s): Provincetown, Massachusetts

Summary: Near breaking up with her lover, ''Ginny'' takes a vacation with her pal Naomi to Provincetown. Staying at the Lavender House, a Victorian bed and breakfast owned by Samantha ''Sam'' Flynn, they meet a small group of other lodgers, among them Joan DiMaio. When ''Ginny'' discovers Joan's dead body on an early morning jog she becomes a murder suspect. Joan had been an activist reporter outing closeted lesbians and gays and thus had many potential enemies. ''Ginny'' and Naomi look for clues to clear her name and in the process discover they both had slept with Joan as had other lodgers. When she uncovers a hidden notebook ''Ginny'' thinks she knows who the real killer is until another death occurs which leaves her looking in another direction.

Where it's reviewed:
Lambda Book Report, July 1992, page 21

Other books by the same author:
Long Goodbyes, 1993 (Virginia Kelley series)
In the Game, 1991 (debut novel)

Other books you might like:
Eleanor Taylor Bland, *Dead Time*, 1992
    Debut novel in a detective mystery series with a female heroine.
Gar Anthony Haywood, *Going Nowhere Fast*, 1994
    Debut novel of the life of a wife and her retired police detective husband as a couple of amateur detectives in a mystery series.
Penny Mickelbury, *Keeping Secrets*, 1994
    Debut novel in a murder mystery series with lesbian characters.
Barbara Neely, *Blanche on the Lam*, 1992
    Debut novel in a contemporary murder mystery series with an amateur detective as the heroine.
Valerie Wilson Wesley, *When Death Comes Stealing*, 1994
    Debut novel in a murder mystery series featuring an ex-policewoman who has become a private detective.

7

NIKKI BAKER, African American

Long Goodbyes

(Tallahassee: Naiad Press, 1993)

Story type: Adult; Lesbian/Contemporary
Series: Virginia Kelley
Subject(s): Murder; Mystery and Detective Stories; Interpersonal Relations
Age range(s): Adult
Major character(s): Virginia ''Ginny'' Kelly, Detective—Amateur, Businesswoman (securities analyst), Lesbian; Rosalee ''Rosey'' Paschen, Lawyer, Abuse Victim (incest), Caucasian (lesbian); Mary Ellen ''Spike'' McMann, Restauranteur, Lesbian, Caucasian
Time period(s): 1990s (1992)
Locale(s): Blue River, Ohio

Summary: Returning home for her 10-year high school reunion, ''Ginny'' finds herself rekindling her feelings of first love for her classmate ''Rosey.'' Her curiosity at seeing her again is aroused even more when ''Rosey'' calls her in Chicago and says she has something important she must tell her at the reunion. Staying at her parent's home ''Ginny'' endures tensions from her mother and father who wish she were different. At the reunion another female classmate ''Spike'' confesses having had a crush on her and they wind up in bed. When ''Rosey'' disappears after also winding up in bed with ''Ginny'' she roams the town looking for her. ''Ginny's'' search uncovers secrets from the past and leads to her life being endangered when she discovers a murderer in her midst.

Where it's reviewed:
African American Review, Spring 1994, page 155
Lambda Book Reports, November 1993, page 27
Publishers Weekly, October 4, 1993, page 69

Other books by the same author:
Lavender House Murder, 1992 (Virginia Kelley series)
In the Game, 1991 (debut novel)

Other books you might like:
Eleanor Taylor Bland, *Dead Time*, 1992
    Debut novel in a detective mystery series with a female heroine.
Gar Anthony Haywood, *Going Nowhere Fast*, 1994
    Debut novel of the life of a wife and her retired police detective husband as a couple of amateur detectives in a mystery series.
Penny Mickelbury, *Keeping Secrets*, 1994
    Debut novel in a murder mystery series with lesbian characters.
Barbara Neely, *Blanche on the Lam*, 1992
    Debut novel in a contemporary murder mystery series with an amateur detective as the heroine.
Valerie Wilson Wesley, *When Death Comes Stealing*, 1994
    Debut novel in a murder mystery series featuring an ex-policewoman who has become a private detective.

8

TONI CADE BAMBARA, African American

The Salt Eaters

(New York: Random House, 1980)

Subject(s): Interpersonal Relations; Psychology; Supernatural
Age range(s): Adult
Major character(s): Velma Henry, Activist, Mother, African American; Minnie Ransom, Healer, Herbalist, African American
Time period(s): 1970s
Locale(s): Georgia

Summary: Velma, an activist in her community, has lost her ''center'' and tries to commit suicide. She is now in Southwest Community Infirmary, sitting on a stool opposite Minnie Ransom, a spiritual community healer who has come to restore her joy of life. Through Velma's wandering mind and psyche, we enter the minds of her family and friends as the two women face each other in a story that blends past, present and future.

About this book: Debut novel.

Where it's reviewed:
Black Scholar, Fall 1982, page 52
Library Journal, April 1, 1980, page 876
New Yorker, May 5, 1980, page 169

Awards the book has won:
American Book Award, 1981

Other books you might like:
Toni Morrison, *Beloved*, 1987
    A mother who escaped slavery kills her baby to keep her former owner from stealing her, and is then haunted and consumed by the baby's ghost.
Gloria Naylor, *Mama Day*, 1988
    Returning to her sea island home, a young woman finds both body and soul threatened by supernatural forces from which she is barely saved by Mama Day.
Alice Walker, *Possessing the Secret of Joy*, 1992
    A woman battling madness after submitting to an African ritual circumcision is aided by an unlikely ally in facing her grief and anger.
Alice Walker, *The Temple of My Familiar*, 1989
    Interwoven lyric tales take place in Africa, Europe and the Americas, in ancient and contemporary times and explore how we affect one another and our world.

9

JACQUELINE TURNER BANKS, African American

Egg-Drop Blues

(Boston: Houghton Mifflin, 1995)

Story type: Young Readers
Subject(s): Brothers; School Life; Twins
Age range(s): Grades 4-8
Major character(s): Judge Jenkins, Twin, Dyslexic, African American; Jury Jenkins, Twin, Student, African American
Time period(s): 1990s
Locale(s): Plank, Kentucky

Summary: Sixth grader Judge's science grade depends on entering the Einstein Rally. His dyslexia makes learning more difficult for him than for his twin brother Jury, and he needs the extra credit. The boys weather some family changes between the egg-drop competition and Jury's games of pom-pom tackle.

Where it's reviewed:
Booklist, April 15, 1995, page 1497
Horn Book Magazine, July 1995, page 483
Library Talk, September 1995, page 36
School Library Journal, August 1995, page 139
Voice of Youth Advocates, June 1995, page 9

Other books by the same author:
The New One, 1994
Project Wheels, 1993 (debut novel)

Other books you might like:
Sharon M. Draper, *Ziggy and the Black Dinosaurs*, 1994
    When their neighborhood playground is destroyed, four 5th grade boys start their own secret club and uncover a mysterious old box of hidden bones.
Joyce Hansen, *Yellow Bird and Me*, 1986
    Missing her best friend who has moved away, a young girl helps a classmate in elementary school overcome stage fright and discover he has dyslexia.
Walter Dean Myers, *Darnell Rock Reporting*, 1994
    Not doing well in school, a 13-year-old joins the school

newspaper and discovers the impact his writing can have and how he can make a difference.

Walter Dean Myers, *Mop, Moondance and Nagasaki Knights*, 1992

Another episode in the lives of two adopted young brothers and their friend, a white young girl on their Little League baseball team.

Harriette Gillem Robinet, *Ride the Red Cycle*, 1980

A boy crippled since the age of two struggles to realize his dream of riding a cycle.

10

JACQUELINE TURNER BANKS, African American

The New One

(Boston: Houghton Mifflin Company, 1994)

Story type: Young Readers
Subject(s): Brothers; School Life; Twins
Age range(s): Grades 4-8
Major character(s): Jury Jenkins, 12-Year-Old, Twin, African American; Judge Jenkins, 12-Year-Old, Twin, African American
Time period(s): 1990s
Locale(s): Plank, Kentucky

Summary: Sixth-graders Jury, Judge, Angela, Faye and Tommy have known each other since kindergarten. When a new girl comes to school, at first Jury is the only one who wants to be friends. Meanwhile at home, their mother's boyfriend Frank begins to get on Jury's and Judge's nerves, especially when it looks like the relationship is getting serious.

Where it's reviewed:
Horn Book Guide, Fall 1994, page 305
Library Talk, September 1994, page 46
Voice of Youth Advocates, October 1994, page 204

Other books by the same author:
Egg-Drop Blues, 1995
Project Wheels, 1993 (debut novel)

Other books you might like:
Candy Dawson Boyd, *Chevrolet Saturdays*, 1993
Struggling with the divorce of his parents and accepting his new stepfather, a young boy has trouble in school and makes mistakes he regrets.
Joyce Hansen, *The Gift Giver*, 1980
A young girl and her fifth grade friends come to like a new boy in their class and are surprised when they discover he is a foster child.
Andrea Davis Pinkney, *Hold Fast to Dreams*, 1995
Two sisters endure prejudice when their family moves to the suburbs and they have to attend separate all-white schools and try to fit in.
Jacqueline Woodson, *Between Madison & Palmetto*, 1993
In their continuing story two 13-year-old best friends are reunited and having to adjust to a lot of change in their lives and in those around them.
Jacqueline Woodson, *Maizon at Blue Hill*, 1992
Another episode in the lives of two young seventh grade

friends where one girl wins an academic scholarship to a white boarding school.

11

JACQUELINE TURNER BANKS, African American

Project Wheels

(Boston: Houghton Mifflin Company, 1993)

Subject(s): Adolescence; Friendship; School Life
Age range(s): Grades 4-8
Major character(s): Angela Collins, 12-Year-Old, Student, African American; Faye Benneck, 12-Year-Old, Student, Caucasian; Jury Jenkins, 12-Year-Old, Twin, African American
Time period(s): 1990s
Locale(s): Plank, Kentucky

Summary: Five kids have been best friends all through grammar school: Angela, Faye, the twins Judge and Jury, and Tommy. Now in sixth grade, Angela notices that things are beginning to change. Faye is getting crushes on boys in school, and even the twins are acting differently around girls. Angela doesn't want her old gang to break up, but what can she do? Working with her friends on a special project to raise money to buy a motorized wheelchair for a classmate, Angela realizes that they are growing up and things won't ever be quite the same.

About this book: Debut novel.

Where it's reviewed:
Booklist, April 1, 1993, page 1430
Kirkus Reviews, March 1, 1993, page 296
School Library Journal, May 1993, page 103

Other books by the same author:
Egg-Drop Blues, 1995
The New One, 1994

Other books you might like:
Candy Dawson Boyd, *Breadsticks and Blessing Places*, 1985
Three sixth-grade girlfriends are involved in their regular routine of activities when one is killed and the others cope with her untimely death.
Eloise Greenfield, *Koya Delaney and the Good Girl Blues*, 1992
A sixth grader caught in the middle when her best friend and her sister have a fight struggles with mixed emotions and knowing who her real friends are.
Joyce Hansen, *The Gift Giver*, 1980
A young girl and her fifth grade friends come to like a new boy in their class and are surprised when they discover he is a foster child.

12

ELEANOR TAYLOR BLAND, African American

Dead Time

(New York: St. Martin's Press, 1992)

Story type: Adult; Police Procedural
Series: Marti MacAlister

Subject(s): Smuggling; Murder; Mystery and Detective Stories

Age range(s): Adult

Major character(s): Marti "Big Mac" MacAlister, Detective—Homicide, Widow(er), African American

Time period(s): 1990s

Locale(s): Lincoln Prairie, Illinois (sixty miles north of Chicago)

Summary: When her policeman husband Johnny is shot to death in an undercover operation, "Big Mac" moves from Chicago to a small town with their teenaged daughter and young son. Working in a new police department with her white partner Vik Jessenovik, "Big Mac" is also still adjusting to her new life. When a woman is murdered at a flophouse, "Big Mac" is on the case. She connects the murder victim to other murders from years past. When more murders occur at the flophouse she fears a serial killer is on the loose. Discovering clues that some runaway youngsters may have witnessed the crime, she makes every effort to find them before the killer does.

About this book: Debut novel

Where it's reviewed:
Armchair Detective, Fall 1992, page 432

Other books by the same author:
Done Wrong, 1995 (Marti MacAlister series)
Gone Quiet, 1994 (Marti MacAlister series)
Slow Burn, 1993 (Marti MacAlister series)

Other books you might like:
Nikki Baker, *In the Game*, 1991
  Debut novel in a murder mystery series with lesbian characters.
Gar Anthony Haywood, *Fear of the Dark*, 1988
  Debut novel in a contemporary murder mystery series with a private detective.
Penny Mickelbury, *Keeping Secrets*, 1994
  Debut novel in a murder mystery series with lesbian characters.
Walter Mosley, *Devil in a Blue Dress*, 1990
  Debut novel in a contemporary murder mystery series with a private detective.
Valerie Wilson Wesley, *When Death Comes Stealing*, 1994
  Debut novel in a murder mystery series featuring an ex-policewoman who has become a private detective.

13

ELEANOR TAYLOR BLAND, African American

Done Wrong

(New York: St. Martin's Press, 1995)

Story type: Adult; Police Procedural

Series: Marti MacAlister

Subject(s): Murder; Mystery and Detective Stories

Age range(s): Adult

Major character(s): Marti "Big Mac" MacAlister, Detective—Homicide, Widow(er), African American

Time period(s): 1990s

Locale(s): Lincoln Prairie, Illinois (sixty miles north of Chicago); Chicago, Illinois

Summary: Marti visits the Jewish widow of one of her late hubands' colleagues and learns there may be a cover up in their husband's deaths. When "Big Mac" shares what she has learned with her white partner Jessenovik he offers to help her investigate. Once in Chicago they examine Johnny's files for clues and as their investigation gets underway so do more murders. "Big Mac" knows Johnny left the answer to his murder in his secret coded deck of cards but they were given to her in a jumble and she hasn't been able to sort them out yet. Drug busts, missing money, murder, and police corruption all unfold as "Big Mac" and her partner track down the clues to finally come face to face with the cop killer Diablo.

Where it's reviewed:
Booklist, June 1, 1995, page 1733
Booklist, June 1, 1995, page 1741
Book World, July 16, 1995, page 6
Los Angeles Times Book Review, June 11, 1995, page 7
Publishers Weekly, May 15, page 58

Other books by the same author:
Gone Quiet, 1994 (Marti MacAlister series)
Slow Burn, 1993 (Marti MacAlister series)
Dead Time, 1992 (debut novel, Marti MacAlister series)

Other books you might like:
Nikki Baker, *In the Game*, 1991
  Debut novel in a murder mystery series with lesbian characters.
Gar Anthony Haywood, *Fear of the Dark*, 1988
  Debut novel in a contemporary murder mystery series with a private detective.
Penny Mickelbury, *Keeping Secrets*, 1994
  Debut novel in a murder mystery series with lesbian characters.
Walter Mosley, *Devil in a Blue Dress*, 1990
  Debut novel in a contemporary murder mystery series with a private detective.
Valerie Wilson Wesley, *When Death Comes Stealing*, 1994
  Debut novel in a murder mystery series featuring an ex-policewoman who has become a private detective.

14

ELEANOR TAYLOR BLAND, African American

Gone Quiet

(New York: St. Martin's Press, 1994)

Story type: Police Procedural

Series: Marti MacAlister

Subject(s): Family Relations; Murder; Mystery and Detective Stories

Age range(s): Adult

Major character(s): Marti "Big Mac" MacAlister, Detective—Homicide, Widow(er), African American; Henry Isaiah Hamilton, Aged Person (seventy), Religious (baptist deacon), African American

Time period(s): 1990s (1994)

Locale(s): Lincoln Prairie, Illinois (Sixty miles north of Chicago)

Summary: Now a ten-year veteran on the Lincoln Prairie police force, "Big Mac" is assigned with her white male partner to what appears to be a routine death case. Reverend Hamilton was found dead in his home by his stepdaughter Denise, a juvenile probation officer. Suspecting something might be wrong when the medical examiner finds the death by suffocation not natural causes "Big Mac" and her partner, Vik Jessenovik, launch into a full investigation to find the killer among the victim's family and friends, including their co-worker Denise. They discover Denise and both her sisters had been molested as children by their stepfather.

Where it's reviewed:
Booklist, June 1, 1994, page 1775
Essence, September 1994, page 61
Publishers Weekly, June 13, 1994, page 53

Other books by the same author:
Done Wrong, 1995 (Marti MacAlister series)
Slow Burn, 1993 (Marti MacAlister series)
Dead Time, 1992 (debut novel, Marti MacAlister series)

Other books you might like:
Gar Anthony Haywood, *Going Nowhere Fast*, 1994
    A debut novel of the life of a wife and her retired police detective husband as amateur detectives in a mystery series.
Yolanda Joe, *Falling Leaves of Ivy*, 1992
    A young woman is murdered and her four closest friends from college become suspects, as the secret they share begins to unravel.
Barbara Neely, *Blanche on the Lam*, 1992
    A debut novel in a contemporary murder mystery series with an amateur detective as the heroine.
Barbara Summers, *The Price You Pay*, 1993
    A young woman in the highly competitive fashion industry finds herself a target as a series of murders occur when a new campaign is launched.
Valerie Wilson Wesley, *When Death Comes Stealing*, 1994
    A debut novel in a murder mystery series featuring an ex-policewoman who has become a private detective.

15

ELEANOR TAYLOR BLAND, African American

Slow Burn

(New York: St. Martin's Press, 1993)

Story type: Police Procedural
Series: Marti MacAlister
Subject(s): Murder; Mystery and Detective Stories; Parenthood
Age range(s): Adult
Major character(s): Marti "Big Mac" MacAlister, Detective—Homicide, Mother, African American
Time period(s): 1990s (1993)
Locale(s): Lincoln Prairie, Illinois (Sixty miles north of Chicago)

Summary: In their latest case homicide detectives "Big Mac" and her white male partner are immersed in the mystery of solving four homicides which at first seemed unrelated. Two bodies were found in a fire at a women's clinic, a young man was murdered across town, and an elderly woman, possibly a witness, is killed. Slowly putting all the pieces together "Big

Mac" and her partner, Vik Jessenovik, discover a link of exploitation and violence involving girls younger than "Big Mac's" own teenaged daughter.

Where it's reviewed:
Booklist, February 15, 1994, page 1057
Book World, October 17, 1993, page 8

Other books by the same author:
Done Wrong, 1995 (Marti MacAlister series)
Gone Quiet, 1994 (Marti MacAlister series)
Dead Time, 1992 (debut novel, Marti MacAlister series)

Other books you might like:
Gar Anthony Haywood, *Going Nowhere Fast*, 1994
    A debut novel of the life of a wife and her retired police detective husband as amateur detectives in a mystery series.
Yolanda Joe, *Falling Leaves of Ivy*, 1992
    A young woman is murdered and her four closest friends from college become suspects, as the secret they share begins to unravel.
Barbara Neely, *Blanche on the Lam*, 1992
    A debut novel in a contemporary murder mystery series with an amateur detective as the heroine.
Barbara Summers, *The Price You Pay*, 1993
    A young woman in the highly competitive fashion industry finds herself a target as a series of murders occur when a new campaign is launched.
Valerie Wilson Wesley, *When Death Comes Stealing*, 1994
    A debut novel in a murder mystery series featuring an ex-policewoman who has become a private detective.

16

CANDY DAWSON BOYD, African American

Breadsticks and Blessing Places

(New York: Macmillan, 1985)

Story type: Young Readers
Subject(s): Death; Friendship; Schools
Age range(s): Grades 6-9
Major character(s): Antoinette Marie "Toni" Douglas, 12-Year-Old, Sister, African American; Susan Denise Lawrence, 12-Year-Old, Accident Victim, African American; Mattie Mae Benson, 12-Year-Old, African American
Time period(s): 1980s
Locale(s): Chicago, Illinois

Summary: Sixth-graders "Toni," Mattie, and Susan enjoy their friendship and normal routine of activities until their lives change when Susan is killed. The grief and confusion of death overtake "Toni," and Mattie tries to help by explaining her experience when her father died.

Other books by the same author:
Chevrolet Saturdays, 1993
Charlie Pippin, 1987
Circle of Gold, 1985 (debut novel)

Other books you might like:
Virginia Hamilton, *Cousins*, 1990
    Concerned that her grandmother might die, a young girl is unprepared for the death of another relative.

Dori Sanders, *Clover*, 1990
When her father is killed on his wedding day, a 10-year-old has to deal with the trauma of her loss and adjust to a new stepmother.

Jacqueline Woodson, *Between Madison & Palmetto*, 1993
Two 13-year-old best friends are reunited and have to adjust to a lot of change in their lives and in those around them.

Jacqueline Woodson, *Last Summer with Maizon*, 1990
The friendship and separation of two youngsters after one suffers the death of her father and the other goes away to boarding school.

Jacqueline Woodson, *Maizon at Blue Hill*, 1992
Another episode in the lives of two young seventh-grade friends where one girl wins an academic scholarship to a white boarding school.

17

CANDY DAWSON BOYD, African American

Charlie Pippin

(New York: Macmillan Publishing Company, 1987)

Story type: Young Readers
Subject(s): Fathers and Daughters; School Life; Vietnam War
Age range(s): Grades 5-9
Major character(s): Chartreuse Marie ''Charlie'' Pippin, 11-Year-Old, Businesswoman, African American
Time period(s): 1980s (1985)
Locale(s): Berkeley, California

Summary: ''Charlie'''s parents had once dreamed of living on the Oregon coast, but all that changed when her father came back from the Vietnam War. Curious about Vietnam and what happened to her father ''Charlie'' joins a school committee on peace and war. Her research uncovers a piece of family history her father had hoped to forget and moves her to visit the Vietnam Memorial, hoping to help him heal old wounds.

Where it's reviewed:
English Journal, September 1993, page 43
Learning: Creative Ideas and Insights for Teachers, February 1993, p65

Awards the book has won:
IRA-CBC Children's Choice, 1988

Other books by the same author:
Chevrolet Saturdays, 1993
Breadsticks and Blessing Places, 1985
Circle of Gold, 1985 (debut novel)

Other books you might like:
Virginia Hamilton, *Plain City*, 1993
A 12-year-old who feels out of place struggles to unearth her past and family history as she gradually discovers more about her long-missing father.

Walter Dean Myers, *Darnell Rock Reporting*, 1994
Not doing well in school, a 13-year-old joins the school newspaper and discovers the impact his writing can have and how he can make a difference.

Walter Dean Myers, *Somewhere in the Darkness*, 1992
An ailing father escapes from prison to prove his inno-

cence to his son by confronting the witness who lied against him.

Eleanora E. Tate, *A Blessing in Disguise*, 1995
Another tale from the Calvary County trilogy where a young girl discovers the father she admired addicted her dying mother to alcohol and drugs.

Joyce Carol Thomas, *The Golden Pasture*, 1986
The exquisite horse a 12-year-old boy finds on his grandfather's farm one summer helps him to understand his difficult father better.

18

CANDY DAWSON BOYD, African American

Chevrolet Saturdays

(New York: Macmillan Publishing Company, 1993)

Story type: Young Readers
Subject(s): Divorce; Remarriage; Stepfathers
Age range(s): Grades 4-7
Major character(s): Joey Davis, 10-Year-Old, Child of Divorced Parents, African American
Time period(s): 1990s
Locale(s): Oakland, California

Summary: Fifth-grader Joey is having a hard time adjusting to the divorce of his parents and his mother's remarriage. When his stepfather buys a new pickup truck, Joey has an opportunity to spend Saturdays working with him in his new contracting business. At first reluctant, Joey soon looks forward to their time together until he absent-mindedly makes a mistake that could have serious consequences. Trying to make amends for his wrongdoing, Joey takes on new responsibilities to gain back his stepfather's trust and his own self-respect.

Where it's reviewed:
Publishers Weekly, January 23, 1995, page 91
Essence, February 1994, page 120
Horn Book Guide, Fall 1993, page 294
Wilson Library Bulletin, January 1994, page 119

Other books by the same author:
Charlie Pippin, 1987
Breadsticks and Blessing Places, 1985
Circle of Gold, 1985 (debut novel)

Other books you might like:
Jacqueline Turner Banks, *The New One*, 1994
Twin brothers disagree about whether to befriend a new girl at school or interfere with their mother's relationship with her boyfriend.

Walter Dean Myers, *Mouse Rap*, 1990
A 14-year-old hears about a hidden treasure in his neighborhood, and his separated parents try getting back together.

Eleanora E. Tate, *A Blessing in Disguise*, 1995
Another tale from the Calvary County trilogy where a young girl discovers the father she admired addicted her dying mother to alcohol and drugs.

Mildred Pitts Walter, *Mariah Keeps Cool*, 1990
A girl trains for a diving competition, tries to figure out her half-sister and plans a surprise for her sister.

Mildred Pitts Walter, *Mariah Loves Rock*, 1988
A girl and her family experience misgivings about the arrival of a half-sister who is coming to live with them.

19

DAVID BRADLEY, African American

The Chaneysville Incident
(New York: Harper & Row, 1981)

Subject(s): Fathers and Sons; Historical; Psychology
Age range(s): Adult
Major character(s): John Washington, Professor, Historian, African American Jack Crawley, Backwoodsman, Foster Parent, African American; Judith Powell, Doctor (psychiatrist), Girlfriend, Caucasian
Time period(s): 1970s (1979)
Locale(s): Philadelphia, Pennsylvania; Pennsylvania (mountains of central Pennsylvania, and some areas south)

Summary: John Washington returns to his home town to comfort a dying friend, Old Jack Crawley, one of the three men who reared him. Taking place during 10 days in March, the story actually spans almost 250 years as John travels mentally and physically through his history, guided by Old Jack's stories. After Old Jack's death, John receives a folio bequeathed by his father, and its contents along with some other clues cause him to reevaluate his own life when he finally understands the circumstances surrounding the deaths of his father, Moses Washington, and his great-grandfather, C.K. Washington. Understanding his feelings for his father, John is better equipped to share every part of his life with Judith, a white woman, who believes in him enough to accompany him on his quest.

Where it's reviewed:
Black Enterprise, July 1981, page 10
Library Journal, May 15, 1981, page 1095
Publishers Weekly, April 9, 1982, page 49

Other books by the same author:
South Street, 1975 (debut novel)

Other books you might like:
Cyrus Colter, *Rivers of Eros*, 1972
   A woman raising her grandchildren must deal with her betrayal of her sister, her daughter's violent death, and the granddaughter she cannot reach.
Leon Forrest, *Divine Days*, 1992
   Voices of the living and the dead are captured by an aspiring playwright in an epic tale referred to as "The Ulysses of the South Side."
Leon Forrest, *There Is a Tree More Ancient than Eden*, 1973
   In a stream of consciousness style the narrator of this first title of the Witherspoon family saga trilogy anguishes about his heritage.
Ernest J. Gaines, *In My Father's House*, 1978
   A civil rights leader and minister is forced to examine who he is and who he was when a stranger emerges from his past.

20

DAVID BRADLEY, African American

South Street
(New York: Grossman Publishers, 1975)

Subject(s): City Life; Interpersonal Relations; Religion
Age range(s): Adult
Major character(s): Adlai Brown, Writer (poet), African American
Time period(s): 1970s
Locale(s): Philadelphia, Pennsylvania

Summary: A young stranger appears at Lightnin' Ed's Bar and Grill and shames numbers' king Leroy Briggs in front of the regulars. The stranger is Adlai Stevenson Brown, a poet who has come to shed the trappings of his middle-class life and live on South Street with the "people" to inspire his work. He finds them here—Leo, the bartender; Big Betsy, a longtime prostitute; Jake, a 75-year-old wino who sleeps in the back room; Rayburn Wallace, a janitor who can't keep his wife happy; Reverend Mr. Peter J. Sloan, whose past eventually catches up with him; and Brother Fletcher, who discovers what a church should be. Brown finds work and becomes part of this community, and finds that when given the opportunity to return to the world of his past, he literally can't cross the bridge.

About this book: Debut novel.

Other books by the same author:
The Chaneysville Incident, 1981

Other books you might like:
Leon Forrest, *Divine Days*, 1992
   An aspiring playwright captures the voices of the living and the dead in an epic tale referred to as "The Ulysses of the South Side."
David Haynes, *Live at Five*, 1996
   A television anchor seeks to re-define his image by broadcasting from the inner city to improve ratings, and finds the "real" story.
Cherry Muhanji, *Her*, 1990
   A young light-skinned woman falls into "the life" of 1950s Detroit and finds a strength to survive within herself and the women around her.
Gloria Naylor, *Bailey's Cafe*, 1992
   A mythical way-station for lost souls, Bailey's cafe has a back door that opens on dimensions unknown.

21

LINDA BROWN BRAGG, African American

Rainbow Roun' Mah Shoulder
(Chapel Hill, NC: Carolina Wren Press, 1982)

Story type: Adult
Subject(s): Conduct of Life; Interpersonal Relations; Religion
Age range(s): Adult
Major character(s): Rebecca Florice Letenielle, Healer (herbalist), African American; Alice Wine, Cook, Friend, African American
Time period(s): 20th century (1915-1954)

Locale(s): New Orleans, Louisiana; Greensboro, North Carolina

Summary: The life of a woman called to heal and help others is told in episodes spanning forty years. Rebecca is first drawn to Father Theodore Canty, who understands her passion and her spiritual side. After moving away to Jacksonville with her husband, she tells him of her talks with God. Mac accuses her of an affair with the Father, and walks away from her, never to be seen again. Rebecca and her friend Alice go to Greensboro to work at a Black college, where she is again drawn to a man of the cloth. Her passionate affair with Reverend Robert Brown proves too dangerous to the married Reverend, who gets himself transferred to Pittsburgh. Rebecca loses her will to live, continuing to work and help the students while quietly destroying herself until Alice discovers the spell and saves her friend. Alice restores Rebecca's health only to fall ill herself. Upon her death, Rebecca seeks out Reverend Brown and discovers that he, too, is gravely ill. Rebecca passes her rainbow of healing and vision on to a young woman of even greater vision.

About this book: Debut novel

Other books by the same author:
Crossing over Jordan, 1995 (written under the name Linda Beatrice Brown)

Other books you might like:
Lorene Cary, *The Price of a Child*, 1995
    Historical tale of a woman who literally walks from slavery to freedom under her slave owner's furious gaze in 1850s Philadelphia.
Helen Elaine Lee, *The Serpent's Gift*, 1994
    Children and grandchildren of two intertwined families endure hardship and triumph as they help each other remember a history beyond their knowing.
Terri McMillan, *Mama*, 1987
    A proud and feisty mother does her best to provide for her five children through three marriages and uncertain times.
Gloria Naylor, *Mama Day*, 1988
    Returning to her sea island home, a young woman finds both body and soul threatened by supernatural forces from which she is barely saved by Mama Day.
Gloria Naylor, *Women of Brewster Place*, 1982
    Seven women's stories who come to live on the dead-end street of Brewster Place and what brings them together in their own redemption.
Richard Perry, *Montgomery's Children*, 1984
    Tales of people living in a small town in central New York interwoven with magic and vision, incest and murder, friendship and sacrifice.

22

CONNIE BRISCOE, African American

Big Girls Don't Cry
(New York: HarperCollins, 1996)

Subject(s): Brothers and Sisters; Interpersonal Relations; Racism
Age range(s): Adult

Major character(s): Naomi Jefferson, African American, Activist, Businesswoman
Time period(s): 20th century (1963-1985)
Locale(s): Washington, District of Columbia

Summary: In Naomi's sheltered childhood the issues of black and white rarely came up, so she didn't always understand her brother Joshua's passion for the civil rights movement. When he is killed in a car accident on the way to a demonstration, the family is shattered and suddenly the differences between black and white are very important. Naomi, too, becomes involved in the civil rights movement in college, and finds after graduation that she still has to prove herself every step of the way in corporate America.

Where it's reviewed:
Kirkus Reviews, March 1, 1996, page 310
Publishers Weekly, March 11, 1996, page 41

Other books by the same author:
Sisters and Lovers, 1994 (debut novel)

Other books you might like:
Linda Brown Bragg, *Rainbow Round' Mah Shoulder*, 1984
    Episodes spanning forty years of the life of a woman who was called to heal and help other people, and her loves and losses.
Bebe Moore Campbell, *Brothers and Sisters*, 1994
    Contemporary account of the life of a career woman as she tries to climb the business ladder and maintain a social life, and of people around her.
David Haynes, *Somebody Else's Mama*, 1995
    The trials and tribulations of a young woman faced with the care of her ill and aging mother-in-law with little help from her family.
Nettie Jones, *Mischief Makers*, 1989
    Three exotically beautiful sisters of mixed race experience the world quite differently both because and in spite of their looks.
Terri McMillan, *Disappearing Acts*, 1989
    A successful professional woman tries to maintain a relationship with a man unable to keep a steady job.
Terry McMillan, *Waiting to Exhale*, 1992
    Contemporary account of the friendship of four women, their relationships with men, and their experiences with family and careers.
Alice Walker, *Meridian*, 1976
    A deserted mother at seventeen, a young girl gets involved in the civil rights movement which changes her life and defines her role in the world.

23

Sisters and Lovers
(New York: Harper Collins, 1994)

Subject(s): Family Relations; Interpersonal Relations; Sisters
Age range(s): Adult
Major character(s): Evelyn DuMont, Mother, Psychologist, African American; Charmaine Perry, Mother, Secretary, African American; Beverly Jordan, Editor, Sister (youngest), African American
Time period(s): 1990s

Locale(s): Washington, District of Columbia

Summary: A contemporary story about the relationships among three sisters and the men in their lives. While being persistent and showing the strength and courage to do what feels right for themselves, Evelyn, Charmaine and Beverly strive to live with integrity and principles as they seek love, follow their dreams, face fears, make mistakes, and deal with disappointments.

About this book: Debut novel.

Where it's reviewed:
Booklist, April 15, 1994, page 1484
Library Journal, April 1, 1994, page 130
Publishers Weekly, March 28, 1994, page 81

Other books you might like:
Tina McElroy Ansa, *Ugly Ways*, 1993
   A contemporary account of three sisters reflecting on their upbringing in a small town and how their lives have evolved.
Steven Corbin, *No Easy Place to Be*, 1989
   Explores the relationships among three sisters in urban New York during the 1920s Harlem Renaissance era.
Nelson George, *Urban Romance*, 1993
   A contemporary relationship of a young male-female couple brought together by mutual friends experiencing love and heartbreak.
Marsha Hunt, *Joy*, 1991
   A childless woman befriends a neighbor girl who sings with her sisters and grows up to become a star. Her untimely death reveals shocking secrets.
Terry McMillan, *Waiting to Exhale*, 1992
   A contemporary account of the friendship of four women, their relationships with men, and their experiences with family and careers.

24

CECIL BROWN, African American

Days Without Weather

(New York: Farrar Straus Giroux, 1983)

Subject(s): Movie Industry; Comedians; Race Relations
Age range(s): Adult
Major character(s): Jonah Drinkwater, Graduate, Entertainer, African American; Clea Menchan, Businesswoman, Caucasian
Time period(s): 1980s
Locale(s): Hollywood, California

Summary: Charged with unlawful conduct, 22-year-old Jonah was booked and arraigned in northern California. Six months later with the help of his uncle Gadge, he is in Hollywood doing a stand up comedy act. Gadge gets Jonah a job at the studio where he works and for a time Jonah lives with him and his wife, but struggling to find his own identity and style as a comedian, Jonah drifts into drugs, supports a boycott of the studio for using racial stereotypes films, and mocks his uncle as a sell out. In an uproar on stage Jonah exposes the hypocrisy and racism of the industry, and to his surprise gains him new fame, putting him in the same position as those he criticized.

Awards the book has won:
American Book Award, 1984

Other books by the same author:
The Life and Loves of Mr. Jiveass Nigger, 1969 (debut novel)

Other books you might like:
Ishmael Reed, *Reckless Eyeballing*, 1986
   Satire on extremist points-of-view and the turmoil caused in a young man's creative life as he is forced to rewrite his work.
Brent Wade, *Company Man*, 1992
   A man attemts to climb the business ladder and preserve his family but faces behind-the-secnes stresses and strains.
John Edgar Wideman, *Hurry Home*, 1970
   A young man becomes a reluctant activist and has an interracial affair during the Civil Rights era.
Dennis Williams, *Crossover*, 1992
   Events in the life of a young man during the Civil Rights era as he becomes a reluctant activist and has an interracial affair.
Al Young, *Sitting Pretty*, 1976
   A man lives in a residence hotel, works odd jobs to pay for his rent and wine, and rolls with the punches through good times and bad.

25

KAY BROWN, African American

Willy's Summer Dream

(New York: Harcourt Brace Jovanovich Gulliver Books, 1989)

Subject(s): Self-Confidence; Single Parent Families; Friendship
Age range(s): Grades 7-9
Major character(s): Willy Palmer, 14-Year-Old, Handicapped, African American
Time period(s): 1980s
Locale(s): New York, New York (Brooklyn)

Summary: What shy Willy has to look forward to this summer is the prospect of changing classes yet again. The principle is sending Willy to a special class and the guys on the playground call him retarded. As summer gets underway Willy meets his West Indian neighbor's niece Katherine. Hanging out together, Willy confesses his problems with his absent father, in making friends and with reading and math, and Katherine offers to tutor him. As they work together, his abilities and self-confidence improve. Later, he helps a 9-year-old in serious trouble, improving his confidence even more. Once back home, his father calls but Willy is more independent and doesn't feel he wants him in his life. In his final triumph, Willy scores big with the guys on the basketball court and starts making new friends.

About this book: This is a debut novel.

Where it's reviewed:
Booklist, February 1, 1990, page 1086
Kirkus Reviews, September 1, 1989, page 1324
Publishers Weekly, November 10, 1989, page 62
School Library Journal, December 1989, page 117

Other books you might like:

Virginia Hamilton, *Sweet Whispers, Brother Rush*, 1982
   A girl caring for her retarded older brother encounters the ghost of her dead uncle and comes to a deeper understanding of her family and herself.

Walter Dean Myers, *Fast Sam, Cool Clyde and Stuff*, 1975
   A teenager recalls significant events from his early life with friends in his Harlem neighborhood from being jailed to his first crush.

Walter Dean Myers, *Won't Know Till I Get There*, 1982
   The summer exploits of a 14-year-old whose his parents decide to adopt a youngster with a juvenile record and the boys get arrested together.

26

LINDA BEATRICE BROWN, African American

Crossing over Jordan

(New York: Ballantine Books, 1995)

Subject(s): Family Relations; Mothers and Daughters; Secrets
Age range(s): Adult
Major character(s): Story Temple Greene, Principal, Mother, African American; Hermine Rose Greene, Businesswoman, Paralegal, African American; Sadie Evelyn Temple, Grandmother, African American
Time period(s): 19th century; 21st century (1865-2012)
Locale(s): Hattenfield, North Carolina; Los Angeles, California

Summary: A saga, spanning four generations from the Civil War era to the early 21st century, about the ties shared by mothers and daughters. Sadie is scarred by the abuses she suffered, and they have an impact on her daughter Story's life. Story's daughter, Hermine, is challenged to overcome her mother's legacy of pain.

Where it's reviewed:
Library Journal, February 15, 1995, page 179
New York Times Book Review, February 19, 1995, page 21
Publishers Weekly, January 23, 1995, page 61

Other books by the same author:
Rainbow Roun' Mah Shoulder, 1984 (debut novel, as Linda Brown Bragg)

Other books you might like:

Arthur Flowers, *Another Good Loving Blues*, 1993
   A Mississippi Delta tale about the life of a "conjure" woman who is haunted by dreams of her abandonment as a child.

Marita Golden, *Long Distance Life*, 1989
   The murder of a young man in the 1980s and the evolution of his family from a 1920s sharecropping background.

Gloria Naylor, *Women of Brewster Place*, 1982
   The stories of seven women who live on the same dead-end street and redeem themselves.

Alice Walker, *The Color Purple*, 1982
   A powerful portrayal of emotional scars, the struggle to be authentic amidst great personal pain, and the transformation power of love.

Helen Elaine Lee, *The Serpent's Gift*, 1994
   Children and grandchildren of two intertwined families endure hardship and triumph as they help each other remember a history beyond their knowing.

27

WESLEY BROWN, African American

Darktown Strutters

(New York: Cane Hill Press, 1994)

Subject(s): Dancing; Freedom; Underground Railroad
Age range(s): Adult
Major character(s): Jim Crow, Dancer, Minstrel, Slave
Time period(s): 19th century (1830-1870)
Locale(s): Louisville, Kentucky; St. Louis, Missouri; New York, New York

Summary: Born into slavery, Jim is allowed to become a minstrel because of his inspired dancing. He travels throughout the South and North with the Featherstone Sisters Traveling Theater, often finding himself on the thin line between anger, violence and laughter in pre- and post-Civil War America.

Where it's reviewed:
New York Times Book Review, December 4, 1994, page 70
Kliatt, July 1994, page 6
Kirkus Review, December 15, 1993, page 1538
Library Journal, January 1994, page 158
Publishers Weekly, January 3, 1994, page 77

Other books by the same author:
Tragic Magic, 1978 (debut novel)

Other books you might like:

Leon Forrest, *Two Wings to Veil My Face*, 1983
   The Witherspoon family saga, from antebellum to contemporary times is concluded in this last volume of a trilogy.

Charles Johnson, *Oxherding Tale*, 1982
   The coming-of-age tale of a light-skinned young man in the plantation South as he struggles to gain his freedom and that of those he loves.

Julius Lester, *Do Lord Remember Me*, 1984
   The life of an eighty-year-old reverend who became known as the "colored Billy Graham."

28

ASHLEY BRYAN, Author/Illustrator, African American

The Cat's Purr

(New York: Atheneum, 1993)

Story type: Young Readers
Subject(s): Folk Tales; Animals; Friendship
Age range(s): Grades 1-3
Time period(s): Indeterminate Past
Locale(s): West Indies

Summary: Once, so the story goes, Cat and Rat lived in huts beside one another and were friends. Rat liked to copy Cat, so, their huts matched, Rat planted the same trees as Cat and wove the same mat for his corner. One day Cat's uncle came for a visit and gave him a small drum, teaching him the special way to play it and warning him that no one else should play it. When Rat hears the sweet sound of the drum, he longs to play it himself, but is warned by Cat not to. Despite his warning, however, Cat catches Rat playing the drum and they argue. Rat shoves the drum down Cat's throat. Swallowing his special drum Cat vows he will eat Rat if he ever catches him, and to this day they are friends no more. Consequently, Cat makes a special drum sound whenever he purrs.

About this book: Based on Elsie Clews Parsons' *Folklore Of the Antilles, French and English* (1936).

Other books by the same author:
The Story of Lightning & Thunder, 1993

Other books you might like:
Patricia C. McKissack, *Fossie and the Fox*, 1986
   The tale of a youngster sent to deliver fresh eggs to a neighbor who outsmarts an egg loving fox along the way trying to prove who he is.
Patricia C. McKissack, *Monkey-Monkey's Trick*, 1988
   An African folktale of a monkey who discovers he is being tricked by a hyena and plays his own trick on the hyena to get his new house built.
Patricia C. McKissack, *Nettie Jo's Friends*, 1989
   Needing to find a sewing needle to make a dress from her doll to be in the wedding with her a child asks three animal friends for help.
Angela Shelf Medearis, *Too Much Talk*, 1995
   Retells a traditional West African folktale of events that occur when a farmer hearing a yam talk runs off screaming in the heat of the day.
Walter Dean Myers, *Mr. Monkey and the Gotcha Bird: An Original Tale*, 1984
   Caught by the Gotcha Bird and afraid of being eaten a monkey uses his wits to outsmart the bird until he is no longer in danger.

29

ASHLEY BRYAN, Author/Illustrator, African American

The Story of Lightning & Thunder

(New York: Atheneum, 1993)

Story type: Young Readers
Subject(s): Folk Tales; Behavior
Age range(s): Grades 1-4
Time period(s): Indeterminate Past
Locale(s): Nigeria

Summary: The story is told that a time long ago thunder and lightning lived as mother and son in a village on the west coast of what is today called Africa. Rain and Ma Sheep Thunder were good friends and if the fields needed moisture Ma Sheep Thunder would go to the mountains and call until her friend Rain came. Once, during the King's procession in the village, he noted how unruly Ma Sheep Thunder's son was he moved them to live on the edge of town. Later, as Son Ram Lightening becomes more and more disruptive, the King banishes, him and his mother to a place far from the village. But when he starts a fire, the King sends him from the earth to live in the sky. Reaching their new home Ma Sheep Thunder often chases after her disobedient Son Ram Lightning when he causes trouble sometimes streaking back to earth striking anything in his path.

About this book: Based on folk stories from Southern Nigeria, West Africa.

Other books by the same author:
The Cat's Purr, 1985

Other books you might like:
Herschel Johnson, *A Visit to the Country*, 1989
   In the country at his grandparents' a child discovers a baby bird, feeds him as he grows and learns to fly, and later returns him to the wild.
Patricia C. McKissack, *A Million Fish. . .More or Less*, 1992
   Fishing in a strange bayou a boy catches a million fish and heads home with them but by the time he arrives his catch has shrunk to only three.
Patricia C. McKissack, *Monkey-Monkey's Trick*, 1988
   An African folktale of a monkey who discovers he is being tricked by a hyena and plays his own trick on the hyena to get his new house built.
Angela Shelf Medearis, *Too Much Talk*, 1995
   Retells a traditional West African folktale of events that occur when a farmer hearing a yam talk runs off screaming in the heat of the day.
Walter Dean Myers, *The Story of the Three Kingdoms*, 1995
   An original fable of how the rulers of the forest, the sea, and the sky were overcome by people telling stories by their fire that gave them wisdom.

30

ANITA RICHMOND BUNKLEY, African American

Black Gold

(New York: Dutton, 1994)

Subject(s): Family Relations; Historical; Interpersonal Relations
Age range(s): Adult
Major character(s): Leela Brandon Alexander Wilder, Niece, Mother, African American; Carey Wilder, Bastard Son, Gambler, African American; Victor Beaufort, Financier, Oil Industry Worker, African American
Time period(s): 19th century; 20th century (1891-1921)
Locale(s): Mexia, Texas

Summary: Leela marries a young landowner, Thomas Jacob ''T.J.'' Wilder, and has his son. When ''T.J.'' dies of tuberculosis, Leela is left on the brink of financial ruin. She makes a deal with wildcatter Victor Beaufort to save her land, and later they become engaged. Carey, ''T.J.'''s half-brother, becomes attracted to Leela. When he is killed, she is accused of his murder and the family secret they share is revealed.

Where it's reviewed:
Publishers Weekly, January 2, 1995, page 71
School Library Journal, November 1994, page 140

Other books by the same author:
Wild Embers, 1995
Emily, the Yellow Rose, 1989 (debut novel)

Other books you might like:
J. California Cooper, *In Search of Satisfaction*, 1994
   Two half-sisters born in the era of the plantation South have to deal with their parents' secret legacy and inheritance.

Rita Dove, *Through the Ivory Gate*, 1992

An unspoken family secret is revealed to a young woman who returns to her home after many years.

Marsha Hunt, *Joy*, 1991

A childless woman befriends a neighbor girl who sings with her sisters and grows up to become a star. Her untimely death reveals shocking secrets.

Paule Marshall, *Daughters*, 1991

A determined young woman struggles in her relationship with her political father. When she returns home for a visit, she makes an important decision.

31

ANITA RICHMOND BUNKLEY, African American

Emily, the Yellow Rose

(Houston: Rinard Publishing, 1989)

Subject(s): Historical; Interpersonal Relations

Age range(s): Adult

Major character(s): Emily D. West, Servant, Abuse Victim, African American; Joshua Kinney, Unemployed, African American; Clabe Ledbeder, Military Personnel, Caucasian

Time period(s): 1830s

Locale(s): New Washington, Texas (Mexican province)

Summary: Eager to earn a passport certifying she is free, Emily agrees to leave New York for the Mexican province of Texas. There she was to serve four years of indentured servitude working as a house servant for the white man who paid for her passage, Colonel Morgan. On arrival she finds herself at the center of an approaching military revolution. A soldier, Clabe, takes a liking to her and rapes her. She meets and falls in love with Joshua, who avenges her being raped. Suspected of plotting a slave revolt, Joshua has to flee and the two lovers are separated. They are reunited after a historic battle between the armies of Generals Sam Houston and Santa Anna.

About this book: Debut novel.

Other books by the same author:
Black Gold, 1994
Wild Embers, 1995

Other books you might like:

Connie Briscoe, *Sisters and Lovers*, 1994

A contemporary story about the lives and struggles of three sisters and the men they become involved with.

Nelson George, *Urban Romance*, 1993

A contemporary relationship of a young couple brought together by mutual friends experiencing love and heartbreak.

Terry McMillan, *Waiting to Exhale*, 1992

Contemporary account of the friendship of four women, their relationships with men, and their experiences with family and careers.

32

ANITA RICHMOND BUNKLEY, African American

Starlight Passage

(New York: Dutton, 1996)

Subject(s): Family Relations; Historical; Underground Railroad

Age range(s): Adult

Major character(s): Kiana Sheridan, Teacher, Genealogist, African American; Rex Tandy, Photojournalist, Historian, African American; Ida Wilson, Stepsister, African American

Time period(s): 1800s; 1990s (1993-1994)

Locale(s): Washington, District of Columbia; Dove Hollow, Tennessee (Smoky Mountains)

Summary: As part of her research for a doctoral dissertation on 19th century Black artisans, Kiana Sheridan tours the Underground Railroad. Kiana's search stretches from 1839 when a Bwerani princess is captured and sold into slavery, to the present day and the oral historians who can tell her what has been passed down to them. She also believes she is the great-great-granddaughter of Soddy Russell, a decorative glassworker whose pieces are now selling for thousands of dollars. Ida, Kiana's stepsister with whom she has had little contact over the years, has an interest in Soddy Glass for her own personal gain. Resentful that Kiana's mother married her father, Ida never made an effort to be a sister or even a friend. As Kiana gets closer finding out the link between her family and Soddy Russell, it is apparent that someone is determined to stop her, and that her life may be in danger. She finds not only the closely guarded secrets of her family's past but those of her own heart.

Other books by the same author:
Wild Embers, 1995
Black Gold, 1994
Emily, the Yellow Rose, 1989 (debut novel)

Other books you might like:

Linda Beatrice Brown, *Crossing over Jordan*, 1995

This saga binds the lives of four generations of mothers and daughters from the Civil War era to the early 21st century.

Lorene Cary, *The Price of a Child*, 1995

A woman walks from slavery to freedom under her slave owner's furious gaze in 1850s Philadelphia.

Leon Forrest, *The Bloodworth Orphans*, 1977

This second book of the Witherspoon trilogy depicts the slave-owning Bloodworth family as told through a narrator.

Leon Forrest, *Two Wings to Veil My Face*, 1983

The Witherspoon family saga from the pre-Civil War south to contemporary times is completed in this last title of the trilogy.

Helen Elaine Lee, *The Serpent's Gift*, 1994

Children and grandchildren of two intertwined families endure hardship and triumph as they help each other remember a history beyond their knowing.

Toni Morrison, *Song of Solomon*, 1977

A young man strikes out on his own in the 1950s to seek buried gold and instead discovers his buried heritage.

33

ANITA RICHMOND BUNKLEY, African American

Wild Embers
(New York: Dutton, 1995)

Story type: Adult; Romance
Subject(s): Historical; Interpersonal Relations; World War II
Age range(s): Adult
Major character(s): Janelle Roy, Nurse, Military Personnel, African American; Lance Fuller, Military Personnel, Pilot, African American; Dalton Graham, Lawyer, Caucasian
Time period(s): 1940s (1943)
Locale(s): Columbus, Ohio; Tuskegee, Alabama

Summary: When her patient dies, a private duty nurse is accused of misconduct by a rich white family. She hires Dalton, a white civil rights attorney to defend her and finds herself attracted to him. Unable to secure a new nursing position, Janelle joins the military where she becomes attracted to pilot Lance. Each keeps secrets of their past from one another and their romance blossoms until Lance sees Janelle with Dalton and breaks off their relationship. Discharged from the military after suffering injuries in an accident, Janelle works helping Dalton gather evidence for a civil rights case, and when her brother goes AWOL she asks Dalton for help. Wounded in action, Lance returns stateside unaware that Janelle has learned his secret.

Where it's reviewed:
Booklist, February 15, 1995, page 1059
Essence, February 1995, page 54
Kirkus Reviews, December 1, 1994, page 1556
Publishers Weekly, December 19, 1994, page 46
Book World, February 26, 1995, page 11

Other books by the same author:
Black Gold, 1994
Emily, the Yellow Rose, 1989 (debut novel)

Other books you might like:
Bebe Moore Campbell, *Brothers and Sisters*, 1994
  Contemporary account of the life of a career woman as she tries to climb the business ladder and maintain a social life, and of the people around her.
Albert French, *Holly*, 1995
  Involved in an interracial affair, a young white girl must flee her family and her community to find safety when she becomes pregnant.
Elaine Perry, *Another Present Era*, 1990
  A young architect drifts away from the lover she shares little with except their light skin and becomes involved with an older white artist.
Dennis Williams, *Crossover*, 1992
  Events in the life of a young man during the Civil Rights era as he becomes a reluctant activist and has an interracial affair.

34

OCTAVIA BUTLER, African American

Clay's Ark
(New York: St. Martin's Press, 1984)

Story type: Science Fiction
Subject(s): Space Exploration; Plague; Survival
Age range(s): Adult
Major character(s): Asa Elias ''Eli'' Doyle, Scientist, Spouse, Alien; Doctor Blake Jason Maslin, Widow(er) (interracial marriage), Father, Caucasian
Time period(s): 21st century (2021)
Locale(s): California (southern desert)

Summary: After World War III, the Earth starship *Clay's Ark* is sent on a mission to the planet Proxima Centauri II. Sabotaged within thirty miles of its return to Earth, the ship blows up with Eli as its sole survivor. With him as a host body, Eli has brought the first extraterrestrial life to Earth. For four years Eli lives on the desert ranch where he was once befriended by a white family. Infected by the plague he carried, the family has died with only the daughter, Meda, and her two sisters-in-law surviving. Fathering mutant children with the women, when more host bodies are needed, they capture people on the road. Now they have kidnapped white Doctor Blake Maslin and his 16-year-old interracial daughters Rahney and her twin sister Keira who is ill with leukemia. After being infected, the Maslins make a daring escape and the chase is on to bring them back to the ranch before they spread the organism and start an epidemic.

Where it's reviewed:
Ms., March 1986, page 74
School Library, Journal, December 1984, page 104

Other books by the same author:
Dawn, 1987 (Xenogenesis Trilogy)
Wild Seed, 1980 (Patternist series)
Survivor, 1978 (Patternist series)
Mind of My Mind, 1977 (Patternist series)
Patternmaster, 1976 (debut novel; Patternist series)

Other books you might like:
Samuel R. Delany, *Stars in My Pocket Like Grains of Sand*, 1984
  Futuristic fiction of the lives of two men brought together in a sexual relationship after one's world is destroyed and he is the lone survivor.
Percival Everett, *Zulus*, 1990
  On a barren planet in the future, a white woman is raped and seeks refuge with the rebels because her fertility is a threat to the government.
Nichelle Nichols, *Saturn's Child*, 1995
  Debut science fiction novel of adventures of a young woman genetically created of parents from different planets and endowed with special powers.

35

OCTAVIA BUTLER, African American

Dawn

(New York: Warner Books, 1987)

Story type: Adult
Series: Xenogenesis Trilogy
Subject(s): Genetic Engineering; Survival
Age range(s): Adult
Major character(s): Lilith Iyapo, Captive, Mother, African American; Jdahya, Alien (Oankali), Father, Teacher; Nikanj, Alien (Ooloi, a third gender), Healer, Student
Time period(s): Indeterminate Future (250 years after Earth destroyed)
Locale(s): Spaceship

Summary: Lilith is awakened to learn from Jdahya that humans destroyed earth centuries ago. She, along with some other humans, were rescued by the Oankali, an asexual race of extraterrestrial gene traders who are rebuilding earth. The humans were collected as trade partners for genetic engineering and will become extinct unless Lilith mates with an Ooloi, Nikanj, to be the mother of a new breed.

Where it's reviewed:
Hungry Mind Review, Fall 1995, page 55

Other books by the same author:
Parable of the Sower, 1993
Imago, 1989 (Xenogenesis Trilogy)
Adulthood Rites, 1987 (Xenogenesis Trilogy)
Patternmaster, 1976 (debut novel Patternist series)

Other books you might like:
Percival Everett, *Zulus*, 1990
    On a barren planet in the future, a white woman is raped and seeks refuge with the rebels because her fertility is a threat to the government.
Nichelle Nichols, *Saturn's Child*, 1995
    Debut science fiction novel of adventures of a young woman genetically created from parents of different planets and endowed with special powers.

36

OCTAVIA BUTLER, African American

Kindred

(New York: Doubleday, 1979)

Story type: Science Fantasy
Subject(s): Mental Telepathy; Race Relations; Time Travel
Age range(s): Adult
Major character(s): Dana Franklin, Time Traveller, Writer, African American; Rufus Weylin, 5-Year-Old, Caucasian
Time period(s): 1970s (1976); 1880s (1815)
Locale(s): Los Angeles, California; Baltimore, Maryland (rural)

Summary: Four months after the two writers met, 22-year-old Dana and her 34-year-old white co-worker Kevin were married, much to the dismay of their families. They had lived in their new home for only two days when the first strange occurrence happens: Dana vanishes before Kevin's eyes.

When she reappears wet and muddied, Dana tells Kevin of saving a small red-haired white boy from drowning in a river. She thinks she was gone only a few minutes until Kevin tells her she disappeared and reappeared in a matter of a few seconds. Later that day when Dana vanishes again and rescues the same red-haired white youngster Rufus, now a few years older, she discovers she has travelled back in time to the 19th century slavery era in rural Maryland. Reappearing minutes later when Dana uncontrollably vanishes once more the next morning she takes Kevin with her but she reappears alone. After eight days at home alone when she vanishes again Dana discovers years have passed since Kevin was left behind on the Weylin plantation and he has since gone north. Her ancestral connection to Rufus apparent, Dana hopes this time she can stay on the plantation long enough for Kevin to return so she can try to save them with what she has now been able to discover.

Where it's reviewed:
Belles Lettres, Spring 1989, page 23
Callaloo, Spring 1991, page 495
Ms., March 1986, Page 74

Other books by the same author:
Parable of the Sower, 1993
Dawn, 1987 (*Xenogenesis Trilogy*)
Clay's Ark, 1984
Wild Seed, 1980 (*Patternist Series*)
Patternmaster, 1976 (debut novel; *Patternist Series*)

Other books you might like:
Linda Beatrice Brown, *Crossing over Jordan*, 1995
    Saga of the ties binding the lives of four generations of mothers and daughters from the Civil War era to the early 21st century.
J. California Cooper, *Family*, 1991
    A young girl's narrative of her life in the plantation south and events in the lives of her children by her slave owner's son and of her grandchildren.
Leon Forrest, *Two Wings to Veil My Face*, 1983
    The Witherspoon family saga from the plantation south before the civil war to contemporary times is completed in this last title in their trilogy.
John Edgar Wideman, *Damballah*, 1981
    First title of the Homewood trilogy portraying the intergenerational history of a family from the 1840s-1960s in Pennsylvania.

37

OCTAVIA BUTLER, African American

Parable of the Sower

(New York: Warner Books, 1993)

Story type: Adult
Subject(s): Coming of Age; Survival
Age range(s): Adult
Major character(s): Lauren Oya Olamina, 15-Year-Old, Empath, African American
Time period(s): 21st century (2024)
Locale(s): Robledo, California (20 miles outside Los Angeles)

Summary: Hyperempathetic Lauren fears, yet prepares for, the day when her walled-in community will be invaded. When her family is killed during the invasion she escapes. Believing in the destiny of "earthseed" she journeys in a world of uncertainty and upheaval searching for a place to start her own colony.

Where it's reviewed:
Booklist, April 1, 1995, page 1399
Kliatt, May 1995, page 12
New York Times Book Review, January 29, 1995, page 24
School Library Journal, December 1994, page 27
Black Scholar, Fall 1994, page 52

Other books by the same author:
Dawn, 1987 (Xenogenesis Trilogy)
Clay's Ark, 1984
Kindred, 1979
Patternmaster, 1976 (Patternist series)

Other books you might like:
Percival Everett, *Zulus*, 1990
    On a barren planet in the future, a white woman is raped and seeks refuge with the rebels because her fertility is a threat to the government.
Nichelle Nichols, *Saturn's Child*, 1995
    Debut science fiction novel of the adventures of a young woman genetically created from parents of different planets and endowed with special powers.

38

OCTAVIA BUTLER, African American

Wild Seed
(New York: Doubleday, 1980)

Story type: Adult
Series: Patternist
Subject(s): Mental Telepathy; Mythology
Age range(s): Adult
Major character(s): Anyanwu, Immortal, Telepath, Healer (300-year-old); Doro, Immortal, Telepath, Mutant (4,000-year-old)
Time period(s): 17th century; 19th century (1690-1840)
Locale(s): Africa; Europe; New York, American Colonies

Summary: Depicts the origins of the Patternists to create a race of superhumans. Doro breeds his children in "seed villages" in Africa shipping them to the New World as part of his breeding program. Anyanwu is a powerful healer he had not discovered before, a "wild seed" whom he wants to breed and control. Changing shapes in host bodies, she is able to escape him to establish her own community before he finds her again.

About this book:

Other books by the same author:
Parable of the Sower, 1993
Clay's Ark, 1984
Survivor, 1978 (Patternist series)
Mind of My Mind, 1977 (Patternist series)
Patternmaster, 1976 (debut novel, Patternist series)

Other books you might like:
Nichelle Nichols, *Saturn's Child*, 1995
    Debut science fiction novel of adventures of a young woman genetically created of parents from different planets and endowed with special powers.

39

OCTAVIA BUTLER, African American

Adulthood Rites
(New York: Warner Books, 1988)

Series: Xenogenesis Trilogy
Subject(s): Genetic Engineering; Survival
Age range(s): Adult
Major character(s): Akin, African American, Child, Genetically Altered Being
Time period(s): Indeterminate Future
Locale(s): Earth

Summary: Lilith has given birth to Akin, a hybrid of alien and human. Saving the Earth, the alien Oankali have set up trade settlements for mating with humans. Humans, rejecting this arrangement, have set up their own resister villages. Akin is abducted by a raiding party of resisters and begins to develop sympathetic feelings for them. He is later rescued and sent to the home ship Chkahichdahk, where he convinces the Oankali to allow the humans to settle on Mars. Akin returns to the resister village to find it set aflame, and he escapes with those willing to go to Mars to save humanity.

Where it's reviewed:
Black American Literature Forum, Summer 1989, page 389
Essence, August 1988, page 658
Kirkus Reviews, May 1, 1988, page 658
Library Journal, June 15, 1988, page 70
Publishers Weekly, May 6, 1988, page 98

Other books by the same author:
Parable of the Sower, 1993
Imago, 1989 (Xenogenesis Trilogy)
Dawn, 1987 (Xenogenesis Trilogy)
Clay's Ark, 1984
Patternmaster, 1976 (debut novel, Patternist series)

Other books you might like:
Percival Everett, *Zulus*, 1990
    On a barren planet in the future, a white woman is raped and seeks refuge with the rebels because her fertility is a threat to the government.
Nichelle Nichols, *Saturn's Child*, 1995
    Debut science fiction novel of adventures of a young woman genetically created of parents from different planets and endowed with special powers.

40

JEANNETTE FRANKLIN CAINES, African American
STEVEN KELLOGG, Illustrator, Caucasian

Abby
(New York: Harper and Row, 1973)

Story type: Young Readers

Subject(s): Adoption; Brothers and Sisters
Age range(s): Grades 1-2
Major character(s): Abby, African American, Adoptee, Sister (younger)
Time period(s): 1970s
Locale(s): United States (unidentified city)

Summary: Looking at her baby book, preschooler Abby asks her mother questions about being adopted. She also asks her older brother Kevin what he said when he first saw her and why he doesn't like her being a girl. Abby is reassured that Kevin loves her and soon they are reading her baby book together. Kevin wants to take Abby to school for show and tell about being adopted. After Kevin leaves to go play with his friends, Abby suggests to her mother that they adopt a boy for Kevin.

About this book: Debut novel.

Other books by the same author:
I Need a Lunch Box, 1988
Chilly Stomach, 1986
Just Us Women, 1982
Window Wishing, 1980
Daddy, 1977

Other books you might like:
Lucille Clifton, *My Brother Fine with Me*, 1975
An 8-year-old sister helping her 5-year-old brother pack to run away discovers how lonely she is without him and is happier when he decides not to leave.
Angela Johnson, *One of Three*, 1991
The youngest of three sisters describes some of the many things they share together and when she gets to spend time alone with her parents.
Angela Johnson, *Tell Me a Story, Mama*, 1989
A little girl wanting her mama to tell her a story about when she was little has memorized the stories she's heard and tells them herself.
Dolores Johnson, *What Will Mommy Do When I'm at School?*, 1990
A child about to start school worries her mom will be lonely without her.
John Steptoe, *My Special Best Words*, 1974
A child tells about her daily routine of living her life with her 1-year-old baby brother, their daddy, and their babysitter.

41

JEANNETTE FRANKLIN CAINES, African American
PAT CUMMINGS, Illustrator, African American

Chilly Stomach
(New York: Harper and Row, 1986)

Story type: Young Readers
Subject(s): Fear; Parent and Child; Secrets
Age range(s): Grades 1-2
Major character(s): Sandy, Child, Niece, Caucasian
Time period(s): 1980s
Locale(s): United States (unidentified city)

Summary: Young white Sandy feels uncomfortable and gets a chilly stomach when her uncle Jim visits and he hugs and kisses her. It feels very different from when her mommy and daddy hug and kiss her. Fearing telling her parents about how she feels if uncle says he's going to spend the night she asks if she can stay over at her friend Jill's house. Jill has an uncle who hugs and kisses her too but she doesn't feel uncomfortable like Sandy. Sandy confides her secret about her uncle to Jill who says she'll tell her mother about it for her. When Sandy goes back home she wonders if her parents will believe her if she tells them how she feels and if Jill's mother will tell them about it.

Other books by the same author:
I Need a Lunch Box, 1988
Just Us Women, 1982
Window Wishing, 1980
Daddy, 1977
Abby, 1973 (debut)

Other books you might like:
John Steptoe, *Daddy Is a Monster. . .Sometimes*, 1980
A young sister and brother discussing what makes their daddy mad and turns him into a monster surprise him when they ask him why it happens.

42

JEANNETTE FRANKLIN CAINES, African American
RONALD HIMLER, Illustrator

Daddy
(New York: Harper and Row, 1977)

Story type: Young Readers
Subject(s): Fathers and Daughters; Divorce
Age range(s): Grades 1-2
Major character(s): Windy, Child of Divorced Parents, African American
Time period(s): 1970s
Locale(s): United States (unidentified city)

Summary: Sometimes Windy gets wrinkles in her stomach at night and at school worrying about her daddy. On Saturday her wrinkles go away when he comes to get her to go to his apartment. Along the way they laugh and play games together. At his apartment Paula greets her with a big hug and when they go grocery shopping she and daddy have to read the labels to Paula who refuses to wear her glasses in public. Her daddy colors with Windy and makes up her face with his shaving cream. They make a special dessert together for dinner and Paula makes her dresses. Windy can hardly wait until next Saturday when daddy comes to get her again.

Other books by the same author:
I Need a Lunch Box, 1988
Chilly Stomach, 1986
Just Us Women, 1982
Window Wishing, 1980
Abby, 1973 (debut)

Other books you might like:
Valerie Flournoy, *The Best Time of Day*, 1978
A child with a busy day of activities ahead with his mom, babysitter, friends, and relatives, looks forward to his daddy getting home from work.

Eloise Greenfield, *First Pink Light*, 1976
A child wants to stay awake until his daddy comes home so he can hide and surprise him but falls asleep waiting in a chair and daddy takes him to bed.

Dolores Johnson, *Papa's Stories*, 1994
Enjoying the stories her papa tells from her books a kindergartner says she'll teach him to read when she discovers he doesn't know how.

Ianthe Thomas, *Willie Blows a Mean Horn*, 1981
Proud of his jazz musician papa a young boy spends special times with him at the club where he plays and thinks of becoming a musician like his papa.

Sharon Dennis Wyeth, *Always My Dad*, 1995
A young girl remembers the summer she and her three younger brothers spent at their grandparents when their dad visited and how much she misses him.

43

JEANNETTE FRANKLIN CAINES, African American
PAT CUMMINGS, Illustrator, African American

I Need a Lunch Box
(New York: Harper and Row, 1988)

Story type: Young Readers
Subject(s): Brothers and Sisters; Wishes
Age range(s): Grades 1-2
Major character(s): Unnamed Character, Child, Brother, African American
Time period(s): 1980s
Locale(s): United States (unidentified city)

Summary: A preschooler wants to have a lunchbox like his older sister Doris. When their dad took them to buy new shoes last week he saw the lunch box he wants in the store window. Getting home he sees all the new things Doris is getting to be ready for school. He imagines all the things he could keep in his lunch box and dreams of what he would do if he had a lunch box for every day in the week. On the day Doris starts school he feels sad when their mommy gives her her lunch box until his daddy gives him his special surprise.

Other books by the same author:
Chilly Stomach, 1986
Just Us Women, 1982
Window Wishing, 1980
Daddy, 1977
Abby, 1973 (debut)

Other books you might like:
Lucille Clifton, *Everett Anderson's Year*, 1974
Activities in a young child's life are depicted for the twelve calendar months in a series of poems capturing his joys, sorrows, and confusions.

Angela Johnson, *One of Three*, 1991
The youngest of three sisters describes some of the many things they share together and when she gets to spend time alone with her parents.

Brian Pinkney, *Max Found Two Sticks*, 1994
A young boy uses two twigs to play rhythms on buckets, hatboxes, bottles, and garbage cans until a drummer tosses him a pair of drum sticks.

Alice Walker, *Finding the Green Stone*, 1991
A young brother and sister have identical green stones and when the brother's is lost his sister, parents, and neighbors rally to help him find it.

Mildred Pitts Walter, *Two and Too Much*, 1990
Trying to help his mama a 7-year-old watches his 2-year-old sister who gets into all kinds of things until she tires herself out and falls asleep.

44

JEANNETTE FRANKLIN CAINES, African American
PAT CUMMINGS, Illustrator, African American

Just Us Women
(New York: Harper and Row, 1982)

Story type: Young Readers
Subject(s): Aunts and Uncles; Adventure and Adventurers
Age range(s): Grades 1-2
Major character(s): Unnamed Character, Child, African American, Sister
Time period(s): 1980s
Locale(s): North Carolina (roadways)

Summary: A youngster narrates her adventures when Aunt Martha gets a new car and they drive to North Carolina together. She tells of their preparations for the trip, the extra road maps they're taking, and the special lunches they pack. Along the way they get to stop at roadside markets, walk in the rain, and talk with farmers on the back roads. After stopping to take pictures they eat in a fancy restaurant and later pick wild mushrooms. When they finally arrive and everyone wonders what took them so long they explain they had a lot of girl talk to do, it was their special time for just us women.

Awards the book has won:
Reading Rainbow Book, 1984

Other books by the same author:
I Need a Lunch Box, 1988
Chilly Stomach, 1986
Window Wishing, 1980
Daddy, 1977
Abby, 1973 (debut)

Other books you might like:
Elizabeth Fitzgerald Howard, *Aunt Flossie's Hats (and Crab Cakes Later)*, 1991
Visits to their great-great-aunt Flossie's are special times for two young girls and they always look forward to eating crab cakes afterwards.

Angela Johnson, *Tell Me a Story, Mama*, 1989
A little girl wanting her mama to tell her a story about when she was little has memorized the stories she's heard and tells them herself.

June Jordan, *Kimako's Story*, 1981
A 7-year-old takes on the responsibility of caring for her neighbors big Airedale dog and gets to see more of her city surroundings.

Gloria Jean Pinkney, *Back Home*, 1992
Raised in the city an 8-year-old visits her relatives for the

first time in her memory in the place where she was born in the country.

45

JEANNETTE FRANKLIN CAINES, African American
KEVIN BROOKS, Illustrator, African American

Window Wishing

(New York: Harper and Row, 1980)

Story type: Young Readers
Subject(s): Grandparents; Vacations; Brothers and Sisters
Age range(s): Grades 1-2
Time period(s): 1980s
Locale(s): United States

Summary: A girl and her young brother Bootsie have a special grandma. They spend their vacations with their grandma Mag who wears sneakers all the time and often lets them walk barefoot. They fish together, shop, and share special treats. Grandma Mag even lets them set the table with mix-matched forks that she's saved over the years. Going downtown together with Grandma Mag they window wish. Each has special wish days and on Grandma's Saturday wish day they picnic at the cemetery where their Grandpa is buried. On Sunday they read comics together and for his birthday Bootsie is promised a special week of wishes for every day.

Other books by the same author:
I Need a Lunch Box, 1988
Chilly Stomach, 1986
Just Us Women, 1982
Daddy, 1977
Abby, 1973 (debut)

Other books you might like:
Donald Crews, *Bigmama's*, 1991
　Recalls the summer exploits of a youngster in the 1940s when he, his brother, sisters, and parents visit his grandparents in the country.
Valerie Flournoy, *The Patchwork Quilt*, 1985
　When her grandma becomes ill a youngster and her mama work on her quilt until she recovers and puts the finishing touches on it herself.
Valerie Flournoy, *Tanya's Reunion*, 1995
　A youngster traveling with her grandma to the family farm for a reunion discovers a special memento for her grandma of days gone by.
Eloise Greenfield, *Grandmama's Joy*, 1980
　Worried when she see's her grandmama sad a child learns why and tries the best way she knows how to put a smile back on her face again.
Francine Haskins, *Things I Like about Grandma*, 1992
　A child enjoys her special relationship with her grandma as they do things together and the fun times they have watching sports with granddaddy.

46

BARBARA CAMPBELL, African American

A Girl Called Bob and a Horse Called Yoki

(New York: Dial, 1982)

Subject(s): Friendship; Family Relations; Honesty
Age range(s): Grades 4-6
Major character(s): Barbara Ann ''Bobby'' Weathers, 8-Year-Old, African American; Charles ''Chuckie'' Williams, 10-Year-Old, African American
Time period(s): 1940s (1942)
Locale(s): St. Louis, Missouri

Summary: The war has started, and Barbara's dad has joined the navy and gone away. Barbara, nicknamed ''Bob'', has a best friend named Shirley. Shirley wants ''Bob'' to be baptized with her this Easter but ''Bob'' is unsure if she is ready for the new responsibility. When she and school mate Chuckie hide the grocer's horse Yoki to save him from the glue factory ''Bob'' worries even more about being ready for baptism. ''Bob'' consoles Shirley when her dad is killed in the war, which makes her concerned about her own dad. With baptism approaching ''Bob'' decides to be honest and confess the truth about hiding Yoki. On Easter she is in store for a special reward: her dad comes home on leave and ''Bob'' looks forward to their being together.

About this book: Debut novel.

Where it's reviewed:
Booklist, August 1982, page 1521
New York Times Book Review, July 4, 1982, page 13
School Library Journal, April 1982, page 67

Other books you might like:
Eloise Greenfield, *Koya Delaney and the Good Girl Blues*, 1992
　A sixth grader, caught in the middle when her best friend and her sister have a fight, struggles with mixed emotions about knowing who her real friends are.
Joyce Hansen, *The Gift Giver*, 1980
　A young girl and her fifth grade friends come to like a new boy in their class and are surprised when they discover he is a foster child.
Emily Moore, *Just My Luck*, 1982
　Dreaming of buying her own puppy a 9-year-old teams up with a schoolmate to solve the mystery of a missing dog so she can get the reward money.
Connie Porter, *Meet Addy: An American Girl*, 1993
　A 9-year-old girl and her mother escape a life of cruel slavery to freedom in Philadelphia during the Civil War.
Mildred D. Taylor, *Song of the Trees*, 1975
　First of a series of stories about the Logan family in the 1930s in rural Mississippi as they struggle to make ends meet and keep their land intact.

47

BEBE MOORE CAMPBELL, African American

Brothers and Sisters

(New York: G.P. Putnam's Sons, 1994)

Subject(s): Friendship; Interpersonal Relations; Race Relations
Age range(s): Adult
Major character(s): Esther Jackson, Banker (regional operations manager), Businesswoman (middle management), African American; Mallory Post, Banker (commercial loan officer), Businesswoman (vice president), Caucasian
Time period(s): 1990s (1992)
Locale(s): Los Angeles, California

Summary: Esther wants to advance in her banking career and, when the bank president hires a new executive, she is optimistic he might be able to help her succeed. Two situations may impact Esther's career goals. First, her friend Mallory accuses the new executive of sexual harassment. Second, a new teller hired by Esther is suspected of taking money.

Where it's reviewed:
Kirkus Reviews, June 1, 1994, page 716
Library Journal, August 1994, page 124
Publishers Weekly, July 4, 1994, page 51

Other books by the same author:
Your Blues Ain't Like Mine, 1992 (debut novel)

Other books you might like:
Connie Briscoe, *Sisters and Lovers*, 1994
    This contemporary story is about the lives and struggles of three sisters and the men they become involved with.
Nelson George, *Urban Romance*, 1993
    This story tells the contemporary relationship of a young couple brought together by mutual friends as they experience love and heartbreak.
Brent Wade, *Company Man*, 1992
    Behind-the-scenes stresses and strains faced by a man attempting to climb the career ladder and preserve his family.
Terry McMillan, *Waiting to Exhale*, 1992
    This contemporary account is about the friendship of four women, their relationships with men, and their experiences with family and careers.

48

BEBE MOORE CAMPBELL, African American

Your Blues Ain't Like Mine

(New York: G.P. Putnam's Sons, 1992)

Subject(s): Family Relations; Prejudice; Race Relations
Age range(s): Adult
Major character(s): Delotha Todd, Mother, Businesswoman, African American; Ida Long, Bastard Daughter, Activist, African American; Lily Cox, Spouse, Mother, Caucasian
Time period(s): 1900s (1950-1980)
Locale(s): Hopewell, Mississippi; Chicago, Illinois

Summary: This story covers the evolution and aftermath of 30 years of race relations in a small town. Delotha's 15-year-old son, Armstrong, is murdered in a small southern town for reportedly offending a caucasian woman, Lily Cox. Lily confides in Ida about the incident and they both hide the truth when Lily's husband Floyd gets tried for the murder. Delotha returns to Chicago after her son's murder becomes an international news event. His murder haunts Delotha throughout her life, especially when she has another son. Ida by accident, discovers the secret of her caucasian father and why the truth was kept from her. Revealing it can have a major impact on the town and its people.

About this book: This is the debut novel of the author.

Where it's reviewed:
Bloomsbury Review, July 1994, page 3
Black Scholar, Summer 1993, page 97

Other books by the same author:
Brothers and Sisters, 1994

Other books you might like:
Cyrus Colter, *A Chocolate Soldier*, 1988
    This story unfolds another story whereby a tale is told of a young idealist who murders his caucasian employer and he himself is killed by a mob lynching.
Albert French, *Billy*, 1993
    When a 10-year-old boy is sentenced to death in the electric chair for killing a caucasian teenaged female, racial hatreds ignite in Mississippi during the 1930s.
Ernest J. Gaines, *A Lesson before Dying*, 1993
    This historical fiction set in Louisiana during the 1940s relates the impact a young man's pending execution for murder has on the community and on his family and friends.
Marita Golden, *Long Distance Life*, 1989
    These episodes relate the murder of a young grandson in the 1980s and the evolution of his family from a sharecropping background of the 1920s.

49

XAM WILSON CARTIER, African American

Be-Bop, Re-Bop

(New York: Ballantine Books, 1987)

Subject(s): Divorce; Family Relations; Self-Reliance
Age range(s): Adult
Major character(s): Unnamed Character, Divorced Person, African American, Unemployed
Time period(s): 1980s
Locale(s): St. Louis, Missouri; San Francisco, California

Summary: A young mother, the narrator of this novel, faces the challenge of living life on her own with a four-year-old daughter in tow. Trying to find the courage to leave her abusive marriage, she fortifies herself with the memories of her parents' struggles as she was growing up. She remembers her father's wisdom and support and her mother's desire for a better life. Armed with a family history of struggle and survival, she leaves.

About this book: Debut novel.

Other books by the same author:
Muse-Echo Blues, 1991

Other books you might like:

Alice Childress, *A Short Walk*, 1973
A woman escapes an abusive marriage and journeys to Harlem in the 1940s.

Terry McMillan, *Waiting to Exhale*, 1992
Contemporary account describes the friendship of four women, their relationships with men, and their experiences with family and careers.

Paule Marshall, *Daughters*, 1991
A determined young woman struggles in her relationship with her political father and when she returns home for a visit makes an important decision.

Gloria Naylor, *Women of Brewster Place*, 1982
These seven stories describe the women who live on the dead-end street of Brewster Place and what brings them together in their own redemption.

Ntozake Shange, *Liliane: Resurrection of the Daughter*, 1994
A young woman in psychotherapy reveals how she coped with family upheavals, romances and friendships, as well as racism and bigotry.

50

XAM WILSON CARTIER, African American

Muse-Echo Blues
(New York: Harmony Books, 1991)

Subject(s): Musicians
Age range(s): Adult
Major character(s): Kat, Composer, Musician, African American
Time period(s): 1990s
Locale(s): San Francisco, California

Summary: Kat is suffering an acute case of composer's block. She finds inspiration in the life and times of fantasy soul sister Kitty, who mixes and mingles with jazz greats of the 1940s.

About this book: This work is presented in a stylistic jazz improvisation of prose.

Where it's reviewed:
Essence, June 1992, page 54
Library Journal, April 15, 1991, page 124
Publishers Weekly, March 22, 1991, page 72

Other books by the same author:
Be-Bop, Re-Bop, 1987 (debut novel)

Other books you might like:

Walter Mosley, *RL's Dream*, 1995
An aging blues musician befriends a young caucasian woman who is haunted by an incestuous past. This story recounts exploits from the musician's past as they become friends.

Elaine Perry, *Another Present Era*, 1990
A young architect drifts away from the lover she has little to share with except their light skin and she becomes involved with an older caucasian white artist.

51

LORENE CARY, African American

The Price of a Child
(New York: Alfred A. Knopf, 1995)

Subject(s): Historical; Underground Railroad
Age range(s): Adult
Major character(s): Mercer Gray, Mother, Slave, African American
Time period(s): 1850s (1855)
Locale(s): Philadelphia, Pennsylvania

Summary: Ginnie finds an opportunity to literally walk away from slavery to freedom under her owner's furious gaze. Befriended by the Quick family, she reinvents herself as Mercer Gray, lecturing in the cause of abolition, falling in love, and planning to rescue the baby she left behind.

About this book: This is the author's debut novel.

Where it's reviewed:
Essence, July 1995, page 56
Library Journal, April 15, 1995, page 111
New York Times Book Review, June 18, 1995, page 12

Other books you might like:

Barbara Chase-Riboud, *The President's Daughter*, 1994
This work chronicles the life of Harriet Hemings, the daughter of miscegenation in the interracial affair of President Thomas Jefferson. It relates her passing for white.

J. California Cooper, *Family*, 1991
This is a narrative of a young girl's life during the plantation era of the South. Included are the events in the lives of her children by her slave owner's son and the lives of her grandchildren.

Leon Forrest, *Two Wings to Veil My Face*, 1983
This last title in the Witherspoon family's saga during the plantation era of the South before the Civil War to contemporary times.

Toni Morrison, *Beloved*, 1987
This is a story about a mother who escapes from slavery and who kills her baby to keep her former owner from stealing her. She is then haunted and consumed by the baby's ghost.

Dorothy West, *The Wedding*, 1995
This saga about five generations of two families with mixed race ancestry, relates the events in the lives of children from a new contemporary generation.

52

BARBARA CHASE-RIBOUD, African American

Echo of Lions
(New York: Morrow, 1989)

Subject(s): Freedom; Historical; Race Relations
Age range(s): Adult
Major character(s): Sengbe "Joseph Cinque" Pieh, Father, Spouse, African (Mende); President John Quincy Adams, Aged Person (seventy-three), Historical Figure (sixth US President), Caucasian; Kaweli "James Covey", Sailor (gunner), Linguist, African (Mende)

Time period(s): 1800s (1839-1842)
Locale(s): Africa (Mendeland); Hartford, Connecticut; Washington, District of Columbia

Summary: This epic tale is about the "only successful slave rebellion in the history of America and American jurisprudence" aboard the historic schooner the *Amistad*. Kidnapped from his African homeland, Sengbe Pieh, or "Joseph Cinque," leads a mutiny aboard the schooner and attempts to sail back to Africa. Deceived by their kidnappers, the schooner drifts into the New York harbor where the Africans are detained and put on trial. Hearing of their plight, Kaweli, also known as " James Covey," himself an African, comes to serve as their interpreter. When their case reaches the Supreme Court, President John Quincy Adams successfully argues their defense.

Where it's reviewed:
Essence, February 1989, page 30
New York Times Book Review, May 14, 1989, page 22
Publishers Weekly, December 16, 1988, page 68

Other books by the same author:
The President's Daughter, 1994
Valide, 1986
Sally Hemings, 1979 (debut novel)

Other books you might like:
Charles Johnson, *Middle Passage*, 1990
   A young man mistakenly stows away on a slave ship bound for Africa, where he must endure storms, mutiny, and illness before the journey ends.
Louise Meriwether, *Fragments of the Ark*, 1994
   This historical tale is about a South Carolina slave who steals a Confederate gunboat, delivers it to the Union Navy, and later becomes its captain.

53

BARBARA CHASE-RIBOUD, African American

The President's Daughter
(New York: Crown Publishers, 1994)

Subject(s): Historical; Race Relations; Identity
Age range(s): Adult
Major character(s): Harriet Hemings, Daughter (Jefferson's illegitimate), Historical Figure, African American (passes for white); Sally Hemings, Historical Figure, Mother (of seven children), African American; President Thomas Jefferson, Father (seven children by Sally Heming), Political Figure (third President of the U.S.), Historical Figure
Time period(s): 1800s
Locale(s): Monticello, Virginia; Philadelphia, Pennsylvania

Summary: This story chronicles the life of Harriet Hemings, daughter of miscegenation in the interracial affair of President Thomas Jefferson with his mistress Sally Hemings. At age twenty-one Harriet leaves her father's plantation and crosses the "color line" to pass for white. She reveals her secret at age seventy-five to her granddaughter after having dealt all her life with society's "colorphobia."

About this book: Sally Hemings is the subject of the author's debut novel.

Where it's reviewed:
Booklist, September 1, 1994, page 23
Kirkus Reviews, July 15, 1994, page 930
Publishers Weekly, August 8, 1994, page 363

Other books by the same author:
Echo of Lions, 1989
Valide, 1986
Sally Hemings, 1979 (debut novel)

Other books you might like:
J. California Cooper, *Family*, 1991
   This is a narrative of a young girl's life during plantation era of the South. Included are the events in the lives of her children by her slave owner's son and the lives of her grandchildren.
Leon Forrest, *Two Wings to Veil My Face*, 1983
   This last title of their trilogy tells of the Witherspoon family's saga during the plantation era of the South before the Civil War to contemporary times.
Charles Johnson, *Oxherding Tale*, 1982
   This coming-of-age tale is about a light-skinned young man during the plantation era of the South as he struggles to gain his freedom and the freedom of those he loves.
Toni Morrison, *Beloved*, 1987
   This story tells about a mother who escapes from slavery, and who kills her baby to keep her former owner from stealing her. She is then haunted and consumed by the baby's ghost.
Dorothy West, *The Wedding*, 1995
   This saga about five generations of two families with mixed race ancestry, relates the events in the lives of children from a new contemporary generation.

54

BARBARA CHASE-RIBOUD, African American

Sally Hemings
(New York: Viking Press, 1979)

Subject(s): Historical; Family Relations; Race Relations
Age range(s): Adult
Major character(s): Sally Hemings, Historical Figure, Mother, African American; President Thomas Jefferson, Father (seven children by Sally), Historical Figure (third U.S. President), Caucasian; Nathan Langdon, Lawyer (census recorder), Caucasian
Time period(s): 18th century; 19th century (1787-1835)
Locale(s): Albemarle County, Virginia; Monticello, Virginia; Paris, France

Summary: Chronicles the life and interracial affair of Sally Hemings, the mistress of President Thomas Jefferson in his crime of miscegenation, and how census records were falsified to hide their crime. Over their thirty-eight year relationship they had seven children, among them Harriet Hemings, the subject of a later novel by this author.

About this book: Debut novel.

Awards the book has won:
Janet Heidinger Kafka Prize for Excellence in Fiction, 1979

Other books by the same author:
The President's Daughter, 1994

Echo of Lions, 1989
Valide, 1986

Other books you might like:
J. California Cooper, *Family*, 1991
   A young girl's narrative of her life in the plantation South and events in the lives of her children by her slave owner's son and of her grandchildren.
Leon Forrest, *Two Wings to Veil My Face*, 1983
   The Witherspoon family saga from the plantation South before the civil war to contemporary times is completed in this last title in the trilogy.
Charles Johnson, *Oxherding Tale*, 1982
   The coming-of-age tale of a light-skinned young man in the plantation South as he struggles to gain his freedom and that of those he loves.
Toni Morrison, *Beloved*, 1987
   A mother who escaped slavery kills her baby to keep her former owner from stealing her, and is then haunted and consumed by the baby's ghost.
Dorothy West, *The Wedding*, 1995
   Saga of five generations of two families of mixed race ancestry, and events in the lives of children from a new contemporary generation.

55

ALICE CHILDRESS, African American

A Hero Ain't Nothin' but a Sandwich
(New York: Putnam, 1973)

Subject(s): Family Relations; Drugs; Peer Pressure
Age range(s): Grades 7-9
Major character(s): Benjie Johnson, 13-Year-Old, Addict, African American
Time period(s): 1970s
Locale(s): New York, New York (Harlem)

Summary: Abandoned by his father and resentful of his mother's boyfriend, Benjie is a troubled youngster. Ditching school he hangs out with friends at Tiger's apartment where Kenny baits him into taking drugs. Afraid of appearing ''chicken,'' Benjie feels the drugs won't affect him and he can stop whenever he wants. Soon he is hooked. After a stay at the hospital in detox Benjie wants to do better but has a hard time. When Kenny dies from an overdose and Benjie's mother insists he goes to the funeral, Benjie wonders what she would think if she knew Kenny was the one who pressured him into drugs. Seemingly making peace with his mother's boyfriend after he saves Benjie's life he wants him for his dad yet leaves him stranded waiting for Benjie to show up at the treatment center.

About this book: Debut novel (juvenile). Author died in 1994.
Awards the book has won:
Coretta Scott King Honor Book, 1974
Other books by the same author:
Those Other People, 1989 (young adults)
Rainbow Jordan, 1981 (young adults)
Other books you might like:
Jess Mowry, *Way Past Cool*, 1992
   Two rival gangs must put aside their differences to solve

their common problem when a drug dealer tries to stir up trouble between them.
Walter Dean Myers, *Scorpions*, 1988
   A gun changes the lives of a young boy and his Puerto Rican friend when they are forced into being involved with a street gang.

56

ALICE CHILDRESS, African American

Rainbow Jordan
(New York: Coward, McCann and Geoghegan, 1981)

Subject(s): Mothers and Daughters; Foster Homes; Teen Relationships
Age range(s): Grades 8-10
Major character(s): Rainbow Jordan, 14-Year-Old, Foster Child, African American; Josephine ''Josie'' Lamont, Foster Parent, Housewife, African American
Time period(s): 1980s
Locale(s): United States

Summary: Her parents were teenagers when Rainbow was born, and after a short marriage they separated. Now Rainbow is fourteen and more like a sister than a daughter to her mother, and her father lives out of state. Left alone much of the time, ''Rainey'' is several times placed in the Lamonts' home by Social Services. With her own marriage disintegrating, Josie Lamont is determined to help Rainbow find her way around her boyfriend's pressure to have sex.

About this book: Author died in 1994.
Where it's reviewed:
Children's Literature Association Quarterly, Summer 1988, page 70
MS., August 1987, page 160
School Library Journal, December 1990, page 40
Awards the book has won:
Coretta Scott King Honor Book, 1982
Other books by the same author:
Those Other People, 1989 (young adults)
A Hero Ain't Nothin' but a Sandwich, 1973 (debut novel, young adult)
Other books you might like:
Tina McElroy Ansa, *Baby of the Family*, 1989
   Coming-of-age tale set in the 1950s of a young girl who was born in a small town with the gift of a thin veil (caul) over her face.
Virginia Hamilton, *A Little Love*, 1984
   A teenage girl has an emptiness food cannot fill: she misses her father, and in her search for him she finds new strengths in herself.
Ntozake Shange, *Betsey Brown*, 1985
   Exploits of a young girl coming-of-age in an era of school integration, the worries of her family and the discoveries she makes at her new school.
Charlotte Sherman, *One Dark Body*, 1993
   Incidents in the life of a young girl, abandoned at birth, dealing with the return of her mother and her friend's entry into manhood.

A.J. Verdelle, *The Good Negress*, 1995
A young country girl who moves to the city wants more from life than cooking, cleaning, and washing, and is encouraged to reach higher by her teacher.

57

ALICE CHILDRESS, African American

A Short Walk

(New York: Coward, McCann and Geoghegan, 1979)

Subject(s): Foster Families; Interpersonal Relations; Parenthood
Age range(s): Adult
Major character(s): Cora James, Orphan, Mother, African American; Kojie Anderson, Maintenance Worker, Widow(er), African American; Cecil Green, Activist, Father, African American
Time period(s): 1900s; 1940s
Locale(s): Charleston, South Carolina; New York, New York (Harlem)

Summary: Cora learns that her real mother died giving birth to her, her real father is white, and the couple who gave her their name and raised her are really her foster parents. After her foster father dies Cora accepts a marriage proposal from Kojie, an older prosperous widower and moves into his home. Kojie abuses Cora so she escapes to New York where she runs into her first love, Cecil, who is active in the Garvey movement. Rekindling their attraction for one another Cora becomes pregnant and gives birth to their illegitimate daughter Delta. As the years pass Cora learns to make a living for herself and Delta, and faces the realities of life and parenthood.

About this book: Author died in 1994.

Other books by the same author:
Those Other People, 1989 (young adult)
Rainbow Jordan, 1981 (young adult)
A Hero Ain't Nothin' but a Sandwich, 1973 (debut novel, young adult)

Other books you might like:
Linda Brown Bragg, *Rainbow Round' Mah Shoulder*, 1984
Episodes spanning forty years of the life of a woman who was called to heal and help other people, and her loves and losses.
Arthur Flowers, *Another Good Loving Blues*, 1993
A Mississippi Delta tale of exploits in the life of a "conjure" woman haunted by dreams of the mother who abandoned her as a child.
Marita Golden, *Long Distance Life*, 1989
Episodes in the murder of a young grandson in the 1980s and the evolution of his family from a sharecropping background of the 1920s.
Terri McMillan, *Mama*, 1987
A proud and feisty mother does her best to provide for her five children through three marriages and uncertain times.
Paule Marshall, *Praisesong for the Widow*, 1983
Disturbed by dreams, a middle-aged widow away on a trip finds self-renewal and returns with a plan to connect her past and improve her future.

58

ALICE CHILDRESS, African American

Those Other People

(New York: G.P. Putnam's Sons, 1989)

Subject(s): Homosexuality/Lesbianism; Racism; Rape
Age range(s): Grades 8-12
Major character(s): Jonathan Barnett, 17-Year-Old, Homosexual, Caucasian; Theodora Lynn, 15-Year-Old, Abuse Victim, Caucasian; Tyrone Tate, 14-Year-Old, Student, African American
Time period(s): 1980s
Locale(s): Minitown

Summary: Jonathan is uncomfortable with his own homosexuality, and so takes a break between high school and college to figure things out. When the opportunity arises to student-teach in a new computer program at Minitown High School, he moves to the small town and tries to get along. Also trying to get along in all-white Minitown are the Tates and their kids Tyrone and Susan, who are just trying to get their piece of the American Dream. When Theodora Lynn levels accusations of attempted rape at a popular teacher, Tyrone and Jonathan find they are the only witnesses. Ugly hatreds erupt as a cross is burned next to the Tates' home and Jonathan receives threatening phone calls. Jonathan must make a decision whether or not to appear before the board and admit who he is and what he knows.

About this book: Author died in 1994.

Where it's reviewed:
Booklist, January 1, 1989, page 778
Horn Book Magazine, May 1989, page 153
Kirkus Reviews, December 15, 1988, page 1810
Publishers Weekly, November 25, 1988, page 67
School Library Journal, February 1989, page 99

Other books by the same author:
Rainbow Jordan, 1981
A Hero Ain't Nothin' but a Sandwich, 1973 (debut novel, young adult)

Other books you might like:
David Haynes, *Right by My Side*, 1993
A high school student writes down his experiences in order to figure things out about his father, his mother and himself.
Jacqueline Woodson, *From the Notebooks of Melanin Sun*, 1995
A 13-year-old boy's world is turned upside down and he has to confront his prejudices when his mother tells him she is in love with a white woman.

59

DEBBI CHOCOLATE, African American
MELODYE ROSALES, Illustrator, African American

On the Day I Was Born

(New York: Scholastic Inc., 1995)

Story type: Young Readers
Subject(s): Babies; Fathers and Sons; Parenthood

Age range(s): Grades 1-2
Major character(s): ''Pine'', Child (boy), Nephew, African American
Time period(s): 1990s
Locale(s): United States (unidentified city)

Summary: Following the African tradition a newborn baby, nicknamed Pines, is welcomed into the family. The child's father holds him to the heavens in the full moon's light. Among the gifts ''Pine'' receives are a kofia, or crown, as well as a kente cloth to wear when he is older. As they feast the family talks about who ''Pine'' resembles. He is blessed and given his name.

About this book: Inspired by the 1977 Alex Haley film *Roots*. Contains a list with meanings of African Adinka symbols created by the Asante peoples of Ghana.

Other books by the same author:
Elizabeth's Wish, 1994 (NEATE book 2)
NEATE to the Rescue, 1992 (NEATE book 1)

Other books you might like:
Lucille Clifton, *Everett Anderson's Nine Month Long*, 1978
With a new stepfather a young boy now anticipates the arrival of a new stepbrother or sister and experiences the ups and downs of waiting.
Eloise Greenfield, *She Come Bringing Me That Little Baby Girl*, 1974
Jealous at first when his mama brings him a baby sister a young boy later feels a new sense of responsibility and pride as a big brother.
John Steptoe, *Birthday*, 1972
On his eighth birthday the firstborn of the community celebrates with his family and friends and wishes for their future together.
Mildred Pitts Walter, *My Mama Needs Me*, 1983
When his newborn baby sister arrives home a young boy is overcome by feelings of responsibility until his mama lets him know it's still ok to play.

60

MAXINE CLAIR, African American

Rattlebone

(New York: Farrar, Straus and Giroux, 1994)

Subject(s): City Life; Coming of Age; Family Relations
Age range(s): Grades 9-Adult
Major character(s): Irene Wilson, Teenager, African American; Pearlean ''Pearl'' Wilson, Mother, Spouse, African American; James ''Shorty'' Wilson, Construction Worker, Father, African American
Time period(s): 1950s
Locale(s): Rattlebone, Missouri

Summary: This story portrays Irene's eventful life in a small town from third grade to high school. It encompasses her teacher's affair with her father, the unwed pregnancy of a classmate, the town's catastrophic plane crash, her sorority interview, and the future's prospects for her parents and herself.

About this book: This is the author's debut novel.

Where it's reviewed:
Kirkus Reviews, March 15, 1994, page 320
Publishers Weekly, April 18, 1994. page 43

Awards the book has won:
Black Caucus of the A.L.A., First Novelist Award, 1995

Other books you might like:
Tina McElroy Ansa, *Baby of the Family*, 1989
This coming-of-age tale set in the 1950s tells of a young girl who is born in a small town with the gift of a thin veil (caul) over her face.
Thulani Davis, *1959*, 1992
This coming-of-age story about a 12-year-old girl recounts events that changed her life and others around her during the historic civil rights movement.
Ntozake Shange, *Betsey Brown*, 1985
This coming-of-age story is about the exploits of a young girl during an era of school integration. It relates the worries of her family and the discoveries she makes at her new school.
Charlotte Sherman, *One Dark Body*, 1993
This story relates the incidents in the life of a young girl abandoned at birth. It deals with the return of her mother and her friend's entry into manhood.
A.J. Verdelle, *The Good Negress*, 1995
A young country girl who wants more from life than cooking, cleaning, and washing moves to the city. She is encouraged by her teacher to strive for higher goals.

61

LUCILLE CLIFTON, African American
JOHN STEPTOE, Illustrator, African American

All Us Come Cross the Water

(New York: Holt, Rinehart and Winston, 1973)

Story type: Young Readers
Subject(s): Africa; Self-Perception; Identity
Age range(s): Grades 2-4
Major character(s): Jim ''Ujamaa'', Child, Brother, African American
Time period(s): 1970s
Locale(s): United States (unidentified city)

Summary: His teacher asks everyone to tell where their people came from and when she calls on Ujamaa he won't say anything. Great-grandmama tells him that in 1855 her grandmother and her mother were brought from Whydah in Dahomey and that his father's people look like Ashanti people from the south of Ghana. His grown-up neighbor Tweezer explains how people came from different parts of Africa and how some of them weren't slaves. This gives Ujamaa a lot to think about. The next day Ujamaa is ready to tell the class where his people came from.

Other books by the same author:
Three Wishes, 1976
My Brother Fine with Me, 1975
The Boy Who Didn't Believe in Spring, 1973
Don't You Remember?, 1973
Good, Says Jerome, 1973

Other books you might like:

Debbi Chocolate, *On the Day I Was Born*, 1995

A newborn is welcomed into the family in an African ceremony where relatives gather, the child is raised to the heavens, blessed and named.

Eloise Greenfield, *Africa Dream*, 1977

Dreaming she has crossed the ocean to long-ago Africa a child shops in the marketplace, reads with magic eyes, and is welcomed by relatives.

Phil Mendez, *The Black Snowman*, 1989

A magic kente cloth helps a boy learn a lesson in self-respect and pride in his heritage while saving his younger brother from a fire.

Faith Ringgold, *Aunt Harriet's Underground Railroad in the Sky*, 1992

Flying in the sky a sister and her younger brother discovering the underground railroad to freedom must retrace its route to be reunited.

62

LUCILLE CLIFTON, African American
THOMAS DIGRAZIA, Illustrator, Caucasian

Amifika

(New York: E.P. Dutton, 1977)

Story type: Young Readers
Subject(s): Parent and Child; Family Life
Age range(s): Grades 2-3
Major character(s): Amifika, Child, Cousin, African American
Time period(s): 1970s
Locale(s): United States (unidentified city)

Summary: Young Amifika worries that, with his father coming home from the army, the family's small, two-room apartment won't have enough space. His mother says she is going to get rid of some things her husband won't even remember. Amifika fears he is one of those things because, if he can't remember his father, why would his father remember him? The young boy awakens in his father's arms and realizes that they do remember each other.

Other books by the same author:

My Friend Jacob, 1980
Three Wishes, 1976
My Brother Fine with Me, 1975
The Boy Who Didn't Believe in Spring, 1973
Don't You Remember?, 1973

Other books you might like:

Eloise Greenfield, *First Pink Light*, 1976

A child wants to stay awake until his daddy comes home so he can hide and surprise him but falls asleep waiting in a chair and daddy takes him to bed.

Dolores Johnson, *Papa's Stories*, 1994

Enjoying the stories her papa tells from her books a kindergartner says she'll teach him to read when she discovers he doesn't know how.

Dolores Johnson, *Your Dad Was Just Like You*, 1993

Talking with his grandpa after making his dad mad a young boy discovers just how much they are alike and why his dad was so upset with him.

John Steptoe, *Daddy Is a Monster. . .Sometimes*, 1980

A young sister and brother discussing what makes their daddy mad and turns him into a monster surprise him when they ask him why it happens.

Sharon Dennis Wyeth, *Always My Dad*, 1995

A young girl remembers the summer she and her three younger brothers spent at their grandparents when their dad visited and how much she misses him.

63

LUCILLE CLIFTON, African American
BRINTON TURKLE, Illustrator, Caucasian

The Boy Who Didn't Believe in Spring

(New York: E.P. Dutton, 1973)

Story type: Young Readers
Subject(s): Spring; Discovery and Exploration; City Life
Age range(s): Grades 2-3
Major character(s): King Shabazz, Child, Student, African American
Time period(s): 1970s
Locale(s): United States (unidentified city)

Summary: In school young King Shabazz' teacher tells the class spring is coming just like his mama has been saying at home. He doesn't believe them and tells his white pal Tony there is no such thing as spring. Together the two boys go off looking for spring. Everyone says spring is just around the corner so they look there but spring isn't there. Searching and searching they discover an abandoned car in a vacant lot. On their way toward it they find a patch of blooming yellow flowers and inside the car they discover a nest of bird's eggs. The boys now have evidence "it's spring."

Other books by the same author:

My Friend Jacob, 1980
Amifika, 1977
Three Wishes, 1976
My Brother Fine with Me, 1975
All Us Come Cross the Water, 1973

Other books you might like:

Elizabeth Fitzgerald Howard, *Mac and Marie and the Train Toss Surprise*, 1993

A 9-year-old waits beside the railroad tracks with his young sister for their uncle working in the dining car to toss them a special gift.

Dolores Johnson, *What Kind of Baby-Sitter Is This?*, 1991

Upset when his mom leaves him with an elderly babysitter a child discovers she likes baseball as much as he does and they become friends.

Herschel Johnson, *A Visit to the Country*, 1989

In the country at his grandparents a child discovers a baby bird, feeds him as he grows and learns to fly, and later returns him to the wild.

Angela Shelf Medearis, *The Adventures of Sugar and Junior*, 1995

Exploits of a young girl and a Latino neighbor boy as they become friends while baking cookies, going to monster movies, and sharing ice cream.

64

LUCILLE CLIFTON, African American
EVALINE NESS, Illustrator, Caucasian

Don't You Remember?

(New York: E.P. Dutton, 1973)

Story type: Young Readers
Subject(s): Promises; Birthdays
Age range(s): Grades 1-2
Major character(s): Desire Mary Tate, 4-Year-Old, Sister, African American
Time period(s): 1970s
Locale(s): United States (unidentified city)

Summary: No one seems to remember the promises they've made to soon-to-be 5-year-old Tate. Not her daddy, who promises to take her to the plant with him "next time." Nor her mom who works in a bakery and promises to bring her a cake with her name on it. Even her older brothers 12-year-old Sammy, 13-year-old Louis and 15-year-old Marvin would always be promising her something later she never got. Sulking in her room, Tate hears a knock on her door and soon her dreams come true.

Awards the book has won:
Coretta Scott King Honor Book, 1974

Other books by the same author:
My Friend Jacob, 1980
Amifika, 1977
Three Wishes, 1976
My Brother Fine with Me, 1975
The Boy Who Didn't Believe in Spring, 1973

Other books you might like:
Pat Cummings, *Carousel*, 1994
    Upset her daddy isn't home for her birthday, a young girl dreams of riding the zebra on the carousel she receives as her present from him.
Eloise Greenfield, *Me and Neesie*, 1975
    A child and her imaginary friend share times together until she goes to school and returning home discovers her friend is no longer around.
Angela Johnson, *Julius*, 1993
    Her granddaddy surprises a child by bringing her her very own pig from Alaska and she shares things she learns with her friends.
John Steptoe, *Birthday*, 1972
    On his eighth birthday the firstborn of the community celebrates with his family and friends and wishes for their future together.
John Steptoe, *My Special Best Words*, 1974
    A child tells about her daily routine of living with her 1-year-old baby brother, their daddy, and their babysitter.

65

LUCILLE CLIFTON, African American
ANN GRIFALCONI, Illustrator, Caucasian

Everett Anderson's 1-2-3

(New York: Holt, Rinehart and Winston, 1977)

Story type: Young Readers
Series: Everett Anderson
Subject(s): Mothers and Sons; Remarriage
Age range(s): Grades 1-2
Major character(s): Everett Anderson, Child, African American
Time period(s): 1970s
Locale(s): United States (unidentified city)

Summary: A new someone, Mr. Perry, has come into his mama's life and Everett's. A neighbor in their building, he drives a bus and likes talking to Everett's mama. Everett thinks about how one can have fun alone, as he does sometimes. He also thinks of how he's gotten used to doing things with his mama, just the two of them at dinner, flying kites, going to the market. Worrying about what would happen if it weren't just the two of them, his mama talks to Everett about missing his daddy, and how being just the two of them can be lonely. On a walk together Everett and Mr. Perry talk about his mama being happy and Everett getting to know him for himself not someone to take his daddy's place. Everett realizes there are times when one, two, or three can be just right.

About this book: Story in rhyme.

Other books by the same author:
Everett Anderson's Goodbye, 1984
Everett Anderson's Nine Month Long, 1978
Everett Anderson's Friend, 1976
Everett Anderson's Christmas Coming, 1971
Some of the Days of Everett Anderson, 1970 (debut)

Other books you might like:
Angela Johnson, *One of Three*, 1991
    The youngest of three sisters describes some of the many things they share together and the times she got to spend alone with her parents.
Lessie Jones Little, *I Can Do It Myself*, 1978
    Wanting to buy his mother a special present on his own for her birthday, a child faces a scary bulldog in the neighborhood on his way to get it. Co-author: Eloise Greenfield.

66

LUCILLE CLIFTON, African American
EVALINE NESS, Illustrator, Caucasian

Everett Anderson's Christmas Coming

(New York: Holt, Rinehart and Winston, 1971)

Story type: Young Readers
Series: Everett Anderson
Subject(s): Christmas; Wishes
Age range(s): Grades 1-2
Major character(s): Everett Anderson, Child, African American
Time period(s): 1970s

Locale(s): United States (unidentified city)

Summary: Counting down to Christmas with five more days to go, Everett keeps in the spirit of the season. He loves the sights and sounds of the holiday. From his apartment window he watches gentle snowflakes fall. Wishing his daddy were there, he thinks of the toys he'd want. Everett snoops around the apartment trying to find his presents before the party guests arrive. He marvels at the Christmas tree and smiles happily when the time arrives for him to open his presents.

About this book: Story in rhyme.

Other books by the same author:
Everett Anderson's Nine Month Long, 1978
Everett Anderson's 1-2-3, 1977
Everett Anderson's Friend, 1976
Everett Anderson's Year, 1974
Some of the Days of Everett Anderson, 1970 (debut)

Other books you might like:
Elizabeth Fitzgerald Howard, *Chita's Christmas Tree*, 1989
    A child and her papa share a special time together as they ride to the woods in their horse drawn buggy to pick out their Christmas tree.
Phil Mendez, *The Black Snowman*, 1989
    A magic kente cloth helps a boy learn a lesson in self-respect and pride in his heritage while saving his younger brother from a fire.

67

LUCILLE CLIFTON, African American
ANN GRIFALCONI, Illustrator, Caucasian

Everett Anderson's Friend
(New York: Holt, Rinehart and Winston, 1976)

Story type: Young Readers
Series: Everett Anderson
Subject(s): Friendship
Age range(s): Grades 1-2
Major character(s): Everett Anderson, Child, African American
Time period(s): 1970s
Locale(s): United States (unidentified city)

Summary: Young Everett is excited that a new family is moving into the apartment next door. He hopes to have some new playmates. Soon he discovers his new neighbor is Maria and her whole family of girls. Disappointed, he would rather play games and spend time with his pals Joe and Kirk. One day when Everett forgets his key, Maria invites him into her apartment where he meets her mother and eats her little pies, calles tacos. Everett and Maria become friends and they both spend time with Joe and Kirk.

About this book: Story in rhyme.

Other books by the same author:
Everett Anderson's Goodbye, 1984
Everett Anderson's Nine Month Long, 1978
Everett Anderson's 1-2-3, 1977
Everett Anderson's Year, 1974
Everett Anderson's Christmas Coming, 1971

Other books you might like:
Angela Johnson, *The Girl Who Wore Snakes*, 1993
    A girl thinks snakes are beautiful and one day she finds someone else who thinks so, too.
Dolores Johnson, *The Best Bug to Be*, 1992
    A child in a school play is disappointed being a bumblebee until she perfects her part and on the night of the play gets the most applause.
Angela Shelf Medearis, *The Adventures of Sugar and Junior*, 1995
    Exploits of a young girl and a Latino neighbor boy as they become friends while baking cookies, going to monster movies, and sharing ice cream.
Belinda Rochelle, *When Jo Louis Won the Title*, 1994
    Dreading going to a new school because classmates make fun of her name a young girl learns from her grandfather how she got her special name.
John Shearer, *Billy Jo Jive, Super Private Eye: The Case of the Missing Ten Speed Bike*, 1976
    Debut mystery series where a young boy solving cases involving his young neighbors and friends meets the young girl who becomes his partner.

68

LUCILLE CLIFTON, African American
ANN GRIFALCONI, Illustrator, Caucasian

Everett Anderson's Nine Month Long
(New York: Holt, Rinehart and Winston, 1978)

Story type: Young Readers
Series: Everett Anderson
Subject(s): Babies; Brothers and Sisters; Stepfamilies
Age range(s): Grades 1-2
Major character(s): Everett Anderson, African American, Stepson
Time period(s): 1970s
Locale(s): United States (unidentified city)

Summary: His mother has remarried and Everett has a stepfather, Mr. Tom Perry. Now there's a new baby on the way. The new family has so much love to share and Everett thinks it's an ok idea to have a new baby brother or sister to give it to. Each day Everett watches as the new baby grows in his mother and she smiles and hums. But Everett is a little uncertain about the whole thing. Reassured by Mr. Perry that he will always be his mother's special one, her firstborn, Everett feels confident again. The last days of waiting pass and the arrival of baby Evelyn Perry occurs.

About this book: Story in rhyme.

Other books by the same author:
Everett Anderson's 1-2-3, 1977
Everett Anderson's Friend, 1976
Everett Anderson's Year, 1974
Everett Anderson's Christmas Coming, 1971
Some of the Days of Everett Anderson, 1970 (debut)

Other books you might like:
Debbi Chocolate, *On the Day I Was Born*, 1995
    A newborn is welcomed into the family in an African

ceremony where relatives gather, the child is raised to the heavens, blessed and named.

Eloise Greenfield, *She Come Bringing Me That Little Baby Girl*, 1974

Jealous at first when his mama brings him a baby sister, a young boy later feels a new sense of responsibility and pride as a big brother.

Mildred Pitts Walter, *My Mama Needs Me*, 1983

When his newborn baby sister arrives home, a young boy is overcome by feelings of responsibility until his mama lets him know it's still OK to play.

69

LUCILLE CLIFTON, African American
ANN GRIFALCONI, Illustrator, Caucasian

Everett Anderson's Year

(New York: Holt, Rinehart and Winston, 1974)

Story type: Young Readers
Subject(s): Family Life; Seasons; Poetry
Age range(s): Grades 1-2
Major character(s): Everett Anderson, Child, African American
Time period(s): 1970s
Locale(s): United States (unidentified city)

Summary: A year in youn Everett's life is described in a series of poems, one for each month. Everett thinks about winter, spring rain, holidays and his birthday, and his mom and dad. He ends the year with questions about what's life all about.

Other books by the same author:
Everett Anderson's Nine Month Long, 1978
Everett Anderson's 1-2-3, 1977
Everett Anderson's Friend, 1976
Everett Anderson's Christmas Coming, 1971
Some of the Days of Everett Anderson, 1970 (debut)

Other books you might like:
Jeannette Franklin Caines, *I Need a Lunch Box*, 1988
A preschooler wanting a lunch box like his older sister's imagines all the things he could keep in it and dreams of having one for every day.
Donald Crews, *Shortcut*, 1992
A group of youngsters take a shortcut home following the railroad tracks. A train appears forcing them to run for safety.
Angela Johnson, *When I Am Old with You*, 1990
A young child depicts all the things he wants to do with his granddaddy when he gets old and how they will rest together in their rocking chairs.
Lessie Jones Little, *I Can Do It Myself*, 1978
Wanting to buy his mother a special present on his own for her birthday, a child faces a scary bulldog in the neighborhood on his way to get it. Co-author: Eloise Greenfield.
Brian Pinkney, *Max Found Two Sticks*, 1994
A young boy uses two twigs to play rhythms on buckets, hatboxes, bottles, and garbage cans until a drummer tosses him a pair of drum sticks.

70

LUCILLE CLIFTON, African American
STEPHANIE DOUGLAS, Illustrator, African American

Good, Says Jerome

(New York: E.P. Dutton, 1973)

Story type: Young Readers
Subject(s): Brothers and Sisters; Fear; Moving, Household
Age range(s): Grades 1-2
Major character(s): Jerome, Child, Brother, African American
Time period(s): 1970s
Locale(s): United States (unidentified city)

Summary: The family is moving and young Jerome doesn't want to go. His older sister Janice Marie tries to reassure him about his fears. Telling him they'll keep their memories from the old place and make new friends, she assures he they'll always have one another. Questioning her about what black is Jerome also wants to know what if his teacher might hate him. In their new house he wonders if they are lost and is afraid of the monster he saw. He is also curious to know who dies, where they go, and if girls are smarter than boys. Supportive Janice Marie manages answering his questions to Jerome's satisfaction.

Other books by the same author:
My Friend Jacob, 1980
Amifika, 1977
My Brother Fine with Me, 1975
The Boy Who Didn't Believe in Spring, 1973
All Us Come Cross the Water, 1973

Other books you might like:
Elizabeth Fitzgerald Howard, *Mac and Marie and the Train Toss Surprise*, 1993
A 9-year-old waits beside the railroad tracks with his young sister for their uncle working in the dining car to toss them a special gift.
Angela Johnson, *The Leaving Morning*, 1992
The impressions of what the day was like for herself and her younger brother when their daddy and pregnant mama moved them away from their home.
Belinda Rochelle, *When Jo Louis Won the Title*, 1994
Dreading going to a new school because classmates make fun of her name a young girl learns from her grandfather how she got her special name.

71

LUCILLE CLIFTON, African American
MONETA BARNETT, Illustrator, African American

My Brother Fine with Me

(New York: Holt, Rinehart and Winston, 1975)

Story type: Young Readers
Subject(s): Brothers and Sisters; Loneliness
Age range(s): Grades 2-3
Major character(s): Wayne "Baggy", 5-Year-Old, Brother, African American; Johnetta, 8-Year-Old, Sister, African American
Time period(s): 1970s

Locale(s): United States (unidentified city)

Summary: For three years Johnetta was an only child until her brother Wayne, who she calls ''Baggy,'' was born. Now eight Johnetta is eager to help ''Baggy'' pack his belongings so he can fulfill his plan to run away to become a brave warrior. For five years now she's had to watch out for him, babysit with him, and spend time with him. Now when he leaves she feels ''free at last.'' But soon Johnetta feels lonely for her brother. Even if he was in the way she misses him now that he's not there, things just aren't going to be the same without him. Much to her surprise when she goes outside ''Baggy'' is sitting on the steps worrying about being lonely for her if he ran away. Both are happier when he decides he'd better stay home and be a warrior taking care of the family.

Other books by the same author:
My Friend Jacob, 1980
Amifika, 1977
Three Wishes, 1976
The Boy Who Didn't Believe in Spring, 1973
All Us Come Cross the Water, 1973

Other books you might like:
Jeannette Franklin Caines, *Abby*, 1973
An adopted preschooler questions her mother and older brother about when she first came there and suggests they adopt another brother.
Elizabeth Fitzgerald Howard, *Mac and Marie and the Train Toss Surprise*, 1993
A 9-year-old waits beside the railroad tracks with his young sister for their uncle working in the dining car to toss them a special gift.
Faith Ringgold, *Aunt Harriet's Underground Railroad in the Sky*, 1992
Flying in the sky a sister and her younger brother discovering the underground railroad to freedom must retrace its route to be reunited.
Alice Walker, *Finding the Green Stone*, 1991
A young brother and sister have identical green stones and when the brother's is lost his sister, parents, and neighbors rally to help him find it.
Mildred Pitts Walter, *Two and Too Much*, 1990
Trying to help his mama a 7-year-old watches his 2-year-old sister who gets into all kinds of things until she tires herself out and falls asleep.

72

LUCILLE CLIFTON, African American
THOMAS DIGRAZIA, Illustrator, Caucasian

My Friend Jacob
(New York: E.P. Dutton, 1980)

Story type: Young Readers
Subject(s): Friendship; Mentally Handicapped
Age range(s): Grades 1-3
Major character(s): Sam, 8-Year-Old, African American
Time period(s): 1980s
Locale(s): United States (unidentified city)

Summary: His next door white neighbor, older Jacob, is young Sam's very best friend. Together they play basketball, watch

cars go by, and go to the grocery store. At first Sam's mothers cautioned him about being careful playing with Jacob and not having him tag along all the time, but now she doesn't do that anymore. Sam helps Jacob remember things he forgets, like red is for stop and green is for go. He's also teaching him how to knock at the door before just walking in. Jacob has a hard time remembering to knock and Sam becomes frustrated saying maybe it's too hard for him to do. Seeing Sam's disappointment Jacob tries harder until he gets it right.

Other books by the same author:
Amifika, 1977
Three Wishes, 1976
My Brother Fine with Me, 1975
The Boy Who Didn't Believe in Spring, 1973
Don't You Remember?, 1973

Other books you might like:
Angela Johnson, *The Girl Who Wore Snakes*, 1993
A girl thinks snakes are beautiful and one day she finds someone else who thinks so, too.
Dolores Johnson, *The Best Bug to Be*, 1992
A child in a school play is disappointed being a bumblebee until she perfects her part and on the night of the play gets the most applause.
Angela Shelf Medearis, *The Adventures of Sugar and Junior*, 1995
Exploits of a young girl and a Latino Neighbor boy as they become friends while baking cookies, going to monster movies, and sharing ice cream.
Ray Prather, *Double Dog Dare*, 1975
Two boys climbing in a tree are scared by a mean dog and dare each other to get down first until the lost dog's owner appears and rewards them.
Harriette Gillem Robinet, *Jay and the Marigold*, 1976
A white youngster in a wheelchair with cerebral palsy envies things his twin sister and others can do and discovers abilities he has of his own.

73

LUCILLE CLIFTON, African American
EVALINE NESS, Illustrator, Caucasian

Some of the Days of Everett Anderson
(New York: Holt, Rinehart and Winston, 1970)

Story type: Young Readers
Series: Everett Anderson
Subject(s): City Life; Play; Parent and Child
Age range(s): Grades 1-2
Major character(s): Everett Anderson, 6-Year-Old, African American
Time period(s): 1970s
Locale(s): United States

Summary: Some of the days in 6-year-old ebony Everett's life are full of fun. Others filled with rain cause him to have to remember not to lose his umbrella. Many of his days are filled with adventures, including the time he was lost for hours and hours. Not afraid of the dark, Everett is aware of the sirens passing by in the street. He also enjoys special comfort times with his mama and getting to ride on his daddy's back. At nightfall he pretends the stars are where his apartment ends.

About this book: Debut.

Awards the book has won:
*School Library Journal One Of the Best Books Of the Year,
1970*

Other books by the same author:
Everett Anderson's Nine Month Long, 1978
Everett Anderson's 1-2-3, 1977
Everett Anderson's Friend, 1976
Everett Anderson's Year, 1974
Everett Anderson's Christmas Coming, 1971

Other books you might like:
Donald Crews, *Shortcut*, 1992
   A group of youngsters taking a shortcut home, following
   the railroad tracks, are frightened when a train appears
   forcing them to run for safety.
Pat Cummings, *Clean Your Room, Harvey Moon!*, 1991
   His mom tells a young boy he has to clean his room before
   watching TV and he discovers a treasure trove of things
   he'd forgotten he had.
Wade Hudson, *I Love My Family*, 1993
   A young boy recalls his enjoyable summer family reunions
   with his father's relatives and looks forward to his
   mother's family reunion.
Dolores Johnson, *What Kind of Baby-Sitter Is This?*, 1991
   Upset when his mom leaves him with an elderly babysitter,
   a child discovers she likes baseball as much as he does and
   they become friends.
John Steptoe, *My Special Best Words*, 1974
   A child tells about her daily routine of living her life with
   her 1-year-old baby brother, their daddy, and their
   babysitter.

74

LUCILLE CLIFTON, African American
STEPHANIE DOUGLAS, Illustrator, African American

Three Wishes

(New York: Viking Press, 1974)

Subject(s): Wishes; Magic
Age range(s): Grades 1-2
Major character(s): Zenobia ''Nobie'', Child, African American
Time period(s): 1970s
Locale(s): United States

Summary: Out for a walk with her best friend Victor, young
''Nobie'' spots a shiny penny in the snow. Victor says it's a
lucky penny and she's got three wishes. Halfway joking
''Nobie'' wishes it wasn't so cold and like magic the sun
comes out. Back in her apartment ''Nobie'' and Victor argue
about believing the penny is lucky, and she wishes he would
leave. Like magic he gets his coat and runs out. Coming to see
what's the matter her mama fusses with her about being
unfriendly. Realizing she's now wasted two of her wishes she
asks her mama if she could have any wish what would it be.
Much to her surprise her mama says she'd wish for good
friends. Going outside ''Nobie'' sits down and thinks of all
the good times she's had with Victor and wishes he was still

her good friend. Like magic Victor comes smiling down the
street. ''Nobie's'' convinced she has a lucky penny.

Other books by the same author:
My Friend Jacob, 1980
Amifika, 1977
My Brother Fine with Me, 1975
Don't You Remember?, 1973
All Us Come Cross the Water, 1973

Other books you might like:
Angela Johnson, *Shoes Like Miss Alice's*, 1995
   Her babysitter shows a child a good time with her different
   pairs of shoes for dancing, walking, napping, and then they
   sit drawing barefooted.
Patricia C. McKissack, *Mirandy and Brother Wind*, 1988
   Folk tale of a young girl desperately wanting to win her
   first cakewalk dance contest so she makes a wish to the
   wind and dances with her friend.
Phil Mendez, *The Black Snowman*, 1989
   A magic kente cloth helps a boy learn a lesson in self-
   respect and pride in his heritage while saving his younger
   brother from a fire.
Alice Walker, *Finding the Green Stone*, 1991
   A young brother and sister have identical green stones and
   when the brother's is lost his sister, parents, and neighbors
   rally to help him find it.

75

CYRUS COLTER, African American

A Chocolate Soldier

(New York: Thunder's Mouth Press, 1988)

Subject(s): Conduct of Life; Guilt; Psychological Thriller
Age range(s): Adult
Major character(s): Meshach Coriolanus Barry, Student, Reli-
   gious, African American; Rollo Ezekiel ''Cager'' Lee,
   Student (idealist), African American
Time period(s): 1900s (1920-1980)
Locale(s): Valhalla, Tennessee

Summary: Meshach, an elderly man, recounts the story of
Rollo, a former classmate whom he regards as a hero. When
Rollo is on the verge of flunking college, he takes a job as a
house servant. He murders the elderly white matron who
employs him and is killed by a mob lynching. Meshach wants
desperately to find meaning in his own life, but sees himself
falling short of his ideal.

Where it's reviewed:
Essence, August 1988, page 24
Library Journal, May 15, 1988, page 91
Publishers Weekly, April 15, 1988, page 82

Other books by the same author:
City of Light, 1993
Night Studies, 1979
The Hippodrome, 1973
Rivers of Eros, 1972 (debut novel)

Other books you might like:
Bebe Moore Campbell, *Your Blues Ain't Like Mine*, 1992
   These episodes describe the lives of individuals affected

by the murder of a 15-year-old boy for reportedly offending a white woman in a small southern town.

Albert French, *Billy*, 1993

When a 10-year-old boy is sentenced to death in the electric chair for killing a teenaged girl, racial hatreds ignite in 1930's Mississippi.

Ernest J. Gaines, *A Lesson before Dying*, 1993

This historical fiction set in Louisiana during the 1940s shows the impact a young man's pending execution for murder has on the community and on his family and friends.

76

CYRUS COLTER, African American

City of Light

(New York: Thunder's Mouth Press, 1993)

Subject(s): Identity; Mothers and Sons; Prejudice

Age range(s): Adult

Major character(s): Paul Kessey, Activist, Researcher, African American; Saturn Marie Kessey, Mother, Spouse, African American; Cecile Stephanie Cambon-Fournier, Doctor, Spouse, French

Time period(s): 1900s

Locale(s): Paris, France

Summary: In Paris, Paul meets Cecile, a married internist with two children. After their affair begins, Cecile suddenly changes and has bad dreams. She suspects her husband knows of her affair yet is surprised to see him one morning when she leaves Paul's place. The encounter changes all their lives.

Where it's reviewed:

Booklist, August 1993, page 2035

Kirkus Reviews, July 1, 1993, page 802

Publishers Weekly, August 16, 1993, page 99

Other books by the same author:

A Chocolate Soldier, 1988

Night Studies, 1979

The Hippodrome, 1973

Rivers of Eros, 1972 (debut novel)

Other books you might like:

Percival Everett, *Suder*, 1983

A young man who fears he may be on the verge of going insane like his mother decides to run away from his wife and son.

Elaine Perry, *Another Present Era*, 1990

A young architect drifts away from her lover and becomes involved with an older Caucasian artist.

Darryl Pinckney, *High Cotton*, 1992

An unnamed narrator reveals the complexities of growing up in the upper-middle class as a young man in the ''talented tenth'' generation.

Charlotte Sherman, *One Dark Body*, 1993

This story recounts incidents in the life of a young girl abandoned at birth and deals with the return of her mother and her friend's entry into manhood.

Dorothy West, *The Wedding*, 1995

Saga about five generations of two families with mixed race ancestry.

77

CYRUS COLTER, African American

Night Studies

(Chicago: Swallow Press, 1979)

Subject(s): Race Relations; Interpersonal Relations; Psychology

Age range(s): Adult

Major character(s): John Calvin Knight, Activist, Crime Victim, African American; Griselda Graves, Widow(er), Caucasian; Mary Dee Adkins, Student, Wealthy, African American

Time period(s): 18th century; 20th century

Locale(s): Chicago, Illinois; Paris, France

Summary: During the Civil Rights Movement John worked with Martin Luther King, Jr. Five years after Dr. Kings assasination, John, at thirty-five, heads the national Black Peoples Congress. When the organization relocates from San Francisco to Chicago a white widow, Griselda, deserts her boyfriend to work for the cause. Studying art in Paris, Mary Dee is forced to leave her white boyfriend and return home to Chicago when her wealthy father dies. All three lives converge in Chicago where they develop lasting relationship.

Other books by the same author:

City of Light, 1993

A Chocolate Soldier, 1988

The Hippodrome, 1973

Rivers of Eros, 1972 (debut novel)

Other books you might like:

David Bradley, *The Chaneysville Incident*, 1981

Returning home to comfort a dying man, a professor must solve the dual mysteries of his father's death and the dark secret of his family's past.

Ernest J. Gaines, *In My Father's House*, 1978

A civil rights leader and minister examines who he is and who he was when a stranger emerges from his past.

Julius Lester, *And All Our Wounds Forgiven*, 1994

A white secretary recalls her affair with a reknowned civil rights leader when she visits his wife's sick bed.

Toni Morrison, *Tar Baby*, 1981

Two young lovers from different backgrounds experience the conflicts wrought by social and cultural circumstances played out in the realm of the heart.

Duane Smith, *The Nubian*, 1994

The twenty year episodes from a young man's life describe his relationship with his mysterious Afrocentric uncle who the government convicts.

78

CYRUS COLTER, African American

Rivers of Eros

(Chicago: Swallow Press, 1972)

Subject(s): Family Relations; Human Behavior; Psychology

Age range(s): Adult

Major character(s): Clotilda Pilgrim, Seamstress, Grandmother, African American; Addie Parker, 17-Year-Old,

Granddaughter, African American; Lester Parker, 12-Year-Old, Grandson, African American

Time period(s): 1970s (1971)
Locale(s): Chicago, Illinois

Summary: Clotilda runs a boardinghouse and takes in sewing to earn a living to support herself and her grandchildren. She is haunted by her past and the violent murder of her daughter, elements for which she feels she must atone and which she also believes contribute to her inability to connect with her granddaughter Addie. As Addie slips farther and farther from Clotilda's reach, neither Addie's little brother Lester nor the other boarders in the house can make things right.

About this book: Debut novel.

Other books by the same author:
City of Light, 1993
A Chocolate Soldier, 1988
Night Studies, 1979
The Hippodrome, 1973

Other books you might like:
Linda Beatrice Brown, *Crossing over Jordan*, 1995
    Saga of the ties binding the lives of four generations of mothers and daughters from the Civil War era to the early 21st century.
Devorah Major, *An Open Weave*, 1995
    Richly textured story of a blind grandmother who weaves astonishing cloths, her epileptic visionary daughter, and strong-willed granddaughter.
Paule Marshall, *Praisesong for the Widow*, 1983
    Disturbed by dreams, a middle-aged widow away on a trip finds self-renewal and returns with a plan to connect her past and improve her future.
Toni Morrison, *The Bluest Eye*, 1970
    A young girl growing up in the 1940s believes she deserves the ill that befalls her, and that having blue eyes would change everything.

79

J. CALIFORNIA COOPER, African American

Family
(New York: Doubleday, 1991)

Subject(s): Family Relations; Race Relations; Slavery
Age range(s): Adult
Major character(s): Clora, 12-Year-Old, Mother (six children), African American
Time period(s): 1800s (1844)
Locale(s): South

Summary: Clora, "dead-but-not-gone," narrates the tale of her life being born into slavery of African American parents. Her mother killed her slave owner and then committed suicide when Clora was twelve. Clora was taken by the slave owner's son with whom she had six children. Eventually committing suicide herself, Clora continues to tell the story of what happens in the lives of her four surviving children and in the lives of her grandchildren. With events spanning years before and after the Civil War, Clora weaves a tale showing the interconnectedness of the human family beyond racial distinctions.

About this book: Debut novel.
Where it's reviewed:
Essence, May 1991, page 52
Publishers Weekly, November 2, 1990, page 64
School Library Journal, August 1991, page 209

Other books by the same author:
In Search of Satisfaction, 1994

Other books you might like:
Lorene Cary, *The Price of a Child*, 1995
    This historical tale is about a woman who literally walks away from slavery to freedom under her owner's furious gaze in Philadelphia during the 1850s.
Barbara Chase-Riboud, *The President's Daughter*, 1994
    This story chronicles the life of Harriet Hemings, the daughter of miscegenation in the interracial affair of President Thomas Jefferson. It relates her passing for white.
Leon Forrest, *Two Wings to Veil My Face*, 1983
    This last title of their trilogy tells of the Witherspoon family's saga during the plantation era of the South before the Civil War to contemporary times.
Toni Morrison, *Beloved*, 1987
    A mother escapes from slavery and kills her baby to keep her former owner from stealing her. She is haunted and consumed by the baby's ghost.
Dorothy West, *The Wedding*, 1995
    This saga about five generations of two families with mixed race ancestry relates the events in the lives of children from a new contemporary generation.

80

J. CALIFORNIA COOPER, African American

In Search of Satisfaction
(New York: Doubleday, 1994)

Subject(s): Family Relations; Race Relations; Sisters
Age range(s): Adult
Major character(s): Josephus Josephus, Father, African American; Ruth Mae Jones, Sister (half-sister), African American; Yingyang Krupt, Sister (half-sister), African American
Time period(s): 19th century; 20th century (1879-1925)
Locale(s): Yoville, South (legal township)

Summary: This is the tale of two half-sisters, Ruth Mae and Yinyang who are born during the plantation era of the South from the same father but different mothers, one being caucasian. With a secret legacy and inheritance from their parents, they search for satisfaction in their separate lives in a small township owned by caucasians.

Where it's reviewed:
Kirkus Reviews, July 15, 1994, page 831
Library Journal, September 1, 1994, page 213
Publishers Weekly, September 12, 1994, page 83

Other books by the same author:
Family, 1991 (debut novel)

Other books you might like:
Anita Richmond Bunkley, *Black Gold*, 1994
    A young woman who is on the brink of ruin before the

historic oil boom in Texas during the 1920s, finds herself accused of murder. Through all this, a family secret is revealed.

Marsha Hunt, *Joy*, 1991

A childless woman befriends a neighbor girl who sings with her sisters. The girl grows up to become a star and when she dies, her untimely death reveals shocking secrets.

81

JAMES EARL HARDY, African American

B-Boy Blues

(Boston: Alyson Publications, 1994)

Subject(s): Homosexuality/Lesbianism; Friendship; Romance

Age range(s): Adult

Major character(s): Mitchell ''Mitch'' Sylvester Crawford, Journalist, Homosexual, African American; Raheim Errol Rivers, Courier (''B-boy''), Father (unwed), Homosexual; Eugene ''Gene'' Roberts, Homosexual, Crime Victim, African American

Time period(s): 1990s (1993)

Locale(s): New York, New York

Summary: In a dance bar, Mitch spots hip-hop ''B-boy'' Raheim. They flirt and exchange phone numbers. After establishing a sexual relationship, Raheim hits Mitch and storms out of his life. Separated, they both realize that they love one another and that some changes will have to occur if they want to make their lives and love work.

About this book: This is the author's debut novel.

Where it's reviewed:

Lambda Book Report, November 1994, page 23

Advocate, October 4, 1994, page 75

Kirkus Reviews, September 15, 1994, page 1221

Booklist, October 15, 1994, page 402

Entertainment Weekly, November 25, 1994, page 70

Other books you might like:

Steven Corbin, *Fragments That Remain*, 1993

This story depicts a contemporary actor's life as he deals with racism, sexism, homophobia, bigotry, an interracial relationship, and secrets from his past.

Steven Corbin, *100 Days from Now*, 1994

This story is a about the courtship and interracial relationship of two men who both test HIV-positive. One of the men has yet to tell his family he is gay and is in love.

Larry Duplechan, *Eight Days a Week*, 1985

Debut novel in a series about a young man's life, in which a gay interracial love story evolves.

82

STEVEN CORBIN, African American

Fragments That Remain

(Boston: Alyson Publications, 1993)

Story type: Gay/Lesbian Fiction

Subject(s): Family Relations; Interpersonal Relations; Race Relations

Age range(s): Adult

Major character(s): Skylar Edward Whyte, Actor, Homosexual, African American; Evan Cabot, Model, Father (bisexual), Caucasian; Aubrey Hutchinson, Designer, Homosexual, African American

Time period(s): 1960s; 1990s

Locale(s): New York, New York

Summary: Skylar's life has been burdened with racism, sexism, homophobia, and bigotry. Now famous and nominated for an Academy Award, he recalls when his beloved gay uncle Aubrey took him to see his first ''colored'' movie star, encouraging him to follow his dreams. He also showed him his first gay bar. Skylar is haunted by nightmares of Aubrey's accidental death in a house fire. He is told the truth about Aubrey's death on his father's deathbed. After their father's funeral, Skylar hears his drug-addicted younger brother wants to go into rehabilitation. Skylar learns a secret from Evan's past that will impact any future he might have with his caucasian lover.

Where it's reviewed:

Booklist, February 15, 1994, page 1059

Awards the book has won:

Lambda Literary Award Finalist, Gay Men's Fiction, 1994

Other books by the same author:

100 Days from Now, 1994

No Easy Place to Be, 1989 (debut novel)

Other books you might like:

Larry Duplechan, *Eight Days a Week*, 1985

This is the debut novel in series about a young man's gay life in which an interracial love story evolves.

James Hardy, *B-Boy Blues*, 1994

This contemporary gay love story is about two men attracted to one another in a dance bar. They learn that love is something you have to work at.

83

STEVEN CORBIN, African American

A Hundred Days From Now

(Boston: Alyson Publications, 1994)

Story type: Gay/Lesbian Fiction

Subject(s): AIDS (Disease); Family Relations; Interpersonal Relations

Age range(s): Adult

Major character(s): Dexter Baldwin, Homosexual, Writer, African American; Sergio Alberto Gutierrez, Wealthy (bisexual), Publisher, Mexican (Anglo Amer/Caucasian mother)

Time period(s): 1990s

Locale(s): Los Angeles, California

Summary: Dexter has achieved some notoriety as a screenwriter. Stopping in a bar for a drink he meets a wealthy Mexican named Sergio who recognizes him from the cover of a London magazine. After a seven week courtship of wining and dining, Sergio confesses being HIV-positive, only to learn later that Dexter is also HIV-positive. Falling in love Sergio takes Dexter on a holiday trip with his family to Hawaii. He confesses about his sexuality to his family, of which only his twin brother knew. Confessing his love, Dexter tells Sergio his intention to stay with him and care for him during his illness.

Where it's reviewed:
Kirkus Reviews, April 1, 1994, page 414
Lambda Book Report, July 1994, page 20
Publishers Weekly, May 23, 1994, page 79

Other books by the same author:
Fragments That Remain, 1993
No Easy Place to Be, 1989 (debut novel)

Other books you might like:
Larry Duplechan, *Eight Days a Week*, 1985
This is the debut novel in a series about a young man's gay life in which a gay interracial love story evolves.
James Hardy, *B-Boy Blues*, 1994
This contemporary gay love story is about two men attracted to one another in a dance bar. They learn that love is something you have to work at.
E. Lynn Harris, *Just as I Am*, 1994
This story is about the bisexual affairs of a young man. It includes how his life impacts the woman who loves him, and how they comfort a friend dying with AIDS.

84

STEVEN CORBIN, African American

No Easy Place to Be
(New York: Simon and Schuster, 1989)

Subject(s): Family Relations; Race Relations; Sisters
Age range(s): Adult
Major character(s): Miriam Brooks, Activist, Nurse, African American; Velma Brooks, Sister (middle), Writer, African American; Louise Brooks, Dancer, Sister (youngest), African American
Time period(s): 1910s; 1920s (1919-1929)
Locale(s): New York, New York (Harlem)

Summary: Three sisters, Miriam, Velma, and Louise, seek their way in life during the historic Harlem Renaissance period. The eldest, Miriam, finds her first love to be a woman; Velma aspires to join the ranks of a new literary vanguard; and the youngest, Louise, marries and passes for white.

About this book: This is the author's debut novel.

Where it's reviewed:
Essence, July 1989, page 20
Library Journal, January 1989, page 100
Publishers Weekly, January 20, 1989, page 136

Other books by the same author:
100 Days from Now, 1994
Fragments That Remain, 1993

Other books you might like:
Tina McElroy Ansa, *Ugly Ways*, 1993
This contemporary account is about three sisters reflecting on their upbringing in a small town and how their lives have evolved.
Connie Briscoe, *Sisters and Lovers*, 1994
This contemporary story is about the lives and struggles of three sisters and the men they become involved with.

Marsha Hunt, *Joy*, 1991
A childless woman befriends a neighbor girl who sings with her sisters. The girl grows up to become a star and when she dies, her untimely death reveals shocking secrets.

85

DONALD CREWS, Author/Illustrator, African American

Bigmama's
(New York: Greenwillow Books, 1991)

Story type: Young Readers
Subject(s): Grandparents; Country Life; Summer
Age range(s): Grades 1-3
Major character(s): Donald Crews, Child, Brother, African American
Time period(s): 1940s
Locale(s): Cottondale, Florida

Summary: The excitement and joy of a summer trip to his grandparents' farm are recalled by Donald. Greeted at the train station by uncle Slank he, his brother, sisters and their mama are driven along dirt roads until they reach "Bigmama's" house in the country. Exploring the house and finding nothing changed, they are all soon out roaming in the yard. They stop at the well, the shed, the barn, the stable, and out at the pond. At dinner the family reminisces and makes plans for their stay. When night falls, they see millions of stars and can hardly sleep thinking of what lies ahead.

Other books by the same author:
Shortcut, 1992

Other books you might like:
Jeannette Franklin Caines, *Window Wishing*, 1980
The exploits of a young sister and brother spending their vacation with their fun grandma who takes them downtown together where they window wish.
Valerie Flournoy, *Tanya's Reunion*, 1995
A youngster traveling with her grandma to the family farm for a reunion discovers a special memento for her grandma of days gone by.
Eloise Greenfield, *Grandmama's Joy*, 1980
Worried when she see's her grandmama sad a child learns why and tries the best way she knows how to put a smile back on her face again.
Francine Haskins, *Things I Like about Grandma*, 1992
A child enjoys her special relationship with her grandma as they do things together and the fun times they have watching sports with granddaddy.
Wade Hudson, *I Love My Family*, 1993
A young boy recalls his enjoyable summer family reunions with his father's relatives and looks forward to his mother's family reunion.
Gloria Jean Pinkney, *Back Home*, 1992
Raised in the city an 8-year-old visits her relatives for the first time in her memory in the place where she was born in the country.

86

DONALD CREWS, Author/Illustrator, African American

Shortcut

(New York: Greenwillow Books, 1992)

Story type: Young Readers
Subject(s): Trains; Fear
Age range(s): Grades 1-2
Major character(s): Donald Crews, Child, Brother, African American
Time period(s): 1940s
Locale(s): Cottondale, Florida

Summary: On a summer visit to his grandparents' Donald and the other children decide to take a shortcut home following the railroad tracks. They know they should take the road but they decide to take the shortcut. Laughing and playing along the way they hear a train whistle in the distance which becomes louder and louder and they have to jump off the tracks into a steep slope. Walking home in silence it will be long time before they can talk about what happened and they will never take the shortcut again.

About this book: Sequel to *Bigmama's*.

Other books by the same author:
Bigmama's, 1991

Other books you might like:
Lucille Clifton, *Everett Anderson's Year*, 1974
 Activities in a young child's life are depicted for the twelve calendar months in a series of poems capturing his joys, sorrows, and confusions.
Lucille Clifton, *Some of the Days of Everett Anderson*, 1970
 Living in the city, a 6-year-old boy's days are filled with activity from playing in the sunshine, to hearing sirens pass by, to times with his parents.
Elizabeth Fitzgerald Howard, *Mac and Marie and the Train Toss Surprise*, 1993
 A 9-year-old waits beside the railroad tracks with his young sister for their uncle working in the dining car to toss them a special gift.
Wade Hudson, *I Love My Family*, 1993
 A young boy recalls his enjoyable summer family reunions with his father's relatives and looks forward to his mother's family reunion.

87

RICARDO CORTEZ CRUZ, African American

Straight Outta Compton

(Boulder, CO: Fiction Collective Two & University of Colorado, 1992)

Story type: Young Adult
Subject(s): City Life; Drugs; Gangs
Age range(s): Grades 10-Adult
Major character(s): Rooster, Gang Member, Teenager, African American; Clive, Gang Member, Teenager, African American
Time period(s): 1990s
Locale(s): Compton, California

Summary: This rap-style novel focuses on the lives of Rooster and Clive-nem, who grow up together on the mean streets of Compton. Clive is like a big brother to Rooster, but Rooster changes, becoming obsessed with women. Clive wants to break from Compton for reasons of his own. He and Rooster split up, fall into rival gangs and begin to hate each other. Whirled together in wonderment and anger, these young men are courageous, bold, living hard and fast on a very thin edge.

About this book: Debut novel

Where it's reviewed:
American Book Review, July 1993, page 17
Los Angeles Times Book Review, November 22, 1992, page 6
Library Journal, September 1, 1992, page 21
Nature, December 21, 1992, page 784

Awards the book has won:
Charles & Mildred Nilon Excellence in Minority Fiction Award, 1992

Other books you might like:
Jess Mowry, *Way Past Cool*, 1992
 Two rival gangs must put aside their differences to solve their common problem when a drug dealer tries to stir up trouble between them.
Walter Dean Myers, *Scorpions*, 1988
 A gun changes the lives of a young boy and his Puerto Rican friend when they are forced into being involved with a street gang.
Walter Dean Myers, *Won't Know Till I Get There*, 1982
 The summer exploits of a 14-year-old whose parents decide to adopt a youngster with a juvenile record and what happens when the boys get arrested together.

88

PAT CUMMINGS, Author/Illustrator, African American

Carousel

(New York: Bradbury Press, 1994)

Story type: Young Readers
Subject(s): Fathers and Daughters; Birthdays; Dreams and Nightmares
Age range(s): Grades 1-3
Major character(s): Alex, Child, Niece, African American
Time period(s): 1990s
Locale(s): United States (unidentified city)

Summary: Even on her birthday Alex doesn't like getting her hair braided or getting all dressed up, especially since her daddy isn't home yet. Opening her presents, Alex fusses and wants to wait for him. When she opens the present from her daddy, she finds a lovely carousel. But she is angry that he broke his promise to be there and when she speaks her mind, is sent to bed. Picking up her carousel in her anger, she accidently breaks the zebra off. Later, her dreams are filled with thoughts about the carousel animals escaping through her window and riding the zebra. When morning comes, daddy gives her a big hug and kiss, noticing the broken zebra and promising to fix it later. Happily heading for breakfast Alex wants to show her daddy her other gifts.

Other books by the same author:
Petey Moroni's Camp Runamok Diary, 1992

Clean Your Room, Harvey Moon!, 1991
C.L.O.U.D.S., 1986
Jimmy Lee Did It, 1985 (debut)

Other books you might like:
Jeannette Franklin Caines, *Daddy*, 1977
Saturdays are special for a child when her father comes to get her to visit with him and they share laughs and fun together all day.
Lucille Clifton, *Don't You Remember?*, 1973
A soon-to-be 5-year-old is disappointed that everyone in the family keeps breaking their promises to her until they give her a birthday surprise.
June Jordan, *Kimako's Story*, 1981
A 7-year-old takes on the responsibility of caring for her neighbors big Airedale dog and gets to see more of her city surroundings.
John Steptoe, *Birthday*, 1972
On his eighth birthday the firstborn of the community celebrates with his family and friends and wishes for their future together.
Sharon Dennis Wyeth, *Always My Dad*, 1995
A young girl remembers the summer she and her three younger brothers spent at their grandparents when their dad visited and how much she misses him.

89

PAT CUMMINGS, Author/Illustrator, African American

Clean Your Room, Harvey Moon!
(New York: Bradbury Press, 1991)

Story type: Young Readers
Subject(s): Cleanliness; Mothers and Sons
Age range(s): Grades 1-2
Major character(s): Harvey Moon, Child, African American
Time period(s): 1990s
Locale(s): United States (unidentified city)

Summary: On Saturday morning young Harvey has settled in front of the television to watch his favorite shows when his mother comes in saying he has to clean his room. Facing his room, he really doesn't see what all the fuss is about. Tossing dirty clothes in the hall, discovering things he doesn't even recognize, and grabbing up stuff off the floor, Harvey finds a treasure trove of things he'd forgotten he had. After several hours tired Harvey realizes he's missed all his TV shows and lunch and he's starving. Putting a few more things away he calls to his mom that he's finished. She's amazed at what he's gotten done when she looks into his room. Saying he can watch TV now and she's fixed him some lunch, she suggests together after that they get started cleaning up the lumps of stuff she sees he's tried hiding.

About this book: Story in rhyme.

Other books by the same author:
Carousel, 1994
Petey Moroni's Camp Runamok Diary, 1992
C.L.O.U.D.S., 1986
Jimmy Lee Did It, 1985 (debut)

Other books you might like:
Lucille Clifton, *Some of the Days of Everett Anderson*, 1970
Living in the city a 6-year-old boy's days are filled with activity from playing in the sunshine, to hearing sirens pass by, to times with his parents.
Dolores Johnson, *What Kind of Baby-Sitter Is This?*, 1991
Upset when his mom leaves him with an elderly babysitter a child discovers she likes baseball as much as he does and they become friends.
June Jordan, *Kimako's Story*, 1981
A 7-year-old takes on the responsibility of caring for her neighbors big Airedale dog and gets to see more of her city surroundings.
June Jordan, *New Life: New Room*, 1975
The story of the changes that occur for a 6-year-old, her 9 and 10-year-old brothers, and their daddy in a small apartment when momma gets pregnant.
Brian Pinkney, *Max Found Two Sticks*, 1994
A young boy uses two twigs to play rhythms on buckets, hatboxes, bottles, and garbage cans until a drummer tosses him a pair of drum sticks.

90

PAT CUMMINGS, Author/Illustrator, African American

Petey Moroni's Camp Runamok Diary
(New York: Bradbury Press, 1992)

Story type: Young Readers
Subject(s): Camps and Camping; Animals
Age range(s): Grades 1-3
Major character(s): Petey Moroni, Writer, Camper, African American
Time period(s): 1990s
Locale(s): United States (unidentified camp site)

Summary: Spending two weeks at summer Camp Runamok seems like a lot of fun to young Petey and each day he records in his diary what happens. Mysteriously things are disappearing like one boy's hot dog and another girl's fruit-flavored pastries. Two 6-year-olds say they saw a masked monster with sharp claws running off with food but nobody believes them. One of their teachers says they have raccoons. That night they leave a trap for the raccoon and begin hiding their food only to discover the raccoon has outsmarted them. After a camp meeting they decide to try other ways of trapping the raccoon and keeping their food safe, and someone even suggests they just eat everything up themselves. No matter what they do the raccoon won't be caught and before Petey knows it camp is ending and they'll have to wait until next summer to catch that raccoon.

Other books by the same author:
Carousel, 1994
Clean Your Room, Harvey Moon!, 1991
C.L.O.U.D.S., 1986
Jimmy Lee Did It, 1985 (debut)

Other books you might like:
Angela Johnson, *Julius*, 1993
Her granddaddy surprises a child by bringing her her very own pig from Alaska and she shares things she learns with her friends.

John Shearer, *Billy Jo Jive and the Case of the Midnight Voices*, 1982

Fifth mystery series title where a young boy and his young girl partner investigate and solve cases involving their young neighbors and friends.

91

CHRISTOPHER PAUL CURTIS, African American

The Watsons Go to Birmingham—1963

(New York: Delacorte Press, 1995)

Story type: Young Readers
Subject(s): Brothers and Sisters; Family Life; Prejudice
Age range(s): Grades 5 and Up
Major character(s): Kenny Watson, 10-Year-Old, Brother, African American; Byron Watson, 13-Year-Old, Brother, African American; Joetta Watson, 5-Year-Old, Sister, African American
Time period(s): 1960s (1963)
Locale(s): Flint, Michigan; Birmingham, Alabama

Summary: Kenny loves his little sister Joetta, although sometimes she is a pest and a tattletale. He alternately adores and fears his older brother Byron who is the "official juvenile delinquent" in the family now that he's thirteen. A series of adventures keeps Byron in trouble with his parents, who decide to drive the kids to Grandma Sands' house in Alabama, where Byron will stay until the end of summer. What starts out as an adventure in their spiffed-up car ends as a horrific initiation to racism when a Birmingham church is bombed.

About this book: Debut novel.

Where it's reviewed:
Booklist, August 1995, page 1946

Awards the book has won:
Coretta Scott King Honor Book, 1996
Newbery Honor Book, 1995

Other books you might like:
Joyce Hansen, *The Gift Giver*, 1980
    A young girl and her fifth grade friends come to like a new boy in their class and are surprised when they discover he is a foster child.
Mildred D. Taylor, *The Friendship*, 1987
    Another episode from the lives of the young Logan children in segregated rural Mississippi as they witness a confrontation caused by racial custom.
Mildred D. Taylor, *The Gold Cadillac*, 1987
    Two young sisters learn their first lessons about segregation and bigotry on a drive to Mississippi in their family's new Cadillac.
Mildred D. Taylor, *Let the Circle Be Unbroken*, 1981
    A continuation of the Logan family stories from the Depression era in rural Mississippi where racial antagonisms and conflicts prevail.

92

OSSIE DAVIS, African American

Just Like Martin

(New York: Simon and Schuster Books For Young Readers, 1992)

Story type: Young Adult
Subject(s): Historical; Civil Rights Movement; Fathers and Sons
Age range(s): Grades 6 and Up
Major character(s): Isaac Stone Jr., 14-Year-Old, Activist, African American; Isaac Stone Sr., Veteran, Carpenter, African American
Time period(s): 1960s (1963)
Locale(s): Alabama (unidentified city)

Summary: Being Junior Assistant Pastor and president of the Young People's Bible Class at Holy Oak Baptist church gave Isaac Jr. a lot of responsibility. On the eve of the congregation preparing to leave for the historic civil rights march on Washington, Isaac Jr. hopes his father will change his mind and let him attend. Isaac Sr., a Korean war veteran, does not believe in the nonviolent movement and has said he could not go. Now a widower, Isaac Sr. lives alone with his son and is not about to let him risk his life in a cause he does not believe in. Months later after a bombing kills two children at the church, a peaceful demonstration turns into a riot where father and son are attacked, and President Kennedy is assassinated, Isaac Sr. begins seeing things differently. He confesses to his son his deeds from the war, and returning to the church meets Martin Luther King Jr. in the hopes of learning more about his ideals.

About this book: Debut novel

Where it's reviewed:
Kliatt, July 1995, page 8
Publishers Weekly, January 16, 1995, page 456
New York Times Book Review, February 21, 1993, page 23

Other books you might like:
Virginia Hamilton, *A Little Love*, 1984
    A teenage girl has an emptiness food cannot fill. She misses her father, and in her search for him she finds new strengths in herself.
David Haynes, *Right by My Side*, 1993
    A high school student writes down his experiences in order to figure things out about his father, his mother and himself.
Mildred D. Taylor, *The Road to Memphis*, 1990
    Another incident from the lives of the Logan family in segregated Mississippi where racial hostilities erupt and new relationships unfold.
Mildred Pitts Walter, *The Girl on the Outside*, 1982
    A student and her white classmate see school integration from very different viewpoints.
Brenda Wilkinson, *Not Separate, Not Equal*, 1987
    Chosen among a group of six to integrate a Georgia high school, a teenage girl experiences hatred and racism and the beginning of civil rights.

93

THULANI DAVIS, African American

1959

(New York: Grove Weidenfeld, 1992)

Subject(s): Civil Rights Movement; Coming of Age; Race Relations
Age range(s): Grades 8-Adult
Major character(s): Katherine ''Willie'' Tarrant, Activist, Student—Junior High, African American; Dixon Tarrant, Activist, Professor, African American; Marian Alexander, Activist, Student—Junior High, African American
Time period(s): 1950s (1959)
Locale(s): Turner, Virginia

Summary: The impact of the historic civil rights movement is seen through the eyes of twelve-year-old ''Willie''. She recounts events including incidents of violence and sex which changed her life and the lives of those around her.

About this book: This is the author's debut novel.

Where it's reviewed:
Essence, May 1992, page 60
Newsweek, March 9, 1992, page 60
Publishers Weekly, December 6, 1991, page 56

Other books you might like:
Tina McElroy Ansa, *Baby of the Family*, 1989
    This coming-of-age tale is about a young girl who is born with supernatural powers.
Maxine Clair, *Rattlebone*, 1994
    This story is about the events in the life of a young girl coming of age in a small town in the 1950s.
Ntozake Shange, *Betsey Brown*, 1985
    This coming-of-age story is about the exploits of a young girl during an era of school integration. It relates the worries of her family and the discoveries she makes at her new school.
Charlotte Sherman, *One Dark Body*, 1993
    This story relates the incidents in the life of a young girl abandoned at birth. It deals with the return of her mother and her friend's entry into manhood.
A.J. Verdelle, *The Good Negress*, 1995
    A young country girl who wants more from life than cooking, cleaning, and washing moves to the city. She is encouraged by her teacher to strive for higher goals.

94

SAMUEL R. DELANY, African American

Dhalgren

(New York: Gregg Press, 1977)

Story type: Science Fiction
Subject(s): Interpersonal Relations; Outcasts; Race Relations
Age range(s): Adult
Major character(s): Kid, Biracial, Writer (poet)
Time period(s): 1970s
Locale(s): Bellona, Fictional Country

Summary: Gargantuan science fiction account set in the near future featuring Kid, a bi-racial (Indian/white) bisexual drifter who arrives in Bellona and becomes tangled in the city's web and the world of the Scorpions, a band of violent lowlife enforcers led by the Dragon Lady and white ex-pimp Nightmare. While he searches for himself and deals with the violence of the city around him, Kid creates a book of poems, *Brass Orchids*.

About this book: Copyrighted in 1974, this was originally published with typographical errors in 1975.

Other books by the same author:
The Mad Man, 1995 (gay fiction)
They Fly at Ciron, 1993 (fantasy)
The Tides of Lust, 1973 (pornographic, also published as *Equinox* (1973))
Babel-17, 1966 (science fiction)
The Jewels of Aptor, 1962 (debut novel (science fiction))

Other books you might like:
Cyrus Colter, *City of Light*, 1993
    Exploits in the life of a young Chicago man who travels to Paris writing letters to his deceased mother about his plight of being light-skinned.
Steven Corbin, *Fragments That Remain*, 1993
    Depicts a contemporary actor's life as he deals with racism, sexism, homophobia, bigotry, an interracial relationship, and secrets from the past.
Percival Everett, *Zulus*, 1990
    On a barren planet in the future, a white woman is raped and seeks refuge with the rebels because her fertility is a threat to the government.

95

SAMUEL R. DELANY, African American

The Mad Man

(New York: Masquerade Books, 1995)

Subject(s): Murder; Interpersonal Relations; Outcasts
Age range(s): Adult
Major character(s): John Marr, Student—College, African American, Homosexual
Time period(s): 1980s; 1990s (1980-1994)
Locale(s): New York, New York

Summary: Sexually explicit episodes abound in John's recounting of a fifteen year period from his gay life. A graduate student in philosophy, he is encouraged by a Jewish professor to conduct research for his doctorate on an extraordinary philosophy prodigy Timothy Hasler, a gay 29-year-old Korean American stabbed to death some years ago. John moves into an upstairs apartment in the same building where Tim once lived. He uncovers the unsavory details of Hasler's life while he himself roams the streets for several years, engaging in sexual acts with countless men. One of them, ''Mad Man Mike,'' was with Hasler the night he was murdered. John is distraught when he witnesses another man's murder and shocked when ''Mad Man Mike'' returns to his apartment and rapes him.

Other books by the same author:
Hogg, 1995 (pornographic)
They Fly at Ciron, 1993 (fantasy)

The Tides of Lust, 1973 (pornographic, also published as *Equinox* (1973))

The Towers of Toron, 1964 (science fiction, second novel in Fall of the Towers trilogy)

The Jewels of Aptor, 1962 (debut novel, science fiction)

Other books you might like:

Steven Corbin, *100 Days from Now*, 1994
The courtship and interracial relationship of two men who are both HIV-positive, one who has yet to tell his family he is gay and in love.

Melvin Dixon, *Vanishing Rooms*, 1991
The interwoven lives of a young man when his white male lover is gang raped and murdered, the woman he reaches out to, and one of the killers.

James Hardy, *B-Boy Blues*, 1994
Contemporary gay love story of two men attracted to one another in a dance bar and who come to learn love is something you have to work at.

96

SAMUEL R. DELANY, African American

Stars in My Pocket Like Grains of Sand
(New York: Bantam Books, 1984)

Story type: Adult; Science Fiction
Subject(s): Interpersonal Relations
Age range(s): Adult
Major character(s): Rat Korga, Survivor, Homosexual, African American; Marq Dyeth, Homosexual, Diplomat, African American
Time period(s): Indeterminate Future
Locale(s): Rhyonon, Planet—Imaginary; Velm, Planet—Imaginary

Summary: Species, human and alien, occupy a universe of planetary worlds. The interstellar agency, the Web, in charge of the general information about the universe is near to being torn apart by a conflict between the Family and the Sygn over how to prevent a Cultural Fugue. Besides humans the Xlvare the single species with a means of interstellar travel in the galaxy yet no communications has been established with them. Someone undergoing the brain process of radical anxiety termination at the Institute becomes known as a RAT and could have their labor sold. When his world is destroyed the lone survivor Rat Korga is rescued to a world where he meets another male Marq and they engage in a sexual relationship until mysteriously Rat Korga is taken away. Falling in love with Rat Korga, Marq is left wondering if the Xlvare destroyed his world and if they will ever see one another again.

About this book: First novel in a science fiction diptych

Other books by the same author:
Babel-17, 1966 (science fiction)
Empire Star, 1966 (science fiction)
The Ballad of Beta-2, 1965 (science fiction)
Captives of the Flame, 1963 (Fall of the Towers trilogy, also published as *Out of the Dead City* (1968))
The Jewels of Aptor, 1962 (debut novel; science fiction)

Other books you might like:

Octavia Butler, *Dawn*, 1987
First title in the science fiction Xenogenesis trilogy where humans have been captured for genetic engineering and mating among aliens.

Octavia Butler, *Wild Seed*, 1980
Science fiction series prequel depicting the origins of the Patternists to create a race of superhumans.

Nichelle Nichols, *Saturn's Child*, 1995
Debut science fiction novel of the adventures of a young woman genetically created from parents of different planets and endowed with special powers.

97

SAMUEL R. DELANY, African American

They Fly at Ciron
(New York: Tom Doherty Associates Book, 1993)

Story type: Adult; Fantasy
Subject(s): Mythology; Survival; War
Age range(s): Adult
Major character(s): Rahm of Ciron, Human (villager); Kire of Myetra, Human, Military Personnel (Lieutenant); Vortcir of Hi-Vator, Mythical Creature (winged one)
Time period(s): Indeterminate
Locale(s): Ciron, Mythical Place

Summary: Recounts the mythical tale of Ciron, a small village attacked by armies from the distant empire of Myetra. Wandering in the Cironian mountains, Lieutenant Kire encounters a naked villager, Rahm, who reveals his village has no weapons and fears the man-beast flying creatures of Hi-Vator. Rahm is befriended by Vortcir, a winged one, and they come to realize they must join forces if they are to endure the attack of the Myetra armies. Their ruins remain as monuments of tribute with memories which assure their endurance for later generations.

About this book: Expanded version of earlier short story.

Where it's reviewed:
Booklist, December 15, 1994, page 740
Kirkus Reviews, November 1, 1994, page 1448
Lambda Book Report, May 1995, page 47
New York Times Book Review, January 1, 1995, page 22

Other books by the same author:
Triton, 1976 (science fiction)
Dhalgren, 1974 (science fiction)
Nova, 1968 (science fiction)
The Einstein Intersection, 1967 (also published as *A Fabulous, Formless Darkness* (1968))
City of a Thousand Suns, 1965 (third novel in *Fall of the Towers* trilogy)

Other books you might like:

Octavia Butler, *Wild Seed*, 1980
Science fiction series prequel depicting the origins of the Patternists to create a race of superhumans.

Nichelle Nichols, *Saturn's Child*, 1995
Debut science fiction novel of adventures of a young woman genetically created from parents of different planets and endowed with special powers.

98

SAMUEL R. DELANY, African American

Triton

(New York, Bantam Books, 1976)

Story type: Science Fiction
Subject(s): Sex Roles; Interpersonal Relations; Self-Acceptance
Age range(s): Adult
Major character(s): Bron Helstrom, Researcher, Human (blond Martian)
Time period(s): 21st century (2112)
Locale(s): Tethys, Planet—Imaginary (Triton)

Summary: The Outer Satellites and the Inner Worlds are at war. The only Outer Satellite that has managed to stay out of the war is Triton on Neptune, the last major moon of the solar system. Its inhabitants reside in co-ops of either mixed-sex groups of male/female/straight/gay, single sex groups with nonspecified sexual preference, gay male groups, or heterosexual male or female groups. Thirty-seven-year-old blond Martian Bron lives at Serpent's House, an all-male co-op of nonspecified sexual preference. Moving there to "get away from women and sex" Bron diplomatically refuses sex with a seventy-something homosexual, only to later become mesmerized by and sexually involved with a thirty-four-year-old blond Ganymede actress known as The Spike. Following a trip to Earth where The Spike rejects his advances Bron returns to Triton where he undergoes a sexual refixation, becoming a bisexual female with a propensity for males, and discovers a different sense of alienation.

Other books by the same author:
They Fly at Ciron, 1993 (fantasy)
Stars in My Pocket Like Grains of Sand, 1984 (science fiction)
Dhalgren, 1977 (science fiction)
Babel-17, 1966 (science fiction)
The Jewels of Aptor, 1962 (science fiction, debut novel)

Other books you might like:
Nichelle Nichols, *Saturn's Child*, 1995
 Debut science fiction novel of adventures of a young woman genetically created of parents from different planets and endowed with special powers.

99

MELVIN DIXON, African American

Trouble the Water

(Boulder: University of Colorado, 1989)

Story type: Adult
Subject(s): Adolescence; Family Relations; Fathers and Sons
Age range(s): Adult
Major character(s): Jordan Henry, Professor, African American; Jake Williams, Father, Maintenance Worker, African American; Harriet Henry, Grandmother (Jordan's), African American
Time period(s): 1960s; 1980s
Locale(s): Pee Dee, North Carolina

Summary: Harriet's only daughter died giving birth to her grandson Jordan. Jordan becomes caught up in his grandmother's web of revenge against his father Jake. He finds himself destined to return home in his grandmother's plot after running away twenty years earlier.

About this book: This is the author's debut novel. Dixon died in 1992.

Where it's reviewed:
Booklist, October 15, 1989, page 426
Kirkus Reviews, August 15, 1989, page 1186
New York Times Book Review, September 24, 1989, page 48

Awards the book has won:
Ferro-Gumley Award for Best Male Fiction of the Year, 1992
Nilon Award, 1989

Other books by the same author:
Vanishing Rooms, 1991
Red Leaves, 1990

Other books you might like:
Reginald McKnight, *I Get on the Bus*, 1990
 A young man tries to avoid making decisions at home, so he joins the Peace Corps. When he travels to Senegal he becomes involved in a new intrigue.
John Edgar Wideman, *Philadelphia Fire*, 1990
 A self-exiled writer returns to Philadelphia to investigate a police bombing and the killing of adults and children.
Duane Smith, *The Nubian*, 1994
 Episodes from a young man's life and his relationship with a mysterious Afrocentric uncle whom the government convicts.

100

MELVIN DIXON, African American

Vanishing Rooms

(New York: Dutton Book, 1991)

Story type: Adult; Gay/Lesbian Fiction
Subject(s): Murder; Interpersonal Relations; City Life
Age range(s): Adult
Major character(s): Jesse Durand, Homosexual, Dancer, African American; Ruella "Rooms" McPhee, Dancer, Secretary, African American; Lonnie Russo, 15-Year-Old, Student—High School, Caucasian (Italian)
Time period(s): 1970s (1975-1976)
Locale(s): New York, New York (Greenwich Village)

Summary: Graduating college Jessie and his white lover Metro move to New York where Jessie pursues a dancing career and Metro becomes a journalist. When Metro is brutally murdered Jessie's life goes into a tailspin. Shocked and upset Jessie reaches out to Ruella a dancer he has just met and comes to nickname Rooms. Aware that Jessie and Metro were lovers Rooms lets herself become emotionally and sexually involved in Jessie's life. She is also struggling with her relationship to her older brother who is in prison on a drug conviction. Ultimately just friends, Jessie and Rooms develop other love relationships while putting their energies into their dance careers.

About this book: Author died in 1992.

Other books by the same author:
Red Leaves, 1990
Trouble the Water, 1989 (debut novel)

Other books you might like:
Steven Corbin, *Fragments That Remain*, 1993
Depicts a contemporary actor's life as he deals with racism, sexism, homophobia, bigotry, an interracial relationship, and secrets from the past.
Larry Duplechan, *Captain Swing*, 1993
Now in his mid-30s and coping with tragic losses in his life, the gay character from the author's debut novel is unsure about risking love again.
James Hardy, *B-Boy Blues*, 1994
Contemporary gay love story of two men attracted to one another in a dance bar, who come to learn love is something you have to work at.
E. Lynn Harris, *Just as I Am*, 1994
Bisexual affair of a young man, the impact on the woman who loves him, and their comforting a friend dying with AIDS.
Canaan Parker, *The Color of Trees*, 1992
A contemporary gay coming-of-age story reflecting on the first sexual experiences of a young boy from Harlem sent to private boarding school.

101

RITA DOVE, African American

Through the Ivory Gate

(New York: Vintage Books, 1992)

Subject(s): Coming of Age; Secrets
Age range(s): Adult
Major character(s): Virginia King, Actress, African American
Time period(s): 1970s
Locale(s): Akron, Ohio

Summary: This is a portrait of Virginia's childhood days and about her growing up to become an actress. After spending many years with her memories she returns to her home town only to have an unspoken family secret revealed to her.

About this book: This is the author's debut novel.

Where it's reviewed:
Kirkus Reviews, July 15, 1992, page 866
Library Journal, August 1992, page 146
Publishers Weekly, August 3, 1992, page 58

Other books you might like:
Anita Richmond Bunkley, *Black Gold*, 1994
A young woman who is on the brink of ruin before the historic oil boom in Texas during the 1920, finds herself accused of murder. Through all this, a family secret is revealed.
J. California Cooper, *In Search of Satisfaction*, 1994
This family saga is about two half-sisters born in the era of the plantation South. They have to deal with their parent's secret legacy and inheritance.
Marsha Hunt, *Joy*, 1991
A childless woman befriends a neighbor girl who sings with her sisters. The girl grows up to become a star and

when she dies, her untimely death reveals shocking secrets.
Paule Marshall, *Daughters*, 1991
A determined young woman struggles in her relationship with her political father and when she returns home for a visit she makes an important decision.

102

SHARON M. DRAPER, African American

Tears of a Tiger

(New York: Atheneum, 1994)

Story type: Young Adult
Subject(s): Accidents; Suicide; Interpersonal Relations
Age range(s): Grades 8-10
Major character(s): Andrew "Andy" Jackson, Basketball Player, Accident Victim, African American; Robert Orlando "Rob" Washington, Basketball Player, Accident Victim, African American
Time period(s): 1990s
Locale(s): United States

Summary: The Hazelwood High School Tigers basketball team has won another victory. Andy drives away from the game with Rob, the captain of the team, and two other classmates to celebrate. He plans on dropping everyone off and then going to his girlfriend's. Drinking along the way Andy loses control of the car and has a crash that kills Rob. Grief-stricken Andy has a hard time readjusting to life and school after the accident. When he reaches out for help only Keisha seems to understand his pain and bouts of depression. His therapist says he is stable yet his grades continue to suffer and finally he and Keisha have a fight and break up. Depressed and confused, Andy is in danger with no one to turn to.

About this book: This is the author's debut novel.

Where it's reviewed:
Booklist, November 1, 1994, page 492
Publishers Weekly, October 31, 1994, page 64
School Library Journal, February 1995, page 112
Voice of Youth Advocates, February 1995, page 338

Other books by the same author:
Ziggy and the Black Dinosaurs, 1994

Other books you might like:
Walter Dean Myers, *Fallen Angels*, 1988
The life-changing experiences of a 17-year-old high school graduate who enlists in the Army and is transported on a tour of duty in Vietnam.
Walter Dean Myers, *Hoops*, 1981
A talented teenaged basketball player is befriended by an ex-pro player who became an alcoholic after his career ended in a gambling scandal.
Joyce Carol Thomas, *Marked by Fire*, 1982
Friends and family help a young girl overcome the effects of a tornado and a physical assault which nearly breaks her will.
Brenda Wilkinson, *Ludell's New York Time*, 1980
Moving from Georgia to New York City in her senior year a teenager struggles to adjust to life in 1960s Harlem.

Jacqueline Woodson, *From the Notebooks of Melanin Sun*, 1995

A 13-year-old boy's world is turned upside down and he has to confront his prejudices when his mother tells him she is in love with a white woman.

103

SHARON M. DRAPER, African American
JAMES E. RANSOME, Illustrator, African American

Ziggy and the Black Dinosaurs
(Orange, New Jersey: Just Us Books, Inc., 1994)

Story type: Young Readers
Subject(s): Clubs; Cemeteries; Friendship
Age range(s): Grades 3-4
Major character(s): Ziggy, 10-Year-Old, 5th Grader, African American
Time period(s): 1990s
Locale(s): Cincinnati, Ohio

Summary: When the neighborhood basketball court is destroyed a group of friends Ziggy, Rashawn, Rico, and Jerome start their own club, the Black Dinosaurs. Rashawn donates his plastic dinosaur to be their mascot and the boys build their clubhouse in Ziggy's backyard. Complete with a secret password the boys set about their first mission; each must bring one official treasure to the clubhouse to bury. Digging the burial hole, the boys discover a mysterious old box with bones in it. Wondering how it got there and what it means, the boys begin looking for clues. In the process they discover who destroyed their basketball court, why an old neighborhood man has been writing weird notes and singing strange songs, and what historical events took place right in Ziggy's own backyard.

Where it's reviewed:
Children's Bookwatch, February 1995, page 3
School Library Journal, March 1995, page 202

Other books by the same author:
Tears of a Tiger, 1994 (debut novel)

Other books you might like:
Virginia Hamilton, *Junius over Far*, 1985
When his grandfather returns to his Caribbean island home, a disturbing letter prompts a young boy and his father to journey to rescue him.
Virginia Hamilton, *The Mystery of Drear House*, 1987
A house that was a station on the Underground Railroad has secret passageways and hidden treasure which must be saved before it is too late.
Walter Dean Myers, *Mouse Rap*, 1990
Summer exploits of a 14-year-old when he hears about a hidden treasure in his neighborhood and his separated parents try getting back together.
Walter Dean Myers, *Tales of a Dead King*, 1983
Journeying to Egypt to participate in an archaeological dig, two white teenagers are intrigued by the mysterious disappearance of the dig's director.
Eleanora E. Tate, *The Secret of Gumbo Grove*, 1987
A youngster upsets her community and her parents when

she spreads stories she's heard about the town ancestors buried in the church cemetery.

104

TANANARIVE DUE, African American

The Between
(New York: Harper Collins, 1995)

Subject(s): Family Relations; Psychological Thriller; Supernatural
Age range(s): Adult
Major character(s): Hilton James, Social Worker, Spouse, African American; Dede James, Judge, Spouse, African American
Time period(s): 1990s
Locale(s): Florida (Dade County)

Summary: When Hilton was a boy, his grandmother gave her own life to rescue him from drowning in the ocean. As his thirty-ninth birthday approaches, Hilton's wife begins to receive racist hate mail and threats to their family. Hilton suffers from nightmares. He begins to lose his grip on reality as he desperately tries to protect and hold on to the people and the life he loves.

About this book: This is the author's debut novel.

Where it's reviewed:
Essence, June 1995, page 52
Library Journal, June 1, 1995, page 158
Publishers Weekly, April 24, 1995, page 60

Other books you might like:
Leon Forrest, *Divine Days*, 1992
An aspiring playwright captures the voices of the living and the dead in an epic tale referred to as *The Ulysses of the South Side*.
Gloria Naylor, *Mama Day*, 1988
Returning to her sea island home, a young woman finds both body and soul threatened by supernatural forces. She is saved by Mama Day.
Ntozake Shange, *Liliane: Resurrection of the Daughter*, 1994
In psychotherapy, a young woman reveals how she coped with family upheavals, romances, friendships, racism, and bigotry.
Ray Shell, *Iced*, 1993
A man reflects in his diary about his accomplishments in life as well as his regrets of descending into the white-smoke world of crack cocaine.
Brent Wade, *Company Man*, 1992
Behind-the-scene stresses and strains faced by a man attempting to climb the business ladder and preserve his family.

105

LARRY DUPLECHAN, African American

Blackbird
(New York: St. Martin's Press, 1986)

Story type: Gay/Lesbian Fiction
Series: Johnnie Ray Rousseau

Subject(s): Coming of Age; Family Relations; Friendship
Age range(s): Adult
Major character(s): Johnnie Ray Rousseau, 17-Year-Old, Homosexual, African American
Time period(s): 1970s (1974)
Locale(s): California (an unidentified town 90 miles outside Los Angeles)

Summary: At 17, Johnnie Ray Rousseau has his first sexual experiences, with both a female classmate and a man he meets at the local junior college. When a classmate's father brutally beats his son for being gay, Johnnie Ray's pastor betrays Johnnie Ray's confidence and tells his homophobic parents he is gay. He survives their subjecting him to a religious exorcism and other traumas. Johnnie Ray graduates from high school and goes away to college looking for acceptance and the gay love of his life.

About this book: This second title of the Johnnie Ray Rousseau series is generally acknowledged as the "first contemporary African American gay coming-out novel."

Where it's reviewed:
Booklist, November 1, 1986, page 385
Kirkus Reviews, September 15, 1986, page 1392
Publishers Weekly, July 19, 1989, page 57

Other books by the same author:
Captain Swing, 1993 (Johnnie Ray Rousseau series)
Tangled Up in Blue, 1989
Eight Days a Week, 1985 (debut novel, Johnnie Ray Rousseau series)

Other books you might like:
April Sinclair, *Coffee Will Make You Black*, 1995
    This coming-of-age story is about a young girl in Chicago during the 1960s. She questions her sexuality when she recognizes her feelings for the school nurse.
Jacqueline Woodson, *Autobiography of a Family Photo*, 1995
    This story is about a teenage girl in New York, who has a gay brother and a half-white brother. She experiences family violence, and she questions her own sexuality.

106

LARRY DUPLECHAN, African American

Captain Swing

(Boston: Alyson Publications, 1993)

Story type: Adult; Gay/Lesbian Fiction
Series: Johnnie Ray Rousseau
Subject(s): Family Relations; Fathers and Sons; Interpersonal Relations
Major character(s): Johnnie Ray Rousseau, Singer, Homosexual, African American; Lance Rousseau, Patient, Divorced Person, African American; Nigel Thibodeaux, 18-Year-Old, Homosexual, African American
Time period(s): 1990s (1993)
Locale(s): St. Charles, Louisiana

Summary: Johnnie Ray journeys back home to his homophobic father's deathbed and is disappointed to discover nothing has changed about his father's feelings. After the death of his lover Keith in a hit-and-run accident, Johnnie Ray is still grieving. Surprised at his attraction to his young second

cousin Nigel, Johnnie Ray lets himself be seduced and asks Nigel if he would like to come live with him in Los Angeles.

Where it's reviewed:
Booklist, September 1, 1993, page 33
Kirkus Reviews, August 1, 1993, page 952
Lambda Book Report, November 1993, page 24

Other books by the same author:
Tangled Up in Blue, 1989
Blackbird, 1986 (Johnnie Ray Rousseau series)
Eight Days a Week, 1985 (debut novel, Johnnie Ray Rousseau series)

Other books you might like:
Steven Corbin, *Fragments That Remain*, 1993
    Depicts a contemporary actor's life as he deals with racism, sexism, homophobia, bigotry, an interracial relationship, and secrets from the past.
James Hardy, *B-Boy Blues*, 1994
    Contemporary gay love story of two men attracted to one another in a dance bar who come to learn love is something you have to work at.

107

LARRY DUPLECHAN, African American

Tangled Up in Blue

(New York: St. Martin's Press, 1989)

Subject(s): AIDS (Disease); Interpersonal Relations; Marriage
Age range(s): Adult
Major character(s): Maggie Elizabeth Taylor Sullivan, Spouse (pregnant), Physical Fitness Expert, Caucasian; Daniel Christopher Taylor Sullivan, Spouse (bisexual), Lawyer, Caucasian; Crockett Miller, Homosexual, Writer, Caucasian
Time period(s): 1980s (1985)
Locale(s): Los Angeles, California

Summary: When Maggie and Daniel met on a double date, it was love at first sight and they were engaged six months later. Now married a year, Maggie is expecting their first child. She learns their close friend Crockett has been diagnosed with AIDS-related complex (ARC). When Maggie discovers Daniel has been tested for AIDS, and he and Crockett were former lovers, she fears for her marriage, her own health and the baby's health.

Where it's reviewed:
Kirkus Reviews, January 1, 1989, page 5
Publishers Weekly, January 6, 1989, page 91

Other books by the same author:
Captain Swing, 1993 (Johnnie Ray Rousseau series)
Blackbird, 1986
Eight Days a Week, 1985 (debut novel, Johnnie Ray Rousseau series)

Other books you might like:
E. Lynn Harris, *Just as I Am*, 1994
    This story is about the bisexual affairs of a young man. It includes how his life impacts the woman who loves him, and how they comfort a friend dying with AIDS.

108

LOUIS EDWARDS, African American

Ten Seconds

(Saint Paul: Graywolf Press, 1991)

Story type: Adult
Subject(s): Coming of Age; Family Relations; Secrets
Age range(s): Adult
Major character(s): Edward "Eddie" James Franklin, Father, Worker, African American; Betty Franklin, Mother, Sister (oldest), African American; Coco, Sister (youngest), Teenager, African American
Time period(s): 1980s (1981)
Locale(s): South End, Texas

Summary: During a track meet Eddie, nearly thirty, daydreams about his life. He relives his past and anticipates his future as a husband and father. As he reflects on his years of adolescence, his family and friends, his marriage to Betty and their kids, he also remembers the family secret he keeps with his young sister-in-law, Coco.

About this book: This is the author's debut novel.

Where it's reviewed:
Essence, September 1991, page 50
Library Journal, May 1, 1991, page 105
Publishers Weekly, May 3, 1991, page 69

Other books you might like:
Melvin Dixon, *Trouble the Water*, 1989
    A young man returns home twenty years later in a plot of revenge between his grandmother and his father.
Trey Ellis, *Home Repairs*, 1993
    A young man captures his coming-of-age exploits in his journal. He searches for love and he finds success in his career.
Nelson George, *Urban Romance*, 1993
    This contemporary story tells of the relationship of a young couple brought together by mutual friends as they experience love and heartbreak.
Reginald McKnight, *I Get on the Bus*, 1990
    A young man tries to avoid making decisions at home, so he joins the Peace Corps. When he travels to Senegal, he becomes involved in a new intrigue.
Dennis Williams, *Crossover*, 1992
    This story relates the events in the life of a young man during the Civil Rights era. He becomes a reluctant activist and he has an interracial affair.

109

GRACE EDWARDS-YEARWOOD, African American

In the Shadow of the Peacock

(New York: McGraw Hill Book Company, 1988)

Subject(s): Mothers and Daughters; Racism
Age range(s): Adult
Major character(s): Celia, Student, Secretary, African American; Frieda, Mother, Widow(er), African American
Time period(s): 20th century (1943-1964)
Locale(s): New York, New York (Harlem)

Summary: Born on the street the night of a riot in which her father was killed, Celia's life has always been closely guarded by her mother Frieda. Controlling in her fear for herself and her daughter, Frieda tries to protect them both from a world that has taken her husband's life. Celia strikes out in spite of her mother's fears, discovering her own voice, her own love and her part in the struggle for civil rights.

About this book: Debut novel.

Other books you might like:
Doris Jean Austin, *After the Garden*, 1987
    The story of a woman caught between her strict grandmother and the free-spirited love of her life and his family in the urban north of the 50s. (Author died in 1994)
Cherry Muhanji, *Her*, 1990
    A young light-skinned woman falls into "the life" of 1950s Detroit and finds a strength in herself and the women around her necessary to her survival.
Alice Walker, *Meridian*, 1976
    A deserted mother at seventeen, a young girl gets involved in the civil rights movement which changes her life and defines her role in the world.

110

TREY ELLIS, African American

Home Repairs

(New York: Simon and Schuster, 1993)

Subject(s): Coming of Age; Interpersonal Relations; School Life
Age range(s): Adult
Major character(s): Austin McMillan, Television Personality, Adoptee, African American
Time period(s): 1970s; 1980s (1979-1988)
Locale(s): Andover, New Hampshire; Stanford, California; New York, New York

Summary: On the eve of a prep school dance, 16-year-old Austin worries about his lack of success with girls. In the hope of learning what he's been doing wrong, he starts a journal of past memories and present events. The journal evolves to span ten years of the exploits in his life. He discovers sex, falls in and out of love, graduates from college, travels abroad, becomes a host on a TV home repair show, meets Playboy mogul Hugh Hefner, and finds a close relationship.

Where it's reviewed:
Essence, August 1993, page 52
New Yorker, September 6, 1993, page 117
Publishers Weekly, May 3, 1993, page 292

Other books by the same author:
Platitudes, 1988 (debut novel)

Other books you might like:
Louis Edwards, *Ten Seconds*, 1991
    This story is about the memories in a young man's life as he anticipates his future as a husband and father, and reflects on the family secret he has kept.
Nelson George, *Urban Romance*, 1993
    This contemporary story tells the relationship of a young couple brought together by mutual friends as they experience love and heartbreak.

Reginald McKnight, *I Get on the Bus*, 1990

A young man tries to avoid making decisions at home, so he joins the Peace Corps. When he travels to Senegal, he becomes involved in a new intrigue.

Dennis Williams, *Crossover*, 1992

This story relates the events in the life of a young man during the Civil Rights era. He becomes a reluctant activist and he has an interracial affair.

111

TREY ELLIS, African American

Platitudes

(New York: Vintage Books, 1988)

Subject(s): Creative Writing; Interpersonal Relations
Age range(s): Adult
Major character(s): Dewayne Wellington, Divorced Person, Writer, African American; Isshee Ayam, Writer, African American
Time period(s): 1980s (1984-1985)
Locale(s): New York, New York

Summary: This is a story within a story. Dewayne shares his creative writing by corresponding with another author Isshee, seeking her advice. Reshaping his teen-age characters into her own parallel story, Isshee sends them back to him. As their creative stories about the teenagers evolve, so does a story about their own relationship. Discovering themselves and each other in their characters, they finally decide to meet face-to-face.

About this book: This is the author's debut novel.

Where it's reviewed:
Essence, June 1988, page 36
New Yorker, February 13, 1989, page 93
Publishers Weekly, July 1, 1988, page 72

Other books by the same author:
Home Repairs, 1993

Other books you might like:
Louis Edwards, *Ten Seconds*, 1991

This story is about the memories in a young man's life as he anticipates his future as a husband and father, and reflects on the family secret he has kept.

Nelson George, *Urban Romance*, 1993

This contemporary story tells the relationship of a young couple brought together by mutual friends as they experience love and heartbreak.

Toni Morrison, *Tar Baby*, 1981

Two young lovers from different backgrounds experience the conflicts wrought by social and cultural circumstances.

Albert Murray, *The Spyglass Tree*, 1991

A young man, one of the ''talented tenth,'' attends college in Mobile county. He gets involved with new friends, while learning about himself.

Ntozake Shange, *Liliane: Resurrection of the Daughter*, 1994

In psychotherapy, the exploits of a young woman's life reveal how she copes with family upheavals, romances, friendships, racism, and bigotry.

112

PERCIVAL EVERETT, African American

Cutting Lisa

(New York: Ticknor and Fields, 1986)

Story type: Adult
Subject(s): Cheating; Family Relations; Fathers and Sons
Age range(s): Adult
Major character(s): John Livesey, Aged Person (retired doctor), Widow(er) (grandfather), Caucasian
Time period(s): 1980s
Locale(s): Yachats, Oregon

Summary: John spends the summer in a small town with his son Elgin, his daughter-in-law Lisa, and his granddaughter. Both Elgin and Lisa seem unhappy she is pregnant, and John discovers the reason—Elgin had a vasectomy a year ago. John suspects who Lisa had an affair with and he considers taking matters into his own hands.

Where it's reviewed:
Booklist, October 1, 1986, page 188
Kirkus Reviews, September 1, 1986, page 1309

Other books by the same author:
God's Country, 1994
For Her Dark Skin, 1990
Zulus, 1990
Walk Me to the Distance, 1985
Suder, 1983 (debut novel)

Other books you might like:
John Edgar Wideman, *Reuben*, 1987

This story relates the exploits of an aged lawyer and the various clients he represents in the Pittsburgh community of Homewood during the 1980s.

113

PERCIVAL EVERETT, African American

For Her Dark Skin

(Seattle: Owl Creek Press, 1990)

Story type: Adult
Subject(s): Mythology; Revenge
Major character(s): Jason, Hero, African American; Medea, Royalty, Sorceress, African American
Time period(s): 1990s
Locale(s): Mythical Place (Colchis); Corinth, Greece

Summary: In this contemporary treatment of classic mythology, Jason goes in search of the Golden Fleece, and is aided by the Princess of Colchis, Medea, a sorceress. She despises him, but is under Cupid's spell and so falls in love with Jason, bearing him twin sons. When he decides to leave Medea and marry young Creusa, the daughter of King Creon, Medea sends a secretly poisoned wedding gift, killing the girl. Before Jason can return for his sons, Medea kills them and escapes by magic.

Other books by the same author:
God's Country, 1994
Zulus, 1990

Cutting Lisa, 1986
Walk Me to the Distance, 1985
Suder, 1983 (debut novel)

Other books you might like:
Samuel R. Delany, *They Fly at Ciron*, 1993
    Tale of mythological creatures and humans who fear one another yet come to be allies against others who would destroy them by war.

114

PERCIVAL EVERETT, African American

God's Country

(Boston: Faber and Faber, 1994)

Story type: Satire
Subject(s): Adventure and Adventurers; American West; Frontier and Pioneer Life
Age range(s): Adult
Major character(s): Curt Marder, Rancher, Gambler, Caucasian; Bubba, Frontiersman, Scout, African American; Jake, Child (girl), Caucasian
Time period(s): 1800s (1871)
Locale(s): West

Summary: Having lost his farm, his wife and his dog, a white man, Curt, hires a tracker, Bubba, to recover what is rightfully his. Subsequently Curt finds himself in all sorts of difficulties. He survives only through Bubba's abilities to cope in this old west story.

Where it's reviewed:
Library Journal, May 1, 1994, page 136
New York Times Book Review, June 5, 1994, page 43
Publishers Weekly, April 18, 1994, page 46

Other books by the same author:
For Her Dark Skin, 1990
Zulus, 1990
Cutting Lisa, 1986
Walk Me to the Distance, 1985
Suder, 1983 (debut novel for adults)

Other books you might like:
Ishmael Reed, *Japanese by Spring*, 1993
    This satire of academic life and race relations is told through the exploits of a professor who will endure any insult to get tenure.

115

PERCIVAL EVERETT, African American
DIRK ZIMMER, Illustrator, German

The One That Got Away

(New York: Clarion Books, 1992)

Story type: Young Readers
Subject(s): American West; Folk Tales
Age range(s): Grades 1-2
Time period(s): Indeterminate Past
Locale(s): United States (unidentified western region)

Summary: A story from the old west of a group of cowboys rounding up ones. The first one they caught was strong and put up a hard fight until it was wrestled into the corral. Hunting for more ones the cowboys look in canyons and near waterholes. Finally they discover an entire herd of ones and round them up into the corral with the first one. Nightfall comes and one jumps the fence and gets away. The cowboys discover one is missing the next morning and they ride out to find it. They search high and low and spot the big one on a steep mountaintop. Climbing the mountain they discover they need a stairway to get across the path and when they do finally reach to top of the mountain there is no one there. On the way back to the corral they talk about the eight other ones they have but when they get back to the corral they discover they had not a single one.

About this book: Debut (Young Readers).

Other books by the same author:
Suder, 1983 (debut novel (adults))

Other books you might like:
Ashley Bryan, *The Story of Lightning & Thunder*, 1993
    A West African folktale about Ma Sheep Thunder and her disobedient Son Ram Lightning who caused them to be banished from the earth to the sky.
Elizabeth Fitzgerald Howard, *Papa Tells Chita a Story*, 1995
    A child asks her beloved papa to tell her the story of when he was the bravest soldier and carried the message and won the war.
Angela Shelf Medearis, *Too Much Talk*, 1995
    Retells a traditional West African folktale of events that occur when a farmer hearing a yam talk runs off screaming in the heat of the day.
Walter Dean Myers, *The Story of the Three Kingdoms*, 1995
    An original fable of how the rulers of the forest, the sea, and the sky were overcome by people telling stories by their fire that gave them wisdom.
Faith Ringgold, *Aunt Harriet's Underground Railroad in the Sky*, 1992
    Flying in the sky a sister and her younger brother discovering the underground railroad to freedom must retrace its route to be reunited.

116

PERCIVAL EVERETT, African American

Suder

(New York: Viking Press, 1983)

Subject(s): Mental Illness; Mothers and Sons
Age range(s): Adult
Major character(s): Craig Suder, Baseball Player, Brother, African American
Time period(s): 1900s
Locale(s): Seattle, Washington

Summary: A few years after the integration of baseball, Craig Suder is third baseman for the Seattle Mariners. When he hits a slump, his coach puts him on the disabled roster telling him to take some time off. He begins to wonder if he's going insane just as his mother did when he was ten-years-old. He decides to run away when he suspects his wife of having an affair with their white neighbor. On his journey, he encounters a homosexual landlord, a murdering drug smuggler, and a child runaway.

About this book: This is the author's debut novel for adults.

Where it's reviewed:
Library Journal, July 1983, page 1381
Publishers Weekly, June 17, 1983, page 63
Time, August 22, 1983, page 70

Other books by the same author:
God's Country, 1994
For Her Dark Skin, 1990
Zulus, 1990
Cutting Lisa, 1986
Walk Me to the Distance, 1985

Other books you might like:
Cyrus Colter, *City of Light*, 1993
  This story is about the exploits of a young Chicago man who travels to Paris and writes letters to his deceased mother about hther about the plight of being light-skinned.

117

PERCIVAL EVERETT, African American

Walk Me to the Distance

(New York: Ticknor and Fields, 1985)

Subject(s): Interpersonal Relations; Mental Illness; Mothers and Sons
Age range(s): Adult
Major character(s): David Larsen, Brother, Veteran (Vietnam), Caucasian; Chloe Sixbury, Aged Person, Mother, Caucasian; Patrick Sixbury, Mentally Ill Person, Caucasian
Time period(s): 1970s (1975)
Locale(s): Savannah, Georgia; Slut's Hole, Wyoming

Summary: Returning from the Vietnam War, David, a white southerner, is in search of himself. His parents are dead and he is estranged from his only sister, so he buys a car and heads out west. In Wyoming, he has car trouble and he rents a room from Chloe, an elderly woman rancher. Chloe's retarded son Patrick disappears and the police investigate because they think he might have been murdered. David hides the secret of Patrick's whereabouts, and stays with Chloe, who seems to be preparing for her own demise.

Where it's reviewed:
Kirkus Reviews, December 15, 1984, page 1156
Publishers Weekly, December 21, 1984, page 81

Other books by the same author:
God's Country, 1994
For Her Dark Skin, 1990
Zulus, 1990
Cutting Lisa, 1986
Suder, 1983 (debut novel)

Other books you might like:
Arthur Flowers, *De Mojo Blues*, 1985
  This story depicts a Vietnam veteran dishonorably discharged for murder with his buddies. He now wants to become trained in the ways of hoodoo and conjuring.

118

PERCIVAL EVERETT, African American

Watershed

(Saint Paul: Graywolf Press, 1996)

Subject(s): Indian Reservations; Race Relations; Rivers
Age range(s): Adult
Major character(s): Robert Hawks, Scientist, African American
Time period(s): 1990s
Locale(s): Denver, Colorado (Plata Reservation)

Summary: On a fishing trip to put some distance between himself and Karen, his neurotic girlfriend, Robert finds himself inadvertently involved in a dispute over Native American treaty rights when two FBI agents are found murdered at a lake near the cabin where he is staying. A hydrologist by trade, he is able to use his natural curiosity and his knowledge of the land to uncover some very shady dealings.

Other books by the same author:
God's Country, 1994
For Her Dark Skin, 1990
Zulus, 1990
Walk Me to the Distance, 1985
Suder, 1983

Other books you might like:
David Haynes, *Live at Five*, 1996
  A television anchor seeks to re-define his image by broadcasting from the inner city to improve ratings, and finds the "real" story.
Clarence Major, *Painted Turtle: Woman with Guitar*, 1988
  A man tells the story of a young Indian woman alienated from her culture and finding her identity as a performer on the cantina circuit.
John A. Williams, *Jacob's Ladder*, 1987
  An army Major is involved in a CIA coup when the African country he once lived in as a boy gains access to nuclear power.

119

PERCIVAL EVERETT, African American

Zulus

(Sag Harbor, NY: The Permanent Press, 1990)

Story type: Adult
Subject(s): Loneliness; Survival
Major character(s): Alice Achitophel, Clerk, Outcast, Caucasian; Kevin Peters, Guide, Rebel, African American
Time period(s): Indeterminate Future
Locale(s): United States

Summary: Alice is a 300-pound woman living in the city some years after a thermo-nuclear war. She is the last woman alive who is not sterile, a fact she has kept to herself for 13 years because it poses a threat to the government. When she is raped, she seeks refuge outside the city in the rebel camps. Kevin Peters guides Alice and two other people to a camp where Alice is held captive by rebels who only want her baby. In a surrealistic episode, Alice explodes and walks out of her own body, leaving its pieces behind. She finds Kevin, and they return to the city where they live together. Alice assumes a new identity and returns to work, secretly planning to help the rebel cause. Kevin disappears, and Alice finally finds him struggling to remedy the problems of the society gone awry on a dying planet.

Other books by the same author:
God's Country, 1994
For Her Dark Skin, 1990
Cutting Lisa, 1986
Walk Me to the Distance, 1985
Suder, 1983 (debut novel)

Other books you might like:
Octavia Butler, *Dawn*, 1987
First title in the science fiction Xenogenesis trilogy where humans have been captured for genetic engineering and mating among aliens.
Octavia Butler, *Parable of the Sower*, 1993
Science fiction tale of a young girl journeying into an insecure world to start her own "earthseed" colony when her family is killed.

120

DWAYNE J. FERGUSON, Author/Illustrator, African American

Captain Africa: The Battle for Egyptica
(Trenton, New Jersey: Africa World Press Inc., 1992)

Story type: Young Readers
Subject(s): Adventure and Adventurers; Science Fiction; Fantasy
Age range(s): Grades 5-8
Major character(s): Prince Najee M'witu, Adventurer ("Captain Africa"), African, Royalty; Princess Johari Wilmanzu, Royalty, African; Buni, Friend, Inventor, African American
Time period(s): Indeterminate Future
Locale(s): Egyptica, Africa

Summary: Prince Najee M'witu has a secret life—when he dons the costume of Captain Africa and holds evil at bay. Attracted to the beautiful Princess Johari, Najee must keep his secret for just a while longer. His inventor friend Buni has always seen to it that he has the tools he needs, and now he needs all the help he can get. Terror Supreme is plotting to destroy the people of Africa and use all the resources of the continent—gold, diamonds, and more—to take over the world. Armed with the wisdom of his ancestors and the power of the Black Flame, Captain Africa must fight Terror Supreme face to face.

About this book: Debut.

Other books you might like:
Virginia Hamilton, *The Gathering*, 1981
Four children time-travel to Dustland and battle Mal, an entity who controls the future but whose immense power has gone awry.
Walter Dean Myers, *Mojo and the Russians*, 1977
A group of twelve-year-olds try to save their friend from a voodoo spell and discover if their neighbors are spies for the Russians.
Walter Dean Myers, *The Nicholas Factor*, 1983
Spy adventure of a young white boy who finds himself in the jungles of Peru when he is asked to infiltrate a suspected neo-Nazi organization.
Walter Dean Myers, *Tales of a Dead King*, 1983
Journeying to Egypt to participate in an archaeological dig, two white teenagers are intrigued by the mysterious disappearance of the dig's director.

121

VALERIE FLOURNOY, African American
GEORGE FORD JR., Illustrator, African American

The Best Time of Day
(New York: Random House, 1978)

Story type: Young Readers
Subject(s): Parent and Child; Family Life
Age range(s): Grades 1-2
Major character(s): William, Child, African American
Time period(s): 1970s
Locale(s): United States (unidentified city)

Summary: He knows he has a busy day ahead when William wakes up hearing his father's car drive away. Sometimes he thinks morning is the best time of day. At the community center with his babysitter, William has lots of fun playing and being with friends. After lunch is nap time, which isn't a good time of the day. When evening comes William knows it's his favorite time of day because that's when daddy comes home and just before bedtime, the family talks about their busy day.

Other books by the same author:
Celie and the Harvest Fiddle, 1995
Tanya's Reunion, 1995
The Twins Strike Back, 1994
The Patchwork Quilt, 1985

Other books you might like:
Jeannette Franklin Caines, *Daddy*, 1977
Saturdays are special for a child when her father comes to get her to visit with him and they share laughs and fun together all day.
Eloise Greenfield, *First Pink Light*, 1976
A child wants to stay awake until his daddy comes home so he can hide and surprise him but falls asleep waiting in a chair and daddy takes him to bed.
Dolores Johnson, *Papa's Stories*, 1994
Enjoying the stories her papa tells from her books a kindergartner says she'll teach him to read when she discovers he doesn't know how.
Ianthe Thomas, *Willie Blows a Mean Horn*, 1981
Proud of his jazz musician papa a young boy spends special times with him at the club where he plays and thinks of becoming a musician like his papa.
Sharon Dennis Wyeth, *Always My Dad*, 1995
A young girl remembers the summer she and her three younger brothers spent at their grandparents when their dad visited and how much she misses him.

122

VALERIE FLOURNOY, African American
JERRY PINKNEY, Illustrator, African American

The Patchwork Quilt
(New York: Dial Books For Young Readers, 1985)

Story type: Young Readers
Subject(s): Family Life; Grandparents; Quilts
Age range(s): Grades 2-4
Major character(s): Tanya Franklin, Child, Sister, African American
Time period(s): 1980s
Locale(s): United States (unidentified city)

Summary: Unable to play outside, Tanya wanders off to talk with grandma. Sitting in her favorite soft chair grandma has a lot of scraps of materials of all textures and colors in her lap. She explains to Tanya how her mother had made her a quilt when she was just about Tanya's age. Saying she wants to help grandma make the quilt Tanya is shocked to learn it may take over a year to make the masterpiece grandma wants. Grandma gathered scraps and worked on the quilt for several months until winter arrived. Then she and Tanya's mama begin working on the quilt together in the evenings. After Christmas grandma took sick. With grandma still recovering Tanya and her mama begin working on the quilt together. It's not until summer that grandma is able to work on the quilt again and she put the finishing touches on it. That night the masterpiece is unveiled and the family remembers the past year of work that went into it. Tanya is especially touched when she sees the corner patch in the last row with her name on it from mama and grandma.

Awards the book has won:
American Library Association Notable Book, 1985
Reading Rainbow Feature Selection, 1984

Other books by the same author:
Celie and the Harvest Fiddle, 1995
Tanya's Reunion, 1995
The Twins Strike Back, 1994
The Best Time of Day, 1978 (debut (young readers))

Other books you might like:
Jeannette Franklin Caines, *Window Wishing*, 1980
A young sister and brother spending their vacation with their fun grandma who takes them downtown together where they window wish.
Donald Crews, *Bigmama's*, 1991
Recalls the summer exploits of a youngster in the 1940s when he, his brother, sisters, and parents visit his grandparents in the country.
Eloise Greenfield, *Grandmama's Joy*, 1980
Worried when she see's her grandmama sad a child learns why and tries the best way she knows how to put a smile back on her face again.
Eloise Greenfield, *William and the Good Old Days*, 1993
A boy's grandma is recovering from an illness and he thinks about the good times they had together in the past before he lets go to see new days ahead.
Francine Haskins, *Things I Like about Grandma*, 1992
A child enjoys her special relationship with her grandma as

they do things together and the fun times they have watching sports with granddaddy.

123

VALERIE FLOURNOY, African American
JERRY PINKNEY, Illustrator, African American

Tanya's Reunion
(New York: Dial Books For Young Readers, 1995)

Story type: Young Readers
Subject(s): Family Relations; Farm Life; Grandparents
Age range(s): Grades 2-4
Major character(s): Tanya Franklin, Child, Sister, African American
Time period(s): Indeterminate Past
Locale(s): Virginia (rural)

Summary: With her older brothers going away to football camp and her grandma needing to arrive early for the family reunion, Tanya gets to accompany her alone on the bus trip. On their long journey Grandma shares stories about her Virginia home. When Tanya gets homesick, Grandma tells her stories about her relatives and the history of the family farm. Exploring with her 7-year-old cousin Keisha, Tanya finds a special memento for her grandma in the orchard. Camping out on the porch that night in their sleeping bags, grandma tells the girls about the night sounds on the farm.

About this book: Sequel to *The Patchwork Quilt*.

Awards the book has won:
Coretta Scott King Award, 1996

Other books by the same author:
Celie and the Harvest Fiddle, 1995
The Twins Strike Back, 1994
The Patchwork Quilt, 1985
The Best Time of Day, 1978 (debut (young readers))

Other books you might like:
Jeannette Franklin Caines, *Window Wishing*, 1980
The exploits of a young sister and brother spending their vacation with their fun grandma who takes them downtown together where they window wish.
Donald Crews, *Bigmama's*, 1991
Recalls the summer exploits of a youngster in the 1940s when he, his brother, sisters, and parents visit his grandparents in the country.
Eloise Greenfield, *Grandmama's Joy*, 1980
Worried when she see's her grandmama sad, a child learns why and tries the best way she knows how to put a smile back on her face again.
Francine Haskins, *Things I Like about Grandma*, 1992
A child enjoys her special relationship with her grandma as they do things together and the fun times they have watching sports with granddaddy.
Gloria Jean Pinkney, *Back Home*, 1992
Raised in the city, an 8-year-old visits her relatives in the place where she was born in the country, though she has no memories of it.

124

ARTHUR FLOWERS, African American

Another Good Loving Blues

(New York: Viking, 1993)

Subject(s): Interpersonal Relations; Mothers and Daughters; Occult

Age range(s): Adult

Major character(s): Melvira Dupree, Occultist (''conjure''), African American; Lucas Bodeen, Musician, African American; Effie Dupree, Mother, Occultist (''conjure''), African American

Time period(s): 1900s (1918)

Locale(s): Sweetwater, Arkansas

Summary: This story is about exploits in the life of Melvira, a ''conjure'' woman of the Mississippi Delta. She meets and comes to love Lucas, yet she is still haunted by dreams of her mother Effie who abandoned Melvira as a child.

Where it's reviewed:
Booklist, January 15, 1993, page 876
Essence, July 1993, page 46
Publishers Weekly, November 30, 1992, page 35

Other books by the same author:
De Mojo Blues, 1985 (debut novel)

Other books you might like:
Linda Beatrice Brown, *Crossing over Jordan*, 1995
    This saga is about the binding ties in the lives of four generations of mothers and daughters from the Civil War era to the early 21st century.
Toni Morrison, *Beloved*, 1987
    A mother who escaped slavery kills her baby to keep her former owner from stealing her, and is then haunted and consumed by the baby's ghost.
Jewell Parker Rhodes, *Voodoo Dreams: A Novel of Marie Laveau*, 1993
    In New Orleans, a young woman becomes entangled with a voodoo doctor who makes her famous before she is forced to destroy him for her own survival.

125

ARTHUR FLOWERS, African American

De Mojo Blues

(New York: E.P. Dutton, 1985)

Subject(s): Interpersonal Relations; Occult; Vietnam War

Age range(s): Adult

Major character(s): Tucept HighJohn, African American, Occultist (hoodoo), Veteran (Vietnam)

Time period(s): 1960s; 1970s (1969-1974)

Locale(s): Memphis, Tennessee

Summary: Tucept, Willie D., and Mike are court-martialed and discharged from the military after being charged with murdering a fellow soldier in Vietnam. Reflecting on his tour of duty, Tucept not only recalls he was given a ''spirit root'' of his namesake ''HighJohn de Conqueror'' but also he was told about the *Lost Book of Hoodoo*. He seeks out a teacher to train him in hoodoo and he becomes an apprentice. When he

completes his study he begins his own private practice of conjury and visions.

About this book: This is the author's debut novel.

Where it's reviewed:
Essence, June 1986, page 32
Kirkus Reviews, November 15, 1985, page 1206
Publishers Weekly, November 8, 1985, page 56

Other books by the same author:
Another Good Loving Blues, 1993

Other books you might like:
Percival Everett, *Walk Me to the Distance*, 1985
    A young Vietnam veteran, searching for purpose in his life, becomes involved in the lives of an elderly woman and her retarded son.
Gloria Naylor, *Mama Day*, 1988
    Returning to her sea island home, a young woman finds both body and soul threatened by supernatural forces. She is barely saved by Mama Day.
Jewell Parker Rhodes, *Voodoo Dreams: A Novel of Marie Laveau*, 1993
    A young woman in New Orleans becomes entangled with a voodoo doctor who makes her famous. She is forced to destroy him for her own survival.

126

LEON FORREST, African American

The Bloodworth Orphans

(New York: Random House, 1977)

Series: Witherspoon Trilogy

Subject(s): Family Relations; Race Relations; Interpersonal Relations

Age range(s): Adult

Major character(s): Nathaniel Turner Witherspoon, Storyteller, African American

Time period(s): 1970s

Locale(s): United States (unidentified city)

Summary: Continuing to search for understanding his heritage in the second title of the trilogy on the Witherspoon family saga, Nathaniel views the lives and relationships of the orphans and bastards in the Bloodsworth slave-owning family. He overheard the scandalizing stories of illegitimate sons Bloodworth sired by Regal Pettibone's stepmother Rachel from his Aunt Hattie Breedlow Wordlaw's twin sister, gossip Stella Jefferson. During prayer hour in Rachel's home Nathaniel and Regal bear witness to the testifying, rejoicing, and pleading of the faithful- and Nathaniel is tormented by the voices of his deceased mother and Aunt Breedlove, who was not his blood aunt yet had helped raise him. Afterwards Nathaniel contemplates what is in store for his life as an incestuous web engulfs others around him. To his amazement when he is later arrested at his friend Saltport's, Nathaniel encounters an orphan Noah who knows tales of the Bloodworth clan.

Other books by the same author:
Divine Days, 1992
Two Wings to Veil My Face, 1983 (*Witherspoon Trilogy*)

There Is a Tree More Ancient than Eden, 1973 (debut novel in the *Witherspoon Trilogy*)

Other books you might like:

Linda Beatrice Brown, *Crossing over Jordan*, 1995
Saga of the ties binding the lives of four generations of mothers and daughters from the Civil War era to the early 21st century.

Richard Perry, *Montgomery's Children*, 1984
Tales of people living in a small town in central New York interwoven with magic and vision, incest and murder, friendship and sacrifice.

John Edgar Wideman, *Damballah*, 1981
First title of the Homewood trilogy portraying the inter-generational history of a family from the 1840s-1960s in Pennsylvania.

| 127 |

LEON FORREST, African American

Divine Days
(Chicago: Another Chicago Press, 1992)

Story type: Adult
Subject(s): Death; Interpersonal Relations
Age range(s): Adult
Major character(s): Joubert Antoine Jones, Stepson, Writer, African American; Deloretto ''Imani'' Holloday, Artist, Single Mother, African American; Sugar-Groove, Travel-ler, African American
Time period(s): 1960s (1966)
Locale(s): New Orleans, Louisiana (Forest County)

Summary: This epic tale, referred to as ''The Ulysses of the South Side,'' follows the events in Joubert's life over a seven-days. After a stint in the army, Joubert, an aspiring play-wright, tends bar in his stepmother's tavern. As his life unfolds during this time, he captures voices of the living and the dead. Included among them are suicide victims Imani and Joubert's deceased mentor, Sugar-Groove.

Where it's reviewed:
Library Journal, June 1, 1995, page 521
Publishers Weekly, December 12, 1994, page 60
New York Times Book Review, February 5, 1995, page 28
Book World, January 29, 1995, page 12
Tribune Books (Chicago), March 5, 1995, page 8

Other books by the same author:
Two Wings to Veil My Face, 1983 (Witherspoon Trilogy)
The Bloodworth Orphans, 1977 (Witherspoon Trilogy)
There Is a Tree More Ancient than Eden, 1973 (debut novel, Witherspoon Trilogy)

Other books you might like:
Tananarive Due, *The Between*, 1995
A man endures nightmares and his sense of reality wavers as he desperately tries to protect his family from the psychotic who stalks them.

Helen Elaine Lee, *The Serpent's Gift*, 1994
The children and grandchildren of two intertwined fami-lies endure hardship. They triumph as they help each other remember a history beyond their realm.

Walter Mosley, *RL's Dream*, 1995
An aging blues musician befriends a young caucasian woman haunted by an incestuous past. This story recounts exploits from the past as they become friends.

Gloria Naylor, *Bailey's Cafe*, 1992
Bailey's Cafe, a mythical waystation for lost souls, has a back door which opens on to dimensions unknown.

John Edgar Wideman, *Reuben*, 1987
This story relates the exploits of an aged lawyer and the various clients he represents in the Pittsburgh community of Homewood during the 1980s.

| 128 |

LEON FORREST, African American

There Is a Tree More Ancient than Eden
(New York: Random House, 1973)

Series: Witherspoon Trilogy
Subject(s): Family Relations; Race Relations; Self-Perception
Age range(s): Adult
Major character(s): Nathaniel Turner Witherspoon, Story-teller, African American
Time period(s): 1970s
Locale(s): United States

Summary: The first title in a trilogy on the Witherspoon family saga introduces people and events over two centuries. In a stream of consciousness style and beginning with the death of his mother, the narrator Nathaniel, searches for meaning in his life and his heritage. Among his ponderings are the impact of his Aunt ''Breedy,'' his father, and a savage lynching and mutilation of a naked man barely past 30 by white soldiers and a crowd of white participants. Brooding in anguish over his birthright, he beseeches the lord to tell him what he is coming to.

About this book: Debut novel.

Other books by the same author:
Divine Days, 1992
Two Wings to Veil My Face, 1983 (Witherspoon Trilogy)
The Bloodworth Orphans, 1977 (Witherspoon Trilogy)

Other books you might like:
Linda Beatrice Brown, *Crossing over Jordan*, 1995
Saga of the ties binding the lives of four generations of mothers and daughters from the Civil War era to the early 21st century.

Helen Elaine Lee, *The Serpent's Gift*, 1994
Children and grandchildren of two intertwined families endure hardship and triumph as they help each other re-member a history beyond their knowing.

Dorothy West, *The Wedding*, 1995
Saga of five generations of two families of mixed race ancestry, and events in the lives of children from a new contemporary generation.

John Edgar Wideman, *Damballah*, 1981
First title of the Homewood Trilogy portraying the inter-generational history of a family from the 1840s-1960s in Pennsylvania.

129

LEON FORREST, African American

Two Wings to Veil My Face
(New York: Random House, 1983)

Series: Witherspoon Trilogy
Subject(s): Family Relations; Race Relations
Age range(s): Adult
Major character(s): Nathaniel Turner Witherspoon, Student, Writer, African American; Sweetie Reed Witherspoon, Aged Person, Religious (of Nathaniel), African American; Jericho Witherspoon, Judge, Lawyer, African American
Time period(s): 19th century; 20th century (1860-1950)
Locale(s): South (Reed Plantation)

Summary: From the plantation era of the South before the Civil War to contemporary times, the Witherspoon family saga is shared by ninety-one-year-old Sweetie Reed. As she tells this family legacy to her grandson Nathaniel, it gives meaning to his own life. Among her reminiscences are episodes about Nathaniel's legendary hero grandfather, Judge Jericho Witherspoon, and the impact of his funeral.

Where it's reviewed:
Callaloo, Spring 1993, page 419

Other books by the same author:
Divine Days, 1992
The Bloodworth Orphans, 1977 (Witherspoon Trilogy)
There Is a Tree More Ancient than Eden, 1973 (debut novel, Witherspoon Trilogy)

Other books you might like:
Lorene Cary, *The Price of a Child*, 1995
    This historical tale is about a woman who literally walks away from slavery to freedom under her owner's furious gaze in Philadelphia during the 1850s.
Barbara Chase-Riboud, *The President's Daughter*, 1994
    This work chronicles the life of Harriet Hemings, the daughter of miscegenation in the interracial affair of President Thomas Jefferson. It relates her passing for white.
J. California Cooper, *Family*, 1991
    This is a narrative in a young girl's life in the plantation era of the South. Included are events in the lives of her children by her slave owner's son and the lives of her grandchildren.
Toni Morrison, *Beloved*, 1987
    This story tells about a mother who escapes from slavery and who kills her baby to keep her former owner from stealing her. She is then haunted and consumed by the baby's ghost.
Dorothy West, *The Wedding*, 1995
    This saga, about five generations of two families with mixed race ancestry, relates the events in the lives of children from a new contemporary generation.

130

ALBERT FRENCH, African American

Billy
(New York: Viking, 1993)

Subject(s): Murder; Race Relations; Death
Age range(s): Adult
Major character(s): Billy Lee Turner, Bastard Son, 10-Year-Old, African American; Lori Pasko, 15-Year-Old, Caucasian; Cinder Turner, Single Mother, Worker, African American
Time period(s): 1930s (1937)
Locale(s): Mississippi (Banes County)

Summary: At sixteen, Cinder gives birth to her son Billy. Ten years later, racial hatreds are sparked when Billy is sentenced to death in the electric chair for killing a teenaged girl.

Where it's reviewed:
Booklist, April 1, 1995, page 1403
Publishers Weekly, January 2, 1995, page 71
Book World, July 9, 1995, page 12
Black Scholar, Spring 1995, page 69
New York Times Book Review, February 12, 1995, page 36

Other books you might like:
Bebe Moore Campbell, *Your Blues Ain't Like Mine*, 1992
    These episodes describe the lives of individuals affected by the murder of a 15-year-old boy for reportedly offending a white woman in a small southern town.
Cyrus Colter, *A Chocolate Soldier*, 1988
    A young idealist murders his Caucasian employer and is himself killed by a mob lynching.
Ernest J. Gaines, *A Lesson before Dying*, 1993
    This historical fiction set in Louisiana during the 1940s shows the impact a young man's pending execution for murder has on the community and his family and friends.

131

ALBERT FRENCH, African American

Holly
(New York: Viking, 1995)

Subject(s): Family Relations; Interpersonal Relations; Race Relations
Age range(s): Adult
Major character(s): Holly Rachelle Hill, Sister, Caucasian; Elias Euritides Owens, Composer, Artist (painter), African American
Time period(s): 1940s (1944-1945)
Locale(s): Supply, North Carolina

Summary: Holly, a poor, white nineteen-year-old, finds her world changed during World War II. Her boyfriend and her brother join the military; one never returns home and the other comes back but is not the same person. Holly and her girl-friend ''explore life'' with local boys and soldiers, but she doesn't feel loved until she meets Elias. Elias, an African American veteran, and Holly fall in love as Elias warns her of the dangers of an interracial relationship. Holly and Elias try to keep their affair secret until Holly gets pregnant. They realize that they must leave town in order to be together forever.

Where it's reviewed:
Booklist, April 15, 1995, page 1479
Kirkus Reviews, February 15, 1995, page 171
Library Journal, April 15, 1995, page 114
New York Times Book Review, June 4, 1995, page 12
Publishers Weekly, February 27, 1995, page 85

Other books by the same author:
Billy, 1993 (debut novel)

Other books you might like:
Julius Lester, *And All Our Wounds Forgiven*, 1994
  A white secretary recalls her affair to a reknowned civil rights leader when she visits his wife's sick bed.
Toni Morrison, *Tar Baby*, 1981
  Two young lovers from different backgrounds experience the conflicts wrought by social and cultural circumstances.
Richard Perry, *No Other Tale to Tell*, 1994
  With their community watching in silence, a young girl gives birth to an idiot son by a white youngster her family had raised.
Dennis Williams, *Crossover*, 1992
  This story relates the events in the life of a young man during the Civil Rights era. He becomes a reluctant activist and he has an interracial affair.

132

ERNEST J. GAINES, African American

The Autobiography of Miss Jane Pittman
(New York: Dial Press, 1971)

Subject(s): Civil Rights Movement; Historical; Race Relations
Age range(s): Adult
Major character(s): Jane Pittman, Aged Person (110-Year-Old), Slave, African American; Ned Douglass, Foster Child, African American, Veteran (Spanish-American War); Joe Pittman, African American, Horse Trainer, Husband
Time period(s): 19th century; 20th century (1860s-1960s)
Locale(s): Louisiana

Summary: When Jane is eleven years old, the Civil War ends and she heads north. On the way, she takes responsibility for Ned, a small boy whose mother and sister are murdered by nightriders. Eventually abandoning her journey north, Jane settles in Louisiana, where she falls in love with a horse tamer named Joe. They share seven or eight peaceful years together until he is killed by a black stallion Jane had seen in her dreams. Ned returns from the Spanish-American War with dreams of building a school. He is killed by someone Jane knows, who also eventually dies, convinced that Jane has worked a spell on him. In the 1960s, at age 110, Jane takes up the cause of a young slain civil rights leader.

Other books by the same author:
A Lesson before Dying, 1993
A Gathering of Old Men, 1983
In My Father's House, 1978
A Long Day in November, 1971 (debut novel, young readers)
Catherine Carmier, 1964 (debut novel, adult)

Other books you might like:
Julius Lester, *Do Lord Remember Me*, 1984
  Saga of the life and times of an eighty-year-old reverend who became known as the "colored Billy Graham."
Lorene Cary, *The Price of a Child*, 1995
  Historical tale of a woman who literally walks from slavery to freedom under her slave owner's furious gaze in 1850s Philadelphia.

133

ERNEST J. GAINES, African American

A Gathering of Old Men
(New York: Alfred A. Knopf, 1983)

Story type: Adult
Subject(s): Courage; Race Relations; Murder
Age range(s): Adult
Major character(s): Mathu, Aged Person, Farmer, African American; Candy Marshall, Landowner, Caucasian; Sheriff Mapes, Lawman, African American
Time period(s): 1970s
Locale(s): Bayonne, Louisiana

Summary: When Cajun farmer Beau Boutan is found shot dead in Mathu's yard, Candy, a young white woman, tells everyone she did it. She gathers more than a dozen old men with recently fired shotguns at the scene and each man claims responsibility for the death when the sheriff arrives. As the men explain their motives, they illuminate the complex relationships between the races and tell of the conflict between old and the new ways.

Other books by the same author:
In My Father's House, 1978
The Autobiography of Miss Jane Pittman, 1971
A Long Day in November, 1971 (debut novel, young readers)
Of Love and Dust, 1967
Catherine Carmier, 1964 (debut novel, adults)

Other books you might like:
Toni Morrison, *Jazz*, 1992
  A working class couple face the trauma of putting their lives back together after the husband murders the girl with whom he was having an affair.
Richard Perry, *No Other Tale to Tell*, 1994
  With their community watching in silence, a young girl gives birth to an idiot son by a white youngster her family had raised.

134

ERNEST J. GAINES, African American

In My Father's House
(New York: Alfred A. Knopf, 1978)

Subject(s): Fathers and Sons; Human Behavior; Psychology
Age range(s): Adult
Major character(s): Reverend Phillip Martin, Activist, African American, Religious; Robert X, Drifter
Time period(s): 1970s (1970)
Locale(s): St. Adrienne, Louisiana; Baton Rouge, Louisiana

Summary: A young unkempt man who calls himself Robert X arrives in St. Adrienne, rents a room and is then seen walking all over town in any kind of weather. Other than saying he is going to meet someone, he has little to say to anyone. The townspeople are suspicious of him and speculate about his presence. Reverend Phillip Martin is an honored and respected member of the community, a civil rights activist who has changed many things in St. Adrienne for the better. The young stranger turns up at a party at Martin's home and watches him. When their eyes finally meet, Martin collapses and the stranger leaves. Upon hearing that the stranger is in jail, Reverend Martin goes to bail him out and thus begins a journey into his own past and the life he thought he had left behind.

Other books by the same author:
A Lesson before Dying, 1993
A Gathering of Old Men, 1983
The Autobiography of Miss Jane Pittman, 1971
A Long Day in November, 1971 (debut novel, young readers)
Catherine Carmier, 1964 (debut novel, adult)

Other books you might like:
Cyrus Colter, *A Chocolate Soldier*, 1988
    A story within a story where a tale is told of a young idealist who murders his white employer and is himself killed by a mob lynching.
Louis Edwards, *Ten Seconds*, 1991
    The memories about his life of a young man anticipating his future as a husband and father, and reflecting on the family secret he's kept.
Gwendolyn Parker, *These Same Long Bones*, 1994
    A man loses his direction following the death of his daughter, and must make a courageous decision that affects those in the community he loves.
Brent Wade, *Company Man*, 1992
    Confessions of the behind-the-scenes stresses and strains faced by a man attempting to climb the business ladder and preserve his family.
Alice Walker, *Meridian*, 1976
    A deserted mother at seventeen, a young girl gets involved in the civil rights movement which changes her life and defines her role in the world.

135

ERNEST J. GAINES, African American

A Lesson before Dying
(New York: Knopf, 1993)

Subject(s): Historical; Friendship; Self-Perception
Age range(s): Adult
Major character(s): Jefferson, Convict, African American; Grant Wiggins, Professor, African American
Time period(s): 1940s (1948)
Locale(s): Bayonne, Louisiana

Summary: Jefferson is on death row for the killing of a white liquor store owner during a robbery. Preparing for his execution, his family has asked Professor Grant to visit him. Grant, hesitant to go at first, comes to develop a friendship with Jefferson as they each search to understand their own lives.

About this book: This work has won two awards.

Where it's reviewed:
African American Review, Fall 1994, page 489
Antioch Review, Winter 1995, page 116
Black Scholar, Spring 1995, page 65
Kliatt, November 1994, page 8
New York Times Book Review, December 4, 1994, page 89

Awards the book has won:
Black Caucus of the A.L.A., Literary Award for Fiction, 1994
National Book Critics Circle Award, 1994

Other books by the same author:
A Gathering of Old Men, 1983
In My Father's House, 1978
The Autobiography of Miss Jane Pittman, 1971
A Long Day in November, 1971 (debut novel, young readers)
Catherine Carmier, 1964 (debut novel, adults)

Other books you might like:
Bebe Moore Campbell, *Your Blues Ain't Like Mine*, 1992
    These episodes describe the lives of individuals affected by the murder of a 15-year-old boy for reportedly offending a white woman in a small southern town.
Cyrus Colter, *A Chocolate Soldier*, 1988
    This story unfolds another story whereby a tale is told of a young idealist who murders his caucasian employer and he himself, is killed by a mob lynching.
Albert French, *Billy*, 1993
    When a 10-year-old boy is sentenced to death in the electric chair for killing a caucasian, teenaged female, racial hatreds ignite in Mississippi during the 1930s.

136

NELSON GEORGE, African American

Urban Romance
(New York: G.P. Putnam's Sons, 1993)

Story type: Adult
Subject(s): City Life; Interpersonal Relations
Age range(s): Adult
Major character(s): Dwayne Robinson, Critic, Writer, African American; Danielle Embry, Editor, Writer, African American
Time period(s): 1980s
Locale(s): New York, New York

Summary: Dwayne and Danielle are brought together by mutual friends, and they develop a relationship that changes their lives. Together they learn about love, friendship, family, and heartbreak. While their relationship develops, the lives of those around them evolve in different ways.

About this book: This is the author's debut novel.

Where it's reviewed:
Publishers Weekly, February 27, 1995, page 101
Village Voice, January 3, 1995, page 76

Other books you might like:
Connie Briscoe, *Sisters and Lovers*, 1994
    This contemporary story is about the lives and struggles of three sisters and the men they become involved with.

Bebe Moore Campbell, *Brothers and Sisters*, 1994

This contemporary account of a career woman's life shows her attempt to climb the business ladder as she maintains a social life, and relationships with the people around her.

Trey Ellis, *Home Repairs*, 1993

A young man captures his coming-of-age exploits in his journal. He searches for love and finds success in his career.

Terry McMillan, *Waiting to Exhale*, 1992

Contemporary account of the friendship of four women, their relationships with men, and their experiences with family and careers.

137

JAN SPIVEY GILCHRIST, Author/Illustrator, African American

Indigo and Moonlight Gold

(New York: Black Butterfly Children's Books, 1993)

Story type: Young Readers
Subject(s): Mothers and Daughters; Change
Age range(s): Grades 1-2
Major character(s): Autrie, Child, Sister, African American
Time period(s): 1990s
Locale(s): United States (unidentified city)

Summary: She and her mother share special times talking and laughing together after Autrie's daddy and her brothers have gone to sleep. Afterwards when they each want to be alone Autrie goes out on the porch while her mama gazes out the window. In the moonlight Autrie looks back at her mama and thinks she looks as beautiful as a painting. She remembers the story mama told her about girls growing up and how things change. Autrie just wants to lift her arms to the clouds and freeze time right where it is. She knows change will come and she has to be strong. Feeling her mama's watchful eyes on her she knows night will turn into day and that little girls sometimes become mamas who sit with a watchful eye over their daughters.

About this book: Debut novel.

Other books you might like:

Valerie Flournoy, *The Patchwork Quilt*, 1985

When her grandma becomes ill a youngster and her mama work on her quilt until she recovers and puts the finishing touches on it herself.

Angela Johnson, *Tell Me a Story, Mama*, 1989

A little girl wanting her mama to tell her a story about when she was little has memorized the stories she's heard and tells them herself.

Dolores Johnson, *What Will Mommy Do When I'm at School?*, 1990

Her mom has never been without her and a child about to start school worries her mom with be lonely without her to do things with.

138

MARITA GOLDEN, African American

And Do Remember Me

(New York: Doubleday, 1992)

Subject(s): Family Relations; Interpersonal Relations; Sexual Abuse
Age range(s): Adult
Major character(s): Jessie Foster, Abuse Victim (incest), Activist, African American; Lincoln Sturgis, Activist, Professor, African American
Time period(s): 1960s; 1990s
Locale(s): South (Mississippi Delta); New York, New York (Harlem)

Summary: Hitchhiking as she runs away from home, Jessie meets Lincoln, a young civil rights worker who invites her to join him in the cause. They develop a friendship and later a romance, but when Lincoln proposes marriage she is unable to accept and their lives separate. Her father, who raped her when she was a child, suffers a stroke and is in a coma. Jessie is forced to face her old demons, and when she returns home confronts her mother for not protecting her from her father.

Where it's reviewed:
Black Scholar, Summer 1994, page 75

Other books by the same author:
Long Distance Life, 1989
A Woman's Place, 1988 (debut novel)

Other books you might like:

Carolivia Herron, *Thereafter Johnnie*, 1991

This story is about the incestuous relationship between a father and daughter.

Walter Mosley, *RL's Dream*, 1995

An aging blues musician befriends a young caucasian woman haunted by an incestuous past. This story recounts exploits from the musician's past.

139

MARITA GOLDEN, African American

Long Distance Life

(New York: Doubleday, 1989)

Subject(s): Family Relations; Brothers; Mothers and Daughters
Age range(s): Adult
Major character(s): Naomi Reeves Johnson, Aged Person, Landlord, African American; Esther Johnson, Activist, Single Mother, African American; Logan Spencer, Bastard Son (Esther's), Doctor, African American
Time period(s): 1920s; 1980s
Locale(s): Spring Hope, North Carolina; Washington, District of Columbia

Summary: Naomi's youngest grandson, Nathaniel, has been murdered. Following his funeral she ponders death and reflects on her eighty-year-old life and her family. From her southern sharecropping upbringing in the 1920s, her migration to Washington, D.C., her rise from domestic work to buying property, her becoming middle class, her marriage and widowhood, her only daughter Esther's plight to the suffering of her only grandchildren, Logan and Nathaniel, she seems what the future may hold for her great-grandchildren. The journey she shares shows the transformation of lives and a culture.

Other books by the same author:
And Do Remember Me, 1992
A Woman's Place, 1988 (debut novel)

Other books you might like:
Linda Beatrice Brown, *Crossing over Jordan*, 1995
  This saga is about the binding ties in the lives of four generations of mothers and daughters from the Civil War era to the early 21st century.
Bebe Moore Campbell, *Your Blues Ain't Like Mine*, 1992
  These episodes describe the lives of individuals affected by the murder of a 15-year-old boy accused of offending a white woman in a small southern town.
Cyrus Colter, *A Chocolate Soldier*, 1988
  A story within a story where a tale is told of a young idealist who murders his white employer and is himself killed by a mob lynching.
Julius Lester, *Do Lord Remember Me*, 1984
  Saga of the life and times from the late 1870s plantation era of an eighty-year-old reverend who became known as the "colored Billy Graham."
Dori Sanders, *Her Own Place*, 1993
  This story is about the remembrances of a senior citizen's exploits as a daughter, wife, mother, and grandmother prior to World War II and including contemporary times.

140

MARITA GOLDEN, African American

A Woman's Place

(New York: Ballantine Books, 1986)

Subject(s): Friendship; Interpersonal Relations; Family Relations
Age range(s): Adult
Major character(s): Crystal Jefferson, Writer, Sister, African American; Faith Hamilton, Sister (youngest), Pregnant Teenager, African American (Muslim); Serena, Social Worker, African American
Time period(s): 1960s; 1980s
Locale(s): Boston, Massachusetts; Nairobi, Kenya

Summary: During the 1960s three young girls become close friends when they room together at Winthrop University in Boston. Each searches for her own place in the world and a life of fulfillment. Faith, embracing the Muslim faith, changes her name to Aisha, marries an older man Rasheed Ali, and has four children. Crystal evolves as a renowned poet from her days at Winthrop. Along the way she marries Neil, a white documentary filmmaker. Their interracial relationship is troubled by her family's reaction, especially that of her father and brother. In their struggles together they witness Neil's parent's divorce, his mother's lesbian lover, his father's alcoholism, and Crystal's miscarriage. In Serena's journey from Winthrop, she travels to Africa where she falls in love with a Kenyan editor who is killed. She begins an affair with a wealthy Nigerian businessman, who has four wives and sev-

eral children. She has a child with him and he gives her money to buy land for a women's farming cooperative. Serena's return to the U.S. leads to a reunion with Faith/Aisha and Crystal.

About this book: Debut novel.

Other books by the same author:
And Do Remember Me, 1992
Long Distance Life, 1989

Other books you might like:
Connie Briscoe, *Sisters and Lovers*, 1994
  Contemporary story about the lives and struggles of three sisters and the men with whom they become involved.
Steven Corbin, *No Easy Place to Be*, 1989
  Explores the relationships among three sisters in urban New York during the 1920s Harlem Renaissance era.
Terry McMillan, *Waiting to Exhale*, 1992
  Contemporary account of the friendship of four women, their relationships with men, and their experiences with family and careers.
Gloria Naylor, *Women of Brewster Place*, 1982
  The story of seven women who come to live on the dead-end street of Brewster Place and what brings them together in their own redemption.
Alice Walker, *The Color Purple*, 1982
  Abused by her father and then by her husband, a woman finds love with her husband's lover and discovers a sense of her own identity and self-worth.

141

JEWELLE GOMEZ, African American

Gilda Stories

(Ithaca: Firebrand Books, 1991)

Story type: Adult; Gay/Lesbian Fiction
Subject(s): Vampires; Immortality
Major character(s): Gilda, Teenager, Vampire, African American; Gilda, Businesswoman (300-year-old), Vampire, Caucasian; Bird, Businesswoman, Vampire, Indian (Lakota)
Time period(s): 19th century; 21st century (1850-2050)
Locale(s): New Orleans, Louisiana

Summary: Spanning two-centuries coast-to-coast this is the tale of a plantation girl who is rescued by a white vampire, Gilda. Gilda's female partner, Bird, is a vampire who is a Lakota. When the girl, who also takes the name Gilda, is brought into the life of a vampire she is taught lessons of survival by Bird, and her journey has many unexpected moments and events.

About this book: Debut novel.

Where it's reviewed:
Necrofile, Spring 1992, page 23
Black Scholar, Fall 1992, page 68
Lambda Book Report, July 1992, page 6

Awards the book has won:
Lambda Literary Award, Lesbian Fiction, 1991
Lambda Literary Award, Lesbian Science Fiction/Fantasy, 1991

Other books you might like:

Linda Beatrice Brown, *Crossing over Jordan*, 1995
Saga of the ties binding the lives of four generations of mothers and daughters from the Civil War era to the early 21st century.

J. California Cooper, *Family*, 1991
A young girl's narrative of her life in the plantation south and events in the lives of her children by her slave owner's son and of her grandchildren.

Arthur Flowers, *Another Good Loving Blues*, 1993
A Mississippi Delta tale of exploits in the life of a "conjure" woman haunted by dreams of the mother who abandoned her as a child.

Helen Elaine Lee, *The Serpent's Gift*, 1994
Children and grandchildren of two intertwined families endure hardship and triumph as they help each other remember a history beyond their knowing.

Jewell Parker Rhodes, *Voodoo Dreams: A Novel of Marie Laveau*, 1993
In New Orleans, a young woman becomes entangled with a voodoo doctor who makes her famous before she is forced to destroy him for her own survival.

142

ELOISE GREENFIELD, African American
CAROLE BYARD, Illustrator, African American

Africa Dream

(New York: John Day Co., 1977)

Story type: Young Readers
Subject(s): Africa; Dreams and Nightmares
Age range(s): Grades 1-2
Major character(s): Unnamed Character, Child, African American
Time period(s): 1970s
Locale(s): United States (unidentified city)

Summary: A child dreams she has crossed the ocean and gone all the way to long-ago Africa. On her journey she goes to the city, where she shops for beautiful things in the marketplace. She reads strange words in old books and rides through crowds on a donkey's back. Her long-ago granddaddy welcomes her home. She eats mangoes, dances to the drums of her uncles, sings with new-old friends, and walks with her cousins. Turning into a baby, she rocks in the arms of her long-ago grandma. face.

Awards the book has won:
Coretta Scott King Award, 1978

Other books by the same author:
Darlene, 1980
Grandmama's Joy, 1980
First Pink Light, 1976
Me and Nessie, 1975
She Come Bringing Me That Little Baby Girl, 1974

Other books you might like:

Lucille Clifton, *All Us Come Cross the Water*, 1973
Wanting to answer his teacher's question about where his people came from a boy asks his family and a neighbor before speaking up in class.

Patricia C. McKissack, *Mirandy and Brother Wind*, 1988
Folk tale of a young girl desperately wanting to win her first cakewalk dance contest who makes a wish to the wind and dances with her friend.

Phil Mendez, *The Black Snowman*, 1989
A magic kente cloth helps a boy learn a lesson in self-respect and pride in his heritage while saving his younger brother from a fire.

Faith Ringgold, *Aunt Harriet's Underground Railroad in the Sky*, 1992
Flying in the sky a sister and her younger brother discovering the underground railroad to freedom must retrace its route to be reunited.

John Steptoe, *Mufaro's Beautiful Daughters: An African Tale*, 1987
The folktale of two young African sisters appearing before the King so he can choose the one he wants to become his wife the Queen.

143

ELOISE GREENFIELD, African American
GEORGE FORD JR., Illustrator, African American

Darlene

(New York: Methuen, 1980)

Story type: Young Readers
Subject(s): Physically Handicapped; Cousins
Age range(s): Grades 1-2
Major character(s): Darlene, Child, Niece, African American
Time period(s): 1980s
Locale(s): United States (unidentified city)

Summary: Anxiously awaiting her mother's return, young wheel-chair bound Darlene is reluctant to play with her cousin until she realizes it will help pass the time. Surprisingly, she finds herself having fun in spite of herself. Singing along to Uncle Eddie's guitar, the girls hear the doorbell. Darlene's mama has arrived to take her home. Thinking of all the fun she's had with cousin Joanne and Uncle Eddie, Darlene decides she doesn't want to go home.

Other books by the same author:
William and the Good Old Days, 1993
Grandpa's Face, 1988
Grandmama's Joy, 1980
Africa Dream, 1977
First Pink Light, 1976

Other books you might like:

Lucille Clifton, *Don't You Remember?*, 1973
A soon-to-be 5-year-old is disappointed that everyone in the family keeps breaking their promises to her until they give her a birthday surprise.

Lucille Clifton, *My Friend Jacob*, 1980
A young boy shares special times with his neighbor and best friend a white mentally handicapped older boy he plays ball with and helps remember things.

Harriette Gillem Robinet, *Jay and the Marigold*, 1976
A white youngster in a wheelchair with cerebral palsy envies things his twin sister and others can do and discovers abilities he has of his own.

144

ELOISE GREENFIELD, African American
MONETA BARNETT, Illustrator, African American

First Pink Light

(New York: Thomas Y. Crowell Co., 1976)

Story type: Young Readers
Subject(s): Mothers and Sons; Fathers and Sons; Bedtime
Age range(s): Grades 1-3
Major character(s): Tyree, Child, African American
Time period(s): 1970s
Locale(s): United States (unidentified city)

Summary: Tyree plays under his mama's table while she does homework. Bedtime arrives, but Tyree wants to stay up until his dad comes home from taking care of Tyree's grandma. Mama lets Tyree wait up in the big chair with his pillow and pajamas. By the time dad arrives, Tyree is fast asleep.

Other books by the same author:
William and the Good Old Days, 1993
Grandpa's Face, 1988
Darlene, 1980
Africa Dream, 1977
Me and Nessie, 1975

Other books you might like:
Jeannette Franklin Caines, *Daddy*, 1977
    Saturdays are special for a child when her father comes to get her to visit with him and they share laughs and fun together all day.
Valerie Flournoy, *The Best Time of Day*, 1978
    A child with a busy day of activities ahead with his mom, babysitter, friends, and relatives looks forward to his daddy getting home from work.
Dolores Johnson, *Your Dad Was Just Like You*, 1993
    Talking with his grandpa after making his dad mad a young boy discovers just how much they are alike and why his dad was so upset with him.
Ianthe Thomas, *Willie Blows a Mean Horn*, 1981
    Proud of his jazz musician papa, a young boy spends special times with him at the club where he plays and thinks of becoming amusician like his papa.
Sharon Dennis Wyeth, *Always My Dad*, 1995
    A young girl remembers the summer she and her three younger brothers spent with their grandparents when their dad visited and how much she misses him.

145

ELOISE GREENFIELD, African American
CAROLE BYARD, Illustrator, African American

Grandmama's Joy

(New York: Philomel Books, 1980)

Story type: Young Readers
Subject(s): Grandparents; Moving, Household; Death
Age range(s): Grades 2-4
Major character(s): Rhondy, Child, African American
Time period(s): 1980s
Locale(s): United States (unidentified city)

Summary: Worried when she notices how sad her grandmama is, Rhondy can't figure out what the matter is. Watching grandmama take clothes from the closet and stuff them into a big box, Rhondy decides to make her smile with one of her dress-up singing shows. Even that doesn't seem to help, for soon grandmama gets a faraway, sad look in her eyes. Starting to cry, grandmama tells Rhondy they have to move away. Worried, Rhondy asks grandmama if she will still be her joy after they move. Grandmama looks at her and gives her a big hug. Rhondy knows everything will be alright since she's still grandmama's joy and grandmama is her joy.

Other books by the same author:
William and the Good Old Days, 1993
Grandpa's Face, 1988
Darlene, 1980
Africa Dream, 1977
Me and Nessie, 1975

Other books you might like:
Jeannette Franklin Caines, *Window Wishing*, 1980
    The exploits of a young sister and brother spending their vacation with their fun grandma who takes them downtown together where they window wish.
Donald Crews, *Bigmama's*, 1991
    Recalls the summer exploits of a youngster in the 1940s when he, his brother, sisters, and parents visit his grandparents in the country.
Valerie Flournoy, *The Patchwork Quilt*, 1985
    When her grandma becomes ill a youngster and her mama work on her quilt until she recovers and puts the finishing touches on it herself.
Valerie Flournoy, *Tanya's Reunion*, 1995
    A youngster traveling with her grandma to the family farm for a reunion discovers a special memento for her grandma of days gone by.
Francine Haskins, *Things I Like about Grandma*, 1992
    A child enjoys her special relationship with her grandma as they do things together and the fun times they have watching sports with granddaddy.

146

ELOISE GREENFIELD, African American
FLOYD COOPER, Illustrator, African American

Grandpa's Face

(New York: Philomel Books, 1988)

Story type: Young Readers
Subject(s): Grandparents; Actors and Actresses
Age range(s): Grades 2-4
Major character(s): Tamika, Child, African American
Time period(s): 1980s
Locale(s): United States (unidentified city)

Summary: Close to her grandpa, young Tamika loves their special times together, their talk-walks, and looking into his gentle face. One of Tamika's favorite places to go is the theatre where grandpa is an actor in the summer. Going to grandpa's dressing room one day Tamika becomes frightened when she see's his face turn angry while he practices reading his lines. Later, when Tamika is in trouble for spilling her milk, they go off for a talk-walk toward the park. Along the way Tamika confesses how grandpa's new mean face scared her but grandpa reassures her he could never look at her like that and once again Tamika feels safe seeing grandpa's smiling face.

Awards the book has won:
American Library Association Notable Book, 1988
School Library Journal Best Book of the Year, 1988

Other books by the same author:
William and the Good Old Days, 1993
Darlene, 1980
Grandmama's Joy, 1980
Africa Dream, 1977
First Pink Light, 1976

Other books you might like:
Angela Johnson, *When I Am Old with You*, 1990
   A young child depicts all the things he wants to do with his granddaddy when he gets old and how they will rest together in their rocking chairs.
Angela Shelf Medearis, *Poppa's New Pants*, 1995
   Sleeping in the farm's spooky kitchen a child hearing noises and seeing ghosts during the night gets a surprise when learning the truth the next morning.
Belinda Rochelle, *When Jo Louis Won the Title*, 1994
   Dreading going to a new school because classmates make fun of her name a young girl learns from her grandfather how she got her special name.

147

ELOISE GREENFIELD, African American

Koya Delaney and the Good Girl Blues
(New York: Scholastic Inc., 1992)

Subject(s): Sisters; School Life; Friendship
Age range(s): Grades 3-6
Major character(s): Koya Delaney, 11-Year-Old, Sister, African American
Time period(s): 1990s
Locale(s): United States (unidentified city)

Summary: Sixth grader Koya and her younger sister Loritha are pals and best friends. Loritha is on the double dutch team with Koya's other best friend Dawn. When Dawn and Loritha have a fight Koya is left in the middle to sort out her feelings. Koya's cousin, Delbert Jr., has become a pop music star and is coming to town for a concert. Koya's classmates begin treating her differently when they learn the famous Del is her cousin, leaving her with some mixed feelings about who her real friends are. Koya's parents attempt to give her some guidance for dealing with emotions.

Where it's reviewed:
Essence, December 1992, page 108
Journal of Reading, April 1993, page 590
Reading Teacher, February 1993, page 412

Other books by the same author:
Talk about a Family, 1978
Sister, 1974

Other books you might like:
Jacqueline Turner Banks, *Project Wheels*, 1993
   As a sixth grader and her friends raise money to buy a motorized wheelchair for a classmate, she realizes their relationships are changing.
Joyce Hansen, *The Gift Giver*, 1980
   A young girl and her fifth grade friends come to like a new boy in their class and are surprised when they discover he is a foster child.
Vaunda Micheaux Nelson, *Mayfield Crossing*, 1993
   The new kids at an elementary school encounter prejudice for the first time and only baseball has the possibility for drawing people together.
Connie Porter, *Addy Learns a Lesson: A School Story*, 1993
   After escaping slavery, a girl and her mother arrive in Philadelphia, where she goes to school and learns a lesson in true friendship.
Ethel Footman Smothers, *Moriah's Pond*, 1995
   A continuation of events from the lives of the Footman family when three sisters spend a summer with their great-grandmother.

148

ELOISE GREENFIELD, African American
MONETA BARNETT, Illustrator, African American

Me and Neesie
(New York: Thomas Y. Crowell Co., 1975)

Story type: Young Readers
Subject(s): Friendship; Behavior
Age range(s): Grades 2-3
Major character(s): Janell, Child, African American
Time period(s): 1970s
Locale(s): United States (unidentified city)

Summary: Neesie is Janell's invisible friend. While mama cornrows her hair Janell watches as Neesie laughs and jumps around, and she yells at her to stop it. When mama tells her to stop talking to herself and says she doesn't want to hear another word about Janell's make believe friend. The next morning leaving for school Janell watches as Neesie waves goodbye from their window. Getting home from school she looks all over for Neesie and Janell tells mama she can't find her anywhere. As mama reads her a story Janell reflects on her times with Neesie and begins thinking of what the next day in school will bring.

Awards the book has won:
American Library Association Notable Children's Book, 1975
Reading Rainbow Selection, 1984

Other books by the same author:
William and the Good Old Days, 1993
Grandpa's Face, 1988
Darlene, 1980
Grandmama's Joy, 1980
Africa Dream, 1977
First Pink Light, 1976
Me and Nessie, 1975
She Come Bringing Me That Little Baby Girl, 1974

Other books you might like:
Lucille Clifton, *Don't You Remember?*, 1973
A soon-to-be 5-year-old is disappointed that everyone in the family keeps breaking their promises to her until they give her a birthday surprise.
Eloise Greenfield, *Darlene*, 1980
In a wheelchair a young girl unexpectedly has fun at her uncle's house playing with her young cousin changing her mind about wanting to go home.
Dolores Johnson, *The Best Bug to Be*, 1992
A child in a school play is disappointed being a bumblebee until she perfects her part and on the night of the play gets the most applause.
Patricia C. McKissack, *Fossie and the Fox*, 1986
The tale of a youngster sent to deliver fresh eggs to a neighbor who outsmarts an egg loving fox along the way trying to prove who he is.
Angela Shelf Medearis, *The Adventures of Sugar and Junior*, 1995
Exploits of a young girl and a Hispanic neighbor boy as they become friends while baking cookies, going to monster movies, and sharing ice cream.

149

ELOISE GREENFIELD, African American
JOHN STEPTOE, Illustrator, African American

She Come Bringing Me That Little Baby Girl

(New York: J.B. Lippincott, 1974)

Story type: Young Readers
Subject(s): Brothers and Sisters; Babies; Jealousy
Age range(s): Grades 1-2
Major character(s): Kevin, Child, Brother, African American
Time period(s): 1970s
Locale(s): United States (unidentified city)

Summary: Glad to see his mother return from the hospital Kevin is not too happy she has brought him a baby sister and not a brother. His mama and daddy seem to only have time for the new baby and everyone keeps ignoring him. Kevin also doesn't like how loud his new baby sister cries and she has all those wrinkles in her face. Staring out the window he is surprised when his mama brings the baby to him and says she's going to need his help in taking care of her. When his uncle Roy tells him what it was like being his mother's big brother he begins changing his mind about the baby. Feeling a new sense of importance and responsibility Kevin proudly invites his friends Debra and Kenny over to see his new little sister.

Awards the book has won:
Irma Simonton Black Award, 1974
American Library Association Notable Book, 1974

Other books by the same author:
William and the Good Old Days, 1993
Grandpa's Face, 1988
Darlene, 1980
Grandmama's Joy, 1980
Africa Dream, 1977

First Pink Light, 1976
Me and Nessie, 1975

Other books you might like:
Debbi Chocolate, *On the Day I Was Born*, 1995
A newborn is welcomed into the family in an African ceremony where relatives gather, the child is raised to the heavens, blessed and named.
Lucille Clifton, *Everett Anderson's Nine Month Long*, 1978
With a new stepfather a young boy now anticipates the arrival of a new stepbrother or sister and experiences the ups and downs of waiting.
Alice Walker, *Finding the Green Stone*, 1991
A young brother and sister have identical green stones and when the brother's is lost his sister, parents, and neighbors rally to help him find it.
Mildred Pitts Walter, *My Mama Needs Me*, 1983
When his newborn baby sister arrives home a young boy is overcome by feelings of responsibility until his mama lets him know it's still ok to play.
Mildred Pitts Walter, *Two and Too Much*, 1990
Trying to help his mama a 7-year-old watches his 2-year-old sister who gets into all kinds of things until she tires herself out and falls asleep.

150

ELOISE GREENFIELD, African American

Sister

(New York: Thomas Y. Crowell, 1974)

Subject(s): Sisters; Mothers and Daughters; Family Relations
Age range(s): Grades 3-6
Major character(s): Doretha Freeman, 13-Year-Old, Sister (youngest), African American
Time period(s): 1970s
Locale(s): United States (unidentified city)

Summary: Four years ago Doretha began keeping a diary she now reads through looking for insights into her life and her older sister Alberta. Her memories include fun times shared with her father before his death when she was ten, and happy days of Alberta and her mother. They also include the untimely death of her father when she was ten and the major changes in her life afterward. In the end Doretha, now thirteen, comes to recognize she can be her own person and her life doesn't have to be the same as her sister's.

About this book: Debut novel.

Where it's reviewed:
Booklist, September 1, 1974, page 41
Choice, November 1977, page 1178
Kirkus Reviews, May 15, 1974, page 535

Other books by the same author:
Koya Delaney and the Good Girl Blues, 1992
Talk about a Family, 1978

Other books you might like:
Virginia Hamilton, *Cousins*, 1990
Concerned that her grandmother might die, a young girl is unprepared for the death of another relative.
Angela Johnson, *Humming Whispers*, 1995
Recounts the life of a young girl living with an older sister

who has schizophrenia and her fear that she too may have the mental illness.

Ethel Footman Smothers, *Moriah's Pond*, 1995
A continuation of events from the lives of the Footman family when three sisters spend a summer with their great-grandmother.

Eleanora E. Tate, *Just an Overnight Guest*, 1980
A young girl and her older sister are surprised when their mother takes in a baby whose mother is said to be poor white trash.

151

ELOISE GREENFIELD, African American
JAMES CALVIN, Illustrator

Talk about a Family
(New York: J.B. Lippincott, 1978)

Subject(s): Family Relations; Brothers and Sisters; Family Problems
Age range(s): Grades 3-6
Major character(s): Genetta "Genny" James, Child, African American
Time period(s): 1970s
Locale(s): United States

Summary: Their mother and father are not getting along well and Genny, her younger sister Kim and her older brother Mac are looking forward to their older brother Larry coming home from the military so he can fix things. Genny has arranged for a surprise party for Larry in their neighbor Mr. Parker's yard and Kim draws pictures for decorations. Still arguing, their parents set their differences aside and the party is perfect. However, afterwards their father announces he is moving out. Genny is distraught when Larry admits he can't make things right with their parents. Visiting Mr. Parker she begins thinking about how families differ and the importance of her sister and brothers for her.

Where it's reviewed:
Booklist, March 1, 1978, page 1105
Essence, October 1984, page 142
School Library Journal, May 1978, page 67

Other books by the same author:
Koya Delaney and the Good Girl Blues, 1992
Sister, 1974

Other books you might like:
Candy Dawson Boyd, *Chevrolet Saturdays*, 1993
Struggling with the divorce of his parents and accepting his new stepfather, a young boy has trouble in school and makes mistakes he regrets.

Dori Sanders, *Clover*, 1990
When her father is killed on his wedding day to a white woman, a 10-year-old has to deal with the trauma of her loss and adjust to a new stepmother.

Ethel Footman Smothers, *Down in the Piney Woods*, 1992
Episodes in the life of the Footman family as the six children all come to live together for the first time sharing life in the country.

Ethel Footman Smothers, *Moriah's Pond*, 1995
A continuation of events from the lives of the Footman

family when three sisters spend a summer with their great-grandmother.

Eleanora E. Tate, *Just an Overnight Guest*, 1980
A young girl and her older sister are surprised when their mother takes in a baby whose mother is said to be poor white trash.

152

ELOISE GREENFIELD, African American
JAN SPIVEY GILCHRIST, Illustrator, African American

William and the Good Old Days
(New York: Harper Collins, 1993)

Story type: Young Readers
Subject(s): Grandparents; Illness
Age range(s): Grades 2-3
Major character(s): William, Child
Time period(s): 1990s
Locale(s): United States

Summary: Thinking about his grandma's illness, William blames it on the fly he saw in her restaurant. After chasing it with the swatter, she got real sick and had to be taken to the hospital. William doesn't think she'll ever be the way she used to be in the good old days, and someone else has the restaurant now. Noticing how tired she seems when he visits her, William is happy to hear she wants to come to his house and help him plant a garden. He begins thinking of the spring, starts letting go of the old days, and looks toward their new good days ahead.

Other books by the same author:
Grandpa's Face, 1988
Darlene, 1980
Grandmama's Joy, 1980
Africa Dream, 1977
First Pink Light, 1976

Other books you might like:
Jeannette Franklin Caines, *Window Wishing*, 1980
The exploits of a young sister and brother spending their vacation with their fun grandma who takes them downtown together where they window wish.

Donald Crews, *Bigmama's*, 1991
Recalls the summer exploits of a youngster in the 1940s when he, his brother, sisters, and parents visit his grandparents in the country.

Valerie Flournoy, *The Patchwork Quilt*, 1985
When her grandma becomes ill a youngster and her mama work on her quilt until she recovers and puts the finishing touches on it herself.

Francine Haskins, *Things I Like about Grandma*, 1992
A child enjoys her special relationship with her grandma as they do things together and the fun times they have watching sports with granddaddy.

153

BONNIE GREER, African American

Hanging by Her Teeth

(New York: Serpent's Tail, 1994)

Story type: Adult
Subject(s): Abandonment; Fathers and Daughters; Growing Up
Age range(s): Adult
Major character(s): Lorraine Williams, African American, Traveller (bisexual)
Time period(s): 1990s
Locale(s): Chicago, Illinois; New York, New York; Europe

Summary: Her journey to find the father who abandoned her when she was a child takes Lorraine from her Chicago home to New York and abroad to Europe. Over the years she has written to her father, a travelling blues man who remembers "seeing" his daughter as a young woman before she was ever born. Her travels in Europe bring her face-to-face with her blind father and the realization of what she has been looking for for many years.

About this book: Debut novel.

Other books you might like:
Alice Childress, *A Short Walk*, 1973
   Saga of events in the childhood and adulthood life of a woman who escapes an abusive marriage and journeys to Harlem in the 1940s.
Melvin Dixon, *Trouble the Water*, 1989
   Running away from home a young man returns twenty years later in a plot of revenge which developed between his grandmother and his father.
Charles Johnson, *Faith and the Good Thing*, 1974
   The tale of a young woman who follows her mother's deathbed wish and goes in search of the good thing, and her ghost embodies a werewitch.
Paule Marshall, *Daughters*, 1991
   A determined young woman struggles in her relationship with her political father and when she returns home for a visit makes an important decision.
Ntozake Shange, *Liliane: Resurrection of the Daughter*, 1994
   In psychotherapy a young woman reveals how she coped with family upheavals, romances and friendships, and racism and bigotry.

154

NIKKI GRIMES, African American
CHARLES LILLY, Illustrator

Growin'

(New York: Dial Press, 1977)

Story type: Young Readers
Subject(s): Friendship; School Life; Secrets
Age range(s): Grades 4-6
Major character(s): Yolanda "Pump" Jackson, 5th Grader, African American; Jim Jim, 5th Grader, African American
Time period(s): 1970s
Locale(s): New York, New York

Summary: When her father is killed in an accident and she and her mother move to a new neighborhood, Pump Jackson thinks that there will be nobody to share her poetry with. Her mother just doesn't seem to understand and she doesn't know anyone at the new school. Then she meets Jim Jim, and she finds a real friend.

About this book: Debut novel (juvenile).

Other books by the same author:
Portrait of Mary, 1994 (young adults)

Other books you might like:
Mildred Pitts Walter, *Mariah Loves Rock*, 1988
   As fifth grade comes to an end, a girl and her family experience misgivings about the arrival of a half-sister who is coming to live with them.
Johnniece Marshall Wilson, *Robin on His Own*, 1990
   A boy grieving his mother's death struggles to make the adjustment when the aunt who has stayed with him gets married and moves away.
Camille Yarbrough, *The Shimmershine Queens*, 1989
   A fifth grade girl learns to stand up for herself and make her own dreams come true when a new teacher comes to her school.

155

NIKKI GRIMES, African American

Portrait of Mary

(New York: Harcourt Brace & Company, 1994)

Subject(s): Historical; Religion; Saints
Age range(s): Grades 8-Adult
Major character(s): Mary, 15-Year-Old, Fiance(e), Religious
Time period(s): 1st century
Locale(s): Bethlehem, Judea; Capernaum, Judea

Summary: Mary will soon marry the carpenter Joseph. An angel of the Lord appears to her to tell her she will bear the son of God who will be the redemption of Jerusalem. At first Joseph is skeptical, but when an angel appears to him as well, he trusts in his faith and he takes Mary with him to Bethlehem for the census. The child is born and Mary is unsure what her baby's life will be like—how much of him is hers, how much God's? Mary watches him grow into a man, then sees him die after being accused of blasphemy. She mourns his loss, and is astounded when the tomb in which he was buried is suddenly empty. He appears to her in a vision and she realizes what the angel said was true.

Other books by the same author:
Growin', 1977 (debut novel, young readers)

Other books you might like:
Joyce Carol Thomas, *Marked by Fire*, 1982
   Friends and family help a young girl overcome the effects of a tornado and a physical assault which nearly breaks her will.
Thulani Davis, *1959*, 1992
   Coming-of-age a 12-year-old girl recounts events that changed her life and others around her during the historic civil rights movement.
Julius Lester, *Othello, a Novel*, 1995
   A reconceptualization with modern dialogue of Shake-

speare's play where a mercenary general and a white noblewoman fall in love and tragedy awaits.

`156`

VIRGINIA HAMILTON, African American

Arilla Sun Down
(New York: Greenwillow Books, 1976)

Subject(s): Birthdays; Family Relations; Identity
Age range(s): Grades 4-7
Major character(s): Arilla Adams, 12-Year-Old, Sister, Interracial; Jack Sun Run Adams, 16-Year-Old, Interracial
Time period(s): 1970s
Locale(s): Midwest (an unidentified small town)

Summary: Twelve-year-old Arilla isn't quite sure where she fits in. She doesn't look like her light-skinned mother or like her half-Native American father. She feels different in school, although her classmates have secret crushes on her older brother, Sun, who has fully embraced his Cherokee heritage. When Sun is injured riding his horse, Arilla gets the help that saves his life. When her father makes one of his periodic disappearances, Arilla figures out where he has gone and brings him back home. She begins to better understand her family and her own identity.

Where it's reviewed:
Booklist, July 15, 1976, page 1596
Horn Book Magazine, December 1976, page 611
Kirkus Reviews, July 1, 1976, page 739

Awards the book has won:
American Library Association Notable Book, 1976

Other books by the same author:
Plain City, 1995
Cousins, 1990
M.C. Higgins, the Great, 1974 (Newbery Medal, National Book Award)
The Planet of Junior Brown, 1971
Zeely, 1967 (debut novel, Young Readers)

Other books you might like:
Eleanora E. Tate, *Thank You, Dr. Martin Luther King, Jr.!*, 1990
    Continuing the *Calvary County Trilogy*, this tale explores the life of a fourth-grade girl who is "color struck," wanting to be white.
Walter Dean Myers, *Darnell Rock Reporting*, 1994
    Not doing well in school, a 13-year-old joins the school newspaper and discovers the impact his writing can have and how he can make a difference.
Ethel Footman Smothers, *Down in the Piney Woods*, 1992
    Episodes in the life of the Footman family as the six children all come to live together for the first time sharing life in the country.
Sharon Dennis Wyeth, *The World of Daughter McGuire*, 1994
    Exploits in the lives of a racially mixed 11-year-old and her younger brother trying to make friends at a new school and enduring racial slurs.
Camille Yarbrough, *The Shimmershine Queens*, 1989
    A fifth-grade girl learns to stand up for herself and make

her own dreams come true when a new teacher comes to her school.

`157`

VIRGINIA HAMILTON, African American
LAMBERT DAVIS, Illustrator, African American

The Bells of Christmas
(New York: Harcourt Brace Jovanovich, 1989)

Story type: Young Readers
Subject(s): Christmas; Family Life; Historical
Age range(s): Grades 3 and Up
Major character(s): Jason Bell, 12-Year-Old, African American
Time period(s): 1890s
Locale(s): Springfield, Ohio (beside the historic National Road)

Summary: It's Christmas Eve, and Jason and his family are preparing for the Great Day when Uncle Levi, his wife Etta, and their daughter Tisha will arrive to celebrate. Jason sits beside the National Road, watching for their wagon and hoping it will snow so he can ride in the sleigh. The tree is trimmed, the meal is prepared, and Christmas Day brings the best surprise of all!

Where it's reviewed:
Booklist, February 15, 1994, page 1095

Other books by the same author:
Plain City, 1995 (Young Readers)
Drylongso, 1992 (Young Readers)
Cousins, 1990 (Young Readers)
The Mystery of Drear House, 1987 (Young Readers)
Zeely, 1967 (debut novel; Young Readers)

Other books you might like:
Connie Porter, *Addy's Surprise: A Christmas Story*, 1993
    A young girl and her mother prepare for Christmas without the rest of the family; they don't have much, but they get the best gift of all.
Mildred Pitts Walter, *Have a Happy. . .*, 1989
    Upset because his birthday falls on Christmas, and worried about money because his father is out of work, an 11-year-old carves animals for Kwanzaa.

`158`

VIRGINIA HAMILTON, African American

Cousins
(New York: Philomel Books, 1990)

Story type: Young Readers
Subject(s): Cousins; Death; Grandparents
Age range(s): Grades 3-7
Major character(s): Cammy, Cousin, Granddaughter, African American; Patty Ann, Cousin, African American; Gram Tut, Grandmother, Aged Person (94-Year-Old)
Time period(s): 1980s
Locale(s): Ohio

Summary: Cammy loves her Gram Tut and sneaks in to visit her at the Care home when she can. Cammy is annoyed that her cousins don't come for a visit, particularly Patty Ann, who is pretty, smart and spoiled. What would it be like if "perfect" Patty Ann just disappeared?

Where it's reviewed:
Publishers Weekly, January 4, 1993, page 74

Other books by the same author:
Junius over Far, 1985 (Young Readers)
The Magical Adventures of Pretty Pearl, 1984 (Young Readers)
Sweet Whispers, Brother Rush, 1982 (Young Readers)
The Gathering, 1981 (Young Readers)
Zeely, 1967 (debut novel; Young Readers)

Other books you might like:
Candy Dawson Boyd, *Breadsticks and Blessing Places*, 1985
When one of three sixth-grade girlfriends is killed, the others cope with her untimely death.
Harriette Gillem Robinet, *Children of the Fire*, 1991
A young girl witnesses the Great Chicago Fire of 1871 and is forever changed.
Dori Sanders, *Clover*, 1990
When her father is killed on his wedding day, a 10-year-old has to deal with the trauma of her loss and adjust to a new stepmother.
Jacqueline Woodson, *Between Madison & Palmetto*, 1993
Two 13-year-old best friends are reunited and have to adjust to a lot of change in their lives.
Jacqueline Woodson, *Last Summer with Maizon*, 1990
The friendship and separation of two youngsters after one suffers the death of her father and the other goes away to boarding school.

159

VIRGINIA HAMILTON, African American
JERRY PINKNEY, Illustrator, African American

Drylongso
(New York: Harcourt Brace Jovanovich, 1992)

Story type: Young Readers
Subject(s): Drought; Farm Life
Age range(s): Grades 3-7
Major character(s): Lindy, Child, African American; Drylongso, Drifter, Young Man, African American
Time period(s): 1970s (1975)
Locale(s): Midwest

Summary: The drought has parched their farmland, but Lindy's mom and dad still get by. A wall of dust sweeps the landscape, bringing before it a young man, Drylongso, and with him the hope of better times.

Where it's reviewed:
Multicultural Review, September 1993, page 81
Booklist, February 15, 1994, page 1095
New York Times Book Review, November 22, 1992, page 34

Other books by the same author:
Plain City, 1995 (Young Readers)
Cousins, 1990 (Young Readers)
The Magical Adventures of Pretty Pearl, 1984 (Young Readers)
Dustland, 1980 (Young Readers)

Zeely, 1967 (debut novel; Young Readers)

Other books you might like:
Harriette Gillem Robinet, *Children of the Fire*, 1991
A young girl witnesses the Great Chicago Fire of 1871 and is forever changed.
Ethel Footman Smothers, *Down in the Piney Woods*, 1992
Episodes in the life of the Footman family as the six children all come to live together for the first time, sharing life in the country.
Mildred D. Taylor, *The Well: David's Story*, 1995
Episode of the boyhood of two brothers from an early generation of the Logan family in rural Mississippi facing racial bigotry.

160

VIRGINIA HAMILTON, African American

Dustland
(New York: Greenwillow Books, 1980)

Story type: Young Readers
Series: Justice Trilogy
Subject(s): Aliens; Teleportation
Age range(s): Grades 5 and Up
Major character(s): Justice Douglass, 11-Year-Old, Empath, Time Traveller; Thomas Douglass, 13-Year-Old, Brother, African American; Dorian Jefferson, 13-Year-Old, Healer, African American
Time period(s): Indeterminate Future; 1970s
Locale(s): Alternate Earth; Midwest

Summary: Together they make up the unit: Thomas, the magician; Dorian, the healer; Justice, the Watcher and the balance of power; and Levi, brother of Justice and twin of Thomas. Traveling into the future to a barren place they named Dustland, they come across Miacis, a golden four-legged creature who becomes attached to them, and the Bambnua, a winged female Slaker who speaks to Justice by telepathy. When Thomas runs away taking Levi with him, it is Miacis who brings them back so that the unit may return home.

Other books by the same author:
Drylongso, 1992 (Young Readers)
Junius over Far, 1985 (Young Readers)
The Magical Adventures of Pretty Pearl, 1984 (Young Readers)
Justice and Her Brothers, 1978 (Justice trilogy; Young Readers)
Zeely, 1967 (debut novel; Young Readers)

Other books you might like:
Walter Dean Myers, *The Nicholas Factor*, 1983
Spy adventure of a young white boy who finds himself in the jungles of Peru when he is asked to infiltrate a suspected neo-Nazi organization.
Walter Dean Myers, *Tales of a Dead King*, 1983
Journeying to Egypt to participate in an archaeological dig, two white teenagers are intrigued by the mysterious disappearance of the dig's director.

161

VIRGINIA HAMILTON, African American

The Gathering

(New York: Greenwillow Books, 1981)

Story type: Young Readers
Series: Justice Trilogy
Subject(s): Aliens; Teleportation
Age range(s): Grades 5 and Up
Major character(s): Justice Douglass, 11-Year-Old, Time Traveller, African American; Thomas Douglass, 13-Year-Old, Time Traveller, African American; Dorian Jefferson, 13-Year-Old, Time Traveller, African American
Time period(s): Indeterminate Future; 1970s
Locale(s): Alternate Earth; Midwest (Greene county)

Summary: Linked by their supersensory powers, Justice, Thomas, Levi and Dorian time-travel to the future in Dustland. They meet other children there: Duster, and his companions Siv and Glass. They battle an entity known as Mal, who controls the future but whose immense power has gone awry, and discover and fulfill the purpose of their presence in Dustland.

Awards the book has won:
American Library Association Notable Book, 1981

Other books by the same author:
Plain City, 1995 (Young Readers)
Cousins, 1990 (Young Readers)
The Mystery of Drear House, 1987 (Young Readers)
Dustland, 1980 (Young Readers)
Zeely, 1967 (debut novel; Young Readers)

Other books you might like:
Walter Dean Myers, *The Nicholas Factor*, 1983
   Spy adventure of a young white boy who finds himself in the jungles of Peru when he is asked to infiltrate a suspected neo-Nazi organization.
Walter Dean Myers, *The Righteous Revenge of Artemis Bonner*, 1992
   Wild west adventure of a young man out to avenge his uncle's murder and to locate his treasure before the killer and his companion.

162

VIRGINIA HAMILTON, African American

Junius over Far

(New York: Harper & Row, 1985)

Story type: Young Readers
Subject(s): Adventure and Adventurers; Family Relations; Grandparents
Age range(s): Grades 6 and Up
Major character(s): Junius Rawlings, 14-Year-Old, African American; Damius Rawlings, Businessman, Father, African American; Jackabo Rawlings, Grandfather, Aged Person, African American
Time period(s): 1980s
Locale(s): Williamson, Caribbean (Snake Island); United States

Summary: Grandfather Jackabo, who raised Junius since he was a baby, has returned to his Caribbean island home. Now each day Junius rushes home from school in hopes he has written a letter. Far away on Snake Island, Jackabo lives on the dilapidated Rawlings Estate, owned by his childhood companion and old enemy, Burtie Rawlings. When Burtie suddenly disappears, Jackabo becomes more and more disoriented. When his next letter to Junius arrives referring to guns, pirates and kidnapping, Junius and his father journey to rescue him.

Where it's reviewed:
Social Studies, March 1995, page 92

Awards the book has won:
Coretta Scott King Award, 1986
Newbery Honor Book, 1986

Other books by the same author:
Plain City, 1995 (Young Readers)
Drylongso, 1992 (Young Readers)
Cousins, 1990 (Young Readers)
The Mystery of Drear House, 1987 (Young Readers)
Zeely, 1967 (debut novel; Young Readers)

Other books you might like:
Sharon M. Draper, *Ziggy and the Black Dinosaurs*, 1994
   When their neighborhood playground is destroyed, four 5th grade boys start their own secret club and uncover a mysterious old box of hidden bones.
Walter Dean Myers, *Mouse Rap*, 1990
   Summer exploits of a 14-year-old when he hears about a hidden treasure in his neighborhood and his separated parents try getting back together.
Walter Dean Myers, *Tales of a Dead King*, 1983
   Journeying to Egypt to participate in an archaeological dig, two white teenagers are intrigued by the mysterious disappearance of the dig's director.
Harriette Gillem Robinet, *Mississippi Chariot*, 1994
   A resourceful 12-year-old son of a sharecropper plans to get his falsely convicted father off of the chain gang in 1930's Mississippi.
Joyce Carol Thomas, *The Golden Pasture*, 1986
   The exquisite horse a 12-year-old boy finds on his grandfather's farm one summer helps him to understand his difficult father better.

163

VIRGINIA HAMILTON, African American

Justice and Her Brothers

(New York: Greenwillow Books, 1978)

Series: Justice Trilogy
Subject(s): Brothers and Sisters; Extrasensory Perception; Twins
Age range(s): Grades 5 and Up
Major character(s): Justice Douglass, 11-Year-Old, Empath, African American; Thomas Douglass, 13-Year-Old, African American, Twin; Dorian Jefferson, 13-Year-Old, African American, Twin
Time period(s): 1970s
Locale(s): Midwest (unidentified small town)

Summary: Justice doesn't understand why her identical twin brothers are so different from one another, almost like mirror images. Thomas likes to control everything and everyone; he seems angry most of the time and picks on her, while Levi is always kind to her. Since their mother is away during the day in a degree-completion program, Thomas and Levi have to let their kid sister tag along on their adventures. This summer Justice becomes aware that she and her brothers and their friend Dorian are more than just ordinary kids, and their extra-sensory powers can be a blessing and a burden.

Where it's reviewed:
Booklist, October 1, 1978, page 294
Horn Book Magazine, October 1978, page 517
Publishers Weekly, October 30, 1978, page 50

Awards the book has won:
Coretta Scott King Honor Book, 1979

Other books by the same author:
Drylongso, 1992 (young readers)
Junius over Far, 1985 (young readers)
The Magical Adventures of Pretty Pearl, 1984 (young readers)
The Gathering, 1981 (book 3 *Justice Trilogy*, young readers)
Dustland, 1980 (book 2 *Justice Trilogy*, young readers)
Zeely, 1967 (debut novel, young readers)

Other books you might like:
Jacqueline Turner Banks, *Egg-Drop Blues*, 1995
 A sixth grader's science grade is low because of his dyslexia, so he and his twin brother enter a competition for extra credit.
Angela Johnson, *Humming Whispers*, 1995
 Recounts the life of a young girl living with an older sister who has schizophrenia and her fear that she too may have the mental illness.
Johnniece Marshall Wilson, *Oh, Brother*, 1988
 A sixth-grader doesn't understand why his older brother keeps taking his bike. When the bike is stolen, it is all his brother's fault.

164

VIRGINIA HAMILTON, African American

A Little Love

(New York: Philomel Books, 1984)

Story type: Young Adult
Subject(s): Adolescence; Family Relations
Age range(s): Grades 8-12
Major character(s): Sheema Hadley, 17-Year-Old, Student—High School, African American
Time period(s): 1980s (1982)
Locale(s): Ohio

Summary: Granmom and Granpop Jackson have lovingly raised Sheema since her mother passed away, but there is an emptiness in Sheema that all the food in the world cannot fill—she misses the father she never knew. When she finishes Harrison Joint Vocational School, she and her boyfriend Forrest set out to find Terhan Cruze Hadley. Searching for him, Sheema finds new strengths in herself.

Awards the book has won:
Coretta Scott King Honor Book, 1985
Newbery Honor Book, 1985

Other books by the same author:
Plain City, 1995 (Young Readers)
A White Romance, 1987 (Young Adults)
Willie Bea and the Time the Martians Landed, 1983 (Young Adults)
Sweet Whispers, Brother Rush, 1982 (Young Adults)
Zeely, 1967 (debut novel; Young Readers)

Other books you might like:
Ossie Davis, *Just Like Martin*, 1992
 A religiously active son and his war veteran father disagree over the civil rights movement until events occur that help them to work together.
David Haynes, *Right by My Side*, 1993
 A high school student writes down his experiences in order to figure things out about his father, his mother and himself.
Walter Dean Myers, *Fallen Angels*, 1988
 The life-changing experiences of a 17-year-old high school graduate who enlists in the Army and is transported on a tour of duty in Vietnam.
Joyce Carol Thomas, *Marked by Fire*, 1982
 Friends and family help a young girl to overcome the effects of a tornado and a physical assault which nearly breaks her will.
Rita Williams-Garcia, *Like Sisters on the Homefront*, 1994
 An unwed 14-year-old mother again pregnant has an abortion and when sent to her relatives in the South she develops a new sense of family and self.

165

VIRGINIA HAMILTON, African American

M.C. Higgins, the Great

(New York: Macmillan Publishing Co., 1974)

Subject(s): Brothers and Sisters; Family Relations; Interpersonal Relations
Age range(s): Grades 4-7
Major character(s): M.C. Higgins, Brother (oldest), African American; Lurhetta Outlaw, Adventurer, Runaway, African American
Time period(s): 1970s
Locale(s): Sarah's Mountain (three miles inland from the Ohio River)

Summary: Sitting atop a 40-foot pole outside of his house on Sarah's Mountain, M.C. watches over his younger brothers and sisters while his parents are away at work in Harenton. He dreams of his family leaving the mountain where they have been for generations to escape the perils of strip mining. From atop his pole he sees two strangers enter his world; one is the "dude" who is recording people's voices and who M.C. believes will make his mother a singing star. The other is Lurhetta, a girl about M.C.'s age who is wandering on her own, camping out where she can find a spot. When Lurhetta disappears without saying goodbye, M.C. is disappointed and angry, but realizes that safety for his own family will never be found in fleeing the hills.

About this book: Virginia Hamilton is the first individual to win the National Book Award and the Newbery Award for the same title.

Where it's reviewed:
Booklist, September 1, 1974, page 41
Choice, November 1975, page 1132
Horn Book Magazine, October 1974, page 143

Awards the book has won:
Newbery Award, 1975
National Book Award, 1975

Other books by the same author:
Plain City, 1995
Cousins, 1990
Arilla Sun Down, 1976
The Planet of Junior Brown, 1971
Zeely, 1967 (debut novel, young readers)

Other books you might like:
Ethel Footman Smothers, *Down in the Piney Woods*, 1992
    Episodes in the life of the Footman family as the six children all come to live together for the first time sharing life in the country.
Ethel Footman Smothers, *Moriah's Pond*, 1995
    A continuation of events from the lives of the Footman family when three sisters spend a summer with their great-grandmother.
Mildred D. Taylor, *The Friendship*, 1987
    Another episode from the lives of the young Logan children in segregated rural Mississippi as they witness a confrontation caused by racial custom.

166

VIRGINIA HAMILTON, African American

The Magical Adventures of Pretty Pearl

(New York: Harper & Row, 1983)

Story type: Young Readers
Subject(s): Magic; Folk Tales; Growing Up
Age range(s): Grades 6 and Up
Major character(s): Pretty Pearl Perry, Child, African American
Time period(s): 1800s
Locale(s): Georgia

Summary: Pretty Pearl, a spirited young African god child eager to show off her powers, travels to the New World where, disguised as a human, she lives among a band of free blacks who have created their own separate world deep inside a vast forest. Pretty's best god brother gives her a magical necklace to help her in time of need, and tells her three god rules which must never be broken. Pretty learns that there is no act without consequence, even for a god child.

Awards the book has won:
Coretta Scott King Honor Book, 1984

Other books by the same author:
Plain City, 1995 (Young Readers)
Drylongso, 1992 (Young Readers)
Cousins, 1990 (Young Readers)
The Bells of Christmas, 1989 (Young Readers)

Zeely, 1967 (debut novel; Young Readers)

Other books you might like:
Joyce Hansen, *The Captive*, 1994
    Historical fiction of the life of a royal African boy who is kidnapped and illegally sold as a slave and is later rescued by a sea captain.
Harriette Gillem Robinet, *Children of the Fire*, 1991
    A young girl witnesses the Great Chicago Fire of 1871 and is forever changed.
Mildred D. Taylor, *The Well: David's Story*, 1995
    Episode of the boyhood of two brothers from an early generation of the Logan family in rural Mississippi facing racial bigotry.
Mildred Pitts Walter, *Trouble's Child*, 1985
    Expected to marry and to succeed her grandmother as the island's midwife, a girl dreams of leaving the island to attend high school.

167

VIRGINIA HAMILTON, African American

The Mystery of Drear House

(New York: Greenwillow Books, 1987)

Story type: Young Readers
Series: Dies Drear Chronicle
Subject(s): Mystery and Detective Stories; Underground Railroad; Treasure
Age range(s): Grades 4-7
Major character(s): Thomas Small, Child, African American; Pesty Darrow, Adoptee, Friend (Neighbor), African American; Professor Walter Small, Father, Historian, African American
Time period(s): 1980s
Locale(s): Ohio

Summary: In this suspenseful sequel Mrs. Darrow frightens Thomas' great-grandmother Jeffers by coming through a secret passageway in their house, which used to be a station on the Underground Railroad. Professor Smalls catalogs a hidden treasure while the Darrow men search for it in vain. Pesty Darrow and Thomas Smalls help in a brilliant plan that will save the treasure before it is stolen or destroyed.

About this book: Sequel to The House of Dies Drear

Other books by the same author:
Drylongso, 1992 (Young Readers)
Junius over Far, 1986 (Young Readers)
Dustland, 1980 (Young Readers)
The House of Dies Drear, 1968 (Young Readers)
Zeely, 1967 (debut novel; Young Readers)

Other books you might like:
Sharon M. Draper, *Ziggy and the Black Dinosaurs*, 1994
    When their neighborhood playground is destroyed, four 5th grade boys start their own secret club and uncover a mysterious old box of hidden bones.
Walter Dean Myers, *Mouse Rap*, 1990
    Summer exploits of a 14-year-old when he hears about a hidden treasure in his neighborhood and his separated parents try getting back together.

Walter Dean Myers, *The Nicholas Factor*, 1983
Spy adventure of a young white boy who finds himself in the jungles of Peru when he is asked to infiltrate a suspected neo-Nazi organization.

Walter Dean Myers, *Tales of a Dead King*, 1983
Journeying to Egypt to participate in an archaeological dig, two white teenagers are intrigued by the mysterious disappearance of the dig's director.

Eleanora E. Tate, *The Secret of Gumbo Grove*, 1987
A youngster upsets her community and her parents when she spreads stories she's heard about the town ancestors buried in the church cemetery.

168

VIRGINIA HAMILTON, African American

Plain City
(New York: Blue Sky Press, 1993)

Story type: Young Readers
Subject(s): Fathers and Daughters; Growing Up; Identity
Age range(s): Grades 3-7
Major character(s): Buhlaire Sims, 12-Year-Old, Student, African American
Time period(s): 1990s (1993)
Locale(s): Plain City, Midwest

Summary: Buhlaire doesn't seem to fit in, perhaps because she is Bluezy Sims' daughter, or maybe because she's a Water House kid; could it be because she looks different than everyone else? Someone told her her father was Missing in Action, but she doesn't know what that means. Suddenly everything seems topsy-turvy when Buhlaire realizes she's been letting people tell her things without thinking for herself, and in a snowy field above her frozen town, something happens that changes Buhlaire forever.

Where it's reviewed:
Publishers Weekly, February 6, 1995, page 86
Booklist, September 15, 1993, page 151
Kirkus Reviews, September 1, 1995, page 1144
Publishers Weekly, August 30, 1993, page 97

Other books by the same author:
Drylongso, 1992 (Young Readers)
Cousins, 1990 (young readers)
The Magical Adventures of Pretty Pearl, 1984 (young readers)
Dustland, 1980 (young readers)
Zeely, 1967 (debut novel; juvenile)

Other books you might like:
Candy Dawson Boyd, *Charlie Pippin*, 1987
Curious about her father's involvement in the Vietnam conflict, an enterprising sixth-grader joins a school group to learn more.

Walter Dean Myers, *Darnell Rock Reporting*, 1994
Not doing well in school, a 13-year-old joins the school newspaper and discovers the impact his writing can have and how he can make a difference.

Harriette Gillem Robinet, *Mississippi Chariot*, 1994
A resourceful 12-year-old son of a sharecropper plans to

get his falsely convicted father off of the chain gang in 1930's Mississippi.

Eleanora E. Tate, *A Blessing in Disguise*, 1995
Another tale from the Calvary County trilogy where a young girl discovers the father she admired addicted her dying mother to alcohol and drugs.

Joyce Carol Thomas, *The Golden Pasture*, 1986
The exquisite horse a 12-year-old boy finds on his grandfather's farm one summer helps him to understand his difficult father better.

169

VIRGINIA HAMILTON, African American

The Planet of Junior Brown
(New York: Macmillan Company, 1971)

Subject(s): City Life; Friendship; Homeless
Age range(s): Grades 7-9
Major character(s): Junior Brown, 13-Year-Old, Musician, African American; Buddy Clark, 13-Year-Old, Streetperson, African American; Mr. Pool, Maintenance Worker, Teacher, African American
Time period(s): 1970s
Locale(s): New York, New York

Summary: Buddy and Junior Brown have been cutting eighth grade for two months. They have been in the school in a hidden basement constructed by Mr. Pool, the janitor, who has made a model of the solar system there and teaches them math and astronomy. Outside of this small shared space, Junior Brown's life is dominated by his overbearing, neurotic mother and is relieved only by his Friday piano lessons. Buddy has no home and makes do on the street, working a job to earn money to take care of other homeless kids. One day they are caught; Mr. Pool is in trouble with his boss and Buddy and Junior Brown are sent to the Vice-Principal's office. Junior Brown's tenuous grasp on reality weakens, and it is up to Buddy to help him.

Where it's reviewed:
Booklist, May 1, 1973, page 838
Horn Book Magazine, February 1972, page 81
Kirkus Reviews, September 1, 1971, page 954
New York Times Book Review, May 21, 1978, page 51

Awards the book has won:
Newbery Honor Book, 1972

Other books by the same author:
Plain City, 1995
Cousins, 1990
The Mystery of Drear House, 1987
Arilla Sun Down, 1976
Zeely, 1967 (debut novel, young readers)

Other books you might like:
Angela Johnson, *Humming Whispers*, 1995
Recounts the life of a young girl living with an older sister who has schizophrenia and her fear that she too may have the mental illness.

Emily Moore, *Whose Side Are You On?*, 1988
When her math tutor mysteriously disappears, a sixth-

grade girl sets out to find him and discovers things aren't always what they seem.

170

VIRGINIA HAMILTON, African American

Sweet Whispers, Brother Rush
(New York: Philomel Books, 1982)

Story type: Young Adult
Subject(s): Adolescence; Family Relations; Ghosts
Age range(s): Grades 7-10
Major character(s): Teresa ''Tree'' Pratt, 14-Year-Old, African American; Dabney ''Dab'' Pratt, Mentally Challenged Person, 17-Year-Old, African American Viola ''Muh Vy'', Nurse, Single Mother, African American
Time period(s): 1970s
Locale(s): Midwest (a small town); Ohio

Summary: Caring for her older retarded brother when her mother is working away from home is an enormous responsibility for teenage ''Tree.'' One afternoon she encounters her uncle's ghost, and through him learns about her family's history and tragedies.

Awards the book has won:
Coretta Scott King Honor Book, 1983
Newbery Honor Book, 1983

Other books by the same author:
Plain City, 1995 (young readers)
A White Romance, 1987 (young adult)
A Little Love, 1984 (young adult)
Willie Bea and the Time the Martians Landed, 1983 (young adult)
Zeely, 1967 (debut novel; young readers)

Other books you might like:
Ossie Davis, *Just Like Martin*, 1992
    A religiously active son and his war veteran father disagree over the civil rights movement until events occur that help them to work together.
David Haynes, *Right by My Side*, 1993
    A high school student writes down his experiences in order to figure things out about his father, his mother and himself.
Angela Johnson, *Toning the Sweep*, 1993
    A young girl prepares a special gift for her grandmother dying of cancer and honors the spirit of the deceased grandfather she never knew.
Joyce Carol Thomas, *Marked by Fire*, 1982
    Friends and family help a young girl overcome the effects of a tornado and a physical assault which nearly breaks her will.
Rita Williams-Garcia, *Like Sisters on the Homefront*, 1994
    An unwed 14-year-old mother, pregnant again, has an abortion and when sent to her relatives in the South, develops a new sense of family and self.

171

VIRGINIA HAMILTON, African American

A White Romance
(New York: Philomel Books, 1987)

Story type: Young Adult
Subject(s): Drugs; Friendship; Race Relations
Age range(s): Grades 7-12
Major character(s): Talley Barbour, Student—High School, Runner, African American
Time period(s): 1980s
Locale(s): Midwest

Summary: When her high school becomes a ''magnet'' and white students are bused-in, Talley doesn't expect to become best friends with Didi, a white girl who shares her passion for running. When Didi becomes involved with heavy-metal rocker Roady Dean, Talley is a little envious. Drawn to Roady's charismatic friend David, Tally becomes involved in a romance of her own, and learns something very important.

Other books by the same author:
Plain City, 1995 (young readers)
A Little Love, 1984 (young adult)
Willie Bea and the Time the Martians Landed, 1983 (young adult)
Sweet Whispers, Brother Rush, 1982 (young adult)
Zeely, 1967 (debut novel; young readers)

Other books you might like:
Mildred D. Taylor, *The Road to Memphis*, 1990
    Another incident from the lives of the Logan family in segregated Mississippi where racial hostilities erupt and new relationships unfold.
Mildred Pitts Walter, *Because We Are*, 1983
    After trouble with a white teacher, an honor student is transferred to a segregated high school where she finds different kinds of challenges.
Mildred Pitts Walter, *The Girl on the Outside*, 1982
    A student and her white classmate see school integratio from very different viewpoints.
Valerie Wilson Wesley, *Where Do I Go from Here?*, 1993
    Having trouble at a snooty mostly-white prep school a teenager learns from another scholarship student that she must make decisions for her own life.
Brenda Wilkinson, *Not Separate, Not Equal*, 1987
    Chosen among a group of six to integrate a Georgia high school, a teenage girl experiences hatred and racism and the beginning of civil rights.

172

VIRGINIA HAMILTON, African American

Willie Bea and the Time the Martians Landed
(New York: Greenwillow Books, 1983)

Story type: Young Adult
Subject(s): Aliens; Farm Life; Halloween
Age range(s): Grades 6 and Up

Major character(s): Willie Bea Mills, 12-Year-Old, Sister, African American; Big Wing, 14-Year-Old, Mentally Challenged Person, African American
Time period(s): 1930s (1938)
Locale(s): Xenia, Ohio

Summary: Willie Bea is excited—her whole family is gathered ''over home'' at Grand and Gramp's house across the road for a big Sunday dinner. It's Halloween and after dinner Aunt Leah returns, upset because she's heard on the radio that Martians have landed! Willie Bea investigates the presence of Martians in her own backyard and is saved by Big on the night of the famous Orson Welles radio broadcast.

Other books by the same author:
Plain City, 1995 (young readers)
A White Romance, 1987 (young adult)
A Little Love, 1984 (young adult)
Sweet Whispers, Brother Rush, 1982 (young adult)
Zeely, 1967 (debut novel; young readers)

Other books you might like:
Angela Johnson, *Toning the Sweep*, 1993
    A young girl prepares a special gift for her grandmother dying of cancer and honors the spirit of the deceased grandfather she never knew.
Mildred D. Taylor, *Let the Circle Be Unbroken*, 1981
    A continuation of the Logan family stories from the Depression era in rural Mississippi where racial antagonisms and conflicts prevail.
Joyce Carol Thomas, *Marked by Fire*, 1982
    Friends and family help a young girl overcome the effects of a tornado and a physical assault which nearly breaks her will.

173

JOYCE HANSEN, African American

The Captive

(New York: Scholastic Inc., 1994)

Story type: Young Readers
Subject(s): Historical; Slavery
Age range(s): Grades 5 and Up
Major character(s): Kofi, 12-Year-Old, Royalty, African (Ashanti); Kwesi, Brother (of Kofi), African (Ashanti)
Time period(s): 1780s; 1790s (1788-1790)
Locale(s): Africa (Ashanti kingdom); Salem, Massachusetts, American Colonies

Summary: Kofi and his brother Kwesi are kidnapped by slavers. When Kofi is released to bring back a reward to rescue his brother, he ends up being enslaved again. This time he is taken away on a slave ship bound for the American Colonies. Illegally bought by a farmer, Kofi and his companions, another African and a British indentured servant, run away. The three boys are rescued by sea captain Paul Cuffe whose African father had been enslaved as a youngster. On a visit to Captain Cuffe's home, Kofi is reunited with an Ashanti girl he knew from Africa. They later marry and devote their lives to helping fugitives who have escaped from slavery.

About this book: Based on the autobiography *The Life of Olaudah Equiano, or Gustavus Vassa, the African*

Where it's reviewed:
Horn Book Guide, Fall 1994, page 310
Publishers Weekly, July 3, 1995, page 62
Social Education, April 1995, page 219

Awards the book has won:
Coretta Scott King Honor Book, 1995

Other books by the same author:
Out from This Place, 1988 (sequel)
Which Way Freedom?, 1986
Yellow Bird and Me, 1986 (sequel)
The Gift Giver, 1980 (debut novel)

Other books you might like:
Virginia Hamilton, *The Magical Adventures of Pretty Pearl*, 1983
    A spirited young African god child travels to the New World where she lives among free blacks and learns that every act has its consequence.
Walter Dean Myers, *The Righteous Revenge of Artemis Bonner*, 1992
    Wild west adventure of a young man out to avenge his uncle's murder and locate his treasure.
Connie Porter, *Meet Addy: An American Girl*, 1993
    A 9-year-old girl and her mother escape from a life of cruel slavery to freedom in Philadelphia during the Civil War.
Harriette Gillem Robinet, *Children of the Fire*, 1991
    A young girl witnesses the Great Chicago Fire of 1871 and is forever changed.
Harriette Gillem Robinet, *If You Please, President Lincoln*, 1995
    Having escaped slavery on Christmas Day in 1863, a 14-year-old joins a group of former slaves on their way to an island off the coast of Haiti.

174

JOYCE HANSEN, African American

The Gift Giver

(New York: Houghton Mifflin, 1980)

Story type: Young Readers
Subject(s): Friendship; Foster Children; City Life
Age range(s): Grades 4-7
Major character(s): Doris Williams, 10-Year-Old, Sister, African American; Amir, 12-Year-Old, Foster Child, African American
Time period(s): 1980s
Locale(s): New York, New York (Harlem)

Summary: Fifth graders Doris and her friends have a new boy in their class, Amir. Amir didn't play basketball, lodies, hookey, talk about other people, lie, cheat or do much of anything Doris and her friends did. Little by little he begins to find a place in their group, motivating the boys into winning their big basketball game against the sixth graders, going to the library with one of the boys to help him raise his grades, bringing food to a runaway boy, and saving the group when they get lost. When Doris' father loses his job and she takes on the responsibility of caring for her baby brother while her mother works, Amir visits to keep her company showing her more of his drawing talent. Everyone is surprised to find out

Amir is a foster child and sorry when they discover their new friend has to move away.

About this book: Debut novel.

Where it's reviewed:
Learning, February 1993, page 64

Other books by the same author:
The Captive, 1994
Out from This Place, 1988 (sequel to *Which Way Freedom*)
Which Way Freedom?, 1986
Yellow Bird and Me, 1986 (sequel to *The Gift Giver*)

Other books you might like:
Jacqueline Turner Banks, *The New One*, 1994
  Five fifth-graders who call themselves "the posse" disagree about whether to befriend a new girl because she seems different.
Candy Dawson Boyd, *Chevrolet Saturdays*, 1993
  Struggling with the divorce of his parents and accepting his new stepfather, a young boy has trouble in school and makes mistakes he regrets.
Christopher Paul Curtis, *The Watsons Go to Birmingham—1963*, 1995
  The ordinary interactions and everyday hijinks of the "weird" Watsons are drastically changed when they visit Grandma in 1960s Alabama.
Mildred Pitts Walter, *Mariah Keeps Cool*, 1990
  A girl trains for a diving competition, tries to figure out her half-sister and plans a surprise for her sister.
Mildred Pitts Walter, *Mariah Loves Rock*, 1988
  As fifth grade comes to an end, a girl and her family experience misgivings about the arrival of a half-sister who is coming to live with them.

175

JOYCE HANSEN, African American

Out from This Place

(New York: Walker and Company, 1988)

Story type: Young Adult
Series: Walker's American History for Young Readers
Subject(s): Historical; Reconstruction; Survival
Age range(s): Grades 5-8
Major character(s): Easter, 14-Year-Old, Slave, African American; Jason, 8-Year-Old, Slave, African American
Time period(s): 1860s (1862-1866)
Locale(s): Santa Elena, South Carolina (Sea Island); New Canaan, South Carolina (Sea Island)

Summary: A year has passed since Easter left young Jason behind when she and Obi ran away from slavery. Separated from Obi on their journey, Easter returns for Jason and discovers he has been sold as a special servant in a plantation house. She and Jason escape with other runaways from the plantation. When they cross the river to the protection of the Union army, the government promises them wages and land when the war ends if they will work in the fields. Years pass while Easter longs to search for Obi and learns to read and write. She and Jason stay together until the war ends and Jason gets a job in a traveling medicine show. Before discov-

ering what has become of Obi, Easter rejects a marriage proposal and leaves to go north for an education.

About this book: Sequel to *Which Way Freedom?*

Where it's reviewed:
Book Report, November 1992, page 64
English Journal, October 1992, page 85

Other books by the same author:
The Captive, 1994
Which Way Freedom?, 1986
Yellow Bird and Me, 1986 (sequel)
The Gift Giver, 1980 (debut novel)

Other books you might like:
Thulani Davis, *1959*, 1992
  Coming-of-age, a 12-year-old girl recounts events that changed her life and others around her during the historic Civil Rights Movement.
Walter Dean Myers, *Glory Field*, 1994
  Family saga of generations of descendents of an African boy kidnapped at the age of eleven and enslaved in the American Colonies.
Mildred D. Taylor, *Roll of Thunder, Hear My Cry*, 1976
  Among a cycle of stories about the Logan family in rural segregated Mississippi during the 1930s and 1940s struggling to survive.
Joyce Carol Thomas, *When the Nightingale Sings*, 1992
  Despite her mean-spirited foster mother's attempts to demean her, a 14-year-old girl has a song to sing and a destiny to fulfill.
A.J. Verdelle, *The Good Negress*, 1995
  A young country girl, moved to the city, wants more from life than cooking, cleaning and washing and is encouraged to reach higher by her teacher.

176

JOYCE HANSEN, African American

Which Way Freedom?

(New York: Walker and Company, 1986)

Story type: Young Adult
Series: Walker's American History for Young Readers
Subject(s): Historical; Slavery
Age range(s): Grades 5-8
Major character(s): Obidiah "Obi" Jennings, Slave, Runaway, African American
Time period(s): 1860s (1861-1864)
Locale(s): South Carolina (thirty miles from Charleston); Fort Pillow, Tennessee (site of a Civil War battle)

Summary: Around the age of six or seven Obi was taken from his mother and sold in the Charleston slave market. He worked on the Jennings tobacco farm with 7-year-old Jason and 13-year-old Easter. As the Civil War heats up the Jennings decide to sell their three slaves and escape before the Union soldiers can arrive. Using a handmade reed boat Obi escapes across the river and joins the Union Army. After a historic battle Obi vows to return across the river for Jason and Easter.

Where it's reviewed:
Book Report, January 1994, page 24

Book Report, November 1992, page 65
English Journal, October 1992, page 85

Awards the book has won:
Coretta Scott King Honor Book, 1987
American Library Association Notable Book, 1986

Other books by the same author:
The Captive, 1994
Out from This Place, 1988
Yellow Bird and Me, 1986
The Gift Giver, 1980 (debut novel)

Other books you might like:
Thulani Davis, *1959*, 1992
Coming-of-age, a 12-year-old girl recounts events that changed her life and others around her during the historic Civil Rights Movement.
Walter Dean Myers, *Glory Field*, 1994
Family saga of generations of descendents of an African boy kidnapped at the age of eleven and enslaved in the American Colonies.
Mildred D. Taylor, *Roll of Thunder, Hear My Cry*, 1976
Among a cycle of stories about the Logan family in rural, segregated Mississippi during the 1930s and 1940s, struggling to survive.
Joyce Carol Thomas, *When the Nightingale Sings*, 1992
Despite her mean-spirited foster mother's attempts to demean her, a 14-year-old girl has a song to sing and a destiny to fulfill.
A.J. Verdelle, *The Good Negress*, 1995
A young country girl, moved to the city, wants more from life than cooking, cleaning and washing and is encouraged to reach higher by her teacher.

177

JOYCE HANSEN, African American

Yellow Bird and Me

(New York: Clarion Books, 1986)

Story type: Young Readers
Subject(s): School Life; Friendship
Age range(s): Grades 4-7
Major character(s): Doris Williams, 6th Grader, Sister, African American; James "Yellow Bird" Towers, 11-Year-Old, 6th Grader, African American
Time period(s): 1980s
Locale(s): New York, New York (Harlem)

Summary: Her best friend Amir moved from the neighborhood with his foster family. Now Doris writes him letters and hopes to some day visit him in upstate New York. Meanwhile their friend Yellow Bird pesters her to help him with his homework and she discovers that Yellow Bird, often the class clown, is quite smart but has trouble reading. When they get a chance to be in a school play, they work together and, with the help of the new drama teacher, succeed and discover why Yellow Bird has trouble reading: he has dyslexia.

About this book: Sequel to *Gift Giver*.

Other books by the same author:
The Captive, 1994
Out from This Place, 1988 (sequel)

Which Way Freedom?, 1986
The Gift Giver, 1980 (debut novel)

Other books you might like:
Jacqueline Turner Banks, *Egg-Drop Blues*, 1995
A sixth grader's science grade is low because of his dyslexia, so he and his twin brother enter a competition for extra credit.
Walter Dean Myers, *Darnell Rock Reporting*, 1994
Not doing well in school, a 13-year-old joins the school newspaper and discovers the impact his writing can have and how he can make a difference.
Walter Dean Myers, *Me, Mop, and the Moondance Kid*, 1988
Two young brothers share a close friendship with a young white girl on their Little League baseball team and hope she gets adopted like they did.
Harriette Gillem Robinet, *Ride the Red Cycle*, 1980
A boy crippled since the age of two struggles to realize his dream of riding a cycle.
Jacqueline Woodson, *Between Madison & Palmetto*, 1993
In their continuing story two 13-year-old best friends are reunited and have to adjust to a lot of change in their lives and in those around them.

178

GARY HARDWICK, African American

Cold Medina

(New York: Dutton, 1996)

Subject(s): Drugs; Mystery and Detective Stories; Police Procedural
Age range(s): Adult
Major character(s): Tony Hill, Detective—Police, Spouse, Father
Time period(s): 1990s
Locale(s): Detroit, Michigan

Summary: Tony joins the police force on the wave of affirmative action and rises to detective, heading the elite Special Crimes unit. While he investigates a series of drug related killings, crucial evidence is leaked to the press and mishandled in the crime lab. Tony and his partner Jim follow every lead until Tony, almost killed in a shoot out, is exhausted and quits the force. His resignation refused, off duty Tony begins to make some new connections in the case and before long follows a major lead exposing police corruption bringing him face-to-face with the killer.

About this book: This is a debut novel.

Other books you might like:
Eleanor Taylor Bland, *Dead Time*, 1992
This debut novel in a detective mystery series includes a female heroine.
Gar Anthony Haywood, *Fear of the Dark*, 1988
This debut novel in a contemporary murder mystery series includes a private detective.
Hugh Holton, *Presumed Dead*, 1994
This debut novel in a contemporary murder mystery series includes a Chicago detective.

Walter Mosley, *Devil in a Blue Dress*, 1990
This debut novel in a contemporary murder mystery series includes a private detective.
Vallerie Wilson Wesley, *When Death Comes Stealing*, 1994
This debut novel in a murder mystery series features an ex-policewoman who has become a private detective.

179

E. LYNN HARRIS, African American

And This Too Shall Pass

(New York: Doubleday, 1996)

Subject(s): Homosexuality/Lesbianism; Interpersonal Relations; Secrets
Age range(s): Adult
Major character(s): Zurich Robinson, Football Player (celibate), African American, Religious; Mia Miller, Journalist (heterosexual), African American, Alcoholic; Sean Elliott, Homosexual, Sportswriter, African American
Time period(s): 1990s
Locale(s): Chicago, Illinois

Summary: Rookie quarterback Zurich Robinson is on the brink of what promises to be a great career with the NFL Chicago Cougars. Mia Miller is on her own way up as a female sportscaster. Granted the first exclusive interview with Zurich, Mia is attracted by his good looks, intelligence and charm. Zurich rebuffs Mia's sexual advances. When Mia is brutally assaulted she leads the police to believe that Zurich is responsible. Sean Elliott, an athlete-turned-sportswriter, also interviews Zurich and finds himself attracted to the athlete. It is the unconditional love of Zurich's grandmother, MamaCee, that puts a healing touch on all their lives.

Other books by the same author:
Just as I Am, 1994 (sequel to *Invisible Life*)
Invisible Life, 1991

Other books you might like:
David Haynes, *Live at Five*, 1996
A television anchor seeks to re-define his image by broadcasting from the inner city to improve ratings, and finds the ''real'' story.
Steven Corbin, *Fragments That Remain*, 1993
Depicts a contemporary actor's life as he deals with racism, sexism, homophobia, bigotry, an interracial relationship, and secrets from the past.
Brent Wade, *Company Man*, 1992
Behind-the-scenes stresses and strains faced by a man attempting to climb the business ladder and preserve his family.

180

E. LYNN HARRIS, African American

Invisible Life

(Atlanta: Consortium Press, 1991)

Subject(s): AIDS (Disease); Interpersonal Relations; Self-Acceptance
Age range(s): Adult

Major character(s): Raymond Wilson Tyler Jr., Lawyer (bisexual), African American; Quinn Mathis, Spouse (bisexual), African American, Stock Broker; Nicole Marie Springer, Actress (heterosexual), Singer, African American
Time period(s): 1990s
Locale(s): New York, New York

Summary: In his senior year in college, while continuing a relationship with his high school sweetheart, Raymond has his first bisexual relationship with Kelvin, a football player. With a promising law career ahead, Raymond no longer considers himself straight but is not sure if he is completely gay. After a rocky beginning Raymond is falling in love with Quinn, a married man and father he meets in a gay bar. When he is introduced to Nicole, they develop a romantic attraction for one another. Torn between his feelings for both Quinn and Nicole, Raymond realizes he has to tell Nicole about himself, especially after an old friend contracts AIDS.

About this book: Debut novel.

Other books by the same author:
Just as I Am, 1994 (sequel to Invisible Life)

Other books you might like:
Larry Duplechan, *Tangled Up in Blue*, 1989
The impact of AIDS when a wife discovers her husband and a friend who's infected had a bisexual affair, with non-African American characters.

181

E. LYNN HARRIS, African American

Just as I Am

(New York: Doubleday, 1994)

Subject(s): AIDS (Disease); Interpersonal Relations; Self-Acceptance
Age range(s): Adult
Major character(s): Raymond Wilson Tyler Jr., Lawyer (bisexual), African American; Nicole Marie Springer, Actress (heterosexual), Singer (African American); Kyle Benton, Homosexual (AIDS victim), African American
Time period(s): 1990s
Locale(s): Atlanta, Georgia; Chicago, Illinois; New York, New York

Summary: Raymond and Nicole are resuming their individual lives after breaking up. Raymond has an affair with a famous football player, and Nicole has an interracial affair. They are brought together at the deathbed of their gay friend Kyle, and later they both find love with secret admirers from their pasts.

About this book: This is a sequel to the debut novel.

Where it's reviewed:
Lambda Book Report, May 1995, page 39

Other books by the same author:
Invisible Life, 1992 (debut novel)

Other books you might like:
Larry Duplechan, *Tangled Up in Blue*, 1989
A wife discovers her husband and a friend who is infected with AIDS had a bisexual affair.

182

FRANCINE HASKINS, Author/Illustrator, African American

Things I Like about Grandma

(San Francisco: Children's Book Press, 1992)

Story type: Young Readers
Subject(s): Grandparents; Interpersonal Relations
Age range(s): Grades 1-2
Time period(s): 1990s
Locale(s): United States

Summary: A child describes her special relationship with her grandma and the things they do together. She especially likes grandma telling her stories of the "old days" and about when her mommy was little like her. They enjoy making a patchwork quilt together that tells stories of the family, and working in grandma's garden. The weekend is a special time when they bake goodies and go to church chatting with friends. They do errands and shop and visit the hairdresser together, ride the bus and share a special lunch. They laugh and have fun when she gets to try on grandma's wig and earrings, and she enjoys doing "boy things" with granddaddy like watching sports on TV.

Other books by the same author:
I Remember "121", 1991 (biography (young readers))

Other books you might like:
Jeannette Franklin Caines, *Window Wishing*, 1980
   The exploits of a young sister and brother spending their vacation with their fun grandma who takes them downtown together where they window wish.
Donald Crews, *Bigmama's*, 1991
   Recalls the summer exploits of a youngster in the 1940s when he, his brother, sisters, and parents visit his grandparents in the country.
Valerie Flournoy, *Tanya's Reunion*, 1995
   A youngster traveling with her grandma to the family farm for a reunion discovers a special memento for her grandma of days gone by.
Eloise Greenfield, *Grandmama's Joy*, 1980
   Worried when she see's her grandmama sad, a child learns why and tries the best way she knows how to put a smile back on her face again.
Eloise Greenfield, *William and the Good Old Days*, 1993
   A boy's grandma is recovering from an illness and he thinks about the good times they had together in the past before he lets go to see new days ahead.

183

DAVID HAYNES, African American

Heathens

(St. Paul: New Rivers Press, 1996)

Subject(s): City Life; Family Relations; Interpersonal Relations
Age range(s): Adult
Major character(s): Verda Gabriel, Mother, Grandmother, African American; Marcus Gabriel, Husband, Teacher, Afri-

can American; LaDonna Gabriel, Mother, Prisoner, African American
Time period(s): 1990s
Locale(s): St. Paul, Minnesota

Summary: LaDonna is an entrepreneur always looking for an angle. She writes a bad check for a real estate deal she'd hoped would make her $10,000 richer and winds up doing 20 days in Shakopee Women's Detention Center, plus an extra 5 days for putting a curse on the judge. Her mother-in-law figures this is her chance to get rid of LaDonna for good so she hires her son a maid hoping she will lure her him away from LaDonna. Meanwhile, undaunted, LaDonna launches Madame LaDonna's cosmetics from her cell.

About this book: Minnesota Voices Project Number 72.

Awards the book has won:
Minnesota Voices Project, 1996

Other books by the same author:
Live at Five, 1996
Somebody Else's Mama, 1995
Right by My Side, 1993 (debut novel, young adult)

Other books you might like:
Helen Elaine Lee, *The Serpent's Gift*, 1994
   Children and grandchildren of two intertwined families endure hardship and triumph as they help each other remember a history beyond their knowing.
Gloria Naylor, *Women of Brewster Place*, 1982
   The story of seven women who come to live on the dead-end street of Brewster Place and what brings them together in their own redemption.
Richard Perry, *Montgomery's Children*, 1984
   Tales of people living in a small town in central New York interwoven with magic and vision, incest and murder, friendship and sacrifice.

184

DAVID HAYNES, African American

Live at Five

(Minneapolis: Milkweed Editions, 1996)

Subject(s): Interpersonal Relations; Single Parent Families; Television
Age range(s): Adult
Major character(s): Brandon Wilson, Television Personality, African American; Nita Sallis, Single Mother, Student, African American
Time period(s): 1990s
Locale(s): St. Paul, Minnesota

Summary: Brandon Wilson anchors a television news show ranking fifth out of five stations. Dexter Rayburn, the new producer, is determined to raise the ratings so he hires a new news director to revamp the set and update the equipment and decides to re-package his anchor. This means that Brandon will be living and broadcasting from the inner city, looking for the "real" story. Brandon moves into the basement of an apartment building run by Nita, a young single mother of three who also works and goes to school at night. Instead of finding the desperation, violence and anger he had expected, Brandon instead finds decent people doing their best to get by.

After a week of broadcasting interviews with neighborhood personalities, Dexter is ready to pull the series unless Brandon finds something sensational. It is Nita who comes to the rescue with a media circus and the images to fit the bill.

Other books by the same author:

Heathens, 1996

Somebody Else's Mama, 1995

Right by My Side, 1993 (debut novel, young adult)

Other books you might like:

E. Lynn Harris, *And This Too Shall Pass*, 1996
   The lives of a rookie quarterback, a female sportscaster, a gay journalist and a lawyer intersect when the quarterback is falsely accused of assault.

John Edgar Wideman, *Philadelphia Fire*, 1990
   Intrigued by a police bombing and killing of adults and children a self-exiled writer returns to Philadelphia to investigate.

John Edgar Wideman, *Reuben*, 1987
   Exploits of an aged lawyer and the varied clients he puts his talents to work for in the Pittsburgh community of Homewood during the 1980s.

185

DAVID HAYNES, African American

Right by My Side

(New York: New Rivers Press, 1993)

Story type: Young Adult

Subject(s): Coming of Age; Family Relations; Fathers and Sons

Age range(s): Grades 8-Adult

Major character(s): Marshall Field Finney, Student—High School, African American; Sam Finney, Father, Maintenance Worker, African American

Time period(s): 1990s

Locale(s): Washington Park, Missouri (suburb of St. Louis)

Summary: When his mother abruptly leaves home, Marshall begins to write down his experiences so he can 'run it by again' and try to figure things out about his father, his mother and himself.

About this book: Debut novel for young adults.

Where it's reviewed:

Booklist, January 15, 1994, page 867

Booklist, February 15, 1994, page 1043

School Library Journal, December 1993, page 149

Awards the book has won:

Minnesota Voices Project Winner, 1992

Young Adult Library Services Association, Best Books for YA, 1994

Other books you might like:

Ossie Davis, *Just Like Martin*, 1992
   A religiously active son and his war veteran father disagree over the civil rights movement until events occur that help them to work together.

Virginia Hamilton, *A Little Love*, 1984
   A teenage girl has an emptiness food cannot fill. She

misses her father, and in her search for him she finds new strengths in herself.

Virginia Hamilton, *Sweet Whispers, Brother Rush*, 1982
   A girl caring for her retarded older brother encounters the ghost of her dead uncle and comes to a deeper understanding of her family and herself.

Walter Dean Myers, *Won't Know Till I Get There*, 1982
   The summer exploits of a 14-year-old whose parents decide to adopt a youngster with a juvenile record and the boys get arrested together.

Lionel Newton, *Getting Right with God*, 1994
   In fantastical chats with God and Satan, a teenage boy figures out his feelings about adolescence, sex, love, religion and doing the right thing.

Lionel Newton, *Things to Be Lost*, 1995
   A young boy understands his ailing father as seemingly no one else does, ultimately killing what he loves most, suffering both guilt and loss.

Brenda Wilkinson, *Not Separate, Not Equal*, 1987
   Chosen among a group of six to integrate a Georgia high school, a teenage girl experiences hatred and racism and the beginning of civil rights.

186

DAVID HAYNES, African American

Somebody Else's Mama

(Minneapolis: Milkweed Editions, 1995)

Subject(s): Family Relations; Marriage; Mothers

Age range(s): Adult

Major character(s): Paula Johnson, Spouse (of Al's), Teacher, African American; Al Johnson, Political Figure, Spouse (of Paula's), African American; Xenobia Mae Kezee, Aged Person, Mother (of Al's), African American

Time period(s): 1990s

Locale(s): River Ridge, Missouri

Summary: Paula's ill and aging mother-in-law, Xenobia Mae, arrives from St. Paul, causing her to face the memory of her own mother's lonely death. Her husband Al, a candidate for mayor, offers her little help in handling the feuding between her twin sons and taking care of the cantankerous old woman who would rather go home.

About this book: This is the author's debut novel.

Where it's reviewed:

Booklist, April 15, 1995, page 1479

Kirkus Reviews, March 1, 1995, page 253

New York Times Book Review, June 18, 1995, page 21

Publishers Weekly, April 10, 1995, page 55

Other books you might like:

Connie Briscoe, *Sisters and Lovers*, 1994
   This contemporary story is about the lives and struggles of three sisters and the men with whom they become involved.

Bebe Moore Campbell, *Brothers and Sisters*, 1994
   This contemporary account of a career woman's life shows her attempt to climb the business ladder as she maintains a social life, and relationships with the people around her.

Terry McMillan, *Waiting to Exhale*, 1992
> This contemporary account is about the friendship of four women, their relationships with men, and their experiences with family and careers.

187

GAR ANTHONY HAYWOOD, African American

Bad News Travels Fast
(New York: G. P. Putnam's Sons, 1995)

Story type: Adult; Amateur Detective
Series: Loudermilks
Subject(s): Family Relations; Murder; Mystery and Detective Stories
Major character(s): Dottie Loudermilk, Aged Person, Mother, African American; Joe Loudermilk, Aged Person, Father, African American; Eddie Loudermilk, Activist, Brother (middle son), African American
Time period(s): 1990s (1995)
Locale(s): Washington, District of Columbia

Summary: Dottie and Joe look forward to a visit to the nation's capital. Their visit is less than enjoyable when they witness their son Eddie argue with a man who is later found dead. Arrested for the murder, Eddie proclaims his innocence, and his parents are determined to help him prove it. With the aid of their lawyer daughter, they locate a key piece of evidence pointing toward high-ranking government officials and come to realize they may all be in over their heads.

Where it's reviewed:
Library Journal, July 1995, page 127
Publishers Weekly, June 12, 1995, page 51
Book World, August 20, 1995, page 11

Other books by the same author:
Going Nowhere Fast, 1994 (Loudermilk series)
You Can Die Trying, 1993 (Aaron Gunner series)
Not Long for This World, 1990 (Aaron Gunner series)
Fear of the Dark, 1988 (debut novel, Aaron Gunner series)

Other books you might like:
Nikki Baker, *In the Game*, 1991
> Debut novel in a murder mystery series with lesbian characters.
Eleanor Taylor Bland, *Dead Time*, 1992
> Debut novel in a detective mystery series with a female heroine.
Penny Mickelbury, *Keeping Secrets*, 1994
> Debut novel in a murder mystery series with lesbian characters.
Barbara Neely, *Blanche on the Lam*, 1992
> Debut novel in a contemporary murder mystery series with an amateur detective as the heroine.
Valerie Wilson Wesley, *When Death Comes Stealing*, 1994
> Debut novel in a murder mystery series featuring an ex-policewoman who has become a private detective.

188

GAR ANTHONY HAYWOOD, African American

Fear of the Dark
(New York: St. Martin's Press, 1988)

Story type: Private Detective; Adult
Series: Aaron Gunner
Subject(s): Crime and Criminals; Murder; Mystery and Detective Stories
Age range(s): Adult
Major character(s): Aaron Gunner, Detective—Private, Maintenance Worker, African American
Time period(s): 1980s
Locale(s): Los Angeles, California

Summary: In this debut novel in the Aaron Gunner series, Gunner is hired to find the man who killed two men in the Acey Deuce bar. After being framed for the murder of the gunman, Gunner discovers the assassin's connection with a local political campaign and a black-power organization.

About this book: This is the author's debut novel in the Aaron Gunner series.

Awards the book has won:
Shamus Awards: Best First P.I. Novel, 1987

Other books by the same author:
Bad News Travels Fast, 1995 (Loudermilks series)
You Can Die Trying, 1993 (Aaron Gunner series)
Not Long for This World, 1990 (Aaron Gunner series)

Other books you might like:
Nikki Baker, *In the Game*, 1991
> This debut novel begins a murder mystery series with lesbian characters.
Penny Mickelbury, *Keeping Secrets*, 1994
> This debut novel begins a murder mystery series with lesbian characters.
Walter Mosley, *Devil in a Blue Dress*, 1990
> This debut novel begins a contemporary murder mystery series with a private detective.
Barbara Neely, *Blanche on the Lam*, 1992
> This debut novel begins a contemporary murder mystery series with an amateur detective as the heroine.
Valerie Wilson Wesley, *When Death Comes Stealing*, 1994
> This debut novel begins a murder mystery series featuring an ex-policewoman who becomes a private detective.

189

GAR ANTHONY HAYWOOD, African American

Going Nowhere Fast
(New York: G.P. Putnam's Sons, 1994)

Story type: Amateur Detective; Adult
Series: Loudermilks
Subject(s): Family Relations; Murder; Mystery and Detective Stories
Age range(s): Adult
Major character(s): Dottie Loudermilk, Aged Person, Mother, African American; Joe Loudermilk, Aged Person, Father, African American

Time period(s): 1990s (1994)
Locale(s): Grand Canyon, Arizona

Summary: Looking to enjoy the open road during retirement, Dottie and Joe purchase an upscale *Airstream* motor home. Reaching the Grand Canyon they are shocked when they return one morning from a jog to find a dead man on their toilet and their grown son hiding in the closet. As the mystery unfolds Dottie becomes more and more intrigued. When she and Joe and their son are under suspicion for the murder, she takes the lead in getting to the bottom of things. With the park rangers, sheriff, FBI, and the mob involved in this who-done-it, Dottie and Joe flush out the killer.

About this book: This is the second title in the Loudermilks' series.

Where it's reviewed:
Armchair Detective, Fall 1994, page 490
New York Times Book Review, November 13, 1994, page 19
Tribune Books (Chicago), December 11, 1994, page 6

Other books by the same author:
Bad News Travels Fast, 1995 (Loudermilks series)
You Can Die Trying, 1993 (Aaron Gunner series)
Not Long for This World, 1990 (Aaron Gunner series)
Fear of the Dark, 1988 (debut novel; Aaron Gunner series)

Other books you might like:
Nikki Baker, *In the Game*, 1991
    This debut novel begins a murder mystery series with lesbian characters.
Eleanor Taylor Bland, *Dead Time*, 1992
    This debut novel begins a detective mystery series with a female heroine.
Walter Mosley, *Devil in a Blue Dress*, 1990
    This debut novel begins a contemporary murder mystery series with a private detective.
Barbara Neely, *Blanche on the Lam*, 1992
    This debut novel begins a contemporary murder mystery series with an amateur detective as the heroine.
Valerie Wilson Wesley, *When Death Comes Stealing*, 1994
    This debut novel begins a murder mystery series featuring an ex-policewoman who becomes a private detective.

190

GAR ANTHONY HAYWOOD, African American

Not Long for This World

(New York: St. Martin's Press, 1990)

Story type: Private Detective; Adult
Series: Aaron Gunner
Subject(s): Crime and Criminals; Gangs; Mystery and Detective Stories
Age range(s): Adult
Major character(s): Aaron Gunner, Detective—Private, Maintenance Worker, African American
Time period(s): 1990s
Locale(s): Los Angeles, California

Summary: Darryl Lovejoy is killed in a drive-by shooting, the apparent victim of the kids he was trying to help. A gang member is in custody, and his attorney enlists the aid of a reluctant Gunner to clear her client.

About this book: This is the second title in the Aaron Gunner series.

Other books by the same author:
Bad News Travels Fast, 1995 (Loudermilks series)
You Can Die Trying, 1993 (Aaron Gunner series)
Fear of the Dark, 1988 (debut novel, Aaron Gunner series)

Other books you might like:
Nikki Baker, *In the Game*, 1991
    This debut novel begins a murder mystery series with lesbian characters.
Yolanda Joe, *Falling Leaves of Ivy*, 1992
    A young woman is murdered and her four closest friends from college become suspects, as the secret shared among them begins to unravel.
Walter Mosley, *Devil in a Blue Dress*, 1990
    This debut novel begins a contemporary murder mystery series with a private detective.
Barbara Summers, *The Price You Pay*, 1993
    A young woman in the highly competitive fashion industry finds herself as a target for murder. A series of murders occur when a new market campaign is launched.
Valerie Wilson Wesley, *When Death Comes Stealing*, 1994
    This debut novel begins a murder mystery series featuring an ex-policewoman who becomes a private detective.

191

GAR ANTHONY HAYWOOD, African American

You Can Die Trying

(New York: St. Martin's Press, 1993)

Story type: Private Detective; Adult
Series: Aaron Gunner
Subject(s): Crime and Criminals; Murder; Mystery and Detective Stories
Age range(s): Adult
Major character(s): Aaron Gunner, Detective—Private
Time period(s): 1990s
Locale(s): Los Angeles, California

Summary: After a highly publicized dismissal from the police department, an ex-cop-turned-security-guard commits suicide during a seemingly routine burglary in Hollywood. Gunner is hired to investigate the incident that got the guard dismissed, and to prove that he was set up.

About this book:

Where it's reviewed:
Black Scholar, Winter 1995, page 62
Guardian Weekly, April 16, 1995, page 28

Other books by the same author:
Bad News Travels Fast, 1995 (Loudermilks series)
Not Long for This World, 1990 (Aaron Gunner series)
Fear of the Dark, 1988 (debut novel, Aaron Gunner series)

Other books you might like:
Eleanor Taylor Bland, *Dead Time*, 1992
    This debut novel begins a detective mystery series with a female heroine.

Penny Mickelbury, *Keeping Secrets*, 1994
> This debut novel begins a murder mystery series with lesbian characters.

Walter Mosley, *Devil in a Blue Dress*, 1990
> This debut novel begins a contemporary murder mystery series with a private detective.

Barbara Neely, *Blanche on the Lam*, 1992
> This debut novel begins a contemporary murder mystery series with an amateur detective as the heroine.

Valerie Wilson Wesley, *When Death Comes Stealing*, 1994
> This debut novel begins a murder mystery series featuring an ex-policewoman who becomes a private detective.

192

NATHAN HEARD, African American

House of Slammers
(New York: Macmillan Publishing Company, 1983)

Subject(s): Ethics; Prisoners and Prisons; Race Relations
Age range(s): Adult
Major character(s): William "Beans" Butler, Convict, Student—College, African American
Time period(s): 1980s
Locale(s): Newark, New Jersey (in prison)

Summary: Serving a sentence for armed robbery, Beans Butler is a different man than the one who walked into the prison five years ago. He has educated himself and earned a scholarship to a correspondence university. More importantly, he feels a different sense of responsibility to his fellow man. Now with only a few months to go, Beans hears that the prisoners are planning a demonstration for better living conditions and they want him to write up their grievances. Although he knows his involvement could ruin his chances at parole, he feels bound to help. He must deal with the factions inside the prison: the Muslims, the neo-Nazis, and the black nationalists, and get them to put aside their differences for their common good. In this uncompromising novel of prison life, Beans must face the consequences of his decision.

Other books by the same author:
A Cold Fire Burning, 1974
To Reach a Dream, 1972
Howard Street, 1968 (debut novel)

Other books you might like:
Chester Himes, *Plan B*, 1993
> A political visionary plots to avenge racial injustice by anonymously arming the common black man to overthrow white society.

Cyrus Colter, *A Chocolate Soldier*, 1988
> A story within a story where a tale is told of a young idealist who murders his white employer and is himself killed by a mob lynching.

Melvin Van Peebles, *Panther*, 1995
> Recounts an urban rebellion of the sixties that became the historic Black Panther movement and plots of the FBI and police to destroy them.

John Edgar Wideman, *Philadelphia Fire*, 1990
> Intrigued by a police bombing and killing of adults and children a self-exiled writer returns to Philadelphia to investigate.

193

NATHAN HEARD, African American

To Reach a Dream
(New York: Dial Press, 1972)

Subject(s): City Life; Graphic Novel; Prisoners and Prisons
Age range(s): Adult
Major character(s): Bart Enos, Convict, Con Artist, African American
Time period(s): 1970s
Locale(s): Newark, New Jersey

Summary: Bart Enos grew up on the streets of Newark with pimps and holdup men as his heros. He wanted the fancy cars, the women and the money for himself. When he is involved as the driver in a series of robberies, he is finally arrested and sentenced to prison. Having served his time, he is back on the streets trying to look out for number one. The opportunity presents itself to con a rich widow out of her money with his youth and sexual charm, but his plan is altered by the appearance of the widow's daughter. A sexual triangle develops and explodes as mother, daughter and lover each pay a high price.

Other books by the same author:
House of Slammers, 1983
A Cold Fire Burning, 1974
Howard Street, 1968 (debut novel)

Other books you might like:
Reginald McKnight, *I Get on the Bus*, 1990
> Trying to avoid making decisions at home, a young man joins the Peace Corps and travels to Senegal, becoming involved in new intrigue.

John Edgar Wideman, *Hurry Home*, 1970
> In search of himself, a law school graduate marries the woman who helped him succeed then abandons her to go abroad, returning three years later.

194

CAROLIVIA HERRON, African American

Thereafter Johnnie
(New York: Random House, 1991)

Subject(s): Family Relations; Fathers and Daughters
Age range(s): Adult
Major character(s): Johnnie Snowdon, Daughter (born of incest), Teenager, African American; John Christopher Snowdon, Father ("Grandfather"), African American; Patricia Snowdon, Abuse Victim (incest), Mother (of Johnnie), African American
Time period(s): 1970s; 1990s
Locale(s): Washington, District of Columbia

Summary: John's incestuous relationship with his daughter, Patricia, begets Johnnie, creating a confusing granddaughter/daughter/sister relationship. In escaping her father's abuse, Patricia shares a love relationship with another woman.

About this book: This is the author's debut novel.

Where it's reviewed:
Callaloo, Spring 1995, page 472

Other books you might like:

Marita Golden, *And Do Remember Me*, 1992

A young girl raped by her father runs away from home. She later finds the courage to return home when he suffers a stroke and she confronts her mother.

Walter Mosley, *RL's Dream*, 1995

An aging blues musician befriends a young, caucasian woman haunted by an incestuous past. This story recounts exploits from the musician's past as they become friends.

195

VY HIGGINSEN, African American
TANYA BOLDEN, Co-Author, African American

Mama, I Want to Sing

(New York: Scholastic Inc., 1995)

Story type: Young Adult
Subject(s): Singing; Mothers and Daughters
Age range(s): Grades 6 and Up
Major character(s): Doris Winter, Singer, African American; Geraldine Winter, Mother, Widow(er), African American
Time period(s): 1940s (1946)
Locale(s): New York, New York (Harlem)

Summary: Young Doris was a talented singer in the church choir where her father was pastor. Suffering a heart attack her father passed away and she and her mother Geraldine were left to carry on. Geraldine took a paying position in the church and reconverted their home to take in boarders. Grieving over her father's death and leaving the choir Doris begins spending more time with her new friends Berry, DeeDee, and Gail. Upset and hoping Doris will lose her interest in popular non-secular music, Geraldine sends her to visit relatives in the South. Thinking of the encouraging words of her father to pursue her singing talent and dreams Doris forms a singing group with the girls and when they win the Apollo Amateur Night their lives are forever changed.

About this book: Debut novel

Where it's reviewed:

Kliatt, September 1995, page 10
Children's Book Review Service, November 1992, page 35
Publishers Weekly, November 9, 1992, page 88
Voice of Youth Advocates, October 1992, page 140

Other books you might like:

Walter Dean Myers, *Crystal*, 1987

On the brink of a promising career in modeling a 16-year-old realizes there is more than glamour to the industry and has to decide what path to choose.

Walter Dean Myers, *Motown and Didi: A Love Story*, 1984

Each dreaming of making a better life for themselves two teenagers meet when the young boy rescues the young girl from street hoodlums.

Joyce Carol Thomas, *When the Nightingale Sings*, 1992

Despite her mean-spirited foster mother's attempts to demean her, a 14-year-old girl has a song to sing and a destiny to fulfill.

Valerie Wilson Wesley, *Where Do I Go from Here?*, 1993

Having trouble at a snooty mostly-white prep school a teenager learns from another scholarship student she must make decisions for her own life.

Rita Williams-Garcia, *Blue Tights*, 1988

Struggling to find friends and acceptance a young girl born out-of-wedlock follows her mother's footsteps in her passion for dancing.

196

CHESTER HIMES, African American

Plan B

(Jackson, Mississippi: University Press of Mississippi, 1993)

Subject(s): Racism; Rebellion; Terrorism
Age range(s): Adult
Major character(s): Tomsson Black, Revolutionary, Convict, African American
Time period(s): 1960s
Locale(s): New York, New York (Harlem)

Summary: Tommson Black earns a degree in political science, travels the world, and serves time for raping a white woman. Racism has poisoned his family so he implements a plan that will allow black people to overthrow white society and avenge racial injustice. A man in Harlem receives a long box with an M-14 automatic weapon inside and a mysterious note saying to learn the weapon and be ready, for freedom is near. More guns are delivered anonymously to many other residents, all containing the same cryptic instructions. A riot breaks out in Harlem and many people are killed. Guilty whites publicly mourn the deaths of the citizens of Harlem, while racially motivated violence escalates as a black man is lynched in Central Park.

About this book: Published posthumously; author died in 1984

Other books by the same author:

Blind Man With a Pistol, 1969
Cotton Comes to Harlem, 1965
The Crazy Kill, 1959
Cast the First Stone, 1953
If He Hollars Let Him Go, 1945 (debut novel)

Other books you might like:

Wesley Brown, *Darktown Strutters*, 1994

A traveling minstrel dances the thin line between anger, violence and laughter in pre- and post-Civil War America.

Nathan Heard, *House of Slammers*, 1983

A convict who educated and changed himself during his sentence becomes involved in a prison demonstration for better conditions.

Ishmael Reed, *Flight to Canada*, 1976

In this satire, three slaves escape but later return to the plantation after the slave owner is murdered by his sister's ghost.

Melvin Van Peebles, *Panther*, 1995

Recounts an urban rebellion of the sixties that became the historic Black Panther movement and plots of the FBI and police to destroy them.

197

HUGH HOLTON, African American

Chicago Blues

(New York: Tom Doherty Associates, 1996)

Subject(s): Crime and Criminals; Mystery and Detective Stories; Police Procedural

Age range(s): Adult

Major character(s): Commander Larry Cole, Detective—Homicide, African American; Reggie Stanton, Bodyguard, African American; Antonio "Tuxedo Tony" DeLisa, Organized Crime Figure

Time period(s): 1990s

Locale(s): Chicago, Illinois

Summary: Mob boss "Tuxedo Tony" orders a hit on a U.S. senator who is launching an investigation on organized crime. His two hit men are brutally murdered before they can complete the job. When Commander Larry Cole investigates the murders he discovers that former colleague Reggie Stanton is now the senator's bodyguard. Reggie could have been involved in some vigilante murders 15 years ago, but the investigation was somehow buried. Suddenly Reggie is up against a professional assassin hired by "Tuxedo Tony" to finish the job on the senator as betrayals pile up like bodies.

Other books by the same author:
Windy City, 1995
Presumed Dead, 1994 (debut novel)

Other books you might like:
Eleanor Taylor Bland, *Dead Time*, 1992
    Debut novel in a detective mystery series with a female heroine.
Eleanor Taylor Bland, *Done Wrong*, 1995
    Fourth title in a detective mystery series with a female heroine.
Gar Anthony Haywood, *Fear of the Dark*, 1988
    Debut novel in a contemporary murder mystery series with a private detective.
Walter Mosley, *Devil in a Blue Dress*, 1990
    Debut novel in a contemporary murder mystery series with a private detective.
Walter Mosley, *A Red Death*, 1991
    Second title in a contemporary murder mystery series with a private detective.

198

HUGH HOLTON, African American

Presumed Dead

(New York: Tom Doherty Associates, 1994)

Subject(s): Police Procedural; Mystery and Detective Stories

Age range(s): Adult

Major character(s): Commander Larry Cole, Detective—Homicide, African American

Time period(s): 1990s

Locale(s): Chicago, Illinois

Summary: When a drug bust goes wrong on Seagull Island behind the National Science and Space Museum, Larry Cole begins to investigate strange happenings on the so-called "Haunted Island." When he discovers that 188 people have disappeared from the museum grounds over the years, he enlists the help of two writers and his team of detectives. He doesn't expect to fall in love with Edna, the beautiful detective backing him up. And he doesn't expect to be the target for the next disappearance.

About this book: Debut novel.

Other books by the same author:
Chicago Blues, 1996
Windy City, 1995

Other books you might like:
Eleanor Taylor Bland, *Done Wrong*, 1995
    Fourth title in a detective mystery series with a female heroine.
Eleanor Taylor Bland, *Slow Burn*, 1993
    Second title in a detective mystery series with a female heroine.
Gar Anthony Haywood, *Fear of the Dark*, 1988
    Debut novel in a contemporary murder mystery series with a private detective.
Gar Anthony Haywood, *You Can Die Trying*, 1993
    Third title in a contemporary murder mystery series with a private detective.
Walter Mosley, *White Butterfly*, 1992
    Third title in a contemporary murder mystery series with a private detective.

199

HUGH HOLTON, African American

Windy City

(New York: Tom Doherty Associates, 1995)

Subject(s): Crime and Criminals; Mystery and Detective Stories; Police Procedural

Age range(s): Adult

Major character(s): Deputy Chief Larry Cole, Detective—Homicide, Father, African American; Margo DeWitt, Businesswoman, Wealthy, Caucasian; Neil DeWitt, Businessman, Wealthy, Caucasian

Time period(s): 1990s

Locale(s): Chicago, Illinois

Summary: When a personal friend and fellow officer is murdered and his white fiance is considered the prime suspect, Deputy Chief Larry Cole begins his own investigation to find out what really happened. He discovers that his friend's murder scene matches that in a book by a local mystery writer, and recent child murders are similar in situation and sequence to those described in a novel by another local writer. Cole's investigation eventually leads him to Neil and Margo DeWitt, a wealthy white couple who apparently have more than a small interest in crime fiction. Cole, his team of detectives, and the "brain trust" of local mystery fiction writers must unearth the murderers quickly because if the child murderer continues to follow the sequence in the novel, Cole's own son will be next.

Other books by the same author:
Chicago Blues, 1996

Presumed Dead, 1994 (debut novel)

Other books you might like:
Eleanor Taylor Bland, *Dead Time*, 1992
   Debut novel in a detective mystery series with a female heroine.
Gar Anthony Haywood, *Fear of the Dark*, 1988
   Debut novel in a contemporary murder mystery series with a private detective.
Walter Mosley, *Devil in a Blue Dress*, 1990
   Debut novel in a contemporary murder mystery series with a private detective.*ACD AUT

200

ELIZABETH FITZGERALD HOWARD, African American
JAMES E. RANSOME, Illustrator, African American

Aunt Flossie's Hats (and Crab Cakes Later)
(New York: Clarion Books, 1991)

Story type: Young Readers
Subject(s): Aunts and Uncles; Sisters
Age range(s): Grades 1-3
Major character(s): Susan, Child, Sister (older), African American; Sarah, Child, Sister (younger)
Time period(s): 1990s
Locale(s): Baltimore, Maryland

Summary: Sunday afternoons young Susan and Sarah go to their great-great-aunt Flossie's house. Joining her for tea and cookies, the girls have a great time playing in her hatboxes and listening to her stories about the many hats they find. Looking at one of the hats, Aunt Flossie tells them about the great fire in Baltimore long ago. Another hat reminds her of the big parade when the Great War ended. And a very special hat reminds them of their favorite story when they were with Aunt Flossie and her hat blew off and afterwards the family went to a restaurant for crab cakes.

Other books by the same author:
Papa Tells Chita a Story, 1995
Mac and Marie and the Train Toss Surprise, 1993
Chita's Christmas Tree, 1989
The Train to Lulu's, 1988 (debut)

Other books you might like:
Jeannette Franklin Caines, *Just Us Women*, 1982
   A young niece narrates the adventures she had with her aunt when they made a trip together in her aunt's new car and all their special memories.
Angela Johnson, *Shoes Like Miss Alice's*, 1995
   Her babysitter shows a child a good time with her different pairs of shoes for dancing, walking, and other activities.
Gloria Jean Pinkney, *Back Home*, 1992
   Raised in the city an 8-year-old visits her relatives for the first time in her memory in the place where she was born in the country.
Gloria Jean Pinkney, *The Sunday Outing*, 1994
   Enjoying watching trains at the station an 8-year-old is excited when her relatives invite her to come visit them on her first train trip.

201

ELIZABETH FITZGERALD HOWARD, African American
FLOYD COOPER, Illustrator, African American

Chita's Christmas Tree
(New York: Bradbury Press, 1989)

Story type: Young Readers
Series: Chita
Subject(s): Christmas; Fathers and Daughters
Age range(s): Grades 1-3
Major character(s): Chita, Child, Cousin, African American
Time period(s): Indeterminate Past
Locale(s): Baltimore, Maryland

Summary: The day before Christmas is very special for young Chita because she and her papa go into the woods to pick their tree for Santa Claus to bring. Riding in their buggy pulled by Henry their horse Chita and papa pass downtown and along the way stop to eat at the waffle man's street wagon. Off into the deep woods they search and search until Chita finds just the right tree. Papa then carves her name in it so Santa Claus will know which one to bring. Back home Chita busies herself in the kitchen with mama and makes a special cookie for papa. Aunts, uncles, and cousins come for the Christmas eve dinner and party. After their ''goodnights'' papa helps Chita hang her sock by the fireplace before she goes to bed. Morning arrives and rushing downstairs Chita discovers before anything else a beautifully decorated tree with her named carved on it.

Awards the book has won:
American Library Association Notable Book, 1990
Booklist ''Best of the 80s''

Other books by the same author:
Papa Tells Chita a Story, 1995
Mac and Marie and the Train Toss Surprise, 1993
Aunt Flossie's Hats (and Crab Cakes Later), 1991
The Train to Lulu's, 1988 (Debut)

Other books you might like:
Lucille Clifton, *Everett Anderson's Christmas Coming*, 1971
   A story in rhyme of a young boy counting down the last five days to Christmas, thinking of the toys he wants, and wishing his daddy were there.
Dolores Johnson, *Papa's Stories*, 1994
   Enjoying the stories her papa tells from her books a kindergartner says she'll teach him to read when she discovers he doesn't know how.
Phil Mendez, *The Black Snowman*, 1989
   A magic kente cloth helps a boy learn a lesson in self-respect and pride in his heritage while saving his younger brother from a fire.

African American Titles

202

ELIZABETH FITZGERALD HOWARD, African American
GAIL GORDON CARTER, Illustrator

Mac and Marie and the Train Toss Surprise

(New York: Four Winds Press, 1993)

Story type: Young Readers
Subject(s): Surprises; Brothers and Sisters; Trains
Age range(s): Grades 1-4
Major character(s): Mac, 9-Year-Old, Brother, African American
Time period(s): Indeterminate Past
Locale(s): United States (between Baltimore and Washington)

Summary: Ever since he can remember, Mac and his little sister Marie have lived close to the train tracks between Baltimore and Washington. His dream is to some day work on the railroad and go everywhere, maybe even California. Uncle Clem, who now works in the dining car on the Seaboard Florida Limited, has written the children that when a train passes their house, he's going to toss something special to them. Waiting for the train, Marie is impatient and Mac checks his watch. As the train flashes by, a package comes hurtling into the air towards them. Excitedly they retrieve it and hurry home to discover Uncle Clem's special gift.

Other books by the same author:
Papa Tells Chita a Story, 1995
Aunt Flossie's Hats (and Crab Cakes Later), 1991
Chita's Christmas Tree, 1989
The Train to Lulu's, 1988 (debut)

Other books you might like:
Lucille Clifton, *The Boy Who Didn't Believe in Spring*, 1973
Everyone says spring is coming and a youngster and his white pal don't believe them so they go searching for evidence to discover spring.
Lucille Clifton, *Good, Says Jerome*, 1973
Moving to a new place he doesn't want to go a child's older sister reassures him and answers his questions about things he doesn't understand.
Lucille Clifton, *My Brother Fine with Me*, 1975
An 8-year-old sister helping her 5-year-old brother pack to runaway discovers how lonely she is without him and is happier when he decides not to leave.
Donald Crews, *Shortcut*, 1992
A group of youngsters taking a shortcut home following the railroad tracks are frightened when a train appears forcing them to run for safety.
Angela Shelf Medearis, *The Adventures of Sugar and Junior*, 1995
Exploits of a young girl and a Hispanic neighbor boy as they become friends while baking cookies, going to monster movies, and sharing ice cream.

203

ELIZABETH FITZGERALD HOWARD, African American
FLOYD COOPER, Illustrator, African American

Papa Tells Chita a Story

(New York: Simon and Schuster Books For Young Readers, 1995)

Story type: Young Readers
Series: Chita
Subject(s): Fathers and Daughters; War; Storytelling
Age range(s): Grades 1-3
Major character(s): Chita, Child, Cousin, African American
Time period(s): Indeterminate Past
Locale(s): United States (unidentified city)

Summary: Sitting close to papa after supper in her own chair Chita wants him to tell her the story of when he was the bravest soldier and carried the message and won the war. Papa begins by telling her he joined the army during the Spanish War in Cuba to earn enough money to go to medical school. The colonel one day called all the men together saying they need reinforcements and more supplies and he wants someone very brave to carry a secret message to their troops across the island. Papa was given a sleek dark horse, Majestic, to ride, a map, a canteen of water, and an oilskin pouch with a letter inside to deliver. On the journey he faced many dangers, among them a swamp alligator and a giant eagle. Finally reaching the campsite papa safely delivered his colonel's letter. At the end of papa's story Chita gets his old soldier's hat and belt, and his bronze medal to look at before he takes her off to bed.

Other books by the same author:
Mac and Marie and the Train Toss Surprise, 1993
Aunt Flossie's Hats (and Crab Cakes Later), 1991
Chita's Christmas Tree, 1989
The Train to Lulu's, 1988 (debut)

Other books you might like:
Percival Everett, *The One That Got Away*, 1992
Western tale of a group of cowboys rounding up ones into a corral and when one jumps the fence what happens when they go searching for it.
Angela Johnson, *Julius*, 1993
Her granddaddy surprises a child by bringing her her very own pig from Alaska and she shares things she learns with her friends.
Dolores Johnson, *Papa's Stories*, 1994
Enjoying the stories her papa tells from her books a kindergartner says she'll teach him to read when she discovers he doesn't know how.
Faith Ringgold, *Aunt Harriet's Underground Railroad in the Sky*, 1992
Flying in the sky a sister and her younger brother discovering the underground railroad to freedom must retrace its route to be reunited.

204

ELIZABETH FITZGERALD HOWARD, African American
ROBERT CASILLA, Illustrator

The Train to LuLu's

(New York: Bradbury Press, 1988)

Story type: Young Readers
Subject(s): Trains; Sisters; Self-Reliance
Age range(s): Grades 1-2
Major character(s): Beppy, Child, Sister, African American
Time period(s): 1930s
Locale(s): United States (between Boston and Baltimore)

Summary: Summer vacation will really begin for Beppy and her younger sister Babs when they arrive at their Aunt Lulu's in Baltimore. Their first train trip will take nine hours and the sisters will be on their own. Mommy has packed their meals and the conductors will watch out for them to be sure they get off at the right station. Babs brings her teddy bear and the girls excitedly board the train. Along the journey they enjoy the scenery and entertain themselves with paper dolls, crayons, and books. The two eventually drift off to sleep and awaken when the conductor calls their station. Happily stepping off the train in Baltimore they are first greeted by aunts and uncles and their cousin, before finally spotting Great-Aunt Lulu coming with her white, white hair.

About this book: Debut

Other books by the same author:
Papa Tells Chita a Story, 1995
Mac and Marie and the Train Toss Surprise, 1993
Aunt Flossie's Hats (and Crab Cakes Later), 1991
Chita's Christmas Tree, 1989

Other books you might like:
Donald Crews, *Shortcut*, 1992
  A group of youngsters taking a shortcut home following the railroad tracks are frightened when a train appears, forcing them to run for safety.
Angela Johnson, *One of Three*, 1991
  The youngest of three sisters describes some of the many things they share together when she gets to spend time alone with her parents.
Gloria Jean Pinkney, *The Sunday Outing*, 1994
  Enjoying watching trains at the station an 8-year-old is excited when her relatives invite her to come visit them on her first train trip.

205

WADE HUDSON, African American
CAL MASSEY, Illustrator

I Love My Family

(New York: Scholastic, Inc., 1993)

Story type: Young Readers
Subject(s): Family Relations; Reunions; Summer
Age range(s): Grades 1-2
Major character(s): Unnamed Character, Child, African American
Time period(s): 1990s

Locale(s): North Carolina (unidentified city)

Summary: An unnamed child tells of his enjoyable summer visits for reunions at his father's relatives in North Carolina. Along with his parents and young sister Andrea he enjoys seeing his out-of-town cousins and his aunts and uncles. He enjoys playing basketball with the guys and his uncle who says he was a Harlem Globetrotter. At the reunion the family's oldest relative who's almost 100-years-old babysits the youngest, a newborn. The relatives swim, play baseball, pick fruit, sing and dance, and at night grandpa tells scary stories. There's lots of good food and eating and they always put up the poster of the family tree. As the reunion comes to a close a photographer takes pictures of each family and the whole family together. No one wants to say good-by when it's over and he looks forward to coming back again next summer and remembers there will also be another reunion with his mother's family at Thanksgiving.

Other books by the same author:
Afro-Bets Kids I'm Gonna Be!, 1992 ((non-fiction))

Other books you might like:
Lucille Clifton, *Some of the Days of Everett Anderson*, 1970
  Living in the city a 6-year-old boy's days are filled with activity from playing in the sunshine, to hearing sirens pass by, to times with his parents.
Donald Crews, *Bigmama's*, 1991
  Recalls the summer exploits of a youngster in the 1940s when he, his brother, sisters, and parents visit his grandparents in the country.
Donald Crews, *Shortcut*, 1992
  A group of youngsters taking a shortcut home following the railroad tracks are frightened when a train appears forcing them to run for safety.
Valerie Flournoy, *Tanya's Reunion*, 1995
  A youngster traveling with her grandma to the family farm for a reunion discovers a special memento for her grandma of days gone by.
Gloria Jean Pinkney, *Back Home*, 1992
  Raised in the city an 8-year-old visits her relatives for the first time in her memory in the place where she was born in the country.

206

MARSHA HUNT, African American

Free

(New York: Dutton, 1992)

Story type: Adult
Subject(s): Friendship; Historical; Race Relations
Major character(s): Theodore "Teenotchy" Simms, Gardener, Housekeeper, African American; Alexander Blake, Homosexual, Nobleman, Caucasian (English)
Time period(s): 1910s (1913)
Locale(s): Germantown, Pennsylvania

Summary: After his mother's murder, Teenotchy Simms works for her former employer as a domestic, and finds additional work at a stable to be close to the horses he likes so much. He meets Alexander, a young white man from England who is about his own age; their friendship transcends the barriers of class, race and social proprieties.

Where it's reviewed:
Kliatt, May 1994, page 9
Publishers Weekly, April 4, 1994, page 66

Other books by the same author:
Joy, 1991

Other books you might like:
Larry Duplechan, *Blackbird*, 1986
   A contemporary gay coming-of-age episode recounting a young man's first sexual experiences in high school.
Larry Duplechan, *Eight Days a Week*, 1985
   Debut novel in a series about a young gay man, who becomes involved in an interracial relationship.
Canaan Parker, *The Color of Trees*, 1992
   A contemporary gay coming-of-age story reflecting on the first sexual experiences of a young boy from Harlem sent to private boarding school.
Dennis Williams, *Crossover*, 1992
   Events in the life of a young man during the Civil Rights era as he becomes a reluctant activist and has an interracial affair.

207

MARSHA HUNT, African American

Joy
(New York: Dutton, 1991)

Subject(s): Family Relations; Secrets; Sisters
Age range(s): Adult
Major character(s): Baby Palatine Ross, Housewife, Neighbor, African American; Joy Clarissa Bang, Entertainer, Neglected Child, African American
Time period(s): 1980s
Locale(s): San Francisco, California

Summary: Learning of Joy's untimely death, mother figure Baby Palatine remembers the times and secrets she shared with Joy, her ''God-sent child.'' Joy had lived next door as a little girl and sang with her two sisters in a group. Their records topped the charts. Upon arriving in New York for Joy's funeral, Baby Palatine discovers that in spite of all they shared, Joy had kept her biggest secrets to herself.

About this book: This is the author's debut novel.

Other books by the same author:
Free, 1992

Other books you might like:
Tina McElroy Ansa, *Ugly Ways*, 1993
   This contemporary account is about three sisters reflecting on their upbringing in a small town and how their lives have evolved.
Linda Beatrice Brown, *Crossing over Jordan*, 1995
   This saga is about the binding ties in the lives of four generations of mothers and daughters from the Civil War era to the early 21st century.
Rita Dove, *Through the Ivory Gate*, 1992
   This coming-of-age story is about a young woman who

returns to her home after being away many years. An unspoken family secret is revealed to her.
Toni Morrison, *Beloved*, 1987
   This story tells about a mother who escapes from slavery and who kills her baby to keep her former owner from stealing her. She is then haunted and consumed by the baby's ghost.
Ntozake Shange, *Liliane: Resurrection of the Daughter*, 1994
   In psychotherapy, the exploits of a young woman's life reveal how she coped with family upheavals, romances, friendships, racism, and bigotry.

208

KRISTIN HUNTER, African American
HAROLD FRANKLIN, Illustrator, African American

Boss Cat
(New York, Charles Scribner's Sons, 1971)

Subject(s): Animals; Family Life
Age range(s): Grades 3-4
Major character(s): Tyrone Tanner, 10-Year-Old, Brother (oldest), African American
Time period(s): 1970s
Locale(s): United States (unidentified city)

Summary: The family has mixed feelings when dad brings home a cat given to him by one of his customers at work. Baby Jewl is too young to care much; the twins, five-year-olds Puddin' and Dumplin' are excited along with their older brother Tyrone; but mom is none too happy. Given the name Pharaoh, the cat pounces on the TV, claws at furniture, destroys mom's wig, and hides under the bed until mom convinces dad to get rid of it. Upset, the kids have to accept that Pharaoh is gone when dad takes him outside and returns alone. When mom is later frightened by a mouse, she sends Tyrone and his dad searching to bring Pharaoh back to catch it. When Pharaoh returns and gets right to work catching mice mom is so grateful she lets him sit on her favorite chair.

Where it's reviewed:
Booklist, February 15, 1972, page 506
Choice, November 1977, page 1178
Kirkus Reviews, November 15, 1971, page 1212
Publishers Weekly, December 13, 1971, page 43

Other books by the same author:
The Soul Brothers and Sister Lou, 1968 (young adults)
God Bless the Child, 1964 (debut novel, adult)

Other books you might like:
Sharon M. Draper, *Ziggy and the Black Dinosaurs*, 1994
   When their neighborhood playground is destroyed, four 5th grade boys start their own secret club and uncover a mysterious old box of hidden bones.
Walter Dean Myers, *Me, Mop, and the Moondance Kid*, 1988
   Two young brothers share a close friendship with a white young girl on their Little League baseball team and hope she gets adopted like they did.
Connie Porter, *Addy's Surprise: A Christmas Story*, 1993
   A young girl and her mother prepare for Christmas without the rest of the family; they don't have much, but they get the best gift of all.

Harriette Gillem Robinet, *Ride the Red Cycle*, 1980
> A boy crippled since the age of two struggles to realize his dream of riding a cycle.

Mildred Pitts Walter, *Have a Happy. . .*, 1989
> Upset because his birthday falls on Christmas, and worried about money because his father is out of work, an 11-year-old carves animals for Kwanzaa.

209

The Lakestown Rebellion
(New York: Charles Scribner's Sons, 1978)

Story type: Adult
Subject(s): Determination; Dishonesty; Race Relations
Major character(s): Abraham "Abe" Lakes, Political Figure, Spouse, African American; Ronald P. "Fess" Roaney, Veteran, Activist, African American
Time period(s): 1960s (1965)
Locale(s): Lakestown, New Jersey

Summary: Back in 1929 Freedom George Lakes won independence for the town that now bears his name. His son Abe is Lakestown's mayor. In the hope of furthering a political career, light-skinned Abe agrees with a group of wealthy white politicians to construct a highway through Lakestown. He soon learns from the mother of his illegitimate daughter, a maid in one of the politicians' homes, that he is being tricked. She also reveals the politicians' plans to the local doctor and his best friend, Fess, and they try thinking of a way to stop construction. Before long the whole town is in an uproar, and Abe's political future does not look bright. Citizens, young and old, are determined to save their town with or without his help.

Other books by the same author:
The Survivors, 1975
The Landlord, 1966
God Bless the Child, 1964 (debut novel, adult)

Other books you might like:
Cyrus Colter, *City of Light*, 1993
> This novel portrays the exploits of a young Chicago man who travels to Paris and writes letters to his deceased mother about his plight of being light-skinned.

Ernest J. Gaines, *In My Father's House*, 1978
> A civil rights leader/minister examines who he is and who he was when a stranger emerges from his past.

C. Eric Lincoln, *The Avenue, Clayton City*, 1988
> This novel depicts the lives of people in a segregated town, among them a Dr. and his biracial wife, her white lover and what pushes her towards murder.

Richard Perry, *No Other Tale to Tell*, 1994
> While a community watches in silence, a young girl gives birth to an idiot son fathered by a white boy her family raised.

Brent Wade, *Company Man*, 1992
> This novel reveals the behind-the-scenes stresses and strains faced by a man attempting to climb the business ladder and preserve his family.

210

KRISTIN HUNTER, African American

Lou in the Limelight
(New York: Charles Scribner's Sons, 1981)

Subject(s): Family Relations; Singing; Interpersonal Relations
Age range(s): Grades 10-12
Major character(s): Louretta "Lou" Hawkins, 16-Year-Old, Singer, African American
Time period(s): 1980s
Locale(s): United States (unidentified northern city); New York, New York; Las Vegas, Nevada

Summary: A hit record for the singing foursome Lou, Frank, David and Ulysses, leads to bookings in New York and Las Vegas. Their agent, Marty Ross, gets their parents' permission to take them on tour and they go to New York, where drugs are introduced and he attempts to trick Lou into sleeping with one of his backers. When they return home for the holidays, the group discovers that they are seriously in debt to Marty. Things only get worse when they go to Las Vegas. Help arrives in the person of Lou's mother's best friend, who, along with the district attorney investigating organized crime, helps rescue the group. With a new agent and on tour in the South, Lou is taken ill and decides to quit the group. While recovering, she discovers relatives she never knew and learns more about her mother's background, helping her to understand her mother better.

About this book: This is the sequel to *The Soul Brothers and Sister Lou*.

Where it's reviewed:
English Journal, April 1987, page 26

Awards the book has won:
Coretta Scott King Honor Book, 1982

Other books by the same author:
Boss Cat, 1971 (young readers)
The Soul Brothers and Sister Lou, 1968 (young adult)
God Bless the Child, 1964 (debut novel, adult)

Other books you might like:
Vy Higginsen, *Mama, I Want to Sing*, 1995
> Recounts events in the life of a talented singer from a young girl singing in the church choir to a renowned award winning star.

Walter Dean Myers, *Crystal*, 1987
> On the brink of a promising career in modeling, a 16-year-old realizes there is more than glamour to the industry and has to decide what path to choose.

Joyce Carol Thomas, *When the Nightingale Sings*, 1992
> Despite her mean-spirited foster mother's attempts to demean her, a 14-year-old girl has a song to sing and a destiny to fulfill.

Rita Williams-Garcia, *Blue Tights*, 1988
> Struggling to find friends and acceptance a young girl born out-ofwedlock follows her mother's footsteps in her passion for dancing.

211

KRISTIN HUNTER, African American

The Survivors
(New York: Charles Scribner's Sons, 1975)

Subject(s): Interpersonal Relations; Survival; City Life
Age range(s): Adult
Major character(s): Lena Ricks, Businesswoman, Spouse, African American; ''B.J.'' Brown, 13-Year-Old, Runaway, African American; James J. Riggs, Alcoholic, Father, African American
Time period(s): 1970s
Locale(s): United States

Summary: Owner of her own dressmaking shop, Lena has made a good life for herself after leaving her alcoholic husband James more than twenty years ago. Working late over the weekend and not cleaning up the shop, Lena is unnerved when she returns to find things are in good order with the trash put out and the windows washed. When a strange youngster, ''B.J.'' shows up with her morning coffee right on schedule from the neighborhood deli, Lena is suspicious of who he is and how he knows her routine. Soon the mysterious ''B.J.'' has worked his way into Lena's life and is liked by her customers. When Lena visits his school to find out why he was suspended she returns to her shop to discover she has been robbed and ''B.J.'' has disappeared. After changing the locks on the doors. Lena searches for ''B.J.'' and discovers he is more a part of her life and past than she ever imagined.

Other books by the same author:
The Lakestown Rebellion, 1978
The Landlord, 1966
God Bless the Child, 1964 (debut novel, adult)

Other books you might like:
Anita Richmond Bunkley, *Black Gold*, 1994
    A young woman on the brink of ruin before the historic oil boom in 1920s Texas finds herself accused of murder and a family secret is revealed.
Melvin Dixon, *Trouble the Water*, 1989
    Running away from home, a young man returns twenty years later in a plot of revenge which developed between his grandmother and his father. Author died in 1992.
Marsha Hunt, *Joy*, 1991
    A childless woman befriends a neighbor girl who sings with her sisters and grows up to become a star whose untimely death reveals shocking secrets.
Gloria Naylor, *Women of Brewster Place*, 1982
    The story of seven women who come to live on the dead-end street of Brewster Place and what brings them together in their own redemption.
Dori Sanders, *Her Own Place*, 1993
    Remembrances of exploits in a senior citizen's life of daughter, wife, mother, and grandmother from before WWII to contemporary times.

212

DARIUS JAMES, African American

Negrophobia: An Urban Parable
(New York: Carol Publishing Group, 1992)

Subject(s): Allegories; Fantasy; Race Relations
Age range(s): Adult
Major character(s): Bubbles Brazil, Student, Teenager, Caucasian
Time period(s): 1990s (1992)
Locale(s): New York, New York (Manhattan's upper west side)

Summary: This is an allegorical tale of a grotesque racial and sexual vision. Bubbles, a white teenager, experiences possible nightmare effects of a voodoo spell and drugs. She finds herself in situations where people are transformed in a surreal world of explicit racial and sexual episodes.

About this book: This is the author's debut novel.

Where it's reviewed:
Essence, January 1993, page 50
Los Angeles Times Book Review, December 27, 1992, page 2
Locus, September 1992, page 60
Publishers Weekly, June 28, 1993, page 72
Village Voice, January 19, 1993, page 56

Other books you might like:
Tananarive Due, *The Between*, 1995
    A man endures nightmares and a sense of reality wavers as he desperately tries to protect his family from the psychotic who stalks them.
Arthur Flowers, *Another Good Loving Blues*, 1993
    This Mississippi Delta tale is about the exploits of a ''conjure'' woman's life which is haunted by dreams of her mother who abandoned her as a child.
Carolivia Herron, *Thereafter Johnnie*, 1991
    This story is about the incestuous relationship between a father and daughter, and their child.
Ntozake Shange, *Liliane: Resurrection of the Daughter*, 1994
    In psychotherapy, the exploits of a young woman's life reveal how she coped with family upheavals, romances, friendships, racism, and bigotry.
Ray Shell, *Iced*, 1993
    A man reflects in his diary about his accomplishments in life, as well as his regrets of descending into the white-smoke world of crack cocaine.

213

LANCE JEFFERS, African American

Witherspoon
(Michigan: The George A. Flippin Press, 1983)

Subject(s): Psychology; Race Relations; Self-Perception
Age range(s): Adult
Major character(s): Lucius Witherspoon, Religious, African American; James Corwul, Religious, Terrorist, African American; Willie Armstrong, Convict, African American
Time period(s): 1960s (1967)
Locale(s): Quiver, South

Summary: Willie Armstrong has been sentenced to death for killing two white men. Reverend Lucius Witherspoon goes to the prison to tell Armstrong that if he will beg for his life on TV, the governor will grant him a pardon. Armstrong instead curses the white man with his last breath. Witherspoon questions his own manhood as he and his fellow pastors meet to discuss racial problems in their community. James Corwul, in favor of drawing the line and ''burning down the town'', stands alone. But when racial incidents mount and his friend Corwul is killed, Witherspoon finds that he too can take action and stand as a man.

About this book: Author died in 1985.

Other books you might like:
David Bradley, *The Chaneysville Incident*, 1981
Returning home to comfort a dying man, a professor must solve the dual mysteries of his father's death and the dark secret of his family's past.
Cyrus Colter, *A Chocolate Soldier*, 1988
As a story within a story, a young idealist murders his white employer and is himself killed by a mob lynching.
Albert French, *Billy*, 1993
A 10-year-old child sentenced to death in the electric chair for killing a white teenager, sparking racial hatred in 1930's Mississippi.
Ernest J. Gaines, *A Lesson before Dying*, 1993
This historical fiction set in 1940's Louisiana describes the impact a young man's pending execution for murder has on the community and his family and friends.

214

YOLANDA JOE, African American

Falling Leaves of Ivy
(Stamford: Longmeadow Press, 1992)

Story type: Adult
Subject(s): Friendship; Murder; Police Procedural
Age range(s): Adult
Major character(s): Michelle DuBois Howard, Student—College; Elizabeth Nickelson, Student—College, Businesswoman, Caucasian; Kevin ''Kayo'' Watson, Student—College, Businessman, African American
Time period(s): 1980s
Locale(s): New Haven, Connecticut (Yale University); New York, New York (Manhattan)

Summary: Four friends in an interracial group, Elizabeth, Michelle, Kayo, and Connor, share a tragic secret from their student days at Yale. As they start their separate careers in Manhattan, Michelle, who is having a secret interracial affair, threatens the others and is murdered. They all become suspects in her murder and their past secret begins to unravel.

About this book: This is the author's debut novel.

Where it's reviewed:
Booklist, November 1, 1992, page 488
Booklist, November 1, 1992, page 495
Black Scholar, Winter 1993, page 43

Other books you might like:
Eleanor Taylor Bland, *Dead Time*, 1992
This debut novel begins a detective mystery series with a female heroine.
Eleanor Taylor Bland, *Slow Burn*, 1993
This is the second title in a detective mystery series with a female heroine.
Barbara Neely, *Blanche on the Lam*, 1992
This debut novel begins a contemporary murder mystery series with an amateur detective as the heroine.
Barbara Summers, *The Price You Pay*, 1993
A young woman in the highly competitive fashion industry finds herself as a target for murder. A series of murders occurs when a new market campaign is launched.
Valerie Wilson Wesley, *When Death Comes Stealing*, 1994
This debut novel begins a murder mystery series featuring an ex-policewoman who becomes a private detective.

215

ANGELA JOHNSON, African American
JAMES E. RANSOME, Illustrator, African American

Do Like Kyla
(New York: Orchard Books, 1990)

Story type: Young Readers
Subject(s): Sisters; Family Life
Age range(s): Grades 1-2
Major character(s): Unnamed Character, Child, Sister, African American
Time period(s): 1990s
Locale(s): United States (unidentified city)

Summary: A little sister tells of the many things she does in her day being just like her older sister young Kyla. As their day starts she follows big sister Kyla standing at their window and tapping at the birds. They dress, eat, read, go window shopping, and walk home in the snow together. At the end of the day they gaze out their window together for sleeping birds.

Other books by the same author:
The Leaving Morning, 1992
One of Three, 1991
When I Am Old with You, 1991
The Girl Who Wore Snakes, 1990
Tell Me a Story, Mama, 1989 (debut)

Other books you might like:
Jeannette Franklin Caines, *Abby*, 1973
An adopted preschooler questions her mother and older brother about when she first came home and suggests they adopt another brother.
Elizabeth Fitzgerald Howard, *Aunt Flossie's Hats (and Crab Cakes Later)*, 1991
Visits to their great-great-aunt Flossie's are special times for two young girls and they always look forward to eating crab cakes afterwards.
Elizabeth Fitzgerald Howard, *The Train To LuLu's*, 1988
For summer vacation two young sisters take their first train trip in the 1930s on a nine hour ride between Boston and Baltimore.

John Steptoe, *My Special Best Words*, 1974
 A child tells about her daily routine of living life with her 1-year-old brother, their daddy, and their babysitter.
Mildred Pitts Walter, *Two and Too Much*, 1990
 Trying to help his mama, a 7-year-old watches his 2-year-old sister who gets into all kinds of things until she tires herself out and falls asleep.

216

ANGELA JOHNSON, African American
JAMES E. RANSOME, Illustrator, African American

The Girl Who Wore Snakes
(New York: Orchard Books, 1993)

Story type: Young Readers
Subject(s): Animals; Aunts and Uncles
Age range(s): Grades 1-2
Major character(s): Ali, Child, African American
Time period(s): 1990s
Locale(s): United States (unidentified city)

Summary: When a man from the zoo visits her class, young Ali is the only one interested in Sylvia, the snake. She wears her all day at school, around her neck, her arms, her legs. When Sylvia goes home to the zoo, Ali becomes the girl who wore the snake. One day Ali gets some snakes of her own, wearing them at home and at school. Nobody seems to think the snakes are as beautiful as Ali does. One day she visits her aunts and finds someone who loves the snakes as much as she does.

Other books by the same author:
Shoe's Like Miss Alice's, 1995
Julius, 1993
One of Three, 1991
Do Like Kyla, 1990
Tell Me a Story, Mama, 1989 (Debut)

Other books you might like:
Lucille Clifton, *Everett Anderson's Friend*, 1976
 Hoping he will have some new guys to play with when a family moves in the building a young boy learns to be friends with the new girl next door.
Lucille Clifton, *My Friend Jacob*, 1980
 A young boy shares special times with his neighbor and best friend, a white mentally handicapped older boy.
Dolores Johnson, *The Best Bug to Be*, 1992
 A child in a school play is disappointed being a bumblebee until she perfects her part and on the night of the play gets the most applause.
Angela Shelf Medearis, *The Adventures of Sugar and Junior*, 1995
 Exploits of a young girl and a Latino neighbor boy as they become friends while baking cookies, going to monster movies, and sharing ice cream.
Belinda Rochelle, *When Jo Louis Won the Title*, 1994
 Dreading going to a new school because classmates make fun of her name a young girl learns from her grandfather how she got her special name.

217

ANGELA JOHNSON, African American

Humming Whispers
(New York: Orchard Books, 1995)

Story type: Young Readers
Subject(s): Sisters; Mental Illness; Orphans
Age range(s): Grades 5 and Up
Major character(s): Sophie, 14-Year-Old, Dancer, African American; Nicole, Mentally Challenged Person, African American
Time period(s): 1990s
Locale(s): Cleveland, Ohio

Summary: Ten years ago when their parents were killed in a car accident young Sophic and her older sister Nicole came to live with their Aunt Shirley. Now 14-year-old Sophie worries about hearing voices and that she may be showing signs of schizophrenia at the same age as her now 24-year-old sister Nicole. Sophie is also concerned about how items in the mall seem to mysteriously end up in a box she keeps under her bed. She and Nicole enjoy watching planes fly overhead at the airport and listening to the sounds of Nicole's boyfriend playing his saxophone. They also enjoy the family ritual of spending birthdays picnicking in the cemetery at their parent's grave. One day when looking in the mirror Sophie is not sure who the person is looking back at her and she knows she is changing.

Where it's reviewed:
Booklist, February 15, 1995, page 1072
Book World, May 7, 1995, page 14
Publishers Weekly, January 23, 1995, page 71
School Library Journal, April 1995, page 154
Voice of Youth Advocates, June 1995, page 95

Other books by the same author:
Toning the Sweep, 1993 (debut novel; young adult)

Other books you might like:
Harriette Gillem Robinet, *Ride the Red Cycle*, 1980
 A boy crippled since the age of two struggles to realize his dream of riding a cycle.
Ethel Footman Smothers, *Moriah's Pond*, 1995
 A continuation of events from the lives of the Footman family when three sisters spend a summer with their great-grandmother.
Mildred Pitts Walter, *Trouble's Child*, 1985
 Expected to marry and to succeed her grandmother as the island's midwife, a girl dreams of leaving the island to attend high school.
Jacqueline Woodson, *Between Madison & Palmetto*, 1993
 In their continuing story two 13-year-old best friends are reunited and have to adjust to a lot of change in their lives and in those around them.
Jacqueline Woodson, *I Hadn't Meant to Tell You This*, 1994
 A popular young girl who becomes friends with a new white young girl in her school discovers a family secret about her new friend.

218

ANGELA JOHNSON, African American
DAV PILKEY, Illustrator, Caucasian

Julius
(New York: Orchard Books, 1993)

Story type: Young Readers
Subject(s): Animals
Age range(s): Grades 1-2
Major character(s): Maya, Child, African American
Time period(s): 1990s
Locale(s): United States (unidentified city)

Summary: On one of her granddaddy's visits from Alaska, he brings Maya a special present, a pig named Julius. Her parents have no use for Julius but Maya loves him, so they let him stay. With Julius around there's never enough food, and he loves rolling around in the flour to get Maya to bake cookies for him. Totally disrupting the household Julius like to stay up late watching TV and he always plays records when everybody wants to read. As their relationship develops, Maya learns a few things from Julius, and Julius learns manners.

Awards the book has won:
Children's Book of the Month Club Selection, 1993

Other books by the same author:
Shoe's Like Miss Alice's, 1995
The Leaving Morning, 1992
One of Three, 1991
When I Am Old with You, 1991
Do Like Kyla, 1990

Other books you might like:
Lucille Clifton, *Don't You Remember?*, 1973
 A soon-to-be 5-year-old is disappointed that everyone in the family keeps breaking their promises to her until they give her a birthday surprise.
Pat Cummings, *Petey Moroni's Camp Runamok Diary*, 1992
 At a two-week summer camp a young boy and his friends try catching the raccoon they've discovered has been stealing their food.
Percival Everett, *The One That Got Away*, 1992
 Western tale of a group of cowboys rounding up ones into a corral and when one jumps the fence what happens when they go searching for it.
June Jordan, *Kimako's Story*, 1981
 A 7-year-old takes on the responsibility of caring for her neighbors big Airedale dog and gets to see more of her city surroundings.
Patricia C. McKissack, *A Million Fish. . .More or Less*, 1992
 Fishing in a strange bayou a boy catches a million fish and heads home with them but by the time he arrives his catch has shrunk to only three.

219

ANGELA JOHNSON, African American
DAVID SOMAN, Illustrator

The Leaving Morning
(New York: Orchard Books, 1992)

Story type: Young Readers
Subject(s): Moving, Household; Brothers and Sisters; Parent and Child
Age range(s): Grades 1-2
Major character(s): Unnamed Character, Child, Sister, African American
Time period(s): 1990s
Locale(s): United States (unidentified city)

Summary: An older sister describes what it was like for her and her younger brother when their parents moved the family away from their home. Telling how they had packed days before and said goodbye to friends, neighbors, and many cousins, she remembers the movers truck arriving. She and her brother woke up early and went to the deli across the street for hot cocoa. They sat on the steps watching the movers in their blue outfits. One of the upstairs neighbors gave her a moving hat and told her to be watchful in their new place. Sitting in the empty apartment between daddy and pregnant mama holding hands their daddy told them they would soon be someplace they love. She knows she's left something behind of herself as the family waves goodbye to leave.

Other books by the same author:
Shoe's Like Miss Alice's, 1995
One of Three, 1991
When I Am Old with You, 1991
Do Like Kyla, 1990
Tell Me a Story, Mama, 1989 (Debut)

Other books you might like:
Lucille Clifton, *Good, Says Jerome*, 1973
 Moving to a new place he doesn't want to, a child's older sister reassures him and answers his questions about things he doesn't understand.
Eloise Greenfield, *Grandmama's Joy*, 1980
 Worried when she see's her grandmama sad a child learns why and tries the best way she knows how to put a smile back on her face again.
June Jordan, *New Life: New Room*, 1975
 The story of the changes that occur for a 6-year-old, her 9 and 10-year-old brothers, and their daddy in a small apartment when momma gets pregnant.

220

ANGELA JOHNSON, African American
DAVID SOMAN, Illustrator

One of Three
(New York: Orchard Books, 1991)

Story type: Young Readers
Subject(s): Sisters; Family Life; Parent and Child
Age range(s): Grades 1-2
Time period(s): 1990s

Locale(s): United States

Summary: The youngest of three sisters tells about her life with her older sisters Eva and Nikki. Their doing things together including walking to school, rain or shine. How if she asks long enough Eva and Nikki sometimes let her play hopscotch with them. On Saturdays how the threesome sits outside the bakery smelling smells. In a taxi on snowy days they squeeze in to keep warm with mama and their aunt and grandma. Looking just like their mama and smiling just like their daddy the youngest likes how they hold hands in the stores and ride the subway together. Being one of three is mostly fun until Eva and Nikki say she can't come along and leave her behind at home. Although she's lonely and misses her sisters she has special times with mama and daddy, and happily becomes one of a different kind of three.

Other books by the same author:
Shoe's Like Miss Alice's, 1995
The Leaving Morning, 1992
When I Am Old with You, 1991
Do Like Kyla, 1990
Tell Me a Story, Mama, 1989 (Debut)

Other books you might like:
Jeannette Franklin Caines, *Abby*, 1973
　　An adopted preschooler questions her mother and older brother about when she first came there and suggests they adopt another brother.
Jeannette Franklin Caines, *I Need a Lunch Box*, 1988
　　A preschooler wanting a lunch box like his older sister's imagines all the things he could keep in it and dreams of having one for every day.
Lucille Clifton, *Everett Anderson's 1-2-3*, 1977
　　A new man comes into his mama's life and a young boy discovers some times are just right for being one alone or for being with others.
Lucille Clifton, *My Brother Fine with Me*, 1975
　　An 8-year-old sister helping her 5-year-old brother pack to runaway discovers how lonely she is without him and is happier when he decides not to leave.
Elizabeth Fitzgerald Howard, *The Train To LuLu's*, 1988
　　For summer vacation two young sisters take their first train trip in the 1930s on a nine hour ride between Boston and Baltimore.

221

ANGELA JOHNSON, African American
KEN PAGE, Illustrator

Shoes Like Miss Alice's
(New York: Orchard Books, 1995)

Story type: Young Readers
Subject(s): Babysitters
Age range(s): Grades 1-2
Time period(s): 1990s
Locale(s): United States (unidentified city)

Summary: A child tells what happens when her babysitter, Miss Alice, arrives. Not too anxious to be left alone with the older woman, she nonetheless waves goodbye to her mama out the window. Before she has time to think about what they're going to do, Miss Alice has turned on the radio and is dancing all about showing off her dancing shoes. Invited to join Miss Alice she's soon dancing along and having a good time. It seems Miss Alice has a pair of shoes for every occasion and the two pass a very pleasant time together after all.

Other books by the same author:
Julius, 1993
One of Three, 1991
When I Am Old with You, 1991
Do Like Kyla, 1990
Tell Me a Story, Mama, 1989 (Debut)

Other books you might like:
Lucille Clifton, *Three Wishes*, 1974
　　Finding a shiny penny in the snow she thinks is lucky a young girl makes three wishes, all of which convince her to believe in magic.
Eloise Greenfield, *Me and Neesie*, 1975
　　A child and her imaginary friend share times together until she goes to school, and returning home, discovers her friend is no longer around.
Elizabeth Fitzgerald Howard, *Aunt Flossie's Hats (and Crab Cakes Later)*, 1991
　　Visits to their great-great-aunt Flossie's are special times for two young girls and they always look forward to eating crab cakes afterwards.
Dolores Johnson, *What Kind of Baby-Sitter Is This?*, 1991
　　Upset when his mom leaves him with an elderly babysitter a child discovers she likes baseball as much as he does and they become friends.
Patricia C. McKissack, *Mirandy and Brother Wind*, 1988
　　Folk tale of a young girl desperately wanting to win her first cakewalk dance contest so makes a wish to the wind and dances with her friend.

222

ANGELA JOHNSON, African American
DAVID SOMAN, Illustrator

Tell Me a Story, Mama
(New York: Orchard Books, 1989)

Story type: Young Readers
Subject(s): Mothers and Daughters; Storytelling
Age range(s): Grades 1-2
Time period(s): 1980s
Locale(s): United States

Summary: A little girl asks her mama to tell her a story about when she was little. Mama doesn't have to say much because the little girl has already memorized the stories and tells them herself. There was the time when mama and aunt Jessie were hollered at by a mean lady with a bulldog. Then there were the special times she had with mama and grandmama. There was that time she found a stray dog without a tail, and the train trip she took with aunt Jessie to St. Louis to be with great-aunt Rosetta. The last story she remembers is the story of how much grandmama cried when mama moved away. Telling mama how much she enjoys her telling stories she asks if she will do it again tomorrow.

Awards the book has won:
School Library Journal Best Book of the Year, 1989

Other books by the same author:
Shoe's Like Miss Alice's, 1995
The Leaving Morning, 1992
One of Three, 1991
When I Am Old with You, 1991
Do Like Kyla, 1990

Other books you might like:
Jeannette Franklin Caines, *Abby*, 1973
   An adopted preschooler questions her mother and older
   brother about when she first came to them and suggests
   they adopt another brother.
Jeannette Franklin Caines, *Just Us Women*, 1982
   A young niece narrates the adventures she had with her
   aunt when they made a trip together in her aunt's new car
   and all their special memories.
Valerie Flournoy, *The Patchwork Quilt*, 1985
   When her grandma becomes ill, a youngster and her mama
   work on her quilt until she recovers and puts the finishing
   touches on it herself.
Jan Spivey Gilchrist, *Indigo and Moonlight Gold*, 1993
   Sharing special times with her mama a child remembers
   the story she told about girls growing up and things changing under a mama's watchful eye.

`223`

ANGELA JOHNSON, African American

Toning the Sweep

(New York: Orchard Books, 1993)

Story type: Young Adult
Subject(s): Family Relations; Death; Parent and Child
Age range(s): Grades 6 and Up
Major character(s): Emily, 14-Year-Old, African American;
   Ola Werren, Aged Person (grandmother), Cancer Patient,
   African American; Diane, Mother, African American
Time period(s): 1990s
Locale(s): Little Rock, California

Summary: Her grandmother Ola is dying of cancer and Emmie
and her mother Diane plan to bring her back to stay with them
in Cleveland. Diane has never liked her mother's desert home.
Emmie, on the other hand, has always liked spending time in
the desert with her grandmother Ola. On this trip Emmie
decides to make a video as a gift for her grandmother. As she
records the video of all her grandmother's friends, Emmie
discovers a lot about her grandmother and the deceased
grandfather she never knew. Thinking about how people die
and are remembered Emmie plans a special ritual ceremony in
the desert for her grandfather and is joined by her mother in
honoring his spirit.

About this book: Debut novel for young adults.

Where it's reviewed:
English Journal, November 1994, page 99
Kliatt, November 1994, page 10
Language Arts, October 1994, page 463

Awards the book has won:
Coretta Scott King Award, 1994

*Young Adult Library Services Association, Best Books for
   YAs, 1994*

Other books by the same author:
Humming Whispers, 1995 (young readers)

Other books you might like:
Virginia Hamilton, *Sweet Whispers, Brother Rush*, 1982
   A girl caring for her retarded older brother encounters the
   ghost of her dead uncle and comes to a deeper understand-
   ing of her family and herself.
Virginia Hamilton, *Willie Bea and the Time the Martians
   Landed*, 1983
   On their farm in Ohio, a family is caught up in the fear
   generated by the 1938 Orson Welles "Martians have
   landed" broadcast.
Walter Dean Myers, *Motown and Didi: A Love Story*, 1984
   Dreaming of making a better life for themselves, two
   teenagers meet when the young boy rescues the young girl
   from street hoodlums.
Mildred D. Taylor, *Let the Circle Be Unbroken*, 1981
   A continuation of the Logan family stories from the Depression era in rural Mississippi where racial antagonisms
   and conflicts prevail.
Rita Williams-Garcia, *Like Sisters on the Homefront*, 1994
   An unwed 14-year-old mother, pregnant again has an abortion and when sent to her relatives in the South, develops a
   new sense of family and self.

`224`

ANGELA JOHNSON, African American
DAVID SOMAN, Illustrator

When I Am Old with You

(New York: Orchard Books, 1990)

Story type: Young Readers
Subject(s): Grandparents; Old Age
Age range(s): Grades 1-2
Time period(s): 1990s
Locale(s): United States

Summary: Sitting beside his grandfather in a rocking chair a
child tells of all the things he wants to do with him when he
grows older: playing with the dog, fishing, playing cards, and
watching the lightning bugs. Together they will explore the
old cedar chest for used clothes, look at old family pictures,
have breakfast on the porch, invite people over and roast corn
over the fire. At the ocean they will walk in the hot sand,
throw rocks in the waves, and wear big hats in the afternoon.
They will ride on granddaddy's tractor, take long walks together speaking to everybody, and at the end of their walks
they will rest in their rocking chairs.

Awards the book has won:
Coretta Scott King Honor Book, 1991

Other books by the same author:
Shoe's Like Miss Alice's, 1995
Julius, 1993
One of Three, 1991
Do Like Kyla, 1990
Tell Me a Story, Mama, 1989 (Debut)

Other books you might like:

Lucille Clifton, *Everett Anderson's Year*, 1974
Activities in a young child's life are depicted for the twelve calendar months in a series of poems capturing his joys, sorrows, and confusions.

Eloise Greenfield, *Grandpa's Face*, 1988
Seeing her beloved grandpa's face turn angry while he practices his lines in a play frightens a child until he reassures her.

Dolores Johnson, *Your Dad Was Just Like You*, 1993
Talking with his grandpa after making his dad mad a young boy discovers just how much they are alike and why his dad was so upset with him.

Angela Shelf Medearis, *Poppa's New Pants*, 1995
Sleeping in the farm's spooky kitchen a child hearing noises and seeing ghosts during the night gets a surprise when learning the truth the next morning.

Belinda Rochelle, *When Jo Louis Won the Title*, 1994
Dreading going to a new school because classmates make fun of her name a young girl learns from her grandfather how she got her special name.

225

CHARLES JOHNSON, African American

Faith and the Good Thing

(New York: Viking, 1974)

Subject(s): Interpersonal Relations; Folk Tales; Superstition
Age range(s): Adult
Major character(s): Faith Cross, Crime Victim, Prostitute, African American
Time period(s): Indeterminate Past
Locale(s): Hatten County, Georgia; Chicago, Illinois

Summary: On her death bed, Faith's mother tells her ''girl, you get yourself a good thing.'' Puzzled, faith seeks the advice of the local werewitch Swamp Woman, who says Faith should move to Chicago. But Chicago proves cruel to Faith; she is mugged and raped, and she gets into prostitution and drugs. Eventually she marries hoping for ''a good thing'' in her husband, but it still eludes her. An old flame re-enters her life and things seem to just get worse.

About this book: Debut novel.

Other books by the same author:
Middle Passage, 1990
Oxherding Tale, 1982

Other books you might like:

Arthur Flowers, *Another Good Loving Blues*, 1993
A Mississippi Delta tale of exploits in the life of a ''conjure'' woman haunted by dreams of the mother who abandoned her as a child.

Jewelle Gomez, *Gilda Stories*, 1991
Vampire tales of a plantation girl who is rescued and brought into the life by a white vampire and her partner, another female vampire.

Carolivia Herron, *Thereafter Johnnie*, 1991
The incestuous relationship between a father and daughter, and their child who was their granddaughter/daughter/sister.

Gloria Naylor, *Mama Day*, 1988
Returning to her sea island home, a young woman finds both body and soul threatened by supernatural forces from which she is barely saved by Mama Day.

Ntozake Shange, *Liliane: Resurrection of the Daughter*, 1994
In psychotherapy the exploits in a young woman's life reveal how she coped with family upheavals, romances and friendships, and racism and bigotry.

226

CHARLES JOHNSON, African American

Middle Passage

(New York: Atheneum, 1990)

Subject(s): Coming of Age; Historical; Sailing
Age range(s): Adult
Major character(s): Rutherford Calhoun, Stowaway, Thief, African American
Time period(s): 1830s (1830)
Locale(s): New Orleans, Louisiana; At Sea (Atlantic Ocean)

Summary: To escape marriage and his impending debts, Rutherford stows away on the *Republic*, only to discover it is a slave ship bound for Africa. Aboard ship he survives storms, mutiny, and illness. Now finding himself a changed man, Rutherford is ready to marry, raise a family, and even make amends with his brother in Illinois.

About this book: This story won the National Book Award in 1990.

Where it's reviewed:
Commonwealth, December 2, 1994, page 28

Awards the book has won:
National Book Award, 1990

Other books by the same author:
Oxherding Tale, 1982
Faith and the Good Thing, 1974 (debut novel)

Other books you might like:

Barbara Chase-Riboud, *Echo of Lions*, 1989
Africans kidnapped aboard the schooner *Amistad* cause a mutiny, President John Quincy Adams argues their defense before the Supreme Court.

Louise Meriwether, *Fragments of the Ark*, 1994
This historical tale is about a South Carolina slave who steals a Confederate gunboat, delivers it to the Union Navy, and later becomes its captain.

227

CHARLES JOHNSON, African American

Oxherding Tale

(Bloomington: Indiana University Press, 1982)

Subject(s): Coming of Age; Identity; Self-Perception
Age range(s): Adult
Major character(s): Andrew Hawkins, Bastard Son, Slave, African American; Minty, Seamstress, Slave, African American; George Hawkins, Servant (butler), Slave
Time period(s): 19th century (1837-1862)

Locale(s): Hodges, South Carolina

Summary: One fateful night, George, the butler, and his white plantation owner get drunk and decide to go home to each other's wife. Their wives never quite recover from this deception, and nine months later Andrew is born to his white mother. Light-skinned Andrew is foresaken by his white mother who leaves his upbringing to his white step-father and then banishes Andrew's father George to the plantation fields. Andrew is educated by a tutor and is sent off to earn wages at a neighboring mine at age twenty. In the hopes of earning enough money to buy the freedom of his father George, his step-mother, and the girl he loves, Minty, Andrew leaves the plantation. He falls captive to the sexual exploits of the mistress at the mine. He later passes for white to escape slavery, marries a white doctor's daughter, and discovers Minty on the slave auction block, diseased and near death.

Other books by the same author:
Middle Passage, 1990
Faith and the Good Thing, 1974 (debut novel)

Other books you might like:
Barbara Chase-Riboud, *The President's Daughter*, 1994
    Chronicles the life of Harriet Hemings, the daughter of miscegenation in the interracial affair of President Thomas Jefferson and his slave Sally.
Cyrus Colter, *City of Light*, 1993
    This story recounts the exploits of a young Chicago man who travels to Paris, when he writes letters to his deceased mother about his plight of being light-skinned.
J. California Cooper, *Family*, 1991
    This is a young girl's narrative of her life during the plantation era of the South. Included are the events in the lives of her children by her slave owner's son and the lives of her grandchildren.
Leon Forrest, *Two Wings to Veil My Face*, 1983
    This last title in their trilogy tells of the Witherspoon family's saga from the plantation era of the South before the Civil War to contemporary times.
Toni Morrison, *Beloved*, 1987
    This story tells about a mother who escapes from slavery and then kills her baby to keep her former owner from stealing her. She is then haunted and consumed by the baby's ghost.

228

DOLORES JOHNSON, Author/Illustrator, African American

The Best Bug to Be
(New York: Macmillan, 1992)

Story type: Young Readers
Subject(s): Theater; School Life
Age range(s): Grades 1-2
Major character(s): Kelly, African American, Dancer, Singer
Time period(s): 1990s
Locale(s): United States (unidentified city)

Summary: Kelly tries out for the school play and tells her teacher she can dance and sing. She gets the part of a bumblebee but, to Kelly, her classmates seem to have better roles, playing the cymbals in the ladybug band, being a webbed footed toad in a froggy pond, or being Queen of the butterflies. In spite of her disappointment at being a bumblebee, her parents try to reassure her and encourage her to be the best bumblebee she can be. On the night of the play, her classmates get the jitters but Kelly's performance is right on key and draws the loudest applause from the audience.

Other books by the same author:
Papa's Stories, 1994
Your Dad Was Just Like You, 1993
What Kind of Baby-Sitter Is This?, 1991
What Will Mommy Do When I'm at School, 1990 (Debut)

Other books you might like:
Lucille Clifton, *Everett Anderson's Friend*, 1976
    Hoping he will have some new guys to play with when a family moves in the building a young boy learns to be friends with the new girl next door.
Lucille Clifton, *My Friend Jacob*, 1980
    A young boy shares special times with his neighbor and best friend a white mentally handicapped older boy he plays ball with and helps remember things.
Eloise Greenfield, *Me and Neesie*, 1975
    A child and her imaginary friend share times together until she goes to school and returning home discovers her friend is no longer around.
Angela Johnson, *The Girl Who Wore Snakes*, 1993
    A girl thinks snakes are beautiful and one day she finds someone else who thinks so, too.
Angela Shelf Medearis, *The Adventures of Sugar and Junior*, 1995
    Exploits of a young girl and a LAtino neighbor boy as they become friends while baking cookies, going to monster movies, and sharing ice cream.

229

DOLORES JOHNSON, Author/Illustrator, African American

Papa's Stories
(New York: Macmillan, 1994)

Story type: Young Readers
Subject(s): Fathers and Daughters; Literacy
Age range(s): Grades 1-3
Major character(s): Kari, Child, African American
Time period(s): 1990s
Locale(s): United States (unidentified city)

Summary: As a little girl, Kari would wait for her father to return home every day from work so she could crawl into his lap and have a story read to her. Sometimes the stories they would change but Kari didn't mind because they were always interesting. An older neighbor girl visits one day and begins to read Kari's books aloud. but Kari says she's not reading them like papa does. When she discovers that her father cannot read, he tells her why he never learned. She promises to teach him what she learns in school, but one day, Papa surprises Kari as he slowly reads from one of her books and tells her explains how her mother has been helping him learn.

Other books by the same author:
Your Dad Was Just Like You, 1993
The Best Bug to Be, 1992

What Kind of Baby-Sitter Is This?, 1991
What Will Mommy Do When I'm at School, 1990 (debut)

Other books you might like:
Jeannette Franklin Caines, *Daddy*, 1977
    Saturdays are special for a child when her father comes to get her to visit with him and they share laughs and fun together all day.
Valerie Flournoy, *The Best Time of Day*, 1978
    A child with a busy day of activities ahead with his mom, babysitter, friends, and relatives, looks forward to his daddy getting home from work.
Elizabeth Fitzgerald Howard, *Papa Tells Chita a Story*, 1995
    A child asks her beloved papa to tell her the story of when he was the bravest soldier and carried the message and won the war.
Dolores Johnson, *Your Dad Was Just Like You*, 1993
    Talking with his grandpa after making his dad mad a young boy discovers just how much they are alike and why his dad was so upset with him.
Sharon Dennis Wyeth, *Always My Dad*, 1995
    A young girl remembers the summer she and her three younger brothers spent at their grandparents when their dad visited and how much she misses him.

230

DOLORES JOHNSON, Author/Illustrator, African American

What Kind of Baby-Sitter Is This?

(New York: Macmillan, 1991)

Story type: Young Readers
Subject(s): Babysitters; Sports/Baseball
Age range(s): Grades 1-2
Major character(s): Kevin, Child, Baseball Player, African American
Time period(s): 1990s
Locale(s): United States

Summary: Young Kevin is very upset on the night his mother leaves him with a babysitter, elderly Mrs. Lovey Pritchard. Mrs. Pritchard assures his mom everything will be alright but Kevin begs and pleads with her not to leave him. Afterwards he decides he's going to leave himself and storms out of the kitchen. When the baby sitter fails to come after him, he goes to see why. He finds Mrs. Pritchard excitedly watching of all things not a soap opera but a baseball game. She puts on a baseball cap, has some baseball cards on the couch, and is waving a baseball pennant for the Badgers, a team Kevin knows can't win. After the Badgers win she turns the TV off and starts reading a book, much to Kevin's surprise, about baseball. Crawling closer to her on the couch she reads louder so Kevin can hear. When mom gets back Kevin has an idea. He thinks the babysitter Aunt Lovey should move in with them, she's not just a babysitter she's become his friend.

Other books by the same author:
Papa's Stories, 1994
Your Dad Was Just Like You, 1993
The Best Bug to Be, 1992
What Will Mommy Do When I'm at School, 1990 (Debut)

Other books you might like:
Lucille Clifton, *The Boy Who Didn't Believe in Spring*, 1973
    Everyone says spring is coming and a youngster and his white pal don't believe them so they go searching for evidence to discover spring.
Pat Cummings, *Clean Your Room, Harvey Moon!*, 1991
    His mom tells a young boy he has to clean his room before watching TV and he discovers a treasure trove of things he'd forgotten he had.
Angela Johnson, *Shoes Like Miss Alice's*, 1995
    Her babysitter shows a child a good time with her different pairs of shoes for dancing, walking, napping, and when they sit drawing barefooted.
Ray Prather, *No Trespassing*, 1974
    When their baseball gets hit over the cranky neighbor's fence three boys have to come up with some imaginative ideas for getting it back.

231

DOLORES JOHNSON, Author/Illustrator, African American

What Will Mommy Do When I'm at School?

(New York: Macmillan, 1990)

Story type: Young Readers
Subject(s): Mothers and Daughters; Family Life
Age range(s): Grades 1-2
Time period(s): 1990s
Locale(s): United States

Summary: About to start school, a child worries about what her mom will do without her since she's never left her alone before. She wonders if her mom will miss her and hopes she won't be scared alone. She reminisces about all the things they do together and when daddy gets home she suggests maybe he stay home since she can't any more. She assures she'll tell her everything she does in school and bring her pictures. Maybe her new friends can be mom's new friends too. Mom eases her worry when she tells her she won't be lonely because she's starting a new job and they'll both have new things to tell each other when they get home.

About this book: Debut

Other books by the same author:
Papa's Stories, 1994
Your Dad Was Just Like You, 1993
The Best Bug to Be, 1992
What Kind of Baby-Sitter Is This?, 1991

Other books you might like:
Jeannette Franklin Caines, *Abby*, 1973
    An adopted preschooler questions her mother and older brother about when she first came to them and suggests they adopt another brother.
Jan Spivey Gilchrist, *Indigo and Moonlight Gold*, 1993
    Sharing special times with her mama, a child remembers the story she told about girls growing up and things changing under a mama's watchful eye.
Eloise Greenfield, *Me and Neesie*, 1975
    A child and her imaginary friend share times together until

she goes to school, and returning home, discovers her friend is no longer around.

Angela Johnson, *Tell Me a Story, Mama*, 1989
A little girl wanting her mama to tell her a story about when she was little has memorized the stories she's heard and tells them herself.

June Jordan, *Kimako's Story*, 1981
A 7-year-old takes on the responsibility of caring for her neighbors' big Airedale dog and gets to see more of her city surroundings.

232

DOLORES JOHNSON, Author/Illustrator, African American

Your Dad Was Just Like You

(New York: Macmillan Publishing Company, 1993)

Story type: Young Readers
Subject(s): Fathers and Sons; Grandparents
Age range(s): Grades 1-3
Major character(s): Peter, Child, African American
Time period(s): 1990s
Locale(s): United States

Summary: Young Peter asks his grandpa if he can move in with him because his dad's mad at him again. Taking Peter on a walk to think things through grandpa surprises him by revealing how much his dad was like him when he was a boy. Grandpa recalls knock knock jokes, the games he played, his friends, and his special love for running. When he tells Peter about a special race and the trophy his dad won, Peter realizes its the one he just broke, running through the house. Understanding his dad better Peter returns home, glues the broken trophy back together, and takes it to his dad with a knock knock joke.

Other books by the same author:
Papa's Stories, 1994
The Best Bug to Be, 1992
What Kind of Baby-Sitter Is This?, 1991
What Will Mommy Do When I'm at School, 1990 (Debut)

Other books you might like:
Lucille Clifton, *Amifika*, 1977
Hearing his mother say his father is returning from the army a child fears he will not remember him and that he will be in the way.

Eloise Greenfield, *First Pink Light*, 1976
A child wants to stay awake until his daddy comes home so he can hide and surprise him but falls asleep waiting in a chair and daddy takes him to bed.

Angela Johnson, *When I Am Old with You*, 1990
A young child depicts all the things he wants to do with his granddaddy when he gets old and how they will rest together in their rocking chairs.

John Steptoe, *Daddy Is a Monster. . .Sometimes*, 1980
A young sister and brother discussing what makes their daddy mad and turns him into a monster surprise him when they ask him why it happens.

Sharon Dennis Wyeth, *Always My Dad*, 1995
A young girl remembers the summer she and her three younger brothers spent at their grandparents when their dad visited and how much she misses him.

233

HERSCHEL JOHNSON, African American
ROMARE BEARDEN, Illustrator, African American

A Visit to the Country

(New York: Harper and Row, 1989)

Story type: Young Readers
Subject(s): Animals; Country Life; Grandparents
Age range(s): Grades 2-3
Major character(s): Mike, Child, African American
Time period(s): 1980s
Locale(s): United States (rural)

Summary: On a visit to his grandparents in the country young Mike discovers a baby bird lying on the ground. Seeing no nest in the trees he takes the bird home, naming it Max. Mike feeds him with an eye dropper and before long he's grown into a red cardinal. Healthy now, Max flies wildly around and even tries eating the decorative cherries on the hats of some ladies who come for Sunday tea. After he crashes into the picture window trying to get outside, Mike decides it might be time to put him back into the wild. He takes him to the creek and sadly releases him. The next day Mike and grandpa head to the railroad tracks to watch the trains and who should go flying by but Max.

About this book: Debut

Other books you might like:
Ashley Bryan, *The Story of Lightning & Thunder*, 1993
A West African folktale about Ma Sheep Thunder and her disobedient Son Ram Lightning who caused them to be banished from the earth to the sky.

Lucille Clifton, *The Boy Who Didn't Believe in Spring*, 1973
Everyone says spring is coming and a youngster and his white pal don't believe them so they go searching for evidence to discover spring.

Patricia C. McKissack, *A Million Fish. . .More or Less*, 1992
Fishing in a strange bayou a boy catches a million fish and heads home with them but by the time he arrives his catch has shrunk to only three.

Gloria Jean Pinkney, *Back Home*, 1992
Raised in the city an 8-year-old visits her relatives for the first time she can remember in the place where she was born in the country.

234

NETTIE JONES, African American

Fish Tales

(New York: Random House, 1983)

Subject(s): Psychology; Growing Up; Interpersonal Relations
Age range(s): Adult
Major character(s): Lewis Jones, Abuse Victim, Divorced Person, Caucasian
Time period(s): 20th century
Locale(s): Detroit, Michigan; New York, New York

Summary: Lewis Jones was raped at 12 and aborted a pregnancy at 16. As an adult she endures bad relationships, including one with the man who raped her; engages in sexual orgies;

and pursues a man who is unfaithful to her. On th edge of a breakdown, she recalls the sight of a woman neighbor, naked, shouting and gesturing wildly while her husband tried to calm her, a vision that seemingly reflects Lewis' own life.

About this book: Debut novel.

Other books by the same author:
Mischief Makers, 1989

Other books you might like:
Bonnie Greer, *Hanging by Her Teeth*, 1994
   This novel reveals the bisexual experiences and abortion of a young woman growing up and the search for the father who abandoned her.
Carolivia Herron, *Thereafter Johnnie*, 1991
   A story of an incestuous relationship between a father and daughter and the child, who was their granddaughter/daughter/sister.
Charles Johnson, *Faith and the Good Thing*, 1974
   This is the tale of a young woman who follows her mother's deathbed wish and goes in search of the "good thing," a quest that has many tragic turns.
Ntozake Shange, *Liliane: Resurrection of the Daughter*, 1994
   While in psychotherapy a young woman reveals how she coped with family upheavals, romances and friendships, and racism and bigotry through her exploits.
Jacqueline Woodson, *Autobiography of a Family Photo*, 1995
   A teenager in New York, who has a gay brother and a half-white brother, experiences family violence and questions her sexuality sexuality.

235

NETTIE JONES, African American

Mischief Makers

(New York: Weidenfeld & Nicolson, 1989)

Subject(s): Family; Identity; Racism
Age range(s): Adult
Major character(s): Lilly Masaube, Femme Fatale, Student, Native American (Chippewa); Blossom Rose Masaube, Blind Person, Healer, Native American (Chippewa); Puma Masaube, Mother, Native American (Chippewa)
Time period(s): 20th century (1924-1945)
Locale(s): Traverse City, Michigan

Summary: Raphael de Baptiste, a light-skinned woman, leaves Detroit to travel farther north and become a nurse. She settles in Leelanau County, where she meets Mishe Masaube, a Chippewa Indian, who marries her and fathers three strikingly beautiful daughters—Blossom Rose, Lilly and Puma. Raphael dies as a son is still-born. The girls grow up with a strong sense of their own identity, and experience the world differently both because of and in spite of their looks. Lilly, mistaken for white, is killed in a race riot when a brick is hurled through a car window. Blinded by a gunshot when she was young, Blossom Rose becomes a herbalist and masseuse, seeing and healing with her hands what others cannot see with their eyes. Puma, the youngest, uses her looks to marry a rich man and bear his children.

Other books by the same author:
Fish Tales, 1983 (debut novel)

Other books you might like:
Tina McElroy Ansa, *Ugly Ways*, 1993
   Contemporary account of three sisters reflecting on their upbringing in a small town and how their lives have evolved.
Steven Corbin, *No Easy Place to Be*, 1989
   Explores the relationships among three sisters in urban New York during the 1920s Harlem Renaissance era.
Terry McMillan, *Waiting to Exhale*, 1992
   Contemporary account of the friendship of four women, their relationships with men, and their experiences with family and careers.
Devorah Major, *An Open Weave*, 1995
   Richly textured story of a blind grandmother who weaves astonishing cloths, her epileptic visionary daughter, and strong-willed granddaughter.
Cherry Muhanji, *Her*, 1990
   A young light-skinned woman falls into "the life" of 1950s Detroit and finds a strength in herself and the women around her necessary to her survival.
Ntozake Shange, *Sassafrass, Cypress and Indigo*, 1982
   Three distinct sisters find their separate way from their working class upbringing in South Carolina as their mother gives them support.

236

JUNE JORDAN, African American

His Own Where

(New York: Thomas Y. Crowell Company, 1971)

Subject(s): Adolescence; Interpersonal Relations; Love
Age range(s): Grades 9-12
Major character(s): Buddy Rivers, 16-Year-Old, Student, African American; Angela Figueroa, 16-Year-Old, Student, African American
Time period(s): 1970s
Locale(s): New York, New York (Brooklyn)

Summary: As his father lays dying in the hospital, Buddy visits him every day, and one day meets Angela, whose mother is a nurse there. He and Angela become friends and their lives intertwine. When Angela is beaten by her father, it is Buddy who takes her to the hospital even though everyone at first assumes he is the one that hurt her. She is sent to a shelter and then to a Catholic Home for Girls. When she comes home for a visit, she and Buddy run away and try to make a new life for themselves.

About this book: Debut novel, young adults.

Awards the book has won:
National Book Award for Children's Books Finalist, 1972
Young Adult Library Services Association, Best Books for YA, 1971

Other books you might like:
David Haynes, *Right by My Side*, 1993
   A high school student writes down his experiences in order to figure things out about his father, his mother and himself.
Walter Dean Myers, *Motown and Didi: a Love Story*, 1984
   Each dreaming of making a better life for themselves, two

teenagers meet when the young boy rescues the young girl from street hoodlums.

Brenda Wilkinson, *Ludell and Willie*, 1977

As she prepares to graduate from high school, a girl must care for the grandmother that raised her and alter her own plans for the future.

Sapphire, *Push*, 1996

Raped by her father, a teenager gives birth to their second child, struggles to learn to read and write and is determined to make a better life.

Jervey Tervalon, *Understand This*, 1994

High school lovers, a male and female couple, find themselves headed in different directions, one to college and the other quitting school.

`237`

JUNE JORDAN, African American
KAY BURFORD, Illustrator

Kimako's Story
(Boston: Houghton Mifflin, 1981)

Story type: Young Readers
Subject(s): City Life; Responsibility; Animals, Treatment of
Age range(s): Grades 1-3
Major character(s): Kimako Anderson, 7-Year-Old, Sister, African American
Time period(s): 1980s
Locale(s): New York, New York

Summary: One of her special times for 7-year-old Kimako is sitting outside on the stoop having her mother corn-row her hair, except when she brushes too hard. Now that time is gone because her mother has begun working so Kimako wears her hair in an Afro. Living in an apartment in the city is not much fun for Kimako since she can't see much from her windows facing other buildings and staying inside watching TV with her baby brother is dull. One of the things she does enjoy is making up poetry puzzles. A neighbor, 17-year-old Bobby, who sometimes teases her about marrying him rescues a stray puppy naming him Bucks. Bucks grows into a big Airedale and Bobby is going a way to a wedding so he asks Kimako if she'll take care of him for the week. Taking care of Bucks is quite a responsibility and one Kimako really enjoys since it gets her out of the house and around more of the city neighborhood. She feels like she is on vacation with all the places they go, things they see, and what they do together. And the experience even gives her a new plan for her upcoming birthday and she writes a new poetry puzzle.

Other books by the same author:
New Life: New Room, 1975
His Own Where, 1971

Other books you might like:
Jeannette Franklin Caines, *Just Us Women*, 1982

A young niece narrates the adventures she had with her aunt when they made a trip together in her aunt's new car and all their special memories.

Pat Cummings, *Clean Your Room, Harvey Moon!*, 1991

His mom tells a young boy he has to clean his room before watching TV and he discovers a treasure trove of things he'd forgotten he had.

Pat Cummings, *Carousel*, 1994

Upset her daddy isn't home for her birthday a young girl dreams of riding the zebra on the carousel she receives as her present from him.

Angela Johnson, *Julius*, 1993

Her granddaddy surprises a child by bringing her her very own pig from Alaska and she shares things she learns with her friends.

Gloria Jean Pinkney, *The Sunday Outing*, 1994

Enjoying watching trains at the station an 8-year-old is excited when her relatives invite her to come visit them on her first train trip.

`238`

JUNE JORDAN, African American
RAY CRUZ, Illustrator, Latino American

New Life: New Room
(New York: Thomas Y. Crowell, 1975)

Story type: Young Readers
Subject(s): Brothers and Sisters; Family Life; Change
Age range(s): Grades 2-4
Time period(s): 1970s
Locale(s): United States (unidentified city)

Summary: The Robinson's small apartment is going to have a new addition, mamma is pregnant. Rudy and Tyrone now share a room together and their sister Linda sleeps on the couch. The parents decide to move into the boys room and switch their bigger bedroom into one for all the children. Rudy and Tyrone don't like giving up their old room and Linda was used to her things being in the living room. After family discussion everyone agrees to give it a try. With poster paint to brighten things up, the room takes on a new appearance, and everyone celebrates. They try sleeping in the new room and discover other adjustments they have to make but by the time mamma gets home from the hospital all is well.

Other books by the same author:
Kimako's Story, 1981
His Own Where, 1971

Other books you might like:
Lucille Clifton, *Everett Anderson's Nine Month Long*, 1978

With a new stepfather a young boy now anticipates the arrival of a new stepbrother or sister and experiences the ups and downs of waiting.

Pat Cummings, *Clean Your Room, Harvey Moon!*, 1991

His mom tells a young boy he has to clean his room before watching TV and he discovers a treasure trove of things he'd forgotten he had.

Eloise Greenfield, *She Come Bringing Me That Little Baby Girl*, 1974

Jealous at first when his mama brings him a baby sister a young boy later feels a new sense of responsibility and pride as a big brother.

Angela Johnson, *The Leaving Morning*, 1992

The impressions of what the day was like for herself and her younger brother when their daddy and pregnant mama moved them away from their home.

Mildred Pitts Walter, *My Mama Needs Me*, 1983

When his newborn baby sister arrives home a young boy is

overcome by feelings of responsibility until his mama lets him know it's still ok to play.

239

JOHN R. KEENE JR., African American

Annotations

(New York: New Directions, 1995)

Story type: Adult
Subject(s): Coming of Age; Identity
Time period(s): 1950s; 1960s
Locale(s): St. Louis, Missouri

Summary: Through a series of short passages on a variety of topics both large and small, unnamed narrator(s) explore questions of identity from many angles—including race, social class, and sexuality—and tell the story of a boy growing up in St. Louis.

About this book: Debut novel

Where it's reviewed:
Publishers Weekly, September 4, 1995, page 61

Other books you might like:
Xam Wilson Cartier, *Muse-Echo Blues*, 1991
    A jazz improvisation prose style tale of a young woman suffering an acute case of composer's block who finds inspiration from a fantasy soul sister.
Ricardo Cortez Cruz, *Straight Outta Compton*, 1992
    This rap-style novel tells the story of Rooster and Clive, growing up together in the streets of Compton, living hard and fast on a very thin edge.

240

JOHN OLIVER KILLENS, African American

The Cotillion, or, One Good Bull Is Half the Herd

(New York: Trident Press, 1971)

Story type: Humor
Subject(s): Interpersonal Relations; Race Relations; Self-Acceptance
Age range(s): Adult
Major character(s): Ben Ali Lumumba, Writer, African American; Yoruba Evelyn Lovejoy, 18-Year-Old, Debutante, African American
Time period(s): 1960s
Locale(s): New York, New York (Harlem)

Summary: Yoruba's working class West Indies mother has longed for the day her daughter would attend a debutante cotillion. Now that it's come, she is beside herself and cannot understand why Yoruba is being so difficult about her hairstyle and choice of an escort. Yoruba and escort Ben Ali upset the traditional decorum at the cotillion, this year with a plantation theme, by arriving in African clothing.

About this book: Author died 1987.

Other books by the same author:
Great Black Russian: A Novel on the Life and Times of Alexander Pushkin, 1989 (published posthumously)

'Sippi, 1967
And Then We Heard Thunder, 1962
Youngblood, 1954 (debut novel)

Other books you might like:
Connie Briscoe, *Sisters and Lovers*, 1994
    Contemporary story about the lives and struggles of three sisters and the men with whom they become involved.
Alice Childress, *A Short Walk*, 1973
    Events in the childhood and adulthood of a woman who escapes an abusive marriage and journeys to Harlem in the 1940s.
Trey Ellis, *Platitudes*, 1988
    The parallel stories created by two writers who are corresponding about teenaged characters and who develop their own personal relationship.
Nettie Jones, *Mischief Makers*, 1989
    Three exotically beautiful sisters of mixed race experience the world quite differently both because and in spite of their looks.
Ntozake Shange, *Liliane: Resurrection of the Daughter*, 1994
    In psychotherapy, a young woman reveals how she coped with family upheavals, romances and friendships, and racism and bigotry.

241

HELEN ELAINE LEE, African American

The Serpent's Gift

(New York: Atheneum, 1994)

Subject(s): Family Relations; Intergenerational Saga
Age range(s): Adult
Major character(s): LaRue Smalls, Adventurer, Storyteller, African American; Vesta Smalls, Care Giver, Spinster, African American; Ouida Staples, Handicapped, Lesbian, African American
Time period(s): 20th century (1900-1980)
Locale(s): Black Oak, South

Summary: Following the dramatic death of Ouida's father, the lives of two families are intertwined. As they face trials and challenges, LaRue helps Ouida and his sister Vesta triumph through the healing of his stories.

About this book: This is the author's debut novel.

Where it's reviewed:
Black Scholar, Summer 1994, page 25
Library Journal, December 1994, page 164
School Library Journal, April 1995, page 166

Other books you might like:
Linda Beatrice Brown, *Crossing over Jordan*, 1995
    This saga is about the binding ties in the lives of four generations of mothers and daughters from the Civil War era to the early 21st century.
J. California Cooper, *Family*, 1991
    This is a young girl's narrative of her life during the plantation era of the South. Included are the events in the lives of her children by her slave owner's son and the lives of her grandchildren.
Leon Forrest, *Two Wings to Veil My Face*, 1983
    This last title in their trilogy tells of the Witherspoon

family saga from the plantation era of the South before the Civil War to contemporary times.

Gloria Naylor, *Bailey's Cafe*, 1992

Bailey's Cafe, a mythical waystation for lost souls, has a back door which opens onto dimensions unknown.

Dorothy West, *The Wedding*, 1995

This saga about five generations of two families with mixed race ancestry, relates the events in the lives of children from a new contemporary generation.

242

JULIUS LESTER, African American

And All Our Wounds Forgiven

(New York: Arcade Publishing, 1994)

Subject(s): Civil Rights Movement; Historical; Race Relations
Age range(s): Adult
Major character(s): John Calvin Marshall, Activist, Professor, African American; Andrea Williams Marshall, Activist, Spouse, African American; Elizabeth "Lisa" Adams, Activist, Secretary, Caucasian
Time period(s): 20th century (1954-1988)
Locale(s): Nashville, Tennessee; Alabama; Michigan

Summary: Social change was needed to eradicate a national evil during the historic civil rights movement. In the wake of the movement, John, a rising activist leader, had an affair with his white secretary Lisa. Lisa reflects back on their times together and thanks about the legacy of accomplishments John left behind.

Where it's reviewed:
Kirkus Reviews, May 1, 1994, page 581
Library Journal, June 15, 1994, page 95
New York Times Book Review, August 7, 1994, page 14
Publishers Weekly, May 2, 1994, page 282

Other books by the same author:
Do Lord Remember Me, 1984 (debut novel)

Other books you might like:
Albert French, *Holly*, 1995

A young white girl involved in an interracial affair must flee her family and her community to find safety when she becomes pregnant.

Dennis Williams, *Crossover*, 1992

This story recounts the events in the life of a young man during the Civil Rights era. He becomes a reluctant activist and he has an interracial affair.

243

JULIUS LESTER, African American

Do Lord Remember Me

(New York: Hold, Rinehart and Winston, 1984)

Subject(s): Family Relations; Farm Life; Fathers and Sons
Age range(s): Adult
Major character(s): Joshua Smith, Aged Person, Religious, African American
Time period(s): 1980s
Locale(s): Nashville, Tennessee

Summary: Eighty-year-old Reverend Smith, once known as the "Singing Evangelist" and the "Colored Billy Graham," suffers an ulcer, a heart attack and a stroke. His memories of his youth in Mississippi during the time of slavery, segregation and the civil rights movement, his marriage to Carlotta for fifty-six years, his two sons, Josh and Carl, and the events of his life are told in this story of his final day.

About this book: This is the author's debut novel for adults.

Other books by the same author:
And All Our Wounds Forgiven, 1994

Other books you might like:
Wesley Brown, *Darktown Strutters*, 1994

A traveling minstrel dances the thin line between anger, violence and laughter in pre- and post-Civil War America.

Marita Golden, *Long Distance Life*, 1989

These episodes relate the murder of a young grandson in the 1980s and the evolution of his family from a sharecropping background of the 1920s.

Walter Mosley, *RL's Dream*, 1995

An aging blues musician befriends a young caucasian woman haunted by an incestuous past. This story recounts exploits from the musician's past as they become friends.

Dori Sanders, *Her Own Place*, 1993

This story is about the remembrances of a senior citizen's exploits as a daughter, wife, mother, and grandmother prior to World War II, including contemporary times.

244

JULIUS LESTER, African American

Othello, a Novel

(New York: Scholastic, 1995)

Story type: Young Adult
Subject(s): Historical; Interpersonal Relations; Jealousy
Age range(s): Grades 7-12
Major character(s): Othello, Mercenary, Spouse, African Desdemona, Noblewoman, Spouse, English
Time period(s): 15th century (late 14th century); 16th century (early 15th century)
Locale(s): England

Summary: A reconceptualization of William Shakespeare's play with modernized dialogue moves the action from Italy to Elizabethan England and alters the racial identity of soldier Iago and his wife. Falling in love General Othello, a middle-aged African, and a young white noblewoman Desdemona marry secretly. Outraged Desdemona's father wants the King to annul their marriage and soon envious Iago is scheming to disrupt the marriage with his suggestions to Othello of Desdemona's infidelity. When Othello is manipulated into a jealous rage by Iago tragedy awaits.

About this book: Debut novel

Other books you might like:
Walter Dean Myers, *Legend of Tarik*, 1981

A medieval story where a young boy survives when his family is killed by a white warrior and two wise men give him special gifts to seek revenge.

Walter Dean Myers, *Motown and Didi: A Love Story*, 1984

Each dreaming of making a better life for themselves two

teenagers meet when the young boy rescues the young girl from street hoodlums.

245

C. ERIC LINCOLN, African American

The Avenue, Clayton City

(New York: William Morrow and Company, 1988)

Subject(s): City Life; Family Relations; Race Relations
Age range(s): Adult
Major character(s): Walter Pinkney Tait, Doctor, Spouse, African American; Ramona Tait, Housewife, Spouse, African American; Hoyt ''Cap'n'' Butler, Businessman, Landowner, Caucasian
Time period(s): 1920s; 1930s (1919-1938)
Locale(s): Clayton City, South

Summary: Dr. Tait came to town almost twenty years ago with his bride Ramona. Reclusive Ramona did not engage in the neighborhood's social activities; she preferred staying home playing the piano and, in later years, drinking. Accused of getting his daughter Makeda pregnant, Dr. Tait admits it but divulges that she is actually the daughter of a member of one of the town's influential white families who had an affair with Ramona.

About this book: Debut novel.

Other books you might like:
Bebe Moore Campbell, *Your Blues Ain't Like Mine*, 1992
    Episodes in the lives of individuals affected by the murder of a 15-year-old boy for reportedly offending a white woman in a small southern town.
Toni Morrison, *Jazz*, 1992
    A working class couple face the trauma of trying to put their lives back together when the husband murders the girl with whom he was having an affair.
Gloria Naylor, *Bailey's Cafe*, 1992
    A mythical waystation for lost souls, Bailey's cafe has a back door that opens on dimensions unknown.
Richard Perry, *Montgomery's Children*, 1984
    Tales of people living in a small town in central New York interwoven with magic and vision, incest and murder, friendship and sacrifice.
John Edgar Wideman, *Damballah*, 1981
    First title of the Homewood trilogy portraying the intergenerational history of a family from the 1840s-1960s in Pennsylvania.

246

LESSIE JONES LITTLE, African American
ELOISE GREENFIELD, Illustrator, African American
CAROLE BYARD, Illustrator, African American

I Can Do It Myself

(New York: Harper Collins Publishers, 1978)

Story type: Young Readers
Subject(s): Birthdays; Mothers and Sons; Brothers
Age range(s): Grades 1-3
Major character(s): Donny, Child, Brother, African American

Time period(s): 1970s
Locale(s): United States (unidentified city)

Summary: Today is his mother's birthday and young Donny has a special present he wants to buy for her. Setting out alone with his wagon, Donny braves the bulldog down the street to get to the nursery where he buys the special plant he's arranged for at a discount. On his way home, the barking bulldog scares Donny so badly that he tips his wagon over and spills the plant. Managing to get the dog back into his yard, and the plant back in his wagon, Donny proudly gives his special birthday present to his mother.

About this book: Debut. Author began writing at age sixty-seven in 1974.

Other books you might like:
Jeannette Franklin Caines, *I Need a Lunch Box*, 1988
    A preschooler wanting a lunch box like his older sister's imagines all the things he could keep in it and dreams of having one for every day.
Lucille Clifton, *Everett Anderson's Year*, 1974
    Activities in a young child's life are depicted for the twelve calendar months in a series of poems capturing his joys, sorrows, and confusions.
Lucille Clifton, *Everett Anderson's 1-2-3*, 1977
    A new man comes into his mama's life and a young boy discovers some times are just right for being one alone or for being with others.
Pat Cummings, *Clean Your Room, Harvey Moon!*, 1991
    His mom tells a young boy he has to clean his room before watching TV and he discovers a treasure trove of things he'd forgotten he had.
Mildred Pitts Walter, *My Mama Needs Me*, 1983
    When his newborn baby sister arrives home a young boy is overcome by feelings of responsibility until his mama lets him know it's still ok to play.

247

CLARENCE MAJOR, Author/Illustrator, African American

Emergency Exit

(New York: Fiction Collective, 1979)

Story type: Adult
Subject(s): Family Relations; Interpersonal Relations; Imagination
Age range(s): Adult
Major character(s): James Ingram, Father, Husband, African American; Deborah Ingram, Mother, Wife, African American; Rosalyn Carter, Girlfriend, African American
Time period(s): 1970s
Locale(s): Inlet, Connecticut

Summary: An unnamed narrator skips through the fragments, thoughts and episodes in the lives of people in a small town in Connecticut that has just passed the Threshold Law, stating that all men must carry all women across all thresholds at all times. Light-skinned Jim Ingram distances himself from his wife Deborah and takes up with Ros Carter. Daughter Julie tries to sort out her feelings about her father's leaving her mother. The narrator comments on the characters, the form of the novel, himself, and his relationship with these characters.

Other books by the same author:
Painted Turtle: Woman with Guitar, 1988
Such Was the Season, 1987
Dirty Bird Blues, 1996
Reflex and Bone Structure, 1975
No, 1973
All-Night Visitors, 1969 (debut novel)

Other books you might like:
Tananarive Due, *The Between*, 1995
  A man endures nightmares and a wavering sense of reality as he desperately tries to protect his family from the psychotic who stalks them.
Trey Ellis, *Platitudes*, 1988
  The novel reveals parallel stories created by two creative writers who are corresponding about teenaged characters, and who develop their own personal relationship.
John R. Keene Jr., *Annotations*, 1995
  Impressions and meditations of a boy growing up in St. Louis are shared in this poetic, highly allusive word-tapestry.
Reginald McKnight, *I Get on the Bus*, 1990
  Trying to avoid making decisions at home, a young man joins the Peace Corps and travels to Senegal, becoming involved in new intrigue.
Ishmael Reed, *Reckless Eyeballing*, 1986
  This is a satire on extremist points-of-view and the turmoil caused in a young man's life who as a creative writer is being forced to rewrite his work.
Melvin Van Peebles, *Don't Play Us Cheap: A Harlem Party*, 1973
  Trying to pass the test to become full-fledged devils two white imps are racially transformed and attempt to wreck a Harlem party.

248

CLARENCE MAJOR, African American

My Amputations
(New York: Fiction Collective, 1986)

Subject(s): Identity; Imagination; Psychology
Age range(s): Adult
Major character(s): Mason Ellis, Imposter, Writer, African American
Time period(s): 1980s
Locale(s): United States (United States, Europe and Africa)

Summary: Episodes in the hallucinatory life of Mason Ellis as a hoodlum, serviceman, bank robber and lecturer. Mason is a writer and claims that another man, possibly the Author, has stolen his manuscript. This man has taken the name of Clarence McKay to hide his identity. Mason kidnaps McKay and assumes his identity, conning $50,000 a year from the Magnan-Rockford Foundation. He travels the globe lecturing but never really answering any questions as his paranoia becomes greater about being found out. He imagines detectives are following him and ends up in Ghana, where a chieftain tells him he has come to the end of his running.

Other books by the same author:
Painted Turtle: Woman with Guitar, 1988
Dirty Bird Blues, 1996

Emergency Exit, 1979
Reflex and Bone Structure, 1975
All-Night Visitors, 1969 (debut novel)

Other books you might like:
Tananarive Due, *The Between*, 1995
  A man endures nightmares and a wavering sense of reality as he desperately tries to protect his family from the psychotic who stalks them.
Reginald McKnight, *I Get on the Bus*, 1990
  Trying to avoid making decisions at home, a young man joins the Peace Corps and travels to Senegal, becoming involved in new intrigue.
Ray Shell, *Iced*, 1993
  In his diary, a man reflects on his accomplishments in life as well as his regrets at descending into the white-smoke world of crack cocaine.

249

CLARENCE MAJOR, African American

No
(New York: Emerson Hall Publishers, Inc., 1973)

Subject(s): Growing Up; Identity; Psychology
Age range(s): Adult
Major character(s): Moses Westby, Researcher, Husband, African American
Time period(s): 1960s
Locale(s): Chickamauga, Georgia; New York, New York

Summary: Moses, the narrator, reviews his past in order to come to terms with his identity. He recalls his childhood in Chickamauga surviving under various names, his first sexual escapades and the unusual people that filled his world. Presently he works in New York analyzing riot statistics and encounters Oni Dunn, a woman he was "married" to in his past. They run away together to a Latin country where Moses dreams he jumps into a bullring in the middle of a bullfight and touches the bull's head. He interpets this as a symbol of his new freedom and perhaps a new beginning.

Other books by the same author:
Painted Turtle: Woman with Guitar, 1988
Such Was the Season, 1987
My Amputations, 1986
Dirty Bird Blues, 1996
All-Night Visitors, 1969 (debut novel)

Other books you might like:
Percival Everett, *Zulus*, 1990
  On a barren planet in the future, a white woman is raped and seeks refuge with rebels because her fertility is a threat to the government.
John R. Keene Jr., *Annotations*, 1995
  Impressions and meditations of a boy growing up in St. Louis are shared in this poetic, highly allusive word-tapestry.
Ishmael Reed, *Flight to Canada*, 1976
  In this satire three slaves escape and later escape and later return to the plantation after the slave owner is murdered by his sister's ghost.

Ishmael Reed, *Reckless Eyeballing*, 1986

This is a satire on extremist points-of-view and the turmoil caused in a young man's life who as a creative writer is being forced to rewrite his work.

250

CLARENCE MAJOR, African American

Painted Turtle: Woman with Guitar

(Los Angeles: Sun & Moon Press, 1988)

Subject(s): Coming of Age; Indians of North America; Musicians

Age range(s): Adult

Major character(s): Painted Turtle, Musician, Singer, Zuni Indian; Baldwin ''Baldy'' Saiyataca, Musician, Native American (Navajo/Hopi)

Time period(s): 20th century (1930s-1980s)

Locale(s): Southwest (Arizona, Colorado, New Mexico)

Summary: Baldy chronicles the life of Painted Turtle and how her alienation from her own Zuni culture forces her away from her people. Raped at age 13, she gives birth to twins, which is considered a curse. After unsuccessfully trying to drown them, Painted Turtle is placed for a short time in a mental institution. After a few months she returns to the reservation but realizes she can no longer live there, and begins her quest for identity. After a series of odd jobs she takes up her guitar and becomes a performer. Baldy, who has been sent by their mutual agent to hear her perform and make Painted Turtle more ''marketable'' falls in love with and is eventually transformed by her.

Other books by the same author:

My Amputations, 1986

Such Was the Season, 1987

Emergency Exit, 1979

Dirty Bird Blues, 1996

All-Night Visitors, 1969 (debut novel)

Other books you might like:

Percival Everett, *Watershed*, 1996

On a fishing trip to get away from his neurotic girlfriend, a man finds himself involved in a fight over Native American treaty rights.

Nettie Jones, *Mischief Makers*, 1989

Three exotically beautiful sisters of mixed race experience the world quite differently both because and in spite of their looks.

251

CLARENCE MAJOR, African American

Reflex and Bone Structure

(New York: Fiction Collective, 1975)

Subject(s): Imagination; Literature; Storytelling

Age range(s): Adult

Major character(s): Cora Hull, Actress; Canada Jackson, Revolutionary, Actor, African American; Dale, Actor, African American

Time period(s): 1970s

Locale(s): New York, New York

Summary: The interrelationships of four characters are examined by an undescribed narrator who is one of the characters *and* the author of the novel. Cora, an actress who is always auditioning for plays or in rehearsal, has intimate relationships with the other three characters. Canada Jackson collects weapons and may be part of a black revolutionary group. He is the chief rival of the narrator. Dale is not well defined, as he refuses to focus himself and the narrator (author) has had a difficult time constructing him. The author doesn't really like Dale and often sends him off on long journeys. A bomb explodes and Canada and his revolutionary group are suspected of setting it off. The investigation goes slowly with no apparent success. It is possible that Cora and Dale are the ones who were killed, or perhaps it was in the author's imagination.

Other books by the same author:

My Amputations, 1986

Dirty Bird Blues, 1996

Such Was the Season, 1987

Emergency Exit, 1979

All-Night Visitors, 1969 (debut novel)

Other books you might like:

Toni Cade Bambara, *The Salt Eaters*, 1980

A woman who attempted suicide finds herself in an unusual healing as her psyche travels through time and the minds of friends and family.

Tananarive Due, *The Between*, 1995

A man endures nightmares and a wavering sense of reality as he desperately tries to protect his family from the psychotic who stalks them.

Trey Ellis, *Platitudes*, 1988

The parallel stories created by two creative writers who are corresponding about teenaged characters, and who develop their own personal relationship.

Ray Shell, *Iced*, 1993

In his diary, a man reflects on his accomplishments in life as well as his regrets at descending into the white-smoke world of crack cocaine.

252

CLARENCE MAJOR, African American

Such Was the Season

(San Francisco: Mercury House, Inc., 1987)

Subject(s): Family Relations; Identity; Politics

Age range(s): Adult

Major character(s): Annie Eliza Sommer-Hicks, Widow(er), Aged Person, African American; Adam ''Juneboy'' North, Doctor, Researcher, African American

Time period(s): 1980s

Locale(s): Atlanta, Georgia

Summary: In a conversational narrative, family matriarch Annie Eliza relates that when her grown nephew Juneboy comes to visit, he has either brought good luck or bad luck with him. In Atlanta to deliver a speech at Spelman College, he has also come to learn about the family history he's ignored all his life. In the midst of all this several current family stories begin to reveal themselves. Annie Eliza shares her thoughts as she attends a pretentious dinner at which her daughter-in-law announces she wants to run for state senate, an intrigue in which her Reverend son is involved begins to unravel, and a conspiracy that strikes rather close to home is uncovered.

Other books by the same author:
Dirty Bird Blues, 1996
Painted Turtle: Woman with Guitar, 1988
Emergency Exit, 1979
Reflex and Bone Structure, 1975
All-Night Visitors, 1969 (debut novel)

Other books you might like:
Al Young, *Seduction by Light*, 1988
    A psychic domestic shares her wry observations and spiritual realizations after an earthquake destroys her home in 1980's Santa Monica.
Al Young, *Sitting Pretty*, 1976
    A man living in a residence hotel does odd jobs to pay for his rent and his wine, and rolls with the punches through good times and bad.
Dori Sanders, *Her Own Place*, 1993
    Remembrances of exploits in a senior citizen's life of daughter, wife, mother, and grandmother from before WWII to contemporary times.

253

DEVORAH MAJOR, African American

An Open Weave

(Seattle: Seal Press, 1995)

Story type: Adult
Subject(s): Family Relations; Friendship; Mothers and Daughters
Major character(s): Ernestine Moore, Blind Person, Grandmother, Artisan; Iree, Epileptic, Psychic, African American; Imani, 17-Year-Old, Psychic, African American
Time period(s): 1990s
Locale(s): Buttonhole, West

Summary: Three generations are bound by loyalty and love: Ernestine, the blind matriarch who weaves astonishing cloths; Iree, her epileptic and visionary foster-daughter; and Imani, Iree's psychic 17-year-old daughter. As family and friends prepare to celebrate Imani's birthday, she is away helping her friend Amanda, a motherless girl who is pregnant. To pass the time, the celebrants share pieces of the extended family's richly textured oral history.

About this book: Debut novel

Where it's reviewed:
Library Journal, September 1, 1995, page 208
Publishers Weekly, July 31, 1995, page 71

Other books you might like:
Linda Beatrice Brown, *Crossing over Jordan*, 1995
    Saga of the ties binding the lives of four generations of mothers and daughters from the Civil War era to the early 21st century.
Helen Elaine Lee, *The Serpent's Gift*, 1994
    Children and grandchildren of two intertwined families

endure hardship and triumph as they help each other remember a history beyond their knowing.
Dorothy West, *The Wedding*, 1995
    Saga of five generations of two families of mixed race ancestry, and events in the lives of children from a contemporary generation.
John Edgar Wideman, *Damballah*, 1981
    First title of the Homewood trilogy portraying the intergenerational history of a family from the 1840s-1960s in Pennsylvania.

254

PAULE MARSHALL, African American

Daughters

(New York: Atheneum, 1991)

Subject(s): Coming of Age; Family Relations; Fathers and Daughters
Age range(s): Adult
Major character(s): Ursa Beatrice Mackenzie, Businesswoman, African American; Primus ''PM'' Mackenzie, Father (of Ursa), Political Figure (Prime Minister), West Indian; Vincereta ''Viney'' Daniels, Girlfriend, Mother, African American
Time period(s): 20th century (1943-1988)
Locale(s): New York, New York; West Indies

Summary: Ursa, a young woman from an affluent upbringing, has ended an intimate relationship and has had an abortion. When events trouble her closest friend, Viney, she comes to the aid of her family. Ursa struggles in her relationship with her father, who is Prime Minister of the West Indies. While visiting her parents in the West Indies during a political campaign, she makes a decision that changes their lives.

Where it's reviewed:
Black Scholar, Fall 1992, page 48
Christian Science Monitor, December 22, 1992, page 13
New York Times Book Review, November 8, 1992, page 64
Village Voice Literary Supplement, October 1992, page 24

Other books by the same author:
Praisesong for the Widow, 1983
The Chosen Place, the Timeless People, 1969
Brown Girl, Brownstones, 1959 (debut novel)

Other books you might like:
Anita Richmond Bunkley, *Black Gold*, 1994
    A young woman who is on the brink of financial ruin before the 1920s oil boom in Texas finds herself accused of murder.
Bebe Moore Campbell, *Brothers and Sisters*, 1994
    This contemporary account of a career woman's life shows her attempt to climb the business ladder and maintain a social life.
Rita Dove, *Through the Ivory Gate*, 1992
    When a young woman returns to her home after being away many years, a family secret is revealed to her.
Gloria Naylor, *Mama Day*, 1988
    Returning to her sea island home, a young woman finds both body and soul threatened by supernatural forces. She is saved by Mama Day.

Richard Perry, *No Other Tale to Tell*, 1994

With their community watching in silence, a young girl gives birth to a son by a youngster her family raised.

255

PAULE MARSHALL, African American

Praisesong for the Widow

(New York: G.P. Putnam's Sons, 1983)

Subject(s): Identity; Interpersonal Relations; Self-Acceptance
Age range(s): Adult
Major character(s): Avatara "Avey" Johnson, Mother, Widow(er), African American
Time period(s): 1970s (1970)
Locale(s): North White Plains, New York; Tatem, North Carolina; Grenada

Summary: After her husband dies of a stroke, "Avey" takes a cruise to the Caribbean. During this voyage she experiences an unsettling dream about the days of her summer childhood in the South, when her great-aunt told her tales of her ancestry. Disturbed by the dream she gets off the ship in Grenada, where she has another disturbing dream in her hotel about her husband. Coming to terms about their marriage and his death, "Avey" is urged by an old man to travel with him to his home on the island of Carriacou. There she finds a new sense of self. She leaves with a clear plan for connecting her past and improving her life when she returns home.

Other books by the same author:
Daughters, 1991
The Chosen Place, the Timeless People, 1969
Brown Girl, Brownstones, 1959 (debut novel)

Other books you might like:
Linda Beatrice Brown, *Crossing over Jordan*, 1995

This saga is about the binding ties in the lives of four generations of mothers and daughters from the Civil War era to the early 21st century.
J. California Cooper, *In Search of Satisfaction*, 1994

This family saga is about two half-sisters born in the era of the plantation South. They have to deal with their parent's secret legacy and inheritance.
Gloria Naylor, *Linden Hills*, 1985

Linden Hills symbolizes success, but two boys doing odd jobs see firsthand the lust, pain, hypocrisy, and valor of its residents.
Gloria Naylor, *Mama Day*, 1988

Returning to her sea island home, a young woman finds her body and soul threatened by supernatural forces. She is barely saved by Mama Day.

256

DINDGA McCANNON, Author/Illustrator, African American

Peaches

(New York: Lothrop, Lee and Shepard Co., 1974)

Subject(s): Family Relations; Growing Up; Death
Age range(s): Grades 4-7

Major character(s): Millicent "Peaches" Johnson, Student, 14-Year-Old, African American
Time period(s): 1970s
Locale(s): New York, New York (Harlem)

Summary: An only child, "Peaches" never saw her father. Her mother Hallelujah has married her stepfather Bent, and "Peaches" lives across the street from them with her grandmother "Ma." "Peaches" and her cousins Dee-Dee and Bumpsi share a lot, including the time they were caught shoplifting. In 7th grade "Peaches" is selected for an advanced class, allowing her to skip the 8th grade. When "Ma" wins money on the numbers she sends 12-year-old "Peaches," with Dee-Dee, and Bumpsi on their first camping trip. When they return "Peaches" discovers someone has been spreading rumors about why she was away, her neighbor Gloria decides to kiss her, and she is almost raped by a classmate's older brother and his pal. Starting junior high "Peaches" meets the soon to be love of her life "Zoom." Caught carrying a gun "Zoom" is given probation to go live with his father down South and before he leaves he asks "Peaches" to marry him. When "Ma" falls ill and goes to the hospital "Peaches" is left to go stay with her mother and stepfather, and before long face the trauma of her beloved grandmother's death.

About this book: This is a debut novel.

Where it's reviewed:
Booklist, January 15, 1975, page 508
Kirkus Reviews, November 1, 1974, page 1151
School Library Journal, January 1975, page 55

Other books by the same author:
Wilhemina Jones, Future Star, 1980 (young adults)

Other books you might like:
Eloise Greenfield, *Sister*, 1974

At age nine a youngster began keeping a diary she reads now at thirteen which helps her realize her life can be different than her older sister's.
Virginia Hamilton, *Cousins*, 1990

Concerned that her grandmother might die, a young girl is unprepared for the death of another relative.
Brenda Wilkinson, *Ludell*, 1975

Events in the life of a young girl raised by her strict grandmother as she comes of age and falls in love for the first time.
Jacqueline Woodson, *Last Summer with Maizon*, 1990

The friendship and separation of two youngsters after one suffers the death of her father and the other goes away to boarding school.
Johnniece Marshall Wilson, *Robin on His Own*, 1990

A boy grieving his mother's death struggles to make the adjustment when the aunt who has stayed with him gets married and moves away.

257

DINDGA MCCANNON, African American

Wilhemina Jones, Future Star
(New York: Delacorte Press, 1980)

Subject(s): Mothers and Daughters; Coming of Age; Interpersonal Relations
Age range(s): Grades 10-12
Major character(s): Wilhemina Orphelia "Willi" Jones, 16-Year-Old, Artist, African American; Theophilus J. "Skeeter" Marcus, Military Personnel, Divorced Person, African American; Orphelia, Mother (of "Willi"), African American
Time period(s): 1970s
Locale(s): New York, New York

Summary: More than anything Willi wants to be a serious artist. Her mother wants her to do something practical where she can make a living. Unbeknownst to her mother, 16-year-old Willi has an older boyfriend, Skeeter, who has been drafted into the military and is about to be sent to Vietnam. Home on leave he pledges his love for her and convinces Willi to have sex for the first time. Entering her first art exhibition Willi comes away with a prize and the friendship of fellow artist Bill, who helps her get her first one woman showing. Discharged from the military Skeeter comes home and asks Willi to live with him. When Orphelia learns of their plans to live together she angrily puts Willi out of the house only to bring her back for two weeks until she reaches eighteen. When she does move out Orphelia vows never to speak to her again.

Where it's reviewed:
Booklist, May 15, 1980, page 1358
Kirkus Reviews, September 1, 1980, page 1167
School Library Journal, May 1980, page 77

Other books by the same author:
Peaches, 1974 (debut novel, young readers)

Other books you might like:
David Haynes, *Right by My Side*, 1993
   A high school student writes down his experiences in order to figure things out about his father, his mother and himself.
Vy Higginsen, *Mama, I Want to Sing*, 1995
   Recounts events in the life of a talented singer from a young girl singing in the church choir to a renowned award winning star.
Walter Dean Myers, *Crystal*, 1987
   On the brink of a promising career in modeling, a 16-year-old realizes there is more than glamour to the industry and has to decide what path to choose.
Joyce Carol Thomas, *When the Nightingale Sings*, 1992
   Despite her mean-spirited foster mother's attempts to demean her, a 14-year-old girl has a song to sing and a destiny to fulfill.
Rita Williams-Garcia, *Blue Tights*, 1988
   Struggling to find friends and acceptance, a young girl born out-of-wedlock follows her mother's footsteps in her passion for dancing.

258

DIANE MCKINNEY-WHETSTONE, African American

Tumbling
(New York: William Morrow and Company, 1996)

Subject(s): Family Relations; Secrets
Age range(s): Adult
Major character(s): Noon, African American, Wife, Abuse Victim; Herbie, African American, Father, Railroad Worker; Fannie, Adoptee, Psychic, African
Time period(s): 1940s; 1950s (1940s-1950s)
Locale(s): Philadelphia, Pennsylvania

Summary: When someone leaves a baby girl on their doorstep, Noon and Herbie take her in and raise her as their own. The child grows up to be outspoken, independent, and gifted with second sight. Unable to be intimate with his wife Noon, Herbie finds comfort in the arms of a jazz singer named Ethel. Six years later another girl is left on their doorstep—Ethel's 6-year-old niece Liz. Ethel wants her to have the good Christian upbringing that she herself cannot provide. Fannie is fiercely loyal to her new sister and the two seem inseparable. For years Ethel's only contact with Liz is the money she sends her every month. Over the years Liz' hate for the woman who abandoned her grows, even as Fannie tries to convince her she was always loved. When their community is threatened by the planned construction of a road, many members sell out even though Fannie's sight tells her there will be no road. Finally, it is the people of the community who pull together and begin to heal themselves and their neighborhood.

About this book: Debut novel.

Other books you might like:
Doris Jean Austin, *After the Garden*, 1987
   The novel portrays a woman caught between her strict grandmother and the free-spirited love of her life and his family in the urban north of the 50s.
David Bradley, *South Street*, 1975
   A stranger appears at Lightnin' Ed's Bar, where the lives of local preachers, hustlers and hoodlums intersect.
Devorah Major, *An Open Weave*, 1995
   This richly textured story portrays a blind grandmother who weaves astonishing cloths, her epileptic visionary daughter, and strong-willed granddaughter.
Rosalyn McMillan, *Knowing*, 1996
   A woman tries to cope with illness and struggles to start her own business despite her husband's lack of support.

259

PATRICIA C. MCKISSACK, African American
FREDRICK L. MCKISSACK, Illustrator, Caucasian
JOHN THOMPSON, Illustrator, Caucasian

Christmas in the Big House, Christmas in the Quarters
(New York: Scholastic Inc., 1994)

Story type: Young Readers
Subject(s): Historical; Race Relations; Christmas
Age range(s): Grades 3 and Up

Time period(s): 1850s (1859)
Locale(s): Virginia (rural plantation)

Summary: Set in Virginia region where the first American Christmas was observed in the Jamestown Colony and many of the present day holiday traditions originated, the book relates events in the plantation lives of slave owners and their servants during the Christmas holiday of 1859. The story depicts the "last Yuletide celebration before the Southern Rebellion." The narrator brings to life holiday revelers in the slave owner's Big House where there is plenty of food and warm hospitality, and in the slave quarters where people are cramped in one-room cabins with dirt floors. When the holiday festivities come to a close, those in the Big House and in the Quarters anticipate the different lives the new year will bring.

About this book: Contains references and a bibliography

Awards the book has won:
Coretta Scott King Award, 1995
NCSS-CBC Notable Children's Book, 1994

Other books by the same author:
A Million Fish—More or Less, 1992
Nettie Jo's Friends, 1989
Mirandy and Brother Wind, 1988
Monkey-Monkey's Trick, 1988
Flossie and the Fox, 1986

Other books you might like:
Virginia Hamilton, *The Bells of Christmas*, 1989
    In this historic account of Christmas 1890, a 12-year-old boy and his family prepare for the Great Day.
Joyce Hansen, *Out from This Place*, 1988
    The plight of a young girl as she and her loved ones run away from slavery and what becomes of them when freedom arrives and the Civil War ends.
Joyce Hansen, *Which Way Freedom?*, 1986
    Unable to read or write, a youngster escapes slavery and when he joins the Union Army he vows to return to rescue the friends he left behind.
Connie Porter, *Addy's Surprise: A Christmas Story*, 1993
    A young girl and her mother prepare for Christmas without the rest of the family; they don't have much, but they get the best gift of all.
Harriette Gillem Robinet, *If You Please, President Lincoln*, 1995
    Having escaped slavery on Christmas Day in 1863, a 14-year-old joins a group of former slaves on their way to an island off the coast of Haiti.

260

PATRICIA C. MCKISSACK, African American
RACHEL ISADORA, Illustrator, Caucasian

Flossie and the Fox
(New York: Dial Books for Young Readers, 1986)

Story type: Young Readers
Subject(s): Folk Tales; Animals
Age range(s): Grades 2-4
Major character(s): Flossie Finley, Child, African American
Time period(s): Indeterminate Past

Locale(s): Tennessee (rural)

Summary: Young Flossie's grandmother gives her a basket of fresh eggs to take to a neighbor. She warns Flossie a fox is on the loose who loves eggs and has been scaring the neighbor's chickens and their hunting dogs have been unable to catch him. Flossie has never seen a fox and she heeds her grandmother's warning that he is quick and sly. When Flossie meets the fox, she proves to be more sly than he is.

Awards the book has won:
School Library Journal Best Book of the Year, 1986

Other books by the same author:
A Million Fish. . .More Or Less, 1992
Nettie Jo's Friends, 1989
Mirandy and Brother Wind, 1988
Monkey-Monkey's Trick, 1988

Other books you might like:
Ashley Bryan, *The Cat's Purr*, 1985
    The West Indies folktale of the Cat and the Rat who were once friends living next to each other until an incident ended their friendship.
Percival Everett, *The One That Got Away*, 1992
    Western tale of a group of cowboys rounding up ones into a corral and when one jumps the fence what happens when they go searching for it.
Angela Johnson, *Julius*, 1993
    Her granddaddy surprises a child by bringing her her very own pig from Alaska and she shares things she learns with her friends.
Walter Dean Myers, *Mr. Monkey and the Gotcha Bird: An Original Tale*, 1984
    Caught by the Gotcha Bird and afraid of being eaten, a monkey uses his wits to outsmart the bird until he is no longer in danger.
John Steptoe, *Mufaro's Beautiful Daughters: An African Tale*, 1987
    The folktale of two young African sisters appearing before the King so he can choose the one he wants to become his wife the Queen.

261

PATRICIA C. MCKISSACK, African American
DENA SCHUTZER, Illustrator

A Million Fish. . .More or Less
(New York: Alfred A. Knopf, Inc., 1992)

Story type: Young Readers
Subject(s): Fishing; Storytelling
Age range(s): Grades 1-3
Major character(s): Hugh Thomas, Child, African American
Time period(s): 1990s
Locale(s): Jackson Pointe (Fictional city)

Summary: Fishing in Bayou Clapateaux one morning young Hugh is greeted by Papa-Daddy and Elder Abbajon. They recall for him their weird adventures in the bayou and then drift off into the fog. At the end of the day he arrives at Papa-Daddy and Elder Abbajon's houseboat with just three fish and his tale of catching "more or less" a million fish.

Other books by the same author:
Nettie Jo's Friends, 1989
Mirandy and Brother Wind, 1988
Monkey-Monkey's Trick, 1988
Flossie and the Fox, 1986

Other books you might like:
Ashley Bryan, *The Story of Lightning & Thunder*, 1993
  A West African folktale about Ma Sheep Thunder and her disobedient Son Ram Lightning who caused them to be banished from the earth to the sky.
Pat Cummings, *Petey Moroni's Camp Runamok Diary*, 1992
  At a two-week summer camp a young boy and his friends try catching the raccoon they've discovered has been stealing their food.
Percival Everett, *The One That Got Away*, 1992
  Western tale of a group of cowboys rounding up ones into a corral and when one jumps the fence what happens when they go searching for it.
Angela Johnson, *Julius*, 1993
  Her granddaddy surprises a child by bringing her her very own pig from Alaska and she shares things she learns with her friends.
Herschel Johnson, *A Visit to the Country*, 1989
  In the country at his grandparents a child discovers a baby bird, feeds him as he grows and learns to fly, and later returns him to the wild.

262

PATRICIA C. MCKISSACK, African American
JERRY PINKNEY, Illustrator, African American

Mirandy and Brother Wind
(New York: Alfred A. Knopf, 1988)

Story type: Young Readers
Subject(s): Folk Tales; Contests; Dancing
Age range(s): Grades 2-4
Major character(s): Mirandy, Child, African American
Time period(s): Indeterminate Past
Locale(s): United States (unidentified rural location)

Summary: The junior cakewalk dance is coming and Mirandy wishes Brother Wind would be her partner so she'd be sure to win the contest. She asks grandmama Beasley and neighbors how to catch the wind and none of them has an answer. Mr. Jessup at the corner store suggests how she can catch the wind but when she tries it the wind just breezes away. She goes to the conjure woman Mis Poinsettia for advice. With only a few hours before her first cakewalk contest Mirandy desperately traps the wind in the barn's henhouse. Arriving at the dance and learning Orlinda has refused to be her friend Ezel's dance partner Mirandy says they are going to win the contest. She rushes to the barn to make a wish to the captured Brother Wind. For weeks afterwards people were talking about how she and Ezel won the cakewalk contest, as grandmama Beasley said looking like they were dancing with the wind.

About this book: Inspired by the historic cakewalk dance of American slaves

Awards the book has won:
Coretta Scott King Award, 1989

Caldecott Honor Book, 1989

Other books by the same author:
A Million Fish. . .More or Less, 1992
Nettie Jo's Friends, 1989
Monkey-Monkey's Trick, 1988
Flossie and the Fox, 1986

Other books you might like:
Lucille Clifton, *Three Wishes*, 1974
  Finding a shiny penny in the snow she thinks is lucky a young girl makes three wishes all of which happen convincing her to believe in magic.
Eloise Greenfield, *Africa Dream*, 1977
  Dreaming she has crossed the ocean to long-ago Africa a child shops in the marketplace, reads with magic eyes, and is welcomed by relatives.
Angela Johnson, *Shoes Like Miss Alice's*, 1995
  Her babysitter shows a child a good time with her different pairs of shoes for dancing, walking, napping, and when they sit drawing barefooted.
Phil Mendez, *The Black Snowman*, 1989
  A magic kente cloth helps a boy learn a lesson in self-respect and pride in his heritage while saving his younger brother from a fire.
Faith Ringgold, *Aunt Harriet's Underground Railroad in the Sky*, 1992
  Flying in the sky a sister and her younger brother discovering the underground railroad to freedom must retrace its route to be reunited.

263

PATRICIA C. MCKISSACK, African American
PAUL MEISEL, Illustrator

Monkey-Monkey's Trick
(New York: Random House, 1988)

Story type: Young Readers
Subject(s): Animals; Folk Tales
Age range(s): Grades 1-3
Time period(s): 1980s
Locale(s): Africa (unidentified city)

Summary: Monkey-Monkey needs a new house before the rainy season. He asks his animal friends to help him but everyone is busy. Monkey-Monkey starts building his house alone when along comes hyena who says he will help. Knowing the hyena is full of tricks Monkey-Monkey refuses. Working all day on his house Monkey-Monkey does not get very far and so he accepts the help of a beautiful creature in exchange for a pot of stew. Monkey-Monkey's house is finally built but only after tricks and spells and more than one pot of stew.

About this book: Based on an African folktale.

Other books by the same author:
A Million Fish. . .More or Less, 1992
Nettie Jo's Friends, 1989
Mirandy and Brother Wind, 1988
Flossie and the Fox, 1986

Other books you might like:

Ashley Bryan, *The Story of Lightning & Thunder*, 1993
   A West African folktale about Ma Sheep Thunder and her
   disobedient Son Ram Lightning who caused them to be
   banished from the earth to the sky.
Ashley Bryan, *The Cat's Purr*, 1985
   The West Indies folktale of the Cat and the Rat who were
   once friends living along side one another and the incident
   which ended their friendship.
Percival Everett, *The One That Got Away*, 1992
   Western tale of a group of cowboys rounding up ones into
   a corral and when one jumps the fence what happens when
   they go searching for it.
Walter Dean Myers, *Mr. Monkey and the Gotcha Bird: An
   Original Tale*, 1984
   Caught by the Gotcha Bird and afraid of being eaten a
   monkey uses his wits to outsmart the bird until he is no
   longer in danger.
John Steptoe, *Mufaro's Beautiful Daughters: An African
   Tale*, 1987
   The folktale of two young African sisters appearing before
   the King so he can choose the one he wants to become his
   wife the Queen.

264

PATRICIA C. MCKISSACK, African American
SCOTT COOK, Illustrator

Nettie Jo's Friends

(New York: Alfred A. Knopf, 1989)

Story type: Young Readers
Subject(s): Animals; Dolls and Dollhouses
Age range(s): Grades 1-3
Major character(s): Nettie Jo, Child, Cousin, African American
Time period(s): Indeterminate Past
Locale(s): Briarsville, Fictional Country

Summary: The wedding is tomorrow and Nettie Jo is to be
flower girl. Mama puts the finishing touches on her dress
when Nettie Jo says she wants Annie Mae, her doll, to go to
the wedding too. Mama says the doll is to old and scraggly-
looking. Nettie Jo convinces mama to let her take Annie Mae
if the doll has a new dress but the problem is no one has time
to make the dress and Nettie Jo can't find sewing needle to do
it herself. Nettie Jo goes off looking everywhere when she
comes upon a rabbit and asks for her help. Instead of helping
her the rabbit hurries away. The exact same thing happens to
Nettie Jo when she comes up on a Fox and a Panther needing
her help. Disappointed, she and Annie Mae head back home.
It seems certain Nettie Jo won't be going to the wedding since
she can't take her best friend. Later that night she hears a big
racket and along comes the rabbit, the fox and the panther to
give her the sewing needle she needs. Hugging her doll, Annie
Mae Nettie Jo hums "here comes the bride."

Other books by the same author:

A Million Fish. . .More or Less, 1992
Mirandy and Brother Wind, 1988
Monkey-Monkey's Trick, 1988
Flossie and the Fox, 1986

Other books you might like:

Ashley Bryan, *The Story of Lightning & Thunder*, 1993
   A West African folktale about Ma Sheep Thunder and her
   disobedient Son Ram Lightning who caused them to be
   banished from the earth to the sky.
Ashley Bryan, *The Cat's Purr*, 1985
   The West Indies folktale of the Cat and the Rat who were
   once friends living along side one another and the incident
   which ended their friendship.
Valerie Flournoy, *The Best Time of Day*, 1978
   A child with a busy day of activities ahead with his mom,
   babysitter, friends, and relatives, looks forward to his
   daddy getting home from work.
Angela Johnson, *Julius*, 1993
   Her granddaddy surprises a child by bringing her her very
   own pig from Alaska and she shares things she learns with
   her friends.
John Steptoe, *Mufaro's Beautiful Daughters: An African
   Tale*, 1987
   The folktale of two young African sisters appearing before
   the King so he can choose the one he wants to become his
   wife the Queen.

265

REGINALD MCKNIGHT, African American

I Get on the Bus

(Boston: Little, Brown and Company, 1990)

Story type: Adult
Subject(s): Africa; Self-Perception
Age range(s): Adult
Major character(s): Evan Norris, Volunteer, African Ameri-
   can; Wanda Wright, Psychologist, African American; Am-
   inata Gueye, Student, African
Time period(s): 1990s (1990)
Locale(s): Senegal

Summary: Evan joins the Peace Corps to avoid any real
decisions at home. He goes to Senegal but quits after three
months and begins to drift in and out of feverish "trips on the
bus." During this time he tries to sort out his feelings about
two very different women in his life—Wanda, a psychologist
in America and Aminata, an African student from Senegal.
He gets involved in an African intrigue where he tries to
figure out who he can trust. He also hopes to discover the truth
before it is too late.

About this book: This is the author's debut novel.

Other books you might like:

Melvin Dixon, *Trouble the Water*, 1989
   A young man returns home after twenty years in a plot of
   revenge between his grandmother and his father.
Tananarive Due, *The Between*, 1995
   A man endures nightmares and his sense of reality wavers
   as he desperately tries to protect his family from the
   psychotic who stalks them.
Louis Edwards, *Ten Seconds*, 1991
   This story is about the memories in a young man's life as
   he anticipates his future as a husband and father, and
   reflects on the family secret he has kept.

John Edgar Wideman, *Philadelphia Fire*, 1990
  A self-exiled writer returns to Philadelphia to investigate a
  police bombing and the killing of adults and children.
Dennis Williams, *Crossover*, 1992
  This story relates the events in the life of a young man
  during the Civil Rights era. He becomes a reluctant activist
  and he has an interracial affair.

266

TERRY MCMILLAN, African American

Disappearing Acts

(New York: Washington Square Press, 1989)

Story type: Adult
Subject(s): Interpersonal Relations
Age range(s): Adult
Major character(s): Zora Banks, Epileptic, Singer (song-
  writer), African American; Franklin Swift, Construction
  Worker, African American, Alcoholic (single)
Time period(s): 1980s
Locale(s): Brooklyn, New York

Summary: Although hardworking and skillful, Franklin has
trouble finding steady employment. His self-confidence is
undermined, putting a strain on his new relationship with
Zora. Zora's musical career is ready to take off. She tries
being patient with Franklin, but after their son is born she
finds she has been strained to the limit.

Other books by the same author:
Waiting to Exhale, 1992
Mama, 1987 (debut novel)

Other books you might like:
Connie Briscoe, *Sisters and Lovers*, 1994
  This contemporary story is about the lives and struggles of
  three sisters and the men they become involved with.
Bebe Moore Campbell, *Brothers and Sisters*, 1994
  This contemporary account of a career woman's life shows
  her attempt to climb the business ladder as she maintains a
  social life and her relationships with the people around her.
Nelson George, *Urban Romance*, 1993
  This contemporary story tells the relationship of a young
  couple brought together by mutual friends as they experience love and heartbreak.
Brenda Lane Richardson, *Chesapeake Song*, 1993
  Two successful people unable to see that problems in their
  marriage mirror those of their parents come to learn the
  importance of love.

267

TERRY MCMILLAN, African American

How Stella Got Her Groove Back

(New York: Viking, 1996)

Subject(s): Independence; Interpersonal Relations; Love
Age range(s): Adult
Major character(s): Stella Payne, Banker (investment analyst),
  Divorced Person, African American; Winston Shake-

speare, Hotel Worker, Jamaican; Quincy Payne, 11-Year-
Old, Student, African American
Time period(s): 1990s (1995)
Locale(s): Negril, Jamaica; Alamo, California (San Francisco
  Bay area)

Summary: While her son Quincy is away in Colorado visiting
his dad, Stella, a successful analyst for an investment banking
firm, decides on the spur of the moment to take a vacation in
Jamaica. Her practial sister Angela thinks she is out of her
mind while her other sister Vanessa applauds her at finally
doing something to liven up her life. Once in Jamaica, Stella
enjoys the resort activities at the Castle Beach Negril and is
enchanted by Winston, a young Jamaican she meets one
morning at breakfast. He rekindles in her feelings she had
almost forgotten existed, and makes her feel better than she
has in years. Her only problem is that he's half her age, a fact
that doesn't seem to bother him in the least. Her vacation
over, Stella returns to California and discovers that her job has
been eliminated but to her surprise she feels relieved. Maybe
this is the nudge she needs to get off the corporate fast track
and get back into textile art. During all this, Stella can't get
Winston out of her mind and people are remarking on how
well and happy she looks. Following another quick trip to
Jamaica, this time with Quincy and his cousin, Stella sends
Winston a ticket to visit her in California. He makes her
happy, encourages her to be herself, and just loves her—now
the problem is that his visit may not be long enough.

Other books by the same author:
Waiting to Exhale, 1992
Disappearing Acts, 1989
Mama, 1987 (debut novel)

Other books you might like:
Connie Briscoe, *Sisters and Lovers*, 1994
  This is a contemporary story about the lives and struggles
  of three sisters and the men with whom they become
  involved.
Bebe Moore Campbell, *Brothers and Sisters*, 1994
  This contemporary account describes the life of a career
  woman as she climbs the business ladder and maintains a
  social life.
E. Lynn Harris, *And This Too Shall Pass*, 1996
  The lives of a rookie quarterback, a female sportscaster, a
  gay journalist, and a lawyer intersect when the quarterback
  is falsely accused of assault.
David Haynes, *Somebody Else's Mama*, 1995
  This novel describes the trials and tribulations of a young
  woman faced with the care of her ill and aging mother-in-
  law with little help from her family.
Al Young, *Seduction by Light*, 1988
  A psychic domestic shares her wry observations and spiritual realizations after an earthquake destroys her home in
  1980's Santa Monica.
Toni Morrison, *Sula*, 1973
  A friendship evolves between two girls that first sustains
  and then injures as they become women and freedom
  clashes with convention.
Cherry Muhanji, *Her*, 1990
  A young light-skinned woman falls into "the life" of
  1950's Detroit and finds a strength in herself and the
  women around her in order to survive.

Gloria Naylor, *Women of Brewster Place*, 1982
  In this novel, seven women and their stories come alive on the dead-end street of Brewster Place, and what brings them together in their own redemption.

268

TERRY MCMILLAN, African American

Mama

(New York: Washington Square Press, 1987)

Subject(s): Family Relations; Loneliness
Age range(s): Adult
Major character(s): Mildred Peacock, Housekeeper, Mother, African American; Freda Peacock, Writer, Alcoholic, African American
Time period(s): 20th century (1965-1985)
Locale(s): Point Haven, Michigan; Los Angeles, California

Summary: In spite of unsteady employment, Mildred does her best to provide for her five children. She always insists that things are to be clean and look respectable even if they are a bit worn. When her eldest daughter, Freda, moves to California looking for a better life, most of the family soon follows. Mildred weathers their experiences with college, love, drugs, jail, marriage and children before finally returning to Point Haven to take care of her ailing father.

About this book: This is the author's debut novel.

Where it's reviewed:
Publishers Weekly, December 6, 1993, page 70

Awards the book has won:
American Book Award, 1987

Other books by the same author:
Waiting to Exhale, 1992
Disappearing Acts, 1989

Other books you might like:
Connie Porter, *All-Bright Court*, 1991
  A young boy, who lives near a steel mill and attends a private school, learns a great deal from his family and neighbors' love and commitment to life.
Linda Raymond, *Rocking the Babies*, 1994
  Two elderly women volunteer to be hospital care givers to drug exposed babies. Both have secret reasons for being there.
Alice Walker, *The Color Purple*, 1982
  Abused by her father and then by her husband, a woman finds love with her husband's lover and discovers a sense of her own identity and self-worth.

269

TERRY MCMILLAN, African American

Waiting to Exhale

(New York: Viking Penguin, 1992)

Story type: Adult
Subject(s): Friendship; Interpersonal Relations
Age range(s): Adult

Major character(s): Bernadine Harris, Accountant, Spouse, African American; Savannah Jackson, Businesswoman, Single Mother, African American; Gloria Matthews, Businesswoman, African American
Time period(s): 1990s (1990)
Locale(s): Phoenix, Arizona

Summary: The lives and friendships of four distinctive women come to life in this story of female camaraderie. The heroines, Bernadine, Savannah, Gloria and Robin, laugh, cry and support one another while they each look for the man of their dreams. This story reveals the strengths and vulnerabilities of women searching for fulfillment and happiness in their lives.

About this book: This story was made into a motion picture.

Where it's reviewed:
Publishers Weekly, October 10, 1994, page 68
Belles Lettres, Fall 1992, page 56
Essence, October 1992, page 77
New York Times Book Review, November 3, 1993, page 33
School Library Journal, November 1992, page 142

Other books by the same author:
Disappearing Acts, 1989
Mama, 1987 (debut novel)

Other books you might like:
Connie Briscoe, *Sisters and Lovers*, 1994
  This contemporary story is about the lives and struggles of three sisters and the men they become involved with.
Bebe Moore Campbell, *Brothers and Sisters*, 1994
  This contemporary account of a career woman's life shows her attempt to climb the business ladder as she maintains a social life, and relationships with the people around her.
Nelson George, *Urban Romance*, 1993
  This contemporary story tells the relationship of a young couple brought together by mutual friends as they experience love and heartbreak.
Sandra Kitt, *All Good Things*, 1984
  This story tells of a romantic triangle involving a young career woman surviving a divorce and making a new life for herself when her ex-husband returns.
Brenda Lane Richardson, *Chesapeake Song*, 1993
  Even though two successful people are unable to see that their marital problems mirror those of their parents, they come to learn the importance of love.
Eric Jerome Dickey, *Sister, Sister*, 1996
  Contemporary account of three women, the men in their lives, and the friendship that sustains the ups and downs of their relationships.

270

ANGELA SHELF MEDEARIS, African American
NANCY POYDAR, Illustrator

The Adventures of Sugar and Junior

(New York: Holiday House, 1995)

Story type: Young Readers
Subject(s): Friendship; Neighbors and Neighborhoods
Age range(s): Grades 1-2

Major character(s): Santiago Antonio ''Junior'' Remirez Jr., Child, Neighbor, Hispanic; Sugar, Child, Neighbor, African American
Time period(s): 1990s
Locale(s): United States (unidentified city)

Summary: When a new family moves into his apartment complex, young Junior Ramirez introduces himself to Sugar Johnson. Becoming friends, the two share many exploits: playing basketball, baking cookies, going to the movies, and buying ice cream cones.

Other books by the same author:
Treemonisha, 1996
Poppa's New Pants, 1995
Too Much Talk, 1995
The Singing Man, 1994

Other books you might like:
Lucille Clifton, *The Boy Who Didn't Believe in Spring*, 1973
Everyone says spring is coming and a youngster and his pal don't believe them, so they go searching for evidence.
Lucille Clifton, *Everett Anderson's Friend*, 1976
Hoping he will have some new guys to play with when a family moves in the building a young boy learns to be friends with the new girl next door.
Lucille Clifton, *My Friend Jacob*, 1980
A young boy shares special times with his neighbor and best friend, a mentally handicapped older boy he plays ball with and helps to remember things.
Angela Johnson, *The Girl Who Wore Snakes*, 1993
A girl thinks snakes are beautiful and one day she finds someone else who thinks so, too.
Dolores Johnson, *The Best Bug to Be*, 1992
A child in a school play is disappointed being a bumblebee until she perfects her part and on the night of the play gets the most applause.

271

ANGELA SHELF MEDEARIS, African American
JOHN WARD, Illustrator, African American

Poppa's New Pants
(New York: Holiday House, 1995)

Story type: Young Readers
Subject(s): Clothes; Family Life
Age range(s): Grades 2-3
Major character(s): George, Child, Nephew, African American
Time period(s): Indeterminate Past
Locale(s): United States (rural)

Summary: Young George lives with his grandma Tiny and Poppa her husband on their farm. When Big Mama and aunt Viney, come to visit, George is relegated to a pallet in the kitchen. Awakened in the night by noises in the spooky kitchen, George hides under his covers when he thinks he sees a ghost. When the voice of grandma Tiny awakes him the next morning to get dressed for church he and the others get a funny surprise.

Other books by the same author:
Treemonisha, 1996

The Adventures of Sugar and Junior, 1995
Too Much Talk, 1995
The Singing Man, 1994

Other books you might like:
Donald Crews, *Bigmama's*, 1991
Recalls the summer exploits of a youngster in the 1940s when he, his brother, sisters, and parents visit his grandparents in the country.
Eloise Greenfield, *Grandpa's Face*, 1988
Seeing her beloved grandpa's face turn angry while he practices his lines in a play frightens a child until he reassures her.
Elizabeth Fitzgerald Howard, *Mac and Marie and the Train Toss Surprise*, 1993
A 9-year-old waits beside the railroad tracks with his young sister for their uncle working in the dining car to toss them a special gift.
Angela Johnson, *When I Am Old with You*, 1990
A young child depicts all the things he wants to do with his granddaddy when he gets old and how they will rest together in their rocking chairs.
Herschel Johnson, *A Visit to the Country*, 1989
In the country at his grandparents a child discovers a baby bird, feeds him as he grows and learns to fly, and later returns him to the wild.

272

ANGELA SHELF MEDEARIS, African American
TEREA SHAFFER, Illustrator, African American

The Singing Man
(New York: Holiday House, 1994)

Story type: Young Readers
Subject(s): Africa; Folk Tales; Musicians
Age range(s): Grades 1-4
Major character(s): Banzar, Musician, Son, African American
Time period(s): Indeterminate Past
Locale(s): Lagos, Nigeria

Summary: In their manhood ceremonies three brothers in a small village announce to their people what they have chosen as their life's work. Swanga desires to become a farmer working in the fields with his father, while Taki wants to become a blacksmith selling his wares in the marketplace. But Banzar who loves music, wants to become a musician. His choice is unacceptable and he is told he must leave the village. On the road Banzar meets an old blind man, Sholo, who travels from village to village singing about the history of African people. As they travel together, Banzar learns everything Sholo has to teach. When Sholo dies Banzar sadly stops playing his flute until he realizes only he knows what Sholo has taught and he must not let it vanish. Going from town to town as a praise singer Banzar becomes very famous, even becoming the King's personal musician. Seeing his brothers in the marketplace he speaks to them but they no longer recognize him. Arriving again with his procession of musicians and servants, Banzar entertains and surprises everyone when he reveals his identity.

About this book: Based on a folktale told by the West African Yoruba people in Nigeria.

Other books by the same author:
Treemonisha, 1996
The Adventures of Sugar and Junior, 1995
Poppa's New Pants, 1995
Too Much Talk, 1995

Other books you might like:
Elizabeth Fitzgerald Howard, *Papa Tells Chita a Story*, 1995
    A child asks her beloved papa to tell her the story of when he was the bravest soldier and carried the message and won the war.
Patricia C. McKissack, *Mirandy and Brother Wind*, 1988
    Folk tale of a young girl, desperately wanting to win her first cakewalk dance contest, who makes a wish to the wind and dances with her friend.
Phil Mendez, *The Black Snowman*, 1989
    A magic kente cloth helps a boy learn a lesson in self-respect and pride in his heritage while saving his younger brother from a fire.
Walter Dean Myers, *The Golden Serpent*, 1980
    The fable of a wise man living with a young boy in the mountains of India whom the King summons to solve the mystery of the golden serpent.
Brian Pinkney, *Max Found Two Sticks*, 1994
    A young boy uses two twigs to play rhythms on buckets, hatboxes, bottles, and garbage cans until a drummer tosses him a pair of drum sticks.

273

ANGELA SHELF MEDEARIS, African American
STEFANO VITALE, Illustrator, Italian

Too Much Talk
(Cambridge, Mass.: Candlewick Press, 1995)

Story type: Young Readers
Subject(s): Folk Tales; Fables
Age range(s): Grades 1-2
Time period(s): Indeterminate Past
Locale(s): Ghana

Summary: A traditional West African tale is retold of a farmer who is surprised hearing his yam and his dog talk to him. Running away up and down the hills screaming in shock the farmer meets a fisherman who asks why he is running in the heat of the day. Telling his story the fisherman says it can't be true, but then they get surprised when they hear his fish talk. This cumulative tale ends when all the characters run to the chief's house telling their story. The chief sends them on their way saying they are talking foolish, but when his chair speaks up and agrees, the chief jumps up screaming and has never been seen again.

About this book: This story is based on a folktale from Accra in Ghana, West Africa.

Other books by the same author:
Treemonisha, 1996
The Adventures of Sugar and Junior, 1995
Poppa's New Pants, 1995
The Singing Man, 1994

Other books you might like:
Ashley Bryan, *The Story of Lightning & Thunder*, 1993
    A West African folktale about Ma Sheep Thunder and her disobedient Son Ram Lightning who caused them to be banished from the earth to the sky.
Ashley Bryan, *The Cat's Purr*, 1985
    The West Indies folktale of the Cat and the Rat who were once friends living alongside one another and the incident which ended their friendship.
Percival Everett, *The One That Got Away*, 1992
    Western tale of a group of cowboys rounding up "ones" into a corral and when one jumps the fence what happens as they go searching for it.
Patricia C. McKissack, *Monkey-Monkey's Trick*, 1988
    An African folktale of a monkey who discovers he is being tricked by a hyena and plays his own trick on the hyena to get his new house built.
Walter Dean Myers, *The Golden Serpent*, 1980
    The fable of a wise man living with a young boy in the mountains of India whom the King summons to solve the mystery of the golden serpent.

274

PHIL MENDEZ, African American
CAROLE BYARD, Illustrator, African American

The Black Snowman
(New York: Scholastic Inc., 1989)

Story type: Young Readers
Subject(s): Brothers; Self-Respect; Magic
Age range(s): Grades 1-3
Major character(s): Jacob Miller, Child, Brother, African American
Time period(s): 1980s
Locale(s): United States (unidentified city)

Summary: Jacob awakens from a dream in which a storyteller in Africa wraps himself in a magic kente cloth, which he keeps even after he is sold into slavery. Entering the kitchen the next morning, Jacob nixes his brother's plans to Christmas shop by telling him they're too poor. He begins to rage about being black, feeling that everything about it is bad. Later, the brothers build a snowman from the trampled snow that's turned black. Using steel wool for hair, buttons for eyes, and a funny old hat, Peewee discovers a colorful cloth in the trash that will be perfect on their black snowman. It's the magic kente cloth. When the snowman comes to life, he challenges Jacob's idea that black is bad and has him mesmerized with new thoughts about being black. Next morning, Peewee comes up with a plan to raise some money for Christmas; they'll collect cans from the building across the street. After he's gone, Jacob hears an explosion and sees that fire has broken out in the building where Peewee went. On the street the snowman appears at Jacob's side and together they find Peewee. The snowman wraps the brothers in the protective magic of the kente and, while he melts, majestic African warriors appear showing Jacob the way to safety.

About this book: Debut novel.

Other books you might like:

Lucille Clifton, *All Us Come Cross the Water*, 1973

Wanting to answer his teacher's question about where his people came from a boy asks his family and a neighbor before speaking up in class.

Lucille Clifton, *Three Wishes*, 1974

Finding a shiny penny in the snow she thinks is lucky a young girl makes three wishes all of which happen convincing her to believe in magic.

Eloise Greenfield, *Africa Dream*, 1977

Dreaming she has crossed the ocean to long-ago Africa a child shops in the marketplace, reads with magic eyes, and is welcomed by relatives.

Faith Ringgold, *Aunt Harriet's Underground Railroad in the Sky*, 1992

Flying in the sky a sister and her younger brother discovering the underground railroad to freedom must retrace its route to be reunited.

275

LOUISE MERIWETHER, African American

Fragments of the Ark

(New York: Pocket Books, 1994)

Subject(s): Civil War; Historical
Age range(s): Adult
Major character(s): Peter Mango, Sea Captain, Slave, African American; Rain Mango, Mother, Slave, African American
Time period(s): 1860s (1861-1868)
Locale(s): Charleston, South Carolina

Summary: Peter organizes a handful of runaway slaves and their families to steal the Confederate gunboat *Suwanee* and deliver it to the Union. As a captain in the Union Navy, Peter with his brothers-in-arms are subject to white supremacy. They are also plagued with the possibility of having to face their former slave owners as they pursue their dreams of family and freedom.

Where it's reviewed:
Publishers Weekly, January 2, 1995, page 71
School Library Journal, November 1994, page 142

Other books by the same author:
Daddy Was a Number Runner, 1970 (debut novel)

Other books you might like:

Barbara Chase-Riboud, *Echo of Lions*, 1989

Africans kidnapped aboard the schooner *Amistad* mutiny. President John Quincy Adams argues their defense before the Supreme Court.

Charles Johnson, *Middle Passage*, 1990

A young man mistakenly stows away on a slave ship bound for Africa, where he must endure storms, mutiny, and illness before the journey ends.

276

PENNY MICKELBURY, African American

Keeping Secrets

(Tallahassee: Naiad Press, 1994)

Story type: Lesbian/Contemporary; Police Procedural
Series: Gianna Maglione
Subject(s): Interpersonal Relations; Murder; Mystery and Detective Stories
Age range(s): Adult
Major character(s): M. Montgomery "Mimi" Patterson, Journalist, Lesbian, African American; Giovanna "Gianna" Maglione, Police Officer, Lesbian, Italian American; Tyler Carson, Homosexual, Journalist, Caucasian
Time period(s): 1990s (1991)
Locale(s): Washington, District of Columbia

Summary: Tyler, the city editor, assigns "Mimi," an investigative reporter, to check on a series of murders of wealthy homosexual professionals. She finds herself falling for "Gianna," the Lieutenant leading the murder investigation. As their interracial romance develops it brings them face-to-face with the killer.

About this book: This is the author's debut novel.

Where it's reviewed:
Booklist, March 15, 1994, page 1331
Bloomsbury Review, January 1994, page 23
Lambda Book Report, March 1994, page 35
Publishers Weekly, January 31, 1994, page 82

Other books by the same author:
Night Songs, 1995

Other books you might like:

Nikki Baker, *In the Game*, 1991

This debut novel begins a murder mystery series with lesbian characters.

Eleanor Taylor Bland, *Dead Time*, 1992

This debut novel begins a detective mystery series with a female heroine.

Gar Anthony Haywood, *Going Nowhere Fast*, 1994

This debut novel begins a mystery series with a wife as an amateur detective and her retired, police detective husband.

Barbara Neely, *Blanche on the Lam*, 1992

This debut novel begins a contemporary murder mystery series with an amateur detective as the heroine.

Valerie Wilson Wesley, *When Death Comes Stealing*, 1994

This debut novel begins a murder mystery series featuring an ex-policewoman who becomes a private detective.

277

PENNY MICKELBURY, African American

Night Songs

(Tallahassee: Naiad Press, 1995)

Story type: Adult; Lesbian/Contemporary
Series: Gianna Maglione
Subject(s): Interpersonal Relations; Murder; Mystery and Detective Stories

Major character(s): M. Montgomery ''Mimi'' Patterson, Journalist, Lesbian, African American; Giovanna ''Gianna'' Maglione, Police Officer, Lesbian, Italian American
Time period(s): 1990s (1995)
Locale(s): Washington, District of Columbia

Summary: Their relationship almost ended before it began when ''Mimi'' and ''Gianna'' first met and found themselves chasing the same story, one as an investigative reporter and the other as a high ranking policewoman. Now the lovers once again find themselves investigating the same crime cases, only this time their relationship is discovered by co-workers as well. ''Mimi'' at first didn't know what kind of story she might be chasing only that her two sources, street prostitutes, said it was potentially big and now they had disappeared. At police headquarters ''Gianna'' has discovered there may be a serial killer on the loose who has been hunting and killing such women for sport with a Daniel Boone type hunting knife. An eye witness account puts ''Mimi'' in danger when she comes to the rescue, and ''Gianna'' is surprised when a murder occurs so close to home.

Where it's reviewed:
Booklist, February 15, 1995, page 1063
Lambda Book Report, March 1995, page 37
Library Journal, February 1, 1995, page 103

Other books by the same author:
Keeping Secrets, 1994 (debut novel)

Other books you might like:
Nikki Baker, *In the Game*, 1991
   Debut novel in a murder mystery series with lesbian characters.
Eleanor Taylor Bland, *Dead Time*, 1992
   Debut novel in a detective mystery series with a female heroine.
Gar Anthony Haywood, *Fear of the Dark*, 1988
   Debut novel in a contemporary murder mystery series with a private detective.
Walter Mosley, *Devil in a Blue Dress*, 1990
   Debut novel in a contemporary murder mystery series with a private detective.
Valerie Wilson Wesley, *When Death Comes Stealing*, 1994
   Debut novel in a murder mystery series featuring an ex-policewoman who has become a private detective.

278

EMILY MOORE, African American

Just My Luck
(New York: E. P. Dutton, 1982)

Subject(s): Friendship; Family Relations; Mystery and Detective Stories
Age range(s): Grades 4-6
Major character(s): Olivia, 9-Year-Old, African American, Detective; Jeffrey Dingle, 9-Year-Old, Child Of Divorced Parents, African American
Time period(s): 1980s
Locale(s): New York, New York

Summary: Her big dream is to have a puppy, but 9-year-old Olivia is having no luck convincing her parents she is ready

for the responsibility. Everyone in the family except her, seems to be involved in something important. Things begin to change when she meets 9-year-old Jeffrey, her landlady's nephew. When Jeffrey starts school, Olivia is assigned to be his buddy and before long she can't get rid of him. After she embarrasses him in front of the other kids, Jeffrey avoids Olivia until his aunt's dog turns up missing and they agree to work together to find her. Olivia is hoping to get the reward so she can buy her own puppy and Jeffrey is eager to be her detective-sidekick and be friends again. Just as they think they have the dognapping mystery solved a new turn of events changes their direction and Olivia and Jeffrey have to decide how important friendship really is.

Where it's reviewed:
Booklist, March 1, 1983, page 908
Horn Book Magazine, Fall 1983, page 47
School Library Journal, January 1983, page 77

Other books by the same author:
Whose Side Are You On?, 1988
Something to Count On, 1980 (debut novel)

Other books you might like:
Sharon M. Draper, *Ziggy and the Black Dinosaurs*, 1994
   When their neighborhood playground is destroyed, four 5th grade boys start their own secret club and uncover a mysterious old box of hidden bones.
Virginia Hamilton, *The Mystery of Drear House*, 1987
   A house that was a station on the Underground Railroad has secret passageways and hidden treasure which must be saved before it is too late.
Joyce Hansen, *Yellow Bird and Me*, 1986
   Missing her best friend who has moved away, a young girl helps a classmate in elementary school overcome stage fright and discover he has dyslexia.
Walter Dean Myers, *Mojo and the Russians*, 1977
   A group of twelve-year-olds try to save their friend from a voodoo spell and discover if their neighbors are for the Russians.
Eleanora E. Tate, *The Secret of Gumbo Grove*, 1987
   A youngster upsets her community and her parents when she spreads stories she's heard about the town ancestors buried in the church cemetery.

279

EMILY MOORE, African American

Something to Count On
(New York: E.P. Dutton, 1980)

Subject(s): Divorce; Family Relations; School Life
Age range(s): Grades 4-7
Major character(s): Lorraine Maybe, 10-Year-Old, Artist, African American
Time period(s): 1970s
Locale(s): New York, New York (the Bronx)

Summary: Since Lorraine's dad has moved to Queens, it seems he is always breaking his promises to come and get Lorraine and her little brother Jason to spend the weekend. Lorraine gets in trouble at school for fighting even though she didn't start it. The bright spot is her new fifth grade teacher,

Mr. Hamilton, who likes Lorraine and likes the drawings she does.

About this book: Debut novel.

Where it's reviewed:
Horn Book Magazine, June 1980, page 301
Kirkus Reviews, July 1, 1980, page 837
Publishers Weekly, April 11, 1980, page 77
Reading Teacher, March 1981, page 735
School Library Journal, October 1980, page 149

Other books by the same author:
Whose Side Are You On?, 1988
Just My Luck, 1982

Other books you might like:
Candy Dawson Boyd, *Chevrolet Saturdays*, 1993
Struggling with the divorce of his parents and accepting his new stepfather, a young boy has trouble in school and makes mistakes he regrets.
Eloise Greenfield, *Talk about a Family*, 1978
Distraught about her parent's breaking up, a youngster comes to realize how families differ and the importance of her younger sister and older brothers.
Camille Yarbrough, *The Shimmershine Queens*, 1989
A fifth grade girl learns to stand up for herself and make her own dreams come true when a new teacher comes to her school.

280

EMILY MOORE, African American

Whose Side Are You On?

(New York: Farrar Straus Giroux, 1988)

Subject(s): Friendship; Peer Pressure; School Life
Age range(s): Grades 5-8
Major character(s): Barbra, 11-Year-Old, Twin, African American; T.J. Brodie, 11-Year-Old, Tutor, African American
Time period(s): 1980s
Locale(s): New York, New York

Summary: When Barbra gets a failing grade in math, her mother decides she needs a tutor. The tutor turns out to be pesky T.J., who has been teasing Barbra as long as she can remember. The two become friends and Barbra's math grades are improving when all of a sudden T.J. disappears and nobody will tell her where he's gone. After some investigation on her own Barbra discovers T.J.'s whereabouts and accuses his grandfather of sending him away. When she finds out more about it, Barbra learns that things are not always what they seem.

Where it's reviewed:
Booklist, February 1, 1990, page 1098
Horn Book Magazine, January 1989, page 73
Kirkus Reviews, July 15, 1988, page 1062
Publishers Weekly, September 14, 1990, page 129
School Library Journal, October 1988, page 147

Other books by the same author:
Just My Luck, 1982
Something to Count On, 1980 (debut novel)

Other books you might like:
Candy Dawson Boyd, *Chevrolet Saturdays*, 1993
Struggling with the divorce of his parents and accepting his new stepfather, a young boy has trouble in school and makes mistakes he regrets.
Virginia Hamilton, *Plain City*, 1993
A 12-year-old who feels out of place, struggles to unearth her past and family history as she gradually discovers more about her long-missing father.
Walter Dean Myers, *Mojo and the Russians*, 1977
A group of twelve-year-olds try to save their friend from a voodoo spell and try to discover if their neighbors are for the Russians.

281

TONI MORRISON, African American

Beloved

(New York: Alfred A. Knopf, 1987)

Subject(s): Family Relations; Mothers and Daughters; Slavery
Age range(s): Adult
Major character(s): Sethe Suggs, Mother, Slave, African American; Beloved, Spirit, 2-Year-Old, African American; Denver Suggs, Care Giver, Young Woman, African American
Time period(s): 19th century (1850-1874)
Locale(s): Cincinnati, Ohio; Kentucky (unidentified city)

Summary: After arriving in Ohio via the underground railroad, Sethe is followed by her former owner. She kills her two-year-old daughter rather than allow her to be returned to slavery. Her house is haunted by the baby's spirit, Beloved, who is driven out but returns as a young woman of twenty. Sethe becomes consumed with this spirit-made-flesh, and she deteriorates both physically and mentally. Denver, Sethe's living daughter, tries to provide for the family. The women of the community drive out the spirit, but it may be too late for Sethe.

About this book: The author received the Nobel Prize for Literature in 1994.

Where it's reviewed:
African American Review, Fall 1994, page 423
African American Review, Summer 1994, page 189
African American Review, Summer 1994, page 223
African American Review, Winter 1994, page 571
Critique, Winter 1995, page 96

Awards the book has won:
American Book Award, 1988
Pulitzer Prize, 1988

Other books by the same author:
Jazz, 1992
Tar Baby, 1981
Song of Solomon, 1977
Sula, 1973
The Bluest Eye, 1970 (debut novel)

Other books you might like:
Lorene Cary, *The Price of a Child*, 1995
This historical tale is about a woman who literally walks

away from slavery to freedom under her owner's furious gaze in Philadelphia during the 1850s.

J. California Cooper, *Family*, 1991

This is a young girl's narrative of her life during the plantation era of the South. Included are the events in the lives of her children and grandchildren.

Barbara Chase-Riboud, *The President's Daughter*, 1994

This work chronicles the life of Harriet Hemings, possibly the daughter of President Thomas Jefferson through an interracial affair.

Leon Forrest, *Two Wings to Veil My Face*, 1983

The Witherspoon family saga, from antebellum to contemporary times, is concluded in this last volume of the trilogy.

Dorothy West, *The Wedding*, 1995

Saga about five generations of two families with mixed race ancestry.

282

TONI MORRISON, African American

The Bluest Eye
(New York: Pocket Books, 1970)

Subject(s): Child Abuse; Loneliness; Self-Perception
Age range(s): Adult
Major character(s): Claudia MacTeer, 9-Year-Old, Sister, African American; Frieda MacTeer, 10-Year-Old, Sister, African American; Pecola Breedlove, 11-Year-Old, Abuse Victim
Time period(s): 1940s (1940-1941)
Locale(s): Lorain, Ohio

Summary: Narrated by young Claudia, this is the story of Pecola Breedlove, a girl who is convinced she is ugly because of her dark skin. Neglected and abused by her parents and picked on by other children, Pecola thinks that if only she were beautiful, if only she had lovely blue eyes, perhaps her parents wouldn't fight and someone would love her. Pecola is raped by her father, and becomes pregnant, and is suspended from school. Claudia and Frieda plant marigold seeds, believing that if they survived, Pecola's baby would be all right. But the baby comes too soon and Pecola retreats into madness with only an imaginary friend for company who tells her that her eyes are the bluest in the world.

About this book: Debut novel.

Other books by the same author:
Jazz, 1992
Beloved, 1987
Tar Baby, 1981
Song of Solomon, 1977
Sula, 1973

Other books you might like:
Cyrus Colter, *Rivers of Eros*, 1972

A woman raising her grandchildren must deal with her betrayal of her sister, her daughter's violent death, and the granddaughter she cannot reach.

Albert French, *Holly*, 1995

Involved in an interracial affair a young white girl must

flee her family and her community to find safety when she becomes pregnant.

Nettie Jones, *Mischief Makers*, 1989

Three exotically beautiful sisters of mixed race experience the world quite differently both because and in spite of their looks.

283

TONI MORRISON, African American

Jazz
(New York: Knopf, 1992)

Story type: Adult
Subject(s): Family Relations; Marriage
Age range(s): Adult
Major character(s): Violet Trace, Businesswoman, Spouse, African American; Joe Trace, Salesman, Spouse, African American; Dorcas Manfred, Student, African American
Time period(s): 1920s (1926)
Locale(s): New York, New York

Summary: This story rich in imagery and metaphor, is told from the voice of an unknown observer. The storyteller reveals events in the life of a working class couple, Violet and Joe, in the 1920s. Joe murders Dorcus, a young girl with whom he was having an affair. Traumatized by what has happened, Joe and Violet try putting their life back together.

About this book: The author received the Nobel Prize for Literature in 1994.

Where it's reviewed:
Callaloo, Spring 1995, page 451
Cressent, December 1994, page 11
Journal of American Studies, December 1994, page 423

Other books by the same author:
Beloved, 1987
Tar Baby, 1981
Song of Solomon, 1977
Sula, 1973
The Bluest Eye, 1970 (debut novel)

Other books you might like:
Gloria Naylor, *Linden Hills*, 1985

Linden Hills symbolizes success, but two boys doing odd jobs see firsthand the lust, pain, the hypocrisy, and valor of its residents.

Brenda Lane Richardson, *Chesapeake Song*, 1993

Even though two successful people are unable to see that their marital problems mirror those of their parents, they come to learn the importance of love.

John Edgar Wideman, *Reuben*, 1987

This story relates the exploits of an aged lawyer and the various clients he represents in the Pittsburgh community of Homewood during the 1980s.

284

TONI MORRISON, African American

Song of Solomon
(New York: Alfred A. Knopf, 1977)

Subject(s): Family Relations; Intergenerational Saga; Race Relations

Age range(s): Adult

Major character(s): Macon "Milkman" Dead III, Son, Traveller, African American; Macon Dead II, Father, Wealthy, African American; Pilate, Aunt, Sister, African American

Time period(s): 1950s; 1960s (1950s-1960s)

Locale(s): Midwest (southern rim of the Great Lakes)

Summary: Milkman is the son of Macon Dead, the richest black man in town who believes there is nothing more important than ownership. He hires his son to collect the rents on the properties he owns. This allows Milkman to spend time in the home of his Aunt Pilate, Macon's sister, whom he has been forbidden to see. Independ and mystical, Pilate recognizes the importance of freedom, love, integrity and responsibility, and encourages the spiritual growth of Milkman. When Macon sends his son on a journey to recover gold that Pilate supposedly abandoned years ago, he finds something far more valuable—his past and his family history.

Awards the book has won:
National Book Critics Circle, 1978

Other books by the same author:
Jazz, 1992
Beloved, 1987
Tar Baby, 1981
Sula, 1973
The Bluest Eye, 1970 (debut novel)

Other books you might like:
Helen Elaine Lee, *The Serpent's Gift*, 1994
    Children and grandchildren of two intertwined families endure hardship and triumph as they help each other remember a history beyond their knowing.
Richard Perry, *Montgomery's Children*, 1984
    Tales of people living in a small town in central New York interwoven with magic and vision, incest and murder, friendship and sacrifice.
Tina McElroy Ansa, *The Hand I Fan With*, 1996
    Contemporary story of a successful woman who finally finds—with a ghost who has been dead for 100 years—the love and companionship she was searching for.

285

TONI MORRISON, African American

Sula
(New York: Alfred A. Knopf, 1973)

Subject(s): Friendship; Human Behavior; Psychology

Age range(s): Adult

Major character(s): Nel Wright, Wife, Mother, African American; Sula Peace, Femme Fatale, Wanderer, African American

Time period(s): 20th century (1919-1965)

Locale(s): Medallion, Ohio

Summary: The story of two girls, Nel and Sula, who grow up together sharing everything—perceptions, judgements, yearnings, secrets, and even crime. Both from very different households, each seems to balance the other. When conventional Nel marries Jude, independent Sula leaves town to go to college and to travel. Returning 10 years later accompanied by a plague of robins, Sula is regarded as evil and is blamed for all the bad luck that falls upon the town. Upon her death the townspeople expect that things will change for the better, but tragedy continues to befall them and Nel realizes she has lost the strongest relationship in her life.

Other books by the same author:
Jazz, 1992
Beloved, 1987
Tar Baby, 1981
Song of Solomon, 1977
The Bluest Eye, 1970 (debut novel)

Other books you might like:
Alice Childress, *A Short Walk*, 1973
    Saga of events in the childhood and adulthood life of a woman who escapes an abusive marriage and journeys to Harlem in the 1940s.
Grace Edwards-Yearwood, *In the Shadow of the Peacock*, 1988
    A young girl strikes out in spite of her mother's fears, discovering her own voice, her own love and her part in the struggle for civil rights.
Cherry Muhanji, *Her*, 1990
    A young light-skinned woman falls into "the life" of 1950s Detroit and finds a strength in herself and the women around her necessary to her survival.
Gloria Naylor, *Linden Hills*, 1985
    Linden Hills symbolizes success, but two boys doing odd jobs see firsthand the lust and pain, the hypocrisy and valor of its residents.
Alice Walker, *The Color Purple*, 1982
    Abused by her father and then by her husband, a woman finds love with her husband's lover and discovers a sense of her own identity and self-worth.

286

TONI MORRISON, African American

Tar Baby
(New York: Alfred A. Knopf, 1981)

Subject(s): Family Relations; Interpersonal Relations

Age range(s): Adult

Major character(s): Son, Sailor, African American; Jadine, Model, Student, African American

Time period(s): 1970s

Locale(s): Caribbean (Isle des Chevaliers); Eloe, Florida; New York, New York

Summary: A life of surface calm is broken only by sudden bursts of sparring between retired, white millionaire Valerian Street and his young wife, Margaret. Sydney and Ondine, a servant couple, see to every detail in the house. Their Sorbonne-educated niece, Jadine, is intrigued by a ragged starving street man who is discovered in Margaret's closet. Attracted to each other, Jadine and the man strive to hold and understand one another, each feeling the weight of their separate worlds. She perceives his vision of reality as a threat to her freedom, and he perceives her as the classic lure, the tar baby set out to entrap him.

About this book: The author received the Nobel Prize for Literature in 1994.

Where it's reviewed:
Spectator, January 1, 1994, page 20
Dissent, Summer 1994, page 426
Modern Fiction Studies, January 1, 1994, page 20

Other books by the same author:
Jazz, 1992
Beloved, 1987
Song of Solomon, 1977
Sula, 1973
The Bluest Eye, 1970 (debut novel)

Other books you might like:
Bebe Moore Campbell, *Brothers and Sisters*, 1994
    This contemporary account of a career woman's life shows her attempt to climb the business ladder as she maintains a social life, and relationships with the people around her.
Trey Ellis, *Platitudes*, 1988
    The parallel stories created by two writers who are corresponding about their teenaged characters, and the personal relationship they develop.
Nelson George, *Urban Romance*, 1993
    This contemporary story tells the relationship of a young couple brought together by mutual friends as they experience love and heartbreak.
Terry McMillan, *Waiting to Exhale*, 1992
    This contemporary account is about the friendship of four women, their relationships with men, and their experiences with family and careers.
Brenda Lane Richardson, *Chesapeake Song*, 1993
    Even though two successful people are unable to see that their marital problems mirror those of their parents, they come to learn the importance of love.

287

WALTER MOSLEY, African American

Black Betty

(New York: W.W. Norton, 1994)

Story type: Private Detective; Adult
Series: Easy Rawlins
Subject(s): Family Relations; Murder; Mystery and Detective Stories
Age range(s): Adult
Major character(s): Ezekiel "Easy" Rawlins, African American, Detective—Private, African American; Elizabeth "Black Betty" Eady, Housekeeper, Mother, African American; Albert Cain, Father, Wealthy, Caucasian
Time period(s): 1960s (1961)
Locale(s): Los Angeles, California

Summary: Easy, a private detective, is hired to find Black Betty, housekeeper for the Cain family, who is missing after the death of her wealthy white employer. His search unveils a web of hatreds and secrets. Along the way, Easy clashes with police and is forced to protect his own family and friends, including his convict buddy and sidekick "the Mouse."

Where it's reviewed:
Booklist, January 15, 1995, page 857
Publishers Weekly, November 7, 1994, page 41
Publishers Weekly, May 29, 1995, page 82
New York Times Book Review, December 4, 1994, page 69
Bloomsbury Review, November 1994, page 3

Other books by the same author:
RL's Dream, 1995
White Butterfly, 1992 (Easy Rawlins series)
A Red Death, 1991 (Easy Rawlins series)
Devil in a Blue Dress, 1990 (debut novel, Easy Rawlins series)

Other books you might like:
Eleanor Taylor Bland, *Dead Time*, 1992
    This debut novel begins a detective mystery series with a female heroine.
Gar Anthony Haywood, *Fear of the Dark*, 1988
    This novel begins a contemporary murder mystery series with a private detective.
Gar Anthony Haywood, *Going Nowhere Fast*, 1994
    This novel begins a mystery series about an amateur detective and her retired police detective husband.
Penny Mickelbury, *Keeping Secrets*, 1994
    This debut novel begins a murder mystery series with lesbian characters.
Valerie Wilson Wesley, *When Death Comes Stealing*, 1994
    This debut novel begins a murder mystery series featuring an ex-policewoman who becomes a private detective.

288

WALTER MOSLEY, African American

Devil in a Blue Dress

(New York: W.W. Norton, 1990)

Story type: Private Detective; Adult
Series: Easy Rawlins
Subject(s): Missing Persons; Murder; Mystery and Detective Stories
Age range(s): Adult
Major character(s): Ezekiel "Easy" Rawlins, Worker, Detective—Private, African American; Daphne Monet, Abuse Victim (incest), Companion, African American (passing for white)
Time period(s): 1940s (1948)
Locale(s): Los Angeles, California

Summary: Easy, having lost his job as a factory worker and needing money for his mortgage, takes on the job of finding Daphne, a missing woman. Daphne, escaping her true identity as Ruby Hanks and her incestuous relationship with her father, has been passing for white. Easy becomes the target for the police and for the man searching for Daphne, "the devil in a blue dress." Entering the underworld to unravel the truth, Easy becomes implicated in past crimes while a string of murders occurs.

About this book: This is the author's debut novel. The book was made into a motion picture.

Where it's reviewed:
Publishers Weekly, August 28, 1995, page 111
Times Educational Supplement, December 23, 1994, page 19
Armchair Detective, Spring 1993, page 53
Village Voice Literary Supplement, October 1992, page 23

Other books by the same author:
RL's Dream, 1995
Black Betty, 1994 (Easy Rawlins series)
White Butterfly, 1992 (Easy Rawlins series)
A Red Death, 1991 (Easy Rawlins series)

Other books you might like:
Eleanor Taylor Bland, *Dead Time*, 1992
    This debut novel begins a detective mystery series with a female heroine.
Gar Anthony Haywood, *Fear of the Dark*, 1988
    This debut novel begins a contemporary murder mystery series with a private detective.
Penny Mickelbury, *Keeping Secrets*, 1994
    This debut novel begins a murder mystery series with lesbian characters.
Barbara Neely, *Blanche on the Lam*, 1992
    This debut novel begins a contemporary murder mystery series with an amateur detective as the heroine.
Valerie Wilson Wesley, *When Death Comes Stealing*, 1994
    This debut novel begins a murder mystery series featuring an ex-policewoman who becomes a private detective.

289

WALTER MOSLEY, African American

A Little Yellow Dog
(New York: W.W. Norton and Co., 1996)

Series: Easy Rawlins
Subject(s): Mystery and Detective Stories; Murder; Drugs
Age range(s): Adult
Major character(s): Ezekiel "Easy" Rawlins, Maintenance Worker, African American, Detective—Private; Idabell Turner, African American, Teacher, Animal Lover
Time period(s): 1960s (1963)
Locale(s): Los Angeles, California

Summary: Since working for two years for the Board of Education supervising the custodial crew at a high school "Easy" figures to put life in the streets behind him, but the school's new principal makes it clear he does not want "Easy" around. Coming to work early one morning "Easy" finds one of the teachers, Mrs. Idabell Turner, has locked herself in her classroom. Opening the door to him he discovers she has brought her small Chihuahua-like dog, Pharaoh, which is against school policy. Idabell explains her husband is angry with the dog and asks "Easy" to watch him for her. Following an intimate sexual episode, "Easy" agrees and takes the dog to hide it in the school's hopper room. Later, a dead body is discovered on school property. While an investigation gets underway "Easy" looks for Idabell and discovers she's left the school saying her dog's had an accident, but he still has the dog. Looking for the missing Idabell

at her home "Easy" discovers another body, which looks like the dead body at the school. The police are getting suspicious of him, Idabell is no where to be found, and the dog growls at him. "Easy" decides he'd better try to figure out what's going on and save his job. His old street smarts give "Easy" an edge as he discovers a drug connection and what a frightened Idabell fears.

Other books by the same author:
RL's Dream, 1995
Black Betty, 1994 (*Easy Rawlins Series*)
White Butterfly, 1992 (*Easy Rawlins Series*)
A Red Death, 1991 (*Easy Rawlins Series*)
Devil in a Blue Dress, 1990 (debut novel, *Easy Rawlins Series*)

Other books you might like:
Eleanor Taylor Bland, *Dead Time*, 1992
    This debut novel in a detective mystery series includes a female heroine.
Gary Hardwick, *Cold Medina*, 1996
    This debut novel features a Detroit detective heading an elite Special Crimes Unitto catch a serial killer.
Gar Anthony Haywood, *Fear of the Dark*, 1988
    This debut novel in a contemporary murder mystery series includes a private detective.
Hugh Holton, *Presumed Dead*, 1994
    This debut novel in a contemporary murder mystery series features a Chicago detective.
Valerie Wilson Wesley, *When Death Comes Stealing*, 1994
    This debut novel in a murder mystery series features an ex-policewoman who has become a private detective.

290

WALTER MOSLEY, African American

A Red Death
(New York: W.W. Norton, 1991)

Story type: Private Detective
Series: Easy Rawlins
Subject(s): Murder; Mystery and Detective Stories; Stealing
Age range(s): Adult
Major character(s): Ezekiel "Easy" Rawlins, Criminal, Detective—Private, African American; Reginald Arnold Lawrence, Government Official (IRS agent), Caucasian; Darryl T. Craxton, Government Official (FBI agent), Caucasian
Time period(s): 1950s (1953)
Locale(s): Los Angeles, California

Summary: "Easy" Rawlins is accused of income tax evasion. IRS agent Lawrence threatens to launch an investigation into properties "Easy" owns but FBI Agent Craxton offers immunity if he agrees to infiltrate union organizers. To save himself, "Easy" must discover where certain secret documents have been hidden and who committed several murders.

About this book:

Where it's reviewed:
Times Educational Supplement, December 23, 1994, page 19
Village Voice Literary Supplement, October 1992, page 23
Village Voice Literary Supplement, October 1992, page 24

Other books by the same author:
RL's Dream, 1995
Black Betty, 1994 (Easy Rawlins series)
White Butterfly, 1992 (Easy Rawlins series)
Devil in a Blue Dress, 1990 (debut novel, Easy Rawlins series)

Other books you might like:
Gar Anthony Haywood, *Fear of the Dark*, 1988
    This debut novel begins a contemporary murder mystery series with a private detective.
Yolanda Joe, *Falling Leaves of Ivy*, 1992
    A young woman is murdered and her four closest friends from college become suspects, and the secret shared among them begins to unravel.
Penny Mickelbury, *Keeping Secrets*, 1994
    This debut novel begins a murder mystery series with lesbian characters.
Barbara Neely, *Blanche on the Lam*, 1992
    This debut novel begins a contemporary murder mystery series with an amateur detective as the heroine.
Barbara Summers, *The Price You Pay*, 1993
    A young woman in the highly competitive fashion industry finds herself as a target for murder. A series of murders occur when a new market campaign is launched.

291

WALTER MOSLEY, African American

RL's Dream
(New York: W.W. Norton, 1995)

Subject(s): Child Abuse; Friendship; Interpersonal Relations
Age range(s): Adult
Major character(s): Atwater "Soupspoon" Wise, Aged Person (seventies), Musician, African American; Kiki Waters, Abuse Victim (incest), Receptionist, Caucasian; Robert LeRoy "RL" Johnson, Musician (singer), African American
Time period(s): 1980s
Locale(s): New York, New York (Bowery)

Summary: Evicted into the street and ill, "Soupspoon" is rescued by his white neighbor Kiki. "Soupspoon" discovers Kiki drinks too much and is haunted by nightmares from her abusive past. Kiki loses her job because she falsifies an insurance policy for "Soupspoon" when he is diagnosed with cancer. "Soupspoon" decides to publish his memories and exploits with musician "RL" Johnson. He tries to find work again by singing the blues.

About this book:

Where it's reviewed:
Booklist, June 1, 1995, page 1684
Los Angeles Times Book Review, August 6, 1995, page 3
Publishers Weekly, May 29, 1995, page 65
Book World, August 20, 1995, page 7

Awards the book has won:
Black Caucus of the A.L.A., Literary Award for Fiction, 1996

Other books by the same author:
Black Betty, 1994 (Easy Rawlins series)
White Butterfly, 1992 (Easy Rawlins series)

A Red Death, 1991 (Easy Rawlins series)
Devil in a Blue Dress, 1990 (debut novel, Easy Rawlins series)

Other books you might like:
Xam Wilson Cartier, *Muse-Echo Blues*, 1991
    A young woman suffering from an acute case of composer's block receives inspiration from a fantasy soul sister and the jazz of the 1940s.
Leon Forrest, *Divine Days*, 1992
    In an epic tale referred to as *The Ulysses of the South Side*, an aspiring playwright captures the voices of the living and the dead.
Marita Golden, *And Do Remember Me*, 1992
    A young girl, raped by her father, runs away from home. She later finds the courage to return home when he suffers a stroke and she confronts her mother.
Julius Lester, *Do Lord Remember Me*, 1984
    This saga is about the life and times of an eighty-year-old reverend who became known as the "colored Billy Graham."

292

WALTER MOSLEY, African American

White Butterfly
(New York: W.W. Norton, 1992)

Story type: Private Detective; Adult
Series: Easy Rawlins
Subject(s): Family Relations; Murder; Mystery and Detective Stories
Age range(s): Adult
Major character(s): Ezekiel "Easy" Rawlins, Father (of Edna), Detective—Private, African American; Cyndi "White Butterfly" Starr, Stripper, Student—College, Caucasian (aka Robin Garnett); Vernor Garnett, Lawyer, Father (of Robin/Cyndi), Caucasian
Time period(s): 1950s (1956)
Locale(s): Los Angeles, California

Summary: Private detective "Easy" Rawlins, now married and a father, becomes involved in a case of serial killings. When a white woman gets murdered, he discovers this woman's dual identities as Robin, the daughter of the powerful city prosecutor Vernor Garnett, and a stripper known as Cyndi Starr the "White Butterfly." His investigation reveals the secrets of Robin/Cyndi. As he tracks down the killer his life, business and marriage are in jeopardy.

About this book:

Where it's reviewed:
Books Magazine, November 1994, page 14
Times Educational Supplement, December 23, 1994, page 19

Other books by the same author:
RL's Dream, 1995
Black Betty, 1994 (Easy Rawlins series)
A Red Death, 1991 (Easy Rawlins series)
Devil in a Blue Dress, 1990 (debut novel, Easy Rawlins series)

Other books you might like:

Nikki Baker, *In the Game*, 1991
> This debut novel begins a murder mystery series with lesbian characters.

Eleanor Taylor Bland, *Dead Time*, 1992
> This debut novel begins a detective mystery series with a female heroine.

Gar Anthony Haywood, *Fear of the Dark*, 1988
> This debut novel begins a contemporary murder mystery series with a private detective.

Gar Anthony Haywood, *Going Nowhere Fast*, 1994
> This debut novel begins with a wife as an amateur detective and her retired police detective husband.

Valerie Wilson Wesley, *When Death Comes Stealing*, 1994
> This debut novel begins a murder mystery series featuring an ex-policewoman who has become a private detective.

293

JESS MOWRY, African American

Children of the Night

(Los Angeles: Holloway House, 1991)

Story type: Young Adult
Subject(s): City Life; Drugs; Self-Respect
Age range(s): Grades 9-Adult
Major character(s): Ryo, 13-Year-Old, African American; Chipmunk, 13-Year-Old, African American; Big Bird, Drug Dealer, 15-Year-Old, African American
Time period(s): 1980s
Locale(s): Oakland, California

Summary: Growing up poor in Oakland, Ryo and Chipmunk want to be ''somebody,'' and that means having money. So they go about getting it the only way they know how—by working for Big Bird, who controls the crack trade in their neighborhood. When Chipmunk disappears, Ryo discovers that the cost of dealing drugs is way too high.

About this book: This is the author's debut novel.

Where it's reviewed:
Wilson Library Bulletin, September 1992, page 96

Other books by the same author:
Six Out Seven, 1993
Way Past Cool, 1992

Other books you might like:

Ricardo Cortez Cruz, *Straight Outta Compton*, 1992
> This rap-style novel tells the story of two young men growing up together in the streets of Compton, living hard and fast on a very thin edge.

Walter Dean Myers, *Scorpions*, 1988
> A gun changes the lives of a young boy and his Puerto Rican friend when they are forced into being involved with a street gang.

Walter Dean Myers, *Won't Know Till I Get There*, 1982
> A 14-year-old's parents decided to adopt a youngster with a juvenile record, and the boys get arrested together.

294

JESS MOWRY, African American

Six Out Seven

(New York: Farrar Straus Giroux, 1993)

Subject(s): Coming of Age; Gangs; Self-Reliance
Age range(s): Grades 8-Adult
Major character(s): Corbitt Wainwright, Student, Runaway, African American
Time period(s): 1990s
Locale(s): New Crossing, Michigan; Oakland, California

Summary: Leaving rural Mississippi for better opportunities in California, Corbitt meets kids living on the streets, struggling to survive. He is respected for his ''African-ness,'' and his personal integrity. In return, he learns to trust his own heart.

Where it's reviewed:
Kliatt, January 1995, page 10
Publishers Weekly, September 19, 1994, page 66

Other books by the same author:
Way Past Cool, 1992
Children of the Night, 1991 (debut novel)

Other books you might like:

Lionel Newton, *Getting Right with God*, 1994
> In fantastical chats with God and Satan, a teenage boy figures out his feelings about adolescence, sex, love, religion and his doing the right thing.

Walter Dean Myers, *Scorpions*, 1988
> A gun changes the lives of a young boy and his Puerto Rican friend when they are forced into being involved with a street gang.

Walter Dean Myers, *Won't Know Till I Get There*, 1982
> The summer exploits of a 14-year-old whose parents decide to adopt a youngster with a juvenile record and the boys get arrested together.

295

JESS MOWRY, African American

Way Past Cool

(New York: Farrar Straus Giroux, 1992)

Story type: Young Adult
Subject(s): City Life; Coming of Age; Gangs
Age range(s): Grades 9-Adult
Major character(s): Gordon, Gang Member, 13-Year-Old, African American; Deek, Drug Dealer, 16-Year-Old, African American
Time period(s): 1990s
Locale(s): Oakland, California

Summary: Fiercely loyal to each other and ''the rules'' that govern their life-and-death world, Gordon and his gang the Friends struggle to hold a few blocks of ragged turf. When a drug dealer named Deek tries to stir up trouble between the Friends and their neighboring rival gang, the Crew, the two groups must put aside their differences to solve their common problem.

Where it's reviewed:
American Visions, June 1994, page 32
Booklist, October 1, 1993, page 335
Journal of Reading, April 1994, page 596

Other books by the same author:
Six Out Seven, 1993
Children of the Night, 1991 (debut novel)

Other books you might like:
Ricardo Cortez Cruz, *Straight Outta Compton*, 1992
  This rap-style novel tells the story of two young men growing up together in the streets of Compton, living hard and fast on a very thin edge.
Walter Dean Myers, *Scorpions*, 1988
  A gun changes the lives of a young boy and his Puerto Rican friend when they are forced into being involved with a street gang.
Walter Dean Myers, *Won't Know Till I Get There*, 1982
  The summer exploits of a 14-year-old whose parents decide to adopt a youngster with a juvenile record where the boys get arrested together.
Lionel Newton, *Getting Right with God*, 1994
  In fantastical chats with God and Satan, a teenage boy figures out his feelings about adolescence, sex, love, religion and doing the right thing.

296

CHERRY MUHANJI, African American

Her

(San Francisco: Aunt Lute Books, 1990)

Subject(s): Identity; Interpersonal Relations; Homosexuality/ Lesbianism
Age range(s): Adult
Major character(s): Kali, 17-Year-Old, Mother, African American
Time period(s): 1950s; 1960s (1950s-1960s)
Locale(s): Detroit, Michigan

Summary: A young and naive bride, light-skinned Kali "Sunshine" comes to Detroit to live with her husband's family. She keeps to herself as she has done all her life; she is too light-skinned for some, not light enough for others. While she awaits the birth of her baby, Kali looks out of the window at the nightlife on John R Street where folks come to have some fun and forget the day's troubles. After a huge argument with her mother-in-law, Kali takes her baby and moves in with Wintergreen, who owns and sings in her own club. Kali's descent into "the life" and her experiences there cause the neighborhood women to gather together. Kali's own strength is her salvation, and an affirmation of survival to the women who know her.

About this book: Debut novel.

Awards the book has won:
Ferro-Grumley, 1991

Other books you might like:
Tina McElroy Ansa, *Ugly Ways*, 1993
  Contemporary account of three sisters reflecting on their upbringing in a small town and how their lives have evolved.

Grace Edwards-Yearwood, *In the Shadow of the Peacock*, 1988
  A young girl strikes out in spite of her mother's fears, discovering her own voice, her own love and her part in the struggle for civil rights.
Nettie Jones, *Mischief Makers*, 1989
  Three exotically beautiful sisters of mixed race experience the world quite differently both because and in spite of their looks.
Toni Morrison, *Sula*, 1973
  Evolution of a friendship between two girls that first sustains and then injures as they become women and freedom clashes with convention.
Gloria Naylor, *Women of Brewster Place*, 1982
  The story of seven women who come to live on the dead-end street of Brewster Place and what brings them together in their own redemption.
Elaine Perry, *Another Present Era*, 1990
  A young architect drifts away from the lover she shares little with except their light skin and becomes involved with an older white artist.

297

ALBERT MURRAY, African American

The Seven League Boots

(New York: Pantheon Books, 1995)

Subject(s): Bands; Interpersonal Relations; Musicians
Age range(s): Adult
Major character(s): Scooter, Traveller, Musician, African American
Time period(s): 1920's
Locale(s): New York, New York; Los Angeles, California; Europe

Summary: Scooter graduates from college and is asked by legendary jazz musician and composer, Bossman, to be a temporary bass player in his traveling band. Although schooled in the humanities, Scooter has a gift for jazz improvisation. He travels from coast to coast, makes records and hones his skills while he saves his money for graduate school. Then he decides to take a break from the road to see if he can make it on his own. He meets movie actress, Jewel Templeton, who enables him to go to Europe and continue the journey of self that began as a small boy dreaming in a chinaberry tree.

Other books by the same author:
The Spyglass Tree, 1991
Train Whistle Guitar, 1974 (debut novel)

Other books you might like:
Xam Wilson Cartier, *Muse-Echo Blues*, 1991
  Inspiration from a fantasy soul sister and the jazz of the 1940s comes to a young woman suffering from an acute case of composer's block.
Helen Elaine Lee, *The Serpent's Gift*, 1994
  Children and grandchildren of two intertwined families endure hardship and triumph as they help each other remember a history beyond their knowing.
Toni Morrison, *Song of Solomon*, 1977
  Coming-of-age story set in the 1950s of a young man

striking out on his own to seek buried gold; instead he discovers his buried heritage.

298

ALBERT MURRAY, African American

The Spyglass Tree

(New York: Pantheon Books, 1991)

Subject(s): Coming of Age; Interpersonal Relations
Age range(s): Adult
Major character(s): Scooter, Student—College, African American; Hortense Hightower, Entertainer (dancer and jazz singer), African American; Giles Cunningham, Restauranteur (employs Hortense), African American
Time period(s): 1930s
Locale(s): Montgomery, Alabama

Summary: Scooter reminisces about growing up in Mobile County. Aided by a network of supportive adults, Scooter attends college in Montgomery. When his friend Giles is threatened by a local white businessman, Scooter is enlisted to ride shotgun with Hortense.

Where it's reviewed:
Reference Services Review, Issue 3, 1995, page 25
Book World, December 20, 1992, page 12
New York Times Book Review, January 3, 1993, page 20
Voice of Youth Advocates, April 1993, page 28

Other books by the same author:
Train Whistle Guitar, 1974 (debut novel)

Other books you might like:
Trey Ellis, *Platitudes*, 1988
  Parallel stories created by two writers who are corresponding about their teenaged characters, develop their own personal relationship.
Darryl Pinckney, *High Cotton*, 1992
  An unnamed narrator reveals the complexities of growing up in the upper-middle class as a young man in the ''talented tenth'' generation.
Dennis Williams, *Crossover*, 1992
  This story relates the events in the life of a young man during the Civil Rights era. He becomes a reluctant activist and has an interracial affair.

299

WALTER DEAN MYERS, African American

Adventure in Granada

(New York: Puffin Books, Viking Penguin, 1985)

Story type: Young Readers
Series: Arrow Adventure
Subject(s): Adventure and Adventurers; Mystery and Detective Stories; Brothers
Age range(s): Grades 5-9
Major character(s): Ken Arrow, 14-Year-Old, Brother, Caucasian; Chris Arrow, 17-Year-Old, Brother, Caucasian; Pedro Barcia, 14-Year-Old, Peddler, Gypsy
Time period(s): 1980s
Locale(s): Granada, Spain

Summary: Teenaged Ken and Chris arrive in Spain with their mother. They meet Pedro, a 14-year-old Gypsy. Pedro goes to church and sees a mysterious woman standing near the altar holding the famous Cruzada Cross. When she vanishes with the cross, Pedro thinks he is witnessing a miracle and she must be a saint. With the cross missing and Pedro on the scene, the police accuse him of theft. Ken and Chris try to help Pedro find the cross. After their lives are threatened and Pedro is kidnapped, the boys solve the crime.

Other books by the same author:
The Nicholas Factor, 1983 (young readers)
Tales of a Dead King, 1983 (young readers)
Legend of Tarik, 1981 (young adults)
Mojo and the Russians, 1977 (young readers)
Fast Sam, Cool Clyde and Stuff, 1976 (debut novel, young adults)

Other books you might like:
Virginia Hamilton, *Junius over Far*, 1985
  When his grandfather returns to his Caribbean island home, a disturbing letter prompts a young boy and his father to journey to rescue him.
Virginia Hamilton, *The Mystery of Drear House*, 1987
  A house that was a station on the Underground Railroad has secret passageways and hidden treasure which must be saved before it is too late.
Harriette Gillem Robinet, *Mississippi Chariot*, 1994
  A resourceful 12-year-old son of a sharecropper plans to get his falsely convicted father off of the chain gang in 1930's Mississippi.
Eleanora E. Tate, *The Secret of Gumbo Grove*, 1987
  A youngster upsets her community and her parents when she spreads stories she's heard about the town ancestors buried in the church cemetery.

300

WALTER DEAN MYERS, African American

Ambush in the Amazon

(New York: Puffin Books, Viking Penguin, 1986)

Story type: Young Readers
Series: Arrow Adventure
Subject(s): Adventure and Adventurers; Mystery and Detective Stories; Brothers
Age range(s): Grades 5-9
Major character(s): Ken Arrow, 14-Year-Old, Brother, Caucasian; Chris Arrow, 17-Year-Old, Brother, Caucasian; Tarija Numa, 14-Year-Old, Student, Quechuan
Time period(s): 1980s
Locale(s): Los Cauchos, Peru

Summary: Ken and Chris go up the Amazon river to meet their guide, Tarija. On the night before her arrival, Chris is attacked in his tent by a huge unidentified animal. Tarija learns the villagers fear a mythical monster has returned and so leave gifts in a clearing to appease it. The villagers make Tarija a sacrifice to the monster, who carries her off into the jungle. To rescue her, Ken and Chris venture into the jungle alone, where they discover more than one monster.

Other books by the same author:
The Righteous Revenge of Artemis Bonner, 1992 (young readers)
The Nicholas Factor, 1983 (young readers)
Tales of a Dead King, 1983 (young readers)
Mojo and the Russians, 1977 (young readers)
Fast Sam, Cool Clyde and Stuff, 1976 (debut novel, young adults)

Other books you might like:
Sharon M. Draper, *Ziggy and the Black Dinosaurs*, 1994
When their neighborhood playground is destroyed, four fifth grade boys start their own secret club and uncover a mysterious old box of hidden bones.
Virginia Hamilton, *Junius over Far*, 1985
When his grandfather returns to his Caribbean island home, a disturbing letter prompts a young boy and his father to journey to rescue him.
Emily Moore, *Whose Side Are You On?*, 1988
When her math tutor mysteriously disappears, a sixth-grade girl sets out to find him and discovers things aren't always what they seem.
Eleanora E. Tate, *The Secret of Gumbo Grove*, 1987
A youngster upsets her community and her parents when she spreads stories she's heard about the town ancestors buried in the church cemetery.

301

WALTER DEAN MYERS, African American

Brainstorm

(New York: Franklin Watts, 1977)

Subject(s): Science Fiction; Space Travel; Time Travel
Age range(s): Grades 7-10
Major character(s): Ron Viacom, 14-Year-Old, African American, Space Explorer
Time period(s): 2070s (2076)
Locale(s): Earth; Planet—Imaginary (Suffes)

Summary: During rain storms FORTIA, the army of the world, discovers a powerful ray is being projected at Earth from a distant planet Suffes. The mysterious ray strikes inhabitant's of cities and steals their minds leaving them in a state of helpless infancy. Unable to block the ray FORTIA decides to send a space crew through a time warp to reach Suffes in three days to stop the rain bringing the ray. To enter the time warp will age the crew fifteen years. Training since age nine now at fourteen Captain Ron Viacom is chosen to head the crew on the spaceship *Odyssey*. Something goes terribly wrong with their ship on entering the time warp and when they arrive at Suffes they are not a day older. The young Captain and his crew have their orders—stop the rain, and if that fails destroy Suffes.

Where it's reviewed:
Center for Children's Books. Bulletin, April 1978, page 132
School Library Journal, November 1977, page 60

Other books by the same author:
Won't Know Till I Get There, 1982 (young adult)
Hoops, 1981 (young adult)
Legend of Tarik, 1981 (young adult)

The Young Landlords, 1979 (young adult)
Fast Sam, Cool Clyde and Stuff, 1976 (debut novel, young adult)

Other books you might like:
Virginia Hamilton, *Willie Bea and the Time the Martians Landed*, 1983
On their farm in Ohio, a family is caught up in the fear generated by the 1938 Orson Welles ''Martians have landed'' broadcast.

302

WALTER DEAN MYERS, African American

Crystal

(New York: Viking Kestrel, 1987)

Story type: Young Adult
Subject(s): Models, Fashion; Family Relations; Suicide
Age range(s): Grades 9-12
Major character(s): Crystal Brown, 16-Year-Old, Model, African American; Rosa ''Rowena'' DeLea, 18-Year-Old, Model, Caucasian
Time period(s): 1980s
Locale(s): New York, New York

Summary: With the approval of her parents and support of an agent, 16-year-old Crystal is becoming a familiar face in the modeling industry. During an assignment, she meets and becomes friends with ''Rowena.'' The pressures of keeping up both her school work and her career are taking a toll on Crystal. She tells her mother she wants to quit the business but, seeing how upset her mother becomes, she changes her mind. Suffering a declining career, ''Rowena'' attempts suicide and when Crystal visits her in the hospital she sees where modeling could lead. Crystal knows she has to make a difficult decision and explain it to her parents.

Other books by the same author:
Motown and DiDi: A Love Story, 1984 (young adult)
Won't Know Till I Get There, 1982 (young adult)
Hoops, 1981 (young adult)
Legend of Tarik, 1981 (young adult)
Fast Sam, Cool Clyde and Stuff, 1976 (debut novel; young adult)

Other books you might like:
Vy Higginsen, *Mama, I Want to Sing*, 1995
Recounts events in the life of a talented singer from the church choir to stardom. r.
Joyce Carol Thomas, *When the Nightingale Sings*, 1992
Despite her foster mother's attempts to demean her, a 14-year-old girl has a song to sing and a destiny to fulfill.
Valerie Wilson Wesley, *Where Do I Go From Here?*, 1993
At a snooty prep school, a teenager learns from another scholarship student that she must make decisions for herself.
Rita Williams-Garcia, *Blue Tights*, 1988
Struggling to find friends and acceptance a young girl born out-of-wedlock follows her mother's footsteps in her passion for dancing.
Rita Williams-Garcia, *Fast Talk on a Slow Track*, 1991
A young man returns to his fierce competition with a rival

Latino door-to-door salesman before reluctantly deciding to become a college freshman.

303

WALTER DEAN MYERS, African American

Darnell Rock Reporting
(New York: Delacorte Press, 1994)

Story type: Young Readers
Subject(s): School Newspapers; Homeless; Brothers and Sisters
Age range(s): Grades 5-8
Major character(s): Darnell Rock, 13-Year-Old, Student—Junior High, African American; Tamika Rock, 13-Year-Old, Student—Junior High, African American
Time period(s): 1990s (1994)
Locale(s): United States (urban city)

Summary: Darnell decides to join the school newspaper. One of his teachers suggests he write human interest stories. Taking the suggestion, Darnell meets a homeless man who was once in the military and writes a story about him with a proposal that gets the attention of the City Council. His sister Tamika is so proud of Darnell she wants to read his story during school announcements, and the whole family accompanies him when he speaks before the City Council. Darnell is overwhelmed by the celebrity and impact of his writing and sees how one person can make a difference.

Where it's reviewed:
Horn Book Guide, Spring 1995, page 81
Los Angeles Book Review, January 1, 1995, page 10
Emergency Librarian, March 1995, page 57
Voice of Youth Advocates, October 1994, page 212
Book Report, January 1995, page 48

Other books by the same author:
Mouse Rap, 1990 (Young Readers)
Me, Mop, and the Moondance Kid, 1988 (Young Readers)
The Nicholas Factor, 1983 (Young Readers)
Tales of a Dead King, 1983 (Young Readers)
Fast Sam, Cool Clyde and Stuff, 1976 (debut novel; young adult)

Other books you might like:
Jacqueline Turner Banks, *Egg-Drop Blues*, 1995
   A sixth grader's science grade is low because of his dyslexia, so he and his twin brother enter a competition for extra credit.
Candy Dawson Boyd, *Charlie Pippin*, 1987
   Curious about her father's involvement in the Vietnam conflict, an enterprising sixth-grader joins a school group to learn more.
Joyce Hansen, *Yellow Bird and Me*, 1986
   Missing her best friend who has moved away, a young girl helps a classmate in elementary school overcome stage fright and discovers he has dyslexia.
Andrea Davis Pinkney, *Hold Fast to Dreams*, 1995
   Two sisters endure prejudice when their family moves to the suburbs and they have to attend separate all-white schools and try to fit in.

Eleanora E. Tate, *The Secret of Gumbo Grove*, 1987
   A youngster upsets her community and her parents when she spreads stories she's heard about the town ancestors buried in the church cemetery.

304

WALTER DEAN MYERS, African American

Duel in the Desert
(New York: Puffin Books, Viking Penguin, 1986)

Story type: Young Readers
Series: Arrow Adventure
Subject(s): Adventure and Adventurers; Mystery and Detective Stories; Brothers
Age range(s): Grades 5-9
Major character(s): Ken Arrow, 14-Year-Old, Brother, Caucasian; Chris Arrow, 17-Year-Old, Brother, Caucasian; Mussa Ahmed Tawfik, 14-Year-Old, Guide, Moroccan
Time period(s): 1980s
Locale(s): Morocco, Egypt

Summary: Once again, 14-year-old and 17-year-old white brothers, Ken and Chris experience adventure. The brothers go to Goulimime where they meet Mussa who is Ken's age. When they arrive Mussa invites them to travel out to desert field site to stay overnight. Chris awakens in the middle of the night drenched in blood and his camera broken. The following day they witness a funeral procession of blue-faced Tuaregs and Chris has a knife thrown at him by an angry camel trader. While sneaking a look at hidden camel herds Chris and Mussa get chased by Senegalese traders with whips and make a dramatic dash for their Land Rover jeep to escape when Ken drives it over the hill. And their adventures are just beginning.

Other books by the same author:
The Righteous Revenge of Artemis Bonner, 1992 (young readers)
The Nicholas Factor, 1983 (young readers)
Tales of a Dead King, 1983 (young readers)
Mojo and the Russians, 1977 (young readers)
Fast Sam, Cool Clyde and Stuff, 1976 (debut novel, young adults)

Other books you might like:
Sharon M. Draper, *Ziggy and the Black Dinosaurs*, 1994
   When their neighborhood playground is destroyed, four 5th grade boys start their own secret club and uncover a mysterious old box of hidden bones.
Emily Moore, *Whose Side Are You On?*, 1988
   When her math tutor mysteriously disappears, a sixth-grade girl sets out to find him and discovers things aren't always what they seem.
Eleanora E. Tate, *The Secret of Gumbo Grove*, 1987
   A youngster upsets her community and her parents when she spreads stories she's heard about the town ancestors buried in the church cemetery.

WALTER DEAN MYERS, African American

Fallen Angels
(New York: Scholastic Inc., 1988)

Story type: Young Adult

Subject(s): Vietnam War; Military Life; Interpersonal Relations

Age range(s): Grades 8-Adult

Major character(s): Richard "Richie" Perry, 17-Year-Old, Military Personnel, African American

Time period(s): 1960s (1967-1968)

Locale(s): Chu Lai, Vietnam; Tam Ky, Vietnam

Summary: Richie joins the Army after high school graduation. Assigned to his first unit after basic training, a doctor says his knee injury is too bad for combat duty. When his medical paperwork is delayed he gets transported to Vietnam. Once dreaming of going to college, now Richie just hopes he can survive when his company goes on patrol. In a few short months of his one-year tour of duty Richie experiences the sadness of the death of his commanding officer, the trauma of killing his first soldier, fear for his life when he gets wounded, the anxiety of going back into combat, the horror of having to strip and burn dead bodies of GIs, and the alarm of being separated from most of his unit in a combat zone. Writing stateside to his mother and younger brother Richie anxiously awaits the end of the Vietnam War and longs to get back home.

Where it's reviewed:

Book Report, January 1994, page 24

Voice of Your Advocates, June 1994, page 68

English Journal, September 1993, page 43

Awards the book has won:

Coretta Scott King Award, 1989

Young Adult Library Services Association, Best Books for YAs, 1988

Other books by the same author:

Scorpions, 1988 (young adult)

Crystal, 1987 (young adult)

Motown and DiDi: A Love Story, 1984 (young adult)

The Outside Shot, 1984 (young adult)

Fast Sam, Cool Clyde and Stuff, 1976 (debut novel; young adult)

Other books you might like:

Ossie Davis, *Just Like Martin*, 1992

A religiously active son and his war veteran father disagree over the civil rights movement until events occur that help them to work together.

Sharon M. Draper, *Tears of a Tiger*, 1994

A teenager escaping a car accident in which his friend is killed and others are injured has difficulty learning to live with the trauma.

Virginia Hamilton, *A Little Love*, 1984

A teenage girl has an emptiness food cannot fill. She misses her father, and in her search for him she finds new strengths in herself.

Rita Williams-Garcia, *Fast Talk on a Slow Track*, 1991

A young man returns to his fierce competition with a rival Latino door-to-door salesman before reluctantly deciding to become a college freshman.

Jacqueline Woodson, *From the Notebooks of Melanin Sun*, 1995

A 13-year-old boy's world is turned upside down and he has to confront his prejudices when his mother tells him she is in love with a white woman.

WALTER DEAN MYERS, African American

Fast Sam, Cool Clyde and Stuff
(New York: Viking Press, 1975)

Subject(s): Friendship; Family Relations; City Life

Age range(s): Grades 7-10

Major character(s): Francis "Stuff" Williams, Teenager, African American

Time period(s): 1970s

Locale(s): New York, New York (Harlem)

Summary: Six years after he was first the new kid on the block, 18-year-old Stuff reflects on events in his life as he became the young friend of Sam, Clyde and his sister Kitty, and Gloria and Maria. Looking back he ponders what led to the number of times the police jailed him with Sam and Clyde when they were teenagers. Stuff also remembers the sadness when Clyde and Kitty's father died and the uproar Kitty created when her mother later began to date. Along the way, the group decides to form themselves into a club of sorts to help each other out when they needed someone to care for them and to talk to. As the group deals with the threat of drugs, family breakups, and lighter moements, everyone supports each other. Stuff realizes he has never again come across a whole group of such good people.

About this book: Debut novel for young adults.

Where it's reviewed:

Horn Book Magazine, August 1975, page 388

New York Times Book Review, May 4, 1975, page 28

School Library Journal, March 1975, page 108

Awards the book has won:

Coretta Scott King Honor Book, 1976

American Library Association Notable Book, 1975

Other books by the same author:

Motown and DiDi: A Love Story, 1984 (young adult)

Won't Know Till I Get There, 1982 (young adult)

Hoops, 1981 (young adult)

Legend of Tarik, 1981 (young adult)

The Young Landlords, 1979 (young adult)

Other books you might like:

Ossie Davis, *Just Like Martin*, 1992

A religiously active son and his war veteran father disagree over the civil rights movement until events occur that help them to work together.

David Haynes, *Right by My Side*, 1993

A high school student writes down his experiences in order to figure things out about his father, his mother and himself.

Mildred D. Taylor, *The Road to Memphis*, 1990

Another incident from the lives of the Logan family in

segregated Mississippi where racial hostilities erupt and new relationships unfold.

Brenda Wilkinson, *Ludell's New York Time*, 1980
Moving from Georgia to New York City in her senior year, a teenager struggles to adjust to life in 1960s Harlem.

Jacqueline Woodson, *From the Notebooks of Melanin Sun*, 1995
A 13-year-old boy's world is turned upside down and he has to confront his prejudices when his mother tells him she is in love with a white woman.

307

WALTER DEAN MYERS, African American

Glory Field

(New York: Scholastic Inc., 1994)

Story type: Young Adult
Subject(s): Historical; Race Relations; Family Relations
Age range(s): Grades 7-10
Major character(s): Muhammad Bilal, 11-Year-Old, Kidnap Victim, African; Malcolm Lewis, Nephew, Musician, African American
Time period(s): 16th century (1753); 20th century (1994)
Locale(s): Sierra Leone; Curry Island, South Carolina; New York, New York (Harlem)

Summary: Kidnapped in Africa in 1753 at the age of eleven and enslaved in the American Colonies, Muhammad was the son of a farmer. The lives of his generations of descendants span from the 16th to 20th century. At the end of the Civil War the government parceled out land to his family, the Lewises, who wanted to stay and farm it as they had done as slaves. Thanking the heavens their eight-acre parcel became known as the glory field. Spanning over two hundred years, the Lewis family saga reaches from sites in South Carolina to Chicago and Harlem. Shackles worn by an enslaved Muhammad as a boy pass on to his descendant Malcolm in 1994.

Where it's reviewed:
Booklist, October 1, 1994, page 319
Los Angeles Times Book Review, January 1, 1995, page 10
New York Times Book Review, November 13, 1994, page 42
School Library Journal, November 1994, page 121
Voice of Youth Advocates, October 1994, page 214

Awards the book has won:
Young Adult Library Services Association, Best Books for YA, 1995

Other books by the same author:
Fallen Angels, 1988 (Young Adults)
Scorpions, 1988 (Young Adults)
Motown and DiDi: A Love Story, 1984 (Young Adults)
The Outside Shot, 1984 (Young Adults)
Fast Sam, Cool Clyde and Stuff, 1976 (debut novel; young adult)

Other books you might like:
Ossie Davis, *Just Like Martin*, 1992
A religiously active son and his war veteran father disagree over the civil rights movement until after events occur that help them to work together.

Virginia Hamilton, *Sweet Whispers, Brother Rush*, 1982
A girl caring for her retarded older brother encounters the ghost of her dead uncle and comes to a deeper understanding of her family and herself.

Mildred D. Taylor, *Let the Circle Be Unbroken*, 1981
A continuation of the Logan family stories from the Depression era in rural Mississippi where racial antagonisms and conflicts prevail.

Brenda Wilkinson, *Not Separate, Not Equal*, 1987
Chosen among a group of six to integrate a Georgia high school, a teenage girl experiences hatred and racism.

308

WALTER DEAN MYERS, African American
ALICE PROVENSEN, Illustrator, Caucasian
MARTIN PROVENSEN, Illustrator, Caucasian

The Golden Serpent

(New York: Viking Press, 1980)

Story type: Young Readers
Subject(s): Fables; Storytelling
Age range(s): Grades 1-3
Major character(s): Ali, Child, African American; Pundabi, Aged Person (wise), African American
Time period(s): Indeterminate Past
Locale(s): India

Summary: Living on a mountaintop in India with a wise man, young Ali comes each day to the village to receive food and hear the questions people want answered by the wise man. One day the King declares that he wants the wise man, Pundabi, to solve a mystery and has him brought to the palace. Standing before the King he is told that the King himself does not know what the mystery is but that if Pundabi does not solve it the King will know him for a fraud and put him in jail. Shaken and afraid Pundabi and Ali walk the streets of the village hoping their eyes will reveal the mystery. Returning to the palace later, Pundabi is unable to solve the mystery but knows it involves the King's golden serpent. When the King returns to the village to find the golden serpent stolen from him, Pundabi and Ali leave for their own village but Ali still does not understand the wisdom of Pundabi's words to the King.

Other books by the same author:
The Story of the Three Kingdoms, 1995
Mr. Monkey and the Gotcha Bird: An Original Tale, 1984

Other books you might like:
Angela Shelf Medearis, *The Singing Man*, 1994
West African folktale of how a boy's life evolves as he becomes a famous praise singer singing the history of the African people.

Angela Shelf Medearis, *Too Much Talk*, 1995
Retells a traditional West African folktale of events that occur when a farmer hearing a yam talk runs off screaming in the heat of the day.

John Steptoe, *Mufaro's Beautiful Daughters: An African Tale*, 1987
The folktale of two young African sisters appearing before the King so he can choose the one he wants to become his wife the Queen.

309

WALTER DEAN MYERS, African American

The Hidden Shrine
(New York: Puffin Books, Viking Penguin, 1985)

Story type: Young Readers
Series: Arrow Adventure
Subject(s): Adventure and Adventurers; Mystery and Detective Stories; Brothers
Age range(s): Grades 5-9
Major character(s): Ken Arrow, 14-Year-Old, Brother, Caucasian; Chris Arrow, 17-Year-Old, Brother, Caucasian; Won Li, 16-Year-Old, Chinese
Time period(s): 1980s
Locale(s): Hong Kong, China

Summary: White 14-year-old Ken and his 17-year-old brother Chris learn from their Chinese friend Won Li in Hong Kong that artifacts are being stolen from the temples. For over a week they ask a lot of questions, trying to figure out who might be the thieves when their lives are threatened by a speeding boat. Diving into the water to escape, the three boys realize the danger they might be in. Now the boys plan to flush out the thieves by planting a false story in the newspaper about an ancient statue going on exhibit at the oldest Hong Kong temple and waiting to see who shows up. What shows up is danger, when the boys follow the clues.

Other books by the same author:
The Righteous Revenge of Artemis Bonner, 1992 (young readers)
The Nicholas Factor, 1983 (young readers)
Tales of a Dead King, 1983 (young readers)
Mojo and the Russians, 1977 (young readers)
Fast Sam, Cool Clyde and Stuff, 1976 (debut novel, young adults)

Other books you might like:
Sharon M. Draper, *Ziggy and the Black Dinosaurs*, 1994
When their neighborhood playground is destroyed, four 5th grade boys start their own secret club and uncover a mysterious old box of hidden bones.
Virginia Hamilton, *The Mystery of Drear House*, 1987
A house that was a station on the Underground Railroad has secret passageways and hidden treasure which must be saved before it is too late.
Emily Moore, *Whose Side Are You On?*, 1988
When her math tutor mysteriously disappears, a sixth-grade girl sets out to find him and discovers things aren't always what they seem.
Eleanora E. Tate, *The Secret of Gumbo Grove*, 1987
A youngster upsets her community and her parents when she spreads stories she's heard about the town ancestors buried in the church cemetery.

310

WALTER DEAN MYERS, African American

Hoops
(New York: Delacorte Press, 1981)

Story type: Young Adult
Series: Lonnie Jackson
Subject(s): Sports/Basketball; Interpersonal Relations; Gambling
Age range(s): Grades 7-12
Major character(s): Lonnie Jackson, 17-Year-Old, Basketball Player, African American; Calvin "Spider" F. Jones, Coach, Alcoholic, African American
Time period(s): 1980s
Locale(s): New York, New York (Harlem)

Summary: In his day "Cal/Spider" Jones had a promising professional basketball career until he sold out to gamblers. Now an alcoholic on the streets, he wants to get back in the game by coaching a street team of players in a tournament of champions. Lonnie, a talented player on the team, is suspicious of "Cal" until they get to know one another. When "Cal" really helps the team develop and then disappears, Lonnie searches for him and discovers gamblers are still trying to run his life. In the playoff game "Cal" and Lonnie have to choose if they are going to let the gamblers win or their team win, a choice which could have dangerous consequences.

Where it's reviewed:
Voice of Youth Advocates, June 1994, page 68

Awards the book has won:
Young Adult Library Services Association, Best Books for YAs, 1981

Other books by the same author:
Glory Field, 1994 (young adult)
Scorpions, 1988 (young adult)
Fallen Angels, 1988 (young adult)
Crystal, 1987 (young adult)
Fast Sam, Cool Clyde and Stuff, 1976 (debut novel; young adult)

Other books you might like:
Ossie Davis, *Just Like Martin*, 1992
A religiously active son and his war veteran father disagree over the civil rights movement until after events occur that help them to work together.
Sharon M. Draper, *Tears of a Tiger*, 1994
A teenager escaping a car accident in which his friend is killed and others are injured has difficulty learning to live with the trauma.
David Haynes, *Right by My Side*, 1993
A high school student writes down his experiences in order to figure things out about his father, his mother and himself.
Rita Williams-Garcia, *Fast Talk on a Slow Track*, 1991
A young man returns to his fierce competition with a rival Latino door-to-door salesman before reluctantly deciding to become a college freshman.
Jacqueline Woodson, *From the Notebooks of Melanin Sun*, 1995

A 13-year-old boy's world is turned upside down and he has to confront his prejudices when his mother tells him she is in love with a white woman.

311

WALTER DEAN MYERS, African American

It Ain't All for Nothing
(New York: Viking Press, 1978)

Subject(s): Fathers and Sons; Responsibility; Stealing
Age range(s): Grades 5-8
Major character(s): Tippy, 12-Year-Old, African American, Abuse Victim; Lonnie, Single Father, Alcoholic, African American
Time period(s): 1970s
Locale(s): New York, New York (Harlem)

Summary: His mother died giving birth to him and after a brief time of staying with his father, Tippy was raised by his grandmother on his mother's side. Angered over her daughter's death and that Tippy's father Lonnie was doing a poor job of raising a baby Grandma Carrie was glad to take him in. Now twelve years later at over seventy Grandma Carrie falls ill of old age and Tippy has to return to live with his father. He soon learns Lonnie is an unemployed, alcoholic womanizer who also uses drugs, steals, and doesn't want to be called daddy. Before long Tippy himself is drinking, getting beaten by his father, and becoming an accomplice in his father's crimes. When Tippy realizes he has to take responsibility for his own life and escape the life of his father he makes a tough decision that changes both their lives.

Where it's reviewed:
Booklist, September 1, 1978, page 40
Horn Book Magazine, October 1978, page 518
Kirkus Reviews, October 15, 1978, page 1143

Other books by the same author:
The Righteous Revenge of Artemis Bonner, 1992 (young readers)
Somewhere in the Darkness, 1992 (young readers)
Mouse Rap, 1990 (young readers)
Tales of a Dead King, 1983 (young readers)
Fast Sam, Cool Clyde and Stuff, 1976 (debut novel, young adults)

Other books you might like:
Candy Dawson Boyd, *Chevrolet Saturdays*, 1993
   Struggling with the divorce of his parents and accepting his new stepfather, a young boy has trouble in school and makes mistakes he regrets.
Virginia Hamilton, *Junius over Far*, 1985
   When his grandfather returns to his Caribbean island home, a disturbing letter prompts a young boy and his father to journey to rescue him.
Harriette Gillem Robinet, *Mississippi Chariot*, 1994
   A resourceful 12-year-old son of a sharecropper plans to get his falsely convicted father off of the chain gang in 1930's Mississippi.
Eleanora E. Tate, *A Blessing in Disguise*, 1995
   Another tale from the *Calvary County Trilogy* where a

young girl discovers the father she admired addicted her dying mother to alcohol and drugs.
Joyce Carol Thomas, *The Golden Pasture*, 1986
   The exquisite horse a 12-year-old boy finds on his grandfather's farm one summer helps him to understand his difficult father better.

312

WALTER DEAN MYERS, African American

Legend of Tarik
(New York: Viking Press, 1981)

Story type: Young Adult
Subject(s): Middle Ages; Revenge; Legends
Age range(s): Grades 7-10
Major character(s): Tarik Ntah, Captive, Orphan, African; Artia "El Muerte" Akwara, Mercenary, Warrior, Caucasian
Time period(s): Indeterminate Past (medieval)
Locale(s): Africa

Summary: A medieval story of a young boy Tarik being held captive and watching helplessly as his merchant family are killed at the hands of a white warrior "El Muerte." Left for dead, Tarik survives and is brought back to health by two wise men, Dacao and Nongo, whose loved ones have also been killed by "El Muerte." Together they mentor and train Tarik to be a warrior and endow him with a magic sword, a powerful crystal of truth, and a magnificent horse. When Tarik leaves them on his journey to kill "ElMuerte" he is joined by a young girl Stria, also mentored by Dacao and Nongo. Reaching the land of "El Muerte" Tarik kills his cousin and "El Muerte" then captures and kills the two wise men who had befriended Tarik. Tarik and Stria maneuver to battle face-to-face to the death with "El Muerte."

Awards the book has won:
Young Adult Library Services, Best Books for Young Adults, 1981
NCSS-CBC Notable Children's Trade Book, 1982

Other books by the same author:
Glory Field, 1994 (young adult)
Scorpions, 1988 (young adult)
Motown and DiDi: A Love Story, 1984 (young adult)
The Outside Shot, 1984 (young adult)
Fast Sam, Cool Clyde and Stuff, 1976 (debut novel; young adult)

Other books you might like:
Julius Lester, *Othello, a Novel*, 1995
   A reconceptualization with modern dialogue of Shakespeare's play where a mercenary general and a white noblewoman fall in love and tragedy awaits.

313

WALTER DEAN MYERS, African American
RODNEY PATE, Illustrator

Me, Mop, and the Moondance Kid
(New York: Delacorte Press, 1988)

Story type: Young Readers
Subject(s): Sports; Adoption; Friendship
Age range(s): Grades 4-6
Major character(s): Tommy ''T.J.'' Jackson, 11-Year-Old, Adoptee, African American; Billy ''Moondance Kid'' Jackson, Child, Adoptee, African American; Olivia ''Mop'' Parrish, 11-Year-Old, Adoptee, Caucasian
Time period(s): 1980s (1988)
Locale(s): United States (unidentified urban city)

Summary: When their parents are killed in a car accident ''T.J.'' and his younger brother, nicknamed the ''Moondance Kid,'' are raised by nuns at the Dominican Academy. They are close friends there with a white youngster, Miss Olivia Parrish, who they nickname ''Mop.'' Six months ago the brothers were adopted by the Williams. With the Academy about to be closed, ''Mop'' hopes to get adopted by the Kennedys who coach the Elks, a Little League baseball team she and the brothers play on. When the Elks get in the playoffs against their rivals the Eagles, ''T.J.,'' ''Moondance,'' and ''Mop'' give it their all to win.

Awards the book has won:
American Library Association Notable Book, 1988

Other books by the same author:
The Righteous Revenge of Artemis Bonner, 1992 (Young Readers)
Mop, Moondance and Nagasaki Knights, 1992 (Young Readers)
Mouse Rap, 1990 (Young Readers)
The Nicholas Factor, 1983 (Young Readers)
Fast Sam, Cool Clyde and Stuff, 1976 (debut novel; young adult)

Other books you might like:
Jacqueline Turner Banks, *The New One*, 1994
   Twin brothers disagree about whether to befriend a new girl at school or interfere with their mother's relationship with her boyfriend.
Sharon M. Draper, *Ziggy and the Black Dinosaurs*, 1994
   When their neighborhood playground is destroyed, four 5th grade boys start their own secret club and uncover a mysterious old box of hidden bones.
Joyce Hansen, *Yellow Bird and Me*, 1986
   Missing her best friend who has moved away, a young girl helps a classmate in elementary school overcome stage fright and discover he has dyslexia.
Vaunda Micheaux Nelson, *Mayfield Crossing*, 1993
   The new kids at an elementary school encounter prejudice for the first time and only baseball has the possibility for drawing people together.
Mildred D. Taylor, *The Well: David's Story*, 1995
   Episode of the boyhood of two brothers from an early generation of the Logan family in rural Mississippi facing racial bigotry.

314

WALTER DEAN MYERS, African American

Mojo and the Russians
(New York: Viking Press, 1977)

Subject(s): Supernatural; Friendship
Age range(s): Grades 5-8
Major character(s): Michael Dean, 12-Year-Old, African American; Drucilla, Occultist, African American; Willie, African American, Maintenance Worker (janitor)
Time period(s): 1970s
Locale(s): New York, New York

Summary: Racing against Kitty on his bicycle Dean speeds around a corner just as Drucilla crosses the street in front of him and hits her. Known in the neighborhood for her Mojo powers of voodoo Drucilla is angered and promises to put a spell on Dean. Along with his friends Kitty, Kwami, Leslie, Wayne, Anthony, and their white friend Judy, Dean tries to think of a way to stop Drucilla. When they go to talk with her boyfriend Willie they discover Russians are coming to visit him on a regular basis. They develop an elaborate plan to find out if Willie and Drucilla are perhaps spies for the Russians and how they can use the information to get Drucilla to leave Dean alone. Once the FBI discovers them their parents are called to get them out of jail.

Where it's reviewed:
Booklist, October 15, 1977, page 379
Kirkus Reviews, October 15, 1977, page 1098
School Library Journal, November 1977, page 74

Other books by the same author:
The Righteous Revenge of Artemis Bonner, 1992 (young readers)
Mouse Rap, 1990 (young readers)
The Nicholas Factor, 1983 (young readers)
Tales of a Dead King, 1983 (young readers)
Fast Sam, Cool Clyde and Stuff, 1976 (debut novel, young adult)

Other books you might like:
Sharon M. Draper, *Ziggy and the Black Dinosaurs*, 1994
   When their neighborhood playground is destroyed, four 5th grade boys start their own secret club and uncover a mysterious old box of hidden bones.
Virginia Hamilton, *The Mystery of Drear House*, 1987
   A house that was a station on the Underground Railroad has secret passageways and hidden treasure which must be saved before it is too late.
Joyce Hansen, *The Gift Giver*, 1980
   A young girl and her fifth grade friends come to like a new boy in their class and are surprised when they discover he is a foster child.
Harriette Gillem Robinet, *Mississippi Chariot*, 1994
   A resourceful 12-year-old son of a sharecropper plans to get his falsely convicted father off of the chain gang in 1930's Mississippi.
Ethel Footman Smothers, *Down in the Piney Woods*, 1992
   Episodes in the life of the Footman family as the six children all come to live together for the first time sharing life in the country.

315

WALTER DEAN MYERS, African American

Mop, Moondance and Nagasaki Knights

(New York: Delacorte Press, 1992)

Story type: Young Readers
Subject(s): Sports; Interpersonal Relations; Homeless
Age range(s): Grades 4-6
Major character(s): Tommy "T.J." Jackson, 11-Year-Old, Adoptee, African American; Billy "Moondance Kid" Jackson, Child, Adoptee, African American; Olivia "Mop" Parrish, 11-Year-Old, Adoptee, Caucasian
Time period(s): 1980s
Locale(s): Lincoln Park, New Jersey

Summary: In another episode with "T.J." his younger brother "Moondance" and their white friend "Mop," the three youngsters have now all been adopted. Their baseball team the Elks has won the championship and an international tournament is about to get underway. Teams have been invited from Mexico, France and Japan to play against the Elks and their rivals, the Eagles and the Hawks. Greg, a new member of the Elks is hitting the ball very well and the team hopes they can win the tournament prize of a trip to Japan. "Moondance" is saddened to learn the United States had once dropped an atomic bomb on the home of the Japan team, the Nagasaki Knights. When Greg misses practice, "T.J." goes looking for him and discovers the boy and his mother have been hiding a secret about where they live.

About this book: Sequel to *Me, Mop, and the Moondance Kid.*

Where it's reviewed:
Booklist, October 1, 1992, page 341
Emergency Librarian, May 1993, page 29
Horn Book Magazine, November 1992, page 739
Horn Book Guide, Spring 1993, page 74

Other books by the same author:
Darnell Rock Reporting, 1994 (young readers)
Somewhere in the Darkness, 1992 (young readers)
Me, Mop, and the Moondance Kid, 1988 (young readers)
Tales of a Dead King, 1983 (young readers)
Fast Sam, Cool Clyde and Stuff, 1976 (debut novel; young adult)

Other books you might like:
Jacqueline Turner Banks, *Egg-Drop Blues*, 1995
 A sixth grader's science grade is low because of his dyslexia, so he and his twin brother enter a competition for extra credit.
Jacqueline Turner Banks, *The New One*, 1994
 Twin brothers disagree about whether to befriend a new girl at school or interfere with their mother's relationship with her boyfriend.
Sharon M. Draper, *Ziggy and the Black Dinosaurs*, 1994
 When their neighborhood playground is destroyed, four 5th grade boys start their own secret club and uncover a mysterious old box of hidden bones.
Joyce Hansen, *Yellow Bird and Me*, 1986
 Missing her best friend who has moved away, a young girl helps a classmate in elementary school overcome stage fright and discover he has dyslexia.

Vaunda Micheaux Nelson, *Mayfield Crossing*, 1993
 The new kids at an elementary school encounter prejudice for the first time and only baseball has the possibility for drawing people together.

316

WALTER DEAN MYERS, African American

Motown and Didi: A Love Story

(New York: Viking Kestrel, 1984)

Story type: Young Adult
Subject(s): Drugs; City Life; Teen Relationships
Age range(s): Grades 7-12
Major character(s): DiDi Johnson, 17-Year-Old, Student—High School, African American; Frank "Motown" Williams, 17-Year-Old, Runaway, African American
Time period(s): 1980s
Locale(s): New York, New York

Summary: When her brother becomes a junkie, teenaged DiDi goes to the police to turn in his drug pusher and soon her life is in danger. She is dragged into a building by three hoodlums but "Motown" comes to her rescue and she escapes by running away. Later looking for "Motown" to thank him, DiDi discovers he lives in an abandoned apartment building. Since his parents were killed in a fire on a ferry "Motown" had lived in several foster homes before running away to make it on his own. Working at odd jobs and donating blood, he is saving his money to rent a decent apartment. Each wanting a better life DiDi and "Motown" are attracted to one another and fall in love.

Where it's reviewed:
Voice of Youth Advocates, June 1994, page 68
English Journal, September 1993, page 52

Awards the book has won:
Coretta Scott King Award, 1985

Other books by the same author:
Glory Field, 1994 (young adult)
Fallen Angels, 1988 (young adult)
Crystal, 1987 (young adult)
The Outside Shot, 1984 (young adult)
Fast Sam, Cool Clyde and Stuff, 1976 (debut novel; young adult)

Other books you might like:
Vy Higginsen, *Mama, I Want to Sing*, 1995
 Recounts events in the life of a talented singer from a young girl singing in the church choir to a renowned award winning star.
Angela Johnson, *Toning the Sweep*, 1993
 A young girl prepares a special gift for her grandmother dying of cancer and honors the spirit of the deceased grandfather she never knew.
Julius Lester, *Othello, a Novel*, 1995
 A reconceptualization with modern dialogue of Shakespeare's play where a mercenary general and a white noblewoman fall in love and tragedy awaits.
Valerie Wilson Wesley, *Where Do I Go From Here?*, 1993
 Having trouble at a snooty mostly-white prep school a

teenager learns from another scholarship student she must make decisions for her own life.

Rita Williams-Garcia, *Fast Talk on a Slow Track*, 1991
  A young man returns to his fierce competition with a rival Latino door-to-door salesman before reluctantly deciding to become a college freshman.

317

WALTER DEAN MYERS, African American

Mouse Rap
(New York: Harper and Row, 1990)

Story type: Young Readers
Subject(s): Treasure; Friendship; Family Relations
Age range(s): Grades 5-8
Major character(s): Frederick "The Mouse" Douglass, Basketball Player, 10th Grader, African American
Time period(s): 1990s
Locale(s): New York, New York (Harlem)

Summary: When summer arrives, "The Mouse," his pal Styx and the guys, and their friends Sheri, Beverly, and Ceil are eager for action. When a newscaster broadcasts the story of a bundle of money being hidden in their neighborhood years ago by the Tiger Moran gang, they form a search party—The Harlem Treasure Crew. As luck would have it, Gramps, Sheri's grandfather, had worked for Moran and thinks he knows exactly where their office was located. He also knows where they might locate old members of the Moran gang, Sudden Sam and Katie Donahue. Katie has passed away but not before she told her young grandson Eugene, "The Booster," about the gang's hideout. While the search for the money is on, "The Mouse" gets involved in a romantic triangle with Beverly and Styx, his separated mother and father may be getting back together, and the girls convince the guys to join them in a talent contest.

Where it's reviewed:
Kliatt Young Adult Paperback Book Guide, November 1992, page 10

Other books by the same author:
Darnell Rock Reporting, 1994 (young readers)
The Righteous Revenge of Artemis Bonner, 1992 (young readers)
Somewhere in the Darkness, 1992 (young readers)
Tales of a Dead King, 1983 (young readers)
Fast Sam, Cool Clyde and Stuff, 1976 (debut novel; young adult)

Other books you might like:
Candy Dawson Boyd, *Chevrolet Saturdays*, 1993
  Struggling with the divorce of his parents and accepting his new stepfather, a young boy has trouble in school and makes mistakes he regrets.
Sharon M. Draper, *Ziggy and the Black Dinosaurs*, 1994
  When their neighborhood playground is destroyed, four 5th grade boys start their own secret club and uncover a mysterious old box of hidden bones.
Virginia Hamilton, *The Mystery of Drear House*, 1987
  A house that was a station on the Underground Railroad

has secret passageways and hidden treasure which must be saved before it is too late.

Jacqueline Woodson, *Between Madison & Palmetto*, 1993
  In their continuing story, two 13-year-old best friends are reunited and have to adjust to a lot of change in their lives and in those around them.

318

WALTER DEAN MYERS, African American
LESLIE MORRILL, Illustrator, Caucasian

Mr. Monkey and the Gotcha Bird: An Original Tale
(New York: Delacorte Press, 1984)

Story type: Young Readers
Subject(s): Animals
Age range(s): Grades 1-3
Time period(s): Indeterminate Past
Locale(s): Mythical Place

Summary: A monkey captured by the Gotcha Bird is afraid of being eaten. He has to use his wits to outsmart the bird until he can flee from danger. An unwitting lion helps the monkey and gets a fine dinner in the bargain.

Other books by the same author:
The Story of the Three Kingdoms, 1995
The Golden Serpent, 1980

Other books you might like:
Ashley Bryan, *The Story of Lightning & Thunder*, 1993
  A West African folktale about Ma Sheep Thunder and her disobedient Son Ram Lightning who caused them to be banished from the earth to the sky.
Ashley Bryan, *The Cat's Purr*, 1985
  The West Indies folktale of the Cat and the Rat who were once friends living along side one another and the incident which ended their friendship.
Patricia C. McKissack, *Flossie and the Fox*, 1986
  The tale of a youngster sent to deliver fresh eggs to a neighbor who outsmarts an egg loving fox along the way trying to prove who he is.
Patricia C. McKissack, *Monkey-Monkey's Trick*, 1988
  An African folktale of a monkey who discovers he is being tricked by a hyena and plays his own trick on the hyena to get his new house built.

319

WALTER DEAN MYERS, African American

The Nicholas Factor
(New York: Viking Press, 1983)

Story type: Young Readers
Subject(s): Adventure and Adventurers; Neo-Nazis; Spies
Age range(s): Grades 6 and Up
Major character(s): Gerald McQuillen, 17-Year-Old, Student—College, Caucasian; John Martens, Spy (National Security Agency), African American; Jennifer Wells, 16-Year-Old, Student—College, Caucasian
Time period(s): 1980s

Locale(s): California (unidentified city); Lima, Peru

Summary: When his father is killed in a race car accident, Gerald and his mother suffer their loss together. Gerald has been drifting in his freshman year at college looking for direction and was curious when the Dean asked him to meet with someone interested in the school's activities. He meets with John who turns out to be an agent for the National Security Agency wanting Gerald to infiltrate the Crusade Society on campus looking for neo-Nazi activity. Soon Gerald is swept up in a spy adventure taking him to the Amazon jungle of Peru along with Jennifer, another member of the Crusade Society. Together they discover their mission for the Crusade Society is not what it appeared when their companion Andwele, a fellow Crusader from the Cameroons, becomes ill, a jungle village of Indians begins dying, and they uncover incriminating evidence. Escaping towards Lima, Gerald and Jennifer hope to find safety if they can contact John before members of the Crusade Society locate them.

Where it's reviewed:
Journal of Youth Services in Libraries, Winter 1993, page 202

Other books by the same author:
The Righteous Revenge of Artemis Bonner, 1992 (young readers)
Somewhere in the Darkness, 1992 (young readers)
Mouse Rap, 1990 (young readers)
Tales of a Dead King, 1983 (young readers)
Fast Sam, Cool Clyde and Stuff, 1976 (debut novel; young adult)

Other books you might like:
Virginia Hamilton, *Dustland*, 1980
    Four children, all possessing extraordinary mental powers, are projected far into the future to a bleak region called Dustland.
Virginia Hamilton, *The Gathering*, 1981
    Four children time-travel to Dustland and battle Mal, an entity who controls the future but whose immense power has gone awry.
Virginia Hamilton, *The Mystery of Drear House*, 1987
    A house that was a station on the Underground Railroad has secret passageways and hidden treasure which must be saved before it is too late.

320

WALTER DEAN MYERS, African American

The Outside Shot
(New York: Delacorte Press, 1984)

Story type: Young Adult
Series: Lonnie Jackson
Subject(s): Sports/Basketball; College Life; Interpersonal Relations
Age range(s): Grades 7-12
Major character(s): Lonnie Jackson, Student—College, Basketball Player, African American; Sherry Jewett, Student—College, Runner, African American
Time period(s): 1980s
Locale(s): Montclare, Indiana

Summary: Born and raised in Harlem, in this episode of his life Lonnie wins a basketball scholarship to a small, predominantly white school in Indiana. He feels the pressures of a freshman as he tries to excel in basketball, succeed in a new part-time job in the physical therapy department, deal with difficult coursework, and make new friends. When Sherry introduces herself to him in one of his classes he is surprised to learn she is also an athlete on the track team. Attracted to her, Lonnie feels somewhat awkward around Sherry and is unsure about how to show his feelings for her. He feels more comfortable on the basketball court until he gets implicated in an investigation about gambling on the games and his future hangs in the balance.

About this book: Sequel to *Hoops*.

Where it's reviewed:
English Journal, September 1993, page 52

Awards the book has won:
Parents' Choice Award, 1984

Other books by the same author:
Glory Field, 1994 (Young Adult)
Scorpions, 1988 (Young Adult)
Fallen Angels, 1988 (Young Adult)
Motown and DiDi: A Love Story, 1984 (Young Adult)
Fast Sam, Cool Clyde and Stuff, 1976 (debut novel; young adult)

Other books you might like:
Ossie Davis, *Just Like Martin*, 1992
    A religiously active son and his war veteran father disagree over the civil rights movement until events occur that help them to work together.
Sharon M. Draper, *Tears of a Tiger*, 1994
    A teenager escaping a car accident in which his friend is killed and others are injured has difficulty learning to live with the trauma.
David Haynes, *Right by My Side*, 1993
    A high school student writes down his experiences in order to figure things out about his father, his mother and himself.
Valerie Wilson Wesley, *Where Do I Go From Here?*, 1993
    Having trouble at a snooty mostly-white prep school a teenager learns from another scholarship student she must make decisions for her own life.
Rita Williams-Garcia, *Fast Talk on a Slow Track*, 1991
    A young man returns to his fierce competition with a rival Latino door-to-door salesman before reluctantly deciding to become a college freshman.

321

WALTER DEAN MYERS, African American

The Righteous Revenge of Artemis Bonner
(New York: HarperCollins Publishers, 1992)

Story type: Young Readers
Subject(s): Revenge; Treasure; Friendship
Age range(s): Grades 5-9
Major character(s): Artemis Bonner, 15-Year-Old, Nephew, African American; Frolic D. "Laughing Bear" Brown, 12-Year-Old, Orphan, Native American (half Cherokee)

Time period(s): 1880s (1882)
Locale(s): Tombstone, Arizona

Summary: When he journeys from his home in New York City to the wild west of Arizona, 15-year-old Artemis is out to seek revenge for the murder of his uncle Ugly Ned Bonner. His mother's sister has asked for Artemis' help to bring his uncle's killer, Catfish Grimes, to justice. In return she promises to pay him well and to give him a map to his uncle's hidden treasure which he can keep for his own if he finds it before Catfish Grimes does. Hunting for the treasure, Catfish Grimes and his companion Lucy Featherdip take Artemis to territories in New Mexico, Mexico, California, Washington, and Alaska. Along the way he meets a trusty young sidekick, Frolic, and they share the adventure together as brothers. In an unexpected conclusion they discover what happened to the treasure and how they might get it back.

Where it's reviewed:
Kliatt, January 1995, page 11
Journal of Youth Services in Libraries, Summer 1995, page 418

Other books by the same author:
Darnell Rock Reporting, 1994 (young readers)
Somewhere in the Darkness, 1992 (young readers)
Mouse Rap, 1990 (young readers)
Tales of a Dead King, 1983 (young readers)
Fast Sam, Cool Clyde and Stuff, 1976 (debut novel; young adult)

Other books you might like:
Joyce Hansen, *The Captive*, 1994
Historical fiction of the life of a royal African boy who is kidnapped and illegally sold as a slave and is later rescued by a sea captain.
Virginia Hamilton, *The Gathering*, 1981
Four children time-travel to Dustland and battle Mal, an entity who controls the future but whose immense power has gone awry.
Harriette Gillem Robinet, *Mississippi Chariot*, 1994
A resourceful 12-year-old son of a sharecropper plans to get his falsely convicted father off of the chain gang in 1930's Mississippi.
Joyce Carol Thomas, *The Golden Pasture*, 1986
The exquisite horse a 12-year-old boy finds on his grandfather's farm one summer helps him to understand his difficult father better.
Mildred Pitts Walter, *Justin and the Best Biscuits in the World*, 1986
A 10-year-old, sure that cleaning and keeping house is "women's work," visits his beloved grandfather's ranch and learns some manly skills.

322

WALTER DEAN MYERS, African American

Scorpions

(New York: Harper and Row Publishers, 1988)

Story type: Young Adult
Subject(s): Gangs; Friendship; Family Relations
Age range(s): Grades 9-12

Major character(s): Jamal Hicks, 12-Year-Old, Student—Junior High, African American; Sassy Hicks, 8-Year-Old, 3rd Grader, African American; Tito Cruz, 12-Year-Old, Student—Junior High, Puerto Rican
Time period(s): 1980s
Locale(s): New York, New York (Harlem)

Summary: With their older brother Randy in jail for murder, Jamal and Sassy watch as their mother visits him and tries to raise money for his appeal. Teenaged Randy had been the leader of a street gang called the Scorpions and now he wants Jamal to take his place. Young Jamal and his closest friend Tito have never been involved in gangs and they vow to stick together no matter what. Once Randy's sidekick, Mack, brings Jamal a gun to show he is ready to take over the Scorpions, things begin to change. Jamal and Tito feel the power having a gun gives them and they also feel scared of what could happen. Sassy finds out about the gun but does not tell her mother, as she hopes Jamal will get rid of it. When some of the Scorpions challenge Jamal, he and Tito take the gun to a meeting in the park that changes their lives forever.

Where it's reviewed:
Booklist, October 15, 1994, page 415
English Journal, September 1995, page 32

Awards the book has won:
American Library Association Notable Book, 1988
Newbery Honor Book, 1989

Other books by the same author:
Glory Field, 1994 (young adult)
Fallen Angels, 1988 (young adult)
Motown and DiDi: A Love Story, 1984 (young adult)
The Outside Shot, 1984 (young adult)
Fast Sam, Cool Clyde and Stuff, 1976 (debut novel; young adult)

Other books you might like:
Sharon M. Draper, *Tears of a Tiger*, 1994
A teenager escaping a car accident in which his friend is killed and others are injured has difficulty learning to live with the trauma.
David Haynes, *Right by My Side*, 1993
A high school student writes down his experiences in order to figure things out about his father, his mother and himself.
Jess Mowry, *Children of the Night*, 1991
Two young boys wanting money so they can "be somebody", go to work for the neighborhood crack dealer, only to discover the cost is way too high.
Jess Mowry, *Way Past Cool*, 1992
Two rival gangs must put aside their differences to solve their common problem when a drug dealer tries to stir up trouble between them.
Rita Williams-Garcia, *Fast Talk on a Slow Track*, 1991
A young man returns to his fierce competition with a rival Latino door-to-door salesman before reluctantly deciding to become a college freshman.
Jacqueline Woodson, *From the Notebooks of Melanin Sun*, 1995
A 13-year-old boy's world is turned upside down and he has to confront his prejudices when his mother tells him she is in love with a white woman.

323

WALTER DEAN MYERS, African American

Somewhere in the Darkness
(New York: Scholastic Inc., 1992)

Story type: Young Readers
Subject(s): Fathers and Sons; Crime and Criminals
Age range(s): Grades 5 and Up
Major character(s): Jimmy Little, 14-Year-Old, 10th Grader, African American; Cephus ''Crab'' Little, Father, Fugitive, African American
Time period(s): 1990s
Locale(s): New York, New York; Marion, Arkansas

Summary: Raised by his dead mother's friend, Mama Jean, and now in the tenth grade, Jimmy is having a hard time in school. When Jimmy gets home from school one day a neighbor tells him a man is looking for him. To his surprise the man is his father, ''Crab,'' who has been in prison for almost nine years. Mama Jean welcomes ''Crab'' but is worried when he says he wants to take Jimmy away on a trip with him. Traveling across country together, Jimmy discovers his father is ill and has escaped from prison to tell him he did not commit the crime for which he was convicted. ''Crab'' wants to prove his innocence to Jimmy by taking him to Arkansas to find the witness who lied about him. The long trip takes its toll on ''Crab'' and he seeks the healing of a conjure man once they arrive. Captured by the police, ''Crab'' gets confined to the hospital with Jimmy by his side.

Where it's reviewed:
Books for Keeps, January 1995, page 11
Junior Bookshelf, February 1995, page 41
School Librarian, February 1995, page 32

Awards the book has won:
Coretta Scott King Honor Book, 1993

Other books by the same author:
The Righteous Revenge of Artemis Bonner, 1992 (young readers)
Mouse Rap, 1990 (young readers)
The Nicholas Factor, 1983 (young readers)
Tales of a Dead King, 1983 (young readers)
Fast Sam, Cool Clyde and Stuff, 1976 (debut novel; young adult)

Other books you might like:
Candy Dawson Boyd, *Charlie Pippin*, 1987
Curious about her father's involvement in the Vietnam conflict, an enterprising sixth-grader joins a school group to learn more.
Virginia Hamilton, *Plain City*, 1993
A 12-year-old who feels out of place struggles to unearth her past and family history as she gradually discovers more about her long-missing father.
Harriette Gillem Robinet, *Mississippi Chariot*, 1994
A resourceful 12-year-old son of a sharecropper plans to get his falsely convicted father off of the chain gang in 1930's Mississippi.
Eleanora E. Tate, *A Blessing in Disguise*, 1995
Another tale from the Calvary County trilogy where a young girl discovers that the father she admired has addicted her dying mother to alcohol and drugs.

324

WALTER DEAN MYERS, African American
ASHLEY BRYAN, Illustrator, African American

The Story of the Three Kingdoms
(New York: Harper Collins, 1995)

Story type: Young Readers
Subject(s): Fables; Animals; Human Behavior
Age range(s): Grades 1-2
Time period(s): Indeterminate Past
Locale(s): Mythical Place

Summary: An original fable telling of three kingdoms on earth and what happens when people meet their rulers. One kingdom is ruled by the giant Elephant, another by the powerful Shark, and one by the fierce Hawk. The Elephant thinks his kingdom of the forest and himself the greatest on earth. In the sea, which covers most of the earth, the Shark sees himself as the most powerful and his as the greatest kingdom on earth. The fierce Hawk in the sky, sees himself and his kingdom as the greatest on earth. They argue amongst themselves as to who rules the greatest kingdom. The people on earth, not as strong as the elephant, nor as fierce as the shark, nor able to fly like the hawk, walk about with their eyes cast down. But soon they begin to use their intelligence to capture the elephant, the shark and the hawk and force all to share their kingdoms with the people. In these ways the people become the masters of the earth ruling the forest, the sea, and the air. They now hold their heads high and never forget to sit by the fire telling their stories.

Other books by the same author:
Mr. Monkey and the Gotcha Bird: An Original Tale, 1984
The Golden Serpent, 1980

Other books you might like:
Ashley Bryan, *The Story of Lightning & Thunder*, 1993
A West African folktale about Ma Sheep Thunder and her disobedient Son Ram Lightning who caused them to be banished from the earth to the sky.
Percival Everett, *The One That Got Away*, 1992
Western tale of a group of cowboys rounding up ''ones'' into a corral and when one jumps the fence what happens when they go searching for it.

325

WALTER DEAN MYERS, African American

Tales of a Dead King
(New York: William Morrow and Company, 1983)

Story type: Young Readers
Subject(s): Mystery and Detective Stories; Archaeology; Egyptian Antiquities
Age range(s): Grades 6 and Up
Major character(s): John Robie, Teenager, Nephew, Caucasian; Karen Lacey, Teenager, Student—High School, Caucasian

Time period(s): 1980s
Locale(s): Aswan, Egypt

Summary: Interested in archaeology, John is excited when his parents send him on a trip to meet his great-uncle, Egyptologist Dr. Erich Leonhardt, for the first time. When John arrives in Aswan he meets Karen, another teenager whom the Dr. has selected to join in the archaeological dig. They are both disappointed at the dingy hotel the Doctor has arranged for them and shocked to find he has disappeared without a trace and owes the hotel money. Questioned by the police, the teenagers decide to stay in Aswan to search for the Doctor. In their search Karen discovers a snake in her bed, they read the notebooks the Doctor left behind, someone begins following them, and a dagger is thrown at them in the marketplace.

Other books by the same author:
Darnell Rock Reporting, 1994 (young readers)
Somewhere in the Darkness, 1992 (young readers)
Mouse Rap, 1990 (young readers)
The Nicholas Factor, 1983 (young readers)
Fast Sam, Cool Clyde and Stuff, 1976 (debut novel; young adult)

Other books you might like:
Virginia Hamilton, *Dustland*, 1980
    Four children, all possessing extraordinary mental powers, are projected far into the future to a bleak region called Dustland.
Virginia Hamilton, *The Mystery of Drear House*, 1987
    A house that was a station on the Underground Railroad has secret passageways and hidden treasure which must be saved before it is too late.
Eleanora E. Tate, *The Secret of Gumbo Grove*, 1987
    A youngster upsets her community and her parents when she spreads stories she's heard about the town ancestors buried in the church cemetery.

326

WALTER DEAN MYERS, African American

Won't Know Till I Get There

(New York: Viking Press, 1982)

Story type: Young Adult
Subject(s): Adoption; Old Age; Interpersonal Relations
Age range(s): Grades 7-10
Major character(s): Stephen ''Steve'' Gerard Perry, 14-Year-Old, African American; Earl Goins, 13-Year-Old, Foundling, African American
Time period(s): 1980s
Locale(s): New York, New York

Summary: Diary accounts of the summer Steve's parents announce they are considering adopting a foster child. He thinks it could be a good idea until he discovers the boy has a criminal record. Earl has been arrested for disturbing the peace, vandalism, and armed robbery. Wanting to prove he is tough too, when Steve introduces Earl to his friends he spray paints a subway car and gets caught in the act. The transit police arrest them all. Steve's parents are dismayed since he has never been in any trouble before and they are grateful when the judge only sentences them to community service in a senior citizens' house. Exploits with the senior citizens fill the summer days. They hit a snag in the adoption proceedings when Earl's mother wants to visit their home. She has the right to deny the adoption and she's done it before. Over the summer Steve and Earl come to be like brothers and are nervous over the outcome of her visit.

Awards the book has won:
Parents' Choice Award, 1982

Other books by the same author:
Glory Field, 1994 (young adult)
Scorpions, 1988 (young adult)
Fallen Angels, 1988 (young adult)
The Outside Shot, 1984 (young adult)
Fast Sam, Cool Clyde and Stuff, 1976 (debut novel; young adult)

Other books you might like:
David Haynes, *Right by My Side*, 1993
    A high school student writes down his experiences in order to figure things out about his father, his mother and himself.
Angela Johnson, *Toning the Sweep*, 1993
    A young girl prepares a special gift for her grandmother dying of cancer and honors the spirit of the deceased grandfather she never knew.
Joyce Carol Thomas, *Marked by Fire*, 1982
    Friends and family help a young girl overcome the effects of a tornado and a physical assault which nearly breaks her will.
Rita Williams-Garcia, *Like Sisters on the Homefront*, 1994
    An unwed 14-year-old mother, pregnant again has an abortion and when she is sent to her relatives in the South, develops a sense of family and self.
Jacqueline Woodson, *From the Notebooks of Melanin Sun*, 1995
    A 13-year-old boy's world is turned upside down and he has to confront his prejudices when his mother tells him she is in love with a white woman.

327

WALTER DEAN MYERS, African American

The Young Landlords

(New York: Viking Press, 1979)

Subject(s): Business Enterprises; Tenant/Landlord Relations; Teen Relationships
Age range(s): Grades 7-10
Major character(s): Paul Williams, 15-Year-Old, Landlord, African American; Gloria Wiggins, 15-Year-Old, Landlord, African American
Time period(s): 1970s
Locale(s): New York, New York (Harlem)

Summary: During their summer vacation, with Gloria's leadership, Paul and his friends Dean, Bubba, Omar and Jeannie form themselves into an Action Group. Among their goals is to do something about the neighborhood's rundown building at 356 Stratford Arms, aka The Joint. When they find the absentee landlord and complain about conditions at the building he sells it to them for one dollar, giving them the responsibility of fixing it up. Now landlords, the group finds themselves in a business they know nothing about. Also that summer, one of their classmates, Chris, is accused of robbery and the group comes to his defense, looking for evidence to prove his innocence. Warned to stay out of police business, they nevertheless put themselves on the line by setting up a sting to buy stolen merchandise and becoming targets of gunfire when they sneak into a warehouse where they think the stolen property is being hidden.

Where it's reviewed:
English Journal, May 1980, page 91
New York Times Book Review, January 6, 1980, page 20
School Library Journal, October 1979, page 160

Awards the book has won:
Coretta Scott King Award, 1980
American Library Association Notable Book, 1979

Other books by the same author:
Motown and DiDi: A Love Story, 1984
Won't Know Till I Get There, 1982
Legend of Tarik, 1981
Brainstorm, 1977
Fast Sam, Cool Clyde and Stuff, 1976 (debut novel)

Other books you might like:
Ossie Davis, *Just Like Martin*, 1992
  A religiously active son and his war veteran father disagree over the civil rights movement until after events occur that help them to work together.
Virginia Hamilton, *Sweet Whispers, Brother Rush*, 1982
  A girl caring for her retarded older brother encounters the ghost of her dead uncle and comes to a deeper understanding of her family and herself.
David Haynes, *Right by My Side*, 1993
  A high school student writes down his experiences in order to figure things out about his father, his mother and himself.
Brenda Wilkinson, *Ludell's New York Time*, 1980
  Moving from Georgia to New York City in her senior year a teenager struggles to adjust to life in 1960s Harlem.

328

GLORIA NAYLOR, African American

Bailey's Cafe

(New York: Harcourt Brace Jovanovich, 1992)

Subject(s): Human Behavior; Outcasts; Storytelling
Age range(s): Adult
Major character(s): Bailey, Cook, Restauranteur, African American; Eve, Businesswoman, African American; Gabriel, Store Owner, African American
Time period(s): 1940s (1948)
Locale(s): San Francisco, California

Summary: Bailey owns a cafe that never closes. It is situated between Eve's boardinghouse, which has a beautiful garden, and Gabriel's pawnshop, which is never open. Bailey introduces the people who pass through this mythical waystation for lost souls. They tell their stories of innocence lost, survival, and future hopes.

Where it's reviewed:
Lambda Book Report, January 1994, page 42
Los Angeles Times Book Review, October 24, 1993, page 10
Tribune Books (Chicago), November 28, 1993, page 8

Other books by the same author:
Mama Day, 1988
Linden Hills, 1985
Women of Brewster Place, 1982 (debut novel)

Other books you might like:
Leon Forrest, *Divine Days*, 1992
  In an epic tale referred to as *The Ulysses of the South Side*, an aspiring playwright captures the voices of the living and the dead.
Helen Elaine Lee, *The Serpent's Gift*, 1994
  The children and grandchildren of two intertwined families endure hardship and they triumph as they help each other remember a history beyond their realm.

329

GLORIA NAYLOR, African American

Linden Hills

(New York: Ticknor & Fields, 1985)

Subject(s): Interpersonal Relations; Identity
Age range(s): Adult
Major character(s): Luther Nedeed, Landowner, Undertaker, African American; Lester Tilson, Writer, African American; Willie Mason, African American, Writer
Time period(s): 1970s
Locale(s): Linden Hills (Fictional city)

Summary: Linden Hills symbolizes success to the people who live there, and for those people who apply for the thousand-year leases from Luther Nedeed. Doing odd jobs to earn Christmas money, Lester and Willie see firsthand the lust, pain, hypocrisy and valor of these residents who have "sold the silver mirror of their soul."

Other books by the same author:
Bailey's Cafe, 1992
Mama Day, 1988
Women of Brewster Place, 1982 (debut novel)

Other books you might like:
Nelson George, *Urban Romance*, 1993
  This contemporary story tells relationship of a young couple brought together by mutual friends as they experience love and heartbreak.
Terri McMillan, *Disappearing Acts*, 1989
  A successful professional woman tries to maintain a relationship with a man who is unable to keep a steady job.
Terry McMillan, *Waiting to Exhale*, 1992
  This contemporary account is about the friendship of four women, their relationships with men, and their experiences with family and careers.
Brenda Lane Richardson, *Chesapeake Song*, 1993
  Even though two successful people are unable to see that their marital problems mirror those of their parents, they come to learn the importance of love.

330

GLORIA NAYLOR, African American

Mama Day

(New York: Ticknor & Fields, 1988)

Subject(s): Family Relations; Supernatural
Age range(s): Adult
Major character(s): Miranda "Mama" Day, Healer, Aged Person, African American; Ophelia "Cocoa" Andrews, Granddaughter, Spouse, African American; George Andrews, Businessman, Spouse, African American
Time period(s): 1980s (1980)
Locale(s): Willow Springs, South

Summary: On a visit to her sea island home with her new husband, Cocoa finds both her body and soul threatened by supernatural forces. These forces of the past and the present challenge all the knowledge of her proud and independent great-aunt Miranda.

Where it's reviewed:
African American Review, Summer 1994, page 173
African American Review, Fall 1993, page 405
Emergency Librarian, January 1994, page 81
Emergency Librarian, March 1994, page 95

Other books by the same author:
Bailey's Cafe, 1992
Linden Hills, 1985
Women of Brewster Place, 1982 (debut novel)

Other books you might like:
Tananarive Due, *The Between*, 1995
   A man endures nightmares and his sense of reality wavers as he desperately tries to protect his family from the psychotic who stalks them.
Arthur Flowers, *De Mojo Blues*, 1985
   This story depicts a Vietnam veteran dishonorably discharged for murder with his buddies. He now wants to become trained in the ways of hoodoo and conjuring.
Paule Marshall, *Daughters*, 1991
   A determined young woman struggles in her relationship with her political father and when she returns home for a visit she makes an important decision.

331

GLORIA NAYLOR, African American

Women of Brewster Place

(New York: Viking Press, 1982)

Story type: Adult
Subject(s): City Life; Interpersonal Relations; Self-Acceptance
Age range(s): Adult
Major character(s): Mattie Michael, Aged Person, Single Mother, African American
Time period(s): 1960s (after 1960)
Locale(s): Brewster Place (Fictional city)

Summary: Among the seven women's stories told when they come to live on the dead-end street of Brewster Place, Mattie's is pivotal. As an unwed mother, she raises her son alone, only to be forsaken by him when he kills someone and then jumps bail. As a result, she loses the home that she used as collateral to set him free and moves to Brewster Place. There she meets her neighbors: Cora Lee, a young unwed mother with several children; Kiswana aka Melanie, a young activist who rejects her affluent Linden Hills upbringing; Lorraine and Theresa, a lesbian couple; Lucielia, a young mother who loses her daughter; and Mattie's childhood friend, Etta Mae. When Lorraine is brutally gang-raped, she loses her mind and kills her friend Ben, the building's janitor. In redemption, the women symbolically tear down the dead-end wall where her blood was spilled.

About this book: This is the author's debut novel, which won an award and was also made into a movie.

Awards the book has won:
American Book Award, 1983

Other books by the same author:
Bailey's Cafe, 1992
Mama Day, 1988
Linden Hills, 1985

Other books you might like:
Linda Beatrice Brown, *Crossing over Jordan*, 1995
   This saga is about the binding ties in the lives of four generations of mothers and daughters from the Civil War era to the early 21st century.
Marita Golden, *And Do Remember Me*, 1992
   A young girl raped by her father, runs away from home. She later finds the courage to return home when he suffers a stroke and she confronts her mother.
Terri McMillan, *Mama*, 1987
   A proud and feisty mother does her best to provide for her five children through three marriages and uncertain times.
John Edgar Wideman, *Reuben*, 1987
   This story relates the exploits of an aged lawyer and the various clients he represents in the Pittsburgh community of Homewood during the 1980s.

332

BARBARA NEELY, African American

Blanche Among the Talented Tenth

(New York: St. Martin's Press, 1994)

Story type: Amateur Detective; Adult
Series: Blanche White
Subject(s): Interpersonal Relations; Murder; Mystery and Detective Stories
Age range(s): Adult
Major character(s): Blanche White, Heroine, Housekeeper, African American
Time period(s): 1990s (1994)
Locale(s): Amber Cove, Maine

Summary: When Blanche arrives with her kids for a holiday at an exclusive resort in Maine, she learns that a guest has had a fatal accident. As she meets the other guests, they draw her into an intrigue of murder, suicide, and secrets from the past. She manages to meet a new man, get knocked unconscious, and commune with her ancient ancestors. With her wit, insight and intelligence, Blanche unravels the mystery.

About this book: This is the second title of the Blanche White series.

Other books by the same author:
Blanche on the Lam, 1992 (debut novel, Blanche White series)

Other books you might like:
Eleanor Taylor Bland, *Dead Time*, 1992
This debut novel begins a detective mystery series with a female heroine.
Gar Anthony Haywood, *Going Nowhere Fast*, 1994
This debut novel begins a mystery series about an amateur detective and her retired police detective husband.
Yolanda Joe, *Falling Leaves of Ivy*, 1992
A young woman is murdered and her four closest friends from college become suspects, as the secret shared among them begins to unravel.
Penny Mickelbury, *Keeping Secrets*, 1994
This debut novel begins a murder mystery series with lesbian characters.
Valerie Wilson Wesley, *When Death Comes Stealing*, 1994
This debut novel begins a murder mystery series featuring an ex-policewoman who becomes a private detective.

333

BARBARA NEELY, African American

Blanche on the Lam
(New York: St. Martin's Press, 1992)

Story type: Amateur Detective
Series: Blanche White
Subject(s): Family Relations; Murder; Mystery and Detective Stories
Age range(s): Adult
Major character(s): Blanche White, Heroine, Housekeeper, African American; Everett Hancock, Spouse, Caucasian; Cousin Mumsfield, Caucasian
Time period(s): 1990s (1992)
Locale(s): Farleigh, North Carolina

Summary: Resourceful Blanche takes a job as a housekeeper with the Hancock family, hiding to avoid her own trouble with the law. She finds herself involved in murder, as a suspect and as an amateur detective, when she uncovers a tale of family deceit, greed, alcoholism, fraud, infidelity, and madness.

About this book: This is the author's debut novel.

Where it's reviewed:
Essence, April 1992, page 54
Kirkus Reviews, December 15, 1991, page 1560
Publishers Weekly, January 20, 1992, page 50

Other books by the same author:
Blanche Among the Talented Tenth, 1994 (Blanche White series)

Other books you might like:
Nikki Baker, *In the Game*, 1991
This debut novel begins a murder mystery series with lesbian characters.

Eleanor Taylor Bland, *Dead Time*, 1992
This debut novel begins a detective mystery series with a female heroine.
Gar Anthony Haywood, *Going Nowhere Fast*, 1994
This debut novel begins a mystery series about an amateur detective and her retired police detective husband.
Barbara Summers, *The Price You Pay*, 1993
A young woman in the highly competitive fashion industry finds herself a target for murder when a new marketing campaign is launched.
Valerie Wilson, *When Death Comes Stealing*, 1994
This debut novel begins a murder mystery series featuring an ex-policewoman who becomes a private detective.

334

VAUNDA MICHEAUX NELSON, African American
LEONARD JENKINS, Illustrator

Mayfield Crossing
(New York: G. P. Putnam's Sons, 1993)

Story type: Young Readers
Subject(s): Sports/Baseball; Race Relations; School Life
Age range(s): Grades 3-6
Major character(s): Meg Turner, 9-Year-Old, Baseball Player, African American
Time period(s): 1960s (1960)
Locale(s): Mayfield Crossing

Summary: It's the end of summer, and the kids in Mayfield Crossing are looking forward to attending Parkview Elementary School with its huge ball field of thick, green grass. They are treated as outsiders and it seems nobody wants them there. They aren't even allowed to play ball. In Mayfield nobody ever thought of black and white, but the kids at Parkview certainly seem to notice. Meg and her friends are able to hold their own and Meg's brother Billie figures out a way to let baseball join all the kids together.

About this book: Debut novel

Where it's reviewed:
Instructor, January 1995, page 88
Language Arts, September 1995, page 372
Quill & Quire, December 1992, page 29

Other books by the same author:
Possibles, 1995

Other books you might like:
Joyce Hansen, *Yellow Bird and Me*, 1986
Missing her best friend who has moved away, a young girl helps a classmate in elementary school overcome stage fright and discover he has dyslexia.
Walter Dean Myers, *Me, Mop, and the Moondance Kid*, 1988
Two young brothers share a close friendship with a white young girl on their Little League baseball team and hope she gets adopted like they did.
Walter Dean Myers, *Mop, Moondance and Nagasaki Knights*, 1992
Another episode in the lives of two adopted young brothers and their friend, a white young girl on their Little League baseball team.

Andrea Davis Pinkney, *Hold Fast to Dreams*, 1995
Two sisters endure prejudice when their family moves to the suburbs and they have to attend separate all-white schools and try to fit in.

Jacqueline Woodson, *Maizon At Blue Hill*, 1992
Another episode in the lives of two young seventh grade friends where one girl wins an academic scholarship to a white boarding school.

335

LIONEL NEWTON, African American

Getting Right with God
(New York: Dutton, 1994)

Subject(s): Coming of Age; City Life; Conduct of Life
Age range(s): Grades 9-Adult
Major character(s): Lucas Martin, Student, Teenager, African American; Roar Taylor, Drug Dealer, Teenager, African American
Time period(s): 1990s
Locale(s): Chicago, Illinois

Summary: Dealing with adolescence, sex, love, and religion, Lucas Martin finds himself in fantastical chats with God and Satan who appear to him as two drag queens. Lucas must decide between hanging out with his best friend Roar, who deals in drugs, playing basketball in the court outside his house, or playing practical jokes or just doing the right thing.

About this book: This is the author's debut novel.

Where it's reviewed:
Book World, March 5, 1995, page 12
Publishers Weekly, January 2, 1995, page 71

Other books by the same author:
Things to Be Lost, 1995

Other books you might like:
Jess Mowry, *Six Out Seven*, 1993
A young Mississippi boy meets street kids struggling to survive in California. He discovers that he can only count on his own integrity.

David Haynes, *Right by My Side*, 1993
A high school student writes down his experiences in order to figure things out about his father, his mother and himself.

336

LIONEL NEWTON, African American

Things to Be Lost
(New York: Dutton, 1995)

Subject(s): Coming of Age; Family Relations
Age range(s): Grades 10-Adult
Major character(s): Randall Roberts, Artist, 12-Year-Old, African American; Frank Roberts, Religious, Doctor (Psychiatrist), African American
Time period(s): 1990s
Locale(s): Midtown, Illinois

Summary: Bright and curious, Randall is as perceptive about the adult world as he is of his own. He understands his ailing father as seemingly no one else does, perhaps because he has been reading his father's journal. Entering into a secretive relationship with his father through the journal and with their religious conversations, ultimately Randall must decide to kill what he loves most and to suffer guilt as well as loss.

Where it's reviewed:
Booklist, December 15, 1994, page 736
Black Scholar, Spring 1995, page 71
Bookworld, August 31, 1995, page 8
Kirkus Reviews, November 1, 1994, page 1437
Los Angeles Times Book Review, June 4, 1995, page 6

Other books by the same author:
Getting Right with God, 1994

Other books you might like:
Jess Mowry, *Six Out Seven*, 1993
A young Mississippi boy meets street kids struggling to survive in California. He discovers that he can only count on his own integrity.

David Haynes, *Right by My Side*, 1993
A high school student writes down his experiences in order to figure things out about his father, his mother and himself.

337

NICHELLE NICHOLS, African American
MARGARET WANDER BONANNO, Co-Author, African American

Saturn's Child
(New York: G. P. Putnam's Sons, 1995)

Story type: Adult; Science Fiction
Subject(s): Family Relations; Interpersonal Relations; Genetic Engineering
Major character(s): Dr. Nyota Domonique, Scientist (space explorer), Telepath, African American; Tetrok, Scientist (space explorer), Royalty, African American; Saturna, Telepath, Genetically Altered Being, African American
Time period(s): 21st century (2089-2109)
Locale(s): Titan, Saturn

Summary: An expedition has been approved by the Earth Space Council to Saturn's largest moon Titan to study it at close range and determine if it would make a good extension colony someday. Nyota has been selected to command the voyage on her ship the *Dragon's Egg*, unaware that inhabitants from the unknown planet, Fazis, are already exploring Titan and awaiting the Earthians arrival. A highly evolved scientifically advanced culture with telepathic abilities, the Fazians have sent their Ruler's son Tetrok to their off world colony on Titan to further explore the newly charted star system. The Earthians and Fazians meet face-to-face for the first time when Nyota's crew arrives and discovers the colony on Titan. With their mutual telepathic abilities scientists Nyota and Tetrok are drawn to one another and develop a close relationship agreeing to an experiment to genetically create a new species of their own child. When their governments disapprove of the idea they are forced to conceal their efforts and are even led to believe they were unsuccessful until twenty years later when their child Saturna becomes known. Saturna has some very special powers and is eager to know her Fazian father Tetrok and her Earthian mother Nyota for the first time in her life.

About this book: Debut novel.

Other books you might like:

Octavia Butler, *Dawn*, 1987

First title in the science fiction Xenogenesis trilogy where humans have been captured for genetic engineering and mating among aliens.

Octavia Butler, *Wild Seed*, 1980

Science fiction series prequel depicting the origins of the Patternists to create a race of superhumans.

338

CANAAN PARKER, African American

The Color of Trees
(Boston: Alyson Publications, 1992)

Story type: Young Adult; Gay/Lesbian Fiction
Subject(s): Coming of Age; Friendship; Interpersonal Relations
Major character(s): Peter Joseph Givens, 13-Year-Old, Homosexual, African American; Thomas Jerrett "T.J." Adams, Teenager, Homosexual, Caucasian
Time period(s): 1960s (1968)
Locale(s): Green River, Connecticut

Summary: Peter, a 13-year-old from Harlem, attends an elite private boys' boarding school on scholarship. Uncomfortable around yet attracted to "T.J.," the son of a wealthy family from the East, Peter develops a friendship that blossoms into his first sexual experience and love. The affair survives jealousies, attractions to other boys, the uncertainties of racial difference, and tensions from other friendships. When "T.J." transfers in his senior year, Peter is left visibly heartbroken. Now an adult, Peter reflects back on his coming-of-age years with "T.J."

About this book: Debut novel.

Where it's reviewed:
Black Scholar, Summer 1993, page 100
Los Angeles Times Book Review, January 24, 1993, Page 9
Publishers Weekly, November 23, 1992, page 58

Other books you might like:

Randall Kenan, *A Visitation of Spirits*, 1989

Unable to find understanding and self-acceptance, a 16-year-old who discovered his homosexuality with a schoolmate, is led to suicide by a demon.

Larry Duplechan, *Blackbird*, 1986

A contemporary gay coming-of-age episode recounting a young man's first sexual experiences in high school.

339

GWENDOLYN PARKER, African American

These Same Long Bones
(New York: Houghton Mifflin Company, 1994)

Story type: Adult
Subject(s): Grief; Loneliness; Small Town Life
Major character(s): Sirus McDougald, Banker, Father, African American; Aileen McDougald, Mother, African American
Time period(s): 1940s (1947)
Locale(s): Durham, North Carolina (Hay-Ti section of town)

Summary: Sirus McDougald, a man regarded as the pillar of a close-knit community, loses his footing following the death of his young daughter, and must rally himself to make a courageous decision reflecting his sense of responsibility to the people he loves.

About this book: Debut novel.

Where it's reviewed:
Belles Lettres, Spring 1995, page 97
Kliatt, September 1995, page 13
Library Journal December 1994, page 164
Publishers Weekly, April 10, 1995, page 60
New York Times Book Review, June 18, 1995, page 32

Other books by the same author:
I Know What the Red Clay Looks Like, 1994

Other books you might like:

Richard Perry, *Montgomery's Children*, 1984

Tales of people living in a small town in central New York interwoven with magic and vision, incest and murder, friendship and sacrifice.

340

GORDON PARKS, African American

Shannon
(Boston: Little, Brown & Company, 1981)

Subject(s): Greed; Interpersonal Relations
Age range(s): Adult
Major character(s): Kevin O'Farrell, Engineer, Husband, Irish American; Shannon Sullivan, Wife, Mother, Irish American; Hannibal Jones, Graduate, Veteran, African American
Time period(s): 1910s (1913)
Locale(s): New York, New York

Summary: Kevin O'Farrell, a brilliant young engineer, marries the daughter of a munitions tycoon. Hannibal Jones, who once risked his life to save Kevin, is denied work because of his dark skin, so he joins the service in order to provide for his wife Phoebe. Kevin and Shannon try to help Phoebe while Hannibal is overseas, but they are unaware of Kevin's mean-spirited brother's actions and are powerless to change the consequences. More tragedy strikes when Shannon is unable to cope after the loss of their first-born child, slips into madness, and refuses to believe the baby is dead.

Other books by the same author:
The Learning Tree, 1963 (debut novel)

Other books you might like:
Doris Jean Austin, *After the Garden*, 1987
The story of a woman caught between her strict grandmother and the free-spirited love of her life and his family in the urban north of the 1950s.
Anita Richmond Bunkley, *Black Gold*, 1994
A young woman on the brink of ruin before the historic oil boom in 1920s Texas finds herself accused of murder and a family secret is revealed.
Diane McKinney-Whetstone, *Tumbling*, 1996
A childless couple take in two abandoned girls in 1940s Philadelphia and almost loses everything when their neighborhood is threatened by developers.

341

ALEXS D. PATE, African American

Losing Absalom

(Minneapolis: Coffee House Press, 1994)

Subject(s): Cancer; City Life; Family Relations
Age range(s): Adult
Major character(s): Absalom Goodman, Cancer Patient, Father, African American; Gwen Goodman, Housewife, African American, Spouse; Sonny Goodman, Businessman
Time period(s): 1980s
Locale(s): Philadelphia, Pennsylvania

Summary: Something unexpected awaits Sonny when he joins his family at his father's hospital bed. Absalom, his father, is dying of cancer and his wife Gwen, his son and his daughter are by his bedside. His ghostly spirit watches over them and sees their lives as they endure violence and try to survive in the inner city.

About this book: This is the author's debut novel.

Where it's reviewed:
Choice, October 1994, page 281
Library Journal, April 1, 1994, page 134
Publishers Weekly, March 14, 1994, page 65
Los Angeles Times Book Review, July 3, 1994, page 6

Awards the book has won:
Black Caucus of the A.L.A., First Novelist Award, 1994

Other books you might like:
Lionel Newton, *Things to Be Lost*, 1995
A young boy understands his ailing father as seemingly no one else does. Ultimately he kills what he loves most, suffering both guilt and loss.

342

ELAINE PERRY, African American

Another Present Era

(New York: Farrar Straus Giroux, 1990)

Subject(s): Interpersonal Relations; Identity; Futuristic Fiction
Age range(s): Adult
Major character(s): Wanda Higgins DuBois, Architect, Daughter, African American; Sterling Cronheim, Artist, German American; Bradley, Businessman, African American
Time period(s): Indeterminate Future
Locale(s): New York, New York

Summary: Lovers Wanda and Bradley, having little in common, begin drifting apart. Architect Wanda's life takes on a new texture when she meets an older artist, Sterling. They share her passion for architecture as well as his memories of Berlin and Paris.

About this book: This is the author's debut novel.

Where it's reviewed:
Essence, August 1990, page 50
Kirkus Reviews, May 1, 1990, page 604
Library Journal, July 1990, page 132

Other books you might like:
Connie Briscoe, *Sisters and Lovers*, 1994
This contemporary story is about the lives and struggles of three sisters and the men with whom they become involved.
Xam Wilson Cartier, *Muse-Echo Blues*, 1991
A young woman suffering from an acute case of composer's block receives inspiration from a fantasy soul sister and the jazz of the 1940s.
Cyrus Colter, *City of Light*, 1993
This story is about exploits in the life of a young Chicago man who travels to Paris and writes letters to his deceased mother about his plight of being light-skinned.
Charles Johnson, *Oxherding Tale*, 1982
This coming-of-age tale is about a light-skinned young man during the plantation era of the South as he struggles to gain his freedom and the freedom of those he loves.

343

RICHARD PERRY, African American

Changes

(New York: Bobbs-Merrill Company, Inc., 1974)

Subject(s): Fantasy; Psychology; Race Relations
Age range(s): Adult
Major character(s): Bill Taylor, Professor, Husband, African American; Noddaman Bukay, Patient, Scientist, African American
Time period(s): 1960s (1968)
Locale(s): New Holland, New York

Summary: In a time when the whole country is changing, Bill Taylor is going through some changes of his own. There is trouble at home, where his marriage is on shaky ground and at the college where he teaches. A young African student is accused of murdering an elderly white man. In the midst of all of this, Bill's brother sends him a newspaper clipping written by a man who, after serving in the World War, was imprisoned for vagrancy and then transferred to Midstown State Hospital. Bill's brother suggests that perhaps there is a story here. When his wife Rachel and their son go to Baltimore, Bill goes to Midstown State Hospital to visit the author of the letter. He meets Bukay, a man who claims to have invented the white race. Since the Supreme One has indicated that the white race is a failure, scientist Bukay must make everyone on the planet black. But changes do not come without cost.

About this book: Debut novel.

Other books by the same author:
No Other Tale to Tell, 1994
Montgomery's Children, 1984

Other books you might like:
Tananarive Due, *The Between*, 1995
    A man endures nightmares and a wavering sense of reality as he desperately tries to protect his family from the psychotic who stalks them.
Percival Everett, *Suder*, 1983
    The escapades of a young man who fears he may be on the verge of going insane like his mother, and decides to run away from his wife and son.
Nathan Heard, *To Reach a Dream*, 1972
    A young man just out of prison seeks to con a rich widow out of her money but gets involved in a sexual triangle where everyone pays a price.

`344`

RICHARD PERRY, African American

Montgomery's Children

(New York: Harcourt Brace Jovanovich, 1984)

Subject(s): Interpersonal Relations; Magic; Small Town Life
Age range(s): Adult
Major character(s): Norman Fillis, Maintenance Worker, Psychic, African American; Gerald Fletcher, Abuse Victim, African American; Josephine Moore, Abuse Victim, African American
Time period(s): 20th century (1948-1980)
Locale(s): Montgomery, New York

Summary: These interwoven tales are about families living in a small town in central New York. Gerald seeks relief from his father's beatings; Josephine discovers a secret about her past; and Norman, seeing a lot but saying very little, prefers to perfect his ability to fly.

Where it's reviewed:
Publishers Weekly, March 1, 1985, page 79
Village Voice Literary Supplement, October 1985, page 27

Other books by the same author:
No Other Tale to Tell, 1994
Changes, 1974 (debut novel)

Other books you might like:
Connie Porter, *All-Bright Court*, 1991
    A young boy living near a steel mill attends private school, but learns more from his family and neighbors' love and commitment to life.

`345`

RICHARD PERRY, African American

No Other Tale to Tell

(New York: William Morrow, 1994)

Story type: Adult
Subject(s): Family Relations; Intergenerational Saga; Race Relations
Age range(s): Adult
Major character(s): Carla March, Mother, Storyteller, African American; Phoenix March, Mentally Challenged Person, African American; Maximillian ''Max'', Father, Religious, Caucasian
Time period(s): 19th century; 20th century (1869-1980)
Locale(s): Kingston, New York

Summary: This is a tale of interconnections within a community. As the community watches, Carla's family takes in and raises a white boy ''Max,'' who becomes a holy boy. Carla gives birth to Phoenix, an idiot son fathered by ''Max.'' The community is haunted by a prophecy and a legend of its historical past. Carla brings them out of their silence to tell their tales and to live in the present.

Where it's reviewed:
Library Journal, May 15, 1994, page 100
New York Times Book Review, August 28, 1994, page 17
Publishers Weekly, May 2, 1994, page 285

Other books by the same author:
Montgomery's Children, 1984
Changes, 1974 (debut novel)

Other books you might like:
Albert French, *Holly*, 1995
    A young white girl involved in an interracial affair, must flee her family and her community to find safety when she becomes pregnant.
Ernest J. Gaines, *A Gathering of Old Men*, 1983
    In the 1970s when a Cajun farmer from Louisiana is found shot, many people claim to have done it. Each person tell their own story.
Toni Morrison, *Jazz*, 1992
    A working class couple face the trauma of putting their lives back together after the husband murders the girl with whom he was having an affair.
John Edgar Wideman, *Reuben*, 1987
    This story relates the exploits of an aged lawyer and the various clients he represents in the Pittsburgh community of Homewood during the 1980s.

`346`

GARY PHILLIPS, African American

Violent Spring

(Portland, Oregon: West Coast Crime, 1994)

Story type: Private Detective
Series: Ivan Monk
Subject(s): Murder; Mystery and Detective Stories
Age range(s): Adult

Major character(s): Ivan Monk, Detective—Private, Brother, African American
Time period(s): 1990s
Locale(s): Los Angeles, California

Summary: In the aftermath of the Rodney King verdict, the Reginald Denny beating, and the killing of Latasha Harlins by a Korean grocer, Los Angeles is a city trying to heal and build anew. At a groundbreaking ceremony for a shopping complex in South Central a bulldozer unearths a dead body. The corpse is Korean liquor store owner Bong Kim Suh, who had been shot execution style and dumped in the ground over a year ago. Eager for the murder to be solved, the Korean-American Merchants Group hires private detective Monk Ivan, who for three years has been dating Judge Jill Kodama. When another murder occurs and Monk uncovers Kim Suh's private notebook about dealings of Jiang Holdings he realizes the extent powerful people are involved and his life is in serious jeopardy.

About this book: Debut novel.

Other books you might like:
Gar Anthony Haywood, *Fear of the Dark*, 1988
   Debut novel in a contemporary murder mystery series with a private detective.
Hugh Holton, *Presumed Dead*, 1994
   Debut novel in a contemporary murder mystery series featuring a Chicago detective.
Walter Mosley, *Devil in a Blue Dress*, 1990
   Debut novel in a contemporary murder mystery series with a private detective.
Valerie Wilson Wesley, *When Death Comes Stealing*, 1994
   Debut novel in a murder mystery series featuring an ex-policewoman who has become a private detective.

347

DARRYL PINCKNEY, African American

High Cotton
(New York: Farrar Straus Giroux, 1992)

Subject(s): Coming of Age; Family Relations; Identity
Age range(s): Adult
Major character(s): Unnamed Character, Handyman, Secretary, African American; Eustace, Businessman, Grandfather, African American
Time period(s): 1960s; 1980s
Locale(s): Indianapolis, Indiana; New York, New York; South

Summary: An unnamed young man narrates this story. He tells of the complexities in the world of the upper-middle class "talented tenth" generation and their families. Exploring his own identity, the narrator reveals a deep relationship with his grandfather Eustace, who also shares the exploits of his own life from another era.

About this book: This is the author's debut novel.

Where it's reviewed:
Essence, August 1992, page 44
Publishers Weekly, December 6, 1991, page 55
Wall Street Journal, February 5, 1992, page A9

Other books you might like:
Cyrus Colter, *City of Light*, 1993
   This story is about the exploits in the life of a young Chicago man who travels to Paris and writes letters to his deceased mother about his plight of being light-skinned.
Charles Johnson, *Oxherding Tale*, 1982
   This coming-of-age tale is about a light-skinned young man during the plantation era of the South as he struggles to gain his freedom and the freedom of those he loves.
Albert Murray, *The Spyglass Tree*, 1991
   A young man, one of the "talented tenth," attends college in Mobile County. He gets involved with new friends, while learning about himself.
Connie Porter, *All-Bright Court*, 1991
   A young boy living near a steel mill attends private school, but learns more from his family and neighbors' love and commitment to life.
Dennis Williams, *Crossover*, 1992
   This story relates the events in the life of a young man during the Civil Rights era. He becomes a reluctant activist and he has an interracial affair.

348

ANDREA DAVIS PINKNEY, African American

Hold Fast to Dreams
(New York: Morrow Junior Books, 1995)

Story type: Young Readers
Subject(s): Prejudice; Race Relations; Sisters
Age range(s): Grades 5-8
Major character(s): Deirdre "Camera Dee" Willis, Photographer, Student—Junior High, African American; Lindsay Willis, Athlete, Student—Junior High, African American; Weber "Web" Coile, 12-Year-Old, Student—Junior High, Caucasian
Time period(s): 1990s
Locale(s): Wexford, Connecticut

Summary: When their family moves from Baltimore to Connecticut, Dee and her younger sister Lindsay struggle to adjust in their separate all-white schools. Amidst stares and whispers they try to fit in by going out for the popular sport lacrosse. At her private school Lindsay shows her talent and makes the team. A star player she nonetheless has to endure prejudiced behavior from teammates. Unable to make the team at her own school, Dee concentrates on her aptitude for taking pictures. Befriended by a white classmate, "Web," and encouraged to let her talent shine she enters her photographs in a school event by her nickname "Camera Dee." Dee and Lindsay discover they are not the only ones being mistreated when they learn of the prejudiced behavior their father was subjected to on his new job. His ordeal gives them some fresh insights about dealing with prejudiced behavior and holding fast to dreams.

About this book: Debut novel

Where it's reviewed:
Booklist, February 15, 1995, page 1085
New York Times Book Review, June 4, 1995, page 25
Publishers Weekly, May 22, 1995, page 60
School Library Journal, April 1995, page 136

Voice of Youth Advocates, August 1995, page 164

Other books you might like:

Jacqueline Turner Banks, *The New One*, 1994
Twin brothers disagree about whether to befriend a new girl at school or interfere with their mother's relationship with her boyfriend.

Walter Dean Myers, *Darnell Rock Reporting*, 1994
Not doing well in school, a 13-year-old joins the school newspaper and discovers the impact his writing can have and how he can make a difference.

Vaunda Micheaux Nelson, *Mayfield Crossing*, 1993
The new kids at an elementary school encounter prejudice for the first time and only baseball has the possibility for drawing people together.

Eleanora E. Tate, *Just an Overnight Guest*, 1980
A young girl and her older sister are surprised when their mother takes in a baby whose mother is said to be poor white trash.

Jacqueline Woodson, *Maizon at Blue Hill*, 1992
Another episode in the lives of two young seventh grade friends where one girl wins an academic scholarship to a white boarding school.

349

BRIAN PINKNEY, Author/Illustrator, African American

Max Found Two Sticks
(New York: Simon & Schuster, 1994)

Story type: Young Readers
Subject(s): Music
Age range(s): Grades 1-2
Major character(s): Max, Child, African American
Time period(s): 1990s
Locale(s): United States (unidentified city)

Summary: Sitting on the stoop of his building, Max sees two twigs fall and picks them up. Grandpa asks what he is going to do with the sticks and instead of answering Max begins to tap out a rhythm on his thighs imitating the sound of birds in flight. Arriving home later his mother asks him what he's doing with his grandpa's cleaning bucket and Max answers her by beating out another rhythm like the sound of rain on the windows. As his friends pass, they ask Max what he's doing with his mothers hatboxes and his only reply is to play a rhythm like the beat of marching band drummers. On his way to work Max's father asks him what he's doing with soda bottles and he answers with a sound like the church bell chimes. Twins ask him what he is doing with garbage cans and he bangs out a rhythm like the sound of the trains. While everyone watches, a marching band suddenly appears. As one of the last drummers pass him, he tosses Max a spare pair of drum sticks with a wink and a nod, and Max doesn't miss a beat.

About this book: Debut novel.

Other books you might like:

Jeannette Franklin Caines, *I Need a Lunch Box*, 1988
A preschooler wanting a lunch box like his older sister's imagines all the things he could keep in it and dreams of having one for every day.

Lucille Clifton, *Everett Anderson's Year*, 1974
Activities in a young child's life are depicted for the twelve calendar months in a series of poems capturing his joys, sorrows, and confusions.

Pat Cummings, *Clean Your Room, Harvey Moon!*, 1991
His mom tells a young boy he has to clean his room before watching TV and he discovers a treasure trove of things he'd forgotten he had.

350

GLORIA JEAN PINKNEY, African American
JERRY PINKNEY, Illustrator, African American

Back Home
(New York: Dial Books For Young Readers, 1992)

Story type: Young Readers
Subject(s): Country Life; Relatives; Family Relations
Age range(s): Grades 2-4
Major character(s): Ernestine Avery Powell, 8-Year-Old, Niece, African American
Time period(s): Indeterminate Past
Locale(s): Lumberton, North Carolina

Summary: 8-year-old Ernestine visits her aunt Beula, uncle June, and cousin Jack. She meets Jack and sees his new goat. Uncle June makes Ernestine and Jack over to the small abandoned farmhouse where she was born. After Sunday church the family visits her grandmama Zulah's grave and Jack holds her hand so she won't be scared. As she packs for her return home, Jack tells her he's decided to give his goat the name she suggested. Regretting her trip was so short, Ernestine looks forward to coming back.

About this book: Debut novel.

Awards the book has won:
ALA Notable Book Award, 1993

Other books by the same author:
The Sunday Outing, 1994 (prequel to *Back Home*)

Other books you might like:

Jeannette Franklin Caines, *Just Us Women*, 1982
A young niece narrates the adventures she had with her aunt when they made a trip together in her aunt's new car.

Donald Crews, *Bigmama's*, 1991
Recalls the summer exploits of a youngster in the 1940s when he, his brother, sisters, and parents visit his grandparents in the country.

Valerie Flournoy, *Tanya's Reunion*, 1995
A youngster traveling with her grandma to the family farm for a reunion discovers a special memento for her grandma.

Elizabeth Fitzgerald Howard, *Aunt Flossie's Hats (and Crab Cakes Later)*, 1991
Visits to their great-great-aunt Flossie's are special times for two young girls and they always look forward to eating crab cakes afterwards.

Wade Hudson, *I Love My Family*, 1993
A young boy recalls his enjoyable summer family reunions with his father's relatives and looks forward to his mother's family reunion.

Herschel Johnson, *A Visit to the Country*, 1989
In the country at his grandparents,' a child discovers a baby bird, feeds him as he grows and learns to fly, and later returns him to the wild.

351

GLORIA JEAN PINKNEY, African American
JERRY PINKNEY, Illustrator, African American

The Sunday Outing

(New York: Dial Books For Young Readers, 1994)

Story type: Young Readers
Subject(s): Trains; Parent and Child; Relatives
Age range(s): Grades 2-4
Major character(s): Ernestine Avery Powell, 8-Year-Old, Niece, African American
Time period(s): Indeterminate Past
Locale(s): United States

Summary: Teased by her friends that she is never going on a train ride, 8-year-old Ernestine eagerly visits the train station with her great-aunt Odessa. Aunt Odessa shares stories with her about great-uncle Ariah who worked for the railroad. Invited by her relatives to visit them at her birthplace in the country, Ernestine is sad when her parents say they cannot afford her ticket. She suggests something she can do without so her parents can send her to the country and they agree to do without some things themselves so she can go. Nervous about making the trip alone she is excited when the family receives a telegram from her uncle June saying he'll pick her up at the station. At the station her parents and Aunt Odessa reassure her she's going to have a great trip and, finding a window seat, she begins her journey south.

About this book: Prequel to *Back Home*.

Awards the book has won:
New York Times Best Illustrated Book

Other books by the same author:
Back Home, 1992 (debut)

Other books you might like:
Valerie Flournoy, *Tanya's Reunion*, 1995
A youngster traveling with her grandma to the family farm for a reunion discovers a special memento for her grandma of days gone by.
Elizabeth Fitzgerald Howard, *Aunt Flossie's Hats (and Crab Cakes Later)*, 1991
Visits to their great-great-aunt Flossie's are special times for two young girls and they always look forward to eating crab cakes afterwards.
Elizabeth Fitzgerald Howard, *The Train to LuLu's*, 1988
For summer vacation two young sisters take their first train trip in the 1930s on a nine hour ride between Boston and Baltimore.
June Jordan, *Kimako's Story*, 1981
A 7-year-old takes on the responsibility of caring for her neighbors' big Airedale dog and gets to see more of her city surroundings.

352

BENITA PORTER, African American

Colorstruck

(New York: B.Q. Press, 1990)

Subject(s): Identity; Race Relations; Twins
Age range(s): Adult
Major character(s): Clothilde ''Chloe'' Bechet, Entertainer, African American, Sister; Solomon Bechet, Director, African American, Brother
Time period(s): 20th century (1909-1936)
Locale(s): New York, New York; Los Angeles, California

Summary: Having lost their merchant marine father in an accident at sea, 8-year-old twins Chloe and Solomon also loose their mother to illness and are uprooted from their New Orleans home. From their earliest years they are aware of skin color discrimination but as they grow older, the twins learn its deep impact on their lives. Raised in Harlem by their great uncle Rupe and Creole grandmother, Maman, Chloe and Solomon are given a sense of self-worth and esteem. While growing up the twins begin a process of determining how they want to live their lives in a segregated society where they could easily pass for white.

About this book: Debut novel.

Other books you might like:
Barbara Chase-Riboud, *The President's Daughter*, 1994
Chronicles the life of Harriet Hemings passing for white, the daughter of miscegenation in the interracial affair of President Thomas Jefferson.
Cyrus Colter, *City of Light*, 1993
Exploits in the life of a young Chicago man who travels to Paris writing letters to his deceased mother about his plight of being light-skinned.
Albert French, *Holly*, 1995
Involved in an interracial affair a young white girl must flee her family and her community to find safety when she becomes pregnant.
Elaine Perry, *Another Present Era*, 1990
A young architect drifts away from the lover she shares little with except their light skin and becomes involved with an older white artist.
Dorothy West, *The Wedding*, 1995
Saga of five generations of two families of mixed race ancestry, and events in the lives of children from a new contemporary generation.

353

CONNIE PORTER, African American
MELODYE ROSALES, Illustrator, African American

Addy Learns a Lesson: A School Story

(Middleton, WI: Pleasant Company, 1993)

Story type: Young Readers
Series: American Girls Collection - Addy
Subject(s): Freedom; Friendship; School Life
Age range(s): Grades 2-5

Major character(s): Addy Walker, 9-Year-Old, Student, African American; Sarah Moore, 9-Year-Old, Student, African American; Harriet Davis, 9-Year-Old, Student, African American
Time period(s): 1860s (1864)
Locale(s): Philadelphia, Pennsylvania

Summary: Addy and her mother arrive in Philadelphia with other fugitive slaves and are met by Sarah and her mother, who help them get settled in a new life. Addy's mother gets a job in a dressmaker's shop, and she and Addy live in a garret above the shop. Addy goes to school for the first time and learns to read. She wants to be friends with Harriet, a popular girl who has beautiful dresses, but discovers that Sarah is her true friend.

Where it's reviewed:
School Library Journal, January 1994, page 116
Children's Book Watch, November 1993, page 4
Horn Book Guide, Spring 1994, page 81

Other books by the same author:
Addy Saves the Day: A Summer Story, 1994 (American Girls Collection)
Changes for Addy: A Winter Story, 1994 (American Girls Collection)
Happy Birthday, Addy! A Springtime Story, 1994 (American Girls Collection)
Addy's Surprise: A Christmas Story, 1993 (American Girls Collection)
Meet Addy: An American Girl, 1993 (Debut novel; American Girls Collection)

Other books you might like:
Eleanora E. Tate, *Thank You, Dr. Martin Luther King, Jr.!*, 1990
 Continuing the Calvary County trilogy, this tale explores the life of a fourth grade girl who is ''color struck'' wanting to be white.
Joyce Hansen, *Which Way Freedom?*, 1986
 Unable to read or write, a youngster escapes slavery and when he joins the Union Army he vows to return to rescue the friends he left behind.
Harriette Gillem Robinet, *Children of the Fire*, 1991
 A young girl witnesses the Great Chicago Fire of 1871 and is forever changed.
Harriette Gillem Robinet, *If You Please, President Lincoln*, 1995
 Having escaped slavery on Christmas Day in 1863, a 14-year-old joins a group of former slaves on their way to an island off the coast of Haiti.

354

CONNIE PORTER, African American
BRADFORD BROWN, Illustrator

Addy Saves the Day: A Summer Story

(Middleton, WI: Pleasant Company, 1994)

Story type: Young Readers
Series: American Girls Collection - Addy
Subject(s): Civil War; Friendship; Slavery
Age range(s): Grades 2-5

Major character(s): Addy Walker, 10-Year-Old, Student, African American; Harriet Davis, 9-Year-Old, Student, African American
Time period(s): 1860s (1864)
Locale(s): Philadelphia, Pennsylvania

Summary: The Civil War has ended, and families that were separated are trying to reunite. The church puts on a fundraiser to help families hurt by the war. Addy and her schoolmate Harriet seem to feud over everything, including fundraising ideas, until a tragedy causes them to set their differences aside and work together. When their cash box is stolen, Addy saves the day and gets a very special reward.

Where it's reviewed:
Booklist, November 1, 1994, page 500
School Library Journal, November 1994, page 107
Horn Book Guide, Spring 1995, page 69

Other books by the same author:
Changes for Addy: A Winter Story, 1994 (American Girls Collection)
Happy Birthday, Addy! A Springtime Story, 1994 (American Girls Collection)
Addy Learns a Lesson: A School Story, 1993 (American Girls Collection)
Addy's Surprise: A Christmas Story, 1993 (American Girls Collection)
Meet Addy: An American Girl, 1993 (Debut novel; American Girls Collection)

Other books you might like:
Joyce Hansen, *Out from This Place*, 1988
 The plight of a young girl as she and her loved ones run away from slavery and what becomes of them when freedom arrives and the Civil War ends.
Joyce Hansen, *Which Way Freedom?*, 1986
 Unable to read or write, a youngster escapes slavery and when he joins the Union Army he vows to return to rescue the friends he left behind.
Harriette Gillem Robinet, *Children of the Fire*, 1991
 A young girl witnesses the Great Chicago Fire of 1871 and is forever changed.
Harriette Gillem Robinet, *If You Please, President Lincoln*, 1995
 Having escaped slavery on Christmas Day in 1863, a 14-year-old joins a group of former slaves on their way to an island off the coast of Haiti.

355

CONNIE PORTER, African American
MELODYE ROSALES, Illustrator, African American

Addy's Surprise: A Christmas Story

(Middleton, WI: Pleasant Company, 1993)

Story type: Young Readers
Series: American Girls Collection - Addy
Subject(s): Christmas; Freedom; Friendship
Age range(s): Grades 2-5
Major character(s): Addy Walker, 9-Year-Old, African American
Time period(s): 1860s (1864)

Locale(s): Philadelphia, Pennsylvania

Summary: Addy's mother works for a dressmaker, and Addy helps out by delivering packages and saving her tips. Christmas is coming and they know it will be hard without Poppa and Sam and Esther. When Addy spots a red scarf in a second-hand shop, she at first decides to get it for Momma, then she decides to give her money to the Freedman's Fund in the hope that somehow it will help her Poppa and Sam. Addy's Christmas surprise for her mother is quite different than she planned, and her own surprise is greater than she could have dreamed.

Other books by the same author:

Addy Saves the Day: A Summer Story, 1994 (American Girls Collection)

Changes for Addy: A Winter Story, 1994 (American Girls Collection)

Happy Birthday, Addy! A Springtime Story, 1994 (American Girls Collection)

Addy Learns a Lesson: A School Story, 1993 (American Girls Collection)

Meet Addy: An American Girl, 1993 (Debut novel; American Girls Collection)

Other books you might like:

Virginia Hamilton, *The Bells of Christmas*, 1989
  In this historic account of Christmas 1890, a 12-year-old boy and his family prepare for the Great Day.

Mildred Pitts Walter, *Have a Happy. . .*, 1989
  Upset because his birthday falls on Christmas and worried about money because his father is out of work, an 11-year-old carves animals for Kwanzaa.

Joyce Hansen, *Which Way Freedom?*, 1986
  Unable to read or write, a youngster escapes slavery and when he joins the Union Army he vows to return to rescue the friends he left behind.

Harriette Gillem Robinet, *If You Please, President Lincoln*, 1995
  Having escaped slavery on Christmas Day in 1863, a 14-year-old joins a group of former slaves on their way to an island off the coast of Haiti.

356

CONNIE PORTER, African American

All-Bright Court

(Boston: Houghton Mifflin Company, 1991)

Subject(s): Interpersonal Relations; Labor and Labor Classes; Neighbors and Neighborhoods

Age range(s): Adult

Major character(s): Samuel Taylor, Father, Worker (steelworker), African American; Mary Kate Taylor, Housewife, Mother, African American; Michael ''Mikey'' Taylor, Child, Student, African American

Time period(s): 1960s; 1970s (1960-1977)

Locale(s): Lackawanna, New York

Summary: Mikey, a gifted student, receives a scholarship to attend a private grammar school. The school is located a long bus ride away from where he lives in the shadow of a steel mill. His family and neighbors share tragedies and happiness,

and keep their hopes alive through their love and commitment to life.

About this book: This is the author's debut novel (adults).

Where it's reviewed:
Belles Lettres, Winter 1991, page 7
New York Times Book Review, October 27, 1991, page 12
Publishers Weekly, July 13, 1992, page 53

Other books you might like:

Gloria Naylor, *Women of Brewster Place*, 1982
  Seven women who come to live on the dead-end street of Brewster Place tell their stories of what brings them together in their own redemption.

Darryl Pinckney, *High Cotton*, 1992
  An unnamed narrator reveals the complexities of growing up in the upper-middle class as a young man in the ''talented tenth'' generation.

Terri McMillan, *Mama*, 1987
  A proud and feisty mother does her best to provide for her five children through three marriages and uncertain times.

Richard Perry, *Montgomery's Children*, 1984
  These tales of people living in a small town in central New York are interwoven with magic and vision, incest and murder, friendship and sacrifice.

357

CONNIE PORTER, African American
BRADFORD BROWN, Illustrator

Changes for Addy: A Winter Story

(Middleton, WI: Pleasant Company, 1994)

Story type: Young Readers

Series: American Girls Collection - Addy

Subject(s): Family Relations; Freedom; Death

Age range(s): Grades 2-5

Major character(s): Addy Walker, 10-Year-Old, Student, African American

Time period(s): 1860s (1865)

Locale(s): Philadelphia, Pennsylvania

Summary: The Civil War has ended, and Addy is fervently hoping her family can be reunited. Her hopes begin to dwindle until word comes that Uncle Solomon, Auntie Lula and baby Esther have started out for Philadelphia. Addy searches the city for them. Her search is rewarded, but the reunion is mixed with joy and sorrow. Freedom has cost her family dearly. As Addy prepares for the Emancipation Celebration at church, she wonders if she even believes the words she is supposed to read. Her mother reminds Addy that their family will always be together in her heart.

Other books by the same author:

Addy Saves the Day: A Summer Story, 1994 (American Girls Collection)

Happy Birthday, Addy! A Springtime Story, 1994 (American Girls Collection)

Addy Learns a Lesson: A School Story, 1993 (American Girls Collection)

Addy's Surprise: A Christmas Story, 1993 (American Girls Collection)

Meet Addy: An American Girl, 1993 (debut novel; American Girls Collection)

Other books you might like:

Joyce Hansen, *Out from This Place*, 1988
  The plight of a young girl as she and her loved ones run away from slavery and what becomes of them when freedom arrives and the Civil War ends.

Joyce Hansen, *Which Way Freedom?*, 1986
  Unable to read or write, a youngster escapes slavery and when he joins the Union Army he vows to return to rescue the friends he left behind.

Harriette Gillem Robinet, *Children of the Fire*, 1991
  A young girl witnesses the Great Chicago Fire of 1871 and is forever changed.

Harriette Gillem Robinet, *If You Please, President Lincoln*, 1995
  Having escaped slavery on Christmas Day in 1863, a 14-year-old joins a group of former slaves on their way to an island off the coast of Haiti.

358

CONNIE PORTER, African American
BRADFORD BROWN, Illustrator

Happy Birthday, Addy! A Springtime Story
(Middleton, WI: Pleasant Company, 1994)

Story type: Young Readers
Series: American Girls Collection - Addy
Subject(s): Birthdays; Freedom; Prejudice
Age range(s): Grades 2-5
Major character(s): Addy Walker, 9-Year-Old, Student, African American; M'dear Golden, Aged Person, Blind Person, African American
Time period(s): 1860s (1864)
Locale(s): Philadelphia, Pennsylvania

Summary: Addy finds a wise and inspiring friend in the boarding house where she and her parents live. M'dear is old enough to be Addy's grandmother, and although she is blind, she seems to see things that others do not. She helps Addy learn to jump rope "double dutch" by listening to the rhythm of the ropes. When M'dear learns that Addy does not know when her birthday is, she encourages her to choose her own day, and tells her that she will know when that special day comes. When M'dear falls ill, Addy and her friend Sarah go to get her some medicine, and come face-to-face with prejudice they cannot understand. Addy's special day arrives, and the whole town celebrates.

Where it's reviewed:
Booklist, November 1, 1994, page 500
Horn Book Guide, Spring 1995, page 70
School Library Journal, November 1994, page 106
Magazine of History, Fall 1994, page 58

Other books by the same author:
Addy Saves the Day: A Summer Story, 1994 (American Girls Collection)
Changes for Addy: A Winter Story, 1994 (American Girls Collection)

Addy Learns a Lesson: A School Story, 1993 (American Girls Collection)
Addy's Surprise: A Christmas Story, 1993 (American Girls Collection)
Meet Addy: An American Girl, 1993 (debut novel; American Girls Collection)

Other books you might like:

Joyce Hansen, *Out from This Place*, 1988
  The plight of a young girl as she and her loved ones run away from slavery and what becomes of them when freedom arrives and the Civil War ends.

Joyce Hansen, *Which Way Freedom?*, 1986
  Unable to read or write, a youngster escapes slavery and when he joins the Union Army he vows to return to rescue the friends he left behind.

Harriette Gillem Robinet, *Children of the Fire*, 1991
  A young girl witnesses the Great Chicago Fire of 1871 and is forever changed.

Harriette Gillem Robinet, *If You Please, President Lincoln*, 1995
  Having escaped slavery on Christmas Day in 1863, a 14-year-old joins a group of former slaves on their way to an island off the coast of Haiti.

Eleanora E. Tate, *Thank You, Dr. Martin Luther King, Jr.!*, 1990
  Continuing the Calvary County trilogy, this tale explores the life of a fourth grade girl who is "color struck" wanting to be white.

359

CONNIE PORTER, African American
MELODYE ROSALES, Illustrator, African American

Meet Addy: An American Girl
(Middleton, WI: Pleasant Company, 1993)

Story type: Young Readers
Series: American Girls Collection - Addy
Subject(s): Family Relations; Freedom; Slavery
Age range(s): Grades 2-5
Major character(s): Addy Walker, 9-Year-Old, Slave, African American
Time period(s): 1860s (1864)
Locale(s): North Carolina

Summary: During the Civil War, Addy and her family work hard on the Stevens plantation, but times are hard. Addy's parents plan to escape to freedom in Philadelphia, but before they can implement their plan, Addy's father and older brother are sold away. Addy and her mother escape in disguise, traveling by night and resting by day until they arrive at a "safe house." A white woman feeds and clothes them then takes them to the coast where they can catch a ship to freedom.

About this book: Debut novel (juvenile).

Where it's reviewed:
Reading Teacher, October 1994, page 157
School Library Journal, January 1994, page 116
Essence, December 1993, page 122

Other books by the same author:
Addy Saves the Day: A Summer Story, 1994 (American Girls Collection)
Changes for Addy: A Winter Story, 1994 (American Girls Collection)
Happy Birthday, Addy! A Springtime Story, 1994 (American Girls Collection)
Addy Learns a Lesson: A School Story, 1993 (American Girls Collection)
Addy's Surprise: A Christmas Story, 1993 (American Girls Collection)

Other books you might like:
Joyce Hansen, *The Captive*, 1994
Historical fiction of the life of a royal African boy who is kidnapped and illegally sold as a slave and is later rescued by a sea captain.
Harriette Gillem Robinet, *If You Please, President Lincoln*, 1995
Having escaped slavery on Christmas day in 1863, a 14-year-old joins a group of former slaves on their way to an island off the coast of Haiti.
Joyce Hansen, *Which Way Freedom?*, 1986
Unable to read or write, a youngster escapes slavery and when he joins the Union Army he vows to return to rescue the friends he left behind.

360

RAY PRATHER, Author/Illustrator, African American

Double Dog Dare

(New York: Macmillan Publishing Company, Inc., 1975)

Story type: Young Readers
Subject(s): Friendship; Behavior
Age range(s): Grades 1-2
Major character(s): Eddie, Child, African American
Time period(s): 1970s
Locale(s): United States (unidentified city)

Summary: Eddie and his friend Ruby find a quarter, which they use to buy ice cream. But the ice cream ends up on the ground and Eddie chases Ruby to the trees. They climb one tree, daring each other to go higher. Then a mean-looking stray dog comes by, and the scared boys can't figure out how to get down without being attacked. But the dog's owner comes by, and everything works out.

Other books by the same author:
No Trespassing, 1974
New Neighbors, 1975
Anthony and Sabrina, 1973 (debut)

Other books you might like:
Lucille Clifton, *The Boy Who Didn't Believe in Spring*, 1973
Everyone says spring is coming, but a youngster and his white pal don't believe them. So they go searching for evidence to discover spring.
Lucille Clifton, *My Friend Jacob*, 1980
A young boy shares special times with his neighbor and best friend, a white mentally handicapped older boy. They play ball and the boy helps his neighbor remember things.

Donald Crews, *Shortcut*, 1992
A group of youngsters take a shortcut home following the railroad tracks. A a train appears, forcing them to run for safety.
Angela Shelf Medearis, *The Adventures of Sugar and Junior*, 1995
Exploits of a young girl and a Latino neighbor boy as they become friends while baking cookies, going to monster movies, and sharing ice cream.
John Steptoe, *Train Ride*, 1970
With little to do on a summer day a group of boys go to the city alone on the train, leaving the scared girls behind.

361

RAY PRATHER, African American

No Trespassing

(New York: Macmillan, 1974)

Story type: Young Readers
Subject(s): Friendship; Resourcefulness
Age range(s): Grades 1-2
Major character(s): Jay, Child, Baseball Player, African American
Time period(s): 1970s
Locale(s): United States (unidentified city)

Summary: Playing baseball Jay's friend Willie Jr. hits the ball into Miss Riley's yard, the cranky neighbor lady. Now they've got to figure out how to get it back without her seeing them. Their friend Charlie comes along and since he's smaller they ask him to crawl under the fence and get the ball. Miss Riley comes out chasing him with her cane and the boys run away to Willie Jr.'s next door. Jay tries a fishing pole but it's not long enough and Miss Riley comes yelling out of the house again. Before she can get to the fence someone shouts somebody's stealing peaches in her backyard. Heading off to the backyard Jay and Willie Jr. dash into the yard grabbing their ball and pole. Later meeting up with Charlie they asks him where he got such a neat idea and this time they invite him to play ball.

Other books by the same author:
Double Dog Dare, 1975
New Neighbors, 1975
Anthony and Sabrina, 1973 (debut)

Other books you might like:
Lucille Clifton, *The Boy Who Didn't Believe in Spring*, 1973
Everyone says spring is coming and a youngster and his white pal don't believe them so they go searching for evidence to discover spring.
Donald Crews, *Shortcut*, 1992
A group of youngsters taking a shortcut home following the railroad tracks are frightened when a train appears forcing them to run for safety.
Pat Cummings, *Petey Moroni's Camp Runamok Diary*, 1992
At a two-week summer camp a young boy and his friends try catching the raccoon they've discovered has been stealing their food.
Dolores Johnson, *What Kind of Baby-Sitter Is This?*, 1991
Upset when his mom leaves him with an elderly babysitter

a child discovers she likes baseball as much as he does and they become friends.

LINDA RAYMOND, African American

Rocking the Babies
(New York: Viking, 1994)

Subject(s): Family Relations; Interpersonal Relations; Mothers
Age range(s): Adult
Major character(s): Martha Howard, Aged Person, Child-Care Giver, African American; Nettie Lee Johnson, Aged Person, Child-Care Giver, African American; Yolanda Johnson, Addict, Pregnant Teenager, African American
Time period(s): 1990s
Locale(s): Dayton, Ohio

Summary: Nettie Lee meets Martha when she volunteers as a hospital care giver to babies exposed to drugs. As they come to know one another, Nettie discovers Martha's secret hope of healing the wound of losing her son when he was a baby. Nettie is hiding a secret about one of the hospital babies she is caring for, while she also raises her young grandson abandoned by her addict daughter, Yolanda.

About this book: This is the author's debut novel.

Where it's reviewed:
Kirkus Reviews, July 1, 1994, page 878
Library Journal, September 1, 1994, page 216
Publishers Weekly, August 8, 1994, page 363

Other books you might like:
Linda Beatrice Brown, *Crossing over Jordan*, 1995
    This saga is about the binding ties in the lives of four generations of mothers and daughters from the Civil War era to the early 21st century.
Marita Golden, *Long Distance Life*, 1989
    These episodes relate the murder of a young grandson in the 1980s and the evolution of his family from a sharecropping background of the 1920s.
Terri McMillan, *Mama*, 1987
    A proud and feisty mother does her best to provide for her five children through three marriages and uncertain times.
Dori Sanders, *Her Own Place*, 1993
    This story is about the remembrances of a senior citizen's exploits as daughter, wife, mother, and grandmother prior to World War II and including contemporary times.

ISHMAEL REED, African American

Flight to Canada
(New York: Random House, 1976)

Story type: Satire
Subject(s): Race Relations; Interpersonal Relations; Civil War
Age range(s): Adult
Major character(s): Raven Quickskill, Runaway, Slave, African American; Arthur Swille, Plantation Owner, Caucasian

Time period(s): 1860s (Civil War era)
Locale(s): Richmond, Virginia; Buffalo, New York; Niagara Falls, Ontario, Canada

Summary: Satirical tale mixing the modern era into the escape of three slaves who run away and the extent to which their slave owner, Arthur Swille, goes to capture them. Nebraska Tracers, Inc., Swille's slave catchers, arrive in Emancipation City to repossess escapee Raven Quickskill who slips away. Raven witnesses Lincoln's assassination during a live broadcast on television. Raven's Native American lover Princess Quaw Quaw Tralaralara jumps into Niagara Falls while her husband argues with Raven on a yacht. Swille is murdered by either his sister's ghost or his wife, and Raven returns to the plantation, which has been willed to one of the former slave servants, Uncle Robin. When Harriet Beecher Stowe phones Uncle Robin, whom she had interviewed for her famous book *Uncle Tom's Cabin*, about collaborating again he informs her the now published poet of *Flight To Canada*, Raven Quickskill, will be doing the book on him.

Other books by the same author:
Japanese by Spring, 1993
Reckless Eyeballing, 1986
Last Days of Louisiana Red, 1974
Mumbo Jumbo, 1972
Freelance Pallbearers, 1967 (debut novel)

Other books you might like:
Wesley Brown, *Darktown Strutters*, 1994
    A traveling minstrel dances the thin line between anger, violence and laughter in pre- and post-Civil War America.
Lorene Cary, *The Price of a Child*, 1995
    Historical tale of a woman who literally walks from slavery to freedom under her slave owner's furious gaze in 1850s Philadelphia.
Leon Forrest, *There Is a Tree More Ancient than Eden*, 1973
    In a stream of consciousness style, the narrator of this first title of the Witherspoon Family Saga trilogy anguishes about his heritage.
Julius Lester, *Do Lord Remember Me*, 1984
    Saga of the life and times from the late 1870s plantation era of an eighty year old reverend who became known as the "colored Billy Graham."

ISHMAEL REED, African American

Japanese by Spring
(New York: Atheneum, 1993)

Story type: Satire
Subject(s): Prejudice; Race Relations; Universities and Colleges
Age range(s): Adult
Major character(s): Benjamin "Chappie" Puttbutt III, Professor, Administrator, African American; Robert Bass Jr., Racist, Student—College, Caucasian; Doctor Yamato, Tutor, Administrator, Japanese
Time period(s): 1990s (1990-1992)
Locale(s): Oakland, California

Summary: Professor Puttbutt will endure almost anything, including the racist insults of his student Robert Bass Jr., to get tenure at his college. He feels threatened when the college wants to hire ecologist April Jokujoku, a radical feminist lesbian poet. He is angered when he finds out he will not receive tenure. When his tutor in Japanese, Dr. Yamato, becomes the new President at the college, Puttbutt gets revenge. Haunted by his past as a military cadet, he also finds himself entangled with Dr. Yamato in a military plot involving his family.

Where it's reviewed:

Black Scholar, Summer 1993, page 101
Multicultural Review, June 1993, page 56
New York Times Book Review, December 5, 1993, page 62

Other books by the same author:

Flight to Canada, 1976
Last Days of Louisiana Red, 1974
Mumbo Jumbo, 1972
Yellow Back Radio Broke Down, 1969
Freelance Pallbearers, 1967 (debut novel)

Other books you might like:

Cyrus Colter, *City of Light*, 1993
This story is about the exploits in the life of a young Chicago man who travels to Paris and writes letters to his deceased mother about his plight of being light-skinned.
Tananarive Due, *The Between*, 1995
A man endures nightmares and his sense of reality wavers as he desperately tries to protect his family from the psychotic who stalks them.
Percival Everett, *God's Country*, 1994
In this satirical western, a white man hires a tracker to recover his farm, wife and dog. He survives only because of the tracker's abilities to cope.
Ray Shell, *Iced*, 1993
A man reflects in his diary about his accomplishments in life as well as his regrets of descending into the white-smoke world of crack cocaine.
Brent Wade, *Company Man*, 1992
These confessions are about the behind-the-scenes stresses and strains faced by a man attempting to climb the business ladder and preserve his family.

365

ISHMAEL REED, African American

The Last Days of Louisiana Red

(New York: Random House, 1974)

Story type: Satire
Series: PaPa LaBas
Subject(s): Mystery and Detective Stories; Murder; Family Relations
Age range(s): Adult
Major character(s): Ed Yellings, Businessman, African American, Father; PaPa LaBas, Aged Person (70-Year-Old), African American, Detective—Private
Time period(s): 1970s
Locale(s): Berkeley, California

Summary: Men are inflicting psychological stress on one another, driving one another to high blood pressure and hardening of the arteries, and doing the usual stabbing, raping, and mugging. It had to be stopped and businessman Ed Yellings is determined to give this Louisiana Red the Business. With his New Orleans recipe he opens Solid Gumbo Works and soon customers are flocking to his doors. Ed's formula is working but his home life is suffering. His wife Ruby deserts him for a political career, leaving him with the children—Wolf, Street, and Minnie. When Ed is murdered, a young 70-year-old PaPa LaBas is sent to put his affairs in order and uncover the killer(s). The eldest son, Wolf, works closely with LaBas while his younger brother Street is arrested and escapes to become a fugitive. Their baby sister Minnie has been converted into the Moocher movement by T Feeler and a white intellectual Max Kasavubu. In his investigation LaBas delves into the rivalries of "Minnie the Moocher" and the possibility Ed was killed by someone he knew. When Street reappears, a fire erupts at Solid Gumbo Works, other murders occur and LaBas uncovers the new formula Ed was developing and tries to put all the pieces together to solve the case. Successful and returning to his position in New York at the Ted Cunningham Institute he learns an important associate has been killed.

Other books by the same author:

Japanese by Spring, 1993
Reckless Eyeballing, 1986
Mumbo Jumbo, 1972
Yellow Back Radio Broke Down, 1969
Freelance Pallbearers, 1967 (debut novel)

Other books you might like:

Arthur Flowers, *De Mojo Blues*, 1985
Depicts a Vietnam veteran dishonorably discharged for murder with his buddies who now wants to become trained in the ways of hoodoo and conjuring.
Jewell Parker Rhodes, *Voodoo Dreams: A Novel of Marie Laveau*, 1993
In New Orleans, a young woman becomes entangled with a voodoo doctor who makes her famous before she is forced to destroy him for her own survival.
Duane Smith, *The Nubian*, 1994
The twenty year episodes from a young man's life and his relationship with his mysterious Afrocentric uncle who the government convicts.

366

ISHMAEL REED, African American

Mumbo Jumbo

(New York: Doubleday, 1972)

Story type: Satire
Series: PaPa LaBas
Subject(s): Mystery and Detective Stories; Murder; Religion
Age range(s): Adult
Major character(s): PaPa LaBas, Aged Person (70-Year-Old), Detective—Private, African American; Hinckle Von Vampton, Aged Person, Librarian, Caucasian
Time period(s): 1920s; 1970s (1971)
Locale(s): New Orleans, Louisiana; New York, New York

Summary: Starting in New Orleans an epidemic of Jes Grew is sweeping America, to some a plague to others an anti-plague. The ancient mysteries of HooDoo threaten Judeo-Christian culture and its purveyors. Under the guise of "bringing stability to the Caribbean" Haiti falls under attack. At the age of 50 PaPa LaBas, HooDoo priest and head of the Mumbo Jumbo Kathedral, becomes involved in recovering the missing ancient HooDoo Text which can establish Jes Grew as the dominant spiritual force in American culture. Once in the possession of the Knights Templar librarian Hinckle Von Vampton, leader of the anti-Jes Grew movement, The Text has now become lost. With murders occurring LaBas discovers where the box containing The Text is to be found. Decades later at age 100 LaBas has again been invited to recount his exploits as a "jacklegged detective of the metaphysical" who was on a crucial case of the 1920s.

Other books by the same author:
Japanese by Spring, 1993
Reckless Eyeballing, 1986
Flight to Canada, 1976
Last Days of Louisiana Red, 1974
Freelance Pallbearers, 1967 (debut novel)

Other books you might like:
Arthur Flowers, *De Mojo Blues*, 1985
  Depicts a Vietnam veteran dishonorably discharged for murder with his buddies who now want to become trained in the ways of hoodoo and conjuring.
Jewell Parker Rhodes, *Voodoo Dreams: A Novel of Marie Laveau*, 1993
  In New Orleans, a young woman becomes entangled with a voodoo doctor who makes her famous before she is forced to destroy him for her own survival.
Duane Smith, *The Nubian*, 1994
  The twenty year episodes from a young man's life and his relationship with his mysterious Afrocentric uncle who the government convicts.

367

ISHMAEL REED, African American

Reckless Eyeballing
(New York: St. Martin's Press, 1986)

Story type: Satire
Subject(s): Creative Writing; Prejudice; Race Relations
Age range(s): Adult
Major character(s): Ian Ball, Writer, African American; Flower Phantom, Criminal, African American; Tremonisha Smarts, Crime Victim, Writer, African American
Time period(s): 1980s (1986)
Locale(s): New York, New York

Summary: When his supportive director is killed by white racists, Ian is faced with the reality of drastically rewriting his second play in hopes of getting it produced. His producer brings in a new director, Tremonisha, who was victimized by a masked intruder, the Flower Phantom. Cutting off the hair of his victims, the Flower Phantom leaves behind a chrysanthemum and he tells his victims why they deserve his wrath. Ian and Tremonisha rewrite his play and it receives critical ac-

claim. While the police think they have solved the identity of the Flower Phantom, Ian returns home where his mother recollects a secret she has been keeping from Ian. They discover new evidence pointing in another direction.

Where it's reviewed:
Black Scholar, May 1987, page 37
New York Times Book Review, March 23, 1986, page 11
Publishers Weekly, January 24, 1986, page 62

Other books by the same author:
Flight to Canada, 1976
Last Days of Louisiana Red, 1974
Mumbo Jumbo, 1972
Yellow Back Radio Broke Down, 1969
Freelance Pallbearers, 1967 (debut novel)

Other books you might like:
Trey Ellis, *Platitudes*, 1988
  Parallel stories created by two writers are corresponding about teenaged characters, and they develop their own personal relationship.
Charles Johnson, *Oxherding Tale*, 1982
  This coming-of-age tale is about a light-skinned young man during the plantation era of the South as he struggles to gain his freedom and the freedom of those he loves.
Gloria Naylor, *Linden Hills*, 1985
  Linden Hills symbolizes success, but two boys doing odd jobs see firsthand the lust, pain, hypocrisy, and valor of its residents.
Brent Wade, *Company Man*, 1992
  These confessions are about the behind-the-scenes stresses and strains faced by a man attempting to climb the business ladder and preserved his family.

368

ISHMAEL REED, African American

The Terrible Threes
(New York: Atheneum, 1989)

Story type: Satire
Series: Nance Saturday
Subject(s): Politics; Social Classes
Age range(s): Adult
Major character(s): Nance Saturday, Driver, Detective— Private, Caucasian; Reverend Clement Jones, Political Figure (White House Chief of Staff), African American
Time period(s): 1990s
Locale(s): New York, New York; Washington, District of Columbia

Summary: President Dean Clift, former model, has been removed from office. Admiral Matthews carries on the affairs of state aided by Reverend Jones, a faith healer and televangelist, Robert Krantz, the White House communications officer and ex-television producer, and a man known as the King of Beer. When the Admiral dies suddenly and the King of Beer drops out of sight, Jones begins talking to people only he can see and borrows a computerized superhero robot from Hollywood to do his dirty work. Operation Two Birds is revealed as a plan to rid the world of its "surplus" people and blame it on Nigeria. A Black Peter impersonator is bamboozled when the real Black Peter surfaces and begins doing good deeds. And Nance Saturday, detective-turned-cabbie, cruises the streets looking for a fare.

Other books by the same author:
Japanese by Spring, 1993
Reckless Eyeballing, 1986
The Terrible Twos, 1982
Last Days of Louisiana Red, 1974
Freelance Pallbearers, 1967 (debut novel)

Other books you might like:
Melvin Dixon, *Trouble the Water*, 1989
  Running away from home a young man returns twenty years later in a plot of revenge which developed between his grandmother and his father.
Percival Everett, *Suder*, 1983
  The escapades of a young man who fears he may be on the verge of going insane like his mother, who decides to run away from his wife and son.
Clarence Major, *My Amputations*, 1986
  Hallucinatory tale in which a man assumes the identity of his kidnap victim and travels the globe in search of a lost manuscript.
Clarence Major, *Reflex and Bone Structure*, 1975
  An author is involved in relationships with the characters in his own novel in this episodic metaphysical detective story.
John Edgar Wideman, *Philadelphia Fire*, 1990
  Intrigued by a police bombing and killing of adults and children, a self-exiled writer returns to Philadelphia to investigate.

369

ISHMAEL REED, African American

The Terrible Twos
(New York: St. Martin's/Marek, 1982)

Story type: Satire
Series: Nance Saturday
Subject(s): Politics; Santa Claus; Social Classes
Age range(s): Adult
Major character(s): Oscar Zumwalt, Businessman, Fugitive, Caucasian; Nance Saturday, Criminologist, Spouse, Caucasian
Time period(s): 1980s (1980-1990)
Locale(s): New York, New York; Washington, District of Columbia

Summary: In this satirical social commentary, a California court awards exclusive rights to Santa Claus to Oscar Zumwalt's North Pole Development Corporation. The President's wife is electrocuted by a paranoid anti-social spruce tree when she turns on the annual Christmas tree lights. Santa delivers a speech declaring Americans are emotional two-year-olds, throwing tantrums and immune to reason. When Nance Saturday is hired to find a missing hit man he finds himself bewildered by Santa Claus' story of body snatching, an incapacitated President is put in a sanitorium, and he thinks he sees a man flying above the roof of a building in a bishop's hat and gown.

Other books by the same author:
Japanese by Spring, 1993
The Terrible Threes, 1989
Mumbo Jumbo, 1972
Yellow Back Radio Broke Down, 1969
Freelance Pallbearers, 1967 (debut novel)

Other books you might like:
Percival Everett, *Suder*, 1983
  The escapades of a young man who fears he may be on the verge of going insane like his mother, who decides to run away from his wife and son.
Percival Everett, *Watershed*, 1996
  On a fishing trip to get away from his neurotic girlfriend, a man finds himself involved in a fight over Native American treaty rights.
Clarence Major, *My Amputations*, 1986
  Hallucinatory tale in which a man assumes the identity of his kidnap victim and travels the globe in search of a lost manuscript.
Clarence Major, *Painted Turtle: Woman with Guitar*, 1988
  A man tells the story of a young Indian woman alienated from her culture and finding her identity as a performer on the cantina circuit.
Clarence Major, *Reflex and Bone Structure*, 1975
  An author is involved in relationships with the characters in his own novel in this episodic metaphysical detective story.
John Edgar Wideman, *Philadelphia Fire*, 1990
  Intrigued by a police bombing and killing of adults and children, a self-exiled writer returns to Philadelphia to investigate.

370

JEWELL PARKER RHODES, African American

Voodoo Dreams: A Novel of Marie Laveau
(New York: St. Martin's Press, 1993)

Subject(s): Fiction; Interpersonal Relations; Occult
Age range(s): Adult
Major character(s): Marie Laveau, Occultist (voodooienne), Historical Figure, African American; Marie, Occultist (voodooienne), Healer, African American; John, Con Artist, Occultist (voodooienne), African American
Time period(s): 19th century (1812-1881)
Locale(s): New Orleans, Louisiana

Summary: Raised in the Louisiana bayou by her grandmother, Marie travels to New Orleans to find her *Maman*. She becomes entangled with John, a voodoo doctor. He uses her to further his own interests before falling victim to his own devices. Marie triumphs over him for her and her daughter's survival.

About this book: This is the author's debut novel.

Where it's reviewed:
Library Journal, April 15, 1994, page 140
New York Times Book Review, January 30, 1994, page 24
Publishers Weekly, September 27, 1993, page 44

Other books you might like:

Barbara Chase-Riboud, *Valide*, 1986

This historical account is about a 14-year-old American creole sold into an 18th century Turkish harem who becomes the mother of the Sultan.

Arthur Flowers, *De Mojo Blues*, 1985

This story depicts a Vietnam veteran dishonorably discharged for murder with his buddies. He now wants to become trained in the ways of hoodoo and conjuring.

Toni Morrison, *Beloved*, 1987

This story tells about a mother who escapes from slavery and who kills her baby to keep her former owner from stealing her. She is then haunted and consumed by the baby's ghost.

Gloria Naylor, *Mama Day*, 1988

Returning to her sea island home, a young woman finds both body and soul threatened by supernatural forces from which she is barely saved by Mama Day.

`371`

BRENDA LANE RICHARDSON, African American

Chesapeake Song

(New York: Amistad Press, Inc., 1993)

Subject(s): Family Relations; Marriage
Age range(s): Adult
Major character(s): Tamra Wells Lane, Mother, Scientist, African American; Charles Lane, Businessman, Farmer, African American
Time period(s): 1990s (1990)
Locale(s): Nanticoke, Maryland

Summary: Tamra and Charles are two successful people who have difficulty seeing how their own marital problems mirror their parents' patterns of successes and failures. They finally realize that even though love alone cannot hold a marriage together, it is an important key to understanding a relationship.

About this book: This is the author's debut novel.

Where it's reviewed:
Belles Lettres, Summer 1994, page 15
Essence, May 1994, page 64
Publishers Weekly, October 4, 1993, page 64

Other books you might like:

Nelson George, *Urban Romance*, 1993

This contemporary story tells the relationship of a young couple brought together by mutual friends as they experience love and heartbreak.

Terri McMillan, *Disappearing Acts*, 1989

A successful professional woman tries to maintain a relationship with a man unable to keep a steady job.

Terry McMillan, *Waiting to Exhale*, 1992

This contemporary account is about the friendship of four women, their relationships with men, and their experiences with family and careers.

Gloria Naylor, *Linden Hills*, 1985

Linden Hills symbolizes success, but two boys doing odd jobs see firsthand the lust, pain, hypocrisy, and valor of its residents.

`372`

FAITH RINGGOLD, Author/Illustrator, African American

Aunt Harriet's Underground Railroad in the Sky

(New York: Crown Publishers, 1992)

Story type: Young Readers
Series: Lightfoot Family
Subject(s): Underground Railroad; Brothers and Sisters; Historical
Age range(s): Grades 2-4
Major character(s): Cassie Louise Lightfoot, Child, Sister, African American
Time period(s): 1990s
Locale(s): New York, New York

Summary: Young Cassie and her baby brother Be Be come across an old train in the sky. Be Be gets on the train, leaving Cassie behind. Cassie meets the conductor, aunt Harriet Tubman, who explains how every one hundred years the train follows the underground railroad route to freedom and what Cassie must do if she wants to reunite with Be Be. On her journey Cassie escapes from a plantation, is befriended by many agents of the underground railroad, travels through woods and swamps, and is hidden in a wagon's secret compartment until she reaches the safety of Canada's Niagara Falls. Reunited, the children now know what their ancestors survived for the sake of freedom.

About this book: Includes a biographical sketch of Harriet Tubman and a reading list.

Other books by the same author:
Bonjour Lonnie, 1996
My Dream of Martin Luther King, 1996
Dinner at Aunt Connie's House, 1993
Tar Beach, 1991 (debut)

Other books you might like:

Lucille Clifton, *All Us Come Cross the Water*, 1973

Wanting to answer his teacher's question about where his people came from a boy asks his family and a neighbor before speaking up in class.

Lucille Clifton, *My Brother Fine with Me*, 1975

An 8-year-old sister helping her 5-year-old brother pack to run away discovers how lonely she is without him and is happier when he decides not to leave.

Eloise Greenfield, *Africa Dream*, 1977

Dreaming she has crossed the ocean to long-ago Africa a child shops in the marketplace, reads with magic eyes, and is welcomed by relatives.

Elizabeth Fitzgerald Howard, *Papa Tells Chita a Story*, 1995

A child asks her beloved papa to tell her the story of when he was the bravest soldier and carried the message and won the war.

Patricia C. McKissack, *Mirandy and Brother Wind*, 1988

Folk tale of a young girl desperately wanting to win her first cakewalk dance contest who makes a wish to the wind and dances with her friend.

373

FAITH RINGGOLD, Author/Illustrator, African American

Bonjour Lonnie

(New York: Hyperion Books For Children, 1996)

Story type: Young Readers
Subject(s): Orphans; Family Relations; Historical
Age range(s): Grades 2-4
Major character(s): Lonnie, Child, Orphan, African American
Time period(s): 1990s
Locale(s): United States (unidentified city); Paris, France

Summary: A lovebird alights on Lonnie's window, telling him of it's magic; it seems people find find their loved ones when he is around. The bird flies away and Lonnie is transported from his orphanage to the streets of Paris. He searches all over Paris for the lovebird, who finally appears to him. The bird leads Lonnie to a courtyard where he ''meets'' his grandfather and White grandmother, his father and his Jewish mother. They each tell their story, the tragic journeys of their lives, explaining how Lonnie was orphaned and smuggled into the U.S. when the Nazi's occupied Paris in World War II. Suddenly Lonnie is in the home of Aunt Connie and Uncle Bates, who want to adopt him, and they all thank the love bird for bringing them together.

About this book: Includes biographical sketches of historical people named in the text and a bibliography. Lonnie was first introduced in *Dinner at Aunt Connie's House*.

Other books by the same author:
Aunt Harriet's Underground Railroad in the Sky, 1995
My Dream of Martin Luther King, 1996
Dinner at Aunt Connie's House, 1993
Tar Beach, 1991 (debut)

Other books you might like:
Jeannette Franklin Caines, *Abby*, 1973
    An adopted preschooler questions her mother and older brother about when she first came there and suggests they adopt another brother.

374

HARRIETTE GILLEM ROBINET, African American

Children of the Fire

(New York: Atheneum, 1991)

Story type: Young Readers
Subject(s): Historical; Fires; Race Relations
Age range(s): Grades 4-6
Major character(s): Hallelujah, 11-Year-Old, Orphan, African American
Time period(s): 1890s (1891)
Locale(s): Chicago, Illinois

Summary: The weather has been windy and dry, and many fires have broken out all over the city; Hallelujah is excited— she will be allowed to go watch the next one. What starts out as an exciting spectacle turns frightening as Hallelujah sees the damage that is done to homes and families, black and white, rich and poor. Hallelujah finds ways to help people during and after the fire and is herself forever changed.

Awards the book has won:
Friends of American Writers, 1992

Other books by the same author:
If You Please, President Lincoln, 1995
Mississippi Chariot, 1994
Ride the Red Cycle, 1980
Jay and the Marigold, 1976 (debut novel)

Other books you might like:
Virginia Hamilton, *Cousins*, 1990
    Concerned that her grandmother might die, a young girl is unprepared for the death of another relative.
Virginia Hamilton, *Drylongso*, 1992
    As a great wall of dust moves across their drought-stricken farm, a family's distress is relieved by a young man called Drylongso.
Connie Porter, *Addy Learns a Lesson: A School Story*, 1993
    After escaping slavery, a girl and her mother arrive in Philadelphia, where she goes to school and learns a lesson in true friendship.
Connie Porter, *Addy Saves the Day: A Summer Story*, 1994
    Working on a church fund-raiser to help families separated by the Civil War, two girls catch a thief and one gets a very special reward.
Connie Porter, *Changes for Addy: A Winter Story*, 1994
    After the Civil War ends, a young girl hopes her family can be reunited in freedom in Philadelphia, but the future holds both happiness and heartache.

375

HARRIETTE GILLEM ROBINET, African American

If You Please, President Lincoln

(New York: Atheneum Books for Young Readers, 1995)

Story type: Young Readers
Subject(s): Historical; Slavery; Self-Respect
Age range(s): Grades 3-7
Major character(s): Moses Lincoln Christmas, 14-Year-Old, Slave, African American
Time period(s): 1860s (1864)
Locale(s): Annapolis, Maryland; Haiti (Isle a Vache)

Summary: When his Aunt Rebekah dies on Christmas Day, 14-year-old Moses escapes slavery and flees to Annapolis. There he is tricked aboard a clipper ship bound for an island in the Republic of Haiti, where he and several hundred other newly freed and runaway slaves were to set up a colony and raise cotton. On the torturous journey to Cow Island, Moses becomes a leader among the passengers, and learns his worth from a blind man named Goshen, and helps get them rescued once they reach their destination.

Where it's reviewed:
Booklist, August 1995, page 1947
Publishers Weekly, June 26, 1995, page 107
School Library Journal, June 1995, page 132
Voice of Your Advocates, October 1995, page 223

Other books by the same author:
Mississippi Chariot, 1994
Children of the Fire, 1991
Ride the Red Cycle, 1980

Jay and the Marigold, 1976 (debut novel)

Other books you might like:

Joyce Hansen, *The Captive*, 1994
Historical fiction of the life of a royal African boy who is kidnapped and illegally sold as a slave and is later rescued by a sea captain.

Connie Porter, *Meet Addy: An American Girl*, 1993
A 9-year-old girl and her mother escape a life of cruel slavery and journey to freedom in Philadelphia during the Civil War.

Connie Porter, *Addy Saves the Day: A Summer Story*, 1994
Working on a church fund-raiser to help families separated by the Civil War, two girls catch a thief and one gets a very special reward.

Connie Porter, *Changes for Addy: A Winter Story*, 1994
After the Civil War ends, a young girl hopes her family can be reunited in freedom in Philadelphia, but the future holds both happiness and heartache.

376

HARRIETTE GILLEM ROBINET, African American
GERTRUDE S. SCOTT, Illustrator

Jay and the Marigold
(Chicago: Children's Press, 1976)

Story type: Young Readers
Subject(s): Cerebral Palsy; Physically Handicapped; Friendship
Age range(s): Grades 1-2
Major character(s): Jay, 8-Year-Old, Handicapped, Caucasian
Time period(s): 1970s
Locale(s): United States (unidentified city)

Summary: Young, blond, blue eyed Jay has cerebral palsy and is unable to walk. In a wheelchair he envies his twin sister Janie and her friends for the many things they can do, playing dodge ball, riding their bicycles, and having a good time together. On one lonely day Jay discovers the tiny sprigs of a green plant sprouting in the corner of the concrete steps. Nurturing the plant he watches it grow and thinks of his own life. A new boy Pedro, who is tall and brown, moves on Jay's street. Jay watches as the kids refuse to play with Pedro and soon he and Pedro become friends. Before long when the kids accept Pedro he includes Jay in their games. By the time school begins Jay and his marigold plant are both blooming.

About this book: Debut novel.

Other books you might like:

Lucille Clifton, *The Boy Who Didn't Believe in Spring*, 1973
Everyone says spring is coming and a youngster and his white pal don't believe them so they go searching for evidence to discover spring.

Lucille Clifton, *My Friend Jacob*, 1980
A young boy shares special times with his neighbor and best friend, a white mentally handicapped older boy he plays ball with and helps remember things.

Eloise Greenfield, *Darlene*, 1980
In a wheelchair a young girl unexpectedly has fun at her uncle's house playing with her young cousin changing her mind about wanting to go home.

377

HARRIETTE GILLEM ROBINET, African American

Mississippi Chariot
(New York: Atheneum, 1994)

Story type: Young Readers
Subject(s): Race Relations; Resourcefulness; Farm Life
Age range(s): Grades 4-7
Major character(s): Abraham Lincoln Jackson, 12-Year-Old, African American; Andrew Jackson "Hawk" Baker, 12-Year-Old, Caucasian
Time period(s): 1930s (1936)
Locale(s): Sleepy Corners, Michigan

Summary: His daddy is on a chain gang for a crime he didn't commit, and Shortning is determined to find a way to get him free. His plan begins with a rumor, the lifeblood of their small town. Shortning rescues white Hawk Baker from drowning, and the two boys begin a friendship that transcends 1930's Mississippi.

Where it's reviewed:
Booklist, November 15, 1994, page 591
Kirkus Reviews, November 15, 1994, page 1541
School Library Journal, December 1994, page 112
Voice of Youth Advocates, June 1995, page 98
Childrens Book Review Service, December 1994, page 47

Other books by the same author:
If You Please, President Lincoln, 1995
Children of the Fire, 1991
Ride the Red Cycle, 1980
Jay and the Marigold, 1976 (debut novel)

Other books you might like:

Virginia Hamilton, *Junius over Far*, 1985
When his grandfather returns to his Caribbean island home, a disturbing letter prompts a young boy and his father to journey to rescue him.

Virginia Hamilton, *Plain City*, 1993
A 12-year-old who feels out of place struggles to unearth her past and family history as she gradually discovers more about her long-missing father.

Walter Dean Myers, *The Righteous Revenge of Artemis Bonner*, 1992
Wild west adventure of a young man out to avenge his uncle's murder and to locate his treasure before the killer and his companion.

Walter Dean Myers, *Somewhere in the Darkness*, 1992
An ailing father escapes from prison to prove his innocence to his son by their confronting the witness who lied against him for murder.

Harriette Gillem Robinet, *Children of the Fire*, 1991
A young girl witnesses the Great Chicago Fire of 1871 and is forever changed.

378

HARRIETTE GILLEM ROBINET, African American
DAVID BROWN, Illustrator, African American

Ride the Red Cycle

(Boston: Houghton Mifflin Company, 1980)

Story type: Young Readers
Subject(s): Physically Handicapped; Bicycles and Bicycling; Independence
Age range(s): Grades 3-5
Major character(s): Jerome Johnson, 11-Year-Old, Handicapped, African American
Time period(s): 1980s
Locale(s): United States

Summary: Crippled since the age of two, Jerome struggles to realize his dream of escaping his wheelchair and riding a cycle all by himself.

Other books by the same author:
If You Please, President Lincoln, 1995
Mississippi Chariot, 1994
Children of the Fire, 1991
Jay and the Marigold, 1976 (debut novel)

Other books you might like:
Jacqueline Turner Banks, *Egg-Drop Blues*, 1995
A sixth grader's science grade is low because of his dyslexia, so he and his twin brother enter a competition for extra credit.
Joyce Hansen, *Yellow Bird and Me*, 1986
Missing her best friend who has moved away, a young girl helps a classmate in elementary school overcome stage fright and discovers he has dyslexia.
Angela Johnson, *Humming Whispers*, 1995
Recounts the life of a young girl living with an older sister who has schizophrenia and her fear that she too may have the mental illness.
Joyce Carol Thomas, *The Golden Pasture*, 1986
The exquisite horse a 12-year-old boy finds on his grandfather's farm one summer helps him to understand his difficult father better.
Mildred Pitts Walter, *Justin and the Best Biscuits in the World*, 1986
A 10-year-old sure that cleaning and keeping house is "women's work," visits his beloved grandfather's ranch and learns some manly skills.

379

DORI SANDERS, African American

Clover

(Chapel Hill, North Carolina: Algonquin Books of Chapel Hill, 1990)

Story type: Young Readers
Subject(s): Family Relations; Farm Life; Race Relations
Age range(s): Grades 5-8
Major character(s): Clover Hill, 10-Year-Old, Stepdaughter, African American; Gaten Hill, Father, Principal, African American; Sara Kate Colson Hill, Stepmother, Designer, Caucasian

Time period(s): 1980s
Locale(s): Round Hill, South Carolina

Summary: Clover's father Gaten is killed in a car accident within hours of his wedding to Sara Kate, a white woman Clover barely knows. Gaten's relatives want to raise Clover themselves and Sara Kate's relatives feel Clover should not be her responsibility. Sara Kate disagrees with them all and wants to raise Clover herself on Gaten's farm. Dealing with their grief and loss and getting to know one another, Clover and Sara Kate try to build a family together.

About this book: Debut novel (Young Readers).

Where it's reviewed:
Booklist, June 1, 1993, page 1865

Awards the book has won:
Lillian Smith Award For Outstanding Writing About the South, 1991

Other books you might like:
Candy Dawson Boyd, *Breadsticks and Blessing Places*, 1985
Three sixth-grade girlfriends are involved in their regular routine of activities when one is killed and the others cope with her untimely death.
Virginia Hamilton, *Cousins*, 1990
Concerned that her grandmother might die, a young girl is unprepared for the death of another relative.
Eleanora E. Tate, *The Secret of Gumbo Grove*, 1987
A youngster upsets her community and her parents when she spreads stories she's heard about the town ancestors buried in the church cemetery.
Jacqueline Woodson, *Between Madison & Palmetto*, 1993
Two 13-year-old best friends are reunited and have to adjust to a lot of change in their lives.
Jacqueline Woodson, *Last Summer with Maizon*, 1990
The friendship and separation of two youngsters after one suffers the death of her father and the other goes away to boarding school.

380

DORI SANDERS, African American

Her Own Place

(Chapel Hill: Algonquin Books of Chapel Hill, 1993)

Subject(s): Individuality; Family Life; Race Relations
Age range(s): Adult
Major character(s): Mae Lee Barnes, Aged Person, Divorced Person, African American
Time period(s): 1980s (1986)
Locale(s): Rising Ridge, South Carolina

Summary: Mae Lee, a retiree shares remembrances and present-day events from her life's lessons of survival and determination. She follows in her father's footsteps to become a farmer, she becomes a World War II bride and then she becomes an abandoned wife. As a proud mother of five and a grandmother, she integrates the hospital auxiliary, and she becomes a Braves fan, and an elegant hostess. Now she finds herself embarking on a new episode of vulnerability in her life as she takes a male roomer into her new home.

About this book: This is the author's debut novel.

Where it's reviewed:
American Book Review, February 1994, page 22
Kliatt, September 1994, page 12
New York Times Book Review, May 29, 1994, page 20

Other books you might like:
Marita Golden, *Long Distance Life*, 1989
  These episodes relate the murder of a young grandson in the 1980s and the evolution of his family from a sharecropping background of the 1920s.
Julius Lester, *Do Lord Remember Me*, 1984
  This saga is about the life and times of an eighty-year-old reverend who became known as the "colored Billy Graham."
Linda Raymond, *Rocking the Babies*, 1994
  Two older women volunteer to be hospital care givers to drug exposed babies. Both have a secret reason for being there.

381

SAPPHIRE, African American

Push
(New York: Alfred A. Knopf, 1996)

Story type: Young Adult
Subject(s): Family Problems; Rape; Self-Perception
Age range(s): Adult
Major character(s): Claireece Precious Jones, 16-Year-Old, Abuse Victim, African American
Time period(s): 1980s (1983); 1990s (1991)
Locale(s): New York, New York (Harlem)

Summary: Raped by her father, Precious became a mother and sister at the age of twelve when she gave birth to a child with Down's Syndrome. Sexually abused by her mother and father, never learning to read or write, living on welfare, and obese at sixteen she is pregnant again by her father. When a teacher befriends her, she gets into an alternative school and struggles to make a better life for herself and her babies.

About this book: Debut novel.

Other books you might like:
Walter Dean Myers, *Sweet Illusions*, 1986
  Episodes in the lives of several pregnant youngsters who gravitate to a counseling center to decide how to deal with their situations and futures.
Jervey Tervalon, *Understand This*, 1994
  High school lovers, a male and female couple, find themselves headed in different directions, one to college and the other quitting school.
Rita Williams-Garcia, *Like Sisters on the Homefront*, 1994
  An unwed 14-year-old mother, pregnant again, has an abortion and, when sent to her relatives in the South, she develops a new sense of family and self.
Jacqueline Woodson, *Autobiography of a Family Photo*, 1995
  New York life of a teenage girl, who has a gay brother and a half-white brother, experiences family violence, and questions her sexuality.

382

DARIECK SCOTT, African American

Traitor to the Race
(New York: Dutton, 1995)

Subject(s): Homosexuality/Lesbianism; Interpersonal Relations; Self-Acceptance
Age range(s): Adult
Major character(s): Kenneth Gabriel, Actor, Homosexual, African American; Evan Marcialis, Actor, Homosexual, Caucasian
Time period(s): 1990s
Locale(s): New York, New York

Summary: Kenneth and his white lover Evan are both actors, but while Evan is a regular on a television soap opera, unemployed Kenneth fills his hours with sexual fantasies which they sometimes re-enact as Games. When Kenneth's cousin Hammett is gang raped and murdered, he begins questioning his own racial identity and the fact that he has a white lover but few connections with other black men. In a dance/music/riot to protest the murder of Hammett and try to heal the community, Kenneth is swept away, hardly recognizing his own reflection.

About this book: This is the author's debut novel.

Other books you might like:
Steven Corbin, *Fragments That Remain*, 1993
  Depicts a contemporary actor's life as he deals with racism, sexism, homophobia, bigotry, an interracial relationship, and secrets from the past.
Steven Corbin, *100 Days from Now*, 1994
  The courtship and interracial relationship of two men who are both HIV-positive, one who has yet to tell his family he is gay and in love.
Melvin Dixon, *Vanishing Rooms*, 1991
  Lives intersect in this story about a young man and his white male lover who is gang-raped and murdered.
Larry Duplechan, *Captain Swing*, 1993
  Now in his mid-30s and coping with tragic losses in his life the gay character in this debut novel is unsure about taking risks in order to love again.
Larry Duplechan, *Tangled Up in Blue*, 1989
  This novel describes the impact of AIDS when a woman discovers that her husband has had a bisexual affair with a friend who's infected.
E. Lynn Harris, *Invisible Life*, 1992
  A young man experiences his first bisexual relationships in college, moves to New York to pursue a law career, and searches to find the one he loves.

383

NTOZAKE SHANGE, African American

Betsey Brown
(New York: St. Martin's Press, 1985)

Subject(s): Coming of Age; Family Relations; Race Relations
Age range(s): Grades 8-Adult

Major character(s): Elizabeth "Betsey" Brown, 13-Year-Old, Sister (oldest), African American; Jane Brown, Mother, Social Worker, African American; Greer Brown, Doctor, Father, African American

Time period(s): 1950s (1959)

Locale(s): St.Louis, Missouri

Summary: Betsey, the eldest of five children, turns thirteen the year that school integration becomes law. When she attends for the first time a predominantly white public school across town, she feels invisible among her white classmates and teachers. She learns she knows more than her teachers about the contributions of her own culture. While her mother, Jane, fears for the safety of her children in this new social climate, her father, Greer, wants them to know their history and culture and be prepared to face racism.

Where it's reviewed:

Essence, June 1985, page 36
Ms., June 1985, page 70
Publishers Weekly, March 22, 1985, page 53

Other books by the same author:

Liliane: Resurrection of the Daughter, 1994
Sassafrass, Cypress and Indigo, 1982 (debut novel)

Other books you might like:

Tina McElroy Ansa, *Baby of the Family*, 1989
  This coming-of-age tale is about a young girl who was born with supernatural powers.

Maxine Clair, *Rattlebone*, 1994
  This story is about the events in the life of a young girl coming of age in a small town in the 1950s.

Thulani Davis, *1959*, 1992
  This coming-of-age story about a 12-year-old girl recounts events that changed her life and others around her during the historic civil rights movement.

Charlotte Sherman, *One Dark Body*, 1993
  This story relates the incidents in the life of a young girl abandoned at birth. It deals with the return of her mother and her friend's entry into manhood.

A.J. Verdelle, *The Good Negress*, 1995
  A young country girl who wants more from life than cooking, cleaning, and washing, moves to the city. She is encouraged by her teacher to strive for higher goals.

384

NTOZAKE SHANGE, African American

Liliane: Resurrection of the Daughter

(New York: St. Martin's Press, 1994)

Series: Jean Stevenson

Subject(s): Coming of Age; Interpersonal Relations; Self-Acceptance

Age range(s): Adult

Major character(s): Liliane Lincoln, Artist, Patient, African American

Time period(s): 1960s

Locale(s): New York, New York (Queens); Michigan (unidentified city); East St. Louis, Missouri

Summary: The complexities of Liliane's life—past and present—are revealed in psychotherapy sessions, in stories told by Liliane herself, and in stories told by the many voices of her friends and lovers. Interacting with those closest to her, Liliane deals with the loss of her mother, comes to grips with her anger toward her father, struggles in her romances and friendships, battles racism and bigotry, and copes with making her way in the world.

Where it's reviewed:

Booklist, September 1, 1994, page 3
Kirkus Reviews, September 1, 1994, page 1158

Other books by the same author:

Betsey Brown, 1985
Sassafrass, Cypress and Indigo, 1982 (debut novel)

Other books you might like:

Trey Ellis, *Platitudes*, 1988
  Parallel stories created by two writers are corresponding about teenaged characters, and they develop their own personal relationship.

Ray Shell, *Iced*, 1993
  A man in his diary reflects about his accomplishments in life as well as his regrets at descending into the white-smoke world of crack cocaine.

Jervey Tervalon, *Understand This*, 1994
  Two high school male-female lovers find themselves headed in different directions as one goes to college and the other quits school.

Brent Wade, *Company Man*, 1992
  These confessions are about the behind-the-scenes stresses and strains faced by a man attempting to climb the business ladder and preserve his family.

Jacqueline Woodson, *Autobiography of a Family Photo*, 1995
  This story is about a teenage girl in New York, who has a gay brother and a half-white brother. She experiences family violence, and she questions her own sexuality.

385

NTOZAKE SHANGE, African American

Sassafrass, Cypress and Indigo

(New York: St. Martin's, 1982)

Story type: Adult

Subject(s): Interpersonal Relations; Sisters

Major character(s): Sassafrass, Artisan (oldest sister), African American; Cypress, Dancer (middle sister), African American; Indigo, Musician (youngest sister), African American

Time period(s): 1970s

Locale(s): Charleston, South Carolina; Los Angeles, California; New York, New York

Summary: The interwoven tale of the lives of three sisters from South Carolina. Venturing to the east coast, Cypress develops her talent as dancer and along the way has an affair with another woman before finding a man she feels is perfect. The youngest sister Indigo has created a world of make believe with her dolls until she discovers expression with the violin. Sassafrass journeys to the west coast with an abusive boyfriend and they later move to a commune where Sassafrass becomes pregnant by someone else. The girl's mother reflects on days gone by with their deceased father and is there giving support to her daughters as they make their own way in the world.

About this book: This is the author's debut novel.

Other books by the same author:
Liliane: Resurrection of the Daughter, 1994
Betsey Brown, 1985 (young adult)

Other books you might like:
Tina McElroy Ansa, *Ugly Ways*, 1993
   Contemporary account of three sisters reflecting on their upbringing in a small town and how their lives have evolved.
Connie Briscoe, *Sisters and Lovers*, 1994
   Contemporary story about the lives and struggles of three sisters and the men with whom they become involved.
Steven Corbin, *No Easy Place to Be*, 1989
   Explores the relationships among three sisters in urban New York during the 1920s Harlem Renaissance era.
Terry McMillan, *Waiting to Exhale*, 1992
   Contemporary account of the friendship of four women, their relationships with men, and their experiences with family and careers.

386

JOHN SHEARER, African American
TED SHEARER, Illustrator, West Indian

Billy Jo Jive and the Case of the Midnight Voices

(New York: Delacorte Press, 1982)

Story type: Young Readers
Series: Billy Jo Jive
Subject(s): Mystery and Detective Stories; Missing Persons; Camps and Camping
Age range(s): Grades 2-3
Major character(s): Billy Jo Jive, Child, Detective—Amateur, African American; Susie Sunset, Child, Detective—Amateur, African American
Time period(s): 1980s
Locale(s): United States (campsite)

Summary: Vacationing at Camp Mountain Lake, young crime fighters Jive and his partner Susie have a new mystery to solve. In their bunkhouse, with a thundering rain falling, Jive and the guys are awakened by moans and groans echoing in the campground. Only Jive is fearless enough to get up and investigate and when two campers are discovered to be missing, he recruits his pal Susie to help him find them. One is discovered next morning, wandering dazed and confused and the other's parents have moved him to a rival camp. At the big bonfire jamboree that night everyone gathers happily until a frightening loud sound scares them all away. Investigating the camp records and participating in a late night stakeout lead to a confession as Jive and Susie wrap up another case.

Other books by the same author:
Billy Jo Jive and the Case of the Midnight Voices, 1982
Billy Jo Jive and the Case of the Missing Pigeons, 1978
The Case of the Sneaker Snatcher, 1977 (Billy Jo Jive)
Billy Jo Jive, Super Private Eye: The Case of the Missing Ten Speed Bike, 1976

Billy Jo Jive and the Walkie-Talkie Caper, 1981

Other books you might like:
Pat Cummings, *Petey Moroni's Camp Runamok Diary*, 1992
   At a two-week summer camp a young boy and his friends try catching the raccoon they've discovered has been stealing their food.
Sharon M. Draper, *Ziggy and the Black Dinosaurs*, 1994
   When their neighborhood playground is destroyed, four 5th grade boys start their own club and uncover a mysterious box of bones.
Teresa Reed, *Keisha the Fairy Snow Queen*, 1995
   A 10-year-old worried about classmates cheating on a test is magically transported to another time where she must solve a mystery.

387

JOHN SHEARER, African American
TED SHEARER, Illustrator, West Indian

Billy Jo Jive, Super Private Eye: The Case of the Missing Ten Speed Bike

(New York: Delacorte Press, 1976)

Story type: Young Readers
Series: Billy Jo Jive
Subject(s): Mystery and Detective Stories; Stealing; Crime and Criminals
Age range(s): Grades 2-3
Major character(s): Billy Jo Jive, Child, Detective—Amateur, African American; Susie Sunset, Child, African American, Detective—Amateur
Time period(s): 1970s
Locale(s): United States (unidentified city)

Summary: Out riding his bike, Jive spots Sunset crying on the curb. It seems the racing bike she "borrowed" from her brother has been stolen. He is due back soon and needs his racer to compete in the annual race he's won two years in a row. The two set off together, picking up clues throughout the neighborhood until the night they catch the thief red-handed. Sammy returns, none the wiser regarding his stolen bike. Sunset congratulates Jive on his great work and Jive heads home thinking Sunset a pretty good partner.

Other books by the same author:
Billy Jo Jive and the Case of the Midnight Voices, 1982
Billy Jo Jive and the Case of the Missing Pigeons, 1978
The Case of the Sneaker Snatcher, 1977 (Billy Jo Jive)
Billy Jo Jive and the Walkie-Talkie Caper, 1981

Other books you might like:
Lucille Clifton, *Everett Anderson's Friend*, 1976
   Hoping he will have some new guys to play with when a family moves in the building a young boy learns to be friends with the new girl next door.
Sharon M. Draper, *Ziggy and the Black Dinosaurs*, 1994
   When their neighborhood playground is destroyed, four 5th grade boys start their own secret club and uncover a mysterious box of bones.
Emily Moore, *Just My Luck*, 1982
   Dreaming of buying her own puppy, a 9-year-old teams up

with a schoolmate to solve the mystery of a missing dog so she can get the reward money.

Teresa Reed, *Keisha the Fairy Snow Queen*, 1995
A 10-year-old, worried about classmates cheating on a test, is magically transported to another time where she must solve a mystery.

RAY SHELL, African American

Iced

(New York: Random House, 1993)

Subject(s): City Life; Drugs
Age range(s): Adult
Major character(s): Cornelius Washington, Addict, African American
Time period(s): 1990s (1992)
Locale(s): New York, New York

Summary: In his diary, 44-year-old Cornelius reflects on his prior successes in college and business. He also tells in explicit language, his descent into the elusive white-smoke world of crack cocaine—a world filled with guilt-crazies and regret.

About this book: This is the author's debut novel.

Where it's reviewed:
Library Journal, October 1, 1994, page 48
New Yorker, July 18, 1994, page 81
Publishers Weekly, July 13, 1994, page 52

Other books you might like:
Tananarive Due, *The Between*, 1995
A man endures nightmares and his sense of reality wavers as he desperately tries to protect his family from the psychotic who stalks them.
Ishmael Reed, *Japanese by Spring*, 1993
This satire of academic life and race relations is told in the exploits in a professor's life who will endure any insult to get tenure.
Ntozake Shange, *Liliane: Resurrection of the Daughter*, 1994
In psychotherapy, the exploits of a young woman's life reveal how she coped with family upheavals, romances, friendships, racism, and bigotry.
Brent Wade, *Company Man*, 1992
These confessions are about the behind-the-scenes stresses and strains faced by a man attempting to climb the business ladder and preserve his family.

CHARLOTTE SHERMAN, African American

One Dark Body

(New York: Harper Collins Publishers, 1993)

Subject(s): Coming of Age; Identity; Mothers and Daughters
Age range(s): Grades 8-Adult
Major character(s): Septeema "Raisin" Barnett, Student, African American; Nola Barnett, Mother, African American; Sin-Sin DuBois, Friend, Student, African American
Time period(s): 1960s (1963)

Locale(s): Pearl, Washington

Summary: Abandoned at birth and raised by foster parents, "Raisin" grapples with the reappearance of her mother Nola. She struggles with the myths and dreams inherited in her blood. She deals with her friend Sin-Sin's initiation into manhood in the magical woods just outside of town.

Where it's reviewed:
Library Journal, October 1, 1993, page 52
Belles Lettres, Summer 1993, page 19
Los Angeles Times Book Review, June 27, 1993, page 11
Women's Review of Books, July 1993, page 23

Other books by the same author:
Touch, 1995

Other books you might like:
Maxine Clair, *Rattlebone*, 1994
This story is about the events in the life of a young girl coming-of-age in a small town in the 1950s.
Thulani Davis, *1959*, 1992
This coming-of-age story about a 12-year-old girl recounts events that changed her life and others around her during the historic civil rights movement.
Ntozake Shange, *Betsey Brown*, 1985
Exploits of a young girl coming-of-age in an era of school integration, the worries of her family and the discoveries she makes at her new school.
A.J. Verdelle, *The Good Negress*, 1995
A young country girl who wants more from life than cooking, cleaning, and washing, moves to th city. She is encouraged by her teacher to strive for higher goals.

CHARLOTTE SHERMAN, African American

Touch

(New York: HarperCollins, 1995)

Story type: Adult
Subject(s): AIDS (Disease); Friendship; Interpersonal Relations
Major character(s): Rayna Sargent, Artist, Social Worker, African American
Time period(s): 1990s (1993)
Locale(s): Seattle, Washington

Summary: An artist who supports herself as a crisis-line counselor, Rayna insulates herself from the reality of others' pain. When she discovers an old friend is in the last stages of AIDS, she doesn't know how to reach out to him. At work, it is discovered that one of the doctors is sterilizing women who have HIV without their consent. Angry at being confronted by AIDS from all directions, Rayna feels that as a heterosexual woman she is somehow exempt. Then she meets Theodore, a gentle man to whom she may want to open herself to love. Everything falls apart when Rayna receives her own HIV diagnosis, and must deal with fears she never knew she had.

Where it's reviewed:
Library Journal, September 1, 1995, page 2
MS., September 1995, page 78

Other books by the same author:
One Dark Body, 1993 (debut novel)

Other books you might like:
Larry Duplechan, *Tangled Up in Blue*, 1989
  The impact of AIDS when a wife discovers her husband
  and a friend who's infected had a bisexual affair, with non-
  African American characters.
E. Lynn Harris, *Just as I Am*, 1994
  Bisexual affairs of a young man, the impact on the woman
  who loves him, and their comforting a friend dying with
  AIDS.

`391`

APRIL SINCLAIR, African American

Ain't Gonna Be the Same Fool Twice
(New York: Hyperion, 1996)

Series: Jean Stevenson
Subject(s): Growing Up; Interpersonal Relations; Self-Acceptance
Age range(s): Adult
Major character(s): Jean Eloise "Stevie" Stevenson, Graduate, Receptionist, African American (bisexual)
Time period(s): 1970s (1971-1975)
Locale(s): Chicago, Illinois; San Francisco, California

Summary: Stevie leaves her Chicago home to go to college.
On graduation Stevie treats herself to a first-time trip to San
Francisco, where she engages in sexual experimentation. The
news of her beloved grandmother's illness takes Stevie back
to Chicago where she confides her sexuality to Grandma.
Grandma is not shocked and shares some words of wisdom.
Returning to San Francisco, Stevie concludes, "Grandma was
right. My sexuality has been a journey. And I'm still on the
road."

Other books by the same author:
Coffee Will Make You Black, 1994 (debut novel)

Other books you might like:
Steven Corbin, *No Easy Place to Be*, 1989
  Explores the relationships among three sisters in urban
  New York during the 1920s Harlem Renaissance era.
Bonnie Greer, *Hanging by Her Teeth*, 1994
  This novel reveals the bisexual experiences of a young girl
  growing up and her search for the father who abandoned
  her.
Cherry Muhanji, *Her*, 1990
  A young light-skinned woman falls into "the life" of
  1950s Detroit and finds strength in herself and the women
  around in order to survive.
Jacqueline Woodson, *Autobiography of a Family Photo*, 1995
  New York life of a teenage girl, who has a gay brother and
  a half-white brother, experiences family violence, and
  questions her sexuality.

`392`

APRIL SINCLAIR, African American

Coffee Will Make You Black
(New York: Avon Books, 1994)

Story type: Young Adult
Subject(s): Coming of Age; Family Relations; Friendship
Age range(s): Adult
Major character(s): Jean Eloise "Stevie" Stevenson, Student—High School, Girlfriend; Carlene Zenobia "Carla" Perkins, Student—High School, Girlfriend, African American; Diane Horn, Nurse, Lesbian, Caucasian
Time period(s): 1960s; 1970s (1965-1970)
Locale(s): Chicago, Illinois

Summary: This story portrays "Stevie's" urban Chicago life
from ages eleven to sixteen when she reaches high school.
Over the disapproval of her mother, she develops a close
friendship with Carla. After deciding to have sex with her first
boyfriend, "Stevie" realizes she has a crush on Diane, the
white school nurse who she believes is a lesbian. After Diane
spends some time with her and they talk, "Stevie" is unsure
about her own sexuality.

About this book: debut novel

Where it's reviewed:
Ms., January 1994, page 73
New Yorker, May 2, 1994, page 109
Publishers Weekly, November 22, 1993, page 50

Other books you might like:
Jacqueline Woodson, *Autobiography of a Family Photo*, 1995
  This story is about a teenage girl in New York, who has a
  gay brother and a half-white brother. She experiences
  family violence, and she questions her own sexuality.
Larry Duplechan, *Blackbird*, 1986
  A contemporary gay coming-of-age episode ecounting the
  first sexual experiences in high school of the young man
  from the author's debut novel.
Virginia Hamilton, *A White Romance*, 1987
  A high school student befriends a white girl who shares her
  love of running, and becomes romantically involved with a
  drug dealer.
June Jordan, *His Own Where*, 1971
  Poetic urban love story of a 16-year-old and the girl he
  meets at a hospital where his father lays dying.
Dindga McCannon, *Wilhemina Jones, Future Star*, 1980
  The life of a young dedicated artist includes her struggle
  with her mother, her first sexual experience, winning an art
  prize and being engaged.

`393`

DUANE SMITH, African American

The Nubian
(College Park, GA: Azimuth Press, 1994)

Story type: Adult
Subject(s): Family Relations; Drugs; Self-Perception

Major character(s): Emanuel ''Manny'' Aaron Castle, Nephew, African American; Derek Andrew Alston, Businessman, Uncle, African American
Time period(s): 1990s (1991-1999); 21st century (2016)
Locale(s): Atlanta, Georgia; Washington, District of Columbia

Summary: The son of a Congressman father and lawyer mother, 11-year-old ''Manny'' and his older sister, Asia, were off from school when their Uncle Derek visited their home in Atlanta. With his father away in Washington so much, ''Manny'' was drawn to his uncle. He soon discovers his Afrocentric uncle's mysterious powers and his beliefs about self-perception and the connection of the spirit, the soul, and the physical world. Home alone one day Derek accidentally discovers confidential government documents misplaced by his brother-in-law. Years later when Derek becomes involved in a scheme to stop drug trafficking and the government learns about his research developments, his partner is mysteriously killed and Derek faces criminal charges. At the time a teenage, ''Manny,'' suffering from the trauma of a car accident, could not believe his uncle was guilty. Now some twenty years later he still reflects on the important life lessons he learned from his uncle and can only wonder why Derek's conviction was never appealed.

About this book: Debut novel.

Other books you might like:
Melvin Dixon, *Trouble the Water*, 1989
   Running away from home a young man returns twenty years later in a plot of revenge which developed between his grandmother and his father.
Leon Forrest, *Divine Days*, 1992
   Voices of the living and the dead are captured by an aspiring playwright in anepic tale referred to as ''The Ulysses of the South Side.''
Helen Elaine Lee, *The Serpent's Gift*, 1994
   Children and grandchildren of two intertwined families endure hardship and triumph as they help each other remember a history beyond their knowing.
Melvin Van Peebles, *Panther*, 1995
   Recounts an urban rebellion of the sixties that became the historic Black Panther movement and plots of the FBI and police to destroy them.

394

ETHEL FOOTMAN SMOTHERS, African American

Down in the Piney Woods
(New York: Alfred Knopf, 1992)

Story type: Young Readers
Subject(s): Family Life; Brothers and Sisters; Race Relations
Age range(s): Grades 3-8
Major character(s): Annie Moriah ''Annie Rye'' Footman, 10-Year-Old, Sister, African American; Josh Lampkin, Farmer, Father, Caucasian
Time period(s): 1950s
Locale(s): Climax, Georgia

Summary: The six children in the Footman family have the same mother but two different fathers. The eldest sisters were raised by their great-grandmother, and now their mother and

father them all to live together. Not fond of the idea, nevertheless, sharing adventures together, the children grow closer. They are shocked one night when they are awakened to find a cross burning outside their door. A man who carries a grudge against their father is thought to be responsible, and is later surprised when he saves the accused man's daughter.

About this book: Debut novel

Where it's reviewed:
Publishers Weekly, January 31, 1994, page 90
Essence, December 1992, page 108
Language Arts, February 1992, page 132

Other books by the same author:
Moriah's Pond, 1995 (sequel)

Other books you might like:
Virginia Hamilton, *Drylongso*, 1992
   As a great wall of dust moves across their drought-stricken farm, a family's distress is relieved by a young man called Drylongso.
Mildred D. Taylor, *The Friendship*, 1987
   Another episode from the lives of the young Logan children in segregated rural Mississippi as they witness a confrontation caused by racial custom.
Mildred D. Taylor, *The Gold Cadillac*, 1987
   Two young sisters learn their first lessons about segregation and bigotry on a drive to Mississippi in their family's new Cadillac.
Mildred D. Taylor, *Mississippi Bridge*, 1990
   A young white boy witnesses bigotry and segregation in a rural Mississippi farm community as well as the devastation of a fatal bus accident.
Mildred D. Taylor, *The Well: David's Story*, 1995
   Episode of the boyhood of two brothers from an early generation of the Logan family in rural Mississippi facing racial bigotry.

395

ETHEL FOOTMAN SMOTHERS, African American

Moriah's Pond
(New York: Alfred A. Knopf, 1995)

Story type: Young Readers
Series: Footman Family
Subject(s): Sisters; Race Relations; Interpersonal Relations
Age range(s): Grades 3-8
Major character(s): Annie Moriah ''Annie Rye'' Footman, 10-Year-Old, Sister, African American; Brat Footman, 12-Year-Old, Sister, African American; Maybaby Footman, 14-Year-Old, Sister, African American
Time period(s): 1950s
Locale(s): Georgia (rural Mitchell county)

Summary: Another episode in the lives of the Footman family when three of the sisters spend a summer with their great-grandmother, Moriah. The youngest, 10-year-old Annie Rye, recounts her adventures with her older sisters Brat and Maybaby. The sisters enjoy swimming in the pond, listening to their elders talk about the olden days, and helping Moriah on wash day. They endure getting their hair straightened, greasing their ashy legs, and the unwanted attentions of Betty

Jean the lonely youngster from the white family Moriah works for. Betty Jean, who once couldn't stop talking about the sisters, is later silent when her actions result in Brat being whipped. Brat also suffers with Maybaby a serious eye infection when the sisters disobey Moriah and swim in the pond after it gets polluted. Annie Ray learns the harm harboring a grudge can have and tries to heal her feelings towards Betty Jean.

About this book: Sequel to *Down In the Piney Woods*.

Where it's reviewed:
Booklist, January 15, 1995, page 930
Kirkus Reviews, February 1995, page 232
Los Angeles Times Book Reviews, February 26, 1995, page 9
Publishers Weekly, January 23, 1994, page 70
School Library Journal, February 1995, page 100

Other books by the same author:
Down in the Piney Woods, 1992 (debut novel)

Other books you might like:
Angela Johnson, *Humming Whispers*, 1995
    Recounts the life of a young girl living with an older sister who has schizophrenia and her fear that she too may have the mental illness.
Mildred D. Taylor, *The Friendship*, 1987
    Another episode from the lives of the young Logan children in segregated rural Mississippi as they witness a confrontation caused by racial custom.
Mildred D. Taylor, *The Gold Cadillac*, 1987
    Two young sisters learn their first lessons about segregation and bigotry on a drive to Mississippi in their family's new Cadillac.
Mildred D. Taylor, *Mississippi Bridge*, 1990
    A young white boy witnesses bigotry and segregation in a rural Mississippi farm community and the devastation of a fatal bus accident.
Mildred D. Taylor, *The Well: David's Story*, 1995
    Episode of the boyhood of two brothers from an early generation of the Logan family in rural Mississippi facing racial bigotry.

396

JOHN STEPTOE, Author/Illustrator, African American

Birthday
(New York: Holt, Rinehart and Winston, 1972)

Story type: Young Readers
Subject(s): Birthdays
Age range(s): Grades 1-2
Major character(s): Javaka Shatu, 8-Year-Old, African American
Time period(s): 1970s
Locale(s): Yoruba (Fictional community)

Summary: Javaka feels today is going to be the best day of his life, it's his eighth birthday. He's the firstborn child in this new place his parents have come to with farms around. His daddy always tells him before they came there they lived in old America where people didn't treat him like a man. Javaka knows the place they live in now is named after a nation of people in Africa. On his way to school Javaka thinks about

how nice it is where he lives and he has lots of friends. In school the teacher asks everyone if they know who's birthday it is and of course they do. Javaka invites them all to his house for a celebration after school. A good time is had by all, the food is good and so is the friendship. In the early morning hours as the party ends everyone shouts "Wa-linkum salaam!" (peace be with you).

Other books by the same author:
Daddy Is a Monster. . .Sometimes, 1980
My Special Best Words, 1974
Train Ride, 1971
Uptown, 1970
Stevie, 1969 (debut)

Other books you might like:
Debbi Chocolate, *On the Day I Was Born*, 1995
    A newborn is welcomed into the family in an African ceremony where relatives gather, the child is raised to the heavens, blessed and named.
Lucille Clifton, *Don't You Remember?*, 1973
    A soon-to-be 5-year-old is disappointed that everyone in the family keeps breaking their promises to her until they give her a birthday surprise.
Pat Cummings, *Carousel*, 1994
    Upset her daddy isn't home for her birthday a young girl dreams of riding the zebra on the carousel she receives as her present from him.

397

JOHN STEPTOE, Author/Illustrator, African American

Daddy Is a Monster. . .Sometimes
(New York: J. B. Lippincott, 1980)

Story type: Young Readers
Subject(s): Fathers; Brothers and Sisters; Behavior
Age range(s): Grades 2-4
Major character(s): Bweela, Child, Sister, African American
Time period(s): 1980s
Locale(s): United States (unidentified city)

Summary: Bweela and her young brother Javaka discuss how their daddy can turn into a monster.sometimes. Sometimes when they play with their food in the restaurant, their room's a little messy, they make a little noise, or have a little accident their daddy gets mad and becomes a monster. He once got mad when a lady gave them some ice cream after they'd already eaten the cones he bought for them. After reading them a bedtime story and tucking them in their daddy can get mad if they want a glass of water or want to go to the bathroom. They surprise him when they ask why he's a monster.sometimes, and he says it probably happens because he's got monster kids!

Other books by the same author:
Mufaro's Beautiful Daughters: An African Tale, 1987
My Special Best Words, 1974
Birthday, 1972
Train Ride, 1971
Uptown, 1970

Other books you might like:

Jeannette Franklin Caines, *Chilly Stomach*, 1986
  When her uncle comes to visit and hugs and kisses her, a
  child feels uncomfortable. She fears telling her parents, so
  she confides in a friend.
Lucille Clifton, *Amifika*, 1977
  Hearing his mother say his father is returning from the
  army a child fears he will not remember him and that he
  will be in the way.
Dolores Johnson, *Your Dad Was Just Like You*, 1993
  Talking with his grandpa after making his dad mad a
  young boy discovers just how much they are alike and why
  he dad was so upset with him.

<hr>

398

JOHN STEPTOE, Author/Illustrator, African American

Marcia
(New York: Viking Press, 1976)

Story type: Young Readers
Subject(s): Coming of Age; Conduct of Life; Interpersonal
  Relations
Age range(s): Grades 6-10
Major character(s): Marcia Williams, 14-Year-Old, Student,
  African American; Danny Walker, 14-Year-Old, Student,
  African American
Time period(s): 1970s
Locale(s): New York, New York (Brooklyn)

Summary: Marcia, a junior high school student, has got the
growing up blues. She talks to her friend Millie about boys
and sex and how confusing everything is. Then she meets
Danny, whose brother is Jeffry the Junkie. Danny is nothing
like his brother—he is captain of the basketball team and
doesn't go near drugs. Marcia confides in her friend Millie
that Danny wants sex and finds out that Millie's boyfriend
Poppo is pressuring her, too. Marcia finally talks to her
mother about it before things go too far and learns that she can
make her own decisions.

About this book: Debut novel; young readers.

Other books you might like:

Nikki Grimes, *Growin'*, 1977
  After her father is killed in an accident and she and her
  mother move, a young girl starting over in a new school
  finds a real friend.
Emily Moore, *Whose Side Are You On?*, 1988
  When her math tutor mysteriously disappears, a sixth-
  grade girl sets out to find him and discovers things aren't
  always what they seem.
Mildred Pitts Walter, *Lillie of Watts Takes a Giant Step*, 1971
  A girl faces a series of crises going to junior high school
  for the first time but finds a new friend, new heroes and a
  new pride in herself.
Brenda Wilkinson, *Ludell*, 1975
  Events in the life of a young girl raised by her strict
  grandmother as she comes of age and falls in love for the
  first time.

399

JOHN STEPTOE, Author/Illustrator, African American

Mufaro's Beautiful Daughters: An African Tale
(New York: Lothrop, Lee and Shepard, 1987)

Story type: Young Readers
Subject(s): Folk Tales; Sisters; Africa
Age range(s): Grades 1-3
Major character(s): Nyasha, Child, Sister, African American;
  Manyara, Child, Sister, African American
Time period(s): Indeterminate Past
Locale(s): Africa (unidentified region)

Summary: Everyone agrees the two young sisters Nyasha and
Manyara are beautiful. They are the daughter's of Mufaro and
live in a small village outside the city where a great king lives.
Jealous and spiteful Manyara says someday she is going to be
queen and make Nyasha her servant. Now the King wants to
choose a wife and the most worthy and beautiful daughters in
the land are invited to appear before him. Manyara tries
convincing her father that only she should be sent before the
King. That night Manyara sneaks out of the village into the
forest to make her way to the city so she might be first to
appear before the King. Discovering her footprints leading
toward the city the next morning the villagers leave in a
wedding party headed to appear before the King. At the city
gates Manyara rushes wildly towards them sobbing and begs
her father not to let Nyasha into the King's chamber for she
has seen a great monster there, a snake with five heads.
Leaving her sister behind to be comforted by their father
Nyasha bravely opens the doors to the King's chamber where
she sees a garden snake. Before her eyes the snake is transformed into the young King Nyoka who tells Nyasha how he
wants her to be his wife.

About this book: Inspired by G.M. Theal's *Kaffir Folktales*
(1895). Author died in 1989.

Awards the book has won:
Coretta Scott King Award, 1988
Caldecott Honor Book, 1988

Other books by the same author:
Daddy Is a Monster. . .Sometimes, 1980
My Special Best Words, 1974
Birthday, 1972
Train Ride, 1971
Uptown, 1970

Other books you might like:

Eloise Greenfield, *Africa Dream*, 1977
  Dreaming she has crossed the ocean to long-ago Africa a
  child shops in the marketplace, reads with magic eyes, and
  is welcomed by relatives.
Patricia C. McKissack, *Flossie and the Fox*, 1986
  The tale of a youngster sent to deliver fresh eggs to a
  neighbor outsmarts an egg loving fox along the way trying
  to prove who he is.
Patricia C. McKissack, *Nettie Jo's Friends*, 1989
  Needing to find a sewing needle to make a dress for her
  doll, a child asks three animal friends for help.

Angela Shelf Medearis, *The Singing Man*, 1994

West African folktale of how a boy's life evolves as he becomes a famous praise singer singing the history of the African people.

Walter Dean Myers, *The Golden Serpent*, 1980

The fable of a wise man living with a young boy in the mountains of India who the King summons to solve the mystery of the golden serpent.

400

JOHN STEPTOE, Author/Illustrator, African American

My Special Best Words
(New York: Viking Press, 1974)

Story type: Young Readers
Subject(s): Brothers and Sisters; Single Parent Families; Family Life
Age range(s): Grades 1-2
Major character(s): Bweela, Child, Sister, African American
Time period(s): 1970s
Locale(s): United States (unidentified city)

Summary: Life with her 1-year-old brother Javaka can be quite something for Bweela. After all he doesn't even know how to make stink on the pot yet, he lets nasty stuff hang out of his nose, and he plays in the water getting his clothes wet. He also likes to mess with Bweela's cat. Every time Bweela goes to the bathroom she takes Javaka and tries showing him how things are done. At breakfast with daddy before going to their babysitter's Javaka eats so slow Bweela has to tell him to hurry up. The babysitter lives on the corner from their house and sometimes she takes them for a ride to the store in her red car. After daddy gets home from work he makes their supper. Taking their bath together before bed Bweela is excited when Javaka wants her to help him get on the toilet for the first time. It's quite an accomplishment even if he does pee some on the floor and on her leg, and daddy is pleased too.

Other books by the same author:
Mufaro's Beautiful Daughters: An African Tale, 1987
Daddy Is a Monster. . .Sometimes, 1980
Birthday, 1972
Train Ride, 1971
Uptown, 1970

Other books you might like:
Jeannette Franklin Caines, *Abby*, 1973

An adopted preschooler questions her mother and older brother about when she first came there and suggests they adopt another brother.

Lucille Clifton, *Some of the Days of Everett Anderson*, 1970

Living in the city a 6-year-old boy's days are filled with activity from playing in the sunshine, to hearing sirens pass by, to times with his parents.

401

JOHN STEPTOE, Author/Illustrator, African American

Train Ride
(New York: Harper and Row, 1970)

Story type: Young Readers
Subject(s): City Life; Friendship; Summer
Age range(s): Grades 1-3
Major character(s): Charlie, Child, Brother, African American
Time period(s): 1970s
Locale(s): United States

Summary: Once his big brother took him to the city and now young Charlie brags he knows how to get there on his own. The guys think it's a good idea to take the train alone to the city but the girls are scared, so they stay behind. Off the train the guys stroll down streets filled with movie houses, some of them dirty movies, and lots of stores. They see more white people than are in their own neighborhood, and they find an arcade to spend time in. After spending all their money they realize how late it is and worry how they'll get home. The token booth man takes pity on them letting them go to the trains free but when they get back home they're afraid to go into their apartments because they know they're parents are going to give them a beating.

Other books by the same author:
Mufaro's Beautiful Daughters: An African Tale, 1987
Daddy Is a Monster. . .Sometimes, 1980
My Special Best Words, 1974
Birthday, 1972
Uptown, 1970

Other books you might like:
Ray Prather, *Double Dog Dare*, 1975

Two boys climbing in a tree are scared by a mean dog and dare each other to get down first until the lost dog's owner appears and rewards them.

Ray Prather, *No Trespassing*, 1974

When their baseball gets hit over the cranky neighbor's fence three boys have to come up with some imaginative ideas for getting it back.

402

BARBARA SUMMERS, African American

The Price You Pay
(New York: Amistad Press, 1993)

Subject(s): Business Enterprises; Murder; Mystery and Detective Stories
Age range(s): Adult
Major character(s): Nicole ''Nicky'' Knight, Model, Student—College, African American; Christina ''Tina'' Thompson, Businesswoman, African American; Vanessa Seymour, Businesswoman, Caucasian
Time period(s): 1990s (1992)
Locale(s): New York, New York; Paris, France

Summary: Among a diverse cast of characters ''Nicky'', a new young model, is welcomed into the highly competitive fashion industry. She finds a strong rivalry existing between

"Tina" and Vanessa as they pursue business in the same market. A series of murders occur when a market campaign is launched and "Nicky" finds her life in jeopardy.

About this book: This is the author's debut novel.

Where it's reviewed:
Essence, July 1994, page 46
Library Journal, December 1993, page 177
Publishers Weekly, January 17, 1994, page 408

Other books you might like:
Eleanor Taylor Bland, *Dead Time*, 1992
   This debut novel begins a detective mystery series with a female heroine.
Eleanor Taylor Bland, *Slow Burn*, 1993
   This is the second title in a detective mystery series with a female heroine.
Yolanda Joe, *Falling Leaves of Ivy*, 1992
   A young woman is murdered and her four closest friends from college become suspects, and the secret shared among them begins to unravel.
Barbara Neely, *Blanche on the Lam*, 1992
   This debut novel begins a contemporary murder mystery series with an amateur detective as the heroine.
Valerie Wilson Wesley, *When Death Comes Stealing*, 1994
   This debut novel begins a murder mystery series featuring an ex-policewoman who has become a private detective.

403

ELEANORA E. TATE, African American

A Blessing in Disguise
(New York: Delacorte Press, 1995)

Story type: Young Readers
Series: Calvary County
Subject(s): Fathers and Daughters; Family Relations; Drugs
Age range(s): Grades 5 and Up
Major character(s): Zambia Renelda Brown, 12-Year-Old, Crime Victim, African American; Vernon "Snake" LaRange, Businessman, Drug Dealer, African American
Time period(s): 1990s
Locale(s): Deacons Neck, South Carolina (Calvary County)

Summary: Raised by her uncle and aunt, 12-year-old Zambia longs to live with her father, "Snake," who owns a local nightclub. She is excited to learn "Snake" is opening a new nightclub in her neighborhood. Her neighbors are outraged because they know the nightclub is a front for drug dealing and prostitution. Zambia is saddened and confused when she discovers that "Snake" was responsible for her mother's becoming an alcoholic and drug addict.

About this book: Sequel to *Thank You, Dr. Martin Luther King, Jr.!*

Where it's reviewed:
Booklist, January 1, 1995, page 822
Kirkus Reviews, February 15, 1995, page 233
Publishers Weekly, December 5, 1994, page 77
School Library Journal, February 1995, page 115
Voice of Youth Advocates, April 1995, page 28

Other books by the same author:
Thank You, Dr. Martin Luther King, Jr.!, 1990 (sequel; young adult)
The Secret of Gumbo Grove, 1987 (young adult)
Just an Overnight Guest, 1980 (debut novel)

Other books you might like:
Candy Dawson Boyd, *Charlie Pippin*, 1987
   Curious about her father's involvement in the Vietnam conflict, an enterprising sixth-grader joins a school group to learn more.
Candy Dawson Boyd, *Chevrolet Saturdays*, 1993
   Struggling with the divorce of his parents and accepting his new stepfather, a young boy has trouble in school and makes mistakes he regrets.
Virginia Hamilton, *Plain City*, 1993
   A 12-year-old who feels out of place struggles to unearth her past and family history as she gradually discovers more about her long-missing father.
Walter Dean Myers, *Somewhere in the Darkness*, 1992
   An ailing father escapes from prison to prove his innocence to his son by confronting the witness who lied against him.
Jacqueline Woodson, *I Hadn't Meant to Tell You This*, 1994
   A young girl discovers a family secret about her new friend.

404

ELEANORA E. TATE, African American

Just an Overnight Guest
(New York: Dial Press, 1980)

Story type: Young Readers
Subject(s): Family Relations; Cousins; Sisters
Age range(s): Grades 4 and Up
Major character(s): Margie Carson, 9-Year-Old, Sister, African American; Ethel Hardisen, 4-Year-Old, Cousin, African American
Time period(s): 1980s
Locale(s): Nutbrush, Missouri

Summary: Margie and her older sister had heard the town gossip about Ethel's mother, Miz Mary, being poor white trash. To their surprise their mother announces Ethel is going to stay with them while her mother goes on a short trip out of town. Margie is soon angry with Ethel when she wets Margie's bed, breaks her favorite seashells, wears her clothes, causes a scene in the movies, and tries stealing her mother's affections. Ethel's mother stays away longer than expected and upon discovering Ethel had never had any real toys and that her mother had been abusive, Margie begins feeling sorry for her and tries to be kinder. When her father returns from a business trip, Margie is again angered with Ethel for trying to also steal his affection. Hurt and upset, Margie is shocked when she learns Ethel is going to be staying for a long time and is in fact a member of the family: her cousin.

About this book: Debut novel.

Other books by the same author:
A Blessing in Disguise, 1995 (sequel; young adult)

Thank You, Dr. Martin Luther King, Jr.!, 1990 (sequel; young adult)
The Secret of Gumbo Grove, 1987 (young adult)

Other books you might like:
Joyce Hansen, *The Gift Giver*, 1980
A young girl and her fifth grade friends come to like a new boy in their class and are surprised when they discover he is a foster child.
Andrea Davis Pinkney, *Hold Fast to Dreams*, 1995
Two sisters endure prejudice when their family moves to the suburbs and they have to attend separate all-white schools and try to fit in.
Ethel Footman Smothers, *Moriah's Pond*, 1995
A continuation of events from the lives of the Footman family when three sisters spend a summer with their great-grandmother.
Mildred Pitts Walter, *Mariah Keeps Cool*, 1990
A girl trains for a diving competition, tries to figure out her half-sister and plans a surprise for her sister.
Jacqueline Woodson, *Between Madison & Palmetto*, 1993
In their continuing story two 13-year-old best friends are reunited and having to adjust to a lot of change in their lives and in those around them.

405

ELEANORA E. TATE, African American

The Secret of Gumbo Grove

(New York: Franklin Watts, 1987)

Story type: Young Readers
Series: Calvary County
Subject(s): Race Relations; Family Relations; Segregation
Age range(s): Grades 5 and Up
Major character(s): Raisin Stackhouse, 11-Year-Old, Student—Junior High, African American; Effie Pfluggins, Aged Person (widow), Secretary, African American
Time period(s): 1980s
Locale(s): Gumbo Grove, South Carolina (Calvary County)

Summary: Intrigued by history, Raisin is talked into helping Miss Effie clean up the old church cemetery. Miss Effie, now eighty-eight, has been maintaining the church records as secretary for many decades. As she and Raisin work side by side she begins to share stories of the past and of who is buried in the cemetery. When she gives Raisin a name to research, Raisin finds herself in the middle of a mysterious historical controversy. Telling her friends what she has learned, Raisin gets the community and her parents upset, and soon the TV media cover the story. Miss Effie is threatened with losing her position as church secretary and Raisin becomes so involved she misses her opportunity to compete in the Miss Ebony Pageant.

Awards the book has won:
Parent's Choice Gold Seal Award, 1987

Other books by the same author:
A Blessing in Disguise, 1995
Thank You, Dr. Martin Luther King, Jr.!, 1990
Just an Overnight Guest, 1980 (debut novel)

Other books you might like:
Sharon M. Draper, *Ziggy and the Black Dinosaurs*, 1994
When their neighborhood playground is destroyed, four 5th grade boys start their own secret club and uncover a mysterious old box of hidden bones.
Virginia Hamilton, *The Mystery of Drear House*, 1987
A house that was a station on the Underground Railroad has secret passageways and hidden treasure which must be saved before it is too late.
Walter Dean Myers, *Darnell Rock Reporting*, 1994
Not doing well in school, a 13-year-old joins the school newspaper and discovers the impact his writing can have and how he can make a difference.
Walter Dean Myers, *Tales of a Dead King*, 1983
Journeying to Egypt to participate in an archaeological dig, two white teenagers are intrigued by the mysterious disappearance of the dig's director.
Andrea Davis Pinkney, *Hold Fast to Dreams*, 1995
Two sisters endure prejudice when their family moves to the suburbs and they have to attend separate all-white schools and try to fit in.

406

ELEANORA E. TATE, African American

Thank You, Dr. Martin Luther King, Jr.!

(New York: Franklin Watts, 1990)

Story type: Young Readers
Series: Calvary County
Subject(s): Identity; Self-Acceptance; School Life
Age range(s): Grades 5 and Up
Major character(s): Mary Elouise Avery, 9-Year-Old, Sister, African American; Brandy Howell, 9-Year-Old, 4th Grader, Caucasian
Time period(s): 1990s
Locale(s): Gumbo Grove, South Carolina (Calvary County)

Summary: Mary Elouise's father was killed in a car accident when she was two. She and her mother, brothers and sister live in a resort town near an Air Force base where children from around the world attend school with her. She most admires and wants to be best friends with a new white girl, Brandy, whose parents are wealthy. When her mother is told Mary Elouise is "color struck," wanting to be white, she can hardly believe it yet recognizes the signs that had been there all along. Once her grandmother realizes what Mary Elouise is experiencing she sets on a course of action to give her pride in herself and her ancestry.

About this book: Sequel to *The Secret of Gumbo Grove*.

Where it's reviewed:
Journal of Reading, April 1993, page 590

Awards the book has won:
National Counc. for the Social Studies, Notable Children's Trade, 1990

Other books by the same author:
A Blessing in Disguise, 1995 (sequel)
The Secret of Gumbo Grove, 1987
Just an Overnight Guest, 1980 (debut novel)

Other books you might like:
Joyce Hansen, *The Gift Giver*, 1980
A young girl and her fifth grade friends come to like a new boy in their class and are surprised when they discover he is a foster child.
Connie Porter, *Addy Learns a Lesson: A School Story*, 1993
After escaping slavery, a girl and her mother arrive in Philadelphia, where she goes to school and learns a lesson in true friendship.
Connie Porter, *Happy Birthday, Addy! A Springtime Story*, 1994
A 9-year-old girl learns that freedom isn't always easy in 1860's Philadelphia, and finds inspiration in a new friend in her bording house.
Jacqueline Woodson, *Maizon at Blue Hill*, 1992
Another episode in the lives of two young seventh grade friends where one girl wins an academic scholarship to a white boarding school.

407

MILDRED D. TAYLOR
MAX GINSBURG, Illustrator

The Friendship

(New York: Dial Books For Young Readers, 1987)

Story type: Young Readers
Series: Logan Family
Subject(s): Interpersonal Relations; Race Relations; Friendship
Age range(s): Grades 3-5
Major character(s): Cassie Logan, 9-Year-Old, Sister, African American; Tom Bee, Aged Person, African American; John Wallace, Businessman, Caucasian
Time period(s): 1930s (1933)
Locale(s): Strawberry, Mississippi

Summary: Cassie recalls from her youth a time when she and her three brothers were obliged to go to the store for an elderly neighbor woman. Their parents had warned that the store owned by the white Wallace family was "off limits" yet they could not refuse to go. Intrigued by all they saw once inside they were also dismayed by the way they were treated by the white storeowner's sons. The bad treatment extends to Tom Bee, even though he once saved the life of the store's owner.

Awards the book has won:
Coretta Scott King Award, 1988
Boston Globe/Horn Book Award, 1987

Other books by the same author:
The Well: David's Story, 1995 (young readers)
Mississippi Bridge, 1990 (young readers)
The Gold Cadillac, 1987 (young readers)
Song of the Trees, 1975 (debut novel; young readers)

Other books you might like:
Christopher Paul Curtis, *The Watsons Go to Birmingham—1963*, 1995
The ordinary interactions and everyday hijinks of the "weird" Watsons are drastically changed when they visit Grandma in 1960s Alabama.

Vaunda Micheaux Nelson, *Mayfield Crossing*, 1993
The new kids at an elementary school encounter prejudice for the first time and only baseball has the possibility for drawing people together.
Ethel Footman Smothers, *Down in the Piney Woods*, 1992
Episodes in the life of the Footman family as the six children all come to live together for the first time, sharing life in the country.
Ethel Footman Smothers, *Moriah's Pond*, 1995
A continuation of events from the lives of the Footman family when three sisters spend a summer with their great-grandmother.
Eleanora E. Tate, *Thank You, Dr. Martin Luther King, Jr.!*, 1990
Continuing the Calvary County trilogy, this tale explores the life of a fourth grade girl who is "color struck" wanting to be white.

408

MILDRED D. TAYLOR, African American
MICHAEL HAYS, Illustrator

The Gold Cadillac

(New York: Dial Books For Young Readers, 1987)

Story type: Young Readers
Subject(s): Family Relations; Race Relations; Segregation
Age range(s): Grades 3-5
Major character(s): Lois, Child, Sister, African American; Wilbert, Spouse, Father, African American
Time period(s): 1950s (1950)
Locale(s): Toledo, Ohio

Summary: When her father, Wilbert, brings home a brand new Cadillac Coupe de Ville, Lois and her young sister are overjoyed and don't understand why their mother is so upset. Neighbors and relatives admire the new car and the sisters are proud to ride in it even if their mother refuses. When their father decides to drive on a visit to relatives in Mississippi the sisters wonder why everyone advises against it. On the journey they learn about the segregated South and bigotry when they see signs forbidding them to eat, drink, or sleep in certain places and when police arrest their father in a small town along the way.

Awards the book has won:
Christopher Award, 1988

Other books by the same author:
The Well: David's Story, 1995 (young readers)
Mississippi Bridge, 1990 (young readers)
The Friendship, 1987 (young readers)
Song of the Trees, 1975 (debut novel; Young Readers)

Other books you might like:
Christopher Paul Curtis, *The Watsons Go to Birmingham—1963*, 1995
The ordinary interactions and everyday hijinks of the "weird" Watsons are drastically changed when they visit Grandma in 1960s Alabama.
Vaunda Micheaux Nelson, *Mayfield Crossing*, 1993
The new kids at an elementary school encounter prejudice

for the first time and only baseball has the possibility for drawing people together.

Ethel Footman Smothers, *Down in the Piney Woods*, 1992
Episodes in the life of the Footman family as the six children all come to live together for the first time sharing life in the country.

Ethel Footman Smothers, *Moriah's Pond*, 1995
A continuation of events from the lives of the Footman family when three sisters spend a summer with their great-grandmother.

Eleanora E. Tate, *Thank You, Dr. Martin Luther King, Jr.!*, 1990
Continuing the Calvary County trilogy, this tale explores the life of a fourth grade girl who is "color struck" wanting to be white.

409

MILDRED D. TAYLOR, African American

Let the Circle Be Unbroken
(New York: Dial Press, 1981)

Story type: Young Adult
Series: Logan Family
Subject(s): Family Relations; Interpersonal Relations; Race Relations
Age range(s): Grades 7-9
Major character(s): Cassie Logan, 10-Year-Old, Sister, African American; Stacey Logan, 13-Year-Old, Brother, African American; Suzella Rankin, 15-Year-Old, Cousin, African American
Time period(s): 1930s (1934-1935)
Locale(s): Strawberry, Mississippi

Summary: The saga of the Logan family continues in this story focused on incidents in their lives during the Depression era. Racial hostilities abound in their rural community and they witness the conviction by an all white jury of an innocent young friend for murder. When union organizers arrive to try to help local farmers, more trouble occurs. Struggling to raise money to keep their farm, Cassie and Stacey's father leaves home to work for the railroad. When their cousin, Bud, visits unexpectedly he announces he has married a white woman and wants their teenaged daughter Suzella, who can pass for white, to spend some time on the farm. Once Suzella arrives, Cassie feels she and Stacey are drifting apart and is heartbroken when he runs away from home to work in the cane fields. The family launch an all out search in the hope of bringing Stacey back home safely.

About this book: Sequel to *Roll of Thunder, Hear My Cry.*

Where it's reviewed:
Booklist, June 1, 1993, page 1865

Awards the book has won:
Coretta Scott King Award, 1982
Young Adult Library Services Association, Best Books for YAs, 1981

Other books by the same author:
The Road to Memphis, 1990 (young adult)
Roll of Thunder, Hear My Cry, 1976 (young adult)
Song of the Trees, 1975 (debut novel; young readers)

Other books you might like:
Virginia Hamilton, *Willie Bea and the Time the Martians Landed*, 1983
On their farm in Ohio, a family is caught up in the fear generated by the 1938 Orson Welles "Martians have landed" broadcast.

Angela Johnson, *Toning the Sweep*, 1993
A young girl prepares a special gift for her grandmother dying of cancer and honors the spirit of the deceased grandfather she never knew.

Walter Dean Myers, *Glory Field*, 1994
Family saga of generations of descendants of an African boy kidnapped at the age of eleven and enslaved in the American Colonies.

Joyce Carol Thomas, *Marked by Fire*, 1982
Friends and family help a young girl to overcome the effects of a tornado and a physical assault which nearly breaks her will.

Rita Williams-Garcia, *Like Sisters on the Homefront*, 1994
An unwed 14-year-old mother again pregnant has an abortion and when sent to her relatives in the South she develops a new sense of family and self.

410

MILDRED D. TAYLOR, African American
MAX GINSBURG, Illustrator

Mississippi Bridge
(New York: Dial Books For Young Readers, 1990)

Story type: Young Readers
Series: Logan Family
Subject(s): Interpersonal Relations; Race Relations; Segregation
Age range(s): Grades 3-5
Major character(s): Jeremy Simms, 10-Year-Old, Caucasian; Josias Williams, Farmer, Passenger, African American; Stacey Logan, 10-Year-Old, Brother, African American
Time period(s): 1930s
Locale(s): Mississippi

Summary: Another episode from the lives of rural Mississippi farmers seen this time from the eyes of a young white boy Jeremy. In the pouring rain, Stacey Logan and his sister and brothers accompany their grandmother to await the bus to visit her ill sister. A neighbor Josias is also waiting for the bus to go get himself a new job in the lumbermill. The bus is full and when a white family, the Amoses, arrive late the driver demands grandmother Logan and Josias give up their seats to them. Following after Josias in the fog and rain, Jeremy runs towards the bridge just as the bus speeds across, hitting the guardrail and plunging down into the river. Josias sends Jeremy for help and jumps into the water to find survivors. When the Logan children return past the bridge and see the accident, Jeremy tells them about how their grandmother was put off the bus and they race home to find her.

Awards the book has won:
Christopher Award, 1991

Other books by the same author:
The Well: David's Story, 1995 (Young Readers)
The Gold Cadillac, 1987 (Young Readers)

The Friendship, 1987 (Young Readers)
Song of the Trees, 1975 (debut novel; Young Readers)

Other books you might like:

Christopher Paul Curtis, *The Watsons Go to Birmingham—1963*, 1995
The ordinary interactions and everyday hijinks of the ''weird'' Watsons are drastically changed when they visit Grandma in 1960s Alabama.

Vaunda Micheaux Nelson, *Mayfield Crossing*, 1993
The new kids at an elementary school encounter prejudice for the first time and only baseball has the possibility for drawing people together.

Ethel Footman Smothers, *Down in the Piney Woods*, 1992
Episodes in the life of the Footman family as the six children all come to live together for the first time sharing life in the country.

Ethel Footman Smothers, *Moriah's Pond*, 1995
A continuation of events from the lives of the Footman family when three sisters spend a summer with their great-grandmother.

Eleanora E. Tate, *Thank You, Dr. Martin Luther King, Jr.!*, 1990
Continuing the Calvary County trilogy, this tale explores the life of a fourth grade girl who is ''color struck'' wanting to be white.

411

MILDRED D. TAYLOR, African American

The Road to Memphis

(New York: Dial Books, 1990)

Story type: Young Adult
Series: Logan Family
Subject(s): Interpersonal Relations; Race Relations; Segregation
Age range(s): Grades 9-12
Major character(s): Cassie Logan, 17-Year-Old, Student—High School, African American; Stacey Logan, Worker, African American; Solomon Bradley, Lawyer, Convict, African American
Time period(s): 1940s (1941)
Locale(s): Strawberry, Mississippi; Jackson, Mississippi; Memphis, Tennessee

Summary: A continuation of episodes from the lives of the Logan family in segregated Mississippi. Cassie, now attending high school in Jackson, lives with relatives and helps out in her cousin's cafe. Stacey, now twenty, has also left home for Jackson to work in a box factory with his friends, Moe and Little Willie. On a return visit home with Stacey to rural Strawberry, Moe gets into a confrontation, seriously injuring some white boys and is hunted by the police. Escaping back to Jackson with the help of a white neighbor, Cassie, Stacey, and two other friends drive Moe on to Memphis where he might safely catch a train for Chicago. Moe had hoped someday he and Cassie would be more than just friends, maybe even marry, but now on the run he fears that may never happen. Confused about her feelings for Moe, Cassie discovers for the first time a new excitement when she meets Solomon, a lawyer, businessman, and ex-con in his mid-twenties. Solo-

mon comes to Cassie's aide when the war breaks out by helping Moe get a train ticket, and, tenderly kissing her, he gives her a gift as she leaves for Jackson.

Where it's reviewed:
English Journal, February 1993, page 85

Awards the book has won:
Coretta Scott King Award, 1991

Other books by the same author:
Let the Circle Be Unbroken, 1981 (young adult)
Roll of Thunder, Hear My Cry, 1976 (young adult)
Song of the Trees, 1975 (debut novel; young readers)

Other books you might like:

Ossie Davis, *Just Like Martin*, 1992
A religiously active son and his war veteran father disagree over the civil rights movement until after events occur that help them to work together.

Virginia Hamilton, *A White Romance*, 1987
A high school student befriends a white girl who shares her love of running, and becomes romantically involved with a drug dealer.

Joyce Carol Thomas, *When the Nightingale Sings*, 1992
Despite her mean-spirited foster mother's attempts to demean her, a 14-year-old girl has a song to sing and a destiny to fulfill.

Valerie Wilson Wesley, *Where Do I Go From Here?*, 1993
Having trouble at a snooty mostly-white prep school a teenager learns from another scholarship student she must make decisions for her own life.

Brenda Wilkinson, *Not Separate, Not Equal*, 1987
Chosen among a group of six to integrate a Georgia high school, a teenage girl experiences hatred and racism and the beginning of civil rights.

412

MILDRED D. TAYLOR, African American

Roll of Thunder, Hear My Cry

(New York: Dial, 1976)

Series: Logan Family
Subject(s): Race Relations; Family Relations; Self-Reliance
Age range(s): Grades 7-9
Major character(s): Cassie Logan, 9-Year-Old, Sister, African American; Stacey Logan, 12-Year-Old, Brother, African American
Time period(s): 1930s (1933-1934)
Locale(s): Mississippi (rural)

Summary: Among a cycle of stories about the Logan family in rural segregated Mississippi. Cassie's family owns a large parcel of farm land which a white landowner, Harlan Granger, wants to buy back as part of his family's original plantation property. Times are hard and Cassie's father David has to work off the farm during parts of the year to make enough money to meet expenses. Selling the land is not an option. Ku Klux Klan nightriders are terrorizing families and when David returns he brings an older man, Mr. Morrison, to stay with the family for protection. The family's concern for their safety increases when a number of events occur, among them—the boycott Cassie's mother organizes against a white storeowner which looses her her school teacher's job, outspoken Cassie irritating a white classmate, and Stacey's secret prank on a spiteful white bus driver. When a white mob comes looking for Stacey's classmate, "T.J." Avery, after a robbery in town David and Mr. Morrison make a sacrifice that saves his life.

Where it's reviewed:
English Journal, September 1988, page 96
Horn Book Magazine, November 1990, page 779
Reading Teacher, March 1987, page 618
Social Studies, March 1987, page 89

Awards the book has won:
Coretta Scott King Honor Book, 1977
Newbery Award, 1977

Other books by the same author:
The Road to Memphis, 1990 (young adult)
Let the Circle Be Unbroken, 1981 (young adult)
Song of the Trees, 1975 (debut novel, young readers)

Other books you might like:
Walter Dean Myers, *Glory Field*, 1994
    Family saga of generations of descendants of an African boy kidnapped at the age of eleven and enslaved in the American Colonies.
Mildred Pitts Walter, *Because We Are*, 1983
    After trouble with a white teacher, an honor student is transferred to a segregated high school where she finds different kinds of challenges.
Brenda Wilkinson, *Not Separate, Not Equal*, 1987
    Chosen among a group of six to integrate a Georgia high school, a teenage girl experiences hatred and racism and the beginning of the Civil Rights Movement.

413

MILDRED D. TAYLOR, African American
JERRY PINKNEY, Illustrator, African American

Song of the Trees
(New York: Dial Press, 1975)

Series: Logan Family
Age range(s): Grades 4 and Up
Major character(s): Cassie Logan, 8-Year-Old, Sister, African American; Stacey Logan, 11-Year-Old, Brother, African American; Christopher-John Logan, 7-Year-Old, Brother, African American; Little Man Logan, 6-Year-Old, Brother, African American
Time period(s): 1930s
Locale(s): Mississippi (rural)

Summary: The first episode of stories about the Logan family in rural Mississippi during the Depression era. The children's father has gone to work on the railroad in Louisiana and their Mama and grandmother, Big Ma, are making ends meet until his return. Out in the woods the kids discover many of their beloved trees have been marked "X" and they overhear their white neighbor, Mr. Andersen, say he's going to cut the trees down. Shocked and upset they are dismayed when Big Ma is pressured to let Mr. Andersen buy the trees. Stacey is sent off on horseback to bring his father home and when he returns with David things change, upsetting Mr. Andersen's plans.

About this book: Debut novel for young readers.

Where it's reviewed:
Booklist, July 15, 1975, page 1193
Horn Book Magazine, August 1975, page 384
Kirkus Reviews, May 1, 1975, page 514
School Library Journal, April 1975, page 60

Awards the book has won:
Coretta Scott King Honor Book, 1976
Council on Interracial Books Award, African American, 1973

Other books by the same author:
The Well: David's Story, 1995 (young readers)
Mississippi Bridge, 1990 (young readers)
The Friendship, 1987 (young readers)
The Gold Cadillac, 1987 (young readers)
Roll of Thunder, Hear My Cry, 1976 (young adults)

Other books you might like:
Sharon M. Draper, *Ziggy and the Black Dinosaurs*, 1994
    When their neighborhood playground is destroyed, four 5th-grade boys start their own secret club and uncover a mysterious old box of hidden bones.
Connie Porter, *Meet Addy: An American Girl*, 1993
    A 9-year-old girl and her mother escape a life of cruel slavery to freedom in Philadelphia during the Civil War.
Harriette Gillem Robinet, *Ride the Red Cycle*, 1980
    A boy crippled since the age of two, struggles to realize his dream of riding a cycle.
Mildred Pitts Walter, *Justin and the Best Biscuits in the World*, 1986
    A 10-year-old, sure that cleaning and keeping house is "women's work," visits his beloved grandfather's ranch and learns some manly skills.

414

MILDRED D. TAYLOR, African American

The Well: David's Story
(New York: Dial Books For Young Readers, 1995)

Story type: Young Readers
Series: Logan Family
Subject(s): Race Relations; Brothers; Country Life
Age range(s): Grades 4-6
Major character(s): David Logan, 10-Year-Old, Brother, African American; Hammer Logan, 13-Year-Old, Brother, African American; Charlie Simms, 14-Year-Old, Caucasian
Time period(s): 1900s (1909)
Locale(s): Mississippi (rural)

Summary: The focus of this episode of the Logan family stories is on a boyhood incident between David and his older brother Hammer. When all the wells in their part of rural Mississippi run dry except the Logans' they generously share their water with their neighbors, even those white neighbors who are bigots, among them the Simms family. The young Simms boy Charlie, who has been taunting the brothers, one day finds himself stranded on the road when his wagon overturns. Angrily demanding they help him, Charlie slaps David for being unable to hold his wagon up longer; defending his brother, Hammer knocks Charlie down hitting his head on a rock. The brothers fear Charlie is dead and run away for safety. The neighborly Logan family and the bigoted Simms family must come to terms over the incident.

Where it's reviewed:
Booklist, December 15, 1994, page 754
Publishers Weekly, January 2, 1995, page 77
School Library Journal, February 1995. page 100
Horn Book Magazine, July 1995, page 461

Other books by the same author:
Mississippi Bridge, 1990 (young readers)
The Gold Cadillac, 1987 (young readers)
The Friendship, 1987 (young readers)
Song of the Trees, 1975 (debut novel; young readers)

Other books you might like:
Sharon M. Draper, *Ziggy and the Black Dinosaurs*, 1994
    When their neighborhood playground is destroyed, four 5th grade boys start their own secret club and uncover a mysterious old box of hidden bones.
Virginia Hamilton, *Drylongso*, 1992
    As a great wall of dust moves across their drought-stricken farm, a family's distress is relieved by a young man called Drylongso.
Virginia Hamilton, *The Magical Adventures of Pretty Pearl*, 1983
    A spirited young African god child travels to the New World where she lives among free blacks and learns that every act has its consequence.
Walter Dean Myers, *Me, Mop, and the Moondance Kid*, 1988
    Two young brothers share a close friendship with a white young girl on their Little League baseball team and hope she gets adopted like they did.
Harriette Gillem Robinet, *Children of the Fire*, 1991
    A young girl witnesses the Great Chicago Fire of 1871 and is forever changed.
Mildred Pitts Walter, *Trouble's Child*, 1985
    Expected to marry and to succeed her grandmother as the island's midwife, a girl dreams of leaving the island to attend high school.

415

JERVEY TERVALON, African American

Understand This

(New York: William Morrow, 1994)

Story type: Young Adult
Subject(s): City Life; Coming of Age; Interpersonal Relations
Age range(s): Adult
Major character(s): Francois Williams, Runner, Student—High School, African American; Margot, Student—High School, Girlfriend, African American
Time period(s): 1990s (1994)
Locale(s): Los Angeles, California

Summary: Even though Francois and Margot are in love, they head in different directions. Margot is planning to leave her south central neighborhood to go to college. She is determined to try and make it. Francois, who has been keeping the secret of witnessing the shooting of a drug dealer, drops out before graduating so he can be on his own. After their break up, they try unsuccessfully getting back together. When

Margot visits from college, she secretly watches her love, Francois, from a distance.

About this book: This is the author's debut novel.

Where it's reviewed:
Essence, April 1994, page 56
Library Journal, November 15, 1993, page 101
New York Times Book Review, March 20, 1994, page 18

Awards the book has won:
New Voices Award, Quality Paperbacks, 1994

Other books you might like:
David Haynes, *Right by My Side*, 1993
    A high school student writes down his experiences in order to figure things out about his father, his mother and himself.
June Jordan, *His Own Where*, 1971
    Poetic urban love story of a 16-year-old and the girl he meets at a hospital where his father lays dying.
Walter Dean Myers, *Motown and Didi: A Love Story*, 1984
    Dreaming of making a better life for themselves, two teenagers meet when the young boy rescues the girl from street hoodlums.
Joyce Carol Thomas, *Bright Shadow*, 1983
    A young woman's peaceful world is turned upside down by a gruesome murder and the person who can help her has troubles of his opwn.

416

IANTHE THOMAS, African American
ANN TOULMIN-ROTHE, Illustrator

Willie Blows a Mean Horn

(New York: Harper & Row, 1981)

Story type: Young Readers
Subject(s): Music; Fathers and Sons
Age range(s): Grades 1-2
Time period(s): 1980s
Locale(s): United States

Summary: Musician Willie ''The Jazz King'' Hawk's young son tells how proud he is of his horn-playing papa. When his papa plays he says the people start moving and swaying and shout for more. Waiting for his papa at the club where he plays the boy has a special seat to watch from and gets to come backstage. Tired as the night comes to a close, the boy rests outside while papa says his goodbyes. By the time they drive home he's asleep and papa carries him in to bed. Awakening, he asks what it means when someone says you ''blow a mean horn.'' The boy drifts back off to sleep knowing his papa ''plays a mean horn.''

Other books by the same author:
Hi, Mrs. Mallory!, 1979
Eliza's Daddy, 1976
My Street's a Morning Cool Street, 1976
Walk Home Tired Billy Jenkins, 1974
Lordy Aunt Hattie, 1973 (debut)

Other books you might like:
Jeannette Franklin Caines, *Daddy*, 1977
    Saturdays are special for a child when her father comes to

get her to visit with him and they share laughs and fun together all day.

Valerie Flournoy, *The Best Time of Day*, 1978
A child with a busy day of activities ahead with his mom, babysitter, friends, and relatives, looks forward to his daddy getting home from work.

Eloise Greenfield, *First Pink Light*, 1976
A child wants to stay awake until his daddy comes home so he can hide and surprise him but falls asleep waiting in a chair and daddy takes him to bed.

Sharon Dennis Wyeth, *Always My Dad*, 1995
A young girl remembers the summer she and her three younger brothers spent at their grandparents when their dad visited and how much she misses him.

417

JOYCE CAROL THOMAS, African American

The Golden Pasture
(New York: Scholastic, Inc., 1986)

Story type: Young Readers
Subject(s): Fathers and Sons; Grandparents; Horsemanship
Age range(s): Grades 4-6
Major character(s): Carlton Lee Jefferson, 12-Year-Old, African American; Grayson Jefferson, Grandfather, Cowboy, African American; Samuel Jefferson, Father, African American
Time period(s): 1950s
Locale(s): Golden Pasture, Oklahoma

Summary: Carlton Lee enjoys spending summers on his grandfather's farm. He enjoys life there and finds it is a welcome break from his father's inexplicable temper. One summer he discovers a beautiful horse in a remote part of the farm; the horse may bring Carlton Lee, his father and his grandfather closer together.

Other books by the same author:
When the Nightingale Sings, 1992
Bright Shadow, 1983
Marked by Fire, 1982 (debut novel)

Other books you might like:
Candy Dawson Boyd, *Charlie Pippin*, 1987
Curious about her father's involvement in the Vietnam conflict, an enterprising sixth-grader joins a school group to learn more.

Virginia Hamilton, *Junius over Far*, 1985
When his grandfather returns to his Caribbean island home, a disturbing letter prompts a young boy and his father to journey to rescue him.

Walter Dean Myers, *The Righteous Revenge of Artemis Bonner*, 1992
Wild west adventure of a young man out to avenge his uncle's murder and to locate his treasure before the killer and his companion.

Harriette Gillem Robinet, *Ride the Red Cycle*, 1980
A boy crippled since the age of two struggles to realize his dream of riding a cycle.

Mildred Pitts Walter, *Justin and the Best Biscuits in the World*, 1986
A 10-year-old sure that cleaning and keeping house is

"women's work" visits his beloved grandfather's ranch and learns some manly skills.

418

JOYCE CAROL THOMAS, African American

Marked by Fire
(New York: Avon Books, 1982)

Story type: Young Adult
Subject(s): Family Relations; Growing Up; Singing
Age range(s): Grades 7-12
Major character(s): Abyssinia "Abby" Jackson, 10-Year-Old, Singer, African American
Time period(s): 20th century (1951-1971)
Locale(s): Ponca City, Oklahoma

Summary: Born on the heels of a tornado, Abby is everybody's pride and joy. She is good in school, reads to her elders, has the gift of song, and is loved by all. When a tornado hits the town, destroying her father's business, he leaves the family, unable to bear the loss of all he worked for. Abby's will is nearly broken when she is physically assaulted by someone she trusted and later is targeted by a malicious neighbor. Only the love of her family and her love for life can help her survive.

About this book: This is the author's debut novel.

Awards the book has won:
American Book Award, 1982

Other books by the same author:
When the Nightingale Sings, 1992
The Golden Pasture, 1986
Bright Shadow, 1983
Water Girl, 1986 (sequel to *Marked by Fire*)

Other books you might like:
Sharon M. Draper, *Tears of a Tiger*, 1994
A teenager escaping a car accident in which his friend is killed and others are injured has difficulty learning to live with the trauma.

Virginia Hamilton, *A Little Love*, 1984
A teenage girl has an emptiness food cannot fill: she misses her father, and in her search for him she finds new strengths in herself.

Virginia Hamilton, *Sweet Whispers, Brother Rush*, 1982
A girl caring for her retarded older brother encounters the ghost of her dead uncle and comes to a deeper understanding of her family and herself.

Virginia Hamilton, *Willie Bea and the Time the Martians Landed*, 1983
On their farm in Ohio, a family is caught up in the fear generated by the 1938 Orson Welles "Martians have landed" broadcast.

Jacqueline Woodson, *From the Notebooks of Melanin Sun*, 1995
A 13-year-old boy's world is turned upside down and he has to confront his prejudices when his mother tells him she is in love with a white woman.

419

JOYCE CAROL THOMAS, African American

When the Nightingale Sings

(New York: HarperCollins, 1992)

Story type: Young Adult
Subject(s): Orphans; Self-Respect; Singing
Age range(s): Grades 7-10
Major character(s): Marigold, Singer, Orphan, African American
Time period(s): 1990s
Locale(s): Sweet Earth, South

Summary: Marigold lives with Cousin Ruby and her disagreeable twin daughters. She waits on them hand and foot, and in addition is supposed to help the girls learn to sing, while being told she cackles like a hen herself. When the Rose of Sharon Baptist Church holds a Great Gospel Invitation to find someone who can succeed Queen Mother Rhythm, the twins enter and Marigold is allowed to accompany them. There she finds her family and her destiny.

Where it's reviewed:
Kliatt, July 1994, page 12
Publishers Weekly, January 31, 1994, page 90

Other books by the same author:
The Golden Pasture, 1986
Bright Shadow, 1983
Marked by Fire, 1982 (debut novel)

Other books you might like:
Vy Higginsen, *Mama, I Want to Sing*, 1995
    Recounts events in the life of a talented singer from a young girl singing in the church choir to a renowned award winning star.
Walter Dean Myers, *Crystal*, 1987
    On the brink of a promising career in modeling, a 16-year-old realizes there is more than glamour to the industry and has to decide what path to choose.
Mildred D. Taylor, *The Road to Memphis*, 1990
    Another incident from the lives of the Logan family in segregated Mississippi where racial hostilities erupt and new relationships unfold.
Valerie Wilson Wesley, *Where Do I Go From Here?*, 1993
    Having trouble at a snooty, mostly-white prep school, a teenager learns from another scholarship student that she must make decisions for her own life.
Rita Williams-Garcia, *Blue Tights*, 1988
    Struggling to find friends and acceptance, a young girl born out-of-wedlock follows her mother's footsteps in her passion for dancing.

420

MELVIN VAN PEEBLES, African American

Don't Play Us Cheap: A Harlem Party

(New York: Bantam Books, 1973)

Subject(s): Conduct of Life; Good and Evil; Supernatural
Age range(s): Adult

Major character(s): Trinity, Supernatural Being, African American; David, Aged Person (50-Year-Old), Supernatural Being, African American
Time period(s): 1970s
Locale(s): New York, New York

Summary: The Devil has declared war on people having a good time. Trouble-making imps can become full-fledged devils if they pass the test of wrecking parties on earth. Two white imps, Trinity and David, appear out of thin air before Earnestine, who is having her twentieth birthday party. Trinity and Earnestine become bewitched with one another and Trinity is dissuaded from disrupting her party. Racially transformed, David appears as an older man to rescue Trinity from himself. David warns Trinity that if they fail to break up the party before it ends, they will be turned into the human beings they are pretending to be.

About this book: Translation of *Le Fete A Harlem* originally published in French (1967) adapted from the play *Harlem Party*.

Other books by the same author:
Panther, 1995
Just an Old Sweet Song, 1976
Sweet Sweetback's Baadasssss Song, 1971 (adapted from screenplay)
The True American: A Folk Fable, 1976 (originally published in 1965 in French as *Un Americaine En Enfer*.)
A Bear for the FBI, 1968 (debut novel, originally published in 1964 in French as *Un Ours Pour Le F.B.I.*)

Other books you might like:
Percival Everett, *For Her Dark Skin*, 1990
    Jason gains the Golden Fleece aided by the sorceress Medea in this contemporary treatment of the classic tale of ambition, passion and revenge.
David Haynes, *Heathens*, 1996
    When a woman goes to jail for selling real estate she doesn't own, her husband falls apart and her mother-in-law tries to find her replacement.
Kristin Hunter, *The Lakestown Rebellion*, 1978
    To further his career, a mayor sacrifices his town to wealthy white politicians. When the citizens learn of the plan, they work to sabotage it.
Richard Perry, *Changes*, 1974
    A young professor's problems at work and at home turn upside down when he meets a man who is going to turn everyone in the world black.

421

MELVIN VAN PEEBLES, African American

Just an Old Sweet Song

(New York: Ballantine Books, 1976)

Subject(s): Family Relations; Race Relations; Parenthood
Age range(s): Adult
Major character(s): Priscilla Simmons, Office Worker, African American, Mother; Nate Simmons, Maintenance Worker (plumber), African American, Father
Time period(s): 1970s

African American Titles

Locale(s): Detroit, Michigan; Georgia (unidentified rural town)

Summary: When his farm-woman mother-in-law comes to visit, Nate is apprehensive, wondering what she might think of the family's city life. She is sick and wants Nate to move the family to her farm in the South but Nate fears the racial situation. However, when Mattie's health deteriorates further, he decides to take her home and take the family with him for a vacation on the farm. Everyone seems to benefit from their time in the country. When Mattie passes away, the family has to decide what to do about the farm she has left them as their inheritance.

Other books by the same author:
Sweet Sweetback's Baadasssss Song, 1971 (adapted from screenplay)
Don't Play Us Cheap: A Harlem Party, 1973 (originally published in 1967 in French as *Le Fete A Harlem*)
The True American: A Folk Fable, 1976 (originally published in 1965 in French as *Un Americaine En Enfer.*)
A Bear for the FBI, 1968 (debut novel (originally published in 1964 in French as *Un Ours Pour Le F.B.I.*))

Other books you might like:
J. California Cooper, *In Search of Satisfaction*, 1994
The family saga of two half-sisters born in the era of the plantation south having to deal with their parents' secret legacy and inheritance.
Terri McMillan, *Mama*, 1987
A proud and feisty mother does her best to provide for her five children through three marriages and uncertain times.
Clarence Major, *Such Was the Season*, 1987
A family matriarch shares her keen and humorous insights as her family becomes involved in family history, politics and conspiracy.
Gloria Naylor, *Women of Brewster Place*, 1982
The story of seven women who come to live on the dead-end street of Brewster Place and what brings them together in their own redemption.
Dorothy West, *The Wedding*, 1995
Saga of five generations of two families of mixed race ancestry, and events in the lives of children from a new contemporary generation.

422

MELVIN VAN PEEBLES, African American

Panther

(New York: Thunder's Mouth Press, 1995)

Story type: Adult
Subject(s): City Life; Historical; Race Relations
Major character(s): Narrator, Researcher, Student—College, Caucasian; Judge Taylor, Activist, Veteran, African American
Time period(s): 1960s (1967-1968)
Locale(s): Oakland, California

Summary: An unnamed white researcher working on a doctoral dissertation about the historic Black Panther movement conducts a series of interviews with witnesses of events that took place during the sixties. In the course of the interviews a story unfolds of the urban rebellion ignited by Huey Newton and Bobby Seale in their efforts to save their community from neglect, police brutality, drugs, the decay of poverty, and lack of self-respect. FBI and police involvement in plots to destroy the Black Panthers are exposed as characters find themselves caught in a web of destruction. Among the characters Judge, a military veteran and college student, who becomes a member of the Black Panthers, is instrumental in discovering a destructive plot to increase the influx of powerful drugs into the community.

Where it's reviewed:
Booklist, May 15, 1995, page 1633
Booklist, May 15, 1995, page 1638
Black Scholar, Spring, 1995, page 73
Library Journal, July 1995, page 124

Other books by the same author:
Just an Old Sweet Song, 1976
Sweet Sweetback's Baadasssss Song, 1971 (adapted from screenplay)
Don't Play Us Cheap: A Harlem Party, 1973 (originally published in French (1967))
The True American: A Folk Fable, 1976 (originally published in French (1965))
A Bear for the FBI, 1968 (debut novel)

Other books you might like:
Ray Shell, *Iced*, 1993
In his diary, a man reflects on his accomplishments in life as well as his regrets at descending into the white-smoke world of crack cocaine.
Duane Smith, *The Nubian*, 1994
The twenty year episodes from a young man's life and his relationship with his mysterious Afrocentric uncle who the governmentconvicts.
John Edgar Wideman, *Philadelphia Fire*, 1990
Intrigued by a police bombing and killing of adults and children a self-exiled writer returns to Philadelphia to investigate.

423

MELVIN VAN PEEBLES, African American

The True American: A Folk Fable

(New York: Doubleday, 1976)

Story type: Satire
Subject(s): Race Relations; Devil; Folk Tales
Age range(s): Adult
Major character(s): George Abraham ''Abe'' Carver, Convict, Veteran, African American; Roscoe L. ''Dogface'' Booker, African American, Worker, Convict; Dave Stock, Scout, Businessman, Caucasian
Time period(s): 1930s (1938); 1960s (1961)
Locale(s): Hell; Georgia; Chicago, Illinois

Summary: A narrator tells the tale of how Abe, winds up a convict, dies, and goes to Hell where he meets ''Dogface,'' a convict who had once forced him into an escape. In Hell for a while now, ''Dogface'' has the lay of the land so he shares his knowledge with Abe. Soon Abe is enrolled in classes where he's learning to read and write and where he becomes friends with Dave, a white scout who died over a hundred years ago during the frontier era. Wanting to escape Hell, Abe and Dave strike a deal with the devil to return them to earth to the exact spot where they died. After eight months on earth Abe has gotten killed and is returned to Hell, while Dave finds a job and a girlfriend. Greeted back in Hell by "Dogface," who has gotten a promotion from the furnaces, Abe realizes he still wants to be on earth and tricks the Devil to get back. Twenty years later at the end of World war II Abe musters from the military a buck sergeant and luckily finds a job as an elevator operator, while Dave is discharged as a decorated colonel and becomes an advertising executive. After years apart they encounter one another on an elevator and brings Dave face-to-face with his time in Hell. For Abe their meeting motivates him to become an activist Freedom Rider where others come to see him as the true American.

About this book: Translation of *Un Americaine en Enfer* originally published in French (1965).

Other books by the same author:
Just an Old Sweet Song, 1976
Sweet Sweetback's Baadasssss Song, 1971 (adapted from screenplay)
Don't Play Us Cheap: A Harlem Party, 1973 (originally published in 1967 in French as *Le Fete a Harlem*)
A Bear for the FBI, 1968 (debut novel,originally published in 1964 in French as *Un Ours pour le F.B.I.*)

Other books you might like:
Cyrus Colter, *A Chocolate Soldier*, 1988
    A story within a story where a tale is told of a young idealist who murders his white employer and is himself killed by a mob lynching.
Gloria Naylor, *Bailey's Cafe*, 1992
    A mythical waystation for lost souls, Bailey's cafe has a back door that opens on dimensions unknown.
Richard Perry, *No Other Tale to Tell*, 1994
    With their community watching in silence, a young girl gives birth to an idiot son by a white youngster her family has taken in and raised.
Ray Shell, *Iced*, 1993
    In his diary, a man reflects on his accomplishments in life as well as his regrets at descending into the white-smoke world of crack cocaine.
Brent Wade, *Company Man*, 1992
    Confessions of the behind-the-scenes stresses and strains faced by a man attempting to climb the business ladder and preserve his family.

424

A.J. VERDELLE, African American

The Good Negress
(Chapel Hill: Algonquin Books of Chapel Hill, 1995)

Subject(s): Coming of Age; Family Relations; Mothers and Daughters
Age range(s): Grades 8-Adult
Major character(s): Denise "Neesey" Palms, Sister, Teenager, African American; Martha Jones Dambridge, Aged Person, Grandmother, African American; Gloria Pearson, Teacher, African American

Time period(s): 1960s (1963)
Locale(s): Detroit, Michigan

Summary: A young country girl "Neesey" lives by the lessons handed down by her grandmother, Martha Jones. When she moves to the city, she has her first sexual experience. "Neesey" wants more from her life than cooking, cleaning and washing for her mother and her family. Her teacher Gloria befriends her and challenges her to reach for her higher potential.

About this book: This is the author's debut novel.

Where it's reviewed:
Black Scholar, Spring 1995, page 73
Essence, April 1995, page 56
New York Times Book Review, May 14, 1995, page 16

Awards the book has won:
Black Caucus of the A.L.A., Honor Book in Fiction, 1996

Other books you might like:
Tina McElroy Ansa, *Baby of the Family*, 1989
    This coming-of-age tale set in the 1950s tells of a young girl who is born in a small town with the gift of a thin veil (caul) over her face.
Maxine Clair, *Rattlebone*, 1994
    This story is about the events in the life of a young girl coming-of-age in a small town in the 1950s.
Thulani Davis, *1959*, 1992
    This coming-of-age story about a 12-year-old girl recounts events that changed her life and others around her during the historic civil rights movement.
Ntozake Shange, *Betsey Brown*, 1985
    This coming-of-age story is about the exploits of a young girl during an era of school integration. It relates the worries of her family and the discoveries she makes at her new school.
Charlotte Sherman, *One Dark Body*, 1993
    This story relates the incidents in the life of a young girl abandoned at birth. It deals with the return of her mother and her friend's entry into manhood.

425

BRENT WADE, African American

Company Man
(Chapel Hill, NC: Algonquin Books of Chapel Hill, 1992)

Subject(s): Business Enterprises; Interpersonal Relations; Race Relations
Age range(s): Adult
Major character(s): William "Billy" Covington, Businessman, Spouse, African American; Paula Covington, Businesswoman, Spouse, African American; Paul "Pee Wee/ Zip" Walker, Friend, Homosexual, African American
Time period(s): 1990s
Locale(s): Baltimore, Maryland

Summary: Writing a confessional diary to "Pee Wee/Zip," his childhood friend, a business executive details the behind-the-scenes stresses and strains he experiences in his corporate position. "Billy/Bill" reveals the marital problems and racism which lead him to attempt suicide.

About this book: This is the author's debut novel.

Where it's reviewed:
Black Scholar, Summer 1992, page 76
Kliatt, July 1993, page 15
Publishers Weekly, January 18, 1993, page 466

Other books you might like:
Bebe Moore Campbell, *Brothers and Sisters*, 1994
    This contemporary account of a career woman's life shows her attempt to climb the business ladder and maintain a social life.
Tananarive Due, *The Between*, 1995
    A man endures nightmares and his sense of reality wavers as he desperately tries to protect his family from the psychotic who stalks them.
Ishmael Reed, *Japanese by Spring*, 1993
    Academic life and race relations are satirized in the story of a professor who will endure any insult to get tenure.
Ntozake Shange, *Liliane: Resurrection of the Daughter*, 1994
    In psychotherapy, a young woman reveals how she coped with family upheavals, romances, friendships, racism, and bigotry. sm, and bigotry.
Ray Shell, *Iced*, 1993
    A man reflects in his diary about his accomplishments in life as well as his regrets of descending into the white-smoke world of crack cocaine.

426

ALICE WALKER, African American

The Color Purple
(New York: Harcourt Brace Jovanovich, 1982)

Story type: Adult
Subject(s): Letters; Self-Perception; Sisters
Major character(s): Celie, Abuse Victim, Lesbian, African American; Shug Avery, Singer, Bisexual, African American; Nettie, Sister, Religious, African American
Time period(s): 20th century (1920s-1940s)
Locale(s): Georgia; Africa

Summary: The lives of two sisters as told through a series of letters. Celie, the older sister, is sexually abused and bears two children that are immediately taken away. Nettie becomes a missionary and travels to Africa with the couple who adopt Celie's children. Celie is married to an older man but falls in love with Shug Avery, her husband's former lover. Eventually she leaves her abusive husband and moves to Memphis to live with Shug, where she starts her own clothing business. Celie inherits her parents' house and store, so she returns to Georgia and finds that both she and her former husband have changed and can now truly honor and appreciate each other.

Where it's reviewed:
African American Review, Fall 1994, page 411
Booklist, October 15, 1994, page 416
English Journal, September 1995, page 32

Awards the book has won:
American Book Award, 1983
Pulitzer Prize, 1983

Other books by the same author:
Possessing the Secret of Joy, 1992

The Temple of My Familiar, 1989
Meridian, 1976
The Third Life of Grange Copeland, 1970 (debut novel; adults)

Other books you might like:
J. California Cooper, *Family*, 1991
    A young girl's narrative of her life in the antebellum South and events in the lives of her children and grandchildren.
J. California Cooper, *In Search of Satisfaction*, 1994
    Two half-sisters born in the antebellum South have to deal with their parent's secret legacy and inheritance.
Carolivia Herron, *Thereafter Johnnie*, 1991
    The incestuous relationship between a father and daughter.
Brenda Lane Richardson, *Chesapeake Song*, 1993
    Two successful people unable to see that problems in their marriage mirror patterns of their parents, come to learn the importance of love.
Jacqueline Woodson, *Autobiography of a Family Photo*, 1995
    New York life of a teenage girl, who has a gay brother and a half-white brother, experiences family violence, and questions her sexuality.

427

ALICE WALKER, African American
CATHERINE DEETER, Illustrator

Finding the Green Stone
(New York: Harcourt Brace Jovanovich, 1991)

Story type: Young Readers
Subject(s): Brothers and Sisters; Behavior; Conduct of Life
Age range(s): Grades 2-3
Major character(s): Johnny Oaks, Child, Brother, African American; Katie Oaks, Child, Sister, African American
Time period(s): 1990s
Locale(s): United States (unidentified city)

Summary: Johnny and Katie have identical iridescent green stones. After behaving badly by saying unkind things to his neighbor and his parents, Johnny discovers he has lost his precious stone. Saddened, Johnny accuses Katie of taking his stone, even after she had let him play with her's. During their search Johnny apologizes for the mean things he has said to everyone and soon the entire community is helping him look for his stone. Johnny realizes he is the only one who can find his stone and when he thanks everyone for their help the rock he thought he held is transformed into his bright green stone.

Other books by the same author:
To Hell with Dying, 1988 (debut (young readers))

Other books you might like:
Jeannette Franklin Caines, *I Need a Lunch Box*, 1988
    A preschooler wanting a lunch box like his older sister's imagines all the things he could keep in it and dreams of having one for every day.
Lucille Clifton, *My Brother Fine with Me*, 1975
    An 8-year-old sister helping her 5-year-old brother pack to runaway discovers how lonely she is without him and is happier when he decides not to leave.
Lucille Clifton, *Three Wishes*, 1974
    Finding a shiny penny in the snow she thinks is lucky, a

young girl makes three wishes. All the wishes come true, convincing her to believe in magic.

Elizabeth Fitzgerald Howard, *Mac and Marie and the Train Toss Surprise*, 1993

A 9-year-old waits beside the railroad tracks with his young sister for their uncle working in the dining car to toss them a special gift.

Faith Ringgold, *Aunt Harriet's Underground Railroad in the Sky*, 1992

Flying in the sky, a sister and her younger brother discovering the underground railroad to freedom must retrace its route to be reunited.

428

ALICE WALKER, African American

Meridian

(New York: Harcourt Brace Jovanovich, 1976)

Subject(s): Civil Rights; Psychology; Race Relations
Age range(s): Adult
Major character(s): Meridian Hill, Activist, Revolutionary, African American; Truman Held, Activist, Artist, African American; Lynne Rabinowitz, Activist, Wife, Caucasian
Time period(s): 1960s; 1970s
Locale(s): Chickokema, Georgia; New York, New York; Atlanta, Georgia

Summary: Meridian, a high-school dropout and deserted wife and mother at 17, finds her only satisfaction in working with civil rights volunteers registering voters. When a scholarship enables her to break away and attend college in Atlanta, she gives away her baby and leaves. Meridian falls in love with Truman, a civil rights worker who does not love her in return. Truman marries a white woman, Lynne, who is also involved in the civil rights struggle but over the years it is Meridian to whom he returns because he feels a bond to her. Meridian becomes a daring and eccentric civil rights worker moving from town to town. Finally she discovers the value of her own life and moves forward, leaving Truman to find his own way.

Other books by the same author:
Possessing the Secret of Joy, 1992
The Temple of My Familiar, 1989
The Color Purple, 1982
The Third Life of Grange Copeland, 1970 (debut novel;adults)

Other books you might like:
Toni Cade Bambara, *The Salt Eaters*, 1980
A woman who attempted suicide finds herself in an unusual healing as her psyche travels through time and the minds of friends and family.
Cyrus Colter, *Rivers of Eros*, 1972
A woman raising her grandchildren must deal with her betrayal of her sister, her daughter's violent death, and the granddaughter she cannot reach.
Grace Edwards-Yearwood, *In the Shadow of the Peacock*, 1988
A young girl strikes out in spite of her mother's fears, discovering her own voice, her own love and her part in the struggle for civil rights.

Ernest J. Gaines, *The Autobiography of Miss Jane Pittman*, 1971
Historical fiction of a 110-year-old woman's life spanning the civil war era to the civil rights movement.

429

ALICE WALKER, African American

Possessing the Secret of Joy

(New York: Harcourt Brace Jovanovich, 1992)

Story type: Adult
Subject(s): Depression; Self-Acceptance; Sexual Abuse
Major character(s): Tashi (Evelyn) Johnson, Mentally Ill Person, African American
Time period(s): 1980s
Locale(s): Africa; United States

Summary: As a young woman, a misguided loyalty to the customs of her African people led Tashi to voluntarily submit to the tsunga's knife and be circumcised. Severely traumatized, she spends the rest of her life battling madness, trying desperately to recognize her own reality and to feel. With the help of a most unlikely ally she studies the mythology behind the mutilation. As her understanding grows, so does her capacity to encounter her overwhelming grief and glowing anger.

Where it's reviewed:
Belles Lettres, Fall 1992, page 57
Black Scholar, Summer 1992, page 85
Kliatt, September 1993, page 15
Library Journal, January 1993, page 58
Publishers Weekly, May 17, 1993, page 76

Other books by the same author:
The Temple of My Familiar, 1989
The Color Purple, 1982
Meridian, 1976
The Third Life of Grange Copeland, 1970 (debut novel; adults)

Other books you might like:
Lorene Cary, *The Price of a Child*, 1995
Historical tale of a woman who literally walks from slavery to freedom under her slave owner's furious gaze in 1850s Philadelphia.
Arthur Flowers, *Another Good Loving Blues*, 1993
A Mississippi Delta tale of exploits in the life of a "conjure" woman haunted by dreams of the mother who abandoned her as a child.
Paule Marshall, *Praisesong for the Widow*, 1983
Disturbed by dreams a middle-aged widow away on a trip finds self-renewal and returns with a plan to connect her past and improve her future.
Linda Raymond, *Rocking the Babies*, 1994
Two aged women volunteering to be hospital care givers to drug exposed babies each have a secret about why they want to be there.

430

ALICE WALKER, African American

The Temple of My Familiar
(New York: Harcourt Brace Jovanovich, 1989)

Story type: Adult
Subject(s): Friendship; Interpersonal Relations; Reincarnation
Major character(s): Suwelo, Professor, African American; Lissie, Aged Person, African American; Carlotta, Professor, African American
Time period(s): 1980s
Locale(s): Berkeley, California

Summary: Interwoven lyric tales take place in Africa, Europe and the Americas in times both ancient and contemporary. Among them are stories of Suwelo, a guerilla history professor, and his love for Fanny, a women's studies professor and masseuse; Aryveda, a rock star who loves both Carlotta, a Latin American refugee and her mother Zede, an artist who makes beautiful feathered capes; and Mr.Hal, a painter who is an eternal familiar to Lissie, a woman who remembers her many lives.

Where it's reviewed:
On the Issues, Spring 1994, page 47
African American Review, Fall 1992, page 507
Kliatt, March 1993, page 27

Other books by the same author:
Possessing the Secret of Joy, 1992
The Color Purple, 1982
Meridian, 1976
The Third Life of Grange Copeland, 1970 (debut novel; adults)

Other books you might like:
Linda Beatrice Brown, *Crossing over Jordan*, 1995
  Saga of the ties binding the lives of four generations of mothers and daughters from the Civil War era to the early 21st century.
Helen Elaine Lee, *The Serpent's Gift*, 1994
  Children and grandchildren of two intertwined families endure hardship and triumph as they help each other remember a history beyond their knowing.
Devorah Major, *An Open Weave*, 1995
  Richly textured story of a blind grandmother who weaves astonishing cloths, her epileptic visionary daughter, and strong-willed granddaughter.
Toni Morrison, *Beloved*, 1987
  A mother who escaped slavery kills her baby to keep her former owner from stealing her, and is then haunted and consumed by the baby's ghost.
Gloria Naylor, *Bailey's Cafe*, 1992
  A mythical waystation for lost souls, Bailey's cafe has a back door that opens on dimensions unknown.

431

ALICE WALKER, African American

The Third Life of Grange Copeland
(New York: Harcourt Brace Jovanovich, 1970)

Subject(s): Family Relations; Psychology; Racism
Age range(s): Adult
Major character(s): Grange Copeland, Farmer, Father, African American; Brownfield Copeland, Son, Abandoned Child, African American; Mem Copeland, Teacher, Wife, African American
Time period(s): 20th century (1920s-1960s)
Locale(s): Georgia; New York, New York

Summary: Grange Copeland, a poor sharecropper hopelessly indebted to a white plantation owner, drinks, abuses his wife and son, and takes up with other women. At first his wife Margaret patiently endures his abuse, but then she begins drinking, too, staying out all hours of the night and has a baby by a white man. Their 15-year-old son Brownfield must care for this half-brother and endure his parents' arguing until Grange leaves for good and Margaret poisons herself and the baby. Brownfield decides to head north, unwittingly following in his father's footsteps. He perpetuates the cycle of violence by abusing his wife and ends up killing her. When Brownfield is released from prison, Grange knows he will destroy his daughter as he destroyed Mem, and sacrifices himself to prevent it.

About this book: This is a debut novel for adults.

Other books by the same author:
Possessing the Secret of Joy, 1992
The Temple of My Familiar, 1989
The Color Purple, 1982
Meridian, 1976

Other books you might like:
Toni Morrison, *The Bluest Eye*, 1970
  A young girl growing up in the 1940s believes she deserves the ill that befalls her, and that having blue eyes would change everything.
Brenda Lane Richardson, *Chesapeake Song*, 1993
  Two successful people, unable to see that problems in their marriage mirror patterns of their parents, come to learn the importance of love.
Dorothy West, *The Wedding*, 1995
  Saga of five generations of two families of mixed race ancestry, and events in the lives of children from a new contemporary generation.

432

MILDRED PITTS WALTER, African American

Because We Are
(New York: Lothrop, Lee & Shepard, 1983)

Story type: Young Adult
Subject(s): Interpersonal Relations; Race Relations; School Life
Age range(s): Grades 7-12

Major character(s): Emma Walsh, Student—High School, 17-Year-Old, African American
Time period(s): 1970s
Locale(s): Brandon Heights, California

Summary: An honor student, Emma is looking forward to her senior year and to being a debutante; she is dating a football star and her plans for college are in place. After a misunderstanding with a white teacher, Emma is transferred to a segregated school where she finds very different challenges.

Awards the book has won:
Coretta Scott King Honor Book, 1984
Newbery Honor Book, 1984

Other books by the same author:
Mariah Keeps Cool, 1990 (Young Readers)
The Girl on the Outside, 1982 (young adult)
Lillie of Watts Takes a Giant Step, 1971 (sequel; young adult)
Lillie of Watts, A Birthday Discovery, 1969 (debut novel (juvenile))

Other books you might like:
Virginia Hamilton, *A White Romance*, 1987
    A high school student befriends a white girl who shares her love of running, and becomes romantically involved with a drug dealer.
Mildred D. Taylor, *The Road to Memphis*, 1990
    Another incident from the lives of the Logan family in segregated Mississippi where racial hostilities erupt and new relationships unfold.
Valerie Wilson Wesley, *Where Do I Go From Here?*, 1993
    At a snooty mostly-white prep school, a teenager learns from another scholarship student that she must make decisions for her own life.
Brenda Wilkinson, *Ludell's New York Time*, 1980
    Moving from Georgia to New York City in her senior year a teenager struggles to adjust to life in 1960s Harlem.
Brenda Wilkinson, *Not Separate, Not Equal*, 1987
    Chosen among a group of six to integrate a Georgia high school, a teenage girl experiences hatred and racism and the beginning of civil rights.

433

MILDRED PITTS WALTER, African American

The Girl on the Outside
(New York: Lothrop, Lee & Shepard, 1982)

Story type: Young Adult
Subject(s): Interpersonal Relations; Race Relations; School Life
Age range(s): Grades 7-12
Major character(s): Eva Collins, 15-Year-Old, Student—High School, African American; Sophia Stuart, 17-Year-Old, Student—High School, Caucasian
Time period(s): 1950s (1957)
Locale(s): Mossville, South

Summary: A white girl, Sophia, has never given much thought to the black people in her life—they've just always been there to serve her and her family. When her high school is scheduled to be integrated, she feels angry without knowing why and is afraid of the "invaders." Eva has been asked to be one

of nine students who will be attending Chatman High School and although her mother is afraid for her safety, Eva feels she will be taking an important step, not only for herself, but for those who will come after her.

About this book: Fictional re-creation of the 1957 integration of Central High School in Little Rock, Arkansas.

Other books by the same author:
Mariah Keeps Cool, 1990 (young readers)
Because We Are, 1983 (young adult)
Lillie of Watts Takes a Giant Step, 1971 (sequel; young adult)
Lillie of Watts, A Birthday Discovery, 1969 (debut novel (juvenile))

Other books you might like:
Ossie Davis, *Just Like Martin*, 1992
    A religiously active son and his war veteran father disagree over the civil rights movement until events occur that help them to work together.
Virginia Hamilton, *A White Romance*, 1987
    A high school student befriends a white girl who shares her love of running, and becomes romantically involved with a drug dealer.
Mildred D. Taylor, *The Road to Memphis*, 1990
    Another incident from the lives of the Logan family in segregated Mississippi where racial hostilities erupt and new relationships unfold.
Valerie Wilson Wesley, *Where Do I Go From Here?*, 1993
    Having trouble at a snooty mostly-white prep school a teenager learns from another scholarship student she must make decisions for her own life.
Brenda Wilkinson, *Not Separate, Not Equal*, 1987
    Chosen among a group of six to integrate a Georgia high school, a teenage girl experiences hatred and racism.

434

MILDRED PITTS WALTER, African American
CAROLE BYARD, Illustrator, African American

Have a Happy. . .
(New York: Lothrop, Lee & Shepard, 1989)

Story type: Young Readers
Subject(s): Birthdays; Family Relations; Holidays
Age range(s): Grades 4-7
Major character(s): Christopher Noel Dodd, 11-Year-Old, Brother, Student
Time period(s): 1980s
Locale(s): United States (unidentified city)

Summary: Feeling sorry for himself because his birthday is on Christmas and will probably get lost in the shuffle, and worried about money because his father is out of work, Christopher keeps busy carving animals for Kwanzaa, an African-American celebration of cultural heritage. The thing he wants most is a bicycle for his birthday, so he can get a paper route and help the family. Christopher sees the principles of Kwanzaa in action as he observes the seven nights with his family.

Other books by the same author:
Mariah Loves Rock, 1988 (young readers)

Justin and the Best Biscuits in the World, 1986 (young readers)

Trouble's Child, 1986 (young readers)

Lillie of Watts, A Birthday Discovery, 1969 (debut novel (juvenile))

Other books you might like:
Virginia Hamilton, *The Bells of Christmas*, 1989
  In this historic account of Christmas 1890, a 12-year-old boy and his family prepare for the Great Day.
Connie Porter, *Addy's Surprise: A Christmas Story*, 1993
  A young girl and her mother prepare for Christmas without the rest of the family; they don't have much, but they get the best gift of all.

435

MILDRED PITTS WALTER, African American
CATHERINE STOCK, Illustrator, African American

Justin and the Best Biscuits in the World
(New York: Lothrop, Lee & Shepard, 1986)

Story type: Young Readers
Subject(s): Grandparents; Ranch Life; Sex Roles
Age range(s): Grades 3-5
Major character(s): Justin, 10-Year-Old, Brother, African American
Time period(s): 1970s
Locale(s): Missouri (Q-T Ranch)

Summary: Justin's sisters and mother always seem to be finding fault with him: he can't make his bed right, he makes a mess in the kitchen, and he can't cook the simplest thing. So when he gets the chance to visit his grandfather's ranch, ride horses and go to a rodeo, he looks forward to forgetting all about ''women's work.''

Awards the book has won:
Coretta Scott King Award, 1987

Other books by the same author:
Mariah Keeps Cool, 1990 (young readers)
Have a Happy. . ., 1989 (young readers)
Trouble's Child, 1986 (young readers)
Lillie of Watts, A Birthday Discovery, 1969 (debut novel (juvenile))

Other books you might like:
Walter Dean Myers, *The Righteous Revenge of Artemis Bonner*, 1992
  Wild west adventure of a young man out to avenge his uncle's murder and to locate his treasure before the killer and his companion.
Harriette Gillem Robinet, *Ride the Red Cycle*, 1980
  A boy crippled since the age of two struggles to realize his dream of riding a cycle.
Ethel Footman Smothers, *Down in the Piney Woods*, 1992
  Episodes in the life of the Footman family as the six children all come to live together for the first time sharing life in the country.
Joyce Carol Thomas, *The Golden Pasture*, 1986
  The exquisite horse a 12-year-old boy finds on his grandfather's farm one summer helps him to understand his difficult father better.

436

MILDRED PITTS WALTER, African American
BONNIE HELENE JOHNSON, Illustrator

Lillie of Watts Takes a Giant Step
(New York: Doubleday & Company, 1971)

Subject(s): Civil Rights Movement; Conformity; School Life
Age range(s): Grades 6-9
Major character(s): Lillie Stevens, 7th Grader, Student, African American
Time period(s): 1968
Locale(s): Los Angeles, California (Watts)

Summary: Lillie is just starting junior high school and finds the changes that it brings difficult to bear. Although her mother works hard as a cleaning woman to support her four children, there is not enough money for Lillie to be able to eat in the cafeteria at lunch, and she is ashamed to be bringing her brown bag. Her best friend from grade school finds other friends, and Lillie is left on her own. She quits eating lunch, and her grades begin to suffer. Lillie meets a new girl who lives in a foster home and has even less than she does. They help form the African-American Culture Club and learn about Martin Luther King and Malcolm X. The club puts on an African fashion show for the school during Black History Week that is a great success, and Lillie has a new pride in herself.

Where it's reviewed:
Kirkus Reviews, October 15, 1971, page 1124
Library Journal, April 15, 1972, page 1611
Publishers Weekly, December 13, 1971, page 43

Other books by the same author:
Mariah Keeps Cool, 1990
Have a Happy. . ., 1989
Justin and the Best Biscuits in the World, 1986
Trouble's Child, 1986
Lillie of Watts, A Birthday Discovery, 1969 (debut novel, young readers)

Other books you might like:
Eloise Greenfield, *Koya Delaney and the Good Girl Blues*, 1992
  A sixth grader caught in the middle when her best friend and her sister have a fight struggles with mixed emotions and knowing who her real friends are.
Virginia Hamilton, *Plain City*, 1993
  A 12-year-old who feels out of place struggles to unearth her past and family history as she gradually discovers more about her long-missing father.
Johnniece Marshall Wilson, *Poor Girl, Rich Girl*, 1992
  A 14-year-old girl gets a number of summer jobs to earn money so she can get contact lenses to replace her big glasses.
Camille Yarbrough, *The Shimmershine Queens*, 1989
  A fifth grade girl learns to stand up for herself and make her own dreams come true when a new teacher comes to her school.

African American Titles

437

MILDRED PITTS WALTER, African American
PAT CUMMINGS, Illustrator, African American

Mariah Keeps Cool
(New York: Bradbury Press, 1990)

Story type: Young Readers
Subject(s): Family Life; Sisters; Sports
Age range(s): Grades 3-5
Major character(s): Mariah Metcalf, 11-Year-Old, Diver, African American
Time period(s): 1980s
Locale(s): United States (unidentified city)

Summary: It's summertime and Mariah and her friends decide to enter the all-city swimming and diving meet. Training for the meet, trying to get along with her half-sister Denise who has come to live with them, and planning a surprise birthday party for her sister Lynn, keeps Mariah quite busy!

Other books by the same author:
Have a Happy. . ., 1989 (Young Readers)
Mariah Loves Rock, 1988 (Young Readers)
Trouble's Child, 1986 (Young Readers)
Lillie of Watts, A Birthday Discovery, 1969 (debut novel (juvenile))

Other books you might like:
Candy Dawson Boyd, *Chevrolet Saturdays*, 1993
Struggling with the divorce of his parents and accepting his new stepfather, a young boy has trouble in school and makes mistakes he regrets.
Joyce Hansen, *The Gift Giver*, 1980
A young girl and her fifth grade friends come to like a new boy in their class and are surprised when they discover he is a foster child.
Ethel Footman Smothers, *Moriah's Pond*, 1995
A continuation of events from the lives of the Footman family when three sisters spend a summer with their great-grandmother.
Eleanora E. Tate, *Just an Overnight Guest*, 1980
A young girl and her older sister are surprised when their mother takes in a baby whose mother is said to be poor white trash.
Jacqueline Woodson, *Last Summer with Maizon*, 1990
The friendship and separation of two youngsters after one suffers the death of her father and the other goes away to boarding school.

438

MILDRED PITTS WALTER, African American
PAT CUMMINGS, Illustrator, African American

Mariah Loves Rock
(New York: Bradbury Press, 1988)

Story type: Young Readers
Subject(s): Growing Up; Rock Music; Stepfamilies
Age range(s): Grades 3-5
Major character(s): Mariah Metcalf, 11-Year-Old, Student, African American

Time period(s): 1980s
Locale(s): United States (unidentified city)

Summary: Mariah is good at sports and is an especially big fan of rock star Sheik Bashara. Sometimes she thinks her older sister, Lynn, is kind of weird because she dresses funny and likes reggae music. But her biggest worry is the arrival of her half-sister Denise, who is coming to live with them. What will she be like?

Other books by the same author:
Mariah Keeps Cool, 1990 (Young Readers)
Justin and the Best Biscuits in the World, 1986 (Young Readers)
Trouble's Child, 1986 (Young Readers)
Lillie of Watts, A Birthday Discovery, 1969 (debut novel (juvenile))

Other books you might like:
Candy Dawson Boyd, *Chevrolet Saturdays*, 1993
Struggling with the divorce of his parents and accepting his new stepfather, a young boy has trouble in school and makes mistakes he regrets.
Joyce Hansen, *The Gift Giver*, 1980
A young girl and her fifth grade friends come to like a new boy in their class and are surprised when they discover he is a foster child.
Ethel Footman Smothers, *Down in the Piney Woods*, 1992
Episodes in the life of the Footman family as the six children all come to live together for the first time sharing life in the country.
Ethel Footman Smothers, *Moriah's Pond*, 1995
A continuation of events from the lives of the Footman family when three sisters spend a summer with their great-grandmother.
Eleanora E. Tate, *Just an Overnight Guest*, 1980
A young girl and her older sister are surprised when their mother takes in a baby whose mother is said to be poor white trash.

439

MILDRED PITTS WALTER, African American
PAT CUMMINGS, Illustrator, African American

My Mama Needs Me
(New York: Lothrop, Lee & Shepard Books, 1983)

Story type: Young Readers
Subject(s): Babies; Mothers and Sons; Responsibility
Age range(s): Grades 2-4
Major character(s): Jason, Child, Brother, African American
Time period(s): 1980s
Locale(s): United States (unidentified city)

Summary: Young Jason's friends want him to come out and play with them but Jason refuses overcome by a sense of responsibility for his new baby sister. He misses out on cookies and milk at his neighbor's and going with Mr. Pompey to feed the ducks at the pond, all because he worries his mom may need him for his new baby sister. He misses out on fun until his mother reassures him that he can play and help with the baby too.

Other books by the same author:
Darkness, 1995
Two and Too Much, 1990
Justin and the Best Biscuits in the World, 1986
Ty's One-Man Band, 1980
Lillie of Watts Takes a Giant Step, 1971

Other books you might like:
Debbi Chocolate, *On the Day I Was Born*, 1995
  A newborn is welcomed into the family in an African ceremony where relatives gather, the child is raised to the heavens, blessed and named.
Lucille Clifton, *Everett Anderson's Nine Month Long*, 1978
  With a new stepfather a young boy now anticipates the arrival of a new stepbrother or sister and experiences the ups and downs of waiting.
Eloise Greenfield, *She Come Bringing Me That Little Baby Girl*, 1974
  Jealous at first when his mama brings him a baby sister a young boy later feels a new sense of responsibility and pride as a big brother.

440

MILDRED PITTS WALTER, African American

Trouble's Child
(New York: Lothrop, Lee & Shepard, 1985)

Story type: Young Readers
Subject(s): Coming of Age; Conformity; Superstition
Age range(s): Grades 4-8
Major character(s): Martha, 14-Year-Old, Granddaughter; Titay, Grandmother, Healer, Midwife
Time period(s): 1980s
Locale(s): Blue Isle, Louisiana

Summary: Martha is struggling with the expectations of others: her grandmother Titay wants Martha to follow in her footsteps to become Blue Isle's midwife and healer, and the island people wait for Martha to show her quilt pattern to announce her readiness for marriage. Martha wants to go to high school, but realizes that means leaving the rhythms and superstitions of island life.

Awards the book has won:
Coretta Scott King Honor Book, 1986
Newbery Honor Book, 1986

Other books by the same author:
Mariah Keeps Cool, 1990 (Young Readers)
Have a Happy..., 1989 (Young Readers)
Justin and the Best Biscuits in the World, 1986 (Young Readers)
Lillie of Watts, A Birthday Discovery, 1969 (debut novel (juvenile))

Other books you might like:
Virginia Hamilton, *The Magical Adventures of Pretty Pearl*, 1983
  A spirited young African god child travels to the New World where she lives among free blacks and learns that every act has its consequence.
Angela Johnson, *Humming Whispers*, 1995
  Recounts the life of a young girl living with an older sister

who has schizophrenia and her fear that she too may have the mental illness.
Eleanora E. Tate, *Thank You, Dr. Martin Luther King, Jr.!*, 1990
  Continuing the Calvary County trilogy, this tale explores the life of a fourth grade girl who is "color struck" wanting to be white.
Mildred D. Taylor, *The Well: David's Story*, 1995
  Episode of the boyhood of two brothers from an early generation of the Logan family in rural Mississippi facing racial bigotry.
Jacqueline Woodson, *Between Madison & Palmetto*, 1993
  In their continuing story two 13-year-old best friends are reunited and having to adjust to a lot of change in their lives and in those around them.

441

MILDRED PITTS WALTER, African American
PAT CUMMINGS, Illustrator, African American

Two and Too Much
(New York: Bradbury Press, 1990)

Story type: Young Readers
Subject(s): Brothers and Sisters; Responsibility; Family Life
Age range(s): Grades 1-2
Major character(s): Brandon, 7-Year-Old, Brother, African American
Time period(s): 1990s
Locale(s): United States

Summary: Company is coming so 7-year-old Brandon has to watch his rambunctious 2-year-old sister Gina while mama cleans. Gina has already been screaming and fussing, she's unzipped the vacuum cleaner bag pulling dirt onto the floor and Brandon doesn't know what to do with her. He spends the day attempting to keep her out of trouble—and isn't very successful—but, he remarks as he's tucking her into bed, she is two and too much.

Other books by the same author:
Darkness, 1995
Ty's One-Man Band, 1980
Mariah Loves Rock, 1988
My Mama Needs Me, 1983

Other books you might like:
Jeannette Franklin Caines, *I Need a Lunch Box*, 1988
  A preschooler, wanting a lunch box like his older sister's, imagines all the things he could keep in it and dreams of having one for every day.
Lucille Clifton, *My Brother Fine with Me*, 1975
  An 8-year-old sister helping her 5-year-old brother pack to runaway discovers how lonely she is without him and is happier when he decides not to leave.
Eloise Greenfield, *She Come Bringing Me That Little Baby Girl*, 1974
  Jealous at first when his mama brings him a baby sister, a young boy later feels a new sense of responsibility and pride as a big brother.

442

VALERIE WILSON WESLEY, African American

Devil's Gonna Get Him

(New York: G. P. Putnam's Sons, 1995)

Story type: Private Detective
Series: Tamara Hayle
Subject(s): Murder; Mystery and Detective Stories; Blackmail
Age range(s): Adult
Major character(s): Tamara Hayle, Detective—Private, Divorced Person, African American; Lincoln E. Storey, Businessman, Wealthy, African American
Time period(s): 1990s
Locale(s): Newark, New Jersey

Summary: Prominent businessman Lincoln Storey hires Tamara to gather information about the man his stepdaughter Alexa has been seeing. Unknown to Storey, the man in question, Brandon Pike, is an old boyfriend of Tamara's. Lincoln invites Tamara to a fundraising party where she can start her surveillance of Brandon. In the midst of the party, Lincoln begins choking and drops dead. Another client soon comes Tamara's way when the police arrest the caterer for Lincoln's murder. When another murder occurs and her own life is threatened, Tamara begins putting the pieces together. Tamara's way when the police arrest the caterer for Lincoln's murder. When another murder occurs and her own life is threatened, Tamara begins putting the pieces together.

Other books by the same author:
When Death Comes Stealing, 1994 (debut novel, adult)

Other books you might like:
Nikki Baker, *In the Game*, 1991
   Debut novel in a murder mystery series with lesbian characters.
Eleanor Taylor Bland, *Dead Time*, 1992
   Debut novel in a detective mystery series with a female heroine.
Gar Anthony Haywood, *Fear of the Dark*, 1988
   Debut novel in a contemporary murder mystery series with a private detective.
Penny Mickelbury, *Keeping Secrets*, 1994
   Debut novel in a murder mystery series with lesbian characters.
Walter Mosley, *Devil in a Blue Dress*, 1990
   Debut novel in a contemporary murder mystery series with a private detective.

443

VALERIE WILSON WESLEY, African American

When Death Comes Stealing

(New York: G.P. Putnam's Sons, 1994)

Story type: Private Detective
Series: Tamara Hayle
Subject(s): Family Relations; Murder; Mystery and Detective Stories
Age range(s): Adult

Major character(s): Tamara Hayle, Divorced Person, Detective—Private, African American; DeWayne Curtis, Businessman, Divorced Person, African American; July Turner, Receptionist, African American
Time period(s): 1990s (1994)
Locale(s): Newark, New Jersey

Summary: A former policewoman, Tamara is now a private detective. When her ex-husband DeWayne's sons are murdered he asks for her help and she reluctantly agrees. In her investigation she is befriended by DeWayne's receptionist July. Tamara discovers buried secrets from his past as she seeks to protect their own son.

About this book: This is the author's debut novel.

Where it's reviewed:
Kirkus Reviews, May 15, 1994, page 670
Library Journal, July 1994, page 132
Publishers Weekly, May 23, 1994, page 80

Other books by the same author:
Devil's Gonna Get Him, 1995 (Tamara Hayle series)

Other books you might like:
Eleanor Taylor Bland, *Dead Time*, 1992
   This debut novel begins a detective mystery series with a female heroine.
Gar Anthony Haywood, *Going Nowhere Fast*, 1994
   This debut novel begins a mystery series with a wife as an amateur detective and her retired police detective husband.
Yolanda Joe, *Falling Leaves of Ivy*, 1992
   A young woman is murdered and her four closest friends from college become suspects, and the secret shared among them begins to unravel.
Barbara Neely, *Blanche on the Lam*, 1992
   This debut novel begins a contemporary murder mystery series with an amateur detective as the heroine.
Barbara Summers, *The Price You Pay*, 1993
   A young woman in the highly competitive fashion industry finds herself as a murder target. A series of murders occur when a new market campaign is launched.

444

VALERIE WILSON WESLEY, African American

Where Do I Go From Here?

(New York: Scholastic, 1993)

Story type: Young Adult
Subject(s): Conduct of Life; Identity; School Life
Age range(s): Grades 7-12
Major character(s): Nia Jones, 15-Year-Old, Student—High School, Orphan; Marcus Garvey Williams, 15-Year-Old, Student—High School, Father
Time period(s): 1990s
Locale(s): Endicott, New Jersey; Newark, New Jersey

Summary: Nia feels she doesn't belong at Endicott Academy, where almost all of the students are white and rich. She is befriended by Marcus, another scholarship student who has managed to fit in and still be himself. When Marcus suddenly disappears, Nia feels deserted but is angered by the rumors that are circulated about him. Defending his name, she gets into a fist fight with a white student and is suspended. She goes home, determined not to return, only to discover she doesn't really fit in with her old friends any more, either. When Nia tracks down Marcus, she begins to understand the decisions she must make for her own life.

About this book: Debut novel (juvenile).

Where it's reviewed:
Booklist, December 15, 1993, page 748
Essence, February 1994, page 121
Kirkus Reviews, December 1, 1993, page 1531
Publishers Weekly, November 8, 1993, page 79
School Library Journal, November 1993, page 126

Other books you might like:
Virginia Hamilton, *A White Romance*, 1987
 A high school student befriends a white girl who shares her love of running, and becomes romantically involved with a drug dealer.
Vy Higginsen, *Mama, I Want to Sing*, 1995
 Recounts events in the life of a talented singer from a young girl singing in the church choir to a renowned award winning star.
Walter Dean Myers, *Crystal*, 1987
 On the brink of a promising career in modeling a 16-year-old realizes there is more than glamour to the industry and has to decide what path to choose.
Walter Dean Myers, *Motown and Didi: A Love Story*, 1984
 Each dreaming of making a better life for themselves two teenagers meet when the young boy rescues the young girl from street hoodlums.
Mildred D. Taylor, *The Road to Memphis*, 1990
 Another incident from the lives of the Logan family in segregated Mississippi where racial hostilities erupt and new relationships unfold.

`445`

DOROTHY WEST, African American

The Wedding
(New York: Doubleday, 1994)

Subject(s): Family Relations; Identity; Interracial Marriage
Age range(s): Adult
Major character(s): Shelby Coles, Young Woman, African American; Lute McNeil, Businessman, Father, African American; Carolyn ''Gram'' Shelby, Grandmother, Caucasian
Time period(s): 1950s (1953)
Locale(s): Martha's Vineyard, Massachusetts

Summary: This saga is about the trials and tribulations of five generations of two families with mixed-race ancestry. This spans from the days of slavery to an era of instituting integration. The white matriarch ''Gram'' looks on at a new generation, seeing the hopes, fears and confusions surfaced in her granddaughter Shelby, a young woman about to marry outside her race. Tragedy awaits as Shelby also becomes attracted to Lute, a man within her race.

About this book: The author is from the legendary Harlem Renaissance era.

Where it's reviewed:
Christian Science Monitor, February 2, 1995, page 11

Essence, February 1995, page 54
New York Times Book Review, February 12, 1995, page 11

Other books by the same author:
The Living Is Easy, 1948 (debut novel)

Other books you might like:
Barbara Chase-Riboud, *The President's Daughter*, 1994
 This work chronicles the life of Harriet Hemings, the daughter of miscegenation in the interracial affair of President Thomas Jefferson. It relates her passing for white.
J. California Cooper, *Family*, 1991
 This is a young girl's narrative of life during the plantation era of the South. Included are the events in the lives of her children by her slave owner's son and the lives of her grandchildren.
Leon Forrest, *Two Wings to Veil My Face*, 1983
 This last title in their trilogy tells of the Witherspoon family's saga during the plantation era of the South before the Civil War to contemporary times.
Charles Johnson, *Oxherding Tale*, 1982
 This coming-of-age tale is about a light-skinned young man in the plantation era of the South as he struggles to gain his freedom and the freedom of those he loves.
John Edgar Wideman, *Damballah*, 1981
 This first title of the Homewood trilogy portrays the intergenerational history of a family from the 1840s-1960s in Pennsylvania.

`446`

JOHN EDGAR WIDEMAN, African American

Damballah
(New York: Avon Books, 1981)

Series: Homewood Trilogy
Subject(s): Family Relations; Intergenerational Saga; Interpersonal Relations
Age range(s): Adult
Major character(s): Lizabeth French Lawson, Mother, Religious, African American; John Lawson, Writer, Student—College, African American; Tommy Lawson, Addict, Thief, African American
Time period(s): 19th century; 20th century (1840s-1960s)
Locale(s): Pittsburgh, Pennsylvania (Homewood community)

Summary: A family tree is traced from the 1840s to the 1960s. In the 1920s, Lizabeth has three sons, among them John and Tommy, who are significantly different and alienated from their community. John is a college student and writer while Tommy is a thief and an addict. With Tommy in prison, John tells him the family saga in letters.

About this book: This is the first title of the Homewood trilogy.

Where it's reviewed:
American Book Review, July 1982, page 12
Kliatt, Winter 1982, page 18
New York Times Book Review, April 11, 1982, page 6

Other books by the same author:
Philadelphia Fire, 1990
Sent for You Yesterday, 1983 (Homewood trilogy)
Hiding Place, 1981 (Homewood trilogy)
A Glance Away, 1967 (debut novel)

Other books you might like:
Linda Beatrice Brown, *Crossing over Jordan*, 1995
This saga is about the binding ties in the lives of four generations of mothers and daughters from the Civil War era to the early 21st century.
Leon Forrest, *Two Wings to Veil My Face*, 1983
The Witherspoon family's saga, from pre-Civil War to contemporary times, is concluded in this last volume of a trilogy.
Marita Golden, *Long Distance Life*, 1989
The murder of a young man in the 1980s and the evolution of his family from a 1920s sharecropping background.
Helen Elaine Lee, *The Serpent's Gift*, 1994
The children and grandchildren of two intertwined families endure hardship and triumph as they help each other remember a history beyond their realm.
Dorothy West, *The Wedding*, 1995
Saga about five generations of two families with mixed race ancestry.

447

JOHN EDGAR WIDEMAN, African American

Hiding Place
(New York: Avon, 1981)

Series: Homewood Trilogy
Subject(s): Survival; Family Relations; Murder
Age range(s): Adult
Major character(s): Tommy Lawson, Fugitive, Cousin, African American; Bess Simpkins, Aged Person, Recluse, African American
Time period(s): 1960s
Locale(s): Pittsburgh, Pennsylvania (Homewood community)

Summary: Continues the story of John Lawson's brother, 25-year-old Tommy. A murder has occurred and Tommy is a suspect. Seeking a place to hide out he goes up on the hill to his aged cousin Bess' place. Called ''Mother Bess'' she has been a recluse struggling to survive by herself since the death of her son Eugene in the war. Tommy's arrival disrupts Mother Bess' routine but in a few days together the two seem to forge a kind of bond. Mother Bess recollects past stories of the family and Tommy confesses he was at the scene of the murder but did not kill anyone. Clement, Mother Bess' delivery boy, discovers she is hiding the one everyone is talking about and that the police are looking for. When Tommy decides to go back and face his accusers, Mother Bess decides it's time to come out of seclusion and she wants to make sure everyone knows of Tommy's innocence.

Other books by the same author:
Philadelphia Fire, 1990
Reuben, 1987
Sent for You Yesterday, 1983 (*Homewood Trilogy*)
Damballah, 1981 (*Homewood Trilogy*)
A Glance Away, 1967 (debut novel)

Other books you might like:
Ernest J. Gaines, *A Lesson before Dying*, 1993
Historical fiction in 1940s Louisiana of the impact a young man's pending execution for murder has on the community and his family and friends.

Marita Golden, *Long Distance Life*, 1989
Episodes in the murder of a young grandson in the 1980s and the evolution of his family from a sharecropping background of the 1920s.
Gwendolyn Parker, *These Same Long Bones*, 1994
A man loses his direction following the death of his daughter, and must make a courageous decision that affects those in the community he loves.
Dori Sanders, *Her Own Place*, 1993
Remembrances of exploits in a senior citizen's life of daughter, wife, mother, and grandmother from before WWII to contemporary times.
John A. Williams, *The Junior Bachelor Society*, 1976
The lives of nine boyhood teammates unfold as they come back together after thirty years to honor their coach and one of them is apprehended for murder.

448

JOHN EDGAR WIDEMAN, African American

Hurry Home
(New York: Harcourt, Brace and World, 1970)

Subject(s): Self-Acceptance; Responsibility; Interpersonal Relations
Age range(s): Adult
Major character(s): Cecil Otis Braithwaite, Graduate, Maintenance Worker, Spouse; Esther Brown Braithwaite, Abuse Victim, Spouse, Maintenance Worker
Time period(s): 1960s (1966-1968)
Locale(s): Washington, District of Columbia; Europe

Summary: Thirty-five-year-old Cecil is in search of who he is and abandons his wife Esther on their wedding night. She believed their life together was preordained by God and had toiled to support Cecil while he finished his law degree. Their son had been stillborn and Esther's aunt was now living with them when Cecil left. In his travels abroad Cecil is befriended by Albert, a drifter searching for the interracial son of his white employer, Charles Webb. When Webb thinks the search might be over and that Cecil is his son, Albert persuades him to leave. Three years later Cecil returns to his wife, finding little has changed in his home as he slips into Esther's bedroom drifting into a dream.

Other books by the same author:
Philadelphia Fire, 1990
Reuben, 1987
Damballah, 1981 (Homewood trilogy)
Lynchers, 1973
A Glance Away, 1967 (debut novel)

Other books you might like:
Cyrus Colter, *City of Light*, 1993
Exploits in the life of a young Chicago man who travels to Paris writing letters to his deceased mother about his plight of being light-skinned.
Melvin Dixon, *Trouble the Water*, 1989
Running away from home a young man returns twenty years later in a plot of revenge which developed between his grandmother and his father.
Louis Edwards, *Ten Seconds*, 1991
The memories about his life of a young man anticipating

his future as a husband and father, and reflecting on the family secret he's kept.

Percival Everett, *Suder*, 1983

> The escapades of a young man who fears he may be on the verge of going insane like his mother, and decides to run away from his wife and son.

Reginald McKnight, *I Get on the Bus*, 1990

> Trying to avoid making decisions at home, a young man joins the Peace Corps and travels to Senegal, becoming involved in new intrigue.

449

JOHN EDGAR WIDEMAN, African American

Philadelphia Fire

(New York: Henry Holt and Company, 1990)

Story type: Adult
Subject(s): Identity; Race Relations; Survival
Age range(s): Adult
Major character(s): Cudjoe, Divorced Person, Writer, African American; Simba ''Simmie'' Mintu, Child, Survivor, African American; Margaret Jones, Mother, Office Worker, African American
Time period(s): 1980s (1985)
Locale(s): Philadelphia, Pennsylvania

Summary: Cudjoe' a self-exiled writer, is prompted to return to Philadelphia when he learns about a police bombing and the killing of six adults and five children at the MOVE organization. Discovering a child may have survived the assault, Cudjoe questions Margaret, a member of the organization. His investigation leads him to question race relations as well as his own identity.

About this book: This book won two awards.

Where it's reviewed:
Essence, January 1991, page 32
Publishers Weekly, August 17, 1990, page 53
Time, October 1, 1990, page 90

Awards the book has won:
American Book Award, 1991
PEN/Faulkner Award for Fiction, 1990

Other books by the same author:
Reuben, 1987
Damballah, 1981 (Homewood trilogy)
Lynchers, 1973
Hurry Home, 1970
A Glance Away, 1967 (debut novel)

Other books you might like:
Melvin Dixon, *Trouble the Water*, 1989

> A young man returns home twenty years later in a plot of revenge between his grandmother and his father.

Reginald McKnight, *I Get on the Bus*, 1990

> A young man tries to avoid making decisions at home so he joins the Peace Corps. When he travels to Senegal he becomes involved in a new intrigue.

450

JOHN EDGAR WIDEMAN, African American

Reuben

(New York: Henry Holt, 1987)

Subject(s): City Life; Interpersonal Relations
Age range(s): Adult
Major character(s): Reuben, Aged Person (hunchbacked dwarf), Lawyer, African American
Time period(s): 1980s (1987)
Locale(s): Pittsburgh, Pennsylvania (Homewood community)

Summary: Living in an unkept trailer on a vacant lot, Reuben has become a hero to those he helps with their legal problems. Some of his clients are the athlete who confides to Reuben he killed a man, and the working mother who wants to get her kidnapped son back. All are residents of the Homewood community. Reuben has seen the ins and outs of life in the community and he strives to help those where his talents can make a difference.

Where it's reviewed:
Essence, March 1988, page 26
Library Journal, November 1, 1987, page 124
Publishers Weekly, September 30, 1988, page 63

Other books by the same author:
Philadelphia Fire, 1990
Damballah, 1981 (Homewood trilogy)
Lynchers, 1973
Hurry Home, 1970
A Glance Away, 1967 (debut novel)

Other books you might like:
Percival Everett, *Cutting Lisa*, 1986

> A retired obstetrician suspects his pregnant daughter-in-law of having an affair and he considers what he might do to resolve the situation.

Leon Forrest, *Divine Days*, 1992

> An aspiring playwright captures voices of the living and the dead in an epic tale referred to as *The Ulysses of the South Side*.

Toni Morrison, *Jazz*, 1992

> A working class couple face the trauma of putting their lives back together after the husband murders the girl with whom he was having an affair.

Gloria Naylor, *Women of Brewster Place*, 1982

> Seven women who come to live on the dead-end street of Brewster Place tell their stories of what brings them together in their own redemption.

Richard Perry, *No Other Tale to Tell*, 1994

> With their community watching in silence, a young girl gives birth to an idiot son by a white youngster her family had raised.

451

JOHN EDGAR WIDEMAN, African American

Sent for You Yesterday

(New York: Allison and Busby, 1983)

Series: Homewood Trilogy

Subject(s): City Life; Family Relations; Interpersonal Relations
Age range(s): Adult
Major character(s): ''Doot'' Lawson, Student—College, African American; Lucy Tate, Adoptee, Addict, African American; Carl French, Addict, Veteran, African American
Time period(s): 1940s; 1970s
Locale(s): Pittsburgh, Pennsylvania (Homewood community)

Summary: The last title of the Homewood trilogy brings ''Doot'' (presumably John Lawson from the trilogy's first title) together with lovers Carl and Lucy. Listening to their stories of the past, ''Doot'' is reminded about Albert Wilkes, an incredible piano player who had an affair with a white woman, killed her white policeman husband and became a fugitive on the run from the law. Seven years later when Wilkes returned to Homewood he sought refuge at the Tate's home. Someone informed the police and they came and shot him. Left to clean up after the killing, Lucy kept a bone fragment which she showed Carl when they first become lovers as teenagers. A veteran of World War II, Carl, Lucy and her adopted albino brother ''Brother'' Tate became addicted to drugs and struggled to get clean. Among their reminiscing with ''Doot'' they also recall ''Brother'' losing his only son in a fire, his ceasing to speak, and his tragic suicide.

Other books by the same author:
Philadelphia Fire, 1990
Reuben, 1987
Hiding Place, 1981 (Homewood trilogy)
Damballah, 1981 (Homewood trilogy)
A Glance Away, 1967 (debut novel)

Other books you might like:
Bebe Moore Campbell, *Your Blues Ain't Like Mine*, 1992
Episodes in the lives of individuals affected by the murder of a 15-year-old boy for reportedly offending a white woman in a small southern town.
Alice Childress, *A Short Walk*, 1973
Saga of events in the childhood and adulthood life of a woman who escapes an abusive marriage and journeys to Harlem in the 1940s.
Leon Forrest, *Divine Days*, 1992
Voices of the living and the dead are captured by an aspiring playwright in an epic tale referred to as ''The Ulysses of the South Side.''
Marita Golden, *Long Distance Life*, 1989
Episodes in the murder of a young grandson in the 1980s and the evolution of his family from a sharecropping background of the 1920s.
Toni Morrison, *Jazz*, 1992
A working class couple face the trauma of trying to put their lives back together when the husband murders the girl with whom he was having an affair.

452

BRENDA WILKINSON, African American

Definitely Cool
(New York: Scholastic Inc., 1993)

Story type: Young Adult
Subject(s): Growing Up; Peer Pressure; School Life
Age range(s): Grades 6 and Up
Major character(s): Roxanne Williams, 12-Year-Old, Student—Junior High, African American
Time period(s): 1990s
Locale(s): New York, New York (Riverdale)

Summary: Roxanne attends Riverdale Junior High, a new school in an upscale neighborhood. She discovers that her new friends are more interested in clothes and chasing boys than in studying and getting good grades. She tries to keep up with them, but when they want her to break the rules, she has to decide what's right for her.

Where it's reviewed:
Booklist, March 15, 1994, page 1361
Essence, February 1994, page 120
Horn Book Guide, Fall 1993, page 306
Journal of Reading, December 1993, page 337

Other books by the same author:
Not Separate, Not Equal, 1984
Ludell's New York Time, 1980
Ludell and Willie, 1976
Ludell, 1975 (debut novel)

Other books you might like:
Angela Johnson, *Toning the Sweep*, 1993
A young girl prepares a special gift for her dying grandmother and honors the spirit of the deceased grandfather she never knew.
Walter Dean Myers, *Won't Know Till I Get There*, 1982
A 14-year-old and his adoptive brother, who has a juvenile record, hang out together during the summer and get arrested together.
Valerie Wilson Wesley, *Where Do I Go From Here?*, 1993
Having trouble at a snooty mostly-white prep school, a teenager learns from another scholarship student that she must make her decisions for her own life.
Rita Williams-Garcia, *Like Sisters on the Homefront*, 1994
An unwed 14-year-old mother has an abortion. Qhen she is sent to her relatives in the South she develops a new sense of family and self.
Jacqueline Woodson, *The Dear One*, 1991
Outraged when her mother announces they're taking in a close friend's unwed, pregnant teenaged daughter, a 12-year-old becomes the baby's namesake.

453

BRENDA WILKINSON, African American

Ludell
(New York: Harper & Row, 1975)

Subject(s): Grandparents; Growing Up
Age range(s): Grades 5-8

Major character(s): Ludell Wilson, 11-Year-Old, Student, African American
Time period(s): 1950s (1955)
Locale(s): Waycross, Georgia

Summary: Ludell has always lived with her grandmother. Her best friend Ruthie Mae lives right next door, and the kids are always back and forth between the two houses. Ludell has her first kiss and her first romance with Ruthie Mae's older brother Willie. Life isn't always easy; her grandmother must work cleaning houses and taking in washing to make ends meet, and Ludell helps out when she is not in school. One summer, Ludell joins Ruthie Mae and her family when they go out to pick cotton in the hot summer sun. And she realizes that Ruthie Mae's older sister who has a baby is perhaps not so different from her own mother, who now lives in New York City.

About this book: Debut novel.

Where it's reviewed:
Booklist, March 15, 1977, page 1102
Horn Book Magazine, April 1976, page 160
Kirkus Reviews, September 15, 1975, page 1068
Publishers Weekly, December 1, 1975, page 66
School Library Journal, December 1975, page 32

Other books by the same author:
Definitely Cool, 1994 (young adults)
Not Separate, Not Equal, 1984 (young adults)
Ludell's New York Time, 1980 (young adults)
Ludell and Willie, 1977 (young adults)

Other books you might like:
Eloise Greenfield, *Koya Delaney and the Good Girl Blues*, 1992
    A sixth grader caught in the middle when her best friend and her sister have a fight struggles with mixed emotions and knowing who her real friends are.
Virginia Hamilton, *Plain City*, 1993
    A 12-year-old who feels out of place struggles to unearth her past and family history as she gradually discovers more about her long-missing father.
Angela Johnson, *Humming Whispers*, 1995
    Recounts the life of a young girl living with an older sister who has schizophrenia and her fear that she too may have the mental illness.
Mildred Pitts Walter, *Lillie of Watts Takes a Giant Step*, 1971
    A girl faces a series of crises going to junior high school for the first time but finds a new friend, new heroes and a new pride in herself.
Mildred Pitts Walter, *Trouble's Child*, 1985
    Expected to marry and to succeed her grandmother as the island's midwife, a girl dreams of leaving the island to attend high school.

454

BRENDA WILKINSON, African American

Ludell's New York Time

(New York: Harper & Row, 1980)

Story type: Young Adult
Subject(s): Growing Up; Love; Teen Relationships

Age range(s): Grades 6 and Up
Major character(s): Ludell Wilson, 18-Year-Old, Student—High School
Time period(s): 1960s
Locale(s): New York, New York

Summary: When the grandmother who raised her passes away, Ludell's mother brings her to New York to finish school at Harlem High. Although some new friends keep trying to fix her up on dates, Ludell is planning to marry her boyfriend Willie as soon as they both graduate. Family problems prevent Willie from making it to New York, so Ludell looks for her first job, discovering that things in the North aren't that much different.

Other books by the same author:
Definitely Cool, 1993
Not Separate, Not Equal, 1984
Ludell and Willie, 1976
Ludell, 1975 (debut novel)

Other books you might like:
Sharon M. Draper, *Tears of a Tiger*, 1994
    A teenager escaping a car accident in which his friend is killed and others are injured has difficulty learning to live with the trauma.
Virginia Hamilton, *A Little Love*, 1984
    A teenage girl has an emptiness food cannot fill: she misses her father, and in her search for him she finds new strengths in herself.
Walter Dean Myers, *Crystal*, 1987
    On the brink of a promising career in modeling a 16-year-old realizes there is more than glamour to the industry and has to decide what path to choose.
Mildred Pitts Walter, *Because We Are*, 1983
    After trouble with a white teacher, an honor student is transferred to a segregated high school where she finds different kinds of challenges.
Rita Williams-Garcia, *Like Sisters on the Homefront*, 1994
    An unwed, 14-year-old mother, again pregnant, has an abortion and when sent to her relatives in the South she develops a new sense of family and self.

455

BRENDA WILKINSON, African American

Not Separate, Not Equal

(New York: Harper and Row, 1987)

Story type: Young Adult
Subject(s): Race Relations; Racism; School Life
Age range(s): Grades 5 and Up
Major character(s): Malene Freeman, Adoptee, 17-Year-Old, African American
Time period(s): 1960s (1965)
Locale(s): Pineridge, Georgia

Summary: Malene's adoptive parents and five other professional couples have volunteered their children to lead the way in integrating Pineridge High School in 1965. The students are met with hostility, threats, and a particularly malicious act that culminates in an explosive situation.

Other books by the same author:
Definitely Cool, 1993
Ludell's New York Time, 1980
Ludell and Willie, 1976
Ludell, 1975 (debut novel)

Other books you might like:
Ossie Davis, *Just Like Martin*, 1992
A religiously active son and his war veteran father disagree over the civil rights movement until after events occur that help them to work together.
Virginia Hamilton, *A White Romance*, 1987
A high school student befriends a white girl who shares her love of running, and becomes romantically involved with a drug dealer.
Mildred D. Taylor, *The Road to Memphis*, 1990
Another incident from the lives of the Logan family in segregated Mississippi where racial hostilities erupt and new relationships unfold.
Mildred Pitts Walter, *The Girl on the Outside*, 1982
A student and her white classmate see school integration from very different viewpoints.
Valerie Wilson Wesley, *Where Do I Go From Here?*, 1993
Having trouble at a snooty mostly-white prep school a teenager learns from another scholarship student she must make decisions for her own life.

456

DENNIS WILLIAMS, African American

Crossover
(New York: Summit Books, 1992)

Subject(s): Coming of Age; Family Relations; Race Relations
Age range(s): Adult
Major character(s): Richard ''Ike'' Isaac, Activist, Student—College, African American; Elizabeth Isaac, Mother, African American; Cheryl Costanza, Girlfriend, Student, Irish Italian
Time period(s): 20th century (1954-1974)
Locale(s): New York, New York

Summary: College student ''Ike'' goes from reluctant activist to graduate law intern during the Civil Rights era. Along the way, he experiences an interracial relationship with Cheryl, witnesses death, and searches for the father who abandoned his family.

About this book: This is the author's debut novel.

Where it's reviewed:
Essence, June 1992, page 54
Kirkus Reviews, November 15, 1991, page 1435
Publishers Weekly, January 1, 1992, page 47

Other books you might like:
Louis Edwards, *Ten Seconds*, 1991
A young man anticipates his future as a husband and father and reflects on the family secret he has kept.
Trey Ellis, *Home Repairs*, 1993
A young man captures his coming-of-age exploits from ages 16-26 in his journal. He searches for love and finds success in his career.

Reginald McKnight, *I Get on the Bus*, 1990
A young man tries to avoid making decisions at home, so he joins the Peace Corps. When he travels to Senegal, he becomes involved in intrigue.
Albert Murray, *The Spyglass Tree*, 1991
A young man, one of the ''talented tenth,'' attends college in Mobile County. He gets involved with new friends while learning about himself.
Darryl Pinckney, *High Cotton*, 1992
An unnamed narrator reveals the complexities of growing up in the upper-middle class as a young man in the ''talented tenth'' generation.

457

JOHN A. WILLIAMS, African American

The Berhama Account
(Far Hills, NJ: New Horizon Press, 1985)

Subject(s): Politics; Campaigns, Political; Interpersonal Relations
Age range(s): Adult
Major character(s): Gary Mandarino, Businessman, Public Relations, Italian
Time period(s): 1980s
Locale(s): Berhama, Caribbean

Summary: The mostly white Berhama United Party (BUP) has hired Mandarino Associates, a public relations firm from the U.S., to help get their Caribbean island's white Prime Minister, Kirkland Trottingham, reelected. The firm's head, Italian Gary Mandarino, has been on the island developing and implementing a strategy for the BUP. Emphasizing the importance of integration for the island's survival Gary has gotten Kirkland to agree to make some concessions in that direction. The Prime Minister and his wealthy supporters are opposed by the mostly non-white Peoples Berhama Party (PBP) and a plot is underway to assassinate the Prime Minister. At the completion of a yacht race a gala celebration party is held where the Prime Minister appears but hand grenades in place for his assassination could cause an explosive ending.

Other books by the same author:
Jacob's Ladder, 1987
Click Song, 1982
The Junior Bachelor Society, 1976
Mothersill and the Foxes, 1975
Captain Blackman, 1972

Other books you might like:
Chester Himes, *Plan B*, 1993
A political visionary plots to avenge racial injustice by anonymously arming the common black man to overthrow white society.
Kristin Hunter, *The Lakestown Rebellion*, 1978
To further his career a mayor sacrifices his town to wealthy white politicians and when the citizens learn they sabotage the plan.
Paule Marshall, *Daughters*, 1991
A determined young woman struggles in her relationship with her political father and when she returns home for a visit makes an important decision.

`458`

JOHN A. WILLIAMS, African American

Captain Blackman
(New York: Doubleday, 1972)

Subject(s): Historical; War; Race Relations
Age range(s): Adult
Major character(s): Captain Abraham Blackman, Military Personnel, African American; Major Ishmael Whittman, Military Personnel, Caucasian
Time period(s): Indeterminate Past; Indeterminate Future
Locale(s): Vietnam

Summary: Conducting a seminar on Black military history to his mixed race command when Captain Blackman is wounded in Vietnam combat he weaves in and out of dreams taking him through every major military battle in history. His dreams incorporate people from his life, including his lover, friends, enemies, and among them his white superior officer Major Ishmael Whittman. In section 1 he encounters historical figures among them Peter Salem, Crispus Attucks, Presidents, and other military leaders as he journeys through the Revolutionary War, the War of 1812, and the Civil War. With the rank of sergeant major in the U.S. Cavalry in section 2 Blackman moves through battles protecting white settlers in Indian territory, the Spanish-American war, and the mass dishonorable discharge of the colored 25th Infantry. World War I, the Spanish Civil war, and World War II occur in sections 3-5. The final section 6 covers the Korean and Vietnam conflicts and moves into the futuristic 21st century where Blackman envisions the U.S. military nuclear power of white oppressors being taken over by his race.

Other books by the same author:
Sons of Darkness, Sons of Light, 1969
The Man Who Cried I Am, 1967
Sissie, 1963
Night Song, 1961
One for New York, 1960 (debut novel later titled *The Angry Ones*)

Other books you might like:
Barbara Chase-Riboud, *Echo of Lions*, 1989
   Mutiny by Africans kidnapped aboard the schooner the *Amistad* leads to President John Quincy Adams arguing their defense before the Supreme Court.
Arthur Flowers, *De Mojo Blues*, 1985
   Depicts a Vietnam veteran dishonorably discharged for murder with his buddies who now wants to become trained in the ways of hoodoo and conjuring.
Charles Johnson, *Middle Passage*, 1990
   A young man mistakenly stows away on a slave ship bound for Africa, where he must endure storms, mutiny, and illness before the journey ends.
Louise Meriwether, *Fragments of the Ark*, 1994
   Historical tale of a South Carolina slave who steals a Confederate gunboat and delivers it to the Union Navy, later becoming its captain.

`459`

JOHN A. WILLIAMS, African American

Click Song
(New York: Houghton Mifflin, 1982)

Subject(s): Business Enterprises; Interpersonal Relations; Race Relations
Age range(s): Adult
Major character(s): Cato Caldwell Douglass, African American, Veteran, Writer; Paul Cummings, Veteran, Writer, Caucasian
Time period(s): 20th century (1939-1982)
Locale(s): New York, New York; Africa; Europe

Summary: Shocked that his white wartime buddy and fellow writer has committed suicide, Cato reflects back over their friendship. The racial tension between them was always evident. Rivals in the competitive literary industry, they both struggled for success. Looking back over the decades, Cato is also looking for answers to the twist of events that led to Paul's death. At the same time, in his own life, Cato's first wife remarries and their son goes off to college. He and Allis, a woman he meets abroad, have a son and he continues his search for a former lover and his child, whom he has never met.

Awards the book has won:
American Book Award, 1983

Other books by the same author:
The Berhama Account, 1985
The Junior Bachelor Society, 1976
Mothersill and the Foxes, 1975
Captain Blackman, 1972
One for New York, 1960 (debut novel later titled *The Angry Ones*)

Other books you might like:
Ernest J. Gaines, *In My Father's House*, 1978
   A civil rights leader and minister is forced to examine who he is and who he was when a stranger emerges from his past.
Gwendolyn Parker, *These Same Long Bones*, 1994
   A man loses his direction following the death of his daughter, and must make a courageous decision that affects those in the community he loves.
Alexs D. Pate, *Losing Absalom*, 1994
   The ghostly presence of a husband and father dying of cancer watches over his wife and children seeing their struggles of life in the inner city.
Brent Wade, *Company Man*, 1992
   Confessions of the behind-the-scenes stresses and strains faced by a man attempting to climb the business ladder and preserve his family.
John Edgar Wideman, *Reuben*, 1987
   Exploits of an aged lawyer and the varied clients he puts his talents to work for in the Pittsburgh community of Homewood during the 1980s.

460

JOHN A. WILLIAMS, African American

Jacob's Ladder
(New York: Thunder's Mouth Press, 1987)

Subject(s): Military Life; Espionage; Africa
Age range(s): Adult
Major character(s): Jacob "Jake" Henry, Military Personnel, Diplomat, African American; Chuma Fasseke, Political Figure, Spouse, African
Time period(s): 1960s
Locale(s): Pandemi, Africa

Summary: His missionary family was stationed in Pandemi when Jake was born before returning to Harlem where his father was a minister. Jake had spent the first decade of his life there and was boyhood buddies with the country's new President Fasseke. President Fasseke had studied in the States, had an interest in Jake's sister which was not returned, and Jake had not seen him since the Korean War some fifteen years ago. Now a military Major, Jake is assigned as the country's attache when their access to nuclear power has become a concern. Trade agreements with the Soviet Union and China threaten American control, and the CIA station chief implements a plan to overthrow President Fasseke. He especially needs to win this operation since his coup of a neighboring country just failed. Jake becomes suspicious of what might be happening and of his role in it.

Other books by the same author:
The Berhama Account, 1985
The Junior Bachelor Society, 1976
Mothersill and the Foxes, 1975
Captain Blackman, 1972
One for New York, 1960 (debut novel later titled *The Angry Ones*)

Other books you might like:
Reginald McKnight, *I Get on the Bus*, 1990
    Trying to avoid making decisions at home, a young man joins the Peace Corps and travels to Senegal, becoming involved in new intrigue.
Ishmael Reed, *The Terrible Threes*, 1989
    Satire on covert operations in government, continuing some characters from author's *The Terrible Twos*.
Duane Smith, *The Nubian*, 1994
    The twenty year episodes from a young man's life and his relationship with his mysterious Afrocentric uncle who the government convicts.
Melvin Van Peebles, *Panther*, 1995
    Recounts an urban rebellion of the sixties that became the historic Black Panther movement and plots of the FBI and police to destroy them.
John Edgar Wideman, *Philadelphia Fire*, 1990
    Intrigued by a police bombing and killing of adults and children a self-exiled writer returns to Philadelphia to investigate.

461

JOHN A. WILLIAMS, African American

The Junior Bachelor Society
(New York: Doubleday, 1976)

Subject(s): Interpersonal Relations; Friendship; Family Life
Age range(s): Adult
Major character(s): Charles "Chappie" Davis, Coach, Hotel Worker, African American; Richard "Bubbles" Wiggins, African American, Worker, Veteran
Time period(s): 1970s
Locale(s): United States (unidentified east coast industrial city)

Summary: A gala celebration is planned to honor 70-year-old coach "Chappie" Davis by the Junior Bachelor Society. For over thirty years he's been like a surrogate father to nine kids and they want to pay their respects. Through the years each of their lives have evolved in various ways. Some stayed in the city, while others have moved distances away. One of the nine, "Moon," is a hustler on the west coast escaping a murder charge. His arrival gets his JBS teammates and coach "Chappie" involved when he gets apprehended by detective Swoop Ferguson, a man who, ironically, coach "Chappie" refused to take into the JBS years ago. Making a deal with Swoop, "Moon" knows there is only one sure way he can save himself.

Other books by the same author:
Jacob's Ladder, 1987
The Berhama Account, 1985
Click Song, 1982
Captain Blackman, 1972
One for New York, 1960 (debut novel later titled *The Angry Ones*)

Other books you might like:
David Bradley, *The Chaneysville Incident*, 1981
    Returning home to comfort a dying man, a professor must solve the dual mysteries of his father's death and the dark secret of his family's past.
Melvin Dixon, *Trouble the Water*, 1989
    Running away from home a young man returns twenty years later in a plot of revenge which developed between his grandmother and his father.
Louis Edwards, *Ten Seconds*, 1991
    The memories about his life of a young man anticipating his future as a husband and father, and reflecting on the family secret he's kept.
Reginald McKnight, *I Get on the Bus*, 1990
    Trying to avoid making decisions at home, a young man joins the Peace Corps and travels to Senegal, becoming involved in new intrigue.
Richard Perry, *Montgomery's Children*, 1984
    Tales of people living in a small town in central New York interwoven with magic and vision, incest and murder, friendship and sacrifice.

462

JOHN A. WILLIAMS, African American

Mothersill and the Foxes
(New York: Doubleday, 1975)

Subject(s): Interpersonal Relations; Behavior; Responsibility
Age range(s): Adult
Major character(s): Odell Mothersill, Social Worker, African American
Time period(s): 1950s; 1960s (1967)
Locale(s): New York, New York

Summary: The sexual exploits began early in Odell's life, with his babysitter and his sister. By fifteen he had found the first love of his life Jennifer Randolph. Now a young man of twenty-five, Odell lives in New York, works as a social worker, and his sexual conquests have not slowed. One of which, with a client's wife Elizabeth Cohen leaves her pregnant. In the process of his life Odell befriends a young woman when her two roommates are brutally murdered, falls in love with his sister's friend who attempts suicide, and for a time lives with a young woman who he learns years later is a lesbian. By age forty-two, an accomplished professional with a doctorate degree, Odell is recognized among the one hundred most eligible bachelors. Into his life comes 18-year-old Candace Cone and unknown to them she brings his past with her. Odell's life is on the line when his relationship with young Candace is revealed by his secretary.

Other books by the same author:
Jacob's Ladder, 1987
The Berhama Account, 1985
Click Song, 1982
Captain Blackman, 1972
One for New York, 1960 (debut novel later titled *The Angry Ones*)

Other books you might like:
Trey Ellis, *Home Repairs*, 1993
The coming-of-age exploits of a young man captured in his journal from ages 16-26 as he searches for love and finds success in his career.
Nelson George, *Urban Romance*, 1993
Contemporary relationship of a young male-female couple brought together by mutual friends experiencing love and heartbreak.
Charles Johnson, *Faith and the Good Thing*, 1974
The tale of a young woman who follows her mother's deathbed wish and goes in search of the good thing, and her ghost embodies a werewitch.
Julius Lester, *And All Our Wounds Forgiven*, 1994
The affair a renowned civil rights leader had with his white secretary is recalled by her when she visits his wife's sick bed.
Ntozake Shange, *Liliane: Resurrection of the Daughter*, 1994
In psychotherapy the exploits in a young woman's life reveal how she coped with family upheavals, romances and friendships, and racism and bigotry.

463

SHERLEY ANNE WILLIAMS, African American

Dessa Rose
(New York: William Morrow, 1986)

Subject(s): Race Relations; Interpersonal Relations; Slavery
Age range(s): Adult
Major character(s): Dessa Rose, Pregnant Teenager, Slave, African American; Ruth Elizabeth ''Rufel'' Sutton, Southern Belle, Revolutionary, Caucasian; Adam Nehemiah, Researcher, Journalist, Caucasian
Time period(s): 1840s (1847-1848)
Locale(s): Alabama (Marengo county)

Summary: Held captive in a cellar sweatbox, pregnant Dessa escapes when Harker, Nathan, and Cully return for her. Before the escape she was being interviewed by white journalist Adam, who was researching a book on slave uprisings and ways of better slave management. Dessa wonders why Rufel, the plantation owner's wife, allows them to hide out on the Sutton's farm. She is shocked and upset to later discover Nathan and Rufel having sex. Harker, has a scheme that will allow them to make enough money to escape West with the help of ''Rufel.'' Suspicious of Rufel Dessa goes along with the scheme and discovers new things about white wom en.

About this book: Debut novel.

Other books you might like:
Lorene Cary, *The Price of a Child*, 1995
Historical tale of a woman who literally walks from slavery to freedom under her slave owner's furious gaze in 1850s Philadelphia.
J. California Cooper, *Family*, 1991
A young girl's narrative of her life in the plantation South and events in the lives of her children by her slave owner's son and of her grandchildren.
Leon Forrest, *Two Wings to Veil My Face*, 1983
The Witherspoon family saga from the plantation South before the Civil War to contemporary times is completed in this last title in their trilogy.
Charles Johnson, *Oxherding Tale*, 1982
The coming-of-age tale of a light-skinned young man in the plantation South as he struggles to gain his freedom and that of those he loves.
Toni Morrison, *Beloved*, 1987
A mother who escaped slavery kills her baby to keep her former owner from stealing her, and is then haunted and consumed by the baby's ghost.

464

SHERLEY ANNE WILLIAMS, African American
CAROLE BYARD, Illustrator, African American

Working Cotton
(San Diego: Harcourt Brace Jovanovich, 1992)

Story type: Young Readers
Subject(s): Migrant Labor; Family Life
Age range(s): Grades 1-3
Major character(s): Shelan, Child, Sister, African American

Time period(s): Indeterminate Past
Locale(s): United States (rural)

Summary: In her family of migrant laborers young Shelan recounts their day working in a cotton field from sunup to sundown. She remembers the bus ride to the fields in the coldest of cold where people stand around open fires trying to get warm. As daybreak arrives her daddy, mamma, and her two older sisters, Jesmarie and Ruise, begin their work with Shelan and her baby sister Leanne close by along side them. Not yet big enough for her own sack of cotton, Shelan helps pile it in the row for her mamma's sack. After lunch, watching her older sisters, Shelan has thoughts of someday being able to pick cotton herself. As the day ends at sundown Shelan's hardworking, tired family heads toward the bus for home.

About this book: Debut (young readers).

Other books you might like:

Jan Spivey Gilchrist, *Indigo and Moonlight Gold*, 1993
Sharing special times with her mama a child remembers the story she told about girls growing up and things changing under a mama's watchful eye.

Angela Johnson, *The Leaving Morning*, 1992
The impressions of what the day was like for herself and her younger brother when their daddy and pregnant mama moved them away from their home.

Angela Johnson, *Tell Me a Story, Mama*, 1989
A little girl wanting her mama to tell her a story about when she was little has memorized the stories she's heard and tells them herself.

465

RITA WILLIAMS-GARCIA, African American

Blue Tights

(New York: E.P. Dutton Lodestar Books, 1988)

Story type: Young Adult
Subject(s): Dancing; Self-Confidence; Mothers and Daughters
Age range(s): Grades 7-10
Major character(s): Joyce Alicia Collins, 15-Year-Old, Bastard Daughter, Dancer
Time period(s): 1980s
Locale(s): New York, New York (Jamaica (Queens))

Summary: Born to a sixteen-year-old, unwed mother and raised by her maiden aunt, Joyce is now nearly that age. Her mother, Minnie, worries Joyce will make the same mistakes she did. Traveling the country to chase her dreams as a dancer, Minnie returned with a new stepfamily to reclaim her child and they became more like sisters than mother and daughter. Outraged when Joyce told her about the advances her new stepfather was making, Minnie nonetheless fled with her daughter. At school Joyce is the butt of her classmates jokes and is struggling to become a dancer as her mother once was. When she joins an independent dance class her talent soars and she lands the lead in an upcoming show. Attracted to the group's drummer, Joyce is upset when they have to separate but it does not crush her new self-confident spirit to be her own person.

About this book: Debut novel.

Where it's reviewed:
Dance, November 1993, page 81

Other books by the same author:
Like Sisters on the Homefront, 1994
Fast Talk on a Slow Track, 1991

Other books you might like:
Virginia Hamilton, *A Little Love*, 1984
A teenage girl has an emptiness food cannot fill: she misses her father, and in her search for him she finds new strengths in herself.

Vy Higginsen, *Mama, I Want to Sing*, 1995
Recounts events in the life of a talented singer from a young girl singing in the church choir to a renowned award winning star.

Walter Dean Myers, *Crystal*, 1987
On the brink of a promising career in modeling a 16-year-old realizes there is more than glamour to the industry and has to decide what path to choose.

Joyce Carol Thomas, *When the Nightingale Sings*, 1992
Despite her mean-spirited foster mother's attempts to demean her, a 14-year-old girl has a song to sing and a destiny to fulfill.

Brenda Wilkinson, *Ludell's New York Time*, 1980
Moving from Georgia to New York City in her senior year a teenager struggles to adjust to life in 1960s Harlem.

466

RITA WILLIAMS-GARCIA, African American

Fast Talk on a Slow Track

(New York: E.P. Dutton Lodestar Books, 1991)

Story type: Young Adult
Subject(s): Self-Perception; College Life; Interpersonal Relations
Age range(s): Grades 7-12
Major character(s): Dinizulu "Denzel" Watson, 18-Year-Old, Salesman, African American; Carmello "Mello", 18-Year-Old, Salesman, Latino
Time period(s): 1990s
Locale(s): New York, New York (Jamaica (Queens))

Summary: Valedictorian in high school, Denzel enters a summer program to get into Princeton. The program shows Denzel just how much he has to learn and his poor grades make him consider not returning in the fall. Once he gets back home following the program, "Denzel" eagerly returns to his summer job selling door-to-door and his fierce competition with rival Latino salesman Mello. A high volume salesman, 18-year-old Mello is also illiterate, an unwed father, and a drug user. Living in two different worlds, the two young men motivate one another until they reach a point of violence. Realizing how much he has going for himself Denzel reluctantly begins his freshman college life by deciding to return to Princeton. no

Where it's reviewed:
Booklist, February 15, 1993, page 1053

Awards the book has won:
Parents' Choice Award, 1991

Young Adult Library Services Association, Best Books for YAs, 1992

Other books by the same author:
Like Sisters on the Homefront, 1994
Blue Tights, 1988 (debut novel)

Other books you might like:
Vy Higginsen, *Mama, I Want to Sing*, 1995
Recounts events in the life of a talented singer from a young girl singing in the church choir to a renowned award winning star.
Walter Dean Myers, *Crystal*, 1987
On the brink of a promising career in modeling, a 16-year-old realizes there is more than glamour to the industry and has to decide what path to choose.
Walter Dean Myers, *Hoops*, 1981
A talented teenaged basketball player is befriended by a ex-pro player who became an alcoholic after his career ended in a gambling scandal.
Walter Dean Myers, *Motown and Didi: A Love Story*, 1984
Each dreaming of making a better life for themselves, two teenagers meet when the young boy rescues the young girl from street hoodlums.
Valerie Wilson Wesley, *Where Do I Go From Here?*, 1993
Having trouble at a snooty mostly-white prep school, a teenager learns from another scholarship student she must make decision for her own life.

467

RITA WILLIAMS-GARCIA, African American

Like Sisters on the Homefront
(New York: E.P. Dutton Lodestar Books, 1994)

Story type: Young Adult
Subject(s): Family Relations; Cousins; Pregnancy
Age range(s): Grades 7-10
Major character(s): Gayle Whitaker, 14-Year-Old, Mother, Pregnant Teenager; Constance "Cookie" Gates, 16-Year-Old, Cousin, Singer
Time period(s): 1990s
Locale(s): New York, New York (Jamaica (Queens)); Columbus, Georgia

Summary: Already the unwed mother of a seven-month-old baby, 14-year-old Gayle has gotten pregnant again by a different boy. Her mother is outraged and immediately takes her to a clinic for an abortion. Returning home her mother packs Gayle's bags and sends her and her baby to live with relatives in Georgia. Streetwise Gayle is none too happy with her country relatives, especially her minister uncle and his religious daughter "Cookie." In addition to being responsible for taking care of her baby, Gayle now has various chores to do, including caring for her dying grandmother. Although Gayle and "Cookie" see life differently they are able to forge a friendship until "Cookie" is swept away by a young college man and Gayle gets revenge on her. When the oral family history is passed on to Gayle from her grandmother's death-bed she develops a new sense of self and keeps "Cookie" from possibly making the same mistake she had.

Where it's reviewed:
Booklist, September 1, 1995, page 75
Publishers Weekly, July 31, 1995, page 82

Awards the book has won:
Coretta Scott King Honor Book, 1996

Other books by the same author:
Fast Talk on a Slow Track, 1991
Blue Tights, 1988 (debut novel)

Other books you might like:
Sharon M. Draper, *Tears of a Tiger*, 1994
A teenager escaping a car accident in which his friend is killed and others are injured has difficulty learning to live with the trauma.
Virginia Hamilton, *Sweet Whispers, Brother Rush*, 1982
A girl caring for her retarded older brother encounters the ghost of her dead uncle and comes to a deeper understanding of her family and herself.
Walter Dean Myers, *Won't Know Till I Get There*, 1982
The summer exploits of a 14-year-old whose parents decide to adopt a youngster with a juvenile record and the boys get arrested together.
Brenda Wilkinson, *Ludell's New York Time*, 1980
Moving from Georgia to New York City in her senior year a teenager struggles to adjust to life in 1960s Harlem.
Jacqueline Woodson, *The Dear One*, 1991
Outraged when her mother announces they're taking in a close friend's unwed, pregnant teenaged daughter a 12-year-old becomes the baby's namesake.

468

JOHNNIECE MARSHALL WILSON, African American

Oh, Brother
(New York: Scholastic Inc., 1988)

Subject(s): Brothers; Family Life
Age range(s): Grades 5-8
Major character(s): Alexander Walker, 6th Grader, Brother, African American; Andrew Walker, 6th Grader, Brother, African American
Time period(s): 1980s
Locale(s): United States (unidentified city)

Summary: Since their little sister Bonnie was born, Alex and his older brother Andrew have shared a room. Alex has just a small space that he keeps very neat, while Andrew's side of the room looks like a disaster. Add to that the fact that Andrew keeps taking Alex's bike without asking and disappearing for hours, even though Alex needs it for his paper route. Then the bike is stolen, and it is all Andrew's fault. No matter what Andrew does to try to make up, Alex stays angry with him. When a fire breaks out across the street, Alex saves the day, putting his differences with his brother behind him.

About this book: Debut novel

Where it's reviewed:
Christian Science Monitor, February 22, 1988, page 26
Kirkus Reviews, December 15, 1987, page 1740
Publishers Weekly, January 20, 1989, page 150
School Library Journal, March 1988, page 201

Other books by the same author:
Poor Girl, Rich Girl, 1992
Robin on His Own, 1990

Other books you might like:
Jacqueline Turner Banks, *Egg-Drop Blues*, 1995
  A sixth grader's science grade is low because of his dyslexia, so he and his twin brother enter a competition for extra credit.
Jacqueline Turner Banks, *The New One*, 1994
  Twin brothers disagree about whether to befriend a new girl at school or interfere with their mother's relationship with her boyfriend.
Mildred D. Taylor, *The Well: David's Story*, 1995
  Episode of the boyhood of two brothers from an early generation of the Logan family in rural Mississippi, where they face racial bigotry.

469

JOHNNIECE MARSHALL WILSON, African American

Poor Girl, Rich Girl
(New York: Scholastic Inc., 1992)

Subject(s): Family Relations; Money; Work
Age range(s): Grades 5-9
Major character(s): Miranda Moses, 14-Year-Old, Student, African American
Time period(s): 1990s
Locale(s): Monroeville

Summary: Miranda wants a pair of contact lenses to replace her big glasses, but her parents say they don't have the money. So Miranda decides to get a summer job to pay for them herself. She babysits for troublesome twin boys, goes to the wilderness as a camp counselor, works as a grocery clerk and finally starts her own business to achieve her goal.

Where it's reviewed:
Booklist, August 1992, page 2014
Kirkus Reviews, May 15, 1992, page 676
Publishers Weekly, March 16, 1992, page 80
School Library Journal, April 1992, page 126

Other books by the same author:
Robin on His Own, 1990
Oh, Brother, 1988 (debut novel)

Other books you might like:
Mildred Pitts Walter, *Lillie of Watts Takes a Giant Step*, 1971
  A girl faces a series of crises going to junior high school for the first time but finds a new friend, new heroes and a new pride in herself.
Mildred Pitts Walter, *Mariah Keeps Cool*, 1990
  A girl trains for a diving competition, tries to figure out her half-sister and plans a surprise for her sister.
Brenda Wilkinson, *Ludell*, 1975
  Events in the life of a young girl raised by her strict grandmother as she comes of age and falls in love for the first time.

470

JOHNNIECE MARSHALL WILSON, African American

Robin on His Own
(New York: Scholastic Inc., 1990)

Subject(s): Death; Growing Up; Mothers and Sons
Age range(s): Grades 4-6
Major character(s): Robin Lazarus, Student, African American; Mr. Lazrus, Teacher, Musician, African American
Time period(s): 1990s
Locale(s): Pennsylvania

Summary: Since his mother's death, Robin's Aunt Belle has stayed with him and his father, watching out for Robin when his father goes to play with his jazz band. Even though Robin has lots of friends and a cat and a parakeet, he is still lonely for his mother. Now Aunt Belle is getting married and will be moving away, and Robin is afraid his father is going to sell their house and move them to an apartment. Left all alone one night, Robin decides to take matters into his own hands.

Where it's reviewed:
Booklist, October 15, 1990, page 443
Kirkus Reviews, September 15, 1990, page 1331
School Library Journal, January 1991, page 97

Other books by the same author:
Poor Girl, Rich Girl, 1992
Oh, Brother, 1988 (debut novel)

Other books you might like:
Candy Dawson Boyd, *Chevrolet Saturdays*, 1993
  Struggling with the divorce of his parents and accepting his new stepfather, a young boy has trouble in school and makes mistakes he regrets.
Christopher Paul Curtis, *The Watsons Go to Birmingham—1963*, 1995
  The ordinary interactions and everyday hijinks of the "weird" Watsons are drastically changed when they visit Grandma in 1960s Alabama.
Virginia Hamilton, *Junius over Far*, 1985
  When his grandfather returns to his Caribbean island home, a disturbing letter prompts a young boy and his father to journey to rescue him.
Virginia Hamilton, *M.C. Higgins, the Great*, 1974
  A boy sits atop a 40-foot pole outside his house and dreams of leaving the mountain where his family has been for generations.
Dori Sanders, *Clover*, 1990
  When her father is killed on his wedding day to a white woman, a 10-year-old has to deal with the trauma of her loss and adjust to a new stepmother.

471

JACQUELINE WOODSON, African American

Autobiography of a Family Photo
(New York: Dutton, 1995)

Story type: Young Adult
Subject(s): City Life; Coming of Age; Family Relations
Age range(s): Adult

African American Titles

Major character(s): Narrator, Teenager, Sister, African American

Time period(s): 1960s; 1970s (1966-1979)

Locale(s): New York, New York (Brooklyn)

Summary: The voice of a nameless young girl recounts episodes in her city life. She grows up with a gay older brother and a half-white baby brother. As she makes sexual discoveries, she questions her own sexuality and resolves to find her own place in the world.

Where it's reviewed:

Ms., November 1994, page 77

New York Times Book Review, February 26, 1995, page 14

Publishers Weekly, December 12, 1994, page 48

Other books you might like:

April Sinclair, *Coffee Will Make You Black*, 1995
   This coming-of-age story is about a young girl in Chicago during the 1960s. She questions her sexuality when she recognizes her feelings for the school nurse.

Alice Childress, *Rainbow Jordan*, 1981
   Examines the pressures in the life of a 14-year-old when her mother leaves her to foster care and her boyfriend expects her to have sex with him.

Walter Dean Myers, *Crystal*, 1987
   On the brink of a promising career in modeling, a 16-year-old realizes there is more than glamour to the industry and has to decide which path to choose.

Charlotte Sherman, *One Dark Body*, 1993
   Incidents in the life of a young girl abandoned at birth dealing with the return of her mother and her friend's entry into manhood.

Joyce Carol Thomas, *Marked by Fire*, 1982
   Friends and family help a young girl overcome the effects of a tornado and a physical assault which nearly breaks her will.

472

JACQUELINE WOODSON, African American

Between Madison & Palmetto

(New York: Delacorte Press, 1993)

Story type: Young Readers

Series: Maizon and Margaret

Subject(s): Friendship; Fathers and Daughters; Interpersonal Relations

Age range(s): Grades 5 and Up

Major character(s): Maizon Singh, 13-Year-Old, 8th Grader, Writer; Margaret Tory, 13-Year-Old, 8th Grader, Sister; Caroline Berg, 13-Year-Old, 8th Grader, Caucasian

Time period(s): 1990s

Locale(s): New York, New York

Summary: A year has passed since Maizon returned from boarding school reuniting with her best friend Margaret. Now attending private school together the girls are experiencing a lot of changes. Changes in their relationship, their bodies, their neighborhood, and their families. Margaret is still adjusting to the death and loss of her father, while Maizon is faced with having to adjust to the return of the father who left her to be raised and adopted by her grandmother when her mother died. While also adjusting to her new feelings for a neighborhood boy and her baby brother's ability to see things, Margaret has a bout with dangerous dieting. Maizon fears for Margaret when she discovers she has been throwing up her food and pleads with her to change.

About this book: Sequel to *Maizon At Blue Hill*.

Where it's reviewed:

Booklist, May 1, 1995, page 1574

Kirkus Reviews, December 1, 1993, page 1532

Publishers Weekly, November 8, 1993, page 28

School Library Journal, November 1993, page 111

Voice of Youth Advocates, June 1994, page 75

Other books by the same author:

I Hadn't Meant to Tell You This, 1994 (Young Readers)

Maizon at Blue Hill, 1992 (sequel; Young Readers)

Last Summer with Maizon, 1990 (debut novel; Young Readers)

Other books you might like:

Jacqueline Turner Banks, *The New One*, 1994
   Twin brothers disagree about whether to befriend a new girl at school or interfere with their mother's relationship with her boyfriend.

Candy Dawson Boyd, *Breadsticks and Blessing Places*, 1985
   Three sixth-grade girlfriends are involved in their regular routine of activities when one is killed and the others cope with her untimely death.

Virginia Hamilton, *Cousins*, 1990
   Concerned that her grandmother might die, a young girl is unprepared for the death of another relative.

Joyce Hansen, *Yellow Bird and Me*, 1986
   Missing her best friend who has moved away, a young girl helps a classmate in elementary school overcome stage fright and discover he has dyslexia.

Eleanora E. Tate, *Just an Overnight Guest*, 1980
   A young girl and her older sister are surprised when their mother takes in a baby whose mother is said to be poor white trash.

473

JACQUELINE WOODSON, African American

The Dear One

(New York: Delacorte Press, 1991)

Story type: Young Adult

Subject(s): Unmarried Mothers; Mothers and Daughters; Friendship

Age range(s): Grades 7-10

Major character(s): Afeni ''Feni'' Harris, Child of an Alcoholic, Child of Divorced Parents, African American; Rebecca, 15-Year-Old, Pregnant Teenager, African American

Time period(s): 1990s

Locale(s): Seton, Pennsylvania

Summary: When her mother wants to take in Rebecca, the unwed, pregnant, teenaged daughter of a college friend, ''Feni'' is outraged. Arriving from Harlem, Rebecca moves into ''Feni's'' room and after a bumpy start the two girls become friends. Meanwhile, Feni is dealing with her parents'

divorce, her father's remarriage, and her mother's alcoholism, while learning about her mother's friends.

Where it's reviewed:
English Journal, November 1993, page 80
Publishers Weekly, January 4, 1993, page 74

Other books by the same author:
From the Notebooks of Melanin Sun, 1995 (young adult)
Last Summer with Maizon, 1990 (debut novel; Young Readers)

Other books you might like:
Virginia Hamilton, *A Little Love*, 1984
A teenage girl has an emptiness food cannot fill: she misses her father. In her search for him she finds new strengths in hersself.
Angela Johnson, *Toning the Sweep*, 1993
A young girl prepares a special gift for her dying grandmother and honors the spirit of the deceased grandfather she never knew.
Mildred D. Taylor, *The Road to Memphis*, 1990
Another incident from the lives of the Logan family in segregated Mississippi where racial hostilities erupt and new relationships unfold.
Brenda Wilkinson, *Definitely Cool*, 1993
At a new school in an upscale neighborhood a youngster discovers her new friends would rather be ''cool'' than study, and end up breaking the rules.
Rita Williams-Garcia, *Like Sisters on the Homefront*, 1994
An unwed, 14-year-old mother, again pregnant, has an abortion. When she is sent to her relatives in the South she develops a new sense of family and self.

474

JACQUELINE WOODSON, African American

From the Notebooks of Melanin Sun
(New York: Blue Sky Press Scholastic Inc., 1995)

Story type: Young Adult
Subject(s): Mothers and Sons; Homosexuality/Lesbianism; Prejudice
Age range(s): Grades 7-12
Major character(s): Melanin ''Mel'' Sun, 13-Year-Old, Writer, African American; Encanta ''EC'' Cedar, Lesbian, Student, African American; Kristin, Lawyer, Lesbian, Caucasian
Time period(s): 1990s
Locale(s): New York, New York (Brooklyn)

Summary: Mel and his mother, a law student, were very close until the day she turned his world upside down, telling him she was in love with a white woman, Kristin. Outraged by his mother's news and fearful his friends and neighbors will find out, the boy isolates himself from EC while continuing to write events of his life in his notebooks. After weeks of little conversation between them, EC pleads with Mel to spend the day with her and Kristin to try and get to know her. Reluctantly Mel agrees in the hope that afterwards EC will stop bringing Kristin around and life can go back to normal.

Where it's reviewed:
Booklist, April 15, 1995, page 1994

Publishers Weekly, May 15, 1995, page 74
School Library Journal, August 1995, page 158
New York Times Book Review, February 26, 1995, page 14
Kirkus Reviews, October 1, 1994, page 1307

Awards the book has won:
Coretta Scott King Honor Book, 1996
Lambda Literary Award, Children's/Young Adult, 1996

Other books by the same author:
The Dear One, 1991 (young adult)
Last Summer with Maizon, 1990 (debut novel; young readers)

Other books you might like:
Sharon M. Draper, *Tears of a Tiger*, 1994
A teenager escapes a car accident in which his friend is killed and others are injured. He then has difficulty learning to live with the trauma.
Walter Dean Myers, *Fallen Angels*, 1988
The life-changing experiences of a 17-year-old high school graduate who enlists in the Army and serves in Vietnam.
Walter Dean Myers, *Hoops*, 1981
A talented teenaged basketball player is befriended by a ex-pro player who became an alcoholic after his career ended in a gambling scandal.
Walter Dean Myers, *Scorpions*, 1988
A gun changes the lives of a young boy and his Puerto Rican friend when they are forced into being involved with a street gang.
Joyce Carol Thomas, *Marked by Fire*, 1982
Friends and family help a young girl to overcome the effects of a tornado and a physical assault which nearly breaks her will.

475

JACQUELINE WOODSON, African American

I Hadn't Meant to Tell You This
(New York: Delacorte Press, 1994)

Subject(s): Child Abuse; Fathers and Daughters; Friendship
Age range(s): Grades 7-12
Major character(s): Marie Victoria, 12-Year-Old, 8th Grader; Elena ''Lena'' Cecilia Bright, 12-Year-Old, Sister, Caucasian
Time period(s): 1990s
Locale(s): Chauncey, Ohio

Summary: Now transformed into an exclusive suburb, once Marie's town had been an all white, poor coal-mining community. Some of the poor whites have begun moving back to the community and Marie is drawn to one when she comes to her class. The other students tease Marie when she hangs around the new white girl ''Lena.'' Soon the two girls discover they have something in common, they both have no mother—''Lena's'' died of breast cancer and Marie's just walked away from the family. Little by little the girls come to share their lives with one another. Swearing Marie to secrecy, ''Lena'' reveals her father has been molesting her and she fears for her younger sister. Marie is at a loss about what to do for ''Lena'' and her younger sister and she becomes even more concerned when ''Lena'' talks of them leaving.

Where it's reviewed:
Essence, February 1995, page 52
Publishers Weekly, November 7, 1994, page 44
New York Times Book Review, November 6, 1994, page 32
Booklist, April 1, 1995, page 1404
Lambda Book Report, September 1994, page 45

Awards the book has won:
Coretta Scott King Honor Book, 1995

Other books by the same author:
Between Madison & Palmetto, 1993 (young readers)
Maizon at Blue Hill, 1992 (sequel; young readers)
Last Summer with Maizon, 1990 (debut novel; young readers)

Other books you might like:
Angela Johnson, *Humming Whispers*, 1995
    Recounts the life of a young girl living with an older sister who has schizophrenia and her fear that she too may have the mental illness.
Eleanora E. Tate, *A Blessing in Disguise*, 1995
    Another tale from the Calvary County trilogy where a young girl discovers that the father she admired has addicted her dying mother to alcohol and drugs.
Eleanora E. Tate, *Just an Overnight Guest*, 1980
    A young girl and her older sister are surprised when their mother takes in a baby whose mother is said to be poor white trash.

476

JACQUELINE WOODSON, African American

Last Summer with Maizon
(New York: Delacorte Press, 1990)

Story type: Young Readers
Series: Maizon and Margaret
Subject(s): Friendship; Death; Change
Age range(s): Grades 5 and Up
Major character(s): Maizon Singh, 11-Year-Old, 6th Grader, Abandoned Child; Margaret Tory, 11-Year-Old, 6th Grader, Sister
Time period(s): 1990s
Locale(s): New York, New York (Brooklyn)

Summary: No stranger to losing a parent, Maizon's mother died giving birth to her and she was abandoned by her father who left her to be raised by her Cheyenne grandmother. Now she is at the side of her best friend, Margaret, who suffers the loss of her father from a heart attack. The girls soon suffer another loss when Maizon is accepted into an out-of-town boarding school, leaving Margaret behind with her baby brother and grieving mother. Saddened by her summer of loss, Margaret writes a prize-winning school poem and starts having an interest in a classmate basketball player. When Maizon calls to say she is coming home, Margaret couldn't be happier and is surprised to discover her baby brother has their neighbor's gift of seeing things before they happen.

About this book: Debut novel (juvenile).

Other books by the same author:
I Hadn't Meant to Tell You This, 1994 (Young Readers)
Between Madison & Palmetto, 1993 (Young Readers)
Maizon at Blue Hill, 1992 (sequel; Young Readers)

Other books you might like:
Candy Dawson Boyd, *Breadsticks and Blessing Places*, 1985
    Three sixth-grade girlfriends are involved in their regular routine of activities when one is killed and the others cope with her untimely death.
Virginia Hamilton, *Cousins*, 1990
    Concerned that her grandmother might die, a young girl is unprepared for the death of another relative.
Joyce Hansen, *The Gift Giver*, 1980
    A young girl and her fifth grade friends come to like a new boy in their class and are surprised when they discover he is a foster child.
Ethel Footman Smothers, *Moriah's Pond*, 1995
    A continuation of events from the lives of the Footman family when three sisters spend a summer with their great-grandmother.
Mildred Pitts Walter, *Mariah Keeps Cool*, 1990
    A girl trains for a diving competition, tries to figure out her half-sister and plans a surprise for her sister.

477

JACQUELINE WOODSON, African American

Maizon at Blue Hill
(New York: Delacorte Press, 1992)

Story type: Young Readers
Series: Maizon and Margaret
Subject(s): Gifted Children; Schools; Self-Confidence
Age range(s): Grades 5 and Up
Major character(s): Maizon Singh, 11-Year-Old, 7th Grader
Time period(s): 1990s
Locale(s): Canton, Connecticut

Summary: In this continuation of two girls' friendship, academically gifted Maizon has won a scholarship to predominately white Blue Hill, a Connecticut boarding school. Leaving her family and best friend Margaret behind in Brooklyn, she journeys away from home for the first time. Maizon writes Margaret letters about her feelings being at Blue Hill but never mails them. She worries of not really fitting in, of dealing with racism and elitism, and missing her family and friends. Earning excellent grades and liked by her teachers, Maizon continues to feel isolated and unhappy until she calls Margaret to say she is coming home. Somewhat sad to leave Blue Hill, a self-confident Maizon knows she must keep looking for her place of belonging.

Where it's reviewed:
Language Arts, March 1994, page 218
Booklist, February 15, 1993, page 1053
School Library Journal, November 1992, page 99
Voice of Youth Advocates, October 1992, page 235

Awards the book has won:
Young Adult Library Services Association, Best Books for YAs, 1993

Other books by the same author:
I Hadn't Meant to Tell You This, 1994 (Young Readers)
Between Madison & Palmetto, 1993 (Young Readers)
Last Summer with Maizon, 1990 (debut novel; Young Readers)

Other books you might like:

Jacqueline Turner Banks, *The New One*, 1994
 Twin brothers disagree about whether to befriend a new
 girl at school or interfere with their mother's relationship
 with her boyfriend.
Candy Dawson Boyd, *Breadsticks and Blessing Places*, 1985
 Three sixth-grade girlfriends are involved in their regular
 routine of activities when one is killed and the others cope
 with her untimely death.
Virginia Hamilton, *Cousins*, 1990
 Concerned that her grandmother might die, a young girl is
 unprepared for the death of another relative.
Vaunda Micheaux Nelson, *Mayfield Crossing*, 1993
 The new kids at an elementary school encounter prejudice
 for the first time and only baseball has the possibility for
 drawing people together.
Andrea Davis Pinkney, *Hold Fast to Dreams*, 1995
 Two sisters endure prejudice when their family moves to
 the suburbs and they have to attend separate all-white
 schools and try to fit in.

478

SHARON DENNIS WYETH, African American
RAUL COLON, Illustrator

Always My Dad

(New York: Alfred A. Knopf, 1995)

Story type: Young Readers
Subject(s): Fathers and Daughters; Family Relations; Country
 Life
Age range(s): Grades 1-3
Major character(s): Unnamed Character, Child, Sister, Afri-
 can American
Time period(s): Indeterminate Past
Locale(s): United States (rural)

Summary: An unnamed young girl spends a happy summer in
the country with her father and grandparents. Then Daddy
announces he's leaving soon, explaining he has a new job
driving a truck cross-country. He says that no matter where he
is he's always her dad. Back home in the city with her mom,
the young girl often dreams of standing in the field with her
dad under a sweet-potato-colored moon.

Other books by the same author:
The World of Daughter McGuire, 1995
Chicken Pox Party, 1990 (Annie K. series)
No Creeps Need Apply, 1989 (Pen Pals 4)

Other books you might like:
Jeannette Franklin Caines, *Daddy*, 1977
 Saturdays are special for a child when her father comes to
 get her to visit with him and they share laughs and fun
 together all day.
Valerie Flournoy, *The Best Time of Day*, 1978
 A child with a busy day of activities ahead with his mom,
 babysitter, friends, and relatives, looks forward to his
 daddy getting home from work.
Eloise Greenfield, *First Pink Light*, 1976
 A child wants to stay awake until his daddy comes home so
 he can hide and surprise him but falls asleep waiting in a
 chair and daddy takes him to bed.

Dolores Johnson, *Papa's Stories*, 1994
 Enjoying the stories her papa tells from her books a kindergartner says she'll teach him to read when she discovers he
 doesn't know how.
Ianthe Thomas, *Willie Blows a Mean Horn*, 1981
 Proud of his jazz musician papa a young boy spends
 special times with him at the club where he plays and
 thinks of becoming a musician like his papa.

479

SHARON DENNIS WYETH, African American

The World of Daughter McGuire

(New York, Delacorte Press, 1994)

Story type: Young Readers
Subject(s): Identity; Prejudice; Family Relations
Age range(s): Grades 4 and Up
Major character(s): Daughter McGuire, 11-Year-Old, Sister
 (oldest), African American (from interracial parents);
 Connie Boggs, 11-Year-Old, Child of Divorced Parents,
 African American; Anna Otake, 11-Year-Old, Japanese
 American
Time period(s): 1990s
Locale(s): Washington, District of Columbia

Summary: Moving to a new city and starting at a new elementary school, Daughter becomes friends with Connie and her
Japanese friend Anna. They decide to start a secret club called
the Explorers like the boys' club called the Avengers. One of
the Avengers, Joey, throws a rock at Daughter and calls her a
"zebra" because her parents are interracial. Upset by the
incident Daughter begins to question who she and her younger brother Satch are and what they should call themselves.
Separated after her father loses his job, their parents seem on
the verge of divorce but, when Satch is hit by a car, things
change. Daughter learns how she got her special name from a
brave ancestor and is courageous enough to stand up to the
Avengers when they turn on Joey, who she learns is also from
a mixed family.

Other books you might like:
Eloise Greenfield, *Talk about a Family*, 1978
 Distraught about her parent's breaking up a youngster
 comes to realize how families differ and the importance of
 her younger sister and older brothers.
Virginia Hamilton, *Arilla Sun Down*, 1976
 An interracial 12-year-old feels she doesn't fit in; she
 "earns" an identity all her own and her family comes to
 grips with its collective past.
Vaunda Micheaux Nelson, *Mayfield Crossing*, 1993
 The new kids at an elementary school encounter prejudice
 for the first time and only baseball has the possibility for
 drawing people together.
Dori Sanders, *Clover*, 1990
 When her father is killed on his wedding day to a white
 woman a 10-year-old has to deal with the trauma of her
 loss and adjust to a new stepmother.
Jacqueline Woodson, *Maizon at Blue Hill*, 1992
 Another episode in the lives of two young seventh grade
 friends where one girl wins an academic scholarship to a
 white boarding school.

480

CAMILLE YARBROUGH, African American

The Shimmershine Queens

(New York: G.P. Putnam's Sons, 1989)

Subject(s): Family Problems; School Life; Self-Perception
Age range(s): Grades 4-7
Major character(s): Angie Peterson, 10-Year-Old, Student, African American
Time period(s): 1980s
Locale(s): New York, New York

Summary: Angie worries that her mother is sick all the time, and that perhaps her father doesn't love her since he has moved away. The kids at school call her ugly because she is dark-skinned. But every day after school she has her dreaming time, when she can do anything and be anything she wants, where she helps people and is a winner. When a new teacher comes to her school, Angie gets to be the lead in a play about African children and learns to stand up for herself and make her own dreams come true.

Where it's reviewed:
Booklist, February 1, 1990, page 1099
Essence, August 1989, page 98
Publishers Weekly, June 29, 1990, page 104

Other books by the same author:
The Little Tree Growin' in the Shade, 1996

Other books you might like:
Eloise Greenfield, *Koya Delaney and the Good Girl Blues*, 1992
    A sixth grader caught in the middle when her best friend and her sister have a fight struggles with mixed emotions and knowing who her real friends are.
Emily Moore, *Something to Count On*, 1980
    A 10-year-old girl always in trouble at school thinks her father doesn't love her when he keeps breaking his promises.
Mildred Pitts Walter, *Lillie of Watts Takes a Giant Step*, 1971
    A girl faces a series of crises going to junior high school for the first time but finds a new friend, new heroes and a new pride in herself.

481

AL YOUNG, African American

Seduction by Light

(New York: Dell Publishing, 1988)

Subject(s): Death; Extrasensory Perception; Love
Age range(s): Adult
Major character(s): Mamie Franklin, Maintenance Worker, Psychic, African American; Burley Cole, Husband, Invalid, African American
Time period(s): 1980s
Locale(s): Santa Monica, California

Summary: Mamie, who was famous in the 1950s for playing domestics in Hollywood films, knows her days are numbered. Ironically, she is now a housekeeper for an eccentric white couple in Beverly Hills. She has always had some psychic powers and now, hovering between life and death in a hospital after an earthquake, she travels out-of-her body to take care of unresolved family business, sharing with us her wry observations of life and humanity until her spirit swims into the light.

Other books by the same author:
Ask Me Now, 1980
Sitting Pretty, 1976
Who Is Angelina?, 1975
Snakes, 1970 (debut novel)

Other books you might like:
Tananarive Due, *The Between*, 1995
    A man endures nightmares and a wavering sense of reality as he desperately tries to protect his family from the psychotic who stalks them.
Helen Elaine Lee, *The Serpent's Gift*, 1994
    Children and grandchildren of two intertwined families endure hardship and triumph as they help each other remember a history beyond their knowing.
Gloria Naylor, *Mama Day*, 1988
    Returning to her sea island home, a young woman finds both body and soul threatened by supernatural forces from which she is barely saved by Mama Day.

482

AL YOUNG, African American

Sitting Pretty

(New York: Holt, Rinehart and Winston, 1976)

Subject(s): Conduct of Life; Interpersonal Relations
Age range(s): Adult
Major character(s): Sidney ''Sitting Pretty'' Prettymon, Divorced Person, Father
Time period(s): 1970s
Locale(s): San Francisco, California

Summary: Sitting Pretty likes to listen to the talk shows on KRZY and call in to offer his point of view. He has called so often, in fact, that the staff know his name and he receives fan mail from other listeners. He lives in a hotel on the San Francisco peninsula, not far from his ex-wife and their grown children. He is in touch with them from time to time, visiting his grandchildren and going to his daughter's house for dinner. He is different from his children in regards to his lifestyle—his children are motivated, fast track people while he is quite the opposite. When the radio station hires him to do some television commercials, Sit becomes somewhat of a celebrity. Good news or bad, Sitting Pretty rolls with the punches, sharing his wry observations along the way.

Other books by the same author:
Seduction by Light, 1988
Bodies and Soul, 1981
Ask Me Now, 1980
Who Is Angelina?, 1975
Snakes, 1970 (debut novel, young adults)

Other books you might like:
Clarence Major, *Such Was the Season*, 1987
    A family matriarch shares her keen and humorous insights as her family becomes involved in family history, politics and conspiracy.

Dori Sanders, *Her Own Place*, 1993
Remembrances of exploits in a senior citizen's life of daughter, wife, mother, and grandmother from before WWII to contemporary times.

483

AL YOUNG, African American

Snakes

(New York: Holt, Rinehart and Winston, 1970)

Subject(s): Coming of Age; Musicians; Drugs
Major character(s): MC Moore, 17-Year-Old, Musician, African American
Time period(s): 1960s
Locale(s): Detroit, Michigan

Summary: MC lives with his grandmother in Detroit, going to high school, playing the guitar and composing his own songs. He and his drummer friend, Shakes, form a jazz/blues band that they call the Masters of Ceremony. Champ, another friend of MC's, encourages them in their exploration of a new sound and gets them into clubs to hear other musicians. After the band competes on a TV talent show and wins, they cut a record which becomes a hit and begin to get a lot of local gigs. As time passes they seldom see Champ, who is living a fast life and using drugs. After graduation the band begins to scatter, and MC leaves his friends and his girl and heads to New York with his guitar.

About this book: Debut novel.

Other books by the same author:
Seduction by Light, 1988 (adult)
Bodies and Soul, 1981
Ask Me Now, 1980
Sitting Pretty, 1976
Who Is Angelina?, 1975

Other books you might like:
David Haynes, *Right by My Side*, 1993
A high school student writes down his experiences in order to figure things out about his father, his mother and himself.
Vy Higginsen, *Mama, I Want to Sing*, 1995
Recounts events in the life of a talented singer, from a young girl singing in the church choir to a renowned award winning star.
Kristin Hunter, *Lou in the Limelight*, 1981
Continuation of the story of a young girl and her friends who form a singing group once they get a hit record and go on their first tour.

484

AL YOUNG, African American

Who Is Angelina?

(New York: Holt, Rinehart and Winston, 1975)

Subject(s): Conduct of Life; Growing Up; Human Behavior

Age range(s): Adult
Major character(s): Angelina Green, Teacher, African American
Time period(s): 1960s
Locale(s): Berkeley, California; Mexico City, Mexico; Detroit, Michigan

Summary: Between teaching jobs and recovering from a broken relationship, Angelina numbs her pain with parties, wine, and dope. But when her apartment is robbed, she decides to take a break and get herself together, borrowing money to go to Mexico for a while. There she meets Watusi, an unpredictable and mysterious American who has an import-export business and with whom she shares a passionate affair. Learning that her father has been hospitalized, she leaves Mexico for her home town of Detroit to be with him. He has been robbed and shot in the now-dangerous neighborhood where Angelina grew up. As he recovers, Angelina examines her roots, decides to quit drinking and smoking and teaches herself to meditate. Soon she discovers she does not need or want to numb herself from life, and returns to Berkeley to start a new teaching job. Watusi appears on her doorstep one day and recounts his adventures in her absence. They share a lovely evening together and Angelina makes a decision that will change her life, feeling for the first time, totally in charge.

About this book: Debut novel for adults.

Other books by the same author:
Seduction by Light, 1988
Ask Me Now, 1980
Sitting Pretty, 1976
Snakes, 1970 (debut novel for young adults)

Other books you might like:
Rita Dove, *Through the Ivory Gate*, 1992
The coming-of-age for a young woman who returns to her home after many years where an unspoken family secret is revealed to her.
Grace Edwards-Yearwood, *In the Shadow of the Peacock*, 1988
A young girl strikes out on her own, in spite of her mother's fears, discovering her own voice, her own love and her part in the struggle for civil rights.
Marita Golden, *A Woman's Place*, 1986
Episodes from the evolving lives of three college roommates searching for their place in the world, and the men they become involved with.
Cherry Muhanji, *Her*, 1990
A young light-skinned woman falls into "the life" of 1950s Detroit and finds a strength in herself and the women around her necessary to her survival.
Ntozake Shange, *Liliane: Resurrection of the Daughter*, 1994
In psychotherapy the exploits in a young woman's life reveal how she coped with family upheavals, romances and friendships, and racism and bigotry.
Alice Walker, *Meridian*, 1976
A deserted mother at seventeen, a young girl gets involved in the civil rights movement which changes her life and defines her role in the world.

Latino Literature

The literary tradition of Latino literature comes from a Spanish language and cultural heritage, and, of course, a colonial heritage, but it is a Spanish heritage none-the-less. It is a very long tradition that dates back to the sixteenth century.

From the early autobiographical and adventure journals of Alvar Núñez Cabeza de Vaca published as *La Relación* in 1542, Pedro de Castañeda's *Relación de la journada de 1540*, and Juan de Oñate's *Proclamación* in 1598, and other writings from Cuba, Texas, California, and the Southwest in general, to the contemporary novels and essays of Rudolfo Anaya of New Mexico and Rosario Ferré of Puerto Rico, a tradition of Latino literature, written and oral, follows a continuum of 500 years. In fact what stands out prominently when one surveys the spectrum of Latino literature, is the continuing connectedness of contemporary autobiographical novels with a tradition established centuries ago by adventurers and immigrants coming to a new land. The impact of cultures colliding, meshing and syncretizing has been constant for 500 years and the human condition obligates that this experience be commemorated in some form. Contemporary Latino writers continue in theme, structure and language, to contemplate, probe and articulate this collective Hispanic heritage, while confronting the one issue that surfaces again and again; cultural survival.

Latino culture, represented in many forms in these novels, is a diverse culture differentiated from the dominant U.S. culture, sometimes subtly, sometimes disagreeably, but always vigorously. Not all Latinos in the U.S. are immigrants. In the Southwest, Latino roots go back to the 16th century, and Cuban, Dominican and Puerto Rican families have journeyed between the islands and the U.S. for over 100 years. Yet, the immigrant experience is still an important literary motif in Latino literature.

Since the mid-19th century, Latinos have been writing stories in English and in Spanish. Yet knowledge about the Latino presence in the U.S. has been almost non-existent, ignored, or misunderstood, causing the literature to be looked upon as a recent phenomenon, when in fact it is not. Although the burgeoning production of Latino novels, essays and short story and poetry collections, appearing in English has been extremely noticeable in recent years, the cultural heritage has always been a literate one, as can be seen by the publication of countless newspapers, in English and Spanish, throughout the country for the past one hundred and fifty years.

The social changes brought about by the Civil Rights Movement in the 1960s was a catalyst that inspired many Latinos to write, publish, and demand access to higher education opportunities. As more and more Latinos entered academia, both as students and later as professors, the study of a Hispanic body of literature became institutionalized and stimulated the creation of energetic literature by recent college-educated writers. The recent increase in the publication of novels, anthologies, and short story collections by a new generation of Latinos is a direct result of the struggles and achievements of the social movements of the 1960s, in conjunction with the influx of fresh immigration from Cuba, Central America, and South America. While a few Latino authors are published by large East Coast publishing houses, the majority of contemporary writers are being published by two main Latino publishers, Arte Público Press and The Bilingual Press. These two presses have contributed tremendously to the public and commercial exposure of the authors represented in this collection.

The development and publication of children's literature follows a similar track. While there have always been books published about Latinos for children and young adults, these tended to be written by non-Latinos and presented a romanticized pastoral view of how a Mexican, Puerto Rican, Cuban or Latin American was supposed to look and act. During the 1970s there was an interest and an increase in the publication of works for Latino children as bilingual curriculum material became more in demand, and this prompted many small presses to seek Latino authors. One such publisher, Children's Book Press, is a non-profit publisher that continues to publish quality books for children to this day. It has only been in recent years that we find a growing volume of books for children written by Latinos that deal with cultural issues relevant and important to Latino children. As more Latino publishing houses flourish, more authors are being published who want to write for the juvenile and young adult. Authors, such as Gary Soto, Nicolasa Mohr, Irene Beltrán Hernández, Judith Ortiz Cofer, and Gloria Velasquez are successfully producing works that present multi-dimensional Latino youth who are dealing with contemporary issues of relevancy to today's Latino young adults.

PUERTO RICAN LITERATURE

The literature, novels and short stories written by Puerto Rican authors reflect the complex cultural identity and social history of the Puerto Rican people, and almost always in relation to the U.S. In 1898 Puerto Rico became a possession of the United States as a result of the Spanish-American War, and in 1917 all Puerto Ricans became citizens of the U.S. Similar to the Spanish Americans of New Mexico, Texas, Arizona and California, these island Spanish-speaking people suddenly found themselves ruled by a government once looked upon as the enemy, with institutions totally foreign to those ingrained in the stable communities of the island, and with no knowledge of their language and culture. English was imposed in the public schools, and it was only in 1949 that Spanish was officially allowed to be the national language of the island. The turmoil of this period under U.S. domination is clearly reflected in the literature.

Puerto Rico had a poor agrarian economy that remained even after the take-over of the U.S. That didn't change at all until after World War II. In the 1940s and 1950s, great social changes occurred on the island—industrialization replaced farms and migration to New York jumped into the millions. To this day there are two Puerto Ricos. One is the island with Latin American cultural traditions and the other is the diffused Puerto Rican community throughout the U.S. with the largest concentration in New York, the Nuyoricans.

As in other parts of the New World, literary production was active in Puerto Rico during the 16th century. Published in 1535 was *Historia General y Natural de las Indias* by Gonzalo Fernández de Oviedo, and in 1690 *Los Infortunios de Alonso Ramírez* was published chronicling the exploits of a carpenter's son who left Puerto Rico at the age of thirteen and traveled the world. During the 19th century, literature production blossomed on the island, partly because of the increase in population from Spain and South America. Manuel Zeno-Gandía is considered to have written the first real novel, *La Charca*, published in 1890, that depicts the harsh rural life of the coffee plantations. In the first half of the 20th century writers were describing the society as "in crisis"; the author Enrique Laguerre, born in 1906, wrote best about this period. His novel *El Laberinto* = *The Labyrinth*, included in this collection, describes the situation of a man in New York who gets involved in the overthrow of a government.

Writers of the 20th century write from two very different cultural and geographical perspectives, depending on where they live; on the island of Puerto Rico or in urban New York. Those living in Puerto Rico can write in English or Spanish, while those living in the mainland write mostly in English. But regardless of the location of the writing, common themes and issues are represented by the authors because culturally they are all American Puerto Ricans. On the island, Spanish is the common language, but English is taught in the schools and many fear that American culture is overpowering the Latino culture. In the U.S., Puerto Ricans are looked upon as a racial underclass and most struggle to maintain a distinct cultural identity. One writer, René Marqués, expresses it this way:

> *This is a really schizophrenic*
> *society. Puerto Ricans have two*
> *languages, two citizenships,*
> *two basic philosophies of life, two*
> *flags, two anthems, two loyalties.*
> *It is very hard for human beings to*
> *deal with all this ambivalence.* [1]

Immigration to the mainland, primarily New York, increased dramatically in the 1950s, about 50,000 a year, and this experience prompted the creation of literature that dealt with the challenge of living in New York. Racial discrimination, unemployment, learning to cope in the streets, these were the social-cultural issues raised in short stories and novels by such writers as Pedro Juan Soto, René Marquéz and Emilio Díaz Valcárcel.

Just a decade later, writers were still writing about these same issues, but also about the question of identity and roots. Many of these writers are represented in this collection, such as Piri Thomas, Jesus Colón, and Nicolasa Mohr. In 1961, Jesus Colón published *A Puerto Rican in New York*, a book probably known by most Puerto Ricans as it describes the struggles and confrontations of a new immigrant in New York.

A new generation of Puerto Rican women writers, Judith Ortiz Cofer, Esmeralda Santiago, and Carmen de Monteflores in the U.S. and Rosario Ferré in Puerto Rico, write about women's oppression in a patriarchal society, but the concepts of identity, linguistic alienation, and cultural heritage continue to be primary concerns in their writings. The contributions of women writers to the overall body of Puerto Rican literature is complex. "They are documenting their own personal histories in light of the larger frame of reference of U.S. multiculturalism. They do not mythify the island of Puerto Rico, nor the past, but explore continuities and divergence's between their own family histories and their present as U.S. Latinas." [2]

Pura Belpré, is the best known writer of children's literature in Puerto Rico and in New York. She became a children's librarian in New York in 1921, the first Latina librarian in the New York Public Library, and she worked towards preserving the folktales and folklore of Puerto Rican culture. Her first book, *Perez and Martina: A Puerto Rican Folktale* was published in 1932 and was followed by many others, which can be found in this collection. Her book *Santiago* received a citation from the Brooklyn Arts Books for Children in 1973. Another well known writer of young adult literature is Nicolasa Mohr, whose book *Nilda*, received many awards. Both of these authors wrote to maintain and to highlight the significance of Puerto Rican culture for children and young adults.

CUBAN AMERICAN LITERATURE

Similar to Puerto Rican literature, Cuban American literature in the United States goes back to the 19th century when José Martí, residing in New York, plotted for Cuba's independence from Spain. Martí, and other Cuban, Dominican and Puerto Rican patriots wrote and published essays, stories and poems in one of the many Spanish language newspapers, such as *El Mensajero Semanal*, *El Mercurio de Nueva York*, or *Las Novedades*, published in New York City during the middle to late 19th century.

But unlike Puerto Rico, Cuba has never had an official political relationship to the United States, although there has always been an immigrating relationship, and several writers resided in New York and published novels and short stories in Spanish in the mid-1800s. A collection of short stories by José María Heredia titled *Cuentos Orientales* was published in New York in 1829. Two novels from this period concerned with the abolition of slavery, Cirilo Villaverde's *Cecilio Valdés or la Loma del Ángel*, first published serially in newspapers, and his *El Penitente*, published in 1889, both described in romantic prose love stories of slaves and relations between the classes. Another writer, Anselmo Suárez y Romero also published in a similar style, *Francisco*, a love story of two Cuban slaves whose master prohibits them from marrying. Written in 1838, it was published posthumously in New York in 1880. Although Spanish language newspapers published in New York from at least 1830 through the turn of the century continued to publish short stories and poetry by Cuban, Dominican and Puerto Rican writers, Cuban American novels in English do not appear in the U.S. until the late 1950s.

Cuban American literature, Cuban exile literature, and Cuban literature blend together at times, cross over, and yet at other times appear as distinctly different genres. According to Rodolfo J. Cortina, "Traditionally, Cuban literature has been written both on the island and abroad. The cases of Heredia, Avellaneda, Casals, Merlin, Martí, Florit, Carpentier, Sarduy, Arenas are but a few examples of this phenomenon. So then, if Cuban literature has often been written in exile, is there a difference between the two? The answer, of course, is no, as long as the writer is considered both as a national author and as an exile after his or her death."[3]

Cuban American literature can be seen as that literature written by a Cuban American who lives and writes in the United States. For example, José Martí lived in New York for 15 years, so he is a writer that fits into all three of the categories mentioned above.

It was as a result of the Castro Revolution that three specific groups of writers can now be identified as having immigrated to the U.S. in the early 1960s. The first group consists of the adults who write mostly in Spanish and whose concern is the denunciation of Castro. The second group came in 1980 during the Muriel Boatlift with Reinaldo Arenas being the most famous from this group, and while they may write in Spanish, but many of their works are now translated into English. The third group includes the younger writers born in the U.S. or those who immigrated as children, grew up here and write mostly in English. This group is also joined by second and third generation Cuban Americans whose families immigrated to Florida and New York in the late 19th and early 20th century. Oscar Hijuelos and José Hijuelos are examples of such writers. Most of the novels in this collection are by authors who fit into the last two of the three categories described above, and almost all write primarily in English.

Younger Cuban American writers are no longer attacking the Castro regime, nor are they all absorbed with writing about exile. Instead some of the themes in this new literature concern living in dual cultures, exploring identities, and maintaining a cultural heritage that is not just Cuban, and not just American. Writing in Spanish but with many of his works available in English, Reinaldo Arenas may be considered the most prominent writer of the Muriel group, and also a link between exile writers and contemporary immigrant writers. Other contemporary writers, such as Roberto Fernández, Virgil Suárez, and Oscar Hijuelos write autobiographical type novels that depict the Cuban communities in Miami and New York. Fernández pokes fun at his community while Suárez and Hijuelos explore the feelings of loss and gain that immigrants experience as they leave their homelands.

Women writers, such as Cristina Garcia, Margarita Engle, and Achy Obejas, specifically characterize the psyche and aura of women's worlds, as mothers, daughters, sisters and lesbians, as they launch into new bicultural lives in the U.S. Assimilation into mainstream American society is a very personal process, yet at the same time involves the whole family. These women writers examine the relations within their families while in the process of both assimilating and sustaining a Cuban identity.

The children's literature by Cuban and Cuban American authors, as with the Puerto Rican works, concentrates primarily on the retelling of early folk and animal tales. Alma Flor Ada is a prolific writer in this area, and also the author of a collection of stories for young adults about her childhood in Cuba.

CHICANO LITERATURE

Because of historical circumstances, Chicano literature has a longer U.S. tradition and has been produced in greater numbers than other Latino literature. People of Mexican descent have been in what is now the Southwestern U.S. since the Spanish settled there in the 1600s. In 1848, after the United States-Mexican War, almost half of Mexico's territory became U.S. territory and the 8,000 or so Spanish-Mexican-Indian people suddenly became United States citizens. After 300 years of speaking Spanish privately and publicly, English became their official language of government and commerce. Chicano literature derives from the early writings of the Spaniards, their memoirs, diaries, autobiographies, and while at first it was an early variant of Mexican literature from the Southwest, in Spanish, it later evolved to the literature of today, persisting to be identified as Chicano or Mexican American and continuing to be written in Spanish, English and in many cases, both.

In the new Southwest a journalistic and literary cultural tradition continued to be maintained by the large number of newspapers published throughout the west, from *El Misisipí* founded in New Orleans in 1808, *El Crepúsculo de la Libertad* in Santa Fe, *La Gaceta de Texas* and *El Mexicano*, all founded in 1813. In California, cities like San Francisco and Los Angeles had *La Estrella de Los Angeles*, *El Clamor Público*, during the 1850s, and *La Crónica* and *La Voz de México* from the 1860s to the 1890s. These newspapers not only provided crucial information to the changing communities during a period of transition from Mexican to Anglo American control, but they also published poetry, fictional sketches, folk tales and legends, and serialized novels. [4]

After the American take over, several conquered Mexicanos wrote their memoirs and autobiographies and these can be seen as precurors to later Chicano testimonies and autobiographical novels. Juan Seguin in Texas wrote *Personal Memoirs* in 1858 and Mariano Vallejo in California wrote his *Recuerdos Historicos y Personales Tocante a la Alta California* in 1875.

Two novels represented here were written in California in the 1880s by Maria Amparo Ruiz de Burton. *Who Would Have Thought It*, originally published in 1872, and *The Squatter and the Don* in 1885, have recently been republished by Arte Público. Maria Amparo Ruiz was of an aristocratic family from Baja California who married Captain Burton in 1849, one year after the signing of the Treaty of Guadalupe Hidalgo. Historical romances, her novels depict the changing society of the proud vanquished Californio families and the loss of their lands by the encroaching Anglo gold-seekers and settlers. As disempowered and as a crushed people the Californios stood helplessly and saw their way of life erode, their language and culture persecuted, and their political rights oppressed. Their own weapon was their words and their language.

In New Mexico, several unpublished novels written by Manuel Salazar and Manuel C. de Baca between 1880 to 1900 have been identified, and Eusebio

Chacón published two novels in Santa Fe in 1892, *El Hijo de la Tempestad* and *Tras la Tormenta la Calma*. With the writings of Chacón, an ethnic folk base to Chicano literature was established in New Mexico. The use of folkloric motifs, as a way to preserve and maintain a language and a Hispanic way of life, is clearly visible in the writings after 1900. An interest in folklore and its relation to the Spanish of the "conquestadores" was propagated by the folklorist Aurelio M. Espinosa and his writings, research and collecting influenced many writers in New Mexico, such as Frey Angelico Chavez, who wrote in the style of "old Spain", retelling Catholic legends and Spanish traditional narratives. During this period there were folkloric narratives by women who, like Maria Amparo Ruiz de Burton were writing to chronicle and record the early Spanish American society of the Southwest. In New Mexico, Cleofas Jaramillo and Fabiola Cabeza de Baca published autobiographical family social histories and in Texas, Jovita Gonzalez, a teacher and folklorist wrote an unpublished novel, *El Caballero*, just recently issued by Arte Público.

After World War II an increase in the publication of Chicano novels written in English occurred. Josephine Niggli, from an ethnically mixed background but raised in Mexico, wrote *Mexican Village* in 1945. It was probably the first Mexican American novel to reach an Anglo audience. In the late 1940s, Mario Suarez published a series of short stories in Arizona journals, and in 1959, José Antonio Villarreal published what is considered to be the first Chicano novel, *Pocho*. Autobiographical in style it is seen as an assimilationist novel and has no Spanish, folk wisdom, or references to grandmothers. Yet, it provides a good portrait of the confusion and personal agony of a young Chicano in California, coming of age, attempting to find his identity and place in society in the years before the start of the second World War.

The significance of the influence of autobiographies and family social histories to the evolution and development of Chicano literature is made clear when Genaro Padilla states, "In autobiographical literature, we see again and again a narrative ground (often a battleground) upon which an individual is contending with social, cultural and ideological forces that simultaneously so disrupt identity as to unfix it, yet, paradoxically, in disrupting identity establish identity as a destablized condition."[5]

In the early 1970s three important writers, two who are still writing today, were introduced to the Chicano community by a small publisher in Berkeley, California, Quinto Sol Publications. Tomás Rivera's *Y no se lo Trago la Tierra*, in 1971, Rudolfo Anaya's *Bless Me Ultima*, in 1972, and Rolando Hinojosa's *Estampas del valle*, in 1972. All three were U.S. born college educated professors who created ordinary common Mexican American characters, complex and comical, socially and racially conscious, speaking in Spanish, English and sharing and participating in preserving a common cultural heritage.

Since the 1970s we have had a renaissance of Chicano literature: poetry, short stories, essays, and novels. California, New Mexico, and Texas are all productive centers of literary creativity. The early Chicano novels that meditated on the pre-Columbian origins of the Mexicano evolved to the immigration novel, to the coming-of-age novel, and now moving into the mystery novel, the gay novel and the romantic novel.

Although not in the same numbers as male writers, Chicana authors have always been published, as can be seen by the works of María Amparo Ruiz de Burton, Cleofas Jaramillo, and Jovita Gonzalez. But in the last couple of decades we have seen a larger number of novels and anthologies by Chicana writers. Chicanas are writing about women's experiences in a culture that was previously dominated by male writers that explored the mythologies of Aztlan yet neglected the individuation of the woman. The process of self-development and coming of age are crucial themes in many Chicana novels. In the early literature Chicanas were absent as full characters, or were portrayed as children or grandmothers, or in one-dimensional images, either as mother/virgin/whore. Contemporary Chicanas are now in charge of creating themselves as fully developed individuals, coming to terms with their psychological and sexual development. Lesbian writers, Cherrie Moraga, Emma Perez, and Gloria Anzaldua, show harsh honesty in exploring Chicano cultural institutions like the Catholic church and its role in subjugating women.

It is important to mention another category of the Chicano novel with samples of it included in this collection. *Literatura chicanesca* is a body of literature that includes short stories and novels about Chicano life but written by non-Chicanos. The novels of Gordon Kahn, Amado Muro, and Danny Santiago are such works, and are included here because of their historical significance.

In the area of children's literature, many new authors and illustrators are now being published. Writers of adult works are finding it important to write for children and Gary Soto, Pat Mora, and Sandra Cisneros have produced quality books for children. Also, Arte Público's division of Piñata Books is publishing young adult works by new writers.

FOOTNOTES:

1. Kal Wagenheim, Cuentos: An Anthology of Short Stories from Puerto Rico (New York, NY: Schocken Books, Inc., 1978), xii.

2. Frances R. Aparicio, "From Ethnicity to Multiculturalism: An Historical Overview of Puerto Rican Literature in the United States," *Handbook of Hispanic Cultures in the United States: Literature and Art*, general editors, Nicolás Kanellos and Claudio Esteva-Fabregat (Houston, TX: Arte Público, 1993), 33.

3. Rodolfo J. Cortina, "History and Development of Cuban American Literature: A Survey," *Handbook of Hispanic Cultures in the United States: Literature and Art*, general editors, Nicolás Kanellos and Claudio Esteva-Fabregat (Houston, TX: Arte Público, 1993), 40.

4. Nicolás Kanellos, "A Socio-Historic Study of Hispanic Newspapers in the United States," *Recovering the U.S. Hispanic Literary Heritage*, ed. by Ramón Gutiérrez and Genaro Padilla (Houston, TX: Arte Público, 1993).

5. Genaro M. Padillo, "Recovering Mexican-American Autobiography," *Recovering the U.S. Hispanic Literary Heritage*, ed. by Ramón Gutiérrez and Genaro Padilla (Houston, TX: Arte Público, 1993), 158.

ADDITONAL RECOMMENDED READINGS:

Herrera-Sobek, María, ed. *Reconstructing a Chicano/a Literary Heritage: Hispanic Colonial Literature of the Southwest*. Tucson, AZ: University of Arizona Press, 1993.

Leal, Luis. "Mexican American Literature: A Historical Perspective", *Modern Chicano Writers, A collection of Critical Essays*. Ed. by Joseph Sommers and Tomás Ybarra-Frausto. Englewood Cliffs, NJ: Prentice-Hall, Inc., 1979.

Zimmerman, Marc. *U.S. Latino Literature: An Essay and Annotated Bibliography*. Chicago, ILL: MARCH/Abrazo Press, 1992

Latino Titles

485

OSCAR ZETA ACOSTA, Mexican American

The Autobiography of a Brown Buffalo
(New York: Vintage Books, 1972)

Subject(s): Growing Up; Law; Identity
Age range(s): Grades 9-Adult
Major character(s): Oscar Zeta Acosta, Lawyer, Chicano
Time period(s): 1960s
Locale(s): California (takes place throughout California.)

Summary: In an autobiographical work and part novel, Oscar Zeta Acosta examines his life as a Robin Hood Chicano lawyer with an appetite for life on the edge. Born in El Paso, Texas, and growing up in Los Angeles, this is his account of coming of age in the sixties, of taking on impossible cases and breaking all courtroom rules, and of searching restlessly for a personal and cultural identity.

About this book: This classic in Chicano literature was republished in 1989.

Where it's reviewed:
Hispanic Journal of Behavioral Sciences, August 1990, page 328

Other books by the same author:
The Revolt of the Cockroach People, 1973 (sequel)

Other books you might like:
Jose Antonio Burciaga, *Spilling the Beans: Loteria Chicana*, 1995
A series of essays, many humorous, recounting experiences from the author's childhood, and explorations into aspects of Chicano culture.
Nash Candelaria, *The Day the Cisco Kid Shot John Wayne*, 1988
These twelve humorous stories portray Chicano Anglo interrelations and conflicts.
Enrique A. Laguerre, *The Labyrinth*, 1984
This is the story of a Puerto Rican man in New York City who goes to night school to earn a law degree and accidentally stumbles into the services of a Caribbean dictator.

Louie Garcia Robinson, *The Devil, Delfina Varela, and the Used Chevy*, 1993
This comical political novel is about the Latino community in San Francisco's Mission District.
Richard Rodriguez, *Hunger of Memory: The Education of Richard Rodriguez, an Autobiography*, 1983
A story about childhood and education and the difficult journey of a "minority student" who must become socially assimilated in order to enjoy academic success.
Laura Del Fuego, *Maravilla*, 1989
Consuelo Contreres, growing up in the housing projects of East Los Angeles, makes her way through turbulent times during the 1960s.
Floyd Salas, *State of Emergency*, 1996
It's the 1960s and a radical professor who finds refuge in the counter-culture is forced to flee the U.S. after beginning an expose of the government.

486

OSCAR ZETA ACOSTA, Mexican American

The Revolt of the Cockroach People
(San Francisco, CA: Straight Arrow Books, 1973)

Subject(s): Politics; Race Relations; Murder
Age range(s): Grades 8-Adult
Major character(s): Oscar Zeta Acosta, Lawyer, Chicano
Time period(s): 1960s; 1970s (1969-1972)
Locale(s): Los Angeles, California

Summary: A personal memoir of the turbulent years that mark the beginning of the Chicano movement in California, this chronicle is a sequel to *The Autobiography of a Brown Buffalo* where Acosta continues his adventures. Deprived and systematically oppressed by the establishment, the Chicanos of East Los Angeles begin to revolt at the end of the sixties. This thriller follows a spontaneous school strike, a riot in St. Basil's Catholic Cathedral on Christmas Eve, some mysterious murders, and the narrator's campaign for Sheriff of Los Angeles County. All of this is seen through the eyes of a brilliant and angry lawyer.

Other books by the same author:
The Autobiography of a Brown Buffalo, 1972

Other books you might like:
Juan Felipe Herrera, *Night Train to Tuxtla*, 1994
  This collection deals with a vast array of subjects, from
  Rodney King and AIDs to zoot suits. There is also a
  section devoted to what Herrera calls ''the swashbuckling
  Chicano sixties''.
Floyd Salas, *What Now My Love*, 1994
  A writer and his two friends flee San Francisco's drug sub-
  culture and a narcotics bust, to travel to the Mexican
  border during the 1960s.
Lucha Corpi, *Eulogy for a Brown Angel: A Mystery Novel*,
  1992
  A Chicana feminist detective solves a murder that occurred
  during the Chicano civil rights movement of the late
  1960s.
Ron Arias, *The Road to Tamazunchale*, 1987
  Don Fausto, old and nearing death in a Los Angeles barrio,
  decides to take a journey through time and space, from the
  Inca world to encounters with undocumented workers in
  California.
Miguel Mendez, *The Dream of Santa Maria de las Piedras*,
  1989
  This is the story of a small rural poor town in the Sonora
  Desert of Mexico, seen through the eyes of the old men
  who gather to reminisce and gossip in the town plaza.
Aristeo Brito, *The Devil in Texas = El Diablo en Texas*, 1990
  This important novel describes the Anglo destruction of a
  Chicano world in Texas, where the devil comes to the
  border town of Presidio.
Nash Candelaria, *Memories of the Alhambra*, 1977
  Jose Rafa disappears, leaving only a receipt for traveler's
  checks and a business card from an L.A. con man who sells
  false genealogies. Has he gone to Mexico to search for
  Spanish ancestors?
Lucha Corpi, *Delia's Song*, 1989
  Participating in the anti-war and civil rights movements of
  the '60s, Delia must find a way to forge her own identity
  and relationships with others.
Edmund Villasenor, *Macho!*, 1973
  This early Chicano novel is about a 17-year-old who
  illegally crosses the U.S. border, cheats his fellow workers,
  becomes a strike breaker and turns criminal in his quest for
  riches and acculturation.

487

ALMA FLOR ADA, Cuban American
LESLIE TRYON, Illustrator

Dear Peter Rabbit = Querido Pedrin

(New York, NY: Maxwell Macmillan International, 1994)

Subject(s): Letters; Animals; Fairy Tale
Age range(s): Grades K-2
Time period(s): Indeterminate Past
Locale(s): United States

Summary: Goldilocks, Baby Bear, Peter Rabbit, and The
Three Little Pigs write letters to each other in this captivating
book. Peter Rabbit is invited to a housewarming party;

Goldilocks meets Little Red Riding Hood and everyone meets
at Goldilocks birthday party!

About this book: Translated by Rosa Zubizarreta.

Where it's reviewed:
Publishers Weekly, February 21, 1994, page 253
School Library Journal, July 1994, page 73

Other books by the same author:
My Name Is Maria Isabel, 1993
The Gold Coin, 1991
Where the Flame Trees Bloom, 1994
Mediopollito = Half-Chicken, 1995

Other books you might like:
Arthur Dorros, *Abuela*, 1991
  A little girl and her grandmother fly all over New York
  City.
Lucia M. Gonzalez, *The Bossy Gallito*, 1994
  A bossy little rooster gets his beak dirty pecking some corn
  while on his way to his uncle's wedding.
Pura Belpre, *The Tiger and the Rabbit and Other Tales*, 1965
  This is a collection of folk tales from Puerto Rico.
Linda Shute, *Rabbit Wishes*, 1995
  Soon after creation, Tio Conejo complains that he wants to
  be large like an elephant or tall like a giraffe.
Pura Belpre, *Dance of the Animals*, 1972
  Senor and Senora Lion, hungry for goat meat, throw a
  party and invite all the animals.
Nicholasa Mohr, *The Song of el Coqui and Other Tales of
Puerto Rico*, 1995
  This collection of three vividly illustrated tales evokes the
  rich ancestral traditions of Puerto Rican culture.

488

ALMA FLOR ADA, Cuban American
NEIL WALDMAN, Illustrator

The Gold Coin

(New York: Antheneum, 1991)

Subject(s): Treasure; Robbers and Outlaws
Age range(s): Grades K-2
Major character(s): Juan, Thief (long-time); Dona Josefa,
  Aged Person (old woman)
Time period(s): Indeterminate Past
Locale(s): Central America (countryside)

Summary: When Juan, who has been a thief for many years,
sees a gold coin in Dona Josefa's hand, he decides to steal her
treasure. He travels all around the countryside trying to catch
up with her, and when he finally does, he discovers a different
kind of treasure.

About this book: This is translated from Spanish by Bernice
Randall.

Where it's reviewed:
Publishers Weekly, January 11, 1991, page 103
Reading Teacher, September 1993, page 46

Other books by the same author:
Dear Peter Rabbit = Querido Pedrin, 1994
Where the Flame Trees Bloom, 1994

Other books you might like:
Gary Soto, *Too Many Tamales*, 1993
  Maria helps her mother make tamales for Christmas Eve
  dinner, but she loses something she must find.
Juanita Havill, *Treasure Nap*, 1992
  Alicia hears the story of Rita, who visits her grandfather in
  the mountains of Mexico.
Omar Castaneda, *Abuela's Weave*, 1993
  A young girl and her grandmother sell their woven fabrics
  at a market in Guatemala.
Harriet Rohmer, *Uncle Nacho's Hat = El Sombrero de Tio
  Nacho*, 1989
  Uncle Nacho does not like his new hat until his niece
  teaches him something.
Pura Belpre, *Ote: A Puerto Rican Folk Tale*, 1969
  Ote must go to the forest in search of food for his wife and
  five children. There he meets a near-sighted devil who
  brings him bad luck.
Fernando Pico, *The Red Comb*, 1994
  A young girl helps save a runaway slave in 19th century
  Puerto Rico
Gary Soto, *The Old Man and His Door*, 1996
  In this humorous tale about an old man who brings a door
  (''la puerta'') instead of a pig (''el puerco'') to a barbecue,
  all turns out well.

489

ALMA FLOR ADA, Cuban American
KIM HOWARD, Illustrator

Mediopollito = Half-Chicken

(New York, NY: Doubleday, 1995)

Subject(s): Animals/Hens; Self-Acceptance; Humor
Age range(s): Grades K-2
Major character(s): Half-Chicken, Chicken (with half a body),
  Mexican
Time period(s): Indeterminate Past
Locale(s): Mexico City, Mexico

Summary: This bilingual retelling of a traditional humorous
tale from Spain is set in colonial Mexico. Half-Chicken, as he
is aptly named, is born with only half a body, and because of
his uniqueness receives a lot of attention. He sets out for
Mexico City to show himself off to the Viceroy. As he travels
he completes several good deeds for water, fire and wind.
When he gets into trouble in Mexico City these elements
come to his rescue.

Where it's reviewed:
Booklist, September 15, 1995, page 165
Horn Book Magazine, November-December 1995, page 749

Other books by the same author:
My Name Is Maria Isabel, 1993
The Gold Coin, 1991
Where the Flame Trees Bloom, 1994
Dear Peter Rabbit = Querido Pedrin, 1994

Other books you might like:
Lucia M. Gonzalez, *The Bossy Gallito*, 1994
  A bossy little rooster gets his beak dirty pecking some corn
  while on his way to his uncle's wedding.

Pura Belpre, *The Tiger and the Rabbit and Other Tales*, 1965
  Collection of folk tales from Puerto Rico.
Linda Shute, *Rabbit Wishes*, 1995
  Soon after creation, Tio Conejo complains that he wants to
  be large like an elephant or tall like a giraffe.
Pura Belpre, *Dance of the Animals*, 1972
  Senor and Senora Lion, hungry for goat meat, throw a
  party and invite all the animals.
Nicholasa Mohr, *The Song of el Coqui and Other Tales of
  Puerto Rico*, 1995
  This collection of three vividly illustrated tales evokes the
  rich ancestral traditions of Puerto Rican culture.
Pat Mora, *The Race of Toad and Deer*, 1995
  Deer thinks he is the biggest and fastest animal in the
  jungle and tries to make the other animals do as he says.
Michael Rose Ramirez, *The Little Ant = La Hormiga
  Chiquita*, 1995
  A little ant with a broken leg seeks restitution from those
  responsible for his injury. This includes animals, humans,
  and even natural events. In the end, the ant learns a lesson.

490

ALMA FLOR ADA, Cuban American
K. DYBLE THOMPSON, Illustrator

My Name Is Maria Isabel

(New York: Atheneum, 1993)

Subject(s): Identity; Schools; Moving, Household
Age range(s): Grades 2-4
Major character(s): Maria Isabel Salazar Lopez, 9-Year-Old,
  3rd Grader
Locale(s): United States (mainland U.S., but city not specified)

Summary: Maria Isabel Salazar Lopez is proud of her name
because of the fact that she is named after relatives who she
loves. But when she begins at a new school, her teacher calls
her Mary Lopez, which is not her full name. Maria Isabel
refuses to answer to this name and begins to have difficulties.
In order to have a part in the school's winter pageant, she must
do something.

About this book: This is translated from Spanish by Ana M.
Cerro.

Where it's reviewed:
Publishers Weekly, April 19, 1993, page 62

Other books by the same author:
Dear Peter Rabbit = Querido Pedrin, 1994
The Gold Coin, 1991
Where the Flame Trees Bloom, 1994

Other books you might like:
Gary Soto, *The Skirt*, 1992
  Fourth-grader Miata loses her mother's folkloric dancing
  skirt and figures out a way to find it.
Gloria Anzaldua, *Friends From the Other Side/Amigos del
  Otro Lado*, 1993
  Prietita helps an undocumented boy and his family hide
  from the migra.
Pura Belpre, *Santiago*, 1969
  Santiago learns to make new friends in a new school.

Gary Soto, *Too Many Tamales*, 1993
Maria helps her mother make tamales for Christmas Eve dinner, but she loses something she must find.
Nicholasa Mohr, *Felita*, 1990
Felita loves her neighborhood and her best friend Gigi, but her world is turned upside down when her family moves to a new neighborhood.
Alma Flor Ada, *Where the Flame Trees Bloom*, 1994
Eleven short stories describe the author's childhood in Cuba.

491

ALMA FLOR ADA, Cuban American
ANTONIO MARTORELL, Illustrator, Puerto Rican

Where the Flame Trees Bloom
(New York: Antheneum, 1994)

Subject(s): Growing Up; Family
Age range(s): Grades 4-6
Major character(s): Alma Flor Ada, Child, Cuban
Time period(s): 20th century (1930-1950)
Locale(s): Cuba

Summary: Like flame trees, Alma Flor Ada's stories blossom beautifully. With eleven stories from her own childhood, Ada writes about her family, friends, and the Cuban hacienda where she grew up. These tales present a strong sense of Cuba, an island close to and yet so different from the United States.

About this book: Eight of these stories were originally written in Spanish and translated by Rosa Zubizarreta.

Where it's reviewed:
Horn Book Magazine, March-April 1995, page 218

Other books by the same author:
Dear Peter Rabbit = Querido Pedrin, 1994
The Gold Coin, 1991
My Name Is Maria Isabel, 1993

Other books you might like:
Fran Leeper Buss, *Journey of the Sparrow*, 1991
Salvadoran refugees, Maria and her brother, are smuggled into the U.S.
Enedina Casarez Vasquez, *Recuerdos de Una Nina*, 1980
These short stories are about growing up in San Antonio, Texas.
Pura Belpre, *Santiago*, 1969
Santiago learns to make new friends in a new school.
Esmeralda Santiago, *When I Was Puerto Rican*, 1993
This autobiographical story is about growing up in Puerto Rico and the U.S.
Judith Ortiz Cofer, *An Island Like You: Stories of the Barrio*, 1995
Twelve stories, set in a barrio of New Jersey, examine the lives of Puerto Rican teenagers who deal with friendship, family, romance and school.
Victor Villasenor, *Walking Stars: Stories of Magic and Power*, 1994
This autobiographical collection of stories recalls the author's parents' and grandparents' lives in Mexico.

492

MARJORIE AGOSIN, Chilean

Happiness: Stories
(Fredonia, NY: White Pine Press, 1993)

Subject(s): Short Stories; Social Classes; Women
Age range(s): Grades 10-Adult
Time period(s): 1980s
Locale(s): Chile (many stories take place in Chile)

Summary: In this collection of short stories, Agosin who is recognized as one of the most provocative Chilean writers of her generation, attempts to challenge and undermine our understanding of reality. Her short pieces, some only two pages long, address history, feminism, identity, and culture with an ironic and often bizarre view.

About this book: This work is translated and has an introduction by Elizabeth Horan.

Where it's reviewed:
Library Journal, February 1, 1994, page 114
Ms. Magazine, March-April 1994, page 78
World Literature Today, Summer 1994, page 542

Other books by the same author:
Brujas y Algo Mas = Witches and Other Things, 1984
Circles of Madness: Mothers of the Plaza de Mayo, 1992
Dear Anne Frank, 1994
A Cross and a Star: Memoirs of a Jewish Girl in Chile, 1995
Hogueras = Bonfires, 1990
Toward the Splendid City, 1994
Landscapes of a New Land: Fiction by Latin American Women, 1989

Other books you might like:
Ana Lydia Vega, *True and False Romances*, 1994
This collection of short stories is about women and romance that take place in Puerto Rico.
Kathleen Ross, *Scents of Wood and Silence: Short Stories by Latin American Women Writers*, 1991
This anthology of short fiction is by Latin American women writers.
Rosario Ferre, *The Youngest Doll*, 1991
This collection of short stories, originally published in Spanish, is about Puerto Rico society.
Kal Wagenheim, *Cuentos: An Anthology of Short Stories from Puerto Rico*, 1978
This collection of short stories is by writers living in Puerto Rico.
Isabel Allende, *Paula*, 1995
Story of Isabel Allende's daughter's illness, coma, treatments, and death at the age of 28.
Isabel Allende, *The Stories of Eva Luna*, 1991
The stories of Eva Luna are twenty-three tales of her life, her loves, and the surrounding political and social events alluded to in *Eva Luna*, but not included in the novel.

493

JACK AGUEROS, Puerto Rican

Dominoes and Other Stories from the Puerto Rican

(Willimatic, CT: Curbstone Press, 1993)

Subject(s): Short Stories; City Life
Age range(s): Grades 10-Adult
Time period(s): 20th century (1940-1990)
Locale(s): New York, New York (Spanish Harlem)

Summary: This collection of short stories is by a poet and playwright who writes about life in the Puerto Rican community of New York covering the years from the 1940's to the 1990's. Dominoes is a sidewalk game played frequently in the streets of the Barrio in New York City.

Where it's reviewed:
Choice, January 1994, page 776
Library Journal, July 1993, page 123
Publishers Weekly, July 19, 1993, page 237

Other books by the same author:
The Immigrant Experience: The Anguish of Becoming American, 1971
Correspondence between the Stonehaulers, 1991

Other books you might like:
Nocholasa Mohr, *El Bronx Remembered: A Novella and Stories*, 1975
  These stories of the Puerto Rican community take place during the 1940s and 1950s.
Piri Thomas, *Stories from El Barrio*, 1978
  These stories are about the childhood years of the author in Spanish Harlem.
Faythe Turner, *Puerto Rican Writers at Home in the U.S.A.: An Anthology*, 1991
  This collection of poetry and prose is written by Puerto Rican authors born and raised in New York City.
Abraham Rodriguez Jr., *The Boy Without a Flag: Tales of the South Bronx*, 1992
  This collection of short stories is about the problems of young Puerto Ricans in the Bronx.
Victor Rodriguez, *Eldorado in East Harlem*, 1992
  Seventeen-year-old Rene is streetwise and he gets involved with a gang committing petty crimes and running drugs.
Judith Ortiz-Cofer, *An Island Like You: Stories of the Barrio*, 1995
  Twelve stories, set in a barrio of New Jersey, examine the lives of Puerto Rican teenagers who deal with friendship, family, romance, and school.

494

NORMA ALARCON, Editor, Mexican American
ANA CASTILLO, Co-Editor, Mexican American
CHERRIE MORAGA, Co-Editor, Mexican American

The Sexuality of Latinas

(Berkeley, CA: Third Woman Press, 1993)

Subject(s): Sexuality; Women; Homosexuality/Lesbianism
Age range(s): Grades 10-Adult
Time period(s): 1980s; 1990s (1984-1993)
Locale(s): United States

Summary: This collection of poems, short stories, and prose examines the often hidden, often subverted, sexuality of Latinas. Confronting family, religion, and social systems, the contributers begin to examine and question Latina sexuality. Well known authors such as Sandra Cisneros, Julia Alvarez, Gloria Anzaldua, and Lucho Corpi are included, along with lesser known writers like Alvina Quintana, Erlinda Gonzales-Berry, and Carmen Tafolla.

About this book: Several essays, stories and poetry in Spanish.

Where it's reviewed:
Journal of Sex Research, February 1990, page 143

Other books by the same author:
The Mixquiahuala Letters, 1986
Loving in the War Years, 1983
So Far from God: A Novel, 1993
The Last Generation, 1993

Other books you might like:
Juanita Ramos, *Companeras: Latina Lesbians: An Anthology*, 1987
  Puerto Rican, Cuban, Chilean, Chicana, Colombian, and other Latina lesbians of different nationalities and with different life experiences, are represented in this anthology.
Margarite Fernandez Olmos, *Pleasure in the Word: Erotic Writings by Latin American Women*, 1993
  A diverse collection of erotic writing by women destroys silence by speaking out about eroticism, love, and violence.
Terri de la Pena, *Margins*, 1992
  This story is about a young lesbian writer who confronts her future and her family about her sexuality.
Alma Luz Villanueva, *Naked Ladies*, 1994
  A novel about the lives of four remarkable women recounts their struggles against prejudices, difficult relationships, and abuse.
Sheila Ortiz Taylor, *Faultline: A Novel*, 1982
  This very funny book is about a lesbian mother of six children, her lover/companion, their 300 rabbits, and a six foot tall Black drag queen baby sitter.
Beatriz Rivera, *African Passions and Other Stories*, 1995
  Narrated with humor, passion, and satire, this collection of short stories focuses on women's obsessive search for love and success.

495

KATHLEEN ALCALA, Mexican American

Mrs. Vargas and the Dead Naturalist

(Corvallis, Oregon: Calyx Books, 1992)

Subject(s): Short Stories; Magic
Age range(s): Grades 10-Adult
Time period(s): 20th century (1900-1980s)
Locale(s): United States; Mexico

Summary: Created as a book of wonders, this collection of short stories contains many about Mexican women coming of age in the United States. Capturing the essence of magical realism, these stories move between worlds to examine the souls of characters with humor, simplicity, and originality. These stories are about interior worlds. They explore the invisible behind the visible, and they all possess a sense of possibility and magic.

Where it's reviewed:
Belles Lettres: A Review of Books by Women, Fall 1992, page 5
off our backs, July 1993, page 12
Publishers Weekly, June 15, 1992, page 96

Other books you might like:
Kleya Forte-Escamilla, *The Storyteller with Nike Airs and Other Barrio Stories*, 1995
 Magical stories of small-town women who battle limited opportunities and emotional hardships, yet manage to survive.
Montserrat Fontes, *First Confession*, 1991
 Cousins Andrea and Victor, spoiled, upper class children, spend a summer together preparing for their First Communion.
Alfredo Vea Jr., *La Maravilla*, 1993
 A young boy grows up on Buckeye Road, a world of marvels in the desert outside the Phoenix city limits, caught between many cultures.
Sabine Ulibarri, *El Condor and Other Stories*, 1989
 A collection of eleven romantic stories for adults that present a world of gypsies, witches, ghosts, and the supernatural.
Sandra Benitez, *A Place Where the Sea Remembers*, 1993
 Written as a series of interrelated magical tales, this novel presents the life of a coastal village in Mexico.
Marjorie Agosin, *Happiness: Stories*, 1993
 This collection of stories, by a Chilean American writer addresses reality, history, feminism, identity, and culture with an ironic and often bizarre view.

496

GIL C. ALICEA, Puerto Rican
CARMINE DESENA, Co-Author

The Air Down Here: True Tales from a South Bronx Boyhood

(San Francisco: Chronicle Books, 1995)

Subject(s): City Life; Drugs; Violence
Age range(s): Grades 6-10
Major character(s): Gil C. Alicea, 16-Year-Old, Puerto Rican
Time period(s): 1990s
Locale(s): New York, New York (takes place in the South Bronx)

Summary: Sixteen-year-old Gil Alicea battles daily with drugs, violence, gangs, school, family, and the media. This book contains 115 short essays and journal entries about the author's life. Gil's voice is strong, and he presents a positive message from the front lines of the inner-city.

About this book: This work contains photographs by Gil C. Alicea.

Where it's reviewed:
Library Journal, October 1, 1995, page 106
Publishers Weekly, August 21, 1995, page 54

Other books you might like:
Nicholasa Mohr, *El Bronx Remembered: A Novella and Stories*, 1975
 These short stories of the Puerto Rican Community takes place during the 1940s and 1950s.
Judith Ortiz Cofer, *An Island Like You: Stories of the Barrio*, 1995
 Twelve stories, set in a barrio of New Jersey, examine the lives of Puerto Rican teenagers who deal with friendship, family, romance, and school.
Jack Agueros, *Dominoes and Other Stories from the Puerto Rican*, 1993
 These stories are about life in New York City.
Abraham Rodriguez Jr., *The Boy Without a Flag: Tales of the South Bronx*, 1992
 These stories are about young people growing up Puerto Rican in New York City.
Victor Rodriguez, *Eldorado in East Harlem*, 1992
 Seventeen year old Rene gets involved with a gang committing petty crimes and running drugs.
Vincent Younis, *Shine Boys: A Story about Santa Fe*, 1995
 A novella narrating the life of an unnamed character growing up in Santa Fe during the late 1950s and his introduction to drugs.

497

ISABEL ALLENDE, Chilean

The House of the Spirits

(New York : A.A. Knopf, 1985.)

Subject(s): Intergenerational Saga; Women; Political Thriller
Age range(s): Grades 10-Adult
Major character(s): Esteban Trueba, Plantation Owner, Political Figure (conservative politician); Clara del Valle Trueba, Spouse (Esteban's wife), Magician (communicates with spirits); Alba Trueba, Granddaughter (of Esteban Trueba), Writer (novel's narrator)
Time period(s): 20th century (1900-1970)
Locale(s): Chile (a South American country like Chile, country of the author)

Summary: The novel traces the Trueba family through four generations, covers eight decades, and ends with the overthrow of the government by the military. It is a complicated political novel with many characters, time periods, and voices. The characters include strong-willed women.

About this book: This was first published in Spanish in 1982.

Where it's reviewed:
Tikkun, January-February 1990, page 66
New York Times Book Review, December 7, 1986, page 84
Christian Science Monitor, June 7, 1985, section B, page b5
Wall Street Journal, June 19, 1985, page 28

Other books by the same author:
Eva Luna, 1988
The Infinite Plan, 1993
Of Love and Shadows, 1987

Paula, 1995
The Stories of Eva Luna, 1991

Other books you might like:

Gabriel Garcia Marquez, *One Hundred Years of Solitude*, 1970
   This intergenerational novel takes place in a fictional city in South America.
Rosario Ferre, *The House on the Lagoon*, 1995
   This intergenerational saga portrays a family living in Ponce, Puerto Rico.
Reinaldo Arenas, *The Doorman*, 1991
   This story about Juan, a young Cuban refugee who becomes a doorman at a luxury apartment building in New York is a parable about freedom.
Victor Villasenor, *Rain of Gold*, 1991
   In this massive novel the author weaves the separate stories of two families, the Gomezs and the Villasenors, as they live in Mexico and later migrate to the U.S.
Marjorie Agosin, *Happiness: Stories*, 1993
   A collection of very short stories by a provocative Chilean writer that challenges and undermines our understanding of reality.
Cristina Garcia, *Dreaming in Cuban, A Novel*, 1992
   A novel that interweaves the stories of three generations of Cuban women and their different responses to the Cuban revolution.
Fernando Alegria, *Paradise Lost or Gained? The Literature of Hispanic Exile*, 1990
   Collection of short stories by Latinos living in exile in the U.S.
Julia Alvarez, *In the Time of the Butterflies*, 1994
   The story of the assassination of three sisters who are fighting to overthrow a dictatorship in the Dominican Republic.
Carole Fernandez, *Sleep of the Innocents*, 1991
   This novel chronicles the lives of women living in a fictional Central American country torn by civil war.

498

ISABEL ALLENDE, Chilean

The Infinite Plan

(New York: Harper Collins, 1993)

Subject(s): Religion; Family Relations; Coming of Age
Major character(s): Gregory Reeves, Lawyer, Veteran (Vietnam), Caucasian
Time period(s): 20th century (1940-1980)
Locale(s): Los Angeles, California (parts of the story take place in Berkeley and San Francisco)

Summary: Set in the urban desolation of the slums of Los Angeles, Allende's modern epic follows the life of Gregory Reeves. *The Infinite Plan* or *The Course That Will Change Your Life* is a pseudo religion created by Charles Reeves, Gregory's father. When no one joins his church, he settles his family in East Los Angeles, the Mexican barrio, and Gregory is almost raised as a Chicano. Disturbed and disillusioned, he goes to Berkeley, is a veteran of the Vietnam War, becomes divorced, and finally seeks therapy. Focused, realistic, and

harsh, the novel examines the treachery of dreams and illusions.

Where it's reviewed:
Library Journal, April 1, 1993, page 128
Booklist, February 15, 1993, page 1010
Publisher Weekly, February 8, 1993, page 74

Other books by the same author:
Eva Luna, 1987
The House of the Spirits, 1985
Of Love and Shadows, 1987
Paula, 1994
The Stories of Eva Luna, 1991

Other books you might like:
Oscar Zeta Acosta, *The Revolt of the Cockroach People*, 1973
   This personal memoir tells of the turbulent years that mark the beginning of the Chicano movement in California and the political activities of East Los Angeles.
Gordon Kahn, *A Long Way from Home*, 1989
   Written forty years before it was published, this novel tells the story of Gilberto, a young Chicano who, after his mother's death, leaves the U.S. for Mexico to find his only remaining family.
Josephina Niggli, *Mexican Village*, 1994
   This is an important collection of ten interrelated short stories about the lives of the people of a small Mexican town, Hidalgo. It was first published in 1945.
Alejandro Morales, *Death of an Anglo*, 1988
   This is the story of Logan, a rebellious and idealistic young doctor who attempts to improve the lives of the Chicano residents of his town.
Floyd Salas, *What Now My Love*, 1994
   A writer and his two friends flee San Francisco's drug subculture and a narcotics bust to travel to the Mexican border during the 1960s.
Lucha Corpi, *Eulogy for a Brown Angel: A Mystery Novel*, 1992
   A Chicana feminist detective solves a murder that occurred during the Chicano civil rights movement of the late 1960s.
Juan Felipe Herrera, *Night Train to Tuxtla*, 1994
   This collection deals with a vast array of subjects, from Rodney King, AIDs, to zoot suits, and a section devoted to what Herrera calls *the swashbuckling Chicano sixties*.

499

ISABEL ALLENDE, Chilean

Paula

(New York: Harper Collins, 1995)

Subject(s): Mothers and Daughters; Death; Family Relations
Age range(s): Grades 10-Adult
Major character(s): Isabel Allende, Child (grows to adulthood), Writer, Chilean
Time period(s): 20th century (1944-1992)
Locale(s): Chile (takes place in Chile, Spain and California)

Summary: This is the story of Isabel Allende's daughter Paula's agonizing illness with porphyria, her descent into a coma, her treatments, and her death at the age of 28. It is also the story of Isabel Allende's life and childhood, and her attempts to conquer and assimilate her painful past. There are descriptions of Chile, her famous uncle Salvador Allende, and of Spanish customs while on a trip to Madrid to stay with her daughter. The book takes the form of an autobiography and also as a letter to a departed child that offers a suspenseful family history.

About this book: Translated by Margaret Sayers Peden.

Where it's reviewed:
Library Journal, July 1995, page 62
New Statesman & Society, September 22, 1995, page 34
Publishers Weekly, May 22, 1995, page 14
Times Literary Supplement, September 29, 1995, page 28

Awards the book has won:
American Library Association Notable Book, 1996

Other books by the same author:
Eva Luna, 1987
The House of the Spirits, 1985 (epic)
Of Love and Shadows, 1987
The Infinite Plan, 1993
The Stories of Eva Luna, 1991

Other books you might like:
Marjorie Agosin, *Happiness: Stories*, 1993
    This collection of very short stories by a provocative Chilean writer challenges and undermines our understanding of reality.
Cristina Garcia, *Dreaming in Cuban, A Novel*, 1992
    This novel interweaves the stories of three generations of Cuban women and their different responses to the Cuban revolution.
Fernando Alegria, *Paradise Lost or Gained? The Literature of Hispanic Exile*, 1990
    Collection of short stories by Latinos living in exile in the U.S.
Julia Alvarez, *In the Time of the Butterflies*, 1994
    This is the story of the assassination of three sisters who are fighting to overthrow a dictatorship in the Dominican Republic.
Carole Fernandez, *Sleep of the Innocents*, 1991
    This novel chronicles the lives of women living in a fictional Central American country torn by civil war.
Carmen C. Esteves, *Green Cane and Juicy Flotsam: Short Stories by Caribbean Women*, 1991
    In this collection of short stories, Caribbean women writers examine questions of race, power, colonialism, poverty, and identity.
Denise Chavez, *Face of an Angel*, 1995
    Sensual story, with many rich characters, about a waitress who works in a Mexican restaurant in a fictional town in New Mexico.
Reinaldo Arenas, *The Palace of the White Skunks*, 1990
    This is the story of Fortunato, a boy raised in poverty by his grandparents, his life as he grows up during the Cuban revolution, and his death.
Pablo Medina, *Exiled Memories: A Cuban Childhood*, 1990
    A collection of the author's memories of growing up in Cuba where he spends summers on his grandfather's sugar cane plantation, La Luisa.

500

ISABEL ALLENDE, Chilean

The Stories of Eva Luna
(New York: Atheneum, 1991)

Subject(s): Magic; Women; Social Classes
Age range(s): Grades 8-Adult
Major character(s): Eva Luna, Storyteller
Time period(s): Indeterminate Past
Locale(s): Argentina

Summary: The stories of Eva Luna are twenty-three tales alluded to in *Eva Luna*, but were not included in the novel. Many of these tales appear to be parodies of the magical realism writing of Latin American authors, such as Garcia Marquez and Mario Vargas Llosa, with female characters that bend tradition and confront society's hypocrisies face to face. Eva Luna tells stories of her life, her loves, and the surrounding political and social events with humor and rich detail.

About this book: Translated by Margaret Sayers Peden.

Where it's reviewed:
Library Journal, November 1, 1991, page 148
Publishers Weekly, November 1, 1991, page 55
Times Literary Supplement, February 8, 1991, page 12

Other books by the same author:
The Infinite Plan, 1993
The House of the Spirits, 1985 (epic)
Of Love and Shadows, 1987
Paula, 1994
Eva Luna, 1987

Other books you might like:
Ana Lydia Vega, *True and False Romances*, 1994
    This is a collection of short stories is about women and romance in Puerto Rico.
Kathleen Ross, *Scents of Wood and Silence: Short Stories by Latin American Women Writers*, 1991
    Short fiction by Latin American women writers is the focus of this anthology.
Rosario Ferre, *The Youngest Doll*, 1991
    These short stories, originally published in Spanish, are about Puerto Rican society.
Kal Wagenheim, *Cuentos: An Anthology of Short Stories from Puerto Rico*, 1978
    Writers living in Puerto Rico have created the works in this anthology.
Marjorie Agosin, *Happiness: Stories*, 1993
    Collected in this volume are short stories by a Chilean writer who attempts to challenge and undermine our understanding of reality.
Diana Velez, *Reclaiming Medusa: Short Stories by Contemporary Puerto Rican Women*, 1988
    Thirteen stories by five well-known Puerto Rican women writers appear in this anthology.
Kathleen Alcala, *Mrs. Vargas and the Dead Naturalist*, 1992
    Short stories, many about Mexican women coming of age in the United States, are here collected as a book of wonders.
Himilce Novas, *Mangos, Bananas, and Coconuts: A Cuban Love Story*, 1996

This tale of a magical yet real love story is an ancient tale, beginning with the love of a man and a woman from different social classes, and the story of the fate of their children.

Graciela Limon, *Song of the Hummingbird*, 1996
Huitzitzilin, Hummingbird in the Nahuatl language, is an Aztec princess who is forced into slavery. As an 82-year-old woman, she now recounts her life story during the Spanish conquest of Mexico.

501

ALURISTA, Editor, Mexican American
ALURISTA ROJAS-URISTA, Co-Editor, Mexican American

Southwest Tales: A Contemporary Collection

(Colorado Springs: Maize Press, 1986)

Subject(s): Short Stories; Anthology
Age range(s): Grades 10-Adult
Time period(s): 1970s; 1980s (1970-1986)
Locale(s): Southwest

Summary: This collection of short stories includes novice authors, as well as early Chicano authors like Mary Helen Ponce, Juan Bruce-Novoa, and Alurista. Chicano literature is very strong in the short fiction genre and this collection reflects that tradition. These short stories present the folktale, the Llorona myth, the religious aspect of the Chicano community, plus other themes and approaches found in the Chicano literary movement.

About this book: This volume is in memory of Tomas Rivera.

Other books you might like:

Gary Soto, *Pieces of the Heart: New Chicano Fiction*, 1993
This collection of short stories is by Chicano writers.

Rudolfo Anaya, *Cuentos Chicanos: A Short Story Anthology*, 1984
This collection of short stories is by Chicano writers.

Tiffany Ana Lopez, *Growing Up Chicano*, 1993
These short stories are by Chicano writers.

Carlota Cardenas de Dwyer, *Chicano Voices*, 1975
This important collection of short stories is from the Southwest.

Rudolfo Anaya, *Voces: An Anthology of Nuevo Mexicano Writers*, 1987
This anthology of poems and short stories is by New Mexican Chicano authors.

Ray Gonzalez, *Mirrors Beneath the Earth: Short Fiction by Chicano Writers*, 1992
This collection of short stories is by contemporary Chicano writers.

502

JULIA ALVAREZ, Dominican American

How the Garcia Girls Lost Their Accents

(Chapel Hill, NC: Algonquin Books, 1991)

Subject(s): Growing Up; Coming of Age; Family Relations
Age range(s): Grades 10-Adult

Major character(s): Carlos Garcia, Father, Doctor, Dominican; Laura ''Mami'' Garcia, Mother, Wife, Dominican
Time period(s): 20th century (1956-1988)
Locale(s): New York, New York; Dominican Republic

Summary: An episodic novel about a family's move to the U.S. and the gradual Americanization of the daughters. Carla, Yolanda, Sandra, and Sofia all attend Catholic schools, college, and become professionals. Yet they are still considered Hispanic in New York, while being called Americanas in the Dominican Republic. The story humorously moves back in time, to the extended family on the island, and forward to the girls' careers and husbands in the U.S. of the 1980s.

Where it's reviewed:
Library Journal, May 1, 1991, page 102
Newsweek, April 20, 1992, page 78
Publishers Weekly, April 5, 1991, page 133
World Literature Today, Summer 1992, page 516

Other books by the same author:
In the Time of the Butterflies, 1994
The Other Side = El Otro Lado, 1995

Other books you might like:

Fernando Alegria, *Paradise Lost or Gained? The Literature of Hispanic Exile*, 1990
This collection by Latino writers addresses the experience of exile and alienation through stories, poems, and essays.

Magali Garcia Ramis, *Happy Days, Uncle Sergio*, 1995
Coming of age novel of a middle class girl in Puerto Rico who dearly loves her uncle Sergio.

Judith Ortiz Cofer, *The Line of the Sun: A Novel*, 1989
A coming of age novel about a middle class girl that takes place in Puerto Rico and Paterson, New Jersey.

Ana Castillo, *So Far from God: A Novel*, 1993
This is the story of Sofi and her four daughters who live in a small fictional town in central New Mexico.

Cristina Garcia, *Dreaming in Cuban, A Novel*, 1992
A novel that interweaves the stories of three generations of Cuban women and their different responses to the Cuban revolution.

Virgil Suarez, *Havana Thursdays: A Novel*, 1995
This is the story of two sisters, their daughters, and how they represent two different manners of dealing with the changes encountered through immigration from a Latino culture.

503

JULIA ALVAREZ, Dominican American

In the Time of the Butterflies

(Chapel Hill, NC: Algonquin Books, 1994)

Subject(s): Politics; Political Prisoners; Women
Age range(s): Grades 10-Adult
Major character(s): Minerva Mirabal, Young Woman, Activist (political), Dominican; Patria Mirabal, Young Woman, Activist (political), Dominican; Maria Teresa Mirabal, Young Woman, Activist (political), Dominican
Time period(s): 20th century (1938-1994)
Locale(s): Dominican Republic

Summary: In the Dominican Republic, the Mirabal sisters, also known as las mariposas, who valiantly stood against the Trujillo regime, are national heroes. In this fictional version of their lives, Minerva and her three sisters become involved in the underground movement against dictator Trujillo. They are imprisoned and suffer horrifically. Eventually they are released, but Trujillo manages to have them eliminated. The fourth Mirabal sister, Dede, lives to tell the story of the Butterflies and keep their memory alive.

Where it's reviewed:
Hispanic, December 1994, page 82
Library Journal, August 1994, page 123
Women's Review of Books, May 1995, page 6
World Literature Today, Autumn 1995, page 789
Americas, March-April 1995, page 60

Other books by the same author:
How the Garcia Girls Lost Their Accents, 1991
The Other Side = El Otro Lado, 1995

Other books you might like:
Demetria Martinez, *Mother Tongue*, 1994
    A young woman falls in love with a Salvadoran political refugee who eventually returns to his country.
Graciela Limon, *In Search of Bernabe*, 1993
    A novel about a mother's search for her son during civil war in El Salvador.
Margarita Engle, *Singing to Cuba*, 1993
    A California woman leaves her husband and children to search for information about family members who disappeared during the Castro revolution.
Virgil Suarez, *The Cutter: A Novel*, 1991
    Julian Campos is required to cut sugarcane in Communist Cuba while waiting permission to leave the island.
Carole Fernandez, *Sleep of the Innocents*, 1991
    This novel chronicles the lives of women living in a fictional Central American country torn by civil war.
Ana Castillo, *Sapogonia: An Anti-Romance in 3/8 Meter*, 1990
    A novel about Sapogonia, a distinct place where all mestizos reside regardless of nationality or race, or possibly because of racial background.

504

JULIA ALVAREZ, Dominican American

The Other Side = El Otro Lado
(New York: Dutton Books, 1995)

Subject(s): Poetry; Family; Coming of Age
Age range(s): Grades 10-Adult
Time period(s): 20th century (1960-1995)
Locale(s): New York

Summary: In this collection of poetry that reads like prose, Julia Alvarez examines love, language, and her past. In sections titled ''Making Up the Past,'' ''The Joe Poems,'' ''The Other Side/El Otro Lado,'' she traces her family's journey to the U.S., presents a love affair, and describes a pilgrimage to the Dominican Republic. Her beautiful, perceptive poetry reads and sounds like prose.

Where it's reviewed:
Library Journal, April 15, 1995, page 80
Publishers Weekly, April 24, 1995, page 65
New York Times Book Review, July 16, 1995, page 20

Other books by the same author:
How the Garcia Girls Lost Their Accents, 1991
In the Time of the Butterflies, 1994
Homecoming: Poems, 1984

Other books you might like:
Judith Ortiz Cofer, *The Latin Deli: Prose and Poetry*, 1994
    Three genres of fiction, poetry , and essays, are represented in this collection, which portray life in Patterson, New Jersey, where the author grew up.
Esmeralda Santiago, *When I Was Puerto Rican*, 1993
    The autobiography of a young girl on the island of Puerto Rico and later in New York.
Norma Elia Cantu, *Canicula: Snapshots of a Girlhood en la Frontera*, 1995
    A collection of short lyrical vignettes, with photographs, that describe the author's growing up in Texas.
Cristina Garcia, *Dreaming in Cuban, A Novel*, 1992
    A novel that interweaves the stories of three generations of Cuban women and their different responses to the Cuban revolution.
Francisca Miranda Schneider, *Sal y Pimienta: A Culinary Education*, 1995
    A collection of personal vignettes that describe the author's childhood in Spain on the eve of the Spanish Civil War and her father's murder by the workers of the Valencia shipyard.

505

ALBA AMBERT, Puerto Rican

A Perfect Silence
(Houston, TX: Arte Publico Press, 1995)

Subject(s): Poverty; Identity; Suicide
Age range(s): Grades 10-Adult
Major character(s): Blanca, Young Woman, Puerto Rican
Time period(s): 20th century (1950-1980)
Locale(s): New York, New York (the South Bronx)

Summary: From the surrealistic world of a mental institution, a Puerto Rican woman attempts to come to terms with her self-destructive past. Abused as both a child and an adult by people and a cruel economic system, Blanca has experienced deprivation, and has been victimized at the hands of family and strangers who determine and control her life. As an adult Blanca must still fight battles to maintain her dual identity.

Where it's reviewed:
Choice, November 1995, page 459
Library Journal, March 1, 1995, page 102
Publishers Weekly, February 27, 1995, page 88

Other books by the same author:
Porque Hay Silencio: Novela, 1987
Puerto Rican Children on the Mainland: Interdisciplinary Perspectives, 1992

Other books you might like:

Maria Espinosa, *Dark Plums*, 1995
> Adrianne, a young girl from Texas, searches for love in Manhattan, falls into an abusive relationship, and eventually works as a prostitute.

Estela Portillo Trambley, *Rain of Scorpions and Other Writings*, 1975
> Collection of short stories by an early Chicana writer that explore the place of women in Mexican society.

Mary Helen Ponce, *Taking Control*, 1987
> Collection of stories portraying domestic and economic oppression of Mexican and Chicana women in the U.S.

Sandra Cisneros, *Woman Hollering Creek and Other Stories*, 1991
> A collection of short stories with strong angry female characters struggling valiantly to make something beautiful of their lives.

Phyllis Tashlik, *Hispanic, Female, and Young*, 1994
> Collection of short stories written by young Latina girls from El Barrio of New York, about the problems of growing up female.

Esmeralda Santiago, *America's Dream*, 1996
> America works as a housekeeper in a hotel on an island off the coast of Puerto Rico until she accepts a job as a nanny in Westchester County, New York and learns of a new life.

506

RUDOLFO ANAYA, Mexican American

Albuquerque
(New York: Warner Books, 1992)

Subject(s): Politics; Family; Folklore
Age range(s): Grades 10-Adult
Major character(s): Abran Gonzalez, Adoptee (son), Boxer, Chicano; Frank Dominic, Businessman, Political Figure
Time period(s): 1990s (1992)
Locale(s): Albuquerque, New Mexico

Summary: An exciting, fast moving novel with many warm and tender characters, about politics and avarice in Albuquerque. At age twenty-one Abran learns that the loving parents who raised him are not his biological parents. On the night he meets his real mother at her deathbed, his world is turned upside down and he's thrust into the realm of dirty city politics on a quest to find his real father. A stimulating story of modern Albuquerque, with a vicious mayoral race, a young Chicano boxer fighting for his pride, and American Indians battling to retain their water rights, all set within the folkloric past of New Mexico.

Where it's reviewed:
World Literature Today, Winter 1994, page 125.
Review of Contemporary Fiction, Fall 1992, page 201
Newsweek, September 1992, page 80
Library Journal, July 1992, page 119
Publishers Weekly, May 25, 1992, page 36

Other books by the same author:
The Adventures of Juan Chicaspatas, 1984
The Anaya Reader, 1995
Bless Me, Ultima, 1972
A Chicano in China, 1986

Lord of the Dawn: The Legend of Quetzalcoatl, 1987
Aztlan: Essays on the Chicano Homeland, 1989

Other books you might like:

Michael Nava, *The Hidden Law*, 1992
> Henry Rios defends a young Chicano accused of murdering a powerful Chicano public official in Los Angeles, and discovers the real murderer.

Louie Garcia Robinson, *The Devil, Delfina Varela, and the Used Chevy*, 1993
> Set in the Mission District of San Francisco, this is a novel about politics, dreams, Latino social affairs, and Delfina, a widow who will do anything for a car.

Nash Candelaria, *Leonor Park*, 1991
> A novel about land and greed in New Mexico on the eve of the Great Depression, and the battle over a father's legacy, a piece of land along the Rio Grande.

Manuel Ramos, *The Ballad of Rocky Ruiz: Death of a Martyr*, 1993
> Luis Montez, middle aged former Chicano activist and lawyer, becomes involved in solving the twenty-year old murder of Rocky Ruiz.

Manuel Ramos, *The Ballad of Gato Guerrero*, 1994
> Felix "Gato" Guerrero, an old friend from way back, calls on Montez to save him and his new love from her husband, a Latino mobster.

507

RUDOLFO ANAYA, Mexican American

The Anaya Reader
(New York: Warner Books, 1995)

Subject(s): Short Stories; Plays; Essays
Age range(s): Grades 10-Adult
Time period(s): 20th century (1940-1995)

Summary: An important collection representative of the diverse writings by Anaya. He is considered the premier author of Chicano literature. These short stories, poems, essays, and plays, have been published elsewhere during the previous twenty-five years. Excerpts from four of his best known novels are included, *Bless me, Ultima*, *Tortuga*, *Albuquerque*, and *Zia Summer*. Anaya's stories, imbued with folkloric beauty, his insightful essays about Chicano literature and culture, and his perceptions about childhood and creative growth, complete this collection. It is a great opportunity for readers to become familiar with the work of a great and prolific writer.

Other books by the same author:
The Adventures of Juan Chicaspatas, 1984
Albuquerque, 1992
Bless Me, Ultima, 1972
A Chicano in China, 1986
Lord of the Dawn: The Legend of Quetzalcoatl, 1987
Aztlan: Essays on the Chicano Homeland, 1989
Zia Summer, 1995
The Legend of La Llorona: A Short Novel, 1984
Tortuga: A Novel, 1979
Tierra, 1989

Other books you might like:

Ray Gonzalez, *Mirrors Beneath the Earth: Short Fiction by Chicano Writers*, 1992
Collection of short stories by Chicano contemporary writers.

Tiffany Ana Lopez, *Growing Up Chicano*, 1993
Short stories by Chicano contemporary writers.

Gary Soto, *Pieces of the Heart: New Chicano Fiction*, 1993
Short stories by Chicano contemporary writers.

Ray Gonzalez, *Currents From the Dancing River: Contemporary Latino Fiction, Nonfiction, and Poetry*, 1994
Short stories by Chicano contemporary writers.

508

RUDOLFO ANAYA, Mexican American

Bless Me, Ultima

(New York: Warner Books, 1972)

Subject(s): Coming of Age; Curanderas; Catholic Religion
Age range(s): Grades 8-Adult
Major character(s): Antonio Marez, 7-Year-Old (boy), Chicano; Ultima, Healer (Curandera), Mexican
Time period(s): 1940s (1940-1945)
Locale(s): New Mexico

Summary: Seven-year-old Antonio learns about life, nature and death, in rural New Mexico. Through his relationship with Ultima, a curandera, the story takes place during and immediately after World War II, a war in which three of Antonio's brothers fight. Ultima, a wonderful curandera, is an aging mysterious healer who works magic among the people of the rural countryside. This story describes evil, violent deaths, religious awakenings, and cruelty in childhood, but is also about life's funny twists and memorable characters.

About this book: The most famous and best-selling Chicano novel, it is considered a Chicano classic.

Where it's reviewed:
Hispanic, September 1994, page 90
Library Journal, May 1, 1989, page 88
Nation, July 18, 1994, page 98

Awards the book has won:
Quinto Sol Award, 1972

Other books by the same author:
The Adventures of Juan Chicaspatas, 1985
The Legend of La Llorona: A Short Novel, 1984
Tortuga: A Novel, 1988
Zia Summer, 1995
Voces: An Anthology of Nuevo Mexicano Writers, 1988
Albuquerque, 1992
The Anaya Reader, 1995
A Chicano in China, 1986
Lord of the Dawn: The Legend of Quetzalcoatl, 1987
Aztlan: Essays on the Chicano Homeland, 1989

Other books you might like:
Montserrat Fontes, *First Confession*, 1991
Cousins Andrea and Victor, spoiled, upper class children, spend a summer together preparing for their First Communion.

Alfredo Vea Jr., *La Maravilla*, 1993
A young boy grows up on Buckeye Road, a world of marvels in the desert outside the Phoenix city limits, caught between many cultures.

Arturo Islas, *The Rain God: A Desert Tale*, 1984
Three generations of the Angel family struggle to live and die with dignity and to understand their family's ghosts.

Ray Gonzalez, *Memory Fever: A Journey Beyond El Paso del Norte*, 1993
A collection of essays and vignettes about growing up in the 60's in El Paso and the surrounding desert.

Sabine Ulibarri, *Tierra Amarilla: Stories of New Mexico = Cuentos de Nuevo Mexico*, 1993
A collection of five short stories and a novella, first published in 1964, that evoke the rural life of a northern New Mexican village.

Orlando Romero, *Nambe—Year One*, 1976
Narrated by Mateo Romero, a resident of Nambe, New Mexico, this story is about the attempts of a gypsy woman to seduce the young hero into leaving his land and traditions.

509

RUDOLFO ANAYA, Editor, Mexican American
ANTONIO MARQUEZ, Co-Editor

Cuentos Chicanos: A Short Story Anthology

(Albuquerque: New America, University of New Mexico Press, 1984)

Subject(s): Anthology; Short Stories
Age range(s): Grades 10-Adult
Time period(s): 1970s; 1980s (1970-1984)
Locale(s): United States

Summary: This short story collection by twenty-one Chicano writers provides insight into the Chicano world during the 1970s and 1980s.

About this book: This is the second revised edition of the work.

Where it's reviewed:
Publishers Weekly, June 5, 1995, page 41
Prairie Schooner, Winter 1994, page 177
Publishers Weekly, March 21, 1994, page 24

Other books by the same author:
Voces: An Anthology of Nuevo Mexicano Writers, 1987
Bless Me, Ultima, 1972
Zia Summer, 1995
The Anaya Reader, 1995
Jalamanta: A Message from the Desert, 1996

Other books you might like:
Gary Soto, *Pieces of the Heart: New Chicano Fiction*, 1993
This is a collection of short stories by Chicano writers.

Tiffany Ana Lopez, *Growing Up Chicano*, 1993
These short stories are by Chicano writers.

Carlota Cardenas de Dwyer, *Chicano Voices*, 1975
This important collection of short stories is from the Southwest.

Ray Gonzalez, *Currents From the Dancing River: Contemporary Latino Fiction, Nonfiction, and Poetry*, 1994
This short stories are by Chicano writers.

Ray Gonzalez, *Mirrors Beneath the Earth: Short Fiction by Chicano Writers*, 1992
This collection of short stories are by Chicano writers.

510

RUDOLFO ANAYA, Mexican American
EDWARD GONZALES, Illustrator, Mexican American

The Farolitos of Christmas
(New York: Hyperion Books for Children, 1995)

Subject(s): Tradition; Christmas; Grandparents
Age range(s): Grades 1-3
Major character(s): Luz, Child, Mexican American
Time period(s): 1940s (1941-1945)
Locale(s): San Juan, New Mexico

Summary: Luz's father has not returned from the war, and her Abuelo is ill. Luz worries that her Abuelo will not be well enough to cut the pinon logs for the *luminarias* that will light the path for the village's traditional Christmas procession. Christmas is only three days away, and Luz must find a new way to carry out the tradition.

Where it's reviewed:
Horn Book Magazine, November-December 1995, page 727
Publishers Weekly, September 18, 1995, page 102
New York Times Book Review, December 17, 1995 , page 28

Other books by the same author:
Bless Me, Ultima, 1972
Albuquerque, 1992
The Anaya Reader, 1995
Bendiceme, Ultima, 1995
A Chicano in China, 1986
The Legend of La Llorona: A Short Novel, 1994
Lord of the Dawn: The Legend of Quetzalcoatl, 1987
Zia Summer, 1995
Tortuga: A Novel, 1979

Other books you might like:
Omar Castaneda, *Abuela's Weave*, 1993
A little girl and her Abuela in Guatamala travel to the marketplace to sell their crafts.

Carmen Lomas Garza, *Family Pictures = Cuadros de Familia*, 1990
A children's book depicting pictures and descriptions of family life and traditions.

Carmen Santiago Nodar, *Abuelita's Paradise*, 1992
After a little girl's grandmother dies, she remembers the stories she once told her.

Gary Soto, *Too Many Tamales*, 1993
Maria helps her mother make tamales for Christmas Eve dinner and in the process loses something important.

Pat Mora, *The Gift of the Poinsettia = El Regalo de la Flor de Nochebuena*, 1995
Carlos is celebrating *Las Posadas* but can't enjoy himself because he's worried that he can't buy a gift for the baby Jesus.

Lulu Delacre, *Vejigantes Masquerade*, 1993
Ramon has always wanted to masquerade in Carnival, so he sews a vejigante costume himself and saves up to buy a devilish mask.

511

RUDOLFO ANAYA, Mexican American

Jalamanta: A Message from the Desert
(New York: Warner Books, 1996)

Subject(s): Magic; Poverty; Religion
Age range(s): Grades 10-Adult
Major character(s): Amado, Leader (later became Jalamanta), Mexican
Time period(s): Indeterminate Past
Locale(s): United States

Summary: After thirty years of being banished to the desert by a government that considered him subversive, Amado has learned the Path to the Sun, and returns to find his people living in squalor. He calls himself Jalamanta, which means ''one who strips away the veils that blind the soul''. His mission is to share what he has learned, and to lead his people to the light. A novel of spiritual insight and man's search for human understanding.

Where it's reviewed:
Library Journal, February 1, 1996, page 64
Publishers Weekly, January 1, 1996, page 58

Other books by the same author:
Albuquerque, 1995
The Anaya Reader, 1995
Bless Me, Ultima, 1972
Zia Summer, 1995
Tierra: Contemporary Short Fiction of New Mexico, 1989

Other books you might like:
Miguel Mendez, *Pilgrims in Aztlan*, 1992
A Chicano classic, first published in Spanish, where an aging veteran of the Mexican Revolution washes cars for tourists while watching the people who come his way and listening to their stories.

Aristeo Brito, *The Devil in Texas: El Diablo en Texas*, 1990
The devil comes to the border town of Presidio in this important novel that describes the Anglo destruction of a Chicano world in Texas.

Ron Arias, *The Road to Tamazunchale*, 1987
Don Fausto, old and nearing death in a Los Angeles barrio, decides to take a journey through time and space from the Inca world to encounters with undocumented workers in California.

Orlando Romero, *Nambe—Year One*, 1976
A resident of the town of Nambe, New Mexico, is being seduced by a gypsy woman to leave his land and traditions.

Graciela Limon, *Song of the Hummingbird*, 1996
Huitzitzilin, Hummingbird in the Nahuatal language, is an Aztec princess who is forced into slavery. As an 82-year-old woman, she recounts her life story during the Spanish conquest of Mexico.

Carlos Miralejos, *Rabid Beasts*, 1993
This science fiction work tells how Jorge Sogaseca, cap-

tain of the space ship Tulumex, saves the Cherokee Nation from dying of exposure to extremely cold weather during a long forced march.

512

RUDOLFO ANAYA, Mexican American

Rio Grande Fall

(New York: Warner Books, Inc., 1996)

Subject(s): Environmental Problems; Witches and Witchcraft; Mystery and Detective Stories
Age range(s): Grades 10-Adult
Major character(s): Sonny Baca, Detective—Private, Chicano
Time period(s): 1990s
Locale(s): Albuquerque, New Mexico (and in surrounding countryside)

Summary: Sonny Baca, private investigator and great grandson of the notorious lawman Elfego Baca, is still caught up in the murder of his cousin Gloria Dominic (*Zia Summer*). He is again pitted against his arch enemy Raven, thought to have been killed in the earlier novel. The battle between the two involves drug smuggling, federal agents, and the Medillin cartel, and it becomes personal when Raven kidnaps Sonny's beautiful girl friend, Rita. Anaya's writing incorporates the folklore of New Mexico, Native American traditions of strength and power, and memorable characters, all set in the ancient Southwest.

Where it's reviewed:
Publishers Weekly, July 29, 1996 , page 73
Kirkus Reviews, July 15, 1996, page

Other books by the same author:
Zia Summer, 1995
Albuquerque, 1992
The Anaya Reader, 1995
Lord of the Dawn: The Legend of Quetzalcoatl, 1987
Aztlan: Essays on the Chicano Homeland, 1989

Other books you might like:
James Roberto Curtis, *Shango*, 1996
    Miguel reads about a stolen skull that leads him to research *santeria* for an ethnography course. He gets involved in a police investigation of ritualistic murder and meets the god, Shango.
Michael Nava, *How Town: A Novel of Suspense*, 1990
    Henry Rios defends a former high school acquaintance from his hometown, accused of murdering a man and also thought to be involved in child pornography.
Lucha Corpi, *Cactus Blood: A Mystery Novel*, 1995
    Gloria Damasco, an apprentice to a private investigator, uses her visionary power to and help solve a murder related to a 15 year old pesticide tank explosion.
Lucha Corpi, *Eulogy for a Brown Angel: A Mystery Novel*, 1992
    A Chicana feminist detective solves a murder that occurred during the Chicano civil rights movement.
Michael Nava, *The Hidden Law*, 1992
    Henry Rios defends a young Chicano accused of murdering a powerful Chicano public official in Los Angeles, and discovers who did the actual killing.

Rolando Hinojosa, *Partners in Crime: A Rafe Buenrostro Mystery*, 1985
    Written in the style of the popular genre this border murder mystery involves Hinojosa's popular characters Jehu Malacara, and Rafe Buenrostro now a lieutenant of the Belken County Homicide Squad.
Manuel Ramos, *The Last Client of Luis Montez*, 1995
    The last client of Denver lawyer Louie Montez is found dead with Montez standing over him. To clear his name Montez becomes entangled in a complicated web that takes him to California and back.
Max Martinez, *White Leg*, 1996
    A fast action murder mystery, after the style of Jim Thompson, about a small town thief in a backwater town in Texas.

513

RUDOLFO ANAYA, Editor, Mexican American

Tierra: Contemporary Short Fiction of New Mexico

(El Paso, TX: Cinco Puntos Press, 1989)

Subject(s): Short Stories; Anthology
Age range(s): Grades 10-Adult
Time period(s): 1980s (1989)
Locale(s): New Mexico

Summary: The well known author Rudolfo Anaya edits this short fiction collection by writers living in New Mexico. Anaya believes that the vast space of earth and sky in New Mexico dictates the rhythm of the people and he calls this space *tierra*, which nourishes creativity. The anthology contains works by well known authors, Latino and non-Latino, representing a broad range of themes and stories, but all exhibit their unique New Mexican point of view. Latino authors in the collection include Sabine R. Ulibarri, Gustavo Sainz, Eduardo Chavez, and Gabriel Melendez.

Where it's reviewed:
Publishers Weekly, September 8, 1989, page 63

Other books by the same author:
Albuquerque, 1992
Bless Me, Ultima, 1972
Aztlan: Essays on the Chicano Homeland, 1989
Zia Summer, 1995
The Anaya Reader, 1995

Other books you might like:
Tey Diana Rebolledo, *Las Mujeres Hablan: An Anthology of Nuevo Mexicana Writers*, 1988
    An anthology, meaning *the women talk*, that contains stories, poems, and memoirs of women writers from New Mexico, in Spanish and English.
Alurista, *Southwest Tales: A Contemporary Collection*, 1986
    A collection of short stories by some early Chicano authors like Mary Helen Ponce, Juan Bruce-Novoa, and Alurista, and also by newer authors.
Carlota Cardenas de Dwyer, *Chicano Voices*, 1975
    An important early collection of short stories from the Southwest by Chicano writers.

Luis Valdez, *Aztlan: An Anthology of Mexican American Literature*, 1972

An early anthology of Chicano literature edited by the director of the Teatro Campesino.

Sabine Ulibarri, *Tierra Amarilla: Stories of New Mexico = Cuentos de Nuevo Mexico*, 1993

A collection of five short stories and a novella, first published in 1964, that evoke the rural life of a northern New Mexican village.

514

RUDOLFO ANAYA, Editor, Mexican American

Voces: An Anthology of Nuevo Mexicano Writers

(Albuquerque: El Norte Publications, 1987)

Subject(s): Anthology; Short Stories
Age range(s): Grades 10-Adult
Time period(s): 1980s (1987)
Locale(s): New Mexico

Summary: This anthology of poems and short stories, by New Mexico's contemporary Chicano writers, represent the artistic expression of the Mexican community. Some contributors are veteran writers like Fray Angelico Chavez and Sabine Ulibarri, while others are from a new generation of writers.

About this book: These stories and poems are in Spanish.

Other books by the same author:
Bless Me, Ultima, 1972
Cuentos Chicanos: A Short Story Anthology, 1984
Albuquerque, 1992
A Chicano in China, 1986
Heart of Aztlan, 1976
Tortuga: A Novel, 1988
Zia Summer, 1995

Other books you might like:
Ray Gonzalez, *Mirrors Beneath the Earth: Short Fiction by Chicano Writers*, 1992
This collection of short stories is by Chicano writers.
Tiffany Ana Lopez, *Growing Up Chicano*, 1993
These short stories by Chicano writers describe growing up Mexian American.
Gary Soto, *Pieces of the Heart: New Chicano Fiction*, 1993
These short stories are by Chicano writers.
Ray Gonzalez, *Mirrors Beneath the Earth: Short Fiction by Chicano Writers*, 1992
Contemporary Chicano authors write these short stories.

515

RUDOLFO ANAYA, Mexican American

Zia Summer

(New York: Warner Books, Inc., 1995)

Story type: Private Detective
Subject(s): Environmental Problems; Witches and Witchcraft; Superstition
Age range(s): Grades 10-Adult

Major character(s): Sonny Baca, Detective—Private (new to the business), Chicano
Time period(s): 1990s (1995)
Locale(s): Albuquerque, New Mexico (and surrounding countryside)

Summary: This exciting, complicated mystery plot involves murder, cult worship of the sun, and a battle over nuclear waste and disposal. Sonny Baca, a great-grandson of the notorious lawman Elfego Baca, sets out to investigate and avenge the murder of his cousin Gloria. Immediately he is in extreme danger, surviving more than one attempt on his life. Still he manages to see his beautiful girl friend Rita and consult with the elders, don Eliseo, Concho, and don Toto, who assist him in his investigation. These characters set in the ancient Southwest will be difficult to forget.

Where it's reviewed:
Publishers Weekly, April 10, 1995, page 56
New York Times Book Review, July 2, 1995, page 15

Other books by the same author:
The Adventures of Juan Chicaspatas, 1984
Albuquerque, 1992
The Anaya Reader, 1995
Bless Me, Ultima, 1972
A Chicano in China, 1986
Lord of the Dawn: The Legend of Quetzalcoatl, 1987
Aztlan: Essays on the Chicano Homeland, 1989

Other books you might like:
Michael Nava, *How Town: A Novel of Suspense*, 1990
Henry Rios defends a former high school acquaintance from his hometown who is accused of murdering a man and also thought to be involved in child pornography.
Lucha Corpi, *Cactus Blood: A Mystery Novel*, 1995
Gloria Damasco, an apprentice to a private investigator, possesses a visionary power and helps solve a murder related to a 15 year old pesticide tank explosion.
Lucha Corpi, *Eulogy for a Brown Angel: A Mystery Novel*, 1992
A Chicana feminist detective solves a murder that occurred during the Chicano civil rights movement.
Michael Nava, *The Hidden Law*, 1992
Henry Rios defends a young Chicano accused of murdering a powerful Chicano public official in Los Angeles, and discovers the true killer.
Rolando Hinojosa, *Partners in Crime: A Rafe Buenrostro Mystery*, 1985
Hinojosa's popular characters Jehu Malacara and Rafe Buenrostro, now a lieutenant of the Belken County Homicide Squad, investigate a murder along the border.
Manuel Ramos, *The Last Client of Luis Montez*, 1996
The last client of Denver lawyer, Louie Montez, is found dead with Montez standing over him. To clear his name, Montez becomes entangled in a complicated web that takes him to California and back.

516

GLORIA ANZALDUA, Mexican American

Borderlands: The New Mestiza = La Frontera

(San Francisco, CA: Spinsters/Aunt Lute, 1987)

Subject(s): Identity; Cultural Identity; Homosexuality/Lesbianism
Age range(s): Grades 10-Adult
Time period(s): 1980s (1987)
Locale(s): Texas (along the Texas-Mexican border)

Summary: In prose and poetry, Anzaldua writes about her childhood along the Texas-Mexican border, describing the experience of being caught between two cultures and belonging to neither. Tracing her history, presenting mythical gods and goddesses, and meditating on the conditions of women, Chicano/as, and lesbians, Anzaldua's work is original and powerful.

Where it's reviewed:
Feminist Studies, Spring 1991, page 135
Library Journal, January 1988, page 40

Awards the book has won:
A Best of 1987 Library Journal selection

Other books by the same author:
Friends from the Other Side/Amigos del Otro Lado, 1993
Making Face, Making Soul = Haciendo Caras: Creative and Critical Perspectives by Feminists of Color, 1990
This Bridge Called My Back: Writings by Radical Women of Color, 1981

Other books you might like:
Cherrie Moraga, *Loving in the War Years: Lo que Nunca Paso por sus Labios*, 1983
  Autobiographical writings about the life of a Chicana lesbian writer growing up in California.
Alicia Gaspar de Alba, *The Mystery of Survival and Other Stories*, 1993
  This first short story collection examines the boundaries between people, beliefs, and cultures.
Sandra Cisneros, *Woman Hollering Creek and Other Stories*, 1991
  Collection of short stories about women living along the Texas-Mexico border.
Norma Elia Cantu, *Canicula: Snapshots of a Girlhood en la Frontera*, 1995
  A collection, with photos, of short stories and vignettes of a young girl growing up along the Texas border.
Denise Chavez, *The Last of the Menu Girls*, 1986
  A collection of interrelated short stories, about a Chicana adolescent girl from southern New Mexico who is looking for her place and identity.
Carla Trujillo, *Chicana Lesbians: The Girls Our Mothers Warned Us About*, 1991
  A diverse collection of short stories, poetry, and prose by Chicana lesbians exploring the intricacies and specifics of culture, family, mixed-race relationships, body and identity.
Emma Perez, *Gulf Dreams*, 1996
  Growing up lesbian in Latino culture occupy the essays, short vignettes, and psychoanalytic discourse of this creative series.
Norma Alarcon, *The Sexuality of Latinas*, 1993
  This collection of poems, short stories, and prose examine the often hidden, often subverted, sexuality of Latinas.

517

GLORIA ANZALDUA, Mexican American
CONSUELO MENDEZ, Illustrator

Friends From the Other Side/Amigos del Otro Lado

(San Francisco: Children's Book Press, 1993)

Subject(s): Illegal Immigrants; Friendship
Age range(s): Grades 1-3
Major character(s): Prietita, 8-Year-Old, Mexican American; Joaquin, Child, Immigrant, Mexican
Time period(s): 1990s (1993)
Locale(s): Texas (Texas-Mexican border)

Summary: Prietita, a Mexican American girl, becomes friends with Joaquin, a boy who lives with his mother on the U.S. side of the border, but live there illegally. She defends him from kids who tease and taunt him. When the INS comes searching for illegal immigrants, Prietita hides Joaquin and his mother at her friend's house.

About this book: This is in bilingual format.

Other books by the same author:
Making Face, Making Soul = Haciendo Caras: Creative and Critical Perspectives by Feminists of Color, 1990
Borderlands: The New Mestiza = La Frontera, 1987
This Bridge Called My Back: Writings by Radical Women of Color, 1981

Other books you might like:
Pura Belpre, *Santiago*, 1969
  Santiago must deal with moving and making new friends.
Fran Leeper Buss, *Journey of the Sparrow*, 1991
  A Salvadoran family is smuggled into Chicago to start a new life.
Gary Soto, *The Skirt*, 1992
  Mia loses her mother's folkloric skirt and must find it within two days.
Enedina Casarez Vasquez, *Recuerdos de Una Nina*, 1980
  These short stories are about growing up in San Antonio, Texas.
Alma Flor Ada, *My Name Is Maria Isabel*, 1993
  Maria moves to a new school and learns not to be shy about her name.
Fernando Pico, *The Red Comb*, 1991
  A young girl helps save a runaway slave in 19th century Puerto Rico.

518

GLORIA ANZALDUA, Mexican American
CRISTINA GONZALEZ, Illustrator, Mexican American

Prietita and the Ghost Woman = Prietita y La Llorona
(San Francisco, CA: Children's Book Press, 1995)

Subject(s): Mothers and Daughters; Medicine
Age range(s): Grades 1-3
Major character(s): Prietita, 8-Year-Old (girl), Mexican American
Time period(s): 1990s
Locale(s): Texas

Summary: Prietita, a young Mexican American girl, goes searching for an herb that will help cure her mother of an illness. She gets lost, but La Llorona, the weeping woman, comes and helps her find her way.

About this book: Bilingual format.

Where it's reviewed:
Skipping Stones, June-August 1996, page 31

Other books by the same author:
Making Face, Making Soul = Haciendo Caras: Creative and Critical Perspectives by Feminists of Color, 1990
Borderlands: The New Mestiza = La Frontera, 1987
This Bridge Called My Back: Writings By Radical Women of Color, 1981
Friends From the Other Side/Amigos del Otro Lado, 1993

Other books you might like:
Alma Flor Ada, *My Name Is Maria Isabel*, 1993
　　Maria Isabel Salazar Lopez is proud of her name and the fact that she is named after a relative who she loves, but when she begins a new school her teacher changes her name.
Fernando Pico, *The Red Comb*, 1994
　　A young girl helps save a runaway slave in 19th century Puerto Rico.
Juan Felipe Herrera, *Calling the Doves = El Canto de las Palomas*, 1995
　　A book depicting the experiences of the author as a young boy growing up as a farm worker in the fields and valleys of California.
Alfred Avila, *Mexican Ghost Tales of the Southwest*, 1994
　　A collection of supernatural tales from the US-Mexico border.
Victor Villasenor, *Walking Stars: Stories of Magic and Power*, 1994
　　This is an autobiographical collection of stories about the author's parents and grandparents in Mexico.
Karen Papagapitos, *Socorro, Daughter of the Desert*, 1993
　　The family of eight-year-old Socorro are farm workers and she helps out as much as she can. When her father becomes ill, Socorro makes tortillas for her mother to sell in the fields.
Diane Gonzales Bertrand, *Alicia's Treasures*, 1996
　　Alicia is invited to spend a weekend at the beach with her brother and she has an exciting adventure.

519

FRANCES R. APARICIO, Editor

Latino Voices
(Brookfield, CN: The Millbrook Press, 1994)

Subject(s): Anthology; Poetry; Short Stories
Age range(s): Grades 7-12
Time period(s): 20th century (1940-1990)
Locale(s): United States

Summary: In this diverse collection of fiction, nonfiction, and poetry by Latino authors, themes such as racial and ethnic division, family, religion, and language are examined. The pieces, some by well known authors such as Sandra Cisneros and Piri Thomas, and other works by newer writers, are specially edited for young adult readers.

Where it's reviewed:
Wilson Library Bulletin, April 1995, page 115

Other books by the same author:
Versiones, Interpretaciones, Creaciones: Instancias de la Traduccion Literaria en Hispanoamerica en el Siglo Veinte, 1991

Other books you might like:
Alma Flor Ada, *Where the Flame Trees Bloom*, 1994
　　These eleven stories are about the childhood of the author in Cuba.
Phyllis Tashlik, *Hispanic, Female, and Young*, 1994
　　These short stories are written by seventh and eighth-grader girls in New York.
Harold Augenbraum, *Growing Up Latino: Memoirs and Stories*, 1993
　　Twenty-five Latinos write stories about growing up in the U.S.
Gary Soto, *A Summer Life*, 1990
　　A short story collection for young adults about Chicanos growing up in the San Joaquin Valley of California.
Victor Villasenor, *Walking Stars: Stories of Magic and Power*, 1994
　　In this collection of stories, some are autobiographical, some about the author's grandparents and parents, and about growing up as the son of Mexican immigrants.
Charles Tatum, *Mexican American Literature*, 1990
　　This anthology of Mexican American literature was written for high school classrooms and contains short stories, poems, and drama, all presented within a historical context.

520

REINALDO ARENAS, Cuban American

The Assault
(New York: Viking, 1994)

Subject(s): Science Fiction; Politics; Revolution
Age range(s): Grades 10-Adult
Major character(s): Stranger, Agent (Bureau of Counterwhispering), Cuban
Time period(s): Indeterminate Future
Locale(s): Cuba

Summary: Set in a society of "degenerate beasts" after "the last big war", Arenas' novel is a fictional exploration of a Castro-era Cuba with a disturbing surreal portrait of political extremes and a society headed toward self-destruction. An allegory, this is the final novel of his *Pentagonia* quintet. Composed of very short chapters, the novel is narrated by an un-named agent of the Bureau of Counterwhispering whose job is to find and execute whisperers against The Glorious Nation.

About this book: This novel is translated by Andrew Hurley.

Where it's reviewed:
Library Journal, June 15, 1994, page 92
Publishers Weekly, May 2, 1994, page 281
Times Literary Supplement, February 10, 1995, page 20

Other books by the same author:
Before Night Falls, 1993
The Doorman, 1991
Farewell to the Sea: A Novel of Cuba, 1986
The Palace of the White Skunks, 1990
Old Rosa: A Novel in Two Stories, 1989

Other books you might like:
Aristeo Brito, *The Devil in Texas: El Diablo en Texas*, 1990
  The devil comes to the border town of Presidio, Texas in this important novel that describes the Anglo destruction of a Chicano world.
Elias Miguel Munoz, *The Greatest Performance*, 1991
  In this poetic novel of exile, two soul-mates recount to each other their stories of living on the margins of family, country, and sexual identity.
Omar Torres, *Fallen Angels Sing*, 1991
  A young Cuban exile becomes involved in a plot to assassinate Fidel Castro.
Roberto Fernandez, *Holy Radishes*, 1995
  This satirical novel depicts the Cuban American community in Florida where exiled Cubans plan the liberation of their homeland while their wives work at a radish plant.
Fernando Alegria, *Paradise Lost or Gained? The Literature of Hispanic Exile*, 1990
  This collection of writings by Latinos addresses the experience of exile and alienation through stories, poems, and essays.
Ramon Ferreira, *The Gravedigger and Other Stories*, 1986
  This collection of disturbing and harsh short stories depicts the underside of Cuban society in the '50s, including political repression, the fear of homosexuality, and the dark side of prejudice.

521

REINALDO ARENAS, Cuban American

Before Night Falls
(New York: Viking Books, 1993)

Subject(s): Prisoners and Prisons; Homosexuality/Lesbianism; Identity
Age range(s): Grades 10-Adult
Major character(s): Reinaldo Arenas, Homosexual, Prisoner (political prisoner), Cuban
Time period(s): 1970s

Locale(s): Havana, Cuba

Summary: This autobiography starts with an introduction titled "The End" where Arena describes almost dying of AIDS in 1987 (he committed suicided in 1990). Caught between a desire to be free and an inability to free himself, this excellent story shows the power of Arena's imagination while also revealing his despair . It is meant to help all Cubans understand the political intolerance of 1970's Cuba. Written while Arenas was imprisoned in Cuba, his sexuality, needs and disappointments, dreams, and illnesses are set against the background of Cuban political turmoil and the gay rights struggle. The narrative traces his birth in Holguin in 1943, his rural childhood and his difficult transition to Havana. He lived in the United States the last ten years of his life.

Where it's reviewed:
New York Review of Books, November 18, 1993, page 23
Publishers Weekly, August 16, 1993, page 92
Times Literary Supplement, December 30, 1994, page 7
World Literature Today, Autumn 1994, page 797
New Yorker, November 29, 1993, page 65

Other books by the same author:
The Assault, 1994
The Doorman, 1991
Farewell to the Sea: A Novel of Cuba, 1986
The Palace of the White Skunks, 1990
Old Rosa: A Novel in Two Stories, 1989

Other books you might like:
Elias Miguel Munoz, *The Greatest Performance*, 1991
  In this poetic novel of exile, two soul-mates recount to each other their stories of living on the margins of family, country, and sexual identity.
Fernando Alegria, *Paradise Lost or Gained? The Literature of Hispanic Exile*, 1990
  This collection of writings by Latinos addresses the experience of exile and alienation through stories, poems, and essays.
Virgil Suarez, *The Cutter: A Novel*, 1991
  Julian Campos is forced by the Cuban Communist regime to work as a "cutter" in the muddy sugarcane fields as he waits to receive permission to leave the island.
Margarita Engle, *Skywriting*, 1995
  Carmen Peregrin's half-brother attempts to escape from Cuba by raft and ends up being arrested and imprisoned.
Gil Cuadros, *City of God*, 1994
  A short novel with a rough account of devastation and empowerment in the age of AIDS, it was written after the death of the author's lover.
Ramon Ferreira, *The Gravedigger and Other Stories*, 1986
  This collection of disturbing and harsh short stories depicts the underside of Cuban society in the '50s, including political repression, the fear of homosexuality, and the dark side of prejudice.
John Rechy, *City of Night*, 1963
  Johnny Rio, born in El Paso, becomes a gay Chicano wanderer, who lives by the statistics of random sexual encounters and orgasms in various cities.

522

REINALDO ARENAS, Cuban

The Doorman
(New York: Grove Press, 1991)

Subject(s): Social Classes; Revolution; Satire
Age range(s): Grades 10-Adult
Major character(s): Juan, Refugee (a doorman), Cuban
Time period(s): 1980s (1987)
Locale(s): New York, New York (Manhattan)

Summary: Juan, a young Cuban refugee, becomes a doorman at a luxury apartment building in New York in this parable about freedom. Alienated from the rich tenants, Juan is instead seduced by their pets, who speak to him and are determined to recruit him to their cause: a revolt against humans and human society.

About this book: Originally published in 1987; translated by Dolores M. Koch.

Where it's reviewed:
Review: Latin American Literature & Arts, July-December '91, page 109
Review of Contemporary Fiction, Spring 1992, page 148

Other books by the same author:
The Assault, 1994
Before Night Falls, 1993
Farewell to the Sea: A Novel of Cuba, 1986
Hallucinations: Being an Account of the Life and Adventures of Friar Servando Teresa de Mier, 1971
Old Rosa: A Novel in Two Stories, 1989
The Palace of the White Skunks, 1990
Singing from the Well, 1987

Other books you might like:
Fernando Alegria, *Paradise Lost or Gained? The Literature of Hispanic Exile*, 1990
  This collection by Latino writers addresses the experience of exile and alienation through stories, poems, and essays.
Isabel Allende, *The House of the Spirits*, 1995
  A complicated political novel about the Trueba family covering eight decades,and ending with the overthrow of the government by the military.
Elias Miguel Munoz, *Crazy Love*, 1989
  An experimental and autobiographical novel about the Cuban American experience.
Virgil Suarez, *Welcome to the Oasis and Other Stories*, 1992
  The Mariel refugees are represented in a novela and short stories that show their culture shock through the eyes of the refugees.

523

REINALDO ARENAS, Cuban American

Old Rosa: A Novel in Two Stories
(New York: Grove Press, 1989)

Subject(s): Revolution; Mental Illness; Homosexuality/Lesbianism
Age range(s): Grades 10-Adult

Major character(s): Old Rosa, Mother, Cuban; Arturo, Son (of Old Rosa), Homosexual, Cuban
Time period(s): 1960s
Locale(s): Cuba

Summary: These two stories converge on the relationship of a Cuban mother and her son. The first story is about Rosa as a young woman and how her life changes when one son joins Castro's army and she finds her younger son in bed with another boy. The second story is about the young son in a Castro camp for homosexuals and the brutality he suffers. Densely charged and lyrically written, this story follows Rosa's growing madness.

Where it's reviewed:
Library Journal, June 15, 1989, page 76
New York Review of Books, March 7, 1991, page 21
Publishers Weekly, May 19, 1989, page 67

Other books by the same author:
Before Night Falls, 1993
The Doorman, 1991
Farewell to the Sea: A Novel of Cuba, 1986
The Palace of the White Skunks, 1990
The Assault, 1994

Other books you might like:
Virgil Suarez, *The Cutter: A Novel*, 1991
  Julian Campos is forced by the Cuban Communist regime to work as a cutter in the muddy sugarcane fields as he waits to receive permission to leave the island.
Margarita Engle, *Skywriting*, 1995
  Carmen Peregrin's half-brother attempts to escape from Cuba by raft and ends up being arrested and imprisoned.
Omar Torres, *Fallen Angels Sing*, 1991
  This is the story of a young exile who gets involved in a plot to assassinate Fidel Castro.
Elias Miguel Munoz, *The Greatest Performance*, 1991
  A poetic novel of exile, this tale has two soul-mates recount to each other their stories of living on the margins of family, country, and sexual identity.
Ramon Ferreira, *The Gravedigger and Other Stories*, 1986
  This collection of disturbing and harsh short stories depict the underside of Cuban society during the '50s, including political repression, fear of homosexuality, and the dark side of prejudice.
Graciela Limon, *In Search of Bernabe*, 1993
  A novel about a mother's search for her son during civil war in El Salvador.

524

REINALDO ARENAS, Cuban American

The Palace of the White Skunks
(New York: Viking, 1990)

Subject(s): Death; Revolution; Poverty
Age range(s): Grades 10-Adult
Major character(s): Fortunato, Young Man, Revolutionary
Time period(s): 1960s
Locale(s): Cuba

Summary: This is the story of Fortunato, a boy raised in poverty by his grandparents, his life as he grows up during the

Cuban revolution, and his death. As a young man he joins the rebel forces, is imprisoned, tortured, and finally executed by the government. His life is related through the voices of his relatives—his grandfather and cousins—and also his own sad voice.

About this book: The translation is by Andrew Hurley.

Where it's reviewed:
Americas (English Edition), January-February 1991, page 60
Library Journal, November 15, 1990, page 90
New York Review of Books, March 7, 1991, page 21
Publishers Weekly, October 19, 1990, page 47

Other books by the same author:
The Assault, 1994
Before Night Falls, 1993
The Doorman, 1991
Farewell to the Sea: A Novel of Cuba, 1986
Singing from the Well, 1987

Other books you might like:
Virgil Suarez, *The Cutter: A Novel*, 1991
    Julian Campos is forced by the Cuban Communist regime to work as a ''cutter'' in the muddy sugarcane fields while he awaits permission to leave the island.
Margarita Engle, *Singing to Cuba*, 1993
    A California woman leaves her husband and children to search for information about family members who disappeared during the Castro revolution.
Margarita Engle, *Skywriting*, 1995
    Carmen Peregrin's half-brother attempts to escape from Cuba by raft and ends up being arrested and imprisoned.
Ramon Ferreira, *The Gravedigger and Other Stories*, 1986
    This collection of disturbing and harsh short stories depicts the underside of Cuban society in the '50s, including political repression, the fear of homosexuality, and the dark side of prejudice.
Gil Cuadros, *City of God*, 1994
    The first half of this book is a short novel and the second half poetry, the author writes after the death of his lover.
Junot Diaz, *Drown, Stories*, 1996
    This collection of ten short stories describes young Latino men being transformed while learning to define their American identity.
Miguel Barnet, *Rachel's Song: A Novel*, 1991
    A famous cabaret dancer, writing of her love affairs and adventures in the theater, recounts the frivolity and injustice of pre-Castro Cuba.

525

MANLIO ARGUETA, Salvadoran
ELLY SIMMONS, Illustrator

Magic Dogs of the Volcanoes = Los Perros Magicos de los Volcanes

(San Francisco: Children's Book Press, 1990)

Subject(s): Animals; Volcanoes; Folk Tales
Age range(s): Grades 2-4
Major character(s): Don Tonio, Salvadoran
Time period(s): Indeterminate Past

Locale(s): El Salvador (story takes place in the villages and volcanoes of El Salvador)

Summary: The magic dogs, or cadejos, who live on the volcanoes of El Salvador, are loved by almost all of the villagers. They rescue children, protect the villagers, and help them stay out of the sun, using their powerful magic. The cadejos seek the magical help of their great-great-grandparents, the volcanoes, when an army of tin soldiers is sent to hunt them.

About this book: This work is in Spanish and English and translated by Stacey Ross.

Where it's reviewed:
Horn Book, September 1991, page 629
Kirkus Reviews, December 1, 1990, page 1667
School Library Journal, February 1991, page 66

Other books by the same author:
Cuzcatlan: Where the Southern Sea Beats, 1987
One Day of Life, 1983

Other books you might like:
Pura Belpre, *The Rainbow-Colored Horse*, 1978
    A beautiful seven-colored horse tramples Tano's maize field. Once caught, he grants three wishes to Pio, Tano's son.
Gary Soto, *Chato's Kitchen*, 1995
    Chato the cat wants to eat some juicy mice, but when he invites them to dinner they outwit him.
Pura Belpre, *Dance of the Animals*, 1972
    Senor and Senora Lion are hungry for goat meat, so they throw a party and invite all the animals.
Omar Castaneda, *Abuela's Weave*, 1993
    A girl and her grandmother make tapestries for an outdoor market.
Alejandro Cruz Martinez, *The Woman Who Outshone the Sun*, 1991
    A Zapotec legend about a beautiful woman with hair so bright that it outshines the sun.
Maria Garcia, *The Adventures of Connie and Diego = Las Aventuras de Connie y Diego*, 1986
    Connie and Diego are different from other people in the Land of Plenty. They have many colors all over their bodies.
Francisco X. Mora, *Juan Tuza and the Magic Pouch*, 1994
    Juan Tuza, a prairie dog, and Pepe, an armadillo, have performed good deeds in the desert. Because of this, they are rewarded with a magic pouch which will grant any wish they make.

526

RON ARIAS, Mexican American

The Road to Tamazunchale

(New York: Anchor Books, 1992)

Subject(s): Magic; Death; Satire
Age range(s): Grades 10-Adult
Major character(s): Don Fausto, Aged Person, Traveller, Mexican American
Time period(s): 1960s
Locale(s): Los Angeles, California

Summary: Don Fausto, an old man approaching death, refuses to fade away, and strikes out on a journey through time and space. An original novel, it was nominated for the National Book Award in 1975, and is considered to be the first Chicano novel to apply a magical realism literary style. The power of Don Fausto's creative imagination takes him from East Los Angeles to Cuzco Peru then back to California where he meets up with a group of undocumented workers, and others, as he prepares to die. Arias oversteps the limits of the traditional narrative.

About this book: Originally published in 1975.

Awards the book has won:
National Book Award nominee, 1975

Other books by the same author:
The Castle, 1976
Five Against the Sea: A True Story of Courage and Survival, 1989

Other books you might like:
John Rechy, *The Miraculous Day of Amalia Gomez: A Novel*, 1991
   This novel follows a day in the life of a Mexican American woman, who lives among poverty, gang warfare, illegal border crossings, yet still has hope.
Miguel Mendez, *Pilgrims in Aztlan*, 1992
   Loreto Maldonado, an aging veteran of the Mexican Revolution, now washes cars for tourists in Tijuana, watching the people who come his way and tell him their stories.
Miguel Mendez, *The Dream of Santa Maria de las Piedras*, 1989
   This is the story of a small, rural, poor town in the Sonora Desert of Mexico, seen through the eyes of the old men who gather to reminisce and gossip in the town plaza.
Leo Romero, *Rita and Los Angeles*, 1995
   In this short story collection, a cast of fascinatingly complex characters grow and evolve, and learn about being outsiders in an alien and hostile world.
Oscar Zeta Acosta, *The Revolt of the Cockroach People*, 1973
   This personal memoir recounts the turbulent years that mark the beginning of the Chicano movement in California when Chicanos were systematically oppressed by the establishment.
Aristeo Brito, *The Devil in Texas = El Diablo en Texas*, 1990
   The devil comes to the border town of Presidio, Texas in this important novel that describes the Anglo destruction of a Chicano world.

527

HAROLD AUGENBRAUM, Editor
ILAN STAVANS, Co-Editor, Mexican American

Growing Up Latino: Memoirs and Stories
(Boston: Houghton Mifflin Co, 1993)

Subject(s): Short Stories; Growing Up; Family Relations
Age range(s): Grades 10-Adult
Time period(s): 20th century (1940-1991)
Locale(s): United States (stories take place from the Southwest to the East Coast)

Summary: In this collection, twenty-five Latino writers describe growing up Latino in the U.S. While several pieces are chapters from novels, they can all be read and understood out of context. Sections of the book include ''Imagining the Family,'' ''Gringolandia,'' and ''Songs of Self-Discovery.''

About this book: Many of the contributors are well-known authors.

Where it's reviewed:
Publishers Weekly, January 11, 1993, page 59
Library Journal, January 1993, page 114

Other books by the same author:
Latinos in English, 1992
Imagining Columbus: The Literary Voyage, 1993
The Hispanic Condition, 1995
The One-Handed Pianist and Other Stories, 1996

Other books you might like:
Ray Gonzalez, *Mirrors Beneath the Earth: Short Fiction by Chicano Writers*, 1992
   This collection of short stories is by Chicano writers.
Gary D. Keller, *Hispanics in the U.S.: An Anthology of Creative Literature*, 1982
   This anthology of short stories and other writings are by Latinos in the U.S.
Nicolas Kanellos, *Short Fiction by Hispanic Writers of the United States*, 1993
   This collection of short stories is by Latinos in the U.S.
Ray Gonzalez, *Currents From the Dancing River: Contemporary Latino Fiction, Nonfiction, and Poetry*, 1994
   Latinos author the short stories in this collection.
Lillian Castillo-Speed, *Latina: Women's Voices from the Borderland*, 1995
   A collection of writings by Latino authors specially edited for young adult readers.
Delia Poey, *Iguana Dreams: New Latino Fiction*, 1992
   This is an anthology of creative fiction by Latino writers in the U.S.

528

ALFRED AVILA, Mexican American

Mexican Ghost Tales of the Southwest
(Houston: Pinata Books, 1994)

Subject(s): Ghosts; Short Stories; Supernatural
Age range(s): Grades 4-8
Time period(s): Indeterminate Past
Locale(s): Southwest

Summary: A collection of supernatural tales from the U.S. Mexico border that reflect the heritage of Mexican Americans. Stories with evil spirits like La Llorona or the weeping woman, the goat devil, owls, witches, and other scary phantoms are related.

Where it's reviewed:
Wilson Library Bulletin, April 1995, page 114

Other books you might like:
Esther De Michael Cervantes, *Barrio Ghosts*, 1988
   These scary short stories are about urban life in the Chicano Community.

Kleya Forte-Escamilla, *The Storyteller with Nike Airs and Other Barrio Stories*, 1995
Stories about the desert with a supernatural twist.

Frances R. Aparicio, *Latino Voices*, 1994
This collection of writings by Latino authors is specially edited for young adult readers.

Victor Villasenor, *Walking Stars: Stories of Magic and Power*, 1994
This collection of autobiographical stories portray the author's ancestors and near family.

Patricia Preciado Martin, *Days of Plenty, Days of Want*, 1988
The past and present meet in this collection of stories where Mexican heritage is in jeopardy of being wiped out.

529

MIGUEL BARNET, Cuban

Rachel's Song: A Novel
(Willamantic, CT: Curbstone Press, 1991)

Subject(s): Dancing; Theater
Age range(s): Grades 10-Adult
Major character(s): Rachel, Dancer, Actor, Cuban
Time period(s): 1920s
Locale(s): Havana, Cuba

Summary: This portrait of pre-Castro Cuba is told through the eyes of Rachel, a famous cabaret dancer, whose story is humorous, surprising, and vivid. Writing of her love affairs and adventures in the theatre, she recounts the frivolity and injustice of the period.

About this book: Translated by W. Nick Hill; originally published 1969.

Where it's reviewed:
Choice, May 1992, page 1398
Library Journal, September 1, 1991, page 227
Publishers Weekly, July 25, 1991, page 46
Review of Contemporary Fiction, Spring 1992, page 150

Other books by the same author:
La Cancion de Rachel, 1985
Gallego, 1985
La Vida Real, 1986
The Documentary Novel, 1979

Other books you might like:
Virgil Suarez, *The Cutter: A Novel*, 1991
Julian Campos is forced by the Cuban Communist regime to work as a cutter in the muddy sugarcane fields while awaiting permission to leave the island.

Cristina Garcia, *Dreaming in Cuban, A Novel*, 1992
A novel that interweaves the stories of three generations of Cuban women and their varied responses to the Cuban revolution.

Carmen C. Esteves, *Green Cane and Juicy Flotsam: Short Stories by Caribbean Women*, 1991
In this collection of short stories, Caribbean women writers examine questions of race, power, colonialism, poverty, and identity.

Margarita Engle, *Singing to Cuba*, 1993
A California woman leaves her husband and children to search for information about family members who disappeared during the Castro revolution.

Ruth Behar, *Bridges to Cuba = Puentes a Cuba*, 1995
An anthology of short stories, essays, poetry, and historical documents exploring the Cuban and Cuban American experience.

530

JOSE BARREIRO

The Indian Chronicles
(Houston, TX: Arte Publico Press, 1993)

Subject(s): Conquest; Slavery; Indians of the West Indies
Age range(s): Grades 10-Adult
Major character(s): Diego Colon, Young Man, Taino Indian
Time period(s): 16th century (1532-1546)
Locale(s): Cuba

Summary: Reworking history from the perspective of a Taino boy, this novel narrates the Indian's discovery of the Europeans. Adopted by Christopher Columbus, Diego Colon keeps a journal where he describes events in his life from 1532-1535, and where he discusses the conquest of Espanola, Cuba, and Puerto Rico. Diego vividly describes the ordeals of native people suffered at the hands of the Spaniards and Christianity. Barreiro maintains accuracy in his exploration of the Taino culture.

About this book: Glossary of Taino and Spanish words included.

Where it's reviewed:
Choice, December 1993, page 600
Library Journal, August 1993, page 144
Parabola, Winter 1993, page 118
Publishers Weekly, July 5, 1993, page 62

Other books by the same author:
Indian Roots of American Democracy, 1992

Other books you might like:
Barbara Mujica, *The Deaths of Don Bernardo*, 1990
This novel that takes the reader into the elegant homes of the rich, the struggling Indian villages of the Andes and presents Bernardo de Alvarez, Peurian plantation owner who murders a man.

Montserrat Fontes, *Dreams of the Centaur*, 1995
Alejo Durcal, son of a slain ranch owner, tries to avenge his father's death, during the period in history when the Yaqui Indians were badly mistreated in Mexico.

Gary D. Keller, *Zapata Lives!*, 1994
The Mexican revolutionary leader Emiliano Zapata has risen from the dead, and he must lead his people in a struggle against economic and social oppression

Tina Juarez, *Call No Man Master*, 1995
Intricately crafted, this historical novel is about a young woman of mixed heritage, Spanish and Indian, and her participation in the events that lead to Mexico's independence from Spain.

Gloria Duran, *Malinche: Slave Princess of Cortez*, 1993
Malinali, born an Aztec princess and sold to the conqueror Cortez, is an ambiguous and controversial figure in Mexican history and this is her story.

Joseph P. Sanchez, *The Aztec Chronicles: The True History of Christopher Columbus, as Narrated by Quilaztli of Texcoco: A Novella*, 1995

A historical novella, based on documentary and bibliographical research, this is narrated by an Aztec historian and attempts to reconstruct the true history of Christopher Columbus.

Graciela Limon, *Song of the Hummingbird*, 1996

Huitzitzilin, Hummingbird in the Nahuatal language, is an Aztec princess who is forced into slavery. As an 82-year-old woman, recounts her life's story during the Spanish conquest of Mexico.

Esteban Montejo, *The Autobiography of a Runaway Slave*, 1993

Based on interviews of a 105-year-old man, this important book in Cuban black literature describes life on a sugar plantation and the experience of being a fugitive.

531

RAYMOND BARRIO, Mexican American

The Plum Plum Pickers
(New York: Harper and Row, 1969)

Subject(s): Migrant Labor; Family; Poverty
Age range(s): Grades 10-Adult
Major character(s): Manuel Gutierrez, Husband, Immigrant (farm worker), Mexican; Lupe Gutierrez, Wife, Immigrant (farm worker), Mexican
Time period(s): 1960s (1969)
Locale(s): California (the Santa Clara Valley of northern California)

Summary: This is the dramatic story of Manuel and Lupe Gutierrez and their children, who are migrant farm workers in California's Santa Clara Valley. The oppressive working and squalid living conditions are vividly depicted. The cast of characters includes a greedy company owner, a stooge Spanish-speaking overseer, and hundreds of fruit pickers caught in the migrant farm labor work cycle. Published in 1969, this novel is considered a classic of the Chicano Movement because it appeared at the height of the United Farm Workers unionization movement.

Other books by the same author:
A Political Portfolio, 1985
The Devil's Apple Corps: A Trauma in Four Acts, 1976
Mexico's Art and Chicano Artists, 1975

Other books you might like:
Tomas Rivera, *Y No Se lo Trago la Tierra.And the Earth Did Not Devour Him*, 1971
Series of short stories and vignettes, in English, about a migrant farm worker boy from Texas.
Jose Antonio Villarreal, *Pocho*, 1959
Considered to be the first key Chicano novel about a Mexican family attempting to assimilate in the Santa Clara Valley of California.
Genaro Gonzalez, *Rainbow's End*, 1988
The story of three generations of the Cavazos family living in the Lower Rio Grande Valley in Texas including their migrant labor and Vietnam hardships.

Helena Maria Viramontes, *Under the Feet of Jesus*, 1995
The hardships suffered by a migrant farm working family, and Estrella a young girl, living in a shack, picking grapes in California's vineyards is recounted in this novel.
Ernesto Galarza, *Barrio Boy*, 1971
Autobiographical, this story examines the early life of a distinguished professor and author who wrote many works about Mexican agricultural workers.

532

RUTH BEHAR, Editor, Cuban

Bridges to Cuba = Puentes a Cuba
(Ann Arbor, MI: The University of Michigan Press, 1995)

Subject(s): Short Stories; Poetry; Essays
Age range(s): Grades 10-Adult
Time period(s): 20th century (1960-1995)
Locale(s): United States

Summary: This diverse collection of short stories, poems, essays, and art breaks literary and intellectual boundaries to show the complexity of culture, identity, and homeland in the Cuban American experience. The authors are from "both sides," Cuba and America. The book is organized into three sections: Reconciliation, Rupture, and Remembering. Many of the writers are well known, such as Gustavo Perez Firmat, Roberto Fernandez, Eliana Rivera and Coco Fusco. Others are not as well known.

About this book: This volume originated as an issue of the Michigan Quarterly Review.

Where it's reviewed:
Michigan Quarterly Review, Fall 1994, page 639

Other books by the same author:
Translated Woman: Crossing the Border with Esperanza's Story, 1993
Women Writing Culture, 1995
Santa Maria del Monte: The Presence of the Past in a Spanish Village, 1986

Other books you might like:
Carolina Hospital, *Cuban American Writers: Los Atrevidos*, 1988
A collection of short stories and poetry by twelve Cuban-American writers, all of whom were born in Cuba and came to the U.S. very young.
Nicolas Kanellos, *Short Fiction by Hispanic Writers of the United States*, 1993
Collection of short stories by Latinos in the U.S., including several Cuban Americans.
Ray Gonzalez, *Currents From the Dancing River: Contemporary Latino Fiction, Nonfiction, and Poetry*, 1994
Collection of short stories and other writings by Latinos in the U.S.
Gustavo Perez Firmat, *Next Year in Cuba: A Cubano's Coming of Age in America*, 1995
A memoir by a professor exploring his biculturalism and his search for identity and roots in America.
Delia Poey, *Iguana Dreams: New Latino Fiction*, 1992
Collection of short stories by Cuban American and other Latino writers in the U.S.

533

PURA BELPRE, Puerto Rican
PAUL GALDONE, Illustrator

Dance of the Animals

(New York: Frederick Warne, 1972)

Subject(s): Animals; Folk Tales
Age range(s): Grades 1-2
Major character(s): Senor Lion, Lion, Puerto Rican; Senora Lion, Lion, Puerto Rican
Time period(s): Indeterminate Past
Locale(s): Puerto Rico (the forest)

Summary: Senor and Senora Lion are hungry for goat meat. They throw a party and invite all the animals, but the goat outwits them.

About this book: A well-loved Puerto Rican folk tale.

Other books by the same author:
The Rainbow-Colored Horse, 1978
Ote: A Puerto Rican Folk Tale, 1969
Santiago, 1969
Juan Bobo and the Queen's Necklace: A Puerto Rican Folk Tale, 1962
Perez and Martina, 1960

Other books you might like:
Gary Soto, *Chato's Kitchen*, 1995
   Chato wants to have mice for dinner, but they outwit him.
Eve Bunting, *Smokey Night*, 1995
   During the Los Angeles riots of 1992 a little cat gets lost.
Jan Romero Stevens, *Carlos and the Squash Plant/Carlos y la Planta de Calabaza*, 1993
   Carlos does not bathe when told by his mother and soon a plant grows out of his ear.
Manlio Argueta, *Magic Dogs of the Volcanoes = Los Perros Magicos de los Volcanes*, 1990
   Ancient volcanoes protect the magic dogs who live on the volcanoes in El Salvador.
Alma Flor Ada, *Dear Peter Rabbit = Querido Pedrin*, 1994
   Goldilocks, Baby Bear, Peter Rabbit, and The Three Little Pigs write letters to each other in this captivating book.
Linda Shute, *Rabbit Wishes*, 1995
   Soon after creation, Tio Conejo complains that he wants to be large like an elephant or tall like a giraffe.

534

PURA BELPRE, Puerto Rican
PAUL GALDONE, Illustrator

Ote: A Puerto Rican Folk Tale

(New York: Pantheon Books, 1969)

Subject(s): Folk Tales; Devil
Age range(s): Grades K-3
Major character(s): Ote, Father (poor)
Time period(s): Indeterminate Past
Locale(s): Puerto Rico (Takes place in the country)

Summary: Ote must go to the forest in search of food for his wife and five children. There he meets a near-sighted devil who brings him bad luck. His youngest son Chiquitin saves the day.

About this book: This is a charming and little-known Puerto Rican folk tale.

Other books by the same author:
Dance of the Animals, 1972
The Rainbow-Colored Horse, 1978
Santiago, 1969
The Tiger and the Rabbit and Other Tales, 1965

Other books you might like:
Manilo Argueto, *Magic Dogs of the Volcanoes = Los Perros Magicos de los Volcanes*, 1990
   The magic dogs, or cadejos, who live on the volcanoes of El Salvador, are loved by the villagers because of their powerful magic.
Gary Soto, *Chato's Kitchen*, 1995
   Chato the lowrider cat wants to eat some juicy mice, but when he invites them to dinner they outwit him.
Lucia M. Gonzalez, *The Bossy Gallito*, 1994
   A bossy little rooster gets his beak dirty pecking some corn while on his way to his uncle's wedding.
Harriet Rohmer, *Uncle Nacho's Hat = El Sombrero de Tio Nacho*, 1989
   Uncle Nacho loves his old, ragged hat, and when his niece gives him a new one Nacho is unable to give up his old one.
Alma Flor Ada, *The Gold Coin*, 1991
   Juan travels the countryside trying to steal the gold coin.
Cruz Martel, *Yagua Days*, 1978
   Adan, born in New York, gets to visit his relatives in Puerto Rico one summer and learns about yagua days.

535

PURA BELPRE, Puerto Rican
CARLOS SANCHEZ, Illustrator

Perez and Martina

(New York: Viking Penguin, 1991)

Subject(s): Animals; Love; Folk Tales
Age range(s): Grades 1-3
Major character(s): Martina, Cockroach (a refined lady cockroach), Spanish; Perez, Mouse (a gallant little mouse), Spanish
Time period(s): Indeterminate Past
Locale(s): Spain

Summary: This traditional Puerto Rican folktale is the story of the courtship and marriage of the Spanish cockroach, Martina, and the gallant mouse, Senor Perez. Although there is an unexpected and sad ending, the colorful illustrations are fascinating and bring the reader back to the story again and again.

About this book: This was First published in 1932 by Frederick Warne and Co., Inc.

Where it's reviewed:
READING TEACHER, February 1993, page 410

Other books by the same author:
Dance of the Animals, 1972
The Rainbow-Colored Horse, 1978

Santiago, 1969
The Tiger and the Rabbit and Other Tales, 1965

Other books you might like:

Manilo Argueto, *Magic Dogs of the Volcanoes = Los Perros Magicos de los Volcanes*, 1990
The magic dogs, or cadejos, who live on the volcanoes of El Salvador, are loved by the villagers because of their powerful magic.

Gary Soto, *Chato's Kitchen*, 1995
Chato the lowrider cat wants to eat some juicy mice, but when he invites them to dinner they outwit him.

Lucia M. Gonzalez, *The Bossy Gallito*, 1994
A bossy little rooster gets his beak dirty pecking some corn while on his way to his uncle's wedding.

Harriet Rohmer, *Uncle Nacho's Hat = El Sombrero de Tio Nacho*, 1989
Uncle Nacho loves his old, ragged hat, and when his niece gives him a new one Nacho is unable to give up his old one.

Alma Flor Ada, *The Gold Coin*, 1991
Juan travels the countryside trying to steal the gold coin.

Nicholasa Mohr, *The Song of el Coqui and Other Tales of Puerto Rico*, 1995
This collection of three vividly illustrated tales evokes the rich ancestral traditions of Puerto Rican culture.

536

PURA BELPRE, Puerto Rican
ANTONIO MORTORELL, Illustrator

The Rainbow-Colored Horse

(New York: Frederick Warne, 1978)

Subject(s): Folk Tales; Animals
Age range(s): Grades K-1
Major character(s): Pio, Child (boy), Puerto Rican; Tano, Father, Puerto Rican
Time period(s): Indeterminate Past
Locale(s): Puerto Rico

Summary: In this retelling of a Puerto Rican folktale, a beautiful seven-colored horse tramples Tano's maize field. Once caught, he grants three wishes to Pio, Tano's son.

Other books by the same author:
Dance of the Animals, 1972
Ote: A Puerto Rican Folk Tale, 1969
Santiago, 1969
Juan Bobo and the Queen's Necklace: A Puerto Rican Folk Tale, 1962
Perez and Martina, 1960

Other books you might like:

Pat Mora, *Listen to the Desert/Oye al Desierto*, 1994
The sounds of the desert are described in both English and Spanish languages.

Jan Romero Stevens, *Carlos and the Squash Plant/Carlos y la Planta de Calabaza*, 1993
Carlos does not bathe when told by his mother and soon a plant grows out of his ear.

Omar Castaneda, *Abuela's Weave*, 1993
A little girl and her grandmother weave tapestries for an outdoor market.

Gary Soto, *Chato's Kitchen*, 1995
Chato, a low-rider cat, prepares dinner for some unexpected guests.

Eve Bunting, *Smokey Night*, 1995
During the Los Angeles riots of 1992 a little cat gets lost.

Arthur Dorros, *Abuela*, 1991
A little girl and her grandmother fly all over New York City.

537

PURA BELPRE, Puerto Rican
SYMEON SHIMIN, Illustrator

Santiago

(New York: Frederick Warne and Company, 1969)

Subject(s): Animals; Friendship
Age range(s): Grades 1-3
Major character(s): Santiago, Child, Puerto Rican
Time period(s): 1960s
Locale(s): New York, New York

Summary: Santiago moves with his family from Puerto Rico to New York. He has to leave his beautiful pet hen, Selina, behind. He tells his friend Ernie about Selina, but Ernie does not believe him. Eventually, Santiago gains a new friend, and learns to bridge the gap between his home and his new city.

Other books by the same author:
Dance of the Animals, 1972
Perez and Martina, 1961
Juan Bobo and the Queen's Necklace : A Puerto Rican Folk Tale, 1962
Ote: A Puerto Rican Folk Tale, 1969

Other books you might like:

Gary Soto, *Too Many Tamales*, 1993
Maria helps her mother make tamales for Christmas Eve dinner.

Gary Soto, *The Skirt*, 1992
Miata loses the beautiful skirt lent her.

Juanita Havill, *Treasure Nap*, 1992
Alicia hears the story about Rita who visits her grandfather in the mountains of Mexico.

Nicholasa Mohr, *Felita*, 1990
Felita loves her neighborhood and her best friend Gigi, but her world is turned upside down when her family moves to a new neighborhood.

Alma Flor Ada, *My Name Is Maria Isabel*, 1993
Maria Isabel Salazar Lopez is proud of her name and the fact that she is named after a relative whom she loves, but when she begins a new school her teacher changes her name.

Cruz Martel, *Yagua Days*, 1976
Adan, born in New York, visits his relatives in Puerto Rico one summer and learns about yagua days.

Karen Papagapitos, *Jose's Basket*, 1990
Because Jose's family is a migrant farm-working family, school starts later and ends earlier for him than for the

other students. His teacher understands and gives him a special gift.

PURA BELPRE, Puerto Rican
TOMIE DE PAOLA, Illustrator

The Tiger and the Rabbit and Other Tales

(Philadelphia: Lippincott, 1965)

Subject(s): Animals; Short Stories; Folk Tales
Age range(s): Grades 3-6
Time period(s): Indeterminate Past
Locale(s): Puerto Rico

Summary: This is a colorful, imaginative collection of folktales from Puerto Rico. Belpre's stories about animals, magic, and ordinary situations are humorous and magical and have been read and told to children in English and in Spanish for generations. In this collection we meet Juan Bobo, La Hormiguita, Senor Billy Goat, the Bed and the Cat, the Mountain Goat, and the Fox.

About this book: This work was first published in 1947. Pura Belpre was known as a great storyteller.

Other books by the same author:
Dance of the Animals, 1972
Juan Bobo and the Queen's Necklace: A Puerto Rican Folk Tale, 1962
Ote: A Puerto Rican Folktale, 1962
Perez and Martinez, 1961
Santiago, 1969

Other books you might like:
Alma Flor Ada, *The Gold Coin*, 1991
   Juan travels the countryside trying to steal the gold coin.
Gary Soto, *Too Many Tamales*, 1993
   Maria helps her mother make tamales for Christmas Eve dinner, but she loses something she must find.
Juanita Havill, *Treasure Nap*, 1992
   Alicia hears the story of Rita, who visits her grandfather in the mountains of Mexico.
Harriet Rohmer, *Uncle Nacho's Hat = El Sombrero de Tio Nacho*, 1989
   Uncle Nacho does not like his new hat until his niece teaches him something.
Manlio Argueta, *Magic Dogs of the Volcanoes = Los Perros Magicos de los Volcanes*, 1990
   The magic dogs, or cadejos, who live on the volcanoes of El Salvador, are loved by the villagers because of their powerful magic.
Alberto Blanco, *The Desert Mermaid = La Sirena Del Desierto*, 1992
   A desert mermaid helps her people rediscover the forgotten songs of their ancestors.
Nicholasa Mohr, *The Song of el Coqui and Other Tales of Puerto Rico*, 1995
   This collection of three vividly illustrated tales evoke the rich ancestral traditions of Puerto Rican culture.

SANDRA BENITEZ, Puerto Rican

A Place Where the Sea Remembers

(Minneapolis, MN: Coffee House Press, 1993)

Subject(s): Family; Magic; City Life
Age range(s): Grades 10-Adult
Major character(s): Marta Rodriguez, 15-Year-Old (girl), Sister, Mexican; Chayo Marroquin, Young Woman, Sister, Mexican
Time period(s): 1980s
Locale(s): Santiago, Mexico (small town along the Pacific coast)

Summary: Written as a series of interrelated stories, this novel presents the life of a coastal village in Mexico. The characters are sensitively and vividly portrayed; the town's bachelor "maestro" who lives with a dominant mother; the local "curandera" who becomes a main character when she becomes intimately involved with two sisters and their unborn children when she places a curse on one of them. These are magical tales. Benitez's prose is lyrical and beautiful as she explores the lives of Mexican women caught in a mystical, fantastic, and often fatalistic world.

Where it's reviewed:
Library Journal, September 1, 1993, page 218
Publishers Weekly, July 19, 1993, page 236

Other books you might like:
Kathleen Alcala, *Mrs. Vargas and the Dead Naturalist*, 1992
   Short stories, capturing the essence of magical realism, examine the lives of Mexican women in this book of wonders.
Himilce Novas, *Mangos, Bananas, and Coconuts: A Cuban Love Story*, 1996
   This tale of a magical yet real love story is an ancient tale, beginning with the love of a man and a woman from different social classes, and the story of the fate of their children.
Rosario Ferre, *The Youngest Doll*, 1991
   Originally published in Spanish, this collection of short stories is about Puerto Rican society.
Helena Maria Viramontes, *Under the Feet of Jesus*, 1995
   This novel is about the hardships of a migrant farm working family, and Estrella, a young girl living in a shack, picking grapes in California's vineyards .
Roberta Fernandez, *Itaglio: Novel in Six Stories*, 1990
   This novel is related in six stories, each about an extraordinary woman, who serves as a role model for the young narrator.
Josephina Niggli, *Mexican Village*, 1994
   This is an important collection of ten interrelated short stories about the lives of the people of a small Mexican town, Hidalgo. It was first published in 1945.
Marcos McPeek Villatoro Jr., *A Fire in the Earth*, 1996
   This epic novel follows Romilia Colonez, descendant of an Indian patriarch who led his clan to claim fertile soil, setting the stage for future trials and tragedies in El Salvador.
Alfredo Vea Jr., *La Maravilla*, 1993
   A young boy caught between many cultures grows up on

Buckeye Road, a melting pot of marvels in the desert outside the Phoenix city limits.

540

T. ERNESTO BETHANCOURT

The Great Computer Dating Caper

(New York: Holiday House, 1984)

Subject(s): Computers; Dating (Social Customs); Money
Age range(s): Grades 6-9
Major character(s): Eddie Ramirez, Student—High School; Jody, Student—High School, Friend
Time period(s): 1980s (1984)
Locale(s): North Hollywood, California

Summary: A hilarious escapade about Eddie Ramirez and his friend Jody who want to raise money to help Eddie's father, so they set up a computer dating service called Data and Dates. They run themselves ragged dating all of the North Hollywood High girls themselves, and must deal with some unforseen problems, including being accused of running a teenage sex-for-profit ring.

Where it's reviewed:
English Journal, December 1985, page 54
Journal of Reading, October 1986, page 89

Other books by the same author:
T.H.U.M.B.B., 1983
The Me Inside of Me, 1985
The Tomorrow Connection, 1984
New York City: Too Far from Tampa Blues, 1975

Other books you might like:
Gary Soto, *Boys at Work*, 1995
  Two boys must earn money to replace a broken discman.
Gary Soto, *Pacific Crossing*, 1992
  Two Chicano teenagers go to Japan for the summer and discover that all families are alike.
Irene Beltran Hernandez, *The Secret of Two Brothers*, 1995
  Two brothers, living in Dallas, fight to improve their future.
Gary Soto, *Summer on Wheels*, 1995
  Two friends ride their bikes from East Los Angeles to Santa Monica and have many adventures along the way.
Jack Agueros, *Dominoes and Other Stories from the Puerto Rican*, 1993
  These stories are about the Puerto Rican barrio in New York.
Danny Santiago, *Famous All over Town*, 1984
  Chato Medina is a teenager who lives in the Chicano barrio of Los Angeles. His disintegrating family, his defiant and doomed friends, and his uncertain future inspire him to succeed in his own way.

541

T. ERNESTO BETHANCOURT

The Me Inside of Me

(Minneapolis: Lerner Publications, 1985)

Subject(s): Money; Wealth

Age range(s): Grades 6-9
Major character(s): Alfredo Flores, 17-Year-Old, Mexican American
Time period(s): 1980s (1985)
Locale(s): Santa Amelia, California (fictional city)

Summary: When 17-year-old Freddie is given a million dollars by a wealthy orphan, he has new problems to deal with. Freddie is a regular, middle class teen until he becomes rich.

Other books by the same author:
The Great Computer Dating Caper, 1984
The Tomorrow Connection, 1984
Dr. Doom, Superstar, 1978
New York City: Too Far from Tampa Blues, 1975

Other books you might like:
Gary Soto, *Crazy Weekend*, 1993
  Two boys capture criminals and have adventures.
Gary Soto, *Pacific Crossing*, 1992
  Two Chicano teenagers go to Japan for the summer and discover that all families are alike.
Irene Beltran Hernandez, *The Secret of Two Brothers*, 1995
  Two brothers, living in Dallas, fight to improve their future.
Gary Soto, *Summer on Wheels*, 1995
  Two friends ride their bikes from East Los Angeles to Santa Monica and have many adventures along the way.
Jim Sagel, *Where the Cinnamon Winds Blow = Donde Soplan Los Vientos de Canela*, 1993
  A magical fantasy, this novel examines ten-year-old Tomas' relationship with his wise and eccentric Tia Zulema and his attempt to reconcile his feelings for the death of his father.

542

T. ERNESTO BETHANCOURT

New York City: Too Far from Tampa Blues

(New York: Holiday House, 1975)

Subject(s): Moving, Household; Friendship; Music
Age range(s): Grades 6-8
Major character(s): Tom, Teenager; Aurelio, Teenager, Italian
Time period(s): 1970s (1975)
Locale(s): New York, New York (Brooklyn)

Summary: Tom moves to New York from Florida. This is his story about living in Brooklyn and making friends with an Italian boy, Aurelio, who like Tom also likes rock music. The boys learn to cope with street life.

Other books by the same author:
The Me Inside of Me, 1985
The Great Computer Dating Caper, 1984
The Tomorrow Connection, 1984
Dr. Doom, Superstar, 1978

Other books you might like:
Gary Soto, *Pacific Crossing*, 1992
  Two Chicano teenagers go to Japan for the summer and discover that all families are alike.

Irene Beltran Hernandez, *The Secret of Two Brothers*, 1995

Two brothers, living in Dallas, fight to improve their future.

Gary Soto, *Summer on Wheels*, 1995

Two friends ride their bikes from East Los Angeles to Santa Monica and have many adventures along the way.

Jack Agueros, *Dominoes and Other Stories from the Puerto Rican*, 1993

These Stories are about the Puerto Rican in New York City.

Nicholasa Mohr, *El Bronx Remembered: A Novella and Stories*, 1975

These stories describe growing up in the Bronx as a Puerto Rican.

Judith Ortiz-Cofer, *An Island Like You: Stories of the Barrio*, 1995

Twelve stories, set in a barrio of New Jersey, examine the lives of Puerto Rican teenagers who deal with friendship, family, romance, and school.

543

T. ERNESTO BETHANCOURT

T.H.U.M.B.B.

(New York: Holiday House, 1983)

Subject(s): Bands; Friendship; Music
Age range(s): Grades 6-9
Major character(s): Tom, Teenager, Student—High School, Italian; Aurelio, Teenager, Student—High School, Italian
Time period(s): 1980s (1983)
Locale(s): New York, New York (takes place in Brooklyn)

Summary: High school students Tom and Aurelio are members of the most inept marching band ever assembled. But Aurelio has a plan to make things more exciting, that includes an entire squad of karate experts, and the boys create T.H.U.M.B.B. — The Hippest Underground Marching Band in Brooklyn. They end up on the national news on St. Patrick's Day.

About this book: This is a sequel to *New York City Too Far from Tampa Blues*.

Where it's reviewed:
Booklist, June 15, 1987, page 1611

Other books by the same author:
The Great Computer Dating Caper, 1984
The Me Inside of Me, 1985
The Tomorrow Connection, 1984
New York City: Too Far from Tampa Blues, 1975

Other books you might like:
Gary Soto, *Boys at Work*, 1995

Two boys must earn money to replace a broken discman.

Gary Soto, *Pacific Crossing*, 1992

Two Chicano teenagers go to Japan for the summer and discover that all families are alike.

Irene Beltran Hernandez, *The Secret of Two Brothers*, 1995

Two brothers, living in Dallas, fight to improve their future.

Gary Soto, *Summer on Wheels*, 1995

Two friends ride their bikes from East Los Angeles to Santa Monica and have many adventures along the way.

Jack Agueros, *Dominoes and Other Stories from the Puerto Rican*, 1993

These stories are about the Puerto Rican barrio in New York.

Jim Sagel, *Where the Cinnamon Winds Blow = Donde Soplan Los Vientos de Canela*, 1993

A magical fantasy influenced by traditional folk tales, the novel examines ten-year-old Tomas's journey toward maturity and self-realization.

544

ALBERTO BLANCO, Mexican American
RODOLFO MORALES, Illustrator

Angel's Kite = La Estrella de Angel

(Emeryville, CA: Children's Book Press, 1994)

Subject(s): Toys
Age range(s): Grades K-2
Major character(s): Angel, Child (little boy), Mexican
Time period(s): Indeterminate Past
Locale(s): United States

Summary: After the church bell disappears, no ones knows how or where, Angel makes a kite with a picture of the town and the church on it. His kite has all the details of the church including the bell. He flies it high and losses it. When it returns, the picture of the bell is no longer on the kite, but it mysteriously appears in it's missing location.

About this book: Bilingual format; translated by Dan Bellm.

Where it's reviewed:
School Library Journal, August 1994, page 181

Other books by the same author:
Dawn of the Senses: Selected Poems of Alberto Blanco, 1995
The Desert Mermaid = La Sirena Del Desierto, 1992

Other books you might like:
Manlio Argueta, *Magic Dogs of the Volcanoes = Los Perros Magicos de los Volcanes*, 1990

The magic dogs, or cadejos, who live on the volcanoes of El Salvador are loved by the villagers because of their powerful magic.

Alejandro Cruz Martinez, *The Woman Who Outshone the Sun*, 1991

This is a Zapotec legend about a beautiful woman with hair so bright that it outshines the sun.

Pura Belpre, *The Rainbow-Colored Horse*, 1978

A beautiful seven-colored horse tramples Tano's maize field. Once caught, he grants three wishes to Pio, Tano's son.

Juanita Havill, *Treasure Nap*, 1992

Mama tells Alicia the story of Rita, who visits her grandfather in the mountains of Mexico and learns to make wooden birdcages.

Cruz Martel, *Yagua Days*, 1978

Adan, born in New York, gets to visit his relatives in Puerto Rico one summer and learn about yagua days. .

Alma Flor Ada, *Mediopollito = Half-Chicken*, 1995

This is a bilingual retelling of a traditional humorous tale from Spain set in colonial Mexico. Half-Chicken is born with only half body, and because of his uniqueness receives a lot of attention.

Karen Papagapitos, *Jose's Basket*, 1990

Because Jose comes from a migrant farm-working family, school starts later and ends earlier for him than for most students. His teacher understands and gives him a special gift.

545

ALBERTO BLANCO, Mexican American
PATRICIA REVAH, Illustrator

The Desert Mermaid = La Sirena Del Desierto

(San Francisco, CA: Children's Book Press, 1992)

Subject(s): Mermaids; Deserts
Age range(s): Grades K-2
Time period(s): Indeterminate Past
Locale(s): United States

Summary: A desert mermaid that lives in an oasis is helping her people by rediscovering the forgotten songs of their ancestors.

About this book: Bilingual format; translated to English by Barbara Paschke.

Where it's reviewed:
Publishers Weekly, June 22, 1992, page 61

Other books by the same author:
Dawn of the Senses: Selected Poems of Alberto Blanco, 1995
Angel's Kite = La Estrella de Angel, 1994

Other books you might like:
Pat Mora, *Listen to the Desert/Oye al Desierto*, 1994
Sounds of the desert in English and Spanish.

Manlio Argueta, *Magic Dogs of the Volcanoes = Los Perros Magicos de los Volcanes*, 1990
Ancient volcanoes protect the magic dogs who live on the volcanoes in El Salvador.

Alejandro Cruz Martinez, *The Woman Who Outshone the Sun*, 1991
This is a Zapotec legend about a beautiful woman with hair so bright that it outshines the sun.

Nicholasa Mohr, *The Song of el Coqui and Other Tales of Puerto Rico*, 1995
This collection of three vividly illustrated tales evokes the rich ancestral traditions of Puerto Rican culture.

Pat Mora, *Desert Is My Mother = Desierto Es Mi Madre*, 1994
This is a beautiful rendition of the relationship between nature and people. The desert is presented as the provider of comfort, food, spirit, and life.

546

MARIA DEL CARMEN BOZA, Editor, Mexican American
BEVERLY SILVA, Co-Editor, Puerto Rican
CARMEN VALLE, Co-Editor, Puerto Rican

Nosotras: Latina Literature Today

(Binghamton, NY: Bilingual Review/Press, 1986)

Subject(s): Anthology; Short Stories; Women
Age range(s): Grades 10-Adult
Time period(s): 1980s (1986)
Locale(s): United States (stories take place throughout the U.S.)

Summary: This collection of creative literature, poetry and short stories, is by U.S. Latinas, representing all of the major Latino groups. Some authors represented are Achy Obejas, Sonia Rivera-Valdes, and Helena Maria Viramontes. The anthology is divided into various themes such as, Kin, Bad Vibes, Sage, and Oppression. It is one of the early collections of literature by Latina women.

About this book: several poems and a few stories are in Spanish.

Other books by the same author:
The Cat and Other Stories, 1986
Glenn Miller y Varias Vidas Despues, 1983
Un Poco De Lo No Dicho, 1980

Other books you might like:
Roberta Fernandez, *In Other Words: Literature by Latinas in the U.S.*, 1994
This anthology of literature is by Latinas in the U.S.

Lillian Castillo-Speed, *Latina: Women's Voices from the Borderlands*, 1995
This collection of short stories is by Latinas.

Bryce Milligan, *Daughters of the Fifth Sun: A Collection of Latina Fiction and Poetry*, 1995
This anthology of poetry and short stories is by Latinas in the U.S.

Evangelina Vigil, *Woman of Her Word: Hispanic Women Write*, 1983
This early collection of creative literature is by Latinas in U.S.

Tey Diana Rebolledo, *Las Mujeres Hablan: An Anthology of Nuevo Mexicana Writers*, 1988
This collection of short stories and poetry is by Chicanas from New Mexico.

Alma Gomez, *Cuentos: Stories by Latinas*, 1983
This is a collection of short stories by Latinas.

547

GIANNINA BRASCHI, Puerto Rican

Empire of Dreams

(London: Yale University Press, 1994)

Subject(s): Humor; Sexuality; Language
Age range(s): Grades 10-Adult
Time period(s): 1980s
Locale(s): New York, New York

Summary: In a series of prose poems, Braschi creates amazing images of New York City with a postmodern twist. Her mastery of language produces a strange and beautiful mixture of poetry, prose, drama, and even a little music. This work is divided into ''Assault on Time,'' ''The Profane Comedy,'' and ''The Intimate Diary of Solitude.'' She infuses her texts with Shakespeare, Beatles songs, and a mixture of cultural influences. With creative images of New York City and wild energy, she invents a lyrical and unique text.

About this book: Translated by Tess O'Dwyer.

Where it's reviewed:
Publishers Weekly, July 18, 1994, page 237
Review of Contemporary Fiction, Spring, 1995, page 168

Other books you might like:
Guillermo Gomez-Pena, *Warrior for Gringostroika: Essays, Performance Texts, and Poetry*, 1993
Included in this richly textured collection are essays, manifestos, performance texts, and poetry, by writer and performance artist Guillermo Gomez-Pena.
John Leguizamo, *Spic-O-Rama: A Dysfunctional Comedy*, 1994
This dysfunctional comedy is a series of satirical performance pieces about an urban Hispanic household by an award-winning one man performance.
Luis Rafael Sanchez, *Macho Camacho's Beat*, 1980
Through the eyes of Santiago, a gay unpublished poet, this novel presents plots and sub-plots, and a vivid depiction of Columbian American culture in Little Colombia Jackson Heights.
Emilio Diaz Valcarcel, *Hot Soles in Harlem*, 1993
A look at New York City, from Harlem to penthouses on Fifth Avenue, through the eyes of a recent Puerto Rican arrival who is shown the city by an unusual character.
Yvonne V. Sapia, *Valentino's Hair*, 1991
Facundo Nieves saves a bit of Valentino's hair and is haunted by its power until his death.
C.M. Mayo, *Sky over el Nido: Stories*, 1995
In these intriguing stories about contemporary cosmopolitan life, wealthy characters effortlessly fly around the world, shopping and picking up a homeless, AIDS-infected man.

548

ARISTEO BRITO, Mexican American

The Devil in Texas = El Diablo en Texas
(Tempe, AZ: Bilingual Press, 1990)

Subject(s): Devil; Historical; Cultural Conflict
Age range(s): Grades 10-Adult
Time period(s): 19th century; 20th century (1880-1970)
Locale(s): Presidio, Texas (the Texas-Mexico border)

Summary: This important novel describes the Anglo destruction of a Chicano world. The devil comes to the border town of Presidio and crosses back and forth across the Rio Grande, each time bringing violence and death. The novel is divided into four historical phases representing four generations of the Uranga family who must confront the devil. This experimental novel brings the world of the border alive through vivid dialogue and dramatic encounters. Presidio, stockade, and prison, meets and defines the experiences of displaced Mexicans due to the Mexican-U.S. war. This volume is printed in both English and Spanish.

About this book: It was first published in Spanish in 1976 and is translated by David William Foster.

Where it's reviewed:
Western American Literature, November 1992, page 250

Awards the book has won:
Western States Book Award, 1990

Other books by the same author:
Cuentos y Poemas, 1974

Other books you might like:
Miguel Mendez, *Pilgrims in Aztlan*, 1992
Loreto Maldonado, an aging veteran of the Mexican Revolution, now washes cars for tourists in Tijuana, watching the people who come his way and tell him their stories.
Jose Antonio Villarreal, *Pocho*, 1959
This is considered to be the first key Chicano novel about a Mexican family attempting to assimilate in the Santa Clara Valley of California.
Tomas Rivera, *Y No Se lo Trago la Tierra.And the Earth Did Not Devour Him*, 1987
Twelve related stories document the spiritual strength of migrant farm workers and reproduces in language the sad and tragic lives of Migrant Labor as they travel the migrant stream.
Genaro Gonzalez, *Rainbow's End*, 1988
This adventure novel depicts dangerous border crossings, confrontations with a magician, and drug smuggling in the lives of the Cavazos family in the lower Rio Grande area of Texas.
Americo Paredes, *George Washington Gomez*, 1990
As he grows up, George Washington Gomez struggles with racism, abuse, and cultural and political clashes, while other Texas Mexicans fight to preserve their language and culture.
Ron Arias, *The Road to Tamazunchale*, 1987
Don Fausto, old and nearing death in a Los Angeles barrio, decides to take a journey through time and space, from the Inca world to encounters with undocumented workers in California.
Miguel Mendez, *The Dream of Santa Maria de las Piedras*, 1989
This is the story of a small, poor, rural town in the Sonora Desert of Mexico, seen through the eyes of the old men who gather to reminisce and gossip in the town plaza.
Carlos Miralejos, *Rabid Beasts*, 1993
This science fiction work tells how Jorge Sogaseca, captain of the space ship Tulumex, saves the Cherokee Nation from dying of exposure to extremely cold weather during a long forced march.

549

BRUCE-NOVOA, Mexican American

Only the Good Times
(Houston, TX: Arte Publico Press, 1995)

Subject(s): Love; Artists and Art
Age range(s): Grades 10-Adult
Major character(s): Paul Valence, Young Man, Student—College, Filmmaker (cinematographer); Ann Marisse, Young Woman, Student—College
Time period(s): 20th century (1960-1980)
Locale(s): California (much of the story takes place in California)

Summary: In this contemporary tale of obsessive love, narrator and cinematographer Paul Valence enters into a lifelong preoccupation with the beautiful Anne Marisse. Starting in adolescence, and enduring for years, the two fail to maintain a lasting relationship. Although Valence has many affairs, he sees his beloved everywhere he focuses his camera and his mind's eye. The popular culture and music of the 60's is the background of this story.

Where it's reviewed:
Library Journal, September 15, 1995, page 91
New York Times Book Review, September 24, 1995, page 26

Other books by the same author:
Chicano Authors: Inquiry by Interview, 1980
Inocencia Perversa: Perverse Innocence, 1977
RetroSpace: Collected Essays on Chicano Literature, Theory, and History, 1990
The Heath Anthology of American Literature, 1994

Other books you might like:
Lucha Corpi, *Delia's Song*, 1988
  A young educated Chicana comes of age politically and sexually during the 1960s.
Oscar Hijuelos, *The Mambo Kings Play Songs of Love*, 1989
  The lives of two brothers, Cesar the bandleader who handles the business, and Nestor the romantic who writes the songs, as they make their way in the New York of the 1950s.
Beatriz Rivera, *African Passions and Other Stories*, 1995
  Narrated with humor, passion, and satire, this collection of short stories focuses on women's obsessive search for love and success.
Benjamin Alire Saenz, *Carry Me Like Water*, 1995
  An involved contemporary novel with many interconnected characters, interracial and gay couples takes place both in El Paso and Palo Alto.
Salas Floyd, *State of Emergency*, 1996
  It's the 1960s and a radical professor who finds refuge in the counter-culture is forced to flee the U.S. after beginning an expose of the government.
Oscar Zeta Acosta, *The Autobiography of a Brown Buffalo*, 1972
  Part novel, more autobiographical, the author, a famous Robin Hood type Chicano lawyer with an appetite for life on the edge, examines his life.

550

EVE BUNTING, Mexican American
DAVID DIAZ, Illustrator

Smoky Night
(New York: Harcourt Brace, 1994)

Subject(s): Animals; Riots
Age range(s): Grades 1-2
Major character(s): Daniel, Child
Time period(s): 1990s (1992)
Locale(s): Los Angeles, California

Summary: Daniel loses his cat during the Los Angeles riot of 1992. Mrs. Kim's cat is also lost, and somehow the two cats come together, just as neighbors come together too.

About this book: The illustrations are striking.

Where it's reviewed:
Horn Book Magazine, July-August 1995, page 434
Publishers Weekly, February 13, 1995, page 16
Wilson Library Bulletin, November 1994, page 118

Awards the book has won:
Caldecott Award 1995

Other books you might like:
Pat Mora, *A Birthday Basket for Tia*, 1992
  Cecilia and her cat select a birthday present for a great aunt.
Jan Romero Stevens, *Carlos and the Squash Plant/Carlos y la Planta de Calabaza*, 1993
  Carlos does not wash up when his mother asks, consequently a plant starts growing out of his ear.
Gary Soto, *Chato's Kitchen*, 1995
  Chato, a low-rider cat, cooks a meal for some unexpected guests.
Manlio Argueta, *Magic Dogs of the Volcanoes = Los Perros Magicos de los Volcanes*, 1990
  Ancient volcanoes protect the magic dogs who live on the volcanoes in El Salvador.
Michael Rose Ramirez, *The Little Ant = La Hormiga Chiquita*, 1995
  In this Mexican folktale a little ant seeks restitution for a broken leg.
Lucia M. Gonzalez, *The Bossy Gallito*, 1994
  On his way to his uncle's wedding, a bossy rooster dirties his beak pecking corn.

551

JOSE ANTONIO BURCIAGA, Mexican American

Spilling the Beans: Loteria Chicana
(Santa Barbara, CA: Joshua Odell Editions, 1995)

Subject(s): Growing Up; Folklore; Humor
Age range(s): Grades 9-Adult
Time period(s): 1940s; 1980s
Locale(s): Southwest (references made to various locations in Southwest)

Summary: This series of essays, many humorous, recounts experiences from the author's childhood, explorations into aspects of Chicano culture, and discussions of the origins of Chicano customs. The author traces the history of the tequila drink ''Margarita'', and also of the Virgin of Guadalupe.

About this book: The author is frequently published in newspapers.

Other books by the same author:
Drink Cultura: Chicanismo, 1993
Weedee Peepo: A Collection of Essays, 1988

Other books you might like:
Mary Helen Ponce, *The Wedding*, 1989
> This comic novel is about Chicano working class life and culture, told through the eyes of a pregnant bride-to-be.

Nash Candelaria, *The Day the Cisco Kid Shot John Wayne*, 1988
> These twelve humorous stories portray Chicano-Anglo interrelations and conflicts.

Al Martinez, *Ashes in the Rain: Selected Essays*, 1990
> Essays are on various subjects by a Pulitzer Prize nominated reporter for the Los Angeles Times.

Norma Elia Cantu, *Canicula: Snapshots of a Girlhood en la Frontera*, 1995
> A series of brief vignettes about growing up that brings into sharp focus the history, lives, and legends of Laredo, Texas.

Americo Paredes, *The Hammon and the Beans and Other Stories*, 1994
> A collection of short stories set in the southern Texas border region with the cultural conflict that has dominated that area since the U.S.-Mexican War.

Jesus Salvador Trevino, *The Fabulous Sinkhole and Other Stories*, 1995
> This first story collection by Trevino, a screenwriter and director, is an entertaining creation of Mexican and Chicano characters, that take place in a fictional town, Arroyo Grande, in Texas.

Guillermo Gomez-Pena, *Warrior for Gringostroika: Essays, Performance Texts, and Poetry*, 1993
> Included in this richly textured collection are essays, manifestos, performance texts, and poetry by writer and performance artist Guillermo Gomez-Pena.

Jesus Salvador Trevino, *The fabulous Sinkhole and Other Stories*, 1995
> This first story collection by Trevino, a screenwriter and director, is an entertaining creation of Mexican and Chicano characters in a fictional town, Arroyo Grande in Texas.

552

FRAN LEEPER BUSS
DAISY CUBIAS, Co-Author

Journey of the Sparrow
(New York: Lodestar books, 1991)

Subject(s): Illegal Immigrants; Refugees
Age range(s): Grades 6-8
Major character(s): Maria, Child (girl), Salvadoran
Time period(s): 1990s (1991)
Locale(s): Chicago, Illinois

Summary: Maria, her brother, and her older sister, Salvadoran refugees, are smuggled into the U.S. and must hide in an apartment building in Chicago. Her father and sister's husband are killed in El Salvador. Eventually they meet good friends, a priest and a midwife, who help them.

Where it's reviewed:
English Journal, November 1993, page 79
Horn Book Magazine, November-December 1991, page 742
Publishers Weekly, September 13, 1991, page 80

Other books by the same author:
La Partera: Study of a Midwife, 1980

Other books you might like:
Gloria Anzaldua, *Friends From the Other Side/Amigos del Otro Lado*, 1993
> A Mexican American girl befriends an undocumented immigrant boy.

Ofelia Dumas Lachtman, *The Girl from Playa Blanca*, 1995
> Elena and her brother Carlos find adventure in Los Angeles as they search for their father.

Irene Beltran Hernandez, *The Secret of Two Brothers*, 1995
> Two brothers, living in Dallas, fight to improve their future.

Gary Soto, *Jesse*, 1994
> Jesse and his brother live together in California's San Joaquin Valley and try to avoid being farm workers.

Irene Beltran Hernandez, *Across the Great River*, 1989
> This novel chronicles the life of illegal immigrant Kata and her family, who must deal with violence, the authorities, a folk healer and labor smugglers.

553

NASH CANDELARIA, Mexican American

The Day the Cisco Kid Shot John Wayne
(Tempe, AZ: Bilingual Press, 1988)

Subject(s): Short Stories; Identity; Growing Up
Age range(s): Grades 10-Adult
Time period(s): 20th century (1940-1988)
Locale(s): New Mexico

Summary: A humorous collection of short stories, from New Mexico, in which the author examines cultural clashes between Latinos and Anglos. With wit, humor, and perceptiveness, Candelaria's stories address individuals who struggle between old ways and new, individuals who live between two cultures. In the title story, a little boy learns to get along with ''aliens'' who have blond hair and don't speak Spanish.

Where it's reviewed:
The American Book Review, January, 1990, page 15

Other books by the same author:
Inheritance of Strangers, 1985
Memories of the Alhambra, 1977
Not by the Sword, 1982
Leonor Park, 1991

Other books you might like:
Rick P. Rivera, *A Fabricated Mexican*, 1995
> A series of comic vignettes about a quiet but mischievous

boy growing up in California, and the antics of his eccentric family during his own search for identity.

Jose Antonio Burciaga, *Spilling the Beans: Loteria Chicana*, 1995

A series of essays, many humorous, recounting experiences from the author's childhood, and explorations into aspects of Chicano culture.

Alberto Alvaro Rios, *The Iguana Killer: Twelve Stories of the Heart*, 1984

Short stories that transform ordinary life into a book of secrets where Mexican and Chicano young boys confront big questions.

Angelico Chavez, *The Short Stories of Fray Angelico Chavez*, 1987

A collection of Chavez's most classic short stories that read like social allegories that address mystery and miracle, age and youth, and cultural clashes.

554

NASH CANDELARIA, Mexican American

Inheritance of Strangers
(Binghamton, NY: Bilingual Press, 1985)

Subject(s): Race Relations; Family Relations; Oppression
Age range(s): Grades 10-Adult
Major character(s): Jose Antonio Rafa, Grandfather, Mexican
Time period(s): 19th century (1848-1890)
Locale(s): New Mexico

Summary: This novel presents the history of New Mexican statehood and Anglo oppression in relation to the struggles of the Rafa family. Jose Antonio relates the historical events of the state to his grandchildren in a series of humorous yet brutally realistic episodes. These rich anecdotes reveal how Chicanos survive when confronting adversity. Along with *Not by the Sword* and *Memories of the Alhambra* this novel makes up part of Candelaria's New Mexico trilogy.

Other books by the same author:
The Day the Cisco Kid Shot John Wayne, 1988
Memories of the Alhambra, 1977
Leonor Park, 1991
Not by the Sword, 1982

Other books you might like:
Montserrat Fontes, *Dreams of the Centaur*, 1995
Alejo Durcal, son of a slain ranch owner, tries to avenge his father's death during the period in history when the Yaqui Indians were badly mistreated in Mexico.

Sylvia Lopez-Medina, *Cantora: A Novel*, 1992
This novel tells the story of four generations of women in Mexico and their lives in America at the turn of the 20th century.

Alejandro Morales, *The Brick People*, 1988
Fictional but historically-based, this novel is about two California families—one proud and one powerful, pitted against each other in the late nineteenth and early twentieth centuries.

Tina Juarez, *Call No Man Master*, 1995
Intricately crafted, this historical novel is about a young woman of mixed heritage, Spanish and Indian, and her

participation in the events that lead to Mexico's independence from Spain.

Genaro Gonzalez, *Rainbow's End*, 1988
This adventure novel presents dangerous border crossings, confrontations with a magician, and drug smuggling in the lives of the Cavazos family in the lower Rio Grande area of Texas.

David Monreal, *Cinco de Mayo: An Epic Novel*, 1993
This historical novel presents the events leading up to the Battle of Puebla on the 5th of May 1862 in Mexico.

Maria Ampara Ruiz de Burton, *The Squatter and the Don*, 1992

A historical romance written from the perspective of the conquered Mexican population, the novel chronicles events following the Treaty of Guadalupe de Hidalgo.

555

NASH CANDELARIA, Mexican American

Leonor Park
(Tempe, AZ: Bilingual Press, 1991)

Subject(s): Family; Property Rights; Prohibition
Age range(s): Grades 10-Adult
Major character(s): Magdalena Armijo Sanchez Castillo Soto, Divorced Person (woman), Aunt, Mexican American; Nicolas Armijo, Brother, Father (of Leonor), Mexican American
Time period(s): 1920s
Locale(s): New Mexico

Summary: A novel about land and greed in New Mexico on the eve of the Great Depression. A powerful woman battles with her brother over their father's legacy; a piece of land along the Rio Grande. The brother's daughter, Leonor, raised by the sister, is the central point of the struggle. Her coming of age is set in this history of New Mexico. Candelaria examines the history of this land and its people, presenting the story of a pueblo rousing from rural life to modern city.

About this book: A sequel to the Rafa family trilogy.

Other books by the same author:
The Day the Cisco Kid Shot John Wayne, 1988
Inheritance of Strangers, 1985
Memories of the Alhambra, 1977
Not by the Sword, 1982

Other books you might like:
Alejandro Morales, *The Brick People*, 1988
A fictional but historically-based novel about two families and the growth of California from the late nineteenth century through the early twentieth century.

Rudolfo Anaya, *Albuquerque*, 1992
An exciting story of modern Albuquerque, with a vicious mayoral race, a young Chicano boxer, American Indians fighting to retain water rights, and the folkloric past of New Mexico.

Roberta Fernandez, *Itaglio: Novel in Six Stories*, 1990
A novel related in six stories, each about an extraordinary woman who serves as a role model for the young narrator.

Americo Paredes, *George Washington Gomez*, 1990
As he grows up, George Washington Gomez struggles

with racism, abuse, and cultural and political clashes, while other Texas Mexicans fight to preserve their language and culture.

NASH CANDELARIA, Mexican American

Memories of the Alhambra

(Palo Alto, CA: Cibola Press, 1977)

Subject(s): Ancestry; Identity; Family Relations
Age range(s): Grades 10-Adult
Major character(s): Jose Antonio Rafa, Aged Person, Mexican
Time period(s): 1960s
Locale(s): Los Angeles, California (parts of the story also take place in New Mexico and Mexico)

Summary: When Jose Rafa disappears, he leaves only a receipt for traveler's checks and a business card from an L.A. con man who sells false genealogies to Chicanos who claim noble ancestry. Jose goes to Mexico to look for his Spanish *conquistador* ancestors. This novel examines the anger felt by many New Mexican Chicanos as they search for an aristocratic identity. Along with *Not by the Sword* and *Inheritance of Strangers* this novel makes up part of Candelaria's New Mexico trilogy.

Other books by the same author:
The Day the Cisco Kid Shot John Wayne, 1988
Inheritance of Strangers, 1985
Leonor Park, 1991
Not by the Sword, 1982

Other books you might like:
Oscar Zeta Acosta, *The Revolt of the Cockroach People*, 1973
  This personal memoir tells of the turbulent years that mark the beginning of the Chicano movement in California and the political activities of East Los Angeles.
Americo Paredes, *George Washington Gomez*, 1990
  As he grows up, George Washington Gomez struggles with racism, abuse, and cultural and political clashes, while other Texas mexicans fight to preserve their language and culture.
Ron Arias, *The Road to Tamazunchale*, 1987
  Don Fausto, old and nearing death in a Los Angeles barrio, decides to take a journey through time and space, from the Inca world to encounters with undocumented workers in California.
Jose Antonio Villarreal, *Pocho*, 1959
  This is considered to be the first key Chicano novel about a Mexican family attempting to assimilate in the Santa Clara Valley of California.
Gordon Kahn, *A Long Way from Home*, 1989
  Written forty years before it was published, this novel tells the story of Gilberto, a young Chicano who, after his mother's death, leaves the U.S. for Mexico to find his only remaining family.
Ofelia Dumas Lachtman, *A Shell for Angela*, 1995
  When nine-year-old Angela Martin sees her father led away by immigration officials, she begins to deny her Mexican heritage and she raises her children to be ignorant of their grandparents.

NASH CANDELARIA, Mexican American

Not by the Sword

(Ypsilanti, MI: Bilingual Press/Editorial Bilinge, 1982)

Subject(s): Ancestors; Identity; Family Relations
Age range(s): Grades 10-Adult
Major character(s): Tercero Rafa, Religious (priest), Landowner, Mexican; Jose Antonio Rafa, Grandfather, Landowner, Mexican
Time period(s): 19th century; 20th century (1846-1954)
Locale(s): United States

Summary: The family of Don Jose Antonio Rafa and Don Francisco struggle with the changes brought about by the annexation of New Mexico by the United States after the U.S.-Mexican War. The adventures of the Rafa family as they cope with the loss of a Mexican way of life is narrated from the perspective of Tercero, who has become a priest and his twin brother Carlos, who is heir to the Rafa property and estate.

About this book: The sequel to this novel is *Inheritance of Strangers*.

Awards the book has won:
American Book Award, 1983

Other books by the same author:
The Day the Cisco Kid Shot John Wayne, 1988
Inheritance of Strangers, 1985
Leonor Park, 1991
Memories of the Alhambra, 1977

Other books you might like:
Montserrat Fontes, *Dreams of the Centaur*, 1995
  The son of a slain ranch owner tries to avenge his father's death during the deportation of the Yaqui Indians during the presidency of Porfirio Diaz.
Sylvia Lopez-Medina, *Cantora: A Novel*, 1992
  This novel tells the story of four generations of women in Mexico and their lives in America at the turn of the 20th century.
Alejandro Morales, *The Brick People*, 1988
  Based on historical events, this novel is about two California families pitted against each other—the powerful Simons and the proud Revueltas during the late nineteenth and early twentieth centuries.
Tina Juarez, *Call No Man Master*, 1995
  Intricately crafted, this historical novel is about a young woman of mixed heritage, Spanish and Indian, and her participation in the events that lead to Mexico's independence from Spain.
Genaro Gonzalez, *Rainbow's End*, 1988
  This adventure novel presents dangerous border crossings, confrontations with a magician, and drug smuggling in the lives of the Cavazos family in the lower Rio Grande area of Texas.
David Monreal, *Cinco de Mayo: An Epic Novel*, 1993
  This historical novel presents the events leading up to the Battle of Puebla on the 5th of May 1862 in Mexico.
Sallie Gallegos, *Stone Horses*, 1996
  This history of the Montez family, living in a rural area in

northern New Mexico in the 1930s and 1940s, follows the extraordinary Eduardo from birth up to his stint in the Navy at eighteen.

558

DANIEL CANO, Mexican American

Pepe Rios

(Houston, TX: Arte Publico Press, 1991)

Subject(s): War; Adventure and Adventurers
Age range(s): Grades 9-Adult
Major character(s): Pepe Rios, Young Man, Traveller, Mexican
Time period(s): 1910s
Locale(s): Mexico

Summary: In this historical novel about the Mexican Revolution of 1910, Pepe Rios searches for peace amidst the chaos and violence of war. The death of Pepe's father propels him across the country to search for love, revenge, and an end to the war. Eventually he is able to cross into the United States. This is an exciting novel about love and war and presents the historical heritage of generations of Mexican immigrants who came to the U.S. because of the war in Mexico.

Where it's reviewed:
American Book Review, August-September 1992, page 22

Other books by the same author:
Shifting Loyalties, 1995

Other books you might like:
Montserrat Fontes, *Dreams of the Centaur*, 1995
    The son of a slain ranch owner tries to avenge his father's death during the deportation of the Yaqui Indians under the presidency of Porfirio Diaz.
Sylvia Lopez-Medina, *Cantora: A Novel*, 1992
    This novel tells the story of four generations of women in Mexico and their lives in America at the turn of the 20th century.
Nash Candelaria, *Not by the Sword*, 1982
    Taking place before the Mexican War of 1846, this novel shows the struggles of the Rafa family in New Mexico and the collapse of the Mexican government.
Nash Candelaria, *Inheritance of Strangers*, 1985
    This sequel to *Not By the Sword*, covers the years after the Mexican War of 1846 until New Mexico statehood, and depicts the Rafa family's struggles against Anglo exploitation.
Victor Villasenor, *Wild Steps of Heaven*, 1996
    Don Juan marries an Indian woman and the continual conflict of their marriage is the history of Mexico; the subjugation of indigenous people by European conquerors.
Gary D. Keller, *Zapata Lives!*, 1994
    The Mexican revolutionary leader Emiliano Zapata has risen from the dead and must lead his people in a struggle against economic and social oppression.

559

DANIEL CANO, Mexican American

Shifting Loyalties

(Houston: Arte Publico Press, 1995)

Subject(s): Vietnam War; Coming of Age; Family Relations
Age range(s): Grades 10-Adult
Major character(s): David Almas, Veteran; Danny Rios, Veteran
Time period(s): 20th century (1950-1980)
Locale(s): California (variously in Southern California, Vietnam, Spain, and Pennsylvania); Vietnam, South

Summary: The lives of five Chicano soldiers and their families before during, and after the Vietnam War are explored in this novel. David, Danny, Charley, Joey, and Manny struggle through post-Vietnam adjustment within their communities and within themselves. Childhood experiences are interspersed with present day relationships, fears, and sadnesses.

Other books by the same author:
Pepe Rios, 1991

Other books you might like:
Ed Vega, *Casualty Report*, 1991
    This short story collection's title story is about a Vietnam veteran.
Oswald Rivera, *Fire and Rain*, 1990
    This is a story of a Marine Corp prison camp riot in Vietnam.
Alejandro Murguia, *Southern Front*, 1990
    Short stories about the combat zone, the Nicaraguan-Costa Rican border, during the rebellion against the Somoza regime in the late 1970s.
Rolando Hinojosa, *The Useless Servants*, 1993
    Set almost entirely in Korea, this novel is made up of the diary entries of Rafe Buenrostro as he is stationed in Korea during the war.
Graciela Limon, *In Search of Bernabe*, 1993
    A mother searches for her son during civil war in El Salvador.
Joe Rodriguez, *The Oddsplayer*, 1989
    Black and Latino soldiers fight the enemy on the battle fields of Vietnam but wars take place in their own ranks as well.
Alejandro Grattan-Dominguez, *The Dark Side of the Dream*, 1995
    A historical novel, this is set right after the outbreak of World War II, when two cousins and their families migrate from Chihuahua to El Paso.

560

NORMA ELIA CANTU, Mexican American

Canicula: Snapshots of a Girlhood en la Frontera

(Albuquerque: University of New Mexico Press, 1995)

Subject(s): Childhood; Coming of Age; Family Relations
Age range(s): Grades 10-Adult

Time period(s): 20th century (1946-1965)
Locale(s): Laredo, Texas; Mexico

Summary: This series of brief vignettes about growing up brings into sharp focus the history, lives, and legends of Laredo, Texas. ''Canicula'' translates as ''dog days'' and refers to the part of the summer in South Texas when the cotton is harvested. These fictional short stories are based on historical photographs, and the author refers to them as fictional autobioethnography.

About this book: Spanish is interspersed throughout the work.

Where it's reviewed:
Prairie Schooner, Winter 1994, page 165
Book World, August 20, 1995, page 8

Other books you might like:
Montserrat Fontes, *First Confession*, 1991
   A story about an upper-class little girl living on the Mexican side of the U.S. Mexico border.
Judith Ortiz Cofer, *Silent Dancing: A Partial Rememberance of a Puerto Rican Childhood*, 1990
   This autobiographical collection of prose, poetry, and short stories is about growing up in Puerto Rico and the U.S.
Tiffany Ana Lopez, *Growing Up Chicano*, 1993
   These short stories are by Chicano writers.
Sandra Cisneros, *The House on Mango Street*, 1986
   These tribulations are about Mexican American young woman growing up.
Enedina Casarez Vasquez, *Recuerdos de Una Nina*, 1980
   These short stories are about growing up in San Antonio, Texas.
Arcadia H. Lopez, *Barrio Teacher*, 1992
   An autobiographical narration by an educator who, despite poverty and turmoil, managed to obtain a university education and teach for forty-six years in San Antonio, Texas.
Gloria Lopez-Stafford, *A Place in El Paso: A Mexican American Childhood*, 1996
   A bittersweet narrative describing the early childhood of the author living in the ''projects'' of El Paso during World War II.
Rolando Hinojosa, *Becky and Her Friends*, 1990
   Narrated by many of her friends, this novel focuses on the strong-willed Becky Escobar, an upwardly-mobile woman who at age thirty-five decides to divorce her husband.

561

CARLOTA CARDENAS DE DWYER, Editor, Mexican American

Chicano Voices
(Boston: Houghton Mifflin, 1975)

Subject(s): Anthology; Short Stories
Age range(s): Grades 9-Adult
Time period(s): 20th century (1917-1975)
Locale(s): United States (western and southwestern U.S.)

Summary: These are stories from writers representative of all states in the Southwest. Chicano social themes, such as El Barrio, La Chicana, and La Causa, define the work.

About this book: This is a key short story collection that is still important today.

Other books you might like:
Ray Gonzales, *Mirrors Beneath the Earth: Short Fiction by Chicano Writers*, 1992
   This is a collection of short stories by Chicano authors.
Gary Soto, *Pieces of the Heart: New Chicano Fiction*, 1993
   This is a collection of short stories by Chicano authors.
Luis Valdez, *Aztlan: An Anthology of Mexican American Literature*, 1972
   A literary collection by Mexican-American authors.
Rudolfo Anaya, *Cuentos Chicanos: A Short Story Anthology*, 1984
   This is a collection of short stories by Chicano writers.
Tiffany Ana Lopez, *Growing Up Chicano*, 1993
   This is a collection of short stories by Chicano writers.
Rudolfo Anaya, *Voces: An Anthology of Nuevo Mexicano Writers*, 1987
   This anthology of poems and short stories is by New Mexican Chicano authors.
Tey Diana Rebolledo, *Las Mujeres Hablan*, 1988
   This collection of short stories and poetry is by Chicanas from New Mexico.

562

LORI M. CARLSON, Editor
CYNTHIA L. VENTURA, Co-Editor, Puerto Rican

Where Angels Glide at Dawn: New Stories from Latin America
(New York: J.B. Lippincott, 1990)

Subject(s): Short Stories; Anthology; Folk Tales
Age range(s): Grades 4-9
Time period(s): Indeterminate Past
Locale(s): South America

Summary: Introduced by Isabel Allende, this collection of stories for younger readers contains a diverse mixture that reflects the climates, geographies, and cultural traditions of Latin America. The stories: the sadness of a El Salvadorian clown, clever magical rabbits from Chile, and snow in San Juan Puerto Rico blend together the scenes and images of Latin America with humor, poetry, politics, and imagination.

About this book: Illustrated by Jose Ortega, these stories have been translated into English by the editors.

Where it's reviewed:
Americas (English Edition), July-August 1991, page 61
Horn Book Magazine, March-April 1991, page 197
Publishers Weekly, September 28, 1990, page 103

Other books by the same author:
American Eyes: New Asian-American Short Stories for Young Adults, 1994
Cool Salsa: Bilingual Poems on Growing up Latino in the United States, 1994

Other books you might like:
Frances R. Aparicio, *Latino Voices*, 1994
   Collection of writings by Latino authors specially edited for young adult readers.

Kleya Forte-Escamilla, *The Storyteller with Nike Airs and Other Barrio Stories*, 1995
  These stories are about the desert, with a supernatural twist.
Alma Flor Ada, *Where the Flame Trees Bloom*, 1994
  Eleven stories from the author's childhood, about her family, friends, and the Cuban hacienda where she grew up.
Victor Villasenor, *Walking Stars: Stories of Magic and Power*, 1994
  This is an autobiographical collection of stories that recall the author's parents' and grandparents' lives in Mexico.

563

OMAR CASTANEDA, Guatemalan
ENRIQUE SANCHEZ, Illustrator

Abuela's Weave
(New York: Lee & Low Books, 1993)

Subject(s): Grandparents; Superstition; Artists and Art
Age range(s): Grades 1-3
Major character(s): Esperanza, Child, Artisan (weaver), Guatemalan Abuela, Grandmother, Artisan (weaver), Guatemalan
Time period(s): Indeterminate Past
Locale(s): Guatemala (in the countryside and an outdoor market in the city)

Summary: Esperanza and her Abuela (grandmother) spend all day weaving tapestries and clothing. At the outdoor market, where they sell their handiwork, crowds gather to admire and buy Esperanza's beautiful fabrics. The story presents a strong relationship between a grandmother and child.

About this book: This work is beautifully illustrated with fabric-like borders on each page.

Where it's reviewed:
Publishers Weekly, March 15, 1993, page 84

Other books by the same author:
Among the Volcanoes, 1991
Remembering to Say Mouth or Face, 1993
Imagining Isabel, 1992

Other books you might like:
Pat Mora, *A Birthday Basket for Tia*, 1992
  Cecilia makes a birthday present for her great aunt.
Gary Soto, *Too Many Tamales*, 1993
  Maria helps her mother make tamales for Christmas Eve dinner.
Arthur Dorros, *Abuela*, 1991
  A little girl and her grandmother fly all over New York City.
Carmen Santiago Nodar, *Abuelita's Paradise*, 1992
  Marita sits in Abuelita's rocking chair and remembers the stories Abuelita told of her life in Puerto Rico.
Leyla Torres, *Saturday Sancocho*, 1995
  Every Saturday Maria Lili helps her grandparents make their traditional chicken sancocho.
Juanita Havill, *Treasure Nap*, 1992
  Mama tells Alicia the story of Rita, who visits her grandfather in the mountains of Mexico and learns to make wooden birdcages.

564

OMAR CASTANEDA, Guatemalan

Among the Volcanoes
(New York: Lodestar Books, 1991)

Subject(s): Family Relations; Rural Life
Age range(s): Grades 6-8
Major character(s): Isabel Pacay, Child, Mayan
Time period(s): 1990s (1991)
Locale(s): Guatemala (rural area of Guatemala)

Summary: Isabel, a teenager, must quit school and take over household responsibilities when her mother becomes ill. She must give up her dream of becoming a teacher.

About this book: This book has a sequel, *Imagining Isabel*.

Where it's reviewed:
Horn Book Magazine, May-June 1991, page 335

Other books by the same author:
Abuela's Weave, 1993
Cunuman, 1987
Remembering to Say Mouth or Face, 1993
Imagining Isabel, 1994

Other books you might like:
Sandra Cisneros, *The House on Mango Street*, 1983
  This is about a young Mexican girl growing up in an urban setting.
Nicholasa Mohr, *Nilda: A Novel*, 1973
  This story is about the life of a Puerto Rican girl living in the barrio of New York City.
Diane Gonzales Bertrand, *Sweet Fifteen*, 1995
  A young girl celebrates her quinceanera and mourns the death of her father.
Gloria Velasquez, *Maya's Divided World*, 1995
  Maya's happy high school world comes apart when her parents announce their divorce.
Irene Beltran Hernandez, *Heartbeat, Drumbeat*, 1992
  Morgana Cruz seeks her cultural identity while caught between the worlds of her Navajo mother and her Mexican father.

565

OMAR CASTANEDA, Guatemalan

Imagining Isabel
(New York: Lodestar Books, 1994)

Subject(s): Coming of Age; Rural Life
Age range(s): Grades 6-9
Major character(s): Isabel Pacay Choy, 16-Year-Old, Mayan
Time period(s): 1990s (1994)
Locale(s): Guatemala (rural area of Guatemala)

Summary: Isabel, a teenager in Guatemala, is newly married and wants to be a teacher. She is invited to attend a government-run teacher-training program in the city and she encounters a difficult time.

About this book: This is a sequel to *Among the Volcanoes*.

Where it's reviewed:
Publishers Weekly, July 11, 1994, page 80

Other books by the same author:
Abuela's Weave, 1993
Among the Volcanoes, 1991
Cunuman, 1987
Remembering to Say Mouth or Face, 1993

Other books you might like:
Sandra Cisneros, *The House on Mango Street*, 1983
 This story is about a young Mexican girl growing up in an urban setting.
Nicholasa Mohr, *Nilda: A Novel*, 1973
 This story is about the life of a Puerto Rican girl living in the barrio of New York City.
Diane Gonzales Bertrand, *Sweet Fifteen*, 1995
 A young girl mourns the death of her father while preparing to celebrate her quinceanera.
Gloria Velasquez, *Maya's Divided World*, 1995
 Maya's happy high school world comes apart when her parents announce their divorce.
Irene Beltran Hernandez, *Heartbeat, Drumbeat*, 1992
 Morgana Cruz seeks her cultural identity while caught between the worlds of her Navajo mother and her Mexican father.

566

OMAR CASTANEDA, Guatemalan

Remembering to Say Mouth or Face
(Boulder, CO: Fiction Collective Two, 1993)

Subject(s): Short Stories; Creation; Mythology
Age range(s): Grades 10-Adult
Time period(s): 1990s (1993)
Locale(s): United States

Summary: These short stories take place both in the U.S. and in Central America. They depict bicultural settings and situations. Several stories are based on the Popol Vuh, the Mayan myth of creation.

About this book: These stories are previously published in various journals.

Where it's reviewed:
Library Journal, October 1, 1993, page 129

Other books by the same author:
Imagining Isabel, 1994
Among the Volcanoes, 1991

Other books you might like:
Kleya Forte-Escamilla, *The Storyteller with Nike Airs and Other Barrio Stories*, 1995
 This collection of short stories is about girls and the supernatural.
Ray Gonzalez, *Currents From the Dancing River: Contemporary Latino Fiction, Nonfiction, and Poetry*, 1994
 This is a collection of creative short fiction by Latino writers in the U.S.
Denis Lynn Daly Heyck, *Barrios and Borderlands: Cultures of Latinos and Latinas in the United States*, 1994
 This anthology of creative literature is by Latino writers in the U.S.

Victor Perera, *Rites, A Guatemalan Boyhood*, 1986
 These autobiographical narratives are about the author's boyhood while living in Guatemala.
Carole Fernandez, *Sleep of the Innocents*, 1991
 This novel chronicles the lives of women living in a fictional Central American country torn by civil war.
Julia Alvarez, *The Other Side = El Otro Lado*, 1995
 A Collection of poetry that reads like prose and examines love, language, and the author's past.

567

ANA CASTILLO, Mexican American

Loverboys, Stories
(New York, NY: W.W. Norton & Company, 1996)

Subject(s): Love; City Life
Age range(s): Grades 10-Adult
Time period(s): 1990s (1996)
Locale(s): Chicago, Illinois (and other parts of the country)

Summary: A first collection of 22 short stories by an established novelist that explore relationships between men and women, men and men, women and women, and the prickly issues of love. The stories range from one-page vignettes to longer narrations. "Loverboys" is about lovers, both male and female, some that have lived little, and some, like several women, who have lived a lot. These stories deal with friendship, and love, among the multitudes, as one character says in the story "Vatolandia." In the title story "Carmen," a bisexual writer and bookstore owner, learns about love from her friends.

Where it's reviewed:
New York Times Book Review, September 8, 1996, page 20
Library Journal, July 1996, page 196
Publisher's Weekly, July 8, 1996, page 73

Other books by the same author:
So Far from God: A Novel, 1993
Sapogonia: An Anti-Romance in 3/8 Meter, 1990
The Mixquiahuala Letters, 1986
Massacre of the Dreamers: Essays on Xicanisma, 1995

Other books you might like:
Ana Lydia Vega, *True and False Romances*, 1994
 Collection of short stories about women and romance that take place in Puerto Rico.
Leo Romero, *Rita and Los Angeles*, 1995
 A short story collection with a cast of complex characters who grow and evolve, and learn about being outsiders in an alien and hostile world.
Alma Luz Villanueva, *Weeping Woman: La Llorona and Other Stories*, 1994
 A collection of stories that examine women who live in a world torn apart by violence, racism, and sexism.
Sandra Cisneros, *Woman Hollering Creek and Other Stories*, 1991
 Collection of short stories about women that take place in Texas and the border area.
Yvonne V. Sapia, *Valentino's Hair*, 1991
 Rudolph Valentino comes into the life of Facundo Nieves

and changes it forever when Nieves saves the hair and its power haunts him until his own death.

Beatriz Rivera, *African Passions and Other Stories*, 1995
  A collection of short stories focusing on women's obsessive search for love and success, where the nature of obsession is examined.

568

ANA CASTILLO, Mexican American

The Mixquiahuala Letters
(Binghamton, NY: Bilingual Press, 1986)

Subject(s): Friendship; Letters; Women
Age range(s): Grades 10-Adult
Major character(s): Teresa, Writer (best friend of Alicia); Alicia, Artist
Time period(s): 1980s (1986)
Locale(s): United States

Summary: This avant garde epistolary novel consists of forty letters, the correspondence between two Latina women, from their youthful travels to Mexico to their middle-years in the United States. These probing letters describe relationships between the sexes and recount travels and struggles in the search for identity. Teresa, a Chicana, writes to to her artist friend Alicia. Together they create a social and cultural document, an examination of love and gender, and a story that is powerful and gripping.

About this book: The author is well known as a playwright also.

Where it's reviewed:
Belles Lettres: A Review of Books by Women, Spring 1993, page 19
Confluencia, Fall 1994, page 67

Awards the book has won:
Before Columbus Foundation's American Book Award, 1986

Other books by the same author:
The Invitation, 1979
Sapogonia: An Anti-Romance in 3/8 Meter, 1990
So Far from God: A Novel, 1993
Women Are Not Roses, 1984
Massacre of the Dreamers: Essays on Xicanisma, 1994

Other books you might like:
Denise Chavez, *Face of an Angel*, 1994
  A humorously and sensuously related long novel that, among other things, shows how women constantly provide service to others, particularly to men.
Estela Portillo Trambley, *Rain of Scorpions and Other Writings*, 1975
  Collection of short stories by an early Chicana writer that explores the place of women in Mexican society.
Sandra Cisneros, *Woman Hollering Creek and Other Stories*, 1991
  Collection of short stories about women that take place in Texas and the border area.
Eliud Martinez, *Voice-Haunted Journey*, 1990
  The entire fictional action of this novel occurs in the mind of Miguel Velasquez, a professor who is writing a novel, during an airplane flight in California.

Gloria Anzaldua, *Borderlands: The New Mestiza = La Frontera*, 1987
  In prose and poetry, Anzaldua writes about her childhood along the Texas-Mexican border, describing the experience of being caught between two cultures.
Tey Diana Rebolledo, *Infinite Divisions: An Anthology of Chicana Literature*, 1993
  An unusual anthology compressed of poetry, plays, and stories about personal identity, from fifty Chicana writers.
Roberta Fernandez, *In Other Words: Literature by Latinas in the US*, 1994
  A large anthology that contains the best and most representative works of contemporary fiction, poetry, drama, and essays written by Latinas in the US.
Julia Alvarez, *The Other Side = El Otro Lado*, 1995
  In this collection of prose poetry, Julia Alvarez examines love, language, and her past.

569

ANA CASTILLO, Mexican American

Sapogonia: An Anti-Romance in 3/8 Meter
(Tempe, AZ: Bilingual Press, 1990)

Subject(s): Women; Lovers; Politics
Age range(s): Grades 10-Adult
Major character(s): Pastora, Young Woman (unconquerable), Mexican (descendant of Mayans); Maximo, Young Man (anti-hero), Spanish (descendant of Conquistadores)
Time period(s): Indeterminate Past
Locale(s): Sapogonia

Summary: In this novel, the author presents Sapogonia, a distinct place where all mestizos reside regardless of nationality or race, or possibly because of racial background. The narrator, Maximo the antihero, is both conqueror and conquered, and enters a destructive relationship with Pastora, a woman whom he cannot dominate. Sapogonia is not identified by modern boundaries.

Where it's reviewed:
Confluencia, Fall 1994, page 67

Other books by the same author:
The Invitation, 1979
So Far from God: A Novel, 1993
Women Are Not Roses, 1984
The Mixquiahuala Letters, 1986

Other books you might like:
Demetria Martinez, *Mother Tongue*, 1994
  Mary meets and shelters a political refugee, falls in love with him, and soon finds that his life is fundamentally different from hers.
Enrique A. Laguerre, *The Labyrinth*, 1984
  This is the story of a Puerto Rican man in New York City who goes to night school to earn a law degree and accidentally stumbles into the services of a Caribbean dictator.
Ana Lydia Vega, *True and False Romances*, 1994
  Collection of short stories about women and romance that take place in Puerto Rico.
Carmen C. Esteves, *Green Cane and Juicy Flotsam: Short Stories by Caribbean Women*, 1991

Collection of short stories by Puerto Rican, Cuban, Jamaican, and Domican women writers.

Diana Velez, *Reclaiming Medusa: Short Stories by Contemporary Puerto Rican Women*, 1988

Thirteen stories by Puerto Rican women writers that address family, marriage, religion, and magic.

Julia Alvarez, *In the Time of the Butterflies*, 1994

The story of the assassination of three sisters who are fighting to overthrow a dictatorship in the Dominican Republic.

570

ANA CASTILLO, Mexican American

So Far from God: A Novel
(New York: W.W. Norton & Co, 1993)

Age range(s): Grades 10-Adult
Major character(s): Sofia, Mother (of four daughters)
Time period(s): Indeterminate Past
Locale(s): Tome, New Mexico

Summary: This is the story of Sofi and her four daughters, Fe, Esperanza, Caridad, and La Loca who live in a small fictional town in central New Mexico. Presented in the style of the telenovela, popular Spanish television soap operas watched by millions in Mexico and South America, it is filled with many characters and sub-plots. The trials and tribulations of Sofi and her daughtes are depicted with humor and, at times, satirical magical realism.

Where it's reviewed:
Belles Lettres: A Review of Books by Women, Fall 1993, page 52
Choice, September 1993, page 112
Commonweal, January 14, 1994, page 37
Library Journal, July 1993, page 118
Publishers Weekly, February 22, 1993, page 81

Other books by the same author:
The Invitation, 1979
The Mixquiahuala Letters, 1986
Sapogonia: An Anti-Romance in 3/8 Meter, 1990
Women Are Not Roses, 1984
Massacre of the Dreamers: Essays on Xicanisma, 1994

Other books you might like:
Luis Rafael Sanchez, *Macho Camacho's Beat*, 1980
Macho Camacho's beat is an inane song that catches the tropical beats of the paradise island of Puerto Rico.
Rudolfo Anaya, *Bless Me, Ultima*, 1972
Story of a young boy's relationship with a curandera while growing up in rural New Mexico.
Denise Chavez, *Face of an Angel*, 1994
An intergenerational story from New Mexico, with Soveida at the center. She works as a waitress and is writing a book about service.
Kathleen Alcala, *Mrs. Vargas and the Dead Naturalist*, 1992
A collection of short stories, many about Mexican women, created as a book of wonders and following the characteristics of magical realism.
Julia Alvarez, *How the Garcia Girls Lost Their Accents*, 1991
An episodic novel about a family, a father, mother, and

four daughters, who move to the U.S. and the gradually become Americanized.

571

RAFAEL CASTILLO, Mexican American

Distant Journeys
(Tempe, AZ: Bilingual Press, 1991)

Subject(s): Identity; Cultural Conflict; Modern Life
Age range(s): Grades 10-Adult
Time period(s): 1980s
Locale(s): Southwest; New York, New York

Summary: Included in this collection are strange and vividly drawn short stories where the characters confront cultural loyalty, academic snobbery, loss, and crisis in identity. These stories are full of irony, humor, and disturbing cultural illusions about the myth of the American Dream. Castillo writes about the Virgin de Guadalupe appearing in improbable places and a Chicano dwarf writes a diary about life in the Lower East Side of New York.

Where it's reviewed:
Hispanic, January-February 1992, page 98

Other books you might like:
Patricia Preciado Martin, *Days of Plenty, Days of Want*, 1988
The past and the present meet in this collection of short stories where Mexican heritage is in jeopardy of being wiped out.
Alberto Alvaro Rios, *Pig Cookies and Other Stories*, 1995
This set of interlocking stories explores the residents of a small Mexican village.
Gary D. Keller, *Zapata Rose in 1992 and Other Tales*, 1992
This collection of satirical stories, by a writer known as an absurdist comedian, is filled with titles such as ''The Mojado Who Offered Up His Tapeworms to the Public Weal.''
Jose Antonio Burciaga, *Spilling the Beans: Loteria Chicana*, 1995
This series of essays, many humorous, recount experiences from the author's childhood, and explorations into aspects of Chicano culture.
Leo Romero, *Rita and Los Angeles*, 1995
This short story collection has a cast of complex characters who grow and evolve, and learn about being outsiders in an alien and hostile world.
Alicia Gaspar de Alba, *The Mystery of Survival and Other Stories*, 1993
These stories are mostly about female characters who explore their cultural boundaries and come to understand their places in the world.
Max Martinez, *A Red Bikini Dream*, 1990
This story collection captures the rhythms and spirit of contemporary American life as it explores self and identity in an increasingly complex nation.

572

LILLIAN CASTILLO-SPEED, Editor, Mexican American

Latina: Women's Voices from the Borderlands

(New York: Simon & Schuster, 1995)

Subject(s): Short Stories; Women; Anthology
Age range(s): Grades 10-Adult
Time period(s): 1990s (1995)
Locale(s): United States (Latino life throughout the U.S.)

Summary: Thirty-one Latina writers are represented in this collection, sharing their personal stories of family, heritage, wisdom, community, and passion. Some well-known writers, including Julia Alvarez, Christina Garcia, and Sandra Cisneros, with other new writers relate their lives as Cuban Americans, Puerto Ricans, and Chicanas.

Where it's reviewed:
Library Journal, July 1995, page 80
Publishers Weekly, July 17, 1995, page 226

Other books by the same author:
Chicana Studies Index, 1992

Other books you might like:
Maria del Carmen Boza, *Nosotras: Latina Literature Today*, 1986
    This is a collection of poetry and short stories by Latina writers.
Roberta Fernandez, *In Other Words: Literature by Latinas in the U.S.*, 1994
    This is an anthology of literature, short stories, and essays.
Evangelina Vigil, *Woman of Her Word: Hispanic Women Write*, 1987
    This is an anthology of writing, poetry and short stories in English and Spanish, by Latinas in the U.S.
Bryce Milligan, *Daughters of the Fifth Sun: A Collection of Latina Fiction and Poetry*, 1995
    A collection of poetry and short fiction by some of the best Latina writers today.
Asuncion Horno-Delgado, *Breaking Boundaries: Latina Writing and Critical Readings*, 1989
    This is an anthology of writings by Chicana, Puerto Rican, Cuban American, and other Latina women.
Tey Diana Rebolledo, *Las Mujeres Hablan: An Anthology of Nuevo Mexicana Writers*, 1988
    This collection of short stories and poetry is by Chicanas from New Mexico.

573

ANGELICO CHAVEZ, Mexican American

The Short Stories of Fray Angelico Chavez

(Albuquerque, NM: University of New Mexico Press, 1987)

Subject(s): Humor; Traditions; Rural Life
Age range(s): Grades 9-Adult
Time period(s): Indeterminate Past
Locale(s): New Mexico

Summary: This collection of Fray Angelico Chavez's most classic short stories presents humorous yet serious cultural and socio-historical evocations of life in New Mexico. These fourteen stories read like social allegories, where the stories address mystery and miracle, age and youth, and cultural conflict. Chavez, a retired Franciscan priest was considered to be one of New Mexico's leading men of letters. He wrote historical scholarship, poetry, and many short stories. All of his stories reflect the rich resources of the informal storytelling tradition of the Mexican community of New Mexico. He died in March of 1996.

About this book: This collection is edited by Genaro M. Padilla.

Where it's reviewed:
New York Times Book Review, October 11, 1987, page 56

Other books by the same author:
But Time and Chance: The Story of Padre Martinez of Taos, 1793-1867, 1981
La Conquistadora: The Autobiography of an Ancient Statue, 1954
From an Altar Screen; El Retablo: Tales From New Mexico, 1957
My Penitente Land: Reflections on Spanish New Mexico, 1974
New Mexico Triptych: Being Three Panels and Three Accounts, 1976

Other books you might like:
Sabine Ulibarri, *Tierra Amarilla: Stories of New Mexico = Cuentos de Nuevo Mexico*, 1993
    This collection of five short stories and a novella, evoke the rural life of a northern New Mexican village of an earlier era, from a young boy's perspective.
Rudolfo Anaya, *The Anaya Reader*, 1995
    Short stories, poetry, essays, plays, and poems, published elsewhere during the previous twenty-five years, is representative of the New Mexico writer.
Patricia Preciado Martin, *Days of Plenty, Days of Want*, 1988
    In this collection of stories the past and present meet, and Mexican heritage is in jeopardy of being wiped out.
Alberto Alvaro Rios, *Pig Cookies and Other Stories*, 1995
    Set earlier in this century, this collection of interrelated short stories takes place in a small village in northern Mexico.
Nash Candelaria, *The Day the Cisco Kid Shot John Wayne*, 1988
    The author examines cultural clashes between Latinos and Anglos in this humorous collection of short stories from New Mexico.
Jim Sagel, *El Santo Queso: Cuentos = The Holy Cheese*, 1990
    Humorously narrated, this collection of short stories is about the clash of cultures between outsiders and traditional New Mexicans.
Orlando Romero, *Nambe—Year One*, 1976
    A resident of the town of Nambe, New Mexico, is being seduced by a gypsy woman to leave his land and traditions.

574

DENISE CHAVEZ, Mexican American

Face of an Angel

(New York: Farrar, Straus, and Giroux, 1994)

Subject(s): Family Relations; Mothers and Daughters; Intergenerational Saga

Age range(s): Grades 10-Adult

Major character(s): Soveida Dosamantes, Waiter/Waitress; Mama Lupita, Grandmother

Time period(s): 19th century; 20th century (1880-1980)

Locale(s): Agua Oscura, New Mexico (a fictional city in New Mexico)

Summary: This is a humorous, sensuous novel with many rich characters. It centers around Soveida, who has worked as a waitress for over twenty years and is writing a book, titled *The Book of Service*, which shows how women constantly provide service to others, particularly men.

Where it's reviewed:

Belles Lettres: A Review of Books by Women, September 1995, page 3
Hispanic, March 1995, page 80
Publishers Weekly, August 15, 1994, page 77
Newsweek, October 17, 1994, page 77

Awards the book has won:

Before Columbus Foundation American Book Award, 1994
Premio Aztlan Award, 1994

Other books by the same author:

The Last of the Menu Girls, 1986

Other books you might like:

Isabel Allende, *The House of the Spirits*, 1985
    The story of a family, particularly the women, in Chile before the revolution.
Sylvia Lopez-Medina, *Cantora: A Novel*, 1992
    This intergenerational story, primarily about women, is about a family's migration from Mexico.
Victor Villasenor, *Rain of Gold*, 1991
    This intergenerational story is about the author's family's migration from Mexico.
Rosario Ferre, *The House on the Lagoon*, 1995
    This is an intergenerational story of a family in Ponce, Puerto Rico.
Alfredo Vea, *La Maravilla*, 1993
    Caught between many cultures, a young boy grows up amidst a world of desert marvels outside the city limits of Phoenix.
Alma Luz Villanueva, *Naked Ladies*, 1994
    This novel reveals the lives of four remarkable women, their struggles against prejudice, and their difficult relationships.

575

DENISE CHAVEZ, Mexican American

The Last of the Menu Girls

(Houston, TX: Arte Publico Press, 1986)

Subject(s): Labor and Labor Classes; Women; Coming of Age

Age range(s): Grades 10-Adult

Major character(s): Rocio Esquibel, Young Woman, Health Care Professional (nurse's aid), Chicana

Time period(s): 1950s

Locale(s): New Mexico

Summary: A collection of interrelated short stories which could be called a novel, about a Chicana adolescent girl from southern New Mexico who is looking for her place, identity, and womanhood. Rocio Esquibel's life is defined through the voices of women who are rarely depicted in fiction, women who occupy secondary positions in society and who tend to blend into the landscape, such as nurses's aids, maids, teachers, and menu girls. Chavez examines these women and makes them holders of great truths, and celebrants of life.

About this book: Title story was winner of the *Puerto Del Sol Fiction Award*, 1985.

Where it's reviewed:

Feminist Studies, Spring 1991, page 135

Other books by the same author:

Face of an Angel, 1994
Shattering the Myth: Plays by Hispanic Women, 1992

Other books you might like:

Gloria Anzaldua, *Borderlands: The New Mestiza = La Frontera*, 1987
    Anzaldua writes about her childhood along the Texas-Mexican border, describing her experience of being caught between two cultures.
Norma Elia Cantu, *Canicula: Snapshots of a Girlhood en la Frontera*, 1995
    A collection, with photos, of short stories and vignettes of a young girl growing up along the Texas border.
Patricia Preciado Martin, *Days of Plenty, Days of Want*, 1988
    A collection of stories where the past and present meet and Mexican heritage is in jeopardy of being wiped out.
Mary Helen Ponce, *Taking Control*, 1987
    Collection of stories portraying domestic and economic oppression of Mexican and Chicana women in the U.S.
Roberta Fernandez, *Itaglio: Novel in Six Stories*, 1990
    A novel related in six stories, each about an extraordinary woman who serves as a role model for the young narrator.
Rolando Hinojosa, *Becky and Her Friends*, 1990
    Narrated by many of her friends, this novel focuses on the strong-willed Becky Escobar, an upwardly-mobile woman who at age thirty-five decides to divorce her husband.

576

SANDRA CISNEROS, Mexican American
TERRY YBANEZ, Illustrator

Hair = Pelitos

(New York: Alfred A. Knopf, 1994)

Subject(s): Family Life; Hair

Age range(s): Grades K-3

Locale(s): Chicago, Illinois

Summary: In this vivid story, excerpted from Sandra Cisneros' *The House on Mango Street*, the narrator examines family and individual differences. Every member of the family has different hair—Papa's hair is like a broom, Nenny's hair is slippery, and Kiki's hair is like fur. But the favorite person of all, Mama, has hair like little candy circles that smells like bread.

About this book: This work is in Spanish and English.

Where it's reviewed:
Horn Book Magazine, November-December 1994, page 716
Publishers Weekly, October 31, 1994, page 61

Other books by the same author:
The House on Mango Sreet, 1988
Woman Hollering Creek and Other Stories, 1991

Other books you might like:
Omar Castaneda, *Abuela's Weave*, 1993
   A little girl and her grandmother sell their crafts at a market in Guatemala.
Carmen Lomas Garza, *Family Pictures = Cuadros de Familia*, 1990
   This work provides descriptions of family life during celebrations and holidays with vivid illustrations.
Arthur Dorros, *Abuela*, 1991
   A little girl and her grandmother fly all over New York City.
Carmen Santiago Nodar, *Abuelita's Paradise*, 1992
   Marita sits in Abuelita's rocking chair and remembers the stories Abuelita told of her life in Puerto Rico.
Pat Mora, *Pablo's Tree*, 1994
   Pablo's grandfather plants a tree at Pablo's birth which they enjoy together.
Leyla Torres, *Saturday Sancocho*, 1995
   Every Saturday, Maria Lili helps her grandparents make their traditional chicken sancocho.

577

SANDRA CISNEROS, Mexican American

The House on Mango Street
(Houston, TX: Arte Publico Press, 1984)

Subject(s): Coming of Age; Identity; City Life
Age range(s): Grades 9-Adult
Major character(s): Esperanza Cordero, Child, Chicana
Time period(s): 1960s
Locale(s): Chicago, Illinois (takes place in a Latino neighborhood of Chicago)

Summary: In this novel, young Esperanza Cordera searches for identity and community in her Latino neighborhood of Chicago. As she reaches adulthood, Esperanza examines violence, oppression, and friendship through writing, narrating the story of her life and the lives of other Mango Street women. The novel covers one crucial year in her life.

About this book: The novel consists of forty-six vignettes that at times read like poetry.

Where it's reviewed:
America, July 18, 1992, page 39
Commonweal, September 13, 1991, page 524
Feminist Studies, Spring 1991, page 135
TLS. Times Literary Supplement, May 15, 1992, page 20

Other books by the same author:
Bad Boys, 1980

My Wicked, Wicked Ways, 1987
Woman Hollering Creek and Other Stories, 1991
Loose Woman: Poems, 1994
Hair = Pelitos, 1994

Other books you might like:
Rosario Ferre, *The House on the Lagoon*, 1995
   This intergenerational story portrays a family from Ponce, Puerto Rico
Esmeralda Santiago, *When I Was Puerto Rican*, 1993
   This autobiographical story portrays a young girl living in poverty in Puerto Rico.
Nicholasa Mohr, *Nilda: A Novel*, 1973
   These autobiographical stories describe a young girl growing up in the Puerto Rican Barrio of New York.
John Rechy, *The Miraculous Day of Amalia Gomez: A Novel*, 1991
   This novel examines poverty and gang warfare as it follows a day in the life of a Mexican-American woman, who lives in the shabby section of Hollywood.
Judith Ortiz Cofer, *Silent Dancing: A Partial Remembrance of a Puerto Rican Childhood*, 1990
   These stories describe growing up in Puerto Rico and U.S.
Denise Chavez, *The Last of the Menu Girls*, 1986
   An adolescent Chicana girl from southern New Mexico searches for her identity and womanhood in this collection of interrelated stories.

578

SANDRA CISNEROS, Mexican American

Woman Hollering Creek and Other Stories
(New York: Random House, 1991)

Subject(s): Short Stories; Women
Age range(s): Grades 10-Adult
Time period(s): 1990s (1991)
Locale(s): Texas

Summary: A collection of short stories with strong, angry female characters struggling valiantly to make something beautiful of their lives. The stories are vivid, ironic, filled with interesting characters such as Rudy Cantu, a drag queen, or the spirit of Emiliano Zapata's wife. Cisneros' powerful, creative use of language, in English and Spanish, conveys strong, intense and passionate situations. The title story, ''Woman Hollering Creek,'' is about a tearful young Mexican bride who must escape an abusive husband and is based on La Llorona, the weeping woman of folklore.

Where it's reviewed:
Library Journal, April 1, 1991, page 149
Newsweek, June 3, 1991, page 60
Publishers Weekly, February 15, 1991, page 76
Times Literary Supplement, August 13, 1993, page 18

Other books by the same author:
The House on Mango Street, 1983
My Wicked, Wicked Ways, 1987
Bad Boys, 1980
Hair = Pelitos, 1994

Other books you might like:

Rosario Ferre, *The Youngest Doll*, 1991
A collection considered by critics as a manifesto of women's rights. The title story, "The Youngest Doll," is one of the author's most successful.

Ana Lydia Vega, *True and False Romances*, 1994
Collection of short stories about women and romance that take place in Puerto Rico.

Alicia Gaspar de Alba, *The Mystery of Survival and Other Stories*, 1993
Stories mostly about female characters who explore and come to understand their places in the world and the cultural boundaries that divide them.

Estela Portillo Trambley, *Rain of Scorpions and Other Writings*, 1975
Collection of short stories by an early Chicana writer that explore the place of women in Mexican society.

Beatriz Rivera, *African Passions and Other Stories*, 1995
A collection of short stories focusing on women's obsessive search for love and success, narrated with humor, passion, and satire.

579

JESUS COLON, Puerto Rican

A Puerto Rican in New York and Other Sketches

(New York: Mainstream Publishers, 1961)

Subject(s): Short Stories; Identity; Politics
Age range(s): Grades 9-Adult
Time period(s): 1940s; 1950s
Locale(s): New York, New York

Summary: This collection of essays and short prose works, many autobiographical, reflect a socially conscious and humanistic point of view. Colon wrote primarily in English, unlike most Puerto Rican writers of his generation, and for this reason his work is considered the precursor to Puerto Rican literature of New York. A major theme in his work was advocacy for the working class.

About this book: Many of these essays were first published in the "Daily Worker", a Communist party publication.

Other books by the same author:
The Way it Was, and Other Writings, 1993

Other books you might like:

Piri Thomas, *Down These Mean Streets*, 1978
This autobiographical novel describes growing up in Spanish Harlem

Emilio Diaz Valcarcel, *Hot Soles in Harlem*, 1993
This exploration of New York characters is from the perspective of a Puerto Rican immigrant.

Faythe Turner, *Puerto Rican Writers at Home in the U.S.A.: An Anthology*, 1991
This collection of poetry and short stories is by Puerto Rican writers in the U.S.

Jack Agueros, *Dominoes and Other Stories from the Puerto Rican*, 1993
This collection of short stories describes life in Spanish Harlem.

580

LUCHA CORPI, Mexican American

Cactus Blood: A Mystery Novel

(Houston, TX: Arte Publico Press, 1995)

Subject(s): Mystery; Supernatural; Dreams and Nightmares
Age range(s): Grades 10-Adult
Major character(s): Gloria Damasco, Detective—Private (in training), Widow(er), Chicana
Time period(s): 1970s; 1980s (1973-1989)
Locale(s): Oakland, California

Summary: Gloria Damasco, recently widowed, decides to become a full time private investigator and serves as an apprentice to Justin Escobar. Together they work their way through the complexities of a murder, that of their good friend Sonny, which is somehow connected to a pesticide tank explosion that occurred fifteen years before, in 1973. The trail leads them to Kingsburg, Fresno, parts of Oakland, and finally to the wine country of Sonoma County. Corpi weaves in the threads of herbs, snakeskins, and poisoned grapes with striking characters, all of whom have remarkable pasts, and ties them together in the end.

Where it's reviewed:
Library Journal, March 1, 1995, page 105
Publishers Weekly, February 6, 1995, page 79

Other books by the same author:
Delia's Song, 1989
Eulogy for a Brown Angel: A Mystery Novel, 1992
Palabras de Mediodia = Noon Words: Poems, 1980

Other books you might like:

Michael Nava, *How Town: A Novel of Suspense*, 1990
Henry Rios defends a former high school acquaintance from his hometown who is accused of murdering a man and is also thought to be involved in child pornography.

Michael Nava, *The Hidden Law*, 1992
Henry Rios defends a young Chicano accused of murdering a powerful Chicano public official in Los Angeles, and discovers who did the actual killing.

Rolando Hinojosa, *Partners in Crime: A Rafe Buenrostro Mystery*, 1985
Written in the style of the popular genre, this border murder mystery involves Hinojosa's popular characters, Jehu Malacara and Rafe Buenrostro (now a lieutenant of the Belken County Homicide Squad).

Rudolfo Anaya, *Zia Summer*, 1995
Sonny Baca is involved in an exciting, complicated mystery plot that involves murder, cult worship of the sun, and a battle over nuclear waste and its disposal in New Mexico.

Rudolfo Anaya, *Albuquerque*, 1992
An exciting story of modern Albuquerque, with a vicious mayoral race, a young Chicano boxer, American Indians fighting to retain their water rights, and the folkloric past of New Mexico.

Manuel Ramos, *The Ballad of Rocky Ruiz: Death of a Martyr*, 1993
Luis Montez, a middle-aged former Chicano activist/lawyer, becomes involved in solving the twenty-year-old murder of Rocky Ruiz.

Manuel Ramos, *The Ballad of Gato Guerrero*, 1994

Felix "Gato" Guerrero, an old friend from way back, calls on Montez to save him and his new love from her husband, a Latino mobster.

581

LUCHA CORPI, Mexican American

Delia's Song

(Houston, TX: Arte Publico Press, 1989)

Subject(s): Identity; Women; Coming of Age
Age range(s): Grades 10-Adult
Major character(s): Delia Trevino, Young Woman, Activist, Chicana
Time period(s): 1970s
Locale(s): Berkeley, California

Summary: In a world of oppression and conflict, Delia must find a way to forge her own identity and relationships with others. She finds it difficult to believe that love and honesty between men and women is possible. Participating in the anti-war and civil rights movements of the '60s, Delia gains the strength to create and impose her own image on reality and to trust love.

Where it's reviewed:
Publishers Weekly, November 4, 1988, page 80
American Book Review, January-February 1990, page 13
Western American Literature, November 1989, page 278

Other books by the same author:
Cactus Blood: A Mystery Novel, 1995
Eulogy for a Brown Angel: A Mystery Novel, 1992
Variaciones Sobre una Tempestad = Variations on a Storm, 1990

Other books you might like:
Juan Felipe Herrera, *Night Train to Tuxtla*, 1994

This collection deals with a vast array of subjects, including Rodney King, AIDS, zoot suits, and what Herrera calls the "swashbuckling Chicano sixties."

Floyd Salas, *What Now My Love*, 1994

A writer and his two friends flee San Francisco's drug subculture and a narcotics bust, to travel to the Mexican border during the 1960s.

Oscar Zeta Acosta, *The Revolt of the Cockroach People*, 1973

This personal memoir tells of the turbulent years that mark the beginning of the Chicano movement in California and the political activities of East Los Angeles.

Laura Del Fuego, *Maravilla*, 1989

Consuelo Contreres, growing up in the housing projects of East Los Angeles, makes her way through turbulent times during the 1960s.

Mary Helen Ponce, *The Wedding*, 1989

Blanca Munoz plans her wedding to Sammy-the-Cricket, as the author shows us an expose of 1950s working class life and culture in a southern California Chicano community.

Richard Vasquez, *Chicano*, 1970

This story about four generations of the Sandoval family who leave Mexico for Los Angeles during the revolution,

focuses on the love affair of Maria Sandoval and her Anglo boyfriend, David.

Denise Chavez, *Face of an Angel*, 1994

This humorous and sensuous novel explores the saga of a family in the fictional New Mexican town of Agua Oscura.

582

LUCHA CORPI, Mexican American

Eulogy for a Brown Angel: A Mystery Novel

(Houston, TX: Arte Publico Press, 1992)

Subject(s): Mystery and Detective Stories; Gangs
Age range(s): Grades 10-Adult
Major character(s): Gloria Damasco, Wife (of a doctor), Activist, Chicana
Time period(s): 1990s
Locale(s): Oakland, California; Los Angeles, California; Napa Valley, California

Summary: While participating in the Chicano Moratorium of 1970 in Los Angeles, Gloria Damasco is witness to police-gang conflicts and the death of a four-year-old boy. Unable to forget the terrible events of that year, Damasco follows the lives of the boy's family, the Cisneros. After many years she is finally able to solve the mystery of the senseless killing. The story is set within the context of recent Mexican American history.

Where it's reviewed:
Publishers Weekly, July 6, 1992, page 41
Western American Literature, August 1993, page 185

Other books by the same author:
Cactus Blood: A Mystery Novel, 1995
Delia's Song, 1989

Other books you might like:
Manuel Ramos, *The Ballad of Gato Guerrero*, 1994

Luis Montez, a divorced lawyer, works at saving Felix "Gato" Guerrero, an old friend from way back, who is being chased by a Latino mobster.

Michael Nava, *How Town: A Novel of Suspense*, 1990

Henry Rios defends a former high school acquaintance from his hometown accused of murder and thought to be involved in child pornography.

Rudolfo Anaya, *Zia Summer*, 1995

Sonny Baca is involved in a mystery that includes murder, cult worship of the sun, and a battle over nuclear waste and its disposal in New Mexico.

Rudolfo Anaya, *Albuquerque*, 1992

An exciting story of modern Albuquerque, with a vicious mayoral race, a young Chicano boxer, American Indians fighting to retain water rights, and the folkloric past of New Mexico.

Manuel Ramos, *The Ballad of Rocky Ruiz: Death of a Martyr*, 1993

Former Chicano activist lawyer, middle aged Luis Montez, becomes involved in solving the twenty-year old murder of Rocky Ruiz.

Manuel Ramos, *The Last Client of Luis Montez*, 1996

The last client of Denver lawyer, Louie Montez, is found

dead with Montez standing over him. To clear his name, Montez becomes entangled in a complicated web thaqt takes him to California and back.

583

ALEJANDRO CRUZ MARTINEZ, Zapotec
FERNANDO OLIVERA, Illustrator, Mexican

The Woman Who Outshone the Sun
(San Francisco: Children's Book Press, 1991)

Subject(s): Magic; Indians of Mexico; Folk Tales
Age range(s): Grades 1-3
Major character(s): Lucia Zenteno, Young Woman
Time period(s): Indeterminate Past
Locale(s): Mexico (takes place in a Zapotec Indian village)

Summary: This story, part of the oral history of the Zapotec Indians, is from a poem by Alejandro Cruz Martinez. Lyrical and moving, it tells of a beautiful woman with hair so bright that it outshines the sun. But the villagers, frightened by the strangeness and magical powers of this woman, are less than friendly.

About this book: This work is in Spanish and English bilingual format.

Where it's reviewed:
Language Arts, March 1993, page 222
Publishers Weekly, January 6, 1992, page 65

Other books you might like:
Manlio Argueta, *Magic Dogs of the Volcanoes = Los Perros Magicos de los Volcanes*, 1990
  The magic dogs, or cadejos, who live on the volcanoes of El Salvador, are loved by the villagers because of their powerful magic.
Gary Soto, *Chato's Kitchen*, 1995
  Chato, the lowrider cat, wants to eat some juicy mice, but when he invites them to dinner they outwit him.
Lucia M. Gonzalez, *The Bossy Gallito*, 1994
  A bossy little rooster gets his beak dirty pecking some corn while on his way to his uncle's wedding.
Harriet Rohmer, *The Legend of Food Mountain*, 1982
  Quetzalcoatl creates the people of the earth but he does not know what to feed them.
Pura Belpre, *Ote: A Puerto Rican Folk Tale*, 1969
  Ote must go to the forest in search of food for his wife and five children. There he meets a near-sighted devil who brings him bad luck.
Richard Garcia, *My Aunt Otilia's Spirits = Los Espiritus de Mi Tia Otilia*, 1978
  When Aunt Otilia comes to visit from Puerto Rico, her spirits make noises during the night. Trying to uncover the mystery behind these noises, her nephew stays awake all night.

584

GIL CUADROS, Mexican American

City of God
(San Francisco: City Lights, 1994)

Subject(s): AIDS (Disease); Homosexuality/Lesbianism; Growing Up
Age range(s): Grades 10-Adult
Time period(s): 20th century (1923-1994)
Locale(s): Los Angeles, California (various locations in California)

Summary: A rough account of devastation and empowerment in the age of AIDS, this collection of writings is sorrowful, painful, and unfiltered. The first half of the book is a short novel and the second half a collection of haunting poetry. The author writes this after the death of his lover while he himself lives with AIDS. He examines his up-bringing, the eroticism of the body, the betrayal of disease, and the remnants of love in a shattered world.

Where it's reviewed:
Lambda Book Report, January-February 1995, page 34
Library Journal, November 1, 1994, page 80
Publishers Weekly, October 31, 1994, page 59

Other books you might like:
John Rechy, *Numbers*, 1984
  Johnny Rio, handsome and trying to escape impending age, travels to Los Angeles in a frenzied attempt to recreate his younger self.
Michael Nava, *The Hidden Law*, 1992
  Henry Rios defends a young Chicano accused of murdering a powerful Chicano public official in Los Angeles, while his long time lover, who has AIDS, leaves him for someone else.
Jaime Manrique, *Latin Moon in Manhattan*, 1992
  Through the eyes of Santiago, a gay unpublished poet, this novel presents plots and sub-plots, and a vivid depiction of Columbian American culture in Little Colombia Jackson Heights.
Reinaldo Arenas, *Before Night Falls*, 1993
  This autobiography describes Arena's almost dying of AIDS in 1987 and the story of his life in Cuba before he came to the United States in 1980, where he later committed suicide in 1990.
John Rechy, *City of Night*, 1963
  Johnny Rio, born in El Paso, becomes a gay Chicano wanderer, who lives by the statistics of random sexual encounters and orgasms in various cities.

585

JAMES ROBERTO CURTIS

Shango
(Houston, TX: Arte Publico, 1996)

Subject(s): Religion; Anthropology; Drugs
Age range(s): Grades 10-Adult
Major character(s): Miguel, Student—College, Cuban American

Time period(s): 1990s
Locale(s): Miami, Florida

Summary: While hanging out on the beach with his Anglo girlfriend, Miguel reads a newspaper article about a stolen skull. This leads him to decide to research ''santeria'' for an ethnography course and he and his professor become involved in a police investigation of a ritualistic murder. Santeria is the Afro-Caribbean religion of his native island and it draws him and a new girlfriend, Ileana, into mysterious cult initiations, dangerous underworld characters, and a confrontation with the terrible god Shango.

Where it's reviewed:
Publishers Weekly, March 25, 1996, page 78

Other books by the same author:
The Cuban-American Experience, 1984
The Mexican Border Cities, 1993

Other books you might like:
Himilce Novas, *Mangos, Bananas, and Coconuts: A Cuban Love Story*, 1996
    This tale of a magical yet real love story is an ancient tale, beginning with the love of a man and a woman from different social classes, and the story of the fate of their children.
Gloria Gonzalez, *The Thirteenth Apostle*, 1993
    Newspaperwoman Geraldine St. Claire investigates the murder of her lover Hal, which leads her to suspect an industrial homicide and also leads her right into the hands of a powerful drug lord.
Thomas Sanchez, *Mile Zero*, 1989
    This exciting novel uses history, voodoo, santeria, folkloric sayings, and tropical culture to create a supernatural mystery and introduce ''Zobop'', possibly a voodoo-inspired killer.
Lucha Corpi, *Cactus Blood: A Mystery Novel*, 1995
    Gloria Damasco, an apprentice to a private investigator, possesses an inexplicable visionary power, and helps solve a murder related to a 15 year old pesticide tank explosion.
Rudolfo Anaya, *Zia Summer*, 1995
    Sonny Baca is involved in an exciting complicated mystery plot that involves murder, cult worship of the sun, and a battle over nuclear waste and disposal in New Mexico.
Sandra Benitez, *A Place Where the Sea Remembers*, 1993
    Written as a series of interrelated magical tales, this novel presents the life of a coastal village in Mexico.
Carolina Garcia-Aguilera, *Bloody Waters*, 1996
    Guadalupe ''Lupe'' Solano, part of Miami's elite, is approached by a young couple for assistance in finding the biological mother of their adopted daughter when she needs a bone-marrow transplant.

586

BEATRIZ DE LA GARZA

The Candy Vendor's Boy and Other Stories

(Houston: Arte Publico Press, 1994)

Subject(s): Short Stories; Identity; Migration
Age range(s): Grades 9-Adult

Time period(s): 1980s
Locale(s): Texas

Summary: The stories in this collection depict realistic characters who struggle with life issues they have no control over, such as war, poverty, racism, and political conflict. Living and growing up in Texas, the characters try to find their identities.

Where it's reviewed:
Publishers Weekly, February 21, 1994, page 248

Other books you might like:
Jose Antonio Burciaga, *Spilling the Beans: Loteria Chicana*, 1995
    This series of essays, many humorous, recounts experiences from the author's childhood in Texas.
Nash Candelaria, *The Day the Cisco Kid Shot John Wayne*, 1988
    These twelve humorous stories portray Chicano-Anglo interrelations and conflicts.
Rolando Hinojosa, *Becky and Her Friends*, 1989
    A novel that follows generations of Anglos and Mexicans in a fictional Rio Grande Valley Texas town.
Victor Villasenor, *Walking Stars: Stories of Magic and Power*, 1994
    These true stories show that life is full of magic that gives strength and power to endure and triumph in everyday life.
Alberto Alvaro Rios, *The Iguana Killer: Twelve Stories of the Heart*, 1984
    In this volume of short stories, the author transforms the stories of ordinary life into a book of secrets.
Sandra Cisneros, *Woman Hollering Creek and Other Stories*, 1991
    This collection of short stories about women takes place in Texas and the border area.
Alma Luz Villanueva, *Weeping Woman: La Llorona and Other Stories*, 1994
    This collection examines women who live in a world torn apart by violence, racism and sexism.

587

TERRI DE LA PENA, Mexican American

Latin Satins

(Seattle, WA: Seal Press, 1994)

Subject(s): Music; Homosexuality/Lesbianism
Age range(s): Grades 10-Adult
Major character(s): Jessica Tamayo, Singer, Lesbian
Time period(s): 1990s
Locale(s): Santa Monica, California

Summary: Jessica, Cindi, Chic, and Rita live together and make up a lesbian salsa band called the Latin Satins trying to make it within the Los Angeles music scene. This novel explores their lives inside and outside of the band, battling racism and homophobia, dealing with work and family and love, and creating music based on their strong bonds of friendship.

About this book: Spanish words are interspersed throughout the text.

Where it's reviewed:
Lambda Book Report, May-June 1995, page 21

Latino Titles

Library Journal, October 1, 1994, page 112
Publishers Weekly, August 1, 1994, page 75

Other books by the same author:
Margins, 1992

Other books you might like:
Cherrie Moraga, *Loving in the War Years: Lo que Nunca Paso por sus Labios*, 1983
This autobiographical work is about a Chicana lesbian writer who grew up California.
Ibis Gomez-Vega, *Send My Roots Rain*, 1991
Carole goes to a small Texas town to paint murals on Church walls and falls in love with a mysterious woman.
Jaime Manrique, *Latin Moon in Manhattan*, 1992
This novel presents bizarre characters, plots and sub-plots, and a vivid depiction of Columbian American culture in Little Columbia, Jackson Heights.
Sheila Ortiz Taylor, *Faultline: A Novel*, 1982
A very funny book about a lesbian mother of six children, her lover/companion, their 300 rabbits, and a six foot tall Black drag queen babysitter.
Emma Perez, *Gulf Dreams*, 1996
A creative series of essays, short vignettes, and psychoanalytic discourse, these are about growing up lesbian in Latino culture.
Sheila Ortiz Taylor, *Southbound: A Sequel to Faultline*, 1990
This humorous lesbian novel, follows professor Arden as she sets out across the country in a hearse with her six kids, her ballet-dancer/live-in babysitter, and her lover, Alice.
Achy Obejas, *We Came All The Way from Cuba So You Could Dress Like This? Stories*, 1994
A collection of seven short stories, set in Chicago, with several gay men and women and outcasts, AIDS patients and immigrants in the 1990s.

588

TERRI DE LA PENA, Mexican American

Margins

(Seattle: Seal Press, 1992)

Subject(s): Mothers and Daughters; Homosexuality/Lesbianism; Family Relations
Age range(s): Grades 10-Adult
Major character(s): Veronica Melendez, Writer (novelist), Lesbian, Chicana
Time period(s): 1990s (1992)
Locale(s): Los Angeles, California (other cities in southern California)

Summary: Veronica Melendez, a writer and part-time student, loses her lover and childhood best friend in a car accident that occurs while Veronica is driving. She must overcome her grief and guilt, make decisions about her future, and tell her parents and older brother about her homosexuality. Besides starting a novel she also starts relationships with two very different women.

Where it's reviewed:
Advocate, June 2, 1992, page 40
Library Journal, March 15, 1992, page 124
Publishers Weekly, March 23, 1992, page 66

Other books by the same author:
Latin Satins, 1994

Other books you might like:
Cherrie Moraga, *Loving in the War Years: Lo que Nunca Paso por sus Labios*, 1983
This autobiographical story is about a Chicana lesbian writer growing up California.
Michael Nava, *How Town: A Novel of Suspense*, 1991
A gay Chicano lawyer solves a murder mystery while unpretentiously depicting a gay relationship.
Ibis Gomez-Vega, *Send My Roots Rain*, 1991
Carole goes to a small Texas town to paint murals on church walls and falls in love with a mysterious woman.
Elias Miguel Munoz, *The Greatest Performance*, 1991
A poetic novel of exile, where two soul-mates recount to each other their stories of living on the margins of family, country, and sexual identity.
Sheila Ortiz Taylor, *Faultline: A Novel*, 1982
A very funny book about a lesbian mother of six children, her lover/companion, their 300 rabbits, and a six foot tall Black drag queen babysitter.
Emma Perez, *Gulf Dreams*, 1996
A creative series of essays, short vignettes, and psychoanalytic discourse describe growing up lesbian in Latino culture.
Sheila Ortiz Taylor, *Southbound: A Sequel to Faultline*, 1990
This humorous lesbian novel, follows professor Arden as she sets out across the country in a hearse with her six kids, her ballet dancer/live-in babysitter, and her lover Alice.
Achy Obejas, *We Came All the Way from Cuba So You Could Dress Like This? Stories*, 1994
A collection of seven short stories, set in Chicago, with several about gay men and women and outcasts, AIDS patients and immigrants in the 1990s.

589

CARMEN DE MONTEFLORES, Puerto Rican

Singing Softly = Cantando Bajito

(San Francisco: Spinsters/Aunt Lute, 1989)

Subject(s): Family Relations; Magic; Women
Age range(s): Grades 10-Adult
Major character(s): Pilar, Grandmother, Puerto Rican Meli, Writer, Puerto Rican (Pilar's granddaughter)
Locale(s): Puerto Rico

Summary: This novel examines the life of Pilar, who has a relationship with the son of a wealthy family. This relationship alienates her from her own family. Pilar's story is told through the eyes of her granddaughter, Meli, who wants to reclaim her relationship with her mother and grandmother through the act of writing.

Where it's reviewed:
Library Journal, July 1989, page 106
Publishers Weekly, May 26, 1989, page 59

Other books you might like:
Magali Garcia Ramis, *Happy Days, Uncle Sergio*, 1995
This coming of age novel is about a middle class girl in Puerto Rico.

Judith Ortiz Cofer, *Silent Dancing: A Partial Remembrance of a Puerto Rican Childhood*, 1990
These stories are about growing up in both Puerto Rico and New Jersey.

Rosario Ferre, *The House on the Lagoon*, 1995
This is an intergenerational story of a family in Ponce, Puerto Rico.

Judith Ortiz Cofer, *The Line of the Sun: A Novel*, 1989
This coming of age novel takes place in Puerto Rico and Paterson, New Jersey.

Sylvia Lopez-Medina, *Cantora: A Novel*, 1992
This novel tells the story of four generations of women in Mexico and their lives in America at the turn of the 20th century.

Isabel Allende, *Paula*, 1995
Isabel Allende, well-known Latino author, renders the story of her daughter's agonizing illness with porphyria, her descent into a coma and her eventual death at an early age.

590

LAURA DEL FUEGO, Mexican American

Maravilla

(Encino, CA: Floricanto Press, 1989)

Subject(s): Growing Up; Identity; City Life
Age range(s): Grades 8-Adult
Major character(s): Consuelo Contreres, Teenager (girl), Chicana
Time period(s): 1960s
Locale(s): San Francisco, California; Los Angeles, California

Summary: Consuelo Contreres, growing up in the housing projects of East Los Angeles, makes her way through turbulent times and strives for self-determination when her friends and family don't understand or care. A thoughtful and sometimes violent story, from East L.A. to the Haight-Ashbury section of San Francisco in the 1960s, this is a story about discovering one's self in the midst of chaos.

Other books you might like:

Acosta Oscar Zeta, *The Autobiography of a Brown Buffalo*, 1972
Part novel, and very much an autobiographical work, Acosta, famous as a Robin Hood Chicano lawyer with an appetite for life on the edge, examines his life.

Floyd Salas, *What Now My Love*, 1994
Fleeing from the San Francisco drug sub-culture and a narcotics bust, a writer and two friends travel from San Francisco to the Mexican border during the turbulent 1960s.

Lucha Corpi, *Delia's Song*, 1988
A young educated Chicana comes of age politically and sexually during the 1960s.

Vincent Younis, *Shine Boys: A Story about Santa Fe*, 1995
This novella narrates the life of an un-named main character growing up in Santa Fe during the late 1950s and his introduction to drugs at a very young age.

Richard Vasquez, *Chicano*, 1970
This novel about four generations of the Sandoval family, who leave Mexico for Los Angeles during the Revolution,

focuses on the love affair of Maria Sandoval and her Anglo boyfriend.

Mary Helen Ponce, *The Wedding*, 1989
Blanca Munoz plans her wedding to Sammy-the-Cricket, as the author shows us an expose of 1950s working class life and culture in a southern California Chicano community.

Estela Portillo Trambley, *Rain of Scorpions and Other Stories*, 1993
An adventure novel, this presents dangerous border crossings, confrontations with a magician, and drug smuggling in the lives of three generations of the Cavazos family in Texas.

591

JUNOT DIAZ, Dominican American

Drown, Stories

(New York, NY: Riverhead Books, 1996)

Subject(s): Identity; Exile; Coming of Age
Age range(s): Grades 10-Adult
Major character(s): Ramon de las Casas, Young Man, Dominican American
Time period(s): 1990s
Locale(s): New York, New York (Dominican Republic, New York, and New Jersey)

Summary: A collection of ten short stories mostly about young Latino men who are experiencing a transformation while learning to define their American identity. Yunior appears in five of the stories, a young man whose family was abandoned by his father for years, until one day he returns to the Dominican to take his family to New Jersey. The story "Negocios" portrays this father, through the love and anger of Yunior, and in the title story a young man is seduced by a male friend while both watch a pornographic film. The language of these young men is that of the outsider, a teenage argot, and Spanish mixed with Black English.

About this book: The story "Ysrael" will appear in Best American Short Stories 1996.

Where it's reviewed:
Publishers Weekly, July 8, 1996, page 71
New York Times Book Review, September 29, 1996, page 9

Other books you might like:

Rafael Zepeda, *Horse Medicine and Other Stories*, 1990
A collection of stories that deal with the world of men, where drinking, swearing, and male one-up-manship is the norm.

Yvonne V. Sapia, *Valentino's Hair*, 1991
Rudolph Valentino comes into the life of Facundo Nieves and changes it forever when Nieves saves the hair and its power haunts him until his own death.

Dagoberto Gilb, *The Last Known Residence of Micke Acuna*, 1994
Mickey Acuna is waiting for something, something arriving through the mail, as he dwells at the YMCA in El Paso.

Dagoberto Gilb, *The Magic of Blood*, 1993
   Short stories, about working-class life, with multi-dimensional characters who lead realistic lives.
Max Martinez, *A Red Bikini Dream*, 1990
   A collection of five short stories that capture the rhythms and spirit of modern life in the U.S. where the characters ponder the question of self and identity in an increasingly complex society.
Ramon Ferreira, *The Gravedigger and Other Stories*, 1986
   These short stories vividly depict the disturbing and harsh underside of Cuban society during the 50s, revealing political repression, fear of homosexuality, and the dark side of racism.
Arturo Islas, *La Mollie and the King of Tears*, 1996
   Louie Mendoza, a jazz musician, waits to hear the diagnosis of his liver, and in the unique street language of Chicanos he narrates his story to a stranger.

592

EMILIO DIAZ VALCARCEL, Puerto Rican

Hot Soles in Harlem
(Pittsburgh: Latin American Literary Press, 1993)

Subject(s): Work; Social Classes; City Life
Age range(s): Grades 10-Adult
Major character(s): Gerardo Sanchez, Immigrant, Puerto Rican; Aleluya, Intellectual, Puerto Rican
Time period(s): 1990s (1993)
Locale(s): New York, New York

Summary: Gerardo meets Aleluya on his first day in New York City, and gets shown the city from the Puerto Rican Barrio in Harlem to the penthouses on Fifth Avenue. Many unusual New York characters are portrayed.

About this book: The title in Spanish *Harlem Todos los Dias* had been published in 1978. It is translated by Tanya T. Fayen.

Where it's reviewed:
Choice, May 1994, page 1440
Library Journal, November 1, 1993, page 147

Other books by the same author:
Schemes in the Month of March, 1979
Mi Mama Me Ama, 1981

Other books you might like:
Piri Thomas, *Down These Mean Streets*, 1967
   The personal and sometimes violent life of a young man growing up in Spanish Harlem in the 1950s.
Ed Vega, *Mendoza's Dreams*, 1987
   These are short stories about Puerto Ricans living in New York City.
Jesus Colon, *A Puerto Rican in New York and Other Sketches*, 1961
   These autobiographical stories and essays are about living in New York City from the 1920s to the mid-1950s.
Jack Agueros, *Dominoes and Other Stories from the Puerto Rican*, 1993
   These stories are about growing up Puerto Rican in New York City.

Jaime Manrique, *Latin Moon in Manhattan*, 1992
   This work is about the life of a gay Columbian poet in New York who knows many crazy characters.

593

ARTHUR DORROS
ELISA KLEVEN, Illustrator

Abuela
(New York: Dutton Children's Books, 1991)

Subject(s): Grandparents; Adventure and Adventurers
Age range(s): Grades 1-3
Major character(s): Rosalba, Child (little girl)
Time period(s): 1980s
Locale(s): New York, New York

Summary: Rosalba's Abuela loves to go on adventures. Together they fly over New York, gliding low to race sailboats, saying buenos dias to people on the street, playing with airplanes, and circling the Statue of Liberty which reminds Abuela of when she first came to this country. Their adventure is vividly illustrated with pictures that shine with energy and color.

About this book: Spanish words throughout; glossary included.

Where it's reviewed:
Horn Book Magazine, November-December 1991, page 726
Publishers Weekly, July 19, 1991, page 55

Other books by the same author:
Radio Man = Don Radio: A Story in English and Spanish, 1993
Tonight Is Carnival, 1991

Other books you might like:
Omar Castaneda, *Abuela's Weave*, 1993
   Esperanza and her Abuela weave tapestries to sell at the market in Guatemala.
Sandra Cisneros, *Hair = Pelitos*, 1994
   Excerpted from the novel *The House on Mango Street* where everyone in the family has different type hair.
Pat Mora, *A Birthday Basket for Tia*, 1992
   Cecilia makes a birthday present for her great aunt.
Gary Soto, *Too Many Tamales*, 1993
   Maria helps her mother make tamales for Christmas Eve dinner.
Carmen Santiago Nodar, *Abuelita's Paradise*, 1992
   Marita sits in Abuelita's rocking chair and remembers the stories Abuelita told of her life in Puerto Rico.

594

ARTHUR DORROS

Radio Man = Don Radio: A Story in English and Spanish
(New York: Harper Collins, 1993)

Subject(s): Migrant Labor; Friendship; Travel
Age range(s): Grades 1-3

Major character(s): Diego, Child, Worker (migrant farmer), Mexican American; David, Child, Worker (migrant farmer)

Locale(s): United States (story takes place in various places across the U.S.)

Summary: This beautifully illustrated story examines the lives of Diego and his family, who are migrant farm workers. They pick melons and cherries in Arizona and apples in Washington. Diego relies on his radio for companionship. When he parts company from a friend in Arizona, Diego makes sure they find each other again.

About this book: This work is in Spanish and English format with the Spanish translation by Sandra Marulanda Dorros.

Where it's reviewed:
Publishers Weekly, September 27, 1993, page 63

Other books by the same author:
Abuela, 1991
Ant Cities, 1987
Me and My Shadow, 1990
Rain Forest Secrets, 1990
Tonight Is Carnival, 1991

Other books you might like:
Carmen Lomas Garza, *Family Pictures = Cuadros de Familia*,
   This work provides descriptions and pictures of family life during celebrations and holidays.
Carmen Santiago Nodar, *Abuelita's Paradise*, 1992
   Marita sits in Abuelita's rocking chair and remembers the stories Abuelita told of her life in Puerto Rico.
Omar Castaneda, *Abuela's Weave*, 1993
   A little girl and her grandmother sell their crafts at a market in Guatemala.
Pat Mora, *Pablo's Tree*, 1994
   Pablo's grandfather plants a tree at Pablo's birth which they enjoy together.
Jan Romero Stevens, *Carlos and the Squash Plant/Carlos y la Planta de Calabaza*, 1993
   Carlos refuses to bathe and his mother warns him about something growing out of his ear.
Juan Felipe Herrera, *Calling the Doves = El Canto de las Palomas*, 1995
   A book depicting the experiences of the author as a young boy growing up as a farm worker in the fields and valleys of California.
Karen Papagapitos, *Socorro, Daughter of the Desert*, 1993
   The family of eight-year-old Socorro are farm workers and she help out as much as she can. When her father becomes ill, Socorro makes tortillas for her mother to sell in the fields.

595

GLORIA DURAN

Malinche: Slave Princess of Cortez

(Hamden, CT: Linnet Books, 1993)

Subject(s): Slavery; Indians of Mexico; Historical
Age range(s): Grades 6 and Up
Major character(s): Malinali, Slave, Royalty (princess), Aztec

Time period(s): 16th century
Locale(s): Tenochtitlan, Mexico

Summary: Malinali, born an Aztec princess and sold to the conqueror Cortez, is an ambiguous and controversial figure in Mexican history. Called Dona Mariana by the conquerors, she became Cortez's translator, confidante, and the mother of two of his children. Was she a traitor to her people, a warrior princess, or simply manipulated by a ruthless man? Malinche is an important figure in Mexican folklore and history. In this novel, Duran attempts to explore Malinali's life and to restore her to a rightful place in history.

Where it's reviewed:
Publishers Weekly, July 12, 1993, page 81

Other books you might like:
Guy Garcia, *Obsidian Sky: A Novel*, 1994
   A doctoral student from Berkeley gets a job at Mexico City's Museum of Anthropology and studies his theory about Aztec ritual and the role of Motecuhzoma, the Aztec king enslaved by Cortes.
Elizabeth Borton de Trevino, *Leona: A Love Story*, 1994
   About Mexico's war for independence, this historical novel is based on the true story of sixteen year old Leona Vicario, who fights to live and love as she chooses.
Alejandro Morales, *The Rag Doll Plagues*, 1992
   Divided into three sections, this novel shows Latino doctors fighting a deadly infectious disease over three centuries, with the first section taking place in the 18th century.
Tina Juarez, *Call No Man Master*, 1995
   This historical novel is about a young woman of mixed heritage, Spanish and Indian, and her participation in the events that lead to Mexico's independence from Spain.
Jose Barreiro, *The Indian Chronicles*, 1993
   Adopted by Christopher Columbus, Diego Colon, a Taino boy, keeps a journal where he describes events in his life from 1532-1535 as he narrates the Indian's discovery of the Europeans.
Graciela Limon, *Song of the Hummingbird*, 1995
   Huitzitzilin, Hummingbird in the Nahuatal language, is an Aztec princess who is forced into slavery. As an 82-year-old woman, she recounts her life story during the Spanish conquest of Mexico.

596

MIGUEL DURAN, Mexican American

Don't Spit on My Corner

(Houston, TX: Arte Publico Press, 1992)

Subject(s): Coming of Age; Crime and Criminals; City Life
Age range(s): Grades 8-Adult
Major character(s): Little Mike, Teenager (boy), Chicano
Time period(s): 1940s
Locale(s): Los Angeles, California

Summary: For Little Mike and his friends coming of age in Los Angeles during World War II, manhood means being "cool" — cruising, drinking, and protecting their turf. Based on Duran's own experiences as a teenage pachuco, this novel is a poignant portrait of Chicano youth headed toward trouble.

This is a genuine depiction of the language, culture and social influences that Chicanos lived with during the 1940s.

Where it's reviewed:
Publishers Weekly, April 20, 1992, page 49

Other books you might like:
Mary Helen Ponce, *The Wedding*, 1989
　　Blanca Munoz plans her wedding to Sammy-the-Cricket, as the author shows us an expose of 1950s working class life and culture in a southern California Chicano community,
Jose Antonio Burciaga, *Spilling the Beans: Loteria Chicana*, 1995
　　A series of essays, many humorous, recount experiences from the author's childhood, and explore aspects of Chicano culture.
Jose Antonio Villarreal, *Pocho*, 1959
　　This story of a Mexican family in the Santa Clara Valley of California before World War II explores the assimilation of the son Richard Rubio.
Lionel G. Garcia, *Hardscrub*, 1990
　　Related from the perspective of eleven-year-old Jim, this novel portrays characters struggling to survive in the tough land of West Texas.
Floyd Salas, *Buffalo Nickel: A Memoir*, 1992
　　This coming-of-age memoir is by a young man who oscillates between his two brothers—Albert, who abuses drugs and is involved in crime, and Edward, intelligent and upwardly mobile.
Ronald L. Ruiz, *Happy Birthday Jesus*, 1994
　　The disturbing story of the violent and turbulent life of a young man raised and abused by his grandmother and how he ends up in prison.

597

MARGARITA ENGLE, Cuban American

Singing to Cuba
(Houston: Arte Publico Press, 1993)

Subject(s): Family Life; Magic; Voyages and Travels
Age range(s): Grades 10-Adult
Major character(s): Gabriel, Prisoner, Uncle, Cuban
Time period(s): 20th century (1950-1992)
Locale(s): United States; Cuba

Summary: A California woman leaves her husband and children to search for information about family members who disappeared during the Castro revolution. She discovers the horrifying reality of her family's suffering. In the style of magical realism, Engle writes a lyrical novel which weaves together her story with the story of her great uncle, Gabriel, imprisoned after the revolution.

Where it's reviewed:
Library Journal, July 1993, page 119
Publishers Weekly, August 2, 1993, page 75

Other books by the same author:
Skywriting, 1995

Other books you might like:
Omar Castaneda, *Remembering to Say Mouth or Face*, 1993
　　These twelve short stories take place in the U.S. and Central America.
Graciela Limon, *In Search of Bernabe*, 1993
　　This novel is about a mother's search for her son during civil war in El Salvador.
Demetria Martinez, *Mother Tongue*, 1994
　　This story is about a young Chicana who falls in love with a Salvadoran refugee, who is tortured as a counter-insurgent in hiss country.
Carmen C. Esteves, *Green Cane and Juicy Flotsam: Short Stories by Caribbean Women*, 1991
　　In this collection of short stories, Caribbean women writers examine questions of race, power, colonialism, poverty, and identity.
Virgil Suarez, *The Cutter: A Novel*, 1991
　　Julian Campos is forced by the Cuban Communist regime to work as a "cutter" in the muddy sugarcane fields while he waits to receive permission to leave the island.
Reinaldo Arenas, *The Assault*, 1994
　　A fictional exploration of Castro-era Cuba, this allegorical novel presents a disturbing surreal portrait of political extremes and a society headed toward self-destruction.

598

MARGARITA ENGLE, Cuban American

Skywriting
(New York: Bantam Books, 1995)

Subject(s): Political Prisoners; Family; Politics
Age range(s): Grades 10-Adult
Major character(s): Carmen Peregrin, Young Woman, Sister (half-sister), Cuban American; Camilo Peregrin, Young Man, Brother (half-brother), Cuban
Time period(s): 1990s (1995)
Locale(s): Cuba

Summary: Carmen Peregrin, raised in the U.S. by her American mother, goes to visit her half-brother in Cuba as an adult. On the day of her arrival he attempts to escape Cuba, by raft, and ends up being arrested and imprisoned. Carmen uses all her influence and power, with support from her extended family throughout the U.S. and Spain, to free her brother. Nevertheless he spends a year in the famous prison, *La Vibora*.

Where it's reviewed:
Library Journal, June 1, 1995, page 158
Publishers Weekly, June 5, 1995, page 52

Other books by the same author:
Singing to Cuba, 1993

Other books you might like:
Graciela Limon, *In Search of Bernabe*, 1993
　　A novel about a mother's search for her son during civil war in El Salvador.
Demetria Martinez, *Mother Tongue*, 1994
　　Story of a young Chicana who falls in love with a Salvadoran refugee who is tortured for allegedly being a counter-insurgent in his country.

Virgil Suarez, *The Cutter: A Novel*, 1991
Julian Campos is forced by the Cuban Communist regime to work as a cutter in the muddy sugarcane fields while he waits to receive permission to leave the island.

Julia Alvarez, *In the Time of the Butterflies*, 1994
The story of the assassination of three sisters who are fighting to overthrow a dictatorship in the Dominican Republic.

Gustavo Perez Firmat, *Next Year in Cuba: A Cubano's Coming of Age in America*, 1995
The author of this memoir explores his biculturalism and his search for identity and roots in America.

599

EDNA ESCAMILL, Mexican American

Daughter of the Mountain: Un Cuento
(San Francisco: Aunt Lute Books, 1991)

Subject(s): Native Americans; Storytelling
Age range(s): Grades 10-Adult
Major character(s): Maggie, Child; Adela Sewa, Grandmother, Storyteller, Yaqui Indian
Time period(s): 1940s; 1950s (1940-1959)
Locale(s): United States (southwest border town)

Summary: Bale and Maggie develop a friendship based upon their common struggle to resist the onslaught of gringos who come to live in their southwest border town. Maggie comes to understand her identity and future through her relationship with her grandmother, a Yaqui Indian, who teaches her spirituality and tools for survival through stories, or cuentos, of the old days.

Where it's reviewed:
Publishers Weekly, July 5, 1991, page 61

Other books by the same author:
The Storyteller with Nike Airs and Other Barrio Stories, 1994

Other books you might like:
Sylvia Lopez-Medina, *Cantora: A Novel*, 1992
Amparo searches her family's past, and learns of the triumphs and tragedies of her grandmother, aunt, and mother.

Ibis Gomez-Vega, *Send My Roots Rain*, 1991
A young woman goes to a Texas border town to paint murals on the church walls.

Rudolfo Anaya, *Bless Me, Ultima*, 1972
A young boy's beliefs are challenged as he grows up in a small rural town in New Mexico.

Montserrat Fontes, *Dreams of the Centaur*, 1995
Alejo Durcal, son of a slain ranch owner, tries to avenge his father's death during the period in history when the Yaqui Indians were badly mistreated in Mexico.

600

MARIA ESPINOSA

Dark Plums
(Houston, TX: Arte Publico Press, 1995)

Subject(s): Identity; Sexual Abuse; Coming of Age
Age range(s): Grades 10-Adult

Major character(s): Adrianne, Young Woman, Prostitute
Time period(s): 1950s
Locale(s): New York, New York

Summary: Adrianne, a young girl from Texas, begins a search for love and self in Manhattan. Wandering the city, she sleeps with strangers, falls into an abusive relationship, and eventually works as a prostitute in order to support her abusive boyfriend, Alfredo. But as Alfredo's treatment becomes increasingly brutal, she must gather the strength to leave him and reclaim her life.

Where it's reviewed:
Library Journal, March 1, 1995, page 102

Other books by the same author:
Longing, 1986

Other books you might like:
Oscar Hijuelos, *The Mambo Kings Play Songs of Love*, 1989
The Castillo brothers, make their way from Havana to New York to play music in the era of the mambo.

Margarite Fernandez Olmos, *Pleasure in the Word: Erotic Writings by Latin American Women*, 1993
This diverse collection of erotic writing by women breaks the silence by speaking out about eroticism, love, and violence.

Phyllis Tashlik, *Hispanic, Female, and Young*, 1994
Collection of short stories written by young Latina girls from El Barrio of New York, about the problems of growing up female.

Abraham Rodriguez Jr., *The Boy Without a Flag: Tales of the South Bronx*, 1992
Collection of short stories about the problems of young Puerto Ricans, both male and female, in the Bronx.

Alba Ambert, *A Perfect Silence*, 1995
From the surrealistic world of a mental institution, a Puerto Rican woman, ponders her abusive past and her self-destructiveness.

Soledad Santiago, *Nightside*, 1994
Anna Eltern, a former nun who runs a shelter for runaway teens, struggles with financial problems and murder, after funding cuts force her to turn away homeless teenagers.

Esmeralda Santiago, *America's Dream*, 1996
America works as a housekeeper in a hotel on an island off the coast of Puerto Rico until she accepts a job as a nanny in Westchester County, New York and learns of another life.

601

MARIA ESPINOSA

Longing
(Houston, TX: Arte Publico Press, 1995)

Subject(s): Sexuality; Alcoholism; Marriage
Age range(s): Grades 10-Adult
Major character(s): Rosa, Spouse (wife of Antonio), Jewish Chilean; Antonio, Alcoholic, Chilean
Time period(s): 1990s
Locale(s): Sausalito, California; Paris, France

Summary: This psychological novel focuses on a young woman's sexuality and her desire for independence from her husband. They meet and start living together in Paris, but later move to New York and eventually end up in Sausalito to be near Rosa's family. She becomes trapped in an unhealthy relationship with Antonio, begins to question her life in a series of fast-moving events and sexual encounters.

Other books by the same author:
Love Feelings, 1967
Dark Plums, 1995

Other books you might like:
Alba Ambert, *A Perfect Silence*, 1995
From the surrealistic world of a mental institution, a Puerto Rican woman attempts to come to terms with her abusive past and her self-destructiveness.
Beatriz Rivera, *African Passions and Other Stories*, 1995
A collection of short stories focusing on women's obsessive search for love and success.
Rosario Ferre, *The Youngest Doll*, 1991
A collection considered by critics as a manifesto of women's rights, where the main story, "The Youngest Doll" is one of the author's most successful.
Alma Luz Villanueva, *Weeping Woman: La Llorona and Other Stories*, 1994
A collection of stories that examine women who live in a world torn apart by violence, racism, and sexism.
Estela Portillo Trambley, *Trini*, 1986
Trini, a Tarahumara woman crosses the border as an undocumented immigrant in order to give birth to her child in the United States.
Esmeralda Santiago, *America's Dream*, 1996
America works as a housekeeper in a hotel on an island off the coast of Puerto Rico until she accepts a job as a nanny in Westchester County, New York and learns of a new life.

602

CARMEN C. ESTEVES, Editor
LIZABETH PARAVISINI-GEBERT, Co-Editor

Green Cane and Juicy Flotsam: Short Stories by Caribbean Women

(New Brunswick, NJ: Rutgers University Press, 1991)

Subject(s): Short Stories; Anthology; Women
Age range(s): Grades 10-Adult
Time period(s): Indeterminate Past
Locale(s): Caribbean (various islands); United States

Summary: In this collection of short stories, Caribbean women examine questions of race, power, colonialism, poverty, and identity. The tradition of folk and fairy tales underlies many of these stories, a tradition readily available to women in domestic spheres. In these stories there is solidarity between women, regardless of class status, and the dispossessed peasantry. Well-known Puerto Rican, Cuban, Jamican, and Dominican writers, such as Rosario Ferre, Olga Nolla, Dora Alonso, Jamaica Kincaid, Ana Lydia Vega, and Jean Rhys, as well as novice writers, are represented in this varied collection.

About this book: Many of these stories have been translated from French and Spanish, but many were also originally written in English.

Where it's reviewed:
Belles Lettres: A Review of Books by Women, Spring 1992, page 21
CHOICE, June 1992, page 1552
Feminist Studies, Spring 1995, page 115
Migration World Magazine, May-June 1992, page 46
Publishers Weekly, November 1, 1991, page 76

Other books by the same author:
Pleasure in the Word: Erotic Writings by Latin American Women, 1993
Remaking a Lost Harmony: Stories from the Hispanic Caribbean, 1995

Other books you might like:
Ana Lydia Vega, *True and False Romances*, 1994
This collection of short stories is about women and romance that take place in Puerto Rico.
Kathleen Ross, *Scents of Wood and Silence: Short Stories by Latin American Women Writers*, 1991
This Anthology of short fiction is by Latin American women writers.
Rosario Ferre, *The Youngest Doll*, 1991
This collection of short stories, originally published in Spanish, is about Puerto Rico society.
Kal Wagenheim, *Cuentos: An Anthology of Short Stories from Puerto Rico*, 1978
This collection of short stories is by a writer living and writing in Puerto Rico.
Diana Velez, *Reclaiming Medusa: Short Stories by Contemporary Puerto Rican Women*, 1988
Thirteen stories, by five well-known Puerto Rican women writers, appear in this anthology.
Isabel Allende, *Paula*, 1995
The story of Isabel Allende's daughter's illness, coma, treatments, and death at the age of 28.
Esmeralda Santiago, *America's Dream*, 1996
America works as a housekeeper in a hotel on an island off the coast of Puerto Rico, until she accepts a job as a nanny in Westchester County, New York, and learns about a new life.

603

CAROLE FERNANDEZ, Puerto Rican

Sleep of the Innocents

(Houston: Arte Publico Press, 1991)

Subject(s): Civil War; Women
Age range(s): Grades 10-Adult
Major character(s): Rosario, Spouse (wife); Anibal, Spouse (husband)
Time period(s): 1980s
Locale(s): Soledad, Fictional Country (war-torn Central American country)

Summary: This novel chronicles the lives of women living in a fictional Central American country torn by civil war. Their family relationships, sexual roles, and expectations in a male-dominated society, come into focus. The influence of American culture on an individual family is focused.

Other books you might like:

Omar Castaneda, *Remembering to Say Mouth or Face*, 1993
 These twelve short stories take place in the U.S. and Central America.

Graciela Limon, *In Search of Bernabe*, 1993
 A novel about a mother's search for her son during civil war in El Salvador.

Demetria Martinez, *Mother Tongue*, 1994
 This story is about a young Chicana who falls in love with a Salvadoran refugee, who is tortured as a counter-insurgent in his country.

Margarita Engle, *Singing to Cuba*, 1993
 A California woman leaves her husband and children to search for information about family members who disappeared during the Castro revolution.

Virgil Suarez, *The Cutter: A Novel*, 1991
 Julian Campos is required to cut sugarcane in Communist Cuba while waiting permission to leave the island.

Marcos McPeek Villatoro, *A Fire in the Earth*, 1996
 This epic novel follows Romilia Colonez, descendant of an Indian patriarch who led his clan to claim fertile soil, setting the stage for future trials and tragedies in El Salvador.

604

ROBERTA FERNANDEZ, Editor, Mexican American

In Other Words: Literature by Latinas in the U.S.

(Houston: Arte Publico Press, 1994)

Subject(s): Anthology; Short Stories; Women
Age range(s): Grades 9-Adult
Time period(s): 1980s; 1990s (1994)
Locale(s): United States (throughout the U.S.)

Summary: This is a large anthology that contains the best and most representative works of contemporary fiction, poetry, drama, and essays written by Latinas in the U.S. These works examine marginality, life in two cultures, the celebration of culture, and Latina feminism.

About this book: This anthology is arranged by genre, and contains an extensive introduction by the editor and an appended bibliography. Some works are in both Spanish and English.

Other books by the same author:
Intaglio: A Novel in Six Stories, 1990
Twenty-five Years of Hispanic Literature in the United States, 1965-1990: An Exhibit, with Accompanying Text, 1992

Other books you might like:

Lillian Castillo-Speed, *Latina: Women's Voices from the Borderlands*, 1995
 This is an anthology of contemporary Latina writers.

Maria del Carmen Boza, *Nosotras: Latina Literature Today*, 1986
 This is a collection of poetry and short stories by Latina writers.

Bryce Milligan, *Daughters of the Fifth Sun: A Collection of Latina Fiction and Poetry*, 1995
 This is an anthology of contemporary Latina writers.

Evangelina Vigil, *Woman of Her Word: Hispanic Women Write*, 1983
 This is a collection of short stories and poetry by Latinas in the U.S.

Tey Diana Rebolledo, *Las Mujeres Hablan: An Anthology of Nuevo Mexicana Writers*, 1988
 This collection of short stories and poetry is by Chicanas from New Mexico.

Alma Gomez, *Cuentos: Stories by Latinas*, 1983
 This is a collection of stories by Hispanic Women.

605

ROBERTA FERNANDEZ, Mexican American

Intaglio: A Novel in Six Stories

(Houston, TX: Arte Publico Press, 1990)

Subject(s): Coming of Age; Women; Magic
Age range(s): Grades 9-Adult
Major character(s): Nenita Cardenas, Young Woman, Mexican American
Time period(s): 20th century (1940-1970)
Locale(s): Texas

Summary: In six stories, each a vivid portrait of an extraordinary woman, Fernandez weaves an inventive novel. Each of the six women serves as a role model for the narrator "the girl" Nenita as she grows up, the eldest of three daughters. Each story has an impact on the narrator, all are interesting and skillfully written depicting the customs and attitudes of Mexican culture. This novel is magical and riveting, exploring the lives of revolutionaries and witches and dressmaker and storytellers.

About this book: Glossary of Spanish words is included.

Where it's reviewed:
Western American Literature, February 1992, page 369

Other books by the same author:
In Other Words: Literature by Latinas in the U.S., 1994

Other books you might like:

Denise Chavez, *The Last of the Menu Girls*, 1986
 A collection of interrelated short stories, about a Chicana adolescent girl from southern New Mexico who is looking for her place, identity, and womanhood.

Patricia Preciado Martin, *Days of Plenty, Days of Want*, 1988
 A collection of stories where the past and the present meet, and Mexican heritage is in jeopardy of being wiped out.

Mary Helen Ponce, *Taking Control*, 1987
 Collection of stories portraying domestic and economic oppression of Mexican and Chicana women in the U.S.

Nash Candelaria, *Leonor Park*, 1992
 A novel about land and greed in New Mexico where a powerful woman battles with her brother over their father's legacy, a piece of land along the Rio Grande.

Patricia Preciado Martin, *El Milagro and Other Stories*, 1996
 A collection of personal and collective memories in the form of short stories, stitched together to form a portrait of the author's family and her life growing up in Arizona.

606

MARGARITE FERNANDEZ OLMOS, Editor, Puerto Rican
LIZABETH PARAVISINI-GEBERT, Co-Editor

Remaking a Lost Harmony: Stories from the Hispanic Caribbean

(Fredonia, NY: White Pine Press, 1995)

Subject(s): Short Stories; Anthology
Age range(s): Grades 10-Adult
Time period(s): 20th century (1960-1995)
Locale(s): Caribbean

Summary: An anthology of twenty-five stories from the Caribbean written after the 1959 Cuban Revolution, but with similar themes and situations as found in the writings of authors on the U.S. mainland. These writers from Cuba, Puerto Rico, and the Dominican Republic reflect both the island cultures and social changes that have sparked a search for the ''lost harmony'' of Caribbean and Latin American culture. This collection tries to unite the Caribbean islands, to explore mutual history, and to paint a vivid picture of the landscapes and people. Authors included are Luis Rafael Sanchez, Jose Alcantara Almanzar, Hilma Contreras, and Veronica Lopez Konina.

Where it's reviewed:
Library Journal, June 1, 1995, page 166
Publishers Weekly, April 17, 1995, page 52

Other books by the same author:
Pleasure in the Word: Erotic Writings by Latin American Women, 1993
Contemporary Women Authors of Latin America, 1983
Green Cane and Juicy Flotsam: Short Stories by Caribbean Women, 1991

Other books you might like:
Ana Lydia Vega, *True and False Romances*, 1994
    Collection of short stories about women and romance that take place in Puerto Rico.
Kathleen Ross, *Scents of Wood and Silence: Short Stories by Latin American Women Writers*, 1991
    Anthology of short fiction by Latin American women writers, including the Caribbean.
Kal Wagenheim, *Cuentos: An Anthology of Short Stories from Puerto Rico*, 1978
    Collection of short stories by writers living and writing in Puerto Rico.
Diana Velez, *Reclaiming Medusa: Short Stories by Contemporary Puerto Rican Women*, 1988
    Thirteen stories, by five well-known Puerto Rican women writers, appear in this anthology.
Ruth Behar, *Bridges to Cuba = Puentes a Cuba*, 1995
    A collection of short stories, poems, and essays by Cuban American writers that exhibit literary and intellectual boundaries which show the complexity of culture and identity.

607

ROBERTO FERNANEZ, Cuban

Holy Radishes

(Houston: Arte Publico, 1995)

Subject(s): Satire; City Life; Politics
Age range(s): Grades 10-Adult
Major character(s): Nelly Pardo, Worker (in a radish plant); Rigoletto, Pig
Time period(s): 1960s
Locale(s): Belle Grande, Florida

Summary: This satirical novel depicts the Cuban American community in Florida. While exiled Cubans plan the liberation of their homeland, their wives work at a radish plant and dream about the Xawa Ladies Tennis Club. Nelly Pardo dreams of an Eden called Mondovi and of her truffle-loving pet pig Rigoletto. In this hilarious novel, Fernandez presents a parody of Cuban immigrant life.

Other books by the same author:
Cuentos Sin Rumbos, 1975
La Montana Rusa, 1985
Raining Backwards, 1988

Other books you might like:
Louie Garcia Robinson, *The Devil, Delfina Varela, and the Used Chevy*, 1993
    This comical and political novel is about the Latino community in San Francisco's Mission District.
Lionel G. Garcia, *A Shroud in the Family*, 1994
    This satire is about Texas and Mexican American life in the modern metropolis.
Mary Helen Ponce, *The Wedding*, 1989
    This comic novel is about Chicano working class life and culture, told through the eyes of a pregnant bride-to-be.
Jaime Manrique, *Latin Moon in Manhattan*, 1992
    This novel presents bizarre characters, plots and sub-plots, and a vivid depiction of Columbian American culture in Little Colombia Jackson Heights.
Luis Rafael Sanchez, *Macho Camacho's Beat*, 1980
    This novel paints a distasteful picture of a Puerto Rican society totally controlled by U.S. imperialistic culture.
Jose Yglesias, *Tristan and the Hispanics*, 1989
    A Yale student and the son of Cuban-born screenwriter and a WASP mother, clashes with his Cuban extended family as he makes the funeral arrangements for his paternal grandfather.

608

ROSARIO FERRE, Puerto Rican

The House on the Lagoon

(New York: Farrar, Straus, & Giroux, 1995)

Subject(s): Family Relations; Intergenerational Saga; Marriage
Age range(s): Grades 10-Adult
Major character(s): Isabel Monfort, Spouse (wife), Writer, Corsican; Quintin Mendizabal, Spouse, Businessman, Spanish

Time period(s): 20th century (1917-1978)
Locale(s): San Juan, Puerto Rico (a suburb of San Juan called Alamares)

Summary: This history of a family starts with the arrival in Puerto Rico by Buena Ventura Mendizabal, the grandfather of Quintin. He starts a successful business importing foods for the upper classes. The story is told by Isabel as she works on a novel. The background of the story is the political future of Puerto Rico for independence or statehood.

Where it's reviewed:
Library Journal, August 1995, page 115
Publishers Weekly, July 3, 1995, page 47
San Francisco Chronicle, October 15, 1995, Book Review, page 4

Other books by the same author:
The Youngest Doll, 1991
Sweet Diamond Dust, 1988

Other books you might like:
Gabriel Garcia Marquez, *One Hundred Years of Solitude*, 1970
    An intergenerational saga of a family in a fictional city called Macondo in Columbia.
Juan Garcia Ponce, *The House on the Beach*, 1994
    The story of a family whose life centers in Merida, Mexico, narrated by a woman visitor.
Denise Chavez, *Face of an Angel*, 1994
    An intergenerational saga of a family in Agua Oscura, New Mexico.
Isabel Allende, *The House of the Spirits*, 1986
    Three generations of women relate their lives in an intergenerational novel of Chile.
Magali Garcia Ramis, *Happy Days, Uncle Sergio*, 1995
    This coming of age novel is about a middle-class girl in Puerto Rico.
Judith Ortiz Cofer, *The Line of the Sun: A Novel*, 1989
    This intergenerational story of a family flows back and forth between New York and Puerto Rico.

609

ROSARIO FERRE, Puerto Rican

Sweet Diamond Dust

(New York: Available Press, Ballantine Books, 1988)

Subject(s): Short Stories; Intergenerational Saga
Age range(s): Grades 10-Adult
Time period(s): 20th century
Locale(s): Puerto Rico

Summary: This novel and three stories revolve around life on the island of Puerto Rico. In the main story, *Sweet Diamond Dust*, an intergenerational family obsesses on a sugar plantation, the Diamond Dust Sugar Mills.

About this book: This was originally published in Spanish as *Maldito Amor* and later translated by the author.

Where it's reviewed:
Publishers Weekly, November 25, 1988, page 62

Other books by the same author:
The Youngest Doll, 1991

The House on the Lagoon, 1995

Other books you might like:
Magali Garcia Ramis, *Happy Days, Uncle Sergio*, 1995
    A middle class girl in Puerto Rico comes of age.
Judith Ortiz Cofer, *Silent Dancing: A Partial Remembrance of a Puerto Rican Childhood*, 1990
    These stories describe growing up in Puerto Rico and the U.S.
Diana Velez, *Reclaiming Medusa: Short Stories by Contemporary Puerto Rican Women*, 1988
    Latino women living in Puerto Rico author this collection of stories.
Ana Lydia Vega, *True and False Romances*, 1994
    Collection of short stories about women and romance that take place in Puerto Rico.
Carmen C. Esteves, *Green Cane and Juicy Flotsam: Short Stories by Caribbean Women*, 1991
    Collection of short stories by Puerto Rican, Cuban, Jamaican, and Dominican women writers.
Nicholasa Mohr, *Nilda; A Novel*, 1973
    This story portrays the life of a Puerto Rican girl growing up in the 1940's in a New York barrio.
Roberto Santiago, *Boricuas: Influential Puerto Rican Writers—an Anthology*, 1995
    Controversial writers of the nineteenth and twentieth centuries comprise this anthology.

610

ROSARIO FERRE, Puerto Rican

The Youngest Doll

(Lincoln: University of Nebraska Press, 1991)

Subject(s): Short Stories; Women
Age range(s): Grades 10-Adult
Time period(s): 1970s
Locale(s): Puerto Rico

Summary: This short story collection was originally published in Spanish under the title *Papeles de Pandora*. This collection is considered by critics as a manifesto of women's rights, and the main story, ''The Youngest Doll'' is one of the author's most successful stories. The stories use the vernacular to present the aunt, the working class woman, servants, and the dialogue between social classes.

About this book: This collection is translated by the author.

Where it's reviewed:
Nation, May 6, 1991, page 597

Other books by the same author:
The House on the Lagoon, 1995
Sweet Diamond Dust, 1988

Other books you might like:
Pedro Juan Soto, *Spiks*, 1970
    These short stories are about Puerto Rican women in New York.
Kal Wagenheim, *Cuentos: An Anthology of Short Stories from Puerto Rico*, 1978
    This is an anthology of short stories from Puerto Rico.
Diana Velez, *Reclaiming Medusa: Short Stories by Contemporary Puerto Rican Women*, 1988

This is a collection of short stories by Puerto Rican women.

Magali Garcia Ramis, *Happy Days, Uncle Sergio*, 1995
This coming of age novel is about a middle-class girl in Puerto Rico.

Kathleen Ross, *Scents of Wood and Silence: Short Stories by Latin American Women Writers*, 1991
This is an anthology of short fiction by Latin American women writers.

Ana Lydia Vega, *True and False Romances*, 1994
Puerto Rican women, with their romances, deposit their stories in this collection.

611

RAMON FERREIRA, Cuban

The Gravedigger and Other Stories
(Maplewood, NJ: Waterfront Press, 1986)

Subject(s): Terror; Racism; Race Relations
Age range(s): Grades 10-Adult
Time period(s): 1950s; 1960s (1950-1960)
Locale(s): Cuba

Summary: This collection of short stories vividly depicts the underside of Cuban society during the '50s. Ferreira, born in Spain and raised in Cuba, has lived in Puerto Rico for over thirty years. His tales are disturbing and harshly told, narrating the crumbling away of old traditions, the darker side of racial prejudice, and the tyrannical rules of a macho society. Several stories reflect the political repression of the times, under the Batista government and also the changes under Castro. These tales are sharp, cunningly contrived, and unforgettable.

About this book: Translated by the author and Kal Wagenheim.

Other books by the same author:
Papa, Cuentame un Cuento, 1989
Teatro, 1993
Los Malos Olores de Este Mundo, 1969

Other books you might like:
Ruth Behar, *Bridges to Cuba = Puentes a Cuba*, 1995
This is an anthology of short stories, essays, poetry, and historical documents that explore the Cuban and Cuban American experience.

Virgil Suarez, *The Cutter: A Novel*, 1991
Julian Campos is forced by the Cuban Communist regime to work as a "cutter" in the muddy sugarcane fields while awaiting permission to leave the island.

Cristina Garcia, *Dreaming in Cuban, A Novel*, 1992
This novel interweaves the stories of three generations of Cuban women and their different responses to the Cuban revolution.

Reinaldo Arenas, *Before Night Falls*, 1993
In this autobiography Arena describes almost dying of AIDS in 1987 and of his life in Cuba before he came to the United States in 1980, where he later committed suicide in 1990.

Reinaldo Arenas, *The Doorman*, 1991
Juan, a young Cuban refugee, becomes a doorman at a luxury apartment building in New York. This parable about freedom shows that Juan is seduced by the pets of the rich tenants.

Marcos McPeek Villatoro, *A Fire in the Earth*, 1996
This epic novel follows Romilia Colonez, descendant of an Indian patriarch who led his clan to claim fertile soil, setting the stage for future trials and tragedies in El Salvador.

Margarita Engle, *Singing to Cuba*, 1993
A California woman leaves her husband and children to search for information about family members who disappeared during the Castro revolution.

612

MONTSERRAT FONTES, Mexican American

Dreams of the Centaur
(New York: W.W. Norton, 1995)

Subject(s): Death; Family; Coming of Age
Age range(s): Grades 10-Adult
Major character(s): Alejo Durcal, Prisoner (son), Mexican; Felipa Durcal, Mother (of Alejo)
Time period(s): 1900s (1900-1910)
Locale(s): Mexico

Summary: This fast-paced novel follows Alejo Durcal, son of a slain ranch owner, as he tries to avenge his father's death and journeys through love, murder, prison, war, and death. The novel examines Alejo's relationship with his mother, Felipa, and his observations of the mounting persecution and deportation of the Yaqui Indians during the presidency of Porfirio Diaz.

Where it's reviewed:
Publishers Weekly, December 4, 1995, page 53

Other books by the same author:
First Confession, 1991

Other books you might like:
Victor Villasenor, *Rain of Gold*, 1991
Intergenerational chronicle of the author's family migration to the U.S. from Mexico.

Sylvia Lopez-Medina, *Cantora: A Novel*, 1992
This novel tells the story of four generations of women in Mexico and their lives in America at the turn of the 20th century.

Nash Candelaria, *Not by the Sword*, 1982
Taking place before the Mexican War of 1846, this novel depicts the struggles of a family in New Mexico, and with the collapse of the Mexican government.

Nash Candelaria, *Inheritance of Strangers*, 1985
Sequel to *Not By the Sword*, it covers the years after the Mexican War of 1846 until New Mexico statehood, presenting the struggles of the Rafa family against Anglo exploitation.

Marcos McPeek Villatoro, *A Fire in the Earth*, 1996
This epic novel follows Romilia Colonez, descendant of an Indian patriarch who led his clan to claim fertile soil, setting the stage for future trials and tragedies in El Salvador.

Jose Barreiro, *The Indian Chronicles*, 1993

Adopted by Christopher Columbus, Diego Colon, a Taino boy, keeps a journal where he describes events in his life from 1532-1535 where he narrates the Indian's discovery of the Europeans.

Gary D. Keller, *Zapata Lives!*, 1994

The Mexican revolutionary leader Emiliano Zapata has risen from the dead and must lead his people in a struggle against economic and social oppression.

613

MONTSERRAT FONTES, Mexican American

First Confession

(New York: W.W. Norton, 1991)

Subject(s): Catholic Religion; Cousins
Age range(s): Grades 10-Adult
Major character(s): Andrea Durcal, Child, 9-Year-Old; Victor Escalante, Child, 9-Year-Old
Time period(s): 20th century (1947-1960)
Locale(s): Mexico (a town in Mexico right across the Texas border)

Summary: Upper-class spoiled children, cousins Andrea and Victor, spend a summer together preparing for their First Communion. Tragedy follows them from the first day, until they grow up and become distant from each other as adults.

Where it's reviewed:
Library Journal, December 1990, page 162
Publishers Weekly, November 9, 1990, page 45

Other books by the same author:
Dreams of the Centaur, 1995

Other books you might like:
Rudolfo Anaya, *Bless Me, Ultima*, 1972
A young boy's beliefs are challenged as he grows up in a small town in New Mexico.
Sandra Cisneros, *The House on Mango Street*, 1986
The tribulations of a Mexican American young woman growing up.
Magali Garcia Ramis, *Happy Days, Uncle Sergio*, 1995
This coming of age novel is about a middle-class girl in Puerto Rico.
Alfredo Vea Jr., *La Maravilla*, 1993
In this extraordinary novel, Buckeye Road, a world of marvels outside the Phoenix city limits, is portrayed as an American outback caught between many cultures.
Alma Flor Ada, *Where the Flame Trees Bloom*, 1994
Eleven stories from the author's childhood about her family, friends, and the Cuban hacienda where she grew up.
Gloria Lopez-Stafford, *A Place in El Paso: A Mexican American Childhood*, 1996
A bittersweet narrative describes the early childhood of the author living in the projects of El Paso during World War II.

614

KLEYA FORTE-ESCAMILLA, Mexican American

The Storyteller with Nike Airs and Other Barrio Stories

(San Francisco: Aunt Lute Books, 1994)

Subject(s): Short Stories; Supernatural
Age range(s): Grades 7 and Up
Time period(s): Indeterminate Past
Locale(s): Southwest (small town life)

Summary: In this collection of short stories, the author presents the voices of small-town women who battle limited opportunities and emotional hardships, and yet manage to survive. She explores themes of communication, hunger, loss, and identity. These stories have realistic depictions of grandmothers, sisters, aunts, with the bilingual voices and bicultural lives typical of Latinas and Chicanas in the U.S.

Where it's reviewed:
Lambda Book Report, May-June 1995, page 22

Other books you might like:
Alfred Avila, *Mexican Ghost Tales of the Southwest*, 1994
This is a collection of supernatural tales from the U.S.-Mexico border.
Esther De Michael Cervantes, *Barrio Ghosts*, 1988
These short stories are about urban life in the Chicano community.
Gary Soto, *A Summer Life*, 1990
This collection of very short stories is about young boys growing up in rural California.
Victor Villasenor, *Walking Stars: Stories of Magic and Power*, 1994
This autobiographical collection of stories is about the author's parents and grandparents in Mexico.
Frances R. Aparicio, *Latino Voices*, 1994
This collection of writing by Latino authors is specially edited for young adult readers.
Alma Flor Ada, *Where the Flame Trees Bloom*, 1994
Eleven short stories describe the author's growing up in Cuba.

615

ERNESTO GALARZA, Mexican American

Barrio Boy

(Notre Dame, IN: University of Notre Dame Press, 1971)

Subject(s): Coming of Age; Education; Family Relations
Age range(s): Grades 9-Adult
Major character(s): Ernesto Galarza, Young Man (boy), Immigrant, Mexican
Time period(s): 20th century (1910-1930)
Locale(s): Sacramento, California; Mexico

Summary: A fictionalized autobiography, this story recounts the author's journey from Mexico to Sacramento, California during the time of the Mexican Revolution. He describes his birth and early years in Jalcoctan and the migration which took a couple of years to complete. His father dies in Mexico and his mother dies in the U.S. during the influenza epidemic of 1917. As a very young man he's left by himself, yet he manages to graduate from high school, attend Stanford University and become a distinguished professor and scholar.

Where it's reviewed:
Los Angeles Times, June 28, 1984, page 7
New York Times, June 25, 1984, page 13

Other books by the same author:
Farm Workers and Agri-Business in California, 1947-1960, 1977
Kodachromes in Rhyme: Poems, 1982
Merchants of Labor: The Mexican Bracero Story, 1964
Spiders in the House and Workers in the Field, 1970
Mexican-Americans in the Southwest, 1970

Other books you might like:
Richard Rodriguez, *Hunger of Memory: The Education of Richard Rodriguez, an Autobiography*, 1982
This story of the author's childhood and education portrays the difficult journey of a ''minority student'' who must become socially assimilated in order to enjoy academic success.
Arcadia H. Lopez, *Barrio Teacher*, 1992
This autobiographical narration is by an educator who, despite poverty and turmoil, manages to obtain a university education and teach for forty-six years in San Antonio, Texas.
Esmeralda Santiago, *When I Was Puerto Rican*, 1993
This autobiographical story is about a young girl living in poverty in Puerto Rico who comes to the U.S. and eventually attends Harvard University.
Victor Villasenor, *Rain of Gold*, 1991
In this massive novel the author weaves the separate stories of two families, the Gomez's and Villasenors, as they live in Mexico and later migrate to the U.S.
Americo Paredes, *George Washington Gomez*, 1990
As he grows up, George Washington Gomez struggles with racism, abuse, and cultural and political clashes, while other Texas Mexicans fight to preserve their language and culture.
Edmund Villasenor, *Macho!*, 1973
This early Chicano novel is about a 17-year-old who illegally crosses the U.S. border, cheats his fellow workers, becomes a strike breaker and turns criminal in his quest for riches and acculturation.
Salvador Guerrero, *Memorias: A West Texas Life*, 1991
This is the autobiography of a man growing up in west Texas whose history was similar to that experienced by many Mexican Americans from Texas during this time period.

616

SALLIE GALLEGOS, Mexican American

Stone Horses

(Albuquerque, NM: U. of New Mexico Press, 1996)

Subject(s): Fathers and Sons; Brothers; Family Relations
Age range(s): Grades 9-Adult
Major character(s): Eduardo Ricardo Montez, Young Man, Mexican American
Time period(s): 20th century (1926-1944)

Locale(s): New Mexico

Summary: In the style of early 20th century literature, this novel relates the history of the Montez family living in a rural area of northern New Mexico. Eduardo is one of eight children and the third son in the family. From his birth until he joins the Navy in 1944 at age eighteen Eduardo is an extraordinary little boy and young man. Not one of his mother's favorite sons, she sends him to live with his paternal grandparents at age four, where he's pampered and indulged by his aunt and uncle. Yet he grows into a sensitive young man. Gallegos incorporates the customs and traditions of the region into the plot of this novel, including a description of the pentitentes' procession, an encampment of gypsies, and the life of ranchers in rural New Mexico.

Other books you might like:
Rudolfo Anaya, *Bless Me, Ultima*, 1972
Antonio, a seven-year-old boy, through his relationship with Ultima, a curandera, learns about life, nature, and death in rural New Mexico during World War II.
Sabine Ulibarri, *El Condor and Other Stories*, 1989
Eleven romantic stories for adults, this collection presents a world of gypsies, witches, ghosts, and the supernatural.
Angelico Chavez, *The Short Stories of Fray Angelico Chavez*, 1987
Edited by Genaro M. Padilla, this collection of short stories is by an early New Mexico writer and folklorist.
Sabine R. Ulibarri, *Tierra Amarilla: Stories of New Mexico = Cuentos de Nuevo Mexico*, 1993
This collection of five short stories and a novella, evoke the rural life of a northern New Mexican village of an earlier era, from a young boy's perspective.
Alberto Alvaro Rios, *Pig Cookies and Other Stories*, 1995
Set earlier in this century, this collection of interrelated short stories takes place in a small village in northern Mexico.
Nash Candelaria, *Leonor Park*, 1991
This novel is about land and greed in New Mexico on the eve of the Great Depression and the battle of a brother and sister over a father's legacy, a piece of land alongside the Rio Grande.

617

CRISTINA GARCIA, Cuban American

Dreaming in Cuban, A Novel

(New York: Ballantine Books, 1992)

Subject(s): Revolution; Family; Grandparents
Age range(s): Grades 10-Adult
Major character(s): Celia del Pino, Grandmother (63-year-old), Revolutionary, Cuban; Pilar, Granddaughter (of Celia del Pino), Artist (punk), Cuban American
Time period(s): 20th century (1960-1992)
Locale(s): Brooklyn, New York

Summary: Interwoven among the stories here are the lives of three generations of Cuban women and their varied responses to the Cuban revolution. Celia del Pino remains in Cuba, a Castro supporter, and her Americanized granddaughter Pilar, born in Cuba when the revolution was 11 days old but now living in the U.S., misses her grandmother. Garcia examines generational fissures, political and geographical divisions.

Where it's reviewed:
Library Journal, June 1, 1993, page 224
Publishers Weekly, January 13, 1992, page 46
Times Literary Supplement, December 25, 1992, page 19
Women's Review of Books, June 1992, page 11

Other books by the same author:
Cars of Cuba, 1995
Sonar en Cubano, 1993

Other books you might like:
Margarita Engle, *Singing to Cuba*, 1993
    A California woman leaves her husband and children to search for information about family members who disappeared during the Castro revolution.
Judith Ortiz Cofer, *The Line of the Sun: A Novel*, 1989
    An intergenerational story of a young girl coming of age in the United States but with a clear reliance on her Puerto Rican culture.
Julia Alvarez, *How the Garcia Girls Lost Their Accents*, 1991
    An episodic novel about a family's move to the U.S., and the gradual Americanization of the daughters.
Himilce Novas, *Mangos, Bananas, and Coconuts: A Cuban Love Story*, 1996
    This tale of a magical yet real love story is an ancient tale beginning with the love of a man and a woman from different social classes, and the story of the fate of their children.

618

GUY GARCIA, Mexican American

Obsidian Sky: A Novel
(New York: Simon & Schuster, 1994)

Subject(s): Indians of Mexico; Travel
Age range(s): Grades 10-Adult
Major character(s): Brian Mendoza, Student—College (doctoral student), Chicano (very Anglicized)
Time period(s): 1990s
Locale(s): Mexico City, Mexico

Summary: Brian Mendoza, a doctoral student from Berkeley, gets a job at Mexico City's Museum of Anthropolgy. He has a theory about Aztec ritual and the role of Motecuhzoma, the Aztec king enslaved by Cortes, that gets him sucked into a political controversy amidst the civil unrest that is developing in Mexico. An interesting sub-plot is the author's use and knowledge of Aztec mythology.

Where it's reviewed:
Library Journal, May 15, 1994, page 98
Publishers Weekly, April 11, 1994, page 54
Review-Latin American Literature and Arts, Fall 1995, page 83

Other books by the same author:
Skin Deep, 1988

Other books you might like:
Gary D. Keller, *Zapata Lives!*, 1994
    A story about the Mexican revolutionary leader Emiliana

Zapata who rises from the dead to lead his people in a struggle against economic and social oppression.
Montserrat Fontes, *Dreams of the Centaur*, 1995
    A fast-paced novel about the son of a slain ranch owner, who tries to avenge his father's death.
Rudolfo Anaya, *Zia Summer*, 1995
    Sonny Baca is involved in a mystery that involves murder, cult worship of the sun, and a battle over nuclear waste and disposal in New Mexico.
Alejandro Morales, *The Rag Doll Plagues*, 1992
    Divided into three sections, this novel depicts Latino doctors fighting deadly infectious diseases over three centuries in Mexico and the U.S.

619

LIONEL G. GARCIA, Mexican American

Hardscrub
(Houston, TX: Arte Publico Press, 1990)

Subject(s): Family Relations; Fathers and Sons; Coming of Age
Age range(s): Grades 10-Adult
Major character(s): Jim Jones, 11-Year-Old (boy)
Time period(s): 20th century (1950-1970)
Locale(s): Texas (in the drought-ridden landscape of West Texas)

Summary: Related from the perspective of eleven-year-old Jim, this novel portrays characters struggling to survive in the tough land of West Texas. Jim's father spends time in prison for killing a man, but even after this experience he continues his abusive behavior towards his two sons, wife and daughter. His drinking, brawling, and wandering threaten to undermine Jim's identity in this violent and turbulent household.

Where it's reviewed:
Publishers Weekly, December 1, 1989, page 52

Awards the book has won:
Texas Institute of Letters' Jesse Jones Award
Texas Literary Award

Other books by the same author:
To a Widow with Children, 1994
I Can Hear the Cowbells Ring, 1994
Leaving Home, 1995 (PEN Southwest Award winner)
A Shroud in the Family, 1994

Other books you might like:
Alfredo Vea Jr., *La Maravilla*, 1993
    A young boy grows up on Buckeye Road, a world of marvels in the desert outside the Phoenix city limits, caught between many cultures.
Maria Espinosa, *Dark Plums*, 1995
    Adrianne, a young girl from Texas, searches for love in Manhattan, falls into an abusive relationship, and eventually works as a prostitute.
Hugo Martinez-Serros, *The Last Laugh and Other Stories*, 1988
    Set in urban Chicago, this collection presents the stories of two brothers, Lazaro and Jaime, who work physically hard alongside their father.

Floyd Salas, *Buffalo Nickel: A Memoir*, 1992
This coming-of-age memoir is by a young man who oscillates between his two brothers—Albert, who abuses drugs and is involved in crime, and Edward, intelligent and upwardly mobile.

Alma Luz Villanueva, *Naked Ladies*, 1994
The lives of four remarkable women and their struggles against prejudices, difficult relationships, and abuse is told in this novel.

Max Martinez, *White Leg*, 1996
In this fast-paced murder mystery, a small-time thief in a backwater Texas town kills a Texas Ranger and three other people during one of his hold-ups.

620

LIONEL G. GARCIA, Mexican American

I Can Hear the Cowbells Ring
(Houston, TX: Arte Publico Press, 1994)

Subject(s): Short Stories; Family Relations; Humor
Age range(s): Grades 8-Adult
Time period(s): 1930s; 1940s (1930-1940)
Locale(s): San Diego, Texas

Summary: This collection of delightful autobiographical vignettes reconstructs life in a small rural town of southern Texas. With humor and nostalgia, Garcia describes the antics of a multitude of vivid, memorable characters; his uncles Tio Nano, Matias, and insane Merce. We also meet the lonely Father Zavala who solicits sins from the children during confession, his mother Marillita, his brother who could not be cured of swearing, and his grandmother Maria, the wonderful cook. These short stories are brought together by warmth, love and the caring found in the extended family and village life.

Where it's reviewed:
Library Journal, September 15, 1994, page 71

Other books by the same author:
Hardscrub, 1990
Leaving Home, 1985
A Shroud in the Family, 1987
To a Widow with Children, 1994

Other books you might like:
Nash Candelaria, *The Day the Cisco Kid Shot John Wayne*, 1988
A humorous collection of short stories from New Mexico in which the author examines cultural clashes between Latinos and Anglos.

Gloria Lopez-Stafford, *A Place in El Paso: A Mexican American Childhood*, 1996
This bittersweet narrative describes the early childhood of the author living in the *projects* of El Paso during World War II.

Norma Elia Cantu, *Canicula: Snapshots of a Girlhood en la Frontera*, 1995
A collection, with photos, of short stories and vignettes of a young girl growing up along the Texas border.

Rolando Hinojosa, *Becky and Her Friends*, 1990
Narrated by many of her friends, this novel focuses on the

strong-willed Becky Escobar, an upwardly-mobile woman who at age thirty-five decides to divorce her husband.

Americo Paredes, *The Hammon and the Beans and Other Stories*, 1994
Set in the southern Texas border region, this collection of short stories explores the cultural conflict that has dominated that area since the U.S.-Mexican War.

Jesus Salvador Trevino, *The Fabulous Sinkhole and Other Stories*, 1995
This first story collection by Trevino, a screenwriter and director, is an entertaining creation of Mexican and Chicano characters, that take place in a fictional town, Arroyo Grande, in Texas.

621

LIONEL G. GARCIA, Mexican American

To a Widow with Children
(Houston, TX: Arte Publico Press, 1994)

Subject(s): Family Relations; Humor; Rural Life
Age range(s): Grades 9-Adult
Major character(s): Maria, Widow(er), Mother (of four children), Mexican American
Time period(s): 19th century; 20th century (1867-1920)
Locale(s): San Diego, Texas

Summary: This delightful magical story takes place in a small sleepy town in Texas along the Mexican border. Maria's four children are wise, mischievous and manipulative, and seem to be at the center of everything that happens in town. The local sheriff is plotting to get them placed in an orphanage when a former Mexican revolutionary comes into town with an extraordinary bicycle, falls in love with Maria, and becomes involved in the revenge and gossip of the town.

Where it's reviewed:
Library Journal, April 1, 1994, page 131
Publishers Weekly, February 28, 1994, page 74

Other books by the same author:
Hardscrub, 1990
I Can Hear the Cowbells Ring, 1994
Leaving Home, 1985
A Shroud in the Family, 1987

Other books you might like:
Louie Garcia Robinson, *The Devil, Delfina Varela, and the Used Chevy*, 1993
Set in the Mission District of San Francisco, this is a novel about politics, dreams, Latino social affairs, and Delfina, a widow who will do anything for a car.

Mary Helen Ponce, *The Wedding*, 1989
This is a tongue-in-cheek expose of working class life and culture in a southern California Chicano community as Blanca Munoz plans her wedding to Sammy-the-Cricket.

Nash Candelaria, *The Day the Cisco Kid Shot John Wayne*, 1988
The author examines cultural clashes between Latinos and Anglos in this humorous collection of short stories from New Mexico.

Gloria Lopez-Stafford, *A Place in El Paso: A Mexican American Childhood*, 1996

This bittersweet narrative describes the early childhood of the author living in the "projects" of El Paso during World War II.

Sandra Benitez, *A Place Where the Sea Remembers*, 1993
Written as a series of interrelated magical tales, this novel presents the life of a coastal village in Mexico.

Josephina Niggli, *Mexican Village*, 1994
This is an important collection of ten interrelated short stories is about the lives of the people of a small Mexican town, Hidalgo, and was first published in 1945.

622

MARIA GARCIA, Mexican American
MALAQUIAS MONTOYA, Illustrator, Mexican American

The Adventures of Connie and Diego = Las Aventuras de Connie y Diego
(San Francisco, CA: Children's Book Press, 1986)

Subject(s): Prejudice; Identity; Brothers and Sisters
Age range(s): Grades K-2
Major character(s): Connie, Twin (girl); Diego, Twin (boy)
Time period(s): Indeterminate Past
Locale(s): United States

Summary: Connie and Diego are different from other people in the Land of Plenty. They have many colors all over their bodies. Because they are not accepted, they journey through the forest and across the wide ocean to find people like themselves. Eventually they meet a fierce tiger who helps them understand where they really belong.

About this book: The book is in Spanish and English and translated by Alma Flor Ada.

Where it's reviewed:
Horn Book Magazine, January-February 1988, page 91

Other books you might like:
Harriet Rohmer, *Atariba and Niguayona: A Story from the Taino People of Puerto Rico*, 1988
Niguayona embarks upon a journey through the forest to save his friend.

Sandra Cisneros, *Hair = Pelitos*, 1994
Everyone in the family has different hair and a different personality.

Manilo Argueta, *Magic Dogs of the Volcanoes = Los Perros Magicos de los Volcanes*, 1990
The magic dogs must call upon their ancestors to battle some tin soldiers.

Alejandro Cruz Martinez, *The Woman Who Outshone the Sun*, 1991
This Zapotec legend is about a beautiful woman with hair so bright that it outshines the sun.

Jan Romero Stevens, *Carlos and the Cornfield: Story = Carlos y la Milpa de Maiz: Cuento*, 1995
A young boy learns to make things right after realizing his mistake in planting corn.

Omar Castaneda, *Abuela's Weave*, 1993
A girl and her grandmother make tapestries for an outdoor market.

623

RICHARD GARCIA, Mexican American
ROBIN CHERIN, Illustrator

My Aunt Otilia's Spirits = Los Espiritus de Mi Tia Otilia
(San Francisco: Children's Book Press, 1987)

Subject(s): Magic; Aunts and Uncles
Age range(s): Grades 1-3
Major character(s): Aunt Otilia, Puerto Rican
Time period(s): Indeterminate Past
Locale(s): San Francisco, California

Summary: When Aunt Otilia comes to visit from Puerto Rico, her spirits make noises during the night. Her nephew wants to discover the mystery behind Aunt Otilia's noises, so he stays awake one night and sees some very strange things.

About this book: This work is in Spanish and English and is translated by Jesus Guerrero Rea

Where it's reviewed:
Booklist, June 15, 1987, page 1611
Publishers Weekly, May 29, 1987, page 75
School Library Journal, June 1987, page 74

Other books you might like:
Alberto Blanco, *Angel's Kite = La Estrella de Angel*, 1994
After the church bell disappears, Angel makes a kite with a picture of the town and the church on it.

Carmen Lomas Garza, *Family Pictures = Cuadros de Familia*, 1990
This work contains descriptions and pictures of family life during celebrations and holidays.

Carmen Santiago Nodar, *Abuelita's Paradise*, 1992
Marita sits in Abuelita's rocking chair and remembers the stories Abuelita told of her life in Puerto Rico.

Arthur Dorros, *Abuela*, 1991
A little girl and her grandmother fly all over New York City.

Juanita Havill, *Treasure Nap*, 1992
A little girl hears the story of Rita who visits her grandfather in the mountains of Mexico.

Alejandro Cruz Martinez, *The Woman Who Outshone the Sun*, 1991
A Zapotec legend about a beautiful woman with hair so bright that it outshines the sun.

Manlio Argueta, *Magic Dogs of the Volcanoes = Los Perros Magicos de los Volcanes*, 1990
The magic dogs must call upon their ancestors to battle some tin soldiers.

624

MAGALI GARCIA RAMIS, Puerto Rican

Happy Days, Uncle Sergio
(Fredonia, NY: White Pine Press, 1995)

Subject(s): Coming of Age; Family Relations
Age range(s): Grades 10-Adult
Major character(s): Lidea, Child (only daughter); Adres, Brother

Time period(s): 1950s
Locale(s): Santurce, Puerto Rico

Summary: This story covers the education and growth of a young middle class girl during the 1950s in Puerto Rico. Her uncle Sergio, a nationalist and political activist, immigrates to the U.S. and represents the tie between Puerto Rico and New York.

About this book: This work is translated by Carmen C. Esteves.

Where it's reviewed:
Library Journal May 15, 1995, page 94
Callaloo, Summer 1994, page 862

Other books by the same author:
Felices Dias, Tio Sergio, 1986
La Ciudad Que Me Habita, 1993
La Familia de Todos Nosotros, 1976

Other books you might like:
Rosario Ferre, *The House on the Lagoon*, 1995
   This intergenerational story portrays a family in Ponce, Puerto Rico.
Judith Ortiz Cofer, *The Line of the Sun: A Novel*, 1989
   A young girl comes of age against the backdrop of Puerto Rico and Paterson, New Jersey.
Montserrat Fontes, *First Confession*, 1991
   An upper class little girl lives on the Mexican side of the U.S.-Mexico border.
Alma Flor Ada, *Where the Flame Trees Bloom*, 1994
   These eleven stories portray the childhood of their Cuban author.
Oscar Hijuelos, *The Mambo Kings Play Songs of Love*, 1989
   The Castillo brothers make their way from Havana to New York to play music in the era of the mambo and become night stars of the dance halls.

625

CAROLINA GARCIA-AGUILERA, Cuban American

Bloody Waters
(New York, NY: Putnam, 1996)

Subject(s): Mystery and Detective Stories; Adoption; Murder
Age range(s): Grades 10-Adult
Major character(s): Guadalupe Solano, Detective—Private, Wealthy, Cuban
Time period(s): 1990s
Locale(s): Miami, Florida

Summary: Guadalupe "Lupe" Solano, part of Miami's elite, is approached by a young couple for assistance in finding the biological mother of their adopted daughter. The lawyer who arranged the illegal-adoption is no help and now their daughter needs a bone-marrow transplant if she's to survive. Solano's Miami connections produce results but not without repercussions, such as a hostile woman and murder. The eccentric family of the detective is also introduced, like her father who's waiting for the fall of Castro, her body-building cousin, and her sister who's a nun.

Where it's reviewed:
Publisher Weekly, January 8, 1996, page 61

Library Journal, February 1, 1996, page 102

Other books you might like:
Esmeralda Santiago, *America's Dream*, 1996
   America works as a housekeeper in a hotel on an island off the coast of Puerto Rico, until she accepts a job as a nanny in Westchester County, New York, and learns about a new life.
Soledad Santiago, *Streets of Fire*, 1996
   This murder mystery with a Latina police officer, Francesca Colon, involves all the elements of big city dirty politics, police corruption, suspicious deaths, and tense ethnic community relations.
Roberto Fernandez, *Holy Radishes*, 1995
   This satirical novel depicts the Cuban American community in Florida where exiled Cubans plan the liberation of their homeland while their wives work at a radish plant.
Virgil Suarez, *Havana Thursdays: A Novel*, 1995
   This is the story of two sisters, their daughters, and how they represent two different manners of dealing with the changes encountered through immigration from a Latino culture.
Rudolfo Anaya, *Albuquerque*, 1992
   This exciting story of modern Albuquerque includes a vicious mayoral race, a young Chicano boxer, American Indians fighting for their water rights and the folkloric past of New Mexicio.
Gloria Gonzalez, *The Thirteenth Apostle*, 1993
   Suspecting an industrial homicide, newspaperwoman Geraldine St. Claire teams up with a charter-boat skipper to investigate the murder of his friend and her lover, Hal.

626

CARMEN LOMAS GARZA, Mexican American

Family Pictures = Cuadros de Familia
(San Francisco: Children's Book Press, 1990)

Subject(s): Traditions; Family; Artists and Art
Age range(s): Grades 1-3
Time period(s): 1940s
Locale(s): Texas

Summary: In this book, Carmen Lomas Garza's beautiful and detailed paintings are combined with descriptions of her life as a girl in a Texas border town. She explains and illustrates traditions, such as the Cakewalk, the Fair in Reynosa, making tamales, and celebrates family bonds.

About this book: Stories are told to Harriet Rohmer by the author in bilingual text.

Where it's reviewed:
Publishers Weekly, July 13, 1990, page 54
School Arts, May-June 1995, page 42

Other books by the same author:
A Piece of My Heart = Pedacito de Mi Corazon: The Art of Carmen Lomas Garza, 1994

Other books you might like:
Enedina Casarez Vasquez, *Recuerdos de Una Nina*, 1980
   These short stories are about growing up in San Antonio, Texas.

Alma Flor Ada, *My Name Is Maria Isabel*, 1993
Maria moves to a new school and learns not to be shy about her name.

Gary Soto, *The Skirt*, 1992
Fourth-grader Miata loses her mother's folkloric dancing skirt and figures out a way to find it.

Gary Soto, *Too Many Tamales*, 1993
Maria helps her mother make tamales for Christmas Eve dinner, but she loses something she must find before her mother finds out.

Sandra Cisneros, *Hair = Pelitos*, 1994
A picture book excerpted from *The House on Mango Street* shows every member of the family has different hair.

Gina Macaluso Rodriguez, *Green Corn Tamales = Tamales de Elote*, 1994
A Latino family makes green corn tamales every year, but there's a twist to this tale—not everybody wants to help.

627

CARMEN LOMAS GARZA, Author/Illustrator, Mexican American

In My Family = En Mi Familia

(San Francisco, CA: Children's Book Press, 1996)

Subject(s): Family Relations; Cultures and Customs; Folklore
Age range(s): Grades K-3
Time period(s): 1950s
Locale(s): Kingsville, Texas

Summary: Another book by the artist Carmen Lomas Garza with beautifully detailed paintings of growing up along the Texas-Mexico border. In this book Garza presents her family and illustrates some family traditions, such as the a birthday barbecue, making Easter "cascarones" eggs, making empanadas, and the giving of the blessing on her cousin's wedding day.

Other books by the same author:
Family Pictures = Cuadros de Familia, 1990
A Piece of My Heart = Pedacito de Mi Corazon: The Art of Carmen Lomas Garza, 1994

Other books you might like:
Gary Soto, *Too Many Tamales*, 1993
Maria helps her mother make tamales for Christmas Eve dinner, but she loses something she must find before her mother finds out.

Sandra Cisneros, *Hair = Pelitos*, 1994
A picture book excerpted from *The House on Mango Street* portrays every member of the family with different hair.

Karen Papagapitos, *Jose's Basket*, 1990
Jose's journal is like his mother's basket, which is made from grasses and twigs from their travels, and is also full of memories.

Ofelia Dumas Lachtman, *Pepita Talks Twice = Pepita Habla Dos Veces*, 1995
Pepita must learn on her own, the value of speaking two languages, Spanish and English.

Gina Macaluso Rodriguez, *Green Corn Tamales = Tamales de Elote*, 1994

A Latino family makes green corn tamales every year, but there's a twist to this tale, not everyone wants to help.

Alberto Blanco, *Angel's Kite = La Estrella de Angel*, 1994
After the church bell disappears, Angel makes a kite with a picture of the town and the church on it.

628

ALICIA GASPAR DE ALBA, Mexican American

The Mystery of Survival and Other Stories

(Tempe, AZ: Bilingual Press, 1993)

Subject(s): Short Stories; Homosexuality/Lesbianism
Age range(s): Grades 10-Adult
Time period(s): 1980s
Locale(s): United States; Mexico

Summary: This is the first short story collection by the poet Gaspar de Alba. These eleven stories examine the boundaries between people, beliefs, and cultures. Her characters explore and come to understand their places in the world and the cultural boundaries that divide them, learning to find answers in cultural traditions and personal memory.

About this book: Two stories are completely in Spanish.

Where it's reviewed:
Library Journal, June 15, 1993, page 99
Publishers Weekly, June 14, 1993, page 64

Other books by the same author:
Three Times a Woman: Chicana Poetry, 1989

Other books you might like:
Gloria Anzaldua, *Borderlands: The New Mestiza = La Frontera*, 1987
In prose and poetry, Anzaldua writes about her childhood along the Texas-Mexican border, caught between two cultures, belonging to neither.

Estela Portillo Trambley, *Rain of Scorpions and Other Writings*, 1975
This collection of short stories by an early Chicana writer explores the place of women in Mexican society.

Sandra Cisneros, *Woman Hollering Creek and Other Stories*, 1991
This collection of short stories about women takes place in Texas and the border area.

Norma Elia Cantu, *Canicula: Snapshots of a Girlhood en la Frontera*, 1995
A collection containing photos, short stories, and vignettes about growing up along the Texas border.

Lillian Castillo-Speed, *Latina: Women's Voices from the Borderlands*, 1995
This collection of short stories is by contemporary Latinas in the U.S.

Alma Luz Villanueva, *Naked Ladies*, 1994
This novel tells the stories of four remarkable women, their struggles against prejudice and their difficult relationships.

629

DAGOBERTO GILB, Mexican American

The Last Known Residence of Mickey Acuna

(Fayetteville, AK: University of Arkansas Press, 1994)

Subject(s): Men
Age range(s): Grades 10-Adult
Major character(s): Mickey Acuna, Streetperson (homeless man), Chicano
Time period(s): 1990s
Locale(s): El Paso, Texas

Summary: Mickey Acuna is waiting for something, something arriving through the mail, as he dwells at the YMCA in El Paso. There he meets a cast of characters, all living a fantasy life and also waiting for something to happen, as they pass their time working out, playing handball, and drinking beer. Gilb's characters are the marginal citizens of society, the invisible men that walk unseen through the streets of most U.S cities.

Where it's reviewed:
World Literature Today, Autumn 1995, page 794
Library Journal, September 15, 1994, page 90
Publishers Weekley, August 8, 1994, page 378

Other books by the same author:
The Magic of Blood, 1993
Winners on the Pass Line, 1985

Other books you might like:
Leo Romero, *Rita and Los Angeles*, 1995
    This short story collection has a cast of complex characters who grow and evolve, and learn about being outsiders in an alien and hostile world.
Manuel Ramos, *The Ballad of Gato Guerrero*, 1994
    Luis Montez is a divorced lawyer works at saving Felix ''Gato'' Guerrero, an old friend from way back, who is being chased by a Latino mobster.
Max Martinez, *A Red Bikini Dream*, 1990
    The rhythms and spirit of modern life in the U.S. are captured in this collection of five short stories where the characters ponder self and identity in an increasingly complex society.
Ed Vega, *Mendoza's Dreams*, 1987
    Populated by strange, loveable characters, this collection includes stories about a hunched back circus clown, an innocent virgin, and an angel attempting to earn respect in heaven.
Luis Alberto Urrea, *In Search of Snow*, 1994
    Mike McGirk, a blue collar Don Quixote, searches for love and life in the Arizona desert, and learns about family from Bobo Garcia.
Rafael Zepeda, *Horse Medicine and Other Stories*, 1990
    This collection of nine stories deals with the world of men. In ''Horse Medicine,'' several men, with kids and wives, participate in rodeos and live with horses.
Genaro Gonzalez, *Only Sons*, 1991
    The main characters in this collection, all male, are trying to define their social relationships. Gonzalez explores ambivalent emotions, cultural values, and family traditions.

630

DAGOBERTO GILB, Mexican American

The Magic of Blood

(New York: Grove Press, 1993)

Subject(s): Short Stories
Age range(s): Grades 10-Adult
Time period(s): 1990s (1993)
Locale(s): California; Texas

Summary: In this collection of short stories, Dagoberto Gilb presents harsh, realistic stories about working-class life. Powerful, brutal, and yet beautifully crafted, his stories perfectly capture the nuances of ordinary life and make it resonate with unexpected meaning. He writes about blue-collar workers who live hard lives, but who are multi-dimensional characters with dreams, aspirations, and humor.

Where it's reviewed:
Library Journal, September 15, 1993, page 108
Nation, June 7, 1993, page 772
Studies in Short Fiction, Spring 1995, page 248
Wilson Library Bulletin, December 1993, page 95

Awards the book has won:
PEN's Ernest Heminway Foundation Award, 1993
Texas Institute of Letters' Jesse Jones Award, 1993

Other books by the same author:
The Last Known Residence of Mickey Acuna, 1994
Winners on the Pass Line, 1985

Other books you might like:
Ed Vega, *Mendoza's Dreams*, 1987
    A collection of stories, populated by strange, loveable characters: a hunched back circus clown, an innocent virgin, and an angel attempting to earn respect in heaven.
Virgil Suarez, *Welcome to the Oasis and Other Stories*, 1992
    A novella and five stories, about Latino characters who struggle to integrate into the American culture while maintaining their heritage.
John Rechy, *The Miraculous Day of Amalia Gomez: A Novel*, 1991
    This novel follows a day in the life of a Mexican American woman who lives with poverty, gang warfare, and illegal border crossings, yet still has hope.
Rick P. Rivera, *A Fabricated Mexican*, 1995
    In a series of comic vignettes, Ricky Coronado, a quiet but mischevious boy, reports on the antics of his eccentric family and his own search for identity.
Genaro Gonzalez, *Rainbow's End*,
    An adventure novel with dangerous border crossings, confrontations with a magician, and drug smuggling.
Rafael Zepeda, *Horse Medicine and Other Stories*, 1990
    This collection of nine stories deals very much with the world of men. In ''Horse Medicine'' several men, with kids and wives, participate in rodeos and live with horses.

631

FRANCISCO GOLDMAN, Guatemalan

The Long Night of White Chickens
(New York, NY: Atlantic Monthly, 1992)

Subject(s): War; Social Classes; Mystery and Detective Stories
Age range(s): Grades 10-Adult
Major character(s): Roger Graetz, Young Man, Guatemalan (father is Jewish)
Time period(s): 1980s
Locale(s): Guatemala

Summary: While Roger is being raised in the U.S. by his wealthy Guatemalan mother, thirteen-year-old Flor de Mayo Puac, a beautiful Guatemalan orphan, comes to live in his home. After her return to Guatemala she becomes the director of an orphanage and is murdered. Determined to find her murderers, Roger and his best friend Luis Moya Martinez, become entangled in dangerous political difficulties as they discover the secret romantic and political life of Flor in a war torn country.

Where it's reviewed:
Times Literary Supplement, January 15, 1993, page 21
Choice, January 1993, page 792
Library Journal, June 1, 1992, page 176
Publishers Weekly, April 13, 1992, page 42
New York Times Book Review, August 16, 1992, page 20

Other books you might like:
Gloria Gonzalez, *The Thirteenth Apostle*, 1993
  Suspecting an industrial homicide newspaperwoman Geraldine St. Claire teams up with a charter-boat skipper to investigate the murder of his friend and her lover, Hal.
Julia Alvarez, *In the Time of the Butterflies*, 1994
  This is the story of the assassination of three sisters who are fighting to overthrow a dictatorship in the Dominican Republic.
Carole Fernandez, *Sleep of the Innocents*, 1991
  This novel chronicles the lives of women living in a fictional Central American country torn by civil war.
Reinaldo Arenas, *The Palace of the White Skunks*, 1990
  This is the story of Fortunato, a boy raised in poverty by his grandparents, his life as he grows up during the Cuban revolution, and his death.
Victor Perera, *Rites, A Guatemalan Boyhood*, 1986
  These are autobiographical narratives of the Jewish boyhood of the author as he was growing up in Guatemala, before moving to the U.S.
Floyd Salas, *State of Emergency*, 1996
  It's the 1960s and a radical professor who finds refuge in the the counter-culture is forced to flee the U.S. after beginning an expose of the government.
Marcos McPeek Villatoro, *A Fire in the Earth*, 1996
  This epic novel follows Romilia Colonez, descendant of an Indian patriarch who led his clan to claim fertile soil, setting the stage for future trials and tragedies in El Salvador.

632

ALMA GOMEZ, Editor, Puerto Rican
CHERRIE MORAGA, Co-Editor, Chilean
MARIANA ROMO-CARMONA, Co-Editor, Chilean

Cuentos: Stories by Latinas
(New York: Kitchen Table, Women of Color Press, 1983)

Subject(s): Anthology; Short Stories
Age range(s): Grades 10-Adult
Time period(s): 20th century (1950-1983)
Locale(s): Mexico; South America

Summary: This anthology contains stories by Latinas in the U.S. and Latin America. The editors intended this collection for the bi-cultural reader.

About this book: Spanish is interspersed through some English stories, while others are entirely in Spanish.

Other books by the same author:
This Bridge Called My Back: Writings by Radical Women of Color, 1981
The Last Generation, 1993
Loving in the War Years: Lo que Nunca Paso por sus Labios, 1983

Other books you might like:
Lillian Castillo-Speed, *Latina: Women's Voices From the Borderlands*, 1995
  This collection of short fiction is by Latinas in the U.S.
Evangelina Vigil, *Woman of Her Word: Hispanic Women Write*, 1987
  This is an anthology of Latina writings.
Roberta Fernandez, *In Other Words: Literature by Latinas in the U.S.*, 1994
  This collection of short fiction is by Latinas in the U.S.
Bryce Milligan, *Daughters of the Fifth Sun: A Collection of Latina Fiction and Poetry*, 1995
  This anthology of fiction and poetry is by Latinas in the U.S.
Tey Diana Rebolledo, *Infinite Divisions: An Anthology of Chicana Literature*, 1993
  This anthology of historical and contemporary literature is by Mexican American women.
Tey Diana Rebolledo, *Las Mujeres Hablan*, 1988
  This collection of short stories and poetry is by Chicanas from New Mexico.
Maria del Carmen Boza, *Nosotras: Latina Literature Today*, 1986
  This is a collection of poetry and short stories by Latina writers.

633

GUILLERMO GOMEZ-PENA, Mexican American

Warrior for Gringostroika: Essays, Performance Texts, and Poetry
(Saint Paul, MN: Graywolf Press, 1993)

Subject(s): Prose; Poetry; Drama
Age range(s): Grades 10-Adult
Time period(s): 1980s

Locale(s): United States

Summary: This richly textured collection of essays, manifestos, performance texts, and poetry, charts the work of writer and performance artist Guillermo Gomez-Pena. His work encourages one to examine, and to cross and recross, the border, conveying a new internationalism, a borderless ethos.

About this book: Gomez-Pena received a MacArthur Genius Award for his work.

Where it's reviewed:
Choice, March 1994, page 1138
Library Journal, November 1, 1993, page 92
Performing Arts Journal, January 1991, page 111

Other books you might like:
John Leguizamo, *Spic-O-Rama: A Dysfunctional Comedy*, 1994
   A series of satirical performance pieces that examine Latino family and identity.
Jose Antonio Burciaga, *Spilling the Beans: Loteria Chicana*, 1995
   A series of essays, many humorous, recounting experiences from the author's childhood, that explore aspects of Chicano culture.
Luis Valdez, *Luis Valdez—Early Works: Actos, Bernabe, and Pensamiento Serpentino*, 1990
   Collection of early works, including one-act plays, by the director of the Teatro Campesino.
Jesus Salvador Trevino, *The Fabulous Sinkhole and Other Stories*, 1995
   This first story collection by Trevino, a screenwriter and director, is an entertaining creation of Mexican and Chicano characters that takes place in the fictional town of Arroyo Grande, Texas.

634

IBIS GOMEZ-VEGA, Mexican American

Send My Roots Rain
(San Francisco: Aunt Lute Books, 1991)

Subject(s): Identity; Religion; Homosexuality/Lesbianism
Age range(s): Grades 10-Adult
Major character(s): Carole Rio, Artist (outsider in town), Lesbian
Time period(s): 1990s
Locale(s): Texas (small Texas border town)

Summary: Carole Rio, fleeing her past, enters a small southwestern border town to paint murals on the church walls. The first thing she learns is that the church has burned down. Her visit brings about a truce between the priest and the town's healer, and helps Carole discover the source of her own problems, as well as her sexual identity.

About this book: This novel was First Runner-up in the 1990 Spinsters/Aunt Lute Fiction Contest.

Where it's reviewed:
Lambda Book Report, May-June 1992, page 34

Other books you might like:
Cherrie Moraga, *Loving in the War Years: Lo que Nunca Paso por sus Labios*, 1983

This autobiographical story is about a Chicana lesbian writer growing up in California.
Terri de la Pena, *Margins*, 1992
   The story of a young lesbian writer who confronts her future and her family about her sexuality.
Terri de la Pena, *Latin Satins*, 1994
   A story that chronicles the rise of a Chicana lesbian singing group in the Los Angeles area.
Carla Trujillo, *Chicana Lesbians: The Girls Our Mothers Warned Us About*, 1991
   A diverse collection of short stories, poetry, and prose by Chicana lesbians exploring the intricacies and specifics of culture, family, mixed-race relationships, body, and identity.
Sheila Ortiz Taylor, *Faultline: A Novel*, 1982
   This humorous book describes a lesbian mother of six children, her lover-companion, their 300 rabbits, and a six foot tall black drag queen babysitter.
Emma Perez, *Gulf Dreams*, 1996
   Growing up lesbian in Latino culture occupy the essays, short vignettes, and psychoanalytic discourse of this creative series.
Norma Alarcon, *The Sexuality of Latinas*, 1993
   This collection of poems, short stories, and prose examines the often hidden, often subverted, sexuality of Latinas.

635

DIANE GONZALES BERTRAND, Mexican American

Alicia's Treasures
(Houston, TX: Pinata Books, 1996)

Subject(s): Brothers and Sisters; Beaches; Identity
Age range(s): Grades 2-4
Major character(s): Alicia Inez Ramos, 10-Year-Old, Child, Mexican American
Time period(s): 1990s (1996)
Locale(s): Port Aransas, Texas

Summary: Alicia is invited to spend a weekend at the beach with her brother's girlfriend's family. It is an exciting adventure for her, as she builds sand castles, catches a fish, tastes salt water, and learns many things about the ocean, about family, and about herself.

Where it's reviewed:
Booklist, May 1, 1996, page 1505

Other books by the same author:
Sweet Fifteen, 1995

Other books you might like:
Gloria Velasquez, *Maya's Divided World*, 1995
   Maya's parents are divorcing, and Maya struggles with depression, loss, and disillusionment.
Irene Beltran Hernandez, *Heartbeat, Drumbeat*, 1992
   Morgana Cruz seeks her cultural identity while caught between the worlds of her Navajo mother and Mexican father.
Alma Flor Ada, *My Name Is Maria Isabel*, 1993
   Maria Isabel Salazar Lopez is proud of her name and the fact that she is named after a relative who she loves, but

when she begins a new school her teacher changes her name.

Karen Papagapitos, *Socorro, Daughter of the Desert*, 1993
The family of eight-year-old Socorro are farm workers and she helps out the family as much as she can. When her father becomes ill, Socorro and makes tortillas for her mother to sell in the fields.

Gary Soto, *The Skirt*, 1992
Fourth-grader Miata loses her mother's folkloric dancing skirt and figures out a way to find it.

Fernando Pico, *The Red Comb*, 1991
A young girl helps save a runaway slave in 19th century Puerto Rico.

636

DIANE GONZALES BERTRAND, Mexican American

Sweet Fifteen
(Houston: Arte Publico Press, 1995)

Subject(s): Family Relations; Coming of Age; Quinceanera
Age range(s): Grades 7-9
Major character(s): Stephanie Bonillo, 15-Year-Old; Rita Navarro, Businesswoman, Seamstress
Time period(s): 1990s (1995)
Locale(s): San Antonio, Texas

Summary: Stephanie has just experienced the loss of her father, and is about to have her quinceanera, a special party given on a girl's fifteenth birthday. Rita gives her a job in her shop and through their friendship helps her get through a difficult period. Although she doesn't want to go through with the celebration, her quinceanera does help her grow and adapt to loss and a new situation. This novel examines the stress felt by teenagers from traditional Latino families caught up in modern-day life.

Where it's reviewed:
School Library Journal, September 1995, Page 218
Booklist, June 1, 1995, page 1750

Other books you might like:
Omar Castaneda, *Imagining Isabel*, 1994
Isabel, a teenager in Guatemala recently married, wants to become a teacher.

Omar Castaneda, *Among the Volcanoes*, 1991
Isabel, a teenager in Guatemala, must quit school to take care of her ill mother.

Gloria Velasquez, *Maya's Divided World*, 1995
Maya's happy high school world comes apart when her parents announce their divorce.

Gloria Velasquez, *Juanita Fights the School Board*, 1994
Juanita is expelled from high school and with help from her friends fights back.

Karen Papagapitos, *Socorro, Daughter of the Desert*, 1993
The family of eight-year-old Socorro are farm workers and she helps out as much as she can. When her mother falls ill, Socorro makes tortillas for her mother to sell in the fields.

Elizabeth Borton de Trevino, *Leona: A Love Story*, 1994
About Mexico's war for independence, this historical novel is based on the true story of sixteen-year-old Leona Vicario, who fights to live and love as she chooses.

637

GENARO GONZALEZ, Mexican American

Only Sons
(Houston, TX: Arte Pubilico Press, 1991)

Subject(s): Fathers and Sons; Family Relations; Short Stories
Age range(s): Grades 10-Adult
Time period(s): 1970s
Locale(s): Texas

Summary: The main characters in this collection, all male, are trying to define their social relationships, particularly with fathers or other men. Gonzalez explores ambivalent emotions, cultural values, and traditions that are passed on from parents and family. In ''Real Life'' a young man faces the death of the aunt who raised him, and in ''Home of the Brave'' a Vietnam veteran returns to Texas a hero, admired by his father and family, and makes an important decision about where to turn next.

Where it's reviewed:
American Book Review, February-March 1994, page 23

Other books by the same author:
Rainbow's End, 1988

Other books you might like:
Dagoberto Gilb, *The Magic of Blood*, 1993
A powerful collection that presents harsh, realistic stories about working-class life in Texas and California.

Rafael Zepeda, *Horse Medicine and Other Stories*, 1990
Nine stories, with Mexican, American Indian and Vietnam veteran characters, deal very much with the world of men.

Rick P. Rivera, *A Fabricated Mexican*, 1995
This series of comic vignettes is about a quiet but mischevious boy growing up in California, the antics of his eccentric family and his own search for identity.

Alberto Alvaro Rios, *The Iguana Killer: Twelve Stories of the Heart*, 1984
These short stories transform ordinary life into a book of secrets where young Mexican and Chicano boys confront big questions.

Salvador Guerrero, *Memorias: A West Texas Life*, 1991
This autobiography is about man growing up in west Texas whose history is similar to that experienced by many Mexican Americans from Texas during the same time period.

Aristeo Brito, *The Devil in Texas: El Diablo en Texas*, 1990
This important novel describes the Anglo destruction of a Chicano world in Texas, where the devil comes to the border town of Presidio.

Rafael Castillo, *Distant Journeys*, 1991
The short stories in this collection are full of irony, humor, and disturbing cultural illusions about the myth of the American Dream.

Junot Diaz, *Drown, Stories*, 1996
A collection of ten short stories about young Latino men who undergo a transformation while trying to define their American identity.

638

GENARO GONZALEZ, Mexican American

Rainbow's End

(Houston, TX: Arte Publico Press, 1988)

Subject(s): Illegal Immigrants; Drugs; Vietnam War
Age range(s): Grades 10-Adult
Major character(s): Heraclio Cavazos, Immigrant, Mexican
Time period(s): 20th century (1940-1988)
Locale(s): Texas (along the US-Mexico border)

Summary: This adventure novel includes dangerous border crossings, confrontations with a magician, and drug smuggling. It is the story of three generations of the Cavazos family living in the Lower Rio Grand Valley of Texas. Heraclio Cavazos swims across the Rio Grande into the U.S. and starts a family who share the many common experiences of the 1950s and 1960s from migrant labor camps, the Vietnam war, and illicit drug smuggling.

Where it's reviewed:
Nation, November, 1988, page 502

Other books by the same author:
Only Sons, 1991

Other books you might like:
Ed Vega, *Casualty Report*, 1991
    Short stories, about Latino life in New York, including one about a frustrated Vietnam veteran.
Joe Rodriguez, *The Oddsplayer*, 1988
    A novel about the Vietnam war where Black and Latino soldiers fight the enemy on the battlefield and also within their own ranks.
John Rechy, *The Miraculous Day of Amalia Gomez: A Novel*, 1991
    A day in the life of a Mexican-American woman, who lives in the shabby section of Hollywood, amidst poverty, gang warfare, and illegal border crossings.
Dagoberto Gilb, *The Magic Blood*, 1993
    A powerful collection that presents harsh, realistic stories about working-class life in Texas and California.
Victor Villasenor, *Rain of Gold*, 1991
    This is an intergenerational saga of a family's migration from Mexico to the U.S.

639

GLORIA GONZALEZ

The Thirteenth Apostle

(New York: Saint Martin's Press, 1993)

Subject(s): Mystery and Detective Stories; Murder; Drugs
Age range(s): Grades 10-Adult
Major character(s): Geraldine St. Claire, Journalist (newspaperwoman), Gambler
Time period(s): 1990s (1993)
Locale(s): Florida

Summary: Newspaperwoman Geraldine St. Claire teams up with a charter-boat skipper to investigate the murder of his friend and her lover, Hal. Their investigation leds them to suspect an industrial homicide and also leads her right into the

hands of the henchmen of the famous drug baron, Marco Luis Delcampo. St. Claire cooks up a dangerous plan to get herself inside Delcampo's operation. A fast-paced mystery tale.

Where it's reviewed:
Publishers Weekly, May 3, 1993, page 298

Other books by the same author:
Gaucho: A Novel, 1977
A Deadly Rhyme, 1986
The Glad Man, 1993

Other books you might like:
Rudolfo Anaya, *Zia Summer*, 1995
    Sonny Baca is involved in an exciting complicated mystery plot that involves murder, cult worship of the sun, and a battle over nuclear waste and disposal in New Mexico.
Manuel Ramos, *The Ballad of Gato Guerrero*, 1994
    Luis Montez is a divorced lawyer at work saving Felix ''Gato'' Guerrero, an old friend from way back, who is being chased by a Latino mobster.
Soledad Santiago, *Nightside*, 1994
    Anna Eltern, a former nun who runs a shelter for runaway teens, struggles with financial problems and murder, after funding cuts force her to turn away homeles teenagers.
Lucha Corpi, *Cactus Blood: A Mystery Novel*, 1995
    Gloria Damasco, an apprentice to a private investigator, possesses an inexplicable visionary power, and helps solve a murder related to a 15 year old pesticide tank explosion.
Rolando Hinojosa, *Partners in Crime: A Rafe Buenrostro Mystery*, 1985
    Written in the style of the popular genre, this border murder mystery involves Hinojosa's popular characters Jehu Malacara and Rafe Buenrostro now a lieutenant of the Belken County Homicide Squad.
Lucha Corpi, *Eulogy for a Brown Angel: A Mystery Novel*, 1992
    A Chicana feminist detective solves a murder that occurred during the Chicano civil rights movement of the late 1960s.
Steven Lopez, *Third and Indiana*, 1994
    The title of this novel refers to the corner where fourteen-year-old Gabriel hands out crack to passing motorists. Diablo, his boss, begins making demands when Gabriel's accounts come up short.

640

LUCIA M. GONZALEZ
LULU DELACRE, Illustrator, Puerto Rican

The Bossy Gallito

(New York: Scholastic, Inc, 1994)

Subject(s): Animals; Folk Tales
Age range(s): Grades 1-3
Major character(s): Gallito, Rooster
Time period(s): Indeterminate Past
Locale(s): Cuba

Summary: A bossy little rooster, ''un Gallito Mandon,'' is on his way to his uncle's wedding, when he gets his beak dirty after pecking at some corn. The elegant Gallito can't go to the wedding in this state, so he orders a cast of unwilling characters to clean his beak for him. This retelling of a Cuban folktale is rhythmic, written in both Spanish and English. Illustrations emphasize tropical setting.

About this book: This Spanish title is *El Gallo de Bodas* and has a glossary and cultural notes in the back of book.

Where it's reviewed:
Horn Book Magazine, September-October 1994, page 602

Other books by the same author:
Arroz con Leche: Popular Songs and Rhymes from Latin America, 1989

Other books you might like:
Pura Belpre, *Dance of the Animals*, 1972
This Puerto Rican folktale featuring a cast of animals.
Gary Soto, *Chato's Kitchen*, 1995
Chato the cat wants to eat some mice, but they outwit him.
Pura Belpre, *The Tiger and the Rabbit and Other Tales*, 1965
A collection of folktales from Puerto Rico.
Manlio Argueta, *Magic Dogs of the Volcanoes = Los Perros Magicos de los Volcanes*, 1990
The magic dogs, or cadejos, who live on the volcanoes of El Salvador, are loved by the villagers because of their powerful magic.
Pat Mora, *The Race of Toad and Deer*, 1995
Deer thinks he is the biggest and the fastest animal in the jungle, and always tries to make the other animals do as he says.
Alma Flor Ada, *Mediopollito = Half-Chicken*, 1995
This is a bilingual retelling of a traditional humourous tale from Spain set in colonial Mexico. Half-Chicken is born with only half a body and because of his uniqueness receives a lot of attention.

641

LUCIA M. GONZALEZ, Puerto Rican

Vejigantes Masquerade
(New York: Scholastic INC, 1993)

Subject(s): Poverty; Traditions; Determination
Age range(s): Grades K-3
Major character(s): Ramon, Child (little boy), Puerto Rican
Time period(s): Indeterminate Past
Locale(s): Puerto Rico

Summary: Ramon has always wanted to masquerade in Carnival, but his family is poor, and he cannot afford to buy a costume. So he sews a vejigante costume himself and saves up his money to buy a devilish mask. But when Ramon participates in the celebration, his costume is ripped.

About this book: Written in Spanish and English

Where it's reviewed:
Publishers Weekly, January 11, 1993, page 63

Other books by the same author:
The Bossy Gallito, 1994

Other books you might like:
Rudolfo Anaya, *The Farolitos of Christmas*, 1995
Luz worries that her Abuelo will not be well enough to cut the pinon logs for the *luminarias* that will light the way for the Christmas posadas.

Omar Castaneda, *Abuela's Weave*, 1993
A young girl and her grandmother sell their woven fabrics at a market in Guatemala.
Juanita Havill, *Treasure Nap*, 1992
Alicia hears the story of Rita, who visits her grandfather in the mountains of Mexico, and learns to make wooden birdcages.
Pura Belpre, *Ote: A Puerto Rican Folk Tale*, 1969
Ote must go to the forest in search of food for his wife and five children. There he meets a near-sighted devil who brings him bad luck.
Karen Papagapitos, *Jose's Basket*, 1990
Because Jose's family is a migrant farm-working family, school starts later and ends earlier for him than for most students. His teacher understands and gives him a special gift.
Pura Belpre, *Santiago*, 1969
Santiago learns to make new friends in a new school.
Francisco X. Mora, *La Gran Fiesta*, 1993
Greedy Crow over-decorates his Christmas tree for *La Gran Fiesta de Navidad* until it collapses under a load of fruits, cookies, candies, and other goodies.

642

RAY GONZALEZ, Editor, Mexican American

Currents From the Dancing River: Contemporary Latino Fiction, Nonfiction, and Poetry
(New York: Harcourt Brace, 1994)

Subject(s): Anthology; Short Stories; Essays
Age range(s): Grades 10-Adult
Time period(s): 1990s
Locale(s): United States (stories take place throughout the U.S.)

Summary: This anthology contains the contemporary writings of outstanding Latino writers living in the U.S. today. 135 works in three genres, poetry, fiction, and nonfiction are presented by Mexican American, Cuban American and Puerto Rican authors. Included are such writers as Judith Ortiz Cofer, Aristeo Brito, Alma Luz Villanueva, Virgil Suarez, Christina Garcia, Rosemary Catacolos, Alberto Rios, and Victor Hernandez Cruz. Also well-known essayists such as Ruben Martinez and Ilan Stavans are represented.

Where it's reviewed:
Library Journal, August 1994, page 91
World Literature Today, Spring 1995, page 368

Other books by the same author:
Mirrors Beneath the Earth: Short Fiction by Chicano Writers, 1992
Memory Fever: A Journey Beyond El Paso Del Norte, 1993
Without Discovery: A Native Response to Columbus, 1992

Other books you might like:
Gary D. Keller, *Hispanics in the U.S.: An Anthology of Creative Literature. Vol. 2*, 1982
This collection of poetry and short stories is by Latino writers.

Nicolas Kanellos, *Short Fiction by Hispanic Writers of the United States*, 1993
This collection of short stories is by Latino writers.

Harold Augenbraum, *Growing Up Latino: Memoirs and Stories*, 1993
Twenty-five Latinos write stories about growing up in the U.S.

Denis Lynn Daly Heyck, *Barrios and Borderlands: Cultures of Latinos and Latinas in the United States*, 1994
This anthology of creative literature is by Latino writers in the U.S.

Delia Poey, *Iguana Dreams: New Latino Fiction*, 1992
This anthology of creative fiction is by Latinos in the U.S.

643

RAY GONZALEZ, Mexican American

Memory Fever: A Journey Beyond El Paso del Norte

(Seattle: Broken Moon Press, 1993)

Subject(s): Short Stories; Deserts; Coming of Age
Age range(s): Grades 10-Adult
Time period(s): 20th century (1960-1990)
Locale(s): El Paso, Texas (stories take place in the surrounding area)

Summary: This collection contains essays and vignettes about growing up in the 1960s in El Paso and the surrounding desert. What emerges is an individual aware of his place in history, his environment, and his sense of identity growing up near the Mexican border.

About this book: The author is primarily a poet.

Where it's reviewed:
Publishers Weekly, April 12, 1993, page 57

Other books by the same author:
Currents From the Dancing River: Contemporary Latino Fiction, Nonfiction, and Poetry, 1994
Mirrors Beneath the Earth: Short Fiction by Chicano Writers, 1992
From the Restless Roots, 1986

Other books you might like:
Virgil Elizondo, *The Future Is Mestizo: Life Where Cultures Meet*, 1988
This biography describes growing up Catholic in San Antonio, Texas.

Anaya Rudolfo, *Aztlan: Essays on the Chicano Homeland*, 1989
Through essay various authors cover history, ethnic identity, and religion.

Benjamin Alire Saenz, *Flowers for the Broken: Stories*, 1992
This collection of stories, set in the Southwest, reveal lives of loneliness, anger, fear and ambition.

Gary Soto, *Pieces of the Heart: New Chicano Fiction*, 1993
This collection of short stories is by Chicanowriters.

Juan Felipe Herrera, *Night Train to Tuxtla*, 1994
This collection deals with a vast array of subjects, from Rodney King, and AIDs, to zoot suits, along with a section devoted to what Herrera calls *the swashbuckling Chicano sixties*.

644

RAY GONZALEZ, Mexican American

Mirrors Beneath the Earth: Short Fiction by Chicano Writers

(East Haven, CT: Curbstone Press, 1992)

Subject(s): Anthology; Short Stories; Family Relations
Age range(s): Grades 10-Adult
Time period(s): 1990s (1992)
Locale(s): United States (stories take place throughout the U.S.)

Summary: Both well-known and lesser-known Chicano authors wrote this anthology of thirty-one stories. Their stories depict the varied experiences of the Chicano in the U.S., revealing the strong influence of traditional values and family myths.

Where it's reviewed:
Library Journal, October 15, 1992, page 102
Publishers Weekly, September 28, 1992, page 69
World Literature Today, Winter 1994, page 137

Other books by the same author:
Currents From the Dancing River: Contemporary Latino Fiction, Nonfiction, and Poetry, 1994
Memory Fever: A Journey Beyond El Paso del Norte, 1993
From the Restless Roots, 1986

Other books you might like:
Gary Soto, *Pieces of the Heart: New Chicano Fiction*, 1993
This collection of short stories is by Chicano writers.

Rudolfo Anaya, *Cuentos Chicanos: A Short Story Anthology*, 1984
This collection of short stories is by Chicano writers.

Tiffany Ana Lopez, *Growing Up Chicano*, 1993
These short stories are by Chicano writers.

Carlota Cardenas de Dwyer, *Chicano Voices*, 1975
This important collection of short stories is from the Southwest.

Rudolfo Anaya, *Voces: An Anthology of Nuevo Mexicano Writers*, 1987
This anthology of poems and short stories is by New Mexican Chicano authors.

Tey Diana Rebolledo, *Infinite Divisions: An Anthology of Chicana Literature*, 1993
This is an anthology of historical and contemporary writing by Mexican American women.

645

ALEJANDRO GRATTAN-DOMINGUEZ, Mexican American

The Dark Side of the Dream

(Houston, TX: Arte Publico Press, 1995)

Subject(s): World War II; Emigration and Immigration; Cousins
Age range(s): Grades 10-Adult
Major character(s): Miguel Salazar, Veteran (young man), Immigrant, Mexican; Francisco Salazar, Young Man, Immigrant, Mexican

Time period(s): 1940s; 1950s (1941-1955)
Locale(s): El Paso, Texas

Summary: A historical novel set right after the outbreak of World War II, this is about two cousins and their families who migrate from Chihuahua to El Paso. The first part of the novel is about Miguel's participation in the army's all-Latino rifle company, the company that fought the Battle of the Rapido River in Italy during the war, and lost most of its men. The second half of the novel tells the story of Francisco's involvement in a farmworker strike that occurred in South Texas during the 1950s.

Where it's reviewed:
Publishers Weekly, September 18, 1995, page 110

Other books you might like:
Americo Paredes, *The Hammon and the Beans and Other Stories*, 1994
    Set in the southern Texas border region, this collection of short stories explores the cultural conflict that has dominated that area since the U.S.-Mexican War.
Gloria Lopez-Stafford, *A Place in El Paso: A Mexican American Childhood*, 1996
    This bittersweet narrative describes the early childhood of the author living in the "projects" of El Paso during World War II.
Edmund Villasenor, *Macho!*, 1973
    This early Chicano novel is about a 17-year-old who illegally crosses the U.S. border, cheats his fellow workers, becomes a strike-breaker and turns criminal in his quest for riches and acculturation.
Rolando Hinojosa, *The Useless Servants*, 1993
    This novel is made up of the diary entries, which serve Rafe Buenrostro, stationed in Korea during the war, as a survival tool where he describes his every day experiences.
Joe Rodriguez, *The Oddsplayer*, 1988
    A novel about the Vietnam war, this describes how Black and Latino soldiers fight the enemy on the battlefield and also within their own ranks.
Daniel Cano, *Shifting Loyalties*, 1995
    The lives of five Chicano soldiers and their families before, during and after the Vietnam War are explored in this novel.
Americo Paredes, *The Hammon and the Beans and Other Stories*, 1994
    Set in the southern Texas border region, this collection of short stories explores the cultural conflict that has dominated the area since the U.S.-Mexican War.

646

SALVADOR GUERRERO, Mexican American

Memorias: A West Texas Life
(Lubbock, TX: Texas Tech University Press, 1991)

Subject(s): Growing Up; Identity; Veterans
Age range(s): Grades 9-Adult
Major character(s): Salvador Guerrero, Child (boy), Mexican American
Time period(s): 20th century (1920-1986)
Locale(s): San Angelo, Texas

Summary: This is the autobiography of a young man growing up in west Texas during the first half of the twentith century. It reads like fiction and its significance is that it chronicles the history experienced by many Mexican Americans from Texas during this time period. Guerrero, in his estimation, achieved part of the American Dream. He fought in World War II, was an early and active member of the GI Forum, was active in the Boy Scouts, and was the first Latino elected to the County Commission of Ector County.

About this book: Foreword by Arnoldo De Leon

Where it's reviewed:
Southwestern Historical Quarterly, January, 1994, page 566
Western Historical Quarterly, Spring 1994, page 111

Other books you might like:
Ernesto Galarza, *Barrio Boy*, 1971
    Autobiographical, this story examines the early life of a distinguished professor and author who wrote many works about Mexican agricultural workers.
Richard Rodriguez, *Hunger of Memory: The Education of Richard Rodriguez, an Autobiography*, 1982
    This is the story of the author's childhood and education, the difficult journey of a *minority student* who must become socially assimilated in order to enjoy academic success.
Norma Elia Cantu, *Canicula: Snapshots of a Girlhood en la Frontera*, 1995
    This series of brief vignettes about growing up brings into sharp focus the history, lives, and legends about Laredo, Texas.
Enedina Casarez Vasquez, *Recuerdos de Una Nina*, 1980
    These are short stories about growing up in San Antonio, Texas.
Arcadia H. Lopez, *Barrio Teacher*, 1992
    An autobiographical narration by an educator who, despite poverty and turmoil, managed to obtain a university education and teach for forty-six years in San Antonio, Texas.
Americo Paredes, *George Washington Gomez*, 1990
    As he grows up, George Washington Gomez struggles with racism, abuse, and cultural and political clashes, while other Texas Mexicans fight to preserve their language and culture.

647

JUANITA HAVILL
ELIVIA SAVADIER, Illustrator

Treasure Nap
(Boston: Houghton Mifflin Company, 1992)

Subject(s): Grandparents; Family Relations; Mothers and Daughters
Age range(s): Grades K-2
Major character(s): Alicia, Child, Mexican American; Mama, Mother, Mexican American
Time period(s): Indeterminate Past
Locale(s): Mexico (story takes place in Mexico and the U.S.)

Summary: It is too hot to sleep, so Mama tells Alicia a story. She tells the story of Rita, who visits her grandfather in the mountains of Mexico. Rita learns to make wooden birdcages, to sit so still birds fly near her, and to play the pito, a flute which sounds like chirping birds when played.

About this book: This work is available in Spanish as *El Paraiso de Abuelita*.

Where it's reviewed:
Publishers Weekly, February 10, 1992, page 81

Other books by the same author:
Jamaica and Brianna, 1993
Jamaica's Find, 1986
The Magic Fort, 1991
Sato and the Elephants, 1993

Other books you might like:
Pat Mora, *A Birthday Basket for Tia*, 1992
    Cecilia creates, with the help of her cat, a birthday gift for her great Aunt.
Arthur Dorros, *Abuela*, 1991
    A little girl and her grandmother fly all over New York City.
Omar Castaneda, *Abuela's Weave*, 1993
    A young girl and her grandmother sell their woven fabrics at a market in Guatemala.
Harriet Rohmer, *Atariba and Niguayona: A Story from the Taino People of Puerto Rico*, 1988
    This Taino legend portrays a young boy and his search for the caimoni tree.
Carmen Santiago Nodar, *Abuelita's Paradise*, 1992
    Marita sits in Abuelita's rocking chair and remembers the stories Abuelita told of her life in Puerto Rico.
Leyla Torres, *Saturday Sancocho*, 1995
    Every Saturday, Maria Lili helps her grandparents make their traditional chicken sancocho.

648

IRENE BELTRAN HERNANDEZ, Mexican American

Across the Great River
(Houston: Arte Publico Press, 1989)

Subject(s): Illegal Immigrants; Coming of Age; Curanderas
Age range(s): Grades 6 and Up
Major character(s): Kata, Child, Immigrant, Mexican; Anita, Healer, Mexican
Time period(s): 1980s
Locale(s): Texas (takes place in Mexico and the U.S.); Mexico

Summary: This novel chronicles a period in the life of Kata and her family, who enter the United States from Mexico illegally. Kata deals with violence, authorities, a folk healer, and labor smugglers. Her story is told with the innocence and directness of a young girl who must deal with the harsh realities of life at an early age.

Where it's reviewed:
Book Report, January 1995, page 28

Other books by the same author:
Heartbeat, Drumbeat, 1992
The Secret of Two Brothers, 1995

Other books you might like:
Ofelia Dumas Lachtman, *The Girl from Playa Blanca*, 1995
    Elena and her brother Carlos find adventure in Los Angeles as they search for their father.
Omar Castaneda, *Imagining Isabel*, 1994
    Isabel, a teenager in Guatemala recently married, wants to become a teacher.
Omar Castaneda, *Among the Volcanoes*, 1991
    Isabel, a teenager in Guatemala, must quit school to take care of her ill mother.
Gloria Velasquez, *Juanita Fights the School Board*, 1994
    Juanita is expelled from high school and with help from her friends fights back.
Nicholasa Mohr, *Nilda: A Novel*, 1973
    These autobiographical stories portray the life of a Puerto Rican Girl living in the barrio of New York City.
Alma Flor Ada, *Where the Flame Trees Bloom*, 1994
    These eleven stories describe the author's growing up in Cuba.

649

IRENE BELTRAN HERNANDEZ, Mexican American

Heartbeat, Drumbeat
(Houston: Arte Publico Press, 1992)

Subject(s): Spiritualism; Coming of Age; Rituals
Age range(s): Grades 7-12
Major character(s): Morgana Cruz, Teenager; Eagle Eyes, Lawyer, Native American (Navajo)
Time period(s): 1990s
Locale(s): United States

Summary: Morgana Cruz is caught between the worlds of her Navajo mother and her Mexican father. She is having difficulty finding her cultural identity and weaves through several personal and cultural conflicts. When her Navajo spiritual teacher dies, she is brought closer to her Native American heritage through a mysterious man named Eagle Eyes, a young Indian lawyer seeking his own identity.

Where it's reviewed:
Publishers Weekly, June 29, 1992, page 64
Western American Literature, August 1994, page 158

Other books by the same author:
Across the Great River, 1989

Other books you might like:
Sandra Cisneros, *The House on Mango Street*, 1983
    A young Mexican American girl grows up in an urban setting.
Nicholasa Mohr, *Nilda: A Novel*, 1973
    This work is about the life of a Puerto Rican girl in the Spanish barrio of New York City.
Diane Gonzales Bertrand, *Sweet Fifteen*, 1995
    A young girl celebrates her quinceano and mourns the death of her father.
Gloria Velasquez, *Maya's Divided World*, 1995
    Maya's happy high school world comes apart when her parents announce their divorce.

Gloria Velasquez, *Juanita Fights the School Board*, 1994
Juanita is expelled from school and with the help of a friend fights back.

Karen Papagapitos, *Socorro, Daughter of the Desert*, 1993
The family of eight-year-old Socorro are farm workers and she helps out the family as much as she can. When her father becomes ill, Socorro makes tortillas for her mother to sell in the fields.

650

IRENE BELTRAN HERNANDEZ, Mexican American

The Secret of Two Brothers

(Houston, TX: Pinata Books, 1995)

Subject(s): Family; Child Abuse; Brothers
Age range(s): Grades 6-9
Major character(s): Beaver Torres, Prisoner (former), Brother, Chicano; Cande Torres, Teenager, Brother, Chicano
Time period(s): 1990s
Locale(s): San Antonio, Texas

Summary: Beaver, returning home after doing time in state prison, tries to create a decent life for himself and his younger brother Cande. Cande has been abused by their father and then left to fend for himself. This novel follows Beaver and Cande as they navigate around barriers, bad memories, and temptations, with their love for each other making them strong.

Other books by the same author:
Across the Great River, 1989
Heartbeat, Drumbeat, 1992

Other books you might like:
Abraham Rodriguez Jr., *The Boy Without a Flag: Tales of the South Bronx*, 1992
Collection of short stories about the problems of young Puerto Ricans in the Bronx.

Danny Santiago, *Famous All Over Town*, 1984
Chato Medina, a teenager who lives in the Chicano barrio of Los Angeles, is trying to beat the odds that are stacked against him.

Gary Soto, *Jesse*, 1994
Brothers, Jesse and Abel, move out of their parents home to live alone and attend junior college.

Gil C. Alicea, *The Air Down Here: True Tales from a South Bronx Boyhood*, 1995
Autobiographical stories and essays about living in the Bronx.

Jim Sagel, *Where the Cinnamon Winds Blow = Donde Soplan Los Vientos de Canela*, 1993
A magical fantasy novel about 10-year-old Tomas' relationship with his eccentric *Tia Zulema* and his attempts to reconcile his feelings for the death of his father.

651

JUAN FELIPE HERRERA, Mexican American
ELLY SIMMONS, Illustrator

Calling the Doves = El Canto de las Palomas

(San Francisco, CA: Children's Book Press, 1995)

Subject(s): Growing Up; Farm Life; Family
Age range(s): Grades K-2
Time period(s): 1950s
Locale(s): California

Summary: This book depicts the experiences of the author as a young boy growing up as a farm worker in the fields and valleys of California picking grapes. It was his hardworking parents who inspired him with songs and poetry, and he grew up to be a writer and poet. He remembers his mother singing and his father telling stories.

About this book: Spanish/English bilingual format.

Where it's reviewed:
School Library Journal, February 1996, page 128
Booklist, January 1, 1996, page 823
School Library Journal, December 1995, page 97

Other books by the same author:
Exiles of Desire, 1983
Facegames: Poems, 1987
Memoria(s) from an Exile's Notebook of the Future, 1993
The Roots of a Thousand Embraces: Dialogues, 1994
Akrilica, 1989

Other books you might like:
Carmen Lomas Garza, *Family Pictures = Cuadros de Familia*, 1990
Carmen Lomas Garza, a well-known Chicana artist, presents beautiful and detailed paintings of her childhood in a Texas border town.

Arthur Dorros, *Radio Man = Don Radio: A Story in English and Spanish*, 1993
This beautifully illustrated story is about Diego, who relies on his radio for companionship, and his family who are migrant farm workers.

Gloria Anzaldua, *Friends From the Other Side/Amigos del Otro Lado*, 1993
Prietita helps an undocumented boy and his family hide from the "migra."

Alma Flor Ada, *My Name Is Maria Isabel*, 1993
Maria Isabel Salazar Lopez is proud of her name and the fact that she is named after a relative whom she loves, but when she begins a new school her teacher changes her name.

Karen Papagapitos, *Socorro, Daughter of the Desert*, 1993
The family of eight-year-old Socorro are farm workers and she helps out the family as much as she can. When her father becomes ill, Socorro makes tortillas for her mother to sell in the fields.

Karen Papagapitos, *Jose's Basket*, 1990
Because Jose comes from a migrant farm-working family, school starts later and ends earlier for him than for most students. His teacher understands and gives him a special gift.

652

JUAN FELIPE HERRERA, Mexican American

Night Train to Tuxtla
(Tucson, AZ: The University of Arizona Press, 1994)

Subject(s): Poetry; Prose; Short Stories
Age range(s): Grades 10-Adult
Time period(s): 20th century (1960-1994)
Locale(s): California (some stories take place in Mexico and Central America)

Summary: Though primarily a poet, this powerful collection of Juan Felipe Herrera includes both poetry and short prose pieces that deal with a vast array of subjects, from Rodney King, and AIDs, to zoot suits. The themes presented here have been a driving force in nearly three decades of writing. One section of the book is devoted to what Herrera calls ''the swashbuckling Chicano sixties'' and another to unearthing stories about the Chicano and Latin American experience. The author is looking into new ways of speaking-writing.

Where it's reviewed:
Library Journal, August 1994, page 86
World Literature Today, Summer 1995, page 589

Other books by the same author:
Exiles of Desire, 1983
Facegames: Poems, 1987
Memoria(s) from an Exile's Notebook of the Future, 1993
The Roots of a Thousand Embraces: Dialogues, 1994
Akrilica, 1989

Other books you might like:
Ray Gonzalez, *Memory Fever: A Journey Beyond El Paso del Norte*, 1993
 This collection contains essays and vignettes about growing up in the 60's in El Paso and the surrounding desert.
Rudolfo Anaya, *Aztlan: Essays on the Chicano Homeland*, 1989
 Essays by various Chicano authors on history, ethnic identity, and religion.
Jose Antonio Burciaga, *Spilling the Beans: Loteria Chicana*, 1995
 A series of essays, many humorous, recounting experiences from the author's childhood, that explore aspects of Chicano culture.
Gary Soto, *Pieces of the Heart: New Chicano Fiction*, 1993
 Collection of short stories by contemporary Chicano writers.
Rudolfo A. Anaya, *Cuentos Chicanos: A Short Story Anthology*, 1984
 An early collection of short stories by Chicano writers.
Tiffany Ana Lopez, *Growing Up Chicano*, 1993
 Short stories by Chicano writers about growing up in the U.S.

653

DENIS LYNN DALY HEYCK, Editor

Barrios and Borderlands: Cultures of Latinos and Latinas in the United States
(New York: Routledge, 1994)

Subject(s): Anthology
Age range(s): Grades 10-Adult
Locale(s): United States

Summary: This anthology contains a diverse collection of short stories, poetry, prose, and nonfiction, focusing on the cultural history of Latinos living in the United States. Many contributors, such as Sandra Cisneros, Victor Villasenor, Rudolfo Anaya and Judith Ortiz Cofer, are well-known, while others are new voices. The anthology is divided into sections which focus on themes of family, religion, community, the arts, migration, exile, and cultural identity.

Where it's reviewed:
Library Journal, November 1, 1994, page 91

Other books by the same author:
Life Stories of the Nicaraguan Revolution, 1990

Other books you might like:
Gary D. Keller, *Hispanics in the U.S.: An Anthology of Creative Literature. Vol. 2*, 1982
 This collection of poetry and short stories is by Latino writers.
Nicolas Kanellos, *Short Fiction by Hispanic Writers of the United States*, 1993
 This collection of short stories is by Latino writers.
Harold Augenbraum, *Growing Up Latino: Memoirs and Stories*, 1993
 Twenty-five Latinos write stories about growing up in the U.S.
Ray Gonzalez, *Currents From the Dancing River: Contemporary Latino Fiction, Nonfiction, and Poetry*, 1994
 This is a collection of short stories.
Delia Poey, *Iguana Dreams: New Latino Fiction*, 1992
 This anthology of creative fiction is by Latino writers in the U.S.
Roberta Fernandez, *In Other Words: Literature by Latinas in the U.S.*, 1994
 This collection of short fiction is by Latinas in the U.S.

654

OSCAR HIJUELOS, Cuban American

The Fourteen Sisters of Emilio Montez O'Brien: A Novel
(New York: Farrar, Straus and Giroux, 1993)

Subject(s): Family Relations; Intergenerational Saga
Age range(s): Grades 10-Adult
Major character(s): Emilio Montez O'Brien, Young Man, Irish Cuban
Time period(s): 20th century (1902-1987)
Locale(s): California; Cuba

Summary: Mariela Montez, Cuban, and her Irish husband Nelson O'Brien move to Cobbleton, Pennsylvania at the turn of the century. There she has fourteen children, Margarita in 1902, and last in 1925, Emilio, the only son. This intergenerational saga follows the lives, fortunes and misfortunes, trips to Cuba and back, of the Montez O'Brien family.

Where it's reviewed:
Library Journal, June 1, 1993, page 211
Time, March 29, 1993, page 63
Times Literary Supplement, August 6, 1993, page 19
World Literature Today, Winter 1994, page 127
New Stateman & Society, July 30, 1993, page 39

Other books by the same author:
The Mambo Kings Play Songs of Love, 1989
Mr. Ives' Christmas, 1995
Our House in the Last World: A Novel, 1983

Other books you might like:
Victor Villasenor, *Rain of Gold*, 1991
In this massive novel the author weaves the separate stories of two families, the Gomezs and Villasenors, as they live in Mexico and later migrate to the U.S.
Rosario Ferre, *The House on the Lagoon*, 1995
This is an intergenerational story of an upper class family living in Ponce, Puerto Rico during the early twentieth century.
Cristina Garcia, *Dreaming in Cuban, A Novel*, 1992
This novel interweaves the stories of three generations of Cuban women and their different responses to the Cuban revolution.
Sylvia Lopez-Medina, *Cantora: A Novel*, 1992
This novel tells the story of four generations of women in Mexico and their lives in America at the turn of the 20th century.
Denise Chavez, *Face of an Angel*, 1994
This intergenerational novel explores the life of a family in Agua Oscura, a fictional town, in New Mexico.
Virgil Suarez, *Havana Thursdays: A Novel*, 1995
This is the story of two sisters, their daughters, and how they represent two different manners of dealing with the changes encountered through immigration from a Latino culture.
Julia Alvarez, *How the Garcia Girls Lost Their Accents*, 1991
This episodic novel concerns a family with four daughters who move to the U.S., where the daughters become Americanized.

655

OSCAR HIJUELOS, Cuban American

The Mambo Kings Play Songs of Love
(New York: Farrar, Straus, Giroux, 1989)

Subject(s): Music; Romance; Brothers
Age range(s): Grades 10-Adult
Major character(s): Cesar Castillo, Musician, Brother (older brother), Cuban; Nestor Castillo, Musician (trumpeter), Brother (younger brother), Cuban
Time period(s): 20th century (1949-1980)
Locale(s): New York, New York

Summary: The Castillo brothers, two young musicians, make their way from Havana to New York to play music in the era of the mambo. They become night stars of the dance halls; the Mambo Kings in their moment of youth. Cesar, the bandleader handles the business and Nestor, the romantic writes the songs. A highlight of their career is appearing on the *I Love Lucy* television show on the invitation of Desi Arnaz. Three decades later, they reminisce with nostalgia and deep affection. Their story is told through the eyes of Eugenio, the son of Nestor.

Where it's reviewed:
Newsweek, August 21, 1989, page 60
Publishers Weekly, June 2, 1989, page 68
Time, August 14, 1989, page 68

Awards the book has won:
Pulitzer Prize, 1990

Other books by the same author:
The Fourteen Sisters of Emilio Montez O'Brien: A Novel, 1993
Our House in the Last World: A Novel, 1983
Mr. Ives' Christmas, 1995

Other books you might like:
Jaime Manrique, *Latin Moon in Manhattan*, 1992
This novel presents bizarre characters, plots and sub-plots, and a vivid depiction of Columbian American culture in Little Colombia Jackson Heights.
Luis Rafael Sanchez, *Macho Camacho's Beat*, 1980
Macho Camacho's beat is an inane song that catches the tropical beats of the paradise island of Puerto Rico.
Maria Espinosa, *Dark Plums*, 1995
Adrianne, a young girl from Texas, searches for love and self in Manhattan, but ends up sleeping with strangers and falling into an abusive relationship.
Beatriz Rivera, *African Passions and Other Stories*, 1995
A collection of short stories focusing on women's obsessive search for love and success, narrated with with humor, passion, and satire.
Himilce Novas, *Mangos, Bananas, and Coconuts: A Cuban Love Story*, 1996
This tale of a magical yet real love story is an ancient tale, beginning with the love of a man and a woman from different social classes, and the story of the fate of their children.

656

OSCAR HIJUELOS, Cuban American

Mr. Ives' Christmas
(New York: HarperCollins Publishers, 1995)

Subject(s): Murder; Family; Christmas
Age range(s): Grades 10-Adult
Major character(s): Edward Ives, Artist (commercial), Father
Time period(s): 20th century (1950-1995)
Locale(s): New York, New York

Summary: Edward Ives, a New York commercial artist, mourns the loss of his beloved son, Robert, a Roman Catholic seminarian-to-be who was shot a few days before Christmas. Edward eventually begins to exchange letters with his son's killer, a young Puerto Rican who will soon be released from prison. This delicately drawn, suspenseful, and deeply somber, novel examines Edward's life prior to and following that one bloody moment and reveals his resurrection from his grave of grief.

Where it's reviewed:
Library Journal, November 1, 1995, page 106
Publishers Weekly, September 25, 1995, page 42
Times Literary Supplement, December 8, 1995, page 20

Other books by the same author:
The Fourteen Sisters of Emilio Montez O'Brien: A Novel, 1993
Our House in the Last World: A Novel, 1983
The Mambo Kings Play Songs of Love, 1989

Other books you might like:
Denise Chavez, *Face of an Angel*, 1994
　　The story of Soveida, who has worked as a waitress for over twenty years and is writing a book, titled *The Book of Service*, that shows women constantly providing service to others.
Victor Villasenor, *Rain of Gold*, 1991
　　Intergenerational saga of the authors' family's migration from Mexico to the U.S.
Maria Espinosa, *Dark Plums*, 1995
　　Adrianne, a young girl from Texas, begins a difficult search for love and self in Manhattan.
Yvonne V. Sapia, *Valentino's Hair*, 1991
　　Rudolph Valentino comes into the life of Facundo Nieves and changes it forever when Nieves saves the hair and its power haunts him until his own death.
Jose Yglesias, *Break-In*, 1996
　　Rudy Pardo comes home to find a young, tall, thin black man rifling through his possessions, and this intrusion brings out his racial prejudices.
Alejandro Morales, *Death of an Anglo*, 1988
　　This complicated novel is the story of Logan, a rebellious and idealistic young doctor who attempts to improve the lives of the Chicano residents of his town.

657

ROLANDO HINOJOSA, Mexican American

Becky and Her Friends

(Houston, TX: Arte Publico Press, 1990)

Series: Klail City Death Trip
Subject(s): Women; Identity; Family Relations
Age range(s): Grades 10-Adult
Major character(s): Becky Escobar, Young Woman, Texas Mexican
Time period(s): 20th century (1939-1980)
Locale(s): Klail City, Texas

Summary: Narrated by many of her friends, this novel focuses on the strong-willed Becky Escobar. She is painted as a modern, upwardly-mobile woman who at age thirty-five decides to divorce her husband Ira Escobar. In this novel Hinojosa reveals women's culture and language, and examines sex and male-female relationships. The author continues his famous

series of novels, which follow generations of Anglos and Mexicans in the fictional town of Klail City, Texas.

About this book: Klail City Death Trip series.

Where it's reviewed:
World Literature Today, Spring 1991, page 303

Other books by the same author:
Claros Varones de Belken = Fair Gentlemen of Belken County, 1986
Dear Rafe, 1995
Klail City: A Novel, 1987
The Useless Servants, 1993
Rites and Witnesses: A Comedy, 1982

Other books you might like:
Denise Chavez, *The Last of the Menu Girls*, 1986
　　An adolescent Chicana girl from southern New Mexico is looking for her place, identity, and womanhood in this collection of interrelated short stories.
Norma Elia Cantu, *Canicula: Snapshots of a Girlhood en la Frontera*, 1995
　　A collection, with photos, of short stories and vignettes of a young girl growing up along the Texas border.
Helena Maria Viramontes, *The Moths and Other Stories*, 1985
　　This early collection of stories by a Chicana writer deals with feminist themes, including biology, religion, and culture.
Mary Helen Ponce, *Taking Control*, 1987
　　This collection of stories portrays the domestic and economic oppression of Mexican and Chicana women in the U.S.
Roberta Fernandez, *Itaglio: Novel in Six Stories*, 1990
　　A novel related in six stories, each about an extraordinary woman that serves as a role model for the young narrator.
Denise Chavez, *Face of an Angel*, 1994
　　Humorously and sensuously related, this long novel shows, among other things, how women constantly provide service to others, particularly to men.
Virgil Suarez, *Havana Thursdays: A Novel*, 1995
　　This is the story of two sisters, their daughters, and how they represent two different manners of dealing with the changes encountered through immigration from a Latino culture.

658

ROLANDO HINOJOSA, Mexican American

Claros Varones de Belken = Fair Gentlemen of Belken County

(Tempe, AZ: Bilingual Press, 1986)

Series: Klail City Death Trip
Subject(s): Race Relations; Social Classes; Friendship
Age range(s): Grades 10-Adult
Major character(s): Rafa Buenrostro, Young Man, Veteran, Chicano
Time period(s): 1950s
Locale(s): Klail City, Texas

Summary: This is part four of Hinojosa's *Klail City Death Trip* series and continues the humorous adventures of Rafa

Buenrostro and Jehu Malacara. This novel paints a portrait of Belken County, a South Texas border community, during the 1950s. Rafe returns from the Korean War and Jehu becomes a missionary. Hinojosa reproduces a landscape and an era, always showing the changes threatening the Belken world by the takeover of an Anglo world, with his humorous and tragicomic cast of characters.

About this book: Translated from the Spanish by Julia Cruz.

Where it's reviewed:
The Americas Review, Summer 1993, page 89

Other books by the same author:
Becky and Her Friends, 1990
Klail City: A Novel, 1986
Dear Rafe, 1985
Korean Love Songs From Klail City Death Trip
The Useless Servants, 1993

Other books you might like:
Norma Elia Cantu, *Canicula: Snapshots of a Girlhood en la Frontera*, 1995
  A collection, with photos, of short stories and vignettes of a young girl growing up along the Texas border.
Americo Paredes, *The Hammon and the Beans and Other Stories*, 1994
  Set in the southern Texas border region, this collection of short stories explores the cultural conflict that has dominated that area since the U.S.-Mexican War.
Jesus Salvador Trevino, *The Fabulous Sinkhole and Other Stories*, 1995
  This first story collection by Trevino, a screenwriter and director, is an entertaining creation of Mexican and Chicano characters, that take place in a fictional town, Arroyo Grande, in Texas.
Aristeo Brito, *The Devil in Texas = El Diablo en Texas*, 1990
  The devil comes to the border town of Presidio, Texas in this important novel that describes the Anglo destruction of a Chicano world.
Lionel G. Garcia, *I Can Hear the Cowbells Ring*, 1994
  A collection of delightful autobiographical vignettes that reconstruct life in a small rural town of southern Texas.
Miguel Mendez, *Pilgrims in Aztlan*, 1992
  A Chicano classic, first published in Spanish, this is about an aging veteran of the Mexican Revolution who now washes cars for tourists in Tijuana and listens to their stories.

659

ROLANDO HINOJOSA, Mexican American

Klail City: A Novel

(Houston, TX: Arte Publico Press, 1987)

Series: Klail City Death Trip
Subject(s): Social Classes; Race Relations; Storytelling
Age range(s): Grades 10-Adult
Major character(s): Rafe Buenrostro, Young Man (narrator), Texas Mexican
Time period(s): 20th century (1900-1984)
Locale(s): Klail City, Texas

Summary: The pivotal novel in Hinojosa's Klail City Death Trip series, this one examines power relations as they are expressed by the Texas Mexicans and the Texas Anglos in the lower Rio Grande Valley. Hinojosa uses four generations of articulate storytellers with multiple viewpoints to narrate Chicano culture. Their stories of tragic realism, alienation, and desire are intense and riveting.

About this book: This novel was published in Spanish as *Klail City y Sus Alrededores* in 1976 and won Cuba's Casa de las Americas prize for 1976.

Where it's reviewed:
The Americas Review, Summer 1993, page 89

Other books by the same author:
Becky and Her Friends, 1990
Claros Varones de Belken = Fair Gentlemen of Belken County, 1986
Dear Rafe, 1985
Korean Love Songs From Klail City Death Trip, 1978
The Useless Servants, 1993

Other books you might like:
Lionel G. Garcia, *I Can Hear the Cowbells Ring*, 1994
  A collection of delightful autobiographical vignettes that, with humor and nostalgia, reconstruct life in a small rural town of southern Texas.
Americo Paredes, *The Hammon and the Beans and Other Stories*, 1994
  Set in the southern Texas border region, this collection of short stories explores the cultural conflict that has dominated that area since the U.S.-Mexican War.
Josephina Niggli, *Mexican Village*, 1994
  This important collection of ten interrelated short stories is about the lives of the people of a small Mexican town, Hidalgo, and was first published in 1945.
Aristeo Brito, *The Devil in Texas = El Diablo en Texas*, 1990
  The devil comes to the border town of Presidio, Texas in this important novel that describes the Anglo destruction of a Chicano world.
Louie Garcia Robinson, *The Devil, Delfina Varela, and the Used Chevy*, 1993
  Comical and political, this novel is about the Latino community in San Francisco's Mission District in the 1990s.
Genaro Gonzalez, *Rainbow's End*, 1988
  This adventure novel presents dangerous border crossings, confrontations with a magician, and drug smuggling in the lives of the Cavazos family in the lower Rio Grande area of Texas.

660

ROLANDO HINOJOSA, Mexican American

The Useless Servants

(Houston, TX: Arte Publico Press, 1993)

Subject(s): War; Military Life; Veterans
Age range(s): Grades 10-Adult
Major character(s): Rafe Buenrostro, Military Personnel (soldier), Veteran, Texas Mexican
Time period(s): 1950s
Locale(s): Republic of Korea

Summary: Set almost entirely in Korea, this novel is made up of the diary entries of Rafe Buenrostro as he is stationed in Korea during the war. The diary becomes a survival mechanism for Rafe where he writes about his experiences and his daily duties as a soldier. Detailing the horrors of war, Rafe's chronicle connects him to his later life in Klail City and his concepts of home and identity. As part of the Klail City Death Trip series this war novel is only one piece of the whole and must be read within the context of the whole Texas border series.

Where it's reviewed:
Library Journal, August, 1993, page 151
MELUS, Spring 1995, page 123
Publishers Weekly, July 12, 1993, page 69
World Literature Today, Winter 1995, page 139

Other books by the same author:
Claros Varones de Belken = Fair Gentlemen of Belken County, 1986
Dear Rafe, 1995
Klail City: A Novel, 1987
Becky and Her Friends, 1990
Rites and Witnesses: A Comedy, 1982

Other books you might like:
Ed Vega, *Casualty Report*, 1991
    Short stories about Latino life in New York, this collection includes one about a frustrated Vietnam veteran.
Joe Rodriguez, *The Oddsplayer*, 1988
    In this novel about the Vietnam war, Black and Latino soldiers fight the enemy on the battlefield and also within their own ranks.
Daniel Cano, *Shifting Loyalties*, 1995
    The lives of five Chicano soldiers and their families before, during and after the Vietnam War are explored in this novel.
Alejandro Murguia, *Southern Front*, 1990
    Short stories about the combat zone, the Nicaraguan-Costa Rican border, these are set during the rebellion against the Somoza regime in the late 1970s.
Americo Paredes, *The Hammon and the Beans and Other Stories*, 1994
    Set in the southern Texas border region, this collection of short stories explores the cultural conflict that has dominated that area since the U.S.-Mexican War.
Alejandro Grattan-Dominguez, *The Dark Side of the Dream*, 1995
    A historical novel, this is set right after the outbreak of World War II, when two cousins and their families migrate from Chihuahua to El Paso.

661

ROLANDO HINOJOSA, Mexican American

The Valley

(Tempe, AZ: Bilingual Review Press,1983)

Series: Klail City Death Trip
Subject(s): Short Stories; Social Classes; Prejudice
Age range(s): Grades 10-Adult
Time period(s): 20th century (1920-1950)
Locale(s): Klail City, Texas

Summary: The first volume in Hinojosa's Klail City Death Trip series, this is re-written in English by Hinojosa. This collection of sketches, featuring various viewpoints from characters living in Belken County, Texas, interprets the Chicano culture of the region. The text is divided into four major parts with smaller pieces within each section. This structure creates a composite of the voices of the community, and provides a wide panoramic view of the vital strength of a people, which Hinojosa captures in the many levels of Chicano linguistic expression. It was the Anglo world, assisted by Chicano sellouts, that took over the county and this story is told in the Death Trip series.

About this book: Published in Spanish as *Estampas del Valle y Othras Obrs* in 1973 and received the Premio Quinto Sol Award in 1972.

Other books by the same author:
Becky and Her Friends, 1990
Dear Rafe, 1985
Klail City: A Novel, 1987
The Useless Servants, 1993
Claros Varones de Belken = Fair Gentlemen of Belken County, 1986

Other books you might like:
Lionel G. Garcia, *I Can Hear the Cowbells Ring*, 1994
    With humour and nostalgia, this collection of delightful autobiographical vignettes reconstruct life in a small rural town in southern Texas.
Americo Paredes, *The Hammon and the Beans and Other Stories*, 1994
    Set in the southern Texas border region, this collection of short stories explores the cultural conflict that has dominated that area since the U.S.-Mexican War.
Gloria Lopez-Stafford, *A Place in El Paso: A Mexican American Childhood*, 1996
    A bittersweet narrative describing the early childhood of the author living in the *projects* of El Paso during World War II.
Norma Elia Cantu, *Canicula: Snapshots of a Girlhood en la Frontera*, 1995
    A collection, with photos, of short stories and vignettes of a young girl growing up along the Texas border.
Aristeo Brito, *The Devil in Texas = El Diablo en Texas*, 1990
    The devil comes to the border town of Presidio, Texas in this important novel that describes the Anglo destruction of a Chicano world.
Jesus Salvador Trevino, *The Fabulous Sinkhole and Other Stories*, 1995
    This first story collection by Trevino, a screenwriter and director, is an entertaining creation of Mexican and Chicano characters that take place in a fictional town, Arroyo Grande, in Texas.
Americo Paredes, *George Washington Gomez*, 1990
    As he grows up, George Washington Gomez struggles with racism, abuse, and cultural and political clashes, while other Texas Mexicans fight to preserve their language and culture.

662

ASUNCION HORNO-DELGADO, Editor, Puerto Rican
ELIANA ORTEGA, Co-Editor, Cuban American

Breaking Boundaries: Latina Writing and Critical Readings

(Amherst, MA: The University of Massachusetts Press, 1989)

Subject(s): Women; Anthology
Age range(s): Grades 10-Adult
Time period(s): 1980s
Locale(s): United States

Summary: This volume of literature and literary criticism addresses the extensive body of literature written by Latina women that is virtually unrecognized by institutions of power. This collection attempts to make this literature visible and accessible, to critically evaluate the literary works, and to reevaluate literary categories.

Where it's reviewed:
College Literature, February 1991, page 103
Signs, Winter 1991, page 382

Other books by the same author:
Infinite Divisions: An Anthology of Chicana Literature, 1993
De Cal y Arena, 1975
Siete Poetas, 1978

Other books you might like:
Roberta Fernandez, *In Other Words: Literature by Latinas in the U.S.*, 1994
  This anthology of literature is by Latinas in the U.S.
Lillian Castillo-Speed, *Latina: Women's Voices from the Borderlands*, 1995
  This collection of short stories is by Latinas.
Bryce Milligan, *Daughters of the Fifth Sun: A Collection of Latina Fiction and Poetry*, 1995
  This anthology of poetry and short stories is by Latinas in the U.S.
Evangelina Vigil, *Woman of Her Word: Hispanic Women Write*, 1983
  This early collection of creative literature is by Latinas in U.S.
Tey Diana Rebolledo, *Las Mujeres Hablan*, 1988
  This collection of short stories and poetry is by Chicanas from New Mexico.
Tey Diana Rebolledo, *Infinite Divisions: An Anthology of Chicana Literature*, 1993
  This extensive anthology of Chicana literature is from the 19th century to the present.

663

CAROLINA HOSPITAL, Editor, Cuban American

Cuban American Writers: Los Atrevidos

(Princeton, NJ: Linden Lane Press, 1988)

Subject(s): Short Stories; Anthology; Poetry
Age range(s): Grades 10-Adult
Time period(s): 1980s
Locale(s): United States (several stories take place in Florida)

Summary: This collection of short stories and poetry by twelve Cuban American writers, all of whom were born in Cuba and came to the U.S. very young, examine themes of cultural collision, history, and language, and the exile consciousness. All of them write primarily in English yet consider themselves Cuban writers, and reflect their ties to a Latin American literary cultural tradition. These stories and excerpts from novels also reveal North American cultural traditions. The title of this book *Los Atrevidos* translates to *the daring ones*, coined because these authors are taking a risk and showing a sense of daringness in their writings.

Where it's reviewed:
Americas Review, Summer 1990, page 118

Other books you might like:
Gary D. Keller, *Hispanics in the U.S.: An Anthology of Creative Literature*, 1982
  An anthology of short stories and other writings by Latinos in the U.S.
Nicolas Kanellos, *Short Fiction by Hispanic Writers of the United States*, 1993
  This collection of short stories is by Latinos in the U.S.
Ray Gonzalez, *Currents From the Dancing River: Contemporary Latino Fiction, Nonfiction, and Poetry*, 1994
  This is a collection of short stories and other writings by Latinos in the U.S.
Harold Augenbraum, *Growing Up Latino: Memoirs and Stories*, 1993
  This collection of short stories is by Latino writers.
Faythe Turner, *Puerto Rican Writers at Home in the U.S.A.: An Anthology*, 1991
  This collection of short stories is about living in the U.S. and Puerto Rico.
Ruth Behar, *Bridges to Cuba = Puentes a Cuba*, 1995
  A collection of short stories, poems, and essays, exhibiting literary and intellectual boundaries to show the complexity of culture and identity by Cuban American writers.

664

ARTURO ISLAS, Mexican American

La Mollie and the King of Tears

(Albuquerque, NM: University of New Mexico Press, 1996)

Subject(s): Coming of Age; City Life; Identity
Age range(s): Grades 10-Adult
Major character(s): Louie Mendoza, Musician (jazz musician), Chicano
Time period(s): 1970s (1973)
Locale(s): San Francisco, California

Summary: Louie Mendoza, a jazz musician, finds himself at San Francisco General Hospital, waiting to hear the diagnosis of his liver. In the unique street language of Chicanos, he narrates the story of his life to a stranger, recounting his experiences on the way to the hospital, a shooting, a broken leg, his love for a rich white woman, La Mollie, and what brought him to this point in his life. Shakespeare had a great influence in his life, and *The King of Tears* of the title refers both to King Lear and to Louie.

About this book: This manuscript was completed before Arturo Islas died in 1991.

Where it's reviewed:
San Francisco Examiner & Chronicle, September 22, 1969, page 8

Other books by the same author:
The Rain God: A Desert Tale, 1984
Migrant Souls: A Novel, 1990

Other books you might like:
Luis Alberto Urrea, *In Search of Snow*, 1994
Mike McGirk, a blue collar Don Quixote, searches for love and life in the Arizona desert, and learns about family from Bobo Garcia.
Jesus Salvador Trevino, *The Fabulous Sinkhole and Other Stories*, 1995
This first story collection by Trevino, a screenwriter and director, is an entertaining creation of Mexican and Chicano characters, that take place in a fictional town, Arroyo Grande, in Texas.
Dagoberto Gilb, *The Last Known Residence of Micke Acuna*, 1994
Mickey Acuna is waiting for something, something arriving through the mail, as he dwells at the YMCA in El Paso.
Oscar Zeta Acosta, *The Autobiography of a Brown Buffalo*, 1972
Partly novel, and very much an autobiographical work, the author a famous Robin Hood type Chicano lawyer with an appetite for life on the edge examines his life.
Jose Antonio Burciaga, *Spilling the Beans: Loteria Chicana*, 1995
A series of essays, many humorous, recounting experiences from the author's childhood in Texas.
Alfredo Vea Jr., *The Silver Cloud Cafe*, 1996
In this complicated novel, set in California, Zeferino Del Campo defends a hunchback midget accused of murder.

665

ARTURO ISLAS, Mexican American

Migrant Souls: A Novel

(New York: William Morrow and Company, 1990)

Subject(s): Intergenerational Saga; Homosexuality/Lesbianism; Identity
Age range(s): Grades 10-Adult
Major character(s): Josie Salazar, Divorced Person, Mexican American; Miguel Chico Angel, Homosexual, Writer, Mexican American
Time period(s): 1980s
Locale(s): Texas

Summary: Josie Salazar returns to her Texas home town after her husband leaves her in California. The reasons for her divorce are gradually unraveled in this novel about three generations of the Angel extended family. This is the second novel of a projected trilogy that first introduced the Angel family in *The Rain God*. Josie's close and favorite cousin, Miguel Chico, has become a novelist in California, and con-

tinues to struggle to accept his biculturalism, along with his homosexuality.

Where it's reviewed:
Library Journal, February 1, 1990, page 106
Nation, March 5, 1990, page 313
Publishers Weekly, December 8, 1989, page 40

Other books by the same author:
The Rain God: A Desert Tale, 1984 (Border Regional Library Conference Best Fiction Award 1985)

Other books you might like:
Eliud Martinez, *Voice-Haunted Journey*, 1990
Miguel Velasquez, a professor at a university and a writer, explores an elaborate series of memories and fantasies about his family, as he flys in a plane across California.
Denise Chavez, *Face of an Angel*, 1994
A humorously and sensuously related long novel that among other things shows how women constantly provide service to others, particularly to men.
Richard Rodriguez, *Hunger of Memory: The Education of Richard Rodriguez, an Autobiography*, 1982
This is the story of the author's childhood and education, the difficult journey of a ''minority student'' who must become socially assimilated in order to enjoy academic success
Americo Paredes, *George Washington Gomez*, 1990
As he grows up, George Washington Gomez struggles with racism, abuse, and cultural and political clashes, while other Texas Mexicans fight to preserve their language and culture.
Gloria Lopez-Stafford, *A Place in El Paso: A Mexican American Childhood*, 1996
A bittersweet narrative describing the early childhood of the author living in the *projects* of El Paso during World War II.
Benjamin Alire Saenz, *Carry Me Like Water*, 1995
This involved contemporary novel has many interconnected characters, interracial and gay couples, and it takes place both in El Paso and Palo Alto.

666

ARTURO ISLAS, Mexican American

The Rain God: A Desert Tale

(Palo Alto, CA: Alexandrian Press, 1984)

Subject(s): Short Stories; Family; Religion
Age range(s): Grades 10-Adult
Major character(s): Miguel Angel, Mexican American
Time period(s): 20th century (1940-1984)
Locale(s): Southwest (fictional town in the desert)

Summary: Organized into six parts with different time sequences and flashbacks, this novel presents three generations of the Angel family. They all struggle to live and die with dignity and to understand the family's ghosts. Miguel Angel, also called Miguel Chico, is caught between his Mexican Catholic heritage and his prestigious American education, as he explores the lives of his family members, each of whom has been a vital force in his own life.

About this book: Considered a classic in Chicano literature.

Where it's reviewed:
American Literature, June 1990, page 284

Other books by the same author:
Migrant Souls: A Novel, 1990

Other books you might like:
Alberto Alvaro Rios, *Pig Cookies and Other Stories*, 1995
   A set of interlocking stories that explores the inhabitants of
   a small Mexican village.
Denise Chavez, *Face of an Angel*, 1994
   A humorously and sensuously related novel that shows
   how women constantly provide service to others, particu-
   larly to men.
Rudolfo Anaya, *Bless Me, Ultima*, 1972
   A young boy's beliefs are challenged as he grows up in a
   small town in New Mexico.
Alfredo Vea Jr., *La Maravilla*, 1993
   In this extraordinary novel, Buckeye Road, a world of
   marvels in the desert outside the Phoenix city limits is
   portrayed, an American outback caught between many cul-
   tures.
Richard Rodriguez, *Hunger of Memory: The Education of
Richard Rodriguez, an Autobiography*, 1982
   The story of the author's childhood and education, the
   difficult journey of a *minority student* who must become
   socially assimilated in order to enjoy academic success.
Ofelia Dumas Lachtman, *A Shell for Angela*, 1995
   When nine-year-old Angela Martin sees her father led
   away by immigration officials, she begins to deny her
   Mexican heritage.

667

TINA JUAREZ, Mexican American

Call No Man Master
(Houston, TX: Arte Publico Press, 1995)

Subject(s): Revolution; War; Historical
Age range(s): Grades 10-Adult
Major character(s): Carmen Rangel, Young Woman (mixed
   heritage), Mexican
Time period(s): 19th century (1810-1836)
Locale(s): Mexico; Texas

Summary: Intricately crafted, this historical novel is about a
young woman of mixed heritage, Spanish and Indian, and her
participation in the events that lead to Mexico's independence
from Spain. At age 16 she meets a "norteamericano" who is
committed to the independence movement and flees north
with him. The novel describes historical events and people,
revealing the influences leading to Mexico's freedom from
Spain, the colonization of Texas by Anglo settlers, and the
battle over the Alamo.

Where it's reviewed:
Publishers Weekly, March 6, 1995, page 61
New York Times Book Review, May 21, 1995, page 32

Other books you might like:
Nash Candelaria, *Not by the Sword*, 1982
   Taking place before the Mexican War of 1846, this novel
   shows the struggles taking place in New Mexico, with the

Rafa family, and with the collapse of the Mexican government.
Nash Candelaria, *Inheritance of Strangers*, 1985
   A sequel to *Not by the Sword*, this book covers the years
   after the Mexican War of 1846 to New Mexico statehood,
   presenting the struggles of the Rafa family against Anglo
   exploitation.
Gary D. Keller, *Zapata Lives!*, 1994
   The Mexican revolutionary leader Emiliano Zapato has
   risen from the dead, and he must lead his people in a
   struggle against economic and social oppression.
Daniel Cano, *Pepe Rios*, 1991
   In this historical novel about the Mexican Revolution of
   1910, Pepe Rios searches for peace amidst the chaos and
   violence of war.
Maria Amparo Ruiz de Burton, *Who Would Have Thought
It?*, 1995
   Originally published in 1872, this historical romance is
   about a young Mexican girl who eventually comes to live
   with a New England family.
Jose Barreiro, *The Indian Chronicles*, 1993
   Adopted by Christopher Columbus, Diego Colon, a Taino
   boy, keeps a journal where he describes events in his life
   from 1532-1535 and where he narrates the Indian's discovery of the Europeans.
Jouita Gonzales Mireles, *Caballero: A Historical Novel*, 1996
   Don Santiago is trying to maintain his family's Mexican
   customs and values amidst the Anglo encroachment on his
   homeland in the 1840s, but his daughters fall in love with
   American men.

668

GORDON KAHN

A Long Way from Home
(Tempe, AZ: Bilingual Press, 1989)

Series: Clasicos Chicanos
Subject(s): War; Politics; Communism
Age range(s): Grades 10-Adult
Major character(s): Gilberto Reyes, Young Man, Military Per-
   sonnel, Mexican American
Time period(s): 1950s
Locale(s): California; Mexico

Summary: Gordon Kahn was an important Hollywood screenwriter during the 1930s and 1940s. Written forty years before
it was published, this novel tells the story of Gilberto, a young
Chicano, who after his mother's death leaves the U.S. for
Mexico to find his only remaining family. He eventually
decides to stay in Mexico and joins the Mexican Army. The
novel depicts the political suppression during the McCarthy
period, and the treatment of ethnic minorities during the
1950s.

About this book: Published posthumously as part of Clasicos
Chicanos, the author is not a Chicano but the publishers found
it to be important in understanding Chicano culture and history.

Other books by the same author:
Hollywood on Trial: The Story of the 10 Who Were Indicted,
   1948

Other books you might like:

Ernesto Galarza, *Barrio Boy*, 1971
Autobiographical story of the early life, the flight from Mexico and the settling in Sacramento of a distinguished professor and author who wrote many works about Mexican agricultural workers.

Jose Antonio Villarreal, *Pocho*, 1959
This is the story of a Mexican family in the Santa Clara Valley of California before World War II and the assimilation of the son Richard Rubio.

Americo Paredes, *George Washington Gomez*, 1990
As he grows up, George Washington Gomez struggles with racism, abuse, and cultural and political clashes, while other Texas Mexicans fight to preserve their language and culture.

Ofelia Dumas Lachtman, *A Shell for Angela*, 1995
When nine-year-old Angela Martin sees her father led away by immigration officials, she begins to deny her Mexican heritage and she raises her children to be ignorant of their grandparents.

Miguel Mendez, *Pilgrims in Aztlan*, 1992
A Chicano classic, first published in Spanish, where an aging veteran of the Mexican Revolution washes cars for tourists while watching the people who come his way and listening to their stories.

Ron Arias, *The Road to Tamazunchale*, 1992
Don Fausto, old and nearing death in a Los Angeles barrio, decides to take a journey through time and space, from the Inca world to encounters with undocumented workers in California.

669

NICOLAS KANELLOS, Editor, Puerto Rican

Short Fiction by Hispanic Writers of the United States

(Houston: Arte Publico, 1993)

Subject(s): Anthology; Short Stories
Age range(s): Grades 10-Adult
Time period(s): 20th century (1940-1993)
Locale(s): United States (stories take place throughout the U.S.)

Summary: Well-known Cuban American, Mexican American, and Puerto Rican writers fill this collection with stories depicting Latino culture in all its complexity, while tackling the serious with humor.

Where it's reviewed:
Choice, July-August 1993, page 1771
Publishers Weekly, April 5, 1993, page 70

Other books you might like:

Harold Augenbraum, *Growing Up Latino: Memoirs and Stories*, 1993
This collection of short stories is by Latino writers.

Gary D. Keller, *Hispanics in the U.S.: An Anthology of Creative Literature*, 1982
This collection contains short stories by Latino writers in the U.S.

Ray Gonzalez, *Currents From the Dancing River: Contemporary Latino Fiction, Nonfiction, and Poetry*, 1994
This collection of short stories is by Latino writers in the U.S.

Delia Poey, *Iguana Dreams: New Latino Fiction*, 1992
This is an anthology of creative fiction by Latino writers in the U.S.

670

GARY D. KELLER, Editor, Mexican American
FRANCISCO JIMENEZ, Co-Editor, Mexican American

Hispanics in the U.S.: An Anthology of Creative Literature. Vol. 2

(Ypsilanti, MI: Bilingual Review/Press, 1982)

Subject(s): Short Stories; Anthology; Folklore
Age range(s): Grades 10-Adult
Time period(s): 1980s
Locale(s): United States

Summary: This collection of poetry and short stories, by Latino writers of the United States, reflects Latino values and lifestyles but is universal in theme. It is divided into such sections as ''The Immigrant Experience,'' ''Humor y Folklore,'' ''La Familia y la Religion,'' and ''La Hispana: Portraits and Self-Portraits.''

About this book: The literary success of volume I, published in 1980, prompted the publication of a second volume.

Other books by the same author:
Zapata Lives!, 1994
Zapata Rose in 1992 and Other Tales, 1992

Other books you might like:

Gary Soto, *Pieces of the Heart: New Chicano Fiction*, 1993
This collection of short stories is by Chicano writers.

Tiffany Ana Lopez, *Growing Up Chicano*, 1993
These short stories are by Chicano writers.

Harold Augenbraum, *Growing Up Latino: Memoirs and Stories*, 1993
This important collection of short stories is by Latino authors.

Nicolas Kanellos, *Short Fiction by Hispanic Writers of the United States*, 1993
Latino writers in the U.S. comprise this collection of creative literature.

Ray Gonzalez, *Currents From the Dancing River: Contemporary Latino Fiction, Nonfiction, and Poetry*, 1994
This collection contains short stories.

Delia Poey, *Iguana Dreams: New Latino Fiction*, 1992
This is an anthology of creative fiction by Latino writers in the U.S.

671

GARY D. KELLER, Mexican American

Zapata Lives!

(San Louis Obispo, CA: Maize Press, 1994)

Subject(s): Revolution; Oppression
Age range(s): Grades 10-Adult

Major character(s): Emiliano Zapata, Revolutionary, Zapotec Indian
Time period(s): 1990s (1994)
Locale(s): Mexico
Summary: The Mexican revolutionary leader Emiliano Zapata has risen from the dead, and he must lead his people in a struggle against economic and social oppression. This fictional account echoes the current political situation in southern Mexico.

About this book: A glossary of Spanish terms, photographs, and documents is appended.

Where it's reviewed:
Library Journal, August 1994, page 130

Other books by the same author:
Hispanics in the U.S.: An Anthology of Creative Literature. Vol. 2, 1982
The Man Who Invented the Automatic Jumping Bean, 1974
Tales of El Huitlacoche, 1984
Zapata Rose in 1992 and Other Tales, 1992

Other books you might like:
Montserrat Fontes, *Dreams of the Centaur*, 1995
  The son of a slain ranch owner tries to avenge the death of his father and journeys through love, murder, prison, and war in Mexico.
Sylvia Lopez-Medina, *Cantora: A Novel*, 1992
  This novel tells the story of four generations of women in Mexico and their lives in America at the turn of the 20th century.
Nash Candelaria, *Not by the Sword*, 1982
  Taking place before the Mexican War of 1846, this novel shows the struggles taking place in New Mexico and with the collapse of the Mexican government.
Nash Candelaria, *Inheritance of Strangers*, 1985
  Sequel to *Not By the Sword*, covering the years from the Mexican War of 1846 to New Mexico statehood in 1912.
Guy Garcia, *Obsidian Sky: A Novel*, 1994
  A doctoral student from Berkeley, working in Mexico's Museum of Anthropolgy, gets sucked into a political controversy amidst growing civil unrest.
Victor Villasenor, *Wild Steps of Heaven*, 1996
  Don Juan marries an Indian woman and the continual conflict of their marriage is the history of Mexico; the subjugation of indigenous people by European conquerors.

672

GARY D. KELLER, Mexican American

Zapata Rose in 1992 and Other Tales

(San Louis Obispo, CA: Maize Press, 1992)

Subject(s): Short Stories; Humor; Satire
Age range(s): Grades 9-Adult
Major character(s): Emilio Zapata, Revolutionary (hero of the Mexican Revolution), Zapotec Indian
Time period(s): 20th century (1970-1992)
Locale(s): California; Mexico

Summary: A collection of seven satirical stories, some originally published in journals and familiar to the author's fans. The writer is known as an absurdist comedian, and the stories

have titles such as "The Mojado Who Offered Up His Tapeworms to the Public Weal," and "A Chicano FBI Searching for Carmen Loca in Sal Si Puedes!". The title story depicts the reawakening in 1992 of Emiliano Zapata, the Mexican Indian revolutionary, and the changes his presence creates for indios, campesinos, and mestizos around the Western Hemisphere.

About this book: This is an expanded edition of the original *Tales of El Huitlacoche*.

Where it's reviewed:
Library Journal, December 1992, page 190

Other books by the same author:
Hispanics in the U.S.: An Anthology of Creative Literature. Vol. 2, 1980
The Man Who Invented the Automatic Jumping Bean, 1974
Tales of El Huitlacoch, 1984
Zapata Lives!, 1994
Miguel Mendez in Aztlan: Two Decades of Literary Production, 1995
Hispanics and United States Film: An Overview and Handbook, 1994
Tomas Rivera, 1935-1984: The Man and His Work, 1988

Other books you might like:
Oscar Zeta Acosta, *The Autobiography of a Brown Buffalo*, 1972
  In this largely autobiographical novel, the author examines his life as a famous Robin Hood-style Chicano lawyer who likes life on the edge.
Jose Antonio Burciaga, *Spilling the Beans: Loteria Chicana*, 1995
  A series of essays, many humorous, recounting experiences from the author's childhood that explore aspects of Chicano culture.
Nash Candelaria, *The Day the Cisco Kid Shot John Wayne*, 1988
  A humorous collection of short stories from New Mexico, in which the author examines cultural clashes between Latinos and Anglos.
Rick P. Rivera, *A Fabricated Mexican*, 1995
  In a series of comic vignettes Ricky Coronado, a quiet but mischevious boy, reports on the antics of his eccentric family and his own search for identity.

673

PABLO LA ROSA, Cuban American

Forbidden Fruit and Other Stories

(Houston, TX: Arte Publico Press, 1996)

Subject(s): Exile; Coming of Age; Oppression
Age range(s): Grades 9-Adult
Time period(s): Indeterminate
Locale(s): Florida (some stories take place in Cuba and Mexico)

Summary: This collection of short stories whimsically depicts the coming-of-age experiences of a young man in Cuba before the revolution. In the title story, "The Forbidden Fruit Was a Papaya," an adolescent becomes wary of which "committed in thought" sins he should recite in the confessional

Latino Titles *(right margin tab)*

since the penance dispensed by the priest could be pretty severe. After the move to the U.S., the characters of these stories become marginalized, despite their race, color, or education. In "El Marielito," a black man's bewilderment is emphasized because of political oppression in pre- and post-revolutionary Cuba.

Other books you might like:

Virgil Suarez, *Welcome to the Oasis and Other Stories*, 1992
This collection, a novella and five stories, depicts a new generation of young Latino characters who struggle to integrate into the American culture while maintaining their heritage.

Elias Miguel Munoz, *Crazy Love*, 1989
Experimental and autobiographical, this novel is about the Cuban American experience.

Pablo Medina, *The Marks of Birth*, 1994
The descendant of a well-to-do Cuban family, is forced to flee the island due to political turmoil, and lives a frustrated self-imposed exiled life.

Omar Torres, *Fallen Angels Sing*, 1991
When Miguel Saavedra moves to New York, he is caught up in a web of plots spun by pro- and anti- Castro agents and is soon involved in planning the assassination of Fidel Castro.

Fernando Alegria, *Paradise Lost or Gained? The Literature of Hispanic Exile*, 1990
This collection of writings by Latinos addresses the experience of exile and alienation through stories, poems, and essays.

Ruth Behar, *Bridges to Cuba = Puentes a Cuba*, 1995
Short stories, essays, poetry, and historical documents exploring the Cuban and Cuban American experience make up this anthology.

Junot Diaz, *Drown, Stories*, 1996
This collection of ten short stories describes young Latino men in transformation while learning to define their American identity.

Ramon Ferreira, *The Gravedigger and Other Stories*, 1986
This collection of disturbing and harsh short stories depict the underside of Cuban society in the '50s, including political repression, the fear of homosexuality, and the dark side of prejudice.

674

OFELIA DUMAS LACHTMAN, Mexican American

The Girl from Playa Blanca
(Houston, TX: Pinata Books, 1995)

Subject(s): Adventure and Adventurers; Family; Emigration and Immigration
Age range(s): Grades 6-9
Major character(s): Maria Elena Vargas, Young Woman, Sister, Mexican; Carlos Vargas, Child (boy), Brother, Mexican
Time period(s): 1990s
Locale(s): Los Angeles, California

Summary: When Elena's father suddenly disappears, Elena and her brother Carlos leave their Mexican seaside village for Los Angeles. Elena finds a job with a Mexican American

family where, she enlists the help of friends to solve the mystery of her father's disappearance. With little to go on but her intelligence, Elena and her friends encounter intrigue and crime.

Other books by the same author:
A Shell for Angela, 1995

Other books you might like:

Gloria Velasquez, *Juanita Fights the School Board*, 1994
When Juanita, a poor Mexican American girl, is faced with expulsion from high school, she decides to fight for her rights.

Diane Gonzales Bertrand, *Sweet Fifteen*, 1995
Stephanie's father dies right before her quinceanera, her special fifteenth birthday party.

Irene Beltran Hernandez, *Hearbeat, Drumbeat*, 1992
Morgana Cruz seeks her cultural identity while caught between the worlds of her Navajo mother and Mexican father.

Omar Castaneda, *Imagining Isabel*, 1994
Isabel, a recently married teenager in Guatemala, wants to become a teacher.

Omar Castaneda, *Among the Volcanoes*, 1991
Isabel, a teenager in Guatemala, must quit school to take care of her ill mother.

Jim Sagel, *Where the Cinnamon Winds Blow = Donde Soplan Los Vientos de Canela*, 1993
A magical fantasy novel about ten-year-old Tomas' relationship with his eccentric *Tia Zulema* and his attempts to reconcile his feelings for the death of his father.

675

OFELIA DUMAS LACHTMAN, Mexican American
ALEX PRADO DE LANGE, Illustrator

Pepita Talks Twice = Pepita Habla Dos Veces
(Houston, TX: Pinata Books, 1995)

Subject(s): Bilingualism; Problem Solving
Age range(s): Grades K-2
Major character(s): Pepita, Child (girl), Mexican
Time period(s): Indeterminate Past
Locale(s): United States

Summary: Pepita must learn on her own the value of speaking two languages, Spanish and English. She becomes annoyed when she constantly has to translate for neighbors, friends and relatives, so she decides to stop speaking Spanish. But she soon learns that now she can't speak to her beloved grandmother, who only speaks Spanish, and her dog Lobo who does not understand his English name, Wolf.

About this book: Bilingual format.

Other books by the same author:
A Shell for Angela, 1995
The Girl from Playa Blanca, 1995

Other books you might like:

Alma Flor Ada, *My Name Is Maria Isabel*, 1993
Maria Isabel Salazar Lopez is proud of her name and the fact that she is named after a relative whom she loves, but

when she begins a new school her teacher changes her name.

Karen Papagapitos, *Socorro, Daughter of the Desert*, 1993
The family of eight-year-old Socorro are farm workers and she helps out as much as she can. When her father becomes ill, Socorro makes tortillas for her mother to sell in the fields.

Fernando Pico, *The Red Comb*, 1994
A young girl helps save a runaway slave in 19th century Puerto Rico.

Gary Soto, *The Skirt*, 1992
Fourth-grader Miata loses her mother's folkloric dancing skirt and figures out a way to find it.

Gloria Anzaldua, *Prietita and the Ghost Woman = Prietita y La Llorona*, 1995
Prietita, a young Mexican American girl, goes searching for an herb that will help cure her mother of an illness.

Gloria Anzaldua, *Friends From the Other Side/Amigos del Otro Lado*, 1993
Prietita, a Mexican American girl, becomes friends with Joaquin, an illegal immigrant boy who lives on the U.S. side of the border. She helps him and his family hide from the migra.

676

OFELIA DUMAS LACHTMAN

A Shell for Angela

(Houston, TX: Arte Publico Press, 1995)

Subject(s): Heritage; Identity; Emigration and Immigration
Age range(s): Grades 10-Adult
Major character(s): Angela Martin, Wife (middle-aged), Mexican American
Time period(s): 20th century (1930-1974)
Locale(s): Los Angeles, California (southern California area)

Summary: When nine-year-old Angela Martin sees her father led away by immigration officials, she begins to deny her Mexican heritage. As an adult she raises her children to be ignorant of their Mexican grandparents. Years later, comfortably settled in her suburban Los Angeles home with her Anglo husband, her fear and regret reawakens and she journeys to a fishing village in Mexico to face her denial and the truth about her father.

Where it's reviewed:
Library Journal, March 1, 1995, page 102
Publishers Weekly, January 23, 1995, page 65

Other books by the same author:
Pepita Talks Twice = Pepita Habla Dos Veces, 1995
The Girl from Playa Blanca, 1995
Campfire Dreams, 1987

Other books you might like:
Ana Castillo, *Sapogonia An Anti-Romance in 3/8 Meter*, 1990
A novel about a distinct place where all mestizos reside regardless of nationality or race, or possibly because of racial background.

Demetria Martinez, *Mother Tongue*, 1994
Mary meets and shelters a political refugee, falls in love

with him, and soon finds that his life is fundamentally different from hers.

Jose Antonio Villarreal, *Pocho*, 1959
The story of a Mexican family in the Santa Clara Valley of California before World War II and the assimilation of the son, Richard Rubio.

Richard Rodriguez, *Hunger of Memory: The Education of Richard Rodriguez, an Autobiography*, 1982
The story of the author's childhood and education, the difficult journey of a "minority student" who becomes culturally assimilated in order to enjoy academic success.

Graciela Limon, *The Memories of Ana Calderon: A Novel*, 1994
Ana Calderon begins life in rural southern Mexico, but the burdens of poverty, dreams of a better life and circumstances lead her family to the U.S.

677

ENRIQUE A. LAGUERRE, Puerto Rican

The Labyrinth

(Maplewood, NJ: Waterfront Press, 1984)

Subject(s): City Life; Political Thriller; Dictators
Age range(s): Grades 10-Adult
Major character(s): Porfirio Uribe, Lawyer (poor but industrious), Puerto Rican
Time period(s): 1950s (1950-1959)
Locale(s): New York, New York

Summary: This is the story of a Puerto Rican man in New York City who goes to night school to earn a law degree and accidentally stumbles into the services of a Caribbean dictator of a fictional country called the Santiagan Republic. In actuality it is almost the true but fictionalized story of the Trujillo regime in the Dominican Republic.

About this book: This is considered a classic novel, first published in Spanish in 1959 and chosen book-of-the-month by London's International Book Club, by one of Puerto Rico's most prolific novelists. It is translated from Spanish by William Rose; and is introduced by Estelle Irizarry.

Where it's reviewed:
The New Republic, January 16, 1961, page 18
The San Juan Star, September 16, 1960,

Other books by the same author:
Benevolent Masters, 1986 (*Los Amos Benevolos*)
La Llamarada: Novela, 1968 (originally published in 1935)
Solar Montoya, 1941
Cauce sin Rio, 1991
La Resaca, 1969

Other books you might like:
Bernardo Vega, *Memoirs of Bernardo Vega*, 1984
First published in 1977, this work relates the story of an early 20th century immigrant from Puerto Rico who arrives in New York.

Isabel Allende, *The House of the Spirits*, 1985
This intergenerational story is about a family, particularly the women, in Chile before the revolution.

Gabriel Garcia Marquez, *One Hundred Years of Solitude*, 1970

This historical intergenerational novel is about the corruption in a fictionalized South American country.

Reinaldo Arenas, *The Doorman*, 1991

This story about Juan, a young Cuban refugee who becomes a doorman at a luxury apartment building in New York, is a parable about freedom.

Jesus Colon, *A Puerto Rican in New York and Other Sketches*, 1961

This series of short stories and essays were previously published in *The Daily Worker*, a publication of the Communist Party.

Omar Torres, *Fallen Angels Sing*, 1991

A young Cuban exile becomes involved in a plot to assassinate Fidel Castro.

Reinaldo Arenas, *The Assault*, 1994

A fictional exploration of Castro-era Cuba, this allegorical novel presents a disturbing surreal portrait of political extremes and a society headed toward self-destruction.

678

JOHN LEGUIZAMO, Columbian

Spic-O-Rama: A Dysfunctional Comedy

(New York: Bantam Books, 1994)

Subject(s): Drama; Family; Comedians
Age range(s): Grades 10-Adult
Major character(s): Kraxy Willie, Veteran
Time period(s): 1990s (1992)
Locale(s): New York

Summary: Leguizamo's comedy is a satire of a dysfunctional urban Hispanic household. An award-winning one-man show, it presents the six eccentric members of the Gigante family, to reveal the love, pain, and the frustration of unrealized dreams common to all families.

About this book: Although this is a one person performance book it reads like a story and includes photographs.

Where it's reviewed:
Library Journal, March 1, 1994, page 88
New York Times, November 8, 1992, page H5
Wall Street Journal, November 4, 1992, page A12
New Yorker, November 9, 1992, page 142

Awards the book has won:
Dramatists Guild Hull-Warriner Award for Best Play, 1992
Drama Dsk Award Nomination, 1992

Other books by the same author:
Mambo Mouth: A Savage Comedy, 1993

Other books you might like:
Guillermo Gomez-Pena, *Warrior for Gringostroika: Essays, Performance Texts, and Poetry*, 1993
Solme of this published performance work of Gomez-Pena has been filmed.

Luis Valdez, *Luis Valdez—Early Works: Actos, Bernabe, and Pensamiento Serpentino*, 1990
This collection of short one-act plays, contain some comical, of the Teatro Campesino.

Jose Antonio Burciaga, *Soilling the Beans: Loteria Chicana*, 1995

This is a series of essays, many humorous, recounting experiences from the author's childhood in Texas.

Roberto Fernandez, *Holy Radishes*, 1995

This satirical novel is about a Cuban American community in Florida.

Jaime Manrique, *Latin Moon in Manhattan*, 1992

This novel presents bizarre characters, plots and sub-plots, and a vivid depiction of Columbian American culture in Little Columbia, Jackson Heights from the perspective of a gay poet.

679

GRACIELA LIMON, Mexican American

In Search of Bernabe

(Houston, TX: Arte Publico Press, 1993)

Subject(s): Politics; Family; Salvadorans in the United States
Age range(s): Grades 10-Adult
Major character(s): Luz Delcano, Mother, Salvadoran; Bernabe Delcano, Son, Salvadoran
Time period(s): 1990s (1993)
Locale(s): California; Mexico; El Salvador

Summary: During a period of political turmoil in El Salvador, at the time of the death of Archbishop Romero, Luz Delcano is separated from her son Barnabe. Determined to find him and reunite her family, Luz travels through Mexico and into southern California, then back again to El Salvador. A story of biblical dimensions with strong, memorable characters, Limon's novel is powerful and vivid.

Where it's reviewed:
Library Journal, August, 1993, page 153
Publishers Weekly, July 26, 1993, page 63
New York Times Book Review, November 1993, page 66

Awards the book has won:
American Book Award, 1994

Other books by the same author:
Maria Belen: The Autobiography of an Indian Woman: A Novel, 1990
The Memories of Ana Calderon: A Novel, 1994

Other books you might like:
Demetria Martinez, *Mother Tongue*, 1994
Nineteen year old Mary, depressed and grieving over the death of her mother, meets and shelters political refugee, Jose Luis Romero.

Margarita Engle, *Singing to Cuba*, 1993
A California woman leaves her husband and children to search for information about family members who disappeared during the Castro revolution.

Carole Fernandez, *Sleep of the Innocents*, 1991
This novel chronicles the lives of women living in a fictional Central American country torn by civil war.

Ana Castillo, *Sapogonia: An Anti-Romance in 3/8 Meter*, 1990
A novel about Sapogonia, a distinct place where all mestizos reside regardless of nationality or race, or possibly because of racial background.

Julia Alvarez, *In the Time of the Butterflies*, 1994
The story of the assassination of three sisters who were

fighting to overthrow a dictatorship in the Dominican Republic.

680

GRACIELA LIMON, Mexican American

Maria Belen: The Autobiography of an Indian Woman: A Novel

(New York, NY: Vantage Press, 1990)

Subject(s): Conquest; Indians of Mexico; Women
Age range(s): Grades 10-Adult
Major character(s): Maria de Belen, Aged Person (old woman), Royalty (princess), Aztec
Time period(s): 16th century
Locale(s): Mexico

Summary: This is a fictional autobiography of Dona Maria de Belen Cihuatzintli, also known as Lady Huitzitzilin, an 82-year-old woman living in the Convent of Saint Hieronymus in Mexico during the 16th century, as related to the nun Sor Tiburcia Solares. She narrates the story of the Spanish conquest of Mexico, the destruction of Tenochtitlan, and describes the Slaughter at the Great Temple, when hundreds of Mexicans were killed at the command of Pedro de Alvarado. Limon pays tribute and homage to pre-Colombian women, and this novel celebrates the endurance of the human spirit in the face of catastrophe.

Other books by the same author:
In Search of Bernabe, 1993
Song of the Hummingbird, 1996
The Memories of Ana Calderon: A Novel, 1994

Other books you might like:
Joseph P. Sanchez, *The Aztec Chronicles: The True History of Christopher Columbus, as Narrated by Quilaztli of Texcoco: A Novella*, 1995
This historical novella, tells the true story of Christopher Columbus, through the voice of Quilaztli, an Aztec historian, who served under both Moctezuma I and Moctezuma II.
Jose Barreiro, *The Indian Chronicles*, 1993
Adopted by Christopher Columbus, Diego Colon, a Taino boy, keeps a journal where he describes events in his life from 1532-1535 as he narrates the Indian's discovery of the Europeans.
Gloria Duran, *Malinche: Slave Princess of Cortez*, 1993
The story of Malinali, born an Aztec princess and sold to the conqueror Cortez, is about an ambiguous and controversial figure in Mexican history.
Elizabeth Borton de Trevino, *I, Juan de Pareja*, 1965
This novel tells the story of Juan, who is born a slave and becomes the devoted servant and friend of Diego Velazquez, the famous painter and it examines Spanish court life and class relations.
Tina Juarez, *Call No Man Master*, 1995
Intricately crafted, this historical novel is about a young woman of mixed heritage, Spanish and Indian, and her participation in the events that lead to Mexico's independence from Spain.

Barbara Mujica, *The Deaths of Don Bernardo*, 1990
This novel takes the reader into the elegant homes of the rich, the struggling Indian villages of the Andes and presents Bernardo de Alvarez, a Peruvian plantation owner who murders a man.

681

GRACIELA LIMON, Mexican American

The Memories of Ana Calderon: A Novel

(Houston, TX: Arte Publico Press, 1994)

Subject(s): Emigration and Immigration; Poverty; Women
Age range(s): Grades 10-Adult
Major character(s): Ana Calderon, Young Woman, Mexican
Time period(s): 20th century (1940-1975)
Locale(s): California; Mexico (in southern Mexico and southern California)

Summary: Ana Calderon begins life a joyful child in rural southern Mexico. But the burdens of poverty, dreams of a better life, and fate and circumstance lead her family to the United States. She suffers many challenges and torments, battles unfair circumstances; the loss of a child, imprisonment, and humiliation. But she survives to become a successful businesswoman and eventually learns to love and value herself, and to forgive.

Where it's reviewed:
Library Journal, August 1994, page 130
Publishers Weekly, July 11, 1994, page 64

Other books by the same author:
In Search of Bernabe, 1993
Maria Belen: The Autobiography of an Indian Woman: A Novel, 1990

Other books you might like:
Estela Portillo Trambley, *Trini*, 1986
Trini, a Tarahumara woman, crosses the border as an undocumented immigrant in order to give birth to her child in the United States.
John Rechy, *The Miraculous Day of Amalia Gomez: A Novel*, 1991
This story examines poverty, gang warfare, border crossings, and visions of salvation while following one day in the life of a Mexican-American woman.
Genaro Gonzalez, *Rainbow's End*, 1988
This adventure novel presents dangerous border crossings, confrontations with a magician, and drug smuggling in the lives of three generations of the Cavazos family in Texas.
Mary Helen Ponce, *Taking Control*, 1987
The domestic and economic oppression of Mexican and Chicana women in the U.S. is portrayed in this collection.
Alma Luz Villanueva, *Naked Ladies*, 1994
The lives of four remarkable women and their struggles against prejudices, difficult relationships, and abuse is told in this novel.
Ofelia Dumas Lachtman, *A Shell for Angela*, 1995
When nine-year-old Angela Martin sees her father led away by immigration officials, she begins to deny her Mexican heritage and she raises her children to be ignorant of their grandparents.

Himilce Novas, *Mangos, Bananas, and Coconuts: A Cuban Love Story*, 1996
This tale of a magical yet real love is an ancient tale, beginning with the love of a man and a woman from different social classes, and the story of the fate of their children.

682

GRACIELA LIMON, Mexican American

Song of the Hummingbird

(Houston, TX: Arte Publico Press, 1996)

Subject(s): Magic; Indians of Mexico; Women
Age range(s): Grades 10-Adult
Major character(s): Huitzitzilin, Royalty (princess), Aged Person (woman), Aztec
Time period(s): 16th century
Locale(s): Mexico

Summary: Huitzitzilin, in the Nahuatl language, is the name of Hummingbird, an Aztec princess who is forced into slavery. She recounts her life story during the Spanish conquest of Mexico, to Father Benito. As an 82 year-old-woman, forced to give up her language and culture, she ends her life in a convent. The priest learns of death and destruction, and sees the conquest through the eyes of the conquered, as he listens to the song of Hummingbird. Limon pays tribute and homage to pre-Colombian women, and this novel celebrates the endurance of the human spirit in the face of catastrophe.

Where it's reviewed:
Library Journal, March 15, 1996, page 96

Other books by the same author:
In Search of Bernabe, 1993
Maria Belen: The Autobiography of an Indian Woman: A Novel, 1993
The Memories of Ana Calderon: A Novel, 1994

Other books you might like:
Joseph P. Sanchez, *The Aztec Chronicles: The True History of Christopher Columbus, as Narrated by Quilaztli of Texcoco: A Novella*, 1995
This historical novella, tells the true story of Christopher Columbus, through the voice of Quilaztli, an Aztec historian, who served under both Moctezuma I and Moctezuma II.
Jose Barreiro, *The Indian Chronicles*, 1993
Adopted by Christopher Columbus, Diego Colon, a Taino boy, keeps a journal where he describes events in his life from 1532-1535, narrating the Indian's discovery of the Europeans.
Gloria Duran, *Malinche: Slave Princess of Cortez*, 1993
The story of Malinali, born an Aztec princess and sold to the conqueror Cortez, portrays the life of an ambiguous and controversial figure in Mexican history.
Elizabeth Borton de Trevino, *I, Juan de Pareja*, 1965
This historically accurate novel tells the story of Juan, a slave, devoted servant, and friend of Diego Velazquez, the famous painter. It examines Spanish court life and class relations in detail.

Tina Juarez, *Call No Man Master*, 1995
This intricately crafted historical novel is about a young woman of mixed heritage, Spanish and Indian, and her participation in the events that lead to Mexico's independence from Spain.
Barbara Mujica, *The Deaths of Don Bernardo*, 1990
This novel takes the reader into the elegant homes of the rich, the struggling Indian villages of the Andes and presents Bernardo de Alvarez, a Peruvian plantation owner who murders a man.

683

ARCADIA H. LOPEZ, Mexican American

Barrio Teacher

(Houston, TX: Arte Publico Press, 1992)

Subject(s): Education; Coming of Age; Teachers
Age range(s): Grades 8-Adult
Major character(s): Arcadia H. Lopez, Teacher, Aged Person (80-Year-Old), Mexican
Time period(s): 20th century (1913-1992)
Locale(s): San Antonio, Texas

Summary: This is the autobiography of an educator who, despite poverty and turmoil, manages to obtain a university education and then return to her neighborhood to help other children of poverty. Her descriptions of traveling by oxcart from Mexico to Texas, and finally settling in San Antonio are fascinating. A pioneer in urban and bilingual education, Lopez taught for 46 years, and she shows herself to be full of courage and determination.

Where it's reviewed:
Publishers Weekly, July 20, 1992, page 252

Other books you might like:
Norma Elia Cantu, *Canicula: Snapshots of a Girlhood en la Frontera*, 1995
This series of brief vignettes about growing up brings into sharp focus the history, lives, and legends about Laredo, Texas.
Enedina Casarez Vasquez, *Recuerdos de Una Nina*, 1980
These short stories are about growing up in San Antonio, Texas.
Montserrat Fontes, *First Confession*, 1991
This is a story about an upper class little girl living on the Mexican side of the U.S.-Mexico border.
Richard Rodriguez, *Hunger of Memory: The Education of Richard Rodriguez, an Autobiography*, 1982
This story of the author's childhood and education portrays the difficult journey of a "minority student" who must become socially assimilated in order to enjoy academic success.
Ernesto Galarza, *Barrio Boy*, 1971
This is an autobiographical story of the early life of a distinguished professor and author who wrote many works about Mexican agricultural workers.
Salvador Guerrero, *Memorias: A West Texas Life*, 1991
The autobiography of a man growing up in west Texas has history similar to that experienced by many Mexican Americans from Texas during this time period.

684

STEVEN LOPEZ

Third and Indiana
(New York: Viking, 1994)

Subject(s): Drugs; Money; Mothers and Sons
Age range(s): Grades 10-Adult
Major character(s): Gabriel Santoro, 14-Year-Old, Drug Dealer; Diablo, Drug Dealer, Criminal, Latino
Time period(s): 1990s
Locale(s): Philadelphia, Pennsylvania

Summary: The title of this novel refers to the *badlands* of Philadelphia, the corner where fourteen-year-old Gabriel hands out crack to people in passing cars. He's working for Diablo, a psychotic drug boss, who's now demanding two grand from Gabriel because of a supposed shortage in his accounts. Meanwhile Gabriel's mother, with the help of a priest, rides her bicycle through the dark streets searching for her runaway son. The tough and violent characters in this hopeless scenario command brutal honesty, sympathy and always there's a glimmer of hope.

Where it's reviewed:
American Journalism Review, December 1994, page 49
Library Journal, January 1995, page 162
Publishers Weekly, June 20, 1994, page 93
Times Literary Supplement, July 14, 1995, page 21

Other books you might like:
Victor Rodriguez, *Eldorado in East Harlem*, 1992
    Seventeen year old Rene is streetwise and he gets involved with a gang committing petty crimes and running drugs.
Abraham Rodriguez Jr., *Spidertown*, 1993
    Sixteen year old Miguel is a runner for a drug dealer and struggles to change his life.
Soledad Santiago, *Nightside*, 1994
    Anna Eltern, a former nun who runs a shelter for runaway teens, struggles with financial problems and murder after funding cuts force her to turn away homeless teenagers.
Gloria Gonzalez, *The Thirteenth Apostle*, 1993
    Newspaperwoman Geraldine St. Claire investigates the murder of her lover Hal, which leads her to suspect an industrial homicide and also leads her right into the hands of a powerful drug lord.
Manuel Ramos, *The Last Client of Luis Montez*, 1996
    The last client of Denver lawyer Louie Montez is found dead with Montez standing over him. To clear his name Montez becomes entangled in a complicated web that takes him to California and back.
Soledad Santiago, *Streets of Fire*, 1996
    This murder mystery with a Latina police officer, Francesca Colon, involves all the elements of big-city dirty politics, police corruption, suspicious deaths, and tense ethnic community relations.

685

TIFFANY ANA LOPEZ, Editor, Mexican American

Growing Up Chicano
(New York: Avon, 1993)

Subject(s): Anthology; Short Stories; Growing Up
Age range(s): Grades 10-Adult
Time period(s): 1950s; 1980s
Locale(s): United States (These stories take place throughout the U.S.)

Summary: This anthology contains stories about growing up Chicano in the U.S. They determine to describe the cultural experiences, languages, traditions, and values, that distinguish Chicanos from other Latinos and other Americans. The stories cover such subjects as history, grandparents, school, and rites of passage.

Where it's reviewed:
Publishers Weekly, November 8, 1993, page 58

Other books you might like:
Ray Gonzalez, *Mirrors Beneath the Earth: Short Fiction by Chicano Writers*, 1992
    This is a collection of short stories.
Gary Soto, *Pieces of the Heart: New Chicano Fiction*, 1993
    These short stories are by Chicano writers.
Tey Diana Rebolledo, *Infinite Divisions: An Anthology of Chicana Literature*, 1993
    Mexican American women author this anthology of historical and contemporary writings.
Rudolfo Anaya, *Voces: An Anthology of Nuevo Mexicano Writers*, 1987
    These stories are by Chicano authors living in New Mexico.
Rick P. Rivera, *A Fabricated Mexican*, 1995
    This series of comic vignettes describe a quiet but mischevious boy searching for his identity while growing up in California.

686

SYLVIA LOPEZ-MEDINA, Mexican American

Cantora: A Novel
(Albuquerque: University of New Mexico Press, 1992)

Subject(s): Family Relations; Women; Intergenerational Saga
Age range(s): Grades 10-Adult
Major character(s): Rosario, Grandmother, Mexican; Amparo, Mexican (Rosario's granddaughter)
Time period(s): 20th century (1900-1970)
Locale(s): California; Mexico

Summary: This novel tells the story of four generations of Mexican women. Amparo searches to discover the truth of her family's past, and learns of the triumphs and tragedies of her grandmother, aunt, and mother. To Amparo, the lives of these women sound like a corrido, which is a traditional Spanish ballad of tragedy and love.

Where it's reviewed:
Library Journal, June 15, 1992, page 102

Other books you might like:

Victor Villasenor, *Rain of Gold*, 1991
This is an intergenerational saga of a family's migration from Mexico to the U.S.

Carmen de Monteflores, *Singing Softly = Cantando Bajito*, 1989
This is a novel of women, a grandmother and granddaughter, and their relationship.

Denise Chavez, *Face of an Angel*, 1994
This is an intergenerational novel about a family in Agua Oscura, a fictional New Mexico town.

Alejandro Morales, *The Brick People*, 1992
A historical novel that traces growth in California from the 19th to the 20th century.

Victor Villasenor, *Wild Steps of Heaven*, 1996
Don Juan marries an Indian woman and the continual conflict of their marriage is the history of Mexico; the subjugation of indigenous people by European conquerors.

Isabel Allende, *Paula*, 1995
Well-known Latina author tells the story of her daughter's agonizing illness, coma, and death at an early age.

687

GLORIA LOPEZ-STAFFORD, Mexican American

A Place in El Paso: A Mexican American Childhood

(Albuquerque, NM: University of New Mexico Press, 1996)

Subject(s): Fathers and Daughters; Growing Up; Identity
Age range(s): Grades 9-Adult
Major character(s): Gloria Lopez-Stafford, Child (little girl), Mexican (nicknamed Yoya)
Time period(s): 1940s
Locale(s): El Paso, Texas

Summary: A bittersweet narrative describing the early childhood of the author living in the "projects" of El Paso during World War II. Living with her elderly widowed father in poverty, yet loving her friends and neighbors, Yoya is an energetic cheerful child. Eventually the changes in her life, moving to a new home and the death of her father, become too much for her and she questions her heritage and identity. The language and dialogues are delightful, full of Spanish words, folklore, and customs of the Mexican people of El Paso.

Other books you might like:

Patricia Preciado Martin, *Days of Plenty, Days of Want*, 1988
In this collection of stories past and present meet, and Mexican heritage is in jeopardy of being wiped out.

Norma Elia Cantu, *Canicula: Snapshots of a Girlhood en la Frontera*, 1995
A collection, with photos, of short stories and vignettes of a young girl growing up along the Texas border.

Enedina Casarez Vasquez, *Recuerdos de Una Nina*, 1980
Short stories about growing up in San Antonio, Texas.

Arcadia H. Lopez, *Barrio Teacher*, 1992
Despite poverty and turmoil, this educator managed to obtain a university education and teach for forty-six years in San Antonio, Texas.

Esmeralda Santiago, *When I Was Puerto Rican*, 1993
This autobiographical story is about a young girl living in poverty in Puerto Rico who comes to the U.S. and eventually attends Harvard University.

Sallie Gallegos, *Stone Horses*,
This history of the Montez family, living in a rural area of northern New Mexico during the 1930s and 1940s, follows the extraordinary Eduardo from birth up to his stint in the Navy at age eighteen.

688

JAIME MANRIQUE, Columbian

Latin Moon in Manhattan

(New York: St. Martins Press, 1992)

Subject(s): City Life; Animals; Homosexuality/Lesbianism
Age range(s): Grades 10-Adult
Major character(s): Santiago Martinez, Writer, Young Man (gay), Columbian
Time period(s): 1990s (1992)
Locale(s): New York, New York (takes place in Jackson Heights and New York City)

Summary: This novel presents bizarre characters, plots and sub-plots, and a vivid depiction of Columbian American culture in Little Colombia Jackson Heights. Santiago, a gay unpublished poet lives with his old cat, Mr. O'Donnell who is slowly dying of an enlarged heart. In its examination of drugs, romance, and literary politics, this writer's New York is dangerous, colorful, vibrant, and complex.

Where it's reviewed:

Advocate, February 25, 1992, page 82
Lambda Book Report, May-June 1992, page 21
Review of Contemporary Fiction, Fall 1992, page 203
Publishers Weekly , December 20, 1991, page 64

Other books by the same author:
Colombian Gold, 1983

Other books you might like:

Louie Garcia Robinson, *The Devil, Delfina Varela, and the Used Chevy*, 1993
This is a humorous political novel about unique characters living in the Mission District of San Francisco.

Emilio Diaz Valcarcel, *Hot Soles in Harlem*, 1993
A look at New York City through the eyes of a recent Puerto Rican arrival.

Michael Nava, *How Town: A Novel of Suspense*, 1991
A gay Chicano lawyer solves a murder mystery while unpretentiously depicting a gay relationship.

Roberto Fernandez, *Holy Radishes*, 1995
Satirical novel depicting the Cuban American community in Florida.

Omar Torres, *Fallen Angels Sing*, 1991
A Cuban exile becomes involved in a plot to assassinate Fidel Castro.

Elias Miguel Munoz, *The Greatest Performance*, 1991
Rosa is sent to Spain with her brother while Mario, her best friend, remains in Cuba and suffers for his crime of homosexuality until he finally escapes to the U.S.

John Rechy, *City of Night*, 1963

Johnny Rio, born in El Paso, becomes a gay Chicano wanderer, who lives by the statistics of random sexual encounters and orgasms in various cities.

689

CRUZ MARTEL, Puerto Rican
JERRY PINKNEY, Illustrator

Yagua Days

(New York: The Dial Press, 1978)

Subject(s): Family Life; Tradition
Age range(s): Grades K-2
Major character(s): Adan Riera, Child, Puerto Rican
Time period(s): 1970s
Locale(s): New York, New York; Puerto Rico

Summary: Adan, born in New York, gets to visit his relatives in Puerto Rico one summer. He experiences many new and wonderful things, such as picking fruit from trees, spending time with his newly discovered family, and learning about Yagua days.

About this book: Many words are in Spanish; with a glossary provided in the back.

Other books you might like:

Jan Romero Stevens, *Carlos and the Squash Plant/Carlos y la Planta de Calabaza*, 1993

Carlos doesn't like to bathe and something starts growing in his ear.

Pura Belpre, *The Rainbow-Colored Horse*, 1978

Three wishes are granted when a rainbow-colored horse tramples a maize field.

Juanita Havill, *Treasure Nap*, 1992

Alicia hears the story of Rita, who visits her grandfather in the mountains of Mexico.

Harriet Rohmer, *Uncle Nacho's Hat = El Sombrero de Tio Nacho*, 1989

Uncle Nacho does not like his new hat until his niece teaches him something.

Pura Belpre, *Santiago*, 1969

After moving to a new country, Santiago learns to make new friends in his new school.

Karen Papagapitos, *Jose's Basket*, 1990

Because Jose's family is a migrant farm-working family, school starts later and ends earlier for him than for the other students. His teacher understands and gives him a special gift.

690

PATRICIA PRECIADO MARTIN, Mexican American

Days of Plenty, Days of Want

(Tempe, AZ: Bilingual Press, 1988)

Subject(s): Short Stories; Identity; Heritage
Age range(s): Grades 10-Adult
Time period(s): 20th century (1960-1988)
Locale(s): Arizona

Summary: A collection of stories where the past and the present meet, creating some very interesting results. In one story a woman's lifetime home is destroyed by land developers, and in another, ''Maria de las Trenzas,'' a young girl changes her dull life and her self by cutting off her long braids. In these stories, heritage is often pushed aside by the progress of modern society, reminding us of the importance of the past and how it relates to our freedom and self-expression.

Other books by the same author:

Songs My Mother Sang to Me: An Oral History of Mexican American Women, 1992
El Milagro and Other Stories, 1995
The Legend of the Bellringer of San Agustin = La Leyenda del Campanero de San Agustin, 1980
Images and Conversations: Mexican Americans Recall a Southwestern Past, 1983

Other books you might like:

Sandra Cisneros, *Woman Hollering Creek and Other Stories*, 1991

A collection of short stories with strong, angry female characters struggling valiantly to make something beautiful of their lives.

Alicia Gaspar de Alba, *The Mystery of Survival and Other Stories*, 1993

Stories mostly about female characters who explore and come to understand their places in the world and the cultural boundaries that divide them.

Estela Portillo Trambley, *Rain of Scorpions and Other Writings*, 1975

Collection of short stories by an early Chicana writer that explore the place of women in Mexican society.

Mary Helen Ponce, *Taking Control*, 1987

Collection of stories portraying the domestic and economic oppression of Mexican and Chicana women in the U.S.

Roberta Fernandez, *Itaglio: Novel in Six Stories*, 1990

A novel related in six stories, each about an extraordinary woman who serves as a role model for the young narrator.

691

PATRICIA PRECIADO MARTIN, Mexican American

El Milagro and Other Stories

(Tucson, AZ: University of Arizona, 1996)

Subject(s): Short Stories; Family Relations; Grandparents
Age range(s): Grades 8-Adult
Time period(s): 1940s; 1950s (1940-1950)
Locale(s): Arizona

Summary: A collection of personal and collective memories in the form of short stories, stitched together to form a portrait of the author's family and her life growing up. The stories titled ''The Tortilla Maker,'' ''The Miracle,'' and ''Embroidery'' are tales that connect barrio characters to each other and to their past. These stories are filled with little miracles, ghosts and dreams.

Where it's reviewed:

Library Journal, March 1, 1996, page 108
Publishers Weekly, February 12, 1996, page 72

Other books by the same author:

Days of Plenty, Days of Want, 1988

Songs My Mother Sang to Me: An Oral History of Mexican American Women, 1992

The Legend of the Bellringer of San Agustin = La Leyenda del Campanero de San Agustin, 1980 (bilingual)

Images and Conversations: Mexican Americans Recall a Southwestern Past, 1983

Other books you might like:

Roberta Fernandez, *Itaglio: Novel in Six Stories*, 1990

A novel related in six stories, each about an extraordinary woman who serves as a role model for the young narrator.

Sabine Ulibarri, *The Best of Sabine R. Ulibarri: Selected Stories*, 1993

This collection of tales—magical, imaginative, and humorous—blends fantastical and realistic elements to create unexpected wonders.

Denise Chavez, *The Last of the Menu Girls*, 1986

This collection of interrelated short stories is about an adolescent Chicana girl from southern New Mexico who is looking for her place, identity, and womanhood.

Angelico Chavez, *The Short Stories of Fray Angelico Chavez*, 1987

This collection of short stories by an early New Mexico writer and folklorist is edited by Genaro M. Padilla.

Kathleen Alcala, *Mrs. Vargas and the Dead Naturalist*, 1992

These short stories capture the essence of magical realism and examine the lives of Mexican women in this book of wonders.

Jim Sagel, *El Santo Queso: Cuentos = The Holy Cheese*, 1990

This collection of short stories, some humorously narrated, is about the clash of cultures between outsiders and traditional New Mexicans.

692

AL MARTINEZ, Mexican American

Ashes in the Rain: Selected Essays

(Berkeley, CA: TQS Publications, 1989)

Subject(s): Journalism; Family Life; Humor

Age range(s): Grades 9-Adult

Time period(s): 1980s

Locale(s): Los Angeles, California

Summary: Award winning columnist Al Martinez writes about family, ethnicity, politics, nature, and other topics in this collection of essays, many originally published in the Los Angeles Times. Martinez's essays celebrate life's sweetnesses while at the same time mourn our follies. His essays on family, about his grandchildren and wife, are humorous and loving; his essays about people he's known are touching and sensitive.

Awards the book has won:

National Headliner Award for Best Columnist, 1987

Best Columnist by California Newspaper Publishers Association, 1987

Other books by the same author:

Dancing under the Moon, 1992

Other books you might like:

Jim Sagel, *Dancing to Pay the Light Bill: Essays on New Mexico and the Southwest*, 1992

A collection of humorous essays about language and culture in the Southwest.

Jose Antonio Burciaga, *Spilling the Beans: Loteria Chicana*, 1995

This series of essays, many humorous, recount experiences from the author's childhood in Texas.

Jesus Salvador Trevino, *The Fabulous Sinkhole and Other Stories*, 1995

This first story collection by Trevino, a screenwriter and director, is an entertaining creation of Mexican and Chicano characters that take place in a fictional town, Arroyo Grande, in Texas.

Octavio I. Romano-V., *Geriatric Fu: My First Sixty-Five Years in the United States*, 1990

In a series of humorous essays Romano presents his autobiographical odyssey, ending in 1989 when he retires after teaching for twenty-six years at the University of California, Berkeley.

Francisca Miranda Schneider, *Sal y Pimienta: A Culinary Education*, 1995

These vignettes, interspersed with family recipes, describe the author's childhood during the Spanish Civil War.

693

DEMETRIA MARTINEZ, Mexican American

Mother Tongue

(Tempe, AZ: Bilingual Press, 1994)

Subject(s): Politics; Love; Women

Age range(s): Grades 10-Adult

Major character(s): Maria, Young Woman (19-year-old), Chicana; Jose Luis Romero, Expatriate, Salvadoran

Time period(s): 1980s

Locale(s): Albuquerque, New Mexico

Summary: Nineteen-year-old Mary, depressed and grieving over the death of her mother, meets and shelters political refugee Jose Luis Romero. Although she plans only to help him adjust to his new life, she soon falls in love with this man whose life is so fundamentally different from her own. The story is related 20 years after the events have occurred through the use of diary excerpts, shopping lists, letters and from memory.

Where it's reviewed:

Nation, December 26, 1994, page 809

Progressive, July, 1995, page 39

Awards the book has won:

Western States Book Award for Fiction, 1994

Other books by the same author:

Three Times a Woman: Chicana Poetry, 1989

Other books you might like:

Julia Alvarez, *In the Time of the Butterflies*, 1994

The story of the assassination of three sisters who are fighting to overthrow a dictatorship in the Dominican Republic.

Graciela Limon, *In Search of Bernabe*, 1993
  A novel about a mother's search for her son during civil war in El Salvador.
Margarita Engle, *Singing to Cuba*, 1993
  A California woman leaves her husband and children to search for information about family members who disappeared during the Castro revolution.
Virgil Suarez, *The Cutter: A Novel*, 1991
  Julian Campos is required to cut sugercane in Communist Cuba while waiting permission to leave the island.
Carole Fernandez, *Sleep of the Innocents*, 1991
  This novel chronicles the lives of women living in a fictional Central American country torn by civil war.
Ana Castillo, *Sapogonia: An Anti-Romance in 3/8 Meter*, 1990
  A novel, about Sapogonia, a distinct place where all mestizos reside regardless of nationality or race, or possibly because of racial background.

`694`

ELIUD MARTINEZ, Mexican American

Voice-Haunted Journey
(Tempe, AZ: Bilingual Press, 1990)

Subject(s): Family; Modern Life; Identity
Age range(s): Grades 10-Adult
Major character(s): Miguel Velasquez, Professor, Writer, Mexican American
Time period(s): 1990s (1990)
Locale(s): California

Summary: This first novel of a projected trilogy is the saga of five generations of a Mexican-American family in California. As he explores an elaborate series of memories and fantasies about his family, Miguel Velasquez, a broodingly complex man and a professor at a university, is writing a novel. All of the action occurs in his mind, during an airplane flight: his brother's death, the women in his life, his psyche, and his struggle for identity.

Where it's reviewed:
Melus, Spring 1991, page 121

Other books by the same author:
The Art of Mariano Azuela: Modernism in la Malhora, el Desquite, la Luciernaga, 1980

Other books you might like:
Emilio Diaz Valcarcel, *Hot Soles in Harlem*, 1993
  Gerardo is shown New York City from the Puerto Rican barrio in Harlem to the penthouses on Fifth Avenue with its many unusual characters.
Gustavo Perez Firmat, *Next Year in Cuba: A Cubano's Coming of Age in America*, 1995
  A memoir by a professor exploring his biculturalism and his search for identity and roots in America.
Arturo Islas, *The Rain God: A Desert Tale*, 1984
  Miguel Angel must find his way between his Mexican Catholic heritage and his Western education while living in a mythical southwest.
Ofelia Dumas Lachtman, *A Shell for Angela*, 1995
  When, at nine, Angela sees her father led away by immi-

gration officials, she begins to deny her Mexican heritage and later raises her own children to be ignorant of their grandparents.

`695`

MAX MARTINEZ, Mexican American

A Red Bikini Dream
(Houston, TX: Arte Publico Press, 1990)

Subject(s): Modern Life; Identity; Sexual Behavior
Age range(s): Grades 10-Adult
Time period(s): 1980s (1990)
Locale(s): New York, New York; Texas

Summary: A collection of five short stories that capture the rhythms and spirit of modern life in the U.S. Martinez's stories ponder the question of self and identity in an increasingly complex nation. In the title story, an attractive divorcee drives across the country searching for the sexual encounter of her dreams. In another, a married couple vacation in Texas while searching for some meaning in their lives.

Where it's reviewed:
Review of Contemporary Fiction, Summer 1991, page 239

Other books by the same author:
The Adventures of the Chicano Kid and Other Stories, 1982
Schoolland: A Novel, 1988
White Leg, 1996

Other books you might like:
Dagoberto Gilb, *Magic of Blood*, 1993
  A powerful collection that presents harsh, realistic stories about working-class life in Texas and California.
Ed Vega, *Mendoza's Dreams*, 1987
  A collection of stories populated by strange, loveable characters such as a hunchback circus clown, an innocent virgin, and an angel attempting to earn respect in heaven.
Genaro Gonzalez, *Rainbow's End*, 1988
  An adventure novel that presents dangerous border crossings, confrontations with a magician, and drug smuggling in the lives of three generations of the Cavazos family in Texas.
Maria Espinosa, *Dark Plums*, 1995
  Adrianne, a young girl from Texas, searches for love in Manhattan, falls into an abusive relationship, and eventually works as a prostitute.
Ana Castillo, *Loverboys, Stories*, 1996
  The stories included in this collection range from one-page vignettes to longer narratives; their subjects range from inexperienced to world-weary.
Dagoberto Gilb, *The Last Known Residence of Mickey Acuna*, 1994
  Mickey Acuna is waiting for something to happen. He hangs out at the YMCA in El Paso with a cast of characters living a fantasy life as they too, wait for something to happen.

MAX MARTINEZ, Mexican American

White Leg
(Houston, TX: Arte Publico, 1996)

Subject(s): Mystery and Detective Stories; Crime and Criminals; Kidnapping
Age range(s): Grades 10-Adult
Major character(s): Gil Blue, Worker (blue collar), Thief
Time period(s): 1990s
Locale(s): White Leg, Texas

Summary: A fast action murder mystery after the style of Jim Thompson about a small town thief in a backwater town in Texas. Gil Blue robs convenience stores to support his wife's expensive tastes. During one of his hold-ups he's interruped by a Texas Ranger so he shoots him, along with the store clerk and a young Mexican couple. As he flees the FBI, he discovers his wife is involved in a plan to kidnap the grandson of the local benefactor for blackmailing purposes, and she's also cheating on him. Lot's of sex, violence, and suspense.

Where it's reviewed:
Publishers Weekly, February 12, 1996, page 59

Other books by the same author:
A Red Bikini Dream, 1990
Schoolland: A Novel, 1988

Other books you might like:
Dagoberto Gilb, *The Last Known Residence of Mickey Acuna*, 1994
   Mickey Acuna is waiting for something, something arriving through the mail, as he dwells at the YMCA in El Paso.
Gloria Gonzalez, *The Thirteenth Apostle*, 1993
   Newspaperwoman Geraldine St. Claire investigates the murder of her lover Hal, which leads her to suspect an industrial homicide and also leads her right into the hands of a powerful drug lord.
Soledad Santiago, *Streets of Fire*, 1996
   This murder mystery with a Latina police officer, Francesca Colon, involves all the elements of big city dirty politics, police corruption, suspicious deaths, and tense ethnic community relations.
Thomas Sanchez, *Mile Zero*, 1989
   This exciting novel uses history, voodoo, santeria, folkloric sayings, and tropical culture to create a supernatural mystery and introduce *Zobop*, possibly a voodoo-inspired killer.
Manuel Ramos, *The Last Client of Luis Montez*, 1996
   The last client of Denver lawyer Louie Montez is found dead with Montez standing over him. To clear his name Montez becomes entangled in a complicated web that takes him to California and back.
Steven Lopez, *Third and Indiana*, 1994
   The title of this novel refers to the corner where fourteen-year-old Gabriel hands out crack to people in passing cars. He works for Diablo, who is demanding payment when his accounts come up short.
Soledad Santiago, *Nightside*, 1994
   Anna Eltern, a former nun who runs a shelter for runaway

teens, struggles with financial problems and murder after funding cuts force her to turn away homeless teenagers.
Rafael Yglesias, *Dr. Neruda's Cure for Evil*, 1996
   The three parts of this long novel concern the title character's background, his relationship with one of his patients, and his evaluation of the flawed therapy he offered this patient.
Lionel G. Garcia, *Hardscrub*, 1990
   Related from the perspective of eleven-year-old Jim, this novel portrays characters struggling to survive in the tough land of West Texas.

HUGO MARTINEZ-SERROS, Mexican American

The Last Laugh and Other Stories
(Houston, TX: Arte Publico Press, 1988)

Subject(s): City Life; Brothers; Family Relations
Age range(s): Grades 10-Adult
Time period(s): 1930s; 1940s (1930-1945)
Locale(s): Chicago, Illinois

Summary: A collection of short stories that evoke the culture and atmosphere of World War II in urban Chicago. In these stories the author creates vivid scenes of industrialization, immigration and migration, life in the factories and mills, education indoctrination, and the weariness of priests as they bring religion to the uneducated. Several stories are about brothers, Lazaro and Jaime, who work hard physically alongside their father to help feed their family. In another story David and Victor, once very close brothers, have lives that take separate paths and end tragically.

Where it's reviewed:
Publishers Weekly, June 3, 1988, page 79
Hispania, September 1990, page 671

Other books you might like:
Rick P. Rivera, *A Fabricated Mexican*, 1995
   A series of comic vignettes about a quiet but mischevious boy growing up in California, and the antics of his eccentric family and his own search for identity.
Jose Antonio Burciaga, *Spilling the Beans: Loteria Chicana*, 1995
   A series of essays, many humorous, recounting experiences from the author's childhood and explorations into aspects of Chicano culture.
Dagoberto Gilb, *The Magic of Blood*, 1993
   A powerful collection that presents harsh, realistic stories about working-class life in Texas and California.
Nash Candelaria, *The Day the Cisco Kid Shot John Wayne*, 1988
   A humorous collection of short stories from New Mexico, in which the author examines cultural clashes between Latinos and Anglos.

698

C.M. MAYO, Mexican American

Sky over el Nido: Stories
(Athens, GA: University of Georgia Press, 1995)

Subject(s): Women; Wealth; Satire
Age range(s): Grades 10-Adult
Time period(s): 20th century (1968-1993)
Locale(s): New York, New York; Mexico

Summary: This collection of interrelated short stories combines humor, satire, and sympathy with critical overtones, and with wealthy characters who effortlessly fly around the world. A matron at a wedding dives after a drowning child, a poet drunkenly toys with a pet jaguarundi, and a bored and wealthy businessman takes a homeless man with AIDs, found on a Manhattan sidewalk, on a trip to Europe. Mayo's stories about contemporary cosmopolitan life are surprising and intriguing.

Where it's reviewed:
Publishers Weekly, October 9, 1995, page 77

Awards the book has won:
Flannery O'Connor Award for Short Fiction, 1995

Other books you might like:
Estela Portillo Trambley, *Rain of Scorpions and Other Stories*, 1993
    A novella and eight stories, this collection deals with many feminist themes where the main characters are strong brave women with special gifts.
Sandra Cisneros, *Woman Hollering Creek and Other Stories*, 1991
    This collection of short stories is about women that take place in Texas and the border area.
Himilce Novas, *Mangos, Bananas, and Coconuts: A Cuban Love Story*, 1996
    This tale of a magical yet real love story is an ancient tale, beginning with the love of a man and a woman from different social classes, and the story of the fate of their children.
Max Martinez, *A Red Bikini Dream*, 1990
    The rhythms and spirit of modern life in the U.S. are captured in this collection of five short stories where the characters ponder self and identity in an increasingly complex society.
Yvonne V. Sapia, *Valentino's Hair*, 1991
    Rudolph Valentino comes into the life of Facundo Nieves and changes it forever when Nieves saves the hair and its power haunts him until his own death.
Giannini Braschi, *Empire of Dreams*, 1994
    In a series of prose poems, Braschi creates amazing postmodernist images of New York City. Her lyrical and unique text blends Shakespeare, Beatles songs, and a mixture of cultural influences.

699

PABLO MEDINA, Cuban American

Exiled Memories: A Cuban Childhood
(Austin, TX: University of Texas Press, 1990)

Subject(s): Growing Up; Revolution; Coming of Age
Age range(s): Grades 8-Adult
Time period(s): 20th century (1940-1960)
Locale(s): Cuba

Summary: This work is a collection of the author's memories of growing up in Cuba. Pablo spends summers on his grandfather's sugar cane plantation, La Luisa, which is taken over by the Castro regime after the revolution. Humorous and moving stories about both his maternal and paternal grandparents, their homes both in the country and in the city of Havana, are presented. Medina's memories are vivid and his narration reads like a novel, documenting his childhood and eventual exile.

About this book: Glossary of Spanish terms appended; photographs throughout the book.

Where it's reviewed:
Library Journal, October 1, 1990, p. 98
Journal of Interamerican Studies & World Affairs, Winter '94, p. 145

Other books by the same author:
Arching into the Afterlife, 1991
The Marks of Birth, 1994

Other books you might like:
Gustavo Perez Firmat, *Next Year in Cuba: A Cubano's Coming of Age in America*, 1995
    A memoir exploring biculturalism, identity and the tenuous roots of those in America who cry "Next year in Cuba!" expecting to return to their homeland at any moment.
Victor Perera, *Rites: A Guatemalan Boyhood*, 1986
    Autobiographical narratives of the author's boyhood growing up in Guatemala.
Omar Castaneda, *Remembering to Say Mouth or Face*, 1993
    Short stories, some of which take place in Central America, by a Guatemalan writer now living in the U.S.
Fernando Alegria, *Paradise Lost or Gained? The Literature of Hispanic Exile*, 1990
    A collection of writings by Latinos addressing the experience of exile and alienation through stories, poems, and essays.
Ruth Behar, *Bridges to Cuba = Puentes a Cuba*, 1995
    An anthology of short stories, essays, poetry, and historical documents exploring the Cuban and Cuban American experience.

700

PABLO MEDINA, Cuban American

The Marks of Birth
(New York: Farrar, Straus, and Giroux, 1994)

Subject(s): Family Relations; Coming of Age; Exile
Age range(s): Grades 10-Adult

Major character(s): Anton Garcia Turner, Young Man, Exile, Cuban American
Time period(s): 20th century (1960-1994)
Locale(s): Florida; Cuba

Summary: The descendant of a well-to-do Cuban family, Anton Garcia Turner is forced to flee the island due to political turmoil. Later, during his adolescence in the Bronx and adulthood in New Jersey, Anton lives a frustrated exiled life. The characters in this novel are shadowy and enigmatic, as the author shows us life in self-imposed exile.

Where it's reviewed:
Library Journal, May 15, 1994, page 100
Publishers Weekly, May 9, 1994, page 61

Other books by the same author:
Arching into the Afterlife, 1991
Exiled Memories: A Cuban Childhood, 1990

Other books you might like:
Virgil Suarez, *Welcome to the Oasis and Other Stories*, 1992
    The author creates a new generation of young Cuban characters in this novella and five stories where they struggle to integrate into the American culture while maintaining their heritage.
Elias Miguel Munoz, *Crazy Love*, 1989
    Experimental and autobiographical, this novel is about the Cuban American experience.
Omar Torres, *Fallen Angels Sing*, 1991
    When Miguel Saavedra moves to New York, he is caught up in a web of plots spun by pro- and anti-Castro agents and soon is involved in planning the assassination of Fidel Castro.
Gustavo Perez Firmat, *Next Year in Cuba: A Cubano's Coming of Age in America*, 1995
    The author of this memoir explores his biculturalism and his search for identity and roots in America.
Ruth Behar, *Bridges to Cuba = Puentes a Cuba*, 1995
    This anthology of short stories, essays, poetry, and historical documents explores the Cuban and Cuban American experience.
Reinaldo Arenas, *The Doorman*, 1991
    This story about Juan, a young Cuban refugee who becomes a doorman at a luxury apartment building in New York is a parable about freedom.

701

MIGUEL MENDEZ, Mexican American

The Dream of Santa Maria de las Piedras
(Tempe, AZ: Bilingual Press, 1989)

Subject(s): Rural Life; Traditions; Men
Age range(s): Grades 10-Adult
Major character(s): Timoteo Noragua, Adventurer, Mexican
Time period(s): Indeterminate Past
Locale(s): Santa Maria de las Piedras, Mexico; Arizona

Summary: This is the story of a small rural poor town in the Sonora Desert of Mexico as seen through the eyes of the old men who gather to reminisce and gossip in the town plaza. The old men tell tales about the town's first brothel, the town's colorful characters, and the Noragua family. They

focus on one of the members of the Noragua family who journeys to the United States and meets disillusionment in a whimsical and mythical adventure.

Where it's reviewed:
Cuadernos Americanos, 1996, page 131

Other books by the same author:
Pilgrims in Aztlan, 1992
Cuentos y Ensayos Para Reir y Aprender, 1990
Peregrinos de Aztlan, 1991
Que No Mueran los Suenos, 1991

Other books you might like:
Aristeo Brito, *The Devil in Texas = El Diablo en Texas*, 1990
    An important novel that describes the Anglo destruction of a Chicano world in Texas where the devil comes to the border town of Presidio.
Alberto Alvaro Rios, *Pig Cookies and Other Stories*, 1995
    Set earlier in this century, this collection of interrelated short stories takes place in a small village in northern Mexico.
Alfredo Vea Jr., *La Maravilla*, 1993
    A young boy grows up on Buckeye Road in a world of marvels in the desert outside the Phoenix city limits, caught between many cultures.
Americo Paredes, *The Hammon and the Beans and Other Stories*, 1994
    A collection of short stories set in the southern Texas border deals with the cultural conflict that has dominated that area since the U.S.-Mexican War.
Ron Arias, *The Road to Tamazunchale*, 1987
    Don Fausto, old and nearing death in a Los Angeles barrio, decides to take a journey through time and space, from the Inca world to encounters with undocumented workers in California.
Nash Candelaria, *Memories of the Alhambra*, 1977
    Jose Rafa disappears leaving only a receipt for traveler's checks and a business card from an L.A. con man who sells false genealogies. Has he gone to Mexico to search for Spanish ancestors?

702

MIGUEL MENDEZ, Mexican American

Pilgrims in Aztlan
(Tempe, AZ: Bilingual Press, 1992)

Subject(s): City Life; Poverty; Migrant Labor
Age range(s): Grades 10-Adult
Major character(s): Loreto Maldonado, Aged Person (old man), Veteran, Mexican
Time period(s): 1930s
Locale(s): Tijuana, Mexico; California

Summary: Loreto Maldonado, an aging veteran of the Mexican Revolution, now washes cars for tourists in Tijuana, watching the people who come his way and tell him their stories. A Chicano Classic with four editions published in Spanish, this is the first English edition. A stream of consciousness narration gives expression to the collective voice of millions of Mexican migrant workers who come to the U.S. Narrated in Mexican Spanish and using "calo", pachuco slang, this novel portrays the impact of city life on the traditional Mexican consciousness.

About this book: First published in Spanish in 1974 as *Peregrinos de Aztlan*; translated by David William Foster.

Where it's reviewed:
America, July 18, 1992, page 39
Library Journal, March 15, 1993, page 108

Other books by the same author:
The Dream of Santa Maria de las Piedras, 1989
Cuentos y Ensayos Para Reir y Aprender, 1990
Peregrinos de Aztlan, 1991
Que No Mueran los Suenos, 1991

Other books you might like:
Raymond Barrio, *The Plum Plum Pickers*, 1969
   This is the dramatic story of Manuel and Lupe Gutierrez and their children, migrant farm workers in California's Santa Clara Valley.
Jose Antonio Villarreal, *Pocho*, 1959
   This is considered to be the first key Chicano novel about a Mexican family attempting to assimilate in the Santa Clara Valley of California.
Tomas Rivera, *Y No Se lo Trago la Tierra.And the Earth Did Not Devour Him*, 1987
   These twelve related stories document the spiritual strength of migrant farm workers. This work reproduces in language the sad and tragic lives of migrant workers as they travel the migrant stream.
Gordon Kahn, *A Long Way from Home*, 1989
   Written forty years before it was published this novel tells the story of Gilberto, a young Chicano who after his mother's death leaves the U.S. for Mexico to find his only remaining family.
Aristeo Brito, *The Devil in Texas = El Diablo en Texas*, 1990
   The devil comes to the border town of Presidio, Texas in this important novel that describes the Anglo destruction of a Chicano world.
Ernesto Galarza, *Barrio Boy*, 1971
   Autobiographical, this story examines the early life of a distinguished professor and author who wrote many works about Mexican agricultural workers.
Edmund Villasenor, *Macho!*, 1973
   This early Chicano novel is about a 17-year-old who illegally crosses the U.S. border, cheats his fellow workers, becomes a strike breaker and turns criminal in his quest for riches and acculturation.
Oscar Zeta Acosta, *The Revolt of the Cockroach People*, 1973
   This personal memoir tells of the turbulent years that mark the beginning of the Chicano movement in California and of political activity in East Los Angeles.
Ron Arias, *The Road to Tamazunchale*, 1987
   Don Fausto, old and nearing death in a Los Angeles barrio, journeys through time and space, from the Inca empire to modern California.

BRYCE MILLIGAN, Editor
MARY GUERRO MILLIGAN, Co-Editor, Mexican American

Daughters of the Fifth Sun: A Collection of Latina Fiction and Poetry
(New York: Riverhead Books, 1995)

Subject(s): Anthology; Short Stories; Poetry
Age range(s): Grades 10-Adult
Time period(s): 1990s (1995)
Locale(s): United States (stories take place throughout the U.S.)

Summary: Thirty-two contemporary Latina writers contributed to this collection of poetry and short stories. Well-known established authors include Sandra Cisneros, Ana Castillo, and Cherrie Moraga. Many new younger authors involved in this anthology represent the next generation of Cuban Americans, Puerto Ricans, and Dominican writers.

Where it's reviewed:
Library Journal, September 15, 1995, page 66
Publishers Weekly, July 24, 1995, page 48

Other books by the same author:
Daysleepers & Other Poems, 1984
Litany Sung at Hell's Gate, 1990

Other books you might like:
Lillian Castillo-Speed, *Latina: Women's Voices from the Borderlands*, 1995
   This collection of short fiction is by Latinas.
Evangelina Vigil, *Woman of Her Word: Hispanic Women Write*, 1987
   Latina writings comprise this anthology
Roberta Fernandez, *In Other Words: Literature by Latinas in the U.S.*, 1994
   This collection of short fiction is by Latinas.
Tey Diana Rebolledo, *Infinite Divisions: An Anthology of Chicana Literature*, 1993
   This anthology contains historical and contemporary writings by Mexican American women.
Tey Diana Rebolledo, *Las Mujeres Hablan*, 1988
   Chicanas from New Mexico author this collection of poetry and short-stories.
Alma Gomez, *Cuentos: Stories by Latinas*, 1983
   This is a collection of stories by Hispanic women.
Maria del Carmen Boza, *Nosotras: Latina Literature Today*, 1986
   This is a collection of poetry and short stories by Latina writers.

CARLOS MIRALEJOS

Rabid Beasts
(Woodbridge, VG: Outer Space Press, 1993)

Subject(s): Science Fiction; Indians of North America; Racism
Age range(s): Grades 9-Adult
Major character(s): Quiro, 15-Year-Old, Prisoner, Native American (Cherokee)

Time period(s): Indeterminate
Locale(s): United States

Summary: On the planet Kapiro, Fasalastraba the maximum leader, receives a mind message from Quiro, a Cherokee Indian on planet Earth. The Cherokee Nation is being forced to march 900 miles to a reservation in Oklahoma during extremely cold weather and are dying by the thousands. This cruelty is imposed on them by rabid beasts, a water based scourge of life species, the final survival of billions of years of evolution known as the human species. In universal time that shifts from past to future, this novel tells the story of the saving of the Cherokees by Jorge Sogaseca, captain of the space ship Tulumex, with his team of cyborgs and Kapirons.

Other books you might like:

Ron Arias, *The Road to Tamazunchale*, 1987
    Don Fausto, old and nearing death in a Los Angeles barrio, decides to take a journey through time and space, from the Inca world to encounters with undocumented workers in California.

Aristeo Brito, *The Devil in Texas = El Diablo en Texas*, 1990
    This important novel describes the Anglo destruction of a Chicano world in Texas, where the devil comes to the border town of Presidio.

Alejandro Morales, *The Rag Doll Plagues*, 1988
    Divided into three sections, this novel shows Latino doctors fighting a deadly infectious disease over three centuries in Mexico and in the future United States.

Joseph P. Sanchez, *THe Aztec Chronicles: The True History of Christopher Columbus, as Narrated by Quilaztli of Texcoco: A Novella*, 1995
    A historical novella, based on documentary and biobliographical research, this is narrated by an Aztec historian and attempts to reconstruct the true history of Christopher Columbus.

Montserrat Fontes, *Dreams of the Centaur*, 1995
    Alejo Durcal, son of a slain ranch owner, tries to avenge his father's death, during the period in history when the Yaqui Indians were badly mistreated in Mexico.

705

JOVITA GONZALEZ MIRELES, Mexican American
EVE RALEIGH, Editor, Mexican American
JOSE E. LIMON, Editor, Mexican American
MARIA COTERA, Editor, Mexican American

Caballero: A Historical Novel

(College Station, TX: Texas A&M University Press, 1996)

Subject(s): Romance; Cultures and Customs
Age range(s): Grades 10-Adult
Major character(s): Don Santiago de Mendoza y Soria, Rancher, Father (patriarch), Texas Mexican
Time period(s): 1840s
Locale(s): Texas (southern Texas, along Mexican border)

Summary: This historical novel takes place during and after the U.S. Mexico War of 1846-48 when Mexico lost a large part of its territory to the U.S. Don Santiago is trying to maintain his family with Mexican customs and values, during the American take-over, but his two daughters each fall in love with Americans. The culture conflicts that result are realistically portrayed.

About this book: This novel was written during the 1930s and the manuscript was recently discovered.

Where it's reviewed:
Publishers Weekly, May 20, 1996, page 252

Other books you might like:

Nash Candelaria, *Not by the Sword*, 1982
    The family of Don Jose Antonio Rafa struggles with the changes brought about by the annexation of New Mexico by the United States after the U.S.-Mexican War.

Montserrat Fontes, *Dreams of the Centaur*, 1995
    A fast-paced novel about the son of a slain ranch owner, who tries to avenge his father's death and journeys through love, murder, prison, and war in Mexico .

Alejandro Morales, *The Brick People*, 1988
    A fictional but historically-based novel about two families pitted against each other, the powerful Simons and the proud Revueltas, during the late nineteenth century in California.

Tina Juarez, *Call No Man Master*, 1995
    A historical novel about a young woman of mixed heritage, Spanish and Indian, who at age 16 participated in the events that lead to Mexico's independence from Spain.

David Monreal, *Cinco de Mayo: An Epic Novel*, 1993
    A historical novel that presents the events leading up to the Battle of Puebla on the 5th of May 1862 in Mexico.

706

NICHOLASA MOHR, Puerto Rican

El Bronx Remembered: A Novella and Stories

(New York: Harper & Row, 1975.)

Subject(s): Short Stories; Family Relations; Poverty
Age range(s): Grades 9-12
Time period(s): 1940s; 1950s (1946-1956)
Locale(s): New York, New York (el barrio in the South Bronx)

Summary: This novella and collection of short stories depict the lives of Puerto Rican families in the South Bronx. Neighborhood life is vividly portrayed, telling about realistic situations such as unhappy marriages, illegitimacy, and homosexuality.

About this book: Since these memorable neighborhood characters are well-created and depicted, they stay with the reader for some time. This work has been re-published several times, most recently in 1986.

Where it's reviewed:
English Journal, February 1978, page 98

Awards the book has won:
National Book Award Finalist, 1976

Other books by the same author:
Nilda: A Novel, 1973
In Nueva York, 1977
Rituals of Survival: A Woman's Portfolio, 1985

Other books you might like:

Jack Agueros, *Dominoes and Other Stories from the Puerto Rican*, 1993

These stories are about growing up Puerto Rican in New York City.

Piri Thomas, *Stories from El Barrio*, 1978

These stories are about growing up Puerto Rican in New York City.

Phyllis Tashlik, *Hispanic, Female, and Young*, 1994

This is a collection of short stories written by young Latina girls from El Barrio of New York.

Abraham Rodriguez Jr., *The Boy Without a Flag: Tales of the South Bronx*, 1992

This collection of short stories is about the problems of young Puerto Ricans in the Bronx.

Judith Ortiz-Cofer, *An Island Like You: Stories of the Barrio*, 1995

Twelve stories, set in a barrio of New Jersey, examine the lives of Puerto Rican teenagers who deal with friendship, family, romance, and school.

Pedro Juan Soto, *Spiks*, 1973

These short stories describe Puerto Rican women in New York.

707

NICHOLASA MOHR, Puerto Rican

Felita
(New York: Bantam, 1990)

Subject(s): Moving, Household; Family; Friendship
Age range(s): Grades 4-6
Major character(s): Felita, Child, Puerto Rican
Time period(s): 1970s
Locale(s): New York, New York

Summary: Felita loves her neighborhood and her best friend Gigi, but her world is turned upside down when her family announces that they will be moving to a new neighborhood. Only her grandmother, who moved to New York from Puerto Rico, understands.

About this book: This work, first published in 1979, includes drawings by Ray Cruz.

Where it's reviewed:
Reading Teacher, October 1991, page 100

Awards the book has won:
Notable Children's Book in the Field of Social Studies

Other books by the same author:
El Bronx Remembered: A Novella and Stories, 1986
In Nueva York, 1977
Nilda: A Novel, 1973
Rituals of Survival: A Woman's Portfolio, 1985

Other books you might like:
Alma Flor Ada, *My Name Is Maria Isabel*, 1993
Maria Isabel must defend her name and heritage.
Pura Belpre, *Santiago*, 1969
Santiago moves to a new country and makes new friends.
Gary Soto, *The Skirt*, 1992
Fourth-grader Miata loses her mother's folkloric dancing skirt and figures out a way to find it.

Cruz Martel, *Yagua Days*, 1978
Adan, born in New York, gets to visit his relatives in Puerto Rico one summer and learn about yagua days.
Ofelia Dumas Lachtman, *Pepita Talks Twice = Pepita Habla Dos Veces*, 1995
Pepita is annoyed that she has to translate for neighbors, friends, and relatives. After she stops speaking Spanish to make her point, she learns the value of bilingualism.

708

NICHOLASA MOHR, Puerto Rican

Going Home
(New York: Dial Books, 1986)

Subject(s): Friendship; Homesickness; Family Life
Age range(s): Grades 5-8
Major character(s): Felita, 12-Year-Old, Puerto Rican
Time period(s): 1980s (1986)
Locale(s): New York; Puerto Rico

Summary: When Felita learns that she will be spending two months in Puerto Rico with relatives, she is excited, even though she'll be leaving her family and friends behind. But in Puerto Rico, some girls her own age call her gringa and say she doesn't belong. Felita learns to use her bravery and determination to make a place for herself.

About this book: This is a sequel to *Felita*.

Where it's reviewed:
Horn Book, September 1986, page 591
Publishers Weekly, July 25, 1986, page 190
School Library Journal, August 1986, page 105

Other books by the same author:
El Bronx Remembered: A Novella and Stories, 1975
In Nueva York, 1977
Nilda: A Novel, 1974
Rituals of Survival: A Woman's Portfolio, 1985
Felita, 1990

Other books you might like:
Karen Papagapitos, *Socorro, Daughter of the Desert*, 1993
The family of eight-year-old Socorro are farm workers and she helps out the family as much as she can. When her father becomes ill, Socorro makes tortillas for her mother to sell in the fields.
Alma Flor Ada, *My Name Is Maria Isabel*, 1993
Maria Isabel must defend her name and heritage.
Pura Belpre, *Santiago*, 1969
Santiago moves to a new country and makes new friends.
Gary Soto, *The Skirt*, 1992
Fourth-grader Miata loses her mother's folkloric dancing skirt and figures out a way to find it.
Cruz Martel, *Yagua Days*, 1978
Adan, born in New York, gets to visit his relatives in Puerto Rico one summer and learn about yagua days.

709

NICHOLASA MOHR, Puerto Rican

In Nueva York
(New York: The Dial Press, 1977)

Subject(s): Short Stories; Poverty; City Life
Age range(s): Grades 9-12
Time period(s): 1950s
Locale(s): New York, New York (lower East Side of New York City)

Summary: These eight short stories portray the life of Puerto Ricans in the Lower East Side. Characters like Old Mary, Ramon, Johnny, and Sebastian seem trapped in an existence out of their control. The Nuyorican population is sketched in dreamlike segments as they remember an idealized Puerto Rican paradise, while facing the hostile life of street gangs, ruthless landlords, racist police, and unfair teachers.

About this book: This work was re-published in 1988.

Where it's reviewed:
English Journal, February 1978, page 98

Awards the book has won:
School Library Journal Best Books for Spring, 1977
American Library Association Best Books for Young Adults, 1977

Other books by the same author:
El Bronx Remembered: A Novella and Stories, 1975
Nilda: A Novel, 1973
Rituals of Survival: A Woman's Portfolio, 1985

Other books you might like:
Jack Agueros, *Dominoes and Other stories from the Puerto Rican*, 1993
   These stories are about growing up Puerto Rican in New York City.
Piri Thomas, *Stories from El Barrio*, 1978
   These stories are about growing up Puerto Rican in New York City.
Phyllis Tashlik, *Hispanic, Female, and Young*, 1994
   This collection of short stories is written by young Latina girls from El Barrio of New York.
Abraham Rodriguez Jr., *The Boy Without a Flag: Tales of the South Bronx*, 1992
   This collection of short stories is about the problems of young Puerto Ricans in the Bronx.
Pedro Juan Soto, *Spiks*, 1973
   These short stories depict Puerto Rican women in New York.
Judith Ortiz-Cofer, *An Island Like You: Stories of the Barrio*, 1995
   Twelve stories, set in a barrio of New Jersey, examine the lives of Puerto Rican teenagers who deal with friendship, family, romance, and school.

710

NICHOLASA MOHR, Puerto Rican

Nilda: A Novel
(New York: Bantam Books, 1973)

Subject(s): Coming of Age; Family Relations; City Life
Age range(s): Grades 9-12
Major character(s): Nilda Ramirez, 10-Year-Old, Puerto Rican
Time period(s): 1940s
Locale(s): New York, New York (Puerto Rican barrio of New York City)

Summary: A semi-autobiographical story about a young girl growing up in the Puerto Rican barrio of New York City during World War II. Her life is followed from 1941-1945, until she graduates from high school and faces the death of her mother. Her good friends Benj and Peter make life easier.

About this book: This a classic work for young Puerto Ricans growing up in New York.

Awards the book has won:
New York Times Outstanding Book of the Year, 1974
American Library Association Best Book, 1973

Other books by the same author:
In Nueva York, 1977
El Bronx Remembered: A Novella and Stories, 1975
Rituals of Survival: A Woman's Portfolio, 1985

Other books you might like:
Sandra Cisneros, *The House on Mango Street*, 1983
   This story is about a young Mexican girl growing up in an urban setting.
Judith Ortiz Cofer, *Silent Dancing: A Partial Remembrance of a Puerto Rican Childhood*, 1990
   These stories are about growing up in both Puerto Rico and in New Jersey.
Jack Agueros, *Dominoes and Other stories from the Puerto Rican*, 1993
   These stories are about growing up Puerto Rican in New York City.
Piri Thomas, *Stories from El Barrio*, 1978
   These stories are about growing up Puerto Rican in New York City.
Phyllis Tashlik, *Hispanic, Female, and Young*, 1994
   This is a collection of short stories written by young Latina girls from El Barrio of New York.
Abraham Rodriguez Jr., *The Boy Without a Flag: Tales of the South Bronx*, 1992
   This collection of short stories is about the problems of young Puerto Ricans in the Bronx.

711

NICHOLASA MOHR, Puerto Rican

Rituals of Survival: A Woman's Portfolio
(Houston: Arte Publico, 1985)

Subject(s): Short Stories; Family Relations; Women
Age range(s): Grades 9-Adult
Major character(s): Inez Otero, Spouse, Artist

Time period(s): 1980s (1985)
Locale(s): New York, New York; Puerto Rico

Summary: Strong Latino women, who take charge, dominate the six stories in this collection. So it is not by chance that women's names—Zoraida, Carmela, Lucia—also title the stories.

Other books by the same author:
El Bronx Remembered: A Novella and Stories, 1986
In Nueva York, 1977
Nilda: A Novel, 1986
The Song of el Coqui and Other Tales of Puerto Rico, 1995

Other books you might like:
Gary D. Keller, *Hispanics in the U.S.: An Anthology of Creative Literature*, 1982
Latino authors created this collection of short stories and poetry
Judith Ortiz Cofer, *Silent Dancing: A Partial Remembrance of a Puerto Rican Childhood*, 1990
This autobiographical collection of prose, poetry, and short stories describes growing up in Puerto Rico and the U.S.
Jack Agueros, *Dominoes and Other Stories from the Puerto Rican*, 1993
These short stories reveal life in New York City as a Puerto Rican experiences it.
Phyllis Tashlik, *Hispanic, Female, and Young*, 1994
Poems and short stories, written by teenage girls in New York, comprise this collection.
Abraham Rodriguez Jr., *The Boy Without a Flag: Tales of the South Bronx*, 1992
Problems of young Puerto Ricans in the Bronx reveal themselves in this collection of short stories.
Esmeralda Santiago, *When I Was Puerto Rican*, 1994
This autobiographical story portrays growing up in Puerto Rico and the U.S.

712

NICHOLASA MOHR, Puerto Rican
ANTONIO MARTORELL, Co-Author, Puerto Rican

The Song of el Coqui and Other Tales of Puerto Rico

(New York: Viking, 1995)

Subject(s): Folk Tales; Animals/Frogs and Toads; Animals/ Mules
Age range(s): Grades K-2
Time period(s): Indeterminate Past
Locale(s): Puerto Rico

Summary: This collection of three vividly illustrated tales evokes the rich ancestral traditions of Puerto Rican culture. It includes a story of creation from the Tainos, another about a stowaway hen from the African population of Puerto Rico, and also a story about bandits and slaves from the Spaniards.

Where it's reviewed:
Publishers Weekly, July 10, 1995, page 56

Other books by the same author:
El Bronx Remembered: A Novella and Stories, 1986

In Nueva York, 1977
Nilda: A Novel, 1973
Rituals of Survival: A Woman's Portfolio, 1985
Felita, 1990

Other books you might like:
Pura Belpre, *Ote: A Puerto Rican Folk Tale*, 1969
Ote must go to the forest in search of food for his wife and five children, where he meets a near-sighted devil who brings him bad luck.
Pura Belpre, *Dance of the Animals*, 1972
Senor and Senora Lion, hungry for goat meat, throw a party and invite all the animals.
Lucia M. Gonzalez, *The Bossy Gallito*, 1994
A bossy little rooster, "un gallito mandon", is on his way to his uncle's wedding, when he gets his beak dirty after pecking at some corn.
Pura Belpre, *The Tiger and the Rabbit and Other Tales*, 1965
This collection of folk tales is from Puerto Rico.
Linda Shute, *Rabbit Wishes*, 1995
Soon after creation, Tio Conejo complains that he wants to be large like an elephant or tall like a giraffe.
Alma Flor Ada, *Dear Peter Rabbit = Querido Pedrin*, 1994
Goldilocks, Baby Bear, Peter Rabbit, and The Three Little Pigs write letters to each other in this captivating book.

713

DAVID MONREAL, Mexican American

Cinco de Mayo: An Epic Novel

(Encino, CA: Floricanto Press, 1993)

Subject(s): War; Holidays; Rebellion
Age range(s): Grades 10-Adult
Major character(s): Jorge Huerta, Journalist, Mexican
Time period(s): 1860s
Locale(s): Puebla de Los Angeles, Mexico (Puebla)

Summary: An historical novel that presents the events leading up to the Battle of Puebla on the 5th of May 1862. The story is related from the viewpoint of Jorge Huert a, a twenty-six-year-old journalist for the *Diario de Mexico*, who is se nt to Puebla to report on activities of the French army. Colorful, exciting, a nd inspiring, Monreal's novel is factual and filled with actual historical data and characters.

Other books by the same author:
Cellmates, 1987
The New Neighbor and Other Stories, 1987

Other books you might like:
Daniel Cano, *Pepe Rios*, 1991
In this historical novel about the Mexican Revolution of 1910, Pepe Rios searches for peace amidst the chaos and violence of war.
Montserrat Fontes, *Dreams of the Centaur*, 1995
The son of a slain ranch owner tries to avenge his father's death during the deportation of the Yaqui Indians during the presidency of Porfirio Diaz.
Nash Candelaria, *Inheritance of Strangers*, 1985
This sequel to *Not By the Sword*, covers the years after the Mexican War of 1846 until the date of New Mexico

statehood. It presents the struggles of the Rafa family against Anglo exploitation.

Alejandro Morales, *The Rag Doll Plagues*, 1988
Divided into three sections, this novel shows Latino doctors fighting a deadly infectious disease over three centuries in Mexico and the United States.

Tina Juarez, *Call No Man Master*, 1995
This intricately crafted historical novel is about a young woman of mixed heritage, Spanish and Indian, and her participation in the events that lead to Mexico's independence from Spain.

Victor Villasenor, *Rain of Gold*, 1991
This is an intergenerational saga of a family's migration from Mexico to the U.S.

714

ESTEBAN MONTEJO, Afro-Cuban
MIGUEL BARNET, Editor, Cuban

The Autobiography of a Runaway Slave
(London: Macmillan Caribbean, 1993)

Subject(s): Autobiography; Slavery; War
Age range(s): Grades 10-Adult
Major character(s): Esteban Montejo, Slave, Aged Person (old man), African Cuban
Time period(s): 19th century (1868-1898)
Locale(s): Cuba

Summary: This documentary novel, based on oral testimony from a 105-year-old ex-slave, Esteban Montejo, provides a unique account of slavery before abolition, of the experience of being a runaway, and of life on a sugar plantation and as a soldier. Barnet met Montejo in 1963 and interviewed him for two years. When Montejo ran away he spent over a year and a half in total solitude in the forest. This is only the second narrative of its kind in Cuban black literature; the first was Francisco Manzano's *Autobiography*, published in 1840 in England. It is also an important source for Afro-Cuban history.

About this book: Published in Spanish as *Biografia de un Cimarron*; first English translation published in 1968. This edition has an introduction by Alistair Hennessy. A bibliographic essay on Cuban salvery is also included. It is translated by Jocasta Innes.

Other books you might like:

Barry B. Levine, *Benjy Lopez, A Picaresque Tale of Emigration and Return*, 1980
The life story of a Puerto Rican migrant who learns to play the system in New York and succeeds.

Ernest J. Gaines, *The Autobiography of Miss Jane Pittman*, 1971
An autobiography based on conversations with an ex-slave of 110 years old around the years 1865-1866.

Ruth Behar, *Bridges to Cuba = Puentes a Cuba*, 1995
An anthology of short stories, essays, poetry, and historical documents exploring the Cuban and Cuban American experience.

Pablo Medina, *Exiled Memories: A Cuban Childhood*, 1990
This work is a collection of the author's memories of growing up in Cuba and spending summers on his grandfather's sugar cane plantation before the revolution.

Jose Barreiro, *The Indian Chronicles*, 1993
Adopted by Christopher Columbus, Diego Colon, a Taino boy, keeps a journal where he describes events in his life from 1532-1535 where he narrates the Indian's discovery of the Europeans.

Carolina Hospital, *Cuban American Writers: Los Atrevidos*, 1988
A collection of short stories and poetry by twelve Cuban-American writers, all of whom were born in Cuba and came to the U.S. very young.

Joseph P. Sanchez, *The Aztec Chronicles: The True History of Christopher Columbus, as Narrated by Quilaztli of Texcoco: A Novella*, 1995
This historical novella tells the story of Christopher Columbus from the perspective of Quilaztli, an Aztec historian who served both Moctezuma I and Moctezuma II.

715

FRANCISCO X. MORA, Mexican American

Juan Tuza and the Magic Pouch
(Fort Atkinson, WI: Highsmith Press, 1994)

Subject(s): Animals; Magic; Deserts
Age range(s): Grades K-2
Time period(s): Indeterminate Past
Locale(s): United States

Summary: Juan Tuza, a prairie dog, and Pepe, the armadillo, have performed good deeds in the Mexican desert. Because of this they are rewarded with a magic pouch, which will produce any wish they make.

Other books by the same author:
La Gran Fiesta, 1993
The Tiger and the Rabbit: A Puerto Rican Folk Tale, 1991
The Coyote Rings the Wrong Bell, 1991
The Legend of the Two Moons, 1992

Other books you might like:

Manlio Argueta, *Magic Dogs of the Volcanoes = Los Perros Magicos de los Volcanes*, 1990
Ancient volcanoes protect the magic dogs who live on the volcanoes in El Salvador.

Jan Romero Stevens, *Carlos and the Cornfield: Story = Carlos y la Milpa de Maiz: Cuento*, 1995
A young boy learns to make things right after realizing his mistake in planting corn.

Alberto Blanco, *Angel's Kite = La Estrella de Angel*, 1994
After the church bell disappears, Angel makes a kite with a picture of the town and the church on it.

Nicholasa Mohr, *The Song of el Coqui and Other Tales of Puerto Rico*, 1995
This collection of three vividly illustrated tales evokes the rich ancestral traditions of Puerto Rican culture.

Alma Flor Ada, *Mediopollito = Half-Chicken*, 1995
A bilingual retelling of a traditional humorous tale from Spain, this is set in colonial Mexico. Half-Chicken is born with only half a body, and his uniqueness attracts a lot of attention.

716

FRANCISCO X. MORA, Author/Illustrator, Mexican
American

La Gran Fiesta

(Fort Atkinson, WI: Highsmith Press, 1993)

Subject(s): Greed; Christmas; Humor
Age range(s): Grades K-2
Major character(s): Crow, Crow, Latino
Time period(s): Indeterminate Past
Locale(s): United States (set in a Spanish-speaking area)

Summary: Crow gets his bird friends to decorate his Christmas
tree for *La Gran Fiesta de Navidad* in the *northern tradition*
with fruits, cookies, candies and other goodies. He wants
more and more, but eventually the tree is so loaded that it
collapses. The birds notice that trees without all the food are
more natural and beautiful than is Crow's, and perhaps he was
being too greedy.

About this book: Interspersed with Spanish.

Other books by the same author:
Juan Tuza and the Magic Pouch, 1994
The Tiger and the Rabbit: A Puerto Rican Folk Tale, 1991
The Coyote Rings the Wrong Bell, 1991
The Legend of the Two Moons, 1992

Other books you might like:
Rudolfo Anaya, *The Farolitos of Christmas*, 1995
    Luz worries that her Abuelo will not be well enough to cut
    the pinon logs for the *luminarias* that will light the path for
    the village's traditional Christmas procession.
Gary Soto, *Too Many Tamales*, 1993
    Maria helps her mother make tamales for Christmas Eve
    dinner and in the process loses something important.
Lucia M. Gonzalez, *The Bossy Gallito*, 1994
    A bossy little rooster gets his beak dirty pecking some corn
    while on his way to his uncle's wedding.
Pat Mora, *The Gift of the Poinsettia = El Regalo de la Flor de
    Nochebuena*, 1995
    Carlos is celebrating *Las Posadas* but can't enjoy himself
    because he's worried that he can't buy a gift for the baby
    Jesus.
Alma Flor Ada, *Mediopollito = Half-Chicken*, 1995
    A bilingual retelling of a traditional humorous tale from
    Spain, this is set in colonial Mexico. Half-Chicken is born
    with only half a body, and because of his uniqueness
    receives a lot of attention.
Gina Macaluso Rodriguez, *Green Corn Tamales = Tamales
    de Elote*, 1994
    A Latino family makes green corn tamales every year, but
    not everyone wants to help.

717

PAT MORA, Mexican American
CECILY LANG, Illustrator

A Birthday Basket for Tia

(New York: Macmillan, 1992)

Subject(s): Aunts and Uncles; Birthdays; Animals

Age range(s): Grades 1-2
Major character(s): Cecilia, Child; Tia, Aunt
Time period(s): 1990s (1992)
Locale(s): Southwest

Summary: A cumulative story plot shows a special relationship between a child and an older person. With her cat Chica
helping her, Cecilia searches for a present to give to her great
aunt on her 90th birthday.

About this book: Spanish words are interspersed with English.

Where it's reviewed:
Horn Book, January-February 1993, page 76
Publishers Weekly, August 31, 1992, page 77

Other books by the same author:
Pablo's Tree, 1994
The Desert Is My Mother = El Desierto Es Mi Madre, 1994
Listen to the Desert/Oye al Desierto, 1994

Other books you might like:
Gary Soto, *Too Many Tamales*, 1993
    A child thinks she's lost something important in the batch
    of tamales made for Christmas Eve.
Jan Romero Stevens, *Carlos and the Squash Plant/Carlos y la
    Planta de Calabaza*, 1993
    Carlos does not wash when he is told and grows a plant in
    his ear.
Eve Bunting, *Smoky Night*, 1995
    Two cats, lost during the Los Angeles riots, somehow
    come together.
Gary Soto, *Chato's Kitchen*, 1995
    Chato, a low-riding cat, is hungry for the family of mice
    that moved in next door.
Arthur Dorros, *Abuela*, 1991
    A little girl and her grandmother fly all over New York
    City.
Sandra Cisneros, *Hair = Pelitos*, 1994
    This picture book excerpted from *The House on Mango
    Street* shows every member of the family with different
    hair.
Omar Castaneda, *Abuela's Weave*, 1993
    A girl and her grandmother make tapestries for an outdoor
    market.
Gina Macaluso Rodriguez, *Green Corn Tamales = Tamales
    de Elote*, 1994
    A Latino family makes green corn tamales every year, but
    there's a twist to this tale, not everyone wants to help.

718

PAT MORA, Mexican American
DANIEL LECHON, Illustrator, Mexican American

*The Desert Is My Mother = El Desierto
Es Mi Madre*

(Houston, TX: Arte Publico Press, 1994)

Subject(s): Nature; Deserts; Poetry
Age range(s): Grades K-2
Time period(s): Indeterminate
Locale(s): United States

Summary: In this beautiful rendition of the relationship between nature and people, the desert is presented as the provider of comfort, food, spirit, and life. Latino and Native American people are shown as having a special relationship with nature. Mora's poetic text is delightful in both English and Spanish.

About this book: This book has a bilingual format.

Where it's reviewed:
Publishers Weekly, December 5, 1994, page 76

Other books by the same author:
Agua Santa = Holy Water, 1995
A Birthday Basket for Tia, 1992
Borders, 1986
Listen to the Desert/Oye al Desierto, 1994
Pablo's Tree, 1994

Other books you might like:
Manlio Argueta, *Magic Dogs of the Volcanoes = Los Perros Magicos de los Volcanes*, 1990
  The magic dogs, or cadejos, who live on the volcanoes of El Salvador, are loved by the villagers because of their powerful magic.
Pura Belpre, *Dance of the Animals*, 1972
  Senor and Senora Lion are hungry for goat meat, so they throw a party and invite all the animals.
Harriet Rohmer, *The Legend of Food Mountain*, 1982
  Quetzalcoatl creates the people of the earth and he must find food to feed them. Food Mountain will make the people strong.
Maria Garcia, *The Adventures of Connie and Diego = Las Aventuras de Connie y Diego*, 1986
  Connie and Diego are different from other people in the Land of Plenty, and because they are not accepted, they journey through the forest and across the country looking for acceptance.
Harriet Rohmer, *Atariba and Niguayona: A Story from the Taino People of Puerto Rico*, 1988
  Niguayona embarks upon a journey through the forest to save his friend.
Alberto Blanco, *The Desert Mermaid = La Sirena Del Desierto*, 1992
  A desert mermaid helps her people rediscover the forgotten songs of their ancestors.

719

PAT MORA, Mexican American
CHARLES RAMIREZ BERG, Illustrator, Mexican American
DANIEL LECHON, Illustrator, Mexican American

The Gift of the Poinsettia = El Regalo de la Flor de Nochebuena
(Houston, TX: Pinata Books, 1995)

Subject(s): Christmas; Love; Traditions
Age range(s): Grades K-2
Major character(s): Carlos, Child (little boy), Mexican
Time period(s): Indeterminate Past
Locale(s): United States

Summary: Carlos is getting ready for Christmas and is celebrating Las Posadas, the Mexican tradition of reenacting the pilgrimage of Mary and Joseph as they search for an inn, a "posada." But Carlos can't enjoy himself because he's worried that he can't buy a gift for the baby Jesus. Many traditional folk materials of Christmas—"papel picado," "cascarones" and "pinatas"—are depicted in this beautifully illustrated book.

About this book: Bilingual format; text and music for songs of Las Posadas included.

Other books by the same author:
Agua Santa = Holy Water, 1995
A Birthday Basket for Tia, 1992
Listen to the Desert/Oye al Desierto, 1994
Pablo's Tree, 1994
The Desert Is My Mother = El Desierto Es Mi Madre, 1994

Other books you might like:
Rudolfo Anaya, *The Farolitos of Christmas*, 1995
  Luz worries that her Abuelo will not be well enough to cut the pinon logs for the "luminarias" that will light the path for the village's traditional Christmas procession.
Gary Soto, *Too Many Tamales*, 1993
  Maria helps her mother make tamales for Christmas Eve dinner and in the process loses something important.
Lulu Delacre, *Vejigantes Masquerade*, 1993
  Ramon has always wanted to masquerade in Carnival, so he sews a vejigante costume himself and saves up to buy a devilish mask.
Carmen Lomas Garza, *Family Pictures = Cuadros de Familia*, 1990
  Carmen Lomas Garza, a well known Chicana artist presents beautiful and detailed paintings of her growing up years in a Texas border town.
Gina Macaluso Rodriguez, *Green Corn Tamales = Tamales de Elote*, 1994
  A Latino family makes green corn tamales every year, but there's a twist to this tale, not everyone wants to help.
Francisco X. Mora, *La Gran Fiesta*, 1993
  Greedy Crow over-decorates his Christmas tree for "La Gran Fiesta de Navidad" until it collapses under a load of fruits, cookies, candies, and other goodies.

720

PAT MORA, Mexican American
FRANCISCO X. MORA, Illustrator, Mexican American

Listen to the Desert/Oye al Desierto
(New York: Clarion Books, 1994)

Subject(s): Deserts; Animals
Age range(s): Grades K-1
Time period(s): Indeterminate Past
Locale(s): United States (desert landscape)

Summary: This beautifully illustrated poem and picture book, presents the sounds of the desert and desert animals in both English and Spanish languages. It includes the animal language of the owl, toad, snake, dove, and coyote.

About this book: This book is in bilingual format.

Where it's reviewed:
Horn Book Guide, Fall 1994, page 348

Other books by the same author:
The Desert Is My Mother = El Desierto Es Mi Madre, 1994
Pablo's Tree, 1994
A Birthday Basket for Tia, 1992

Other books you might like:
Jan Romero Stevens, *Carlos and the Squash Plant/Carlos y la Planta de Calabaza*, 1993
  Carlos does not wash up when his mother asks, consequently a plant grows out of his ear.
Eve Bunting, *Smoky Night*, 1995
  During the Los Angeles riots of 1992 a little cat gets lost.
Omar Castaneda, *Abuela's Weave*, 1993
  A girl and her grandmother make tapestries for an outdoor market.
Gary Soto, *Chato's Kitchen*, 1995
  Chato, a lowrider cat, prepares dinner for some unexpected guests.
Michael Rose Ramirez, *The Little Ant = La Hormiga Chiquita*, 1995
  A little ant seeks restitution for his broken leg.
Manlio Argueta, *Magic Dogs of the Volcanoes = Los Perros Magicos de los Volcanes*, 1990
  Ancient volcanoes protect the magic dogs who live on the volcanoes in El Salvador.

721

PAT MORA, Mexican American
CECILY LANG, Illustrator

Pablo's Tree
(New York: Macmillan, 1994)

Subject(s): Trees; Grandparents; Birthdays
Age range(s): Grades K-1
Major character(s): Pablo, 5-Year-Old (boy); Lito, Grandfather
Time period(s): 1990s (1994)
Locale(s): Southwest

Summary: Pablo celebrates all his birthdays with his grandfather. Each year Lito decorates the tree with something special—balloons, streamers, paper lanterns. This is a story of a special relationship between a child and grandparent.

About this book: Spanish words are interspersed throughout the book.

Where it's reviewed:
Horn Book Magazine, November-December 1994, page 723

Other books by the same author:
Listen to the Desert/Oye al Desierto, 1994
The Desert Is My Mother = El Desierto Es Mi Madre, 1994
A Birthday Basket for Tia, 1992

Other books you might like:
Jan Romero Stevens, *Carlos and the Squash Plant/Carlos y la Planta de Calabaza*, 1993
  Carlos does not bathe when told by his mother and soon a plant grows out of his ear.
Omar Castaneda, *Abuela's Weave*, 1993
  A little girl and her grandmother weave tapestries for an outdoor market.

Gary Soto, *Chato's Kitchen*, 1995
  Chato, a lowrider cat, prepares dinner for some unexpected guests.
Eve Bunting, *Smokey Night*, 1995
  During the Los Angeles riots of 1992 a little cat gets lost.
Arthur Dorros, *Abuela*, 1991
  A little girl and her grandmother fly all over New York city.
Sandra Cisneros, *Hair = Pelitos*, 1994
  A picture book excerpted from *The House on Mango Street* shows every member of the family has different hair.
Juanita Havill, *Treasure Nap*, 1992
  Alicia hears the story of Rita, who visits her grandfather in the mountains of Mexico, and learns to make wooden birdcages.

722

PAT MORA, Mexican American
MAYA ITZNA BROOKS, Illustrator, Guatemalan

The Race of Toad and Deer
(New York: Orchard Books, 1995)

Subject(s): Animals/Frogs and Toads; Animals/Deer; Folk Tales
Age range(s): Grades K-2
Major character(s): Tio Sapo, Toad; Tio Venado, Deer
Time period(s): Indeterminate Past
Locale(s): United States

Summary: Deer thinks he is the biggest and the fastest animal in the jungle, and he always tries to make the other animals do what he says. But when Toad challenges him to a race, he is in for a surprise. Beautifully illustrated with vivid colors.

Where it's reviewed:
Publishers Weekly, September 4, 1995, page 68

Other books by the same author:
Agua Santa = Holy Water, 1995
Communion, 1991
The Desert Is My Mother = El Desierto Es Mi Madre, 1994
Listen to the Desert/Oye al Desierto, 1994
Pablo's Tree, 1994

Other books you might like:
Pura Belpre, *Dance of the Animals*, 1972
  Senor and Senora Lion, hungry for goat meat, throw a party and invite all the animals.
Lucia M. Gonzalez, *The Bossy Gallito*, 1994
  A bossy little rooster, "un gallito mandon" is on his way to his uncle's wedding, when he gets his beak dirty after peck ing at some corn.
Gary Soto, *Chato's Kitchen*, 1995
  Chato, a low-rider cat, plans a dinner and invites some nice mice, but they outwit him.
Pura Belpre, *The Tiger and the Rabbit and Other Tales*, 1965
  This collection of folk tales is from Puerto Rico.
Linda Shute, *Rabbit Wishes*, 1995
  Soon after creation, Tio Conejo complains that he wants to be large like an elephant or tall like a giraffe.

Alma Flor Ada, *Mediopollito = Half-Chicken*, 1995
This is a bilingual retelling of a traditional humorous tale from Spain set in colonial Mexico. Half-Chicken, is born with only half a body, and because of his uniqueness receives a lot of attention.

723

CHERRIE MORAGA, Mexican American

The Last Generation
(Boston, MA: South End Press, 1993)

Subject(s): Prose; Homosexuality/Lesbianism; Identity
Age range(s): Grades 10-Adult
Time period(s): 1980s
Locale(s): California

Summary: This collection of prose and poetry by a respected and admired Chicana writer is written as a prayer for the passing of a culture and the triumph of colonialism. Moraga sees herself in an international feminist context and attempts to resurrect history, to speak in cataclysmic times, and to expose the problems of individualism and consumerism.

About this book: The author is also well known as a playwright.

Where it's reviewed:
Lambda Book Report, January-February 1994, page 28
Library Journal, September 1, 1993, page 184
Women's Review of Books, January 1994, page 22
off our backs, June 1994, page 11

Other books by the same author:
Cuentos: Stories by Latinas, 1983
Loving in the War Years: Lo que Nunca Paso por sus Labios, 1983
This Bridge Called My Back: Writings by Radical Women of Color, 1981

Other books you might like:
Julia Alvarez, *The Other Side = El Otro Lado*, 1995
In this collection of poetry, that reads like prose, Julia Alvarez examines love, language, and her past.
Carla Trujillo, *Chicana Lesbians: The Girls Our Mothers Warned Us About*, 1991
A diverse collection of short stories, poetry, and prose by Chicana lesbians exploring the intricacies and specifics of culture, family, mixed-race relationships, body, and identity.
Gloria Anzaldua, *Borderlands: The New Mestiza = La Frontera*, 1987
In prose and poetry, Anzaldua writes about her childhood along the Texas-Mexican border, describing the experience of being caught between two cultures.
Tey Diana Rebolledo, *Infinite Divisions: An Anthology of Chicana Literature*, 1993
Fifty Chicana writers from the past and present write about personal identity in this unusual anthology of poetry, plays, and stories.
Roberta Fernandez, *In Other Words: Literature by Latinas in the U.S.*, 1994
This anthology contains the best and most representative works of contemporary fiction, poetry, drama, and essay written by Latinas in the U.S.

724

ALEJANDRO MORALES, Mexican American

The Brick People
(Houston, TX: Arte Publico Press, 1988)

Subject(s): Family Relations; Labor and Labor Classes; Intergenerational Saga
Age range(s): Grades 10-Adult
Major character(s): Octavio Revueltas, Worker (factory worker), Spouse, Mexican
Time period(s): 19th century; 20th century (1892-1940)
Locale(s): California

Summary: A historically-based novel about two families pitted against each other — the powerful Simons and the proud Revueltas. The story traces the growth of California from the late nineteenth century through the early twentieth century. The "brick people" are the workers, primarily Mexican immigrants, of the Simons Brick Factory in southern California. With attention to historical detail, Morales examines the construction of modern California, and at the same time presents individuals who want to forge their own destinies. This is a true story of California.

Where it's reviewed:
Publishers Weekly, June 3, 1988, page 79
Confluencia, Spring 1992, page 99

Other books by the same author:
Death of an Anglo, 1979
The Rag Doll Plagues, 1992
Old Faces and New Wine, 1981
Reto en el Paraiso, 1983

Other books you might like:
Nash Candelaria, *Leonor Park*, 1992
A novel about land and greed set in New Mexico where a powerful woman battles with her brother over their father's legacy, a piece of land along the Rio Grande.
Victor Villasenor, *Rain of Gold*, 1991
Intergenerational chronicle of the author's family migration to the U.S. from Mexcio during the early 19th century.
Jose Antonio Villarreal, *Pocho*, 1959
The story of a Mexican family in the Santa Clara Valley of California before World War II and the assimilation of the son Richard Rubio.
Richard Vasquez, *Chicano*, 1970
An early Chicano novel about the Sandoval family who leave revolutionary Mexico and settle in a Los Angeles barrio.
Americo Paredes, *George Washington Gomez*, 1990
As he grows up, George Washington Gomez struggles with racism, abuse and cultural and political clashes while other Texas Mexicans fight to preserve their language and culture.

725

ALEJANDRO MORALES, Mexican American

Death of an Anglo
(Tempe, AZ: Bilingual Press, 1988)

Subject(s): Medicine; Murder; Hero
Age range(s): Grades 10-Adult
Major character(s): Logan, Doctor (medical), Caucasian; Eutemio, Writer (narrator of the story), Mexican American
Time period(s): 1970s
Locale(s): Mathis, Texas

Summary: A complicated novel, this is the story of Logan, a rebellious and idealistic young doctor who attempts to improve the lives of the Chicano residents of his town. Eutemio, an ostracized academic and aspiring writer, gains strength and defiance through his contact with Logan, and the two explore the meaning of heroism and commitment. After Logan is murdered, Eutemio continues his work and condemns the injustice of his death.

About this book: This was originally published in Spanish as *La Verdad Sin Voz* and is translated by Judith Ginsberg.

Other books by the same author:
The Brick People, 1988
Old Faces and New Wine, 1981
The Rag Doll Plagues, 1992

Other books you might like:
Dagoberto Gilb, *The Magic of Blood*, 1993
  These short stories about working-class life have multi-dimensional characters who lead realistic lives.
Genaro Gonzalez, *Rainbow's End*, 1988
  An adventure novel, this presents dangerous border crossings, confrontations with a magician, and drug smuggling in the lives of three generations of the Cavazos family in Texas.
Oscar Hijuelos, *Mr. Ives' Christmas*, 1995
  Edward Ives, a New York commercial artist, mourns the loss of his beloved son, and begins to exchange letters with his son's killer, a young Puerto Rican in prison.
Soledad Santiago, *Nightside*, 1994
  Anna Eltern, a former nun, runs a shelter for runaway teens in New York City. Financial problems, funding cuts, and murder are forcing her to turn away teenagers in need.
John Rechy, *The Miraculous Day of Amalia Gomez: A Novel*, 1991
  This novel follows a day in the life of a Mexican-American woman, who lives among poverty, gang warfare, and illegal border crossings, yet still has hope.
Carlos Miralejos, *Rabid Beasts*, 1993
  This science fiction work tells how Jorge Sogaseca, captain of the space ship Tulumex, saves the Cherokee Nation from dying of exposure to extremely cold weather during a long forced march.

726

ALEJANDRO MORALES, Mexican American

The Rag Doll Plagues
(Houston, TX: Arte Publico Press, 1992)

Subject(s): Medicine; Plague; Intergenerational Saga
Age range(s): Grades 10-Adult
Time period(s): 18th century; 21st century (1788-2000)
Locale(s): Los Angeles, California; Mexico

Summary: Divided into three sections, this novel shows Latino doctors fighting a deadly infectious disease over three centuries. In the first section, an 18th century Spanish physician is sent to Mexico to diagnose and cure a deadly plague. The second section is about a doctor in Los Angeles who allows his wife, who has AIDS, to participate in a Mexican Indian healing ritual which he believes may save her life. And the third story is set in the future and presents a plague that ravages residents of Mexico and the U.S.

Where it's reviewed:
Library Journal, January 1992, page 180
Publishers Weekly, October 11, 1991, page 50

Other books by the same author:
The Brick People, 1988
Death of an Anglo, 1979
Old Faces and New Wine, 1981

Other books you might like:
David Monreal, *Cinco de Mayo: An Epic Novel*, 1993
  A historical novel that presents the events leading up to the Battle of Puebla on the 5th of May 1862 in Mexico.
Daniel Cano, *Pepe Rios*, 1991
  In this historical novel about the Mexican Revolution of 1910, Pepe Rios searches for peace amidst the chaos and violence of war.
Montserrat Fontes, *Dreams of the Centaur*, 1995
  The son of a slain ranch owner tries to avenge his father's death during the deportation of the Yaqui Indians during the presidency of Porfirio Diaz.
Guy Garcia, *Obsidian Sky: A Novel*, 1994
  A doctoral student from Berkeley working in Mexico's Museum of Anthropolgy gets sucked into a political controversy amidst growing civil unrest.
Nash Candelaria, *Inheritance of Strangers*, 1985
  A sequel to *Not by the Sword*, this covers the years after the Mexican War of 1846 until the date of New Mexico Statehood presenting the struggles of the Rafa family against Anglo exploitation.
Carlos Miralejos, *Rabid Beasts*, 1993
  This science fiction work tells how Jorge Sogaseca, captain of the space ship Tulumex, saves the Cherokee Nation from dying of exposure to extremely cold weather during a long forced march.

727

AURORA LEVINS MORALES, Puerto Rican
ROSARIO MORALES, Co-Author, Puerto Rican

Getting Home Alive

(Ithaca, NY: Firebrand Books, 1986)

Subject(s): Short Stories; Mothers and Daughters; Women
Age range(s): Grades 10-Adult
Time period(s): 20th century (1950-1986)
Locale(s): United States; Puerto Rico

Summary: A mother and daughter write episodes, short stories, and poems about themselves and each other's lives. The stories reveal nostalgia for Puerto Rico, anger about racism and poverty, and a love for each other.

Other books you might like:

Judith Ortiz Cofer, *Silent Dancing: A Partial Remembrance of a Puerto Rican Childhood*, 1990
These stories are about growing up in both Puerto Rico and in New Jersey.

Faythe Turner, *Puerto Rican Writers at Home in the U.S.A.: An Anthology*, 1991
This collection of poetry and prose is written by Puerto Rican authors born and raised in New York City.

Rosario Ferre, *The Youngest Doll*, 1991
This collection of short stories, originally published in Spanish, is about Puerto Rico society.

Kal Wagenheim, *Cuentos: An Anthology of Short Stories from Puerto Rico*, 1978
This is a collection of short stories that take place in Puerto Rico.

728

BARBARA MUJICA

The Deaths of Don Bernardo

(Encino, CA: Floricanto Press, 1990)

Subject(s): Murder; Money; Indians of South America
Age range(s): Grades 9-Adult
Major character(s): Bernardo de Alvarez, Plantation Owner, Businessman, Peruvian
Time period(s): 1910s (1910-1917)
Locale(s): Peru

Summary: Bernardo de Alvarez, plantation owner and ruthless businessman, deals with large American corporations and at the same time murders a man and contracts a demon. This novel takes the reader into the elegant homes of the rich, the struggling Indian villages of the Andes, and convents and brothels. Based on historical facts, it shows how labor and Indianist movements deplored the exploitation of Peru's indigenous population.

Where it's reviewed:

Americas (English Edition), May-June 1990, page 63

Other books by the same author:

Readings in Spanish Literature, 1975
Antologia de la Literatura Espanola; Edad Media, 1991
Calderon's Characters: An Existential Point of View, 1980

Texto y Vida: Introduccion a la Literatura Hispanoamericana, 1991

Other books you might like:

Montserrat Fontes, *Dreams of the Centaur*, 1995
Alejo Durcal, son of a slain ranch owner, tries to avenge his father's death during the period in history when the Yaqui Indians were badly mistreated in Mexico.

Marcos McPeek Villatoro, *A Fire in the Earth*, 1996
This epic novel follows Romilia Colonez, descendant of an Indian patriarch who claimed fertile land for his clan, setting the stage for future trials and tragedies in El Salvador.

Nash Candelaria, *Inheritance of Strangers*, 1985
A sequel to *Not By the Sword*, this covers the years after the Mexican War of 1846 up until the date of New Mexico statehood, presenting struggles of the Rafa family against Anglo exploitation.

Gary D. Keller, *Zapata Lives!*, 1994
The Mexican revolutionary leader Emiliano Zapato has risen from the dead, and he must lead his people in a struggle against economic and social oppression

Guy Garcia, *Obsidian Sky: A Novel*, 1994
A doctoral student from Berkeley, working in Mexico's Museum of Anthropolgy, gets sucked into a political controversy amidst growing civil unrest.

Estela Portillo Trambley, *Trini*, 1986
Trini, a Tarahumara woman whose indigenous life is wondrous and magical, crosses the boarder as an undocumented immigrant in order to give birth to her child in the United States.

Rosa Martha Villarreal, *Doctor Magdalena: Novella*, 1995
This spiritual odyssey of a modern female doctor is narrated by her Indian ancestors and spans three worlds.

729

ELIAS MIGUEL MUNOZ, Cuban American

Crazy Love

(Houston, TX: Arte Publico Press, 1989)

Subject(s): Coming of Age; Autobiography
Age range(s): Grades 10-Adult
Major character(s): Julian, Brother, Cuban; Geneia, Sister (little sister), Cuban
Time period(s): 1960s
Locale(s): Florida; Cuba

Summary: This experimental novel combines many forms. It is an epistolary novel, a story of a young man coming of age through examining his past, and an autobiography that challenges "the American dream." A mosaic of Cuban American culture, the novel is structured by a musical undercurrent.

Where it's reviewed:

Revista Iberoamericana, July-December 1990, page 1396
Hispania, March 1991, page 90
American Book Review, January-February 1990, page 9
Chasqui-Revista de Literatura Latinoamericana, May 1989, page 96

Other books by the same author:

En Estas Tierras = In This land, 1989
The Greatest Performance, 1991

Other books you might like:

Virgil Suarez, *Welcome to the Oasis and Other Stories*, 1992
   The Mariel refugees represented in a novella and short stories that show culture shock through the eyes of the refugees.

Roberto Fernandez, *Holy Radishes*, 1995
   Satirical novel depicting the exiled Cuban American community in Florida.

Omar Torres, *Fallen Angels Sing*, 1991
   Story of a young exile who gets involved in a plot to assassinate Fidel Castro.

Pablo Medina, *Exiled Memories: A Cuban Childhood*, 1990
   A collection of the author's memories of growing up in Cuba where he spent summers on his grandfather's sugar cane plantation, La Luisa.

Ruth Behar, *Bridges to Cuba = Puentes a Cuba*, 1995
   An anthology of short stories, essays, poetry, and historical documents exploring the Cuban and Cuban American experience.

730

ELIAS MIGUEL MUNOZ, Cuban American

The Greatest Performance

(Houston, TX: Arte Publico Press, 1991)

Subject(s): Exile; Family; Homosexuality/Lesbianism
Age range(s): Grades 10-Adult
Major character(s): Rosa, Young Woman, Cuban; Mario, Young Man, Cuban
Time period(s): 20th century (1960-1980)
Locale(s): United States

Summary: A poetic novel of exile, where two soul-mates recount to each other their stories of living on the margins of family, country, and sexual identity. The two friends, Rosa and Mario alternately narrate their stories. Rosa is sent to Spain with her brother until they are reunited with their family in California, while Mario remains in Cuba and suffers for his crime of homosexuality until he finally escapes to the U.S. We see these two grow into adults with AIDS as a grim fact of life.

Where it's reviewed:
Library Journal, September 15, 1991, page 112
Publishers Weekly, September 6, 1991, page 100
Review of Contemporary Fiction, Spring 1992, page 155

Other books by the same author:
Crazy Love, 1989
En Estas Tierras = In This Land, 1989

Other books you might like:

Arturo Islas, *The Rain God: A Desert Tale*, 1984
   Miguel Chico, is caught between his Mexican Catholic heritage and his prestigious American education.

Terri de la Pena, *Margins*, 1992
   Veronica Melendez loses her lover in a car accident and must make decisions about her future, and tell her parents and older brother about her homosexuality.

Cherrie Moraga, *Loving in the War Years: Lo que Nunca Paso por sus Labios*, 1983

The autobiographical life of a Chicana lesbian writer who grew up in California.

Michael Nava, *How Town: A Novel of Suspense*, 1990
   A gay Chicano lawyer solves a murder mystery while unpretentiously depicting a gay relationship.

Ibis Gomez-Vega, *Send My Roots Rain*, 1991
   Carole goes to a small Texas town to paint murals on Church walls and falls in love with a mysterious woman.

731

ALEJANDRO MURGUIA, Mexican American

Southern Front

(Tempe, AZ: Bilingual Press, 1990)

Subject(s): Short Stories; War
Age range(s): Grades 10-Adult
Major character(s): Ulises, Military Personnel (volunteer), Chicano
Time period(s): 1970s; 1980s (1977-1986)
Locale(s): Nicaragua

Summary: *Southern Front* refers to the area along the Nicaraguan-Costa Rican border. This was the site of the combat zone during the rebellion against the Somoza regime in the late 1970s. This collection of stories about the international volunteers who went to Nicaragua to join the Sandinistas in their fight, focuses on Ulises, a Chicano from Los Angeles. Taking place during the offensive and aftermath of the war, these stories provide a vivid, realistic, examination of the political upheaval and the Nicaraguan Revolution.

Other books by the same author:
Farewell to the Coast, 1980

Other books you might like:

Ed Vega, *Casualty Report*, 1991
   A collection of short stories including one about a Vietnam War veteran.

Graciela Limon, *In Search of Bernabe*, 1993
   A novel about a mother's search for her son during civil war in El Salvador.

Carole Fernandez, *Sleep of the Innocents*, 1991
   This novel chronicles the lives of women living in a fictional Central American country torn by civil war.

Daniel Cano, *Shifting Loyalties*, 1995
   A story of four Chicano soldiers before, during and after the Vietnam War.

Joe Rodriguez, *The Oddsplayer*, 1989
   Black and Latino soldiers fight the enemy on the battle fields of Vietnam but wars take place in their own ranks as well.

732

AMADO MURO

The Collected Stories of Amado Muro

(Austin, TX: Thorpe Springs Press, 1979)

Subject(s): Short Stories; Men; Poverty
Age range(s): Grades 9-Adult
Time period(s): 20th century (1935-1971)

Locale(s): Southwest; Mexico

Summary: Amado Muro was the Mexican American pseudonym for the Anglo American newspaperman and writer Charles Seltzer. Described as "one of the most promising Mexican American writers" during the 1970s, when many of these stories were published in magazines and newspapers of the Southwest, it was not known that he wasn't Mexican. Muro lived on and off in Mexico, married a Mexican woman and settled in El Paso. There he quietly wrote of the people and landscapes of Mexico. His stories reflect his experiences, working as a farm worker, riding the railroads, living in rescue missions and labor camps, and going to sea. Stories like "Cecilia Rosas" and "Mala Torres" are humorous with sensitively developed and memorable characters.

Other books you might like:

Dagoberto Gilb, *The Last Known Residence of Mickey Acuna*, 1994
  Mickey Acuna is waiting for something, something arriving through the mail, as he dwells at the YMCA in El Paso.
Max Martinez, *A Red Bikini Dream*, 1990
  The rhythms and spirit of modern life in the U.S. are captured in this collection of five short stories where the characters ponder self and identity in an increasingly complex society.
Luis Alberto Urrea, *In Search of Snow*, 1994
  Mike McGirk, a blue collar Don Quixote, searches for love and life in the Arizona desert, and learns about family from Bobo Garcia.
Americo Paredes, *The Hammon and the Beans and Other Stories*, 1994
  Set in the southern Texas border region, this collection of short stories explores the cultural conflict that has dominated that area since the U.S.-Mexican War.
Rafael Zepeda, *Horse Medicine and Other Stories*, 1990
  This collection of nine stories deals very much with the world of men. In "Horse Medicine" several men, with kids and wives, participate in rodeos and live with horses.
Dagoberto Gilb, *The Magic of Blood*, 1993
  These short stories about working-class life have multidimensional characters who lead realistic lives.
Jesus Salvador Trevino, *The Fabulous Sinkhole and Other Stories*, 1995
  This first story collection by Trevino, a screenwriter and director, is an entertaining creation of Mexican and Chicano characters, that take place in a fictional town, Arroyo Grande, in Texas.
Josephina Niggli, *Mexican Village*,
  This important collection of ten interrelated short stories recounts the lives of the people of a small Mexican town, Hidalgo. It was first published in 1945.

733

MICHAEL NAVA, Mexican American

The Death of Friends

(New York, NY: Putnam, 1996)

Subject(s): Mystery and Detective Stories; Homosexuality/Lesbianism; AIDS (Disease)

Age range(s): Grades 10-Adult

Major character(s): Henry Rios, Lawyer (gay man), Homosexual, Chicano

Time period(s): 1990s

Locale(s): Los Angeles, California

Summary: Henry Rios, faces a difficult duty when he comes to the side of his former lover, Joss as he dies of AIDs. Meanwhile Rios's college friend and closet homosexual, Chris Chandler, has been murdered, and the accused is his secret young lover, whom Rios must defend. The reality of AIDs and it's impact on the gay community is a central feature of this murder mystery, with Chandler symbolically representing the lives and lies of many gay men.

Where it's reviewed:

Publishers Weekly, July 8, 1996, page 77

Other books by the same author:

How Town: A Novel of Suspense, 1990
The Hidden Law, 1992

Other books you might like:

Manuel Ramos, *The Last Client of Luis Montez*, 1995
  The last client of Denver lawyer Louie Montez is found dead with Montez standing over him. To clear his name Montez becomes entangled in a complicated web that takes him to California and back.
Max Martinez, *White Leg*, 1996
  A fast action murder mystery, after the style of Jim Thompson, about a small town thief in a back watertown in Texas, who robs convenience stores to support his wife's expensive tastes.
Soledad Santiago, *Streets of Fire*, 1996
  This murder mystery with a Latina police officer, Francesca Colon, involves all the elements of big city dirty politics, police corruption, suspicious deaths, and tense ethnic community relations.
Carolina Garcia-Aguilera, *Bloody Waters*, 1996
  Guadalupe "Lupe" Solano, part of Miami's elite, is approached by a young couple for assistance in finding the biological mother of their adopted daughter.
Gil Cuadros, *City of God*, 1994
  The first half of this book is a short novel and the second half is a collection of haunting poetry, the author writes after the death of his lover while he himself lives with AIDS.

734

MICHAEL NAVA, Mexican American

The Hidden Law

(New York: HarperCollins Publishers, 1992)

Subject(s): AIDS (Disease); Crime and Criminals; Homosexuality/Lesbianism

Age range(s): Grades 10-Adult

Major character(s): Henry Rios, Lawyer (man), Homosexual, Chicano; Josh, Lover (man), Homosexual

Time period(s): 1990s (1992)

Locale(s): Los Angeles, California

Summary: Henry Rios is almost inadvertently drawn into defending a young Chicano, who's on probation. He is accused of killing a prestigious Latino public official, one who might have become the next and first Chicano mayor of Los Angeles. During his investigation, Rios encounters stock Latino characters: the Latina city councilwoman, the Chicano Studies professor, and the Anglo middle-aged woman social worker. In a sub-plot, his lover Josh falls in love with someone more understanding and more knowledgeable about AIDs and he moves out of their home.

Where it's reviewed:
Advocate, December 1, 1992, page 107
Lambda Book Report, November-December 1992, page 24
Publishers Weekly, September 7, 1992, page 82

Awards the book has won:
Lambda Award, 1993

Other books by the same author:
Finale, 1989
Goldenboy, 1988
How Town: A Novel of Suspense, 1990
The Little Death, 1986

Other books you might like:
Rolando Hinojosa, *Partners in Crime: A Rafe Buenrostro Mystery*, 1985
  Popular characters Jehu Malacara and Rafe Buenrostro, now a lieutenant of the Belken County Homicide Squad, are involved in a murder mystery.
Lucha Corpi, *Eulogy for a Brown Angel: A Mystery Novel*, 1992
  A Chicana feminist detective solves a murder that occurred during the Chicano civil rights movement of the late 1960s.
Lucha Corpi, *Cactus Blood: A Mystery Novel*, 1995
  Gloria Damasco, an apprentice to a private investigator, uses her visionary power to help solve a murder related to a 15-year-old pesticide tank explosion.
Rudolfo Anaya, *Zia Summer*, 1995
  Sonny Baca is involved in an exciting complicated mystery plot that involves murder, cult worship of the sun, and a battle over nuclear waste and disposal in New Mexico.
Rudolfo Anaya, *Albuquerque*, 1992
  An exciting story of Albuquerque, with a vicious mayoral race, a young Chicano boxer, American Indians fighting to retain water rights, and the folkloric past of New Mexico.
Manuel Ramos, *The Ballad of Rocky Ruiz: Death of a Martyr*, 1993
  Luis Montez, middle aged former Chicano activist and lawyer becomes involved in solving the twenty-year old murder of Rocky Ruiz.
Manuel Ramos, *The Ballad of Gato Guerrero*, 1994
  Felix ''Gato'' Guerrero, an old friend from way back, calls on Montez to save him and his new love from her husband, a Latino mobster.

735

MICHAEL NAVA, Mexican American

How Town: A Novel of Suspense
(New York: Harper & Row, 1990)

Subject(s): Murder; Crime and Criminals; Homosexuality/Lesbianism
Age range(s): Grades 10-Adult
Major character(s): Henry Rios, Lawyer, Homosexual, Chicano; Josh, Lover, Homosexual
Time period(s): 1980s
Locale(s): Los Robles, California (northern California)

Summary: Henry Rios is asked to defend a former high school acquaintance from his hometown, accused of murdering a man and also thought to be involved in child pornography. He accepts the case out of loyalty to his sister and out of curiosity since he once had a crush on the brother of the accused. A subplot of the novel deals with Rios' lover, Josh, who is much younger than him and HIV positive.

Where it's reviewed:
Wilson Library Bulletin, June, 1990, page 121

Other books by the same author:
Finale, 1989
Goldenboy, 1988
The Hidden Law, 1992
The Little Death, 1986

Other books you might like:
Lucha Corpi, *Cactus Blood: A Mystery Novel*, 1995
  Gloria Damasco, an apprentice to a private investigator, possesses an unexplainable visionary power which helps solve a murder related to a 15-year-old pesticide tank explosion.
Lucha Corpi, *Eulogy for a Brown Angel: A Mystery Novel*, 1992
  A Chicana feminist detective solves a murder that occurred during the Chicano civil rights movement of the late 1960s.
Arturo Islas, *The Rain God: A Desert Tale*, 1984
  Miguel Chico, whose uncle is killed in unusual circumstances, is caught between his Mexican Catholic heritage and his prestigious American education.
Rudolfo Anaya, *Zia Summer*, 1995
  Sonny Baca is involved in an exciting and complicated mystery plot that involves murder, cult worship of the sun, and a battle over nuclear waste and its disposal in New Mexico.
Rolando Hinojosa, *Partners in Crime: A Rafe Buenrostro Mystery*, 1985
  This border murder mystery involves Hinojosa's popular characters, Jehu Malacara and Rafe Buenrostro (now a lieutenant of the Belken County Homicide Squad).
Rudolfo Anaya, *Albuquerque*, 1992
  An exciting story of modern Albuquerque, with a vicious mayoral race, a young Chicano boxer, American Indians fighting to retain water rights, and the folkloric past of New Mexico.
Manuel Ramos, *The Ballad of Rocky Ruiz: Death of a Martyr*, 1993

Luis Montez, middle-aged former Chicano activist/lawyer, becomes involved in solving the twenty-year old murder of Rocky Ruiz.

Manuel Ramos, *The Ballad of Gato Guerrero*, 1994
  Felix "Gato" Guerrero, an old friend from way back, calls on Montez to save him and his new love from her husband, a Latino mobster.

736

JOSEPHINA NIGGLI, Scandinavian Mexican

Mexican Village
(Albuquerque, NM: U. of New Mexico Press, 1994)

Subject(s): Rural Life; Cultural Conflict; Identity
Age range(s): Grades 10-Adult
Major character(s): Robert Webster, Young Man (bicultural), Texas Mexican (European and Mexican)
Time period(s): 1920s; 1930s (1920-1930)
Locale(s): Hidalgo, Mexico (Nuevo Leon)

Summary: Niggli is considered to be a border author and her writing is a precursor to Chicano literature. This collection of ten interrelated short stories about the lives of the people of a small Mexican town, Hidalgo, was first published in 1945. The main protagonist, Robert Webster appears in several of the stories, as an enigmatic man who looks Mexican but has an Anglo name and speaks perfect English and Spanish. He comes to Hidalgo to work as the quarry master of a mine but also to search for his ancestoral roots. These stories are written in the romanticized tradition of the times yet they reflect a realistic portrayal of racism and cultural conflict that continue to be themes in contemporary Chicano literature.

About this book: The introduction is by Maria Herrera-Sobek

Other books by the same author:
Mexican Folk Plays, 1939
Step Down, Elder Brother, 1947
A Miracle of Mexico, 1964

Other books you might like:
Alberto Alvaro Rios, *Pig Cookies and Other Stories*, 1995
  Set earlier in this century, this collection of interrelated short stories takes place in a small village in northern Mexico.
Denise Chavez, *Face of an Angel*, 1995
  This sensual story, with many rich characters, is about a waitress who works in a Mexican restaurant in a fictional town in New Mexico.
Sabine Ulibarri, *Tierra Amarilla: Stories of New Mexico = Cuentos de Nuevo Mexico*, 1993
  First published in 1964, this collection of five short stories and a novella evoke the rural life of a northern New Mexican village.
Lionel G. Garcia, *I Can Hear the Cowbells Ring*, 1994
  With humour and nostalgia, this collection of delightful autobiographical vignettes reconstruct life in a small rural town of southern Texas.
Americo Paredes, *The Hammon and the Beans and Other Stories*, 1994
  A collection of short stories set in the southern Texas

border region deal with the cultural conflict that has dominated the area since the U.S.-Mexican War.
Rolando Hinojosa, *Klail City: A Novel*, 1987
  Part of the Klail City Death Trip series, Hinojosa uses four generations of articulate storytellers with multiple viewpoints to narrate the place of Chicano culture in the Texas Rio Grande area.
Sandra Benitez, *A Place Where the Sea Remembers*, 1993
  Written as a series of interrelated stories, this novel presents the life of a coastal village in Mexico where the women are caught in a mystical, fantastic, and often fatalistic world.

737

CARMEN SANTIAGO NODAR, Puerto Rican
DIANE PATERSON, Illustrator

Abuelita's Paradise
(Morton Grove, IL: Albert Whitman and Company, 1992)

Subject(s): Grandparents; Growing Up; Death
Age range(s): Grades 2-4
Major character(s): Marita, Child, Puerto Rican Abuelita, Grandmother (Marita's), Puerto Rican
Time period(s): Indeterminate Past
Locale(s): United States; Puerto Rico

Summary: When Marita's grandmother dies, she is given her abuelita's old plaid blanket and her rocking chair. As Marita rocks in the chair, she remembers the stories her abuelita told her about her Puerto Rican childhood. This journey helps Marita deal with her grandmother's death by understanding that her abuelita has gone to a different kind of paradise.

Where it's reviewed:
Publishers Weekly, September 7, 1992, page 96

Other books you might like:
Omar Castaneda, *Abuela's Weave*, 1993
  A little girl journeys with her grandmother to sell woven crafts at a market in Guatemala.
Juanita Havill, *Treasure Nap*, 1992
  Mama tells Alicia the story of Rita, who visits her grandfather in the mountains of Mexico, and learns to make wooden birdcages.
Pat Mora, *A Birthday Basket for Tia*, 1992
  Cecilia creates, with the help of her cat, a birthday gift for her great aunt.
Arthur Dorros, *Abuela*, 1991
  A little girl and her grandmother fly all over New York City.
Alejandro Cruz Martinez, *The Woman Who Outshone the Sun*, 1991
  A Zapotec legend about a woman whose hair outshines the sun.
Leyla Torres, *Saturday Sancocho*, 1995
  Every Saturday, Maria Lili helps her grandparents make their traditional chicken sancocho.

738

HIMILCE NOVAS, Cuban American

Mangos, Bananas, and Coconuts: A Cuban Love Story

(Houston, TX: Arte Publico Press, 1996)

Subject(s): Romance; Social Classes; Exile
Age range(s): Grades 10-Adult
Major character(s): Esmeralda, Young Woman, Cuban
Time period(s): 1980s
Locale(s): New York, New York (Spanish Harlem); Miami, Florida

Summary: This tale of a magical yet real love story is an ancient one. Beginning with the love of a man and a woman from different social classes, the story follows the fate of their children, separated at birth and living in two different worlds. Juan grows up pampered and spoiled, with a wealthy class of Cubans in Miami, and beautiful, humble Esmeralda grows up in Spanish Harlem. She becomes the pride and wonder of El Barrio, until, one day, a handsome young man is drawn to her church. Circumstances seem to have conspired to bring the two together and they become inseparable.

Where it's reviewed:
Publishers Weekly, February 5, 1996, page 76

Other books by the same author:
Everything You Need to Know about Latino History, 1994
Remembering Selena: A Tribute in Pictures and Words, 1995
The Hispanic 100, 1995

Other books you might like:
Graciela Limon, *The Memories of Ana Calderon: A Novel*, 1994
  Ana Calderon suffers many challenges and torments and battles unfair circumstances; the loss of a child, imprisonment, and, in adulthood, amazing happiness and humiliation.
Isabel Allende, *The Stories of Eva Luna*, 1991
  In twenty-three tales Eva Luna tells of her life, her loves, and the surrounding political and social turmoil in which they take place. They are filled with humor and rich detail.
Ana Lydia Vega, *True and False Romances*, 1994
  This collection of short stories is about women and romance in Puerto Rico.
Kathleen Alcala, *Mrs. Vargas and the Dead Naturalist*, 1992
  Created as a book of wonders, this collection of short stories, many about Mexican women, follow the characteristics of magical realism.
Fernando Alegria, *Paradise Lost or Gained? The Literature of Hispanic Exile*, 1990
  This collection of writings by Latinos addresses the experience of exile and alienation through stories, poems, and essays.
Oscar Hijuelos, *The Mambo Kings Play Songs of Love*, 1989
  The Castillo brothers make their way from Havana to New York to play music in the era of the mambo where they become night stars of the dance halls.
Margarite Fernandez Olmos, *Pleasure in the Word: Erotic Writings by Latin American Women*, 1993
  This diverse collection of erotic writing by women destroys silence by speaking out about eroticism, love, and violence.

739

ACHY OBEJAS, Cuban American

Memory Mambo: A Novel

(Pittsburg, PA: Cleis Press, 1996)

Subject(s): Homosexuality/Lesbianism; Exile; Emigration and Immigration
Age range(s): Grades 10-Adult
Major character(s): Juani Casas, Lesbian (20-year-old), Cuban American
Time period(s): 1990s
Locale(s): Chicago, Illinois

Summary: Juani Casas, a twenty-something lesbian runs her family's laundromat in a Cuban American community of Chicago. Her sexuality is kept secret from her family until her relationship with her lover ends violently. Understanding her family's history, both in Cuba before the revolution and in the United States, becomes very important to Juani, and as she hears stories about Cuba the mythology of exile overcomes her. This novel is about the importance of love and family.

Where it's reviewed:
Publishers Weekly, July 8, 1996, page 79

Other books by the same author:
We Came All the Way from Cuba So You Could Dress Like This? Stories, 1994

Other books you might like:
Jaime Manrique, *Latin Moon in Manhattan*, 1992
  This novel, about a gay poet, presents bizarre characters, plots and sub-plots, and a vivid depiction of Columbian American culture in Little Colombia, Jackson Heights.
Virgil Suarez, *Havana Thursdays: A Novel*, 1995
  This is the story of two sisters, their daughters, and how they represent two ways of dealing with the changes encountered in immigration from a Latino culture.
Terri de la Pena, *Margins*, 1992
  The story of a young lesbian writer who confronts her future and her family about her sexuality.
Emma Perez, *Gulf Dreams*, 1996
  A creative series of essays, short vignettes, and psychoanalytic discourses on growing up lesbian in Latino culture.
Himilce Novas, *Mangos, Bananas, and Coconuts: A Cuban Love Story*, 1996
  This tale of a magical, yet real, love story is an ancient tale of the consummation of the love between a man and a woman from different social classes, and the story of the fate of their children.
Jose Yglesias, *Tristan and the Hispanics*, 1989
  A cynical tale about a Yale graduate, the son of a Cuban-born screenwriter and a WASP mother who must make funeral arrangements for his paternal grandfather.
Sheila Ortiz Taylor, *Faultline: A Novel*, 1982
  A very funny book about a lesbian mother of six children, her lover/companion, their 300 rabbits, and a six foot tall Black drag queen baby sitter.

740

ACHY OBEJAS, Cuban American

We Came All the Way from Cuba So You Could Dress Like This? Stories

(Pittsburgh, PA: Cleis Press, 1994)

Subject(s): Homosexuality/Lesbianism; Women; Emigration and Immigration
Age range(s): Grades 10-Adult
Time period(s): 1990s
Locale(s): Chicago, Illinois

Summary: This collection of seven short stories includes several about gay men and women, outcasts, AIDS patients and immigrants in the 1990s. In one story, ''Wreaks'', a woman always manages to crash her car when her lovers leave her; in ''Above All a Family Man'' an Anglo young man dying of AIDS is in love with a married Mexican man who has children. The title story is about a woman who came to the U.S. with her parents at age 10 in 1963, and how she evolved to become a politically active lesbian, while her father could never let Cuba go. An unconscious humor is found in Obeja's narrations.

Where it's reviewed:
Belles Lettres: A Review of Books by Women, January 1996, page 54
Chicago Review, Spring-Summer 1995, page 158
Lambda Book Report, November-December 1994, page 24
Ms. Magazine, November-December 1994, page 76

Other books by the same author:
Memory Mambo: A Novel, 1996

Other books you might like:
Terri de la Pena, *Margins*, 1992
  A young lesbian writer confronts her future and her family about her sexuality in this story.
Terri de la Pena, *Latin Satins*, 1994
  The rise of a Chicana lesbian singing group in the LA area is chronicled in this story.
Cherrie Moraga, *Loving in the War Years: Lo que Nunca Paso por sus Labios*, 1983
  This is the autobiographical life of a Chicana lesbian writer who grew up California.
Ibis Gomez-Vega, *Send My Roots Rain*, 1991
  Carole goes to a small Texas town to paint murals on church walls and falls in love with a mysterious woman.
Jaime Manrique, *Latin Moon in Manhattan*, 1992
  Through the eyes of Santiago, a gay unpublished poet, this novel presents plots and sub-plots, and a vivid depiction of Columbian American culture in Little Colombia Jackson Heights.
Sheila Ortiz Taylor, *Faultline: A Novel*, 1982
  This very funny book is about a lesbian mother of six children, her lover/companion, their 300 rabbits, and a six foot tall Black drag queen baby sitter.
Sheila Ortiz Taylor, *Southbound: A Sequel to Faultline*, 1990
  This humorous lesbian novel follows professor Arden as she sets out across the country in a hearse with her six kids, her ballet dancer/live-in babysitter, and her lover Alice.

Roberto Fernandez, *Holy Radishes*, 1995
  This satirical novel depicts the Cuban American community in Florida where exiled Cubans plan the liberation of their homeland while their wives work at a radish plant.
Emma Perez, *Gulf Dreams*, 1996
  A creative series of essays, short vignettes, and psychoanalytic discourses on growing up lesbian in Latino culture.

741

JULIAN OLIVARES, Mexican American

Cuentos Hispanos de Los Estados Unidos

(Houston, TX: Arte Publico, 1993)

Subject(s): Anthology; Short Stories
Age range(s): Grades 9-Adult
Time period(s): 1980s
Locale(s): United States

Summary: A collection of short stories, written in Spanish, by Latino authors of the U.S. This anthology was conceived for native Spanish speakers studying Spanish, and for students in intermediate and advanced Spanish language courses. The stories are by Cuban Americans, Chicano, Puerto Rican , and other Latino writers. Each story includes a glossary and theme questions for discussion. Included are stories by Roberto Fernandez, Rosaura Sanchez, Tomas Rivera, Rolando Hinojosa, and many others.

About this book: Complete texts are in Spanish with no English translations.

Where it's reviewed:
Americas, English Edition, July-August 1994, page 63

Other books by the same author:
Decade II: An Anniversary Anthology, 1993
Tomas Rivera: The Complete Works, 1991

Other books you might like:
Fernando Alegria, *Paradise Lost or Gained? The Literature of Hispanic Exile*, 1990
  Collection of short stories by Latinos living in exile in the U.S.
Carolina Hospital, *Cuban American Writers: Los Atrevidos*, 1988
  A first collection of stories by Cuban American writers.
Ray Gonzalez, *Currents From the Dancing River: Contemporary Latino Fiction, Nonfiction, and Poetry*, 1994
  Collection of short stories and other writings by Latinos in the U.S.
Harold Augenbraum, *Growing Up Latino: Memoirs and Stories*, 1993
  Collection of short stories by Latino writers in the United States.
Jose B. Fernandez, *Nuevos Horizintes: Cuentos Chicanos, Puertorriquenos y Cubanos*, 1982
  Eighteen short stories in an intermediate reader by authors who live in the United States.

742

JULIAN OLIVARES, Editor
EVANGELINA VIGIL, Co-Editor, Mexican American

Decade II: An Anniversary Anthology
(Houston: Arte Publico, 1993)

Subject(s): Anthology; Short Stories
Age range(s): Grades 10-Adult
Time period(s): 1980s; 1990s (1980-1993)
Locale(s): United States (stories take place throughout U.S. and also in ficticious locations)

Summary: This anthology contains stories that appeared in *Revista Chicano Riquena/The Americas Review* during the decade 1983-1992. Twenty-seven new voices share coverage with fourteen veteran writers, who were included in the first *Decade* anthology. Collectively, they represent U.S. Latino literature.

About this book: The first *Decade* anthology was published in 1983.

Other books you might like:
Ray Gonzalez, *Mirrors Beneath the Earth: Short Fiction by Chicano Writers*, 1992
    This is a collection of short stories.
Tiffany Ana Lopez, *Growing Up Chicano*, 1993
    These short stories are by Chicano writers.
Gary Soto, *Pieces of the Heart: New Chicano Fiction*, 1993
    These short stories are by Chicano writers.
Ray Gonzalez, *Currents From the Dancing River: Contemporary Latino Fiction, Nonfiction, and Poetry*, 1994
    These short stories are by Chicano writers.
Rudolfo Anaya, *Voces: An Anthology of Nuevo Mexican Writers*, 1987
    These stories describe living in New Mexico.
Delia Poey, *Iguana Dreams: New Latino Fiction*, 1992
    This is an anthology of creative fiction by Latino writers in the U.S.
Nicolas Kanellos, *Short Fiction by Hispanic Writers of the United States*, 1993
    This is a collection of short stories by Latino writers.

743

MARGARITE FERNANDEZ OLMOS, Editor, Puerto Rican
LIZABETH PARAVISINI-GEBERT, Co-Editor

Pleasure in the Word: Erotic Writings by Latin American Women
(Fredonia, NY: White Pine Press, 1993)

Subject(s): Short Stories; Poetry; Sexuality
Age range(s): Grades 10-Adult
Time period(s): 1990s (1993)
Locale(s): United States

Summary: This diverse collection of writing by women breaks the silence by speaking out about eroticism, love, and violence. Seeking pleasure within a politics in Latin America that censures and represses, these writers, some of whom are well known, dare to write freely and with passion. This collection contains the works of Puerto Rican and Cuban writers, such as Isabel Allende, Ana Lydia Vega, Marjorie Agosin and Rosario Ferre.

About this book: First published in Spanish in 1991 as *El Placer de la Palabra: Literataura Erotica Femenina de America Latina*.

Where it's reviewed:
Publishers Weekly, August 23, 1993, page 61
Women's Review of Books, May 1995, page 19

Other books by the same author:
Remaking a Lost Harmony: Stories from the Hispanic Caribbean, 1995
Green Cane and Juicy Flotsam: Short Stories by Caribbean Women, 1991

Other books you might like:
Ana Lydia Vega, *True and False Romances*, 1994
    Collection of short stories about women and romance that take place in Puerto Rico.
Kathleen Ross, *Scents of Wood and Silence: Short Stories by Latin American Women Writers*, 1991
    Anthology of short fiction by Latin American women writers.
Rosario Ferre, *The Youngest Doll*, 1991
    Collection of short stories, originally published in Spanish, about Puerto Rican society.
Kal Wagenheim, *Cuentos: An Anthology of Short Stories from Puerto Rico*, 1978
    Collection of short stories by a writer living and writing in Puerto Rico.
Diana Velez, *Reclaiming Medusa: Short Stories by Contemporary Puerto Rican Women*, 1988
    Thirteen stories, by five well-known Puerto Rican women writers, appear in this anthology.

744

JUDITH ORTIZ COFER, Puerto Rican

An Island Like You: Stories of the Barrio
(New York: Orchid Books, 1995)

Subject(s): Short Stories; City Life; Coming of Age
Age range(s): Grades 6-9
Time period(s): 1990s
Locale(s): Paterson, New Jersey

Summary: These twelve stories, set in a barrio of New Jersey, examine the lives of Puerto Rican teenagers who deal with friendship, family, romance, and school. The interconnected stories are colorful, emotional, and honest, and their characters move toward independence and make decisions about their lives.

Where it's reviewed:
Horn Book Magazine, July-August 1995, page 464
Horn Book Magazine, September-October 1995, page 581
Publishers Weekly, April 17, 1995, page 61

Other books by the same author:
The Latin Deli: Prose and Poetry, 1993
The Line of the Sun: A Novel, 1989
Silent Dancing: A Partial Remembrance of a Puerto Rican Childhood, 1990

Other books you might like:
Nicholasa Mohr, *Rituals of Survival: A Woman's Portfolio*, 1985
  These stories are about strong Puerto Rican women who take control of their lives.
Phyllis Tashlik, *Hispanic, Female, and Young*, 1994
  This collection of short stories is by young Latina girls growing up in New York City.
Jack Agueros, *Dominoes and Other Stories from the Puerto Rican*, 1993
  This collection of short stories is about life in New York City.
Faythe Turner, *Puerto Rican Writers at Home in the U.S.A.: An Anthology*, 1991
  This collection of short stories is about life in the U.S.
Abraham Rodriguez Jr., *The Boy Without a Flag: Tales of the South Bronx*, 1992
  These stories are about young people growing up Puerto Rican in New York City.
Gil C. Alicea, *The Air Down Here: True Tales from a South Bronx Boyhood*, 1995
  Sixteen-year-old Gil Alicea battles daily with drugs, violence, gangs, school and family, and the media in this book of short essays and journal entries.

745

JUDITH ORTIZ COFER, Puerto Rican

The Latin Deli: Prose and Poetry
(New York: W.W. Norton & Co. 1995)

Subject(s): Short Stories; Coming of Age; Poetry
Age range(s): Grades 10-Adult
Time period(s): 20th century (1960-1994)
Locale(s): Paterson, New Jersey

Summary: Ortiz Cofer is a writer of fiction, poetry, and essays, and all three genres are represented in this collection. Life in Patterson, New Jersey, is portrayed in the short stories *El Building* and *American History*. Her characters are young Puerto Rican girls who must face the challenges of growing up with conflicting bicultural values, but who come from a strong supportive community.

Where it's reviewed:
Studies in Short Fiction, Summer 1994, page 502
Parnassus: Poetry in Review, Spring-Fall 1995, page 458
Publishers Weekly, November 8, 1993, page 60
Library Journal, November 1, 1993, page 93

Other books by the same author:
An Island Like You: Stories of the Barrio, 1995
Silent Dancing: A Partial Remembrance of a Puerto Rican Childhood, 1990
The Line of the Sun: A Novel, 1989
Terms of Survival: Poems, 1987

Other books you might like:
Esmeralda Santiago, *When I Was Puerto Rican*, 1993
  This autobiography is about life on the island of Puerto Rico.
Edward Rivera, *Family Installments: Memories of Growing Up Hispanic*, 1982

This humorously related episodes are about growing up in Puerto Rico and in New York.
Nicholasa Mohr, *Rituals of Survival: A Woman's Portfolio*, 1985
  These stories are about strong Puerto Rican women who take control of their lives.
Phyllis Tashlik, *Hispanic, Female, and Young*, 1994
  This collection of short stories is by young Latina girls growing up in New York City.
Julia Alvarez, *The Other Side = El Otro Lado*, 1995
  A collection of poetry that reads like prose and examines love, language, and the author's past.

746

JUDITH ORTIZ COFER, Puerto Rican

The Line of the Sun: A Novel
(Athens, GA: University of Georgia Press, 1989)

Subject(s): Intergenerational Saga; Coming of Age; Women
Age range(s): Grades 10-Adult
Major character(s): Marisol, Young Woman (first person narrator), Puerto Rican; Gusman, Uncle (of Marisol), Puerto Rican; Romana, Mother (of Marisol), Puerto Rican
Time period(s): 20th century (1930-1960)
Locale(s): Salud, Puerto Rico (fictional city); Paterson, New Jersey

Summary: A young girl comes at age in the United States but its her Puerto Rican culture she relies on for support. The first half of this intergenerational novel presents the background heritage of her family. While the second half reveals Marisol maturing into a young woman living in New York. The influence of her Uncle Gusman contributes to her growth and sense of identity.

Where it's reviewed:
Hudson Review, Spring 1990, page 151
Wilson Library Bulletin, October 1989, page 123
Library Journal, May 15, 1989, page 88
Publishers Weekly, April 28, 1989 page 61

Other books by the same author:
An Island Like You: Stories of the Barrio, 1995
Silent Dancing: A Partial Remembrance of a Puerto Rican Childhood, 1990
The Latin Deli: Prose and Poetry, 1993

Other books you might like:
Magali Garcia Ramis, *Happy Days, Uncle Sergio*, 1995
  A young girl comes of age in Puerto Rico.
Rosario Ferre, *The House on the Lagoon*, 1995
  This intergenerational story presents an upper class family in Ponce, Puerto Rico.
Esmeralda Santiago, *When I Was Puerto Rican*, 1993
  In this autobiographical story Santiago shares her experiences growing up in Puerto Rico and the U.S.
Alma Flor Ada, *Where the Flame Trees Bloom*, 1994
  These eleven stories describe the authors childhood in Cuba.
Cristina Garcia, *Dreaming in Cuban, A Novel*, 1992
  A novel that interweaves the stories of three generations of

Cuban women and their different responses to the Cuban revolution.

747

JUDITH ORTIZ COFER, Puerto Rican

Silent Dancing: A Partial Remembrance of a Puerto Rican Childhood
(Houston: Arte Publico Press, 1990)

Subject(s): Childhood; Mothers and Daughters; Grandparents
Age range(s): Grades 10-Adult
Time period(s): 20th century (1955-1970)
Locale(s): Paterson, New Jersey

Summary: This collection of personal narratives, short stories, poetry, and essays present the childhood of Judith Ortiz Cofer as she grows up in both Puerto Rico and Patterson, New Jersey.

Where it's reviewed:
Library Journal, July 1990, page 96
Melus, Summer 1993, page 121
Publishers Weekly, June 8, 1990, page 50

Other books by the same author:
An Island Like You: Stories of the Barrio, 1995
The Latin Deli: Prose and Poetry, 1993
The Line of the Sun: A Novel, 1989

Other books you might like:
Esmeralda Santiago, *When I Was Puerto Rican*, 1993
   This autobiography depicts life on the island of Puerto Rico.
Edward Rivera, *Family Installments: Memories of Growing Up Hispanic*, 1982
   These humorous episodes revolve around growing up in Puerto Rico and in New York.
Nicholasa Mohr, *Rituals of Survival: A Woman's Portfolio*, 1985
   These stories portray strong Puerto Rican women who take control of their lives.
Roberto Santiago, *Boricuas: Influential Puerto Rican Writers—an Anthology*, 1995
   This anthology of essays, fiction, poetry, monologues, and screenplays is by controversial writers from the nineteenth and twentieth centuries.

748

KAREN PAPAGAPITOS

Jose's Basket
(New York, NY: Kapa Press, 1990)

Subject(s): Friendship; Migrant Labor; Mothers and Sons
Age range(s): Grades K-2
Major character(s): Jose, Child (boy), Worker (migrant), Mexican American
Time period(s): 1970s
Locale(s): Arizona

Summary: Because Jose's family is a migrant farm working family that travels from southern Arizona to Central Califor-

nia, Jose starts school later than most students, but he loves school and makes friends with a Vietnamese little girl. When it is time to leave again he is saddened and his teacher gives him a journal with all the names and addresses of the students in his class and is full of memories. This journal is like his mother's basket, which is made from grasses and twigs from their travels, and is also full of memories.

Other books by the same author:
Socorro, Daughter of the Desert, 1993

Other books you might like:
Arthur Dorros, *Radio Man = Don Radio: A Story in English and Spanish*, 1993
   This beautifully illustrated story is about Diego, who relies on his radio for companionship, and his family who are migrant farm workers.
Gloria Anzaldua, *Friends From the Other Side/Amigos del Otro Lado*, 1993
   Prietita helps an undocumented boy and his family hide from the *migra*.
Juan Felipe Herrera, *Calling the Doves = El Canto de las Palomas*, 1995
   A book depicting the experiences of the author as a young boy growing up as a farm worker in the fields and valleys of California.
Karen Papagapitos, *Socorro, Daughter of the Desert*, 1993
   Eight-year-old Socorro belongs to a family of farm workers and she helps them out as much as she can. When her father becomes ill, Socorro makes tortillas for her mother to sell in the fields.
Carmen Lomas Garza, *Family Pictures = Cuadros de Familia*, 1990
   Carmen Lomas Garza, a well known Chicana artist presents beautiful and detailed paintings of her growing up years in a Texas border town.
Pura Belpre, *Santiago*, 1969
   Santiago learns to make new friends in a new school.
Nicholasa Mohr, *Felita*, 1990
   Felita loves her neighborhood and her best friend Gigi, but her world is turned upside down when her family moves to a new neighborhood.

749

KAREN PAPAGAPITOS
RONDI COLLETTE, Illustrator

Socorro, Daughter of the Desert
(New York, NY: Kapa, 1993)

Subject(s): Migrant Labor; Family Life; Ghosts
Age range(s): Grades 2-5
Major character(s): Socorro, 8-Year-Old (girl), Worker (migrant), Mexican American
Time period(s): 1950s
Locale(s): Arizona

Summary: The family of eight-year-old Socorro are farm workers and she helps out as much as she can. When her father becomes ill, along with many other workers, Socorro and her Tia Conchita make tortillas for her mother to sell in the fields to earn extra money. She also entertains her brothers with stories of the desert, including one about a black-clad stranger.

Awards the book has won:
NABE Best Children's Book, 1993
Publishers Marketing Association Benjamin Franklin Award

Other books by the same author:
Jose's Basket, 1990

Other books you might like:
Arthur Dorros, *Radio Man = Don Radio: A Story in English and Spanish*, 1993
This beautifully illustrated story is about Diego, who relies on his radio for companionship, and his family who are migrant farm workers.

Gloria Anzaldua, *Friends From the Other Side/Amigos del Otro Lado*, 1993
Prietita helps an undocumented boy and his family hide from the ''migra''.

Juan Felipe Herrera, *Calling the Doves = El Canto de las Palomas*, 1995
A book depicting the experiences of the author as a young boy growing up as a farm worker in the fields and valleys of California.

Diane Gonzales Bertrand, *Alicia's Treasures*, 1996
Alicia is invited to spend a weekend at the beach with her brother and she has an exciting adventure.

Carmen Lomas Garza, *Family Pictures = Cuadros de Familia*, 1990
Carmen Lomas Garza, a well known Chicana artist, presents beautiful and detailed paintings of her growing up years in a Texas border town.

Juanita Havill, *Treasure Nap*, 1992
Mama tells Alicia the story of Rita, who visits her grandfather in the mountains of Mexico, and learns to make wooden birdcages.

Gary Soto, *The Skirt*, 1992
Fourth-grader Miata loses her mother's folkloric dancing skirt and figures out a way to find it.

Alma Flor Ada, *My Name Is Maria Isabel*, 1993
Maria Isabel moves to a new school where she must defend her name and her heritage.

750

AMERICO PAREDES, Mexican American

George Washington Gomez

(Houston, TX: Arte Publico Press, 1990)

Subject(s): Growing Up; Adventure and Adventurers
Age range(s): Grades 8-Adult
Major character(s): George Washington Gomez, Young Man, Mexican American; Feliciano Garcia, Young Man, Uncle, Mexican American
Time period(s): 1920s; 1930s (1920-1940)
Locale(s): Jonesville, Texas

Summary: The background plot of this novel is the historical struggle of Texas Mexicans to preserve their language and culture. As he grows up, George Washington Gomez struggles with racism, abuse, and cultural and political clashes. After his father is killed by a Texas Ranger, Gualinto, as he's

called by his family, is raised by his mother Maria and his uncle Feliciano. They work hard to give him an education which leads him to marriage with an Anglo woman and to work for the government. Absorbing and sensitively told, this novel examines the life of a boy with an important and ironic name.

Other books by the same author:
Between Two Worlds, 1991
The Hammon and the Beans and Other Stories, 1994
Folklore and Culture on the Texas-Mexican Border, 1993
With His Pistol in His Hand: A Border Ballad and Its Hero, 1958

Other books you might like:
Nash Candelaria, *Leonor Park*, 1991
This novel, set in New Mexico, is about land and greed, where a powerful woman battles with her brother over their father's legacy, a piece of land alongside the Rio Grande.

Jose Antonio Villarreal, *Pocho*, 1959
This is the story of a Mexican family in the Santa Clara Valley of California before World War II and the assimilation of the son Richard Rubio.

Alejandro Morales, *The Brick People*, 1988
Fictional but historically-based, this novel is about two families against each other—the Simons and the Revueltas—during the late nineteenth and early twentieth centuries in California.

Genaro Gonzalez, *Rainbow's End*, 1988
This adventure novel presents dangerous border crossings, confrontations with a magician, and drug smuggling in the lives of the Cavazos family in the lower Rio Grande area of Texas.

Ernesto Galarza, *Barrio Boy*, 1971
Autobiographical, this story examines the early life of a distinguished professor and author who wrote many works about Mexican agricultural workers.

Lionel G. Garcia, *Hardscrub*, 1990
Related from the perspective of eleven-year-old Jim, this novel portrays characters struggling to survive in the tough land of West Texas.

Aristeo Brito, *The Devil in Texas = El Diablo en Texas*, 1990
The devil comes to the border town of Presidio, Texas in this important novel that describes the Anglo destruction of a Chicano world.

751

AMERICO PAREDES, Mexican American

The Hammon and the Beans and Other Stories

(Houston, TX: Arte Publico Press, 1994)

Subject(s): War; Politics; Women
Age range(s): Grades 10-Adult
Time period(s): 19th century; 20th century (1846-1952)
Locale(s): Texas (some stories take place in Japan and Korea)

Summary: This collection of short stories written by the distinguished and well known Dr. Paredes present historical events spanning a hundred year time period. Several of the stories have never before been published and were written in the 1940s and early 1950s. The southern Texas border region and the cultural conflict that has dominated that area since the U.S.-Mexican War is the setting for several of these stories. We find stories, some definitely political, about revolutionaries, guerrilla warriors, and the hated Texas Rangers. There are also stories about racism and the cultural conflict experienced by Mexican American and Black soldiers at war in Korea and living in Japan.

Where it's reviewed:
Publishers Weekly, June 6, 1994, page 61

Other books by the same author:
Between Two Worlds, 1991
Folktales of Mexico, 1970
George Washington Gomez, 1990
Folklore and Culture on the Texas-Mexican Border, 1993
With His Pistol in His Hand: A Border Ballad and Its Hero, 1958

Other books you might like:
Rolando Hinojosa, *The Useless Servants*, 1993
    This novel is made up of the diary entries, which serve as a survival mechanism, by Rafe Buenrostro as he is stationed in Korea during the war, and where he describes his every day experiences.
Nash Candelaria, *Not by the Sword*, 1982
    Set before the Mexican War of 1846 this novel shows the struggles taking place in New Mexico, the Rafa family, and the collapse of the Mexican government.
Nash Candelaria, *The Day the Cisco Kid Shot John Wayne*, 1988
    The author examines cultural clashes between Latinos and Anglos in this humorous collection of short stories from New Mexico.
Genaro Gonzalez, *Rainbow's End*, 1988
    This adventure novel presents dangerous border crossings, confrontations with a magician, and drug smuggling in the lives of the Cavazos family in the lower Rio Grande area of Texas.
Jose Antonio Burciaga, *Spilling the Beans: Loteria Chicana*, 1995
    This series of essays, many humorous, recount experiences from the author's childhood in Texas.
Josephina Niggli, *Mexican Village*, 1994
    This is an important collection of ten interrelated short stories about the lives of the people of a small Mexican town, Hidalgo. It was first published in 1945.
Jesus Salvador Trevino, *The Fabulous Sinkhole and Other Stories*, 1995
    This first story collection by Trevino, a screenwriter and director, is an entertaining creation of Mexican and Chicano characters, that take place in a fictional town, Arroyo Grande, in Texas.
Gloria Lopez-Stafford, *A Place in El Paso: A Mexican American Childhood*, 1996
    This bittersweet narrative describes the author's early childhood in the projects of El Paso during World War II.

VICTOR PERERA, Guatemalan

Rites: A Guatemalan Boyhood
(New York: Harcourt Brace, 1985)

Subject(s): Growing Up; Social Classes; Moving, Household
Age range(s): Grades 8-Adult
Major character(s): Victor Perera, Child, Guatemalan
Time period(s): 20th century (1940-1981)
Locale(s): Guatemala

Summary: These are autobiographical narratives of the author's boyhood while living in Guatemala. His parents, Sephardic Jews, immigrated from Jerusalem to Guatemala and a growing Jewish community. Perera grew up in Guatemala speaking Spanish and attending elementary school there. His family immigrated again to the U.S., but Perera continued to return to Guatemala. He reveals the comical and traumatic experiences from his childhood as we meet some of his childhood friends.

Where it's reviewed:
Library Journal, June 1, 1986, page 120
New York Times Book Review, July 13, 1986, page 19
Publishers Weekly, May 9, 1986, page 242

Other books by the same author:
The Conversion, 1970
The Cross and the Pear Tree: A Sephardic Journey, 1995
Unfinished Conquest: The Guatemalan Tragedy, 1995

Other books you might like:
Omar Castaneda, *Remembering to Say Mouth or Face*, 1993
    This collection of stories, some taking place in Central America, is by a Guatemalan writer living in the U.S.
Fernando Alegria, *Paradise Lost or Gained? The Literature of Hispanic Exile*, 1990
    A collection of literature by Latino writers addressing the experience of exile and alienation through stories, poems, and essays.
Kal Wagenheim, *Cuentos: An Anthology of Short Stories from Puerto Rico*, 1978
    This collection of short stories is by Puerto Rican authors living in Puerto Rico.
Rosario Ferre, *The Youngest Doll*, 1991
    This collection of short stories, originally published in Spanish, is about Puerto Rico society.
Pablo Medina, *Exiled Memories: A Cuban Childhood*, 1990
    This work is a collection of the author's memories of growing up in Cuba, spending summers on his grandfather's sugar cane plantation before the revolution.
Ilan Stavans, *The One-Handed Pianist and Other Stories*, 1996
    Nine short stories, most previously published in journals, explore memory, culture, language, and Judaism in the Latino world. Stavans presents a metaphysical perspective of the world.
Francisco Goldman, *The Long Night of White Chickens*, 1992
    Determined to find the murderers of his cousin, Flor, Roger and his best friend, Luis, become entangled in political difficulties as they discover the secret life of Flor in a war-torn Guatemala.

753

EMMA PEREZ, Mexican American

Gulf Dreams

(Berkeley, CA: Third Woman Press, 1996)

Subject(s): Coming of Age; Homosexuality/Lesbianism; Biography
Age range(s): Grades 10-Adult
Major character(s): Emma Perez, Lesbian, Chicana
Time period(s): 20th century (1950-1995)
Locale(s): Texas

Summary: A creative series of essays, short vignettes, and psychoanalytic discourse on growing up lesbian in a Latino culture. Perez employs non-fiction, fictionalized memoirs, and personal history to create a lesbian cultural space for Chicanas like herself. She explores theories of pain and pleasure, betrayal, and her search for meaning in life.

Other books you might like:

Cherrie Moraga, *Loving in the War Years: Lo que Nunca Paso por sus Labios*, 1983
This is the autobiographical life of a Chicana lesbian writer who grew up in California.

Achy Obejas, *We Came All the Way from Cuba So You Could Dress Like This? Stories*, 1994
These seven short stories, set in Chicago, include several about gay men and women, outcasts, AIDS patients and immigrants in the 1990s.

Sheila Ortiz Taylor, *Faultline: A Novel*, 1982
This very funny book is about a lesbian mother of six children, her lover/companion, their 300 rabbits, and a six foot tall Black drag queen baby sitter.

Sheila Ortiz Taylor, *Southbound: A Sequel to Faultline*, 1990
This humorous lesbian novel follows professor Arden as she sets out across the country in a hearse with her six kids, her ballet dancer/live-in babysitter, and her lover Alice.

Terri de la Pena, *Margins*, 1992
A young lesbian writer confronts her future and her family about her sexuality in this story.

Ibis Gomez-Vega, *Send My Roots Rain*, 1991
Carole goes to a small Texas town to paint murals on church walls and falls in love with a mysterious woman.

Juanita Ramos, *Companeras: Latina Lesbians: An Anthology*, 1987
This anthology includes the writings of Puerto Ricans, Cubans, Chileans, Chicana Colombians, and other Latina lesbians of different nationalities and with different life experiences.

Norma Alarcon, *The Sexuality of Latinas*, 1993
This collection of poems, short stories, and prose examine the often hidden, often subverted, sexuality of Latinas.

Carla Trujillo, *Chicana Lesbians: The Girls Our Mothers Warned Us About*, 1991
A diverse collection of short stories, poetry, and prose by Chicana lesbians exploring the intricacies and specifics of culture, family, mixed-race relationships, body, and identity.

754

GUSTAVO PEREZ FIRMAT, Cuban American

Next Year in Cuba: A Cubano's Coming of Age in America

(New York: Anchor Books, 1995)

Subject(s): Coming of Age; Identity; Biculturalism
Age range(s): Grades 10-Adult
Time period(s): 20th century (1960-1995)
Locale(s): Florida (also takes place in Michigan and North Carolina)

Summary: A memoir by a professor exploring the biculturalism of the author, and his search for identity and roots in America. Every year, at Christmas, his family celebrated with the cry "Next year in Cuba!" expecting to return to Cuba at any moment. After thirty five years in the U.S. that moment has yet to come. In this recollection Perez Firmat brings together the different strands of his life as an exile, searching for both his American and his Cuban heritage.

Where it's reviewed:
Hispanic, August 1995, page 60
Library Journal, August 1995, page 84
Publishers Weekly, July 10, 1995, page 48

Other books by the same author:
Bilingual Blues: Poems, 1981-1994, 1995
The Cuban Condition: Translation and Identity in Modern Cuban Literature, 1989
Life on the Hyphen: The Cuban-American Way, 1994
Literature and Liminality: Festive Readings in the Hispanic Tradition, 1986

Other books you might like:

Victor Perera, *Rites: A Guatemalan Boyhood*, 1986
These autobiographical narratives are about the author's childhood living in Guatemala.

Omar Castaneda, *Remembering to Say Mouth or Face*, 1993
These short stories, some which take place in Central America, are by a Guatemalan writer now living in the U.S.

Fernando Alegria, *Paradise Lost or Gained? The Literature of Hispanic Exile*, 1990
A collection by Latino writers addressing the experience of exile and alienation through stories, poems, and essays.

Ruth Behar, *Bridges to Cuba = Puentes a Cuba*, 1995
An anthology of short stories, essays, poetry, and historical documents exploring the Cuban and Cuban American experience.

Pablo Medina, *Exiled Memories: A Cuban Childhood*, 1990
This work is a collection of the author's memories of growing up in Cuba, spending summers on his grandfather's sugar cane plantation before the revolution.

Pablo Medina, *The Marks of Birth*, 1994
The descendant of a well-to-do Cuban family is forced to flee the island due to political turmoil and lives a frustrated, self-imposed exiled life.

755

FERNANDO PICO, Puerto Rican
MARIA ANTONIA ORDONEZ, Illustrator, Cuban

The Red Comb

(Mahwah, NJ: Bridgewater Books, 1991)

Subject(s): Slavery; Friendship
Age range(s): Grades 1-3
Major character(s): Vitita, Child; Sina Rosa Bultron, Friend (of Vitita), Widow(er), Healer
Time period(s): 19th century (1842-1849)
Locale(s): Caimito, Puerto Rico (a rural district of Rio Piedras)

Summary: When Vitita discovers a runaway slave beneath her porch, she decides to save her from the slave catcher. With the help of her friend, old Sina Rosa, Vitita leaves the slave woman food, essentials, and her own precious red comb as a gift. They must use their wits to save the woman and rid the town of the slave catcher forever.

About this book: This story is based on historical documents with beautiful illustrations by Ordonez. It is translated and adapted by Argentina Palacios.

Where it's reviewed:
Horn Book Magazine, May-June 1995, page 317
Wilson Library Bulletin, June 1995, page 118

Awards the book has won:
Ediciones Huracan of Puerto Rico, 1987

Other books you might like:
Alma Flor Ada, *The Gold Coin*, 1991
    A thief searches for a gold coin but discovers the treasure of friendship.
Gloria Anzaldua, *Friends From the Other Side/Amigos del Otro Lado*, 1993
    Prietita, a Mexican American girl, becomes friends with Joaquin, an illegal immigrant boy who lives with his mother on the U.S. side of the border.
Enedina Casarez Vasquez, *Recuerdos de Una Nina*, 1980
    These short stories are about growing up in San Antonio, Texas.
Alma Flor Ada, *My Name Is Maria Isabel*, 1993
    Maria moves to a new school and learns not to be shy about her name.
Pura Belpre, *Santiago*, 1969
    Santiago must deal with moving and making new friends.
Fran Leeper Buss, *Journey of the Sparrow*, 1991
    A Salvadoran family is smuggled into Chicago to start a new life.

756

CECILE PINEDA, Peruvian American

The Love Queen of the Amazon

(Boston: Little, Brown, and Company, 1992)

Subject(s): Satire; Romance; Sexual Behavior
Age range(s): Grades 10-Adult
Major character(s): Ana Magdelena Orgaz, Young Woman, Prostitute, Peruvian; Federico Orgaz y Orgaz, Writer, Husband (married to Ana Magdelena), Peruvian

Time period(s): Indeterminate Past
Locale(s): Peru

Summary: A parody of a Latin American male-novel that traces the escapades of Ana Magdelena and her husband, Federico Orgaz y Orgaz. For social appearances Ana Magdelena is forced to marry the elderly affluent writer, who it turns out, has lost his fortune. He ignores Ana Magdelena and devotes all his time to his novel *The Love Queen of the Amazon*, which is about the sexual adventures of Ana, her aunt's bordello, and later Ana's brothel established right in her own home.

Where it's reviewed:
Belles Lettres: A Review of Books by Women, Fall, 1992, page 12
Library Journal, February 15, 1992, page 197
New Statesman & Society, February 12, 1993, page 47
Publishers Weekly, January 20, 1992, page 47
Times Literary Supplement, February 12, 1993, page 21

Other books by the same author:
Face, 1985
Frieze, 1986

Other books you might like:
Mario Vargas Llosa, *Aunt Julia and the Scriptwriter*, 1982
    A comical Peruvian novel about a scriptwriter whose real-life episodes mirror his imagination and the writing of a radio serial.
Maria Espinosa, *Dark Plums*, 1995
    Adrianne, a young girl from Texas, begins a search for love and self in Manhattan.
Kathleen Alcala, *Mrs. Vargas and the Dead Naturalist*, 1992
    A collection of short stories, many about Mexican women, created as a book of wonders and following the characteristics of magical realism.
Luis Rafael Sanchez, *Macho Camacho's Beat*, 1980
    Macho Camacho's beat is an inane song that catches the tropical beats of the paradise island of Puerto Rico.
Beatriz Rivera, *African Passions and Other Stories*, 1995
    A collection of short stories focusing on women's obsessive search for love and success, narrated with humor, passion, and satire.
Himilce Novas, *Mangos, Bananas, and Coconuts: A Cuban Love Story*, 1996
    This tale of a magical yet real love story is an ancient tale, beginning with the love of a man and a woman from different social classes, and the story of the fate of their children.

757

DELIA POEY, Editor, Mexican American
VIRGIL SUAREZ, Co-Editor, Cuban American

Iguana Dreams: New Latino Fiction

(New York: Harper Prennial, 1992)

Subject(s): Anthology; Short Stories
Age range(s): Grades 10-Adult
Time period(s): 1980s
Locale(s): United States

Summary: This collection of literature, by Latino authors, gives an individual perspective on the Latino experience. Some of the elements that unify Latino culture are language, specifically the Spanish language and bilingualism; the need for cultural survival or the experiences of assimilation; and urban life in big cities. Even though these are unifying experiences they are experienced differently by Latinos in the U.S. This anthology mirrors these different experiences by some well-known writers like Sandra Cisneros, Rudolfo Anaya, Abraham Rodriguez, Jr., and Cristina Garcia.

About this book: The preface is by Oscar Hijuelos.

Where it's reviewed:
Library Journal, September 15, 1992, page 96
Publishers Weekly, August 3, 1992, page 64

Other books by the same author:
Paper Dance: 55 Latino Poets, 1995
The Cutter: A Novel, 1991
Welcome to the Oasis and Other Stories, 1992
Latin Jazz, 1989

Other books you might like:
Gary D. Keller, *Hispanics in the U.S.: An Anthology of Creative Literature. Vol. 2*, 1982
This collection of poetry and short stories is by Latino writers.
Nicolas Kanellos, *Short Fiction by Hispanic Writers of the United States*, 1993
This collection of short stories is by Latino writers.
Harold Augenbraum, *Growing Up Latino: Memoirs and Stories*, 1993
Twenty-five Latinos write stories describing growing up in the U.S.
Ray Gonzalez, *Currents From the Dancing River: Contemporary Latino Fiction, Nonfiction, and Poetry*, 1994
This collection of creative short fiction is by Latino writers in the US.
Denis Lynn Daly Heyck, *Barrios and Borderlands: Cultures of Latinos and Latinas in the United States*, 1994
This Anthology of creative literature is by Latino writers in the U.S.
Lillian Castillo-Speed, *Latina: Women's Voices from the Borderlands*, 1995
This is a collection of short fiction, specially edited for young adult readers.

758

MARY HELEN PONCE, Mexican American

Hoyt Street: An Autobiography
(Albuquerque, NM: University of New Mexico Press, 1993)

Subject(s): Growing Up; Family Relations; Coming of Age
Age range(s): Grades 10-Adult
Major character(s): Mary Helen Ponce, Child (girl), Mexican American
Time period(s): 1930s; 1940s (1930-1940)
Locale(s): Pacoima, California

Summary: Mary Helen Ponce writes her autobiography as a young girl growing up in a Mexican American neighborhood during the 1930s and 1940s. Her descriptions of her home, parents, sisters, and the local neighbors are vivid and bustling with life. The reader is immersed in the dynamic life of Hoyt Street during the years before World War II through the fresh vision of a child's eyes tempered by adult irony. Her narrative provides a commentary on religion, popular culture, and family.

Where it's reviewed:
Hispanic, July 1995, page 82
Nation, June 7, 1995, page 772

Other books by the same author:
Recuerdo: Short Stories of the Barrio, 1983
The Wedding, 1989
Taking Control, 1987

Other books you might like:
Gloria Lopez-Stafford, *A Place in El Paso: A Mexican American Childhood*, 1996
A bittersweet narrative describing the early childhood of the author living in the "projects" of El Paso during World War II.
Norma Elia Cantu, *Canicula: Snapshots of a Girlhood en la Frontera*, 1995
This collection, with photos, of short stories and vignettes show a young girl growing up along the Texas Mexican border.
Rolando Hinojosa, *Becky and Her Friends*, 1990
Narrated by many of her friends, this novel focuses on the strong-willed Becky Escobar, an upwardly-mobile woman who at age thirty-five decides to divorce her husband.
Denise Chavez, *The Last of the Menu Girls*, 1986
An adolescent Chicana girl from southern New Mexico is looking for her place, identity, and womanhood in this collection of interrelated short stories.
Patricia Preciado Martin, *Days of Plenty, Days of Want*, 1988
The past and present meet in this collection of stories where Mexican heritage is in jeopardy of being wiped out.
Roberta Fernandez, *Itaglio: Novel in Six Stories*, 1990
In each of these six related stories, an extraordinary woman serves as a role model for the young narrator.

759

MARY HELEN PONCE, Mexican American

The Wedding
(Houston, TX: Arte Publico Press, 1989)

Subject(s): Marriage; Traditions; Satire
Age range(s): Grades 10-Adult
Major character(s): Blanca Munoz, Young Woman, Mexican American
Time period(s): 1950s
Locale(s): California (near Los Angeles)

Summary: A tongue-in-cheek expose of working class life and culture in a southern California Chicano community. Blanca Munoz is planning her traditional Mexican wedding to Sammy-the-Cricket, a member of the gang, Los Tacones. The marriage preparations reveal the oppressive customs, mores, and beliefs that entrap and suffocate women's intellectual development.

Where it's reviewed:
Hispanic, December 1990, page 1005
Western American Literature, November 1990, page 262

Other books by the same author:
Hoyt Street: An Autobiography, 1993
Recuerdo: Short Stories of the Barrio, 1983
Taking Control, 1987

Other books you might like:
Jose Antonio Burciaga, *Spilling the Beans: Loteria Chicana*, 1995
　　A series of essays, many humorous, recounting experiences from the author's childhood that explore aspects of Chicano culture.
Nash Candelaria, *The Day the Cisco Kid Shot John Wayne*, 1988
　　A humorous collection of short stories from New Mexico, in which the author examines cultural clashes between Latinos and Anglos.
Sandra Cisneros, *Woman Hollering Creek and Other Stories*, 1991
　　A collection of short stories with strong, angry female characters struggling valiantly to make something beautiful of their lives.
Estela Portillo Trambley, *Rain of Scorpions and Other Writings*, 1975
　　Collection of short stories by an early Chicana writer that explore the place of women in Mexican society.
Louie Garcia Robinson, *The Devil, Delfina Varela, and the Used Chevy*, 1993
　　Set in the Mission District of San Francisco, this is a novel about politics, dreams, Latino social affairs, and Delfina, a widow who will do anything for a car.

760

MICHAEL ROSE RAMIREZ, Mexican American
LINDA DALAL SAWAYA, Illustrator

The Little Ant = La Hormiga Chiquita
(New York, NY: Rizzoli, 1995)

Subject(s): Animals/Ants; Responsibility; Folk Tales
Age range(s): Grades K-2
Time period(s): Indeterminate Past
Locale(s): United States

Summary: A little ant with a broken leg seeks restitution from those responsible. This includes animals, human beings, and even natural events. In the end the ant learns a lesson.

About this book: Bilingual format.

Where it's reviewed:
School Library Journal, March 1996, page 192

Other books you might like:
Lucia M. Gonzalez, *The Bossy Gallito*, 1994
　　A bossy little rooster gets his beak dirty pecking some corn while on his way to his uncle's wedding.
Linda Shute, *Rabbit Wishes*, 1995
　　Soon after creation, Tio Conejo complains that he wants to be large like an elephant or tall like a giraffe.

Pat Mora, *The Race of Toad and Deer*, 1995
　　Deer thinks he is the biggest and the fastest animal in the jungle, and he tries to make the other animals do as he says.
Gary Soto, *Chato's Kitchen*, 1995
　　Chato, a lowrider cat, plans a dinner and invites some nice mice, but they outwit him.
Pura Belpre, *Dance of the Animals*, 1972
　　Senor and Senora Lion, hungry for goat meat, throw a party and invite all the animals.
Alma Flor Ada, *Mediopollito = Half-Chicken*, 1995
　　This bilingual retelling of a traditional humorous tale from Spain is set in colonial Mexico. Half-Chicken is born with only half a body, and his uniqueness attracts a lot of attention.

761

JUANITA RAMOS, Editor, Puerto Rican

Companeras: Latina Lesbians: An Anthology
(New York: Latina Lesbian History Project, 1987)

Subject(s): Anthology; Homosexuality/Lesbianism
Age range(s): Grades 10-Adult
Time period(s): 1970s; 1980s (1987)
Locale(s): United States

Summary: This anthology contains the voices of Puerto Rican, Cuban, Chilean, Chicana Colombian, and other Latina lesbians with different life experiences. The stories and poems, many of which are in Spanish, deal with self-discovery, identity, coming out, family, oppression, and the search for meaning.

About this book: In 1994 a new edition has been issued by Routledge. This anthology is a valuable resource which lists organizations, publications, and periodicals.

Where it's reviewed:
Lambda Book Report, November-December 1994

Other books you might like:
Cherrie Moraga, *Loving in the War Years: Lo que Nunca Paso por sus Labios*, 1983
　　This autobiographical story is about a Chicana lesbian writer growing up in California.
Ibis Gomez-Vega, *Send My Roots Rain*, 1991
　　A woman artist arrives in a small Texas border town to paint murals on the church walls.
Terri de la Pena, *Margins*, 1992
　　The story of a young lesbian writer who confronts her future and her family about her sexuality.
Terri de la Pena, *Latin Satins*, 1994
　　A story that chronicles the rise of a Chicana lesbian singing group in the Los Angeles area.
Tey Diana Rebolledo, *Las Mujeres Hablan: An Anthology of Nuevo Mexicana Writers*, 1988
　　This collection of short stories and poetry is by Chicanas from New Mexico.
Norma Alarcon, *The Sexuality of Latinas*, 1993
　　A collection of poems, short stories, and prose that examine the often hidden, often subverted, sexuality of Latinas.

Carla Trujillo, *Chicana Lesbians: The Girls Our Mothers Warned Us About*, 1991

A diverse collection of short stories, poetry, and prose by Chicana lesbians exploring the intricacies and specifics of culture, family, mixed-race relationships, body, and identity.

Emma Perez, *Gulf Dreams*, 1996

A creative series of essays, short vignettes, and psychoanalytic discourse describe growing up lesbian in Latino culture.

762

MANUEL RAMOS, Mexican American

The Ballad of Gato Guerrero

(New York: St. Martins Press, 1994)

Subject(s): Crime and Criminals; Mystery and Detective Stories
Age range(s): Grades 10-Adult
Major character(s): Luis Montez, Lawyer, Chicano
Time period(s): 1990s (1994)
Locale(s): Denver, Colorado

Summary: Luis Montez is a divorced lawyer trying make ends meet both in his practice and at home. Felix "Gato" Guerrero, an old friend from way back, calls on Montez to save him and his new love Elizabeth, from her husband, a Latino mobster. As it turns out, not only is the mobster after Gato, but his ex-father-in-law, bitter over the death of his daughter, is after him too. Montez fights to protect Gato, while also working to save a tough young Chicano, son of a client.

Where it's reviewed:
Publisher Weekly, April 11, 1994, page 58

Other books by the same author:
The Ballad of Rocky Ruiz: Death of a Martyr, 1993
The Last Client of Luis Montez

Other books you might like:
Michael Nava, *How Town: A Novel of Suspense*, 1990
Henry Rios defends a former high school acquaintance from his hometown accused of murder and thought to be involved in child pornography.
Lucha Corpi, *Cactus Blood: A Mystery Novel*, 1995
Gloria Damasco, an apprentice to a private investigator, uses her visionary power to help solve a murder related to a 15-year-old pesticide tank explosion.
Lucha Corpi, *Eulogy for a Brown Angel: A Mystery Novel*, 1992
A Chicana feminist detective solves a murder that occurred during the Chicano civil rights movement of the late 1960s.
Rudolfo Anaya, *Zia Summer*, 1995
Sonny Baca is involved in a mystery that involves murder, cult worship of the sun, and a battle over nuclear waste and its disposal in New Mexico.
Rudolfo Anaya, *Albuquerque*, 1992
A story of modern Albuquerque, with a vicious mayoral race, a young Chicano boxer, American Indians fighting to retain water rights, and the folkloric past of New Mexico.

763

MANUEL RAMOS, Mexican American

The Ballad of Rocky Ruiz: Death of a Martyr

(New York: St. Martins Press, 1993)

Subject(s): Mystery and Detective Stories; Crime and Criminals
Age range(s): Grades 10-Adult
Major character(s): Luis Montez, Lawyer, Chicano
Time period(s): 1990s (1993)
Locale(s): Denver, Colorado

Summary: When a mysterious Chicana lawyer comes to town, former Chicano activist lawyer, middle aged Luis Montez becomes interested in solving the twenty-year-old murder of Rocky Ruiz. In the course of the investigation one of his friends, a former Chicano radical, is killed and two others receive threatening telephone calls. Montez is a likeable sleuth and he quickly draws the reader into the college radicalism of the late 1960s.

Where it's reviewed:
Hispanic, August 1994, page 40
Library Journal, June 1, 1993, page 196
Publishers Weekly, May 10, 1993, page 55

Awards the book has won:
Colorado Book Award, 1993
University of California Irvine, Chicano/Latino Fiction Award, 1993

Other books by the same author:
The Last Client of Luis Montez, 1996
The Ballad of Gato Guerrero, 1994

Other books you might like:
Michael Nava, *How Town: A Novel of Suspense*, 1990
Henry Rios defends a former high school acquaintance from his hometown. The man is accused of murder and thought to be involved in child pornography.
Lucha Corpi, *Cactus Blood: A Mystery Novel*, 1995
Gloria Damasco, an apprentice to a private investigator, uses her visionary power to help solve a murder related to a 15-year-old pesticide tank explosion.
Lucha Corpi, *Eulogy for a Brown Angel: A Mystery Novel*, 1992
A Chicana feminist detective solves a murder that occurred during the Chicano civil rights movement of the late 1960s.
Rudolfo Anaya, *Zia Summer*, 1995
Sonny Baca is involved in a mystery plot that involves murder, cult worship of the sun, and a battle over nuclear waste and its disposal in New Mexico.
Rudolfo Anaya, *Albuquerque*, 1992
A story of modern Albuquerque, with a vicious mayoral race, a young Chicano boxer, American Indians fighting to retain water rights, and the folkloric past of New Mexico.

764

MANUEL RAMOS, Mexican American

The Last Client of Luis Montez
(New York, NY: St. Martin's Press, 1996)

Subject(s): Family Relations; Crime and Criminals; Mystery and Detective Stories
Age range(s): Grades 10-Adult
Major character(s): Luis Montez, Lawyer (middle-aged), Chicano
Time period(s): 1990s
Locale(s): Denver, Colorado

Summary: The last client of Denver lawyer Louie Montez is found dead with Montez standing over him. To make matters worse, Montez was the last one to see the dead man's sister, who has disappeared, and Montez is charged with a possible double murder. In his efforts to extricate himself from these accusations and prove his innocence, Montez becomes even more entangled in a web that includes crooked cops, an old-wealthy Denver family, a hitch-hiking trip to San Diego, and battles with his family about his ill father.

Where it's reviewed:
Library Journal, March 1, 1996, page 109
Publishers Weekly, January 22, 1996, page 62

Other books by the same author:
The Ballad of Rocky Ruiz: Death of a Martyr, 1993
The Ballad of Gato Guerrero, 1994

Other books you might like:
Rudolfo Anaya, *Zia Summer*, 1995
　　Sonny Baca is involved in an exciting complicated mystery plot that includes murder, cult worship of the sun, and a battle over nuclear waste and its disposal in New Mexico.
Rolando Hinojosa, *Partners in Crime: A Rafe Buenrostro Mystery*, 1985
　　Written in the style of popular genre, this border murder mystery involves Hinojosa's popular characters Jehu Malacara and Rafe Buenrostro, now a lieutenant of the Belken County Homicide Squad.
Rudolfo Anaya, *Albuquerque*, 1992
　　This exciting story of modern Albuquerque has a vicious mayoral race, a young Chicano boxer, American Indians fighting for their water rights, and the folkloric past of New Mexico.
Lucha Corpi, *Cactus Blood: A Mystery Novel*, 1995
　　Gloria Damasco, an apprentice to a private investigator, possesses an inexplainable visionary power, which helps solve a murder related to a 15 year old pesticide tank explosion.
Lucha Corpi, *Eulogy for a Brown Angel: A Mystery Novel*, 1992
　　A Chicana feminist detective solves a murder that occurred during the Chicano civil rights movement.
Gloria Gonzalez, *The Thirteenth Apostle*, 1993
　　Newspaperwoman Geraldine St. Claire investigates the murder of her lover Hal, which leads her to suspect an industrial homicide and also leads her right into the hands of a powerful drug lord.

Michael Nava, *The Death of Friends*, 1996
　　A man faces difficult duties when he comes to the side of his former lover, dying of AIDS and must also defend his college friend, a closet homosexual, who is accused of murder.

765

TEY DIANA REBOLLEDO, Editor, Mexican American
ELIANA RIVERO, Co-Editor, Mexican American

Infinite Divisions: An Anthology of Chicana Literature
(Tucson: The University of Arizona Press, 1993)

Subject(s): Anthology; Women; Short Stories
Age range(s): Grades 10-Adult
Time period(s): 19th century; 20th century (1880-1980)
Locale(s): United States (stories take place primarily in the west and southwest)

Summary: This is an unusual anthology with a historical framework that contains the work of fifty Chicana writers from the past and present. It includes texts about early lives of Mexican American women in stories from the oral tradition found in the WPA Archives in New Mexico. There are chapters with poetry, plays, and stories about personal identity, growing up, relationships, private and public spaces of Chicana reality, myths and archetypes central to Chicana writing.

About this book: There are many bilingual texts.

Where it's reviewed:
CHOICE, January 1994, page 780
Publishers Weekly, May 17, 1993, page 74
Women's Review of Books, November 1993, page 16

Other books by the same author:
Las Mujeres Hablan: An Anthology of Nuevo Mexicana Writers, 1988
Nuestras Mujeres: Hispanas of New Mexico: Their Images and Their Lives, 1582-1992, 1992
Women Singing in the Snow: A Cultural Analysis of Chicana Literature, 1995

Other books you might like:
Roberta Fernandez, *In Other Words: Literature by Latinas in the U.S.*, 1994
　　This anthology of literature is by Latinas in the U.S.
Lillian Castillo-Speed, *Latina: Women's Voices from the Borderlands*, 1995
　　This collection of short stories is by Latinas.
Bryce Milligan, *Daughters of the Fifth Sun: A Collection of Latina Fiction and Poetry*, 1995
　　This anthology of poetry and short stories is by Latinas in the U.S.
Evangelina Vigil, *Woman of Her Word: Hispanic Women Write*, 1983
　　This early collection of creative literature is by Latinas in U.S.
Carla Trujillo, *Chicana Lesbians: The Girls Our Mothers Warned Us About*, 1991
　　A diverse collection of short stories, poetry and prose by Chicana lesbians exploring the intricacies and specifics of

culture, family, mixed-race relationships, body and identity.

Alma Gomez, *Cuentos: Stories by Latinas*, 1983
This is a collection of short stories by Latinas.

766

TEY DIANA REBOLLEDO, Editor, Mexican American
ERLINDA GONZALES-BERRY, Co-Editor, Mexican American
TERESA MARQUEZ, Co-Editor, Mexican American

Las Mujeres Hablan: An Anthology of Nuevo Mexicana Writers

(Albuquerque: El Norte Publications, 1988)

Subject(s): Short Stories; Anthology
Age range(s): Grades 10-Adult
Locale(s): New Mexico

Summary: The title of this anthology translates to *the women talk* and contains the work of women writers from New Mexico. The works are short stories, poems, memoirs, and other pieces, some of which are written in Spanish or Spanish and English. The anthology is divided into thematic sections, and covers themes such as the oral tradition, childhood, family, and neighbors. This collection begins to document the long oral tradition of women in New Mexico.

Where it's reviewed:
American Book Review, January-February 1990, page 1

Other books by the same author:
Infinite Divisions: An Anthology of Chicana Literature, 1993
Women Singing in the Snow: A Cultural Analysis of Chicana Literature, 1995
Nuestras Mujeres: Hispanas of New Mexico: Their Images and Their Lives, 1582-1992, 1992

Other books you might like:
Maria del Carmen Boza, *Nosotras: Latina Literature Today*, 1986
This short story collection is by Latina writers.
Roberta Fernandez, *In Other Words: Literature by Latinas in the U.S.*, 1994
This anthology of literature, short stories, and essays is by Latinas in U.S.
Evangelina Vigil, *Woman of Her Word: Hispanic Women Write*, 1987
This anthology of writing, poetry and short stories in English and Spanish, is by Latinas.
Bryce Milligan, *Daughters of the Fifth Sun: A Collection of Latina Fiction and Poetry*, 1995
This collection of poetry and short fiction is by some of the best Latina writers today.
Asuncion Horno-Delgado, *Breaking Boundaries: Latina Writing and Critical Readings*, 1989
This anthology of writings is by Chicanas, Puerto Rican, Cuban American , and other Latina women.
Lillian Castillo-Speed, *Latina: Women's Voices from the Borderlands*, 1995
This collection of writings is by contemporary Latinas in the U.S.

767

JOHN RECHY, Mexican American

City of Night

(New York: Grove Press, 1963)

Subject(s): City Life; Homosexuality/Lesbianism; Prostitution
Age range(s): Grades 10-Adult
Major character(s): Johnny Rio, Chicano, Homosexual
Time period(s): 1950s
Locale(s): Los Angeles, California (story takes place in El Paso, New York and Los Angeles)

Summary: Johnny Rio, born in El Paso, becomes a gay Chicano wanderer, who lives by the statistics of random sexual encounters and orgasms, traveling from El Paso to New York and other cities. The life of male prostitution is vividly portrayed and Rechy's portrait of an adventurer in the underworld is harsh, unsparing, and eloquent.

Other books by the same author:
Bodies and Souls: A Novel, 1983
Marilyn's Daughter: A Novel, 1988
The Miraculous Day of Amalia Gomez: A Novel, 1991
Rushes: A Novel, 1979
The Vampires, 1971

Other books you might like:
Gil Cuadros, *City of God*, 1994
A rough account of devastation and empowerment in the age of AIDS, this short novel was written after the death of the author's lover.
Michael Nava, *The Hidden Law*, 1992
Henry Rios defends a young Chicano accused of murdering a powerful Chicano public official in Los Angeles, while his long time lover, who has AIDS, leaves him for someone else.
Jaime Manrique, *Latin Moon in Manhattan*, 1992
This novel presents plots and sub-plots, and a vivid depiction of Columbian American culture in Little Colombia Jackson Heights, through the eyes of Santiago, a gay unpublished poet.
Reinaldo Arenas, *Before Night Falls*, 1993
In this autobiography, Arena describes almost dying of AIDS in 1987 and tells the story of his life in Cuba before he came to the United States in 1980, where he later committed suicide in 1990.
Terri de la Pena, *Margins*, 1992
The story of a young lesbian writer who confronts her future and her family about her sexuality.
Emma Perez, *Gulf Dreams*, 1996
A creative series of essays, short vignettes, and psychoanalytic discourses, these are about growing up lesbian in Latino culture.

768

JOHN RECHY, Mexican American

The Miraculous Day of Amalia Gomez: A Novel

(New York: Arcade Publishing, 1991)

Subject(s): Poverty; Gangs; Homosexuality/Lesbianism
Age range(s): Grades 10-Adult
Major character(s): Amalia Gomez, Divorced Person, Mother (single), Mexican American
Time period(s): 1980s
Locale(s): Los Angeles, California; El Paso, Texas

Summary: This novel follows a day in the life of a Mexican American woman who lives in the shabby section of Hollywood. The story examines poverty, gang warfare, border crossings, and visions of salvation. Amalia seems to have nothing but bad luck, twice divorced, the mother of three teenagers, trapped in poverty, surrounded by violence, and continually searching for a secure and loving relationship.

Where it's reviewed:
Library Journal, August 1991, page 147
Publishers Weekly, June 28, 1991, page 87

Other books by the same author:
Bodies and Souls: A Novel, 1983
City of Night, 1963
Marilyn's Daughter: A Novel, 1988
Numbers, 1990
Rushes: A Novel, 1977

Other books you might like:
Abraham Rodriguez Jr., *Spidertown*, 1993
    Sixteen-year-old Miguel is a runner for a drug dealer in New York but struggles to change his life.
Victor Rodriguez, *Eldorado in East Harlem*, 1992
    Seventeen-year-old Rene is streetwise and involved with a gang committing petty crimes and running drugs.
Sandra Cisneros, *The House on Mango Street*, 1984
    Young Esperanza Cordera faces violence and oppression as she searches for identity and community in her Latino neighborhood in Chicago.
Dagoberto Gilb, *The Magic of Blood*, 1993
    Short stories about working-class life, with realistic, multi-dimensional characters.
Genaro Gonzalez, *Rainbow's End*, 1988
    An adventure novel that presents dangerous border crossings, confrontations with a magician, and drug smuggling in the lives of three generations of the Cavazos family in Texas.

769

JOHN RECHY, Mexican American

Numbers

(New York: Grove Press, 1984)

Subject(s): Sexuality; Homosexuality/Lesbianism
Age range(s): Grades 10-Adult
Major character(s): Johnny Rio, Homosexual, Chicano
Time period(s): 1960s

Locale(s): Los Angeles, California

Summary: Johnny Rio, handsome and trying to escape impending age, travels to Los Angeles in a frenzied attempt to recreate his younger self. In ten precious days, he tries to draw the ''numbers,'' the men who will confirm his desirability. Rechy paints well the dark world of anonymous homosexual sex.

About this book: Originally published in 1967; Rechy considers this his favorite novel.

Where it's reviewed:
Journal of Homosexuality, August-September 1993, page 111

Other books by the same author:
City of Night, 1963
Marilyn's Daughter: A Novel, 1988
The Miraculous Day of Amalia Gomez: A Novel, 1991
Rushes: A Novel, 1979
The Vampires, 1971

Other books you might like:
Michael Nava, *How Town: A Novel of Suspense*, 1990
    A Chicano lawyer solves a murder mystery while unpretentiously depicting a gay relationship.
Gil Cuadros, *City of God*, 1994
    A painful short novel and haunting collection of poetry written by the author after the death of his lover and while he himself lives with AIDS.

770

JOHN RECHY, Mexican American

Our Lady of Babylon

(New York, NY: Arcade Publishing, 1996)

Subject(s): Women; Sexuality; Religion
Age range(s): Grades 10-Adult
Major character(s): Madame Bernice, Religious (mystic), European
Time period(s): Indeterminate Past
Locale(s): Europe

Summary: A novel of myth and history set in the late eighteenth century when an unnamed Countess flees her husband's chateau after being accused of murdering him. She ends up in the country at the chateau of Madame Bernice, a mystic who helps her recall memories that extend back to the Wars of the Angels, and to embark on a journey of redemption to vindicate the lives of unjustly blamed women, from Mary Magdalene to La Malinche. In a series of reincarnations, the Lady relives the lives of Eve, Delilah, Salome, Medea, and other fallen women. But evil pursuers, and a wicked Pope, are after the Countess, and through a succession of events, she might elude them.

Where it's reviewed:
Publishers Weekly, May 13, 1996, page 58

Other books by the same author:
Bodies and Souls: A Novel, 1983
Marilyn's Daughter: A Novel, 1988
The Miraculous Day of Amalia Gomez: A Novel, 1991
Rushes: A Novel, 1979
The Vampires, 1971

Other books you might like:

Graciela Limon, *The Memories of Ana Calderon: A Novel*, 1994

Ana Calderon begins life in rural southern Mexico, but the burdens of poverty, dreams of a better life, and circumstance lead her family to the United States.

Alma Luz Villanueva, *Weeping Woman: La Llorona and Other Stories*, 1994

A collection of stories that examine women who live in a world torn apart by violence, racism, and sexism.

Graciela Limon, *Song of the Hummingbird*, 1996

Huitzitzilin, Hummingbird in the Nahuatl language, is an Aztec princess who is forced into slavery. As an 82-year-old woman, she recounts her life story during the Spanish conquest of Mexico.

Gloria Duran, *Malinche: Slave Princess of Cortez*, 1993

Malinali, born an Aztec princess and sold to the conqueror Cortez, is an ambiguous and controversial figure in Mexican history and this is her story.

Rosa Martha Villarreal, *Doctor Magdalena: Novella*, 1995

Narrated through the voice of her Indian ancestors, this novella is a spiritual odyssey of a modern female doctor, spanning three worlds.

Isabel Allende, *The Stories of Eva Luna*, 1991

The stories of Eva Luna are twenty-three tales of her life, her loves, and the surrounding political and social events, alluded to in *Eva Luna*, but not included in the novel.

Estela Portillo Trambley, *Trini*, 1986

Trini, a Tarahumara woman whose indigenous lise is wondrous and magical, crosses the boarder as an undocumented immigrant in order to give birth to her child in the United States.

771

DANIEL REVELES, Mexican American

Enchiladas, Rice, and Beans

(New York, NY: Ballantine Books, 1994)

Subject(s): Short Stories; Humor
Age range(s): Grades 10-Adult
Time period(s): 1990s (1994)
Locale(s): Tecate, California; Mexico (Baha, California - Mexico border town)

Summary: A collection of short stories, or "chismes," about the inhabitants of a small town very close to the California-Mexico border. Humorously narrated, these novellas present colorful local characters, roosters that crow in Spanish, life where miracles happen daily, and "business friendly" Mexico, which means cheap labor and no IRS.

Where it's reviewed:
Publishers Weekly, August 1, 1994, page 74
Library Journal, August 1994, page 137

Other books you might like:

Luis Alberto Urrea, *In Search of Snow*, 1996

Mike McGirk, a blue collar Don Quixote, searches for love and life in the Arizona desert, and learns about family from Bobo Garcia.

Louie Garcia Robinson, *The Devil, Delfina Varela, and the Used Chevy*, 1993

Set in the Mission District of San Francisco this is a novel about politics, dreams, Latino social affairs, and Delfina, a widow who will do anything for a car.

Lionel G. Garcia, *I Can Hear the Cowbells Ring*, 1994

With humour and nostalgia, this collection of delightful autobiographical vignettes reconstruct life in a small rural town of southern Texas.

Jose Antonio Burciaga, *Spilling the Beans: Loteria Chicana*, 1995

This series of essays, many humorous, recount experiences from the author's childhood in Texas.

Jesus Salvador Trevino, *The Fabulous Sinkhole and Other Stories*, 1995

This first story collection by Trevino, a screenwriter and director, is an entertaining creation of Mexican and Chicano characters, that take place in a fictional town, Arroyo Grande, in Texas.

David Rice, *Give the Pig a Chance and Other Stories*, 1996

This collection of stories is about growing up in a bicultural environment in a small town on the Texas-Mexico border.

772

DAVID RICE

Give the Pig a Chance and Other Stories

(Tempe, AZ: Bilingual Press/Editorial Bilingue, 1996)

Subject(s): Short Stories; Humor; Growing Up
Age range(s): Grades 9-Adult
Time period(s): 1990s
Locale(s): Edcouch, Texas

Summary: This collection of fourteen stories about Edcouch, a town on the Mexican-Texas border with a population of 2,683, presents a picture of the blend of cultures in the predominantly Mexican American town. The story "The Circumstances Surrounding My Penis" about a boy's embarrassment is a good example of the sensitivity of the author in portraying growing up in a bicultural environment.

Where it's reviewed:
Publishers Weekly, November 27, 1995, page 63

Other books you might like:

Americo Paredes, *The Hammon and the Beans and Other Stories*, 1994

Set in the southern Texas border region, this collection of short stories explores the cultural conflict that has dominated that area since the U.S.-Mexican War.

Lionel G. Garcia, *I Can Hear the Cowbells Ring*, 1994

With humour and nostalgia, this collection of delightful autobiographical vignettes reconstruct life in a small rural town of southern Texas.

Norma Elia Cantu, *Canicula: Snapshots of a Girlhood en la Frontera*, 1995

This series of brief vignettes about growing up brings into sharp focus the history, lives, and legends about Laredo, Texas.

Jesus Salvador Trevino, *The Fabulous Sinkhole and Other Stories*, 1995

This first story collection by Trevino, a screenwriter and director, is an entertaining creation of Mexican and Chicano characters that takes place in a fictional town, Arroyo Grande, in Texas.

Amado Muro, *The Collected Stories of Amado Muro*, 1979
Amado Muro is the pseudonym for the Anglo American newspaperman Charles Seltzer. His stories reflect his experiences as a farm worker, riding the rails, living in labor camps and going to sea.

Luis Alberto Urrea, *In Search of Snow*, 1994
Mike McGirk, a blue collar Don Quixote, searches for love and life in the Arizona desert, and learns about family from Bobo Garcia.

773

ALBERTO ALVARO RIOS, Mexican American

The Iguana Killer: Twelve Stories of the Heart

(Lewiston, Idaho : Blue Moon and Confluence Press, 1984)

Subject(s): Short Stories; Secrets
Age range(s): Grades 10-Adult
Time period(s): 1980s (1984)
Locale(s): United States

Summary: In this volume of short stories, Alberto Alvaro Rios transforms the stories of ordinary life into a book of secrets. In the title story ''The Iguana Killer'' a Mexican receives a baseball bat from his grandmother that he uses to kill iguanas. Several of these stories are about Mexican and Chicano young boys confronting big questions. Each story is strong and distinct, but they all work together to create a well integrated work that examines a culture in transition.

Awards the book has won:
Western States Book Award, 1984

Other books by the same author:
Pig Cookies and Other Stories, 1995
The Lime Orchard Woman: Poems, 1988
Teodoro Luna's Two Kisses: Poems, 1990
Whispering to Fool the Wind: Poems, 1982

Other books you might like:
Gary Soto, *Summer on Wheels*, 1995
Hector and Mando take a leisurely six-day bike trip, with many adventures, from East L.A. to the beach in Santa Monica.

Ofelia Dumas Lachtman, *The Girl from Playa Blanca*, 1995
Elena and brother Carlos find adventure in Los Angeles as they search for their father.

Irene Beltran Hernandez, *The Secret of Two Brothers*, 1995
Two brothers fight for survival and to improve their future in Dallas, Texas.

Beatriz de la Garza, *The Candy Vendor's Boy and Other Stories*, 1994
The stories in this collection depict realistic characters who struggle with life issues over which they have no control, such as war, poverty, racism, and political conflict.

Nash Candelaria, *The Day the Cisco Kid Shot John Wayne*, 1988
Twelve humorous stories portraying Chicano-Anglo interrelations and conflicts.

774

ALBERTO ALVARO RIOS, Mexican American

Pig Cookies and Other Stories

(San Francisco, CA: Chronicle Books, 1995)

Subject(s): Short Stories; Magic
Age range(s): Grades 10-Adult
Major character(s): Lazaro Luna, Baker, Mexican; Noe, Butcher (a lonely man)
Time period(s): 20th century (covers several decades)
Locale(s): Mexico (a small village in northern Mexico)

Summary: In this collection of interrelated short stories, set earlier in this century in a small village in northern Mexico, the fortunes of extraordinary characters rise and fall in the eyes of their watchful neighbors. The pig cookies, or cochitos in Spanish, are gingerbread cookies that many Mexican American children grow up eating, but that Rios disliked as a child. The world of Rios is enchanting and lyrical, reminiscent of Garcia Marquez, poignant and memorable.

Where it's reviewed:
Hispanic, May 1995, page 80
Library Journal, May 1, 1995, page 134
Publishers Weekly, March 20, 1995, page 54
New York Times Book Review, September 17, 1995, page 25

Other books by the same author:
The Iguana Killer: Twelve Stories of the Heart, 1984
Teodoro Luna's Two Kisses: Poems, 1990
Five Indiscretions: A Book of Poems, 1985
The Lime Orchard Woman: Poems, 1988

Other books you might like:
Arturo Islas, *The Rain God: A Desert Tale*, 1984
Miguel Angel must find his way between his Mexican Catholic heritage and his North American education while living in a mythical southwest.

Rudolfo Anaya, *Bless Me, Ultima*, 1972
A young boy's beliefs are challenged as he grows up in a small rural town in New Mexico.

Denise Chavez, *Face of an Angel*, 1995
Sensual story, with many rich characters, about a waitress who works in a Mexican restaurant in a fictional town in New Mexico.

Alfredo Vea Jr., *La Maravilla*, 1993
A young boy learns about life in an impoverished but symbolically rich community in the desert outside the Phoenix city limits.

Leo Romero, *Rita and Los Angeles*, 1995
A short story collection with a cast of complex characters who grow and evolve, and learn about being outsiders in an alien and hostile world.

775

BEATRIZ RIVERA, Cuban American

African Passions and Other Stories

(Houston, TX: Arte Publico Press, 1995)

Subject(s): Love; Women; Success
Age range(s): Grades 10-Adult

Time period(s): 1990s (1995)
Locale(s): New Jersey (in a Latino barrio)

Summary: A collection of short stories focusing on women's obsessive search for love and success. Rivera examines the nature of obsession with humor, passion, and satire. A succession of strong women, living in the Latino barrio of New Jersey, search for love and prosperity, thinking to find it through lovers. There's one trying to trap a momma's-boy, another pursuing a stereotypical Latin lover, and the list goes on.

Where it's reviewed:
Choice, October 1995, page 295
Library Journal, March 1, 1995, page 102

Other books you might like:
Ana Lydia Vega, *True and False Romances*, 1994
　Collection of short stories about women and romance that take place in Puerto Rico.
Kathleen Ross, *Scents of Wood and Silence: Short Stories by Latin American Women Writers*, 1991
　Anthology of short fiction by Latin American women writers including some residing in the Caribbean.
Rosario Ferre, *The Youngest Doll*, 1991
　A collection considered by critics as a manifesto of women's rights. The title story, ''The Youngest Doll,'' is one of the author's most successful.
Sandra Cisneros, *Woman Hollering Creek and Other Stories*, 1991
　A collection of short stories with strong, angry female characters struggling valiantly to make something beautiful of their lives.
Cecile Pineda, *The Love Queen of the Amazon*, 1992
　A parody of a Latin American men's novel that traces the escapades of Ana Magdelena and her husband, Federico Orgaz y Orgaz.
Ana Castillo, *Loverboys, Stories*, 1996
　The stories included in this collection range from one-page vignettes to longer narratives; their subjects range from inexperienced to world-weary.

776

EDWARD RIVERA, Puerto Rican

Family Installments: Memories of Growing Up Hispanic
(New York: William Morrow & Co, 1982)

Subject(s): Growing Up; Fathers and Sons
Age range(s): Grades 10-Adult
Major character(s): Santos Malanguezes, Child, Student, Puerto Rican; Tego Malanguezes, Brother, Student, Puerto Rican
Time period(s): 20th century (1919-1960)
Locale(s): New York, New York

Summary: This memoir reads like a novel of a youth's family and history, against the backdrop of Puerto Rico and New York. Written in a straight style with comical descriptions, the author describes attending Catholic schools, struggling with the Mafia and Irish nuns, and learning English.

Other books you might like:
Judith Ortiz Cofer, *Silent Dancing: A Partial Remembrance of a Puerto Rican Childhood*, 1990
　These autobiographical narratives portray growing up in Puerto Rico and New Jersey.
Richard Ruiz, *The Hungry American*, 1978
　In this autobiographical story, a Puerto Rican boy searches for success and assimilation.
Judith Ortiz Cofer, *The Line of the Sun: A Novel*, 1989
　This intergenerational story of a family flows back and forth between New York and Puerto Rico.
Victor Rodriguez, *Eldorado in East Harlem*, 1992
　Seventeen year old Rene is streetwise and she gets involved with a gang committing petty crimes and running drugs.
Esmeralda Santiago, *When I Was Puerto Rican*, 1994
　This autobiographical story describes growing up in Puerto Rico and the U.S.
Piri Thomas, *Down These Mean Streets*, 1991
　This autobiographical novel recounts the story of a young Puerto Rican growing up in New York's Spanish Harlem and doing time in prison.
Yvonne V. Sapia, *Valentino's Hair*, 1991
　Rudolph Valentino comes into the life of Facundo Nieves and changes it forever when Nieves saves the hair and its power haunts him until his own death.

777

OSWALD RIVERA, Puerto Rican

Fire and Rain
(New York: Four Walls Eight Windows, 1990)

Subject(s): Vietnam War; Armed Services/Marines; Prisoners and Prisons
Age range(s): Grades 12-Adult
Major character(s): Corporal Dawson, Military Personnel (Marine), Prisoner (in a Marine Corp prison); Chi-Chi Hernandez, Prisoner (in Marine Corp prison), Puerto Rican
Time period(s): 1960s (1969)
Locale(s): Vietnam

Summary: This is a fictionalized story, based on a true incident, of a riot in the U.S. Marine Corps prison in Da Nang, Vietnam, in 1969. The inmates of the prison are primarily Black and Hispanic and they riot over the inhumane treatment they are receiving by the prison guards. The story is brutally and realistically narrated by Corporal Dawson who is also a prisoner.

About this book: The author was a Marine soldier during the Vietnam Conflict.

Where it's reviewed:
Library Journal, October 1, 1990, page 118
Publishers Weekly, September 7, 1990, page 76

Other books you might like:
Daniel Cano, *Shifting Loyalties*, 1995
　This novel is about Chicano soldiers and their families, before, during and after Vietnam.

Ed Vega, *Casualty Report*, 1991
> These short stories are about life in New York, including one about a Vietnam veteran.

Joe Rodriguez, *The Oddsplayer*, 1988
> A novel about the Vietnam War where Black and Latino soldiers fight the enemy on the battlefield and also within their own ranks.

Ronald L. Ruiz, *Happy Birthday Jesus*, 1994
> The disturbing story of the violent and turbulent life of a young man raised and abused by his grandmother and how he ends up in prison.

Reinaldo Arenas, *Old Rosa: A Novel in Two Stories*, 1989
> These two stories converge on the relationship of a Cuban mother and her sons. Rosa's life undergoes major changes when one son joins Castro's army and she finds the other in bed with another man.

778

RICK P. RIVERA, Mexican American

A Fabricated Mexican
(Houston, TX: Arte Publico Press, 1995)

Subject(s): Growing Up; Family; Identity
Age range(s): Grades 8-Adult
Major character(s): Ricky Coronado, Young Man, Mexican American
Time period(s): 20th century (1950-1980)
Locale(s): California

Summary: In a series of comic vignettes, Ricky Coronado, a quiet but mischievous boy, reports on the antics of his eccentric family and his own search for identity. He struggles with his father's suicide, the pressures that his mother places upon him, and growing up in two cultures. Eventually he comes to understand that he must create a new identity for himself. His strong-willed mother holds his family together after the death of his father and is a wonderful example of matriarchal strength.

Where it's reviewed:
Library Journal, April 1, 1995, page 126

Other books you might like:

Oscar Zeta Acosta, *The Autobiography of a Brown Buffalo*, 1972
> In this largely autobiographical novel, the author examines his life as a famous Robin Hood-style Chicano lawyer who likes life on the edge.

Jose Antonio Burciaga, *Spilling the Beans: Loteria Chicana*, 1995
> A series of essays, many humorous, recount experiences from the author's childhood, and explores aspects of Chicano culture.

Dagoberto Gilb, *The Magic of Blood*, 1993
> A powerful collection that presents harsh, realistic stories about working-class life in Texas and California.

Nash Candelaria, *The Day the Cisco Kid Shot John Wayne*, 1988
> A humorous collection of short stories, from New Mexico, in which the author examines cultural clashes between Latinos and Anglos.

Gary D. Keller, *Zapata Rose in 1992 and Other Tales*, 1992
> A collection of seven satirical stories, by a writer known as an absurdist comedian.

Rafael Zepeda, *Horse Medicine and Other Stories*, 1990
> This collection of nine stories deals very much with the world of men. In "Horse Medicine" several men, with kids and wives, participate in rodeos and live with horses.

Hugo Martinez-Serros, *The Last Laugh and Other Stories*, 1988
> The culture and atmosphere of urban Chicago during World War II are brought to life in this collection of short stories.

779

TOMAS RIVERA, Mexican American

The Harvest: Short Stories
(Houston, TX: Arte Publico Press, 1989)

Subject(s): Migrant Labor; Family; Poverty
Age range(s): Grades 9-Adult
Time period(s): 1940s
Locale(s): Texas (throughout the Midwest)

Summary: A poshumous collection of the author's short fiction. Framed within the world of the struggles of migrant farmworkers, Rivera's short stories are myths and parables which relate themes of alienation, death, and community. Written in poetic prose, these characters are memorable and outspoken in their search to establish and maintain a community. The story "Pete Fonseca" is included.

About this book: All the stories are in English and Spanish; edited by Julian Olivares.

Where it's reviewed:
Western American Literature, May 1990, page 74

Other books by the same author:
This Migrant Earth, 1995
Y No Se lo Trago la Tierra.And the Earth Did Not Devour Him, 1987
Always and Other Poems, 1972
Tomas Rivera: The Complete Works, 1991

Other books you might like:

Patricia Preciado Martin, *Days of Plenty, Days of Want*, 1988
> A collection of stories where the past and present meet and Mexican heritage is in jeopardy of being wiped out.

Raymond Barrio, *The Plum Plum Pickers*, 1969
> The dramatic story of Manuel and Lupe Gutierrez and their children, migrant farm workers in California's Santa Clara Valley.

Jose Antonio Villarreal, *Pocho*, 1959
> Considered the first key Chicano novel, this is about a Mexican family attempting to assimilate in the Santa Clara Valley of California.

Genaro Gonzalez, *Rainbow's End*, 1988
> The story of the migrant labor and Vietnam hardships of a family living in the Lower Rio Grande Valley in Texas.

Rolando Hinojosa, *The Valley*, 1983
> A collection of stories that take place in a South Texas border community from the 1930s to 1950s.

780

TOMAS RIVERA, Mexican American

This Migrant Earth
(Houston, TX: Arte Publico Press, 1987)

Subject(s): Migrant Labor; Family; Poverty
Age range(s): Grades 8-Adult
Time period(s): 1940s
Locale(s): Texas

Summary: This English rendition Tomas Rivera's *.y no se lo trago la tierra*, captures Rivera's spirit and poetry. He originally wrote his book in Spanish in 1970 and it was the basis for the modern Chicano literary movement. There have been two literal translations published, with Hinojosa's being the third. This work reproduces the sad and tragic lives of migrant workers as they travel the migrant midwest stream and confront the challenges of abuse, from both man and nature.

Where it's reviewed:
Hispania, March 1991, page 57
Hispania, December 1991, page 903
Western American Literature, May 1990, page 74

Other books by the same author:
Always and Other Poems, 1972
The Harvest: Short Stories, 1988
Tomas Rivera: The Complete Works, 1991
Y No Se lo Trago la Tierra.And the Earth Did Not Devour Him, 1991

Other books you might like:
Raymond Barrio, *The Plum Plum Pickers*, 1969
  The dramatic story of Manuel and Lupe Gutierrez and their children, migrant farm workers in California's Santa Clara Valley.
Jose Antonio Villarreal, *Pocho*, 1959
  Considered the first key Chicano novel, this is about a Mexican family attempting to assimilate in the Santa Clara Valley of California.
Genaro Gonzalez, *Rainbow's End*, 1988
  The story of the migrant labor and Vietnam hardships of a family living in the Lower Rio Grande Valley in Texas.
Miguel Mendez, *Pilgrims in Aztlan*, 1992
  An aging veteran of the Mexican Revolution now washes cars for tourists in Tijuana, watching the people who come his way and tell him stories.
Aristeo Brito, *The Devil in Texas = El Diablo en Texas*, 1990
  An important novel that describes the Anglo destruction of a Chicano world in Texas, where the devil comes to the border town of Presidio.
Rolando Hinojosa, *The Valley*, 1983
  A collection of stories that take place in a South Texas border community from the 1930s to the 1950s.
Norma Elia Cantu, *Canicula: Snapshots of a Girlhood en la Frontera*, 1995
  A collection, with photos, of short stories, and vignettes of a young girl growing up along the Texas border.

781

TOMAS RIVERA, Mexican American

Tomas Rivera: The Complete Works
(Houston, TX: Arte Publico Press, 1991)

Subject(s): Family; Poverty; Migrant Labor
Age range(s): Grades 8-Adult
Time period(s): 1940s
Locale(s): Texas

Summary: The complete works of Tomas Rivera include his famous novel *Y no se lo Trago la Tierra* including two short stories and five vignettes that were not published in the orignial novel; twenty-five poems unpublished at the time of his death; and also his published critical essays. In the Appendix are two works previously unpublished, one of which appears to be an introduction to a novel-in-progress. Rivera is considered to be one of the fathers of Chicano literature, his first novel being published in 1971 and a landmark in Chicano literary history. He was the son of Texas migrant farmworkers, earned higher education degrees, and eventually became the Chancellor of the University of California, Riverside. He died suddenly in 1984.

About this book: Introduction by Julian Olivares.

Where it's reviewed:
Hispania, December 1991, page 903

Other books by the same author:
This Migrant Earth, 1995
The Harvest: Short Stories, 1989
Always and Other Poems, 1972
Y No Se lo Trago La Tierra.And the Earth Did Not Devour Him, 1987 (1970 Quinto Sol Literary Prize winner)

Other books you might like:
Raymond Barrio, *The Plum Plum Pickers*, 1969
  This is the dramatic story of Manuel and Lupe Gutierrez and their children, migrant farm workers in California's Santa Clara Valley.
Jose Antonio Villarreal, *Pocho*, 1959
  This is considered to be the first key Chicano novel about a Mexican family attempting to assimilate in the Santa Clara Valley of California.
Genaro Gonzalez, *Rainbow's End*, 1988
  This adventure novel presents dangerous border crossings, confrontations with a magician, and drug smuggling in the lives of the Cavazos family in the lower Rio Grande area of Texas.
Miguel Mendez, *Pilgrims in Aztlan*, 1992
  A Chicano classic first published in Spanish, this is about an aging veteran of the Mexican Revolution who now washes cars in Tijuana, listening to the stories of the people who come his way.
Aristeo Brito, *The Devil in Texas: El Diablo en Texas*, 1990
  The devil comes to the border town of Presidio, Texas in this important novel that describes the Anglo destruction of a Chicano world.
Rolando Hinojosa, *The Valley*, 1983
  This collection of stories that take place in South Texas border community from the 1930s to 1950s.

Norma Elia Cantu, *Canicula: Snapshots of a Girlhood en la Frontera*, 1995

This series of brief vignettes about growing up brings into sharp focus the history, lives, and legends about Laredo, Texas.

782

TOMAS RIVERA, Mexican American

Y No Se lo Trago la Tierra.And the Earth Did Not Devour Him

(Houston, TX: Arte Publico Press, 1987)

Subject(s): Family; Poverty; Migrant Labor
Age range(s): Grades 9-Adult
Time period(s): 1940s
Locale(s): Texas (includes travel throughout the Midwest)

Summary: Twelve related stories document .the spiritual strength of migrant farm workers. This work reproduces the sad and tragic lives of migrant workers as they travel the migrant midwest stream and confront the challenges of abuse by both man and nature. Rivera writes of men and women who are economically, politically, and socially deprived and yet refuse to suffer or be subdued. Through the vision of a nameless Chicano boy and the voices of many others, the search for a better life is revealed.

About this book: First published in 1970 this is a new translation by Evangelina Vigil-Pinon; a bilingual edition.

Where it's reviewed:
Hispania, March 1991, page 57
American Book Review, January-February 1990, page 11
Western American Literature, February 1989, page 388

Awards the book has won:
First Annual Premio Quinto Sol, 1970

Other books by the same author:
This Migrant Earth, 1995
The Harvest: Short Stories, 1989
Always and Other Poems, 1972
Tomas Rivera: The Complete Works, 1991

Other books you might like:
Raymond Barrio, *The Plum Plum Pickers*, 1969
The dramatic story of Manuel and Lupe Gutierrez and their children, migrant farm workers in California's Santa Clara Valley.
Jose Antonio Villarreal, *Pocho*, 1959
Considered to be the first key Chicano novel about a Mexican family attempting to assimilate in the Santa Clara Valley of California.
Genaro Gonzalez, *Rainbow's End*, 1988
The story of the migrant labor and Vietnam hardships of a family living in the Lower Rio Grande Valley in Texas.
Miguel Mendez, *Pilgrims in Aztlan*, 1992
A Chicano classic, first published in Spanish, where an aging veteran of the Mexican Revolution washes cars for tourists while watching the people who come his way and listening to their stories.
Aristeo Brito, *The Devil in Texas: El Diablo en Texas*, 1990
The devil comes to the border town of Presidio, Texas on

this important novel that describes the Anglo destruction of a Chicano world.

783

LOUIE GARCIA ROBINSON, Mexican American

The Devil, Delfina Varela, and the Used Chevy

(New York: Anchor Books, 1993)

Subject(s): Politics; City Life; Social Classes
Age range(s): Grades 10-Adult
Major character(s): Manny Caballos, Businessman; Ruy Lopez, Gardener; Delfina Varela, Widow(er)
Time period(s): 1990s (1993)
Locale(s): San Francisco, California (Mission District of San Francisco)

Summary: Delfina, a widow, will do anything for a car. Manny, a businessman, dreams of helping to elect a Hispanic to the Board of Supervisors. Ruy is having a love affair like he never dreamed possible. Their lives come together in a humorous drama.

Where it's reviewed:
Hispanic, June 1994, page 72
Library Journal, August 1993, page 155

Other books you might like:
Jorge Amado, *Gabriela Cloves and Cinnamon*, 1962
Humorous escapades of the political and social life of a small town in Bahia, Brazil.
Rolando Hinojosa, *Klail City: A Novel*, 1987
This is about the life of a Mexican American community in a small town in Texas.
Lionel G. Garcia, *A Shroud in the Family*, 1994
This satire is about Texas and Mexican American life in the modern metropolis.
Roberto Fernandez, *Holy Radishes*, 1995
This satirical novel is about a Cuban immigrant community in Florida.
Rudolfo Anaya, *Albuquerque*, 1992
An exciting story of modern Albuquerque, with a vicious mayoral race, a young Chicano boxer, American Indians fighting to retain their water rights, and the folkloric past of New Mexico.
Nash Candelaria, *Leonor Park*, 1991
This novel, set in New Mexico, is about land and greed. A powerful woman battles with her brother over their father's land alongside the Rio Grande.

784

ABRAHAM RODRIGUEZ JR., Puerto Rican

The Boy Without a Flag: Tales of the South Bronx

(Minneapolis: Milkweed Editions, 1992)

Subject(s): Short Stories; City Life; Growing Up
Age range(s): Grades 9-Adult
Time period(s): 1990s (1992)

Locale(s): New York, New York (South Bronx)

Summary: These seven stories portray the difficult lives of young people growing up in the South Bronx in the 1990s. In one story a junior-high Puerto Rican boy refuses to salute the American flag, and in another a teenage mother leaves her baby to go out and party. The author states, ''these are the kids no one likes to talk about.''

Where it's reviewed:
Studies in Short Fiction, Fall 1994, page 709
Library Journal, October 15, 1992, page 103
Publishers Weekly, May 18, 1992, page 63

Other books by the same author:
Spidertown, 1993

Other books you might like:
Edward Rivera, *Family Installments: Memories of Growing Up Hispanic*, 1982
    Humorous episodes reflect growing up in Puerto Rico and in New York.
Nicholasa Mohr, *Rituals of Survival: A Woman's Portfolio*, 1985
    Strong Puerto Rican women, who take control of their lives, dominate these stories.
Jack Agueros, *Dominoes and Other Stories from the Puerto Rican*, 1993
    Living in New York City as a Puerto Rican comprises the subject matter for these short stories.
Phyllis Tashlik, *Hispanic, Female, and Young*, 1994
    Young girls from a New York public school author this collection.
Gil C. Alicea, *The Air Down Here: True Tales from a South Bronx Boyhood*, 1995
    A sixteen-year-old describes his South Bronx boyhood in short stories.

785

ABRAHAM RODRIGUEZ JR., Puerto Rican

Spidertown
(New York: Hyperion, 1993)

Subject(s): Gangs; Drugs; City Life
Age range(s): Grades 10-Adult
Major character(s): Miguel, 16-Year-Old, Gang Member (runner); Spider, Drug Dealer; Firbug, Criminal (professional arsonist)
Time period(s): 1990s
Locale(s): New York, New York (takes place in the South Bronx)

Summary: Sixteen-year-old Miguel is a runner for a drug dealer and struggles to change his life. His love for Christalena, who works an ordinary nine-to-five job, leads him to consider giving up his dangerous profession. Rodriguez presents a realistic and haunting picture of urban youth.

About this book: The title of this novel refers to the South Bronx. Film rights have been negotiated.

Where it's reviewed:
Hispanic, March 1995, page 80
Library Journal, April 15, 1993, page 127

Publishers Weekly, March 29, 1993, page 33

Other books by the same author:
The Boy Without a Flag: Tales of the South Bronx, 1992

Other books you might like:
Piri Thomas, *Down These Mean Streets*, 1978
    This autobiographical novel is set in New York's Spanish Harlem.
Edwin Torres, *Carlito's Way*, 1976
    This story portrays a Puerto Rican criminal and his underworld life.
Jack Agueros, *Dominoes and Other Stories from the Puerto Rican*, 1993
    These stories describe Puerto Rican life in New York.
Victor Rodriguez, *Eldorado in East Harlem*, 1992
    Seventeen year old Rene is streetwise and involved with a gang committing petty crimes and running drugs.
Steven Lopez, *Third and Indiana*, 1994
    The title of this novel refers to the corner where fourteen-year-old Gabriel hands out crack to people in passing cars. His boss, Diablo, becomes demanding when he comes up short in his accounts.
Soledad Santiago, *Nightside*, 1994
    Anna Eltern, a former nun, runs a shelter for runaway teens in New York City. Financial problems, funding cuts, and murder force her to turn away teenagers in need.

786

GINA MACALUSO RODRIGUEZ, Mexican American
GARY SHEPARD, Illustrator

Green Corn Tamales = Tamales de Elote
(Tucson, AZ: Hispanic Books Distributors, 1994)

Subject(s): Family Life; Relatives; Cooks and Cookery
Age range(s): Grades K-2
Major character(s): Nana, Grandmother, Mexican American
Time period(s): Indeterminate Past
Locale(s): United States

Summary: A Latino family makes green corn tamales every year, but there's a twist to this tale. Similar to the story of *The Little Red Hen* or *La Gallinita Roja* this story has a Nana who asks all her relatives who are visiting for help and they all say ''no,'' except one person. In the end they all join in.

About this book: Bilingual format.

Where it's reviewed:
School Library Journal, August 1994, page 182

Other books you might like:
Leyla Torres, *Saturday Sancocho*, 1995
    Every Saturday, Maria Lili helps her grandparents make their traditional chicken sancocho.
Carmen Lomas Garza, *Family Pictures = Cuadros de Familia*, 1990
    Carmen Lomas Garza, a well known Chicana artist, presents beautiful and detailed paintings of her growing up in a Texas border town.
Gary Soto, *Too Many Tamales*, 1993
    Maria helps her mother make tamales for their Christmas Eve dinner, and in the process loses something important.

Omar Castaneda, *Abuela's Weave*, 1993
A young girl and her grandmother sell their woven fabrics at a market in Guatemala.

Jan Romero Stevens, *Carlos and the Cornfield: Story = Carlos y la Milpa de Maiz: Cuento*, 1995
A young boy learns to make things right after realizing his mistake in planting corn.

Lucia M. Gonzalez, *The Bossy Gallito*, 1994
A bossy little rooster gets his beak dirty pecking some corn while on his way to his uncle's wedding.

Francisco X. Mora, *La Gran Fiesta*, 1993
Greedy Crow over-decorates his Christmas tree for "La Gran Fiesta de Navidad" until it collapses under a load of fruits, cookies, candies, and other goodies.

787

JOE RODRIGUEZ, Mexican American

The Oddsplayer
(Houston, TX: Arte Publico Press, 1989)

Subject(s): Revenge; Vietnam War; Military Life
Age range(s): Grades 10-Adult
Time period(s): 1960s
Locale(s): Vietnam

Summary: In this war novel, Rodriguez writes of soldiers from diverse backgrounds and ethnicities, Puerto Ricans, Chicanos, and African Americans, who converge upon their top sergeant in order to overcome his racism and brutality. Various characters relate their life stories, as they plan to seek revenge in a war where the enemy is everywhere, including within their own company.

Where it's reviewed:
Publishers Weekly, October 7, 1988, page 112
Western American Literature, November 1989, page 278
Hispania, March 1991, page 90

Other books you might like:
Ed Vega, *Casualty Report*, 1991
This short story collection's title story is about a Vietnam veteran.

Oswald Rivera, *Fire and Rain*, 1990
A Marine Corp prison camp riot in Vietnam is the focus of this novel.

Alejandro Murguia, *Southern Front*, 1990
These are short stories about the combat zone, the Nicaraguan-Costa Rican border, during the rebellion against the Somoza regime in the late 1970s.

Rolando Hinojosa, *The Useless Servants*, 1993
Set almost entirely in Korea, this novel is made up of the diary entries of Rafe Buenrostro, stationed in Korea during the war.

Alejandro Grattan-Dominguez, *The Dark Side of the Dream*, 1995
A historical novel, this is set after the outbreak of WWII, and relates the migration of two cousins to El Paso from Chihuahua and their participation in the army's all-Latino rifle company.

Daniel Cano, *Shifting Loyalties*, 1995
This novel explores five Chicano soldiers and their families before, during and after the Vietnam War.

788

RICHARD RODRIGUEZ, Mexican American

Hunger of Memory: The Education of Richard Rodriguez, an Autobiography
(New York: Bantam Books, 1982)

Subject(s): Education; Language; Identity
Age range(s): Grades 8-Adult
Major character(s): Richard Rodriguez, Child (boy), Mexican American
Time period(s): 20th century (1950-1982)
Locale(s): Sacramento, California

Summary: This is the story of the author's childhood and education, his difficult journey as a "minority student" who must become socially assimilated in order to enjoy academic success. Rodriguez pays the price for his success with alienation from his past, his parents, and his culture. This work is a profound study of language and discusses bilingual education. Although it is an autobiography, the narration is smooth and reads easily. It is a beautifully written, yet controversial book among Latinos.

About this book: This work has been widely used in college English classes.

Where it's reviewed:
Business Week, October 20, 1989, page E130
Commonweal, March 26, 1993, page 20
English Journal, November 1993, page 83

Other books by the same author:
Days of Obligation: An Argument With My Mexican Father, 1992

Other books you might like:
Victor Perera, *Rites: A Guatemalan Boyhood*, 1986
Autobiographical narratives of the author's boyhood growing up in Guatemala.

Oscar Zeta Acosta, *The Autobiography of a Brown Buffalo*, 1972
In this largely autobiographical novel, the author examines his life as a famous Robin Hood style Chicano lawyer who likes life on the edge.

Ernesto Galarza, *Barrio Boy*, 1971
Autobiographical story of the early life of a distinguished professor and author who wrote many works about Mexican agricultural workers.

Ofelia Dumas Lachtman, *A Shell for Angela*, 1995
When nine-year-old Angela Martin sees her father led away by immigration officials, she begins to deny her Mexican heritage.

Arcadia H. Lopez, *Barrio Teacher*, 1992
An autobiographical narration by an educator who, despite poverty and turmoil, managed to obtain a university education and teach for forty-six years in San Antonio, Texas.

Arturo Islas, *The Rain God: A Desert Tale*, 1984
Organized into six parts with different time sequences and flashbacks, this novel presents three generations of the Angel family living in the Southwest.

789

VICTOR RODRIGUEZ, Puerto Rican

Eldorado in East Harlem

(Houston, TX: Arte Publico Press, 1992)

Subject(s): City Life; Drugs; Crime and Criminals
Age range(s): Grades 10-Adult
Major character(s): Rene, 17-Year-Old (boy), Gang Member
Time period(s): 1960s
Locale(s): New York, New York (East Harlem)

Summary: Seventeen year old Rene is streetwise. He gets involved with a gang committing petty crimes and running drugs. His ghetto adventures bring him close to an illusory Eldorado, but soon enough his daydreams of riches turn into a living nightmare. The 1960s are vividly portrayed through their music and historical events.

Where it's reviewed:
Library Journal, September 1, 1992, page 216
Publishers Weekly, July 27, 1992, page 60

Other books you might like:
Abraham Rodriguez Jr., *The Boy Without a Flag: Tales of the South Bronx*, 1992
  These seven stories portray the difficult lives of young people growing up in the South Bronx in the 1990s.
Piri Thomas, *Down These Mean Streets*, 1978
  Autobiographical novel about a young Puerto Rican man growing up in Spanish Harlem.
Abraham Rodriguez Jr., *Spidertown*, 1993
  Sixteen year old Miguel is a runner for a drug dealer and struggles to change his life.
Jack Agueros, *Dominoes and Other Stories from the Puerto Rican*, 1993
  Short stories about living in New York city as a Puerto Rican.
Phyllis Tashlik, *Hispanic, Female, and Young*, 1994
  Collection of stories and poems written by young girls in a New York public school.
Gil C. Alicea, *The Air Down Here: True Tales from a South Bronx Boyhood*, 1995
  Autobiographical short stories and essays by a sixteen year old Puerto Rican boy.

790

HARRIET ROHMER
JESUS GUERRERO REA, Illustrator
CONSUELO MENDEZ, Illustrator

Atariba and Niguayona: A Story from the Taino People of Puerto Rico

(San Francisco: Children's Book Press, 1988)

Subject(s): Animals; Folk Tales; Friendship
Age range(s): Grades 1-2
Major character(s): Atariba, Child, Puerto Rican; Niguayona, Child, Puerto Rican
Time period(s): Indeterminate Past
Locale(s): Puerto Rico

Summary: Niguayona's best friend, Atariba, is very sick. A macaw tells Niguayona, a young hero from the Taino people of Puerto Rico, that he can cure his friend by bringing her the magical red fruit of the caimoni tree. Niguayona embarks upon a journey through the forest to save his friend.

About this book: This work is in bilingual Spanish and English format and is translated from Spanish by Rosalma Zubizarreta.

Where it's reviewed:
Publishers Weekly, June 10, 1988, page 80
Wilson Library Bulletin, September 1988, page 60

Other books by the same author:
Cuna Song = Cancion de los Cunas, 1976
The Headless Pirate = El pirata sin Cabeza, 1976
How We Came to the Fifth World: A Creation Story from Ancient Mexico, 1988
The Invisible Hunters: A Legend from the Miskito Indians of Nicaragua, 1976
The Legend of Food Mountain, 1982
Uncle Nacho's Hat = El Sombrero de Tio Nacho, 1989

Other books you might like:
Manlio Argueta, *Magic Dogs of the Volcanoes = Los Perros Magicos de los Volcanes*, 1990
  The magic dogs must call upon their ancestors to battle some tin soldiers.
Pura Belpre, *The Rainbow-Colored Horse*, 1978
  A beautiful seven-colored horse tramples Tano's maize field. Once caught, he grants three wishes to Pio, Tano's son.
Pura Belpre, *Dance of the Animals*, 1972
  Senor and Senora Lion are hungry for goat meat, so they throw a party and invite all the animals.
Omar Castaneda, *Abuela's Weave*, 1993
  A young girl and her grandmother sell their woven fabrics at a market in Guatemala.
Juanita Havill, *Treasure Nap*, 1992
  Alicia hears the story of Rita, who visits her grandfather in the mountains of Mexico, and learns to make wooden birdcages.
Maria Garcia, *The Adventures of Connie and Diego = Las Aventuras de Connie y Diego*, 1986
  Connie and Diego are different from other people in the Land of Plenty. They have many colors all over their bodies.
Gary Soto, *The Old Man and His Door*, 1996
  In this humorous tale about an old man who brings a door (la puerta) instead of a pig (el puerco) to a barbecue, all turns out well.
Pat Mora, *The Desert Is My Mother = El Desierto Es Mi Madre*, 1994
  This is a beautiful rendition of the relationship between nature and people. The desert is presented as the provider of comfort, food, spirit, and life.

791

HARRIET ROHMER
GRACIELA CARRILLO, Illustrator

How We Came to the Fifth World: A Creation Story from Ancient Mexico

(San Francisco: Children's Book Press, 1988)

Subject(s): Folk Tales; Creation
Age range(s): Grades 2-4
Time period(s): Indeterminate Past
Locale(s): United States

Summary: In this famous creation story from ancient Mexico, the world is created four times before our present fifth world. Our fifth world can be saved, say Aztec elders, only if people can live together peacefully.

About this book: The multicolored illustrations are based on the original Indian picture writings.

Where it's reviewed:
People Weekly, Aug 22, 1988, page 31
Publishers Weekly, June 10, 1988, page 80
Wilson Library Bulletin, September 1988, page 60

Other books by the same author:
Cuna Song = Cancion de los Cunas, 1976
The Headless Pirate = El Pirata sin Cabeza, 1976
The Invisible Hunters: A Legend from the Miskito Indians of Nicaragua, 1987
Mr. Sugar Came to Town, 1989
Atariba and Niguayona: A Story from the Taino People of Puerto Rico, 1976
Uncle Nacho's Hat = El Sombrero de Tio Nacho, 1989

Other books you might like:
Manlio Argueta, *Magic Dogs of the Volcanoes = Los Perros Magicos de los Volcanes*, 1990
The magic dogs must call upon their ancestors to battle some tin soldiers.
Pura Belpre, *The Rainbow-Colored Horse*, 1978
A beautiful seven-colored horse tramples Tano's maize field. Once caught, he grants three wishes to Pio, Tano's son.
Pura Belpre, *Dance of the Animals*, 1972
Senor and Senora Lion are hungry for goat meat, so they throw a party and invite all the animals.
Omar Castaneda, *Remembering to Say Mouth or Face*, 1993
This collection of stories, includes several works based on the Popol Vuh and creation myths of the Mayas.
Alejandro Cruz Martinez, *The Woman Who Outshone the Sun*, 1991
This Zapotec legend is about a beautiful woman with hair so bright it outshines the sun.
Pat Mora, *The Desert Is My Mother = El Desierto Es Mi Madre*, 1994
This is the beautiful rendition of the relationship between nature and people. The desert is presented as the provider of comfort, food, spirit, and life.

792

HARRIET ROHMER
GRACIELA CARRILLO, Illustrator

The Legend of Food Mountain

(San Francisco: Children's Book Press, 1982)

Subject(s): Folk Tales; Food; Creation
Age range(s): Grades 2-4
Major character(s): Quetzalcoatl, Deity
Time period(s): Indeterminate Past
Locale(s): Mexico (Quetzalcoatl's land is the ''Western Heaven'')

Summary: When the great god, Quetzalcoatl, creates the people of the earth, he does not know what to feed them. Food Mountain will make the people of the earth strong, but in this Mexican folk tale, fulfillment does not come without struggle.

About this book: This work in Bilingual format is translated from Spanish by Alma Flor Ada and Rosalma Zubizarreta.

Where it's reviewed:
Horn Book Magazine, January-February 1988, page 90

Other books by the same author:
The Invisible Hunters: A Legend from the Miskito Indians of Nicaragua, 1987
Mr. Sugar Came to Town, 1989
Atariba and Niguayona: A Story from the Taino People of Puerto Rico, 1976
How We Came to the Fifth World: A Creation Story from Ancient Mexico, 1988
Uncle Nacho's Hat = El Sombrero de Tio Nacho, 1989

Other books you might like:
Manlio Argueta, *Magic Dogs of the Volcanoes = Los Perros Magicos de los Volcanes*, 1990
The magic dogs must call upon their ancestors to battle some tin soldiers.
Pura Belpre, *The Rainbow-Colored Horse*, 1978
A beautiful seven-colored horse tramples Tano's maize field. Once caught, he grants three wishes to Pio, Tano's son.
Pura Belpre, *Dance of the Animals*, 1972
Senor and Senora Lion are hungry for goat meat, so they throw a party and invite all the animals.
Alejandro Cruz Martinez, *The Woman Who Outshone the Sun*, 1991
A Zapotec legend about a beautiful woman with hair so bright that it outshines the sun.
Pat Mora, *The Race of Toad and Deer*, 1995
Deer thinks he is the biggest and the fastest animal in the jungle, and he tries to make the other animals do as he says.

793

HARRIET ROHMER
VEG REISBERG, Illustrator

Uncle Nacho's Hat = El Sombrero de Tio Nacho

(Emeryville, CA: Children's Book Press, 1989)

Subject(s): Animals; Clothes; Folk Tales
Age range(s): Grades K-3
Major character(s): Uncle Nacho, Uncle; Ambrosia, Niece
Locale(s): Nicaragua (the countryside)

Summary: Uncle Nacho loves his old, ragged hat. When his niece, Ambrosia, gives him a new hat as a present, Nacho is unable to give up his old hat. He tries many plans to get rid of his old hat, but it keeps coming back. Finally, Ambrosia proposes a simple solution to his problem.

About this book: This work is bilingual with Spanish and English formats and it contains beautiful and colorful illustrations.

Where it's reviewed:
Horn Book Magazine, May-June 1990, page 362
Publishers Weekly, August 11, 1989, page 458
Wilson Library Bulletin, February 1990, page 82

Other books by the same author:
Brother Anansi and the Cattle Ranch, 1989
Mr. Sugar Came to Town, 1989
Atariba and Niguayona: A Story from the Taino People of Puerto Rico, 1988
How We Came to the Fifth World: A Creation Story from Ancient Mexico, 1988
The Invisible Hunters: A Legend from the Miskito Indians of Nicaragua, 1987
The Legend of Food Mountain, 1987

Other books you might like:
Pat Mora, *A Birthday Basket for Tia*, 1992
    Cecilia creates, with the help of her cat, a birthday gift for her great Aunt.
Arthur Dorros, *Abuela*, 1991
    A little girl and her grandmother fly all over New York City.
Omar Castaneda, *Abuela's Weave*, 1993
    A young girl and her grandmother sell their woven fabrics at a market in Guatemala.
Juanita Havill, *Treasure Nap*, 1992
    Alicia hears the story of Rita, who visits her grandfather in the mountains of Mexico.
Lulu Delacre, *Vejigantes Masquerade*, 1995
    Ramon has always wanted to masquerade at Carnival so he sews a vejigante costume himself to and saves up to buy a devilish mask.
Arthur Dorros, *Radio Man = Don Radio: A Story in English and Spanish*, 1993
    This beautifully illustrated story is about Diego, who relies on his radio for companionship, and his family, who are migrant workers.

794

OCTAVIO I. ROMANO-V,, Mexican American

Geriatric Fu: My First Sixty-Five Years in the United States

(Berkeley, CA: TQS Publications, 1990)

Subject(s): Autobiography; Humor; Personal Odyssey
Age range(s): Grades 10-Adult
Major character(s): Octavio I. Romano-V., Writer, Anthropologist, Mexican American
Time period(s): 20th century (1923-1990)
Locale(s): Berkeley, California

Summary: In a series of humorous essays, Romano presents his autobiographical odyssey. It starts with his seventh month, in the womb of his mother, before his birth in Mexico City, and ends in 1989 when he retires after teaching for twenty-six years at the University of California, Berkeley. Anthropologist, author, editor, publisher, and video producer, Romano describes his experiences during the Great Depression, World War II, his student years at the University of New Mexico, Berkeley, and the modern world. He writes about computers and libraries, his hens, drugs, the fantastic and the humorous.

Other books by the same author:
El Espejo—The Mirror: Selected Chicano Literature, 1972

Other books you might like:
Ernesto Galarza, *Barrio Boy*, 1971
    Autobiographical, this story examines the early life of a distinguished professor and author who wrote many works about Mexican agricultural workers.
Jesus Salvador Trevino, *The Fabulous Sinkhole and Other Stories*, 1995
    This first story collection by Trevino, a screenwriter and director, is an entertaining creation of Mexican and Chicano characters that take place in a fictional town, Arroyo Grande, in Texas.
Jose Antonio Burciaga, *Spilling the Beans: Loteria Chicana*, 1995
    A series of essays, many humorous, recounting experiences from the author's childhood in Texas.
Americo Paredes, *The Hammon and the Beans and Other Stories*, 1994
    Set in the southern Texas border region, this collection of short stories explores the cultural conflict that has dominated that area since the U.S.-Mexican War.
Al Martinez, *Ashes in the Rain: Selected Essays*, 1989
    This is a series of published essays of a Los Angeles Times writer and columnist, with a satirical and humorous twist.
Francisca Miranda Schneider, *Sal y Pimienta: A Culinary Education*, 1995
    These vignettes, interspersed with family recipes, describe the author's childhood during the Spanish Civil War.
Sabine Ulibarri, *Tierra Amarilla: Stories of New Mexico = Cuentos de Nueva Mexico*, 1993
    Five short stories and a novella, first published in 1964, evoke the rural life of a northern New Mexican village, portraying through the eyes of a boy the customs and traditions of an earlier era.

795

LEO ROMERO, Mexican American

Rita and Los Angeles

(Tempe, AZ: Bilingual Press, 1995)

Subject(s): Short Stories; Coming of Age; Growing Up
Age range(s): Grades 10-Adult
Time period(s): 1990s (1995)
Locale(s): Los Angeles, California

Summary: In this short story collection, a cast of fascinatingly complex characters grow and evolve, learning about being outsiders in an alien and hostile world. Haunting landscapes and difficult issues create a collection with depth and resonance. In the title story ''Rita and Los Angeles'', a young boy falls in love with the woman pictured on an orange crate. In another story, a homely single man concocts stories of sexual encounters to entertain his married friends.

Where it's reviewed:
Library Journal, May 15, 1995, page 98
Publishers Weekly, May 29, 1995, page 81

Other books by the same author:
Agua Negra, 1981
Celso, 1985
Going Away Indian, 1990

Other books you might like:
Beatriz de la Garza, *The Candy Vendor's Boy and Other Stories*, 1994
    The stories with realistic characters who struggle with life issues and try to find their identities.
Jose Antonio Burciaga, *Spilling the Beans: Loteria Chicana*, 1995
    A series of essays, many humorous, recounting experiences from the author's childhood in Texas.
Nash Candelaria, *The Day the Cisco Kid Shot John Wayne*, 1988
    Twelve humorous stories protraying Chicano-Anglo inter-relations and conflicts.
Alberto Alvaro Rios, *The Iguana Killer: Twelve Stories of the Heart*, 1984
    In this volume of short stories, the author transforms tales of ordinary life into a book of secrets.
Rick P. Rivera, *A Fabricated Mexican*, 1995
    A series of comic vignettes about a quiet but mischevious boy growing up in California, his search for identity and the antics of his eccentric family.
Jesus Salvador Trevino, *The Fabulous Sinkhole and Other Stories*, 1995
    This first story collection by Trevino, a screenwriter and director, is an entertaining creation of Mexican and Chicano characters who live in the fictional town of Arroyo Grande, Texas.

796

ORLANDO ROMERO, Mexican American

Nambe—Year One

(Berkeley, CA: Tonatiuh International, 1976)

Subject(s): Growing Up; Folklore; Legends
Age range(s): Grades 9-Adult
Major character(s): Mateo Romero, Young Man, Chicano
Time period(s): Indeterminate Past
Locale(s): Nambe, New Mexico

Summary: Narrated by Mateo Romero, resident of the town of Nambe, New Mexico, this story focuses on the attempts of a gypsy woman to seduce the young hero into leaving his land and traditions. Using folklore, dreams, and legends to teach about life, this poetic novel is mythical and follows the tradition of the literature of Rudolfo Anaya.

Other books by the same author:
Adobe: Building and Living with Earth, 1994

Other books you might like:
Rudolfo Anaya, *Bless Me, Ultima*, 1972
    Antonio, a seven-year-old boy, through his relationship with Ultima, a curandera, learns about life, nature and death in rural New Mexico during World War II.
Alfredo Vea Jr., *La Maravilla*, 1993
    A young boy grows up on Buckeye Road, a world of marvels in the desert outside the Phoenix city limits, caught between many cultures.
Sabine Ulibarri, *El Condor and Other Stories*, 1989
    A collection of eleven romantic stories for adults presents a world of gypsies, witches, ghosts, and the supernatural.
Angelico Chavez, *The Short Stories of Fray Angelico Chavez*, 1987
    Edited by Genaro M. Padilla, this collection of short stories is by an early New Mexico writer and folklorist.
Nash Candelaria, *Memories of the Alhambra*, 1977
    Jose Rafa disappears, leaving only a receipt for traveler's checks and a business card from an L.A. con man who sells false genealogies. Has he gone to Mexico to search for Spanish ancestors?
Sallie Gallegos, *Stone Horses*, 1996
    This history of the Montez family, living in a rural area in northern New Mexico in the 1930s and 1940s, follows the extraordinary Eduardo from birth up to his stint in the Navy at eighteen.

797

JORGE RUFFINELLI, Editor, Chilean
FERNANDO ALEGRIA, Co-Editor

Paradise Lost or Gained? The Literature of Hispanic Exile

(Houston: Arte Publico Press, 1990)

Subject(s): Anthology; Essays; Exile
Age range(s): Grades 10-Adult
Time period(s): 1980s
Locale(s): United States

Summary: This collection of literature by Latino writers addresses the experience of exile and alienation through stories, poems, and essays. This exile is not the result of war, but from the journeying of people fleeing to protect their language and their culture. The voices are strong, and tell of nostalgia, secret wishes, cultural assimilation , and solidarity.

About this book: This collection is divided between Spanish and English language.

Where it's reviewed:
Americas, May-June 1993, page 60

Other books by the same author:
Allende: A Novel, 1993
The Chilean Spring, 1980
The Maypole Warriors, 1993

Other books you might like:
Victor Perera, *Rites, A Guatemalan Boyhood*, 1986
These autobiographical narratives are about the author's boyhood while living in Guatemala.
Nicolas Kanellos, *Short Fiction by Hispanic Writers of the United States*, 1993
This is a collection of short stories by Latino writers.
Harold Augenbraum, *Growing Up Latino: Memoirs and Stories*, 1993
Twenty-five Latinos write stories about growing up in the U.S.
Ray Gonzalez, *Currents From the Dancing River: Contemporary Latino Fiction, Nonfiction, and Poetry*, 1994
This is a collection of creative literature by contemporary Latinos.
Delia Poey, *Iguana Dreams: New Latino Fiction*, 1992
This is an anthology of creative fiction by Latino writers in the U.S.
Omar Castaneda, *Remembering to Say Mouth or Face*, 1993
These short stories, some which take place in Central America, are by a Guatemalan writer now living in the U.S.
Isabel Allende, *Paula*, 1995
This is the story of Allende's daughter's agonizing illness (she suffers from porphyria), her descent into a coma, her treatments and her death at the age of 28.

798

RONALD L. RUIZ, Mexican American

Happy Birthday Jesus

(Houston, TX: Arte Publico Press, 1994)

Subject(s): Religion; Crime and Criminals; Prisoners and Prisons
Age range(s): Grades 10-Adult
Major character(s): Jesus Olivas, Criminal, Murderer, Chicano
Time period(s): 1960s
Locale(s): Fresno, California

Summary: The disturbing story of a violent and turbulent life, this novel recreates the making of a sociopath. Raised and abused by his grandmother, Jesus Olivas comes of age in a period of turmoil. A combination of religious fanaticism, poverty, and race hatred create unbelievable violence. In a court trial, Jesus' victimization emerges, yet he falls into the horror of prison life.

Where it's reviewed:
Library Journal, April 15, 1994, page 114
Publishers Weekly, February 14, 1994, page 80

Other books you might like:
Piri Thomas, *Down These Mean Streets*, 1978
This autobiographical novel recounts the story of a young Puerto Rican growing up in New York's Spanish Harlem and doing time in prison.
Floyd Salas, *Buffalo Nickel: A Memoir*, 1992
This coming-of-age portrait includes brutal depictions of inner city life, prison, death, and the struggles of a younger brother yearning for glory.
Oswald Rivera, *Fire and Rain*, 1990
This is a vivid story of a 1969 riot at the U.S. Marine Corps prison in Da Nang, Vietnam, that involved primarily black and Hispanic prisoners.
Lionel G. Garcia, *Hardscrub*, 1990
Related from the perspective of eleven-year-old Jim, this novel portrays characters struggling to survive in the tough land of West Texas.
Esmeralda Santiago, *America's Dream*, 1996
America works as a housekeeper in a hotel on an island off the coast of Puerto Rico, until she accepts a job as a nanny in Westchester County, New York, and learns about a new life.
Maria Espinosa, *Dark Plums*, 1995
Adrianne, a young girl from Texas, searches for love in Manhattan, falls into an abusive relationship, and eventually works as a prostitute.

799

MARIA AMPARO RUIZ DE BURTON, Mexican

The Squatter and the Don

(Houston, TX: Arte Publico Press, 1992)

Subject(s): Capitalism; War; Romance
Age range(s): Grades 10-Adult
Major character(s): Don Mariano Alamar, Landowner (owns a rancho), Californio
Time period(s): 1870s
Locale(s): California

Summary: Originally published in San Francisco in 1885, this novel is the first fictional narrative written in English from the perspective of the conquered Mexican population after the signing of the Treaty of Guadalupe Hildago. The squatters were the Americans who took the ranchos away from the conquered Californios by squatting on their lands. A historical romance, the novel chronicles the disintegration of the old Mexican order, shifts in power relations, and the capitalist development of the California territory. Ruiz de Burton describes calls for justice and a redress of grievances.

About this book: This novel is a *Recovering the U.S. Hispanic Literary Heritage Publication*, edited and introduced by Dr. Rosaura Sanchez and Dr. Beatrice Pita

Where it's reviewed:
Western American Literature, August 1994, page 147

Other books by the same author:
Who Would Have Thought It?, 1995 (originally published in 1872)

Other books you might like:
Nash Candelaria, *Not by the Sword*, 1982
  Taking place before the Mexican War of 1846, this novel shows the struggles taking place in New Mexico with the Rafa family and with the collapse of the Mexican government.
Nash Candelaria, *Inheritance of Strangers*, 1985
  A sequel to *Not by the Sword*, this book covers the years after the Mexican War of 1846 to New Mexico statehood, presenting the struggles of the Rafa family against Anglo exploitation.
Josephina Niggli, *Mexican Village*, 1994
  This important collection of ten interrelated short stories recounts the lives of the people of a small Mexican town, Hidalgo. It was first published in 1945.
Aristeo Brito, *The Devil in Texas = El Diablo en Texas*, 1990
  An important novel, it describes the Anglo destruction of a Chicano world in Texas, where the devil comes to the border town of Presidio.
Ron Arias, *The Road to Tamazunchale*, 1987
  Don Fausto, old and nearing death in a Los Angeles barrio, decides to take a journey through time and space, from the Inca world to encounters with undocumented workers in California.
Alejandro Morales, *The Brick People*, 1988
  Fictional but historically-based, this novel is about two families against each other—the Simons and the Revueltas—during the late nineteenth and early twentieth centuries in California.

`800`

MARIA AMPARO RUIZ DE BURTON, Mexican

Who Would Have Thought It?
(Houston, TX: Arte Publico Press, 1995)

Subject(s): Racism; Cultural Conflict; Romance
Age range(s): Grades 8-Adult
Major character(s): Lola, Child, Orphan, Mexican
Time period(s): 1850s
Locale(s): Connecticut

Summary: This historical romance, originally published in 1872, follows a young Mexican girl as she enters Indian captivity in the Southwest and eventually comes to live with a New England family. The author moved to California in 1847 and witnessed the annexation of California in 1848. Through the use of allegory, satire, and parody, the author shows how culture, perspectives, and identities clash as the novel criticizes the dominant society's opportunism, hypocrisy, and racism.

About this book: This novel is a *Recovering the U.S. Hispanic Literary Heritage Publication*. The introduction is by Dr. Rosaura Sanchez and Dr. Beatrice Pita.

Where it's reviewed:
Publishers Weekly, October 16, 1995, page 54

Other books by the same author:
The Squatter and the Don, 1992 (originally published in 1885)

Other books you might like:
Tina Juarez, *Call No Man Master*, 1995
  This historical novel is about a young woman of mixed heritage, Spanish and Indian, and her participation in the events that lead to Mexico's independence from Spain.
Nash Candelaria, *Not by the Sword*, 1982
  Taking place before the Mexican War of 1846, this novel shows the struggles taking place in New Mexico with the Rafa family and with the collapse of the Mexican government.
Nash Candelaria, *Inheritance of Strangers*, 1985
  A sequel to *Not by the Sword*, this novel covers the years after the Mexican War of 1846 to New Mexico statehood, presenting the struggles of the Rafa family against Anglo exploitation.
Montserrat Fontes, *Dreams of the Centaur*, 1995
  Alejo Durcal, son of a slain ranch owner, tries to avenge his father's death, during the period in history when the Yaqui Indians were badly mistreated in Mexico.
Alejandro Morales, *The Brick People*, 1988
  Based on historical events, this novel is about two California families pitted against each other—the powerful Simons and the proud Revueltas during the late nineteenth and early twentieth centuries.
Jovita Gonzalez Mireles, *Caballero: A Historical Novel*, 1996
  Don Santiago is trying to maintain his family's Mexican customs and values amidst the Anglo encroachment of his homeland in the 1840s, but his daughters fall in love with American men.

`801`

BENJAMIN ALIRE SAENZ

Carry Me Like Water
(New York: Hyperion, 1995)

Subject(s): Race Relations; Homosexuality/Lesbianism; Family Relations
Age range(s): Grades 10-Adult
Major character(s): Diego, Young Man, Deaf Person (also cannot speak), Chicano
Time period(s): 1990s
Locale(s): El Paso, Texas; Palo Alto, California

Summary: In this long involved novel with many interconnected characters and interracial couples, the story takes place both in El Paso and Palo Alto. In El Paso, Diego, a deaf-mute, is writing a long suicide letter, while he misses his long-lost sister Maria Elena who lives in Palo Alto and is married to wealthy and handsome Eddie. Eddie also misses his long-lost gay brother Jacob, and Lizzie, a nurse and best friend to Maria Elena and Eddie has also lost touch with her twin brother. In the end, after several characters die, the survivors reunite in El Paso.

Where it's reviewed:
Library Journal, March 15, 1995, page 99
Publishers Weekly, April 24, 1995, page 57
Virginia Quarterly Review, Winter 1996, p.

Other books by the same author:
Calendar of Dust, 1991 (American Book Award winner)
Dark and Perfect Angels, 1995
Flowers for the Broken: Stories, 1992

Other books you might like:
Graciela Limon, *The Memories of Ana Calderon: A Novel*, 1994
  Ana Calderon begins life in rural southern Mexico, but the burdens of poverty, dreams of a better life, and circumstance lead her family to the United States.
Himilce Novas, *Mangos, Bananas, and Coconuts: A Cuban Love Story*, 1996
  This tale of a magical yet real love story is an ancient tale, beginning with the love of a man and a woman from different social classes, and the story of the fate of their children.
Bruce-Novoa, *Only the Good Times*, 1995
  In this contemporary tale of obsessive love, narrator and cinematographer Paul Valence enters into a lifelong preoccupation with a beautiful woman, starting in adolescence, and enduring for years.
Eliud Martinez, *Voice-Haunted Journey*, 1990
  A professor at a university and a writer, Miguel Velasquez explores an elaborate series of memories and fantasies about his family, as he flys in a plane across California.
Arturo Islas, *Migrant Souls: A Novel*, 1990
  Josie Salazar returns to her Texas home town after her husband leaves her in California, and the reasons for her divorce gradually unravel in this novel about the Angel family.
Alejandro Morales, *Death of an Anglo*, 1988
  Logan, a rebellious and idealistic young doctor, attempts to improve the lives of the Chicano residents of his town.

802

BENJAMIN ALIRE SAENZ, Mexican American

Flowers for the Broken: Stories
(Seattle: Broken Moon Press, 1992)

Subject(s): Short Stories; Growing Up
Age range(s): Grades 9-Adult
Time period(s): 1980s
Locale(s): Southwest (stories take place in El Paso and the southwest)

Summary: These stories are personal, hard-hitting, explosively charged, compassionate and poignant. Saenz examines anger, prejudice, alienation, injustice, and complacency, and his characters walk between promise and loss.

About this book: This collection of short stories is by an author on a Stegner Fellowship at Stanford University.

Where it's reviewed:
Nation, June 7, 1993, page 772

Other books by the same author:
Calendar of Dust, 1991 (received the Before Columbus Foundation American Book Award in 1992)
Carry Me Like Water, 1995
Dark and Perfect Angels, 1995

Other books you might like:
Alurista, *Southwest Tales: A Contemporary Collection*, 1986
  This collection of stories is set in the Southwest.
Ray Gonzalez, *Memory Fever: A Journey Beyond El Paso del Norte*, 1993
  A collection of essays and vignettes about growing up in the 1960s in El Paso and the surrounding desert.
Virgil Elizondo, *The Future Is Mestizo: Life Where Cultures Meet*, 1988
  This is a biography about growing up Catholic in San Antonio, Texas.
Rudolfo Anaya, *Aztlan: Essays on the Chicano Homeland*, 1989
  These essays are by various authors on history, ethnic identity, and religion.
Rudolfo Anaya, *Voces: An Anthology of Nuevo Mexicano Writers*, 1987
  This anthology of poems and short stories is by New Mexican Chicano authors.

803

JIM SAGEL

El Santo Queso: Cuentos = The Holy Cheese: Stories
(Hanover, NH: Ediciones del Norte, 1990)

Subject(s): Short Stories; Folklore; Cultural Conflict
Age range(s): Grades 9-Adult
Time period(s): 1980s
Locale(s): New Mexico

Summary: This captivating collection of short stories, some humorously narrated, is about the clash of cultures. Land developers, scientific and military installations, hippies, and religious cults battle the traditional culture of New Mexico between the pages of this book. Sagel's language vividly captures the dialects of the people and his images are strong. In the title story, ''The Holy Cheese'', a candidate running for the school board is labeled ''the cheese candidate'' because of his involvement in distributing the free cheese of the Reagan administration.

About this book: Contains English and Spanish versions.

Other books by the same author:
Dancing to Pay the Light Bill: Essays on New Mexico and the Southwest, 1992
Mas Que No Love It: Cuentos/Short Stories, 1991
Sabelotodo Entiendelonada and Other Stories, 1988
Tunomas Honey, 1981 (received the Premio Casa de las Americas Award)
Where the Cinnamon Winds Blow = Donde Soplan Los Vientos de Canela, 1993

Other books you might like:
Orlando Romero, *Nambe—Year One*, 1976
  A resident of the town of Nambe, New Mexico, is being seduced by a gypsy woman to leave his land and traditions.
Sabine Ulibarri, *El Condor and Other Stories*, 1989
  A collection of eleven romantic stories for adults presents a world of gypsies, witches, ghosts, and the supernatural.

Angelico Chavez, *The Short Stories of Fray Angelico Chavez*, 1987

> Edited by Genaro M. Padilla, this is a collection of short stories by an early New Mexico writer and folklorist.

Patricia Preciado Martin, *El Milagro and Other Stories*, 1996

> A collection of personal and collective memories in the form of short stories, are stitched together to form a portrait of the author's family and her life growing up in Arizona.

Alberto Alvaro Rios, *Pig Cookies and Other Stories*, 1995

> A collection of interrelated short stories set earlier in this century in a small village in northern Mexico.

Nash Candelaria, *The Day the Cisco Kid Shot John Wayne*, 1988

> A humorous collection of short stories from New Mexico in which the author examines cultural clashes between Latinos and Anglos.

804

JIM SAGEL

Mas Que No Love It: Cuentos/Short Stories

(Albuquerque, NM: West End Press, 1991)

Subject(s): Folklore; Rural Life; Language
Age range(s): Grades 9-Adult
Time period(s): 1980s
Locale(s): New Mexico

Summary: In this collection of short stories, the narrators' voices are familiar and wise, recreating the ordinary, indelible voices of New Mexico. Stories with titles like "Egg Shoes", "The Witch", and "The Late Joe Hurts" reflect the religious and linguistic values of the people of northern New Mexico. Sagel's stories mirror the popular wisdom and living characterizations of a people in a linguistically diverse and dynamic region.

Where it's reviewed:
The American Book Review, August 1992, page 14

Other books by the same author:
Dancing to Pay the Light Bill: Essays on New Mexico and the Southwest, 1982
Sabelotodo Entiendelonada and Other Stories, 1988
El Santo Queso: Cuentos = The Holy Cheese, 1990
Tunomas Honey, 1983 (received the Premio Casa de las Americas Award)
Where the Cinnamon Winds Blow = Donde Soplan Los Vientos de Canela, 1993

Other books you might like:
Orlando Romero, *Nambe—Year One*, 1976

> A resident of the town of Nambe, New Mexico, is being seduced by a gypsy woman to leave his land and traditions.

Sabine Ulibarri, *El Condor and Other Stories*, 1989

> This collection of eleven romantic stories for adults presents a world of gypsies, witches, ghosts, and the supernatural.

Sabine R. Ulibarri, *Tierra Amarilla: Stories of New Mexico = Cuentos de Nuevo Mexico*, 1993

> Five short stories and a novella, first published in 1964,

evoke the rural life of a northern New Mexican village, portraying life, customs and traditions of an earlier era, through the eyes of a boy.

Angelico Chavez, *The Short Stories of Fray Angelico Chavez*, 1987

> This collection of short stories is by an early New Mexico writer and folklorist and is edited by Genaro M. Padilla.

Patricia Preciado Martin, *El Milagro and Other Stories*, 1996

> A collection of personal and collective memories in the form of short stories, are stitched together to form a portrait of the author's family and her life growing up in Arizona.

Alberto Alvaro Rios, *Pig Cookies and Other Stories*, 1995

> This set of interlocking stories explores the inhabitants of a small Mexican village.

Nash Candelaria, *The Day the Cisco Kid Shot John Wayne*, 1988

> The author examines cultural clashes between Latinos and Anglos in this humorous collection of short stories from New Mexico.

805

JIM SAGEL

Where the Cinnamon Winds Blow = Donde Soplan Los Vientos de Canela

(Santa Fe, NM: Red Crane Books, 1993)

Subject(s): Identity; Coming of Age; Magic
Age range(s): Grades 4-9
Major character(s): Tomas, 10-Year-Old, Mexican American; Tia Zuelma, Aunt (great-aunt), Mexican American
Time period(s): 1990s
Locale(s): United States

Summary: A magical fantasy, this novel examines ten-year-old Tomas's relationship with his wise and eccentric Tia Zulema and his attempts to reconcile his feelings for the death of his father. Tomas sets out on a journey toward maturity and self-realization which is influenced by traditional folk tales.

About this book: Spanish and English format

Other books by the same author:
Foreplay and French Fries, 1981
Mas Que No Love It: Cuentos/Short Stories, 1991*OCF
Sabelotodo Entiendelonada and Other Stories, 1988
El Santo Queso: Cuentos = The Holy Cheese: Stories, 1990
Tunomas Honey, 1981

Other books you might like:
Irene Beltran Hernandez, *The Secret of Two Brothers*, 1995

> Two young brothers living in Dallas fight to improve their future.

Frances R. Aparicio, *Latino Voices*, 1994

> Specially edited for young adult readers, this collection is by Latino authors.

Diane Gonzales Bertrand, *Sweet Fifteen*, 1995

> Stephanie's father dies right before her quinceanera, her special fifteenth birthday party.

Victor Villasenor, *Walking Stars: Stories of Magic and Power*, 1994

> In this collection of stories, some are autobiographical,

some about the author's grandparents and parents, and about growing up as the son of Mexican immigrants.

Gary Soto, *A Summer Life*, 1990

This collection of very short stories is about young boys growing up in rural California.

Vincent Younis, *Shine Boys: A Story about Santa Fe*,

This novella narrates the life of an un-named main character growing up in Santa Fe during the late 1950s. It focuses on his introduction to drugs at a very young age.

806

FLOYD SALAS, Mexican American

Buffalo Nickel: A Memoir
(Houston, TX: Arte Publico Press, 1992)

Subject(s): Sports/Boxing; City Life; Coming of Age
Age range(s): Grades 9-Adult
Major character(s): Floyd Salas, Young Man, Boxer, Chicano
Time period(s): 20th century (1930-1950s)
Locale(s): Oakland, California

Summary: This coming-of-age memoir follows a troubled but passionate child through adolescence and into adulthood. Salas oscillates between his two brothers—Albert, who abuses drugs and is involved in crime, and Edward, intelligent and upwardly mobile. He must decide which path his life is to take. This engaging and often shocking novel is a brutal portrait of inner city life and death, and the struggles of a younger brother yearning for glory.

Where it's reviewed:
Library Journal, August 1992, page 101
Nation, January 18, 1993, page 65
Publishers Weekly, June 29, 1992, page 49

Other books by the same author:
State of Emergency, 1996
Lay My Body on the Line: A Novel, 1978
Tattoo the Wicked Cross, 1967
What Now My Love, 1994
Stories and Poems from Close to Home, 1986

Other books you might like:
Miguel Duran, *Don't Spit on My Corner*, 1992
Little Mike and his friends, coming of age in Los Angeles during World War II, spend their time being "cool"—cruising, drinking, and protecting their turf.

Jose Antonio Villarreal, *Pocho*, 1959
This is the story of a Mexican family in the Santa Clara Valley of California before World War II and the assimilation of the son Richard Rubio.

Oscar Zeta Acosta, *The Autobiography of a Brown Buffalo*, 1972
From this part novel/part autobiographical work, the author, a famous Robin Hood type Chicano lawyer with an appetite for life on the edge, examines his life.

Piri Thomas, *Down These Mean Streets*, 1978
This autobiographical novel is about a young Puerto Rican man growing up in Spanish Harlem.

Abraham Rodriguez Jr., *Spidertown*, 1993
Sixteen year old Miguel is a runner for a drug dealer and struggles to change his life.

Americo Paredes, *George Washington Gomez*, 1990
As he grows up, George Washington Gomez struggles with racism, abuse, and cultural and political clashes, while other Texas Mexicans fight to preserve their language and culture.

Lionel G. Garcia, *Hardscrub*, 1990
Related from the perspective of eleven-year-old Jim, this novel portrays characters struggling to survive in the tough land of West Texas.

807

FLOYD SALAS, Mexican American

State of Emergency
(Houston, TX: Arte Publico Press, 1996)

Subject(s): Psychological Thriller; Politics; Drugs
Age range(s): Grades 10-Adult
Major character(s): Roger, Professor (radical)
Time period(s): 1960s
Locale(s): United States (parts of this novel take place in various European countries)

Summary: It is the radical 1960s, the era of political turmoil, free speech, free love, drugs, and paranoia. Roger is a self-styled radical professor who finds refuge in the counter-culture and in the people of other nations. He feels forced to flee the U.S. when he starts writing an expose of government and military efforts to destroy radicals like himself, and he is pursued by secret agents. With his girlfriend Penny they flee to England, Spain, the Canary Islands, Morocco, and France but nevertheless he feels the enemy is always close behind him.

Other books by the same author:
Buffalo Nickel: A Memoir, 1992
Lay My Body on the Line: A Novel, 1978
What Now My Love, 1994
Stories and Poems from Close to Home, 1986
Tatoo the Wicked Cross, 1967

Other books you might like:
Oscar Zeta Acosta, *The Autobiography of a Brown Buffalo*, 1972
Part novel, more autobiographical, the author,a famous Robin Hood type Chicano lawyer with an appetite for life on the edge examines his life.

Laura Del Fuego, *Maravilla*, 1989
Consuelo Contreres, growing up in the housing projects of East Los Angeles, makes her way through turbulent times during the 1960s.

Arturo Islas, *La Mollie and the King of Tears*, 1996
Louie Mendoza, a jazz musician finds himself at San Francisco General Hospital to hear the diagnosis of his liver and in a unique street language, he tells his story to a stranger.

Oscar Zeta Acosta, *Revolt of the Cockroach People*, 1973
A personal memoir recounts the turbulent years that mark the beginning of the Chicano movement in California when the Chicanos of East Los Angeles began to revolt at the end of the sixties.

Lucha Corpi, *Delia's Song*, 1989
Participating in the anti-war and civil rights movements of

the '60s, Delia must find a way to forge her own identity and relationships with others.

Francisco Goldman, *The Long Night of White Chickens*, 1992
Determined to find the murderers of his cousin Flor, Roger and his best friend Luis, become entangled in political difficulties as they discover Flor's secret life in war-torn Guatemala.

Bruce-Novoa, *Only the Good Times*, 1995
In this contemporary tale of obsessive love, narrator and cinematographer, Paul Valence, enters into a lifelong pre-occupation with a beautiful woman, starting in adolescence, and enduring for years.

808

FLOYD SALAS, Mexican American

What Now My Love
(Houston, TX: Arte Publico Press, 1994)

Subject(s): Drugs; Freedom
Age range(s): Grades 10-Adult
Major character(s): Miles, Writer
Time period(s): 1960s
Locale(s): San Francisco, California; Mexico (a border town)

Summary: Fleeing from the San Francisco drug sub-culture and a narcotics bust, a writer and two friends travel to the Mexican border. They discover a questionable freedom in a Mexican border-town underworld. This is a novel of wild flight and pursuit, of freedom and the tyranny of the establishment.

About this book: First published in 1969.

Where it's reviewed:
The Texas Observer, November 25, 1994, page 17

Other books by the same author:
Buffalo Nickel: A Memoir, 1992
Lay My Body on the Line: A Novel, 1978
Stories and Poems from Close to Home, 1986
Tatoo the Wicked Cross, 1967

Other books you might like:
Oscar Zeta Acosta, *The Autobiography of a Brown Buffalo*, 1972
In this largely autobiographical novel, the author examines his life as a famous Robin Hood-style Chicano lawyer who likes life on the edge.

Dagoberto Gilb, *The Magic of Blood*, 1993
Short stories about working-class life, with multi-dimensional characters who lead realistic lives.

John Rechy, *The Miraculous Day of Amalia Gomez: A Novel*, 1991
This novel follows a day in the life of a Mexican-American woman who lives with poverty, gang warfare, and illegal border crossings, yet still has hope.

Piri Thomas, *Down These Mean Streets*, 1967
A confessional autobiography describing street life, gangs, violence, and use of drugs in Spanish Harlem during the 1940's and 1950s.

Laura Del Fuego, *Maravilla*, 1989
Consuelo Contreres, growing up in the housing projects of

East Los Angeles, makes her way through turbulent times during the 1960s.

809

JOSEPH P. SANCHEZ, Mexican American

The Aztec Chronicles: The True History of Christopher Columbus, as Narrated by Quilaztli of Texcoco: A Novella
(Berkeley, CA: TQS Publications, 1995)

Subject(s): Conquest; Indians of Mexico; Historical
Age range(s): Grades 8-Adult
Major character(s): Cristobal Colon, Military Personnel (Admiral), Explorer, Spanish; Quilaztli, Historian, Aztec
Time period(s): 16th century
Locale(s): Mexico

Summary: This historical novella, based on documentary and bibliographical research, attempts to reconstruct the true history of Christopher Columbus. The story is told through the voice of Quilaztli, an Aztec historian, who served under both Moctezuma I and Moctezuma II. In this fictionalized account Quilaztli is instructed by three guardian spriits, Tilini, Tleume and Caudi to write the history of the past, present and future of the encounter between the Discoverer's people and Indian America.

Other books by the same author:
The Rio Abajo Frontier, 1540-1692: A History of Early Colonial New Mexico, 1987
Spanish Bluecoats: The Catalonian Volunteers in Northwestern New Spain, 1767-1810, 1990

Other books you might like:
Tina Juarez, *Call No Man Master*, 1995
Intricately crafted, this historical novel is about a young woman of mixed heritage, Spanish and Indian, and her participation in the events that lead to Mexico's independence from Spain.

Jose Barreiro, *The Indian Chronicles*, 1993
Adopted by Christopher Columbus, Diego Colon, a Taino boy, keeps a journal where he describes events in his life from 1532-1535 where he narrates the Indian's discovery of the Europeans.

Gloria Duran, *Malinche: Slave Princess of Cortez*, 1993
Malinali, born an Aztec princess and sold to the conqueror Cortez, is an ambiguous and controversial figure in Mexican history and this is her story.

Elizabeth Borton de Trevino, *I, Juan de Pareja*, 1965
Spanish court life is detailed in this historically accurate novel that tells the story of Juan, who is born a slave but becomes a devoted servant and friend to the painter Diego Velazquez.

Montserrat Fontes, *Dreams of the Centaur*, 1995
Alejo Durcal, son of a slain ranch owner, tries to avenge his father's death, during the period in history when the Yaqui Indians were badly mistreated in Mexico.

Graciela Limon, *Song of the Hummingbird*, 1996
Huitzitzilin, Hummingbird in the Nahautal language, is an Aztec princess who is forced into slavery. As an 82-year-

old woman, she is recounting her life during the Spanish conquest of Mexico.

Esteban Montejo, *The Autobiography of a Runaway Slave*, 1993

Based on interviews of a 105-year-old man, this important book in Cuban black literature describes slavery on a sugar plantation and the experience of being a fugitive.

LUIS RAFAEL SANCHEZ, Puerto Rican

Macho Camacho's Beat

(New York: Pantheon, 1980)

Subject(s): Identity; Popular Culture; Music
Age range(s): Grades 10-Adult
Time period(s): 1970s
Locale(s): San Juan, Puerto Rico

Summary: This novel, in which not much happens, has the author portraying a distasteful picture of a Puerto Rican society that is totally controlled by a U.S. imperialist culture. *Macho Camacho's Beat* is an inane song, with an English title of *Life Is a Phenomenal Thing*, that catches the tropical beats of a meaningless paradise. The novel, created around the song, presents various narratives about San Juan residents spending a typical late afternoon facing the emptiness of their lives.

About this book: This novel was published in Spanish in Buenos Aires and has never been published in Puerto Rico. The title in Spanish is *La Guaracha del Macho Camacho* published in 1976 and translated to English by Gregory Rabassa

Where it's reviewed:
World Literature Today, Spring 1983 , page 286
Latin American Literary Review , Spring-Summer 1983, page 125

Other books you might like:
Bernardo Vega, *Memoirs of Bernardo Vega*, 1984
First published in 1977, the work relates the story of an early 20th century immigrant from Puerto Rico who arrives in New York.
Emilio Diaz Valcarcel, *Hot Soles in Harlem*, 1993
This exploration of New York characters is from the perspective of a Puerto Rican immigrant.
Rosario Ferre, *The Youngest Doll*, 1991
This collection of short stories, originally published in Spanish, is about Puerto Rico society.
Kal Wagenheim, *Cuentos: An Anthology of Short Stories from Puerto Rico*, 1978
This collection of short stories takes place in Puerto Rico.
Ana Lydia Vega, *True and False Romances*, 1994
This collection of short stories is about women and romance that take place in Puerto Rico.
Oscar Hijuelos, *The Mambo Kings Play Songs of Love*, 1989
The Castillo brothers, two young musicians, make their way from Havana to New York to play music in the era of the mambo.
Virgil Suarez, *Havana Thursdays: A Novel*, 1995
This is the story of two sisters, their daughters, and how

they represent two different manners of dealing with the changes encountered through immigration from a Latino culture.

THOMAS SANCHEZ, Mexican American

Mile Zero

(New York: Alfred A. Knopf, 1989)

Subject(s): Mystery and Detective Stories; Crime and Criminals
Age range(s): Grades 10-Adult
Major character(s): St. Cloud, Expatriate, Caucasian; Justo Tamarindo, Police Officer, Veteran (Vietnam), Cuban American
Time period(s): 1980s
Locale(s): Key West, Florida

Summary: This exciting novel uses history, voodoo, santeria, folkloric sayings, and tropical culture to bring a group of expatriates together on the island of Key West. All of the extraordinary characters have left something behind in another life, like a *shadow life*. Sanchez slowly creates this supernatural mystery by introducing *Zobop*, possibly the voodoo-inspired killer, who is loose on the island. This is a complicated and dense story that is difficult to put down.

Where it's reviewed:
New York Review of Books, December 7, 1989, page 46
New York Times Book Review, October 1, 1989, page 7
Library Journal, September 15, 1989, page 136
Publishers Weekly, August 4, 1989, page 83

Other books by the same author:
Rabbit Boss, 1973
Zoot-Suit Murders: A Novel, 1978
Angels Burning: Native Notes from the Land of Earthquake and Fire, 1987

Other books you might like:
Enrique A. Laguerre, *The Labyrinth*, 1984
This is the story of a Puerto Rican man in New York City who goes to night school to earn a law degree and accidentally stumbles into the services of a Caribbean dictator.
Dagoberto Gilb, *The Last Known Residence of Mickey Acuna*, 1994
Mickey Acuna is waiting for something, something arriving through the mail, as he dwells at the YMCA in El Paso.
Omar Torres, *Fallen Angels Sing*, 1991
When Miguel Saavedra moves to New York, he is caught up in a web of plots spun by pro- and anti-Castro agents and soon he is involved in planning the assassination of Fidel Castro.
Gloria Gonzalez, *The Thirteenth Apostle*, 1993
Newspaperwoman Geraldine St. Claire investigates the murder of her lover Hal, which leads her to suspect an industrial homicide and also leads her right into the hands of a powerful drug lord.
Jose Yglesias, *Break-In*, 1996
Rudy Pardo comes home to find a young tall thin black

man rifling through his possessions, and this intrusion brings out his racial prejudices.

Rafael Yglesias, *The Murderer Next Door*, 1990
When Molly's best friend Wendy is murdered by her husband, Molly will do anything to gain custody of Wendy's daughter.

James Roberto Curtis, *Shango*, 1996
Miguel researches *santeria* in Miami for an ethnography course and becomes involved in a police investigation of a ritualistic murder, which leads him to meet the terrible god Shango.

Carolina Garcia-Aguilera, *Bloody Waters*, 1996
Guadalupe "Lupe" Solano, part of Miami's elite, is approached by a young couple for assistance in finding the biological mother of their adopted daughter when she needs a bone-marrow transplant.

812

DANNY SANTIAGO

Famous All over Town
(New York: Plume Books, 1984)

Subject(s): City Life; Family; Independence
Age range(s): Grades 7-10
Major character(s): Chato Medina, Teenager (boy)
Locale(s): Los Angeles, California (set in the Chicano barrio)

Summary: Chato Medina, a teenager who lives in the Chicano barrio of Los Angeles, wants to beat the odds that are stacked against him. His disintegrating family, his defiant and doomed friends, and his future that he may never see, inspire him to succeed in his own way.

About this book: The author is not a Latino and uses a pseudonym.

Where it's reviewed:
New York Review of Books, August 16, 1984, page 17

Other books you might like:
Kleya Forte-Escamilla, *The Storyteller with Nike Airs and Other Barrio Stories*, 1995
This collection of stories is about girls and the supernatural.

Ofelia Dumas Lachtman, *The Girl from Playa Blanca*, 1995
Elena and her brother Carlos find adventure in Los Angeles as they search for their father.

T. Ernesto Bethancourt, *The Me Inside Me*, 1985
Seventeen-year-old Freddie is a regular middle class teen until he becomes rich.

Tiffany Ana Lopez, *Growing Up Chicano*, 1993
This collection of short stories is by Chicano writers.

Irene Beltran Hernandez, *The Secret of Two Brothers*, 1995
Beaver, returning home after doing time in state prison, tries to create a decent life for himself and his younger brother Cande.

Gary Soto, *Jesse*, 1994
Jesse and his brother live together in Califronia's San Joaquin Valley and try to avoid being farm workers.

Vincent Younis, *Shine Boys: A Story about Santa Fe*, 1995
This novella narrates the life of an unnamed male character

growing up in Santa Fe during the late 1950s and his introduction to drugs at a very young age.

813

ESMERALDA SANTIAGO, Puerto Rican

America's Dream
(New York, NY: HarperCollins, 1996)

Subject(s): Identity; Women; Violence
Age range(s): Grades 10-Adult
Major character(s): America Gonzalez, Mother, Housekeeper, Puerto Rican
Time period(s): 1990s
Locale(s): Vieques, Puerto Rico; New York

Summary: America works as a housekeeper in a hotel on an island off the coast of Puerto Rico. Her life is an uphappy one, with a boyfriend who beats her and a fourteen year old daughter that's growing away from her. She jumps at the opportunity to work as a nanny in Westchester County, New York. In the U.S. America learns about herself, she learns about American life, and she learns to leave her past behind and start a new life.

Where it's reviewed:
Publishers Weekly, March 25, 1996, page 59

Other books by the same author:
When I Was Puerto Rican, 1993
Cuando Era Puertorriquena, 1994

Other books you might like:
Maria Espinosa, *Dark Plums*, 1995
Adrianne, a young girl from Texas, begins a search for love and self in Manhattan. Wandering the city, she sleeps with strangers and falls into an abusive relationship.

Alba Ambert, *A Perfect Silence*, 1995
From the surrealistic world of a mental institution, a Puerto Rican woman, Blanca, attempts to come to terms with her abusive past and her self-destructiveness.

Soledad Santiago, *Nightside*, 1994
Anna Eltern, a former nun, runs a shelter for runaway teens in New York City. Financial problems, funding cuts, and murder are forcing her to turn away teenagers in need.

Phyllis Tashlik, *Hispanic, Female, and Young*, 1994
This collection of short stories is written by young Latina girls from El Barrio of New York, about the problems of growing up female.

Alma Luz Villanueva, *Weeping Woman: La Llorona and Other Stories*, 1994
This collection of stories examines women who live in a world torn apart by violence, racism, and sexism.

Estela Portillo Trambley, *Trini*, 1986
Trini, a Tarahumara woman crosses the border as an undocumented immigrant in order to give birth to her child in the United States.

814

ESMERALDA SANTIAGO, Puerto Rican

When I Was Puerto Rican
(Reading, MA: Addison-Wesley, 1993)

Subject(s): Mothers and Daughters; Emigration and Immigration; Poverty
Age range(s): Grades 9-Adult
Major character(s): Negi, Child (book lover); Mami, Mother
Time period(s): 1950s; 1960s
Locale(s): San Juan, Puerto Rico (rural area outside San Juan)

Summary: This is the story of a young girl's experiences growing up poor, with vivid descriptions of rural and urban Puerto Rico. After moving to New York City at age fourteen, with her mother and six siblings, Negi continues to be a lover of books and learning and eventually attends Harvard University.

Where it's reviewed:
Hispanic, May 1994, page 76
Library Journal, September 15, 1993, page 85
Publishers Weekly, September 13, 1993, page 114

Other books you might like:
Rudolfo Anaya, *Bless Me, Ultima*, 1972
   A young boy's beliefs are challenged as he grows up in a small town in New Mexico.
Sandra Cisneros, *The House on Mango Street*, 1986
   The tribulations of a Mexican American young woman growing up.
Montserrat Fontes, *First Confession*, 1991
   A young girl experiences tragedy while she prepares for her First Communion.
Judith Ortiz Cofer, *Silent Dancing: A Partial Remembrance of a Puerto Rican Childhood*, 1990
   These autobiographical narratives are about growing up in both Puerto Rico and New Jersey.
Alma Flor Ada, *Where the Flame Trees Bloom*, 1994
   These eleven stories are about the childhood of the author in Cuba.
Gloria Lopez-Stafford, *A Place in El Paso: A Mexican American Childhood*, 1996
   A bittersweet narrative describing the early childhood of the author living in the ''projects'' of El Paso during World War II.

815

ROBERTO SANTIAGO, Editor, Puerto Rican

Boricuas: Influential Puerto Rican Writers—An Anthology
(New York: One World/Ballantine Books, 1995)

Subject(s): Anthology; Short Stories; Plays
Age range(s): Grades 10-Adult
Time period(s): 19th century; 20th century (1850-1990)
Locale(s): New York

Summary: This work contains fifty selections of writings by controversial writers from the nineteenth and twentieth centuries chosen for the impact of their work on Puerto Ricans in the U.S. and in Puerto Rico. This diverse anthology of essays, fiction, poetry, monologues, speeches and screenplays reflect the vibrant and original voices of Puerto Rican writers.

About this book: *Boricua* is an affectionate name that Puerto Ricans call one another, a term of cultural affirmation and endearment.

Where it's reviewed:
Hispanic, October 1995, page 80
Library Journal, August 1995, page 74
Publishers Weekly, July 31, 1995, page 76

Other books you might like:
Judith Ortiz Cofer, *Silent Dancing: A Partial Rememberance of a Puerto Rican Childhood*, 1990
   This autobiographical collection of prose, poetry, and short stories is about growing up in Puerto Rico and the U.S.
Jack Agueros, *Dominoes and Other Stories from the Puerto Rican*, 1993
   These short stories are about living in New York City as a Puerto Rican.
Jesus Colon, *A Puerto Rican in New York and Other Sketches*, 1961
   These short stories are about living in New York in the 1940s.
Faythe Turner, *Puerto Rican Writers at Home in the U.S.A.: An Anthology*, 1991
   This collection of short stories is about living in the U.S. and Puerto Rico.
Kal Wagenheim, *Cuentos: An Anthology of Short Stories from Puerto Rico*, 1978
   This is a collection of short stories that take place in Puerto Rico.
Ana Lydia Vega, *True and False Romances*, 1994
   These stories about women and romance, many comically related, take place in Puerto Rico.

816

SOLEDAD SANTIAGO, Puerto Rican

Nightside
(New York: Doubleday, 1994)

Subject(s): Murder; Runaways; Homeless
Age range(s): Grades 9-Adult
Major character(s): Anna Eltern, Young Woman, Social Worker
Time period(s): 1990s (1994)
Locale(s): New York, New York

Summary: Anna Eltern, a former nun who runs a shelter for runaway teens, struggles with financial problems and murder. Funding cuts are forcing her to turn away teenagers in need. A particularly close girl and favorite is murdered, while another that she turned away is arrested for her murder. The resulting scandal leads her on a search to find the real killer. This is a realistic but sordid portrayal of Hell's Kitchen and other dismal areas of New York City.

Where it's reviewed:
Publishers Weekly, November 1, 1993, page 68

Other books by the same author:
Room 9, 1992
Streets of Fire, 1996

Other books you might like:
Victor Rodriguez, *Eldorado in East Harlem*, 1992
    Streetwise seventeen year old Rene gets involved with a gang committing petty crimes and running drugs.
Abraham Rodriguez Jr., *Spidertown*, 1993
    Sixteen year old Miguel is a runner for a drug dealer and struggles to change his life.
Jack Agueros, *Dominoes and Other Stories from the Puerto Rican*, 1993
    Short stories about living in New York City as a Puerto Rican.
Phyllis Tashlik, *Hispanic, Female, and Young*, 1994
    Collection of stories and poems written by young girls in a New York public school.
Gil C. Alicea, *The Air Down Here: True Tales from a South Bronx Boyhood*, 1995
    Autobiographical short stories and essays by a sixteen year old Puerto Rican boy.
Maria Espinosa, *Dark Plums*, 1995
    Adrianne, a young girl from Texas, searches for love and self in Manhattan, but ends up sleeping with strangers and falling into an abusive relationship.
Esmeralda Santiago, *America's Dream*, 1996
    America works as a housekeeper in a hotel on an island off the coast of Puerto Rico, until she accepts a job as a nanny in Westchester County, New York, and learns about a new life.

`817`

SOLEDAD SANTIAGO, Puerto Rican

Room 9
(New York, NY: Doubleday, 1992)

Subject(s): Mystery and Detective Stories; Murder; Political Thriller
Age range(s): Grades 10-Adult
Major character(s): Marie Terranova, Widow(er) (police widow), Administrator (Mayor's assistant), Latina; Raul Vega, Journalist, Cuban American
Time period(s): 1990s
Locale(s): New York, New York

Summary: Room 9 is where the City Hall press corps is housed. When the N.Y.C. Deputy Mayor commits suicide, the implications for the Mayor are great, and his administrative assistant, recently widowed Marie Terranova, must keep the press corps in check. Cuban reporter Raul Vega is romantically interested in Marie and helps her solve the mystery of her husband's death which they learn is linked to City Hall and to fires in city-funded shelters. Marie becomes extremely disappointed by her bosses' hypocrisy and by the plight of the urban poor under his government.

Where it's reviewed:
Publishers Weekly, October 18, 1991, page 54

Other books by the same author:
Nightside, 1994

Streets of Fire, 1996
Undercover, 1988

Other books you might like:
Gloria Gonzalez, *The Thirteenth Apostle*, 1993
    Newspaperwoman Geraldine St. Claire investigates the murder of her lover Hal, which leads her to suspect an industrial homicide and also leads her right into the hands of a powerful drug lord.
Michael Nava, *The Hidden Law*, 1992
    Henry Rios defends a young Chicano accused of murdering a powerful Chicano public official in Los Angeles, while his long time lover, who has AIDS, leaves him for someone else.
Rudolfo Anaya, *Albuquerque*, 1992
    This exciting story of modern Albuquerque includes a vicious mayoral race, a young Chicano boxer, American Indians fighting for their water rights, and the folkloric past of New Mexico.
Manuel Ramos, *The Ballad of Gato Guerrero*, 1994
    Luis Montez is a divorced lawyer at work saving Felix ''Gato'' Guerrero, an old friend from way back, who is being chased by a Latino mobster.
Manuel Ramos, *The Last Client of Luis Montez*, 1996
    The last client of Denver lawyer Louie Montez is found dead with Montez standing over him. To clear his name Montez becomes entangled in a complicated web that takes him to California and back.
Steven Lopez, *Third and Indiana*, 1994
    The title of this novel refers to the corner where fourteen-year-old Gabriel hands out crack to people in passing cars. His boss, Diablo, becomes demanding when he comes up short in his accounts.
Carolina Garcia-Aguilera, *Bloody Waters*, 1996
    Guadalupe ''Lupe'' Solano, part of Miami's elite, is approached by a young couple for assistance in finding the biological mother of their adopted daughter when she needs a bone-marrow transplant.

`818`

SOLEDAD SANTIAGO, Puerto Rican

Streets of Fire
(New York, NY: Dutton, 1996)

Subject(s): Mystery and Detective Stories; Murder; Drugs
Age range(s): Grades 10-Adult
Major character(s): Francesca Colon, Single Mother, Police Officer, Puerto Rican
Time period(s): 1990s
Locale(s): New York, New York

Summary: This murder mystery with a Latina police officer, Francesca Colon, involves all the elements of big city dirty politics, police corruption, and tense ethnic community relations. Besides having to deal with a sexist partner, Colon has personal problems when her daughter becomes pregnant and her son runs away to be with his AIDs-infected father. Latino youth are being killed by policemen and Colon becomes the spokesperson for the police department to the community. Amidst all this the novel does end with a hopeful note.

Where it's reviewed:
Publishers Weekly, April 29, 1996, page 51
Library Journal, June 1, 1996, page 152

Other books by the same author:
Nightside, 1994
Room 9, 1992
Undercover, 1988

Other books you might like:
Steven Lopez, *Third and Indiana*, 1994
 The title of this novel refers to the corner where fourteen-year-old Gabriel hands out crack to people in passing cars. Diablo, his boss, begins making demands on him when his accounts come up short.
Michael Nava, *The Hidden Law*, 1992
 Henry Rios defends a young Chicano accused of murdering a powerful Chicano public official in Los Angeles, while his long time lover, who has AIDS, leaves him for someone else.
Victor Rodriguez, *Eldorado in East Harlem*, 1992
 Streetwise seventeen year old Rene gets involved with a gang committing petty crimes and running drugs.
Phyllis Tashlik, *Hispanic, Female, and Young*, 1994
 Collection of short stories and poems written by young Latina girls in a New York public school.
Gloria Gonzalez, *The Thirteenth Apostle*, 1993
 Newspaperwoman Geraldine St. Claire investigates the murder of her lover Hal, which leads her to suspect an industrial homicide and also leads her right into the hands of a powerful drug lord.
Rudolfo Anaya, *Albuquerque*, 1992
 This exciting story of modern Albuquerque includes a vicious mayoral race, a young Chicano boxer, American Indians fighting for their water rights and the folkloric past of New Mexico.
Max Martinez, *White Leg*, 1996
 A fast action murder mystery about a small town thief in a backwater town in Texas who kills a Texas Ranger and three other people during one of his hold-ups.

819

YVONNE V. SAPIA, Puerto Rican

Valentino's Hair

(Boulder, CO: Fiction Collective Two, 1991)

Subject(s): Fathers and Sons; Secrets; Death
Age range(s): Grades 10-Adult
Major character(s): Facundo Nieves, Businessman (barber), Father, Puerto Rican; Lupe Nieves, Young Man, Son, Puerto Rican
Time period(s): 20th century (1926-1961)
Locale(s): New York, New York

Summary: Rudolph Valentino comes into the life of Facundo Nieves and changes it forever. Nieves shaves and gives Valentino a haircut one month before he's hospitalized and once again before he dies. For unexplainable reasons he saves the hair and its power haunts him until his own death. The incredible story of Valentino's hair is narrated by Facundo to his son Lupe, as the child grows from a little boy to young manhood in the barrio of New York City.

Where it's reviewed:
Library Journal, November 1, 1991, page 133
Publishers Weekly, September 27, 1991, page 52
The American Book Review, August 1992, page 12

Awards the book has won:
Charles & Mildred Nilon Excellence in Minority Fiction Award, 1991

Other books by the same author:
The Fertile Crescent, 1983

Other books you might like:
Oscar Hijuelos, *Mr. Ives' Christmas*, 1995
 Edward Ives, a New York commercial artist, mourns the loss of his beloved son, and begins to exchange letters with his son's killer, a young Puerto Rican who will soon be released from prison.
Enrique A. Laguerre, *The Labyrinth*, 1984
 This is the story of a Puerto Rican man in New York City who goes to night school to earn a law degree and accidentally stumbles into the services of a Caribbean dictator.
Bernardo Vega, *Memoirs of Bernardo Vega*, 1984
 First published in 1977, the work relates the story of an early 20th century immigrant from Puerto Rico who comes to New York.
Rafael Yglesias, *Fearless: A Novel*, 1993
 After he survives a plane crash Max Klein's terror turns into ecstasy and he wants to help everyone. Since he has passed through death, he no longer fears it.
Jesus Colon, *A Puerto Rican in New York and Other Sketches*, 1961
 This series of short stories and essays was previously published in *The Daily Worker*, a publication of the Communist Party.
C.M. Mayo, *Sky Over El Nido: Stories*, 1995
 In these intriguing stories about contemporary cosmopolitan life, wealthy characters effortlessly fly around the world shopping and picking up a homeless AIDs infected man.
Giannina Braschi, *Empire of Dreams*, 1994
 In a series of prose poems, Braschi creates amazing postmodernist images of New York City. Her lyrical and unique text blends Shakespeare, Beatles songs, and a mixture of cultural influences.

820

FRANCISCA MIRANDA SCHNEIDER, Spanish American

Sal y Pimienta: A Culinary Education

(Berkeley, CA: Ariel Books, 1995)

Subject(s): Autobiography; Cooks and Cookery; Growing Up
Age range(s): Grades 10-Adult
Major character(s): Francisca Miranda, Child, Spanish
Time period(s): 20th century (1935-1950)
Locale(s): Spain

Summary: A collection of personal vignettes, of family and places, that describes the childhood of the author growing up in Spain. She was born on the eve of the Spanish Civil War and her father was murdered by the workers of the Valencia shipyard in 1936. These vignettes are interspersed with family recipes and serve to accent the vividness of the time period. As an adult the author settled in Berkeley, California and worked as a bilingual librarian for many years.

Other books you might like:

Victor Perera, *Rites: A Guatemalan Boyhood*, 1986
These are autobiographical narratives of the boyhood of the author while growing up in Guatemala.

Pablo Medina, *Exiled Memories: A Cuban Childhood*, 1990
A collection of the author's memories of growing up in Cuba and spending summers on his grandfather's sugarcane plantation, LaLuisa, before it was taken over by the Castro regime after the revolution.

Norma Elia Cantu, *Canicula: Snapshots of a Girlhood en la Frontera*, 1995
This collection, with photos, includes short stories and vignettes of a young girl growing up along the Texas border.

Judith Ortiz Cofer, *Latin Deli: Prose and Poetry*, 1994
Three genres of fiction, poetry, and essays are represented in this collection which portray life in Patterson, New Jersey, where the author grew up.

Cristina Garcia, *Dreaming in Cuban, A Novel*, 1992
This novel interweaves the stories of three generations of Cuban women and their different responses to the Cuban revolution.

Octavio I, Romano-V., *Geriatric Fu: My First Sixty-Five Years in the United States*,
In a series of humorous essays Romano presents his autobiographical odyssey, ending in 1989 when he retires after teaching for twenty-six years at the University of California, Berkeley.

821

LINDA SHUTE

Rabbit Wishes

(New York: Lothrop, Lee, and Shepard Books, 1995)

Subject(s): Animals; Folk Tales
Age range(s): Grades K-3
Major character(s): Tio Conejo, Rabbit
Locale(s): Cuba (takes place in a tropical forest)

Summary: Soon after Creation, Tio Conejo began to complain. He wanted to be large like an elephant or tall like a giraffe, but Papa Dios, his creator, agreed to grant his wish only if he brought him a feather from the eagle, an egg from the snake, and a tooth from the lion. This retelling of an African Cuban folktale is colorful and lyrical with a surprising ending.

About this book: There are Spanish words throughout and included is a Spanish vocabulary and source notes.

Where it's reviewed:

Publishers Weekly, May 1, 1995, page 59

Other books by the same author:

Clever Tom and the Leprechaun: An Old Irish Story, 1988
Momotaro, the Peach Boy: A Traditional Japanese Tale, 1986

Other books you might like:

Manilo Argueto, *Magic Dogs of the Volcanoes = Los Perros Magicos de los Volcanes*, 1990

The magic dogs, or cadejos, who live on the volcanoes of El Salvador, are loved by the villagers because of their powerful magic.

Gary Soto, *Chato's Kitchen*, 1995
Chato the low-rider cat wants to eat some juicy mice, but when he invites them to dinner they outwit him.

Lucia M. Gonzalez, *The Bossy Gallito*, 1994
A bossy little rooster gets his beak dirty pecking some corn while on his way to his uncle's wedding.

Harriet Rohmer, *Uncle Nacho's Hat = El Sombrero de Tio Nacho*, 1989
Uncle Nacho loves his old, ragged hat, and when his niece gives him a new one, Nacho is unable to give up his old one.

Pura Belpre, *Perez and Martina*, 1932
The love story of a gallant mouse and a lady cockroach.

Pura Belpre, *Ote: A Puerto Rican Folk Tale*, 1969
Ote must go to the forest in search of food for his wife and five children. There he meets a near-sighted devil who brings him bad luck.

822

BEVERLY SILVA, Cuban American

The Cat and Other Stories

(Tempe, AZ: Bilingual Press, 1986)

Subject(s): Short Stories; Animals; Students
Age range(s): Grades 10-Adult
Time period(s): 1980s
Locale(s): San Jose, California

Summary: These fifteen stories are about many things, such as cat lovers, cat haters, the life of the graduate student, small town California, and then life in general. One story deals with the difficulty in writing a thesis.

About this book: The author was born in Los Angeles but has been a resident of San Jose for many years.

Other books by the same author:

Nosotras: Latina Literature Today, 1986
The Second St. Poems, 1983

Other books you might like:

Roberta Fernandez, *In Other Words: Literature by Latinas in the U.S.*, 1994
This anthology of poetry and short stories is by Latinas.

Lillian Castillo-Speed, *Latina: Women's Voices from the Borderlands*, 1995
This anthology of short fiction is by Latinas.

Bryce Milligan, *Daughters of the Fifth Sun: A Collection of Latina Fiction and Poetry*, 1995
This collection of poetry and short stories is by Latinas in the U.S.

Evangelina Vigil, *Woman of Her Word: Hispanic Women Write*, 1983
This anthology of creative literature is by Latinas in the U.S.

Tey Diana Rebolledo, *Infinite Divisions: An Anthology of Chicana Literature*, 1993
Mexican American women author this collection of contemporary and historical writings.

823

GARY SOTO, Mexican American

Baseball in April: and Other Stories
(San Diego: Harcourt Brace Jovanovich, 1990)

Subject(s): Short Stories; Growing Up
Age range(s): Grades 5-8
Time period(s): 1980s
Locale(s): Fresno, California

Summary: This collection of short stories is about the everyday experiences of young people. Small events of day-to-day life—first dates, staying home alone, showing off, and playing baseball, reveal the themes of youth and age, love and friendship, and success and failure.

Where it's reviewed:
English Journal, December 1991, page 86
Horn Book Magazine, July-August 1990, page 458
Publishers Weekly, March 30, 1990, page 64

Other books by the same author:
Crazy Weekend, 1994
Local News, 1993
Pacific Crossing, 1992
The Pool Party, 1993
The Skirt, 1992
Too Many Tamales, 1993
Living up the Street: Narrative Recollections, 1985
Neighborhood Odes, 1992
New and Selected Poems, 1995

Other books you might like:
Kleya Forte-Escamilla, *The Storyteller with Nike Airs and Other Barrio Stories*, 1995
This collection of stories is about girls and the supernatural.
Ofelia Dumas Lachtman, *The Girl from Playa Blanca*, 1995
Elena and her brother Carlos find adventure in Los Angeles as they search for their father.
T. Ernesto Bethancourt, *The Me Inside Me*, 1985
Seventeen-year-old Freddie is a regular middle-class teen until he becomes rich.
Isabel Allende, *Paula*, 1995
Story of Isabel Allende's daughter Paula's agonizing illness with porphyria, her descent into a coma, treatment, and death at the age of 28. It is also the story of Isabel's life and childhood.
Jim Sagel, *Where the Cinnamon Winds Blow = Donde Soplan Los Vientos de Canela*, 1993
A magical fantasy, this novel examines ten-year-old Tomas' relationship with his wise and eccentric Tia Zulema and his attemts to reconcile his feelings for the death of his father.
Gil C. Alicea, *The Air Down Here: True Tales from a South Bronx Boyhood*, 1995
Sixteen-year-old Gil Alicea battles daily with drugs, violence, gangs, school, family, and the media in this book of short essays and journal entries.

824

GARY SOTO, Mexican American
ROBERT CASILLA, Illustrator

Boys at Work
(New York: Delacorte Press, 1995)

Subject(s): Animals; Money; Friendship
Age range(s): Grades 4-6
Major character(s): Rudy Herrera, Child; Alex, Friend (Rudy's best friend)
Time period(s): 1990s
Locale(s): Fresno, California

Summary: When Rudy Herrera accidentaly breaks an expensive Discman that belongs to a neighborhood bully, he must find some way to earn enough money to replace it. But when Rudy and his friend Alex start looking for jobs, they discover that earning money is harder than they thought.

About this book: This is the companion novel to *The Pool Party*.

Where it's reviewed:
Horn Book Magazine, September-October 1995, page 604

Other books by the same author:
Baseball in April: and Other Stories, 1990
Chato's Kitchen, 1995
Crazy Weekend, 1994
Jesse, 1994
Local News, 1993
Pacific Crossing, 1992
The Pool Party, 1993
The Skirt, 1992
A Summer Life, 1990
Taking Sides, 1991
Too Many Tamales, 1993

Other books you might like:
T. Ernesto Bethancourt, *The Me Inside of Me*, 1985
A young boy is given a million dollars and must decide what to do with it.
Pura Belpre, *Santiago*, 1969
Santiago must deal with moving and making new friends.
Gil C. Alicea, *The Air Down Here: True Tales from a South Bronx Boyhood*, 1995
These autobiographical stories and essays are about living in the Bronx.
T. Ernesto Bethancourt, *The Great Computer Dating Caper*, 1984
Eddie Ramirez and his friend Jody want to raise money to help Eddie's father, so they set up a computer dating service.
Vincent Younis, *Shine Boys: A Story about Santa Fe*, 1995
This novella narrates the life of an un-named main character growing up in Santa Fe during the late 1950s and his introduction to drugs at a very young age.
Jim Sagel, *Where the Cinnamon Winds Blow = Donde Soplan Los Vientos de Canela*, 1993
A magical fantasy influenced by traditional folk tales, the novel examines ten-year-old Tomas's journey toward maturity and self-realization.

825

GARY SOTO, Mexican American
SUSAN GUEVARA, Illustrator

Chato's Kitchen

(New York: G.P. Putnam's Sons, 1995)

Subject(s): Animals/Cats; Friendship; Food
Age range(s): Grades K-3
Major character(s): Chato, Cat
Time period(s): Indeterminate Past
Locale(s): United States (the barrio)

Summary: Chato, a low-riding cat with six stripes, is hungry for the family of tiny grey mice who have just moved in next door. He prepares a wonderful meal of fajitas, chiles rellenos, carne asado, and other good food, and invites the mouse family to his house for dinner. Instead of adding mice to his menu, Chato gets a surprise.

About this book: Spanish words throughout the story are defined in a glossary. Illustrations are rich and colorful.

Where it's reviewed:
Horn Book Magazine, September-October 1995, page 591
Publishers Weekly, February 6, 1995, page 84

Other books by the same author:
Baseball in April and Other Stories, 1990
The Cat's Meow, 1987
Local News, 1993
The Skirt, 1992
Too Many Tamales, 1993

Other books you might like:
Eve Bunting, *Smoky Night*, 1995
    Two cats, lost during the Los Angeles riots, somehow come together.
Pura Belpre, *Dance of the Animals*, 1972
    Senor and Senora Lion, hungry for goat meat, throw a party and invite all the animals in the jungle.
Pat Mora, *A Birthday Basket for Tia*, 1992
    Cecilia and her cat select a birthday present for a great aunt.
Lucia M. Gonzalez, *The Bossy Gallito*, 1994
    While on his way to his uncle's wedding, a bossy little rooster gets his beak dirty pecking corn.

826

GARY SOTO, Mexican American

Crazy Weekend

(New York: Scholastic Inc, 1994)

Subject(s): Robbers and Outlaws; Mystery and Detective Stories
Age range(s): Grades 8-12
Major character(s): Hector Beltran, 7th Grader, Chicano; Mando Tafolla, 7th Grader, Chicano
Time period(s): 1990s (1994)
Locale(s): Fresno, California

Summary: Two boys spend the weekend in Fresno, and after photographing a robbery and publishing the picture in the paper, are pursued by the bumbling thieves.

About this book: This is a suspense-filled and funny story.

Where it's reviewed:
Publisher's Weekly, January 31, 1995, page 90

Other books by the same author:
Chato's Kitchen, 1995
Local News, 1993
The Pool Party, 1993
The Skirt, 1993
Pacific Crossing, 1992
Taking Sides, 1991
Baseball in April and Other Stories, 1990
The Cat's Meow, 1987

Other books you might like:
T. Ernesto Bethancourt, *The Me Inside of Me*, 1985
    Seventeen-year-old Freddie is a regular middle-class teen until he becomes rich.
Alfred Avila, *Mexican Ghost Tales of the Southwest*, 1994
    This is a collection of supernatural tales from the U.S.-Mexican border.
Ofelia Dumas Lachtman, *The Girl from Playa Blanca*, 1995
    Elena and her brother Carlos find adventure in Los Angeles as they search for their father.
Tiffany Ana Lopez, *Growing Up Chicano*, 1993
    This is a collection of short stories by Chicano wtiers.
Irene Beltran Hernandez, *The Secret of Two Brothers*, 1995
    Two brothers, living in Dallas, fight to improve their future.
T. Ernesto Bethancourt, *The Great Computer Dating Caper*, 1984
    Eddie Ramirez and his friend Jody want to raise money to help Eddie's father, so they set up a computer dating service.

827

GARY SOTO, Mexican American

Jesse

(New York: Harcourt Brace & Company, 1994)

Subject(s): Coming of Age; Family Relations; College Life
Age range(s): Grades 9-12
Major character(s): Jesse, Student—College, Brother, Mexican American; Abel, Student—College, Brother, Mexican American
Time period(s): 1960s
Locale(s): Fresno, California

Summary: Jesse and Abel, brothers, move out of their parents home to live alone and attend junior college. They dream of a better future without doing farm labor, and also hope to avoid the Vietnam Conflict.

Where it's reviewed:
Wilson Library Bulletin, April 1995, page 115
Horn Book, March-April 1995, page 201

Other books by the same author:
Baseball in April: and Other Stories, 1990

The Skirt, 1992
Taking Sides, 1991
The Pool Party, 1993

Other books you might like:

Diane Gonzales Bertrand, *Sweet Fifteen*, 1995
  A young girl who recently lost her father is befriended by a
  slightly older young woman.
Tiffany Ana Lopez, *Growing Up Chicano*, 1993
  This is an anthology of short fiction about the experiences
  of growing up Chicano.
Irene Beltran Hernandez, *The Secret of Two Brothers*, 1995
  Two brothers, living in Dallas, fight to improve their
  future.
Gloria Velasquez, *Juanita Fights the School Board*, 1994
  Juanita is expelled from high school and she fights back
  with help from her friends.
T. Ernesto Bethancourt, *The Me Inside Me*, 1985
  Seventeen-year-old Freddie is a regular middle-class teen
  until he becomes rich.
Abraham Rodriguez Jr., *The Boy Without a Flag: Tales of the
  South Bronx*, 1992
  These stories portray young people growing up Puerto
  Rican in New York City.

828

GARY SOTO, Mexican American

Local News

(New York: Harcourt Brace Javanovich, 1993)

Subject(s): Short Stories
Age range(s): Grades 7-9
Time period(s): 1990s (1993)
Locale(s): San Joaquin Valley, California (Mexican American
  barrio)

Summary: These everyday-life short stories are about young
Mexican Americans and their family escapades. In one story
Angel has his picture taken by his brother while in the shower
and is blackmailed to do things for him.

Where it's reviewed:
Horn Book, July-August 1993, page 460
Publishers Weekly, April 12, 1993, page 64
Wilson Library Bulletin, May 1994, page 98

Other books by the same author:
Chato's Kitchen, 1995
Crazy Weekend, 1994
The Pool Party, 1993
The Skirt, 1993
Pacific Crossing, 1992
Taking Sides, 1991
The Cat's Meow, 1987

Other books you might like:

Abraham Rodriguez Jr., *The Boy Without a Flag: Tales of the
  South Bronx*, 1992
  This collection of short stories is about the problems of
  young Puerto Ricans in the Bronx.
Kleya Forte-Escamilla, *The Storyteller with Nike Airs and
  Other Barrio Stories*, 1995

This collection of stories is about girls and the supernatu-
ral.
Ofelia Dumas Lachtman, *The Girl from Playa Blanca*, 1995
  Elena and her brother Carlos find adventure in Los Ange-
  les as they search for their father.
T. Ernesto Bethancourt, *The Me Inside Me*, 1985
  Seventeen-year-old Freddie is a regular middle class teen
  until he becomes rich.
Irene Beltran Hernandez, *The Secret of Two Brothers*, 1995
  Beaver returns home after doing time in state prison and
  tries to create a decent life for himself and his younger
  brother Cande.

829

GARY SOTO, Mexican American
JOE CEPEDA, Illustrator, Mexican American

The Old Man and His Door

(New York, NY: Putnam, 1996)

Subject(s): Humor; Marriage; Animals/Pigs
Age range(s): Grades K-2
Major character(s): El Viejo, Aged Person, Mexican Ameri-
  can
Time period(s): Indeterminate Past
Locale(s): United States

Summary: A humorous tale about an absent minded old man,
''el viejo'', who is not listening to his wife when she tells him
to bring ''el puerco'' to a barbecue and instead brings ''la
puerta'', the door. But carrying the door on his back serves
him very well as he travels, and he gets to save a drowning
boy and accumulate many good things to eat. Everyone
enjoys the victuals he brings and in the end there's a very
happy plump pig. Wonderfully illustrated.

About this book: Interspersed with Spanish words; glossary in
back of book.

Where it's reviewed:
Publishers Weekly, April 1, 1996, page 75
School Library Journal, June 1996, page 110
Booklist, April 1, 1996, page 1374

Other books by the same author:
Chato's Kitchen, 1995
Crazy Weekend, 1994
Jesse, 1994
Local News, 1993
Too Many Tamales, 1993

Other books you might like:

Juanita Havill, *Treasure Nap*, 1992
  Mama tells Alicia the story of Rita, who visits her grandfa-
  ther in the mountains of Mexico, and learns to make
  wooden birdcages.
Arthur Dorros, *Abuela*, 1991
  A little girl and her grandmother fly all over New York
  City.
Lucia M. Gonzalez, *The Bossy Gallito*, 1994
  A bossy little rooster gets his beak dirty pecking some corn
  while on his way to his uncle's wedding.
Jan Romero Stevens, *Carlos and the Squash Plant/Carlos y la
  planta de Calabaza*, 1993

Carlos refuses to bathe and his mother warns him about something growing out of his ear.

Carmen Santiago Nodar, *Abuelita's Paradise*, 1992
Marita sits in Abuelita's rocking chair and remembers the stories Abuelita told of her life in Puerto Rico.

Arthur Doors, *Radio Man = Don Radio: A Story in English and Spanish*, 1993
This beautifully illustrated story about Diego, who relies on his radio for companionship, and his family who are migrant farm workers.

Pura Belpre, *Ote: A Puerto Rican Folk Tale*, 1969
Ote must go to the forest in search of food for his wife and five children. There he meets a near-sighted devil who brings him bad luck.

830

GARY SOTO, Mexican American

Pacific Crossing
(San Diego: Harcourt Brace, 1992)

Subject(s): International Relations; Martial Arts; Friendship
Age range(s): Grades 6-8
Major character(s): Lincoln Mendoza, Student—Junior High; Tony Contreras, Student—Junior High
Time period(s): 1990s (1992)
Locale(s): San Francisco, California (also takes place in the countryside of Japan)

Summary: Lincoln and his friend Tony are selected by their principal to spend the summer in Tokyo, Japan. They have studied Shorinji Kempo, a Japanese martial art. In Japan, the two Chicano boys meet Mitsuo, their host brother, who is their age. After they adapt to their Japanese families, they find them similar to their own families back home.

About this book: There is a glossary of Spanish and Japanese words in the back of the book.

Where it's reviewed:
Horn Book Magazine, November-December 1992, page 725
Publishers Weekly, October 5, 1992, page 71

Other books by the same author:
Chato's Kitchen, 1995
Crazy Weekend, 1994
Local News, 1993
The Pool Party, 1993
The Skirt, 1993
Taking Sides, 1991
Baseball in April and Other Stories, 1990
The Cat's Meow, 1987

Other books you might like:
T. Ernesto Bethancourt, *The Me Inside of Me*, 1985
A boy is given a million dollars and must deal with the changes it creates.

Alfred Avila, *Mexican Ghost Tales of the Southwest*, 1994
Tales of mystery and the supernatural.

Ofelia Dumas Lachtman, *The Girl from Playa Blanca*, 1995
Elena and her brother Carlos find adventure in Los Angeles as they search for their father.

Tiffany Ana Lopez, *Growing Up Chicano*, 1993
Anthology of short fiction about the experiences of growing up Chicano.

Irene Beltran Hernandez, *The Secret of Two Brothers*, 1995
Two brothers, living in Dallas, fight to improve their future.

831

GARY SOTO, Editor, Mexican American

Pieces of the Heart: New Chicano Fiction
(San Francisco: Chronicle Books, 1993)

Subject(s): Anthology; Short Stories
Age range(s): Grades 10-Adult
Time period(s): 1990s (1993)
Locale(s): Southwest (west and southwest areas of the U.S.)

Summary: Fifteen authors, including well-known Sandra Cisneros, Alberto Rios, Jack Lopez, and Helena Maria Viramontes are included in this anthology.

About this book: This collection of short stories highlights some of the best of Chicano literature.

Where it's reviewed:
Library Journal, May 15, 1993, page 99
Publishers Weekly, April 5, 1993, page 70
Nation, June 7, 1993, page 772

Other books by the same author:
California Childhood: Recollections and Stories of the Golden State, 1988
Crazy Weekend, 1994
Local News, 1993
Pacific Crossing, 1992
The Pool Party, 1993
The Skirt, 1992
Too Many Tamales, 1993
Living up the Street: Narrative Recollections, 1985
Neighborhood Odes, 1992
New and Selected Poems, 1995

Other books you might like:
Ray Gonzalez, *Currents From the Dancing River: Contemporary Latino Fiction, Nonfiction, and Poetry*, 1994
This is a collection of creative literature by contemporary Latinos.

Ray Gonzalez, *Mirrors Beneath the Earth: Short Fiction by Chicano Writers*, 1992
This is a collection of short stories by Chicano writers.

Rudolfo Anaya, *Cuentos Chicanos: A Short Story Anthology*, 1984
This is a collection of short stories by Chicano writers.

Tiffany Ana Lopez, *Growing Up Chicano*, 1993
This is a collection of short stories by Chicano writers.

Carlota Cardenas de Dwyer, *Chicano Voices*, 1975
This is an important collection of short stories from the Southwest.

Rudolfo Anaya, *Voces: An Anthology of Nuevo Mexicano Writers*, 1987
This anthology of poems and short stories is by New Mexican Chicano authors.

Tey Diana Rebolledo, *Infinite Divisions: An Anthology of Chicana Literature*, 1993
This extensive anthology of Chicana literature covers the 19th century to the present.

832

GARY SOTO, Mexican American
ROBERT CASILLA, Illustrator

The Pool Party
(New York: Delacorte, 1993)

Subject(s): Human Behavior
Age range(s): Grades 3-6
Major character(s): Rudy Herrera, 5th Grader
Time period(s): 1990s (1993)
Locale(s): Fresno, California

Summary: Ten-year-old Rudy gets invited to a swimming pool party at the home of the richest girl in school. Everyone in his family gives him advice on how to behave. He just wants to dive and swim and act like himself.

Where it's reviewed:
Publishers Weekly, June 7, 1993, page 70

Other books by the same author:
Chato's Kitten, 1995
Crazy Weekend, 1994
Local News, 1993
The Skirt, 1993
Pacific Crossing, 1992
Taking Sides, 1991
Baseball in April and Other Stories, 1990
The Cat's Meow, 1987

Other books you might like:
Pura Belpre, *Santiago*, 1969
    Santiago must deal with moving and making new friends.
Lulu Delacre, *Vejigantes Masquerade*, 1993
    Ramon wants to masquerade in Carnival, so he sews a vejigante costume himself and saves up to buy a devilish mask.
Fran Leeper Buss, *Journey of the Sparrow*, 1991
    A Salvadoran family is smuggled into Chicago to start a new life.
Alma Flor Ada, *My Name Is Maria Isabel*, 1993
    Maria moves to a new school and learns not to be shy about her name.
Juan Felipe Herrera, *Calling the Doves = El Canto de las Palomas*, 1995
    This book depicts the experiences of the author as a young boy growing up as a farm worker in the fields and valleys of California.
Karen Papagapitos, *Jose's Basket*, 1990
    Because Jose's family is a migrant farm working family, school starts later and ends earlier for him than for the other students. His teacher understands and gives him a special gift.

833

GARY SOTO, Mexican American
ERIC VELASQUEZ, Illustrator

The Skirt
(New York: Delacorte Press, 1992)

Subject(s): Family Relations; Problem Solving; Dancing
Age range(s): Grades 3-4
Major character(s): Miata, 4th Grader
Time period(s): 1990s (1992)
Locale(s): Sanger, California (rural town in San Joaquin Valley)

Summary: On a Friday afternoon Miata leaves her mother's treasured folkloric dancing skirt on the school bus. With her best friend Ana she figures out a way to get it in time for her performance on Sunday, but her mother also surprises her with a new skirt.

Where it's reviewed:
Horn Book, November-December 1992, page 720
Publishers Weekly, August 24, 1992, page 80

Other books by the same author:
Baseball in April: and Other Stories, 1990
Taking Sides, 1991
Pacific Crossing, 1992
Crazy Weekend, 1994
Local News, 1993
The Pool Party, 1993
Too Many Tamales, 1993
Living up the Street: Narrative Recollections, 1985
Neighborhood Odes, 1992
New and Selected Poems, 1995

Other books you might like:
Enedina Casarez Vasquez, *Recuerdos de Una Nina*, 1980
    These short stories are about growing up in San Antonio, Texas.
Alma Flor Ada, *My Name Is Maria Isabel*, 1993
    Maria moves to a new school and learns not to be shy about her name.
Gloria Anzaldua, *Friends From the Other Side/Amigos del Otro Lado*, 1993
    Prietita helps an undocumented boy and his family hide from the migra.
Pura Belpre, *Santiago*, 1969
    Santiago learns to make new friends in a new school.
Fran Leeper Buss, *Journey of the Sparrow*, 1991
    This story depicts a Salvadoran family smuggled into Chicago in order to start a new life.
Nicholasa Mohr, *Felita*, 1990
    Felita loves her neighborhood and her best friend Gigi, but her world is turned upside down when her family moves to a new neighborhood.
Fernando Pico, *The Red Comb*, 1991
    A young girl helps save a runaway slave in 19th century Puerto Rico.
Karen Papagapitos, *Socorro, Daughter of the Desert*, 1993
    The family of eight-year-old Socorro are farm workers and she helps out as much as she can. When her father falls ill, Socorro makes tortillas for her mother to sell in the fields.

834

GARY SOTO, Mexican American

A Summer Life

(Hanover, NH: University Press of New England, 1990)

Subject(s): Short Stories; Growing Up
Age range(s): Grades 6 and Up
Major character(s): Rick, Brother
Time period(s): 1950s; 1960s (1950-1960)
Locale(s): Fresno, California

Summary: This collection of short stories is about the author's childhood in Fresno, California. These autobiographical stories about the author and his brother Rick are full of their mischief, riding bikes in dusty roads, climbing trees to steal plums, and dating as they grow up.

About this book: The author is well known for his poetry.

Where it's reviewed:
Wilson Library Bulletin, November 1990, page 142
Library Journal, July 1990, page 97
Publishers Weekly, June 8, 1990, page 40

Other books by the same author:
Baseball in April and Other Stories, 1990
The Cat's Meow, 1987
Local News, 1993
The Skirt, 1992
Too Many Tamales, 1993
Living up the Street: Narrative Recollections, 1985
Neighborhood Odes, 1992
New and Selected Poems, 1995

Other books you might like:
Kleya Forte-Escamilla, *The Storyteller with Nike Airs and Other Barrio Stories*, 1995
This collection of stories is about girls and the supernatural.
Ofelia Dumas Lachtman, *The Girl from Playa Blanca*, 1995
Elena and her brother Carlos find adventure in Los Angeles as they search for their father.
Vincent Younis, *Shine Boys: A Story about Santa Fe*, 1995
This novella narrates the story of a young boy growing up in Santa Fe in the 1950's and his early introduction to drugs.
Danny Santiago, *Famous All over Town*, 1984
Chato Medina, a Chicano teenager living in an L.A. barrio, must deal with his disintegrating family, his defiant and doomed friends and his own future.
Jim Sagel, *Where the Cinnamon Winds Blow = Donde Soplan Los Vientos de Canela*, 1993
A magical fantasy, this novel examines ten-year-old Tomas' relationship with his wise and eccentric Tia Zulema and his attempts to reconcile his feelings for the death of his father.

835

GARY SOTO, Mexican American

Summer on Wheels

(New York: Scholastic Inc, 1995)

Subject(s): Bicycles and Bicycling; Adventure and Adventurers; Friendship
Age range(s): Grades 4-7
Major character(s): Hector, Teenager, Chicano; Mando, Teenager, Chicano
Locale(s): Los Angeles, California (East Los Angeles)

Summary: Hector and Mando take a leisurely six-day bike trip from East Los Angeles to the beach in Santa Monica. On the way they stay with relatives and experience many adventures, such as starring in a TV commercial, recording a rap song, and painting a mural.

About this book: This is the sequel to *Crazy Weekend*.

Where it's reviewed:
Wilson Library Bulletin, June 1995, page 120

Other books by the same author:
Crazy Weekend, 1994
Local News, 1993
Pacific Crossing, 1992
The Pool Party, 1993
The Skirt, 1992
Too Many Tamales, 1993
Living up the Street: Narrative Recollections, 1985
Neighborhood Odes, 1992
New and Selected Poems, 1995

Other books you might like:
Kleya Forte-Escamilla, *The Storyteller with Nike Airs and Other Barrio Stories*, 1995
This collection of stories is about girls and the supernatural.
Ofelia Dumas Lachtman, *The Girl from Playa Blanca*, 1995
Elena and her brother Carlos find adventure in Los Angeles as they search for their father.
T. Ernesto Bethancourt, *The Me Inside Me*, 1985
Seventeen-year-old Freddie is a regular middle-class teen until he becomes rich.
Irene Beltran Hernandez, *The Secret of Two Brothers*, 1995
Two brothers fight for survival to improve their future in Dallas, Texas.
T. Ernesto Bethancourt, *New York City: Too Far from Tampa Blues*, 1975
Tom moves from Florida to New York, where he lives in Brooklyn and makes friends with Aurelio. The boys share an interest in rock music and learn to cope with street life.

836

GARY SOTO, Mexican American

Taking Sides

(San Diego: Harcourt Brace, 1991)

Subject(s): Sports/Basketball; Moving, Household
Age range(s): Grades 7-9

Major character(s): Lincoln Mendoza, 14-Year-Old, Student—Junior High, Chicano; Tony Contreras, 14-Year-Old, Student—Junior High, Chicano
Time period(s): 1990s (1991)
Locale(s): San Francisco, California (suburb of San Francisco)

Summary: Lincoln and his mother move to a suburb and he has to change schools. In the up-coming basketball game he will have to play against his old team. His divided loyalties teach him something new.

Where it's reviewed:
Language Arts, March 1993, page 222
Publishers Weekly, September 6, 1991, page 104
Wilson Library Bulletin, October 1991, page 104

Other books by the same author:
Chato's Kitten, 1995
Crazy Weekend, 1994
Local News, 1993
The Pool Party, 1993
The Skirt, 1993
Pacific Crossing, 1992
Baseball in April and Other Stories, 1990
The Cat's Meow, 1987

Other books you might like:
Abraham Rodriguez Jr., *The Boy Without a Flag: Tales of the South Bronx*, 1992
   This collection of short stories is about the problem of young Puerto Ricans in the Bronx.
Kleya Forte-Escamilla, *The Storyteller with Nike Airs and Other Barrio Stories*, 1995
   This collection of stories is about girls and the supernatural.
Ofelia Dumas Lachtman, *The Girl from Playa Blanca*, 1995
   Elena and her brother Carlos find adventure in Los Angeles as they search for their father.
T. Ernesto Bethancourt, *The Me Inside Me*, 1985
   Seventeen-year-old Freddie is a regular middle-class teen until he becomes rich.
Irene Beltran Hernandez, *The Secret of Two Brothers*, 1995
   Two brothers, living in Dallas, fight to improve their future.

837

GARY SOTO, Mexican American
ED MARTINEZ, Illustrator, Argentinean

Too Many Tamales
(New York: G.P. Putnam's Sons, 1993)

Subject(s): Christmas; Food
Age range(s): Grades 1-2
Major character(s): Maria, Child
Time period(s): 1990s (1993)
Locale(s): United States (someplace where it snows)

Summary: Maria helps her mother make tamales for the Christmas Eve dinner. Later she can't remember where she left her mother's ring after trying it on in the kitchen.

Where it's reviewed:
Horn Book, November-December 1993, page 727
Publishers Weekly, August 16, 1993, page 103

Other books by the same author:
Baseball in April: and Other Stories, 1990
Taking Sides, 1991
Pacific Crossing, 1992
Crazy Weekend, 1994
Local News, 1993
The Pool Party, 1993
The Skirt, 1992
Living up the Street: Narrative Recollections, 1985
Neighborhood Odes, 1992
New and Selected Poems, 1995

Other books you might like:
Pat Mora, *A Birthday Basket for Tia*, 1992
   A little girl and a little cat find a birthday present for a 90 year old great aunt.
Gloria Anzaldua, *Friends From the Other Side/Amigos del Otro Lado*, 1993
   Prietita helps an undocumented boy and his family hide from the migra.
Pura Belpre, *Santiago*, 1969
   Santiago learns to make new friends in a new school.
Alma Flor Ada, *The Gold Coin*, 1991
   Juan travels around the countryside trying to steal a gold coin from an old woman.
Rudolfo Anaya, *The Farolitos of Christmas*, 1995
   Luz helps her Abuelo create *farolitos* that will light the path for the village's traditional Christmas procession.
Gina Macaluso Rodriguez, *Green Corn Tamales = Tamales de Elote*, 1994
   A Latino family makes green corn tamales every year, but there's a twist to this tale, not everyone wants to help.
Pat Mora, *The Gift of the Poinsettia = El Regalo de la Flor de Nochebuena*, 1995
   Carlos is celebrating *Las Posadas* but can't enjoy himself because he's worried that he can't buy a gift for the baby Jesus.

838

PEDRO JUAN SOTO, Puerto Rican

Spiks
(New York: Monthly Review Press, 1973)

Subject(s): Short Stories; City Life
Age range(s): Grades 10-Adult
Time period(s): Indeterminate
Locale(s): New York, New York (South Bronx and Spanish Harlem)

Summary: A collection of seven short stories by a well-known Puerto Rican writer. Although the author spent most of his life in the U.S. these stories about the hostile atmosphere of New York City were written in Spanish. In four of the stories a woman is the main protagonist.

About this book: Soto writes in Spanish and only a couple of his novels have been translated to English. This collection is translated by Victoria Ortiz.

Other books by the same author:
Puerto Rico: La Nueva Vida/The New Life, 1966
Hot Land, Cold Season, 1973

Other books you might like:

Jack Agueros, *Dominoes and Other Stories from the Puerto Rican*, 1993
   This collection of short stories describes life in New York City.

Faythe Turner, *Puerto Rican Writers at Home in the U.S.A.: An Anthology*, 1991
   This collection of short stories portrays life in the U.S.

Jesus Colon, *A Puerto Rican in New York and Other Sketches*, 1961
   These short stories are about living in New York in the 1940s.

Roberto Santiago, *Boricuas: Influential Puerto Rican Writers—an Anthology*, 1995
   This anthology of essays, fiction, poetry, monologues, and screenplays is by controversial writers from the nineteenth and twentieth centuries.

Judith Ortiz Cofer, *An Island Like You: Stories of the Barrio*, 1995
   Twelve stories, set in a barrio of New Jersey, examine the lives of Puerto Rican teenagers who deal with friendship, family, romance, and school.

Esmeralda Santiago, *When I Was Puerto Rican*, 1993
   This autobiographical story portrays growing up in Puerto Rico and the U.S.

839

ILAN STAVANS, Mexican Jewish

The One-Handed Pianist and Other Stories
(Albuquerque, NM: University of New Mexico Press, 1996)

Subject(s): Short Stories; Identity
Age range(s): Grades 10-Adult
Time period(s): Indeterminate
Locale(s): New York, New York; Mexico City, Mexico

Summary: Nine short stories, most previously published in journals, explore memory, culture, language, and Judaism in the Latino world. Stavans presents a metaphysical perspective of the world as he creates his characters, some in the tradition of magic realism. In the title story "The One-Handed Pianist" a woman loses movement in her left side and that makes her piano playing one-sided, in "The Death of Yankos" a man shrinks until he disappears.

Where it's reviewed:
Library Journal, February 15, 1996, page 178
Publishers Weekly, January 1, 1996, page 59
New York Times Book Review, May 5, 1996, page 22

Other books by the same author:
Growing Up Latino: Memoirs and Stories, 1993
Tropical Synagogues: Short Stories, 1994
Antiheroes: Mexico y Su Novela Policial, 1993
Bandido: Oscar "Zeta" Acosta and the Chicano Experience, 1995

Other books you might like:
Marjorie Agosin, *Happiness: Stories*, 1993
   This collection of stories by a Chilean American writer addresses reality, history, feminism, identity, and culture with an ironic and often bizarre view.

Fernando Alegria, *Paradise Lost or Gained? The Literature of Hispanic Exile*, 1990
   A collection of literature by Latino writers addresses the experience of exile and alienation through stories, poems, and essays.

Victor Perera, *Rites: A Guatemalan Boyhood*, 1986
   Autobiographical narratives of the boyhood of a Sephardic Jew who immigrates from Jerusalem to Guatemala into a growing Jewish population in Guatemala.

Kathleen Alcala, *Mrs. Vargas and the Dead Naturalist*, 1992
   Short stories, capturing the essence of magical realism, examine the lives of Mexican women in this book of wonders.

C.M. Mayo, *Sky over el Nido: Stories*, 1995
   In these intriguing stories about contemporary cosmopolitan life, wealthy characters effortlessly fly around the world shopping and picking up a homeless AIDS infected man.

840

JAN ROMERO STEVENS, Mexican American
JEANNE ARNOLD, Illustrator

Carlos and the Cornfield: Story = Carlos y la Milpa de Maiz: Cuento
(Flagstaff, AZ: Northland Publishers, 1995)

Subject(s): Farm Life; Money; Responsibility
Age range(s): Grades K-2
Major character(s): Carlos, Child, Mexican
Time period(s): Indeterminate Past
Locale(s): New Mexico (rural New Mexico)

Summary: A young boy learns to make things right after realizing his mistake in planting corn. He wants to earn money with his corn, but doesn't follow the instructions of his father, and only after having to return the money he earned does he complete the job correctly.

About this book: Bilingual format; Translated by Patricia Hinton Davison.

Where it's reviewed:
Booklist, September 1, 1995, page 80
School Library Journal, September, 1995, page 186

Other books by the same author:
Carlos and the Squash Plant = Carlos y la Planta de Calabaza, 1993

Other books you might like:
Omar Castaneda, *Abuela's Weave*, 1993
   A girl and her grandmother make tapestries for an outdoor market.

Pat Mora, *A Birthday Basket for Tia*, 1992
   Cecilia and her cat select a birthday present for a great aunt.

Pat Mora, *Listen to the Desert/Oye al Desierto*, 1994
   Sounds of the desert in English and Spanish.

Manlio Argueta, *Magic Dogs of the Volcanoes = Los Perros Magicos de los Volcanes*, 1990
   Ancient volcanoes protect the magic dogs who live on the volcanoes in El Salvador.

Maria Garcia, *The Adventures of Connie and Diego = Las Aventuras de Connie y Diego*, 1986

Connie and Diego are different from other people in the Land of Plenty. They have many colors all over their bodies.

Lucia M. Gonzalez, *The Bossy Gallito*, 1994

A bossy little rooster gets his beak dirty pecking some corn while on his way to his uncle's wedding.

841

JAN ROMERO STEVENS, Mexican American
JEANNE ARNOLD, Illustrator

Carlos and the Squash Plant/Carlos y la Planta de Calabaza

(Flagstaff, AZ : Northland, 1993)

Subject(s): Cleanliness; Farm Life
Age range(s): Grades 1-2
Major character(s): Carlos, Child, Mexican
Time period(s): Indeterminate Past
Locale(s): New Mexico (rural northern New Mexico)

Summary: Carlos lives on a farm in northern New Mexico. He ignores his mother's warnings about what will happen if he does not bathe. He awakens one morning to find a squash growing out of his ear.

About this book: This story in bilingual format includes a recipe for Calabacitas, a squash dish.

Other books you might like:
Omar Castaneda, *Abuela's Weave*, 1993

A girl and her grandmother make tapestries for an outdoor market.

Pat Mora, *A Birthday Basket for Tia*, 1992

Cecilia and her cat select a birthday present for a great aunt.

Pat Mora, *Listen to the Desert/Oye al Desierto*, 1994

The sounds of the desert are described in both English and Spanish languages.

Manlio Argueta, *Magic Dogs of the Volcanoes = Los Perros Magicos de los Volcanes*, 1990

Ancient volcanoes protect the magic dogs who live on the volcanoes in El Salvador.

Carmen Lomas Garza, *Family Pictures = Cuadros de Familia*, 1994

Carmen Lomas Garza, a well-known Chicana artist presents beautiful and detailed paintings of her growing up years in a Texas border town.

Richard Garcia, *My Aunt Otilia's Spirits = Los Espiritus de Mi Tia Otilia*, 1978

Aunt Otilia's visits bring strange sounds and vibrations that never bother the little boy but one night.

842

VIRGIL SUAREZ, Cuban American

The Cutter: A Novel

(New York: Ballantine Books, 1991)

Subject(s): Communism; Oppression; Grandparents

Age range(s): Grades 10-Adult
Major character(s): Julian Campos, Worker, Refugee, Cuban
Time period(s): 1970s
Locale(s): Havana, Cuba

Summary: Julian Campos is forced by the Cuban Communist regime to work as a cutter in the muddy sugarcane fields. His parents managed to escape to the U.S. five years earlier, but he had to stay behind with his grandmother. Among his many problems are the romantic interests of two women, harassment by police and getting accepted into a group with an escape plan. Even though he knows machetes and stones are no match for machine guns, Julian must risk his life in order to save it.

Where it's reviewed:
Hudson Review, Spring 1992, page 144
Publishers Weekly, January 4, 1991, page 67

Other books by the same author:
Iguana Dreams: New Latino Fiction, 1992
Paper Dance: 55 Latino Poets, 1995
Havana Thursdays: A Novel, 1995
Latin Jazz, 1989
Welcome to the Oasis and Other Stories, 1995

Other books you might like:
Margarita Engle, *Singing to Cuba*, 1993

A California woman leaves her husband and children to search for information about family members who disappeared during the Castro revolution.

Graciela Limon, *In Search of Bernabe*, 1993

A novel about a mother's search for her son during civil war in El Salvador.

Demetria Martinez, *Mother Tongue*, 1994

Story of a young Chicana who falls in love with a Salvadoran refugee who is tortured as a counter-insurgent in his country.

Carmen C. Esteves, *Green Cane and Juicy Flotsam: Short Stories by Caribbean Women*, 1991

In this collection of short stories, Caribbean women writers examine questions of race, power, colonialism, poverty, and identity.

Carole Fernandez, *Sleep of the Innocents*, 1991

This novel chronicles the lives of women living in a fictional Central American country torn by civil war.

Margarita Engle, *Skywriting*, 1995

Carmen Peregrin's half-brother attempts to escape from Cuba by raft and ends up being arrested and imprisoned.

Reinaldo Arenas, *The Palace of the White Skunks*, 1990

This is the story of Fortunato, a boy raised in poverty by his grandparents, his life and his death as he grows up during the Cuban Revolution.

843

VIRGIL SUAREZ, Cuban American

Havana Thursdays: A Novel

(Houston, TX: Arte Publico Press, 1995)

Subject(s): Family Relations; Women; Traditions
Age range(s): Grades 10-Adult

Major character(s): Laura Torres, Housewife, Widow(er), Cuban
Time period(s): 1990s
Locale(s): Miami, Florida

Summary: This is the story of two sisters, their daughters, and how they represent two different manners of dealing with the changes encountered through immigration from a Latino culture. After Laura becomes widowed, her and Maura's family come together every Thursday for family dinners, and also to redefine their relationships, with each other and with their daughters. The author shows how Latino culture is preserved by the women of the family.

Where it's reviewed:
Hispanic, October 1995, page 80

Other books by the same author:
Iguana Dreams: New Latino Fiction, 1992
The Cutter: A Novel, 1991
Latin Jazz, 1989
Welcome to the Oasis and Other Stories, 1992

Other books you might like:
Oscar Hijuelos, *The Fourteen Sisters of Emilio Montez O'Brien: A Novel*, 1993
  An intergenerational saga, this novel follows the lives of Mariela Montez, Cuban, and her Irish husband Nelson O'Brien who move to Cobbleton, Pennsylvania at the turn of the century.
Cristina Garcia, *Dreaming in Cuban, A Novel*, 1992
  This novel interweaves the stories of three generations of Cuban women and their different responses to the Cuban revolution.
Rolando Hinojosa, *Becky and Her Friends*, 1990
  Narrated by many of her friends, this novel focuses on the strong-willed Becky Escobar, a modern, upwardly-mobile woman who at age thirty-five decides to divorce her husband.
Julia Alvarez, *How the Garcia Girls Lost Their Accents*, 1991
  This episodic novel is about a family, the father, mother, and four daughters, their move to the U.S., and the gradual Americanization of the daughters.
Jose Yglesias, *Tristan and the Hispanics*, 1989
  A Yale student, the son of a Cuban-born screenwriter and a WASP mother, clashes with his Cuban extended family as he makes the funeral arrangements for his paternal grandfather.
Junot Diaz, *Drown, Stories*, 1996
  This collection of ten short stories describes young Latino men in transformation while learning to define their American identity.
Achy Obejas, *Memory Mambo: A Novel*, 1996
  A twenty-something lesbian hides her sexuality from her Cuban American family until her relationship with her lover ends violently and she comes to appreciate her heritage and her family.

844

VIRGIL SUAREZ, Cuban American

Welcome to the Oasis and Other Stories
(Houston: Arte Publico Press, 1992)

Subject(s): Short Stories; Cultural Identity; Biculturalism
Age range(s): Grades 8-Adult
Time period(s): 1980s
Locale(s): United States

Summary: In this collection, a novella and five stories, Suarez creates a new generation of young Latino characters who struggle to integrate into the American culture while maintaining their heritage. This original and vibrant collection brings a fresh perspective to our multicultural environment. The characters experience culture clash, linguistic confusion, and continue to search for the American Dream.

Where it's reviewed:
Kirkus Reviews,
The Philadelphia Inquirer,

Awards the book has won:
New York Public Library's Books for the Teen Age, 1992

Other books by the same author:
Iguana Dreams: New Latino Fiction, 1992
Paper Dance: 55 Latino Poets, 1995
The Cutter: A Novel, 1991
Havana Thursdays: A Novel, 1995
Latin Jazz, 1990

Other books you might like:
Gil C. Alicea, *The Air Down Here: True Tales from a South Bronx Boyhood*, 1995
  These autobiographical stories and essays are about living in the Bronx.
Abraham Rodriguez Jr., *The Boy Without a Flag: Tales of the South Bronx*, 1992
  These stories are about young people growing up Puerto Rican in New York City.
Nicolas Kanellos, *Short Fiction by Hispanic Writers of the United States*, 1993
  This collection of short stories is by Latino writers in the U.S.
Jack Agueros, *Dominoes and Other Stories from the Puerto Rican*, 1993
  The collection of short stories is about growing up in the barrio of New York.
Elias Miguel Munoz, *Crazy Love*, 1989
  An experimental and autobiographical novel about the Cuban American experience.
Achy Obejas, *We Came All the Way from Cuba So You Could Dress Like This? Stories*, 1994
  These seven short stories, set in Chicago, include several about gay men and women, and outcasts, AIDS patients and immigrants in the 1990s.
Pablo La Rosa, *Forbidden Fruit and Other Stories*, 1996
  This collection of short stories whimsically depict the coming of age of a young man in Cuba before the revolution and the marginalization experienced by each of the characters in the U.S.

845

PHYLLIS TASHLIK, Editor

Hispanic, Female, and Young

(Houston: Pinata Books, 1994)

Subject(s): Anthology; Coming of Age; Women
Age range(s): Grades 7-10
Time period(s): 1990s (1994)
Locale(s): New York, New York (Spanish Harlem)

Summary: This anthology is a collection of stories and poems written by teenage girls in a New York public school. They come together to read literature by Latinas and to write their own stories for a class titled ''Las Mujeres Hispanas.'' The results are stories describing their culture, families, and fears, as well as magic and mysticism.

About this book: Stories by published authors are included along with the girls stories.

Where it's reviewed:
Wilson Library Bulletin, April 1995, page 115

Other books you might like:
Judith Ortiz Cofer, *Silent Dancing: A Partial Remembrance of a Puerto Rican Childhood*, 1990
  Puerto Rico and New Jersey are the settings for a narrative portraying a childhood.
Nicholasa Mohr, *El Bronx Remembered: A Novella and Stories*, 1975
  A Puerto Rican remembers growing up in the Bronx.
Nicholasa Mohr, *In Nueva York*, 1977
  A Puerto Rican describes growing up in New York.
Abraham Rodriguez Jr., *The Boy Without a Flag: Tales of the South Bronx*, 1992
  This collection of short stories relates the problems of young Puerto Ricans in the Bronx.
Jack Agueros, *Dominoes and Other Stories from the Puerto Rican*, 1993
  This collection of short stories describes growing up in the barrio of New York.
Judith Ortiz, *An Island Like You: Stories of the Barrio*, 1995
  Twelve stories, set in a barrio of New Jersey,examine the lives of Puerto Rican teenagers who deal with friendship, family, romance, and school

846

CHARLES TATUM, Editor, Mexican American

Mexican American Literature

(Orlando: Harcourt, Brace, Jovanovich, 1990)

Subject(s): Anthology; Short Stories; Folklore
Age range(s): Grades 9-12
Time period(s): Indeterminate Past (1528-1990)
Locale(s): United States (stories take place throughout the West and Southwest)

Summary: This anthology of Mexican American Literature was written for high school classrooms and contains short stories, poems, and drama. The various genres are presented within a historical context, including folktales, oral literature, the Spanish and Mexican periods, and ending with the largest section from 1960 to the present.

About this book: Study questions, historical notes, and writing ideas are also presented.

Other books by the same author:
Handbook of Latin American Popular Culture, 1985
Chicano Literature, 1982
Not Just for Children: The Mexican Comic Book in the Late 1960s and 1970s, 1992
New Chicana/Chicano Writing, 1992

Other books you might like:
Gary Soto, *Pieces of the Heart: New Chicano Fiction*, 1993
  This collection of short stories is by Chicano writers.
Tiffany Ana Lopez, *Growing Up Chicano*, 1993
  These short stories are by Chicano writers.
Carlota Cardenas de Dwyer, *Chicano Voices*, 1975
  This is an important collection of short stories from the Southwest.
Ray Gonzalez, *Currents From the Dancing River: Contemporary Latino Fiction, Nonfiction, and Poetry*, 1994
  This collection of short stories is by Latino writers in the U.S.
Frances R. Aparicio, *Latino Voices*, 1994
  This collection of writings by Latino authors is specially edited for young adult readers.
Ray Gonzalez, *Mirrors Beneath the Earth: Short Fiction by Chicano Writers*, 1992
  This collection of short stories is by Chicano writers.

847

CHARLES TATUM, Editor

New Chicana/Chicano Writing

(Tuscon: University of Arizona Press, 1992)

Subject(s): Short Stories; Anthology
Age range(s): Grades 10-Adult
Time period(s): 1980s
Locale(s): United States

Summary: This collection of poetry and fiction represents the range and vitality of new work by Mexican American writers. Well-known writers, such as Gary Soto, Gloria Anzaldua, and Sandra Cisneros, as well as new writers, are represented.

About this book: Many pieces are written bilingually and translations are not provided.

Where it's reviewed:
Library Journal, May 1, 1992, page 82

Other books by the same author:
Mexican American Literature, 1990
Chicano Literature, 1982

Other books you might like:
Gary Soto, *Pieces of the Heart: New Chicano Fiction*, 1993
  This collection of short stories is by Chicano writers.
Tiffany Ana Lopez, *Growing Up Chicano*, 1993
  These short stories are by Chicano writers.
Carlota Cardenas de Dwyer, *Chicano Voices*, 1975
  This important collection of short stories is from the Southwest.

Ray Gonzalez, *Currents From the Dancing River: Contemporary Latino Fiction, Nonfiction, and Poetry*, 1994

These short stories are by Chicano writers.

Ray Gonzalez, *Mirrors Beneath the Earth: Short Fiction by Chicano Writers*, 1992

This collection of short stories is by Chicano writers.

Rudolfo Anaya, *Cuentos Chicanos: A Short Story Anthology*, 1984

This is a collection of short stories by Chicano writers.

848

SHEILA ORTIZ TAYLOR, Mexican American

Faultline: A Novel

(Tallahassee, FL: The NAIAD Press, Inc, 1982)

Subject(s): Family Relations; Homosexuality/Lesbianism; Humor

Age range(s): Grades 10-Adult

Major character(s): Arden Benbow, Professor, Mother (lesbian), Chicana

Time period(s): 1970s

Locale(s): Los Angeles, California

Summary: This very funny book is about a lesbian mother of six children, her lover/companion, their 300 rabbits, and a six foot tall Black drag queen baby sitter. Presented in a multi-voiced, very relaxed narration, this family account of growing up on the San Andreas Fault is very California.

Other books by the same author:
Southbound: The Sequel to Faultline, 1990
Slow Dancing at Miss Polly's, 1989
Spring Forward/Fall Back, 1985

Other books you might like:
Ibis Gomez-Vega, *Send My Roots Rain*, 1991
Carole goes to a small Texas town to paint murals on church walls and falls in love with a mysterious woman.

Jaime Manrique, *Latin Moon in Manhattan*, 1992
This novel presents bizarre characters, plots and sub-plots, and a vivid depiction of Columbian American culture in Little Colombia Jackson Heights from the perspective of a gay poet.

Elias Miguel Munoz, *The Greatest Performance*, 1991
A poetic novel of exile, this tale has two soul-mates recount to each other their stories of living on the margins of family, country, and sexual identity.

Terri de la Pena, *Margins*, 1992
A young lesbian writer confronts her future and her family about her sexuality in this story.

Terri de la Pena, *Latin Satins*, 1994
This story that chronicles the rise of a Chicana lesbian singing group in the LA area.

Achy Obejas, *We Came All The Way from Cuba So You Could Dress Like This? Stories*, 1994
Seven short stories set in Chicago, this collection includes several about gay men and women, outcasts, AIDS patients and immigrants in the 1990s.

Emma Perez, *Gulf Dreams*, 1996
A creative series of essays, short vignettes, and psychoanalytic discourses, these are about growing up lesbian in Latino culture.

849

SHEILA ORTIZ TAYLOR, Mexican American

Southbound: The Sequel to Faultline

(Tallahassee, FL: Niad Press, 1990)

Subject(s): Family Relations; Homosexuality/Lesbianism; Humor

Age range(s): Grades 10-Adult

Major character(s): Arden Benbow, Professor, Mother (lesbian)

Time period(s): 1990s

Locale(s): Los Angeles, California

Summary: Arden Benbow, who loses her UCLA professorship, searches for employment while trying to retain custody of her children. She accepts a job at a college in Florida and sets out across the country with her six kids, her ballet dancer/live-in babysitter, and her lover Alice. This humorous lesbian novel follows Arden as she sets out across the country in a hearse.

About this book: A sequel to *Faultline*.

Other books by the same author:
Faultline: A Novel, 1982
Slow Dancing at Miss Polly's, 1989
Spring Forward/Fall Back, 1985

Other books you might like:
Ibis Gomez-Vega, *Send My Roots Rain*, 1991
Carole goes to a small Texas town to paint murals on Church walls and falls in love with a mysterious woman.

Jaime Manrique, *Latin Moon in Manhattan*, 1992
This novel presents bizarre characters, plots and sub-plots, and a vivid depiction of Columbian American culture in Little Colombia, Jackson Heights from the perspective of a gay poet.

Elias Miguel Munoz, *The Greatest Performance*, 1991
Two soul-mates recount to each oher their stories of living on the margins of family, country, and sexual identity in this poetic novel of exile.

Terri de la Pena, *Margins*, 1992
This is the story of a young lesbian writer who confronts her future and her family about her sexuality.

Terri de la Pena, *Latin Satins*, 1994
The rise of a Chicana lesbian singing group in the LA area is chronicled in this story.

Achy Obejas, *We Came All the Way from Cuba So You Could Dress Like This? Stories*, 1994
These seven short stories, set in Chicago, include several about gay men and women, outcasts, AIDS patients and immigrants in the 1990s.

850

PIRI THOMAS, Puerto Rican

Down These Mean Streets

(New York: Vintage Books, 1991)

Subject(s): Drugs; Prisoners and Prisons; Race Relations

Age range(s): Grades 10-Adult

Major character(s): Piri Thomas, Addict, Drug Dealer, Puerto Rican
Time period(s): 1940s; 1950s (1945-1956)
Locale(s): New York, New York (Spanish Harlem)

Summary: This confessional autobiography describes life in Spanish Harlem during the 1940s and 1950s. Thomas describes his initiation into street life, gangs, violence, and use of drugs. His relationship with his father is also a major issue in his life.

About this book: This is a famous novel, first published in 1967, and made into a movie.

Other books by the same author:
Stories from El Barrio, 1978
Seven Long Times, 1975 (re-published in 1994)
Savior, Savior, Hold My Hand, 1972

Other books you might like:
Lefty Barreto, *Nobody's Hero: A Puerto Rican Story*, 1976
    This is an autobiographical novel about coming of age in the New York Barrio.
Nicholasa Mohr, *Nilda: A Novel*, 1973
    This story is about the life of a Puerto Rican girl growing up in the 1940's in the New York Barrio.
Richard Ruiz, *The Hungry American*, 1978
    This story tells the success of a Puerto Rican young man who leaves the Barrio.
Edwin Torres, *Carlito's Way*, 1976
    This is the story of the underworld life of a Puerto Rican criminal.
Jack Agueros, *Dominoes and Other Stories From the Puerto Rican*, 1993
    These stories are about growing up Puerto Rican in New York City.
Victor Rodriguez, *Eldorado in East Harlem*, 1992
    Streetwise, seventeen-year-old Rene gets involved with a gang committing petty crimes and running drugs.
Abraham Rodriguez Jr., *The Boy Without a Flag: Tales of the South Bronx*, 1992
    These stories describe growing up Puerto Rican in New York City.

851

LEYLA TORRES

Saturday Sancocho

(New York: Farrar, Straus, Giroux, 1995)

Subject(s): Food; Grandparents; Traditions
Age range(s): Grades K-2
Major character(s): Maria Lili, Child (little girl)
Time period(s): Indeterminate Past
Locale(s): Colombia

Summary: Every Saturday, Maria Lili helps her grandparents make their traditional chicken sancocho. This Saturday, they discover that there is nothing in the house except eggs. But Mama Ana has a plan. Taking the eggs, Mama Ana and Maria Lili travel to the market.

About this book: The book includes the recipe.

Where it's reviewed:
Publishers Weekly, April 24, 1995, page 71

Other books by the same author:
Subway Sparrow, 1993

Other books you might like:
Omar Castaneda, *Abuela's Weave*, 1993
    A young girl and her grandmother sell their woven fabrics at a market in Guatemala.
Juanita Havill, *Treasure Nap*, 1992
    Alicia hears the story of Rita, who visits her grandfather in the mountains of Mexico, and learns to make wooden birdcages.
Gary Soto, *Too Many Tamales*, 1993
    Maria helps her mother make tamales for their Christmas Eve dinner, and in the process loses something important.
Gary Soto, *Chato's Kitchen*, 1995
    Chato, a low-rider cat, plans a dinner and invites some nice mice, but they outwit him.
Carmen Lomas Garza, *Family Pictures = Cuadros de Familia*, 1990
    Carmen Lomas Garza, a well known Chicana artist presents beautiful and detailed paintings of her growing up in a Texas border town.
Gina Macaluso Rodriguez, *Green Corn Tamales = Tamales de Elote*, 1994
    A Latino family makes green corn tamales every year, but there's a twist to this tale.

852

OMAR TORRES, Cuban American

Fallen Angels Sing

(Houston: Arte Publico Press, 1991)

Subject(s): Politics; Angels; Emigration and Immigration
Age range(s): Grades 10-Adult
Major character(s): Miguel Saavedra, Writer (poet), Cuban
Time period(s): 1960s; 1970s
Locale(s): New York, New York (parts of the novel take place in Miami)

Summary: When Miguel Saavedra moves to New York, he is caught up in a web of plots spun by pro- and anti- Castro agents. Soon he is involved in planning the assassination of Fidel Castro. His journey leads him from place to place in a surrealistic flow of days. The barriers between dream and reality begin to disappear, and Miguel must confront angels and archangels, good and evil.

About this book: This was originally published in Spanish as, *Apenas un Bolero*.

Where it's reviewed:
American Book Review, February-March 1994, page 23

Other books by the same author:
Al Partir, 1986
Apenas un Bolero: Novela, 1981
De Nunca a Siempre, 1981

Other books you might like:
Enrique A. Laguerre, *The Labyrinth*, 1984
    This is the story of a Puerto Rican man in New York City

who goes to night school to earn a law degree and accidentally stumbles into the services of a Caribbean dictator.

Jaime Manrique, *Latin Moon in Manhattan*, 1992
This novel presents bizarre characters, plots and sub-plots, and a vivid depiction of Columbian American culture in Little Colombia Jackson Heights.

Louie Garcia Robinson, *The Devil, Delfina Varela, and the Used Chevy*, 1993
This humorous political novel is about unique characters living in the Mission District of San Francisco.

Emilio Diaz Valcarcel, *Hot Soles in Harlem*, 1993
This work presents a look at New York City through the eyes of a recent Puerto Rican arrival.

Roberto Fernandez, *Holy Radishes*, 1995
This satirical novel depicts the Cuban American community in Florida.

Pablo Medina, *The Marks of Birth*, 1994
The descendant of a well-to-do Cuban family is forced to flee the island due to political turmoil and lives a frustrated, self-imposed exiled life.

853

ESTELA PORTILLO TRAMBLEY, Mexican American

Rain of Scorpions and Other Stories
(Tempe, AZ: Bilingual Press/Editorial Bilingue, 1993)

Series: Clasicos Chicanos
Subject(s): Women; Short Stories; Family Relations
Age range(s): Grades 10-Adult
Time period(s): 1950s
Locale(s): Texas

Summary: A novella and eight stories, several previously published in the 1975 edition, are revised for this collection. Many of the stories have feminist themes with the main characters being strong brave women with special gifts. In ''Pay the Criers'' a young wife spends her life waiting on a lazy husband; in ''The Paris Gown'' Clotilde devises a plan for escaping an arranged marriage; and in ''Rain of Scorpions,'' revised from its 1975 version and a sort-of-protest work, a community seeks a home outside of Smeltertown, an industrial settlement created by Anglo society.

Other books by the same author:
Trini, 1986
Sor Juana and Other Plays, 1983

Other books you might like:
Sandra Cisneros, *Woman Hollering Creek and Other Stories*, 1991
This collection of short stories about women takes place in Texas and the border area.

John Rechy, *The Miraculous Day of Amalia Gomez: A Novel*, 1991
This story examines poverty, gang warfare, border crossings, and visions of salvation while following one day in the life of a Mexican-American woman.

Alma Luz Villanueva, *Weeping Woman: La Llorona and Other Stories*, 1994
This collection examines women who live in a world torn apart by violence, racism, and sexism.

Graciela Limon, *The Memories of Ana Calderon: A Novel*, 1994
Ana Calderon begins life in rural southern Mexico, but the burdens of poverty, dreams of a better life, and circumstance lead her family to the United States.

Nash Candelaria, *Leonor Park*, 1991
This novel about land and greed in New Mexico on the eve of the Great Depression, recounts the battle between a brother and sister over a father's legacy, a piece of land alongside the Rio Grande.

Ana Castillo, *Loverboys, Stories*, 1996
Stories that range from one-page vignettes to longer narrations about females.

854

ESTELA PORTILLO TRAMBLEY, Mexican American

Trini
(Tempe, AZ: Bilingual Press, 1986)

Subject(s): Emigration and Immigration; Indians of Central America; Magic
Age range(s): Grades 10-Adult
Major character(s): Trini, Teenager (undocumented immigrant), Mother, Indian (Tarahumara)
Time period(s): 1950s
Locale(s): El Paso, Texas; Mexico

Summary: Trini, a Tarahumara woman whose indigenous life is wondrous and magical, crosses the border as an undocumented immigrant in order to give birth to her child in the United States. Experiencing numerous tragedies and betrayals, she ultimately combines her ability to perceive the magical qualities of life with realism and self-sufficiency.

Other books by the same author:
Rain of Scorpions and Other Stories, 1993
Sor Juana and Other Plays, 1983

Other books you might like:
Omar Castaneda, *Imagining Isabel*, 1994
Isabel, a teenager in Guatemala, recently married, wants to become a teacher.

Sandra Cisneros, *Woman Hollering Creek and Other Stories*, 1991
Collection of short stories about women in Texas and the border area.

John Rechy, *The Miraculous Day of Amalia Gomez: A Novel*, 1991
This story examines poverty, gang warfare, border crossings, and visions of salvation while following one day in the life of a Mexican-American woman.

Genaro Gonzalez, *Rainbow's End*, 1988
An adventure novel that presents border crossings, confrontations with a magician, and drug smuggling that are part of the life of the Cavazos family in Texas.

Alba Ambert, *A Perfect Silence*, 1995
Abused as a child and as an adult, a Puerto Rican woman in the South Bronx tries to break the cycle of poverty and oppression.

Alma Luz Villanueva, *Weeping Woman: La Llorona and Other Stories*, 1994

A collection of stories that examine women who live in a world torn apart by violence, racism, and sexism.

Graciela Limon, *The Memories of Ana Calderon: A Novel*, 1994

Ana Calderon begins life in rural southern Mexico, but the burdens of poverty, dreams of a better life and circumstance lead her family to the U.S.

855

ELIZABETH BORTON DE TREVINO, Mexican

El Guero: A True Adventure Story

(New York: Farrar, Straus, Giroux, 1989)

Subject(s): Adventure and Adventurers; Revolution
Age range(s): Grades 5-8
Major character(s): El Guero, Child (boy), Mexican
Time period(s): 1870s
Locale(s): Ensenada, Mexico

Summary: El Guero — the Blond One — son of a respected judge, never suspects that his comfortable life will change. But when political turmoil (Portifirio Diaz becomes President) sends his family into exile, El Guero's life changes dramatically. He and his family encounter many adventures as they flee to Baja California. After they settle he must still confront danger, and use his courage to save his father.

About this book: Bilingual format; stories translated by Thelma Campbell Nelson.

Where it's reviewed:
Horn Book Magazine, September-October 1989, page 624
Journal of Reading, September 1993, page 78
Publishers Weekly, June 30, 1989, page 105
Wilson Library Bulletin , May 1990, page S3

Other books by the same author:
I, Juan de Pareja, 1965
The Hearthstone of My Heart, 1977
The House on Bitterness Street, 1970
Leona: A Love Story, 1994

Other books you might like:
Victor Villasenor, *Walking Stars: Stories of Magic and Power*, 1994
Stories about the author's parents and grandparents' lives in Mexico.
Omar Castaneda, *Among the Volcanoes*, 1991
The story of sixteen year old Isabel, in Guatemala, who must quit school to take care of her ill mother.
Omar Castaneda, *Imagining Isabel*, 1994
A sequel to *Among the Volcanoes*, where Isabel gets married, but still wants to become a school teacher.
Rudolfo Anaya, *The Anaya Reader*, 1995
A collection of short stories, poetry, essays, plays, and poems, published during the previous twenty-five years, representative of the New Mexico writer.
Rudolfo Anaya, *Bless Me, Ultima*, 1972
A young boy's beliefs are challenged as he grows up in a small town in New Mexico.
Angelico Chavez, *The Short Stories of Fray Angelico Chavez*, 1987

Collection of short stories by an early New Mexico writer and folklorist, edited by Genaro M. Padilla.

Patricia Preciado Martin, *Days of Plenty, Days of Want*, 1988
A collection of stories where the past and the present meet, and Mexican heritage is in jeopardy of being wiped out.

856

ELIZABETH BORTON DE TREVINO, Mexican

I, Juan de Pareja

(New York: Farrar, Straus, and Giroux, 1965)

Subject(s): Artists and Art; Slavery
Age range(s): Grades 4-7
Major character(s): Juan de Pareja, Slave, Spanish
Time period(s): 17th century
Locale(s): Spain

Summary: Depicting both the beauty and the cruelty of the time and place, this novel presents the story of Juan, who is born a slave and becomes the devoted servant, and friend of Diego Velazquez, the famous painter. Detailed and historically accurate, the novel examines Spanish court life, class relations, and artistic expression. It advocates the virtues of friendship and devotion and encourages the development of an individual's talents.

About this book: A Spanish edition of this book was published in 1995 and was translated by Enrique R. Trevino Borton.

Where it's reviewed:
Times Educational Supplement, April 1, 1988, page 22
Horn Book Magazine, January-February 1995, page 80

Awards the book has won:
John Newbery Medal, 1966

Other books by the same author:
A Carpet of Flowers = Una Alfombra de Flores, 1975
El Guero: A True Adventure Story, 1989
The Hearthstone of My Heart, 1977
The House on Bitterness Street, 1970

Other books you might like:
Victor Villasenor, *Walking Stars: Stories of Magic and Power*, 1994
Stories about the author's parents' and grandparents' lives in Mexcio.
Gloria Duran, *Malinche: Slave Princess of Cortez*, 1993
Malinali, born an Aztec princess and sold to the conqueror Cortez, is an ambiguous and controversial figure in Mexican history and this is her story.
Tina Juarez, *Call No Man Master*, 1995
This historical novel is about a young woman of mixed heritage, Spanish and Indian, and her participation in the events that lead to Mexico's independence from Spain.
Montserrat Fontes, *Dreams of the Centaur*, 1995
Alejo Durcal, son of a slain ranch owner, tries to avenge his father's death, during the period in history when the Yaqui Indians were badly mistreated in Mexico.
Jose Barreiro, *The Indian Chronicles*, 1993
Adopted by Christopher Columbus, Diego Colon, a Taino boy, keeps a journal where he describes events in his life from 1532-1535 as he narrates the Indian's discovery of the Europeans.

857

ELIZABETH BORTON DE TREVINO, Mexican

Leona: A Love Story

(New York: Farrar Straus Giroux, 1994)

Subject(s): Romance; Social Classes; War
Age range(s): Grades 6-9
Major character(s): Leona Vicario, 16-Year-Old (girl), Criolla (Mexican/Spanish heritage); Andres Quintana Roo, Lawyer (statesman and orator)
Time period(s): 1800s (1808-1812)
Locale(s): Mexico (part of the novel takes in Quintano Roo)

Summary: This historical novel is about Mexico's war for independence and is based on the true story of sixteen-year-old Leona Vicario, who fights to live and love as she chooses. Wealthy and well educated, Leona nevertheless sees the injustice of the Spanish government. She meets Andres, a Mexican patriot, and they fall in love despite class differences. She realizes she must fight for the freedom of Mexico.

Where it's reviewed:
Publishers Weekly, June 27, 1994, page 78

Other books by the same author:
El Guero: A True Adventure Story, 1989
I, Juan de Pareja, 1965

Other books you might like:
Diane Gonzales Bertrand, *Sweet Fifteen*, 1995
    A girl celebrates her fifteenth birthday and tries to deal with her father's death.
Victor Villasenor, *Walking Stars: Stories of Magic and Power*, 1994
    These stories are about the author's parents and grandparents in Mexcio.
Omar Castaneda, *Among the Volcanoes*, 1991
    This story is about a sixteen-year-old Isabel, in Guatemala, who must quit school to take care of her ill mother.
Omar Cantaneda, *Imagining Isabel*, 1994
    A sequel to *Among the Volcanoes*, where Isabel gets married, but still wants to become a school teacher.
Irene Beltran Hernandez, *Heartbeat, Drumbeat*, 1992
    Morgana Cruz seeks her cultural identity while caught between the worlds of her Navajo mother and her Mexican father.
Irene Beltran Hernandez, *Across the Great River*, 1989
    This novel chronicles the life of illegal young immigrant, Kata, who must deal with violence, the authorities, a folk healer and labor smugglers.

858

JESUS SALVADOR TREVINO, Mexican American

The Fabulus Sinkhole and Other Stories

(Houston, TX: Arte Publico Press, 1995)

Subject(s): Short Stories; Humor; Satire
Age range(s): Grades 9-Adult
Time period(s): 1990s (1995)
Locale(s): Arroyo Grande, Texas

Summary: This is a collection of interrelated short stories that take place in a fictional town, Arroyo Grande, in Texas. This first story collection by Trevino, a screenwriter and director, is an entertaining creation of Mexican and Chicano characters, from an aging mariachi band to a gang of lowrider zombies. From the ''The Fabulous Sinkhole'' which gives birth to many of the elements and characters appearing in the later stories, to ''The Great Pyramid of Aztlan'' a tale about a virtual Chicano city in the Arizona desert, these stories present a comical satirical vision of the barrios of Chicanos.

Where it's reviewed:
Hispanic, September 1995, page 72

Other books by the same author:
Birthwrite: Growing Up Hispanic, 1989 (videorecording)
Yo Soy Chicano, 1972 (videorecording)
The Art of Resistance, 1994 (videorecording)

Other books you might like:
Leo Romero, *Rita and Los Angeles*, 1995
    A cast of complex characters who grow and evolve, and learn about being outsiders in an alien and hostile world populate these stories.
Alberto Alvaro Rios, *Pig Cookies and Other Stories*, 1995
    This set of interlocking stories explores the inhabitants of a small Mexican village.
Nash Candelaria, *The Day the Cisco Kid Shot John Wayne*, 1988
    These twelve humorous stories portray Chicano-Anglo interrelations and conflicts.
Alberto Alvaro Rios, *The Iguana Killer: Twelve Stories of the Heart*, 1984
    These are short stories of ordinary life in a book of secrets, several of which are about Mexican and Chicano young boys confronting big questions.
Americo Paredes, *The Hammon and the Beans and Other Stories*, 1994
    Set in the southern Texas border region, this collection of short stories explores the cultural conflict that has dominated that area since the U.S.-Mexican War.
Jose Antonio Burciaga, *Spilling the Beans: Loteria Chicana*, 1995
    This series of essays, many humorous, recount experiences from the author's childhood in Texas.
Lionel G. Garcia, *I Can Hear the Cowbells Ring*, 1994
    With humour and nostalgia, this collection of delightful autobiographical vignettes reconstruct life in a small rural town of southern Texas.
David Rice, *Give the Pig a Chance and Other Stories*, 1996
    This collection of stories is about growing up in a bicultural environment in a small town on the Texas-Mexico border.

859

CARLA TRUJILLO, Editor, Mexican American

Chicana Lesbians: The Girls Our Mothers Warned Us About

(Berkeley, CA: Third Woman Press, 1991)

Subject(s): Homosexuality/Lesbianism; Poetry; Sexuality

Age range(s): Grades 10-Adult
Time period(s): 1980s
Locale(s): United States

Summary: This diverse collection of short stories, poetry, and prose by Chicana lesbians explores, among other topics, the intricacies and specifics of culture, family, mixed-race relationships, the body, and identity. The book is divided into such sections as "The Life," "The Desire," "The Color," and "The Struggle." Writers such as Cherrie Moraga, Terri de la Pena, Emma Perez, Ana Castillo, and Gloria Anzaldua examine what it means to rebel against heterosexuality and to claim one's own sexuality.

About this book: Introduction by Carla Trujillo.

Where it's reviewed:
Signs, Summer, 1993, page 956

Other books you might like:

Juanita Ramos, *Companeras: Latina Lesbians: An Anthology*, 1987
   This anthology includes the writings of Puerto Ricans, Cubans, Chileans, Chicana Colombians, and other Latina lesbians of different nationalities and with differenct life experiences.
Cherrie Moraga, *Loving in the War Years*, 1983
   In this autobiography a Chicana lesbian writer recounts her life growing up in California.
Terri de la Pena, *Margins*, 1992
   A young lesbian writer confronts her future and her family about her sexuality in this story.
Norma Alarcon, *The Sexuality of Latinas*, 1993
   This collection of poems, short stories, and prose examine the often hidden, often subverted, sexuality of Latinas.
Cherrie Moraga, *The Last Generation*, 1993
   Prose and poetry by a much admired Chicana writer, this collection is written as a prayer for the passing of a culture and the triumph of colonialism.
Emma Perez, *Gulf Dreams*, 1996
   A creative series of essays, short vignettes, and psychoanalytic discourses, these are about growing up lesbian in Latino culture.

860

FAYTHE TURNER, Editor

Puerto Rican Writers at Home in the U.S.A.: An Anthology

(Seattle, WA: Open Hand Publishing Inc., 1991)

Subject(s): Anthology; Short Stories; Biculturalism
Age range(s): Grades 10-Adult
Time period(s): 20th century (1978-1991)
Locale(s): New York, New York; Puerto Rico

Summary: This is a collection of Puerto Rican writing, including poetry and short stories, by individuals who were born or who grew up in New York City and who write primarily in English. Many of the writers are well-known today, such as Victor Hernandez Cruz, Miguel Pinero, Nicholasa Mohr, Martin Espada, and Judith Ortiz Cofer, but were not known in the 1970s.

About this book: About a third of this collection is composed of poetry.

Where it's reviewed:
America, July 18, 1992, page 41
Library Journal, May 15, 1991, page 83

Other books you might like:

Gary D. Keller, *Hispanics in the U.S.: An Anthology of Creative Literature. Vol. 2*, 1982
   This collection of short stories and poetry is by Latino authors.
Judith Ortiz Cofer, *Silent Dancing: A Partial Remembrance of a Puerto Rican Childhood*, 1990
   This autobiographical collection of prose, poetry, and short stories describes growing up in Puerto Rico and the U.S.
Jack Agueros, *Dominoes and Other Stories from the Puerto Rican*, 1993
   These short stories depicts life in New York City as a Puerto Rican.
Jesus Colon, *A Puerto Rican in New York and Other Sketches*, 1961
   These short stories describe living in New York in the 1940s.
Roberto Santiago, *Boricuas: Influential Puerto Rican Writers—an Anthology*, 1995
   This anthology of essays, fiction, poetry, monologues, and screenplays exhibits the work of controversial writers from the ninentieth centuries.

861

SABINE ULIBARRI, Mexican American

The Best of Sabine R. Ulibarri: Selected Stories

(Albuquerque, NM: University of New Mexico Press, 1993)

Subject(s): Magic; Supernatural; Folklore
Age range(s): Grades 10-Adult
Time period(s): Indeterminate Past
Locale(s): New Mexico

Summary: This collection of twenty short stories by Sabine R. Ulibarri represents only about one third of the total number of stories he has written to date. Included here are stories considered his most famous and influential works, as well as some yet unpublished stories. His tales are magical, imaginitive, and humorous, blending fantastical and realistic elements to create unexpected wonders. Ulibarri's characters are created with humor and sincerity and are derived from Mexican folk traditions and legends from northern New Mexico. All of the stories are in English and Spanish.

Other books by the same author:
El Condor and Other Stories, 1988
Governor Glu Glu and Other Stories, 1988
Tierra Amarilla: Stories of New Mexico = Cuentos de Nuevo Mexico, 1964
Suenos = Dreams, 1994

Other books you might like:
Rudolfo Anaya, *The Anaya Reader*, 1995
   A collection of short stories, poetry, essays, plays, and

poems, published in the previous twenty-five years, representative of the New Mexico writer.

Rudolfo Anaya, *Bless Me, Ultima*, 1972
   A young boy's beliefs are challenged as he grows up in a small town in New Mexico.

Angelico Chavez, *The Short Stories of Fray Angelico Chavez*, 1987
   Collection of short stories by an early New Mexico writer and folklorist, edited by Genaro M. Padilla.

Kathleen Alcala, *Mrs. Vargas and the Dead Naturalist*, 1992
   Short stories, capturing the essence of magical realism, examine the lives of Mexican women in this book of wonders.

Alberto Alvaro Rios, *Pig Cookies and Other Stories*, 1995
   A collection of interrelated short stories set earlier in this century in a small village in northern Mexico.

Rudolfo Anaya, *Tierra: Contemporary Short Fiction of New Mexico*, 1989
   Collection by New Mexico writers who believe that the vast space of earth and sky in New Mexico dictates the rhythm of the people.

862

SABINE ULIBARRI, Mexican American

El Condor and Other Stories
(Houston, TX: Arte Publico Press, 1989)

Subject(s): Short Stories; Supernatural; Magic
Age range(s): Grades 10-Adult
Time period(s): Indeterminate Past
Locale(s): New Mexico

Summary: A collection of eleven romantic stories for adults that presents a world of gypsies, witches, ghosts, and the supernatural. Traditional New Mexican lore meets the modern world of technology and urbanization to explore the mysteries of humans and nature. The title story is about a retired university professor who becomes an urban guerilla to help the oppressed indigenous of Ecuador.

About this book: All stories are in English and Spanish.

Where it's reviewed:
Review of Contemporary Fiction, Summer, 1991, page 248

Other books by the same author:
The Best of Sabine Ulibarri: Selected Stories, 1993
Tierra Amarilla: Stories of New Mexico = Cuentos de Nuevo Mexico, 1993
Governor Glu Glu and Other Stories, 1988
Primeros Encuentros = First Encounters, 1983

Other books you might like:
Kathleen Alcala, *Mrs. Vargas and the Dead Naturalist*, 1992
   Short stories, capturing the essence of magical realism, examine the lives of Mexican women in this book of wonders.

Alfredo Vea Jr., *La Maravilla*, 1993
   A young boy grows up on Buckeye Road, a world of marvels in the desert outside the Phoenix city limits, caught between many cultures.

Alberto Alvaro Rios, *Pig Cookies and Other Stories*, 1995
   A collection of interrelated short stories set earlier in this century in a small village in northern Mexico.

Denise Chavez, *The Last of the Menu Girls*, 1986
   A collection of short stories, about a Chicana girl from southern New Mexico who is looking for her place, identity, and womanhood.

Patricia Preciado Martin, *Days of Plenty, Days of Want*, 1988
   A collection of stories where the past and the present meet and Mexican heritage is in jeopardy of being wiped out.

863

SABINE R. ULIBARRI, Mexican American

Tierra Amarilla: Stories of New Mexico = Cuentos de Nuevo Mexico
(Albuquerque, NM: University of New Mexico Press, 1993)

Series: Paso por Aqui
Subject(s): Rural Life; Folklore; Satire
Age range(s): Grades 8-Adult
Time period(s): Indeterminate Past
Locale(s): Tierra Amarilla, New Mexico

Summary: This collection of five short stories and a novella, first published in 1964, evoke the rural life of a northern New Mexican village. They portray the life, customs and traditions of an earlier era, from a young boy's perspective. Ulibarri's characters are detailed and carefully drawn. They can be cruel, eccentric, and humorous, but are always unforgettable. An introduction by Erlinda Gonzales-Berry places the writer within the context of a Mexican American literary tradition.

Other books by the same author:
The Best of Sabine Ulibarri: Selected Stories, 1993
El Condor, and Other Stories, 1988
Governor Glu Glu and Other Stories, 1988
Primeros Encuentros = First Encounters, 1983

Other books you might like:
Victor Villasenor, *Rain of Gold*, 1991
   A massive novel where the author weaves the separate stories of two familes, the Gomez's and Villasenors, as they live in Mexico and later migrate to the U.S.

Virgil Elizondo, *The Future Is Mestizo: Life Where Cultures Meet*, 1988
   This is a biography about growing up Catholic in San Antonio, Texas.

Benjamin Alire Saenz, *Flowers for the Broken: Stories*, 1992
   This collection of stories is about loneliness, anger, fear and ambition, and is set in the Southwest.

Tey Diana Rebolledo, *Las Mujeres Hablan*, 1988
   This collection of short stories and poetry is by Chicanas from New Mexico.

864

LUIS ALBERTO URREA, Mexican American

In Search of Snow
(New York: Harper Collins, 1994)

Subject(s): Love; Coming of Age; Family Relations

Age range(s): Grades 10-Adult
Major character(s): Mike McGirk, Young Man, Worker (blue collar), Caucasian; Bobo Garcia, Young Man, Mechanic (ex-prizefighter), Mexican American
Time period(s): 1950s
Locale(s): Arizona

Summary: Mike McGirk, a blue collar Don Quixote, searches for love and life in the Arizona desert. Having spent his life working for his father, who was a small time boxer and gas station operator, Mike doesn't know much about family. After his father's death he is free to find his way, and he then meets Bobo Garcia, who introduces him to a loving and tender family, somthing Mike has never known. Discovering friends and lovers and journeying from one comical adventure to another, Mike struggles with relationships, family, and his own destiny. Urrea's strong characters come dramatically alive in this funny novel.

Where it's reviewed:
Library Journal, February 15, 1994, page 186
Nation, July 18, 1994, page 98
Publishers Weekly, February 7, 1994, page 71

Other books by the same author:
Across the Wire: Life and Hard Times on the Mexican Border, 1993
The Fever of Being: Poems, 1994

Other books you might like:
Dagoberto Gilb, *The Last Known Residence of Mickey Acuna*, 1994
Mickey Acuna is waiting for something, something arriving through the mail, as he hangs out at the YMCA in El Paso.
Oscar Hijuelos, *The Mambo Kings Play Songs of Love*, 1989
The Castillo brothers, two young musicians, make their way from Havana to New York to play music in the era of the mambo; Cesar, the bandleader, handles the business and Nestor writes love songs.
Rafael Zepeda, *Horse Medicine and Other Stories*, 1990
This collection of nine stories deals with the world of men. In ''Horse Medicine'' several men, with kids and wives, participate in rodeos and live with horses.
Dagoberto Gilb, *The Magic of Blood*, 1993
These short stories about working-class life have multidimensional characters who lead realistic lives.
Max Martinez, *A Red Bikini Dream*, 1990
The rhythms and spirit of modern life in the U.S. are captured in this collection of five short stories where the characters ponder self and identity in an increasingly complex society.
Louie Garcia Robinson, *The Devil, Delfina Varela, and the Used Chevy*, 1993
Set in the Mission District of San Francisco this is a novel about politics, dreams, Latino social affairs, and Delfina, a widow who will do anything for a car.
Arturo Islas, *La Mollie and the King of Tears*, 1996
Louie Mendoza, a jazz musician, finds himself at San Francisco General Hospital to hear the diagnosis of his liver ailment. Talking to strangers, he tells his story in his unique street language.

865

ENEDINA CASAREZ VASQUEZ, Mexican American

Recuerdos de Una Nina
(San Anton: Cntro de Commun, Misions Oblat de Maria Inmacula, 1980)

Subject(s): Growing Up; Childhood
Age range(s): Grades 6-9
Time period(s): 1950s
Locale(s): San Antonio, Texas

Summary: These twenty-five vignettes describe people and events in the author's life as she was growing up in San Antonio, Texas. An illustration by the author accompanies each vignette.

About this book: These short stories are in English.

Other books you might like:
Phyllis Tashlik, *Hispanic, Female, and Young*, 1994
Seventh and eighth-grade girls from New York write these short stories.
Gary Soto, *The Skirt*, 1992
A little girl learns to solve her problems.
Alma Flor Ada, *Where the Flame Trees Bloom*, 1994
These eleven stories portray the childhood of this Cuban author.
Norma Elia Cantu, *Canicula: Snapshots of a Girlhood en la Frontera*, 1995
These short stories reveal the author's childhood, growing up on the Texas-Mexican border.
Arcadia H. Lopez, *Barrio Teacher*, 1992
An autobiographical narration by an educator who, despite poverty and turmoil, managed to obtain a university education and teach for forty-six years in San Antonio, Texas.
Gloria Lopez-Stafford, *A Place in El Paso: A Mexican American Childhood*, 1996
This bittersweet narrative describes the early childhood of the author living in the projects of El Paso during World War II.

866

RICHARD VASQUEZ, Mexican American

Chicano
(Garden City, NY: Doubleday, 1970)

Subject(s): Prejudice; Romance; Social Classes
Age range(s): Grades 10-Adult
Major character(s): Maria Sandoval, Young Woman, Chicana; David Stiver, Young Man, Caucasian
Time period(s): 1960s
Locale(s): Los Angeles, California

Summary: This very early Chicano novel is by a pioneer in Chicano literature and tells the story of four generations of the Sandoval family, who leave Mexico during the revolution and settle in Los Angeles. A main focus of the story is the love affair of Maria Sandoval and her Anglo boyfriend, David Stiver. Their relationship, troubled and riddled with illusions, becomes a battleground for ethnic identity. To accept her as an equal he yearns for her to have a Spanish noble ancestry instead of a Mexican one and only after her death does he learn a truth.

Other books by the same author:
Another Land, 1982
The Giant Killer, 1977

Other books you might like:
Victor Villasenor, *Rain of Gold*, 1991
  A massive novel where the author weaves the separate stories of two families, the Gomezs and Villasenors, as they live in Mexico and later migrate to the U.S.
Edmund Villasenor, *Macho!*, 1973
  This early Chicano novel is about a 17-year-old who illegally crosses the U.S. border, cheats his fellow workers, becomes a strike-breaker and turns criminal in his quest for riches and acculturation.
Jose Antonio Villarreal, *Pocho*, 1959
  The story of a Mexican family in the Santa Clara Valley of California before World War II and the assimilation of the son Richard Rubio.
Oscar Zeta Acosta, *The Autobiography of a Brown Buffalo*, 1972
  Partly novel, very much autobiography, this book examines the life of a famous Robin Hood type Chicano lawyer with an appetite for living on the edge.
Laura Del Fuego, *Maravilla*, 1989
  Consuelo Contreres, growing up in the housing projects of East Los Angeles, makes her way through turbulent times during the 1960s.
Eliud Martinez, *Voice-Haunted Journey*, 1990
  Miguel Velasquez, a writer and university professor, explores an elaborate series of memories and fantasies about his family while flying across California in a plane.

867

ALFREDO VEA JR., Mexican American

La Maravilla

(New York: Plume Books, 1993)

Subject(s): Cultural Identity; Family
Age range(s): Grades 10-Adult
Major character(s): Alberto ''Beto'', 9-Year-Old (boy), Grandson, Meztiso (son, Spanish and Yaqui parents); Josephina Valenzuela de Castillo, Grandmother, Healer, Spanish; Manuel, Grandfather, Husband (of Josephina), Yaqui Indian
Time period(s): 20th century (1920-1960)
Locale(s): Phoenix, Arizona

Summary: In this extraordinary novel, Alfredo Vea examines Buckeye Road, a world of marvels in the desert outside the Phoenix city limits, an American outback caught between many cultures. Beto, a young boy at the center of the novel, negotiates Buckeye Road with the help of his aristocratic Spanish grandmother and his Yaqui Indian grandfather. Fascinating characters fill the pages of this novel from mythic dogs to interracial lovers; local prostitutes, Potrice and Sugar Dee; and Vernetta, whose secret slowly unfolds.

Where it's reviewed:
Library Journal, March 1, 1993, page 109

Publishers Weekly, January 18, 1993, page 446

Other books you might like:
Arturo Islas, *The Rain God: A Desert Tale*, 1984
  Organized into six parts with different time sequences and flashbacks, this novel presents three generations of the Angel family living in the Southwest.
Alberto Alvaro Rios, *Pig Cookies and Other Stories*, 1995
  A set of interlocking stories that explore the lives of inhabitants of a small Mexican village.
Denise Chavez, *Face of an Angel*, 1994
  A humorously and sensuously related novel that shows how women constantly provide service to others, particularly to men.
Rudolfo Anaya, *Bless Me, Ultima*, 1972
  A young boy's beliefs are challenged as he grows up in a small town in New Mexico.
Americo Paredes, *George Washington Gomez*, 1990
  As he grows up, George Washington Gomez struggles with racism, abuse, and cultural and political clashes, while other Texas Mexicans fight to preserve their language and culture.

868

ALFREDO VEA JR., Mexican American

The Silver Cloud Cafe

(New York, NY: Dutton)

Subject(s): Emigration and Immigration; Migrant Labor; Mystery and Detective Stories
Age range(s): Grades 10-Adult
Major character(s): Zeferino Del Campo, Lawyer, Chicano
Time period(s): 1950s; 1990s
Locale(s): San Francisco, California

Summary: The settings for this complicated novel are a California migrant labor camp during the 1950s and the San Francisco Mission District in the 1990s. Before Zeferino Del Campo can defend a hunchbacked midget accused of murder, he must trace back to the midget's childhood and to a murder he witnessed in a migrant labor camp. The Silver Cloud Cafe is a dancehall bar where the down-and-out hang out, and where this tale which goes from the Mexican Revolution to the Philippines and across the U.S., unravels. It includes a variety of characters including a gay Filipino, a Mexican stripper, and the San Francisco police.

Where it's reviewed:
Publishers Weekly, August 5, 1996, page 429

Other books by the same author:
La Maravilla, 1993

Other books you might like:
James Roberto Curtis, *Shango*, 1996
  Miguel, a graduate student, becomes involved with *santeria* and a ritualistic murder, cult initiations, and dangerous underworld characters.
Thomas Sanchez, *Mile Zero*, 1989
  This exciting novel uses history, voodooo, santeria, folkloric sayings, and tropical culture to create a supernatural mystery and introduce *Zobop*, possibly a voodoo-inspired killer.

Rudolfo Anaya, *Zia Summer*, 1995
Sonny Baca is embroiled in a complicated mystery plot that involves murder, cult worship of the sun, and a battle over nuclear waste and it's disposal in New Mexico.

Luis Alberto Urrea, *In Search of Snow*, 1994
Mike McGirk, a blue collar Don Quixote, searches for love and life in the Arizona desert, and learns about family from Bobo Garcia.

Arturo Islas, *La Mollie and the King of Tears*, 1996
Louie Mendoza, a jazz musician, is at San Francisco General Hospital. While waiting to hear the diagnosis of his liver exam, he tells his story to strangers in the unique street language of Chicanos.

Oscar Zeta Acosta, *The Autobiography of a Brown Buffalo*, 1972
In this largely autobiographical work, the author, a famous Robin Hood type Chicano lawyer with an appetite for life on the edge, examines his life.

869

ANA LYDIA VEGA, Puerto Rican

True and False Romances
(London, New York: Serpent's Tail, 1994)

Subject(s): Short Stories; Women; Romance
Age range(s): Grades 10-Adult
Time period(s): 1980s
Locale(s): Puerto Rico

Summary: As the title suggests, this is a collection of short stories, and a novella, about romance. These stories portray romantic relationships in a humorous and at times cynical fashion, but also with all the complexities inherent in the affairs of love and marriage. All of the stories take place in Puerto Rico, except for one, where the protagonist goes to France to visit her best friend, and while there observes the unusual marriage of her friend.

About this book: Many of the stories were previously published in Spanish and were translated by Andrew Hurley.

Where it's reviewed:
TLS. Times Literary Supplement, July 29, 1994, page 20
Callaloo, Summer 1994, page 8

Other books by the same author:
Cuentos Calientes, 1992
Esperando a Lolo Otros Delirios Generacionales, 1994
Falsas Cronicas del Sur, 1991

Other books you might like:
Kathleen Ross, *Scents of Wood and Silence: Short Stories by Latin American Women Writers*, 1991
This anthology of short fiction is by Latin American women writers.

Rosario Ferre, *The Youngest Doll*, 1991
This collection of short stories, originally published in Spanish, is about Puerto Rico society.

Carmen C. Esteves, *Green Cane and Juicy Flotsam: Short Stories by Caribbean Women*, 1991
In this collection of short stories, Caribbean women writers examine questions of race, power, colonialism, poverty and identity.

Kal Wagenheim, *Cuentos: An Anthology of Short Stories from Puerto Rico*, 1978
This collection of short stories takes place in Puerto Rico.

Magali Garcia Ramis, *Happy Days, Uncle Sergio*, 1995
This is a coming of age novel about a middle class girl in Puerto Rico.

Judith Ortiz Cofer, *Silent Dancing: A Partial Remembrance of a Puerto Rican Childhood*, 1990
These stories are about growing up in Puerto Rico and the U.S.

Marjorie Agosin, *Happiness: Stories*, 1993
A collection of very short stories by a provocative Chilean writer that challenges and undermines our understanding of reality.

Diana Velez, *Reclaiming Medusa: Short Stories by Contemporary Puerto Rican Women*, 1988
Thirteen stories, by five well-known Puerto Rican women writers, appear in this anthology.

870

ED VEGA, Puerto Rican

Casualty Report
(Houston: Arte Publico Press, 1991)

Subject(s): Short Stories; City Life; Vietnam War
Age range(s): Grades 10-Adult
Time period(s): 1980s
Locale(s): New York, New York

Summary: These ten short stories portray Latino life in New York. "Casualty Report" tells the story of a frustrated Vietnam veteran searching for meaning. These stories draw from both the Spanish and the English literary traditions.

Where it's reviewed:
Library Journal, July, 1991, page 139

Other books by the same author:
The Comeback, 1985
Mendoza's Dreams, 1987

Other books you might like:
Jack Agueros, *Dominoes and Other Stories from the Puerto Rican*, 1993
This collection of short stories portrays life in Spanish Harlem.

Oswald Rivera, *Fire and Rain*, 1990
This story describes a riot in a Marine Corp prison camp during the Vietnam War.

Faythe Turner, *Puerto Rican Writers at Home in the U.S.A.: An Anthology*, 1991
This collection of poetry and short stories is by Puerto Rican writers in the U.S.

Joe Rodriguez, *The Oddsplayer*, 1988
During the Vietnam War, Black and Latino soldiers fight the enemy on the battlefield and also in their own ranks.

Daniel Cano, *Shifting Loyalties*, 1995
The lives of five Chicano soldiers and their families are explored in this novel that takes place before during and after the Vietnam war.

Roberto Santiago, *Boricuas: Influential Puerto Rican Writers—an Anthology*, 1995

Controversial writers from the nineteenth and twentieth centuries comprise this anthology.

871

ED VEGA, Puerto Rican

The Comeback
(Houston: Arte Publico Press, 1985)

Subject(s): Sports; Satire; Identity
Age range(s): Grades 10-Adult
Major character(s): Frank Garboil, Professor (ice-hockey player), Puerto Rican Eskimo; John Chota, Police Officer (undercover), Puerto Rican
Time period(s): 1980S
Locale(s): New York, New York

Summary: This satirical ''ethnic autobiography'' concerns itself with racism and revolutionary politics. As a college ice hockey star, a Puerto Rican Eskimo goes through a dramatic, classic identity crisis and is treated by a team of Freudian therapists.

About this book: Ed Vega is considered to be the most literary of the New York Puerto Rican writers.

Other books by the same author:
Mendoza's Dreams, 1987
Casualty Report, 1991

Other books you might like:
Jorge Prieto, *The Quarterback Who Almost Wasn't*, 1994
  This autobiographical story is about achievement in sports by a young Mexican living in political exile.
Roberto Fernandez, *Holy Radishes*, 1995
  This satirical novel is about a Cuban American community in Florida.
Edward Rivera, *Family Installments: Memories of Growing Up Hispanic*, 1982
  These humorous episodes portray growning up in Puerto Rico and New York.
Jaime Manrique, *Latin Moon in Manhattan*, 1992
  With plots and sub-plots, this novel vividly depicts Columbian American culture in Little Colombia Jackson Heights through the eyes of Santiago, a gay unpublished poet.

872

ED VEGA, Puerto Rican

Mendoza's Dreams
(Houston: Arte Publico Press, 1987)

Subject(s): Short Stories; Satire; City Life
Age range(s): Grades 10-Adult
Major character(s): Ernesto Mendoza, Storyteller
Time period(s): 1980s (1987)
Locale(s): New York, New York (El Barrio of New York)

Summary: This collection of stories, all narrated by Mendoza, is populated by strange, lovable characters such as a hunched-back circus clown, an innocent virgin, an angel attempting to earn respect in heaven, and others who fight against bureaucracies and the system in a series of interrelated stories. The narrator is considered the official chronicler of *the people*, the

Puerto Rican people, and weaves his stories to involve and captivate the reader. He is the type of magician creator that can make dreams come true.

Where it's reviewed:
Kirkus Reviews, February 15, 1987, page 256
Hispania, March 1988, page 97
Short Story Review, Fall 1987, page 12

Other books by the same author:
Casualty Report, 1991
The Comeback, 1985

Other books you might like:
Louie Garcia Robinson, *The Devil, Delfina Varela, and the Used Chevy*, 1993
  This humorous political novel is about unique characters living in the Mission District of San Francisco.
Rolando Hinojosa, *Dear Rafe*, 1985
  This bitter-comic story of the political lives of various characters in the fictional city of Klail City is narrated by Jehu Malacara.
Jesus Salvador Trevino, *The Fabulous Sinkhole and Other Stories*, 1995
  These interconnected short stories of an off-beat and magically real vision are about life in the barrios of Arroyo Grande, Texas.
Leo Romero, *Rita and Los Angeles*, 1995
  This short story collection has a cast of complex characters who grow and evolve, and learn about being outsiders in an alien and hostile world.
Jaime Manrique, *Latin Moon in Manhattan*, 1992
  This novel presents bizarre characters, plots and sub-plots and a vivid depiction of Columbian American culture in Little Columbia, Jackson Heights, from the perspective of a gay poet.

873

GLORIA VELASQUEZ, Mexican American

Juanita Fights the School Board
(Houston: Pinata Books, 1994)

Subject(s): Schools; Race Relations; Friendship
Age range(s): Grades 6-9
Major character(s): Juanita, Student—High School, Mexican American; Sandy Martinez, Psychologist, Latina
Time period(s): 1990s
Locale(s): California

Summary: When Juanita, a poor Mexican American girl, is faced with expulsion from high school, she decides to fight for her rights. With the help of a Latina psychologist, Juanita confronts the powerful school board of her district and discovers that regardless of race or social standing, most people are one when it comes to fairness.

Where it's reviewed:
Wilson Library Bulletin, April 1995, page 114

Other books by the same author:
I Used to Be a Superwoman, 1994
Maya's Divided World, 1995

Other books you might like:

Omar Castaneda, *Imagining Isabel*, 1994
Isabel, a teenager in Guatemala recently married, wants to become a teacher.

Omar Castaneda, *Among the Volcanoes*, 1991
Isabel, a teenager in Guatemala, must quit school to take care of her ill mother.

Ofelia Dumas Lachtman, *The Girl from Playa Blanca*, 1995
Elena and her brother Carlos find adventure in Los Angeles as they search for their father.

Diane Gonzales Bertrand, *Sweet Fifteen*, 1995
Stephanie's father dies right before her quinceasera, her special fifteenth birthday party.

Irene Beltran Hernandez, *Heartbeat, Drumbeat*, 1992
Morgana Cruz seeks her cultural identity while caught between the worlds of her Navajo mother and Mexican father.

Arcadia H. Lopez, *Barrio Teacher*, 1992
An autobiographical narration by an educator who, despite poverty and turmoil, managed to obtain a university education and teach for forty-six years in San Antonio, Texas.

874

GLORIA VELASQUEZ, Mexican American

Maya's Divided World

(Houston, TX: Arte Publico Press, 1995)

Series: Rossevelt High School
Subject(s): Divorce; Schools; Growing Up
Age range(s): Grades 7-10
Major character(s): Maya, Teenager (girl), Mexican American
Time period(s): 1990s
Locale(s): California

Summary: When Maya's parents announce their impending divorce, everyone is shocked, especially Maya who struggles with depression, loss, and disillusionment. Although she had been an excellent student, Maya begins to turn her back on her aspirations, accomplishments, and her old friends and starts hanging out with a rougher crowd.

Where it's reviewed:
Catholic Library World, 1996, page 54

Other books by the same author:
Juanita Fights the School Board, 1994
I Used to Be a Superwoman, 1994
Tommy Stands Alone, 1995

Other books you might like:

Omar Castaneda, *Imagining Isabel*, 1994
Isabel, a teenager in Guatemala, recently married, wants to become a teacher.

Omar Castaneda, *Among the Volcanoes*, 1991
Isabel, a teenager in Guatemala, must quit school to take care of her ill mother.

Ofelia Dumas Lachtman, *The Girl from Playa Blanca*, 1995
Elena and brother Carlos find adventure in Los Angeles as they search for their father.

Diane Gonzales Bertrand, *Sweet Fifteen*, 1995
Stephanie's father dies right before her quinceanera, her special fifteenth birthday party.

Irene Beltran Hernandez, *Heartbeat, Drumbeat*, 1992
Morgana Cruz seeks her cultural identity while caught between the worlds of her Navajo mother and Mexican father.

Judith Ortiz Cofer, *An Island Like You: Stories of the Barrio*, 1995
Twelve stories, set in a barrio of New Jersey, examine the lives of Puerto Rican teenagers who deal with friendship, family, romance, and school.

875

GLORIA VELASQUEZ, Mexican American

Tommy Stands Alone

(Houston, TX: Pinata Books, 1995)

Series: Roosevelt High School
Subject(s): Identity; Homosexuality/Lesbianism; Growing Up
Age range(s): Grades 6-10
Major character(s): Tommy, Teenager (boy), Homosexual
Time period(s): 1990s (1995)
Locale(s): California

Summary: As Tommy begins to realize that he might be gay, he tries to avoid his friends, and starts to cut classes and drink. A suicide attempt lands him in the hospital and leads to a relationship with the counselor Ms. Martinez. Tommy must deal with friends, family, and homophobia in his attempt to claim an identity.

Other books by the same author:
Juanita Fights the School Board, 1994
I Used to Be a Superwoman, 1994
Maya's Divided World, 1995

Other books you might like:

Ofelia Dumas Lachtman, *The Girl from Playa Blanca*, 1995
Elena and brother Carlos find adventure in Los Angeles as they search for their father.

Diane Gonzales Bertrand, *Sweet Fifteen*, 1995
Stephanie's father dies right before her quinceanera, her special fifteenth birthday party.

Irene Beltran Hernandez, *Hearbeat, Drumbeat*, 1992
Morgana Cruz seeks her cultural identity while caught between the worlds of her Navajo mother and Mexican father.

Danny Santiago, *Famous All over Town*, 1984
A teenager who lives in the Chicano barrio of Los Angeles, wants to beat the odds that are stacked against him.

Judith Ortiz Cofer, *An Island Like You: Stories of the Barrio*, 1995
Twelve stories, set in a New Jersey barrio, examine the lives of Puerto Rican teenagers, their friendship, family, romance, and school life.

876

DIANA VELEZ, Editor, Puerto Rican

Reclaiming Medusa: Short Stories by Contemporary Puerto Rican Women
(San Francisco: Spinsters/Aunt Lute, 1988)

Subject(s): Short Stories; Anthology; Women
Age range(s): Grades 10-Adult
Time period(s): 1970s
Locale(s): Puerto Rico

Summary: Thirteen stories, by five well-known Puerto Rican women writers, appear in this anthology. Lively and imaginative, the stories by Rosario Ferre, Carmen Lugo Filippi, Mayra Montero, Carmen Valle, and Ana Lydia Vega, address family, marriage, religion, and magic. The influence by recent Latin American writers is noticeable.

About this book: The Summer 1994 issue of Callaloo has a ten page article on Puerto Rican women writers and includes an interview with Ana Lydia Vega.

Where it's reviewed:
Callaloo, Summer, 1994, page 816

Other books by the same author:
Trumpets from the Islands of Their Eviction, 1987

Other books you might like:
Alma Gomez, *Cuentos: Stories by Latinas*, 1983
    This is a collection of stories by Hispanic women.
Bryce Milligan, *Daughters of the Fifth Sun: A Collection of Latina Fiction and Poetry*, 1995
    This anthology of creative literature is by Latinas in the U.S.
Faythe Turner, *Puerto Rican Writers at Home in the U.S.A.: An Anthology*, 1991
    This collection of writings is by Puerto Rican writers in the U.S.
Kathleen Ross, *Scents of Wood and Silence: Short Stories by Latin American Women Writers*, 1991
    This anthology of short fiction is by Latin American women writers.
Rosario Ferre, *The Youngest Doll*, 1991
    This collection of short stories, originally published in Spanish, is about Puerto Rico society.
Kal Wagenheim, *Cuentos: An Anthology of Short Stories from Puerto Rico*, 1978
    This collection of short stories takes place in Puerto Rico.
Ana Lydia Vega, *True and False Romances*, 1994
    This collection of short stories is about women and romance that take place in Puerto Rico.
Carmen C. Esteves, *Green Cane and Juicy Flotsam: Short Stories by Caribbean Women*, 1991
    This collection of short stories is by Puerto Rican, Cuban, Jamaican, and Domican women writers.

877

ALMA LUZ VILLANUEVA, Mexican American

Naked Ladies
(Tempe, AZ: Bilingual Press, 1994)

Subject(s): Women; Race Relations; Violence
Age range(s): Grades 10-Adult
Major character(s): Alta, Spouse (young woman), Mother, Latina
Time period(s): 1990s
Locale(s): California

Summary: A novel about the lives of four remarkable women and their struggles against prejudices, difficult relationships, and abuse. Alta is attempting to finish college as she raises her two children and deals with a belligerent husband who is a closet homosexual. Katie finds out she has cancer and only six months to live. The title of the novel *Naked Ladies* comes from the wild flowers, that are vulnerable yet resilient, and reflect the life and death battles of these women who are working to maintain strong interracial relationships.

Where it's reviewed:
Publishers Weekly, November 22, 1993, page 59
Women's Review of Books, May 1994, page 25

Other books by the same author:
Bloodroot, 1982
Life Span, 1985
The Ultraviolet Sky, 1988
Weeping Woman: La Llorona and Other Stories, 1994

Other books you might like:
John Rechy, *The Miraculous Day of Amalia Gomez: A Novel*, 1991
    This story examines poverty, gang warfare, border crossings, and visions of salvation while following one day in the life of a Mexican American woman.
Graciela Limon, *The Memories of Ana Calderon: A Novel*, 1994
    Ana Calderon begins life in rural southern Mexico, but the burdens of poverty, dreams of a better life, and circumstance lead her family to the United States.
Alba Ambert, *A Perfect Silence*, 1995
    A Puerto Rican woman brought up in the South Bronx tells her story of being abused as a child and as an adult, and how she tries to break the cycle of poverty and oppression.
Maria Espinosa, *Dark Plums*, 1995
    Adrianne, a young girl from Texas, searches for love in Manhattan, falls into an abusive relationship, and eventually works as a prostitute.
Esmeralda Santiago, *America's Dream*, 1996
    America works as a housekeeper in a hotel on an island off the coast of Puerto Rico, until she accepts a job as a nanny in Westchester County, New York, and learns about a new life.
Graciela Limon, *Song of the Hummingbird*, 1996
    Huitzitzilin, Hummingbird in the Nahuatal language, is an Aztec princess who is forced into slavery. As an 82-year-old woman, she recounts her life story during the Spanish conquest of Mexico.

878

ALMA LUZ VILLANUEVA

Weeping Woman: La Llorona and Other Stories

(Tempe, AZ: Bilingual Press, 1994)

Subject(s): Short Stories; Folk Tales; Women
Age range(s): Grades 10-Adult
Time period(s): 1980s; 1990s (1980-1990)
Locale(s): California

Summary: This collection of short stories examines women who live in a world torn apart by violence, racism, and sexism. Some of the stories are disturbing but the women, whose lives are harmed and distorted, nevertheless have the strength and spirituality to triumph.

Where it's reviewed:
CHOICE, December 1994, page 603
Library Journal, March 1, 1994, page 121
Publishers Weekly, January 17, 1994, page 422

Other books by the same author:
Bloodroot, 1982
Life Span, 1985
Naked Ladies, 1994
Planet, with Mother, May I?, 1993
The Ultraviolet Sky, 1988

Other books you might like:
Ana Lydia Vega, *True and False Romances*, 1994
    These stories about women and romance, many comically related, take place in Puerto Rico.
Kathleen Ross, *Scents of Wood and Silence: Short Stories by Latin American Women Writers*, 1991
    This anthology of short fiction is by Latin American women writers.
Rosario Ferre, *The Youngest Doll*, 1991
    This collection of short stories, originally published in Spanish, is about women in Puerto Rican society.
Lillian Castillo-Speed, *Latina: Women's Voices from the Borderland*, 1995
    This collection of short stories is by contemporary Latinas in the U.S.
Maria Espinosa, *Dark Plums*, 1995
    Adrianne, a young girl from Texas, begins a search for love and self in Mnahattan. Wandering the city, she sleeps with strangers and falls into an abusive relationship.
Esmeralda Santiago, *America's Dream*, 1996
    America works as a housekeeper in a hotel on an island off the coast of Puerto Rico, until she accepts a job as a nanny in Westchester County, New York, and learns about a new life.

879

JOSE ANTONIO VILLARREAL, Mexican American

Pocho

(Garden City, NY: Doubleday & Company, 1959)

Subject(s): Identity; Coming of Age; Heritage
Age range(s): Grades 9-Adult

Major character(s): Richard Rubio, Young Man (the pocho), Mexican American
Time period(s): 1930s; 1940s (1930-1940)
Locale(s): Santa Clara, California

Summary: Published in 1959, this is considered to be the first key novel in the renaissance of Chicano literature. It is the story of a Mexican family migrating to the Santa Clara Valley of California to get away from war-torn Mexico. Richard Rubio, the son and *pocho* of the story, is born in California and considers America his home, while his parents struggle to adapt to Anglo customs and values during the Depression. Issues of assimilation, racism, and denial of ethnic heritage are raised in literature for the first time.

About this book: Considered a classic Chicano novel.

Other books by the same author:
Clemente Chacon: A Novel, 1984
The Fifth Horseman, 1974

Other books you might like:
Raymond Barrio, *The Plum Plum Pickers*, 1969
    This is the dramatic story of Manuel and Lupe Gutierrez and their children, migrant farm workers in California's Santa Clara Valley.
Tomas Rivera, *Y No Se lo Trago la Tierra.And the Earth Did Not Devour Him*, 1971
    Series of short stories and vignettes, in English, about a migrant farm worker boy from Texas.
Richard Vasquez, *Chicano*, 1970
    An early Chicano novel about the Sandoval family who leave revolutionary Mexico and settle in a Los Angeles barrio.
Victor Villasenor, *Rain of Gold*, 1991
    Intergenerational chronicle of the author's family migration to the U.S. from Mexico.
Edmund Villasenor, *Macho!*, 1973
    This early Chicano novel is about a 17-year-old who illegally crosses the U.S. border, cheats his fellow workers, becomes a strike breaker and turns criminal in his quest for riches and acculturation.
Miguel Duran, *Don't Spit on My Corner*, 1992
    Little Mike and his friends, coming of age in Los Angeles during WWII, spend their time being "cool," cruising, drinking and protecting their turf.
Gordon Kahn, *A Long Way from Home*, 1989
    Written forty years before it was published, this novel tells the story of Gilberto, a young Chicano who, after his mother's death, leaves the U.S. for Mexico to find his only remaining family.
Dagoberto Gilb, *The Last Known Residence of Mickey Acuna*, 1994
    Mickey Acuna is waiting for something as he hangs out at the YMCA in El Paso where he meets a cast of characters living a fantasy life as they, too, wait for something to happen.

880

ROSA MARTHA VILLARREAL, Mexican American

Doctor Magdalena: Novella
(Berkeley, CA: TQS Publications, 1995)

Subject(s): Self-Acceptance; Medicine; Fathers and Daughters
Age range(s): Grades 8-Adult
Major character(s): Magdalena Ibarra, Doctor, Daughter, Mexican
Time period(s): Indeterminate Past
Locale(s): Mexico (the story starts in Texas, but occurs mostly in Mexico)

Summary: Narrated through the voice of her Indian ancestors, this novella is the spiritual odyssey of a modern female doctor, spanning three worlds. It is the story of a healer who experiences the folly of her parents' choices and strives toward self-realization and the mystical. Ashamed of the privileged role her doctor father assumes, Magdalena wants to become a doctor to heal the ''human flesh'' of all people.

Other books you might like:

Kathleen Alcala, *Mrs. Vargas and the Dead Naturalist*, 1992
Short stories capturing the essence of magical realism, examine the lives of Mexican women in this book of wonders.

Alejandro Morales, *The Rag Doll Plagues*, 1988
Divided into three sections, this novel shows Latino doctors fighting a deadly infectious disease for over three centuries in Mexico and the United States.

Guy Garcia, *Obsidian Sky: A Novel*, 1994
A contemporary theory about Aztec ritual and the role of Motecuhzoma (Moctezuma), the Aztec king enslaved by Cortes, gets the protagonist sucked into a political controversy in Mexico.

Orlando Romero, *Nambe—Year One*, 1976
This is the story of the attempts of a gypsy woman to seduce the young hero into leaving his land and traditions.

Graciela Limon, *Song of the Hummingbird*, 1996
Huitzitzilin, Hummingbird in the Nahautal language, is an Aztec princess who is forced into slavery. As an 82-year-old woman, she recounts her life's story during the Spanish conquest of Mexico.

Carlos Miralejos, *Rabid Beasts*, 1993
This science fiction work tells how Jorge Sogaseca, captain of the space ship Tulumex, saves the Cherokee Nation from dying of exposure to extremely cold weather during a long forced march.

881

EDMUND VILLASENOR, Mexican American

Macho!
(New York: Bantam Books, 1973)

Subject(s): Growing Up; Farm Life; Emigration and Immigration
Age range(s): Grades 8-Adult
Major character(s): Roberto Garcia, 17-Year-Old (boy), Immigrant, Mexican Indian
Time period(s): 1960s

Locale(s): California; Mexico

Summary: This early Chicano novel, still read and discussed today, is about a Mexican-born Tarascan Indian teenager, Roberto Garcia, who illegally crosses the U.S. border, cheats his fellow workers, becomes a strike-breaker, and finally turns criminal in his unending quest for riches. When he returns to Mexico, his odyssey and acculturation cause him to reject the machismo code of violence. This novel realistically portrays the struggles of the United Farm Workers Union during its early years.

Other books you might like:

Raymond Barrio, *The Plum Plum Pickers*, 1969
This dramatic story of Manuel and Lupe Gutierrez and their children recounts their lives as migrant farm workers in California's Santa Clara Valley.

Jose Antonio Villarreal, *Pocho*, 1959
Considered the first key Chicano novel, this tells the story of a Mexican family attempting to assimilate in the Santa Clara Valley of California.

Tomas Rivera, *Y No Se lo Trago la Tierra.And the Earth Did Not Devour Him*, 1987
Twelve related stories document the spiritual strength of migrant farm workers. This work reproduces in language the sad and tragic lives of migrant workers as they travel the migrant stream.

Helena Maria Viramontes, *Under the Feet of Jesus*, 1995
The hardships suffered by a migrant farm working family and Estrella, a young girl living in a shack picking grapes in California's vineyards, is recounted in this novel.

Miguel Mendez, *Pilgrims in Aztlan*, 1992
Loreto Maldonado, an aging veteran of the Mexican Revolution, now washes cars for tourists in Tijuana, watching the people who come his way and tell him their stories.

Ernesto Galarza, *Barrio Boy*, 1971
Autobiographical, this story examines the early life of a distinguished professor and author who wrote many works about Mexican agricultural workers.

Alejandro Grattan-Dominguez, *The Dark Side of the Dream*, 1995
A historical novel set right after the outbreak of World War II, this story presents two cousins and their families who migrate from Chihuahua to El Paso and a strike of farmworkers in South Texas.

Genaro Gonzalez, *Only Sons*, 1991
The main characters in this collection, all male, are trying to define their social relationships. Gonzalez explores ambivalent emotions, cultural values, and family traditions.

882

VICTOR VILLASENOR, Mexican American

Rain of Gold
(New York: Dell Publishing, 1991)

Subject(s): Family; Romance; Intergenerational Saga
Age range(s): Grades 9-Adult
Major character(s): Lupe Gomez, Child (girl), Mexican; Salvador Villasenor, Young Man, Mexican
Time period(s): 20th century (1900-1930)
Locale(s): California

Summary: A massive novel where the author weaves together the separate stories of two families, the Gomezs and Villasenors, both living in Mexico and later migrating to the U.S. The narration leads to and presents the relationship between the author's father, a volatile bootlegger, and his mother, the beautiful Lupe. Filled with many characters and events, the Mexican southern California of the 1920s and 1930s is well depicted. A collective memoir of a people and a time, the novel honestly and inspiringly explores mystery, passion, death, and miracles.

Where it's reviewed:
Publishers Weekly, December 11, 1995, page 64
Wilson Library Bulletin, April 1995, page 114
Hispania, January-February 1995, page 124
Library Journal, July 1991, page 113

Other books by the same author:
Lluvia de Oro, 1993
Macho!, 1973
Walking Stars: Stories of Magic and Power, 1994
Jury: The People vs. Juan Corona, 1977
Wild Steps of Heaven, 1996

Other books you might like:
Genaro Gonzalez, *Rainbow's End*, 1988
    The story of three generations of the Cavazos family living in the Lower Rio Grande Valley in Texas, including their migrant labor and Vietnam hardships.
Montserrat Fontes, *Dreams of the Centaur*, 1995
    A fast-paced novel set during the Porfirio Diaz regime about the son of a slain ranch owner who tries to avenge his father's death.
Sylvia Lopez-Medina, *Cantora: A Novel*, 1992
    This novel tells the story of four generations of women in Mexico and their lives in America at the turn of the 20th century.
Denise Chavez, *Face of an Angel*, 1994
    Intergenerational novel about a family in Agua Oscura, a fictional town, in New Mexico.
Alejandro Morales, *The Brick People*, 1992
    A historical novel that traces growth in California from the 19th to the 20th century.
Richard Vasquez, *Chicano*, 1970
    An early Chicano novel about the Sandoval family who leave revolutionary Mexico and settle in a Los Angeles barrio.
Edmund Villasenor, *Macho!*, 1973
    This early Chicano novel is about a 17-year-old who illegally crosses the U.S. border, cheats his fellow workers, becomes a strike breaker and turns criminal in his quest for riches and acculturation.

883

VICTOR VILLASENOR, Mexican American

Walking Stars: Stories of Magic and Power

(Houston: Pinata Books, 1994)

Subject(s): Magic; Short Stories; Grandparents
Age range(s): Grades 6 and Up
Time period(s): 20th century (1920-1960)
Locale(s): California (some stories take place in Mexico)

Summary: This is a collection of stories, some autobiographical, some about the author's grandparents and parents, and some about growing up as the son of Mexican immigrants in California. The book is divided into three parts: My Birth to Power and Magic; Stories of My Mother; Stories of My Father. They are true stories that show that life is full of magic that gives strength and power to endure and triumph in everyday life.

About this book: Some of these stories appear in expanded version in *Rain of Gold*.

Where it's reviewed:
Hispanic, January-February 1995, page 124
Publishers Weekly, September 12, 1994, page 92
Wilson Library Bulletin, April 1995, page 114

Other books by the same author:
Macho!, 1993
Rain of Gold, 1991
Jury: The People vs. Juan Corona, 1977

Other books you might like:
Kleya Forte-Escamilla, *The Storyteller with Nike Airs and Other Barrio Stories*, 1995
    This collection of stories is about girls and the supernatural.
Alfred Avila, *Mexican Ghost Tales of the Southwest*, 1994
    This collection of supernatural tales is from the U.S.-Mexico border.
Esther De Michael Cervantes, *Barrio Ghosts*, 1988
    These short stories are about urban life in the Chicano community.
Gary Soto, *A Summer Life*, 1990
    This collection of very short stories is about young boys growing up in rural California.
Beatriz de la Garza, *The Candy Vendor's Boy and Other Stories*, 1994
    This collection of stories depicts realistic characters who struggle with life issues which they have no control over.
Charles Tatum, *Mexican American Literature*, 1990
    The various genres represented in this anthology are presented within a historical context and include short stories, poems, drama, folktales, and oral literature.
Jim Sagel, *Where the Cinnamon Winds Blow = Donde Soplan Los Vientos de Canela*, 1993
    A magical fantasy novel about ten-year-old Tomass relationship eccentric Tua Zulema and his attempts to reconcile his feelings for the death of his father.
Jim Sagel, *Where the Cinnamon Winds Blow = Donde Soplan Los Vientos de Canela*, 1993
    A magical fantasy novel about 10-year-old Tomas' relationship with his eccentric *Tia Zulema* and his attempts to reconcile his feelings for the death of his father.

884

VICTOR VILLASENOR, Mexican American

Wild Steps of Heaven

(New York, NY: Delacorte Press, 1996)

Subject(s): Marriage; Supernatural; Revolution
Age range(s): Grades 9-Adult

Major character(s): Don Juan Jesus Villasenor, Grandfather, Spanish; Dona Margarita Villasenor, Grandmother, Mexican
Time period(s): 1900s (1900-1914)
Locale(s): Mexico

Summary: This sequel to *Rain of Gold* is the story of the paternal grandparents of the author, and their life in Mexico before they immigrated to the United States. Don Juan, a descendent of kings of Spain as he always describes himself, marries an Indian woman, Dona Margarita, and she gives birth to thirteen children. The youngest one, Juan, becomes the father of the author. The continual conflict in this marriage is the history of Mexico, the subjugation of the civilization and culture of indigenous people by the European conquerors. Dona Margarita's beliefs in supernatural and spiritual powers saves her and her family's lives many times over during the Mexican revolution.

About this book: Sequel to *Rain of Gold*

Where it's reviewed:
Hispanic, April 1996, page 72

Other books by the same author:
Lluvia de Oro, 1993
Macho!, 1973
Walking Stars: Stories of Magic and Power, 1994
Jury: The People vs. Juan Corona, 1977
Rain of Gold, 1991

Other books you might like:
Genaro Gonzalez, *Rainbow's End*, 1988
   The story of three generations of the Cavazos family living in the lower Rio Grande Valley in Texas includes their migrant labor and Vietnam hardships.
Montserrat Fontes, *Dreams of the Centaur*, 1995
   The son of a slain ranch owner tries to avenge his father's death during the deportation of the Yaqui Indians during the presidency of Porfirio Diaz.
Sylvia Lopez-Medina, *Cantora: A Novel*, 1992
   This novel tells the story of four generations of women in Mexico and their lives in America at the turn of the 20th century.
Richard Vasquez, *Chicano*, 1970
   This novel about four generations of the Sandoval family, who leave Mexico for Los Angeles during the revolution, focuses on the love affair of Maria Sandoval and her Anglo boyfriend.
Daniel Cano, *Pepe Rios*, 1991
   In this historical novel about the Mexican Revolution of 1910, Pepe Rios searches for peace amidst the chaos and violence of war.

885

MARCOS MCPEEK VILLATORO, Salvadoran American

A Fire in the Earth
(Houston, TX: Arte Publico, 1996)

Subject(s): Family Problems; Earthquakes; Factories
Age range(s): Grades 10-Adult
Major character(s): Romilia Vasquez, Young Woman (Indigenous Native), Mother

Time period(s): 19th century; 20th century (1870-1930)
Locale(s): El Salvador

Summary: The title of this epic novel refers to the earthquake that created a volcanic mound where Romilia is born and where she later tills the land. The story follows the Patricio Colonez family, the husband of Romilia, descendants of an Indian patriarch who led his clan to claim fertile soil, setting the stage for future trials and tragedies. Attempting to fight off foreign business interests, the Colonezes establish a brick factory in the only patch of land not devoted to coffee. Their son Paco also attempts to mitigate exploitation by leading a workers' uprising, that is disastrously crushed by government troops. Romilia eventually must choose between her life of prosperity and the survival of her people.

Where it's reviewed:
Publishers Weekly, February 26, 1996, page 85

Other books you might like:
Demetria Martinez, *Mother Tongue*, 1994
   Mary meets and shelters a political refugee, falls in love with him, and soon finds that his life is fundamentally different from hers.
Graciela Limon, *In Search of Bernabe*, 1993
   A mother searches for her son, lost during the civil war in El Salvador.
Julia Alvarez, *In the Time of the Butterflies*, 1994
   The story of the assassination of three sisters who are fighting to overthrow a dictatorship in the Dominican Republic is the focus of this book.
Francisco Goldman, *The Long Night of White Chickens*, 1992
   Determined to find the murderers of his cousin Flor, Roger and his best friend Luis become entangled in political difficulties as they discover the secret life of Flor in war-torn Guatemala.
Carole Fernandez, *Sleep of the Innocents*, 1991
   This novel chronicles the lives of women living in a fictional Central American country torn by civil war.
Victor Perera, *Rites: A Guatemalan Boyhood*, 1986
   These autobiographical narratives are of the Jewish boyhood of the author while growing up and living in Guatemala, before moving to the U.S.
Carmen de Monteflores, *Singing Softly = Cantando Bajito*, 1989
   This is a novel of women, a grandmother and granddaughter, and their relationship.

886

HELENA MARIA VIRAMONTES, Mexican American

The Moths and Other Stories
(Houston, TX: Arte Publico Press, 1985)

Subject(s): Short Stories; Women; Family Relations
Age range(s): Grades 10-Adult
Time period(s): 1950s
Locale(s): United States

Summary: An early collection of stories by a Chicana writer that attempts to depict the reality of women's lives. These stories are about women of all ages, some weak some strong, struggling in some way to fulfill their potential as original and creative individuals. Viramontes women's conflicts are about Chicano culture and family, the Catholic church, relations with fathers, and the social values that shape their lives. She examines the female body, family dynamics, and artistic creation.

Other books by the same author:
Under the Feet of Jesus, 1995

Other books you might like:
Alicia Gaspar de Alba, *The Mystery of Survival and Other Stories*, 1993
These stories are mostly about female characters who explore and come to understand their places in the world and the cultural boundaries that divide them.
Estela Portillo Trambley, *Rain of Scorpions and Other Writings*, 1975
A novella and eight stories, this collection deals with many with feminist themes where the main characters are strong brave women with special gifts.
Rosario Ferre, *The Youngest Doll*, 1991
This collection, considered by critics as a manifesto of women's rights, includes *The Youngest Doll*, one of the author's most successful stories.
Sandra Cisneros, *Woman Hollering Creek and Other Stories*, 1991
A collection of short stories with strong angry female characters struggling valiantly to make something beautiful of their lives.
Mary Helen Ponce, *Taking Control*, 1987
This collection of stories portrays the domestic and economic oppression of Mexican and Chicana women in the U.S.
Roberta Fernandez, *Itaglio: Novel in Six Stories*, 1990
A novel related in six stories, each is about an extraordinary woman who serves as a role model for the young narrator.
Ana Castillo, *Loverboys, Stories*, 1996
The stories included in this collection range from one-page vignettes to longer narratives; their subjects range from inexperienced to world-weary.

887

HELENA MARIA VIRAMONTES, Mexican American

Under the Feet of Jesus
(New York: Dutton, 1995)

Subject(s): Farm Life; Poverty; Mothers and Daughters
Age range(s): Grades 10-Adult
Major character(s): Estrella, 13-Year-Old, Migrant Worker, Mexican American
Time period(s): 1960s
Locale(s): California

Summary: This novel is about the hardships of a migrant farm working family, living in a shack, picking grapes in California's vineyards. Estrella, a young girl quickly growing old, carries a heavy weight, reflecting on why her father abandoned them, and watching her weary mother juggle her life so her family will be fed. She fights a white girl to defend her mother's decision to live with an older man, Perfecto, who without his help they wouldn't survive. The somber and dismal realities of farm workers' lives are delicately drawn here by Viramontes, including pesticide poisoning, young teenage boys working alone to send money home and the knowledge that social justice is somehow lacking but who is to blame?

Where it's reviewed:
Publishers Weekly, March 20, 1995, page 42
Women's Review of Books, October 1995, page 19

Other books by the same author:
The Moths and Other Stories, 1985

Other books you might like:
Raymond Barrio, *The Plum Plum Pickers*, 1969
This is the dramatic story of Manuel and Lupe Gutierrez and their children, migrant farm workers in California's Santa Clara Valley.
Tomas Rivera, *Y No Se lo Trago la Tierra.And the Earth Did Not Devour Him*, 1971
This series of short stories and vignettes, in English, are about a migrant farm worker boy from Texas.
Jose Antonio Villarreal, *Pocho*, 1959
This is considered to be the first key Chicano novel about a Mexican family attempting to assimilate in the Santa Clara Valley of California.
Alicia Gaspar de Alba, *The Mystery of Survival and Other Stories*, 1993
These stories are mostly about female characters who explore and come to understand their places in the world and the cultural boundaries that divide them.
Sandra Cisneros, *Woman Hollering Creek and Other Stories*, 1991
This collection of short stories has strong, angry female characters struggling valiantly to make something beautiful of their lives.
Ernesto Galarza, *Barrio Boy*, 1971
Autobiographical, this story examines the early life of a distinguished professor and author who wrote many works about Mexican agricultural workers.
Edmund Villasenor, *Macho!*, 1973
This early Chicano novel is about a 17-year-old who illegally crosses the U.S. border, cheats his fellow workers, becomes a strike breaker and turns criminal in his quest for riches and acculturation.
Estela Portillo Trambley, *Rain of Scorpions and Other Stories*, 1993
A novella and eight stories, this collection deals mainly with feminist themes. Many of the major characters are strong, brave women with special gifts.
Sandra Benitez, *A Place Where the Sea Remembers*, 1993
Written as a series of interrelated stories, this novel presents the life of a coastal village in Mexico where the women are caught in a mystical, fantastic, and often fatalistic world.

888

KAL WAGENHEIM, Editor

Cuentos: An Anthology of Short Stories From Puerto Rico
(New York: Shocken Books, 1978)

Subject(s): Short Stories; Anthology
Age range(s): Grades 10-Adult
Time period(s): 1940s; 1960s
Locale(s): Puerto Rico

Summary: Six authors use twelve stories to describe migration from Puerto Rico to the United States. Some of the stories take place in Puerto Rico, while others depict the political-cultural tensions that exist for those living in New York. Geography and culture influence the writing so a different perspective is notable between the Latino writer in Puerto Rico and the Latino writer in the U.S.

About this book: In bilingual format, all stories are printed in English and Spanish.

Other books by the same author:
Clemente!, 1973
The Puerto Ricans: A Documentary History, 1973
Puerto Ricans in the U.S., 1983
A Survey of Puerto Ricans on the U.S. Mainland in the 1970s, 1975

Other books you might like:
Faythe Turner, *Puerto Rican Writers at Home in the U.S.A.: An Anthology*, 1991
This collection of short stories describes living in the U.S. and Puerto Rico.
Esmeralda Santiago, *When I Was Puerto Rican*, 1993
A young girl grows up in Puerto Rico.
Harold Augenbraum, *Growing Up Latino: Memoirs and Stories*, 1993
Twenty-five Latinos write stories about growing up in the U.S.
Diana Velez, *Reclaiming Medusa: Short Stories by Contemporary Puerto Rican Women*, 1988
Women writers in Puerto Rico author this collection of short stories.
Judith Ortiz Cofer, *Silent Dancing: A Partial Remembrance of a Puerto Rican Childhood*, 1990
This autobiographical collection of prose, poetry, and short stories depicts growing up in Puerto Rico and the U.S.
Ana Lydia Vega, *True and False Romances*, 1994
Women and romance in Puerto Rico are portrayed in this collection of short stories.

889

JOSE YGLESIAS, Cuban American

Break-In
(Houston, TX: Arte Publico Press, 1996)

Subject(s): Crime and Criminals; Race Relations; Friendship
Age range(s): Grades 10-Adult

Major character(s): Rudy Pardo, Fire Fighter (retired chief), Widow(er), Cuban American; Munro Perkins, Criminal, Teenager, African American
Time period(s): 1990s
Locale(s): Tampa, Florida

Summary: When 70-year-old ex-fire chief Rudy Pardo comes home to find a young, tall, thin black man rifling through his posessions, the intrusion brings out his racial prejudices. Living alone since the death of his wife and dealing with the problems of his sisters, son and nephew, Pardo wants quick justice and is ready to send the thief to prison. Slowly he is drawn into a complex and polarized relationship with the young burglar, based on some mutual respect, as he wrestles with his views of law and order.

Where it's reviewed:
Publishers Weekly, March 11, 1996, page 44

Other books by the same author:
Home Again, 1987
The Kill Price: A Novel, 1976
Tristan and the Hispanics, 1989

Other books you might like:
Oscar Hijuelos, *Mr. Ives' Christmas*, 1995
Edward Ives, a New York commercial artist, mourns the loss of his beloved son, and begins to exchange letters with his son's killer, a young Puerto Rican who will soon be released from prison.
Rafael Yglesias, *Fearless: A Novel*, 1993
After he survives a plane crash Max Klein's terror turns into ecstasy and he wants to help everyone. Since he has passed through death, he no longer fears it.
Dagoberto Gilb, *The Last Known Residence of Mickey Acuna*, 1994
Mickey Acuna is waiting for something, something arriving through the mail, as he dwells at the YMCA in El Paso.
Luis Alberto Urrea, *In Search of Snow*, 1994
Mike McGirk, a blue collar Don Quixote, searches for love and life in the Arizona desert, and learns about family from Bobo Garcia.
Manuel Ramos, *The Last Client of Luis Montez*, 1996
The last client of Denver lawyer Louie Montez is found dead with Montez standing over him. To clear his name Montez becomes entangled in a complicated web that takes him to California and back.
Gloria Gonzalez, *The Thirteenth Apostle*, 1993
Newspaperwoman Geraldine St. Claire investigates the murder of her lover Hal, which leads her to suspect an industrial homicide and also leads her right into the hands of a powerful drug lord.
Max Martinez, *White Leg*, 1996
This fast action murder mystery is about a small town thief in a backwater town in Texas who kills a Texas Ranger and three other people during one of his hold-ups.
Junot Diaz, *Drown, Stories*, 1996
A collection of ten short stories mostly about young Latino men who are transformed while learning to define their American identity.

890

JOSE YGLESIAS, Cuban American

Tristan and the Hispanics
(New York: Simon and Schuster, 1989)

Subject(s): Social Classes; Family Relations; Traditions
Age range(s): Grades 10-Adult
Major character(s): Tristan Granados, Student—College, Cuban American
Time period(s): 1980s
Locale(s): Tampa, Florida

Summary: Tristan Granados, the son of a Cuban-born screenwriter and a WASP mother, is a Yale undergraduate, sent to Tampa to make funeral arrangements for his paternal grandfather. This cynical tale of the conflicts between two cultures, follows the adventures of Tristan as he tries, among his large extended Cuban family, to arrange for a cremation. Yglesias acidly portrays the pomposity of Anglo materialist culture, while making fun of the extreme assimilationist inclinations of the Cuban immigrant community. Yglesias writes with biting humor.

Where it's reviewed:
Library Journal, March 15, 1989, page 88
Publishers Weekly, January 6, 1989, page 92

Other books by the same author:
Home Again, 1987
The Kill Price: A Novel, 1976
A Wake in Ybor City, 1963
Break-In, 1996

Other books you might like:
Roberto G. Fernandez, *Holy Radishes*, 1995
    This satirical novel depicts the Cuban American community in Florida where exiled Cubans plan the liberation of their homeland while their wives work at a radish plant.
Jaime Manrique, *Latin Moon in Manhattan*, 1992
    Through the eyes of Santiago, a gay unpublished poet, this novel presents plots and sub-plots and a vivid depiction of Columbian American culture in Little Colombia Jackson Heights.
Oscar Hijuelos, *The Fourteen Sisters of Emilio Montez O'Brien: A Novel*, 1993
    An intergenerational saga, this novel follows the lives of Mariela Montez. Cuban, and her Irish husband Nelson O'Brien who move to Cobbleton, Pennsylvania at the turn of the century.
Virgil Suarez, *Havana Thursdays: A Novel*, 1995
    This is the story of two sisters, their daughters, and how they represent two different manners of dealing with the changes encountered through immigration from a Latino culture.
Pablo La Rosa, *Forbidden Fruit and Other Stories*, 1996
    This collection of short stories whimsically depicts the coming-of-age experiences of a young man in Cuba before the revolution.
Carolina Garcia-Aquilera, *Bloody Waters*, 1996
    Guadalupe Solano, one of Miami's elite, is approached by a young couple for assistance in finding the biological mother of their adopted daughter when she needs a bone marrow transplant.

891

RAFAEL YGLESIAS, Cuban American

Dr. Neruda's Cure for Evil
(New York, NY: Warner, 1996)

Subject(s): Psychological Thriller; Family Relations; Sexual Abuse
Age range(s): Grades 10-Adult
Major character(s): Dr. Rafael Neruda, Doctor (psychiatrist), Cuban American; Gene Kenny, Patient, Young Man, Caucasian
Time period(s): 1990s
Locale(s): New York, New York

Summary: A very long (700 pages) novel that examines at length the psychological depth of the primary characters and explores the multiple dimensions of evil. The first section of this three part novel records the life of Dr. Rafael Neruda, the son of a Cuban father and Jewish mother, particularly his relationship with his father, and his growth through therapy. In the second section a patient of Dr. Neruda is introduced, Gene Kenny, who goes through extensive therapy with Dr. Neruda to remedy his neuroses due to the abuse he suffered as a child. He becomes "cured", but then he commits a terrible crime, which implies that his neuroses were somehow helpful to his psychological well being. In the third section of the novel Neruda becomes more intimately involved in Kenny's life, including his work, to determine what went wrong with his therapy. In Kenny's high-tech firm Neruda discovers evil in the persons of the CEO and his cruel daughter, and they seem perfectly happy! A suspenseful novel as Yglesias ponders whether evil is a medical condition or a moral one.

Where it's reviewed:
Publishers Weekly, May 27, 1996, page 1996
Library Journal, May 1, 1996, page 136

Other books by the same author:
The Murderer Next Door, 1990
Fearless: A Novel, 1993
The Game Player, 1978
Hot Properties, 1986
Only Children, 1988

Other books you might like:
Francisco Goldman, *The Long Night of White Chickens*, 1992
    Determined to find the murderers of his cousin Flor, Roger and his best friend Luis become entangled in political difficulties as they discover the secret life of Flor in war-torn Guatemala.
Oscar Hijuelos, *Mr. Ives' Christmas*, 1995
    Edward Ives, a New York commercial artist, mourns the loss of his beloved son and begins to exchange letters with his son's killer, a young Puerto Rican who will soon be released from prison.
John Rechy, *The Miraculous Day of Amalia Gomez: A Novel*, 1991
    This story examines poverty, gang warfare, border cross-

ings, and visions of salvation while following one day in the life of a Mexican American woman.

Alba Ambert, *A Perfect Silence*, 1995
From the surrealistic world of a mental institution, a Puerto Rican woman, Blanca, attempts to come to terms with her abusive past and her self-destructiveness.

Esmeralda Santiago, *America's Dream*, 1996
America works as a housekeeper in a hotel on an island off the coast of Puerto Rico, until she accepts a job as a nanny in Westchester County, New York, and learns about a new life.

Floyd Salas, *State of Emergency*, 1996
Roger, a 1960s radical professor, finds refuge in the counter-culture and in the people of other nations after he writes an expose of the government and is forced to flee the U.S.

Max Martinez, *White Leg*, 1996
This fast-paced murder mystery concerns a small-time thief in a backwater Texas town who kills a Texas Ranger and three other people during one of his hold-ups.

892

RAFAEL YGLESIAS, Cuban American

Fearless: A Novel
(New York: Warner Books, 1993)

Subject(s): Airplane Accidents; Courage; Death
Age range(s): Grades 10-Adult
Major character(s): Max Klein, Architect, Accident Victim (airplane crash), Caucasian
Time period(s): 1990s
Locale(s): New York, New York

Summary: The plane carrying Max Klein crashes in a Southern California cornfield. He survives and somehow his terror is turned into ecstasy and he wants to help everyone. He's passed through death, no longer fears it and he becomes a sort of saint. For weeks he only associates with another survivor, a Latina woman who lost a child in the crash. He tests death again by consciously crashing his Volvo into a wall.

Where it's reviewed:
Library Journal, April 1, 1993, page 134
Publishers Weekly, February 8, 1993, page 76

Other books by the same author:
The Game Player, 1978
Hide Fox, and All After, 1972
Hot Properties, 1986
The Murderer Next Door, 1990
Only Children, 1988

Other books you might like:
Oscar Hijuelos, *Mr. Ives' Christmas*, 1995
Edward Ives, a New York commercial artist, mourns the loss of his beloved son, and begins to exchange letters with his son's killer, a young Puerto Rican who will soon be released from prison.

Himilce Novas, *Mangos, Bananas, and Coconuts: A Cuban Love Story*, 1996
This tale of a magical yet real love story is an ancient tale, beginning with the love of a man and a woman from

different social classes, and the story of the fate of their children.

Dagoberto Gilb, *The Last Known Residence of Mickey Acuna*, 1994
Mickey Acuna is waiting for something, something arriving through the mail, as he dwells at the YMCA in El Paso.

Max Martinez, *A Red Bikini Dream*, 1990
This story collection captures the rhythms and spirit of modern life in the U.S. and explores self and identity in an increasingly complex nation.

Luis Alberto Urrea, *In Search of Snow*, 1994
Mike McGirk, a blue collar Don Quixote, searches for love and life in the Arizona desert, and learns about family from Bobo Garcia.

Yvonne V. Sapia, *Valentino's Hair*, 1991
Rudolph Valentino comes into the life of Facundo Nieves and changes it forever when Nieves saves the hair and its power haunts him until his own death.

893

RAFAEL YGLESIAS, Cuban American

The Murderer Next Door
(New York: Crown Publishers, 1990)

Subject(s): Mystery and Detective Stories; Murder; Child Custody
Age range(s): Grades 10-Adult
Major character(s): Molly Gray, Lawyer
Time period(s): 1980s
Locale(s): New York, New York

Summary: When Molly's best friend, talented artist and musician Wendy Sonnenfeld marries a peculiar acting unsightly man, Molly doesn't understand it at all. When the couple has a baby, childless Molly becomes the doting aunt, until she learns about Ben's moodswings and histrionics. Wendy is suddenly murdered and Ben, it's discovered, is the murderer and a closet transvestite who gets custody of his child. Molly will do anything to protect the baby, including mad and senseless dangerous acts.

Where it's reviewed:
Library Journal, August 1990, page 146
New York Times Book Review, October 14, 1990, page 46
Publishers Weekly, July 6, 1990, page 60
Virginia Quarterly Review, Summer 1991, page 95

Other books by the same author:
Fearless: A Novel, 1993
The Game Player, 1978
Hot Properties, 1986
Only Children, 1988
The Work Is Innocent, 1976

Other books you might like:
Thomas Sanchez, *Mile Zero*, 1989
This exciting novel uses history, voodoo, santeria, folkloric sayings, and tropical culture to create a supernatural mystery and introduces *Zobop*, possibly a voodoo-inspired killer.

Gloria Gonzalez, *The Thirteenth Apostle*, 1993
 Newspaperwoman Geraldine St. Claire investigates the murder of her lover Hal, which leads her to suspect an industrial homicide and also leads her right into the hands of a powerful drug lord.

Soledad Santiago, *Nightside*, 1994
 Anna Eltern, a former nun who runs a shelter for runaway teens, struggles with financial problems and murder after funding cuts force her to turn away homeless teenagers.

Manuel Ramos, *The Last Client of Luis Montez*, 1996
 The last client of Denver lawyer Louie Montez is found dead with Montez standing over him. To clear his name Montez becomes entangled in a complicated web that takes him to California and back.

Francisco Goldman, *The Long Night of White Chickens*, 1992
 Determined to find the murderers of his cousin Flor, Roger and his best friend Luis become entangled in political difficulties as they discover the secret life of Flor in a war-torn Guatemala.

Max Martinez, *White Leg*, 1996
 A fast action murder mystery about a small town thief in a back water town in Texas who kills a Texas Ranger and three other people during one of his hold-ups.

Jose Yglesias, *Break-In*, 1996
 Rudy Pardo comes home to find a young, tall, thin black man rifling through his possessions, and this intrusion brings out his racial prejudices.

894

VINCENT YOUNIS, Mexican American

Shine Boys: A Story about Santa Fe
(Taos, NM: Blinking Yellow Books, 1995)

Subject(s): Drugs; Growing Up; Identity
Age range(s): Grades 7 and Up
Time period(s): 1950s; 1960s (1950-1965)
Locale(s): Santa Fe, New Mexico

Summary: This novella narrates the life of an un-named main character growing up in Santa Fe. Through the voice of this young boy, we're introduced to his best friend Pablito, his "jifita", and the life of Santa Fe including some customs and traditions, during the late 1950s. At a very young age he is introduced to drugs and drug dealing, spending time in juvenile detention, and eventually being forced to join the army by his probation officer.

Other books you might like:
Gil C. Alicea, *The Air Down Here: True Tales from a South Bronx Boyhood*, 1995
 Sixteen-year-old Gil Alicea battles daily with drugs, violence, gangs, school, family, and the media in this book of short essays and journal entries.

Abraham Rodriguez Jr., *The Boy Without a Flag: Tales of the South Bronx*, 1992
 Stories about young people growing up Puerto Rican in New York city.

Miguel Duran, *Don't Spit on My Corner*, 1992
 Little Mike and his friends, coming of age in Los Angeles during World War II, spend their time being "cool", cruising, drinking, and protecting their turf.

Laura Del Fuego, *Maravilla*, 1989
 Consuelo Contreres, growing up in the housing projects of East Los Angeles, makes her way through turbulent times in the 1960s.

Floyd Salas, *What Now My Love*, 1994
 A writer and his two friends flee San Francisco's drug subculture and a narcotics bust, to travel to the Mexican border during the 1960s.

Denise Chavez, *The Last of the Menu Girls*, 1986
 An adolescent Chicana girl from southern New Mexico searches for her identity and womanhood in this collection of interrelated stories.

895

RAFAEL ZEPEDA, Mexican American

Horse Medicine and Other Stories
(Long Beach, CA: Applezaba Press, 1990)

Subject(s): Short Stories; Family Relations; Men
Age range(s): Grades 9-Adult
Time period(s): 1980s
Locale(s): California

Summary: There are nine stories in this collection, each dealing with the world of men. In "Horse Medicine" several men, with kids and wives, participate in rodeos and live with horses; in "Shaft Alley" a young man works in the engine room of a westbound ship that's full of bombs. Drinking, swearing, and male one-up-manship is the norm, until one man is found dead. Zepeda's characters are Mexican, American Indians, and Vietnam veterans, and all seem to be moving, active, and busy in their world of men.

Where it's reviewed:
Western American Literature, November 1991, page 276

Other books you might like:
Dagoberto Gilb, *The Magic of Blood*, 1993
 A powerful collection presents harsh, realistic stories about working-class life in Texas and California.

Ed Vega, *Casualty Report*, 1991
 These short stories, about Latino life in New York, include one about a frustrated Vietnam veteran.

Hugo Martinez-Serros, *The Last Laugh and Other Stories*, 1988
 The culture and atmosphere of urban Chicago during World War II are brought to life in this collection of short stories.

Max Martinez, *A Red Bikini Dream*, 1990
 The rhythms and spirit of modern life in the U.S. are captured in this collection of five short stories where the characters ponder self and identity in an increasingly complex society.

Leo Romero, *Rita and Los Angeles*, 1995
 In this short story collection, a cast of fascinatingly complex characters grow and evolve, and learn about being outsiders in an alien and hostile world.

Genaro Gonzalez, *Only Sons*, 1991
 The main characters in this collection, all male, are trying to define their social relationships. Gonzalez explores ambivalent emotions, cultural values, and family traditions.

Rafael Castillo, *Distant Journeys*, 1991
The short stories in this collection are full of irony, humor, and disturbing cultural illusions about the myth of the American Dream.

Asian American Literature

Even as recently as two decades ago, the average reader was probably not familiar with so-called "Asian American literature." Perhaps the reader could name a single title or author, but to consider it a genre of literature would most likely have been thought of by the general public as somewhat premature.

The first true "breakthrough" title into the mainstream appeared in 1976 with the publication of Maxine Hong Kingston's *The Woman Warrior,* a multi-award winning (including the National Book Critics Circle Award for best nonfiction) memoir on growing up Chinese American in a predominantly white world. According to Bill Moyers in his *A World of Ideas* (volume 2), *The Woman Warrior,* together with Hong Kingston's follow-up work, *China Men,* became "the most widely taught books by a living American author on college campuses during the 1980s." In spite of its undeniable critical, academic, even commercial success, not to mention having a major publishing house behind it (Alfred A. Knopf), *The Woman Warrior,* nor its venerable author, quite became household names.

Then came the surprise success of *The Joy Luck Club* by Amy Tan in 1989. Not until Tan made publishing history with her meteoric rise to the top of the bestseller charts, her history-making seven-digit sales of paperback rights and her subsequent bank-breaking advances did the general public become fully conscious of the Asian American novel—like a brick falling on someone's head. Publishers immediately saw dollar signs. And major houses began to take chances on

brand new, unproven writers with such ethnic hybrid names as Chang-rae Lee, Gish Jen, Cynthia Kadohata, Belle Yang and Gus Lee...and they received almost instant payback. A new niche popular market was born. And it's been growing exponentially ever since.

A Working Definition

In spite of what seems to be a recent (rather splashy) public entry into the publishing mainstream, the concept of "Asian American literature" is hardly a new fad or passing phenomenon. Books written by people of Asian ancestry have been around for over a century, just as considerable numbers of Asian Americans have made their home in the U.S. since the 1850s. And while the term "Asian American literature" might imply a sense of homogeneity, the breadth of included titles cannot be described in a single sentence or even a paragraph, just as the diverse, individual writers cannot be circumscribed by a single narrow definition.

For the purposes of this inaugural edition of *What Do I Read Next? Multicultural Literature,* "Asian American literature" has been approached as an *inclusive* term. These 240 entries are the works of diverse authors of Asian Pacific heritage, including Chinese, Japanese, Korean, Filipino, Vietnamese, Hawaiian, East Indian and South Pacific backgrounds. A few Canadian American writers are also included. And, as a reflection of America's melting pot characteristic, a number of mixed Asian heritage writers such as Chinese Scottish American Ruthanne Lum McCunn and Chinese Eurasian American Diana Chang are listed, as well. Multigenerations of Asian Americans are found here, from fifth-generation Chinese American Frank Chin to Indian American Bharati Mukherjee who immigrated to the U.S. in her twenties and later became a naturalized Canadian citizen.

The thousands of pages represented in these entries arejust as diverse as their authors. This survey of Asian American literature encompasses stories as diverse as Filipino American Carlos Bulosan's immigrant experiences in *America Is in the Heart*, Japanese American Jeanne Wakatsuki Houston's memories of the World War II Japanese internment crisis in *A Farewell to Manzanar*, Japanese American Lydia Minatoya's search for her hyphenated Asian American identity in *Talking to High Monks in the Snow: An Asian American Odyssey,* Sri Lankan Canadian Shyam Selvadurai's fictionalized account of his experiences in his homeland before arriving in America in *Funny Boy*, or Korean American Helie Lee's search for her grandmother's North Korean past in *Still Life With Rice: A Young American Woman Discovers the Life and Legacy of Her Korean Grandmother*. Still others wrote non-ethnic-specific books with or without characters who just might (or might not) happen to be Asian American, such as Lowry Pei's coming-of-age tale, *Family Resemblances,* or Vikram Seth's novel in verse about five friends, *The Golden Gate*, or Cynthia Kadohata's futuristic story, *In the Heart of the Valley of Love.*

While the majority of the entries are of titles published in the last two decades, groundbreaking earlier works such as Chinese Eurasian American Edith Maude Eaton's *Mrs. Spring Fragrance and Other Writings,* collected short stories written (and many originally published) almost a century ago under the pseudonym Sui Sin Far, or Japanese American Monica Sone's *Nisei Daughter,* a memoir of growing up during the 1920s to '40s in Washington State, are also included. [*Not* included among the historically important texts are those that are not readily available because they are either published by an obscure small press or no longer in print such as Korean American Younghill Kang's *East Goes West: The Making of an Oriental Yankee,* originally published in 1937 by Charles Scribner's Sons.]

The works here represent a spectrum for readers as well, from picture books for children to young adult titles to adult literature that includes not only fiction, but drama, history, personal memoirs and poetry. Anthologies are especially helpful in offering a varied overview of types of Asian American literature, sometimes as specific as *Our Feet Walk the Sky: Women of the South Asian Diaspora,* edited by the Women of South Asian Descent Collective, or as broad as *Charlie Chan Is Dead: An Anthology of Contemporary Asian American Fiction,* edited by Jessica Hagedorn.

A Brief Historical Overview

Asian Americans became a piece of the American ethnic pie during the 1850s when large numbers of Chinese laborers entered the U.S. and went to work building the transcontinental railroads, and later tending endless crop fields—work that required long hours of back-breaking, often life-threatening labor for unjustly meager wages. A significant flow of Japanese immigrants followed the Chinese during the turn of the century, while small numbers of Korean and Filipino transplants entered the U.S. during the early decades of the 1900s. Segregated from the already established towns and work camps, these Asian immigrants were forced to establish their own peripheral communities, maintaining their native language and customs. Under such conditions of being overworked, living in impoverished conditions and forced into cultural and linguistic isolation, these immigrants hardly had the time, the means nor possibly the inclination to produce an early generation of writers. In addition, among Asian cultures, "talk story," or the oral tradition, was traditionally the preferred mode of passing on tales from generation to generation.

Not surprisingly, the earliest known published work in English by a writer of Asian heritage was not written by an immigrant laborer, but a Yale University graduate, a young man who was sent to the U.S. by the Chinese government in the 1870s as one of a select group of Chinese boys to receive a Western education. Lee Yan Phou's *When I Was a Boy in China*, published in 1887, was hardly an account of the early Asian American immigrant experience; rather, as its title suggests, it focused on Lee's childhood in China, describing Chinese games and sports, food, traditional ceremonies and folk tales. More importantly, Lee's treatise was the first of more than a century's worth of literature that attempted to dispel the growing stereotypes and misconceptions of Asians—in Lee's case, to reclaim the rich Chinese culture that had been sullied by the racism that gave birth to the insulting "Ching Chong Chinaman"-type epithets and slurs. Even today, the bulk of Asian American literature, on some level, tries to project valid, accurate accounts of the Asian American experience, at the same time fighting the media's caricature images of Asian Americans as the "yellow peril," the Confucius-quoting "Number One Son," the "dragon lady," Fu Manchu, the "inscrutable Oriental," and the like.

Approximately a decade after Lee's autobiographical work appeared, two Chinese English Canadian sisters made literary history with the publication of what is today believed to be the first works of true Asian American fiction. Edith Maude Eaton, writing under the name Sui Sin Far, began publishing various essays, short stories and journalistic articles during the 1880s; in 1896, her short story, "The Gamblers," was the first fiction piece that dealt specifically with the Asian North American experience. [Largely ignored during the last century, Sui Sin Far's works have experienced a revival in the last decade, with inclusion in numerous anthologies as well as a recently published collection of her short stories, *Mrs. Spring Fragrance and Other Writings.*] Edith's sister, Winifred Lillie Eaton, writing as Onoto Watanna, published the novel *Miss Nume of Japan* in 1899; in marked difference to her sister's writings, *Miss Nume,* along with Winifred's later works, were all set in Asia.

Understandably, since the majority of early Asian Americans were of Chinese and Japanese descent, Asian American literature was initially dominated by Chinese American and Japanese American voices. Moreover, due to strict anti-Asian immigration laws from the 1880s to the 1940s, the Asian American community hardly had an opportunity to grow, much less become more diverse.

Although most of the early Asian American writers during the first half of the twentieth century wrote from their own experiences, producing such titles as Etsu Sugimoto's *A Daughter of the Samurai* (1925), Jade Snow Wong's *Fifth Chinese Daughter* (1945) and Lin Yutang's *A Chinatown Family* (1948), these works were, for the most part, far removed from the harsh realities of blatant racism and economic deprivation virtually synonymous with the Asian American

experience at the time. An exception to this group of works was Carlos Bulosan's *American Is in the Heart* (1946) which achingly depicted the author's difficult struggles and failed attempts to establish himself as an accepted member of American society.

With the advent of World War II, a new direction in Asian American literature emerged. Between 1942 and 1945, some 120,000 Americans of Japanese descent, two-thirds of whom were U.S. citizens *by birth*, were incarcerated in 10 concentration camps throughout the West. Caught as scapegoats in a national hysteria against the Japanese following the December 7, 1941 attack on Pearl Harbor and fearing the possibility of Japanese American collusion with the Japanese government, then-President Franklin D. Roosevelt signed Executive Order 9066 which resulted in the cattle-like round-up and unjust imprisonment of Japanese Americans.

Two of the earliest writings about the tragic experience was Mine Okubo's 1946 illustrated memoir *Citizen 13660* and Hisaye Yamamoto's 1950 short story, "The Legend of Miss Sasagawara." Other accounts of the experience would not appear until decades later; the older Japanese Americans were silenced by the traumatic event, surviving emotionally and mentally by telling themselves, "*shigata ga nai* (it can't be helped; nothing can be done)," and hiding what they believed to be a shameful part of the past, "*kodomo no tame ni* (for the sake of the children)." Not until the 1970s was that silence finally broken, resulting in a virtual rush of internment experience-inspired literature, including such notable works as Momoko Iko's play *The Gold Watch,* about a Japanese American family caught in the racist fervor on the eve of the evacuation order, John Okada's novel *No-No Boy,* about a young Japanese American man who refused to take the U.S. loyalty oath and risk his life fighting for the country that unjustly imprisoned him, Yoshiko Uchida's memoir *Desert Exile: The Uprooting of a Japanese American Family,* about the Uchida family's experiences at Camp Topaz, and Ken Mochizuki's children's book, *Baseball Saved Us,* about how a group of young internees endured the tedium of their imprisonment in part by playing baseball behind barbed wire.

Perhaps partially in response to the civil rights movement starting to take shape in the 1960s, U.S. immigration laws were considerably eased by 1965, and a new wave of Asian immigrants began to arrive in considerable numbers. These new citizens-to-be changed the landscape of a predominantly Chinese and Japanese Asian America; a new influx of Koreans, Taiwanese, Filipinos, East Indians, Vietnamese, Cambodians, Laotians, Singaporeans, Sri Lankans, and other South Pacific Islanders arrived on American shores, bringing different languages, age-old traditions, unfamiliar customs, diverse foods and new names to add to the polyglot of American society.

The Asian American community burst forth with previously unheard, long ignored voices. The publication in 1974 of the groundbreaking anthology, *Aiiieeeee! An Anthology of Asian American Writers,* edited by Frank Chin, Jeffery Paul Chan, Lawson Fusao Inada and Shawn Wong, first by a small independent press and later by a major New York publishing giant (Penguin Group), announced to the public the flourishing existence of Asian American literature. As the list of Asian American titles and Asian American authors grew, the academic world was the first to take notice, especially universities in California (where the largest Asian American populations are found) which began to offer classes in Asian American literature. These and other related classes on the Asian American experience eventually evolved into Asian American Studies departments, a trend that is slowly spreading nationwide.

Asian American Literature Today

By the mid-1980s, Asian Americans were reclaiming their life stories and experiences in a trend that continues to grow stronger even today. For the first time, large numbers of Asian Americans were telling their stories, in their own words. Following in the literary footsteps of such early pioneering memoirs as Bulosan's *America Is in the Heart* and Monica Sone's *Nisei Daughter,* which accurately depicted the often harsh realities of life as an immigrant or even as an American-born Asian American, other Asian Americans reclaimed their misrepresented, silenced past in such life-affirming memoirs as Mary Paik Lee's *Quiet Odyssey: A Pioneer Korean Woman in America* and Lydia Minatoya's *Talking to High Monks in the Snow: An Asian American Odyssey,* as well as various anthologies including *Growing Up Asian American,* edited by Maria Hong, *Under Western Eyes: Personal Essays from Asian America,* edited by Garrrett Hongo

and *East to America: Korean American Life Stories,* edited by Elaine H. Kim and Eui-Young Yu.

In the midst of the emergence of more and more Asian American voices, two breakthrough events catapulted Asian American literature into the mainstream market. In March 1988, David Henry Hwang's gender-bender, Tony Award-winning drama, *M. Butterfly,* debuted on Broadway. Based on a story Hwang heard about a French diplomat who was involved in a 20-year affair with a male Chinese spy whom he believed to be a woman, the play became one of the most successful non-musical works in Broadway history. It was produced in three dozen countries around the world and grossed over $35 million. At age 32, Hwang was an international phenomenon. *Time* magazine referred to him as "potential[ly] ... the first important dramatist of American public life since Arthur Miller, and maybe the best of them all." The drama world had a bonafide, bankable Asian American star.

Then came Amy Tan's overnight sensation, *The Joy Luck Club.* Published in 1989 to unheard of success, the novel about the relationships between four Chinese mothers, who meet every week to play mahjong and share their lives, and their four American-born daughters, opened new doors for a proliferation of other writers of Asian descent.

New anthologies collected the neglected older works of such talented writers as Hisaye Yamamoto in *Seventeen Syllables and Other Stories* and Wakako Yamauchi in *Songs My Mother Taught Me: Stories, Plays, and Memoir,* at the same time showcasing the debut pieces of new, unknown names. Asian American women writers found new representation in a significant number of women-only collections, such as *Making Waves: An Anthology of Writings By and About Asian American Women* edited by Asian Women United, *The Forbidden Stitch: An Asian American Women's Anthology* edited by Shirley Geok-lin Lim, *Home to Stay: Asian American Women's Fiction* edited by Sylvia Watanabe and Carol Bruchac, and *Her Mother's Ashes and Other Stories by South Asian Women in Canada and the United States* edited by Nurjehan Aziz.

Moreover, writers who had been previously

published by smaller presses picked up contracts with major publishers. For example, Shawn Wong's debut novel *Homebase* was originally published by independent small press I. Reed Books in 1979, and later went out of print before being reissued by Penguin in 1991; his second novel, *American Knees,* was published by Simon and Schuster in 1995. Lois-Ann Yamanaka's first work *Saturday Night at the Pahala Theatre,* was produced by Bamboo Ridge Press in 1993; three years later, her novel *Wild Meat and the Bully Burgers,* was published by Farrar Straus Giroux.

Fiction writers were not the only writers pushed into the mainstream limelight. Poet Garrett Hongo garnered a Pulitzer Prize nomination with his 1988 collection, *The River of Heaven,* published by Alfred A. Knopf. Professor Ronald Takaki was also nominated for a Pulitzer with his 1989 history text, *Strangers from a Different Shore: A History of Asian Americans,* published by Little, Brown and Company.

The late 1980s and 1990s have also witnessed a near explosion of Asian American titles for children. Veterans Allen Say, Laurence Yep and Ed Young have been joined by newcomers Sheila Hamanaka, Huy Voun Lee, Jeanne M. Lee, Ken Mochizuki and Chyng Feng Sun, to name a few. Many recent children's books are also finding inspiration in new retellings and adaptations of traditional folktales and legends of Asian origin, such as Charlie Chin's *China's Bravest Girl,* based on the legend of the Chinese woman warrior Fa Mu Lan, Demi's *Liang and the Magic Paintbrush,* about a young boy whose drawings come to life, or Nami Rhee's *Magic Spring: A Korean Folktale,* about a kind old couple who discover the fountain of youth.

The young adult market, too, has progressed tremendously in the 1990s, although this section of the publishing sector has the most room for potential growth. Again Laurence Yep has been an established name in the field for over two decades, as has the late Yoshiko Uchida. Joining them are Sook Nyul Choi, with her trilogy—*Year of Impossible Goodbyes, Echoes of the White Giraffe* and *Gathering of Pearls*—about a young Korean girl's experiences during the Korean War and her eventual immigration to the U.S., Marie G. Lee and her three titles—*Finding My Voice, If It Hadn't Been for Yoon Jun* and *Saying Goodbye—*

focusing on growing up Korean American, and Lensey Namioka's more recent works such as *April and the Dragon Lady, Yang the Youngest and His Terrible Ear* and *Yang the Third and Her Impossible Family* about coming of age as a Chinese American.

Just as the Asian American population has grown vastly in the last two decades, Asian American literature has also developed in parallel, constantly adding new authors, new titles, and even founding new Asian American-oriented publishing houses. At the same time, Asian American literature is finding a larger, more encompassing audience without ethnic boundaries.

Ironically, as the field of Asian American literature develops and broadens, it will ultimately outgrow itself because someday, such defined, exclusive ethnic terms as Asian American, African American, Latino or Native American will no longer be necessary in the multicultural American society of the future. And in this potentially tolerant, fluid world, even a reference guide such as this, which is much needed today, will hopefully render itself obsolete.

Publishing information

The majority of the titles listed should be accessible to readers throughout the country's libraries and book stores, since many are published by major presses. Two smaller presses whose titles are widely distributed nationally, University of Washington Press in Seattle, Washington and Coffee House Press in Minneapolis, Minnesota, offer numerous Asian American titles: University of Washington Press specializes in reprinting classics such as Carlos Bulosan's *America Is in the Heart* and Diana Chang's *Frontiers of Love,* while Coffee House focuses on more recent works such as Frank Chin's *Donald Duk* and *Gunga Din Highway* and M. Evelina Galang's *Her Wild American Self.* Three other small presses specifically publish Asian and Asian Pacific American titles only: Bamboo Ridge Press in Honolulu, Hawaii, which specializes in Hawaiian authors, and also offers a literary quarterly, *Bamboo Ridge: The Hawaii Writers' Quarterly;* the recently founded Kaya Production in New York, New York, which focuses on contemporary Asian American writers [Kaya also plans to begin a series of reclaiming out-of-print Asian

American classics, such as Younghill Kang's *East Goes West.*]; and Polychrome Publishing in Chicago, Illinois, which specializes in Asian American children and young adult titles.

Some Favorite Titles

The following is a list of books (organized by audience type, alphabetically by author) from the 240 included entries which were personal favorites. They do not necessarily represent the most critically acclaimed or most commercially successful titles.

For children:

Children of Asian America by the Asian American Coalition

Halmoni and the Picnic by Sook Nyul Choi
Heroes by Ken Mochizuki
Aekyung's Dream by Min Paek
Dumpling Soup by Jama Kim Rattigan
Grandfather's Journey by Alley Say
Mama Bear by Chyng Feng Sun
Ashok by Any Other Name by Sandra Yamate

For young adults:

Finding My Voice by Marie G. Lee
Shizuko's Daughter by Kyoko Mori
American Dragons: Twenty-Five Asian American Voices edited by Laurence Yep

For adults:

Typical American by Gish Jen
Three Filipino Women by F. Sionil Jose
East to America: Korean American Life Stories edited by Elaine H. Kim and Eui-Young Yu
Dancer Dawkins and the California Kid by Willyce Kim
Native Speaker by Chang-rae Lee
Pangs of Love by David Wong Louie
Bombay Talkie by Ameena Meer
Talking to High Monks in the Snow: An Asian American Odyssey by Lydia Minatoya
Jasmine by Bharati Mukherjee
Love, Stars and All That by Kirin Narayan
A Feather on the Breath of God by Sigrid Nunez
The Golden Gate by Vikram Seth
Wild Meat and the Bully Burgers by Lois-Ann Yamanaka

Baba: A Return to China Upon My Father's Shoulders by Belle Yang

Asian American Literary Publications

Amerasia Journal. Los Angeles: The Asian American Studies Center, University of California at Los Angeles.
The Asian Pacific American Journal. New York: The Asian American Writers Workshop.
Asian/Pacific American Women's Journal. Ann Arbor: University of Michigan.
Bamboo Ridge: The Hawaii Writers' Quarterly. Honolulu: Bamboo Ridge Press.

Suggested Literary Criticism Texts

Cheung, King-Kok and Stan Yogi. *Asian American Literature: An Annotated Bibliography.* New York: The Modern Language Association, 1988.

Chin, Frank, Jeffery Paul Chan, Lawson Fusao Inada and Shawn Wong, ed. *Aiiieeeee! An Anthology of Asian American Writers.* New York: Mentor (Penguin Group), 1974.

———. *The Big Aiiieeeee! An Anthology of Chinese American and Japanese American Literature.* New York: Meridian (Penguin Group), 1991.

Hsu, Kai-yu and Helen Palubinskas, eds. *Asian American Authors.* Boston: Houghton Mifflin, 1972.

Kim, Elaine H. *Asian American Literature: An Introduction to the Writings and Their Social Context.* Philadelphia: Temple University Press, 1982.

Lim, Shirley Geok-lin and Amy Ling, ed. *Reading the Literatures of Asian America.* Philadelphia: Temple University Press, 1992.

Wong, Sau-Ling. *Reading Asian American Literature: From Necessity to Extravagance.* Princeton: Princeton University Press, 1993.

Asian American Titles

896

MEENA ALEXANDER

Nampally Road

(San Francisco: Mercury House, 1991)

Subject(s): Multicultural; Identity; Politics
Age range(s): Adult
Major character(s): Mira Kannadical, Professor (teaches English Poetry); Ramu, Professor (fellow university instructor), Lover (Mira's); Durgabai "Little Mother" Gokhale, Doctor (OB-GYN, treats anyone in need)
Time period(s): 1990s
Locale(s): Hyderabad, India

Summary: Mira returns to her native India after graduate school in England, to a new address on Nampally Road, a new lover and new friends. But the post-colonial India she has returned to is governed by a new dictator and corrupt police. Once lost in the poetry of Wordsworth, Mira struggles to define her new life.

About this book: A rather thin, yet extremely dense volume.

Where it's reviewed:
Belles Lettres, Fall 1991, page 46
Kirkus Reviews, November 1, 1990, page 1472
Publishers Weekly, December 14, 1990, page 62

Other books by the same author:
Women in Romanticism: Mary Wollstonecraft, Dorothy Wordsworth and Mary Shelley, 1989 (critical study)
The Storm: A Poem in Five Parts, 1989
House of a Thousand Doors, 1988 (poetry)

Other books you might like:
Chitra Banerjee Divakaruni, *Arranged Marriage*, 1995
A collection of 11 short stories about young Indian and Indian American women, some married, some single, in various stages of claiming their independence.
Bharati Mukherjee, *Jasmine*, 1989
A novel about Jasmine Vijh's odyssey through America, from her arrival from India as a 17-year-old widow to her new life as Jane Ripplemeyer, assumed to be an Iowa housewife.
Nayantara Sahgal, *Mistaken Identity*, 1988
In 1929, Bhusan Singh, the aimless son of a wealthy raja, is arrested, falsely charged with treason and imprisoned. He spends three years in jail, reflecting on his life.
Gita Mehta, *A River Sutra*, 1993
A retired civil servant living along the holy Narmada River comes into contact with numerous travelers and their mesmerizing stories.
Ameena Meer, *Bombay Talkie*, 1994
Sabah heads to India in search of her ethnic identity. What she finds in the wealthy world of her Indian relatives is a liberal Westernized culture bound by strict traditions.

897

JOSE ARUEGO, Adaptor
ARIANE DEWEY, Co-Adaptor

Rockabye Crocodile

(Boston: Greenwillow Books (William Morrow & Company), 1988)

Subject(s): Folk Tales; Good and Evil; Greed
Age range(s): Grades 1-3
Major character(s): Amabel, Boar (cheerful, kind and elderly); Nettie, Boar (mean and selfish), Neighbor (Amabel's); Crocodile, Crocodile, Mother (has baby crocodile)
Time period(s): Indeterminate Past
Locale(s): "in the jungle"

Summary: Amabel and Nettie are two elderly boars who live in the jungle. Amabel is nice, Nettie is mean. Amabel is rewarded for her goodness, especially by the mother crocodile whose baby Amabel cares for. When Nettie hears of Amabel's good fortune, she rudely demands her share, only to be punished for her selfish greed.

About this book: Based on a classic Philippine fable.

Where it's reviewed:
Horn Book Magazine, September 1988, page 611
Kirkus Reviews, September 1, 1988, page 1318
School Library Journal, December 1988, page 79

Other books you might like:

Demi, *The Empty Pot*, 1990

All the children in China must grow a flower from the Emperor's seeds, but Ping cannot. His admission of the fact, earns him a reward.

Demi, *Liang and the Magic Paintbrush*, 1980

When a poor boy who longs to paint is given a brush, it turns out to be magic, bringing to life whatever he paints.

Laurence Yep, *The Shell Woman and the King*, 1993

The magical shell woman saves her husband and her self from the evil, greedy king.

Ai-Ling Louie, *Yeh-Shen: A Cinderella Story from China*, 1982

In spite of the wicked machinations of her stepmother, the beautiful young Yeh-Shen manages to survive her deprived life, marry the king and live happily ever after.

Nami Rhee, *Magic Spring: A Korean Folktale*, 1993

A hardworking, childless, elderly couple find the fountain of youth. Their greedy neighbor rushes to the magic spring and overindulges, leading to a surprise ending.

898

ASIAN AMERICAN COALITION
GENE H. MAYEDA, Illustrator

Children of Asian America

(Chicago: Polychrome Publishing Corporation, 1995)

Subject(s): Multicultural; Difference; Tolerance
Age range(s): Grades 3 and Up
Locale(s): Chicago, Illinois

Summary: A collection of original stories about growing up as an Asian American child, centered around the diverse ethnic Asian communities of Chicago—featuring Asian Americans of Bangladeshi, Cambodian, Chinese, Filipino, Indian, Japanese, Korean, Laotian, Pakistani, Thai, Vietnamese and multiracial heritages.

Other books you might like:

Maria Hong, *Growing Up Asian American*, 1993

These essays, excerpts, and short stories by Americans of Asian descent address issues such as parent-child relationships, self-realization, identity and the discovery of one's cultural heritage.

Min Paek, *Aekyung's Dream*, 1988

Aekyung, a young Korean girl recently in the U.S., dreams about King Sejong who created *Hangul*, the Korean alphabet, and finds new pride in her Korean heritage.

Kate Waters, *Lion Dancer: Ernie Wan's Chinese New Year*, 1990

Young Ernie is about to perform his first Lion Dance through the streets of New York City's Chinatown as part of the Chinese New Year celebration.

Michele Maria Surat, *Angel Child, Dragon Child*, 1983

Young Ut, a recent Vietnamese immigrant, is teased because of her different appearance. Thrown together by the school principal, Ut and a once cruel boy develop a new friendship.

Sheila Hamanaka, *All the Colors of the Earth*, 1994

Children of the world come in many colors, but inside, they're all the same.

899

ASIAN WOMEN UNITED OF CALIFORNIA, Editor

Making Waves: An Anthology of Writings by and about Asian American Women

(Boston: Beacon Press, 1989)

Subject(s): Multicultural; Identity; Emigration and Immigration
Age range(s): Adult
Time period(s): 1870s; 1990s
Locale(s): United States

Summary: The first compilation since the early 1970s of primarily unpublished works by and about Asian American women, *Making Waves* brings together autobiographical writings, short stories, poetry, essays and photography by and about Asian American women whose roots reach back to China, Japan, Korea, the Philippines, India, Pakistan, Vietnam, Cambodia, Burma and Thailand.

About this book: The book's overall introduction, "A Woman-Centered Perspective on Asian American History" is especially interesting and useful. Divided into seven parts ranging from immigration to work to identity to activism, each prefaced by a haunting photo and section introduction, this anthology serves equally well as both a historical and literary text.

Where it's reviewed:
Booklist, June 15, 1989, page 1760
Library Journal, June 15, 1989, page 58
Publishers Weekly, May 19, 1989, page 78

Other books you might like:

Jessica Hagedorn, *Charlie Chan Is Dead: An Anthology of Contemporary Asian American Fiction*, 1993

A collection of 48 works by Asian American writers of different ages, backgrounds and styles.

Shirley Geok-lin Lim, *The Forbidden Stitch: An Asian American Women's Anthology*, 1989

Also edited with Mayumi Tsutakawa and Margarita Donnelly. A rich collection of poetry, short stories, art and reviews focusing on being a contemporary Asian American woman.

Sylvia Watanabe, *Home to Stay: Asian American Women's Fiction*, 1990

Also edited with Carol Bruchac. A collection of short stories that celebrates the literary achievements of Asian American women writers.

Nurjehan Aziz, *Her Mother's Ashes, and Other Stories by South Asian Women in Canada and the United States*, 1994

This anthology highlights the diverse cultures and unique experiences of 21 first-generation North American Women who arrived in Canada and the U.S. by way of South Asia, Africa and the Caribbean.

Women of South Asian Descent Collective, *Our Feet Walk the Sky: Women of the South Asian Diaspora*, 1993

This is the first major compilation that focuses on women of South Asian descent in the U.S. The anthology includes short stories, poetry, personal histories and critical essays.

900

JEANNINE ATKINS
VENANTIUS J. PINTO, Illustrator

Aani and the Tree Huggers

(New York: Lee & Low Books Inc., 1995)

Subject(s): Nature; Heroines; Historical
Major character(s): Aani, Young Woman (young village girl in India); Kalawati, Aged Person (oldest woman in the village)
Time period(s): 1970s
Locale(s): India (a village)

Summary: Aani, a young Indian woman, bravely leads the other women of her village in putting their arms around the many trees of their forest in order to save them from being cut down by unthinking developers.

Where it's reviewed:
School Library Journal, December 1995, Page 94
Smithsonian, November 1995, page 169

Awards the book has won:
Smithsonian Magazine Notable Books for Children, 1995

Other books you might like:
Gita Mehta, *A River Sutra*, 1993
    A retired civil servant living along the holy Narmada River comes into contact with numerous travelers and their mesmerizing stories.
Allen Say, *The Lost Lake*, 1989
    A young boy and his father share a special camping trip.
Demi, *Buddha*, 1996
    The story of the gifted young Prince Siddhartha who leaves his life of luxury and forsakes everything on this earth to seek the Truth of life over death.

901

NURJEHAN AZIZ, Editor

Her Mother's Ashes, and Other Stories by South Asian Women in Canada and the United States

(Toronto: TSAR Publications, 1994)

Subject(s): Multicultural; Identity; Short Stories
Age range(s): Adult

Summary: The anthology features 21 stories by first-generation North American women of South Asian descent, who have arrived in either Canada or the U.S. by way of South Asia, Africa or the Caribbean. While each of the contributors shares the common bond of being of South Asian origin, their stories highlight the many different cultures and unique experiences of the vastly diverse individuals they represent.

Where it's reviewed:
Books in Canada, February 1995, page 37

Other books you might like:
Asian Women United of California, *Making Waves: An Anthology of Writings by and about Asian American Women*, 1989

First major compilation since the early 1970s of primarily unpublished works by and about Asian American women.
Juliet S. Kono, *Sister Stew: Fiction and Poetry by Women*, 1991
    Also edited with Cathy Song. A colorful collection of writings by women of various backgrounds, the majority of whom are either Hawaiian by birth or by adopted residency.
Shirley Geok-lin Lim, *The Forbidden Stitch: An Asian American Women's Anthology*, 1989
    Also edited with Mayumi Tsutakawa and Margarita Donnelly. A rich collection of poetry, short stories, art and reviews focusing on being a contemporary Asian American woman.
Sylvia Watanabe, *Home to Stay: Asian American Women's Fiction*, 1990
    Also edited with Carol Bruchac. A collection of short stories that celebrates the literary achievements of Asian American women writers.
Women of South Asian Descent Collective, *Our Feet Walk the Sky: Women of the South Asian Diaspora*, 1993
    The first major compilation that focuses on women of South Asian descent in the U.S. The anthology includes short stories, poetry, personal histories and critical essays.

902

PETER BACHO

Cebu

(Seattle: University of Washington Press, 1991)

Subject(s): Family Relations; Catholic Religion; Multicultural
Age range(s): Adult
Major character(s): Ben Lucero, Religious (Catholic priest), Filipino American; Clara ''Aunt Clara'' Natividad, Friend (of Lucero's mother), Businesswoman (wealthy, powerfully connected); Ellen Labrado, Assistant (one of Aunt Clara's many), Guide (asked to be Ben's guide)
Time period(s): 1980s; 1990s (with flashbacks to World War II)
Locale(s): Philippines (action split between Cebu and Manila); Seattle, Washington

Summary: Ben Lucero, a Filipino American priest, arrives in the Philippines for the first time to bury his mother in her homeland. As a guest of his Aunt Clara, his mother's lifelong best friend, he experiences the life of the wealthy and powerful, while witnessing the plight of the deprived and oppressed.

Where it's reviewed:
Booklist, September 1, 1991, page 27
Kirkus Reviews, August 1, 1991, page 945
New York Times Book Review, December 15, 1991, page 18

Awards the book has won:
Winner of the American Book Award, Before Columbus Foundation

Other books you might like:
M. Evelina Galang, *Her Wild American Self*, 1996
    A collection of short stories centered on the experiences of Filipina American women of various ages and lifestyles, each in search of her own unique identity.

Jessica Hagedorn, *Dogeaters*, 1990
An autobiographical novel about growing up in Manila in the late 1950s during the turbulent and corrupt Marcos regime.

F. Sionil Jose, *Three Filipino Women: Novellas*, 1992
Three novellas about three remarkable, though ultimately tragic Filipino women: Narita, a politician, Ermita, a high class prostitute, and Malu, a political idealist.

Marianne Villanueva, *Ginseng and Other Tales from Manila*, 1991
Stories inspired by real life events and newspaper articles, focusing on the desperate citizens of a troubled country trying to survive poverty, corruption and loss of freedom.

Bienvenido Santos, *Scent of Apples: A Collection of Short Stories*, 1955
A collection of short stories about the experiences of Filipino men living displaced lives.

903

HIMANI BANNERJI
S. SASSO, Illustrator

Coloured Pictures

(Toronto: Sister Vision, Black Women and Women of Colour Press, 1991)

Subject(s): Multicultural; Emigration and Immigration; Racism

Age range(s): Grades 6-10

Major character(s): Sujata Ghosh, Student (young girl), South Asian Canadian; Samir Ghosh, Brother (Sujata's younger brother), South Asian Canadian; Surindar Singh, Friend (friend of Sujata and Samir); Mr. Stephen ''Big Steve'' Stephenson, Teacher (activist against racism)

Time period(s): 1980s

Locale(s): Toronto, Ontario, Canada

Summary: The Ku Klux Klan opens a local office close to a multiethnic area in Toronto, forcing Sujata and her friends to confront racism first hand. With the help of a driven, activist teacher, both students and parents join forces to keep racism from spreading through their school and city.

Where it's reviewed:
Books in Canada, December 1991, page 38
CM: Canadian Materials for Young People, September 1991, page 217

Other books you might like:
Lori M. Carlson, *American Eyes: New Asian-American Short Stories for Young Adults*, 1994
A collection of 10 short works about young Asian Americans coming of age and coming to terms with an identity comprised of two very different cultures.

Eve Begley Kiehm, *Plantation Child and Other Stories*, 1995
Struggling to survive in the Korean camp section of a Hawaiian sugarcane plantation in the early 1900s, the young Kims still manage to grasp what little is left of their childhood.

Joy Kogawa, *Naomi's Road*, 1986
Young adult story of a Japanese Canadian family that is splintered and scattered as a result of forced evacuation and relocation during World War II.

Laurence Yep, *American Dragons: Twenty-Five Asian American Voices*, 1993
A collection of short stories, poetry and play excerpts from both established Asian American writers and new writers about growing up Asian American.

904

MISHA BERSON, Editor

Between Worlds: Contemporary Asian-American Plays

(New York: Theatre Communications Group, 1990)

Subject(s): Theater; Multicultural
Age range(s): Adult
Time period(s): Indeterminate

Summary: An anthology of diverse plays by six Asian American writers: *Nuit Blanche: A Select View of Earthlings* by Ping Chong, *The Wash* by Philip Kan Gotanda, *Tenement Lover: No Palm Trees/in New York City* by Jessica Hagedorn, *As the Crow Flies* and *The Sound of a Voice* by David Henry Hwang, *And the Soul Shall Dance* by Wakako Yamauchi and *Pay the Chinaman* by Laurence Yep.

About this book: The first published anthology of plays by Asian American writers.

Where it's reviewed:
TDR: The Drama Review, Spring 1993, page 173

Other books you might like:
Philip Kan Gotanda, *Fish Head Soup and Other Plays*, 1995
Four dramas by an extraordinary playwright, focusing on family relations between first-, second- and third-generation Japanese Americans.

Velina Hasu Houston, *The Politics of Life: Four Plays by Asian American Women*, 1993
Edited by Houston; includes works by Wakako Yamauchi, Genny Lim and Houston.

David Henry Hwang, *FOB and Other Plays*, 1990
A collection of six of Hwang's plays, including the Broadway gender-bender sensation, *M. Butterfly*.

Roberta Uno, *Unbroken Thread: An Anthology of Plays by Asian American Women*, 1993
Edited by Uno; includes plays by Genny Lim, Wakako Yamauchi, Momoko Iko, Velina Hasu Houston, Jeannie Barroga and Elizabeth Wong

---

905

CLAIRE HUCHET BISHOP
KURT WIESE, Co-Author

The Five Chinese Brothers

(New York: Sandcastle Books (Putnam & Grosset Group), 1938)

Subject(s): Folk Tales; Brothers; Survival
Age range(s): Grades 1-3
Time period(s): Indeterminate Past
Locale(s): China

Summary: Five Chinese brothers, who look exactly alike, each has an extraordinary talent. When First Chinese Brother is unfairly sentenced to death, the other brothers each call on their special talents to save their brother and prove his innocence.

About this book: Published in 1938, this book remains a children's classic almost six decades later. The 1990 children's book, *The Seven Chinese Brothers*, is another, somewhat different variation of the same Chinese folktale.

Where it's reviewed:
Publishers Weekly, April 28, 1989, page 83
School Library Journal, June 1988, page 51

Other books you might like:
Margaret Mahy, *The Seven Chinese Brothers*, 1990
   Seven identical Chinese brothers, each with an extraordinary power, must call on his special talent to save each other's lives from the cruel emperor.
Ed Young, *Lon Po Po: A Red-Riding Hood Story from China*, 1989
   Three sisters left home alone and told to keep the doors locked, are tricked by a hungry wolf disguised as grandma.
Jeannine Atkins, *Aani and the Tree Huggers*, 1995
   Young Aani leads the other women of the village in putting their arms around the many trees of their forest to save them from being cut down by unthinking developers.
Jeanne M. Lee, *Toad Is the Uncle of Heaven*, 1985
   The Toad asks the King of Heaven for rain. On his journey, he is joined by the Bees, the Rooster and the Tiger. With the help of his friends, Toad convinces the King to provide rain.
Laurence Yep, *The City of Dragons*, 1995
   The boy with the saddest face in the world proves to be a hero in the city of dragons.

906

BARBARA BRENNER
JULIA TAKAYA, Illustrator
JUNE OTANI, Illustrator

Chibi: A True Story from Japan
(New York: Clarion Books (Houghton Mifflin), 1996)

Subject(s): Animals; Historical; Human Behavior
Age range(s): Grades 1-4
Major character(s): Okasan, Duck (brown-and-gold), Mother (okasan is mother in Japanese); Sato, Photographer (newspaper photographer); Chibi, Duck (youngest and tiniest of 10)
Time period(s): 1990s
Locale(s): Tokyo, Japan (the Mitsui Office Park and the Emperor's Gardens)

Summary: A lone duck flies into downtown Tokyo and hatches 10 ducklings. People flock to Mitsui Office Park to watch the ducks' progress, including Mr. Sato, a newspaper photographer who names the tiniest of the ducks Chibi. Okasan transfers her brood across an eight-lane highway to the Emperor's Gardens where they survive a typhoon and make a new life.

About this book: Based on a true story. Thousands of Tokyoites followed the adventures of the lone mother duck determined to raise her brood in the middle of one of the world's busiest cities. So obsessed was the public with Okasan and Chibi that the evening news broadcast a daily "Duck Watch."

Where it's reviewed:
Booklist, February 15, 1996, page 1023
Kirkus Reviews, December 15, 1995, page 1767
Publishers Weekly, January 15, 1996, page 462

Other books by the same author:
Storytelling: Art and Technique, 1996 (adult nonfiction)

Other books you might like:
Jama Kim Rattigan, *Dumpling Soup*, 1993
   Every year the Yang family gathers at Grandma's house from all over Oahu, Hawaii to celebrate New Year's Eve. This year young Marisa will help Grandma make her famous dumpling soup.
Ed Young, *Little Plum*, 1994
   A childless, elderly couple long for a child, even if he were only as big as a plum seed. But even a young man as small as a plum seed can do good deeds if he is brave.
Chiyoko Tomioka, *Rise and Shine, Mariko-chan!*, 1986
   Young Mariko gets up each morning and gets ready for the yellow school bus that will take her to school.
Yoriko Tsutsui, *Anna in Charge*, 1979
   While her mother goes to run an errand, Anna is left in charge of her younger sister, Katy. Katy wanders off while Anna is not looking and Anna quickly goes searching for her.

907

WESLEY BROWN, Editor
AMY LING, Co-Editor

Imagining America: Stories from the Promised Land
(New York: Persea Books, 1991)

Subject(s): Emigration and Immigration; Multicultural; Identity
Age range(s): Adult
Time period(s): 20th century (1900-present)
Locale(s): United States

Summary: A multicultural anthology of 37 short stories about immigration to and migration within the U.S., the so-called "Promised Land." Contributing writers are of varied ethnic backgrounds, including Asian, African, Latino, Native American, Jewish, Middle Eastern and European; together, they are a representative microcosm of the vast diversity and richness that is America.

Where it's reviewed:
Belles Lettres, Spring 1992, page 43
Choice, April 1992, page 1226
School Library Journal, June 1992, page 152
Library Journal, November 15, 1991, page 109
Publishers Weekly, December 20, 1991, page 74

Other books by the same author:
Visions of America: Personal Narratives from the Promised Land, 1993 (anthology)

Other books you might like:

Juliet S. Kono, *Sister Stew: Fiction and Poetry by Women*, 1991

Edited with Cathy Song, this is a colorful collection of writings by women of various backgrounds, the majority of whom are either Hawaiian by birth or by adopted residency.

Diane Glancy, *Two Worlds Walking: Short Stories, Essays, and Poetry by Writers with Mixed Heritages*, 1994

First-of-a-kind anthology that brings together the works of 42 writers, each of mixed ancestry, each ''walking in two worlds,'' trying to discover their ''American'' identities.

Jessica Hagedorn, *Charlie Chan Is Dead: An Anthology of Contemporary Asian American Fiction*, 1993

A collection of 48 works by Asian American writers of different ages, backgrounds and styles.

Bennett Lee, *Many-Mouthed Birds: Contemporary Writings by Chinese Canadians*, 1991

A diverse collection of short stories from some of Canada's leading Asian voices, including Larissa Lai, Evelyn Lau, Sky Lee and Denise Chong.

908

JOSEPH BRUCHAC, Editor

Breaking Silence: An Anthology of Contemporary Asian American Poets

(Greenfield Center, NY: The Greenfield Review Press, 1983)

Subject(s): Multicultural; Identity; Poetry
Age range(s): Adult
Locale(s): United States

Summary: Most likely the first major anthology of all Asian American written poetry, *Breaking Silence* presents the work of some 50 contributors, including such established writers as Jessica Hagedorn, Garrett Hongo, Joy Kogawa, David Mura, Cathy Song and Nellie Wong.

Where it's reviewed:
Western American Literature, Winter 1985, page 322

Other books you might like:

Jeffery Paul Chan, *Aiiieeeee! An Anthology of Asian American Writers*, 1974

Edited by Chin, Inada and Wong, this is *the* anthology of Asian American writing.

Frank Chin, *The Big Aiiieeeee! An Anthology of Chinese American and Japanese American Literature*, 1991

Edited by Chan, Inada and Wong, this is the follow-up to *Aiiieeeee!*.

Jessica Hagedorn, *Charlie Chan Is Dead: An Anthology of Contemporary Asian American Fiction*, 1993

A collection of 48 works by Asian American writers of different ages, backgrounds and styles.

Him Mark Lai, *Island: Poetry and History of Chinese Immigrants on Angel Island, 1910-1940*, 1980

Edited with Genny Lim and Judy Yung. Poetry inscribed by Angel Island detainees on the buildings' walls, during holding periods that sometimes lasted two years.

Walter K. Lew, *Premonitions: The Kaya Anthology of New Asian North American Poetry*, 1995

This is a collection of 73 authors, ranging from the established to the up-and-coming, who are writing in all modes of poetry.

909

MARINA TAMAR BUDHOS

House of Waiting

(New York: Global City Press, 1995)

Subject(s): Multicultural; Emigration and Immigration; Identity
Age range(s): Adult
Major character(s): Sarah Weissberg Singh, Narrator (native New Yorker), Young Woman (of Orthodox Jewish parentage); Roland ''Bump'' Singh, Husband (charismatic, young), Immigrant (Indian from British Guiana); Charles Magalee, Friend (childhood friend of Roland's); Sarita Magalee, Spouse (Charles' young wife)
Time period(s): 1950s
Locale(s): New York, New York; Phoenicia, New York (small town in upstate New York, in the Catskills region)

Summary: Sarah, a young and naive New York Jew, impulsively marries Roland, an Indian immigrant from the Caribbean. Months after the wedding, Roland returns to his native Guiana, embroiled in its political turmoil. As she waits for his return, she creates a new life among Roland's tight community of East Indian transplants.

Where it's reviewed:
Library Journal, July 1995, page 117
Publishers Weekly, July 3, 1995, page 57

Other books you might like:

Chitra Banerjee Divakaruni, *Arranged Marriage*, 1995

A collection of 11 short stories about young Indian and Indian American women, some married, some single, in various stages of claiming their independence.

Ameena Meer, *Bombay Talkie*, 1994

Sabah heads to India in search of her ethnic identity. What she finds in the wealthy world of her Indian relatives is a liberal Westernized culture bound by strict traditions.

Bharati Mukherjee, *Jasmine*, 1989

A novel about Jasmine Vijh's odyssey through America, from her arrival from India as a 17-year-old widow to her new life as Jane Ripplemeyer, assumed to be an Iowa housewife.

Bharati Mukherjee, *The Middleman and Other Stories*, 1988

An award-winning collection of stories about displaced, diverse Americans, from a troubled Vietnam vet to an Iraqi Jew from Queens to a wealthy immigrant Filipina.

Kirin Narayan, *Love, Stars, and All That*, 1994

A delightful novel that follows Gita Das—from immigrant graduate student at Berkeley to esteemed professor—through her bumpy search for her ideal mate.

910

CARLOS BULOSAN

America Is in the Heart

(Seattle: University of Washington Press, 1943)

Subject(s): Autobiography; Emigration and Immigration; Prejudice
Age range(s): Adult
Major character(s): Carlos Bulosan, Writer, Immigrant (itinerant laborer); Leon Bulosan, Brother (oldest brother of Carlos); Macario Bulosan, Brother (older brother of Carlos); Nick, Friend (Carlos' companion worker); Jose, Friend (Nick's brother)
Time period(s): 1920s; 1940s
Locale(s): Philippines; West

Summary: The autobiography of writer and poet Carlos Bulosan, from his boyhood in the Philippines, to his arrival in America, to the difficulties he faced as a migrant laborer. In spite of the prejudices and racism that confronted him daily, Bulosan remained determined to live a life filled with dignity and respect.

About this book: The first autobiography by a Filipino American, who "longed to become a part of America," yet was never fully accepted.

Where it's reviewed:
Educational Leadership, April 1974, page 593

Other books you might like:
Ronyoung Kim, *Clay Walls*, 1987
    The memoir of a young Korean woman and the difficulties and hardships she faces in her new life as an immigrant American.
Ronald Takaki, *Strangers from a Different Shore*, 1989
    Traces the diverse lives of the Japanese, Chinese, Koreans, Filipinos, Asian Indians, Vietnamese, Cambodians and Laotians who have come to the U.S. over the last 150 years.
Mary Paik Lee, *Quiet Odyssey: A Pioneer Korean Woman in America*, 1990
    Edited by Professor Sucheng Lee, this memoir covers nearly a century of change, by one of the country's first Korean American women.
Tooru J. Kanazawa, *Sushi and Sourdough*, 1989
    At the turn of the century, a Japanese immigrant heads for Alaska hoping to strike it rich panning for gold.
Bienvenido Santos, *Scent of Apples: A Collection of Short Stories*, 1955
    A collection of short stories about the experiences of young Filipino American men living displaced lives, torn between their family ties in the Philippines and their struggles to survive in the U.S.

911

LORI M. CARLSON, Editor

American Eyes: New Asian-American Short Stories for Young Adults

(New York: Henry Holt and Company, Inc., 1994)

Subject(s): Multicultural; Identity; Short Stories
Age range(s): Grades 8-Adult
Time period(s): Indeterminate
Locale(s): United States

Summary: A collection of 10 short works about young Asian Americans coming of age and coming to terms with an identity comprised of two very different cultures. Stories range from a young Chinese American girl obsessed with being blonde, an adopted Korean American searching for her biological, Korean parents, and a Vietnamese American boy who loses the girl but rediscovers his family.

About this book: Short, easy to read stories and excerpts from longer works, especially appropriate for young adult readers. Includes a short, witty introduction by Cynthia Kadohata, author of the adult novels, *Floating World* and *In the Heart of the Valley of Love*.

Where it's reviewed:
Horn Book Magazine, July 1995, page 464
Kirkus Reviews, December 15, 1994, page 1559
Publishers Weekly, November 21, 1994, page 78

Other books you might like:
Laurence Yep, *American Dragons: Twenty-Five Asian American Voices*, 1993
    A collection of short stories, poetry and play excerpts from both established Asian American writers and new writers about growing up Asian American.
Asian American Coalition, *Children of Asian America*, 1995
    This collection of original stories about growing up Asian American centers around the diverse ethnic Asian communities of Chicago.
Diane Glancy, *Two Worlds Walking: Short Stories, Essays, and Poetry by Writers with Mixed Heritages*, 1994
    Edited with C.W. Truesdale, this first-of-a-kind anthology brings together the works of 42 writers, each of mixed ancestry, each "walking in two worlds".

912

THERESA HAK KYUNG CHA

Dictee

(New York: Tanam Press, 1982)

Subject(s): Multicultural; Identity; Emigration and Immigration
Age range(s): Adult

Summary: An autobiographical exploration of memory and personal history, presented in a vast spectrum of mediums, including prose, poetry, descriptions of dreams, biography, family history in Korea, French translation exercises, photographs, handwritten notes, calligraphy, letters and more. A groundbreaking work, which pushes the traditional limits of written narrative.

About this book: Cha, a writer, experimental filmmaker and performance and visual artist, was tragically murdered at age 31 on the streets of New York City. She left behind an extraordinary, extensive body of work, of which *Dictee* was her last completed project, released just nine days before her death. The short work, temporarily out of print, has taken on near-cult status; it will be re-released in a new edition from Kaya Production in 1996/'97.

Where it's reviewed:
Village Voice Literary Supplement, June 1993, page 27

Other books you might like:
Joseph Bruchac, *Breaking Silence: An Anthology of Contemporary Asian American Poets*, 1983
One of the first major anthologies of Asian American poetry, featuring the work of some 50 writers.
Myung Mi Kim, *Under Flag*, 1991
A sparse, elliptical poetry collection, dealing with a child and her family's life in Korea under American occupation and her later struggles as a new immigrant in the U.S.
Walter K. Lew, *Premonitions: The Kaya Anthology of New Asian North American Poetry*, 1995
This collection of 73 authors, ranging from established to up-and-comer, features writing in all modes of poetry, including works in non-standard forms and dialects.

913

JEFFERY PAUL CHAN, Editor
FRANK CHIN, Co-Editor
LAWSON FUSAO INADA, Co-Editor
SHAWN WONG, Co-Editor

The Big Aiiieeeee! An Anthology of Chinese American and Japanese American Literature

(New York: Meridian (Penguin Group), 1991)

Subject(s): Multicultural; Identity; Emigration and Immigration
Age range(s): Adult
Time period(s): 1870s; 1990s
Locale(s): United States

Summary: A follow-up to the seminal *Aiiieeeee!*, this anthology highlights over a century of writing by Asian Americans, from the revealing 1875 *An English-Chinese Phrase Book*, used by the first generation of Chinese immigrants, to the most recent stories and essays by prominent contemporary Asian American writers.

Where it's reviewed:
School Library Journal, February 1992, page 121
Booklist, December 1, 1992, page 660

Other books by the same author:
Aiiieeeee! An Anthology of Asian American Writers, 1974

Other books you might like:
Wesley Brown, *Imagining America: Stories from the Promised Land*, 1991
A multicultural anthology of 37 short stories about immi-

gration to and migration within the U.S., the so-called "Promised Land". Edited with Amy Ling.
Wesley Brown, *Visions of America: Personal Narratives from the Promised Land*, 1993
Edited with Amy Ling.
Joseph Bruchac, *Breaking Silence: An Anthology of Contemporary Asian American Poets*, 1983
One of the first major anthologies of Asian American poetry, featuring the work of some 50 writers.
Jessica Hagedorn, *Charlie Chan Is Dead: An Anthology of Contemporary Asian American Fiction*, 1993
A collection of 48 works by Asian American writers of different ages, backgrounds and styles.

914

JENNIFER L. CHAN
WENDY K. LEE, Illustrator

ONE small GIRL

(Chicago: Polychrome Publishing Corporation, 1993)

Subject(s): Play; Games
Age range(s): Grades 1-2
Major character(s): Jennifer Lee, Child (young Chinese American girl)
Time period(s): 1990s (1993)
Locale(s): Chinatown

Summary: Told not to touch anything in either her grandmother's or her uncle's adjacent Chinatown stores, a little girl still manages to have fun.

Where it's reviewed:
Children's Bookwatch, February 1994, page 5

Other books you might like:
Demi, *The Empty Pot*, 1990
When Ping presents an empty pot to the Emperor, he is rewarded for his honesty.
Huy Voun Lee, *At the Beach*, 1994
On a beautiful day at the beach, Xiao Ming learns to write Chinese characters with his mother in the sand.
Huy Voun Lee, *In the Snow*, 1995
During a winter walk through the forest, Xiao Ming's mother teaches him new Chinese characters, using the white snow to draw the picture-like characters.
Sheila Hamanaka, *All the Colors of the Earth*, 1994
Children of the world come in many colors, but inside, they're the same.

915

DIANA CHANG

Frontiers of Love

(Seattle: University of Washington Press, 1956)

Subject(s): Multicultural; Identity; War
Age range(s): Adult
Major character(s): Sylvia Chen, Young Woman, Chinese Caucasian; Chen Liyi, Businessman, Father (Sylvia's), Chinese; Feng Huang, Young Man (idealistic Communist), Friend (of Sylvia); Robert Bruno, Lover (of Mimi

Lambert), Caucasian; Mimi Lambert, Young Woman (Sylvia's father), Chinese Australian

Time period(s): 1940s
Locale(s): Shanghai, China

Summary: The story of a group of young, idealistic friends in Japanese-occupied Shanghai in 1945. Caught between an ancient culture overwhelmed by Western colonialism, each of the friends must try and find his or her own individual place in a society intolerant of its mixed-race citizens.

Where it's reviewed:
Belles Lettres, Spring 1995, page 65

Other books by the same author:
A Woman of Thirty
A Passion for Life
The Only Game in Town
Eye to Eye, 1974
A Perfect Love

Other books you might like:
Sui Sin Far, *Mrs. Spring Fragrance and Other Writings*, 1995
   A collection of short stories, first published at the turn of the century, which represents the first fiction in English by an Asian American, as well as journalistic writings.
Anchee Min, *Red Azalea*, 1994
   The personal memoir of Min's difficult life in China during the Cultural Revolution and her struggle to escape the brutality of her homeland.
Fiona Cheong, *The Scent of the Gods*, 1991
   Young Esha comes of age in Singapore in the late 1960s, a time of political strife between the Chinese government and the local Singaporeans.
Shyam Selvadurai, *Funny Boy*, 1995
   A young boy comes of age and discovers his homosexuality during a time of great political turbulence in his native Sri Lanka.
Margaret Chang, *In the Eye of War*, 1990
   Shao-Shao celebrates his tenth birthday in the final days of the Japanese Occupation of China.

916

HEIDI CHANG, Author/Illustrator

Elaine and the Flying Frog
(New York: Random House (A Stepping Stone Book), 1988)

Subject(s): Multicultural; Prejudice; Friendship
Age range(s): Grades 3-6
Major character(s): Elaine Chow, Student—Elementary School (young girl), Chinese American; Mary Lewis Thorp, Friend (and classmate of Elaine's); Kelleen Burke, Classmate (not friendly or broad-minded); Mrs. Bonovox, Teacher (Elaine and Mary Lewis')
Time period(s): 1980s (1983)
Locale(s): Cedarville, Iowa

Summary: Elaine moves to a small town in Iowa from San Francisco. Suddenly she feels like an outsider, being the only Asian American student in her school. She meets Mary Lewis, a fellow classmate obsessed with frogs, and together they form a strong friendship as they work on a special science project.

About this book: Previously titled *Elaine, Mary Lewis, and the Frogs*.

Other books you might like:
Duncan Chin, *Growing Up on Grove Street 1931-1946*, 1995
   A Chinese American boy's childhood in a small California produce town is captured through wonderful sketches of the places, faces and memories of his diverse past.
Cynthia Chin-Lee, *Almond Cookies and Dragon Well Tea*, 1993
   When Erica visits Nancy's house for the first time, she expects many differences because Nancy is Chinese American, but finds that their two families are more similar than not.
Elaine Hosozawa-Nagano, *Chopsticks from America*, 1994
   Two Japanese American children move to Japan. While they look like "chopsticks among other chopsticks," they are American, which proves to be different from being Japanese.
Joy Kogawa, *Naomi's Road*, 1986
   Young adult story of a Japanese Canadian family that is splintered and scattered as a result of forced evacuation and relocation during World War II.
Min Paek, *Aekyung's Dream*, 1988
   Aekyung, a young Korean girl recently in the U.S., dreams about King Sejong who created *Hangul*, the Korean alphabet, and finds new pride in her Korean heritage.

917

MARGARET CHANG, Adaptor
RAYMOND CHANG, Illustrator
WARWICK HUTTON, Illustrator

The Cricket Warrior: A Chinese Tale
(New York: Margaret K. McElderry Books (Macmillan Publishing Co.), 1994)

Subject(s): Folk Tales; Courage; Filial Piety
Age range(s): Grades 1-4
Major character(s): Cheng Ming, Farmer (poor farmer with failing crops); Wei nian, Son (faithful, hardworking)
Time period(s): Indeterminate Past
Locale(s): China ("a long time ago in China")

Summary: The emperor levies a new tax on his subjects—to be paid in crickets because he loves to watch cricket matches. The farmer Cheng Ming finds a promising cricket, but his son, Wei nian, promptly loses it. The loyal son takes the form of a cricket and saves his family by becoming the court champion.

Where it's reviewed:
Kirkus Reviews, August 15, 1994, page 1123
Publishers Weekly, September 5, 1994, page 110

Other books by the same author:
In the Eye of War, 1990 (young adult)

Other books you might like:
Ed Young, *Little Plum*, 1994
   A childless, elderly couple long for a child, even if he is only as big as a plum seed. When such a child is born, he proves that even a man as small as a plum seed can do great deeds if he is brave.

Demi, *The Magic Tapestry*, 1994

When his mother's heavenly tapestry is stolen by fairies of the Sun Mountain, the youngest son must win it back.

Laurence Yep, *The Shell Woman and the King*, 1993

The magical shell woman saves her husband and herself from the evil, greedy king.

Laurence Yep, *The Boy Who Swallowed Snakes*, 1994

Little Chou swallows a poisonous *ku* snake to prevent evil from spreading.

918

MARGARET CHANG
RAYMOND CHANG, Co-Author

In the Eye of War

(New York: Margaret K. McElderry Books, Macmillan Publishing Co., 1990)

Subject(s): Children and War; Family Relations; World War II
Age range(s): Grades 6 and Up
Major character(s): Li Wu-Jiang "Shao-shao", 10-Year-Old, 5th Grader, Chinese (lives in occupied Shanghai); Chow Yun-lung, Friend (and classmate of Shao-shao); Chen Li-sha, Friend (and classmate of Shao-shao), Daughter (of enemy Japanese sympathizer)
Time period(s): 1940s (August 1944-August 1945)
Locale(s): Shanghai, China (Japanese-occupied during World War II)

Summary: Ten-year-old Shao-shao is the youngest child in a large family living in Japanese-occupied Shanghai during the end of World War II. Everyday life for him means going to school and playing with his friends. Little by little, he comes to realize his family's role in the underground movement as the war draws to an end.

Where it's reviewed:
Booklist, December 1, 1992, page 660

Other books by the same author:
The Cricket Warrior: A Chinese Tale, 1994 (children's story)

Other books you might like:
Lori M. Carlson, *American Eyes: New Asian-American Short Stories for Young Adults*, 1994

A collection of 10 short works about young Asian Americans coming of age and coming to terms with an identity comprised of two very different cultures.

Diana Chang, *Frontiers of Love*, 1956

The story of a group of young, idealistic friends in Japanese-occupied Shanghai in 1945, each caught between an ancient culture overwhelmed by Western colonialism.

Shyam Selvadurai, *Funny Boy*, 1995

A young boy comes of age and discovers his homosexuality during a time of great political turbulence in his native Sri Lanka.

Laurence Yep, *American Dragons: Twenty-Five Asian American Voices*, 1993

A collection of short stories, poetry and play excerpts from both established Asian American writers, as well as writers, about growing up Asian American.

919

FIONA CHEONG

The Scent of the Gods

(New York: W. W. Norton & Company, Inc., 1991)

Subject(s): Coming of Age; Family Relations; Politics
Age range(s): Adult
Major character(s): Esha Su Yen "Chief", Granddaughter, 11-Year-Old, Chinese; Li Shin, Cousin (Esha's oldest male cousin), Resistance Fighter (volunteer cadet), Chinese; Li Yuen, Brother (Li Shin's younger brother), Chinese; Grandmother, Grandmother (family matriarch), Chinese
Time period(s): 1960s (1966-1967)
Locale(s): Singapore

Summary: Eleven-year-old Esha comes of age in Singapore in the late 1960s, a time of growing political strife between the predominantly Chinese government and the local Singaporeans and their supporters. Esha's protected life as the granddaughter of a wealthy Chinese family changes quickly as the realities of the outside stubbornly encroach.

Where it's reviewed:
Los Angeles Times Book Review, July 18, 1993, page 8
New York Times Book Review, July 4, 1993, page 20
World Literature Today, Winter 1993, page 240

Other books you might like:
Wendy Law-Yone, *The Coffin Tree*, 1983

A political coup forces a young woman and her half-brother to flee their native Burma, catapulting them to a difficult, desperate new life in the U.S.

Shyam Selvadurai, *Funny Boy*, 1995

A young boy comes of age and discovers his homosexuality during a time of great political turbulence in his native Sri Lanka.

Jessica Hagedorn, *Dogeaters*, 1990

An autobiographical novel about growing up in Manila in the late 1950s during the turbulent and corrupt Marcos regime.

Diana Chang, *Frontiers of Love*, 1956

This story is about a group of idealistic friends in Japanese-occupied Shanghai in 1945. Each must find his or her own individual place in a society intolerant of its mixed-race citizens.

920

CHARLIE CHIN, Adaptor
TOMIE ARAI, Illustrator

China's Bravest Girl: The Legend of Hua Mu Lan

(San Francisco: Children's Book Press, 1993)

Subject(s): Legends; Parent and Child; Filial Piety
Age range(s): Grades 1-6
Major character(s): Hua Mu Lan, Daughter (warrior)
Time period(s): Indeterminate Past
Locale(s): China

Summary: Disguised as a man, Hua Mu Lan takes her elderly father's place in the Emperor's army and becomes a legendary warrior. Even after years of fighting, none of her comrades realize her true identity. She returns home to her proud parents as a decorated general and resumes her life as a young woman.

About this book: A bilingual book, written in both English and Chinese. The legend of Hua Mu Lan (also Fa Mu Lan) is based on a poem called "Mu Lan Ci," which was recorded during China's Soong Dynasty (960-1279 A.D.). An animated film version of the *Legend of Fa Mu Lan* is due out from Disney in late 1996.

Where it's reviewed:
Booklist, March 1, 1994, page 1264
Horn Book Guide, Spring 1994, page 114
Kirkus Reviews, November 1, 1993, page 1388
Publishers Weekly, October 18, 1993, page 73
School Library Journal, March 1994, page 226

Other books you might like:
Ed Young, *Little Plum*, 1994
   A childless couple long for a child, even if he were as small as a plum seed. When such a child is born, he proves that even a man as small as a plum seed can do great deeds if he is brave.
Demi, *The Magic Tapestry*, 1994
   When his mother's heavenly tapestry is stolen by fairies of Sun Mountain, the youngest son must win it back.
Raymond Chang, *The Cricket Warrior: A Chinese Tale*, 1994
   The Emperor levies a new tax—to be paid in crickets for his cricket matches. When Wei'nian loses his father's promising cricket, the loyal son takes the form of a cricket to save his family.
Amy Tan, *The Moon Lady*, 1992
   Nai-nai tells her granddaughters the story of her trip to see the Moon Lady and be granted a secret wish when she was seven.
Laurence Yep, *The Ghost Fox*, 1994
   A brave boy saves his mother from the evil ghost fox who tries to steal her soul.

921

DUNCAN CHIN, Author/Illustrator

Growing Up on Grove Street 1931-1946
(Capitola, CA: Capitola Book Company, 1995)

Story type: Young Adult
Subject(s): Multicultural; Biography
Age range(s): Grades 3 and Up
Major character(s): Duncan Chin, Child, Chinese American (growing up during Depression)
Time period(s): 1930s; 1940s (1941-1946)
Locale(s): Watsonville, California (South Watsonville, beside the Pajaro River)

Summary: The story of a young Chinese American boy growing up in a small produce town in California is told through wonderful sketches that capture the places, faces and memories of a diverse childhood in a changing multicultural area.

About this book: The book's foreword and afterword, both written by Sandy Lydon (noted Monterey Bay Area history scholar and author of *Chinese Gold: The History of the Chinese in the Monterey Bay Region*), offer an insightful overview of life in small-town California, living among Chinese, Japanese, Slavs, "Okies," "Arkies," "Texies," Mexicans and other working folks, all in pursuit of the American Dream.

Other books you might like:
Ruthanne Lum McCunn, *Chinese American Portraits: Personal Histories 1828-1988*, 1988
   Collected here are profiles of prominent Chinese Americans, from pioneers to politicians.
Ruthanne Lum McCunn, *An Illustrated History of the Chinese in America*, 1979
   This illustrated history book traces the presence of the Chinese in America, from their arrival during the California Gold Rush to their contemporary place in America.
Kate Waters, *Lion Dancer: Ernie Wan's Chinese New Year*, 1990
   Young Ernie is about to perform his first Lion Dance through the streets of New York City's Chinatown as part of the Chinese New Year celebration.
Paul Yee, *Tales from Gold Mountain: Stories of the Chinese in the New World*, 1989
   Illustrated by Simon Ng, this collection of eight tales is about Chinese immigrants in the New World.

922

FRANK CHIN, Editor
JEFFERY PAUL CHAN, Co-Editor
LAWSON FUSAO INADA, Co-Editor
SHAWN WONG, Co-Editor

Aiiieeeee! An Anthology of Asian American Writers
(New York: Mentor (Penguin Group), 1974)

Subject(s): Multicultural; Identity; Emigration and Immigration
Age range(s): Adult
Time period(s): 1930s; 1970s
Locale(s): United States

Summary: Considered *the* seminal anthology of Asian American literature, Aiiieeeee! was the first anthology dedicated solely to American writers of Asian descent. Included are short stories, excerpts from various novels and one act of the first Asian American play ever produced in New York.

About this book: Originally published by Howard University Press. Ironically, during the late 1960s and 70s, it was the African American community who lent the most supportive voice to Asian American writers and their projects, of which *Aiiieeeee!* is just one example.

Where it's reviewed:
Change, November 1989, page 66
Voice of Youth Advocates, April 1992, page 50

Other books by the same author:
The Big Aiiieeeee! An Anthology of Chinese American and Japanese American Literature, 1991 (sequel)

Other books you might like:

Sylvia Watanabe, *Into the Fire: Asian American Prose*, 1996
This collection of short stories and interviews details the diverse journey of Asian Americans from their faraway homelands to new lives in this new country.

Bennett Lee, *Many-Mouthed Birds: Contemporary Writings by Chinese Canadians*, 1991
A diverse collection of short stories from some of Canada's leading Asian American voices, including Larissa Lai, Evelyn Lau, Sky Lee and Denise Chong.

Joseph Bruchac, *Breaking Silence: An Anthology of Contemporary Asian American Poets*, 1983
One of the first major anthologies of Asian American poetry, featuring the work of some 50 writers.

Jessica Hagedorn, *Charlie Chan Is Dead: An Anthology of Contemporary Asian American Fiction*, 1993
A collection of 48 works by writers of different ages, backgrounds and styles, who each happen to be Asian American.

923

FRANK CHIN

The Chickencoop Chinaman and the Year of the Dragon: Two Plays by Frank Chin

(Seattle: University of Washington Press, 1981)

Subject(s): Theater; Identity; Multicultural
Age range(s): Adult

Summary: Two plays by pioneer Frank Chin. The groundbreaking *The Chickencoop Chinaman*, which introduces three unpredictable characters who challenge and satirize existing media stereotypes of Asian Americans, was the first Asian American play to be produced in New York City; it debuted off-Broadway in 1972. *The Year of the Dragon*, about the disintegration of the Chinese American family, appeared off-Broadway in 1974.

About this book: In 1973, fifth-generation Chinese American Frank Chin founded the Asian American Theater Workshop in San Francisco which later became the Asian American Theater Company, one of the five early Asian American theaters in the U.S. Chin angrily left in 1977 after creative differences could not be resolved.

Other books by the same author:

Gunga Din Highway, 1994

The Big Aiiieeeee! An Anthology of Chinese American and Japanese American Literature, 1991

Donald Duk, 1991

The Chinaman Pacific & Frisco R.R. Co., 1988 (short story collection)

Aiiieeeee! An Anthology of Asian American Writers, 1974 (Seminal anthology of Asian American literature, edited with Chan, Wong and Inada.)

Other books you might like:

Misha Berson, *Between Worlds: Contemporary Asian-American Plays*, 1990
Edited by Berson. Anthology includes works by Ping Chong, Philip Kan Gotanda, Jessica Hagedorn, David Henry Hwang, Wakako Yamauchi and Laurence Yep.

Velina Hasu Houston, *The Politics of Life: Four Plays by Asian American Women*, 1993
Edited by Houston. Includes works by Wakako Yamauchi, Genny Lim and Houston.

Roberta Uno, *Unbroken Thread: An Anthology of Plays by Asian American Women*, 1993
Edited by Uno. Includes plays by Genny Lim, Wakako Yamauchi, Momoko Iko, Velina Hasu Houston, Jeannie Barroga and Elizabeth Wong.

924

FRANK CHIN

Donald Duk

(Minneapolis: Coffee House Press, 1991)

Subject(s): Multicultural; Coming of Age; Identity
Age range(s): Adult
Major character(s): Donald Duk, 12-Year-Old (doesn't like his name), Chinese American; King Duk, Father (Donald's), Restauranteur (chef/owner; in Chinatown); Daisy Duk, Mother (Donald's); Arnold Azalea, Friend (Donald's best friend), Classmate (Donald's)
Time period(s): 1980s
Locale(s): San Francisco, California (San Francisco's Chinatown)

Summary: At 12, Donald Duk dislikes his name and is less than comfortable with his Chinese heritage. Chinese New Year is just around the corner, but he's hardly in a festive mood. Little by little, Donald learns to confront his ancestors, discover his own history, and finally comes to appreciate his heritage, free of blatant misconceptions and stereotypes.

Where it's reviewed:

Library Journal, July 1991, Page 168
New York Times Book Review, March 31, 1991, page 9
Publishers Weekly, February 8, 1991, page 52

Other books by the same author:

Gunga Din Highway, 1994

The Big Aiiieeeee! An Anthology of Chinese American and Japanese American Literature, 1991

The Chinaman Pacific & Frisco R.R. Co., 1988 (short story collection)

The Chickencoop Chinaman and the Year of the Dragon: Two Plays by Frank Chin, 1981

Aiiieeeee! An Anthology of Asian American Writers, 1974 (Seminal anthology of Asian American literature, edited with Chan, Wong and Inada.)

Other books you might like:

Steven Lo, *The Incorporation of Eric Chung*, 1989
A comic novel of Eric Chung's rise from immigrant student at Texas Tech to major Texas businessman with Important Connections.

Shawn Wong, *Homebase*, 1991
Rainsford Chan, a 14-year-old, fourth-generation Chinese American orphan, attempts to recreate the stories of his family's 125-year-long history in the U.S.

Louis Chu, *Eat a Bowl of Tea*, 1961
The story of American-born Ben Loy and his Chinese-born wife, Mei Oi, in which their blissful marriage is marred by

infidelity but later reclaimed with a new bond and a happily-ever-after ending.

Darrell H.Y. Lum, *Pass On, No Pass Back!*, 1990
A humorous collection of short stories about growing up in Hawaii.

Milton Murayama, *All I Asking for Is My Body*, 1959
A young Japanese American boy's coming-of-age in Hawaii during the 1930s up until the advent of World War II.

925

CYNTHIA CHIN-LEE
YOU-SHAN TANG, Illustrator

Almond Cookies and Dragon Well Tea

(Chicago: Polychrome Publishing Corporation, 1993)

Subject(s): Multicultural; Friendship
Age range(s): Grades 1-3
Major character(s): Nancy Hong, Child (girl), Chinese; Erica Howard, Child (Nancy's close schoolfriend), Caucasian
Time period(s): 1990s (1993)
Locale(s): United States

Summary: Erica visits Nancy's house where she tastes almond cookies and dragon well tea, sees a family altar and hears a Chinese zither—all for the first time. But rather than the many differences she first expected, Erica realizes that Nancy's home and family and her home and family are not too different from each other.

Other books you might like:

Maria Hong, *Growing Up Asian American*, 1993
These essays, short stories and excerpts by Americans of Asian descent address issues such as parent-child relationships, self-realization, identity and the discovery of one's cultural heritage.

Sandra S. Yamate, *Ashok by Any Other Name*, 1992
Ashok, a young Indian American boy, wishes he had a more ''American'' name, so he tries a new name each day, finally realizing ''Ashok'' is the perfect name for him.

Sandra S. Yamate, *Char Siu Bao Boy*, 1991
Charlie's favorite food, *char sui bao*, causes his classmates to make fun of him until, one day, he brings enough for all of them to taste.

Asian American Coalition, *Children of Asian America*, 1995
A collection of original stories about growing up as an Asian American child, centered around the diverse ethnic Asian communities of Chicago.

926

KAREN CHINN
CORNELIUS VAN WRIGHT, Illustrator
YING-HWA HU, Illustrator

Sam and the Lucky Money

(New York: Lee & Low Books Inc., 1995)

Subject(s): Multicultural; Charity; Holidays
Age range(s): Grades 3 and Up
Major character(s): Sam, Child (young Chinese American boy)

Time period(s): 1990s (1995)
Locale(s): Chinatown

Summary: It's Chinese New Year and Sam is excited about spending his lucky money—New Year's gifts of money in red envelopes called *leisees*. But everything he wants seems to cost more than he has. He's disappointed, until he sees a lonely stranger without shoes and realizes how lucky he truly is.

Awards the book has won:
Pick of the Lists, American Bookseller, 1995

Other books you might like:

Jama Kim Rattigan, *Dumpling Soup*, 1993
Every year the Yang family gathers at Grandma's house from all over Oahu, Hawaii to celebrate New Year's Eve. This year, young Marisa will help Grandma make her famous dumpling soup.

Janet Mitsui Brown, *Thanksgiving at Obaachan's*, 1994
A Japanese American girl loves to visit her grandmother's house for Thanksgiving where the meal is a combination of traditional American and Japanese fare.

Kate Waters, *Lion Dancer: Ernie Wan's Chinese New Year*, 1990
Young Ernie is about to perform his first Lion Dance through the streets of New York City's Chinatown as part of the Chinese New Year celebration.

927

SOOK NYUL CHOI

Echoes of the White Giraffe

(Boston: Houghton Mifflin Company, 1993)

Subject(s): Multicultural; Historical; Korean War
Age range(s): Grades 7-12
Major character(s): Sookan Bak, 15-Year-Old, Korean; Hyunsuk ''Mother'' Bak, Mother (Sookan's mother), Korean; Bokhi, Girlfriend (Sookan's best friend), Student (Sookan's fellow student), Refugee; Junho Min, Friend (special male friend)
Time period(s): 1950s
Locale(s): Pusan, Korea, South; Seoul, Korea, South

Summary: Sookan, the protagonist from *Year of Impossible Goodbyes*, having escaped bombed-out Seoul, is now a teenage war refugee living in Pusan with her mother and younger brother. In spite of her difficult surroundings, she manages to find hope, forging new friendships, especially with one special young man.

About this book: The lyrical title comes from the name of a fellow refugee who lived on the mountain one over from Sookan's temporary home. Baik Rin, whose name meant ''White Giraffe,'' would shout a greeting each morning to his fellow war refugees. Ill and alone, he dies quietly, and is mourned by the refugees who continue to hear the echoes of his morning cheer.

Where it's reviewed:
Booklist, April 1, 1993, page 1424
Kirkus Reviews, April, 1, 1993, page 453
Publishers Weekly, March 22, 1993, page 80
School Library Journal, May 1993, page 104

Children's Bookwatch, June 1993, page 2

Other books by the same author:
Gathering of Pearls, 1994 (sequel)
Halmoni and the Picnic, 1993 (children's story)
Year of Impossible Goodbyes, 1991 (award-winning prequel)

Other books you might like:
K. Connie Kang, *Home Was the Land of Morning Calm: The Saga of a Korean American Family*, 1995
This adult work weaves the saga of one Korean family with the country's turbulent history, from 1900 to the present, from North Korea to Japan and finally to the U.S.

Helie Lee, *Still Life with Rice: A Young American Woman Discovers the Life and Legacy of Her Korean Grandmother*, 1996
A Korean woman survives great hardship in Korea and finally arrives in the U.S. Her Korean American granddaughter tells her story in this adult work of non-fiction.

Marie G. Lee, *Saying Goodbye*, 1994
Ellen has left her small hometown for Harvard University where she comes face-to-face with the reality of racial boundaries and racial tensions and must define her position as a Korean American.

Marie G. Lee, *Finding My Voice*, 1992
A senior in high school, Ellen struggles to find her voice and speak out for what she wants and believes in, especially as she faces the racism in her tiny hometown.

Margaret Chang, *In the Eye of War*, 1990
Shao-shao celebrates his tenth birthday in the final days of the Japanese occupation of China and befriends the daughter of a traitor.

928

SOOK NYUL CHOI

Gathering of Pearls

(Boston: Houghton Mifflin Company, 1994)

Subject(s): Multicultural; Emigration and Immigration; College Life
Age range(s): Grades 7-12
Major character(s): Sookan Bak, Student—College (freshman from Korea), Korean; Ellen Lloyd, Student—College, Roommate (close friend); Marci Gannon, Student—College (Sookan's dormmate and friend)
Time period(s): 1950s (1954-1955)
Locale(s): White Plains, New York (on the campus of Finch College, an all-girls Catholic school)

Summary: Sookan, the protagonist from *Year of Impossible Goodbyes* and *Echoes of the White Giraffe*, arrives at a small all-girls Catholic college from Korea. Her first year at college is a period of great adjustment, trying to find the right balance between her traditional Korean upbringing and the freedom of her new, independent American life.

Where it's reviewed:
Booklist, September 1, 1994, page 33
Kirkus Reviews, August 15, 1994, page 1123
Publishers Weekly, August 8, 1994, page 440

Other books by the same author:
Echoes of the White Giraffe, 1993 (sequel)

Halmoni and the Picnic, 1993 (children's story)
Year of Impossible Goodbyes, 1991 (award-winning prequel)

Other books you might like:
K. Connie Kang, *Home Was the Land of Morning Calm: The Saga of a Korean American Family*, 1995
The saga of one Korean family, interwoven with the country's turbulent history from 1900 to the present, from North Korea to Japan and finally to the U.S.

Helie Lee, *Still Life with Rice: A Young American Woman Discovers the Life and Legacy of Her Korean Grandmother*, 1996
This is the true story of a Korean woman who survives great hardship in Korea and finally arrives in the U.S., as told by her Korean grandmother. (Adult)

Mary Paik Lee, *Quiet Odyssey: A Pioneer Korean Woman in America*, 1990
Edited by Professor Sucheng Lee, this memoir covers nearly a century of change, by one of the country's first Korean American women.

Marie G. Lee, *Saying Goodbye*, 1994
Ellen has left her small hometown for Harvard where she comes face-to-face with the reality of racial boundaries and racial tensions and must define her own position as an aware Korean American.

Marie G. Lee, *Finding My Voice*, 1992
A senior in high school, Ellen struggles to find her voice and speak out for what she wants and believes in, especially as she faces the racism in her tiny hometwon.

929

SOOK NYUL CHOI
KAREN M. DUGAN, Illustrator

Halmoni and the Picnic

(Boston: Houghton Mifflin, 1993)

Subject(s): Multicultural; Emigration and Immigration; Family Relations
Age range(s): Grades 1-4
Major character(s): Yunmi, Child, Korean American; Halmoni, Grandmother (Yunmi's); Anna Marie, Friend (Yunmi's classmate); Helen, Friend (Yunmi's classmate); Mrs. Nolan, Teacher (Yunmi's)
Time period(s): 1990s (1993)
Locale(s): New York, New York

Summary: Yunmi's grandmother has recently arrived from Korea and has difficulty adjusting to life in America. With the help of her friends, Yunmi persuades her grandmother to chaperone the annual Central Park class picnic. There, among Yunmi's friends and teacher, her grandmother finds new acceptance and finally begins to feel at home.

About this book: The word "Halmoni" is Korean for "grandmother."

Where it's reviewed:
Horn Book Guide, Spring 1994, page 64
New York Times Book Review, May 8, 1994, page 20
School Library Journal, November 1993, page 78

Other books by the same author:
Gathering of Pearls, 1994 (sequel)

Echoes of the White Giraffe, 1993 (sequel)
Year of Impossible Goodbyes, 1991 (award-winning prequel)

Other books you might like:

Asian American Coalition, *Children of Asian America*, 1995
A collection of original stories about growing up as an Asian American child, centered around the diverse ethnic Asian communities of Chicago.

Kimiko Sakai, *Sachiko Means Happiness*, 1990
Sachiko is upset when her elderly grandmother does not even recognize her. When she comes to understand what has happened to her grandmother, she learns again how to be her friend.

Min Paek, *Aekyung's Dream*, 1988
Aekyung, a young Korean girl recently in the U.S., dreams about King Sejong who created *Hangul*, the Korean alphabet, and finds new pride in her Korean heritage.

Tran Khanh Tuyet, *The Little Weaver of Thai-Yen Village*, 1977
A young Vietnamese refugee arrives in the U.S. and struggles to adjust to her new life. She starts to weave again, as she did in her home country with her late grandmother.

Michele Maria Surat, *Angel Child, Dragon Child*, 1983
Young Ut, a recent Vietnamese immigrant, is teased because of her different appearance. Thrown together by the school principal, Ut and a once cruel boy develop a new friendship.

930
SOOK NYUL CHOI

Year of Impossible Goodbyes
(New York: Dell Publishing (Bantam Doubleday Dell), 1991)

Subject(s): Multicultural; Historical; Korean War
Age range(s): Grades 7-12
Major character(s): Sookan Bak, Young Woman, Korean; Hyunsuk "Mother" Bak, Mother (Sookan's mother), Korean; Inchun Bak, Brother (Sookan's younger brother), Korean; "Aunt Tiger", Aunt (Sookan and Inchun's aunt), Korean; Kisa, Cousin (Sookan's), Mechanic
Time period(s): 1940s; 1950s
Locale(s): Pyongyang, Korea, North; Seoul, Korea, South

Summary: Ten-year-old Sookan witnesses first-hand the cruel Japanese occupation of her Korean homeland. But the eventual defeat of the Japanese military is followed by only a brief respite, before the Korean War tears the country apart. Sookan and her family realize they must escape from Pyongyang to Seoul if they are to be free.

About this book: Although a work of fiction, this novel offers a historically accurate depiction of the Japanese occupation and war experiences of Koreans.

Where it's reviewed:
Booklist, March 15, 1992, page 1363
Horn Book Guide, Spring 1992, page 63
Quill & Quire, February 1992, page 36
Kirkus Reviews, August 15, 1991, page 1087
Publishers Weekly, June 28, 1991, page 102

Awards the book has won:
ALA Children's Notable Book, 1991

American Library Association Best Book for Young Adults, 1991

Other books by the same author:
Gathering of Pearls, 1994 (sequel)
Echoes of the White Giraffe, 1993 (sequel)
Halmoni and the Picnic, 1993 (children's story)

Other books you might like:

K. Connie Kang, *Home Was the Land of Morning Calm: The Saga of a Korean American Family*, 1995
This adult work weaves the saga of one Korean family with the country's turbulent history, from 1900 to the present, from North Korea to Japan and finally to the U.S.

Helie Lee, *Still Life with Rice: A Young American Woman Discovers the Life and Legacy of Her Korean Grandmother*, 1996
A Korean woman survives great hardship in Korea and finally arrives in the U.S. Her Korean American granddaughter tells her story in this adult work of non-fiction.

Marie G. Lee, *Saying Goodbye*, 1994
Ellen has left her small hometown for Harvard where she comes face-to-face with the reality of racial boundaries and racial tensions and must define her own position as an aware Korean American.

Marie G. Lee, *Finding My Voice*, 1992
A senior in high school, Ellen struggles to find her voice and speak out for what she wants and believes in, especially as she faces the racism in her tiny hometwon.

Margaret Chang, *In the Eye of War*, 1990
Shao-shao celebrates his tenth birthday in the final days of the Japanese occupation of China and befriends the daughter of a traitor.

931
LOUIS CHU

Eat a Bowl of Tea
(Seattle: University of Washington Press, 1961)

Subject(s): Multicultural; Emigration and Immigration; Marriage
Age range(s): Adult
Major character(s): Ben Loy, Spouse (Husband), Chinese; Mei Oi, Spouse (beautiful bride of Ben Loy), Chinese; Wah Gay, Father (Ben Loy's "bachelor" father), Chinese; Ah Song, Gambler (cheat), Rogue (seduces other men's wives), Chinese
Time period(s): 1940s; 1950s
Locale(s): New York, New York (Chinatown)

Summary: American-born Ben Loy and Chinese-born Mei Oi are, at first, blissfully married until Ben Loy finds himself overworked and impotent. Mei Oi, lonely and isolated in the new world, is seduced by Chinatown's scoundrel. The affair is discovered and Ben Loy is avenged by his father. Reunited, Ben Loy and Mei Oi move to San Francisco where they start anew.

About this book: An often comic novel, *Tea* is one of the first works to offer a faithful portrait of New York's Chinatown. The title comes from an old Chinese herbal remedy: eating a bowl of tea is believed to restore a man's potency.

Other books you might like:
Gish Jen, *Typical American*, 1991
    A novel of the Chang family, newly arrived from China, and their often humorous new life in the New World.
Tooru J. Kanazawa, *Sushi and Sourdough*, 1989
    At the turn of the century, a Japanese immigrant heads for Alaska hoping to strike it rich panning for gold.
Steven Lo, *The Incorporation of Eric Chung*, 1989
    A comic novel of Eric Chung's rise from immigrant student at Texas Tech to major Texas businessman with Important Connections.
Shawn Wong, *American Knees*, 1995
    A novel about the amorous adventures of Raymond Ding, a young, recently divorced, Chinese American man.

932

DEMI, Author/Illustrator

Buddha
(New York: Henry Holt and Company, 1996)

Subject(s): Biography; Buddhism
Age range(s): Grades 2-6
Major character(s): Prince Siddhartha, Royalty (gives up birthright), Historical Figure; Devadatta, Cousin (jealous of Siddhartha)
Time period(s): 6th century B.C.
Locale(s): India (kingdom in foothills of Himalayan mountains)

Summary: A gifted young prince, Siddhartha, leaves his life of luxury and forsakes everything on this earth to seek the Truth of life over death. His search leads him to the path of enlightenment and at the age of 35, he becomes the Buddha.

About this book: The prolific Demi is the author and illustrator of over a hundred books for children.

Other books by the same author:
The Magic Tapestry, 1994
Demi's Dragons and Fantastic Creatures, 1993 (an illustrated guide)
Chingis Khan, 1991
The Empty Pot, 1990
Liang and the Magic Paintbrush, 1980

Other books you might like:
Jeannine Atkins, *Aani and the Tree Huggers*, 1995
    Aani bravely leads the other women of her village in putting their arms around the trees of their forest in order to save them from unthinking developers.
Margaret Chang, *The Cricket Warrior: A Chinese Tale*, 1994
    Adapted with Raymond Chang. The dutiful son, Wei Nian, takes the form of a cricket and saves his family by becoming the champion of the Emperor's court.
Charlie Chin, *China's Bravest Girl: The Legend of Hua Mu Lan*, 1993
    Adapted by Chin. Disguised as a man, Hua Mu Lan takes her elderly father's place in the Emperor's army and becomes a legendary warrior.
Ed Young, *Little Plum*, 1994
    In spite of his diminutive size, Little Plum proves to be a powerful young man.

933

DEMI, Author/Illustrator

Chingis Khan
(New York: Henry Holt and Company, 1991)

Subject(s): Biography; Kings, Queens, Rulers, etc.; Courage
Age range(s): Grades 1-4
Major character(s): Temujin "Chingis Khan", Child, Artist (longs to paint), Chinese
Time period(s): 12th century; 13th century (1160-1227, Chingis Khan's lifetime)
Locale(s): Mongolia

Summary: A biography, based on both historical accounts and legends, of the great Mongol warrior and leader, Chingis Khan (aka Ghenghis Khan), who, at the height of his career, controlled the largest empire ever created during the lifetime of one man.

About this book: The prolific Demi is the author and illustrator of over a hundred books for children.

Where it's reviewed:
Hornbook Guide, Spring 1992, page 127
New York Times Book Review, April 26, 1992, page 25
Booklist, October 1, 1991, page 329
Kirkus Reviews, October 1, 1991, page 1286
School Library Journal, October 1991, page 108

Other books by the same author:
Buddha, 1996
The Magic Tapestry, 1994
Demi's Dragons and Fantastic Creatures, 1993 (illustrated guide)
The Empty Pot, 1990
Liang and the Magic Paintbrush, 1980

Other books you might like:
Margaret Chang, *The Cricket Warrior: A Chinese Tale*, 1994
    Adapted with Raymond Chang. The dutiful son, Wei nian, takes the form of a cricket and saves his family by becoming the champion of the Emperor's court.
Charlie Chin, *China's Bravest Girl: The Legend of Hua Mu Lan*, 1993
    Adapted by Chin. Disguised as a man, Hua Mu Lan takes her elderly father's place in the Emperor's army and becomes a legendary warrior.
Jacquelin Singh, *Fat Gopal*, 1984
    The Maharajah's servant, Fat Gopal, receives huge sums of money to measure the earth and to count the stars.
Paul Yee, *Tales from Gold Mountain: Stories of the Chinese in the New World*, 1989
    A collection of eight tales about Chinese immigrants in the New World.
Laurence Yep, *The Man Who Tricked a Ghost*, 1993
    Sung is not afraid of anything—even a ghost determined to scare him to death.

934

DEMI, Author/Illustrator

The Empty Pot

(New York: Henry Holt and Company, 1990)

Subject(s): Folk Tales; Honesty; Kings, Queens, Rulers, etc.
Age range(s): Grades 1-4
Major character(s): Ping, Child (young boy), Gardener (with a very green thumb), Chinese; The Emperor, Ruler (old, searching for successor)
Time period(s): Indeterminate Past (''a very long time ago'')
Locale(s): China

Summary: Anything young Ping plants, blossoms. When the old Emperor announces that the child who grows the most special flower from the Emperor's seeds will become his successor, Ping eagerly participates. But Ping's seed does not sprout and he returns to the palace with an empty pot. Ironically he is justly rewarded for his honesty.

About this book: The prolific Demi is the author and illustrator of over a hundred books for children.

Where it's reviewed:
Booklist, April 1, 1990, page 1545
Hornbook, May 1990, page 342
Kirkus Reviews, March 1, 1990, page 340
Publishers Weekly, February 9, 1990, page 59
School Library Journal, July 1990, page 58

Awards the book has won:
An IRA-CBC Children's Choice
An American Bookseller Pick of the Lists

Other books by the same author:
Buddha, 1996
The Magic Tapestry, 1994
Demi's Dragons and Fantastic Creatures, 1993 (illustrated guide)
Chingis Khan, 1991
Liang and the Magic Paintbrush, 1980

Other books you might like:
Jose Aruego, *Rockabye Crocodile*, 1988
  Edited with Ariane Dewey. Two elderly boars, a crocodile and her baby teach a lesson about goodness, greed and rewards.
Karen Chinn, *Sam and the Lucky Money*, 1995
  Disappointed that everything he wants to buy with his Chinese New Year gift money costs too much, Sam finally realizes how lucky he is when he sees a lonely stranger without shoes.
Jan Freeman Long, *The Bee and the Dream: A Japanese Tale*, 1996
  Shin so believes in the reality of his friend Tasuke's dream of finding gold that he borrows money and sets off to find the treasure.
Ai-Ling Louie, *Yeh-Shen: A Cinderella Story from China*, 1982
  In spite of the wicked machinations of her stepmother, the beautiful young Yeh-Shen manages to survive her deprived life, marry the king and live happily ever after.

Laurence Yep, *The Shell Woman and the King*, 1993
  The magical shell woman saves her husband and herself from the evil, greedy king.

935

DEMI, Author/Illustrator

Liang and the Magic Paintbrush

(New York: Henry Holt and Company, 1980)

Subject(s): Folk Tales; Artists and Art; Greed
Age range(s): Grades 1-3
Major character(s): Liang, Child, Artist (longs to paint), Chinese
Time period(s): Indeterminate Past
Locale(s): China

Summary: Young Liang longs to paint, but cannot afford a brush. One night, a magical figure gives him a magic paintbrush; Liang finds that everything he paints comes to life. With it, he helps needy family and friends. The greedy emperor demands Liang draw him more and more elaborate things, eventually leading to his own demise.

About this book: The prolific Demi is the author and illustrator of over a hundred books for children.

Where it's reviewed:
Booklist, September 15, 1980, page 113
Children's Book Review Service, October 1980, page 14
Kirkus Reviews, November 15, 1980, page 1459
Publishers Weekly, February 26, 1988, page 199
School Library Journal, September 1980, page 68

Awards the book has won:
A Reading Rainbow Selection

Other books by the same author:
Buddha, 1996
The Magic Tapestry, 1994
Demi's Dragons and Fantastic Creatures, 1993 (illustrated guide)
Chingis Khan, 1991
The Empty Pot, 1990 (when Ping presents an empty pot to the Emperor, he is rewarded for his honesty)

Other books you might like:
Charlie Chin, *China's Bravest Girl: The Legend of Hua Mu Lan*, 1993
  Adapted by Chin. Disguised as a man, Hua Mu Lan takes her elderly father's place in the Emperor's army and becomes a legendary warrior.
Jan Freeman Long, *The Bee and the Dream: A Japanese Tale*, 1996
  Shin so believes in the reality of his friend Tasuke's dream of finding gold that he borrows money and sets off to find the treasure.
Nami Rhee, *Magic Spring: A Korean Folktale*, 1993
  A hardworking, childless, elderly couple find the fountain of youth. Their greedy neighbor rushes to the magic spring and overindulges, leading to a surprise ending.
Laurence Yep, *The Boy Who Swallowed Snakes*, 1994
  Little Chou swallows a poisonous *ku* snake to prevent evil from spreading.

Asian American Titles

Laurence Yep, *The City of Dragons*, 1995

The boy with the saddest face in the world proves to be a hero in the city of dragons.

936

DEMI, Author/Illustrator

The Magic Tapestry

(New York: Henry Holt and Company, 1994)

Subject(s): Folk Tales; Courage; Magic
Age range(s): Grades 1-4
Major character(s): Widow, Widow(er) (a poor widow with three sons), Artisan (weaver of beautiful tapestries); Eldest Son, Son (eldest of the weaver widow); Second Son, Son (middle of the weaver widow); Youngest Son, Son (youngest of the weaver widow)
Time period(s): Indeterminate Past (''long ago'')
Locale(s): China (''southern China'')

Summary: A poor widow spends years weaving a tapestry so spectacular that the fairies of Sun Mountain steal it away. She sends each of her three sons one by one to retrieve her life work, but only the youngest son has the courage to succeed.

About this book: The prolific Demi is the author and illustrator of over a hundred books for children.

Where it's reviewed:
Booklist, August 1994, page 2045
Kirkus Reviews, May 15, 1994, page 697
Publishers Weekly, May 2, 1994, page 308
School Library Journal, August 1994, page 150

Other books by the same author:
Buddha, 1996
Demi's Dragons and Fantastic Creatures, 1993 (illustrated guide)
Chingis Khan, 1991
The Empty Pot, 1990
Liang and the Magic Paintbrush, 1980 (young Liang is given a magic paintbrush that brings to life everything he draws)

Other books you might like:
Margaret Chang, *The Cricket Warrior: A Chinese Tale*, 1994
Adapted with Raymond Chang. The dutiful son, Wei nian, takes the form of a cricket and saves his family by becoming the champion of the Emperor's court.
Charlie Chin, *China's Bravest Girl: The Legend of Hua Mu Lan*, 1993
Adapted by Chin. Disguised as a man, Hua Mu Lan takes her elderly father's place in the Emperor's army and becomes a legendary warrior.
Ellin Greene, *Ling-Li and the Phoenix Fairy: A Chinese Folktale*, 1996
Ling-Li creates a wedding robe so beautiful that the magpies carry it away. Ling-Li follows the birds to the Phoenix Fairy who returns the robe with her special blessings.
Ed Young, *Little Plum*, 1994
In spite of his diminutive size, Little Plum proves to be a powerful young man.

937

CHITRA BANERJEE DIVAKARUNI

Arranged Marriage

(New York: Anchor Books (Doubleday), 1995)

Subject(s): Multicultural; Emigration and Immigration; Short Stories
Age range(s): Adult
Time period(s): 1990s (1995)
Locale(s): United States (various major cities); India (various locations)

Summary: A collection of 11 short stories about young Indian and Indian American women, some married, some single, in various stages of claiming independence from their well-meaning but suffocating families and their oppressive patriarchal heritage. Strong and determined, many of Divakaruni's heroines establish themselves with new beliefs, new goals, and new identities in the U.S.

Where it's reviewed:
Ms., July 1995, page 77
New York Times Book Review, July 16, 1995, page 20
Publishers Weekly, June 5, 1995, page 53

Other books by the same author:
Black Candle, 1991 (poetry)
The Reason for Nasturtiums, 1990 (poetry)
Dark Like the River, 1987 (poetry)

Other books you might like:
Bharati Mukherjee, *Jasmine*, 1989
A novel about Jasmine Vijh's odyssey through America, from her arrival from India as a 17-year-old widow to her new life as Jane Ripplemeyer, assumed to be an Iowa housewife.
Bharati Mukherjee, *Wife*, 1975
Dimple Dasgupta marries an engineer bound for the U.S. but her expectations of being a dutiful wife and living glamorously in America fall far short of reality.
Kirin Narayan, *Love, Stars, and All That*, 1994
This delightful novel follows Gita Das—from immigrant graduate student at Berkeley to esteemed professor—through her bumpy search for her ideal mate.
Marina Tamar Budhos, *House of Waiting*, 1995
As Sarah awaits the return of her Indian-Caribbean husband Roland, embroiled in the political turmoil of his native Guiana, she creates a new life among his tight community of East Indian transplants.
Ameena Meer, *Bombay Talkie*, 1994
Sabah heads to India in search of her ethnic identity. What she finds in the wealthy world of her Indian relatives is a liberal Westernized culture bound by strict traditions.

938

M. EVELINA GALANG

Her Wild American Self

(Minneapolis: Coffee House Press, 1996)

Subject(s): Multicultural; Family Relations; Short Stories
Age range(s): Adult

Time period(s): 1990s
Locale(s): United States

Summary: A collection of short stories centered on the experiences of Filipina American women of various ages, different lifestyles, changing goals, and private longings—each in search of her own unique identity.

Where it's reviewed:
Kirkus Reviews, February 1, 1996, page 156
Publishers Weekly, February 26, 1996, page 98

Other books you might like:
Peter Bacho, *Cebu*, 1991
   On his first visit to the Philippines to bury his mother, Filipino American priest Ben Lucero finds all his moral and religious beliefs thrown into question.
Jessica Hagedorn, *Dogeaters*, 1990
   An autobiographical novel about growing up in Manila in the late 1950s during the turbulent and corrupt Marcos regime.
F. Sionil Jose, *Three Filipino Women: Novellas*, 1992
   Three novellas about three remarkable, though ultimately tragic Filipino women: Narita, a politician, Ermita, a high class prostitute, and Malu, a political idealist.
Marianne Villanueva, *Ginseng and Other Tales from Manila*, 1991
   Stories inspired by real life events and newspaper articles, focusing on the desperate citizens of a troubled country trying to survive poverty, corruption and loss of freedom.

939

PHILIP KAN GOTANDA

Fish Head Soup and Other Plays

(Seattle: University of Washington Press, 1995)

Subject(s): Theater; Family Relations; Multicultural
Age range(s): Adult
Time period(s): Indeterminate

Summary: A collection of four plays by premiere Japanese American playwright Philip Kan Gotanda, including the award-winning *The Wash*, about the heart-wrenching disintegration of an older Japanese American couple's marriage, and *Yankee Dawg You Die*, about two actors trying to survive in an industry built on stereotypical portrayals of Asian Americans.

Other books you might like:
Misha Berson, *Between Worlds: Contemporary Asian-American Plays*, 1990
   Edited by Berson; anthology includes works by Ping Chong, Philip Kan Gotanda, Jessica Hagedorn, David Henry Hwang, Wakako Yamauchi and Laurence Yep.
Velina Hasu Houston, *The Politics of Life: Four Plays by Asian American Women*, 1993
   Edited by Houston; includes works by Wakako Yamauchi, Genny Lim and Houston.
David Henry Hwang, *FOB and Other Plays*, 1990
   A collection of six of Hwang's plays, including the Broadway gender-bender sensation, *M. Butterfly*.
Roberta Uno, *Unbroken Thread: An Anthology of Plays by Asian American Women*, 1993

Edited by Uno; includes plays by Genny Lim, Wakako Yamauchi, Momoko Iko, Velina Hasu Houston, Jeannie Barroga and Elizabeth Wong.

940

ELLIN GREENE, Adaptor
ZONG-ZHOU WANG, Illustrator

Ling-Li and the Phoenix Fairy: A Chinese Folktale

(New York: Clarion Books (Houghton Mifflin), 1996)

Subject(s): Folk Tales; Talent; Marriage
Age range(s): Grades 1-3
Major character(s): Ling-Li, Artisan (talented in weaving/embroidery); Manchang, Fiance(e) (Ling-Li's betrothed); Golden Flower, Young Woman (jealous of Ling-Li's talents)
Time period(s): Indeterminate Past
Locale(s): China (mountainous region)

Summary: Ling-Li prepares for her marriage by creating a beautiful wedding robe. A wealthy, jealous village girl tries to steal it, but magpies carry it away. Ling-Li follows the birds to the Phoenix Fairy who returns the robe with her special blessings for Ling-Li's marriage.

Where it's reviewed:
Booklist, February 15, 1996, page 1014
Publishers Weekly, January 8, 1996, page 70

Other books you might like:
Demi, *The Magic Tapestry*, 1994
   When his mother's heavenly tapestry is stolen by fairies of Sun Mountain, the youngest son must win it back.
Laurence Yep, *The Shell Woman and the King*, 1993
   The magical shell woman saves her husband and herself from the evil, greedy king.
Demi, *Liang and the Magic Paintbrush*, 1980
   When a poor boy who longs to paint is given a brush, it turns out to be magic, bringing to life whatever he paints.
Louie Ai-Ling, *Yeh-Shen: A Cinderella Story from China*, 1982
   In spite of the wicked machinations of her stepmother, the beautiful, young Yeh-Shen manages to survive her deprived life, marry the king and live happily ever after.
Ed Young, *Red Thread*, 1993
   One morning, Wei Gu meets an old matchmaker from the spirit world who tells him about the woman fate says he will marry. When the child is not to his liking, he orders his servant to kill her.

941

JESSICA HAGEDORN, Editor

Charlie Chan Is Dead: An Anthology of Contemporary Asian American Fiction

(New York: Penguin Books, 1993)

Subject(s): Identity; Multicultural; Short Stories
Age range(s): Adult

Time period(s): 1870s; 1990s
Locale(s): United States

Summary: This anthology, which includes both short stories and excerpts from larger works, celebrates the diversity of Asian American literature, from the many literary styles to the various ethnic backgrounds, ages, and beliefs of the 48 writers included in this collection.

About this book: Created by a white man named Earl Derr Biggers in 1925, Charlie Chan was one of the ultimate Asian stereotypes, known for his obsequious manner and broken English versions of fortune-cookie pop psychology. The diverse, individual, invincible Asian American voices in this collection prove that such cartoonish Asian Americans never existed in reality.

Where it's reviewed:
Ms., November 1993, page 67
Multicultural Review, December 1993, Page 30
New York Times Book Review, December 19, 1993, page 17

Other books by the same author:
Danger and Beauty, 1993 (poetry and short fiction)
Dogeaters, 1990 (autobiography)

Other books you might like:
Asian Women United of California, *Making Waves: An Anthology of Writings by and about Asian American Women*, 1989
    First major compilation since the early 1970s of primarily unpublished works by and about Asian American women.
Joseph Bruchac, *Breaking Silence: An Anthology of Contemporary Asian American Poets*, 1983
    One of the first major anthologies of Asian American poetry, featuring the work of some 50 writers.
Jeffery Paul Chan, *Aiiieeeee! An Anthology of Asian American Writers*, 1974
    Edited by Chin, Inada and Wong, *the* original anthology of Asian American writing.
Frank Chin, *The Big Aiiieeeee! An Anthology of Chinese American and Japanese American Literature*, 1991
    Edited by Chan, Inada and Wong, this is a follow-up to *Aiiieeeee!*.

942

JESSICA HAGEDORN

Dogeaters

(New York: Penguin Books, 1990)

Subject(s): Coming of Age; Multicultural
Age range(s): Adult
Major character(s): Rio Gonzaga, Student (feisty young schoolgirl), Filipino; Pucha Gonzaga, Cousin (Rio's slightly older cousin), Filipino; Dolores Gonzaga, Mother (Rio's glamorous mother), Filipino; Narcisa "Lola" Divina, Grandmother (Rio's maternal grandmother), Filipino
Time period(s): 1950s; 1960s
Locale(s): Manila, Philippines

Summary: Rio, a feisty young schoolgirl, comes of age in turbulent Manila during the final dictatorship in the Philippines. Her world is populated with American films and movie stars, soda shops, political corruption and turmoil and a never-ending list of eccentric relatives.

About this book: Interspersed through the text are historical excerpts, including random paragraphs from a racist 1946 history book, various newspaper articles and gossip columns. The effect of the so-called "truth" of history makes for an interesting juxtaposition with the "fictionality" of the novel.

Where it's reviewed:
MS., July 1995, page 73

Awards the book has won:
National Book Award nominee, 1990

Other books by the same author:
Charlie Chan Is Dead: An Anthology of Contemporary Asian American Fiction, 1994 (edited by Hagedorn)
Danger and Beauty, 1993 (poetry and short fiction)

Other books you might like:
F. Sionil Jose, *Three Filipino Women: Novellas*, 1992
    Novellas about three remarkable, though ultimately tragic Filipino women: Narita, a politician, Ermita, a high class prostitute, and Malu, a political idealist.
Marianne Villanueva, *Ginseng and Other Tales from Manila*, 1991
    Stories focusing on the desperate citizens of a troubled country trying to survive poverty, government corruption and loss of individual freedom.
Peter Bacho, *Cebu*, 1991
    On his first visit to the Philippines to bury his mother, Filipino American priest Ben Lucero finds all his moral and religious beliefs thrown into question.
M. Evelina Galang, *Her Wild American Self*, 1996
    A collection of short stories centered on the experiences of Filipina American women of various ages and lifestyles, each in search of her own unique identity.
R. Zamora Linmark, *Rolling the R's*, 1995
    A collection of interrelated short stories, many about young Filipino Americans coming to terms with their ethnicity and with their sexuality in Honolulu.

943

KIMIKO HAHN

Earshot

(Brooklyn, NY: Hanging Loose Press, 1992)

Subject(s): Poetry; Multicultural; Identity
Age range(s): Adult

Summary: Poetry collection filled with imaginative, even quirky pieces, incorporating such diverse subjects as language, marriage and Japanese folklore.

Where it's reviewed:
American Poetry Review, November 1992, page 33
Small Press, Winter 1993, page 53
Small Press Book Review, September 1992, page 12

Other books by the same author:
The Unbearable Heart, 1996 (poetry)
Air Pocket, 1989 (debut poetry collection)

Other books you might like:

Joseph Bruchac, *Breaking Silence: An Anthology of Contemporary Asian American Poets*, 1983
> One of the first major anthologies of Asian American poetry, featuring the work of some 50 writers.

Li-Young Lee, *The City in Which I Love You*, 1990
> Award-winning second poetry collection, about relationships between family and lovers.

Walter K. Lew, *Premonitions: The Kaya Anthology of New Asian North American Poetry*, 1995
> This collection of 73 authors, ranging from the up-and-coming to the established, features writing in all modes of poetry, including works in non-standard forms and dialects.

Cathy Song, *Frameless Windows, Squares of Light*, 1988
> Cathy Song's second poetry collection in which she writes of family, friends and nameless strangers.

Cathy Song, *Picture Bride*, 1983
> Award-winning debut poetry collection.

Garrett Hongo, *The Open Boat: Poems from Asian America*, 1993
> A collection of works by 30 Asian American writers, both U.S. and foreign-born, covering over 100 years of the Asian American presence in America.

944

SHEILA HAMANAKA, Author/Illustrator

All the Colors of the Earth

(New York: Morrow Junior Books, 1994)

Subject(s): Identity; Multicultural
Age range(s): Grades 1-3
Locale(s): United States

Summary: Despite outward differences in skin color or diversity in facial characteristics, all children on the inside are basically the same, and each deserves to be loved and cherished.

Where it's reviewed:
AB Bookman's Weekly, December 19, 1994, page 2588
Horn Book Magazine, November 1994, page 760
Instructor, January 1995, page 89

Other books by the same author:
Peace Crane, 1995
The Journey: Japanese Americans, Racism, and Renewal, 1990

Other books you might like:

Sandra S. Yamate, *Ashok by Any Other Name*, 1992
> Ashok, a young Indian American boy, wishes he had a more "American" name, so he tries a new one each day, finally realizing "Ashok" is the perfect name for him.

Sandra S. Yamate, *Char Siu Bao Boy*, 1991
> Charlie's favorite food, *char sui bao*, causes his classmates to make fun of him, until one day he brings enough for all of them to taste.

Cynthia Chin-Lee, *Almond Cookies and Dragon Well Tea*, 1993
> When Erica visits Nancy's house for the first time, she expects many differences because Nancy is Chinese American, but finds that their two families are more similar than not.

Min Paek, *Aekyung's Dream*, 1988
> Aekyung, a young Korean girl recently in the U.S., dreams about King Sejong who created *Hangul*, the Korean alphabet, and finds new pride in her Korean heritage.

Asian American Coalition, *Children of Asian America*, 1995
> A collection of original stories about growing up as an Asian American child, centered around the diverse ethnic communities of Chicago.

945

SHEILA HAMANAKA, Editor

On the Wings of Peace: Writers and Illustrators Speak Out for Peace, in Memory of Hiroshima and Nagasaki

(New York: Clarion Books (Houghton Mifflin), 1996)

Subject(s): Multicultural; Children and War; Nuclear Warfare
Age range(s): Grades 5 and Up
Time period(s): 1990S

Summary: Compiled, with an introduction by Sheila Hamanaka. A beautiful collection of stories, poetry, remembrances and art focusing on the tragedies caused by war, and the hopes for a lasting peace for today's children.

About this book: A book for children of all ages as well as adults. While it deals with the horrors of war, destruction and death, the book also provides committed prayers and fervent hopes that such tragedies never be repeated again.

Where it's reviewed:
Booklist, January 1, 1996, page 810
Horn Book Magazine, November 1995, page 742
School Library Journal, October 1995, page 150

Other books by the same author:
Peace Crane, 1995
All the Colors of the Earth, 1994
The Journey: Japanese Americans, Racism, and Renewal, 1990

Other books you might like:

Toshi Maruki, *Hiroshima No Pika (The Flash of Hiroshima)*, 1980
> Although young Mii and her parents survived the initial blast of the Hiroshima atomic bomb, the horror they endured afterwards was a tragedy beyond description.

Laurence Yep, *Hiroshima*, 1995
> The horror of the Hiroshima bombing, told through the tragic story of two sisters who were on their way to school when the B-29 bomber named *Enola Gay* dropped the first bomb.

946

SHEILA HAMANAKA, Author/Illustrator

Peace Crane

(New York: Morrow Junior Books, 1995)

Subject(s): Children and War; Peace

Age range(s): Grades 1-4
Major character(s): Child, Child (girl)
Time period(s): 1990s (1995)
Locale(s): United States

Summary: After learning about Sadako Sasaki, a young Hiroshima bomb victim who folded thousands of paper cranes in hopes of prolonging her life, a young American girl folds a crane of her own and wishes it could carry her to a peaceful world.

About this book: The Japanese have a tradition of folding paper cranes as a symbol of long life.

Where it's reviewed:
Booklist, September 15, 1995, page 175
Publisher Weekly, July 31, 1995, page 79
School Library Journal , September 1995, page 179

Other books by the same author:
All the Colors of the Earth, 1994
The Journey: Japanese Americans, Racism, and Renewal, 1990

Other books you might like:
Laurence Yep, *Hiroshima*, 1995
    The horror of the Hiroshima bombing, told through the tragic story of two sisters who were on their way to school when the B-29 bomber, the *Enola Gay*, dropped the first atomic bomb.
Toshi Maruki, *Hiroshima No Pika (The Flash of Hiroshima)*, 1980
    Although young Mii and her parents survived the initial blast of the Hiroshima atomic bomb, the horror they endured afterwards was a tragedy beyond description.
Michele Maria Surat, *Angel Child, Dragon Child*, 1983
    Young Ut, a recent Vietnamese immigrant, is teased because of her different appearance. Thrown together by their school principal, Ut and a once cruel boy develop a new friendship.
Tran Khanh Tuyet, *The Little Weaver of Thai-Yen Village*, 1977
    A young Vietnamese refugee arrives in the U.S. and struggles to adjust to her new life. She starts to weave again, as she did in her home country with her late grandmother.

947

OKI S. HAN, Author/Illustrator

Sir Whong and the Golden Pig

(New York: Dial Book for Young Readers (Penguin), 1993)

Subject(s): Folk Tales; Honesty; Cheating
Age range(s): Grades 1-5
Major character(s): Sir Whong, Gentleman (kind, generous, wise), Wealthy; Mr. Oh, Impostor (seeks Whong's money)
Time period(s): Indeterminate Past
Locale(s): Republic of Korea (a village)

Summary: The stranger Mr. Oh requests to borrow a huge sum of money from wealthy Sir Whong in order to help his ill mother. He offers a priceless golden pig as security. Sir Whong generously agrees. But Mr. Oh proves to be a greedy liar and Sir Whong devises his own plan to retrieve his money.

Where it's reviewed:
Reading Teacher, December 1994, page 344
Raading Teacher, March 1995, page 493

Other books you might like:
Ed Young, *Lon Po Po: A Red-Riding Hood Story from China*, 1989
    Three sisters, left alone and told to keep the door locked, are tricked by a hungry wolf disguised as Grandma.
Jan Freeman Long, *The Bee and the Dream: A Japanese Tale*, 1996
    Shin so believes in the reality of his friend Tasuke's dream of finding gold that he borrows money and sets off to find the treasure.
Nami Rhee, *Magic Spring: A Korean Folktale*, 1993
    A hardworking, childless, elderly couple find the fountain of youth. Their greedy neighbor rushes to the magic spring and overindulges, leading to a surprise ending.
Laurence Yep, *The Shell Woman and the King*, 1993
    The magical shell woman saves her husband and herself from the evil, greedy king.
Ai-Ling Louie, *Yeh-Shen: A Cinderella Story from China*, 1982
    In spite of the wicked machinations of her stepmother, the beautiful young Yeh-Shen manages to survive her deprived life, marry the king and live happily ever after.

948

SUZANNE CROWDER HAN
YUMI HEO, Illustrator

The Rabbit's Escape

(New York: Henry Holt and Company, 1995)

Subject(s): Folk Tales; Loyalty; Survival
Age range(s): Grades 1-3
Major character(s): Dragon King of the East Sea, Ruler (underworld king who is ill); Turtle, Turtle (loyal underworld subject); Rabbit, Rabbit (clever land animal)
Time period(s): Indeterminate Past

Summary: The court physician advises the ill Dragon King of the East Sea that in order to recover, he needs the raw liver of a rabbit. The turtle volunteers to bring back a rabbit from the land kingdom. He tricks the rabbit into the underworld, but the rabbit cleverly makes his escape.

Where it's reviewed:
Booklist, May 15, 1995, page 1649
Publishers Weekly, April 3, 1995, page 62
School Library Journal, June 1995, page 101

Other books by the same author:
The Rabbit's Judgment, 1994

Other books you might like:
Chyng Feng Sun, *Square Beak*, 1993
    Square Beak is aptly named. When she is ostracized because she looks diferent from the other chickens in the yard, she begins to wander outide her own small world.
Lina Mao Wall, *Judge Rabbit and the Tree Spirit: A Folktale from Cambodia*, 1991
    Judge rabbit helps a young couple trap the tree spirit who has taken the form of the young husband.

Blia Xiong, *Nine-in-One Grr! Grr!*, 1989
    Bird comes up with a clever trick to prevent earth from being overpopulated with tigers.
Ed Young, *Cat and Rat: The Legend of the Chinese Zodiac*, 1995
    An adaptation of how the twelve animals of the zodiac were selected.
Jeanne M. Lee, *Toad Is the Uncle of Heaven*, 1985
    Toad asks the King of Heaven for rain. On his journey, he is joined by the Bees, the Rooster and the Tiger. With the help of his friends, Toad convinces the King to provide rain.

949

SUZANNE CROWDER HAN, Adaptor
YUMI HEO, Illustrator

The Rabbit's Judgment
(New York: Henry Holt and Company, 1994)

Subject(s): Folk Tales; Survival; Animals
Age range(s): Grades 1-3
Major character(s): Tiger, Tiger (trapped in a deep pit); Unnamed Character, Young Man (saves the trapped tiger); Rabbit, Rabbit (cleverly saves the man)
Time period(s): Indeterminate Past
Locale(s): ''a forest''

Summary: A man is tricked into saving a tiger trapped in a pit, but once freed, the tiger intends to eat his savior. The man insists they get a second opinion, first from a tree then an ox who both advise the tiger to eat him. But the clever rabbit is able to save the man.

About this book: A bilingual book, written in both English and Korean.

Where it's reviewed:
Booklist, June 1, 1994, page 1825
Kirkus Reviews, March 1, 1994, page 305
Publishers Weekly, March 7, 1994, page 70

Other books by the same author:
The Rabbit's Escape, 1995

Other books you might like:
Lina Mao Wall, *Judge Rabbit and the Tree Spirit: A Folktale from Cambodia*, 1991
    Adapted by Cathy Spagnoli. Judge Rabbit helps a young couple trap the tree spirit who has taken the form of the young husband.
Jose Aruego, *Rockabye Crocodile*, 1988
    Two elderly boars, a crocodile and her baby teach a lesson about goodness, greed and rewards. Edited with Ariane Dewey.
Oki S. Han, *Sir Whong and the Golden Pig*, 1993
    When a stranger dupes Sir Whong into a loan using a fake golden pig as security, Sir Whong devises a plan to retrieve his money.
Jeanne M. Lee, *Toad Is the Uncle of Heaven*, 1985
    The Toad asks the King of Heaven for rain. On his journey, he is joined by the Bees, the Rooster and the Tiger. With the help of his friends, Toad convinces the King to provide rain.

Nami Rhee, *Magic Spring: A Korean Folktale*, 1993
    A hardworking, childless, elderly couple find the fountain of youth. Their greedy neighbor rushes to the magic spring and overindulges, leading to a surprise ending.

950

MARIE HARA

Bananaheart and Other Stories
(Honolulu: Bamboo Ridge Press, 1994)

Subject(s): Multicultural; Short Stories
Time period(s): 1890s; 1990s
Locale(s): Hawaii

Summary: Short stories that cover a century of life in Hawaii, including tales about a newly arrived picture bride, a young native woman working in a large foreign house, a young hapa girl searching for her identity and an eccentric old woman convinced that she mysteriously lost a daughter in infancy.

Where it's reviewed:
Women's Review of Books, April 1995, page 21

Other books you might like:
Susan Nunes, *A Small Obligation and Other Stories of Hilo*, 1982
    A collection of interrelated stories about Amy Freitas of Hilo, Hawaii, and her extended family—Japanese on her mother's side and Portuguese on her father's side.
Jessica K. Saiki, *From the Lanai and Other Hawaii Stories*, 1991
    A collection of stories about the Japanese American residents of Lunalilo, Hawaii, including a lonely spinster, a deserted husband and a young woman desperate for stardom.
Jessica K. Saiki, *Once, a Lotus Garden and Other Stories*, 1987
    A first collection of stories, mostly set in wartime Hawaii, about the residents of Lunalilo, including new picture brides from Japan and young schoolgirls and their dreams.
Kathleen Tyau, *A Little Too Much Is Enough*, 1995
    Mahi Wong grows up during post-World War II Hawaii, surrounded by her large family, immersed in a complex, mixed-up culture of Chinese and Hawaiian influences.
Sylvia Watanabe, *Talking to the Dead*, 1992
    Award-winning collection, with stories about a female Chinese Fred Astaire, a grandmother who makes quilts of stolen laundry and a girl longing to leave home any way she can.
Lois-Ann Yamanaka, *Wild Meat and the Bully Burgers*, 1996
    A coming-of-age first novel about Lovey Nariyoshi of Hilo, Hawaii, her best friend Jerome, her adolescent enemies and her eccentric family.

951

MARIA HONG, Editor

Growing Up Asian American
(New York: Avon Books, 1993)

Subject(s): Multicultural; Identity; Coming of Age

Age range(s): Adult
Time period(s): 1800s; 1990s
Locale(s): United States

Summary: A diverse collection of essays, excerpts and short stories about growing up in the U.S., all authored by Americans of Asian descent that address such global issues as parent-child relationships, self-realization and identity and the discovery of cultural heritage.

About this book: Includes a wide variety of contributions, pieces that range from the 1800s to the contemporary, by writers of Chinese, Japanese, Filipino, Korean, Indian, bi- and multi-racial descent.

Where it's reviewed:
Los Angeles Times Book Review, January 15, 1995, page 8
Far Eastern Economic Review, August 3, 1995, page 39

Other books you might like:
Garrett Hongo, *Under Western Eyes: Personal Essays from Asian America*, 1995
    A collection of 15 autobiographical essays from leading Asian American voices, confronting racism, language, family, stereotypes and other social and political issues.
Joanne Faung Jean Lee, *Asian Americans*, 1991
    A collection of oral histories from first- to fourth-generation Asian Americans of Chinese, Filipino, Japanese, Korean, Indian, Southeast Asian and Pacific Island ancestry.
Ruthanne Lum McCunn, *Chinese American Portraits: Personal Histories 1828-1988*, 1988
    Profiles of prominent Chinese Americans, from pioneers to politicians.
Ruthanne Lum McCunn, *An Illustrated History of the Chinese in America*, 1979
    An illustrated history book which traces the presence of Chinese in America, from the arrival of Chinese during the California Gold Rush, to contemporary Chinese Americans.
Ronald Takaki, *Strangers from a Different Shore*, 1989
    Traces the diverse lives of the Japanese, Chinese, Koreans, Filipinos, Asian Indians, Vietnamese, Cambodians and Laotions who have come to the U.S. over the past 150 years.

952

GARRETT HONGO, Editor

The Open Boat: Poems from Asian America

(New York: Anchor Books (Doubleday), 1993)

Subject(s): Poetry; Multicultural; Identity
Age range(s): Adult
Time period(s): Indeterminate Past
Locale(s): United States

Summary: This collection of works by 30 Asian American writers, both U.S. and foreign-born, covers over 100 years of the Asian American presence in America. It includes such diverse subjects as immigration, sojourning, stereotypes, assimilation, anti-Asian sentiment, the internment crisis and multicultural identities.

Where it's reviewed:
Booklist, March 1,1993, page 1152
Kliatt, July 1993, page 23
Library Journal, February 1, 1993, page 84
Publishers Weekly, January 4, 1993, page 69
School Library Journal, August 1993, page 208

Other books by the same author:
Under Western Eyes: Personal Essays from Asian America, 1995 (autobiography)
Volcano: A Memoir of Hawai'i, 1995
The River of Heaven, 1988 (Pulitzer Prize-nomination poetry collection)
Yellow Light, 1982 (debut poetry collection)

Other books you might like:
Joseph Bruchac, *Breaking Silence: An Anthology of Contemporary Asian American Poets*, 1983
    One of the first major anthologies of Asian American poetry, this collection features the work of some 50 writers.
Jeffery Paul Chan, *Aiiieeeee! An Anthology of Asian American Writers*, 1974
    Also edited by Chin, Inada and Wong, this is an original anthology of Asian American writing.
Frank Chin, *The Big Aiiieeeee! An Anthology of Chinese American and Japanese American Literature*, 1991
    Also edited by Chan, Inada and Wong, this anthology is a follow-up to *Aiiieeeee!*.
Jessica Hagedorn, *Charlie Chan Is Dead: An Anthology of Contemporary Asian American Fiction*, 1993
    This is collection of 48 works by Asian American writers of different ages, backgrounds and styles.
Walter K. Lew, *Premonitions: The Kaya Anthology of New Asian North American Poetry*, 1995
    Seventy-three authors, ranging from the established to up-and-comers, writing in all modes of poetry, including works in nonstandard forms and dialects, make this a ground-breaking collection.

953

GARRETT HONGO

The River of Heaven

(New York: Alfred A. Knopf, 1988)

Subject(s): Multicultural; Identity; Poetry
Age range(s): Adult
Time period(s): Indeterminate
Locale(s): United States

Summary: In his award-winning second poetry collection, Hango draws on his diverse background, filling his poems with images of Hawaiian volcanoes, war-torn battlefields, a high school classroom, Chinatown back alleys and California beaches.

Where it's reviewed:
Booklist, May 1, 1988, page 1473
Hudson Review, Spring 1989, page 151
Library Journal, May 1, 1988, page 81
Minnesota Review, Spring 1990, page 155
Publishers Weekly, February 12, 1988, page 81

Awards the book has won:
Lamont Poetry Prize of the Academy of American Poets, 1987
Pulitzer Prize finalist

Other books by the same author:
Under Western Eyes: Personal Essays from Asian America, 1995 (autobiography)
Volcano: A Memoir of Hawai'i, 1995
The Open Boat: Poems from Asian America, 1993 (poetry, edited by Hongo)
Yellow Light, 1982 (debut poetry collection)

Other books you might like:
Joseph Bruchac, *Breaking Silence: An Anthology of Contemporary Asian American Poets*, 1983
One of the first major anthologies of Asian American poetry, this collection features the work of some 50 writers.
Kimiko Hahn, *Earshot*, 1992
This poetry collection includes the imaginative, the quirky and the varied.
Li-Young Lee, *The City in Which I Love You*, 1990
Relationship between family and lovers inhabit the poetry of this award-winning second collection.
Walter K. Lew, *Premonitions: The Kaya Anthology of New Asian North American Poetry*, 1995
This collection of 73 authors ranging from established to up-and-comer, features writing in all modes of poetry.
Cathy Song, *Picture Bride*, 1983
Song's collection debuts as award-winning poetry.

954

GARRETT HONGO, Editor

Under Western Eyes: Personal Essays from Asian America

(New York: Anchor Books (Doubleday), 1995)

Subject(s): Multicultural; Emigration and Immigration; Identity
Age range(s): Adult

Summary: A collection of 15 autobiographical essays from leading Asian American voices, confronting racism, language, family, stereotypes and other social and political issues. Contributors include such writers as Peter Bacho, Jeanne Wakatsuki Houston, Chang-rae Lee, Li-Young Lee, David Mura and Amy Tan.

Where it's reviewed:
Publishers Weekly, July 17, 1995, page 225

Other books by the same author:
Volcano: A Memoir of Hawai'i, 1995
The Open Boat: Poems from Asian America, 1993 (edited by Hongo)
The River of Heaven, 1988 (poetry collection; finalist for the Pulitzer Prize)
Yellow Light, 1982 (poetry collection)

Other books you might like:
Joanne Faung Jean Lee, *Asian Americans*, 1991
A collection of oral histories from Asian Americans of

Chinese, Filipino, Japanese, Korean, Indian, Southeast Asian and Pacific Island ancestry.
Maria Hong, *Growing Up Asian American*, 1993
These essay, excerpts, and short stories by Americans of Asian descent address issues such as parent-child relationships, self-realization, identity and the discovery of one's cultural heritage.
Ruthanne Lum McCunn, *Chinese American Portraits: Personal Histories 1828-1988*, 1988
Profiles of prominent Chinese Americans, from pioneers to politicians.
Ronald Takaki, *Strangers from a Different Shore*, 1989
Traces the diverse lives of the Japanese, Chinese, Koreans, Filipinos, Asian Indians, Vietnamese, Cambodians and Laotions who have come to the U.S. over the past 150 years.
Elaine H. Kim, *East to America: Korean American Life Stories*, 1996
Co-edited with Eui-Young Yu, these are oral histories of 38 Korean Americans, from immigrants to third-generation Americans, including journalists, activists, artists, shopkeepers and students.

955

ELAINE HOSOZAWA-NAGANO
MASAYUKI MIYATA, Illustrator

Chopsticks from America

(Chicago: Polychrome Publishing Corporation, 1994)

Subject(s): Multicultural; Change; Moving, Household
Age range(s): Grades 1-6
Major character(s): Tiffany, 11-Year-Old (young Japanese American girl); Kevin, 5-Year-Old (Tiffany's younger brother)
Time period(s): 1990s (1994)
Locale(s): Japan (Tokyo and Saitama Prefecture)

Summary: Tiffany and Kevin, two Japanese American children, move to Japan because of their father's job. While they look like "chopsticks among other chopsticks," they are American, which proves to be very different from being Japanese. Little by little, the two children adapt, and even enjoy their new environment.

Where it's reviewed:
Children's Book Review Service, August 1995, page 162
Publishers Weekly, July 10, 1995, page 56

Other books you might like:
Allen Say, *Grandfather's Journey*, 1993
A Japanese American man recounts his grandfather's journey from Japan to America and back again, trying to understand his grandfather's feelings of being torn between the love of both countries.
Yoshiko Uchida, *The Forever Christmas Tree*, 1963
Young Takashi learns about a joyous holiday called Christmas from his sister Kaya. They decorate a reclusive neighbor's fir tree and bring their neighborhood together.
Allen Say, *Tree of Cranes*, 1991
Lovely story about a young Japanese boy who learns about Christmas for the first time from his California-born Japanese American mother.

Barbara Brenner, *Chibi: A True Story from Japan*, 1996
Written with Julia Takaya, this is the true story of a lone duck who flies into downtown Tokyo and hatches 10 ducklings.

956

JEANNE WAKATSUKI HOUSTON
JAMES D. HOUSTON, Co-Author

Farewell to Manzanar
(Boston: Houghton Mifflin, 1973)

Subject(s): Internment; Coming of Age; Multicultural
Age range(s): Grades 9-Adult
Major character(s): Jeanne Wakatsuki, Daughter, Japanese American (second-generation); Riku "Mama" Wakatsuki, Mother; Ko "Papa" Wakatsuki, Father, Fisherman
Time period(s): 1940s (1941-1945)
Locale(s): California

Summary: Jeanne Wakatsuki was just 7 years old when Pearl Harbor was bombed. Within months, her father was taken away by the government. Soon thereafter, the rest of the Wakatsuki family was uprooted and unjustly incarcerated at Manzanar. Camp life meant three-and-a-half years behind barbed wire, surviving with 10,000 other Americans of Japanese ancestry.

About this book: Houston began *Farewell to Manzanar* as a personal memoir and a means of dealing with a past that was too painful and difficult to actually voice, except finally through the distance of pen and paper. The result proved to be a landmark postwar historical text, still taught in countless classrooms throughout the country.

Where it's reviewed:
Booklist, February 15, 1992, page 1100
Western Historical Quarterly, July 1986, page 284

Other books you might like:
Mine Okubo, *Citizen 13660*, 1946
The autobiographical account, told through sketches and text, of a Japanese American woman who was reduced to Citizen 13660 and interned during World War II.
Joy Kogawa, *Obasan*, 1982
The story of a Japanese Canadian family that is splintered and scattered as a result of forced evacuation and relocation during World War II.
Yoshiko Uchida, *Desert Exile: The Uprooting of a Japanese-American Family*, 1982
The autobiographical account of a second-generation Japanese American woman from Berkeley, California and her family's internment experiences at Camp Topaz during World War II.
Monica Sone, *Nisei Daughter*, 1953
An account of a second-generation Japanese American woman growing up in Seattle in the 1920s and 1930s, her incarceration during World War II and her new life in the Midwest.
Yoshiko Uchida, *Journey to Topaz: A Story of the Japanese-American Evacuation*, 1985
A young adult novel about the Sakanes, a typical Japanese

American family, and their experiences during World War II in the bleak desert concentration camp called Topaz.

957

VELINA HASU HOUSTON, Editor

The Politics of Life: Four Plays by Asian American Women
(Philadelphia: Temple University Press, 1993)

Subject(s): Theater; Multicultural
Age range(s): Adult
Time period(s): Indeterminate

Summary: An anthology of four plays by three Asian American women playwrights: "12-1-A" and "The Chairman's Wife" by Wakako Yamauchi, "Bitter Cane" by Genny Lim and "Asa Ga Kimashita (Morning Has Broken)" by Velina Hasu Houston.

Where it's reviewed:
Theatre Journal, March 1995, page 151
Amerasia Journal, Issue 3, 1993, page 163
Women's Review of Books, May 1994, page 16

Other books you might like:
Misha Berson, *Between Worlds: Contemporary Asian-American Plays*, 1990
Edited by Berson; anthology includes works by Ping Chong, Philip Kan Gotanda, Jessica Hagedorn, David Henry Hwang, Wakako Yamauchi and Laurence Yep.
Philip Kan Gotanda, *Fish Head Soup and Other Plays*, 1995
Four dramas by an extraordinary playwright, focusing on family relations between first-, second- and third-generation Japanese Americans.
David Henry Hwang, *FOB and Other Plays*, 1990
A collection of six of Hwang's plays, including the Broadway gender-bender sensation, *M. Butterfly*.
Roberta Uno, *Unbroken Thread: An Anthology of Plays by Asian American Women*, 1993
Edited by Uno; includes plays by Genny Lim, Wakako Yamauchi, Momoko Iko, Velina Hasu Houston, Jeannie Barroga and Elizabeth Wong.
Genny Lim, *Paper Angels and Bitter Cane*, 1991
Two important plays are included here, one about Chinese immigrants detained at Angel Island and the other about the virtual imprisonment of Asian laborers on Hawaiian sugar cane plantations.

958

DAVID HENRY HWANG

FOB and Other Plays
(New York: Plume (Penguin Books), 1990)

Subject(s): Theater; Multicultural; Identity
Age range(s): Adult
Time period(s): Indeterminate

Summary: A collection of six plays by ground-breaking Asian American playwright, David Henry Hwang, including his much-produced contemporary classic, *FOB*, the gender-bender Broadway hit, *M. Butterfly*, and the Philip Glass collaboration, *1000 Airplanes on the Roof*.

About this book: Hwang was the first Asian American to find major success on the American stage, including Broadway. His *M. Butterfly*, a Tony-award winning bona-fide hit on the Great White Way, was *the* most critically and commercially successful play ever written by an Asian American.

Other books you might like:

Misha Berson, *Between Worlds: Contemporary Asian-American Plays*, 1990
Edited by Berson; anthology includes works by Ping Chong, Philip Kan Gotanda, Jessica Hagedorn, David Henry Hwang, Wakako Yamauchi and Laurence Yep.

Philip Kan Gotanda, *Fish Head Soup and Other Plays*, 1995
Four dramas by an extraordinary playwright, focusing on family relations between first-, second- and third-generation Japanese Americans.

Velina Hasu Houston, *The Politics of Life: Four Plays by Asian American Women*, 1993
Edited by Houston; includes works by Wakako Yamauchi, Genny Lim and Houston.

Roberta Uno, *Unbroken Thread: An Anthology of Plays by Asian American Women*, 1993
Edited by Uno; includes plays by Genny Lim, Wakako Yamauchi, Momoko Iko, Velina Hasu Houston, Jeannie Barroga and Elizabeth Wong.

959

LAWSON FUSAO INADA

Legends from Camp
(Minneapolis: Coffee House Press, 1992)

Subject(s): Poetry; Internment; Identity
Age range(s): Adult

Summary: Poetry collection by an award-winning, third-generation Japanese American. As a child, Inada was interned during World War II with his parents at Jerome Camp in Arkansas and Amache Camp in Colorado. In spite of the grim realities of imprisonment, Inada's memories are mixed with strains of be-bop and jazz.

Where it's reviewed:

American Book Review, December 1993, page 22
Western American Literature, Spring 1994, page 85
Los Angeles Times Book Review, September 5, 1993, page 6

Other books by the same author:

The Big Aiiieeeee! An Anthology of Chinese American and Japanese American Literature, 1991 (sequel)
Aiiieeeee! An Anthology of Asian American Writers, 1974

Other books you might like:

Joseph Bruchac, *Breaking Silence: An Anthology of Contemporary Asian American Poets*, 1983
One of the first major anthologies of Asian American poetry, featuring the work of some 50 writers.

Mitsuye Yamada, *Camp Notes and Other Poems*, 1976
Poetry collection which draws on Yamada's internment experiences during World War II in Minidoka, Idaho.

Mine Okubo, *Citizen 13660*, 1946
This autobiographical account, told through sketches and

text, is of a Japanese American woman who was reduced to Citizen 13660 and interned during World War II.

Walter K. Lew, *Premonitions: The Kaya Anthology of New Asian North American Poetry*, 1995
This collection of 73 authors, ranging from the established to the up-and-coming, features writing in all modes of poetry, including works in non-standard forms and dialects.

Garrett Hongo, *The Open Boat: Poems from Asian America*, 1993
A collection of works by 30 Asian American writers, both U.S. and foreign-born, covering over 100 years of the Asian American presence in America.

960

GISH JEN

Typical American
(Boston: Houghton Mifflin, 1991)

Subject(s): Multicultural; Family Life; Identity
Age range(s): Adult
Major character(s): Ralph Yifeng Chang, Student (Ph.D. candidate in engineering), Businessman (fast food restaurant owner); Helen Chang, Spouse (Ralph's wife); Theresa Chang, Sister (Ralph's older sister), Doctor
Time period(s): 1980s; 1990s
Locale(s): New York (from New York City to suburbia)

Summary: Yifeng Chang arrives in the U.S., is renamed "Ralph" by an impatient immigration official, and pursues an engineering degree. He is reunited with his older sister, Theresa, marries Helen, and moves to suburbia in search of the American Dream where he discovers fried chicken fast food joints, glamour magazines and con artists.

About this book: The title comes from the phrase, "typical American," which the Changs use in moments of exasperation and disgust at how they initially view Americans—wasteful, lazy, rude, etc. But eventually what begins as an insult quickly turns into a lifestyle goal of wanting to become "typical Americans" with a suburban house, wall-to-wall carpeting, two-car garage, magazine subscriptions and fried chicken for dinner.

Where it's reviewed:

Parnassus, Issue 1, 1992, page 88
Publishers Weekly, January 18, 1991, page 46
Time, June 3, 1991, page 66

Other books by the same author:

Mona in the Promised Land, 1996

Other books you might like:

Cynthia Kadohata, *The Floating World*, 1989
A coming-of-age novel about 12-year-old Olivia, who with her family, moves continuously throughout the Pacific Northwest in search of a better life.

Maxine Hong Kingston, *Tripmaster Monkey: His Fake Book*, 1989
Kingston's first novel about the often comic mishaps and adventures of Wittman Ah Sing, a young Chinese American, in search of his dreams.

Chang-rae Lee, *Native Speaker*, 1995
  A first novel about Korean American Henry Park who is trying to come to terms with both his troubled personal life and his problematic career as a spy.

Steven Lo, *The Incorporation of Eric Chung*, 1989
  A comic novel of Eric Chung's rise from immigrant student at Texas Tech to major Texas businessman with Important Connections.

961

F. SIONIL JOSE

Three Filipino Women: Novellas

(New York: Random House, 1992)

Subject(s): Short Stories
Age range(s): Adult
Time period(s): Indeterminate
Locale(s): Philippines

Summary: Three novellas about three remarkable, though ultimately tragic Filipino women: Narita, a politician trying to escape her poverty-stricken past, Ermita, a very high class prostitute in search of true love, and Malu, a political idealist fighting for her beliefs.

Where it's reviewed:
Multi Cultural Review, October 1992, page 63
World Literature Today, Winter 1994, page 221

Other books by the same author:
Po-On: A Novel, 1984
Tree, 197?
My Brother, My Executioner, 1979
The Pretenders, 1980
Mass: A Novel, 1979

Other books you might like:
Jessica Hagedorn, *Dogeaters*, 1990
  An autobiographical novel about growing up in Manila in the late 1950s during the turbulent and corrupt Marcos regime.
Marianne Villanueva, *Ginseng and Other Tales from Manila*, 1991
  Stories focusing on the desperate citizens of a troubled country trying to survive poverty, government corruption, and loss of individual freedom.
M. Evelina Galang, *Her Wild American Self*, 1996
  A collection of short stories centered on the experiences of Filipina American women of various ages and lifestyles, each in search of her own unique identity.
Peter Bacho, *Cebu*, 1991
  On his first visit to the Philippines to bury his mother, Filipino American priest Ben Lucero finds all his moral and religious beliefs thrown into question.

962

CYNTHIA KADOHATA

The Floating World

(New York: Viking (Penguin Group), 1989)

Subject(s): Intergenerational Saga; Multicultural; Family Life

Age range(s): Adult
Major character(s): Olivia Ann Osaka, Daughter (granddaughter of Hisae), Japanese; Hisae Fujiitano, Grandmother, Immigrant (from Japan), Japanese; Mother Osaka, Mother (Olivia's mother), Daughter (Hisae's daughter), Japanese; Charles ''Charlie-O'' Osaka, Father (Olivia's stepfather), Japanese
Time period(s): 1950s
Locale(s): West

Summary: A coming-of-age novel about an adolescent named Olivia who, with her parents, her three brothers and her tormenting grandmother, lives a traveling life, following the search for available jobs. Her world is filled with motels, empty roads, gas station attendants and constant new faces as her life seems to change day to day.

Where it's reviewed:
Los Angeles Times Book Review, May 2, 1993, page 10

Other books by the same author:
In the Heart of the Valley of Love, 1992 (futuristic)

Other books you might like:
Bharati Mukherjee, *Jasmine*, 1989
  A novel about Jasmine Vijh's odyssey through America, from her arrival from India as a 17-year-old widow to her new life as Jane Ripplemeyer, assumed to be an Iowa housewife.
Fae Myenne Ng, *Bone*, 1993
  A multigenerational saga of a San Francisco Chinese American family.
R.A. Sasaki, *The Loom and Other Stories*, 1991
  A collection of short stories, interwoven to tell the story of three generations of a Japanese American family.
Julie Shigekuni, *A Bridge Between Us*, 1995
  Four generations of women—each a mother and a daughter—of a San Francisco Japanese American family trace their lives from 1900 to the present.
Hisaye Yamamoto, *Seventeen Syllables and Other Stories*, 1988
  Collection of 15 short stories from Yamamoto's almost half-century writing career.
Lowry Pei, *Family Resemblances*, 1986
  A comic coming-of-age novel about 15-year-old Karen Moss who is sent to spend the summer with her eccentric Aunt Augusta.

963

CYNTHIA KADOHATA

In the Heart of the Valley of Love

(New York: Viking Penguin (Penguin Group), 1992)

Subject(s): Futuristic Fiction; Family Life; Survival
Age range(s): Adult
Major character(s): Francie, Young Woman (19-year-old), Niece (of Annie) ''Auntie'' Annie, Businesswoman (operates a delivery business); Rohn, Boyfriend (Auntie Annie's), Businessman (Annie's partner)
Time period(s): 2050s (2052)
Locale(s): Los Angeles, California

Summary: In 2052, America has deteriorated beyond recognition. Francie, 19, lives with her Auntie Annie and Rohn, Annie's boyfriend, in Los Angeles, where the three run a delivery business. When Rohn disappears, Francie and Annie must venture out to the unknown, trying to survive in a desperate environment.

Where it's reviewed:
Book World (Washington Post) August 16, 1992, page 5
Kirkus Reviews, May 15, 1992, page 629
Publishers Weekly, August 3, 1992, page 48

Other books by the same author:
The Floating World, 1989

Other books you might like:
Amy Tan, *The Hundred Secret Senses*, 1995
　　A novel of two half-sisters, one Chinese-born, the other half-Chinese and half-American.
Sigrid Nunez, *A Feather on the Breath of God*, 1995
　　A young woman, the child of a Chinese Panamanian father and a German mother, grows up in a New York housing project trying to make sense of her identity.
Nayantara Sahgal, *Mistaken Identity*, 1988
　　In 1929, Bhusan Singh, the aimless son of a wealthy raja, is arrested, falsely charged with treason and imprisoned. He spends three years in jail, reflecting on his life.
Julie Shigekuni, *A Bridge Between Us*, 1995
　　Four generations of women—each a mother and a daughter—of a San Francisco Japanese American family, trace their lives from 1900 to the present.

964

TOORU J. KANAZAWA

Sushi and Sourdough

(Seattle: University of Washington Press, 1989)

Subject(s): Multicultural; Pioneers; Gold Discoveries
Age range(s): Adult
Major character(s): Matajiro "Mat" Fuse, Pioneer (Alaskan gold prospector), Immigrant, Japanese; Yaso Fuse, Spouse (wife of Matajiro Fuse), Japanese; Kennosuke "Ken" Fuse, Son (oldest son of Mat and Yaso), Japanese American; Joe Toranosuke Thor Fuse, Son (Mat's and Yaso's), Japanese American (first American-born son)
Time period(s): 1890s; 1920s
Locale(s): Seattle, Washington; Alaska (various cities, including Douglas, Juneau, Anchorage, etc.)

Summary: At the turn of the century, Mat Fuse, a Japanese immigrant, heads for Alaska hoping to strike it rich panning for gold. When he finally gives up on his dream of a fast fortune and finds steady work as a barber, Fuse brings over his family from Japan and settles into life as a "sourdough," an Alaskan pioneer.

Where it's reviewed:
Library Journal, November 15, 1989, page 105
Publishers Weekly, October 20, 1989, page 42
Western American Literature, Fall 1991, page 264

Other books you might like:
Sky Lee, *Disappearing Moon Cafe*, 1991
　　One hundred years of the Wong family saga, which begins

in the 1890s when a Chinese man marries a Native Indian, and is uncovered and recorded by his fifth generation descendent.
Ruthanne Lum McCunn, *Thousand Pieces of Gold*, 1981
　　The first biographical novel of Chinese American pioneer woman, Polly Bemis.
Monica Sone, *Nisei Daughter*, 1953
　　An account of a second-generation Japanese American woman growing up in Seattle in the 1920s and '30s, being incarcerated during World War II and her new life in the Midwest.
Carlos Bulosan, *America Is in the Heart*, 1943
　　This autobiography of writer and poet Carlos Bulosan covers his life from his boyhood in the Philippines to his arrival in America where he worked as a migrant laborer.
Bienvenido Santos, *Scent of Apples: A Collection of Short Stories*, 1955
　　These stories capture the experiences of young Filipino American men living displaced lives.

965

K. CONNIE KANG

Home Was the Land of Morning Calm: The Saga of a Korean American Family

(Reading, MA: Addison-Wesley Publishing Company, 1995)

Subject(s): Intergenerational Saga; Korean War; Emigration and Immigration
Age range(s): Adult
Major character(s): K. Connie Kang, Journalist (in Korea and the U.S.); Myong-Hwan Kang, Grandfather (Connie's paternal), Revolutionary (during Japanese Occupation); Joo-han Kang, Father (Connie's), Linguist (translator hired by U.S. govt.); Sok-Won Choe, Mother (Connie's)
Time period(s): 1990s (1995)
Locale(s): Asia (Korea and other locations in Asia); United States (cities in California)

Summary: The saga of one Korean family, interwoven with the country's turbulent history, from 1900 to the present. The Kang clan, once a powerful North Korean family, survives the Japanese occupation, then escapes to the South during the Korean War. The author's immediate family moves to Japan, and finally to the U.S. where they begin another new life.

About this book: Connie Kang, the product of three cultures (Korean, Japanese and American) first arrived in the U.S. to pursue her college education. She became one of the first Korean American journalists in U.S. history. While she has lived and worked in both the U.S. and Korea, she does not feel that she has ever been truly comfortable, or accepted, in either culture: "I am more American than Korean in my mind, but I am more Korean than American in my soul. As for my heart, it is split in half," she writes.

Where it's reviewed:
Los Angeles Times Book Review, August 20, 1995, page 2
Publishers Weekly, June 12, 1995, page 55

Other books you might like:
Ronyoung Kim, *Clay Walls*, 1987
　　The memoir of a young Korean woman and the difficulties

and hardships she faces in her new life as an immigrant American.

Helie Lee, *Still Life with Rice: A Young American Woman Discovers the Life and Legacy of Her Korean Grandmother*, 1996
The true story of a Korean woman who survives great hardship in Korea and finally arrives in the U.S., as told by her Korean American granddaughter.

Mary Paik Lee, *Quiet Odyssey: A Pioneer Korean Woman in America*, 1990
Edited by Professor Sucheng Lee; a memoir that covers nearly a century of change, by one of the country's first Korean American women.

Anchee Min, *Red Azalea*, 1994
The personal memoir of Min's difficult life in China during the Cultural Revolution and her struggle to escape the brutality of her homeland.

966

EVE BEGLEY KIEHM
CHRISTINE JOY PRATT, Illustrator

Plantation Child and Other Stories

(Honolulu: University of Hawai'i Press, 1995)

Subject(s): Multicultural; Emigration and Immigration; Short Stories
Age range(s): Grades 6 and Up
Major character(s): Marita Kim, Daughter (oldest child), Korean American; Pauly Kim, 11-Year-Old (oldest son), Korean American, Brother (of Marita); Blossom Kim, Daughter (second oldest), Korean American, Sister; Joe Kim, Brother (youngest son), Korean American; Puni "Little Sister" Kim, Sister (youngest daughter), Korean American; Abuji "Father" Kim, Father (widowed), Korean American
Time period(s): 20th century (1905-1950)
Locale(s): Hawaii (Korean camp on a sugarcane plantation)

Summary: This is a group of lyrical, interrelated short stories about the members of the Kim family, living in the Korean camp section of a Hawaiian sugarcane plantation in the early 1900's. As the young Kims struggle to survive, they still manage to grasp what little is left of their childhood.

About this book: This haunting collection of stories is suitable even for adults.

Other books you might like:

Lori M. Carlson, *American Eyes: New Asian-American Short Stories for Young Adults*, 1994
This collection of 10 short works portrays young Asian Americans coming of age and coming to terms with an identity comprised of two very different cultures.

Joy Kogawa, *Naomi's Road*, 1986
In this young adult story a Japanese Canadian family splinters and scatters as a result of forced evacuation and relocation during World War II.

Genny Lim, *Paper Angels and Bitter Cane*, 1991
The following two important plays portray the Asain American experience: "Paper Angels", about Chinese immigrants, and "Bitter Cane" about Asian immigrant laborers in Hawaii.

Laurence Yep, *American Dragons: Twenty-Five Asian American Voices*, 1993
This collection of short stories, poetry and play excerpts concerns itself with growing up Asian American, and comes from established as well as new Asian American writers.

Laurence Yep, *Dragonwings*, 1975
Based on actual events, this novel portrays a Chinese American aviator who builds and flies a new machine in 1909.

967

ELAINE H. KIM, Editor
EUI-YOUNG YU, Co-Editor

East to America: Korean American Life Stories

(New York: The New Press, 1996)

Subject(s): Multicultural; Emigration and Immigration; Autobiography
Age range(s): Adult
Time period(s): Indeterminate Past
Locale(s): Los Angeles, California

Summary: A collection of oral histories of 38 diverse Korean Americans, from recent immigrants to third-generation Americans, who offer vastly different, sometimes startling perspectives as a result of their gender, economic background, education, career, religion, etc.

About this book: From the introduction: "It is popularly thought that Asians come West from the East.' Most Korean immigrants, including the ancestors of U.S.-born Korean Americans, moved *east* to America, although their paths have been circuitous rather than linear or unidirectional. Thus, while our title has its shortcomings, it does call into question the centrality of the West."

Where it's reviewed:
Kirkus Reviews, January 1, 1996, page 44
Publishers Weekly, January 15, 1996, page 450

Other books by the same author:
Asian American Literature: An Introduction to the Writings and Their Social Context, 1982

Other books you might like:

K. Connie Kang, *Home Was the Land of Morning Calm: The Saga of a Korean American Family*, 1995
The saga of one Korean family, interwoven with the country's turbulent history, from 1900 to the present, from North Korea to Japan and finally to the U.S.

Ronyoung Kim, *Clay Walls*, 1987
The memoir of a young Korean woman and the difficulties and hardships she faces in her new life as an immigrant American.

Helie Lee, *Still Life with Rice: A Young American Woman Discovers the Life and Legacy of Her Korean Grandmother*, 1996
The true story of a Korean woman who survives great hardship in Korea and finally arrives in the U.S., as told by her Korean American granddaughter.

Mary Paik Lee, *Quiet Odyssey: A Pioneer Korean Woman in America*, 1990

Edited by Professor Sucheng Lee; a memoir that covers nearly a century of change, by one of the country's first Korean American women.

Ronald Takaki, *Strangers from a Different Shore*, 1989

Traces the diverse lives of the Japanese, Chinese, Koreans, Filipinos, Asian Indians, Vietnamese, Cambodians and Laotions who have come to the U.S. over the past 150 years.

968

RONYOUNG KIM (Pseudonym of Gloria Hahn)

Clay Walls

(Seattle: University of Washington Press, 1987)

Subject(s): Multicultural; Emigration and Immigration; Family Relations

Age range(s): Adult

Major character(s): Haesu Chun, Immigrant (from Korea), Daughter (wealthy, marriage is arranged), Korean; Youngjune Chun, Immigrant (from Korea), Husband (Haesu's, small business owner), Korean (from a poor farming family); Faye Inyoung Chun, Daughter (Haesu and Chun's youngest)

Time period(s): 1920s; 1940s

Locale(s): Los Angeles, California (small towns and suburbs in the Los Angeles area)

Summary: Haesu Chun, newly arrived in the U.S. from Korea with her husband, struggles to establish a home in a foreign land. Born into a wealthy family, Haesu is initially ill-prepared for the racism, humiliation and economic hardships she must endure as an immigrant, but through tenacity and fortitude, survives personal tragedy and raises three independent children.

About this book: One of the few literary works that deals with the early Korean American experience (from the 1920s), including the immigrant Korean's long-distance devotion and economic support for the struggling homeland trying desperately to free itself from Japanese occupation.

Where it's reviewed:
Belles Lettres, Fall 1990, page 26

Other books you might like:
K. Connie Kang, *Home Was the Land of Morning Calm: The Saga of a Korean American Family*, 1995

The saga of one Korean family, interwoven with the country's turbulent history, from 1900 to the present, from North Korea to Japan and finally to the U.S.

Elaine H. Kim, *East to America: Korean American Life Stories*, 1996

Co-edited with Eui-Young Yu. The oral histories of 38 Korean Americans, from immigrants to third-generation Americans, including journalists, activists, artists, shopkeepers and students.

Helie Lee, *Still Life with Rice: A Young American Woman Discovers the Life and Legacy of Her Korean Grandmother*, 1996

The true story of a Korean woman who survives great

hardship in Korea and finally arrives in the U.S., as told by her Korean American granddaughter.

Mary Paik Lee, *Quiet Odyssey: A Pioneer Korean Woman in America*, 1990

Edited by Professor Sucheng Lee; a memoir that covers nearly a century of change, by one of the country's first Korean American women.

969

WILLYCE KIM

Dancer Dawkins and the California Kid

(Boston: Alyson Publications, Inc., 1985)

Subject(s): Adventure and Adventurers; Cults

Age range(s): Adult

Major character(s): Dancer Dawkins, Young Woman (searches for estranged lover); Willy "The California Kid" Gutherie, Young Woman (search for life/identity in CA); Jessica Nahale Riggins, Lover (Dancer's estranged lover); Ta Fan the Korean, Cook (Golden Goose owner and chef)

Time period(s): 1980s

Locale(s): San Francisco, California (with flashbacks to Los Angeles and Bangor, ME)

Summary: Dancer Dawkins is searching for her lover Jessica. Little Willy Gutherie is searching for a new life as the California Kid. They collide on a San Francisco road which sets in motion a chain of events that includes meeting a mind-reading Korean American chef and her killer dog, saving the country's vineyards and rescuing Jessica from a dubious cult.

About this book: A rambunctious comic novel, much in the style of a short Tom Robbins creation.

Where it's reviewed:
Library Journal, May 1, 1985, page 65
Women's Review of Books, February 1986, page 8

Other books by the same author:
Dead Heat, 1988 (sequel)

Other books you might like:
Milton Murayama, *All I Asking for Is My Body*, 1959

A young Japanese American boy's coming-of-age in Hawaii during the 1930s up until the advent of World War II.

Lowry Pei, *Family Resemblances*, 1986

A comic coming-of-age novel about 15-year-old Karen Moss who is sent to spend the summer with her eccentric Aunt Augusta.

Sharon Lim-Hing, *The Very Inside: An Anthology of Writing by Asian and Pacific Islander Lesbian and Bisexual Women*, 1994

A collection that includes an array of prose, poetry and art work.

Steven Lo, *The Incorporation of Eric Chung*, 1989

A comic novel of Eric Chung's rise from immigrant student at Texas Tech to major Texas businessman with Important Connections.

Gish Jen, *Typical American*, 1991

The Chang family arrives in the U.S. from China in search of education and safety. What they find is fried chicken

Asian American Titles

fast food joints, glamour magazines, suburbia and con artists.

WILLYCE KIM

Dead Heat

(Boston: Alyson Publications, Inc., 1988)

Subject(s): Adventure and Adventurers; Horse Racing
Age range(s): Adult
Major character(s): Dancer Dawkins, Young Woman (getting over her ex-lover); Willy "The California Kid" Gutherie, Friend (Dancer's close friend), Waiter/Waitress (works in Ta Fan's restaurant); Ta Fan the Korean, Restauranteur (owner of the Golden Goose); Cody Roberts, Jockey; Janes Philips Joyce, Lover (Vinny's, then "The Kid's"); Vinny "The Skull" LaRoca, Organized Crime Figure (head of horse-gambling ring)
Time period(s): 1980s
Locale(s): California (Mainly San Francisco Bay Area)

Summary: Dancer Dawkins is trying to get over a bad break-up. She heads to San Francisco to find solace with old friends, "The Kid" and Ta Fan, and gets indirectly mixed up with gangsters, a gangster's moll, horse racing and gambling, a jockey who can't sleep and a kidnapped dog.

About this book: A follow-up to *Dancer Dawkins and the California Kid*.

Where it's reviewed:
Booklist, September 15, 1988, page 120
Publishers Weekly, September 2, 1988, page 98

Other books by the same author:
Dancer Dawkins and the California Kid, 1985 (debut novel, Dancer Dawkins series)

Other books you might like:
Lowry Pei, *Family Resemblances*, 1986
   A comic coming-of-age novel about 15-year-old Karen Moss who is sent to spend the summer with her eccentric Aunt Augusta.
Lois-Ann Yamanaka, *Wild Meat and the Bully Burgers*, 1996
   This coming-of-age novel is about Lovey Nariyoshi of Hilo, Hawaii, her best friend Jerome, her adolescent enemies and her eccentric family.
R. Zamora Linmark, *Rolling the R's*, 1995
   A collection of interrelated short stories, many about young Filipino Americans coming to terms with their ethnicity and with their sexuality in Honolulu.
Shyam Selvadurai, *Funny Boy*, 1995
   A young boy comes of age and discovers his homsexuality during a time of great political turbulence in his native Sri Lanka.

MAXINE HONG KINGSTON

China Men

(New York: Vintage International (Random House), 1980)

Subject(s): Multicultural; Emigration and Immigration; Historical
Age range(s): Adult
Major character(s): Baba, Father, Immigrant, Chinese American; Ah Goong, Grandfather
Time period(s): 20th century
Locale(s): San Francisco, California (Bay area); China (various locations)

Summary: A history made up of myths and memories of generations of Chinese American men: from the grandfather who worked on the transcontinental railroad, to a father who ran a laundry and danced like Fred Astaire, to a brother who was drafted to serve in Vietnam.

About this book: Almost exactly in the middle of the book is a chapter called "The Laws," which gives the history of the Chinese in America using a timeline. The insertion is almost an admonition or an angry statement, as if to say, look, we Chinese have been here for generations and we've made important contributions to the history of the U.S.

Where it's reviewed:
New York Times Book Review, May 21, 1989, page 50
Village Voice Literary Supplement, May 1989, page 9

Other books by the same author:
Tripmaster Monkey: His Fake Book, 1989
The Woman Warrior: Memoirs of a Girlhood Among Ghosts, 1975

Other books you might like:
Gus Lee, *China Boy*, 1991
   A coming-of-age novel about Kai Ting, the American-born son of an aristocratic Chinese family who fled China to escape the Cultural Revolution.
Belle Yang, *Baba: A Return to China upon My Father's Shoulders*, 1994
   After hearing the story of her father's coming-of-age as a son of the prominent Manchurian House of Yang, the author takes a personal odyssey through northern China of the 1930s and 1940s
Ronald Takaki, *Strangers from a Different Shore*, 1989
   This book traces the diverse lives of the Japanese, Chinese, Koreans, Filipinos, Asian Indians, Vietnamese, Cambodians and Laotians who have come to the U.S. over the past 150 years.
Victor G. Nee, *Longtime Californ': A Documentary Study of an American Chinatown*, 1974
   Co-authored by Brett de Bary Nee, this history of the Chinese in America is told through both narrative and extensive interviews, using the backdrop of San Francisco's Chinatown.
Garrett Hongo, *Under Western Eyes: Personal Essays from Asian America*, 1995
   A collection of 15 autobiographical essays, these are from leading Asian Ameican voices, confronting racism, language, family, stereotypes and other issues.

972

MAXINE HONG KINGSTON

Tripmaster Monkey: His Fake Book

(New York: Alfred A. Knopf, 1989)

Subject(s): Multicultural; Identity; Personal Odyssey
Age range(s): Adult
Major character(s): Wittman Ah Sing, Writer (of plays, poetry, talk story), Chinese; Lance Kamiyama, Friend (Wittman's friend and rival); Tana De Weese, Spouse (may be Wittman's wife); Nanci Lee, Friend (whom Wittman may love), Chinese
Time period(s): 1960s
Locale(s): West

Summary: Kingston's first novel about the often comic mishaps and adventures of Wittman Ah Sing, who is one year out of UC-Berkeley, a slacker before his time. Set in the 1960s, Wittman's dream is to write and stage a spectacular version of several interwoven Chinese novels and fairy tales, faithful versions of ancient Chinese literary and oral traditions.

About this book: The Maxine Hong Kingston/Frank Chin debate has been raging for decades. Chin, also a writer, has heavily criticized Kingston for what he calls ''corrupting'' ancient Chinese myths and legends, such as in her version of ''Fa Mu Lan'' in *The Woman Warrior*. Two distinct camps— the ''fake'' and the ''real,'' as Chin calls them—have emerged from this debate which shows little sign of ever abating. Although Kingston has repeatedly said otherwise, the hero Wittman Ah Sing is believed to be a little-disguised version of Frank Chin. In Chin's latest novel, *Gunga Din Highway*, one of the major characters is said to be a thinly-veiled caricature of Kingston. By the way, for those expecting more of the *Warrior* or *Men* genre, be warned: This is a very different kind of work. The subtitle *His Fake Book* should be an obvious tip that even as a novel, this book will not be a predictable piece of literature.

Where it's reviewed:
The Nation, June 5, 1989 768
USA Today, April 28, 1989, 6D
The New Republic, April 17, 1989, 44
The Boston Globe, April 16, 1989, B51
The New York Times, April 14, 1989, C30

Other books by the same author:
China Men, 1977
The Woman Warrior: Memoirs of a Girlhood Among Ghosts, 1975

Other books you might like:
Cynthia Kadohata, *The Floating World*, 1989
  A coming-of-age novel about 12-year-old Olivia, who with her family, moves continuously throughout the Pacific Northwest in search of a better life.
Frank Chin, *Gunga Din Highway*, 1994
  The Kwan family saga, as told through young Ulysses, who is on a cross-cultural, cross-country odyssey in search of his identity.
Chang-rae Lee, *Native Speaker*, 1995
  A first novel about Korean American Henry Park who is

trying to come to terms with both his troubled personal life and his problematic career as a spy.
Steven Lo, *The Incorporation of Eric Chung*, 1989
  A comic novel of Eric Chung's rise from immigrant student at Texas Tech to major Texas businessman with Important Connections.
Gus Lee, *China Boy*, 1994
  A coming-of-age novel about Kai Ting, the American-born son of an aristocratic Chinese family who fled China for California to escape the Cultural Revolution.

973

MAXINE HONG KINGSTON

The Woman Warrior: Memoirs of a Girlhood Among Ghosts

(New York: Vintage International (Random House), 1976)

Subject(s): Multicultural; Emigration and Immigration
Age range(s): Adult
Major character(s): Maxine Hong, Daughter, Chinese American (second-generation); Fa Mu Lan, Warrior (the mythic woman warrior); Mother Hong, Chinese American (Immigrant), Mother (mother of Maxine)
Time period(s): Indeterminate Past
Locale(s): San Francisco, California (Bay Area); China (various locations)

Summary: The story of a young girl growing up in the San Francisco Bay Area, divided between the stories and myths of her parents' faraway past in China and her own experiences as an immigrant's daughter coming of age in a foreign, Caucasian world.

About this book: *The* Asian American literary work to break into the mainstream, it has also been, on and off, the most-taught text on U.S. college campuses, especially in the last decade. The term ''ghosts'' in the subtitle refers to the Chinese name for Caucasians—white ''ghosts'' because of their pale skin. While the Library of Congress lists the book as ''nonfiction,'' an argument as to the book's proper classification—should it be considered fiction—is still ongoing.

Where it's reviewed:
Booklist, January 1, 1986, page 679
New York Times Book Review, May 21, 1989, page 50
School Library Journal, October 1988, page 41

Awards the book has won:
National Book Critics Circle Award for Best Nonfiction, 1976

Other books by the same author:
Tripmaster Monkey: His Fake Book, 1989
China Men, 1977

Other books you might like:
Maria Hong, *Growing Up Asian American*, 1993
  These essays, excerpts and short stories by Americans of Asian descent, address issues such as parent-child relationships, self-realization, identity and the discovery of one's cultural heritage.
Paul Yee, *Tales from Gold Mountain: Stories of the Chinese in the New World*, 1989

Asian American Titles

This collection of eight stories, illustrated by Simon Ng, recounts the tales of Chinese immigrants in the new world.

Amy Tan, *The Joy Luck Club*, 1989

A novel about the timeless relationship of four Chinese-born mothers and their American-born daughters.

Jade Snow Wong, *Fifth Chinese Daughter*, 1945

An autobiographical account of an American-born Chinese woman growing up in San Francisco's Chinatown between the 1920s and the 1940s.

Lydia Yuri Minatoya, *Talking to High Monks in the Snow: An Asian American Odyssey*, 1992

Minatoya's personal odyssey, which she recounts here, begins in upstate New York in the 50s and continues through Japan, China and Nepal.

974

JOY KOGAWA
MATT GOULD, Illustrator

Naomi's Road

(Toronto: Oxford University Press, 1986)

Subject(s): Internment; Coming of Age; Children and War
Age range(s): Grades 6 and Up
Major character(s): Megumi Naomi Nakane, Daughter, Japanese Canadian (second generation); Stephen Nakane, Brother (Naomi's older), Japanese Canadian; Daddy Nakane, Father (Naomi and Stephen's), Musician (composer and piano player); Obasan, Aunt (Naomi and Stephen's maternal)
Time period(s): 1940s
Locale(s): Vancouver, British Columbia, Canada; Slocan, British Columbia, Canada (internment camp is in this remote town); Granton, Alberta, Canada (a remote relocation ''farm'')

Summary: Naomi is just a little girl when World War II scatters her Japanese Canadian family. Separated from their parents, Naomi and her older brother Stephen are relocated far from their home in the care of a maternal aunt. In spite of bleak wartime circumstances, Naomi manages to find hope in everyday events.

About this book: This young adult work is based on Kogawa's adult novel, *Obasan*. It is the first Canadian novel for young readers to deal with the Japanese Canadian wartime experience. In comparison to the U.S., the Canadian government was more unjust to their citizens of Japanese ancestry. The Nakane family was completely torn apart, with parents disappearing without a trace, children left to be raised by other relatives, grandparents shipped away to die and other family members separated for decades.

Where it's reviewed:
Canadian Children's Literature, Vol. 49, 1988, page 51
Booklist, June 1, 1988, page 1681
Publishers Weekly, March 18, 1988, page 87
Quill & Quire, October 1986, page 17
School Library Journal, May 1988, page 98

Other books by the same author:
Itsuka, 1992 (sequel)
Obasan, 1982

Other books you might like:
Yoshiko Uchida, *Journey Home*, 1978
The story of Yuki and her family continues after their release from Camp Topaz.

Jeanne Wakatsuki Houston, *Farewell to Manzanar*, 1973
In this true story, the U.S. government uproots the Wakatsuki family from their home and incarcerates them at Manzanar, one of 10 U.S. concentration camps for Japanese Americans during World War II.

Mine Okubo, *Citizen 13660*, 1946
Sketches and text reveal the autobiographical account of a Japanese American woman, who was reduced to Citizen Number 13660 and interned during World War II.

Monica Sone, *Nisei Daughter*, 1953
As a second-generation Japanese American woman growing up in Seattle in the 1920s and 1930s, *Nisei Daughter* faces imprisonment during World War II, followed by a new life in the Midwest.

Yoshiko Uchida, *Journey to Topaz: A Story of the Japanese-American Evacuation*, 1985
This young adult novel tells the story about the Sakanes, a typical Japanese American family, and their experiences during World War II in the bleak desert concentration camp called Topaz.

975

JOY KOGAWA

Obasan

(New York: Anchor Books/Doubleday, 1982)

Subject(s): Internment; Coming of Age; Multicultural
Age range(s): Adult
Major character(s): Megumi Naomi Nakane, Daughter, Teacher (of 12- and 13-year-olds), Japanese Canadian (second generation); Isamu ''Uncle'' Nakane, Uncle, Japanese Canadian; Ayako ''Obasan'' Nakane, Aunt, Japanese Canadian; Emily ''Aunt Emily'' Kato, Aunt (Naomi's maternal)
Time period(s): 1940s; 1980s
Locale(s): Canada (various locations)

Summary: When her elderly uncle dies, Naomi, an unmarried schoolteacher, is called back to the remote town of her childhood. There she is reunited with Obasan, her Uncle's widow, and confronted with the shattered memories of her past, of the family that was torn apart and unjustly scattered with the advent of World War II.

About this book: In comparison to the U.S., the Canadian government was even more unjust to their citizens of Japanese ancestry during World War II. The Nakane/Kato family was completely torn apart, with parents disappearing without a trace, children left to be raised by other relatives, grandparents shipped away to die and other family members separated for decades.

Where it's reviewed:
Canadian Literature, Winter 1990, page 41
Dalhousie Review, Summer 1987, page 286
Tulsa Studies in Women's Literature, Fall 1989, page 287

Other books by the same author:
Itsuka, 1992 (sequel)

Other books you might like:
Jeanne Wakatsuki Houston, *Farewell to Manzanar*, 1973
  The true story of the Wakatsuski family, uprooted from their home and incarcerated at Manzanar, one of 10 U.S. concentration camps for Japanese Americans during World War II.
Yoshiko Uchida, *Desert Exile: The Uprooting of a Japanese-American Family*, 1982
  The autobiographical account of a second-generation Japanese American woman from Berkeley, California and her family's internment experiences at Camp Topaz during World War II.
Milton Murayama, *All I Asking for Is My Body*, 1959
  A young Japanese American boy's coming-of-age in Hawaii during the 1930s up until the advent of World War II.
Monica Sone, *Nisei Daughter*, 1953
  An account of a second-generation Japanese American woman growing up in Seattle in the 1920s and 1930s, being incarcerated during World War II and her new life in the Midwest.
Lawson Fusao Inada, *Legends from Camp*, 1992
  As a child, Inada was interned during World War II with his parents. In spite of the grim realities of imprisonment, his memories are mixed with strains of be-bop and jazz.

976

JULIET S. KONO

Hilo Rains
(Honolulu: Bamboo Ridge Press, 1988)

Subject(s): Poetry; Multicultural; Identity
Age range(s): Adult

Summary: A lyrical first collection of poems that draws on such diverse topics as Kono's native Hawaii, the legacy of Asian immigrant sugar cane plantation laborers, the Japanese internment crisis and family obligations.

Other books by the same author:
Tsunami Years, 1995 (poetry collection)
Sister Stew: Fiction and Poetry by Women, 1991 (Edited by Kono and Cathy Song. Anthology featuring mostly Hawaiian contributors.)

Other books you might like:
Joseph Bruchac, *Breaking Silence: An Anthology of Contemporary Asian American Poets*, 1983
  One of the first major anthologies of Asian American poetry, featuring the work of some 50 writers.
Walter K. Lew, *Premonitions: The Kaya Anthology of New Asian North American Poetry*, 1995
  Edited by Lew. A collection of 73 authors ranging from the established to the up-and-comers, writing in all modes of poetry.
Cathy Song, *Frameless Windows, Squares of Light*, 1988
  Cathy Song's second poetry collection in which she writes of family, friends and nameless strangers.
Cathy Song, *Picture Bride*, 1983
  Award-winning debut poetry collection.

977

JULIET S. KONO, Editor
CATHY SONG, Co-Editor

Sister Stew: Fiction and Poetry by Women
(Honolulu: Bamboo Ridge Press, 1991)

Subject(s): Multicultural; Identity; Short Stories
Age range(s): Adult

Summary: A colorful collection of writings by women of various backgrounds, the majority of whom are either Hawaiian by birth or by adopted residency.

Other books by the same author:
Tsunami Years, 1995 (poetry collection)
School Figures, 1994 (poetry collection)
Frameless Windows, Squares of Light, 1988 (poetry collection)
Hilo Rains, 1988 (debut poetry collection)
Picture Bride, 1983 (award-winning debut poetry collection)

Other books you might like:
Asian Women United of California, *Making Waves: An Anthology of Writings by and about Asian American Women*, 1989
  First major compilation since the early 1970s of primarily unpublished works by and about Asian American women.
Shirley Geok-lin Lim, *The Forbidden Stitch: An Asian American Women's Anthology*, 1989
  Also edited with Mayumi Tsutakawa and Margarita Donnelly. A rich collection of poetry, short stories, art and reviews focusing on being a contemporary Asian American woman.
Sylvia Watanabe, *Home to Stay: Asian American Women's Fiction*, 1990
  Also edited with Carol Bruchac. A collection of short stories that celebrates the literary achievements of Asian American women writers.
Kathleen Tyau, *A Little Too Much Is Enough*, 1995
  Mahi Wong grows up during post-World War II Hawaii, surrounded by her large family, immersed in a complex, mixed-up culture of Chinese and Hawaiian influences.
Lois-Ann Yamanaka, *Wild Meat and the Bully Burgers*, 1996
  A coming-of-age first novel about Lovey Nariyoshi of Hilo, Hawaii, her best friend Jerome, her adolescent enemies and her eccentric family.

978

GERALDINE KUDAKA, Editor

On a Bed of Rice: An Asian American Erotic Feast
(New York: Anchor Books (Doubleday), 1995)

Subject(s): Erotica; Multicultural; Identity
Age range(s): Adult
Time period(s): Indeterminate

Summary: The first collection of erotica created by writers of Chinese, Japanese, Korean, Vietnamese, Filipino, Thai, East Indian, Pakistani and Amerasian descent, including essays, short stories, poems, drawings and photographs. Contributors include Frank Chin, Chitra Banerjee Divakaruni, Garrett Hongo, David Henry Hwang (collaborating with the Artist formerly known as Prince!) and Bharati Mukherjee.

Where it's reviewed:
Kirkus Reviews, October 1, 1995, page 1371
Library Journal, November 1, 1995, page 64
Publishers Weekly, October 16, 1995, page 56

Other books you might like:
Bennett Lee, *Many-Mouthed Birds: Contemporary Writings by Chinese Canadians*, 1991
   A diverse collection of short stories from some of Canada's leading Asian American voices, including Larissa Lai, Evelyn Lau, Sky Lee and Denise Chong.
Shirley Geok-lin Lim, *The Forbidden Stitch: An Asian American Women's Anthology*, 1989
   Edited with Mayumi Tsutakawa and Margarita Donnelly. A rich collection of poetry, short stories, art and reviews focusing on being a contemporary Asian American woman.
Jessica Hagedorn, *Charlie Chan Is Dead: An Anthology of Contemporary Asian American Fiction*, 1993
   This collection of 48 works is by Asian American writers of different backgrounds, ages and styles.
Sharon Lim-Hing, *The Very Inside: An Anthology of Writing by Asian and Pacific Islander Lesbian and Bisexual Women*, 1994
   A collection that includes an array of prose, poetry and art work.
Sylvia Watanabe, *Into the Fire: Asian American Prose*, 1996
   This collection of short stories and interviews details the diverse journeys of Asian American's from their faraway homelands to new lives in this new country.

979

HIM MARK LAI, Editor
GENNY LIM, Co-Editor
JUDY YUNG, Co-Editor

Island: Poetry and History of Chinese Immigrants on Angel Island, 1910-1940

(Seattle: University of Washington Press, 1980)

Subject(s): Multicultural; Historical; Poetry
Age range(s): Adult
Time period(s): 20th century (1910-1940)
Locale(s): Angel Island, California

Summary: Angel Island was the West Coast entry point for potential Asian immigrants and returning Asian Americans. An elaborate interrogation process kept people detained there, in limbo, for up to two *years*. In 1970, a park ranger discovered poetry scratched by detainees into the barrack walls; as a result of a local community effort, the buildings were preserved and Angel Island was turned into a state park.

About this book: When the Chinese Exclusion Act of 1882 passed, for the first time in U.S. history a specific ethnic group was denied entry and admittance to the U.S. naturalization process. According to the new immigration laws, only government officials, merchants, students, teachers, visitors and those with proof of U.S. citizenship were allowed to enter the

U.S. In order to gain admittance, potential immigrants were subjected to medical scrutiny and an elaborate questioning process before being released; even after being detained for substantial periods, deportation was not uncommon. The waiting could be just two days or even two years. At any given time, between 200 and 300 males and 30 to 50 females were detained. Evidence of the immigrants' ordeal is recorded in the poetry literally carved into the barrack walls.

Where it's reviewed:
Los Angeles Times Book Review, July 19, 1992, page 14
Multicultural Review, January 1992, page 34
Kliatt, January 1992, page 41

Other books you might like:
Joseph Bruchac, *Breaking Silence: An Anthology of Contemporary Asian American Poets*, 1983
   One of the first major anthologies of Asian American poetry, featuring the work of some 50 writers.
Jeffery Paul Chan, *Aiiieeeee! An Anthology of Asian American Writers*, 1974
   Edited by Chin, Inada and Wong, this is *the* anthology of Asian American writing.
Frank Chin, *The Big Aiiieeeee! An Anthology of Chinese American and Japanese American Literature*, 1991
   Edited by Chan, Inada and Wong, this is a follow-up to *Aiiieeeee!*.
Ronald Takaki, *Strangers from a Different Shore*, 1989
   A groundbreaking history of Asian Americans in the U.S. during the last 150 years.

980

EVELYN LAU

Fresh Girls and Other Stories

(New York: Hyperion (HarperCollins Publishers Ltd.), 1995)

Subject(s): Short Stories; Sexual Behavior
Age range(s): Adult
Locale(s): Canada

Summary: Author Evelyn Lau, a teenage runaway who lived on the streets for two years, writes frankly and unemotionally from personal experience. Lau has said that she left home in order to have the freedom to become a writer, a career that her traditional upbringing would never have allowed. This is a stark collection of 10 stories, mostly about desperate young woman trapped in a life of prostitution, drugs and sexual abuse.

About this book: Lau has won numerous literary awards; in 1992, she became the youngest poet ever to be nominated for the Governor General's Award in her native Canada.

Where it's reviewed:
Booklist, March 1, 1995, page 1179
Kirkus Reviews, January 1, 1995, page 13
Library Journal, February 1, 1995, page 102

Other books by the same author:
In the House of Slaves, 1994 (poetry collection)
Oedipal Dreams, 1992 (poetry collection)
You Are Not Who You Claim, 1990 (poetry collection)
Runaway: Diary of a Street Kid, 1988 (memoir)

Other books you might like:
R. Zamora Linmark, *Rolling the R's*, 1995
A collection of interrelated stories, many about young Filipino Americans coming to terms with their ethnicity and with their sexuality in Honolulu.

981

EVELYN LAU

Runaway: Diary of a Street Kid

(Toronto: Coach House Press, 1995)

Subject(s): Runaways; Sexual Abuse; Autobiography
Age range(s): Adult
Major character(s): Evelyn Lau, 14-Year-Old (girl), Runaway (from strict parents), Chinese Canadian
Time period(s): 1980s (March 22, 1986-January 20, 1988)
Locale(s): Canada (various locations; mostly Vancouver)

Summary: At 14, Evelyn Lau was an honors student, the dutiful daughter of a strict, traditional Chinese family. Lau's parents could not understand her obsession to become a writer; being published in literary magazines and winning awards only served to anger her parents. Searching for freedom and determined that she would become a writer at any price, Lau flees her family, choosing a life of teenage prostitution, drug abuse and homelessness over being creatively stifled. These pages are Lau's frank, often brutal memoirs of her two years on the streets.

About this book: Since the publication of *Runaway* in Canada in 1990, Lau has won numerous literary awards. In 1992, she became the youngest poet ever to be nominated for the Governor General's Award, Canada's highest literary honor.

Where it's reviewed:
Canadian Forum, March 1995, page 22

Other books by the same author:
Other Women, 1996

Other books you might like:
Bennett Lee, *Many-Mouthed Birds: Contemporary Writings by Chinese Canadians*, 1991
A diverse collection of short stories from some of Canada's leading Asian American voices, including Larissa Lai, Evelyn Lau, Sky Lee and Denise Chong.
R. Zamora Linmark, *Rolling the R's*, 1995
A collection interrelated short stories, many about young Filipino Americans coming to terms with their ethnicity and with their sexuality in Honolulu.
Shyam Selvadurai, *Funny Boy*, 1995
A young boy comes of age and discovers his homosexuality during a time of great political turbulence in his native Sri Lanka.

982

WENDY LAW-YONE

The Coffin Tree

(Boston: Beacon Press, 1983)

Subject(s): Emigration and Immigration; Mental Illness; Family Relations

Age range(s): Adult
Major character(s): Unnamed Character, Protagonist, Young Woman (forced to flee Burma for U.S.); Shan, Brother (older, half-brother); Father, Father (absent; of mythical status), Revolutionary (legendary rebel general)
Time period(s): 1970s; 1980s
Locale(s): Burma; New York, New York

Summary: A young woman, the daughter of a powerful political revolutionary, and her half-brother flee their native Burma following a political coup and arrive in New York, ill-prepared to cope with their new lives as near-penniless refugees. Haunted by a life filled with desperation, both sister and brother face great tragedy.

About this book: A powerful first novel confronting alienation and overwhelming mental illness. The sparse language is especially effective, if not haunting.

Other books by the same author:
Irawaddy Tango, 1993

Other books you might like:
Shyam Selvadurai, *Funny Boy*, 1995
A young boy comes of age and discovers his homosexuality during a time of great political turbulence in his native Sri Lanka.
Fiona Cheong, *The Scent of the Gods*, 1991
Eleven-year-old Esha comes of age in Singapore of the late 1960s, a time of growing political strife between the predominantly Chinese government and the local Singaporeans.
Carlos Bulosan, *America Is in the Heart*, 1943
The autobiography of writer and poet Carlos Bulosan, from his boyhood in the Philippines, to his arrival in America, to the difficulties he faced as a migrant laborer.
Jessica Hagedorn, *Dogeaters*, 1990
An autobiographical novel about growing up in Manila in the late 1950s during the turbulent and corrupt Marcos regime.
Bienvenido Santos, *Scent of Apples: A Collection of Short Stories*, 1955
A collection of short stories, some interrelated, about the experiences of young Filipino American men living displaced lives.

983

BENNETT LEE, Editor
JIM WONG-CHU, Co-Editor

Many-Mouthed Birds: Contemporary Writings by Chinese Canadians

(Seattle: University of Washington Press, 1991)

Subject(s): Multicultural; Identity; Short Stories
Age range(s): Adult

Summary: A diverse collection of short stories from some of Canada's leading Asian American voices, including Larissa Lai, Evelyn Lau, Sky Lee and Denise Chong.

Where it's reviewed:
Bookwatch, April 1992, page 8
Publishers Weekly, February 24, 1992, page 45

Quill & Quire, October 1991, page 27

Other books you might like:

Wesley Brown, *Imagining America: Stories from the Promised Land*, 1991
A multicultural anthology of 37 short stories about immigration to and migration within the U.S., the so-called "Promised Land."

Jeffery Paul Chan, *Aiiieeeee! An Anthology of Asian American Writers*, 1974
Also edited by Chin, Inada and Wong. The original anthology of Asian American writing.

Frank Chin, *The Big Aiiieeeee! An Anthology of Chinese American and Japanese American Literature*, 1991
Also edited by Chan, Inada and Wong. Follow-up to *Aiiieeeee!*.

Jessica Hagedorn, *Charlie Chan Is Dead: An Anthology of Contemporary Asian American Fiction*, 1993
A collection of 48 works by Asian American writers of different ages, backgrounds and styles.

Sylvia Watanabe, *Into the Fire: Asian American Prose*, 1996
This collection of short stories and interviews details the diverse journey of Asian American's from their faraway homelands to new lives in a new country.

984

CHANG-RAE LEE

Native Speaker

(New York: Riverhead Books (G.P. Putnam's Sons), 1995)

Subject(s): Multicultural; Identity; Politics
Age range(s): Adult
Major character(s): Henry Park, Spy; Leila Park, Spouse (Henry's estranged wife), Teacher (special education), Caucasian; John Kwang, Political Figure (rising NYC councilman), Korean American
Time period(s): 1970s; 1990s
Locale(s): Ardsley, New York; New York, New York

Summary: Korean American Henry Park is a spy whose life is falling apart: his wife just left him, his son died tragically, and he has yet to make peace with his dead father. He's assigned to spy on John Kwang, a rising Korean American politician who for Park represents the immigrant success story. Park becomes embroiled in the political world, only to learn that nothing is what it seems to be, even his own sense of identity.

Where it's reviewed:
Library Journal, February 1, 1995, page 98
New Yorker, July 10, 1995, page 76
Publishers Weekly, January 9, 1995, page 54

Other books you might like:

Gish Jen, *Typical American*, 1991
The Chang family arrives in the U.S. from China in search of education and safety. What they find is fried chicken fast food joints, glamour magazines, suburbia and con artists.

Aimee Liu, *Face*, 1994
After years of running away, Maibelle Chung returns to her Chinatown roots, finally ready to start facing the dark secrets of her incongruous, inescapable past.

Maxine Hong Kingston, *Tripmaster Monkey: His Fake Book*, 1989
Kingston's first novel about the often comic mishaps and adventures of Wittman Ah Sing, a young Chinese American in search of his dreams.

Sky Lee, *Disappearing Moon Cafe*, 1991
The Wong family saga, which begins in the 1890s when a Chinese man marries a Native Indian, is uncovered and recorded by his fifth generation descendent, a new mother and writer.

Shawn Wong, *American Knees*, 1995
A novel about the amorous adventures of Raymond Ding, a young, recently divorced, Chinese American man.

985

GUS LEE

China Boy

(New York: Signet (Penguin Group), 1991)

Subject(s): Multicultural; Coming of Age; Identity
Age range(s): Adult
Major character(s): Kai "China Boy" Ting, Son (American-born, of aristocracy), Chinese American; T.K. "Ba-Ba" Ting, Father (Kai's), Immigrant (former colonel in Chinese Army), Chinese; Dai-li Mar Ting, Mother (Kai's, dies of cancer), Chinese; Edna Madalyn McGurk Ting, Wife (Caucasian second wife of T.K.), Stepmother (quintessential evil stepmother); C.K. "Dababa" Shim, Uncle (unofficial "uncle" to Kai), Chinese; Toussaint LaRue, Friend (Kai's closest friend); Anthony Cemore Barraza, Coach (Kai's boxing coach and mentor)
Time period(s): 1950s
Locale(s): San Francisco, California

Summary: Soon after Kai Ting, the only American-born son of a once noble Chinese family now living in San Francisco, loses his beloved mother, his father remarries and brings home a cold, uncaring stepmother. Kai finds sanctuary at the YMCA where he learns to fight his battles, not only on the rough city streets, but finally at home with his overdominant stepmother.

Where it's reviewed:
Booklist, January 15, 1992, page 872
Kirkus Reviews, March 15, 1991, page 351
Time, June 3, 1991, page 66
Library Journal, April 1, 1991, page 152
Publishers Weekly, March 22, 1991, page 70

Other books by the same author:
Tiger's Tail, 1996
Honor and Duty, 1994

Other books you might like:

Louis Chu, *Eat a Bowl of Tea*, 1961
The story of American-born Ben Loy and his Chinese-born wife, Mei Oi—their blissful marriage marred by infidelity, later reclaimed with a new bond and a happily-ever-after ending.

Gish Jen, *Typical American*, 1991
A novel of the Chang family, newly arrived from China, and their often humorous new life in the New World.

Maxine Hong Kingston, *Tripmaster Monkey: His Fake Book*, 1989

Kingston's first novel about the often comic mishaps and adventures of Wittman Ah Sing, a young Chinese American, in search of his dreams.

Cynthia Kadohata, *The Floating World*, 1989

A coming-of-age novel about 12-year-old Olivia, who with her family, moves continuously throughout the Pacific Northwest in search of a better life.

Lois-Ann Yamanaka, *Wild Meat and the Bully Burgers*, 1996

A coming-of-age first novel about Lovey Nariyoshi of Hilo, Hawaii, her best friend Jerome, her adolescent enemies and her eccentric family.

986

HELIE LEE

Still Life With Rice: A Young American Woman Discovers the Life and Legacy of Her Korean Grandmother

(New York: Scribner, 1996)

Subject(s): Family Life; Korean War; Intergenerational Saga
Age range(s): Adult
Major character(s): Baek Hongyang, Grandmother (matriarch of the Lee family), Korean; Lee Helie, Granddaughter, Korean American, Rebel (in search of cultural identity)
Time period(s): 20th century (1912-1991)
Locale(s): San Fernando Valley, California; Korea, North (various locations); China (various locations)

Summary: A young Korean American woman, trying to come to terms with her strong ethnic heritage, travels to Korea for the first time. There she discovers her grandmother's legacy of survival, through the Japanese Occupation to life in China, through the Korean War to post-war depression and finally immigration to the U.S.

About this book: A remarkable first work, more so because the story is true.

Where it's reviewed:
Kirkus Reviews, February 1, 1996, page 200
Publishers Weekly, February 5, 1996, page 72

Other books you might like:
K. Connie Kang, *Home Was the Land of Morning Calm: The Saga of a Korean American Family*, 1995

The saga of one Korean family, from their escape from North Korea during the Korean War, to their journey to Japan, and finally the author's move to the U.S.

Ronyoung Kim, *Clay Walls*, 1987

The memoir of a young Korean woman and the difficulties and hardships she faces in her new life as an immigrant American.

Mary Paik Lee, *Quiet Odyssey: A Pioneer Korean Woman in America*, 1990

Edited by Professor Sucheng Lee; a memoir that covers nearly a century of change, by one of the country's first Korean American women.

Elaine H. Kim, *East to America: Korean American Life Stories*, 1996

These are oral histories of 38 Korean Americans, from immigrants to third-generation Americans, including journalists, activists, artists, shopkeepers and students. Co-edited with Eui-Young Yu.

987

HUY VOUN LEE, Author/Illustrator

At the Beach

(New York: Henry Holt and Company, 1994)

Subject(s): Language; Multicultural; Learning
Age range(s): Grades 1-2
Major character(s): Xiao Ming, Child (young boy); Mother, Mother (Xiao Ming's mother)
Time period(s): 1990s (1994)
Locale(s): United States (at the beach)

Summary: During a beautiful day at the beach, Xiao Ming learns to write Chinese characters in the sand with his mother. To Xiao Ming, the characters are much like drawing simple pictures: a person walking to symbolize "man," a person with both arms and legs outstretched to symbolize "big" and so on.

About this book: An ingenious approach to introducing young children to the existence of other writing methods that differ greatly from the English alphabet. The 10 Chinese characters chosen for the story are especially picture-like and easy to learn.

Where it's reviewed:
Publishers Weekly, April 11, 1994, page 64
Horn Book Guide, Fall 1994, page 279

Other books by the same author:
In the Snow, 1995

Other books you might like:
Jama Kim Rattigan, *Dumpling Soup*, 1993

Every year the Yang family gathers at Grandma's house from all over Oahu, Hawaii to celebrate New Year's Eve. This year, young Marisa will help Grandma make her famous dumpling soup.

Sandra S. Yamate, *Ashok by Any Other Name*, 1992

Ashok wishes he had a more "American" name, so he tries a new name each day, finally realizing that "Ashok" is the perfect name for him.

Allen Say, *Tree of Cranes*, 1991

Lovely story about a young Japanese boy who learns about Christmas for the first time from his California-born Japanese American mother.

Jennifer L. Chan, *ONE small GIRL*, 1993

Told not to touch anything in either her grandmother's or her uncle's adjacent Chinatown stores, a little girl still manages to have fun.

988

HUY VOUN LEE, Author/Illustrator

In the Snow

(New York: Henry Holt and Company, 1995)

Subject(s): Language; Multicultural; Learning
Age range(s): Grades 1-2

Major character(s): Xiao Ming, Child (young boy); Mother, Mother (Xiao Ming's)
Time period(s): 1990s (1995)
Locale(s): United States (in the forest)

Summary: During a winter walk through the forest, Xiao Ming's mother teaches him new Chinese characters, using the white snow to draw the picture-like characters.

About this book: An ingenious approach to introducing young children to the existence of other writing methods that differ greatly from the English alphabet. The 10 Chinese characters chosen for the story are especially picture-like and easy to learn.

Where it's reviewed:
Publishers Weekly, September 4, 1995, page 69

Other books by the same author:
At the Beach, 1994

Other books you might like:
Jama Kim Rattigan, *Dumpling Soup*, 1993
Every year the Yang family gathers at Grandma's house from all over Oahu, Hawaii to celebrate New Year's Eve. This year, young Marisa will help Grandma make her famous dumpling soup.
Sandra S. Yamate, *Ashok by Any Other Name*, 1992
Ashok, a young Indian American boy, wishes he had a more ''American'' name, so he tries a new one each day, finally realizing that ''Ashok'' is the perfect name for him.
Allen Say, *Tree of Cranes*, 1991
Lovely story about a young Japanese boy who learns about Christmas for the first time from his California-born Japanese American mother.
Jennifer L. Chan, *ONE small GIRL*, 1993
Told not to touch anything in either her grandmother's or her uncle's adjacent Chinatown stores, a little girl still manages to have fun.

989

JEANNE M. LEE, Author/Illustrator

Silent Lotus

(New York: Farrar, Straus & Giroux, 1991)

Subject(s): Deafness; Dancing; Communication
Age range(s): Grades 1-4
Major character(s): Lotus, Child (beautiful young girl), Handicapped (cannot hear or speak); Mother, Mother (Lotus' mother); Father, Father (Lotus' father)
Time period(s): Indeterminate Past
Locale(s): Vietnam; Cambodia

Summary: Beautiful Lotus is unable to hear or speak. Ostracized by the other children, she is lonely and sad. Her parents take her to the local temple where she sees temple dancers for the first time. Through the dance and movement, she learns to communicate and becomes a famous royal court dancer.

About this book: Vietnamese-born Lee brings to life the thousand-year-old tradition of the Cambodian court ballet.

Where it's reviewed:
Booklist, November 15, 1991, page 630
Horn Book Magazine, January 1992, page 99

Publishers Weekly, October 4, 1991, page 87

Other books you might like:
Chyng Feng Sun, *Square Beak*, 1993
Square Beak is aptly named. She is ostracized because she looks different from the other chickens in the yard and begins to wander outside her own small world.
Min Paek, *Aekyung's Dream*, 1988
Aekyung, a young Korean girl recently in the U.S., dreams about King Sejong who created *Hangul*, the Korean alphabet, and finds new pride in her Korean heritage.
Tran Khanh Tuyet, *The Little Weaver of Thai-Yen Village*, 1977
A young Vietnamese refugee arrives in the U.S. and struggles to adjust to her new life. She starts to weave again, as she did in her home country with her late grandmother.
Michele Maria Surat, *Angel Child, Dragon Child*, 1983
Young Ut, a recent Vietnamese immigrant, is teased because of her different appearance. Thrown together by the school principal, Ut and a once cruel boy develop a new friendship.
Taro Yashima, *Crow Boy*, 1955
Shy Chibi does not fit in with the rest of his classmates, but when the new teacher takes an interest in him, he emerges from his shell and his classmates see his determination and courage.

990

JEANNE M. LEE, Author/Illustrator

Toad Is the Uncle of Heaven

(New York: Henry Holt & Company, 1985)

Subject(s): Folk Tales; Animals; Drought
Age range(s): Grades 1-4
Major character(s): Toad, Toad (seeks to meet King of Heaven); The Bees, Bee (join Toad on his journey); Rooster, Rooster (joins Toad on his journey); Tiger, Tiger (joins Toad on his journey); King of Heaven, Ruler (almighty ruler)
Time period(s): Indeterminate Past (''Once upon a time .'')
Locale(s): Vietnam

Summary: During a drought, the Toad decides to ask the King of Heaven for rain. On his journey, he is joined by the Bees, the Rooster and the Tiger. When they reach heaven, the King tries to get rid of the Toad. But with the help of his friends, the diligent Toad convinces the King to provide rain.

About this book: A Vietnamese folktale as retold by Lee.

Where it's reviewed:
Social Studies, January 1995, page 31

Awards the book has won:
NCSS-CBC Notable Book in the Field of Social Studies

Other books by the same author:
Silent Lotus, 1991

Other books you might like:
Suzanne Crowder Han, *The Rabbit's Escape*, 1995
A rabbit is tricked by the turtle into going to the underworld, but the cleverly sets himself free.

Suzanne Crowder Han, *The Rabbit's Judgment*, 1994
A man is tricked into saving the life of a tiger; a clever rabbit helps the man from being eaten by the ungrateful, hungry tiger.

Lina Mao Wall, *Judge Rabbit and the Tree Spirit: A Folktale from Cambodia*, 1991
Adapted with Cathy Spagnoli. Judge Rabbit helps a young couple trap the tree spirit who has taken the form of the husband.

Blia Xiong, *Nine-in-One Grr! Grr!*, 1989
Bird comes up with a clever trick to prevent Tiger from having the nine cubs every year as promised by the god Shao, thereby preventing earth from being overpopulated with tigers.

Ed Young, *Cat and Rat: The Legend of the Chinese Zodiac*, 1995
An Adaptation of how the 12 animals of the zodiac were selected.

991

JOANN FAUNG JEAN LEE, Editor

Asian Americans

(New York: The New Press, 1991)

Subject(s): Multicultural; Emigration and Immigration; Historical
Age range(s): Adult
Time period(s): 1840s; 1990s

Summary: A collection of oral histories from first- to fourth-generation Asian Americans of Chinese, Filipino, Japanese, Korean, Indian, Southeast Asian and Pacific Island ancestry. Asian Americans of diverse backgrounds reflect on their American identities, discussing issues of racism, education, language, opportunities and their own hopes and dreams.

Where it's reviewed:
Reason, December 1993, page 48

Other books you might like:
Garrett Hongo, *Under Western Eyes: Personal Essays from Asian America*, 1995
A collection of 15 autobiographical essays from leading Asian American voices, confronting racism, language, family, stereotypes and other issues.

Ruthanne Lum McCunn, *Chinese American Portraits: Personal Histories 1828-1988*, 1988
Profiles of prominent Chinese Americans, from pioneers to politicians.

Maria Hong, *Growing Up Asian American*, 1993
These essays, excerpts and short stories by Americans of Asian descent address issues such as parent-child relationships, self-realization, identity and the discovery of one's cultural heritage.

Ronald Takaki, *Strangers from a Different Shore*, 1989
Traces the diverse lives of the Japanese, Chinese, Koreans, Filipinos, Asian Indians, Vietnamese, Cambodians and Laotions who have come to the U.S. over the past 150 years.

Victor G. Nee, *Longtime Californ': A Documentary Study of an American Chinatown*, 1974
With co-author Brett de Bary Nee, Nee presents a history of the Chinese in America told through both narrative and extensive interviews, using the backdrop of San Francisco's Chinatown.

992

LAUREN LEE

Stella: On the Edge of Popularity

(Chicago: Polychrome Publishing Corp., 1994)

Subject(s): Multicultural; Stereotypes; Friendship
Age range(s): Grades 7-12
Major character(s): Stella Sung Ok Kim, 7th Grader (young girl), Korean American; Grandmother, Grandmother (Stella's grandmother); Eileen Englehart, Friend (ex-best friend of Stella); Rachel Weintraub, Friend (Rachel's back-up friend)
Time period(s): 1990s (1994)
Locale(s): Chicago, Illinois

Summary: Stella Kim can't understand how Eileen, once her best friend, can now be so mean-spirited. Stella's other friend Rachel doesn't understand why Stella won't speak up for herself. Little by little, Stella finds her own unique strength, learning a new sense of pride in her rich Korean American heritage.

Where it's reviewed:
Horn Book Guide, Fall 1994, page 321
Publishers Weekly, May 16, 1994, page 65
School Library Journal, September 1994, page 218
Center for Children's Books. Bulletin, July 1994, page 363

Other books you might like:
Laurence Yep, *Ribbons*, 1996
To help her family bring her grandmother to the U.S. from Hong Kong, Robin must sacrifice her dance lessons. But ballet means everything to her.so is her grandmother worth it?

Lensey Namioka, *April and the Dragon Lady*, 1994
The only daughter of a traditional Chinese American household, April feels responsible for her grandmother but, leaving for college soon, she must make her family aware of their responsibilities.

Kyoko Mari, *One Bird*, 1995
At 15, young Megumi is left behind to live with her cold father and difficult grandmother when her unhappy mother suddenly leaves.

Marie G. Lee, *Finding My Voice*, 1992
A senior in high school, Ellen struggles to find her voice and speak out for what she wants and believes in, especially as she faces the racism in her tiny hometown.

Marie G. Lee, *Saying Goodbye*, 1994
Ellen has left her small hometown for Harvard where she comes face-to-face with the reality of racial boundaries and racial tensions and must define her own position as an aware Korean American.

993

LI-YOUNG LEE

The City in Which I Love You

(Brockport, NY: BOA Editions, 1990)

Subject(s): Poetry; Multicultural; Identity
Age range(s): Adult

Summary: Award-winning second poetry collection, about relationships between family and lovers.

Where it's reviewed:
Library Journal, September 1, 1990, page 224
New York Times Book Review, January 27, 1991, page 20
Publishers Weekly, January 4, 1991 page 37

Awards the book has won:
Lamont Poetry Selection of The Academy of American Poets, 1990

Other books by the same author:
The Winged Seed: A Remembrance, 1995 (memoir)
Rose, 1986 (debut poetry collection)

Other books you might like:
Joseph Bruchac, *Breaking Silence: An Anthology of Contemporary Asian American Poets*, 1983
 One of the first major anthologies of Asian American poetry, featuring the work of some 50 writers.
Kimiko Hahn, *Earshot*, 1992
 Imaginative, quirky, varied poetry collection.
Walter K. Lew, *Premonitions: The Kaya Anthology of New Asian North American Poetry*, 1995
 This collection of 73 authors, ranging from the established to the up-and-coming, features writing in all modes of poetry including works in non-standard forms and dialects.
Cathy Song, *Frameless Windows, Squares of Light*, 1988
 Cathy Song's second poetry collection in which she writes of family, friends and nameless strangers.

994

MARIE G. LEE

Finding My Voice

(Boston: Houghton Mifflin, 1992)

Subject(s): Multicultural; Identity; Teen Relationships
Age range(s): Grades 8-12
Major character(s): Ellen Joyce Sung, Student—High School (senior in a small midwest town), Korean American; Jessie, Friend (Ellen's best); Tom "Tomper" Sandel, Boyfriend (Ellen's)
Time period(s): 1990s (1992)
Locale(s): Arkin, Minnesota (small, midwest town where the Sungs are the only Asian American family)

Summary: It's senior year and Ellen wants to spend time with her friends while her parents expect her to study more so she can get into Harvard. Ellen must learn to find her own voice and speak out for what she wants and believes in, especially as she faces blatant racism as the only Asian American in her tiny hometown.

Where it's reviewed:
Booklist, September 1, 1992, page 48
Kirkus Reviews, September 15, 1992, page 1190
Publishers Weekly, July 6, 1992, page 57

Other books by the same author:
Saying Goodbye, 1994 (sequel)
If It Hadn't Been for Yoon Jun, 1993

Other books you might like:
Lauren Lee, *Stella: On the Edge of Popularity*, 1994
 Stella must learn who her true friends are as she defines her own unique place among her classmates at school, and as a second-generation Korean American in the outside world.
Laurence Yep, *Ribbons*, 1996
 To help her family bring her grandmother to the U.S. from Hong Kong, Robin must sacrifice her dance lessons. But ballet means everything to her.is her grandmother worth it?
Kyoko Mari, *One Bird*, 1995
 At 15, young Megumi is left behind to live with her cold father and difficult grandmother when her unhappy mother suddenly leaves.
Lensey Namioka, *April and the Dragon Lady*, 1994
 The only daughter in a traditional Chinese American household, April feels responsible for her grandmother, but, leaving for college soon, she must make her family aware of their responsibilties.

995

MARIE G. LEE

If It Hadn't Been for Yoon Jun

(Boston: Houghton Mifflin, 1993)

Subject(s): Multicultural; Identity; Adoption
Age range(s): Grades 6-10
Major character(s): Alice Larsen, Adoptee, 7th Grader (from a small midwestern town), Korean American; Minna Lund, Friend (one of Alice's two best); Laura Kristiansen, Friend (the other of Alice's two best); Yoon Jun Lee, Immigrant (recently arrived from Korea), 7th Grader, Korean
Time period(s): 1990s (1993)
Locale(s): Bainer, Minnesota (small, midwestern)

Summary: Alice Larsen is a popular seventh-grade cheerleader. Then Yoon Jun Lee arrives from Korea, and Alice's father wants her to be his friend. Although Alice's face may be Korean, she's all-American, having been adopted at birth. Reluctantly, Alice realizes that she may have more to learn from Yoon Jun than he from her.

Where it's reviewed:
Booklist, July 1993, page 1966
Children's Bookwatch, June 1993, page 2
Kirkus Reviews, April 1, 1993, page 459
Publishers Weekly, May 10, 1993, page 72
School Library Journal, April 1993, page 121

Other books by the same author:
Saying Goodbye, 1994 (sequel)
Finding My Voice, 1992 (prequel)

Other books you might like:

Lauren Lee, *Stella: On the Edge of Popularity*, 1994
Stella must learn who her true friends are as she defines her own unique place among her classmates at school, and as a second-generation Korean American in the outside world.

Laurence Yep, *Ribbons*, 1996
To help her family bring her grandmother to the U.S. from Hong Kong, Robin must sacrifice her dance lessons. But ballet means everything to her.so is her grandmother worth it?

Lensey Namioka, *April and the Dragon Lady*, 1994
The only daughter of a traditional Chinese American household, April feels responsible for her grandmother, but, leaving for college soon, she must make her family aware of their responsibilities.

Bette Bao Lord, *In the Year of the Boar and Jackie Robinson*, 1984
Shirley Temple Wong, with her new American name, arrives in Brooklyn. Through new friends and the discovery of baseball, Shirley finds her own special niche in her new home.

Jean Davies Okimoto, *Molly by Any Other Name*, 1990
At 17, adopted Molly begins to question who she is. Her parents help her find her birth mother and a whole new chapter of Molly's life begins.

996

MARIE G. LEE

Saying Goodbye

(Boston: Houghton Mifflin, 1994)

Subject(s): Multicultural; Identity; Stereotypes
Age range(s): Grades 8-12
Major character(s): Ellen Joyce Sung, Student—College (freshman at Harvard), Korean American; Michelle Sung, Sister (Ellen's older sister), Student—College (junior at Harvard), Korean American; Leecia Thomas, Student—College (Harvard), Roommate (Ellen's), African American; Jae-Chun Kim, Student—College (fellow Harvard student), Friend, Korean American
Time period(s): 1990s (1994)
Locale(s): Cambridge, Massachusetts (Harvard University campus); Arkin, Minnesota (Sungs are the only Asian Americans in town)

Summary: Ellen has left her small hometown for Harvard University, where she becomes good friends with her African American roommate and finds new friends among the Korean American students. She comes face-to-face with the reality of racial boundaries and racial tensions, and must define her own position as a newly aware Korean American.

About this book: Sequel to Lee's *Finding My Voice*.

Where it's reviewed:
Center for Children's Books. Bulletin, July 1994, page 364
Horn Book Magazine, July 1994, page 458
Kirkus Reviews, March 15, 1994, page 398
School Library Journal, August 1994, page 168
Children's Bookwatch, July 1994, page 6

Other books by the same author:
Finding My Voice, 1992 (prequel)
If It Hadn't Been for Yoon Jun, 1993

Other books you might like:

Lauren Lee, *Stella: On the Edge of Popularity*, 1994
Stella must learn who her true friends are, as she defines her own unique place among her classmates at school, and as a second-generation Korean American in the outside world.

Laurence Yep, *Ribbons*, 1996
To help her family bring her grandmother to the U.S. from Hong Kong, Robin must sacrifice her dance lessons. But ballet means everything to her.is her grandmother worth it?

Sook Nyul Choi, *Gathering of Pearls*, 1994
Sookan arrives at a small girls Catholic college from Korea. Her first year is a great adjustment, finding the right balance between her traditional upbringing and her new, independent American life.

997

MARY PAIK LEE
SUCHENG CHAN, Editor

Quiet Odyssey: A Pioneer Korean Woman in America

(Seattle: University of Washington Press, 1990)

Subject(s): Family Life; Emigration and Immigration; Intergenerational Saga
Age range(s): Adult
Major character(s): Mary Kuang Sun Paik Lee, Immigrant, Korean American, Spouse (wife of Lee Hung Man); Hung Man "H.M." Lee, Spouse (husband of Mary Paik Lee), Korean American, Immigrant
Time period(s): 1900s; 1990s
Locale(s): California (various cities in both Southern and Northern California)

Summary: The memoir of a Korean American pioneer, who left her native country for America at age 5 in 1905. Through a near century of change, Lee narrates the story of her life, from her early days in Korea, to her childhood as the daughter of immigrant laborers, to her adulthood as wife and mother, farmer, produce merchant, apartment manager and Korean Independence supporter.

About this book: Mary Paik Lee tells her own story, in her own words with detailed insight and outspoken honesty.

Where it's reviewed:
Kliatt, September 1990, page 33
Publishers Weekly, April 13, 1990, page 58
School Library Journal, October 1990, page 152

Other books you might like:

K. Connie Kang, *Home Was the Land of Morning Calm: The Saga of a Korean American Family*, 1995
The saga of one Korean family, from their escape from North Korea during the Korean War, to their journey to Japan, and finally the author's move to the U.S.

Ronyoung Kim, *Clay Walls*, 1987
The memoir of a young Korean woman and the difficulties

and hardships she faces in her new life as an immigrant American.

Helie Lee, *Still Life with Rice: A Young American Woman Discovers the Life and Legacy of Her Korean Grandmother*, 1996

The true story of a Korean woman who survives great hardship in Korea and finally arrives in the U.S., as told by her Korean American granddaughter.

Elaine H. Kim, *East to America: Korean American Life Stories*, 1996

Included here are oral histories of 38 Korean Americans, from immigrants to third-generation Americans, including journalists, activists, artists, shopkeepers and students. Co-edited with Eui-Young Yu

998

SKY LEE

Disappearing Moon Cafe

(Seattle: Seal Press, 1991)

Subject(s): Emigration and Immigration; Intergenerational Saga; Multicultural
Age range(s): Adult
Major character(s): Kae Ying Woo, Writer (Chinese Canadian); Wong Gwei Chang, Pioneer (in the New World); Lee Mui Lan, Spouse (wife of Wong Gwei Chang); Wong Choy Fuk, Son (of Wong Gwei Chang); Chan Fong Mei, Spouse (wife of Wong Choy Fuk)
Time period(s): 1890s; 1980s (1892-1986)
Locale(s): British Columbia, Canada

Summary: The Wong family saga, which begins in the 1890s when a Chinese man marries a Native Indian, is uncovered and recorded by his fifth generation descendant, a new mother and writer. The history that unfolds is filled with long-lost secrets, endless deceptions, even incest.

About this book: The book's title refers to the restaurant founded in the Canadian Wild West by Wong Gwei Chang and run by Lee Mui Lan.

Where it's reviewed:
Library Journal, September 15, 1991, page 110
New York Times Book Review, February 9, 1992, page 18
Publishers Weekly, August 23, 1991, page 42

Other books you might like:
Ruthanne Lum McCunn, *Thousand Pieces of Gold*, 1981
The first biographical novel of Chinese American pioneer woman, Polly Bemis.
Shawn Wong, *Homebase*, 1991
Chinese American Rainsford Chan, orphaned at age 14, recounts the 125 years of his family's history in the U.S.
Paul Yee, *Tales from Gold Mountain: Stories of the Chinese in the New World*, 1989
Illustrated by Simon Ng, this collection of eight tales is about Chinese immigrants in the New World.
Lydia Yuri Minatoya, *Talking to High Monks in the Snow: An Asian American Odyssey*, 1992
Minatoya's personal odyssey, which she recounts here, begins in the 1950s in upstate New York and continues through Japan, China and Nepal.

Amy Tan, *The Hundred Secret Senses*, 1995
A novel of two half-sisters, one Chinese-born, the other half-Chinese and half-American.

999

WALTER K. LEW, Editor

Premonitions: The Kaya Anthology of New Asian North American Poetry

(New York: Kaya Production, 1995)

Subject(s): Poetry; Multicultural; Identity
Age range(s): Adult

Summary: A ground-breaking collection of 73 authors, ranging from the established to up-and-comers, writing in all modes of poetry, including numerous works in nonstandard forms and dialects.

About this book: Founded in 1994, Kaya Production is the first publishing house devoted to producing works of the Asian and Asian American diaspora. Titles range from works by innovative poets, new authors, comprehensive anthologies and a biographical series on performing artists. Kaya's Recovery series will reintroduce out-of-print classics and other lost or neglected works.

Where it's reviewed:
Library Journal, July 1995, page 85

Other books you might like:
Joseph Bruchac, *Breaking Silence: An Anthology of Contemporary Asian American Poets*, 1983
One of the first major anthologies of Asian American poetry, featuring the work of some 50 writers.
Kimiko Hahn, *Earshot*, 1992
This poetry collection includes the imaginative, the quirky and the varied.
Li-Young Lee, *The City in Which I Love You*, 1990
Award-winning second poetry collection about relationships between family and lovers.
Garrett Hongo, *The Open Boat: Poems from Asian America*, 1993
A collection of works by 30 Asian American writers, both U.S. and foreign-born, covering over 100 years of the Asian American presence in America.
Him Mark Lai, *Island: Poetry and History of Chinese Immigrants on Angel Island, 1910-1940*, 1980
Edited with Genny Lim and Judy Yung. Poetry inscribed by Angel Island detainees in the buildings' walls, during holding periods that sometimes lasted two years.

1000

GENNY LIM

Paper Angels and Bitter Cane

(Honolulu: Kalamaku Press, 1991)

Subject(s): Theater; Emigration and Immigration; Multicultural
Age range(s): Adult

Summary: Two important plays about the Asian American experience. *Paper Angels*, a groundbreaking one-act play about Chinese immigrants detained on the West Coast immigration center, Angel Island, debuted in 1980 and was produced by American Playhouse for PBS in 1985. *Bitter Cane* focuses on the virtual imprisonment of Asian immigrant laborers on Hawaiian sugar cane plantations, told through the story of a young Chinese son who follows in the laboring footsteps of his missing father.

About this book: Lim's diverse detainees in *Paper Angels* are a cross-representation of the approximately 175,000 Chinese immigrants who entered the U.S. between 1910 and 1940 through Angel Island in the San Francisco Bay. The unjust Chinese Exclusion Act of 1882 drastically limited Chinese immigration, granting entry only to merchants, students and tourists. Would-be immigrants who did not fit into the designated categories attempted to enter with falsified papers (therefore referred to as ''paper sons''), linking them to Chinese American ''relatives.'' Lim herself is a descendant of an Angel Island detainee.

Other books by the same author:
Island: Poetry and History of Chinese Immigrants on Angel Island, 1910-1940, 1980 (edited with Him Mark Lai and Judy Yung)

Other books you might like:
Misha Berson, *Between Worlds: Contemporary Asian-American Plays*, 1990
   Edited by Berson. Anthology includes works by Ping Chong, Philip Kan Gotanda, Jessica Hagedorn, David Henry Hwang, Wakako Yamauchi and Laurence Yep.
Velina Hasu Houston, *The Politics of Life: Four Plays by Asian American Women*, 1993
   Edited by Houston. Includes works by Wakako Yamauchi, Genny Lim and Houston.
Roberta Uno, *Unbroken Thread: An Anthology of Plays by Asian American Women*, 1993
   Edited by Uno. Includes plays by Genny Lim, Wakako Yamauchi, Momoko Iko, Velina Hasu Houston, Jeannie Barroga and Elizabeth Wong.

1001

SHIRLEY GEOK-LIN LIM, Editor
MAYUMI TSUTAKAWA, Co-Editor
MARGARITA DONNELLY, Co-Editor

The Forbidden Stitch: An Asian American Women's Anthology
(Corvalis, OR: Calyx Books, 1989)

Subject(s): Multicultural; Identity; Emigration and Immigration
Age range(s): Adult
Time period(s): Indeterminate
Locale(s): United States

Summary: A rich collection of poetry, short stories, visual art and reviews which together make up a collage of what it means to be a contemporary Asian American woman.

Where it's reviewed:
Belles Lettres, Winter 1989, page 22

Booklist, February 1, 1989, page 908
Library Journal, May 1, 1989, page 78

Other books you might like:
Asian Women United of California, *Making Waves: An Anthology of Writings by and about Asian American Women*, 1989
   First major compilation since the early 1970s of primarily unpublished works by and about Asian American women.
Women of South Asian Descent Collective, *Our Feet Walk the Sky: Women of the South Asian Diaspora*, 1993
   This compilation is the first that focuses on women of South Asian descent in the U.S. The anthology includes poetry, short stories, personal histories and critical essays.
Nurjehan Aziz, *Her Mother's Ashes, and Other Stories by South Asian Women in Canada and the United States*, 1994
   This anthology highlights the diverse cultures and unique experiences of 21 first-generation North American Women who arrived in Canada or the U.S. by way of South Asia, Africa or the Caribbean.
Jessica Hagedorn, *Charlie Chan Is Dead: An Anthology of Contemporary Asian American Ficiton*, 1993
   This collection of 48 works is by Asian American writers of different ages, backgrounds and styles.
Sylvia Watanabe, *Home to Stay: Asian American Women's Fiction*, 1990
   Edited with Carol Bruchac, this collection of short stories celebrates the literary achievements of Asian American women writers.

1002

SHARON LIM-HING, Editor

The Very Inside: An Anthology of Writing by Asian and Pacific Islander Lesbian and Bisexual Women
(Toronto: Sister Vision Press, 1994)

Subject(s): Multicultural; Identity; Homosexuality/Lesbianism
Age range(s): Adult

Summary: A collection that includes an array of prose, poetry and art work. Writes Aziz in the introduction about how the anthology was conceived: ''I wanted a book of our own that would speak to us about our lives as lesbians and bisexual women and our experiences in the many racist, homophobic communities that we inhabit.''

Where it's reviewed:
Lambda Book Report, September 1994, page 26

Other books you might like:
Asian Women United of California, *Making Waves: An Anthology of Writings by and about Asian American Women*, 1989
   First major compilation since the 1970s of primarily unpublished works by and about Asian American women.
Nurjehan Aziz, *Her Mother's Ashes, and Other Stories by South Asian Women in Canada and the United States*, 1994
   Twenty-one stories by first-generation North American

women of South Asian descent, who have arrived in either Canada or the U.S. by way of South Asia, Africa or the Caribbean.

Geraldine Kudaka, *On a Bed of Rice: An Asian American Erotic Feast*, 1995

The first collection of erotica created by writers of Chinese, Japanese, Korean, Vietnamese, Filipino, Thai, East Indian, Pakistani and Amerasian descent.

Shirley Geok-lin Lim, *The Forbidden Stitch: An Asian American Women's Anthology*, 1989

Also edited with Mayumi Tsutakawa and Margarita Donnelly. A rich collection of poetry, short stories, art and reviews focusing on being a contmporary Asian American woman.

Sylvia Watanabe, *Home to Stay: Asian American Women's Fiction*, 1990

Also edited with Carol Bruchac. A collection of short stories that celebrates the literary achievements of Asian American women writers.

1003

R. ZAMORA LINMARK

Rolling the R's

(New York: Kaya Production, 1995)

Subject(s): Multicultural; Coming of Age; Short Stories
Age range(s): Adult
Time period(s): 1970s
Locale(s): Honolulu, Hawaii

Summary: A debut collection of interrelated short stories, predominantly about the Filipino American community in Honolulu—from young teenagers discovering their sexuality and coming to terms with their ethnicity to older citizens trying to find peace among culture clashes and financial challenges.

Where it's reviewed:
Publishers Weekly, October 23, 1995 page 59

Other books you might like:
Darrell H.Y. Lum, *Pass On, No Pass Back!*, 1990
A humorous collection of short stories about growing up in Hawaii.

Milton Murayama, *All I Asking for Is My Body*, 1959
A young Japanese American boy's coming-of-age in Hawaii during the 1930s up until the advent of World War II.

Kathleen Tyau, *A Little Too Much Is Enough*, 1995
Mahi Wong grows up during post-World War II Hawaii, surrounded by her large family, immersed in a complex, mixed-up culture of Chinese and Hawaiian influences.

Lois-Ann Yamanaka, *Wild Meat and the Bully Burgers*, 1996
A coming-of-age first novel about Lovey Nariyoshi of Hilo, Hawaii, her best friend Jerome, her adolescent enemies and her eccentric family.

Norman Wong, *Cultural Revolution*, 1994
These interrelated stories begin in 1953 in Macao where Wei lives with his overprotective grandmother and ineffectual father. It continues with his emigration to Honolulu and the life he builds there.

1004

AIMEE LIU

Face

(New York: Warner Books, Inc., 1994)

Subject(s): Multicultural; Identity; Photography
Age range(s): Adult
Major character(s): Maibelle Chung, Photographer; Lao "Uncle Li" Li, Businessman (Chinese antiques art dealer); Tommy "Tai" Wah, Writer
Time period(s): 20th century (1950s-1994)
Locale(s): New York, New York (various locations throughout Manhattan)

Summary: Maibelle Chung, in spite of her last name, is a tall, curly red-haired woman with green eyes. Her father is Chinese-born, her mother from the Midwest. After years of running away, Maibelle returns to her Chinatown roots, finally ready to start facing the dark secrets of her incongruous, inescapable past.

About this book: Each section of the novel is introduced with an anonymous photograph of Chinatown; the powerful images capture an indescribable essence of the famous ethnic neighborhood. In the novel, Maibelle is attempting to do just that, to capture the faces of a changing, fading Chinatown, to preserve those images in a book project on which she agrees to collaborate. The included photographs truly add a sense of suspended real life to an otherwise fictional story.

Where it's reviewed:
Belles Lettres, Spring 1995, page 65
Los Angeles Times Book Review, January 8, 1995, page 6

Other books by the same author:
Solitaire: A Narrative, 1979 (nonfiction)

Other books you might like:
Chang-rae Lee, *Native Speaker*, 1995
A first novel about Korean American Henry Park who is trying to come to terms with both his troubled personal life and his problematic career as a spy.

Amy Tan, *The Hundred Secret Senses*, 1995
A novel of two half-sisters, one Chinese-born, the other half-Chinese and American-born.

Sky Lee, *Disappearing Moon Cafe*, 1991
The Wong family saga, which begins in the 1890s when a Chinese man marries a Native Indian, is uncovered and recorded by his fifth generation descendant, a new mother and writer.

Yoji Yamaguchi, *Face of a Stranger*, 1995
Kikue, a Japanese woman, arrives in the U.S. believing she is to be a picture bride. Forced into prostitution instead, she makes plans to secure her freedom and plot revenge on those who deceived her.

1005

STEVEN LO

The Incorporation of Eric Chung

(Chapel Hill: NC, Algonquin Bks of Chapel Hill (Workman Publ. Co),1989)

Subject(s): Emigration and Immigration; Business Enterprises
Age range(s): Adult
Major character(s): Eric Chung, Student—College (in engineering at TX Tech), Businessman (figurehead); Victor Liu, Student—College (graduate student with Eric); Roger Holton, Businessman (entrepreneur)
Time period(s): 1970s; 1980s
Locale(s): Lubbock, Texas; Dallas, Texas

Summary: Eric Chung begins his American life as an engineering graduate student. From Lubbock, he heads to Dallas to climb the corporate ladder. He meets fast-talking Roger Holton, creator of the dubious ''China Business'' who talks a major company into investing, installs Chung as figurehead and quickly disappears.

Where it's reviewed:
Kirkus Reviews, August 1, 1989, page 1102
Publishers Weekly, August 18, 1989, page 51
School Library Journal, April 1990, page 31

Other books you might like:
Gish Jen, *Typical American*, 1991
    The Chang family arrives in the U.S. from China in search of education and safety. What they find is fried chicken fast food joints, glamour magazines, suburbia and con artists.
Bharati Mukherjee, *Wife*, 1975
    Dimple Dasgupta marries an engineer bound for the U.S. but her expectations of being a dutiful wife and living glamorously, fall far short of reality.
Kirin Narayan, *Love, Stars, and All That*, 1994
    A delightful novel that follows Gita Das—from immigrant graduate student at Berkeley to esteemed professor—through her bumpy search for her ideal mate.
Wang Ping, *American Visa*, 1994
    Eleven interrelated stories about young Seaweed, a determined young woman in China during the Cultural Revolution in search of higher education.
Yoji Yamaguchi, *Face of a Stranger*, 1995
    Kikue, a Japanese woman, arrives in the U.S. believing she is to be a picture bride. Forced into prostitution instead, she makes plans to secure her freedom and plot revenge on those who deceived her.

1006

JAN FREEMAN LONG, Adaptor
KAORU ONO, Illustrator

The Bee and the Dream: A Japanese Tale

(New York: Dutton Children's Books (Penguin), 1996)

Subject(s): Folk Tales; Friendship; Dreams and Nightmares
Age range(s): Grades 1-4

Major character(s): Shin, Worker (hardworking peasant); Tasuke, Friend (Shin's co-worker and friend)
Time period(s): Indeterminate Past
Locale(s): Japan (tiny village at the foot of a mountain)

Summary: Shin so believes in the reality of his friend Tasuke's dream of finding gold that he borrows money and sets off to find the treasure. Arriving at the site of the dream, Shin is disappointed, but when he returns home, he finds a tremendous surprise.

Other books you might like:
Nami Rhee, *Magic Spring: A Korean Folktale*, 1993
    A hardworking, childless, elderly couple find the fountain of youth. Their greedy neighbor rushes to the magic spring and overindulges, leading to a surprise ending.
Laurence Yep, *The Shell Woman and the King*, 1993
    The magical shell woman saves her husband and herself from the evil, greedy king.
Laurence Yep, *The City of Dragons*, 1995
    The boy with the saddest face in the world proves to be a hero in the city of dragons.
Oki S. Han, *Sir Whong and the Golden Pig*, 1993
    When a stranger dupes Sir Whong into a loan using a fake golden pig as security, Sir Whong devises a plan to retrieve the money.
Ai-Ling Louie, *Yeh-Shen: A Cinderella Story from China*, 1982
    In spite of the wicked machinations of her stepmother, the beautiful young Yeh-Shen manages to survive her deprived life, marry the king and live happily ever after.

1007

BETTE BAO LORD
MARC SIMONT, Illustrator

In the Year of the Boar and Jackie Robinson

(New York: HarperTrophy (HarperCollins Publishers), 1984)

Subject(s): Multicultural; Emigration and Immigration; Sports/Baseball
Age range(s): Grades 5-7
Major character(s): Shirley Temple ''Bandit'' Wong, Immigrant (goes to Brooklyn, N.Y.), Young Woman, Chinese; Mother Wong, Mother (Shirley's); Father Wong, Father (Shirley's); Mabel, Friend (Shirley's ally), Student (fellow classmate of Shirley's), African American; Ellen Levy, Friend (becomes Shirley's close friend), Student (new girl in school)
Time period(s): 1940s (1947)
Locale(s): Brooklyn, New York

Summary: Shirley Temple Wong, with her new American name, arrives in her new American home. But making friends proves difficult. She discovers baseball and Jackie Robinson, the baseball legend who, in spite of difficult beginnings, became a national hero. And Shirley learns that she, too, can make a difference in her new world.

About this book: According to the Chinese zodiac calendar, 1947 was the Year of the Boar. The work is loosely based on

Lord's own first year in the U.S., which, like Shirley, she spent in Brooklyn, New York.

Where it's reviewed:
Children's Book Review Service, October 1984, page 20
Horn Book Magazine, September 1984, page 592
Kirkus Reviews, September 1, 1984, page J71
Publishers Weekly, July 6, 1984, page 65
Reading Teacher, December 1984, page 339

Other books by the same author:
The Middle Heart, 1996 (adult novel)
Legacies: A Chinese Mosaic, 1990 (adult memoir)
Spring Moon: A Novel of China, 1981
Eighth Moon: The True Story of a Young Girl's Life in Communist China, 1964 (biography)

Other books you might like:
Laurence Yep, *Dragonwings*, 1975
    Eight-year-old Moon Shadow joins his father, whom he has never met, in California where they work together, through many disasters, to achieve their dream—to fly.
Marie G. Lee, *If It Hadn't Been for Yoon Jun*, 1993
    Although Alice Larsen's face may be Korean, she's all-American, having been adopted at birth. She reluctantly befriends Yoon Jun, the new student from Korea, who helps her discover her own heritage.
Sook Nyul Choi, *Gathering of Pearls*, 1994
    Sookan arrives at a small girls Catholic college from Korea. Her first year is a great adjustment, finding the right balance between her traditional upbringing and her new, independent American life.
Lensey Namioka, *Yang the Third and Her Impossible Family*, 1995
    Yingmei tries her best to "be American" while her family clings to Chinese customs.
Lensey Namioka, *Yang the Youngest and His Terrible Ear*, 1992
    Surrounded by a musically talented family, Yingtao struggles to play his violin.

1008

AI-LING LOUIE
ED YOUNG, Illustrator

Yeh-Shen: A Cinderella Story from China
(New York: Philomel Books (G.P. Putnam's Sons), 1982)

Subject(s): Folk Tales; Good and Evil; Greed
Age range(s): Grades 1-4
Major character(s): Yeh-Shen, Orphan (beautiful young girl); Stepmother, Stepmother (Yeh-Shen's wicked stepmother); King, Ruler (local king)
Time period(s): Indeterminate Past
Locale(s): China (a kingdom in Southern China)

Summary: In spite of the wicked machinations of her stepmother, the beautiful young Yeh-Shen manages to survive her deprived life and with the help of a beloved fish and a mysterious old sage, marries the king.

Where it's reviewed:
Booklist, January 15, 1983, page 678
Horn Book Magazine, April 1983, page 160

School Library Journal, December 1982, page 59
Other books you might like:
Demi, *Liang and the Magic Paintbrush*, 1980
    Young Liang is given a magic paintbrush that brings to life everything he touches.
Ellin Greene, *Ling-Li and the Phoenix Fairy: A Chinese Folktale*, 1996
    Ling-Li creates a wedding robe so beautiful that the magpies carry it away. Ling-Li follows the birds to the Phoenix Fairy who returns the robe with her special blessings.
Oki S. Han, *Sir Whong and the Golden Pig*, 1993
    When a stranger dupes Sir Whong into a loan using a fake golden pig as security, Sir Whong devises a plan to retrieve the money.
Nami Rhee, *Magic Spring: A Korean Folktale*, 1993
    A hardworking, childless, elderly couple discover the fountain of youth. Their greedy neighbor rushes to the magic spring and overindulges, leading to a surprise ending.
Laurence Yep, *The Shell Woman and the King*, 1993
    The magical shell woman saves her husband and herself from the evil, greedy king.

1009

DAVID WONG LOUIE

Pangs of Love
(New York: Alfred A. Knopf, Inc., 1991)

Subject(s): Multicultural; Identity; Short Stories
Age range(s): Adult
Time period(s): 1990s
Locale(s): United States

Summary: A first collection of stories that explores the Asian American experience, with a spectrum of characters—from a woman who pretends to speak no English to a young sushi restaurant employee to a mother longing for a Chinese daughter-in-law.

Where it's reviewed:
New York Times Book Review, August 9, 1992, page 24
Publishers Weekly, June 8, 1992, page 61
Parnassus, Issue 1, 1992, page 88

Other books you might like:
Jessica Hagedorn, *Charlie Chan Is Dead: An Anthology of Contemporary Asian American Fiction*, 1993
    A collection of 48 works by Asian American writers of different ages, backgrounds and styles.
Hisaye Yamamoto, *Seventeen Syllables and Other Stories*, 1988
    A collection of 15 short stories from Yamamoto's almost half-century-long writing career.
Sylvia Watanabe, *Talking to the Dead*, 1992
    Award-wining collection, with stories about a female Chinese Fred Astaire, a grandmother who makes quilts of stolen laundry and a girl longing to leave home any way she can.
Kathleen Tyau, *A Little Too Much Is Enough*, 1995
    Mahi Wong grows up in post-World War II Hawaii, sur-

rounded by her large family, immersed in a complex, mixed-up culture of Chinese and Hawaiian influences.

Wang Ping, *American Visa*, 1994

Eleven interrelated stories about young Seaweed, a determined young woman in China during the Cultural Revolution in search of higher education.

1010

DARRELL H.Y. LUM

Pass On, No Pass Back!

(Honolulu: Bamboo Ridge Press, 1990)

Subject(s): Multicultural; Family Life; Short Stories
Age range(s): Adult
Locale(s): Hawaii

Summary: A humorous collection of short stories about young boys growing up in Hawaii, written in pidgin English, the native everyday language of the Islands. Each of the stories is prefaced by a cartoon, depicting the adventures of Booly, Bullette and Burrito, illustrated by Art Kodani.

Other books you might like:

Milton Murayama, *All I Asking for Is My Body*, 1959
A young Japanese American boy's coming-of-age in Hawaii during the 1930s up until the advent of World War II.

Norman Wong, *Cultural Revolution*, 1994
These interrelated stories begin in 1953 in Macao where Wei lives with his overprotective grandmother and ineffectual father. It continues with his emigration to Honolulu and the life he builds there.

Marie Hara, *Bananaheart and Other Stories*, 1994
These stories cover a century of life in Hawaii, with tales of a picture bride, a woman working in a foreign house, a hapa girl searching for identity and an old woman who lost an infant daughter.

Lois-Ann Yamanaka, *Wild Meat and the Bully Burgers*, 1996
A coming-of-age first novel about Lovey Nariyoshi of Hilo, Hawaii, her best friend Jerome, her adolescent enemies and her eccentric family.

R. Zamora Linmark, *Rolling the R's*, 1995
A collection of interrelated stories, many about young Filipino Americans coming to terms with their ethnicity and their sexuality in Honolulu.

1011

MARGARET MAHY
JEAN TSENG, Illustrator
MOU-SIEN TSENG, Illustrator

The Seven Chinese Brothers

(New York: Scholastic Inc., 1990)

Subject(s): Folk Tales; Brothers; Dictators
Age range(s): Grades 1-3
Major character(s): Emperor Ch'in Shih Huang, Ruler (of ancient China)
Time period(s): Indeterminate Past (Once upon a time.)
Locale(s): China

Summary: Seven Chinese brothers, who walk alike, talk alike, even look alike, each possesses an extraordinary, unique power. Each must call on his special power to save each other's lives from the cruel Emperor Ch'in Shih Huang.

Where it's reviewed:
Horn Book Magazine, July 1990, page 465
New York Times Book Review, October 21, 1990, page 41
Publishers Weekly, February 23, 1990, page 217

Awards the book has won:
American Library Association Notable Book

Other books you might like:

Ed Young, *Little Plum*, 1994
A childless couple long for a child, even if he were only as big as a plum seed. When such a child is born, he proves that even a man as small as a plum seed can do great deeds if he is brave.

Claire Huchet Bishop, *The Five Chinese Brothers*, 1938
Five identical Chinese brothers, each with an extraordinary talent, must call on these special talents to save the life of First Chinese Brother.

Margaret Chang, *The Cricket Warrior: A Chinese Tale*, 1994
Adapted with Raymond Chang, this story is about the dutiful son, Wei'nian, who takes the form of a cricket to save his family by becoming the champion of the Emperor's court.

Demi, *Chingis Khan*, 1991
Based on the life of the great Mongol warrior and leader, Chingis Khan.

1012

TOSHI MARUKI, Author/Illustrator

Hiroshima No Pika (The Flash of Hiroshima)

(New York: Lothrop, Lee & Shepard Books, 1980)

Subject(s): World War II; Children and War; Nuclear Weapons
Age range(s): Grades 2-6
Major character(s): Mii, 7-Year-Old (girl), Survivor (of Hiroshima blast); Mother, Mother (Mii's), Survivor (of Hiroshima blast); Father, Father (Mii's), Survivor (of Hiroshima blast)
Time period(s): 1940s (August 6, 1945 after atomic bomb)
Locale(s): Hiroshima, Japan

Summary: When the world's first atomic bomb detonated over the Japanese city of Hiroshima, young Mii was sitting at breakfast with her mother and father. Remarkably, the family survived the blast that day, but the horror they endured afterwards was a tragedy beyond description.

About this book: A brilliantly illustrated depiction of the horrifying event, based on the true life experiences of an anonymous survivor. The book is certainly accessible to young readers with its simple narrative, but it will have a lasting, chilling effect on adult readers, as well.

Where it's reviewed:
Booklist, June 1, 1995, page 1761
Journal of Reading, October 1994, page 158

English Journal, December 1992, page 78

Other books you might like:

Sheila Hamanaka, *On the Wings of Peace: Writers and Illustrators Speak Out for Peace, in Memory of Hiroshima and Nagasaki*, 1996

Compiled by Hamanaka. A collection of stories, poetry, remembrances and art focusing on the tragedies caused by war, and the hopes for a lasting peace for today's children.

Sheila Hamanaka, *Peace Crane*, 1995

After learning about Sadako, a victim of the Hiroshima bombing, a girl imagines a peaceful world.

Michele Maria Surat, *Angel Child, Dragon Child*, 1983

Young Ut, a recent Vietnamese immigrant, is teased because of her different appearance. Thrown together by the school principal, Ut and a once cruel boy develop a new friendship.

Tran Khanh Tuyet, *The Little Weaver of Thai-Yen Village*, 1977

A young Vietnamese refugee arrives in the U.S. and struggles to adjust to her new life. She starts to weave again, as she did in her home country with her late grandmother.

Laurence Yep, *Hiroshima*, 1995

The horror of the Hiroshima bombing, told through the tragic story of two sisters who were on their way to school when the B-29 bomber named *Enola Gay* dropped the first atom bomb.

1013

RUTHANNE LUM MCCUNN

Chinese American Portraits: Personal Histories 1828-1988

(San Francisco: Chronicle Books, 1988)

Subject(s): Emigration and Immigration; Multicultural; Historical

Age range(s): Grades 8-Adult

Time period(s): 1820s; 1980s (1828-1988)

Locale(s): United States

Summary: A historical look at the Chinese American experience, from early pioneers to modern day heroes. Through personal histories, McCunn presents numerous Chinese Americans and their lasting contributions to all aspects of life in the U.S., including China Mary, Alaskan pioneer and prospector, Lue Gim Gong, developer of frost-resistant oranges, and Chin Gee-hee, railroad baron.

About this book: Filled with over 150 historical and contemporary photographs that bear witness to Chinese American contributions. McCunn would go on to write a novel based on the life of one of the profilees, horticulturalist Lue Gim Gong, titled *Wooden Fish Songs*.

Where it's reviewed:

Booklist, November 1, 1992, page 503

Other books by the same author:

Wooden Fish Songs, 1995 (adult novel)

Sole Survivor, 1985 (biographical novel)

Pie-Biter, 1983 (children's story)

Thousand Pieces of Gold, 1981 (biographical novel)

An Illustrated History of the Chinese in America, 1979

Other books you might like:

Victor G. Nee, *Longtime Californ': A Documentary Study of an American Chinatown*, 1974

Co-author Brett de Bary Nee; a history of the Chinese in America told through both narrative and extensive interviews, using the backdrop of San Francisco's Chinatown.

Ronald Takaki, *Strangers from a Different Shore*, 1989

Traces the diverse lives of the Japanese, Chinese, Koreans, Filipinos, Asian Indians, Vietnamese, Cambodians and Laotions who have come to the U.S. over the past 150 years.

Connie Young Yu, *Profiles in Excellence: Peninsula Chinese Americans*, 1986

Biographies of prominent Chinese Americans in the San Francisco Bay Area who have made significant contributions in all fields.

Judy Yung, *Chinese Women of America: A Pictorial History*, 1986

Using interviews, photographs and long-overlooked documents, this text examines the experiences of Chinese American women over a 150-year history.

Judy Yung, *Unbound Feet: A Social History of Chinese Women in San Francisco*, 1995

Yung traces the history of Chinese American women who arrived in America at the turn of the century as the property of their husbands or slaves and how they became active members of American society.

1014

RUTHANNE LUM MCCUNN

An Illustrated History of the Chinese in America

(San Francisco: Design Enterprises of San Francisco, 1979)

Story type: Young Adult; Young Readers

Subject(s): Emigration and Immigration; Multicultural; Historical

Age range(s): Grades 5 and Up

Time period(s): 19th century; 20th century (1828-1988)

Locale(s): United States

Summary: An illustrated history book which traces the presence of the Chinese in America, from the first written proof (a Buddhist priest arrived in Canada and proceeded to Mexico in 458 A.D.), to the arrival of Chinese in large numbers during the California Gold Rush, to the achievements of contemporary Chinese Americans.

About this book: McCunn finds it "alarming" that so many of the book's readers are older students (the book is a popular college text) since the book was written for schoolchildren at a fifth-grade reading level.

Where it's reviewed:

Booklist, February 1, 1985, page 792

Other books by the same author:

Wooden Fish Songs, 1995 (adult novel)

Chinese American Portraits: Personal Histories 1828-1988, 1988

Sole Survivor, 1985

Pie-Biter, 1983 (children's story)

Thousand Pieces of Gold, 1981

Other books you might like:

Victor G. Nee, *Longtime Californ': A Documentary Study of an American Chinatown*, 1974
Co-author Brett de Bary Nee; a history of the Chinese in America told through both narrative and extensive interviews, using the backdrop of San Francisco's Chinatown.

Ronald Takaki, *Strangers from a Different Shore*, 1989
Traces the diverse lives of the Japanese, Chinese, Koreans, Filipinos, Asian Indians, Vietnamese, Cambodians and Laotians who have come to the U.S. over the past 150 years.

Connie Young Yu, *Profiles in Excellence: Peninsula Chinese Americans*, 1986
Biograhies of prominent Chinese Americans in the San Francisco Bay Area who have made significant contributions in all fields.

Judy Yung, *Chinese Women of America: A Pictorial History*, 1986
Using interviews, photographs and long-overlooked documents, this text examines the experiences of Chinese American women over a 150-year history.

Judy Yung, *Unbound Feet: A Social History of Chinese Women in San Francisco*, 1995
Yung traces the history of Chinese American women who arrived in America at the turn of the century as the property of their husbands and how they became active members of American society.

1015

RUTHANNE LUM MCCUNN
YOU-SHAN TANG, Illustrator

Pie-Biter

(San Francisco: Design Enterprises of San Francisco, 1983)

Story type: Historical/American West; Young Readers
Subject(s): Adventure and Adventurers; Emigration and Immigration; Multicultural
Age range(s): Grades 1-6
Major character(s): Hoi "Pie-Biter", Immigrant (young boy from China), Railroad Worker
Time period(s): 1860s (starts in 1865 and covers 20 years)
Locale(s): West

Summary: Hoi, a young Chinese boy, arrives in America in 1865 to work on the railroads. Because his favorite food is American pies, his friends rename him "Pie-Biter." He quickly grows to be a strong young man. When the transcontinental railroad is completed, Pie-Biter establishes himself as a train packer, delivering goods to places not accessible by the new railroads.

About this book: During the late 19th century, railroad companies imported Chinese immigrant laborers to build the transcontinental railroad. This story is based on a true story of a young Chinese laborer who lived and worked in the Pacific Northwest for 20 years.

Where it's reviewed:
Multicultural Review, April 1992, page 36

Children's Literature in Education, September 1994, page 169

Awards the book has won:
American Book Award, 1984

Other books by the same author:
Wooden Fish Songs, 1995 (adult novel)
Chinese American Portraits: Personal Histories 1828-1988, 1988
Sole Survivor, 1985
Thousand Pieces of Gold, 1981
An Illustrated History of the Chinese in America, 1979

Other books you might like:

Paul Yee, *Tales from Gold Mountain: Stories of the Chinese in the New World*, 1989
This collection of eight stories is about Chinese immigrants in the New World.

Laurence Yep, *Dragon's Gate*, 1993
A young adult story about Chinese immigration and the construction of the transcontinental railroad during the mid-19th century.

Laurence Yep, *Dragonwings*, 1975
Eight-year-old Moon Shadow joins his father, whom he has never met, in California where they work together, through many disasters, to achieve their dream—to fly.

Charlie Chin, *China's Bravest Girl: The Legend of Hua Mu Lan*, 1993
Disguised as a man, Hua Mu Lan takes her father's place in the Emperor's army and becomes a legendary warrior, returning home years later, still undiscovered, as a decorate general.

Allen Say, *Grandfather's Journey*, 1993
A Japanese American man recounts his grandfather's journey from Japan to America and back again, trying to understand his grandfather's feelings of being torn between the love of both countries.

1016

RUTHANNE LUM MCCUNN

Thousand Pieces of Gold

(Boston: Beacon Press, 1981)

Subject(s): Emigration and Immigration; American West; Multicultural
Age range(s): Adult
Major character(s): Lalu Nathoy "Polly" Bemis, Slave (forced to immigrate to U.S.), Chinese American (pioneer); Hong King, Saloon Keeper/Owner (Lalu's "master"); Charlie Bemis, Spouse ("wins" Polly in poker game)
Time period(s): 19th century; 20th century (1865-1933)
Locale(s): China (countryside of northern China); West (arrives in San Francisco, settles in Warrens, Idaho)

Summary: When famine strikes northern China in 1871, Lalu Nathoy is sold at age 13, is eventually taken by a slave merchant to America and auctioned off to a seedy saloon keeper. She becomes the prize during a poker game and is "won" by an honest man whom she marries, becoming Polly Bemis, beloved pioneer woman.

About this book: Most likely the first biographical novel of a Chinese American pioneer woman. The book was the basis for a 1991 independent film for American Playhouse, but McCunn was unhappy with the celluloid translation. She told Hong in a 1994 interview, " It was very different. The character names and the title were the same, but everything else was different."

Where it's reviewed:
Biography, Spring 1990, page 143
Los Angeles Times Book Review, March 5, 1989, page 14

Other books by the same author:
Wooden Fish Songs, 1995 (adult novel)
Chinese American Portraits: Personal Histories 1828-1988, 1988
Sole Survivor, 1985 (biographical novel)
Pie-Biter, 1983 (children's story)
An Illustrated History of the Chinese in America, 1979

Other books you might like:
Jade Snow Wong, *Fifth Chinese Daughter*, 1945
An autobiographical account of an American-born Chinese woman growing up in San Francisco's Chinatown between the 1920s to 1940s.
Monica Sone, *Nisei Daughter*, 1953
An account of a second-generation Japanese American woman growing up in Seattle in the 1920s and '30s, being incarcerated during World War II and her new life in the Midwest.
Judy Yung, *Chinese Women of America: A Pictorial History*, 1986
Using interviews, photographs and long overlooked documents, this text examines the experiences of Chinese American women over a 150-year history.
Paul Yee, *Tales from Gold Mountain: Stories of the Chinese in the New World*, 1989
Illustrated by Simon Ng, this collection of eight tales is about Chinese immigrants in the New World.
Maxine Hong Kingston, *The Woman Warrior: Memoirs of a Girlhood Among Ghosts*, 1975
The story of a young girl growing up in the San Francisco Bay Area divided amidst the stories of her parents' faraway past in China and her own experiences in a Caucasian world.

1017

AMEENA MEER

Bombay Talkie

(New York: High Risk Books/Serpent's Tail, 1994)

Subject(s): Multicultural; Personal Odyssey; Family Relations
Age range(s): Adult
Major character(s): Sabah Al-Hussain, Young Woman, Indian American; Adam Al-Hussain, Cousin (Sabah's cousin, "Jimmy's" son), Indian; Syed Jamal Noor "Jimmy" Al-Hussain, Actor (beloved movie star), Indian; Sanjay, Friend (Sabah's close friend), Indian; Rani, Friend (Sabah's childhood friend), Indian American (lives in India)
Time period(s): 1990s (1994)

Locale(s): United States (various locations, including Berkeley, Boston and New York City); India (various locations, including Bombay and Delhi)

Summary: Independent, headstrong Sabah heads to India in search of her ethnic identity. What she finds in the wealthy world of her Indian relatives is a liberal Westernized culture bound by strict traditions, where the latest American tunes play in the trendiest discos, and where wives can still be immolated by dissatisfied husbands.

Where it's reviewed:
Kirkus Reviews, May 15, 1994, page 653
Library Journal, June 11, 1994, page 162
Publishers Weekly, June 20, 1994, page 101

Other books you might like:
Marina Tamar Budhos, *House of Waiting*, 1995
As Sarah awaits the return of her Indian-Caribbean husband Roland, embroiled in the political turmoil of his native Guiana, she creates a new life among his tight community of East Indian transplants.
Chitra Banerjee Divakaruni, *Arranged Marriage*, 1995
A collection of 11 short stories about young Indian and Indian American women, some married, some single, in various stages of claiming their independence.
Bharati Mukherjee, *Jasmine*, 1989
A novel about Jasmine Vijh's odyssey through America, from her arrival from India as a 17-year-old widow to her new life as Jane Ripplemeyer, assumed to be an Iowa housewife.
Bharati Mukherjee, *The Middleman and Other Stories*, 1988
An award-winning collection of stories about displaced, diverse Americans, from a troubled Vietnam vet to an Iraqi Jew from Queens to a wealthy immigrant Filipina.
Kirin Narayan, *Love, Stars, and All That*, 1994
A delightful novel that follows Gita Das—from immigrant graduate student at Berkeley to esteemed professor—through her bumpy search for her ideal mate.

1018

GITA MEHTA

A River Sutra

(New York: Vintage Books (Random House), 1993)

Age range(s): Adult
Major character(s): Narrator, Civil Servant (retired); Mr. Chagla, Clerk (rest home activities leader); Tariq Mia, Teacher (mullah (religious teacher)), Neighbor (older friend of the narrator)
Time period(s): 1990s (1993)
Locale(s): India (along the Narmada River from the town of Rudra)

Summary: A retired civil servant living along the holy Narmada River whose banks are believed to contain 400 billion sacred places, comes into contact with numerous travelers and their mesmerizing stories, including an ascetic monk who gave up unimaginable wealth, a young man possessed by the spirit of a scorned lover and a woman in search of her kidnapped daughter.

Where it's reviewed:
Kliatt, January 1995, page 10
Booklist, January 15, 1994, page 865
Los Angeles Times Book Review, September 11, 1994, page 10
New York Times Book Review, December 5, 1993, page 64
Publishers Weekly, May 30, 1994, page 50

Other books by the same author:
Raj, 1989 (historical novel)
Karma Cola, 1979

Other books you might like:
Chitra Banerjee Divakaruni, *Arranged Marriage*, 1995
A collection of 11 short stories about young Indian and Indian American women, some married, some single, in various stages of claiming their independence.
Ameena Meer, *Bombay Talkie*, 1994
Sabah heads to India in search of her ethnic identity. What she finds in the wealthy world of her Indian relatives is a liberal Westernized culture bound by strict traditions.
Bharati Mukherjee, *Jasmine*, 1989
A novel about Jasmine Vijh's odyssey through America, from her arrival from India as a 17-year-old widow to her new life as Jane Ripplemeyer, assumed to be an Iowa housewife.
Kirin Narayan, *Love, Stars, and All That*, 1994
A delightful novel that follows Gita Das—from immigrant graduate student at Berkeley to esteemed professor—through her bumpy search for her ideal mate.
Meena Alexander, *Nampally Road*, 1991
Mira returns to her native India to a post-colonial governed by a new dictator and corrupt police. Once lost in the poetry of Wordsworth, Mira struggles to define her new life.

1019

ANCHEE MIN

Katherine

(New York: Riverhead Books (G.P. Putnam's Sons), 1995)

Subject(s): Multicultural; Love; Survival
Age range(s): Adult
Major character(s): Katherine, Teacher (teaching English in China); Zebra, Student (Chinese woman in English class); Lion Head, Student (Zebra's young male classmate)
Time period(s): 1980s
Locale(s): China (various locations, including Shanghai and remote villages)

Summary: In post-Mao China, Katherine, a young American, teaches English to a group of Chinese workers. Her life becomes especially entwined with two of her students, Zebra and Lion Head, eventually resulting in a disastrous love triangle. But Zebra and Katherine's relationship survives, and eventually they prove to be each other's salvation.

Where it's reviewed:
Library Journal, March 15, 1995, page 98
New York Times Book Review, September 10, 1995, page 31
Publishers Weekly, March 13, 1995, page 58

Other books by the same author:
Red Azalea, 1994 (memoir)

Other books you might like:
Belle Yang, *Baba: A Return to China upon My Father's Shoulders*, 1994
After hearing the story of her father's coming-of-age as a son of the prominent Manchurian House of Yang, the author takes a personal odyssey through northern China of the 1930s and 1940s.
Diana Chang, *Frontiers of Love*, 1956
This story is about a group of idealistic friends in Japanese-occupied Shanghai in 1945. Each must find his or her own individual place in a society intolerant of its mixed-race citizens.
Lydia Yuri Minatoya, *Talking to High Monks in the Snow: An Asian American Odyssey*, 1992
Minatoya's personal odyssey, which she recounts here, begins in upstate New York in the 1950s and continues through Japan, China and Nepal.
Peter Bacho, *Cebu*, 1991
On his first visit to the Philippines to bury his mother, Filipino American priest, Ben Lucero, finds all his moral and religious beliefs thrown into question.
Amy Tan, *The Hundred Secret Senses*, 1995
A novel of two half-sisters, one Chinese-born, the other half-Chinese and half-American.

1020

ANCHEE MIN

Red Azalea

(New York: Berkley Books (Random House), 1994)

Subject(s): Autobiography; Political Prisoners; Survival
Age range(s): Adult
Major character(s): Anchee Min, Worker (resident of Mao's labor camp), Actress (demoted to studio worker); Yan Sheng, Worker (leader of remote Red Fire Farm), Lover (Min's lesbian lover at farm); The Supervisor, Filmmaker (chief of Shanghai Film Studio), Lover (Min's furtive lover at studio)
Time period(s): 20th century (1957-1984)
Locale(s): Shanghai, China (various locations including remote villages)

Summary: A personal memoir of Min's difficult young life in China during the brutal Cultural Revolution. From Shanghai to an intense labor camp to menial labor in a film studio—until she finally escapes to the U.S.—Min remains a true survivor in spite of nearly impossible odds.

About this book: The book's title refers to the film, *Red Azalea*, a government-sponsored propaganda production about Chairman Mao's wife. Min was one of three potential actresses chosen to train for the lead, but she was ultimately not cast. At the Shanghai Film Studio, Min became friends with actress Joan Chen (of *The Last Emperor* fame); Min publicly credits Chen with helping her finally escape Communist China.

Where it's reviewed:
Kirkus Reviews, December 1, 1993, page 1506

New Yorker, February 21, 1994, page 119
Publishers Weekly, December 20, 1993, page 57

Awards the book has won:
New York Times Notable Book, 1994

Other books by the same author:
Katherine, 1995

Other books you might like:
K. Connie Kang, *Home Was the Land of Morning Calm: The Saga of a Korean American Family*, 1995
    The saga of one Korean family, interwoven with the country's turbulent history, from 1900 to the present, from North Korea to Japan and finally to the U.S.
Paul Yee, *Tales from Gold Mountain: Stories of the Chinese in the New World*, 1989
    Illustrated by Simon Ng, this collection of eight tales is about Chinese immigrants in the New World.
Helie Lee, *Still Life with Rice: A Young American Woman Discovers the Life and Legacy of Her Korean Grandmother*, 1996
    The true story of a Korean woman who survives great hardship in Korea and finally arrives in the U.S., as told by her Korean American granddaughter.
Belle Yang, *Baba: A Return to China upon My Father's Shoulders*, 1994
    The author takes a personal odyssey through northern China of the 1930s and 1940s, following the story of her father's coming-of-age as a son of the prominent Manchurian House of Yang.
Diana Chang, *Frontiers of Love*, 1956
    This story is about a group of idealistic friends in Japanese-occupied Shanghai in 1945. They must each try and find his or her own individual place in a society intolerant of its mixed-race citizens.

1021

LYDIA YURI MINATOYA

Talking to High Monks in the Snow: An Asian American Odyssey
(New York: HarperPerennial (HarperCollins), 1992)

Subject(s): Multicultural; Identity; Coming of Age
Age range(s): Adult
Major character(s): Lydia Yuri Minatoya, Young Woman (in search of cultural identity), Japanese American (second-generation); Miyeko Minatoya, Mother (Lydia's), Immigrant (from Japan), Japanese
Time period(s): 1950s; 1990s
Locale(s): Albany, New York; Okinawa, Japan

Summary: Lydia Minatoya, a second-generation Japanese American, searches for her own answers to what it means to be Asian American. Her personal odyssey begins in upstate New York where the Minatoyas were the only Asian family in the '50s, and continues through Japan, China and Nepal, as her experiences become interwoven with the incredible tales of her Japanese ancestors.

About this book: A rare lyrical, haunting work filled with resonating images and evocative language. One of the most

beautifully written pieces of prose, astonishing for its power to effect.

Where it's reviewed:
Booklist, January 15, 1992, page 904
Kirkus Reviews, December 1, 1991, page 1517
Publishers Weekly, December 13, 1991, page 42
Village Voice, April 14, 1992, page 70

Awards the book has won:
PEN/Jerard Fund Award, 1991

Other books you might like:
Maria Hong, *Growing Up Asian American*, 1993
    These essays, excerpts and short stories by Americans of Asian descent address issues such as parent-child relationships, self-realization, identity and the discovery of one's cultural heritage.
Monica Sone, *Nisei Daughter*, 1953
    An account of a second-generation Japanese American woman growing up in Seattle in the 1920s and 30s, being incarcerated during World War II and her new life in the Midwest.
Ronald Takaki, *Strangers from a Different Shore*, 1989
    A groundbreaking history of Asian Americans in the U.S. during the last 150 years.
Garrett Hongo, *Under Western Eyes: Personal Essays from Asian America*, 1995
    A collection of 15 autobiographical essays from leading Asian American voices, confronting racism, language, family, stereotypes and other social and political issues.
Joanne Faung Jean Lee, *Asian Americans*, 1991
    A collection of oral histories from first- to fourth-generation Asian Americans of Chinese, Filipino, Japanese, Korean, Indian, Southeast Asian and Pacific Island ancestry.

1022

JANET MITSUI BROWN, Author/Illustrator

Thanksgiving at Obaachan's
(Chicago: Polychrome Publishing Corporation, 1994)

Subject(s): Multicultural; Family Life
Age range(s): Grades 1-3
Major character(s): Unnamed Character, Child (young Japanese American girl); Obaachan, Grandmother (the narrator's)
Time period(s): 1990s (1994)
Locale(s): United States

Summary: A young Japanese American girl loves to visit her grandmother's house for Thanksgiving, where the meal is a combination of traditional American and Japanese fare. Although the girl does not speak Japanese and her grandmother does not speak English, they still manage to communicate their great love for one another.

Where it's reviewed:
Publishers Weekly, May 30, 1994, page 55
School Library Journal, August 1994, page 126

Other books you might like:
Jama Kim Rattigan, *Dumpling Soup*, 1993
    Every year the Yang family gathers at Grandma'a house from all over Oahu, Hawaii to celebrate New Year's Eve.

This year, young Marisa will help Grandma make her famous dumpling soup.

Allen Say, *Grandfather's Journey*, 1993
A Japanese American man recounts his grandfather's journey from Japan to American and back again, trying to understand his grandfather's feelings of being torn between the love of both countries.

Kimiko Sakai, *Sachiko Means Happiness*, 1990
Sachiko is upset when her elderly grandmother does not even recognize her. When she finally comes to understand what has happened to her, she learns again how to be her friend.

Sook Nyul Choi, *Halmoni and the Picnic*, 1993
Yunmi's grandmother, newly arrived from Korea, finally begins to feel at home when she chaperones the annual Central Park class picnic for Yunmi and her classmates.

1023

KEN MOCHIZUKI
DOM LEE, Illustrator

Baseball Saved Us
(New York: Lee & Low Books Inc., 1993)

Story type: Young Readers
Subject(s): Multicultural; Racism; Children and War
Age range(s): Grades 1-6
Major character(s): "Shorty", Child, Japanese American (interned during WW II)
Time period(s): 1940s (1942-1945)
Locale(s): West

Summary: "Shorty," a young Japanese American boy, and his family are forcibly relocated to a concentration camp during World War II. There, in order to help the children survive the barbed-wire fences and armed guards, Shorty's father organizes a baseball league. Although small, "Shorty" proves to be a talented player.

About this book: During World War II, some 120,000 Americans of Japanese ancestry were imprisoned in concentration camps throughout the West because they were unjustly perceived to be a national security threat. In 1988, the U.S. government formally apologized, including monetary reparations for loss of property and basic human dignity. This story is based on actual experiences.

Where it's reviewed:
Horn Book Magazine, July 1993, page 453
Publishers Weekly, March 29, 1993, page 55
School Library Journal, June 1993, page 84

Other books by the same author:
Heroes, 1995

Other books you might like:
Asian American Coalition, *Children of Asian America*, 1995
This collection of original stories about growing up as an Asian American child centers around the diverse ethnic Asian communities of Chicago.

Marlene Shigekawa, *Blue Jay in the Desert*, 1993
Living in an American internment camp during WWII, Junior receives a special gift from his grandfather and must discover its significance for himself.

Chyng Feng Sun, *Square Beak*, 1993
Square Beak is aptly named. But because she looks different from the other chickens in the yard, she is ostracized and begins to wander outside her own small world.

1024

KEN MOCHIZUKI
DOM LEE, Illustrator

Heroes
(New York: Lee & Low Books Inc., 1995)

Subject(s): Multicultural; Racism; Hero
Age range(s): Grades 3 and Up
Major character(s): Donnie Okada, Child (young boy), Japanese American; Dad Okada, Father (Donnie's), Veteran (U.S. Army during World War II); Uncle Yoshi Okada, Uncle (Donnie's), Veteran (U.S. Army during Korean War)
Time period(s): 1960s
Locale(s): United States

Summary: Donnie's friends always force him to play the enemy, because as a Japanese American, he looks like "them." But Donnie's father served in World War II and his uncle was in Korea. His friends want him to prove it, but his father and uncle tell him, "real heroes don't brag."

Where it's reviewed:
Kirkus Reviews, March 15, 1995, page 389
Publishers Weekly, March 6, 1995, page 69
School Library Journal, July 1995, page 79

Awards the book has won:
Smithsonian Magazine Notable Books for Children, 1995
Editor's Choice, San Francisco Chronicle, 1996

Other books by the same author:
Baseball Saved Us, 1993

Other books you might like:
Marlene Shigekawa, *Blue Jay in the Desert*, 1993
Living in an American internment camp during World War II, Junior receives a special gift from his grandfather and must discover its significance for himself.

Min Paek, *Aekyung's Dream*, 1988
Aekyung, a young Korean girl recently in the U.S., dreams about King Sejong who created *Hangul*, the Korean alphabet, and finds new pride in her Korean heritage.

Michele Maria Surat, *Angel Child, Dragon Child*, 1983
Young Ut, a recent Vietnamese immigrant, is teased because of her different appearance. Thrown together by their school principal, Ut and a once cruel boy develop a new friendship.

Marie Villanueva, *Nene and the Horrible Math Monster*, 1993
Nene hates math although she's very good at it. When she must represent her class in a competition, she has nightmares of the horrible math monster.

Sandra S. Yamate, *Char Siu Bao Boy*, 1991
Charlie's favorite food, char sui bao, causes his classmates to make fun of him, until one day he brings in enough for all of them to taste.

1025
KYOKO MORI

One Bird
(New York: Henry Holt and Company, 1995)

Subject(s): Divorce; Mothers and Daughters; Friendship
Age range(s): Grades 7-12
Major character(s): Megumi Shimizu, 15-Year-Old (girl), Japanese; Chie Shimizu, Mother (Megumi's), Japanese; Dr. Kumiko Mizutani, Friend (Megumi's confidante and mentor), Veterinarian (interested in wild birds); Toru Uchida, Friend (Megumi's), Teenager; Kyoshi Kato, Friend (childhood, of Megumi's)
Time period(s): 1970s (1976)
Locale(s): Ashiya, Japan (small city near Kobe)

Summary: At 15, young Megumi is left behind to live with her cold father and difficult grandmother when her desperately unhappy mother suddenly leaves the family. With the help of a local veterinarian and an older childhood friend who has also lost his mother, Megumi learns to fight against tradition and establish her own independence.

About this book: In Japan, tradition dictates that children must remain with the father in the case of separation or divorce. Children are not allowed any contact, whether by mail, phone or in person, with the absent mother until they turn 22 years of age.

Where it's reviewed:
Booklist, October 15, 1995, page 396
Children's Book Review Service, October 1995, page 23
Center for Children's Books. Bulletin, January 1996, page 166
Kirkus Reviews, September 15, 1995, page 1355
Publishers Weekly, November 13, 1995, page 62

Other books by the same author:
The Dream of Water, 1995 (memoir)
Shizuko's Daughter, 1993 (young adult)

Other books you might like:
Allen Say, *The Ink-keeper's Apprentice*, 1994
    Determined to become an artist, Sei Koichi convinces famous cartoonist, Noro Shinpei, to take him on as apprentice.
Joy Kogawa, *Naomi's Road*, 1986
    Young adult story of a Japanese Canadian family that is splintered and scattered as a result of forced evacuation and relocation during World War II.
Laurence Yep, *Child of the Owl*, 1977
    Casey is sent to live in San Francisco's Chinatown with her maternal grandmother where she learns of her rich cultural heritage.
Laurence Yep, *Ribbons*, 1996
    To help her family bring her grandmother to the U.S. from Hong Kong, Robin must sacrifice her dance lessons. But ballet means everything to her.is her grandmother worth it?
Jean Davies Okimoto, *Molly by Any Other Name*, 1990
    At 17, adopted Molly begins to question who she is. Her parents help her find her birth mother and a whole new chapter of Molly's life begins.

1026
KYOKO MORI

Shizuko's Daughter
(New York: Fawcett Juniper (Random House), 1993)

Subject(s): Suicide; Mothers and Daughters; Family Relations
Age range(s): Grades 7-12
Major character(s): Yuki Okuda, Young Woman (dealing with mother's suicide), Japanese; Shizuko Matsumoto Okuda, Mother (Yuki's mother), Japanese; Aya Matsumoto, Aunt (Yuki's maternal aunt), Japanese; Hideki Okuda, Father (Yuki's aloof father), Japanese; Hanae Okuda, Stepmother (Yuki's selfish stepmother)
Time period(s): 1960s; 1970s (March 1969-May 1976)
Locale(s): Kobe, Japan

Summary: When her mother suddenly commits suicide, 12-year-old Yuki is left behind to try and piece her life back together. Living with an aloof father and an uncaring stepmother, Yuki must learn to rely on herself and create a new life of independence and quiet strength.

Where it's reviewed:
Belles Lettres, Summer 1994, page 40
Booklist, March 15, 1994, page 1359
Horn Book Guide, Fall 1993, page 311
Kliatt, September 1994, page 10
Publishers Weekly, November 1, 1993, page 49

Awards the book has won:
ALA Best Book for Young Adults, 1993
New York Times Notable Book, 1993

Other books by the same author:
The Dream of Water, 1995 (memoir)
One Bird, 1995 (young adult)

Other books you might like:
Allen Say, *The Ink-keeper's Apprentice*, 1994
    Determined to become an artist, Sei Koichi convinces famous cartoonist, Noro Shinpei, to take him on as an apprentice.
Joy Kogawa, *Naomi's Road*, 1986
    Young adult story of a Japanese Canadian family that is splintered and scattered as a result of forced evacuation and relocation during World War II.
Laurence Yep, *Child of the Owl*, 1977
    Casey is sent to live in San Francisco's Chinatown with her maternal grandmother where she learns of her rich cultural heritage.
Laurence Yep, *Ribbons*, 1996
    To help her family bring her grandmother to the U.S. from Hong Kong, Robin must sacrifice her dance lessons. But ballet means everything to her.is her grandmother worth it?
Jean Davies Okimoto, *Molly by Any Other Name*, 1990
    At 17, adopted Molly begins to question who she is. Her parents help her find her birth mother and whole new chapter of Molly's life begins.

Asian American Titles

1027

TOSHIO MORI

The Chauvinist and Other Stories

(Los Angeles: Asian American Studies Center, U. of California, 1979)

Subject(s): Multicultural; Emigration and Immigration; Short Stories
Age range(s): Adult
Time period(s): 1930s; 1950s
Locale(s): California

Summary: A collection of short stories about the Japanese American experience in California before and after World War II. From established immigrants to desperate American-born citizens, these stories capture a spirit of quiet survival.

Other books by the same author:
Yokohama, California, 1949
Woman from Hiroshima, 1978

Other books you might like:
Monica Sone, *Nisei Daughter*, 1953
 An account of a Japanese American woman growing up in Seattle in the 1920s and 30s, her incarceration during World War II and her new life in the Midwest.
Hisaye Yamamoto, *Seventeen Syllables and Other Stories*, 1988
 Collection of 15 short stories from Yamamoto's almost half-century-long writing career.
Frank Chin, *The Chinaman Pacific & Frisco R.R. Co.*, 1988
 A collection of eight stories about Chinese Americans struggling to establish their identities in a white world governed by unforgiving stereotypes.
Wakako Yamauchi, *Songs My Mother Taught Me: Stories, Plays, and Memoir*, 1994
 This rich collection, by one of the pioneer voices of Asian America, spans 35 years.
Sui Sin Far, *Mrs. Spring Fragrance and Other Writings*, 1994
 A collection of short stories, first published at the turn of the century, which represents the first fiction in English by an Asian American, as well as journalistic writings.

1028

TOSHIO MORI

Yokohama, California

(Seattle: University of Washington Press, 1949)

Subject(s): Multicultural; Emigration and Immigration; Short Stories
Age range(s): Adult
Time period(s): 1930s; 1940s (late 1930s to early 1940s)
Locale(s): Yokohama, California

Summary: A collection of short stories about the Japanese Americans who live on and around Seventh Street, in the fictional community of Yokohama, a small town somewhere in California. The stories capture the spirit of the town's residents, from immigrants to the American-born, living and surviving together in a foreign culture.

About this book: *Yokohama, California* is the first collection of short stories ever published by a Japanese American.

Tragically, only after Mori's death were his stories and writings ''discovered'' and taken seriously; he lived, wrote and died in virtual obscurity.

Where it's reviewed:
Kliatt, Winter 1986, page 30
Reprint Bulletin Book Reviews, Issue 1, 1987, page 15

Other books by the same author:
The Chauvinist and Other Stories, 1979
Woman from Hiroshima, 1978

Other books you might like:
Monica Sone, *Nisei Daughter*, 1953
 An account of a second-generation Japanese American woman growing up in Seattle in the 1920s and 30s, her incarceration during World War II and her new life in the Midwest
Hisaye Yamamoto, *Seventeen Syllables and Other Stories*, 1988
 A collection of 15 short stories from Yamamoto's almost half-century-long writing career.
Wakako Yamauchi, *Songs My Mother Taught Me: Stories, Plays, and Memoir*, 1994
 This rich collection by one of the pioneer voices of Asian America, spans over 35 years.
Sui Sin Far, *Mrs. Spring Fragrance and Other Writings*, 1994
 A collection of short stories, first published at the turn of the century, which represents the first fiction in English by an Asian American, as well as journalistic writings.
Frank Chin, *The Chinaman Pacific & Frisco R.R. Co.*, 1988
 A collection of eight stories about Chinese Americans struggling to establish their identities in a white world governed by unforgiving stereotypes.

1029

DHAN GOPAL MUKERJI
BORIS ARTZYBASHEFF, Illustrator

Gay-Neck: The Story of a Pigeon

(New York: E.P.Dutton & Co., Inc., 1927)

Subject(s): Discovery and Exploration; Animals; Adventure and Adventurers
Age range(s): Grades 6 and Up
Major character(s): Gay-Neck, Pigeon (protagonist's beloved); Unnamed Character, Narrator, Child (boy breeds homing pigeons), Indian; Radja, Friend, 16-Year-Old, Religious (Brahmin priest); Ghond, Teacher, Animal Trainer, Aged Person
Time period(s): 1920s (during World War I)
Locale(s): Calcutta, India

Summary: Gay-Neck, an especially talented pigeon, is the pride of his owner, a young Indian boy from Calcutta. The bird spends a summer in the Himalayan mountains, honing his skills and eventually proves to be a hero transporting secret messages during the final days of World War I.

Awards the book has won:
John Newbery Medal, 1927

Other books by the same author:
Kari the Elephant, 1922

Other books you might like:
Kyoko Mori, *One Bird*, 1995
> This is a coming of age young adult novel about Megumi Shimizu, left to live with her cold father and difficult grandmother when her unhappy mother suddenly leaves the family.

Laurence Yep, *Dragonwings*, 1975
> Based on actual events, this novel portrays a Chinese American aviator who built and flew a flying machine in 1909.

Laurence Yep, *Later, Gator*, 1995
> Teddy brings home a baby alligator for his younger brother Bobby's birthday. When Oscar the alligator disappears, havoc ensues.

1030

BHARATI MUKHERJEE

Jasmine
(New York: Grove Weidenfeld, 1989)

Subject(s): Multicultural; Emigration and Immigration; Identity
Age range(s): Adult
Time period(s): 1980s
Locale(s): United States (various locations); India (various locations)

Summary: Born Jyoti, meaning "light," in a small Indian village, she is renamed Jasmine by her husband. Suddenly widowed at 17, Jasmine escapes to America where she begins an odyssey through the country, eventually landing in Iowa where she becomes Mrs. Jane Ripplemeyer, assumed to be a pregnant banker's wife and the adoptive mother of a Vietnamese refugee.

Where it's reviewed:
Library Journal, July 1989, page 110
New Yorker, October 2, 1989, page 119
Publishers Weekly, January 18, 1991, page 55

Other books by the same author:
The Holder of the World, 1993
The Middleman and Other Stories, 1988 (award-winning collection)
Darkness, 1985
Wife, 1975
The Tiger's Daughter, 1971

Other books you might like:
Chitra Banerjee Divakaruni, *Arranged Marriage*, 1995
> A collection of 11 short stories about young Indian and Indian American women, some married, some single, in various stages of claiming their independence.

Marina Tamar Budhos, *House of Waiting*, 1995
> As Sarah awaits the return of her Indian-Caribbean husband Roland, embroiled in the political turmoil of his native Giuana, she creates a new life among his tight community of East Indian transplants.

Ameena Meer, *Bombay Talkie*, 1994
> Sabah heads to India in search of her ethnic identity. What she finds in the wealthy world of her Indian relatives is a liberal Westernized culture bound by strict traditions.

Kirin Narayan, *Love, Stars, and All That*, 1994
> This delightful novel follows Gita Das—from immigrant graduate student at Berkeley to esteemed professor—through her bumpy search for her ideal mate.

1031

BHARATI MUKHERJEE

The Middleman and Other Stories
(New York: Fawcett Crest (Ballentine/Random House), 1988)

Subject(s): Multicultural; Identity; Short Stories
Age range(s): Adult

Summary: An award-winning collection of stories about displaced, diverse Americans, from a troubled Vietnam vet to an Iraqi Jew from Queens to a wealthy immigrant Filipina.

Awards the book has won:
National Book Critics Circle Award Winner, 1988
New York Times Book Review Notable Book of the Year, 1988

Other books by the same author:
The Holder of the World, 1993
Jasmine, 1989
Darkness, 1985 (short story collection)
Wife, 1975
The Tiger's Daughter, 1971

Other books you might like:
Meena Alexander, *Nampally Road*, 1991
> Mira returns to her native India to a country governed by a new dictator and corrupt police. Once lost in the poetry of Wordsworth, Mira struggles to define her new life.

Marina Tamar Budhos, *House of Waiting*, 1995
> As Sarah awaits the return of her Indian-Caribbean husband Roland, embroiled in the political turmoil of his native Guiana, she creates a new life among his tight community of East Indian transplants.

Chitra Banerjee Divakaruni, *Arranged Marriage*, 1995
> A collection of 11 short stories about young Indian and Indian American women, some married, some single, in various stages of claiming their independence.

Ameena Meer, *Bombay Talkie*, 1994
> Sabah heads to India in search of her ethnic identity. What she finds in the wealthy world of her Indian relatives is a liberal Westernized culture bound by strict traditions.

Kirin Narayan, *Love, Stars, and All That*, 1994
> A delightful novel that follows Gita Das—from immigrant graduate student at Berkeley to esteemed professor—through her bumpy search for her ideal mate.

1032

BHARATI MUKHERJEE

Wife
(New York: Fawcett Crest (Ballentine/Random House), 1975)

Subject(s): Multicultural; Emigration and Immigration; Identity
Age range(s): Adult

Major character(s): Dimple Dasgupta Basu, Young Woman, Immigrant, Indian (immigrates to the U.S.); Amit Basu, Husband (Dimple's), Engineer; Ina Mullick, Friend (Dimple's confidante), Immigrant (very Westernized), Indian; Milt Glasser, Friend (Ina's friend)

Time period(s): 1970s

Locale(s): Bombay, India; New York, New York (Brooklyn and Manhattan)

Summary: Young, naive Dimple Dasgupta marries an engineer bound for the U.S. and embarks on a new American adventure. But her expectations — of being married, of being a dutiful wife, of living a glamorous new life in the U.S. — are far from reality.

Other books by the same author:
The Holder of the World, 1993
Jasmine, 1989
The Middleman and Other Stories, 1988 (award-winning collection)
Darkness, 1985 (short story collection)
The Tiger's Daughter, 1971

Other books you might like:
Marina Tamar Budhos, *House of Waiting*, 1995
  As Sarah awaits the return of her Indian-Caribbean husband Roland, embroiled in the political turmoil of his native Guiana, she creates a new life among his tight community of East Indian transplants.
Chitra Banerjee Divakaruni, *Arranged Marriage*, 1995
  A collection of 11 short stories about young Indian and Indian American women, some married, some single, in various stages of claiming their independence.
Gish Jen, *Typical American*, 1991
  A novel of the Chang family, newly arrived from China, and their often humorous new life in the New World.
Louis Chu, *Eat a Bowl of Tea*, 1961
  The story of American-born Ben Loy and his Chinese-born wife, Mei Oi in which their blissful marriage was marred by infidelity but later reclaimed with a new bond and a happily-after ending.

1033

MILTON MURAYAMA

All I Asking for Is My Body

(Honolulu: University of Hawaii Press, 1959)

Subject(s): Multicultural; Coming of Age
Age range(s): Adult
Major character(s): Kiyoshi Oyama, Son (second son); Toshio Oyama, Son (Kiyoshi's older brother); Father Oyama, Father, Fisherman
Time period(s): 1930s; 1940s
Locale(s): Hawaii (plantation camps)

Summary: An often comic, yet poignant work about the coming of age of young Kiyoshi, living in the Japanese plantation camps of Hawaii during the 1930s and 1940s. While he is expected to be a filial son and help pay off a $6,000 family debt, Kiyoshi cannot help admire his older, outspoken, less dutiful brother.

About this book: Originally published by Supa Press. The title comes from first son Toshio's constant complaint: "All I asking for is my body"—all I ask is that I am finally freed from my impossible filial duties to live my own life. In addition to the book's important historical context (Hawaiian plantation life, Pearl Harbor, etc.), it also focuses on the importance of language among second-generation Asian Americans living in Hawaii. As Kiyoshi remarks, American-born children in Hawaii interchangeably spoke four languages: "good English in school, pidgin English the native Hawaiian pidgin among themselves, good or pidgin Japanese to our parents and the other old folks."

Where it's reviewed:
Nation, September 21, 1992, page 293

Other books you might like:
Gus Lee, *China Boy*, 1991
  A coming-of-age novel about Kai Ting, the American-born son of an aristocratic Chinese family who fled China for California to escape the Cultural Revolution.
Kathleen Tyau, *A Little Too Much Is Enough*, 1995
  Mahi Wong grows up in post-World War II Hawaii surrounded by her large family, immersed in a complex, mixed-up culture of Hawaiian and Chinese influences.
Lois-Ann Yamanaka, *Wild Meat and the Bully Burgers*, 1996
  This coming-of-age first novel is about Lovey Nariyoshi of Hilo, Hawaii, her best friend Jerome, her adolescent enemies and her eccentric family.
Darrell H.Y. Lum, *Pass On, No Pass Back!*, 1990
  A humorous collection of short stories about growing up in Hawaii.
Norman Wong, *Cultural Revolution*, 1994
  These interrelated stories begin in 1953 in Macao where Wei lives with his overprotective grandmother and ineffectual father. It continues with his emigration to Honolulu and the life he builds there.

1034

LENSEY NAMIOKA

April and the Dragon Lady

(San Diego: Browndeer Press (Harcourt Brace & Company), 1994)

Subject(s): Multicultural; Family Relations; Coming of Age
Age range(s): Grades 8-12
Major character(s): April Chen, Student—High School, Chinese American; Grandma Chen, Grandmother (April's grandmother), Chinese American; Gilbert Chen, Father (April's father), Son (Grandma's eldest), Chinese American; Harry Chen, Brother (April's older brother), Chinese American; Steve Daniels, Boyfriend (April's boyfriend)
Time period(s): 1990s (1994)
Locale(s): Seattle, Washington

Summary: As the only daughter in a traditional Chinese American household, 16-year-old April Chen feels responsible for her grandmother, a strong, manipulative woman. But April will soon be leaving for college, and as she struggles to establish her independence, she must make the other family members aware of their own responsibilities.

Where it's reviewed:
Booklist, March 1, 1994, page 1253
Children's Book Review Service, July 1994, page 155
Kirkus Reviews, June 1, 1994, page 778
Publishers Weekly, April 4, 1994, page 81
School Library Journal, April 1994, page 152

Other books by the same author:
Yang the Third and Her Impossible Family, 1995
Yang the Youngest and His Terrible Ear, 1992
The Coming of the Bear, 1992 (young adult)
Island of Ogres, 1989 (young adult)

Other books you might like:
Lauren Lee, *Stella: On the Edge of Popularity*, 1994
    Stella must learn who her true friends are, as she defines
    her own unique place among her classmates at school, and
    as a second-generation Korean American in the outside
    world.
Laurence Yep, *Ribbons*, 1996
    To help her family bring her grandmother to the U.S. from
    Hong Kong, Robin must sacrifice her dance lessons. But
    ballet means everything to her.so is her grandmother worth
    it?
Laurence Yep, *Child of the Owl*, 1977
    Casey is sent to live in San Francisco's Chinatown with her
    maternal grandmother where she learns of her rich cultural
    heritage.
Marie G. Lee, *Finding My Voice*, 1992
    A senior in high school, Ellen struggles to find her voice
    and speak out for what she wants and believes in, espe-
    cially as she faces the racism in her tiny hometown.
Marie G. Lee, *Saying Goodbye*, 1994
    Ellen has left her small hometown for Harvard where she
    comes face-to-face with the reality of racial boundaries
    and racial tensions and must define her position as a
    Korean American.

1035

LENSEY NAMIOKA
KEES DE KIEFTE, Illustrator

Yang the Third and Her Impossible Family

(Boston: Little, Brown and Company, 1995)

Subject(s): Multicultural; Family Relations; Friendship
Age range(s): Grades 4-8
Major character(s): Yingmei ''Mary'' Yang, Student (third
child of Yang family), Chinese American; Yingtao ''Yang
the Youngest'' Yang, Brother (Mary's youngest brother),
Chinese American; Holly Hanson, Student (Mary's popu-
lar schoolmate); Kim O'Meara, Friend (Mary's eventual
friend), Student (Mary's classmate)
Time period(s): 1990s (1995)
Locale(s): Seattle, Washington

Summary: Yingmei Yang wants to ''be American.'' She's
changed her name to Mary, keeps a notebook of American
slang and tries her best to make friends at school. But she
realizes that fitting in means she must first learn to accept her
own family just as they are, even with their traditional Chinese ways.

About this book: Sequel to *Yang the Youngest and His Terrible Ear*

Where it's reviewed:
Booklist, April 15, 1995, page 1500
Horn Book Magazine, May 1995, page 350
School Library Journal, August 1995, page 144
Quill & Quire, April 1995, page 43

Other books by the same author:
April and the Dragon Lady, 1994
Yang the Youngest and His Terrible Ear, 1992
The Coming of the Bear, 1992 (young adult)
Island of Ogres, 1989 (young adult)

Other books you might like:
Lauren Lee, *Stella: On the Edge of Popularity*, 1994
    Stella must learn who her true friends are as she defines her
    own unique place among her classmates at school, and as a
    second-generation Korean American in the outside world.
Bette Bao Lord, *In the Year of the Boar and Jackie Robinson*,
1984
    Shirley Temple Wong, with her new American name, ar-
    rives in Brooklyn. Through new friends and the discovery
    of baseball, Shirley finds her own special niche in her new
    home.
Marie G. Lee, *If It Hadn't Been for Yoon Jun*, 1993
    Alice Larsen learns about her own Korean heritage from a
    recent immigrant student.
Marie G. Lee, *Finding My Voice*, 1992
    A senior in high school, Ellen struggles to find her voice
    and speak out for what she wants and believes in, espe-
    cially as she faces the racism in her tiny hometown.
Laurence Yep, *Ribbons*, 1996
    To help her family bring her grandmother to the U.S. from
    Hong Kong, Robin must sacrifice her dance lessons. But
    ballet means everything to her.is her grandmother worth
    it?

1036

LENSEY NAMIOKA
KEES DE KIEFTE, Illustrator

Yang the Youngest and His Terrible Ear

(Boston: Little, Brown and Company, 1992)

Subject(s): Multicultural; Family Relations; Music
Age range(s): Grades 4-8
Major character(s): Yingtao ''Yang the Youngest'' Yang,
Immigrant, Chinese American; Matthew Conner, Friend
(Yingtao's best friend), Chinese American; Yang the Eldest, Brother (oldest of Yang children), Musician (violin
player), Chinese American; Yang the Second Oldest, Sister (second oldest of Yang children), Musician (viola
player), Chinese American; Mary ''Yang the Third Eldest'' Yang, Sister (third child of Yang family), Musician
(cello player)
Time period(s): 1990s (1992)
Locale(s): Seattle, Washington

Summary: Nine-year-old Yingtao Yang has just moved with
his family from China to Seattle. As he adjusts to his new
American life—making friends and discovering baseball—

he struggles daily with his hated violin as the only untalented member in a family of gifted musicians.

Where it's reviewed:
Booklist, June 1, 1992, page 1762
Horn Book Magazine, July 1992, page 452
Kirkus Reviews, June 1, 1992, page 722
Publishers Weekly, May 18, 1992, page 70
School Library Journal, July 1992, page 74

Other books by the same author:
Yang the Third and Her Impossible Family, 1995
April and the Dragon Lady, 1994
The Coming of the Bear, 1992 (young adult)
Island of Ogres, 1989 (young adult)

Other books you might like:
Bette Bao Lord, *In the Year of the Boar and Jackie Robinson*, 1984
Shirley Temple Wong, with her new American name, arrives in Brooklyn. Through new friends and the discovery of baseball, Shirley finds her own special niche in her new home.
Marie G. Lee, *If It Hadn't Been for Yoon Jun*, 1993
Alice Larsen learns about her own Korean heritage from a recent immigrant student.
Laurence Yep, *Later, Gator*, 1995
When Teddy's mother insists he get a special birthday present for his ''perfect'' younger brother, Teddy comes home with a baby alligator.
Laurence Yep, *Ribbons*, 1996
To help her family bring her grandmother to the U.S. from Hong Kong, Robin must sacrifice her dance lessons. But ballet means everything to her.is her grandmother worth it?

1037

KIRIN NARAYAN

Love, Stars, and All That

(New York: Washington Square Press (Pocket Books), 1994)

Subject(s): Love; Multicultural; Personal Odyssey
Age range(s): Adult
Major character(s): Gita Das, Student—College (grad student, UC-Berkeley), Immigrant (from India); Saroj ''Aunty'' Shah, Aunt (Gita's); Professor Norvin Weinstein, Professor (at Berkeley); Timothy Schilling, Writer (renowned post-Beat poet); Firoze Ganifrockwala, Student—College (Indian grad student, Berkeley)
Time period(s): 1980s; 1990s
Locale(s): Berkeley, California (on and around the University of California, Berkeley campus); Whitney, Vermont (small, liberal-arts college town); India (mainly in Bombay and Delhi)

Summary: A delightful novel that follows immigrant graduate student Gita through her bumpy search for her ideal mate. In Chaitra 2040—that is, March 1984—Gita's beloved Aunty's numerologist has prophesied that Gita will meet *him*. But details are slim and not until years later does Gita realize who her Prince Charming truly is.

Where it's reviewed:
Kliatt, March 1995, page 10
New York Times Book Review, December 25, 1994, page 20
Publishers Weekly, December 12, 1994, page 60

Other books by the same author:
Storytellers, Saints and Scoundrels: Folk Narrative in Hindu Religious Teaching, 1990 (award-winning nonfiction)

Other books you might like:
Ameena Meer, *Bombay Talkie*, 1994
Sabah heads to India in search of her ethnic identity. What she finds in the wealthy world of her Indian relatives is a liberal Westernized culture bound by strict traditions.
Chitra Banerjee Divakaruni, *Arranged Marriage*, 1995
A collection of 11 short stories about young Indian and Indian American women, some married, some single, in various stages of claiming their independence.
Bharati Mukherjee, *Jasmine*, 1989
A novel about Jasmine Vijh's odyssey through America, from her arrival from India as a 17-year-old widow to her new life as Jane Ripplemeyer.
Bharati Mukherjee, *Wife*, 1975
Dimple Dasgupta marries an engineer bound for the U.S. but her expectations of being a dutiful wife and living glamorously in America, fall far short of reality.
Marina Tamar Budhos, *House of Waiting*, 1995
As Sarah awaits the return of her Indian-Caribbean husband Roland, himself embroiled in the political turmoil of his native Guiana, she creates a new life among his tight community of East Indians.

1038

VICTOR G. NEE
BRETT DE BARY NEE, Co-Author

Longtime Californ': A Documentary Study of an American Chinatown

(Boston: Houghton Mifflin, 1972)

Subject(s): Multicultural; Emigration and Immigration; Historical
Age range(s): Adult
Time period(s): 1840s; 1970s
Locale(s): San Francisco, California (Chinatown section of San Francisco)

Summary: An Asian American historical classic, focusing on the Chinese in America—from the first Gold Mountain settlers to contemporary activists and shop owners—told through both personal narratives and extensive interviews, using the backdrop of San Francisco's Chinatown.

About this book: One of the first works to deal exclusively, and extensively, with the history of Chinese Americans in the U.S., a group long denied a voice, especially in Eurocentric textbooks and history lessons.

Where it's reviewed:
Kirkus Reviews, May 15, 1993, page 589
New Yorker, September 10, 1993, page 134
Publishers Weekly, January 30, 1981, page 74

Other books you might like:

Garrett Hongo, *Under Western Eyes: Personal Essays from Asian America*, 1995

A collection of 15 autobiographical essays from leading Asian American voices, confronting racism, language, family, stereotypes and other social and political issues.

Joanne Faung Jean Lee, *Asian Americans*, 1991

A collection of oral histories from Asian Americans of Chinese, Filipino, Japanese, Korean, Indian, Southeast Asian and Pacific Island ancestry.

Ruthanne Lum McCunn, *Chinese American Portraits: Personal Histories 1828-1988*, 1988

Profiles of prominent Chinese Americans, from pioneers to politicians.

Ruthanne Lum McCunn, *An Illustrated History of the Chinese in America*, 1979

An illustrated history book which traces the Chinese in America, from their arrival during the California Gold Rush, to contemporary Chinese Americans.

Judy Yung, *Unbound Feet: A Social History of Chinese Women in San Francisco*, 1995

Yung traces the history of Chinese American women who arrived in America at the turn of the century as the property of their husbands or as slaves, yet became active members of American society.

1039

FAE MYENNE NG

Bone

(New York: Hyperion, 1993)

Subject(s): Multicultural; Family Relations; Suicide
Age range(s): Adult
Major character(s): Leila Fu Louie, Daughter (eldest of three), Teacher (liaison for teachers/parents), Chinese American (bilingual); ''Mah'' Leong, Mother (Leila's mother), Businesswoman (owner of herb shop), Chinese American; Mason Louie, Husband (Leila's husband), Mechanic (foreign car mechanic), Chinese American; Leon Leong, Father (Leila's stepfather), Chinese American; Nina Leong, Daughter (youngest of three), Flight Attendant (New-York based), Chinese American
Time period(s): 1990s
Locale(s): San Francisco, California

Summary: Middle daughter Ona unexpectedly commits suicide, leaving the other Leong family members to try and figure out why. The suicide acts as a pivotal point from which two very different Chinese American generations of parents and children and husbands and wives must reexamine and redefine their relationships with one another.

Where it's reviewed:
Amerasia Journal, No. 1, 1994, page 184
Kliatt, March 1994, page 10
Publishers Weekly, December 20, 1993, page 65
Tribune Books (Chicago), February 13, 1994, page 8
New England Review, Winter 1994, page 169

Other books you might like:

Gish Jen, *Typical American*, 1991

The Chang family arrives in the U.S. from China in search

of education and safety. What they find is fried chicken fast food joints, glamour magazines, suburbia and con artists.

R.A. Sasaki, *The Loom and Other Stories*, 1991

This collection of short stories weaves together the stories of three generations of a Japanese American family.

Julie Shigekuni, *A Bridge Between Us*, 1995

Four generations of women—each a mother and a daughter—of a San Francisco, Japanese American, family trace their lives from 1900 to the present.

Amy Tan, *The Joy Luck Club*, 1989

This novel unravels the timeless relationships of four Chinese-born mothers and their American-born daughters.

Amy Tan, *The Kitchen God's Wife*, 1991

Winnie realizes she must finally share the hidden secrets of her past with her American-born daughter, a past that spans over 50 years and two continents.

1040

SUSAN NUNES

A Small Obligation and Other Stories of Hilo

(Honolulu: Bamboo Ridge Press, 1982)

Subject(s): Multicultural; Family Life; Short Stories
Age range(s): Adult
Major character(s): Amy Freitas, Daughter (Japanese and Portuguese)
Time period(s): 1940s; 1980s
Locale(s): Hilo, Hawaii

Summary: A collection of interrelated stories about young Amy Freitas and her extended family which is Japanese on her mother's side and Portuguese on her father's side, as well as some of the other residents of her Hawaiian hometown, Hilo.

Other books you might like:

Kathleen Tyau, *A Little Too Much Is Enough*, 1995

Mahi Wong grows up in post-World War II Hawaii surrounded by her large family, immersed in a complex, mixed-up culture of Chinese and Hawaiian influences.

Marie Hara, *Bananaheart and Other Stories*, 1994

These stories cover a century of life in Hawaii, with tales of a picture bride, a woman working in a foreign house, a hapa girl searching for identity and an old woman who lost an infant daughter.

Jessica K. Saiki, *From the Lanai and Other Hawaii Stories*, 1991

A collection of stories about the Japanese American residents of Lunalilo, Hawaii, including a lonely spinster, a deserted husband and a young woman desperate for stardom.

Jessica K. Saiki, *Once, a Lotus Garden and Other Stories*, 1987

A first collection of stories, mostly set in wartime Hawaii, about the residents of Lunalilo, including new picture brides from Japan and young schoolgirls and their dreams.

Lois-Ann Yamanaka, *Wild Meat and the Bully Burgers*, 1996

A coming-of-age first novel about Lovey Nariyoshi of

Hilo, Hawaii, her best friend Jerome, her adolescent enemies and her eccentric family.

1041
SIGRID NUNEZ

A Feather on the Breath of God
(New York: HarperCollins Publishers, Inc., 1995)

Subject(s): Multicultural; Coming of Age; Identity
Age range(s): Adult
Major character(s): Young Woman, Young Woman (narrator), Chinese Panamanian German; Carlos Cipriano Chang, Father (of narrator), Chinese Panamanian; Christa Cipriano, Mother (of narrator), German
Time period(s): 1950s; 1990s
Locale(s): New York, New York

Summary: A young woman, the child of a Chinese Panamanian father and a German mother, grows up in a New York housing project trying to make sense of her identity. She survives her adolescence by immersing herself in ballet, escapes to college, and as an adult, teaches English to immigrants, eventually becoming involved with a Russian student.

Where it's reviewed:
New York Times Book Review, January 14, 1995, page 28
Booklist, December 15, 1994, page 738
Kirkus Reviews, October 15, 1994, page 1367
Publishers Weekly, November 14, 1994, page 51
Los Angeles Times Book Review, February 12, 1995, page 1

Other books you might like:
Chang-rae Lee, *Native Speaker*, 1995
   A first novel about Korean American Henry Park who is trying to come to terms with both his troubled personal life and his problematic career as a spy.
Aimee Liu, *Face*, 1994
   After years of running away, Maibelle Chung returns to her Chinatown roots, finally ready to start facing the dark secrets of her incongruous, inescapable past.
Bharati Mukherjee, *Jasmine*, 1989
   A novel about Jasmine Vijh's odyssey through America, from her arrival from India as a 17-year-old widow to her new life as Jane Ripplemeyer, assumed to be an Iowa housewife.
Marina Tamar Budhos, *House of Waiting*, 1995
   As Sarah awaits the return of her Indian-Caribbean husband Roland, embroiled in the political turmoil of his native Guiana, she creates a new life among his tight community of East Indian transplants.
Ameena Meer, *Bombay Talkie*, 1994
   Sabah heads to India in search of her ethnic identity. What she finds in the wealthy world of her Indian relatives is a liberal Westernized culture bound by strict traditions.

1042
JOHN OKADA

No-No Boy
(Seattle: University of Washington Press, 1957)

Subject(s): Internment; Multicultural; Identity
Age range(s): Adult
Major character(s): Ichiro Yamada, Political Prisoner (''no-no boy'' who is imprisoned), Son, Japanese American (second-generation); Mama Yamada, Mother (Ichiro's pro-Japanese), Businesswoman (grocery store owner); Pa Yamada, Father (Ichiro's), Businessman (grocery store owner); Kenji Kanno, Veteran (served in World War II), Friend (Ichiro's), Japanese American
Time period(s): 1940s (just after World War II)
Locale(s): Seattle, Washington

Summary: Ichiro Yamada, a second-generation Japanese American, returns to his home city of Seattle after spending two years in a concentration camp and another two years in jail. He returns home a pariah, for having refused to serve in World War II. He struggles for acceptance, especially from his own self.

About this book: Originally published by Charles E. Tuttle Publishing. During World War II, some 200,000 Americans of Japanese ancestry were imprisoned in concentration camps. The term ''No-No Boy'' refers to the Japanese American young men who, when given the loyalty questionnaire in camp, refused to swear absolute allegiance to the U.S. and refused to serve in the U.S. military. Already having been stripped of their basic civil rights and imprisoned without due process behind barbed wire, a small percentage of Japanese Americans could no longer place their faith in a government that had treated them so wrongly. Of these ''No-No Boys,'' some were eventually deported to Japan (even though most of them had never been there), while others were sent to maximum security camp facilities (such as the barren and isolated Tule Lake camp) or jailed for several years. Although Okada writes with fluency about the ''No-No Boy'' experience, he was not one himself; he served in the U.S. Army during the war.

Where it's reviewed:
Change, November 1989, page 66

Other books you might like:
Joy Kogawa, *Obasan*, 1982
   The story of a Japanese Canadian family that is splintered and scattered as a result of forced evacuation and relocation during World War II.
Monica Sone, *Nisei Daughter*, 1953
   An account of a second-generation Japanese American woman growing up in Seattle in the 1920s and 1930s, being incarcerated during World War II and her new life in the Midwest.
Hisaye Yamamoto, *Seventeen Syllables and Other Stories*, 1988
   A collection of 15 short stories from Yamamoto's almost half-century-long writing career, about the Japanese American experience, including the internment.

Lawson Fusao Inada, *Legends from Camp*, 1992
> As a child, Inada was interned during World War II with his parents. In spite of the grim realities of his imprisonment, Inada's memories are mixed with strains of be-bop and jazz.

Shawn Wong, *Homebase*, 1991
> Chinese American Rainsford Chan, orphaned at age 14, recounts the 125 years of his family's history in the U.S.

1043

JEAN DAVIES OKIMOTO

Molly by Any Other Name
(New York: Scholastic Inc., 1990)

Subject(s): Multicultural; Identity; Adoption
Age range(s): Grades 7-12
Major character(s): Molly Jane Fletcher, Adoptee, Asian, 17-Year-Old (high school student); Roland Hirada, Friend (Molly's best); Ellie Fletcher, Mother (Molly's), Doctor (pediatrician); Paul Fletcher, Father (Molly's), Scientist (research head); Karen Kumai Matsuda, Mother (Molly's birth mother), Artist (painter)
Time period(s): 1990s
Locale(s): Seattle, Washington

Summary: At 17, Molly begins to question who she is. Lovingly raised, she's always known she was adopted. But now she wants to know where she came from. Although at first reluctant, her parents help her finally find her birth mother, and a whole new chapter of Molly's life begins.

Where it's reviewed:
School Library Journal, March 1992, page 164
Journal of Reading, March 1992, page 509
Booklist, January 15, 1991, page 1053
Kirkus Reviews, November 15, 1990, page 1604
School Library Journal, December 1990, page 122

Awards the book has won:
IRA/CBC Young Adults' Choice

Other books by the same author:
Talent Night, 1995

Other books you might like:
Lauren Lee, *Stella: On the Edge of Popularity*, 1994
> Stella must learn who her true friends are, as she defines her own unique place among her classmates at school, and as a second-generation Korean American in the outside world.

Marie G. Lee, *If It Hadn't Been for Yoon Jun*, 1993
> Although Alice Larsen's face may be Korean, she's all-American, having been adopted at birth. She reluctantly befriends Yoon Jun, the new student from Korea, who helps her discover her own heritage.

Marie G. Lee, *Finding My Voice*, 1992
> A senior in high school, Ellen struggles to find her voice and speak out for what she wants and what she believes in, especially as she faces the racism in her tiny hometown.

Lensey Namioka, *April and the Dragon Lady*, 1994
> The only daughter of a traditional Chinese American household, April feels responsible for her grandmother,

but, leaving for college soon, she must make her family aware of their responsibilities.

Laurence Yep, *Child of the Owl*, 1977
> Casey is sent to live in San Francisco's Chinatown with her maternal grandmother where she learns of her rich cultural heritage.

1044

MINE OKUBO, Author/Illustrator

Citizen 13660
(Seattle: University of Washington Press, 1946)

Subject(s): Internment; Autobiography
Age range(s): Grades 8-Adult
Major character(s): Mine Okubo, Artist, Japanese American; Brother, Brother (younger brother of Mine)
Time period(s): 1940s
Locale(s): California; Camp Topaz, Utah (internment camp for Americans of Japanese ancestry during World War II)

Summary: The autobiographical account, told through sketches and text, of a second generation Japanese American woman, who was reduced to Citizen Number 13660 and incarcerated during World War II, first at the Tanforan Assembly Center in San Bruno, California and later at Camp Topaz in Utah.

About this book: The first personal account of the Japanese American internment experience ever published.

Other books you might like:
Jeanne Wakatsuki Houston, *Farewell to Manzanar*, 1973
> The true story of the Wakatuski family, uprooted from their home and incarcerated at Manzanar, one of 10 U.S. concentration camps for Japanese Americans during World War II.

Joy Kogawa, *Obasan*, 1982
> The story of a Japanese Canadian family that is splintered and scattered as a result of forced evacuation and relocation during World War II.

Lawson Fusao Inada, *Legends from Camp*, 1992
> As a child, Inada was interned during World War II with his parents. In spite of the grim realities of his imprisonment, Inada's memories are mixed with strains of be-bop and jazz.

Monica Sone, *Nisei Daughter*, 1953
> An account of a second-generation Japanese American woman being incarcerated during World War II and her new life in the Midwest.

Hisaye Yamamoto, *Seventeen Syllables and Other Stories*, 1988
> A collection of 15 short stories from Yamamoto's almost half-century-long writing career.

1045

MIN PAEK, Author/Illustrator

Aekyung's Dream

(San Francisco: Children's Book Press, 1988)

Subject(s): Emigration and Immigration; Prejudice; Multicultural

Age range(s): Grades 1-6

Major character(s): Aekyung, Immigrant (young schoolgirl), Korean American

Time period(s): 1980s (1988)

Locale(s): United States

Summary: Aekyung, a young Korean girl recently arrived in the U.S., is teased at school for her different features and has not yet made friends. Inspired by a dream about King Sejong who created *Hangul*, the Korean alphabet, Aekyung learns English and begins to adjust to her new life.

About this book: A bilingual book, written in both English and Korean.

Where it's reviewed:

Bookwatch, January 1989, page 7

Kirkus Reviews, December 15, 1988, page 1814

Library Talk, May 1989, page 30

Reading Teacher, April 1990, page 588

School Library Journal, May 1989, page 91

Other books you might like:

Sandra S. Yamate, *Char Siu Bao Boy*, 1991
Charlie's favorite food, *char sui bao*, causes his classmates to make fun of him until one day he brings enough for all of them to taste.

Sandra S. Yamate, *Ashok by Any Other Name*, 1992
Ashok, a young Indian American boy, wishes he had a more ''American'' name, so he tries a new name each day, finally realizing that ''Ashok'' is the perfect name for him.

Michele Maria Surat, *Angel Child, Dragon Child*, 1983
Young Ut, a recent Vietnamese immigrant, is teased because of her different appearance. Thrown together by the school principal, Ut and a once cruel boy develop a new friendship.

Marie Villanueva, *Nene and the Horrible Math Monster*, 1993
Nene hates math although she is very good at it. When she is chosen to represent her class at a competition, she has nightmares of the horrible math monster.

Heidi Chang, *Elaine and the Flying Frog*, 1991
Lonely in her new school after moving to a small town in Iowa, Chinese American Elaine Chow finds friendship as she and a girl with a consuming interest in frogs work on a science project together.

1046

LOWRY PEI

Family Resemblances

(New York: Vintage Contemporaries, 1986)

Subject(s): Coming of Age; Family Life; Love

Age range(s): Grades 6 and Up

Major character(s): Karen, Teenager, 15-Year-Old; Aunt Augusta, Aunt (Karen's eccentric aunt), Teacher (English teacher); George Short, Friend (Karen's summertime romance)

Time period(s): 1980s

Locale(s): New Franklin, Illinois

Summary: Hoping she will get over her latest romance, Karen's parents send her to spend her 15th summer with her unusual, eccentric Aunt Augusta. There in her new environment, Karen makes new friends, finds a new love and learns about growing up from a very independent woman who makes her own rules.

Where it's reviewed:

Kirkus Reviews, February 1, 1986, page 162

Library Journal, April 15, 1986, page 96

Publishers Weekly, February 21, 1986, page 154

Other books you might like:

Willyce Kim, *Dancer Dawkins and the California Kid*, 1985
Dancer and Little Willy Gutherie (a.k.a. The California Kid) collide in San Francisco and set off on a series of unpredictable adventures.

Lois-Ann Yamanaka, *Wild Meat and the Bully Burgers*, 1996
This coming-of-age novel is about Lovey Nariyoshi of Hilo, Hawaii, her best friend Jerome, her adolescent enemies and her eccentric family.

Cynthia Kadohata, *The Floating World*, 1989
A coming-of-age novel about 12-year-old Olivia who, with her family, moves continuously throughout the Pacific Northwest in search of a better life.

Sigrid Nunez, *A Feather on the Breath of God*, 1995
A young woman, the child of a Chinese Panamanian father and a German mother, grows up in a New York housing project trying to make sense of her identity.

1047

WANG PING

American Visa

(Minneapolis: Coffee House Press, 1994)

Subject(s): Short Stories; Emigration and Immigration; Family Relations

Age range(s): Adult

Major character(s): Seaweed, Daughter (oldest of four children), Immigrant (arrives in U.S.); Mother, Mother (Seaweed's); Waipo, Grandmother (Seaweed's, maternal)

Time period(s): 1950s; 1980s

Locale(s): China (various locations including Shanghai, Beijing and remote villages); New York, New York

Summary: Eleven interrelated short stories about Seaweed, a determined young woman in China during the Cultural Revolution in search of higher education. She endures ''reeducation'' at a remote village, gets herself into college and eventually emigrates to the U.S., becoming the sole source of hope for new life for the family she leaves behind.

Other books by the same author:

The Kaya Anthology of New Chinese Poetry, 1996 (edited by Ping)

Other books you might like:

Gish Jen, *Typical American*, 1991

The Changs arrive in the U.S. from China in search of education and safety. What they find is fried chicken fast food joints, glamour magazines, suburbia and con artists.

Anchee Min, *Katherine*, 1995

A novel about the relationship between an American woman and two Chinese students in post-Mao China.

Anchee Min, *Red Azalea*, 1994

The personal memoir of Min's difficult life in China during the Cultural Revolution and her struggle to escape the brutality of her homeland.

Belle Yang, *Baba: A Return to China upon My Father's Shoulders*, 1994

After hearing the story of her father's coming-of-age as a son of the prominent Manchurian House of Yang, the author takes a personal odyssey through northern China of the '30s and '40s.

1048

JAMA KIM RATTIGAN
LILLIAN HSU-FLANDERS, Illustrator

Dumpling Soup

(Boston: Little, Brown and Company, 1993)

Subject(s): Multicultural; Family Life; Holidays
Age range(s): Grades 2-6
Major character(s): Marisa Yang, 7-Year-Old (girl), Hawaiian; Grandma Yang, Grandmother (known for delicious dumplings)
Time period(s): 1990s (New Year's Eve and day before)
Locale(s): Wahiawa, Hawaii (a rural town on Oahu)

Summary: Every year, the extended Yang family gathers from all over the Hawaiian island of Oahu at Grandma's house to celebrate New Year's Eve. This year, young Marisa will help make the dumplings for Grandma's famous dumpling soup.

About this book: Set in Hawaii, a veritable melting pot of diverse races, this book represents a rich mix of customs and cultures through the depiction of the close-knit Yang family. While most of the family is of Korean descent, other members are Japanese, Chinese, native Hawaiian and *haole* (Hawaiian for Caucasians). All together, they create a loving, sharing family who gather annually to celebrate their rich heritages. An exquisitely illustrated, heartwarming work.

Where it's reviewed:

Library Talk, March 1995, page 32
Reading Teacher, November 1994, page 251
Booklist, September 15, 1993, page 160

Awards the book has won:

New Voices, New World Contest winner, 1990

Other books you might like:

Janet Mitsui Brown, *Thanksgiving at Obaachan's*, 1994

A Japanese American girl loves to visit her grandmother's house for Thanksgiving, where the meal is a combination of traditional American and Japanese fare.

Karen Chinn, *Sam and the Lucky Money*, 1995

Disappointed that everything he wants to buy with his Chinese New Year gift money costs too much, Sam finally

realizes how lucky he is when he sees a lonely stranger without shoes.

Sook Nyul Choi, *Halmoni and the Picnic*, 1993

Yunmi's grandmother, newly arrived from Korea, finally begins to feel at home when she chaperones the annual Central Park class picnic for Yunmi and her classmates.

Amy Tan, *The Chinese Siamese Cat*, 1994

Ming Mao tells her five kittens about their illustrious Chinese ancestry.

Kate Waters, *Lion Dancer: Ernie Wan's Chinese New Year*, 1990

Written with Madeline Slovenz-Low, Young Ernie performs his first Lion Dance through the streets of New York City's Chinatown, as part of the Chinese New Year celebration.

1049

NAMI RHEE, Author/Illustrator

Magic Spring: A Korean Folktale

(New York: Whitebird Book (G.P. Putnam's Sons), 1993)

Subject(s): Folk Tales; Honesty; Greed
Age range(s): Grades 1-4
Major character(s): Old Man, Aged Person (kind); Old Woman, Aged Person, Spouse (wife of Old Man); Neighbor, Neighbor (greedy, rich)
Time period(s): Indeterminate Past
Locale(s): Republic of Korea (a village)

Summary: A hardworking, childless elderly couple are led to the fountain of youth by a mysterious bluebird and warned to take just a sip. Their greedy neighbor hears about their discovery, rushes to magic spring and overindulges, leading to a surprise ending.

Where it's reviewed:

Children's Book Review Service, May 1993, page 115
Publishers Weekly, May 31, 1993, page 54
School Library Journal, July 1993, page 82

Other books you might like:

Oki S. Han, *Sir Whong and the Golden Pig*, 1993

When a stranger dupes Sir Whong into a loan using a fake golden pig as security, Sir Whong devises a plan to retrieve the money.

Laurence Yep, *The Shell Woman and the King*, 1993

The magical shell woman saves her husband and herself from the evil, greedy king.

Demi, *Liang and the Magic Paintbrush*, 1980

Young Liang is given a magic paintbrush that brings to life everything he draws.

Amy Tan, *The Chinese Siamese Cat*, 1994

Ming Mao tells her five kittens about their illustrious Chinese ancestry.

Ai-Ling Louie, *Yeh-Shen: A Cinderella Story from China*, 1982

In spite of the wicked machinations of her stepmother, beautiful young Yeh-Shen manages to survive her deprived life, marry the king and live happily ever after.

1050

NAYANTARA SAHGAL

Mistaken Identity

(New York: New Directions Publishing Corp., 1988)

Subject(s): Politics; Prisoners and Prisons; Personal Odyssey
Age range(s): Adult
Major character(s): Bhushan Singh, Political Prisoner (imprisoned for unknown charges), Heir (son of North Indian royal); Sylla, Lover (Bhushan Singh's late-lover); Razia, Lover (Bhushan Singh's), Young Man (adolescent)
Time period(s): 1920s; 1930s (told through flashbacks)
Locale(s): India (various locations in North India)

Summary: In 1929, Bhusan Singh, the aimless son of a wealthy raja, is on a train headed for his family home when he is arrested, falsely charged with treason and imprisoned. Efforts to free him fail; over the next three years, he relives his life, in his memory and through tales he shares with his Communist cell-mates.

Where it's reviewed:
New York Times Book Review, July 12, 1992, page 32
Kirkus Reviews, March 1, 1989, page 329
World Literature Today, Winter 1990, page 194

Other books by the same author:
A Time to Be Happy
This Time of Morning
Storm in Chandigarh, 1969
The Day in Shadow, 1971
A Situation in New Delhi, 1977

Other books you might like:
Meena Alexander, *Nampally Road*, 1991
    Mira returns to her native India now governed by a new dictator and corrupt police. Once lost in the poetry of Wordsworth, Mira struggles to define her new life.
Shyam Selvadurai, *Funny Boy*, 1995
    A young boy comes of age and discovers his homosexuality during a time of great political turmoil in his native Sri Lanka.
Fiona Cheong, *The Scent of the Gods*, 1991
    Young Esha comes of age in Singapore in the late 1960s, a time of political strife between the Chinese government and the local Singaporeans.
Wendy Law-Yone, *The Coffin Tree*, 1983
    A political coup forces a young woman and her older half-brother to flee their native Burma, catapulting them into a difficult, desperate new life in the U.S.

1051

JESSICA K. SAIKI

From the Lanai and Other Hawaii Stories

(St. Paul, MN: New Rivers Press, 1991)

Subject(s): Multicultural; Family Life; Short Stories
Age range(s): Adult
Time period(s): 1990s
Locale(s): Hawaii (mostly in the Japanese American community of Lunalilo)

Summary: Haunting stories, mostly about the residents of Lunalilo, including a lonely spinster, a deserted husband and a young woman desperate for stardom. Other stories explore the interaction between Lunalilo residents and white outsiders, including a woman and her wealthy employers, a young girl and a salesman, and a journalist and a man obsessed with all things Japanese.

Where it's reviewed:
Kirkus Reviews, December 1, 1990, page 1635
Publishers Weekly, January 4, 1991, page 69
School Library Journal, August 1991, page 210

Other books by the same author:
Once, a Lotus Garden and Other Stories, 1987

Other books you might like:
Toshio Mori, *The Chauvinist and Other Stories*, 1979
    Short stories about Japanese Americans in California before and after World War II. From established immigrants to desperate American-born citizens, these stories capture a spirit of survival.
Toshio Mori, *Yokohama, California*, 1949
    The first published collection of short stories by a Japanese American, about the diverse lives of the members of the fictional California community during the 1930s and 1940s.
Kathleen Tyau, *A Little Too Much Is Enough*, 1995
    Mahi Wong grows up in post-World War II Hawaii surrounded by her large family, immersed in a complex, mixed-up culture of Chinese and Hawaiian influences.
Susan Nunes, *A Small Obligation and Other Stories of Hilo*, 1982
    A collection of interrelated stories about Amy Freitas of Hilo, Hawaii, and her extended family—Japanese on her mother's side and Portuguese on her father's side.
Marie Hara, *Bananaheart and Other Stories*, 1994
    These stories cover a century of life in Hawaii, with tales of a picture bride, a woman working in a foreign house, a hapa girl searching for identity and an old woman who lost an infant daughter.

1052

JESSICA K. SAIKI

Once, a Lotus Garden and Other Stories

(St. Paul, MN: New Rivers Press, 1987)

Subject(s): Multicultural; Family Life; Short Stories
Age range(s): Adult
Time period(s): 1930s; 1940s
Locale(s): Lunalilo, Hawaii (Japanese American community)

Summary: A collection of poignant short stories, mostly about the residents of Lunalilo, including new picture brides arriving from Japan, young schoolgirls and their dreams, young working women, the silent, other victims of the Pearl Harbor bombing and numerous lonely men and women.

Other books by the same author:
From the Lanai and Other Hawaii Stories, 1991

Other books you might like:
Kathleen Tyau, *A Little Too Much Is Enough*, 1995
    Mahi Wong grows up in post-World War II Hawaii sur-

rounded by her large family, immersed in a complex, mixed-up culture of Chinese and Hawaiian influences.

Susan Nunes, *A Small Obligation and Other Stories of Hilo*, 1982

A collection of interrelated stories about Amy Freitas of Hilo, Hawaii, and her extended family—Japanese on her mother's side and Portuguese on her father's side.

Hisaye Yamamoto, *Seventeen Syllables and Other Stories*, 1988

A collection of 15 short stories from Yamamoto's almost half-century-long writing career.

Juliet S. Kono, *Sister Stew: Fiction and Poetry by Women*, 1991

Edited with Cathy Song, this is a colorful collection of writings by women of various backgrounds, the majority of whom are either Hawaiian by birth or by adopted residency.

Marie Hara, *Bananaheart and Other Stories*, 1994

These stories cover a century of life in Hawaii, with tales of a picture bride, a woman working in a foreign house, a hapa girl searching for identitiy and an old woman who lost an infant daughter.

1053

KIMIKO SAKAI
TOMIE ARAI, Illustrator

Sachiko Means Happiness

(San Francisco: Children's Book Press, 1990)

Subject(s): Grandparents; Old Age; Mental Illness
Age range(s): Grades 1-3
Major character(s): Sachiko, Child; Sachiko, Grandmother (Alzheimer's victim)
Time period(s): 1990s
Locale(s): United States

Summary: Young Sachiko is frustrated about having to spend time with her elderly grandmother, with whom she shares the same name, who no longer even recognizes her. Sachiko comes to understand what has happened to her grandmother and learns again how to be her friend.

Where it's reviewed:
Booklist, December 1, 1990, page 755
Horn Book Guide, July 1990, page 33
Kirkus Reviews, December 1, 1990, page 1677
Publishers Weekly, November 30, 1990, page 69
School Library Journal, March 1991, page 179

Other books you might like:
Jama Kim Rattigan, *Dumpling Soup*, 1993

Every year the Yang family gathers at Grandma's house from all over Oahu, Hawaii to celebrate New Year's Eve. This year, young Marisa will help Grandma make her famous dumpling soup.

Janet Mitsui Brown, *Thanksgiving at Obaachan's*, 1994

A Japanese American girl loves to visit her grandmother's house for Thanksgiving, where the meal is a combination of traditional American and Japanese fare.

Cynthia Chin-Lee, *Almond Cookies and Dragon Well Tea*, 1993

When Erica visits Nancy's house for the first time, she

expects many differences because Nancy is Chinese American, but finds that their two families are more similar than not.

Karen Chinn, *Sam and the Lucky Money*, 1995

Disappointed that everything he wants to buy with his Chinese New Year gift money costs too much, Sam finally realizes how lucky he is when he sees a lonely stranger without shoes.

Sook Nyul Choi, *Halmoni and the Picnic*, 1993

Yunmi's grandmother, newly arrived from Korea, finally begins to feel at home when she chaperones the annual Central Park class picnic for Yunmi and her classmates.

1054

BIENVENIDO SANTOS

Scent of Apples: A Collection of Short Stories

(Seattle: University of Washington Press, 1955)

Subject(s): Multicultural; Emigration and Immigration; Short Stories
Age range(s): Adult
Time period(s): 1940s; 1950s
Locale(s): United States

Summary: A collection of short stories, some interrelated, about the experiences of young Filipino American men living displaced lives, caught between their emotional ties to their families back in the Philippines, and their valiant attempts to sustain independent, productive lives often as unwelcome immigrants in the U.S.

Where it's reviewed:
Kirkus Reviews, February 1, 1980, page 160

Other books by the same author:
The Man Who (Thought He) Looked Like Robert Taylor, 1983
Villa Magdalena, 1965 (first novel)
Brother, My Brother, 1960 (short story collection)
You Lovely People, 1955 (short story collection)

Other books you might like:
Peter Bacho, *Cebu*, 1991

On his first visit to the Philippines to bury his mother, Filipino American priest Ben Lucero finds all his moral and religious beliefs thrown into question.

Jessica Hagedorn, *Dogeaters*, 1990

An autobiographical novel about growing up in Manila in the late 1950s during the turbulent and corrupt Marcos regime.

F. Sionil Jose, *Three Filipino Women: Novellas*, 1992

Three novellas about three remarkable, though ultimately tragic Filipino women: Narita, a politician, Ermita, a high class prostitute, and Malu, a political idealist.

Marianne Villanueva, *Ginseng and Other Tales from Manila*, 1991

Stories inspired by real life events and newspaper articles, focusing on the desperate citizens of a troubled country trying to survive poverty, corruption and loss of freedom

Carlos Bulosan, *America Is in the Heart*, 1943

This autobiography of writer and poet Carlos Bulosan

covers his life from his boyhood in the Philippines to his arrival in America where he worked as a migrant laborer.

1055

R.A. SASAKI

The Loom and Other Stories

(St. Paul: Graywolf Press, 1991)

Subject(s): Short Stories; Family Relations
Age range(s): Adult
Major character(s): Joanne ''Jo'' Terasaki, Daughter (youngest of four); Linda Terasaki, Daughter (oldest of four); Keiko ''Mom'' Terasaki, Mother, Daughter (of immigrants); ''Dad'' Terasaki, Father (born in U.S., raised in Japan)
Time period(s): 1980s
Locale(s): San Francisco, California (San Francisco Bay Area)

Summary: Nine interrelated stories, mostly about the San Francisco-based Terasaki family, usually filtered through the perception of Jo, the youngest daughter.

Where it's reviewed:
Library Journal, October 15, 1991, page 126
New York Times Book Review, December 8, 1991, page 24
Publishers Weekly, September 6, 1991, page 100

Other books you might like:
Cynthia Kadohata, *The Floating World*, 1989
    A coming-of-age novel about 12-year-old Olivia, who with her family, moves continuously throughout the Pacific Northwest in search of a better life.
Fae Myenne Ng, *Bone*, 1993
    A multigenerational saga of a San Francisco Chinese American family.
Julie Shigekuni, *A Bridge Between Us*, 1995
    Four generations of women—each a mother and a daughter—of a San Francisco Japanese American family trace their lives from 1900 to the present.
Kathleen Tyau, *A Little Too Much Is Enough*, 1995
    Mahi Wong grows up in post-World War II Hawaii surrounded by her large family, immersed in a complex, mixed-up culture of Chinese and Hawaiian influences.
Sigrid Nunez, *A Feather on the Breath of God*, 1995
    A young woman, the child of a Chinese Panamanian father and a German mother, grows up in a New York housing project trying to make sense of her identity.
Amy Tan, *The Joy Luck Club*, 1989
    A novel about the timeless relationship of four Chinese-born mothers and their American-born daughters.

1056

ALLEN SAY, Author/Illustrator

Grandfather's Journey

(Boston: Houghton Mifflin, 1993)

Subject(s): Emigration and Immigration; Voyages and Travels; Multicultural
Age range(s): Grades 1-3

Major character(s): Grandfather, Grandfather, Immigrant (from Japan); Unnamed Character, Young Man, Japanese American
Time period(s): 19th century; 20th century
Locale(s): California; Japan

Summary: A Japanese American man recounts his grandfather's journey from Japan to America, and back to Japan. He comes to understand his grandfather's feelings of being torn by a sense of being home in two very different countries, and longing for one while in the other.

Where it's reviewed:
Booklist, July 1993, page 1974
Horn Book Magazine, September 1993, page 590
Publishers Weekly, August 23, 1993, page 70

Other books by the same author:
Stranger in the Mirror, 1995
Tree of Cranes, 1991
El Chino, 1990 (biography)
The Lost Lake, 1989
A River Dream, 1988

Other books you might like:
Min Paek, *Aekyung's Dream*, 1988
    Aekyung, a young Korean girl recently in the U.S., dreams about King Sejong who create *Hangul*, the Korean alphabet, and finds new pride in her Korean heritage.
Tran Khanh Tuyet, *The Little Weaver of Thai-Yen Village*, 1977
    A young Vietnamese refugee arrives in the U.S. and struggles to adjust to her new life. She starts to weave again, as she did in her home country with her late grandmother.
Michele Maria Surat, *Angel Child, Dragon Child*, 1983
    Young Ut, a recent Vietnamese immigrant, is teased because of her different apperance. Thrown together by the school principal, Ut and a once cruel boy develop a new friendship.
Kimiko Sakai, *Sachiko Means Happiness*, 1990
    Sachiko is upset when her elderly grandmother does not even recognize her. When she finally comes to understand what has happened to her grandmother, she learns again how to be her friend.

1057

ALLEN SAY

The Ink-keeper's Apprentice

(Boston: Houghton Mifflin, 1994)

Subject(s): Coming of Age; Autobiography; Artists and Art
Age range(s): Grades 6 and Up
Major character(s): Sei Koichi, 13-Year-Old, Japanese (schoolboy), Apprentice (to cartoonist Noro Shinpei); Noro Shinpei, Artist (famous cartoonist), Teacher (mentor to Kiyoi and Tokida), Japanese; Tokida, Apprentice (to Noro Shinpei, cartoonist)
Time period(s): 1940s (after World War II)
Locale(s): Tokyo, Japan

Summary: Determined to become an artist, young Sei Koichi convinces the famous cartoonist, Noro Shinpei, to take him on as an apprentice. Under Sensei's (Japanese for ''teacher'') nurturing tutelage, he receives a new name, Kiyoi, and comes of age with a growing independence in postwar Japan.

About this book: This is an autobiographical novel based on Allen Say's own boyhood in Japan, first published in 1979 and reissued in 1994. Appropriate for both young adult and adult readers.

Awards the book has won:
ALA Notable Book for Young Adults, 1994

Other books by the same author:
Stranger in the Mirror, 1995
Grandfather's Journey, 1993
Tree of Cranes, 1991
The Lost Lake, 1989
A River Dream, 1988

Other books you might like:
Joy Kogawa, *Naomi's Road*, 1986
　　Young adult story of a Japanese Canadian family that is splintered and scattered as a result of forced evacuation and relocation during World War II.
Kyoko Mori, *One Bird*, 1995
　　A coming-of-age young adult novel about Megumi Shimizu, left to live with her cold father and difficult grandmother when her unhappy mother suddenly leaves the family.
Kyoko Mori, *Shizuko's Daughter*, 1993
　　When her mother suddenly commits suicide, 12-year-old Yuki is left behind to try and piece her life back together.
Laurence Yep, *Child of the Owl*, 1977
　　Casey is sent to live in San Francisco's Chinatown with her maternal grandmother, where she learns of her rich cultural heritage.
Laurence Yep, *Dragonwings*, 1975
　　A Chinese American aviator designs and flies a machine in 1909. Story is based on actual events.

1058

ALLEN SAY, Author/Illustrator

The Lost Lake

(Boston: Houghton Mifflin, 1989)

Subject(s): Fathers and Sons; Camps and Camping; Wilderness
Age range(s): Grades 1-3
Major character(s): Luke, Child (spending summer with father); "Dad", Father (Luke's)
Time period(s): 1980s (1989)
Locale(s): United States

Summary: Luke and his father embark on a camping trip to "the Lost Lake," where the father used to go with his own father. When they arrive they find that too many others have discovered it, as well. Father and son continue on their journey, sharing new experiences and discovering one another.

Where it's reviewed:
Booklist, October 1, 1989, page 355
Horn Book Magazine, January 1990, page 56
Publishers Weekly, September 8, 1989, page 69

Other books by the same author:
Stranger in the Mirror, 1995
Grandfather's Journey, 1993
Tree of Cranes, 1991
El Chino, 1990 (biography)
A River Dream, 1988

Other books you might like:
Chyng Feng Sun, *Mama Bear*, 1994
　　Mei-Mei saves money to purchase the perfect Christmas present—a giant stuffed bear. When the money she's saved proves not to be enough, she realizes that she's had something more special all along.
Sook Nyul Choi, *Halmoni and the Picnic*, 1993
　　Yunmi's grandmother, newly arrived from Korea, finally begins to feel at home when she chaperones the annual Central Park class picnic for Yunmi and her classmates.
Karen Chinn, *Sam and the Lucky Money*, 1995
　　Disappointed when everything he wants to buy with his Chinese New Year gift money costs too much, Sam finally realizes how lucky he is when he sees a lonely stranger without any shoes.
Cynthia Chin-Lee, *Almond Cookies and Dragon Well Tea*, 1993
　　When Erica visits Nancy's house for the first time, she expects many differences because Nancy is Chinese American, but finds that their two families are more similar than not.

1059

ALLEN SAY, Author/Illustrator

A River Dream

(Boston: Houghton Mifflin, 1988)

Subject(s): Fishing; Wildlife Conservation; Family Life
Age range(s): Grades 1-3
Major character(s): Mark, Child (in bed with a high fever); Uncle Scott, Uncle (sends Mark a special present)
Time period(s): 1980s (1983)
Locale(s): United States

Summary: Mark is in bed with a high fever. His Uncle Scott sends him a metal box for trout flies, which brings back memories of Mark's first fishing trip. He's transported to a sparkling river, meets up with Uncle Scott, and catches his biggest fish ever. But Mark learns that perhaps it's better to "leave the river the way he found it."

Where it's reviewed:
Horn Book Magazine, November 1988, page 778
Kirkus Reviews, October 1, 1988, page 1475
Publishers Weekly, September 9, 1988, page 132

Other books by the same author:
Stranger in the Mirror, 1995
Grandfather's Journey, 1993
Tree of Cranes, 1991
El Chino, 1990 (biography)
The Lost Lake, 1989

Other books you might like:
Yoshiko Uchida, *The Forever Christmas Tree*, 1963
　　Young Takashi learns about a joyous holiday called

Christmas from his sister Kaya. They decorate a reclusive neighbor's fir tree and bring their neighborhood together.

Chiyoko Tomioka, *Rise and Shine, Mariko-chan!*, 1986
Young Mariko gets up each morning and gets ready for the yellow school bus that will take her to school.

Yoriko Tsutsui, *Anna in Charge*, 1979
While her mother goes to run an errand, Anna is left in charge of her younger sister, Katy. Katy wanders off while Anna is not looking and Anna quickly goes searching for her.

Jennifer L. Chan, *ONE small GIRL*, 1993
Told not to touch anything in either her grandmother's or her uncle's adjacent Chinatown stores, a little girl still manages to have fun.

1060

ALLEN SAY, Author/Illustrator

Stranger in the Mirror

(Boston: Houghton Mifflin, 1995)

Subject(s): Self-Perception; Family Life
Age range(s): Grades 1-4
Major character(s): Sam, Child (young boy, loves to skateboard); Jessie, Sister (Sam's younger sister)
Time period(s): 1990s (1995)
Locale(s): United States

Summary: Sam wakes up one day with the face of his elderly grandfather. He has a frustrating time trying to convince his family and friends that he really is still Sam inside. Only when he takes to the skateboard does he feel like his old self again.

Where it's reviewed:
Publishers Weekly, September 11, 1995, page 84

Other books by the same author:
Grandfather's Journey, 1993
Tree of Cranes, 1991
Feast of Lanterns, 1990
El Chino, 1990 (biography)
The Lost Lake, 1989

Other books you might like:
Kimiko Sakai, *Sachiko Means Happiness*, 1990
Sachiko is upset when her elderly grandmother does not even recognize her until she finally comes to understand what has happened to her and she learns how to be her friend again.

Sook Nyul Choi, *Halmoni and the Picnic*, 1993
Yunmi's grandmother, newly arrived from Korea, finally begins to feel at home when she chaperones the annual Central Park class picnic for Yunmi and her classmates.

1061

ALLEN SAY, Author/Illustrator

Tree of Cranes

(Boston: Houghton Mifflin, 1991)

Subject(s): Multicultural; Christmas; Mothers and Sons
Age range(s): Grades 1-3

Major character(s): Young Boy, Child (too young to wear long pants), Japanese; Mama, Mother (young boy's mother)
Time period(s): 1990s (1991)
Locale(s): Japan

Summary: A lovely story about a young Japanese boy who learns about Christmas for the first time from his California-born Japanese American mother as she prepares a special pine tree, decorated with paper cranes.

Where it's reviewed:
Booklist, March 15, 1992, page 1367
Horn Book Magazine, November 1991, page 721
Publishers Weekly, September 13, 1991, page 79

Awards the book has won:
ALA Notable Childrens' Book, 1991
Notable Children's Trade Book (in social studies)

Other books by the same author:
Stranger in the Mirror, 1995
Grandfather's Journey, 1993
El Chino, 1990 (biography)
The Lost Lake, 1989
A River Dream, 1988

Other books you might like:
Yoshiko Uchida, *The Forever Christmas Tree*, 1963
Young Takashi learns about a joyous holiday called Christmas from his sister Kaya. They decorate a reclusive neighbor's fir tree, and bring their neighborhood together.

Chyng Feng Sun, *Mama Bear*, 1994
Mei-Mei saves money to buy the perfect Christmas gift—a stuffed bear. When the money she's saved proves not to be enough, she realizes that she's had something even more special all along.

Kate Waters, *Lion Dancer: Ernie Wan's Chinese New Year*, 1990
Young Ernie is about to experience the most important day of his life. He will perform his first Lion Dance through the street's of New York's Chinatown, as part of the Chinese New Year celebration.

Karen Chinn, *Sam and the Lucky Money*, 1995
Disappointed that everything he wants to buy with his Chinese New Year gift money costs too much, Sam finally realizes how lucky he is when he sees a lonely stranger without shoes.

Elaine Hosozawa-Nagano, *Chopsticks from America*, 1994
Two Japanese American children move to Japan. While they look like "chopsticks among other chopsticks," they are American, which proves to be different from being Japanese.

1062

LISA SEE

On Gold Mountain: The One-Hundred-Year Odyssey of a Chinese-American Family

(New York: St. Martin's Press, 1995)

Subject(s): Emigration and Immigration; Identity; Family Relations

Age range(s): Adult
Major character(s): Fong See, Immigrant (from China), Businessman, Chinese (patriarch of large family); Letticie Pruett "Ticie" See, Wife (second of Fong See), Businesswoman (supported Fong See's success), Caucasian; Fong Yun, Brother (Fong See's youngest), Businessman (sometime partner to Fong See), Chinese; Leo Ming Quan "Eddy" See, Son (fourth of Fong See), Chinese; Florence Jun Oy "Sissee" See, Daughter (the See's only), Chinese
Time period(s): 1860s; 1990s
Locale(s): Los Angeles, California; Dimtao, China (small village, native home of the Fong See family)

Summary: Lisa See's great-great-grandfather arrived in the U.S. from China more than 100 years ago, followed by his son who eventually became one of the most successful Chinese American antiques merchants. The Fong See family history, spanning over a century, is filled with colorful stories of immigrants, multiple wives, concubines, interracial marriages, and more.

About this book: Through telling her family's story, See also provides the historical context of the Chinese American experience.

Other books you might like:

Monica Sone, *Nisei Daughter*, 1953
An account of a second-generation Japanese American woman growing up in Seattle in the 1920s and 1930s, being incarcerated during World War II and her new life in the midwest.

Helie Lee, *Still Life with Rice: A Young American Woman Discovers the Life and Legacy of of Her Korean Grandmother*, 1996
The true story of a Korean woman who survives great hardship in Korea and finally arrives in the U.S., as told by her Korean American granddaughter.

Mary Paik Lee, *Quiet Odyssey: A Pioneer Woman in America*, 1990
Edited by Professor Sucheng Lee. A memoir that covers nearly a century of change, by one of the country's first Korean American women.

Ruthanne Lum McCunn, *Thousand Pieces of Gold*, 1981
The first biographical novel of Chinese American pioneer woman, Polly Bemis.

Lydia Yuri Minatoya, *Talking to High Monks in the Snow: An Asian American Odyssey*, 1992
A young woman searches for her own answers to what it means to be Asian American. A beautifully written piece of prose, astonishing for its power to effect.

1063

SHYAM SELVADURAI

Funny Boy

(New York: William Morrow and Company, Inc.)

Subject(s): Homosexuality/Lesbianism; Coming of Age; Politics
Age range(s): Adult
Major character(s): Arjun "Arjie" Chelvaratnam, Young Man, Sri Lankan (upper-middle class); Nalini

Chelvaratnam, Mother (Arjie's); Shehan Soyza, Lover (young classmate of Arjie's), Homosexual
Time period(s): 1970s; 1980s
Locale(s): Colombo, Sri Lanka

Summary: Arjie, a young boy growing up in an upper-middle-class family in Sri Lanka, is "funny"—he prefers to dress in saris and play with the girls. He comes of age amidst a time of political turbulence marked by the growing tension between two opposing ethnic groups—the Tamils and the Sinhalese—vying for controlling power.

About this book: A lauded first novel which remained on Canadian bestseller lists for over four months.

Where it's reviewed:
Books in Canada, April 1995, page 9
Canadian Forum, January 1995, page 40
Guardian Weekly, November 13, 1994, page 28
Maclean's October 24, 1994, page 55
Observer (London), January 1, 1995, page 18

Awards the book has won:
Smithbooks/Books in Canada First Novel Award

Other books you might like:

Fiona Cheong, *The Scent of the Gods*, 1991
Eleven-year-old Esha comes of age in Singapore of the late 1960s, a time of growing political strife between the predominantly Chinese government and the local Singaporeans.

Wendy Law-Yone, *The Coffin Tree*, 1983
A political coup forces a young woman and her older half-brother to flee their native Burma, catapulting them to a difficult, desperate new life in the U.S.

Carlos Bulosan, *America Is in the Heart*, 1943
The autobiography of writer and poet Carlos Bulosan, from his boyhood in the Philippines, to his arrival in America, to the difficulties he faced as a migrant laborer.

Jessica Hagedorn, *Dogeaters*, 1990
An autobiographical novel about growing up in Manila in the late 1950s during the turbulent and corrupt Marcos regime.

Bienvenido Santos, *Scent of Apples: A Collection of Short Stories*, 1955
A collection of short stories, some interrelated, about the experiences of young Filipino American men living displaced lives.

1064

VIKRAM SETH

Golden Gate: A Novel in Verse

(New York: Vintage International (Random House), 1986)

Subject(s): Love; Friendship
Age range(s): Adult
Major character(s): John Brown, Computer Expert (successful 26-year-old Yuppie); Philip "Phil" Weiss, Activist (for peace, ex-Defense employee), Divorced Person; Janet "Jan" Hayakawa, Artist (sculptor), Musician; Elizabeth "Liz" Dorati, Lawyer (high-power attorney); Ed Dorati, Advertising, Brother (Liz's)
Time period(s): 1980s (1986)

Locale(s): San Francisco, California

Summary: A novel written entirely in verse, about the machinations of love in the modern age. John's lonely, so Jan secretly runs a personal ad on his behalf. John finds Liz. Recently divorced Phil ends up with Liz's younger brother Ed. But nothing is as it seems with these five friends.

About this book: Even the acknowledgments, dedication and table of contents are in verse! A remarkable, unique feat. Originally, the work was rejected by most poetry publishers, but eventually found an editor at Random House who recognized its priceless merit and published it to great acclaim, quickly making Seth a literary sensation.

Where it's reviewed:
Kirkus Reviews, February 15, 1986, page 245
Library Journal, July 1986, page 111
New Yorker, July 14, 1986, page 82
Newsweek, April 14, 1986, page 74

Other books by the same author:
A Suitable Boy, 1993
All You Who Sleep Tonight, 1990 (poetry collection)
The Humble Administrator's Garden, 1985 (poetry collection)
From Heaven Lake: Travels through Sinkiang and Tibet, 1983
Mappings, 1980 (debut poetry collection)

Other books you might like:
Shawn Wong, *American Knees*, 1995
    A hip and sexy novel about the on-and-off-again love affair between politically correct Raymond Ding and independent Aurora Crane.
Willyce Kim, *Dancer Dawkins and the California Kid*, 1985
    Dancer and Little Willy Gutherie (a.k.a. The California Kid) collide in San Francisco and set off on a series of unpredictable adventures.
Willyce Kim, *Dead Heat*, 1988
    A follow-up to *Dancer Dawkins and the California Kid*. Dancer Dawkins, trying to get over a bad break-up, heads to San Francisco for solace with old friends.
Maxine Hong Kingston, *Tripmaster Monkey: His Fake Book*, 1989
    Kingston's first novel about the often comic mishaps and adventures of Wittman Ah Sing, a young Chinese American, in search of his dreams.

1065

MARLENE SHIGEKAWA
ISAO KIKUCHI, Illustrator

Blue Jay in the Desert

(Chicago: Polychrome Publishing Corporation, 1993)

Subject(s): Internment; Children and War
Age range(s): Grades 1-6
Major character(s): Junior, Child (boy, lives in internment camp); Grandpa, Grandfather (Junior's)
Time period(s): 1940s
Locale(s): Camp Poston, Arizona (internment camp)

Summary: Junior and his family live in Camp Poston, an internment camp where Japanese Americans were imprisoned

during World War II. Junior's grandfather is carving him a special blue jay, but young Junior would rather have a bigger, stronger bird. Junior must discover for himself the significance of the blue jay.

Other books you might like:
Ken Mochizuki, *Heroes*, 1995
    Always forced to play the enemy because he looks like "them", Japanese American Donnie enlists his reluctant father and uncle to prove their U.S. military service records.
Ken Mochizuki, *Baseball Saved Us*, 1993
    Living in a World War II internment camp, a Japanese American boy learns to play baseball.
Michele Maria Surat, *Angel Child, Dragon Child*, 1983
    Young Ut, a recent Vietnamese immigrant, is teased because of her different appearance. Thrown together by their school principal, Ut and a once cruel boy develop a new friendship.
Tran Khanh Tuyet, *The Little Weaver of Thai-Yen Village*, 1977
    A young Vietnamese refugee arrives in the U.S. and struggles to adjust to her new life. She starts to weave again, as she did in her home country with her late grandmother.

1066

JULIE SHIGEKUNI

A Bridge Between Us

(New York: Anchor Books (Doubleday), 1995)

Subject(s): Mothers and Daughters; Multicultural; Intergenerational Saga
Age range(s): Adult
Major character(s): Reiko Hito, Grandmother (matriarch of Hito family), Japanese American (daughter of Japanese immigrant); Rio Hito, Grandmother (grandmother to Nomi), Japanese American, Daughter (daughter of Reiko); Tomoe Kanemori Hito, Granddaughter (granddaughter-in-law of Reiko), Spouse (wife of Rio's son, Goro), Japanese American; Nomi Hito, Daughter (daughter of Tomoe and Goro), Japanese American
Time period(s): 20th century (1900-1990)
Locale(s): San Francisco, California (Bay Area); Japan (various locations)

Summary: In a large Victorian home in San Francisco live four generations of Japanese American women. Reiko, the domineering matriarch: Rio, her desperate daughter: Tomoe, the dependable granddaughter-in-law: and Nomi, the rebellious great-granddaughter. Each lives with secrets, yet always remain aware of the invisible, unbreakable bridge that binds them all together.

About this book: Debut novel for the fifth-generation Japanese American author.

Where it's reviewed:
Library Journal, June 1, 1995, page 208
New York Times Book Review, March 19, 1995, page 7
Publishers Weekly, January 2, 1995, page 57

Other books you might like:

Cynthia Kadohata, *The Floating World*, 1989
  This coming-of-age novel is about 12-year-old Olivia, who, with her family, moves continuously throughout the Pacific Northwest in search of a better life.
Fae Myenne Ng, *Bone*, 1993
  A multigenerational saga of a San Francisco Chinese American family.
R.A. Sasaki, *The Loom and Other Stories*, 1991
  A collection of short stories, interwoven to tell the story of three generations of a Japanese American family.
Amy Tan, *The Joy Luck Club*, 1989
  A novel about the timeless relationship of four Chinese-born mothers and their American-born daughters.

1067

R.A. SHIOMI

Yellow Fever

(Toronto: Playwrights Canada, 1984)

Subject(s): Theater; Mystery and Detective Stories
Age range(s): Adult
Major character(s): Sam Shikaze, Detective—Private; Nancy Wing, Journalist (inexperienced); Chuck Chan, Lawyer; Sergeant MacKenzie, Police Officer, Racist
Time period(s): 1970s (March 1973)
Locale(s): Vancouver, British Columbia, Canada (Powell Street in Vancouver)

Summary: In this parody of the hard-boiled detective genre, Sam Shikaze (of the Sam Spade school) is a Japanese American private detective hired to find the missing Cherry Blossom Queen. In the process, he meets all sorts of seedy, disreputable characters.

About this book: A modern Asian American theater classic, *Yellow Fever* debuted at San Francisco's Asian American Theater Company in 1982 and subsequently was produced throughout the U.S. and Canada, including a successful, extended run Off-Broadway. Today, playwright Rick Shiomi is the artistic director at Theater Mu, an Asian American theater based in Minneapolis, Minnesota.

Other books you might like:

Misha Berson, *Between Worlds: Contemporary Asian-American Plays*, 1990
  Edited by Berson; anthology includes works by Ping Chong, Philip Kan Gotanda, Jessica Hagedorn, David Henry Hwang, Wakako Yamauchi and Laurence Yep.
Frank Chin, *The Chickencoop Chinaman and the Year of the Dragon: Two Plays by Frank Chin*, 1981
  In the first of these two plays, Chin challenges media stereotypes of Asian Americans. In the second, he examines the disintegration of the Chinese American family.

1068

JACQUELIN SINGH
DEMI, Illustrator

Fat Gopal

(New York: Harcourt Brace Jovanovich, 1984)

Subject(s): Folk Tales; Problem Solving; Resourcefulness
Age range(s): Grades 1-3
Major character(s): Nawab, Ruler (domain between mountains/sea), Indian; Maharajah, Nobleman (rules land within Nawab's land); Fat Gopal, Servant (Maharajah's court jester)
Time period(s): Indeterminate Past
Locale(s): India

Summary: The ruling Nawab requests the Maharajah to do an impossible task: to measure the earth and to count the stars, the sun's rays and the men on the moon. The Majarajah's servant, Fat Gopal, comes to the rescue and jovially promises the answers in return for huge sums of money to cover his so-called research expenses.

Where it's reviewed:
Social Education, April 1985, page 326

Other books you might like:

Ed Young, *Seven Blind Mice*, 1991
  Seven blind mice, feeling the different parts of an elephant, argue over its appearance.
Demi, *Buddha*, 1996
  The story of the gifted young Prince Siddhartha who leaves his life of luxury and forsakes everything on this earth to seek the Truth of life over death.
Jeannine Atkins, *Aani and the Tree Huggers*, 1995
  Young Aani leads the other women of her village in putting their arms around the many trees in their forest to save them from being cut down by unthinking developers.

1069

DIANNE SNYDER, Adaptor
ALLEN SAY, Illustrator

The Boy of the Three-Year Nap

(Boston: Houghton Mifflin, 1988)

Subject(s): Folk Tales; Mothers and Sons; Marriage
Age range(s): Grades 1-3
Major character(s): Taro "The Boy of the Three-Year Nap", Child (laziest person in the village), Japanese; Widow, Mother (Taro's frustrated mother), Japanese; Merchant, Businessman (wealthy rice merchant)
Time period(s): Indeterminate Past
Locale(s): Nagara River, Japan

Summary: Taro is known throughout the village as its laziest citizen. When a rich merchant moves into town, he hatches a plan to ensure an easy life by convincing the merchant that his daughter must marry Taro. But Taro's mother has plans of her own, and his napping days soon come to an end.

Where it's reviewed:
Kirkus Reviews, April 1, 1988, page 544
Publishers Weekly, March 18, 1988, page 84

School Library Journal, April 1988, page 97

Awards the book has won:
Caldecott Honor Book Medal, 1989
Boston Globe-Horn Book Award, 1989

Other books by the same author:
Stranger in the Mirror, 1995
Grandfather's Journey, 1993
Tree of Cranes, 1991
El Chino, 1990 (biography)
The Lost Lake, 1989 (authored by Say, a young boy and his father share a special camping trip)

Other books you might like:
Amy Tan, *The Chinese Siamese Cat*, 1994
    Ming Mao tells her five kittens about their illustrious Chinese ancestry.
Amy Tan, *The Moon Lady*, 1992
    Nai-Nai tells her granddaughters the story of her trip to see the Moon Lady and be granted a wish when she was seven.
Ed Young, *Cat and Rat: The Legend of the Chinese Zodiac*, 1995
    An adaptation of how the 12 animals of the zodiac were selected.
Laurence Yep, *The Ghost Fox*, 1994
    A brave boy saves his mother from the evil ghost fox who tries to steal her soul.

1070

MONICA SONE

Nisei Daughter
(Seattle: University of Washington Press, 1953)

Subject(s): Multicultural; Coming of Age; Internment
Age range(s): Adult
Major character(s): Kazuko Monica Sone, Daughter, Japanese American (second-generation); "Father" Sone, Father, Hotel Owner (Carrollton Hotel, Seattle), Japanese American (immigrant); Benko Sone, Mother, Japanese American, Immigrant
Time period(s): 1920s; 1950s
Locale(s): Seattle, Washington; Camp Minidoka, Idaho (internment camp for Japanese Americans during World War II); Chicago, Illinois

Summary: The autobiograhical account of a second-generation Japanese American woman growing up in Seattle in the 1920s through the 1940s, her family's incarceration during World War II in Idaho and her new life as a college student in Chicago.

About this book: Originally published by Little, Brown and Company. Sone writes one of the most eloquent passages questioning the Japanese American concentration camp experience: "What was I doing behind a fence like a criminal? If there were accusations to be made, why hadn't I been given a fair trial? Maybe I wasn't considered an American anymore. My citizenship wasn't real, after all. Then what was I?"

Where it's reviewed:
Kliatt, Spring 1980, page 28

Other books you might like:
Jeanne Wakatsuki Houston, *Farewell to Manzanar*, 1973
    The true story of the Wakatsuski family, uprooted from their home and incarcerated at Manzanar, one of 10 U.S. concentration camps for Japanese Americans during World War II.
Joy Kogawa, *Obasan*, 1982
    The story of a Japanese Canadian family that is splintered and scattered as a result of forced evacuation and relocation during World War II.
Mine Okubo, *Citizen 13660*, 1946
    This autobiographical account, told through sketches and text, is of a Japanese American woman who was reduced to Citizen 13660 and interned during World War II.
Hisaye Yamamoto, *Seventeen Syllables and Other Stories*, 1988
    A collection of 15 short stories from Yamamoto's almost half-century-long writing career.
Jade Snow Wong, *Fifth Chinese Daughter*, 1945
    An autobiographical account of an American-born Chinese woman growing up in San Francisco's Chinatown between the 1920s to 1940s.

1071

CATHY SONG

Picture Bride
(New Haven, CT: Yale University Press, 1983)

Subject(s): Poetry; Multicultural; Identity
Age range(s): Adult

Summary: Cathy Song's award-winning debut poetry collection is divided into five sections, each named after flowers. Song draws inspiration from the works of 19th-century Japanese woodcut printmaker Kitagawa Utamaro, modern American artist Georgia O'Keefe, as well as detailed elements of the life that surrounds her.

Where it's reviewed:
American Book Review, January 1986, page 19

Awards the book has won:
Yale Series of Younger Poets, 1982

Other books by the same author:
School Figures, 1994 (poetry collection)
Frameless Windows, Squares of Light, 1988 (poetry collection)

Other books you might like:
Joseph Bruchac, *Breaking Silence: An Anthology of Contemporary Asian American Poets*, 1983
    One of the first major anthologies of Asian American poetry, featuring the work of some 50 writers.
Kimiko Hahn, *Earshot*, 1992
    Imaginative, quirky, varied poetry collection.
Li-Young Lee, *The City in Which I Love You*, 1990
    Award-winning second poetry collection, about relationships between family and lovers.
Walter K. Lew, *Premonitions: The Kaya Anthology of New Asian North American Poetry*, 1995
    This collection of 73 authors, ranging from the established

to the up-and-coming, features writing in all modes of poetry, including works in non-standard form and dialects.

Garrett Hongo, *The Open Boat: Poems from Asian America*, 1993

A collection of works by 30 Asian American writers, both U.S. and foreign-born, covering over 100 years of the Asian American presence in America.

1072

SUI SIN FAR (Pseudonym of Edith Maude Eaton)

Mrs. Spring Fragrance and Other Writings

(Urbana: University of Illinois Press, 1995)

Subject(s): Multicultural; Short Stories
Time period(s): 1880s; 1910s

Summary: A collection of short stories and journalistic writings by Sui Sin Far, whose work was the first ever to focus on the Chinese experience in the U.S. and Canada. Her short stories, many of which have been compiled in this volume, were the first fiction in English by an Asian American.

Where it's reviewed:
Publishers Weekly, June 19, 1995, page 55

Other books you might like:
Sky Lee, *Disappearing Moon Cafe*, 1991
  One hundred years of the Wong family saga, which begins in the 1890s when a Chinese man marries a Native Indian, and is uncovered and recorded by his fifth generation descendent.
Ruthanne Lum McCunn, *Thousand Pieces of Gold*, 1981
  The first biographical novel of Chinese American pioneer woman, Polly Bemis.
Jade Snow Wong, *Fifth Chinese Daughter*, 1945
  An autobiographical account of an American-born Chinese woman growing up in San Francisco's Chinatown between the 1920s to 1940s.
Wakako Yamauchi, *Songs My Mother Taught Me: Stories, Plays, and Memoir*, 1994
  This rich collection, by one of the pioneer voices of Asian America, spans 35 years.

1073

CHYNG FENG SUN
LOLLY ROBINSON, Illustrator

Mama Bear

(Boston: Houghton Mifflin Company, 1994)

Subject(s): Mothers and Daughters; Gifts; Perseverance
Age range(s): Grades 1-4
Major character(s): Mei-Mei, Child (living with her mother), Chinese American; Mother, Mother (Mei-Mei's), Waiter/Waitress (works for Mrs. Wong); Mrs. Wong, Restauranteur (owner of Chinese restaurant)
Time period(s): 1990s (1994)
Locale(s): Chinatown (book jacket says Boston's Chinatown)

Summary: Mei-Mei sees the perfect Christmas present for herself and her mother—a giant stuffed bear. She saves money for the expensive gift, even having a cookie sale. The bear proves too expensive, but in the end, Mei-Mei realizes that she already has something even more special.

Where it's reviewed:
Booklist, September 1, 1994, page 55
Publishers Weekly, August 22, 1994, page 55

Other books by the same author:
Cat and Cat-face, 1996
On a White Pebble Hill, 1994
Square Beak, 1993

Other books you might like:
Jama Kim Rattigan, *Dumpling Soup*, 1993
  Every year the Yang family gathers at Grandma's house from all over Oahu, Hawaii to celebrate New Year's Eve. This year, young Marisa will help Grandma make her famous dumpling soup.
Kate Waters, *Lion Dancer: Ernie Wan's Chinese New Year*, 1990
  Young Ernie is about to experience the most important day of his life. He will perform his first Lion Dance through the streets of New York's Chinatown as part of the Chinese New Year celebration.
Karen Chinn, *Sam and the Lucky Money*, 1995
  Disappointed that everything he wants to buy with his Chinese New Year gift money costs too much, Sam finally realizes how lucky he is when he sees a lonely stranger without shoes.
Janet Mitsui Brown, *Thanksgiving at Obaachan's*, 1994
  A Japanese American loves to visit her grandmother's house for Thanksgiving, where the meal is a combination of traditional Japanese and American fare.
Kimiko Sakai, *Sachiko Means Happiness*, 1990
  Sachiko is upset when her grandmother does not even recognize her. When she finally comes to understand what has happened to her grandmother, Sachiko learns again how to be her friend.

1074

CHYNG FENG SUN
CHIHSIEN CHEN, Illustrator

Square Beak

(Boston: Houghton Mifflin Company, 1993)

Subject(s): Prejudice; Popularity; Difference
Age range(s): Grades 1-4
Major character(s): Square Beak, Chicken (born from a square egg); Lao Lao, Chicken (Square Beak's mother)
Time period(s): Indeterminate Past

Summary: Square Beak is aptly named for her square-shaped beak. Because she looks different from the other chickens in the yard, she is ostracized. She wanders outside her small world, and becomes famous for the beautiful, unusual eggs she is able to lay. But sudden popularity does not necessarily bring her happiness.

Where it's reviewed:
Booklist, April 1, 1993, page 1441
New York Times Book Review, October 17, 1993, page 33
Publishers Weekly, March 1, 1993, page 56

Other books you might like:
Ken Mochizuki, *Heroes*, 1995
> Always forced to play the enemy because he looks like ''them,'' Japanese American Donnie enlists his reluctant father and uncle to prove their U.S. military service records.

Michele Maria Surat, *Angel Child, Dragon Child*, 1983
> Young Ut, a recent Vietnamese immigrant, is teased because of her different appearance. Thrown together by their school principal, Ut and a once cruel boy develop a new friendship.

Sandra S. Yamate, *Char Siu Bao Boy*, 1991
> Charlie's favorite food, char sui bao, causes his classmates to tease him until, one day, he brings in enough for everyone to taste.

Sandra S. Yamate, *Ashok by Any Other Name*, 1992
> Ashok, a young Indian American boy, wishes he had a more ''American'' name, so he tries a new one each day until he finally realizes that ''Ashok'' is the perfect name for him.

Jeanne M. Lee, *Silent Lotus*, 1991
> Beautiful Lotus is unable to hear or speak. When she is ostracized by the local children, her parents take her to see the temple dancers and she begins her training to become one of them.

1075

MICHELE MARIA SURAT
VO-DINH MAI, Illustrator

Angel Child, Dragon Child
(New York: Scholastic Inc., 1983)

Subject(s): Prejudice; Sisters; Multicultural
Age range(s): Grades 1-4
Major character(s): Hoa ''Ut'' Nguyen, Student, Immigrant (from Vietnam), Vietnamese; Chi Hai Nguyen, Sister (Ut's older sister); Little Quang Nguyen, Brother (younger brother of Ut and Chi), Child (preschooler); Raymond, Classmate (Ut's)
Time period(s): 1980s (1983)
Locale(s): United States

Summary: Young Ut has recently arrived in the U.S. from Vietnam with her siblings and father, but the family still waits for their mother. Ut's new life is difficult, as other students tease her about her different appearance. Thrown together by the school principal, Ut develops a new friendship with a once cruel boy.

Where it's reviewed:
Booklist, July 1985, page 1570
Booklist, October 1, 1986, page 280
Children's Library Association Quarterly, Summer 1991, page 58
Instructor, August 1991, page 36
Multicultural Review, April 1992, page 37

Other books you might like:
Sheila Hamanaka, *On the Wings of Peace: Writers and Illustrators Speak Out for Peace, in Memory of Hiroshima and Nagasaki*, 1996
> Compiled by Hamanaka. A collection of stories, poetry,

remembrances and art focusing on the tragedies caused by war, and the hopes for a lasting peace for today's children.

Sheila Hamanaka, *Peace Crane*, 1995
> After learning about Sadako, a victim of the Hiroshima bombing, a girl imagines a peaceful world.

Toshi Maruki, *Hiroshima No Pika (The Flash of Hiroshima)*, 1980
> Although young Mii and her parents survived the initial blast of the Hiroshima atomic bomb, the horror they endured afterwards was a tragedy beyond description.

Tran Khanh Tuyet, *The Little Weaver of Thai-Yen Village*, 1977
> A young Vietnamese refugee arrives in the U.S. and struggles to adjust to her new life. She starts to weave again, as she did in her home country with her late grandmother.

1076

RONALD TAKAKI

Strangers from a Different Shore
(Boston: Little, Brown and Company, 1989)

Subject(s): Multicultural; Emigration and Immigration; Historical
Age range(s): Adult
Time period(s): 1830s; 1980s
Locale(s): United States

Summary: A groundbreaking history of Asian Americans in the U.S. during the last 150 years, told predominantly through the actual narratives of Japanese, Chinese, Korean, Filipino, Asian Indian, Vietnamese, Cambodian and Laotian immigrants. These Asian Americans—from fourth-generation Chinese Americans to Hmong refugees—continue to be perceived as ''strangers,'' even in the place they call ''home.''

Where it's reviewed:
Kirkus Reviews, June 15, 1989, page 906
Library Journal, July 1989, page 93
New Yorker, October 16, 1989, page 132

Awards the book has won:
Pulitzer Prize nomination for nonfiction, 1989
New York Times Notable Book, 1989

Other books by the same author:
A Different Mirror: A History of Multicultural America, 1993
Pau Hana: Plantation Life and Labor in Hawaii, 1983
Iron Cages: Race and Culture in Nineteenth-Century America, 1979
Violence in the Black Imagination, 1971
A Pro-Slavery Crusade, 1970 (a study of the Southern ideological defense of slavery)

Other books you might like:
Victor G. Nee, *Longtime Californ': A Documentary Study of an American Chinatown*, 1974
> With co-author Brett de Bary Nee, Nee presents a history of the Chinese in America told through both narrative and extensive interviews, using the backdrop of San Francisco's Chinatown.

Joanne Faung Jean Lee, *Asian Americans*, 1991
> A collection of oral histories from first- to fourth-genera-

tion Asian Americans of Chinese, Filipino, Japanese, Korean, Southeast Asian and Pacific Island ancestry.

Garrett Hongo, *Under Western Eyes: Personal Essays from Asian America*, 1994

A collection of 15 autobiographical essays from leading Asian American voices, confronting racism, language, family, stereotypes and other social and political issues.

Maria Hong, *Growing Up Asian American*, 1993

These essays, excerpts and short stories by Americans of Asian descent address issues such as parent-child relationships, self-realization, identity and the discovery of one's cultural heritage.

Elaine H. Kim, *East to America: Korean American Life Stories*, 1996

Co-edited with Eui-Young Yu, these oral histories come from 38 Korean Americans, from immigrants to third-generation Americans, including journalists, activists, artists, shopkeepers and students.

1077

AMY TAN
GRETCHEN SHIELDS, Illustrator

The Chinese Siamese Cat
(New York: Macmillan Publishing Company, 1994)

Subject(s): Folk Tales; Multicultural; Animals
Age range(s): Grades 3-6
Major character(s): Ming Miao, Cat (mother-cat of five kittens); Sagwa of China, Cat (ancient ancestor of Ming Mao), Chinese; The Foolish Magistrate, Ruler (decreed ridiculous rules)
Time period(s): Indeterminate Past (from the present to ancient times)
Locale(s): China (in ''the House of the Foolish Magistrate'')

Summary: Ming Miao tells her five kittens about their famous ancestor, Sagwa of China, who one day, during mischievous play, falls into the inkpot and walks all over the Foolish Magistrate's dreaded Scroll of Rules, completely changing their grievous nature. The Magistrate becomes a hero to the grateful people and Sagwa is well rewarded.

About this book: Tan's second children's book.

Where it's reviewed:
Children's Book Review Service, September 1994, page 5
Kirkus Reviews, July 15, 1994, page 997
Publishers Weekly, July 11, 1994, page 78

Other books by the same author:
The Hundred Secret Senses, 1995
The Moon Lady, 1992
The Kitchen God's Wife, 1991
The Joy Luck Club, 1989

Other books you might like:
Barbara Brenner, *Chibi: A True Story from Japan*, 1996
Written with Julia Takaya. The true story of a lone duck who flies into downtown Tokyo and hatches 10 ducklings.
Jeanne M. Lee, *Toad is the Uncle of Heaven*, 1985
The Toad asks the King of Heaven for rain. On his journey, he is joined by the Bees, the Rooster and the Tiger. With

the help of his friends, Toad convinces the King to provide rain.

Dianne Snyder, *The Boy of the Three-Year Nap*, 1988
Lazy Taro hatches a plan to ensure an easy life by convincing a rich merchant that his beautiful daughter must marry Taro.

Ed Young, *Cat and Rat: The Legend of the Chinese Zodiac*, 1995
An adaptation of how the 12 animals of the zodiac were selected.

1078

AMY TAN

The Hundred Secret Senses
(New York: G.P. Putnam's Sons, 1995)

Subject(s): Sisters; Multicultural; Supernatural
Age range(s): Adult
Major character(s): Olivia ''Libby-ah'' Simon, Sister (half-sister of Kwan), Photographer, Chinese American (American-born); Kwan Li, Sister (half-sister of Olivia), Chinese American (Chinese-born); Simon Bishop, Spouse (husband of Olivia), Writer
Time period(s): 20th century (1960s-1990s); 1860s (1864; interwoven over time)
Locale(s): San Francisco, California; Changmian, China (major action in China happens in Changmian, and briefly in Guilin)

Summary: At age 6, Olivia meets for the first time, her adult half-sister Kwan, just arrived from China. Kwan shares with a disbelieving Olivia her stories of the Yin people—people not of this world with whom Kwan is able to communicate. Thirty years later, fate brings Kwan, Olivia and Simon, Olivia's estranged husband, to Kwan's native village in China. There Olivia finally comes to understand Kwan, especially Kwan's unconditional love and loyalty for her, even when Olivia did not always deserve it.

About this book: The title refers to the ability to use one's ''hundred secret senses,'' to think and look beyond the everyday seven senses and to rely on all of one's heart and soul to recognize the extraordinary. Kwan's link to the ''World of Yin'' is due to her familiarity with her hundred secret senses, a skill she is always reminding Olivia to rely on.

Where it's reviewed:
Booklist, September 15, 1995, page 116
Publishers Weekly, September 11, 1995, page 73

Other books by the same author:
The Moon Lady, 1992 (children's book)
The Chinese Siamese Cat, 1994 (children's tale)
The Kitchen God's Wife, 1991
The Joy Luck Club, 1989

Other books you might like:
Aimee Liu, *Face*, 1993
Red-haired, green-eyed Maibelle Chung returns to her Chinatown roots to finally confront the dark secrets of her incongruous, inescapable past.
Belle Yang, *Baba: A Return to China upon My Father's Shoulders*, 1994

The author takes a personal odyssey through northern China of the 1930s and 1940s, following the story of her father's coming-of-age as a son of the prominent Manchurian House of Yang.

Fae Myenne Ng, *Bone*, 1993

A multigenerational saga of a San Francisco Chinese American family.

Anchee Min, *Katherine*, 1995

This novel is about the relationship between an American woman and two Chinese students in post-Mao China.

1079

AMY TAN

The Joy Luck Club

(New York: G.P. Putnam's Sons, 1989)

Subject(s): Mothers and Daughters; Multicultural; Emigration and Immigration

Age range(s): Adult

Major character(s): Suyuan Woo, Friend (founder of the Joy Luck Club), Mother (of June Woo), Chinese American; Jing-mei "June" Woo, Daughter (of Suyuan Woo), Chinese American (American-born); Lindo Jong, Friend (best friend of Suyuan Woo), Mother (of Waverly Jong), Chinese American (immigrant); Waverly Jong, Daughter (of Lindo Jong), Chinese American (American-born); An-Mei Hsu, Chinese American (immigrant), Mother (of Rose Hsu Jordan); Rose Hsu Jordan, Daughter (of An-mei Hsu), Chinese American (American born); Ying-ying St. Clair, Immigrant, Mother (of Lena St. Clair), Chinese American; Lena St. Clair, Daughter (of Ying-ying St.Clair), Chinese American (American born)

Time period(s): 20th century (1930-1989)

Locale(s): San Francisco, California (Bay Area); China (various locations before 1949)

Summary: Since 1949, four Chinese-born women now living in San Francisco gather regularly to play mah-jong and share their lives. Together they make up the Joy Luck Club. They share stories of the old world, each having escaped a secret past, and indulge in the hopes of the New World, nurturing the lives of their four American-born daughters.

About this book: A timeless story of the special relationship between mothers and daughters, this work became the first major breakthrough commercial novel by an Asian American.

Where it's reviewed:

New Yorker, June 26, 1989, page 91
Publishers Weekly, May 4, 1990, page 66
Time, March 27, 1989, page 98

Awards the book has won:

National Book Award finalist, 1989
National Book Critics Circle Award finalist, 1989

Other books by the same author:

The Hundred Secret Senses, 1995
The Moon Lady, 1992 (for children)
The Kitchen God's Wife, 1991
The Chinese Siamese Cat, 1994 (for children)

Other books you might like:

Maxine Hong Kingston, *The Woman Warrior: Memoirs of a Girlhood Among Ghosts*, 1975

The story of a young girl growing up in the San Francisco Bay Area divided amidst the stories of her parents' faraway past in China and her own experiences in a Caucasian world.

Anchee Min, *Red Azalea*, 1994

The personal memoir of Min's difficult life in China during the Cultural Revolution and her struggle to escape the brutality of her homeland.

Fae Myenne Ng, *Bone*, 1993

A multigenerational saga of a San Francisco Chinese American family.

R.A. Sasaki, *The Loom and Other Stories*, 1991

A collection of short stories, interwoven to tell the story of three generations of a Japanese American family.

Julie Shigekuni, *A Bridge Between Us*, 1995

Four generations of women—each a mother and a daughter—of a San Francisco Japanese American family trace their lives from 1900 to the present.

1080

AMY TAN

The Kitchen God's Wife

(New York: G.P. Putnam's Sons, 1991)

Subject(s): Mothers and Daughters; Multicultural; Emigration and Immigration

Age range(s): Adult

Major character(s): Winnie Louie, Businesswoman (flower shop co-owner), Mother (of Pearl Louie), Chinese American (immigrant); Helen "Auntie Helen" Kwong, Businesswoman (flower shop co-owner), Sister (sister-in-law to Winnie Louie), Chinese American (immigrant); Pearl Louie, Daughter (of Winnie), Chinese American (American born)

Time period(s): 20th century (1920-1991)

Locale(s): San Francisco, California (Bay Area); China (various locations from the 1920s to 1949)

Summary: Helen and Winnie share a past that spans over 50 years and two continents, and is filled with hidden secrets. When Helen thinks she's dying and feels she must tell all, Winnie realizes she must be the one to share with Pearl, her American-born daughter, all of her own secrets. Little by little, Winnie reveals the life she led in China, sharing her hard-won knowledge and strength.

Where it's reviewed:

Ms., November 1991, page 76
Publishers Weekly, November 1, 1991, page 20
Time, June 3, 1991, page 67

Other books by the same author:

The Hundred Secret Senses, 1995
The Moon Lady, 1992 (for children)
The Joy Luck Club, 1989
The Chinese Siamese Cat, 1994 (for children)

Other books you might like:

Maxine Hong Kingston, *The Woman Warrior: Memoirs of a Girlhood Among Ghosts*, 1975

The story of a young girl growing up in the San Francisco Bay Area divided amidst the stories of her parents' faraway past in China and her own experiences in a Caucasian world.

Anchee Min, *Red Azalea*, 1994

The personal memoir of Min's difficult life in China during the Cultural Revolution and her struggle to escape the brutality of her homeland.

Fae Myenne Ng, *Bone*, 1993

A multigenerational saga of a San Francisco Chinese American family.

R.A. Sasaki, *The Loom and Other Stories*, 1991

A collection of short stories, interwoven to tell the story of three generations of a Japanese American family.

Julie Shigekuni, *A Bridge Between Us*, 1995

Four generations of women—each a mother as well as a daughter—from a San Francisco Japanese American family trace their lives from 1900 to the present.

1081

AMY TAN
GRETCHEN SHIELDS, Illustrator

The Moon Lady

(New York: Macmillan Publishing Company, 1992)

Subject(s): Folk Tales; Multicultural; Wishes
Age range(s): Grades 3-6
Major character(s): Amah, Child-Care Giver (Ying-ying's nursemaid in China); Ying-ying, Grandmother, Chinese
Time period(s): 1990s (from present to many years ago)
Locale(s): China

Summary: One rainy afternoon, a grandmother tells her three granddaughters a story from her childhood in China. Mischievous and curious, young Ying-ying becomes separated from her family during the Moon Festival and discovers that her one true wish is to be back in the arms of her loved ones.

About this book: This is Tan's first children's book.

Other books by the same author:
The Hundred Secret Senses, 1995
The Chinese Siamese Cat, 1994
The Kitchen God's Wife, 1991
The Joy Luck Club, 1989

Other books you might like:

Oki S. Han, *Sir Whong and the Golden Pig*, 1993

Mr. Oh borrows a huge sum of money from Sir Whong and offers a priceless golden pig as security. Mr. Oh proves to be a greedy liar and Sir Whong devises his own plan for revenge.

Kimiko Sakai, *Sachiko Means Happiness*, 1990

Young Sachiko learns again how to be a friend to her elderly grandmother with whom she shares the same name.

Chyng Feng Sun, *Mama Bear*, 1994

While looking for the perfect Christmas present, Mei-Mei learns she has something more special at home than an expensive toy bear

Taro Yashima, *Crow Boy*, 1955

Award-winning story of shy Chibi who does not fit in with the rest of his schoolmates.

Laurence Yep, *The City of Dragons*, 1995

The boy with the saddest face in the world proves to be a hero in the city of dragons.

1082

CHIYOKO TOMIOKA
YOSHIHARU TSUCHIDA, Illustrator

Rise and Shine, Mariko-chan!

(New York: Scholastic Inc., 1986)

Subject(s): Family Relations
Age range(s): Grades 1-2
Major character(s): Mariko-chan, Child (getting ready for school); Mama, Mother (Mariko's); Oba-san, Grandmother (Mariko's)
Time period(s): 1980s (1986)

Summary: Mariko wakes up every morning to her mother's cheerful call. She shares breakfast with her family, then watches the hustle-bustle of her two older sisters and parents preparing to leave, until finally it's her turn to get ready for the yellow school bus that will take her to school.

About this book: In Japanese, to add ''-chan'' to the end of a name is a term of endearment, usually used for small children.

Where it's reviewed:
Publishers Weekly, August 3, 1992, page 73

Other books you might like:

Jennifer L. Chan, *ONE small GIRL*, 1993

Told not to touch anything in either her grandmother's or her uncle's adjacent Chinatown stores, a little girl manages to have fun.

Demi, *The Empty Pot*, 1990

When Ping presents an empty pot to the Emperor, he is rewarded for his honesty.

Huy Voun Lee, *At the Beach*, 1994

On a beautiful day at the beach, Xiao Ming learns to write Chinese characters with his mother in the sand.

Huy Voun Lee, *In the Snow*, 1995

During a winter walk through the forest, Xiao Ming's mother teaches him new Chinese characters, using the white snow to draw the picture-like characters.

Yoriko Tsutsui, *Anna in Charge*, 1979

While her mother goes to run an errand, Anna is left in charge of her younger sister, Katy. Katy wanders off while Anna is not looking and Anna quickly goes searching for her.

1083

TRAN KHANH TUYET
NANCY HOM, Illustrator

The Little Weaver of Thai-Yen Village

(San Francisco: Children's Book Press, 1977)

Subject(s): Vietnam War; Children and War; Emigration and Immigration

Age range(s): Grades 3-6
Major character(s): Hien, Refugee, Child, Vietnamese; Mother, Mother (Hien's), Vietnamese; Grandmother, Grandmother (Hien's), Vietnamese
Time period(s): 1960s; 1970s (during the Vietnam War)
Locale(s): Thai-Yen Village, Vietnam; United States

Summary: Hien's village is destroyed during the Vietnam War, killing her mother and grandmother. Hien is seriously injured and must go to the U.S. for an operation. Living with an American family, she starts to weave again, as she did with her grandmother, creating blankets to send back to refugees in Vietnam.

About this book: A bilingual book, written in both English and Vietnamese.

Other books you might like:
Michele Maria Surat, *Angel Child, Dragon Child*, 1983
　　Young Ut, a recent Vietnamese immigrant, is teased because of her different appearance. Thrown together by the school principal, Ut and a once cruel boy develop a new friendship.
Toshi Maruki, *Hiroshima No Pika (The Flash of Hiroshima)*, 1980
　　Although young Mii and her parents survived the initial blast of the Hiroshima atomic bomb, the horror they endured afterwards was a tragedy beyond description.
Sheila Hamanaka, *Peace Crane*, 1995
　　After learning about Sadako, a victim of the Hiroshima bombing, a girl imagines a peaceful world.

1084

C.W. TRUESDALE, Editor
DIANE GLANCY, Co-Editor

Two Worlds Walking: Short Stories, Essays, and Poetry by Writers with Mixed Heritages
(Minneapolis: New Rivers Press, 1994)

Subject(s): Identity; Multicultural; Short Stories
Age range(s): Adult
Time period(s): Indeterminate
Locale(s): United States

Summary: A first-of-a-kind anthology that brings together the works of 42 writers, each of mixed ancestry, each ''walking in two worlds,'' trying to discover their ''American'' identities. The contributors' ethnic backgrounds are as diverse as their modes of writing, from Korean Japanese-German Nancy Lee to Chilean-Jewish Barbara Mujica.

Other books you might like:
Wesley Brown, *Imagining America: Stories from the Promised Land*, 1991
　　Also edited with Amy Ling. A multicultural anthology of 37 short stories about immigration to and migration within the U.S., the so-called ''Promised Land.''
Wesley Brown, *Visions of America: Personal Narratives from the Promised Land*, 1993
　　Also edited with Amy Ling.

Juliet S. Kono, *Sister Stew: Fiction and Poetry by Women*, 1991
　　Edited with Cathy Song, this is a colorful collection of writings by women of various backgrounds, the majority of whom are either Hawaiian by birth or by adopted residency.
Bennett Lee, *Many-Mouthed Birds: Contemporary Writings by Chinese Canadians*, 1991
　　A diverse collection of short stories from some of Canada's leading Asian voices, including Larissa Lai, Evelyn Lau, Sky Lee and Denise Chong.
Jessica Hagedorn, *Charlie Chan Is Dead: An Anthology of Contemporary Asian American Fiction*, 1993
　　This collection of 48 works is by Asian American writers of different ages, backgrounds and styles.

1085

YORIKO TSUTSUI
AKIKO HAYASHI, Illustrator

Anna in Charge
(New York: Puffin Books (Penguin Group), 1979)

Subject(s): Responsibility; Sisters
Age range(s): Grades 1-3
Major character(s): Anna Lee, Child (left to watch her baby sister); Katy Lee, Sister (Anna's younger sister)
Time period(s): 1970s (1979)

Summary: While her mother goes to run an errand, Anna is left in charge of her younger sister, Katy. Katy wanders off while Anna is not looking and Anna quickly goes about searching.

Other books you might like:
Jennifer L. Chan, *ONE small GIRL*, 1993
　　Told not to touch anything in either her grandmother's or her uncle's adjacent Chinatown stores, a little girl still manages to have fun.
Huy Voun Lee, *At the Beach*, 1994
　　On a beautiful day at the beach, Xiao Ming learns to write Chinese characters with his mother in the sand.
Huy Voun Lee, *In the Snow*, 1995
　　During a winter walk through the forest, Xiao Ming's mother teaches him new Chinese characters, using the white snow to draw the picture-like characters.
Chiyoko Tomioka, *Rise and Shine, Mariko-chan!*, 1986
　　Young Mariko gets up each morning and gets ready for the yellow school bus that will take her to school.

1086

KATHLEEN TYAU

A Little Too Much Is Enough
(New York: Farrar, Straus and Giroux, 1995)

Subject(s): Coming of Age; Multicultural; Family Relations
Age range(s): Adult
Major character(s): Mahealani Suzanne ''Mahi'' Wong, Young Woman, Chinese Hawaiian; Anna Choy Wong, Mother (Mahi's); Kuhio Wong, Father (Mahi's); Auntie Nona Choy, Aunt (eccentric, maternal)

Time period(s): 1940s; 1950s

Locale(s): Hawaii (mostly centered in Honolulu and Waikiki)

Summary: Mahi Wong grows up in post-World War II Hawaii, surrounded by a large and complicated family of parents, siblings and endless uncles and aunties. She is immersed in a mixed, sometimes confusing Chinese Hawaiian heritage that includes everything from Chinese nine-course banquets, native poi, elaborate luaus, pineapple factories and crackseed.

Where it's reviewed:
Booklist, July 1995, page 1861
Library Journal, June 1, 1995, page 168
Publishers Weekly, June 12, 1995, page 47

Other books you might like:
R. Zamora Linmark, *Rolling the R's*, 1995
    A collection interrelated short stories, many about young Filipino Americans coming to terms with their ethnicity and with their sexuality in Honolulu.
Darrell H.Y. Lum, *Pass On, No Pass Back!*, 1990
    A humorous collection of short stories about growing up in Hawaii.
Milton Murayama, *All I Asking for Is My Body*, 1959
    A young Japanese American boy's coming-of-age in Hawaii during the 1930s up until the advent of World War II.
Yoji Yamaguchi, *Face of a Stranger*, 1995
    Kikue, a Japanese woman, arrived in the U.S. believing she was to be a picture bride. Forced into prostitution instead, she makes plans to gain her freedom and plot revenge on those who deceived her.
Lois-Ann Yamanaka, *Wild Meat and the Bully Burgers*, 1996
    A coming-of-age first novel about Lovey Nariyoshi of Hilo, Hawaii, her best friend Jerome, her adolescent enemies and her eccentric family.

1087

YOSHIKO UCHIDA

Desert Exile: The Uprooting of a Japanese-American Family

(Seattle: University of Washington Press, 1982)

Subject(s): Internment; Multicultural; Coming of Age

Age range(s): Adult

Major character(s): Yoshiko Uchida, Daughter, Japanese American (second-generation); Keiko Uchida, Daughter (older sister of Yoshiko), Japanese American (second-generation); Dwight Takashi Uchida, Father, Businessman (employed by Japanese company), Japanese (first-generation); Iku Umegaki Uchida, Mother, Japanese (first-generation)

Time period(s): 1920s; 1940s

Locale(s): California (Berkeley, Oakland and the Tanforan Assembly Center); Camp Topaz, Utah (internment camp for Americans of Japanese ancestry during World War II)

Summary: The autobiographical account of a second-generation Japanese American woman growing up in Berkeley, California and her family's internment experiences at Camp Topaz during World War II.

Where it's reviewed:
Booklist, September 15, 1982, page 90

Los Angeles Times Book Review, October 31, 1982, page 6
Western Historical Quarterly, October 1983, page 485

Other books by the same author:
The Invisible Thread, 1991 (children's book)
The Happiest Ending, 1985
The Best Bad Thing, 1983 (sequel; young adult)
A Jar of Dreams, 1981 (young adult)
Journey to Topaz: A Story of the Japanese American Evacuation, 1971 (young adult)

Other books you might like:
Jeanne Wakatsuki Houston, *Farewell to Manzanar*, 1973
    The true story of the Wakatsuki family, uprooted from their home and incarcerated at Manzanar, one of 10 U.S. concentration camps for Japanese Americans during World War II.
Joy Kogawa, *Obasan*, 1982
    The story of a Japanese Canadian family that is splintered and scattered as a result of forced evacuation and relocation during World War II.
Mine Okubo, *Citizen 13660*, 1946
    The autobiographical account, told through sketches and text, of a Japanese American woman, who was reduced to Citizen Number 13660 and interned during World War II.
Monica Sone, *Nisei Daughter*, 1953
    An account of a second-generation Japanese American woman growing up in Seattle in the 1920s and '30s, being incarcerated during World War II and her new life in the Midwest.
Hisaye Yamamoto, *Seventeen Syllables and Other Stories*, 1988
    collection of 15 short stories from Yamamoto's almost half-century-long writing career.

1088

YOSHIKO UCHIDA
KAZUE MIZUMURA, Illustrator

The Forever Christmas Tree

(New York: Charles Scribner's Sons, 1963)

Subject(s): Multicultural; Christmas; Friendship

Age range(s): Grades 3-6

Major character(s): Takashi, Child (not old enough to go to school); Kaya, 8-Year-Old, Sister (older of Takashi); Mr. Toda, Neighbor (reclusive, next door), Aged Person

Time period(s): 1960s (December)

Locale(s): Sugi Village, Japan

Summary: Young Takashi hears wonderful stories about a joyous holiday called Christmas from his sister Kaya. As the day approaches, the two create beautiful decorations. On Christmas Eve, they decorate their mean, reclusive neighbor's fir tree. The decorated tree ends up bringing the whole neighborhood together.

About this book: With 27 young adult and children's titles (and two adult works) to her name, Uchida is considered the foremost author of books for young people about the Japanese American experience. Uchida wrote between 1948 and 1991, and passed away in June 1992.

Other books by the same author:
The Invisible Thread, 1991 (children's book)
The Happiest Ending, 1985 (sequel)
The Best Bad Thing, 1983 (sequel; young adult)
A Jar of Dreams, 1981 (young adult)
Journey to Topaz: A Story of the Japanese American Evacuation, 1971 (young adult)

Other books you might like:
Allen Say, *Tree of Cranes*, 1991
 Lovely story about a young Japanese boy who learns about Christmas for the first time from his California-born Japanese American mother.
Kate Waters, *Lion Dancer: Ernie Wan's Chinese New Year*, 1990
 Young Ernie is about to experience the most important day of his life. He will perform his first Lion Dance through the streets of New York's Chinatown as part of the Chinese New Year celebration.
Chyng Feng Sun, *Mama Bear*, 1994
 Mei-Mei saves money to buy the perfect Christmas gift—a stuffed bear. When the money she's saved is not enough, she realizes that she's had something even more special all along.
Karen Chinn, *Sam and the Lucky money*, 1995
 Disappointed that everything he wants to buy with his Chinese New Year gift money costs too much, Sam finally realizes how lucky he is when he sees a lonely stranger without shoes.
Elaine Hosozawa-Nagano, *Chopsticks from America*, 1994
 Two Japanese American children move to Japan. While they look like ''chopsticks among chopsticks,'' they are American, which proves to be different from being Japanese.

1089

YOSHIKO UCHIDA
CHARLES ROBINSON, Illustrator

Journey Home
(New York: Aladdin Books (Macmillan Publishing Company), 1978)

Subject(s): Internment; Anti-Asian Sentiment; Coming of Age
Age range(s): Grades 6-10
Major character(s): Yuki Sakane, Young Woman (leaving internment camp), Japanese American (second generation); ''Mother'' Sakane, Mother (Yuki's), Immigrant, Japanese American; ''Father'' Sakane, Father (Yuki's), Immigrant, Japanese American; Emiko ''Emi'' Kurihara, Friend (fellow camp internee), Young Woman, Japanese American; Grandma Kurihara, Grandmother (Emi's, with whom she lives); Kunisaburo ''Uncle Oka'' Oka, Friend, Aged Person (bitter), Japanese American
Time period(s): 1940s (1944-1945)
Locale(s): Salt Lake City, Utah; Berkeley, California

Summary: Just before the end of World War II, the Sakane family is released from internment camp and sent to live briefly in Salt Lake City. When they are finally allowed to return to their native California, they must face further hardships and difficulties in the place they once called home.

About this book: Sequel to *Journey to Topaz*.

Where it's reviewed:
Booklist, December 15, 1978, page 691
Children's Book Review Service, January 1979, page 50
Center for Children's Books. Bulletin, April 1979, page 146
Kirkus Reviews, January 1, 1979, page 6
School Library Journal, January 1979, page 58

Other books by the same author:
The Invisible Thread, 1991 (children's book)
The Happiest Ending, 1985 (sequel)
The Best Bad Thing, 1983 (sequel; young adult)
A Jar of Dreams, 1981 (young adult)
Journey to Topaz: A Story of the Japanese-American Education, 1971 (prequel)

Other books you might like:
Sheila Hamanaka, *On the Wings of Peace: Writers and Illustrators Speak Out for Peace, in Memory of Hiroshima and Nagasaki*, 1996
 Compiled by Hamanaka. Rich collection of stories, poetry, remembrances and art focusing on the tragedies caused by war, and the hopes for a lasting peace for today's children.
Jeanne Wakatsuki Houston, *Farewell to Manzanar*, 1973
 The true story of the Wakatsuki family, uprooted from their home and incarcerated at Manzanar, one of 10 U.S. concentration camps for Japanese Americans during World War II.
Joy Kogawa, *Naomi's Road*, 1986
 Young adult story of a Japanese Canadian family that is splintered and scattered as a result of forced evacuation and relocation during World War II.
Mine Okubo, *Citizen 13660*, 1946
 The autobiographical account, told through sketches and text, of a Japanese American woman, who was reduced to Citizen Number 13660 and interned during World War II.
Monica Sone, *Nisei Daughter*, 1953
 An account of a second-generation Japanese American woman growing up in Seattle in the 1920s and 1930s, being incarcerated during World War II and her new life in the Midwest.

1090

YOSHIKO UCHIDA
DONALD CARRICK ROBINSON, Illustrator

Journey to Topaz: A Story of the Japanese-American Education
(Berkeley, CA: Creative Arts Book Company, 1971)

Subject(s): Multicultural; Internment; Children and War
Age range(s): Grades 6-10
Major character(s): Yuki Sakane, 12-Year-Old (girl, interned with her family), Japanese American (second generation); Kenichi ''Ken'' Sakane, Brother (Yuki's college-age), Japanese American; ''Mother'' Sakane, Mother (Yuki and Ken's), Japanese American; Emiko ''Emi'' Kurihara, Friend (fellow internee), 12-Year-Old, Japanese American
Time period(s): 1940s (1941-1943)
Locale(s): California (Berkeley and Tanforan Assembly Center); Camp Topaz, Utah (bleak concentration camp in the Utah desert)

Summary: With the advent of World War II, Yuki's family is separated and imprisoned. Her father is taken away by the FBI, and the rest of the family is eventually shipped to Camp Topaz where they must face fierce duststorms, difficult living conditions, and needless tragedy.

About this book: With 27 young adult and children's titles and two adult works to her name, Uchida is considered the foremost author of books for young people about the Japanese American experience. Uchida wrote between 1948 and 1991, and passed away in June 1992.

Where it's reviewed:
Booklist, January 1, 1972, page 395
Book World, November 7, 1971, page 14
Horn Book Magazine, December 1971, page 615
Instructor, November 1971, page 133
Publishers Weekly September 6, 1971, page 51

Other books by the same author:
The Invisible Thread, 1991 (children's book)
The Happiest Ending, 1985 (sequel)
The Best Bad Thing, 1983 (sequel; young adult)
A Jar of Dreams, 1981 (young adult)
Journey Home, 1978

Other books you might like:
Sheila Hamanaka, *On the Wings of Peace: Writers and Illustrators Speak Out for Peace, in Memory of Hiroshima and Nagasaki*, 1996
 Compiled by Hamanaka. Rich collection of stories, poetry, remembrances and art focusing on the tragedies caused by war, and the hopes for a lasting peace for today's children.
Jeanne Wakatsuki Houston, *Farewell to Manzanar*, 1973
 The true story of the Wakatsuki family, uprooted from their home and incarcerated at Manzanar, one of 10 U.S. concentration camps for Japanese Americans during World War II.
Joy Kogawa, *Naomi's Road*, 1986
 Young adult story of a Japanese Canadian family that is splintered and scattered as a result of forced evacuation and relocation during World War II.
Mine Okubo, *Citizen 13660*, 1946
 The autobiographical account, told through sketches and text, of a Japanese American woman, who was reduced to Citizen Number 13660 and interned during World War II.
Monica Sone, *Nisei Daughter*, 1953
 An account of a second-generation Japanese American woman growing up in Seattle in the 1920s and '30s, being incarcerated during World War II and her new life in the Midwest.

1091

YOSHIKO UCHIDA, Adaptor
MARIANNE YAMAGUCHI, Illustrator

The Sea of Gold and Other Tales from Japan

(New York: Charles Scribner's Sons, 1965)

Subject(s): Folk Tales; Short Stories; Multicultural
Age range(s): Grades 6-12
Time period(s): Indeterminate Past

Summary: A collection of 12 diverse folktales, including stories about magic monkeys, foolish cats, a talking bowl, kind old men rewarded for their generosity, mountain gods and vengeful snakes.

Where it's reviewed:
Booklist, December 1, 1965, page 365
Center for Children's Books. Bulletin, December 1966, page 64
Kirkus Reviews, October 1, 1965, page 1043
Language Arts, November 1980, page 900
Library Journal, October 15, 1965, page 4623

Other books by the same author:
The Invisible Thread, 1991 (children's book)
Journey Home, 1978
Journey to Topaz: A Story of the Japanese-American Evacuation, 1971 (prequel)
The Magic Listening Cap: More Folk Tales from Japan, 1955
The Dancing Kettle and Other Japanese Folk Tales, 1949

Other books you might like:
Asian Cultural Centre for Unesco, *Folk Tales From Asia for Children Everywhere*, 1975
 Two volumes of traditional folktales with Asian origins, beautifully illustrated especially for children.
Valorie Slaughter Bejarano, *The Beginning and Other Asian Folktales*, 1995
 A delightful collection of adapted folktales of various Asian origin.
Jeannette Faurot, *Asian-Pacific Folktales and Legends*, 1995
 A diverse collection of over 60 folktales from Asia.
Laurence Yep, *Tongues of Jade*, 1991
 A collection of adaptations of 17 ancient Chinese folktales.
Laurence Yep, *The Rainbow People*, 1989
 A collection of 20 folktales, adapted by Yep from age-old Chinese lore.

1092

ROBERTA UNO, Editor

Unbroken Thread: An Anthology of Plays by Asian American Women

(Amherst, MA: The University of Massachusetts Press, 1993)

Subject(s): Theater; Multicultural
Age range(s): Adult
Time period(s): Indeterminate

Summary: An anthology of diverse plays by six Asian American women playwrights: *Paper Angels* by Genny Lim, *The Music Lessons* by Wakako Yamauchi, *Gold Watch* by Momoko Iko, *Tea* by Velina Hasu Houston, *Walls* by Jeannie Barroga and *Letters to a Student Revolutionary* by Elizabeth Wong.

About this book: The book opens with a well-informed introduction to the history of Asian American women in theater.

Where it's reviewed:
Theatre Journal, March 1995, page 151
Choice, June 1994, page 1594
Women's Review of Books, May 1994, page 16
Bookwatch, March 1994, page 8

Other books you might like:

Misha Berson, *Between Worlds: Contemporary Asian-American Plays*, 1990
  Edited by Berson; anthology includes works by Ping Chong, Philip Kan Gotanda, Jessica Hagedorn, David Henry Hwang, Wakako Yamauchi and Laurence Yep.

Velina Hasu Houston, *The Politics of Life: Four Plays by Asian American Women*, 1993
  Edited by Houston; includes works by Wakako Yamauchi, Genny Lim and Houston

Philip Kan Gotanda, *Fish Head Soup and Other Plays*, 1995
  Four dramas by an extraordinary playwright, focusing on family relations between first-, second-, and third-generation Japanese Americans.

David Henry Hwang, *FOB and Other Plays*, 1990
  A collection of six of Hwong's plays, including the Broadway gender-bender sensation, *M. Butterfly*.

Genny Lim, *Paper Angels and Bitter Cane*, 1991
  Two important plays are included here; one about Chinese immigrants detained at Angel Island and the other about the virtual imprisonment of Asian laborers on Hawaiian sugar cane plantations.

1093

MARIANNE VILLANUEVA

Ginseng and Other Tales from Manila
(Corvalis, OR: Calyx Books, 1991)

Subject(s): Short Stories
Age range(s): Adult
Time period(s): 1980s
Locale(s): Philippines (mostly in Manila)

Summary: A collection of stories, mostly set in Manila, inspired by real life stories and newspaper articles, focusing on the desperate citizens of a troubled country trying to survive poverty, government corruption and loss of individual freedom.

Where it's reviewed:
American Book Review, April 1993, page 18
Small Press, Spring 1992, page 78

Other books by the same author:
Trespassing Innocence, 1989 (poetry collection)

Other books you might like:

Jessica Hagedorn, *Dogeaters*, 1990
  An autobiographical novel about growing up in Manila in the late 1950s during the turbulent and corrupt Marcos regime.

F. Sionil Jose, *Three Filipino Women: Novellas*, 1992
  Three novellas about three remarkable, though ultimately tragic Filipino women: Narita, a politician, Ermita, a high class prostitute, and Malu, a political idealist.

M. Evelina Galang, *Her Wild American Self*, 1996
  A collection of short stories centered on the experiences of Filipina American women of various ages and lifestyles, each in search of her own unique identity.

Peter Bacho, *Cebu*, 1991
  On his first visit to the Philippines to bury his mother,

Filipino American priest Ben Lucero finds all his moral and religious beliefs thrown into question.

1094

MARIE VILLANUEVA
RIA UNSON, Illustrator

Nene and the Horrible Math Monster
(Chicago: Polychrome Publishing Corporation, 1993)

Subject(s): Stereotypes; School Life
Age range(s): Grades 1-5
Major character(s): Maria Elizabeth "Nene" Flores, Child (young Filipina American girl); Mrs. MacKenzie, Teacher (Nene's)
Time period(s): 1990s (1993)
Locale(s): United States

Summary: Nene hates math, but because she works very hard, she still does well. But when she is chosen to represent her class in math in the annual academic competition, she is haunted by nightmares of the horrible math monster. She finally tells her surprised teacher that she much prefers writing to numbers.

Where it's reviewed:
Children's Bookwatch, February 1994, page 5

Other books you might like:

Michele Maria Surat, *Angel Child, Dragon Child*, 1983
  Young Ut, a recent Vietnamese immigrant, is teased because of her different appearance. Thrown together by their school principal, Ut and a once cruel boy develop a new friendship.

Min Paek, *Aekyung's Dream*, 1988
  Aekyung, a young Korean girl recently in the U.S., dreams about King Sejong who created *Hangul*, the Korean alphabet, and finds new pride in her Korean heritage.

Sandra S. Yamate, *Ashok by Any Other Name*, 1992
  Ashok, a young Indian American boy, wishes he had a more "American" name, so he tries a new one each day until he finally realizes that "Ashok" is the perfect name for him.

Sandra S. Yamate, *Char Siu Bao Boy*, 1991
  Charlie's favorite food, char sui bao, causes his classmates to tease him until, one day, he brings in enough for everyone to taste.

Heidi Chang, *Elaine and the Flying Frog*, 1991
  Lonely in her new school after moving to a small Iowa town, Chinese American Elaine finds friendship as she and a girl with a consuming interest in frogs, work on a science project together.

1095

LINA MAO WALL, Adaptor
CATHY SPAGNOLI, Illustrator
NANCY HOM, Illustrator

Judge Rabbit and the Tree Spirit: A Folktale from Cambodia

(San Francisco: Children's Book Press, 1991)

Subject(s): Fairy Tale; Supernatural
Age range(s): Grades 1-6
Major character(s): Husband, Spouse (young husband); Wife, Spouse (waiting for husband); Tree Spirit, Spirit (able to take any form); Judge Rabbit, Mythical Creature (wise sage)
Time period(s): Indeterminate Past (Long ago.)
Locale(s): Cambodia

Summary: A young husband is called off to war, leaving his wife behind. The tree spirit assumes the husband's image and goes to live with the wife. The real husband returns and must seek the aid of Judge Rabbit who helps trap the impostor so that the young couple can live happily ever after.

About this book: A bilingual book, written in both English and Khmer.

Other books you might like:
Blia Xiong, *Nine-in-One Grr! Grr!*, 1989
  Bird comes up with a clever trick to prevent earth from being overpopulated with tigers.
Jeanne M. Lee, *Toad Is the Uncle of Heaven*, 1985
  Toad asks the King of Heaven for rain. On his journey, he is joined by the Bees, the Rooster and the Tiger. With the help of his friends, Toad convinces the King to provide rain.
Suzanne Crowder Han, *The Rabbit's Escape*, 1995
  A rabbit is tricked by the turtle into going to the underworld, but the rabbit cleverly sets himself free.
Suzanne Crowder Han, *The Rabbit's Judgment*, 1994
  A man is tricked into saving the life of a tiger; a clever rabbit keeps the man from being eaten by the ungrateful, hungry tiger.
Laurence Yep, *The Ghost Fox*, 1994
  A brave boy saves his mother from the evil ghost fox who tries to steal her soul.

1096

SYLVIA WATANABE, Editor
CAROL BRUCHAC, Co-Editor

Home to Stay: Asian American Women's Fiction

(Greenfield Center, NY: The Greenfield Press Review, 1990)

Subject(s): Multicultural; Identity; Short Stories
Age range(s): Adult
Time period(s): Indeterminate
Locale(s): United States

Summary: A collection of short stories that celebrate the literary achievements of Asian American women authors. Included are the works of 29 writers who are of Chinese, Malaysian, Vietnamese, Korean, Filipino, Indian, Japanese and Pakistani descent.

Where it's reviewed:
American Book Review, November 1990, page 18
Library Journal, April 1, 1990, page 136
Western American Literature, Summer 1991, page 165

Other books you might like:
Asian Women United of California, *Making Waves: An Anthology of Writings by and about Asian American Women*, 1989
  First major compilation since the early 1970s of primarily unpublished works by and about Asian American women.
Nurjehan Aziz, *Her Mother's Ashes, and Other Stories by South Asian Women in Canada and the United States*, 1994
  This anthology highlights the diverse cultures and unique experiences of 21 first-generation North American women who arrived in Canada or the U.S. by way of South Asia, Africa or the Caribbean.
Women of South Asian Descent Collective, *Our Feet Walk the Sky: Women of the South Asian Diaspora*, 1993
  This is the first major compilation that focuses on women of South Asian descent in the U.S. The anthology includes short stories, poetry, personal histories and critical essays.
Shirley Geok-lin Lim, *The Forbidden Stitch: An Asian American Women's Anthology*, 1989
  Edited with Mayumi Tsutakawa and Margarita Donnelly, this rich collection of poetry, short stories, art and reviews focuses on being a contemporary Asian American woman.
Juliet S. Kono, *Sister Stew: Fiction and Poetry by Women*, 1991
  This colorful anthology collects the writings of women of various backgrounds, the majority of whom are either Hawaiian by birth or adopted residency. Edited with Cathy Song.

1097

SYLVIA WATANABE, Editor
CAROL BRUCHAC, Co-Editor

Into the Fire: Asian American Prose

(Greenfield Center, NY: Greenfield Review Press, 1996)

Subject(s): Multicultural; Identity; Short Stories
Age range(s): Adult
Time period(s): 1930s; 1990s

Summary: A collection of short stories and interviews, detailing the diverse journey of Asian Americans from their faraway homelands to new lives in this new country to which they traveled, or into which they were born. Includes works from established writers such as Jeanne Wakatsuki Houston and Wakako Yamaguchi, as well as never-before-published newcomers.

Other books by the same author:
Home to Stay: Asian American Women's Fiction, 1990 (short story anthology)

Other books you might like:

Asian Women United of California, *Making Waves: An Anthology of Writings by and about Asian American Women*, 1989
   First major compilation since the early 1970s of primarily unpublished works by and about Asian American women.

Wesley Brown, *Imagining America: Stories from the Promised Land*, 1991
   A multicultural anthology of short stories about immigration to and migration within the U.S., the so-called "Promised Land."

Diane Glancy, *Two Worlds Walking: Short Stories, Essays and Poetry by Writers with Mixed Heritages*, 1994
   First-of-a-kind anthology that brings together the work of 42 writers, each of mixed ancestry, each "walking in two worlds" trying to discover their "American" identity.

Jessica Hagedorn, *Charlie Chan Is Dead: An Anthology of Contemporary Asian American Fiction*, 1993
   A collection of 48 works by Asian American writers of different ages, backgrounds and styles.

Shirley Geok-lin Lim, *The Forbidden Stitch: An Asian American Women's Anthology*, 1989
   Also edited with Mayumi Tsutakawa and Margarita Donnelly. A rich collection of poetry, short stories, art and reviews focusing on being a contemporary Asian American woman.

1098

SYLVIA WATANABE

Talking to the Dead
(New York: Doubleday, 1992)

Subject(s): Multicultural; Short Stories
Age range(s): Adult
Time period(s): 1990s
Locale(s): Hawaii

Summary: This collection of lyrical short stories, set in the Hawaiian islands, explores such diverse characters as a female Chinese Fred Astaire, a grandmother who makes quilts from stolen pieces of laundry and a wild young woman longing to leave the islands any way she can.

About this book: The title story, "Talking to the Dead," was a 1991 O. Henry Award winner.

Where it's reviewed:
Booklist, December 1, 1992, page 661
Library Journal, June 1, 1993, page 224
Locus, September 1992, page 64
Publishers Weekly, July 12, 1993, page 76

Awards the book has won:
PEN/Faulkner Award Nominee, Best Books of 1992

Other books by the same author:
Into the Fire: Asian American Prose, 1996 (edited with Carol Bruchac)
Home to Stay: Asian American Women's Fiction, 1990 (edited with Carol Bruchac)

Other books you might like:
Susan Nunes, *A Small Obligation and Other Stories of Hilo*, 1982

This is a collection of interrelated stories about Amy Freitas of Hilo, Hawaii, and her extended family—Japanese on her mother's side and Portuguese on her father's side.

Jessica K. Saiki, *From the Lanai and Other Hawaii Stories*, 1991
   This collection of stories about the Japanese American residents of Lunalilo, Hawaii, reveals a lonely spinster, a deserted husband and a young woman desperate for stardom.

Jessica K. Saiki, *Once, a Lotus Garden and Other Stories*, 1987
   This first collection of stories, mostly set in wartime Hawaii, portrays the residents of Lunalilo, including new picture brides from Japan and young schoolgirls and their dreams.

Kathleen Tyau, *A Little Too Much Is Enough*, 1995
   Mahi Wong grows up during post-World War II Hawaii, surrounded by her large family, immersed in a complex, mixed-up culture of Chinese and Hawaiian influences.

Lois-Ann Yamanaka, *Wild Meat and the Bully Burgers*, 1996
   This first novel is a coming-of-age story about Lovey Nariyoshi of Hilo, Hawaii, her best friend Jerome, her adolescent enemies an her eccentric family.

1099

KATE WATERS
MADELINE SLOVENZ-LOW, Illustrator
MARTHA COOPER, Illustrator

Lion Dancer: Ernie Wan's Chinese New Year
(New York: Scholastic Inc., 1990)

Subject(s): Multicultural; Holidays; City Life
Age range(s): Grades 1-3
Major character(s): Ernie Wan, 6-Year-Old, Chinese American; Jenny Wan, Sister (Ernie's older)
Time period(s): 1990's (Chinese New Year)
Locale(s): New York, New York (Chinatown)

Summary: Young Ernie is about to experience the most important day of his life. He will perform his first Lion Dance through the streets of New York City's Chinatown, as part of the Chinese New Year celebration.

About this book: A colorful book, filled with distinctive photographs that follow a young boy's life through the most important holiday of the Chinese American community.

Other books you might like:
Jama Kim Rattigan, *Dumpling Soup*, 1993
   Every year the Yang family gathers at Grandma's house from all over Oahu, Hawaii to celebrate New Year's Eve. This year, young Marisa will help Grandma make her famous dumpling soup.

Chyng Feng Sun, *Mama Bear*, 1994
   Mei-Mei saves money to buy the perfect Christmas gift—a stuffed bear. When the money she's saved is not enough, she realizes that she's had something even more special all along.

Yoshiko Uchida, *The Forever Christmas Tree*, 1963
  Young Takashi learns about a joyous holiday called Christmas from his sister Kaya. They decorate a reclusive neighbor's fir tree and bring their neighborhood together.
Janet Mitsui Brown, *Thanksgiving at Obaachan's*, 1994
  A Japanese American girl loves to visit her grandmother's house for Thanksgiving, where the meal is a combination of traditional Japanese and American fare.
Allen Say, *Tree of Cranes*, 1991
  Lovely story about a young Japanese boy who learns about Christmas for the first time from his California-born Japanese American mother.

1100

MICHI NISHIURA WEGLYN

Years of Infamy: The Untold Story of America's Concentration Camps

(Seattle: University of Washington Press, 1976)

Subject(s): Internment; World War II; Historical
Age range(s): Adult
Time period(s): 1940s
Locale(s): United States

Summary: In this groundbreaking historical work, Weglyn relies on careful research and documentation to reveal the abuses of power in the highest reaches of the U.S. government—a war hysteria-ridden government that fails to protect the basic rights of over 120,000 Americans of Japanese descent during World War II.

About this book: Both Weglyn and her book have been credited with changing the face of Asian American history. *Years of Infamy* helped release a new social activism among Japanese Americans, urging the community to become more involved in promoting civil and human rights, which eventually led to the redress movement of the late 1980s and early 1990s.

Where it's reviewed:
Booklist, May 15, 1976, page 1312
Choice, September 1776, page 886
Kliatt, Fall 1978, page 47
Kirkus Reviews, March 1, 1976, page 307
Library Journal, July 1976, page 1529

Awards the book has won:
Anisfield-Wolf Award in Race Relations, 1976

Other books you might like:
Jeanne Wakatsuki Houston, *Farewell to Manzanar*, 1973
  In this true story, the U.S. government uproots the Wakatsuki family from their home and incarcerates them at Manzanar, one of 10 U.S. concentration camps for Japanese Americans during World War II.
Mine Okubo, *Citizen 13660*, 1946
  Sketches and text reveal the autobiographical account of a Japanese American woman, who was reduced to Citizen Number 13660 and interned during World War II.
Monica Sone, *Nisei Daughter*, 1953
  As a second-generation Japanese American woman growing up in Seattle in the 1920s and '30s, *Nisei Daughter*

faces imprisonment during World War II, followed by a new life in the Midwest.
Ronald Takaki, *Strangers from a Different Shore*, 1989
  Takaki produces a groundbreaking history of Asian Americans in the U.S. during the last 150 years.
Yoshiko Uchida, *Desert Exile: The Uprooting of a Japanese-American Family*, 1982
  In this autobiographical account, a second generation Japanese American woman from Berkeley, California describes her own, and her family's internment experiences at Camp Topaz during World War II.

1101

WOMEN OF SOUTH ASIAN DESCENT COLLECTIVE,
Editor

Our Feet Walk the Sky: Women of the South Asian Diaspora

(San Francisco: Aunt Lute Books, 1993)

Subject(s): Multicultural; Identity; Short Stories
Age range(s): Adult

Summary: As the first major compilation that focuses on South Asian American and South Asian immigrant women in the U.S., this anthology offers a wide variety of short stories, poetry, personal histories and critical essays, by and about women whose ethnic roots trace back to India, Pakistan, Sri Lanka, Bangladesh and Nepal.

About this book: While South Asians were among the smaller immigration groups during the earlier years of the 20th century, more relaxed immigration laws after 1965 saw the South Asian population grow to become the fourth largest Asian American community in the U.S. In spite of their large growth, the South Asian population remains one of the least studied ethnic groups in the U.S.

Other books you might like:
Asian Women United of California, *Making Waves: An Anthology of Writings by and about Asian American Women*, 1989
  First major compilation since the early 1970s of primarily unpublished works by and about Asian American women.
Juliet S. Kono, *Sister Stew: Fiction and Poetry by Women*, 1991
  Also edited with Cathy Song. A colorful collection of writings by women of various backgrounds, the majority of whom are either Hawaiian by birth or by adopted residency.
Shirley Geok-lin Lim, *The Forbidden Stitch: An Asian American Women's Anthology*, 1989
  Also edited with Mayumi Tsutakawa and Margarita Donnelly. A rich collection of poetry, short stories, art and reviews focusing on being a contemporary Asian American woman.
Sylvia Watanabe, *Home to Stay: Asian American Women's Fiction*, 1990
  Also edited with Carol Bruchac. A collection of short stories that celebrates the literary achievements of Asian American women writers.

Nurjehan Aziz, *Her Mother's Ashes, and Other Stories by South Asian Women in Canada and the United States*, 1994

Twenty-one stories by first-generation North American women of South Asian descent, who have arrived in either Canada or the U.S. by way of South Asia, Africa or the Caribbean.

1102

JADE SNOW WONG

Fifth Chinese Daughter
(Seattle: University of Washington Press, 1945)

Subject(s): Multicultural; Identity; Coming of Age
Age range(s): Adult
Major character(s): Jade Snow Wong, Daughter (fifth), Chinese American (American-born); Mother Wong, Mother, Chinese American, Immigrant; Daddy Wong, Father, Businessman (garment factory owner), Chinese American (immigrant)
Time period(s): 1920s; 1940s
Locale(s): San Francisco, California (Chinatown)

Summary: Jade Snow Wong is the American-born, fifth daughter of Chinese immigrants. Growing up in San Francisco's Chinatown, Jade Snow must come to terms with two diverse worlds: a traditional household which strictly adheres to 19th-century standards of Imperial China, and the western values of the New World with its promises of freedom and individuality.

About this book: Originally published by Harper. One of the first works of Asian American literature, *Fifth Chinese Daughter* has been criticized by Frank Chin and his "Gang of Four" (editors of the *Aiiieeeee* anthologies) as an example of a "Chinatown Book" whose basic formula was " I'm an American because I eat spaghetti and Chinese because I eat chow mein." Chin argued that Wong, as well as other early Chinese American writers, wrote from a "white tradition of Chinese novelty" in which the white culture was "supreme," rather than from the sense of a true "Chinese America."

Where it's reviewed:
Belles Lettres, Fall 1990, page 21
Kliatt, September 1989, page 33

Other books by the same author:
No Chinese Stranger, 1974

Other books you might like:
Gish Jen, *Typical American*, 1991
    The Chang family arrives in the U.S. from China in search of education and safety. What they find is fried chicken fast food joints, glamour magazines, suburbia and con artists.
Maxine Hong Kingston, *The Woman Warrior: Memoirs of a Girlhood Among Ghosts*, 1975
    The story of a young girl growing up in the San Francisco Bay Area divided amidst the stories of her parents' faraway past in China and her own experiences in a Caucasian world.
Gus Lee, *China Boy*, 1991
    A coming-of-age novel about Kai Ting, the American-

born son of an aristocratic Chinese family who fled China for California to escape the Cultural Revolution.
Monica Sone, *Nisei Daughter*, 1953
    An account of a second-generation Japanese American woman growing up in Seattle in the 1920s and 1930s, being incarcerated during World War II and her new life in the Midwest.

1103

NORMAN WONG

Cultural Revolution
(New York: Persea Books, 1994)

Subject(s): Family Life; Coming of Age; Homosexuality/Lesbianism
Age range(s): Adult
Major character(s): Wei Lau, Immigrant (living in Hawaii), Chinese; Marie Lau, Wife (Wei's), Mother (Michael and Julia's); Julia Lau, Daughter (Wei and Marie's oldest child); Michael Lau, Son (Wei and Marie's second child)
Time period(s): 1950s; 1990s
Locale(s): Honolulu, Hawaii (the majority of the short stories take place in Hawaii)

Summary: A collection of interrelated short stories that begins in 1953 Macao, where a sickly Wei lives with his overprotective grandmother and ineffective father. Wei eventually emigrates to Honolulu, gets married, and has two children, Michael and Julia, who come of age amidst ancient family tales, dim sum restaurants and shopping malls.

Where it's reviewed:
Los Angeles Times Book Review, October 15, 1995, page 10
New York Times Book Review, October 22, 1995, page 44
Kirkus Reviews, January 1, 1994, page 18
Library Journal, March 1, 1994, page 122
Publishers Weekly, January 31, 1994, page 75

Other books you might like:
R. Zamora Linmark, *Rolling the R's*, 1995
    A collection of interrelated short stories, many about young Filipino Americans coming to terms with their ethnicity and with their sexuality in Honolulu.
Darrell H.Y. Lum, *Pass On, No Pass Back!*, 1990
    A humorous collection of short stories about growing up in Hawaii.
Milton Murayama, *All I Asking for Is My Body*, 1959
    A young Japanese American boy's coming-of-age in Hawaii during the 1930s up until the advent of World War II.
Kathleen Tyau, *A Little Too Much Is Enough*, 1995
    Mahi Wong grows up during post-World War II Hawaii, surrounded by her large family, immersed in a complex, mixed-up culture of Chinese and Hawaiian influences.
Lois-Ann Yamanaka, *Wild Meat and the Bully Burgers*, 1996
    A coming-of-age first novel about Lovey Nariyoshi of Hilo, Hawaii, her best friend Jerome, her adolescent enemies and her eccentric family.

1104
SHAWN WONG

American Knees
(New York: Simon and Schuster, 1995)

Subject(s): Multicultural; Identity; Love

Age range(s): Adult

Major character(s): Raymond Ding, Administrator (minority affairs director), Chinese American (in his 30s); Aurora "Ro" Crane, Lover (Raymond's), Photojournalist, Japanese (half Japanese, half Caucasian); Brenda Nishitani, Friend (Aurora's best friend); Woodrow "Wood" Ding, Father (Raymond's father); Betty Nguyen, Lover (Raymond's lover after Aurora), Administrator (assistant registrar)

Time period(s): 1990s (1995)

Locale(s): San Francisco Bay Area, California (with occasional flashbacks to Los Angeles and Washington, D.C.)

Summary: Raymond Ding, a divorced Chinese American man in his 30s who prides himself on his strong ethnic identity and his politically correct views, is in love with Aurora Crane, a half-Japanese, half-Caucasian photojournalist in her 20s. In spite of their passionate bond, they must be separate before they can finally come back together.

About this book: A hip, sexy, sometimes satiric jaunt through love and commitment in the 90s.

Where it's reviewed:
Entertainment Weekly, August 11, 1995
Los Angeles Times Book Review, September 10, 1995, page 1
Library Journal, March 1, 1995, page 91
Publishers Weekly, June 26, 1995, page 88

Other books by the same author:
The Big Aiiieeeee! An Anthology of Chinese American and Japanese American Literature, 1991 (sequel)
Homebase, 1991
Aiiieeeee! An Anthology of Asian American Writers, 1974

Other books you might like:
Maxine Hong Kingston, *Tripmaster Monkey: His Fake Book*, 1989
 Kingston's first novel about the often comic mishaps and adventures of Wittman Ah Sing, a young Chinese American, in search of his dreams.
Vikram Seth, *Golden Gate: A Novel in Verse*, 1986
 A novel written entirely in verse, about the machinations of love in the modern age between five friends in San Francisco.
Yoji Yamaguchi, *Face of a Stranger*, 1995
 Kikue, a Japanese woman who arrived in the U.S. believing she was to be a picture bride but instead was forced into prostitution, devises an elaborate plan to secure her freedom.
Lois-Ann Yamanaka, *Wild Meat and the Bully Burgers*, 1996
 A coming-of-age first novel about Lovey Nariyoshi of Hilo, Hawaii, her best friend Jerome, her adolescent enemies and her eccentric family.

1105
SHAWN WONG

Homebase
(New York: Plume (Penguin Group), 1991)

Subject(s): Multicultural; Emigration and Immigration; Identity

Age range(s): Adult

Major character(s): Rainsford Chan, Orphan, Chinese American (fourth-generation)

Time period(s): 1850s; 1970s

Locale(s): United States (the West)

Summary: At 14, fourth-generation Chinese American Rainsford Chan is orphaned. Alone and searching, he recreates his family's 125-year-long history in the U.S., wandering among his male ancestors, learning their stories and experiencing their lives. But even after 125 years, claiming America as "homebase" is still not without difficulty.

About this book: Originally published by I. Reed Books in 1979, the book subsequently went out of print. Ironically, it was only available in a German-language edition for several years until it was reissued in 1991. Although a very short novel, the prose is extremely dense, more reminiscent of epic poetry than straightforward narrative.

Where it's reviewed:
Book World, February 24, 1991, page 12
Los Angeles Times Book Review, January 20, 1991, page 14

Awards the book has won:
Pacific Northwest Booksellers Award
Washington State Governor's Writers Day Award

Other books by the same author:
American Knees, 1995
The Big Aiiieeeee! An Anthology of Chinese American and Japanese American Literature, 1991
Aiiieeeee! An Anthology of Asian American Writers, 1974

Other books you might like:
Frank Chin, *The Chinaman Pacific & Frisco R.R. Co.*, 1988
 A collection of eight stories about Chinese Americans struggling to establish their identities in a white world governed by unforgiving stereotypes.
Carlos Bulosan, *America Is in the Heart*, 1943
 This autobiography of writer and poet Carlos Bulosan covers his life from his boyhood in the Philippines to his arrival in America where he worked as a migrant laborer.
Frank Chin, *The Chickencoop Chinaman and the Year of the Dragon: Two Plays by Frank Chin*, 1981
 In the first of these two plays, Chin challenges media stereotypes of Asian Americans. In the second, he examines the disintegration of the Chinese American famliy.
Frank Chin, *Donald Duk*, 1991
 At 12, Donald Duk dislikes his name and is less than comfortable with his heritage. As the Chinese New Year approaches, he confronts his ancestors, his history and his heritage.

`1106`

BLIA XIONG, Adaptor
CATHY SPAGNOLI, Illustrator
NANCY HOM, Illustrator

Nine-in-One Grr! Grr!

(San Francisco: Children's Book Press, 1989)

Subject(s): Fairy Tale; Animals
Age range(s): Grades 1-3
Major character(s): Tiger, Tiger (the earth's first); Shao, Deity (god); Bird, Bird (clever Eu bird)
Time period(s): Indeterminate Past
Locale(s): Earth

Summary: The earth's first tiger asks the god Shao how many cubs she will have. He promises she will have nine every year, as long as she remembers his words. Bird overhears the prophecy and convinces Tiger that she will have only one cub a year, thereby preventing earth from being overpopulated with tigers.

Other books you might like:

Lina Mao Wall, *Judge Rabbit and the Tree Spirit: A Folktale from Cambodia*, 1991
  Adapted by Cathy Spagnoli. Judge Rabbit helps a young couple trap the tree spirit who has taken the form of the young husband.
Ed Young, *Lon Po Po: A Red-Riding Hood Story from China*, 1989
  Three sisters, left alone and admonished to keep the door locked, are tricked by a hungry wolf disguised as Grandma.
Suzanne Crowder Han, *The Rabbit's Escape*, 1995
  A rabbit is tricked by the turtle into going to the underworld, but the rabbit cleverly sets himself free.
Suzanne Crowder Han, *The Rabbit's Judgment*, 1994
  A man is tricked into saving the life of a tiger; a clever rabbit keeps the man from being eaten by the ungrateful, hungry tiger.
Jeanne M. Lee, *Toad Is the Uncle of Heaven*, 1985
  Toad asks the King of Heaven for rain. On his journey, he is joined by the Bees, the Rooster and the Tiger. With the help of his friends, Toad convinces the King to provide rain.
Laurence Yep, *The Man Who Tricked a Ghost*, 1993
  Sung is not afraid of anything—even a ghost determined to scare him to death.

`1107`

YOJI YAMAGUCHI

Face of a Stranger

(New York: HarperCollins Publishers, 1995)

Subject(s): Prostitution; Identity; Emigration and Immigration
Age range(s): Adult
Major character(s): Kikue, Prostitute (forced into prostitution), Immigrant (to U.S. as "picture bride"), Japanese; Takashi Arai, Migrant Worker (has a hard time keeping a job), Immigrant, Japanese; Shino, Prostitute (forced into prostitution), Friend (Kikue's); Kogoro Doi, Farmer (dull, of very large bulk), Friend (to Takashi)
Time period(s): 1930s
Locale(s): California (China Alley, in an unnamed town outside of San Francisco)

Summary: Kikue, a Japanese woman who arrived in the U.S. believing she was to be a picture bride but instead was forced into prostitution, devises an elaborate plan, not only to secure her freedom, but to plot her revenge against the man whose face was borrowed as the bogus groom in the photograph used to deceive her.

About this book: Due to strict anti-Asian immigration laws, few women from Asia were allowed into the U.S. unless they were already married to a U.S. resident. Japanese, Korean and some Chinese men arranged for "picture brides" — that is, marriages were arranged through a go-between with women from the homeland, sight unseen, except for an exchange of pictures. Many times, to entice eligible women, men sent pictures of themselves when they were younger, or sometimes even pictures of other, more attractive men.

Other books you might like:

Maxine Hong Kingston, *Tripmaster Monkey: His Fake Book*, 1989
  Kingston's first novel about the often comic mishaps and adventures of Wittman Ah Sing, a young Chinese American, in search of his dreams.
Vikram Seth, *Golden Gate: A Novel in Verse*, 1986
  A novel written entirely in verse, about the machinations of love in the modern age between five friends in San Francisco.
Shawn Wong, *American Knees*, 1995
  A novel about the amorous adventures of Raymond Ding, a young, recently divorced Chinese American man.

`1108`

HISAYE YAMAMOTO

Seventeen Syllables and Other Stories

(Latham, NY: Kitchen Table: Women of Color Press, 1988)

Subject(s): Multicultural; Emigration and Immigration; Short Stories
Age range(s): Adult
Time period(s): 20th century (1948-1987)
Locale(s): United States

Summary: A collection of 15 short stories from Yamamoto's almost half-century-long writing career. Although the stories cover diverse subject matter, some of Yamamoto's recurring themes include multicultural and multiethnic interaction, multigenerational conflicts and the difficulties first generation immigrants, especially Japanese American women, face in the New World.

About this book: The definitive collection of Yamamoto's best short stories. Although not a prolific writer despite the length of her long career, Yamamoto is considered to be one of the best Asian American authors, producing the most consistently anthologized stories in the Asian American literary canon.

Where it's reviewed:
Belles Lettres, Winter 1989, page 9

Nation, November 15, 1989, page 566
Publishers Weekly, October 21, 1988, page 54

Awards the book has won:
American Book Award for Lifetime Achievement, 1986 (for author)

Other books you might like:
Asian Women United of California, *Making Waves: An Anthology of Writings by and about Asian American Women*, 1989
A collection of short stories, essays, poetry; the first major compilation of primarily unpublished works by and about Asian American women since the early 1970s.
Wakako Yamauchi, *Songs My Mother Taught Me: Stories, Plays, and Memoir*, 1994
This rich collection, by one of the pioneer voices of Asian America, spans over 35 years.
Shirley Geok-lin Lim, *The Forbidden Stitch: An Asian American Women's Anthology*, 1989
Also edited by Mayumi Tsutakawa and Margarita Donnelly; a collection of poetry, prose, art and reviews by many of the best known Asian American women writers and artists.
David Wong Louie, *Pangs of Love*, 1991
A collection of poignant, memorable stories about families, relationships, history and every day life.
Sylvia Watanabe, *Talking to the Dead*, 1992
This award-winning collection includes stories about a female Fred Astaire, a grandmother who makes quilts of stolen laundry and a girl longing to leave home anyway she can.

1109

LOIS-ANN YAMANAKA

Wild Meat and the Bully Burgers
(New York: Farrar Straus Giroux, 1996)

Subject(s): Multicultural; Family Life; Coming of Age
Age range(s): Adult
Major character(s): Lovey Nariyoshi, Teenager (Japanese American adolescent); Jerome "Jerry", Sidekick (Lovey's best friend); Calhoun Nariyoshi, Sister (Lovey's younger sister); Hubert Nariyoshi, Father (Lovey's eccentric father)
Time period(s): 1970s
Locale(s): Hilo, Hawaii

Summary: A coming-of-age first novel about young Lovey Nariyoshi of Hilo, Hawaii, trying to forge her identity amidst the mish-mash of Japanese American roots, coveted Barbie dolls and pop music, surrounded by her best friend Jerome, her too-popular enemies and her eccentric family.

Where it's reviewed:
Library Journal, March 1, 1996, page 136
New York Times Book Review, December 31, 1995, page 11
Publishers Weekly, October 2, 1995, page 51

Other books by the same author:
Saturday Night at the Pahala Theatre, 1993 (short story collection)

Other books you might like:
Darrell H.Y. Lum, *Pass On, No Pass Back!*, 1990
A humorous collection of short stories about growing up in Hawaii.
Milton Murayama, *All I Asking for Is My Body*, 1959
A young Japanese American boy's coming-of-age in Hawaii during the 1930s up until the advent of World War II.
Susan Nunes, *A Small Obligation and Other Stories of Hilo*, 1982
A collection of interrelated stories about Amy Freitas of Hilo, Hawaii, and her extended family—Japanese on her mother's side and Portuguese on her father's side.
Kathleen Tyau, *A Little Too Much Is Enough*, 1995
Mahi Wong grows up in post-World War II Hawaii surrounded by her large family, immersed in a complex, mixed-up culture of Chinese and Hawaiian influences.
Norman Wong, *Cultural Revolution*, 1994
These interrelated stories begin in 1953 in Macao where Wei lives with his overprotective grandmother and ineffectual father. It continues with his emigration to Honolulu and the life he builds there.

1110

SANDRA S. YAMATE
JANICE TOHINAKA, Illustrator

Ashok by Any Other Name
(Chicago: Polychrome Publishing Corporation, 1992)

Subject(s): Multicultural; Difference; Tolerance
Age range(s): Grades 1-3
Major character(s): Ashok, Child (young boy), Indian American; Mr. Fletcher, Librarian (at Ashok's school)
Time period(s): 1990s (1992)
Locale(s): United States

Summary: Ashok, a young Indian American boy, wishes he had a more obviously "American" name. So each day Ashok tries a new name, from Tom to Walter to Frances, until he realizes with the help of the school librarian that "Ashok" is already the perfect name for him.

Where it's reviewed:
Children's Bookwatch, February 1994, page 5

Other books by the same author:
Char Siu Bao Boy, 1991

Other books you might like:
Marie Villanueva, *Nene and the Horrible Math Monster*, 1993
Nene hates math although she is very good at it. When she is chosen to represent the class in a competition, she begins having nightmares of the horrible math monster.
Min Paek, *Aekyung's Dream*, 1988
Aekyung, a young Korean girl recently in the U.S., dreams about King Sejong who created *Hangul*, the Korean alphabet, and finds new pride in her Korean heritage.
Michele Maria Surat, *Angel Child, Dragon Child*, 1983
Young Ut, a recent Vietnamese immigrant, is teased because of her different appearance. Thrown together by their school principal, Ut and a once cruel boy develop a new friendship.

Ken Mochizuki, *Heroes*, 1995

Always forced to play the enemy because he looks like ''them,'' Japanese American Donnie enlists his reluctant father and uncle to prove their U.S. military service records.

1111

SANDRA S. YAMATE
JOYCE M.W. JENKIN, Illustrator

Char Siu Bao Boy

(Chicago: Polychrome Publishing Corporation, 1991)

Subject(s): Multicultural; Difference; Tolerance
Age range(s): Grades 1-3
Major character(s): Charlie, Child (boy), Chinese American; Grandmother, Grandmother (Charlie's)
Time period(s): 1990s (1991)
Locale(s): United States

Summary: Charlie's favorite food is *char siu bao*, a barbecue pork filled bun. He eats these buns every day, but the other students make fun of him. So he tries bringing ham, tuna or turkey sandwiches instead. One day, Charlie brings in buns for his classmates who have never tasted them, and when they do, the love them.

Other books by the same author:
Ashok by Any Other Name, 1992

Other books you might like:
Marie Villanueva, *Nene and the Horrible Math Monster*, 1993

Nene hates math, although she is very good at it. When she is chosen to represent her class at a competition, she begins to dream of the horrible math monster.

Min Paek, *Aekyung's Dream*, 1988

Aekyung, a young Korean girl recently in the U.S., dreams about King Sejong who created *Hangul*, the Korean alphabet, and finds new pride in her Korean heritage.

Michele Maria Surat, *Angel Child, Dragon Child*, 1983

Young Ut, a recent Vietnamese immigrant, is teased because of her different appearance. Thrown together by their school principal, Ut and a once cruel boy develop a new friendship.

Ken Mochizuki, *Heroes*, 1995

Always forced to play the enemy because he looks like ''them,'' Japanese American Donnie enlists his reluctant father and uncle to prove their U.S. military service records.

Chyng Feng Sun, *Square Beak*, 1993

Square Beak is aptly named. When she is ostracized because she looks different from the other chickens in the yard, she begins to wander outside her own small world.

1112

WAKAKO YAMAUCHI
GARRETT HONGO, Editor

Songs My Mother Taught Me: Stories, Plays, and Memoir

(New York: The Feminist Press at The City University of New York, 1994)

Subject(s): Multicultural; Emigration and Immigration; Short Stories
Age range(s): Adult

Summary: A rich collection of stories, plays and memoir that span over 35 years by one of the pioneer voices of Asian America. Yamauchi is best known for her play, ''And the Soul Shall Dance,'' based on her own short story, about two migrant Japanese American families trying to find a new life in their adopted land.

About this book: As one of the first important voices of Asian American fiction and drama, Yamauchi's stories have been widely anthologized and her plays produced throughout the country. Ironically, in spite of her pioneering status, this collection is her first.

Where it's reviewed:
Belles Lettres, Spring 1995, page 65
Kliatt, November 1994, page 29
New York Times Book Review, October 30, 1994, page 48
Women's Review of Books, December 1994, page 8

Other books you might like:
Toshio Mori, *The Chauvinist and Other Stories*, 1979

Short stories about Japanese Americans in California before and after World War II. From established immigrants to desperate American-born citizens, these stories capture a spirit of survival.

Toshio Mori, *Yokohama, California*, 1949

Short stories dealing with the Japanese American experience from the 1930s to 1940s.

Monica Sone, *Nisei Daughter*, 1953

An account of a second-generation Japanese American woman growing up in Seattle in the 1920s and 30s, being incarcerated during World War II and her new life in the Midwest.

Hisaye Yamamoto, *Seventeen Syllables and Other Stories*, 1988

A collection of 15 short stories from Yamamoto's almost half-century-long writing career.

1113

BELLE YANG, Author/Illustrator

Baba: A Return to China upon My Father's Shoulders

(New York: Harcourt Brace & Company, 1994)

Subject(s): Family Life; Multicultural; Fathers and Daughters
Age range(s): Adult
Major character(s): Joseph ''Baba'' Yang, Son (fourth of 7 children), Grandson (grandson to Great Progenitor); The

Great Progenitor, Grandfather (patriarch of the House of Yang); Nainai Yang, Mother (Baba's mother); Yeye Yang, Father (Baba's father), Son (first son of Yang patriarch)

Time period(s): 20th century (1930s-1990s)

Locale(s): China (Manchuria)

Summary: The author returns to her ancestral homeland, guided by the stories her father—her "Baba"—has told her. There she begins a personal odyssey through northern China of the 1930s and 1940s, following the story of her father's coming-of-age as a son of the prominent Manchurian House of Yang.

About this book: This exquisitely illustrated work is best described as an adult picture book. In a 1995 interview with Hong, Yang explained that *Baba* is part of the greater continuum of the Asian American literary experience. "Writers like Maxine Hong Kingston, Amy Tan and many before them set the stage for a book like *Baba*. Through their writing, they showed a true understanding of Asian Americans. From that point, I'm able to take readers back to China, to show them where we Asian Americans come from."

Where it's reviewed:
Kirkus Reviews, July 15, 1994, page 972
Publishers Weekly, August 22, 1994, page 45

Other books you might like:
Maxine Hong Kingston, *China Men*, 1980
    A history made up of myth and memory of generations of Chinese American men.
Gus Lee, *China Boy*, 1991
    A coming-of-age novel about Kai Ting, the American-born son of an aristocratic Chinese family who fled China for California to escape the Cultural Revolution.
Lydia Yuri Minatoya, *Talking to High Monks in the Snow: An Asian American Odyssey*, 1992
    Minatoya's personal odyssey, which she recounts here, begins in the 1950s in upstate New York and continues through Japan, China and Nepal.
Amy Tan, *The Hundred Secret Senses*, 1995
    A novel of two half-sisters, one Chinese-born, the other half-Chinese and half-American.
Helie Lee, *Still Life with Rice: A Young American Woman Discovers the Life and Legacy of Her Korean Grandmother*, 1996
    This is the true story of a Korean woman who survives great hardship in Korea and finally arrives in the U.S., as told by her Korean granddaughter. (Adult)

1114

TARO YASHIMA, Author/Illustrator

Crow Boy

(New York: Puffin Books (Penguin Group), 1955)

Subject(s): Perseverance; Prejudice; School Life

Age range(s): Grades 1-4

Major character(s): Chibi "Crow Boy", Child (shy, quiet young boy); Mr. Isobe, Teacher (of sixth-grade, helps Chibi)

Time period(s): 1950s (1955)

Locale(s): Japan (a village in Japan)

Summary: Shy Chibi does not fit in with the rest of his schoolmates. During the last school year, the new teacher takes an interest in Chibi, who amazes the teacher with his knowledge about the outdoors, especially his ability to imitate crows. As Chibi emerges from his shell, others take notice of his courage and determination.

Where it's reviewed:
Booklist, September 1, 1983, page 94
Emergency Librarian, January 1984, page 20
Library Journal, October 15, 1973, page 2163
Reading Teacher, May 1979, page 942

Awards the book has won:
Caldecott Honor Book, 1955

Other books you might like:
Ellin Greene, *Ling-Li and the Phoenix Fairy: A Chinese Folktale*, 1996
    Ling-Li creates a wedding robe so beautiful that the magpies carry it away. Ling-Li follows the birds to the Phoenix Fairy who returns the robe with her special blessings.
Min Paek, *Aekyung's Dream*, 1988
    Aekyung, a young Korean girl recently arrived in the U.S., dreams about King Sejong who created *Hangul*, the Korean alphabet, and finds new pride in her Korean heritage.
Michele Maria Surat, *Angel Child, Dragon Child*, 1983
    Young Ut, a recent Vietnamese immigrant, is teased because of her different appearance. Thrown together by the school principal, Ut and a once cruel boy develop a new friendship.

1115

PAUL YEE
SIMON NG, Illustrator

Tales from Gold Mountain: Stories of the Chinese in the New World

(New York: MacMillan Publishing Company, 1989)

Story type: Historical/American West; Young Readers

Subject(s): Emigration and Immigration; Multicultural; American West

Age range(s): Grades 3-8

Time period(s): 19th century (late 1800s)

Locale(s): West; West, Canada

Summary: A collection of eight original tales that draw on the real-life experiences of the Chinese who immigrated to North America in the latter half of the 19th century during the height of the Gold Rush, the building of the transcontinental railroad and the settling of the Wild West.

About this book: These beautifully illustrated stories capture the spirit of Chinese pioneers who battled prejudice, harsh conditions and great adversity to endure and survive in the New World.

Where it's reviewed:
Horn Book Magazine, July 1990, page 459
Kirkus Reviews, February 15, 1990, page 272
School Library Journal, May 1990, page 121

Other books by the same author:
Teach Me to Fly, Skyfighter (children's book)

The Curses of Third Uncle (children's book)
Saltwater City: An Illustrated History of the Chinese in Vancouver

Other books you might like:
Ruthanne Lum McCunn, *Pie-Biter*, 1983
    Children's story about a Chinese boy who arrives in America to work on the railroad.
Laurence Yep, *Dragon's Gate*, 1993
    A young adult story about Chinese immigration and the construction of the transcontinental railroad during the mid-19th century.
Ruthanne Lum McCunn, *Chinese American Portraits: Personal Histories 1828-1988*, 1988
    These are profiles of prominent Chinese Americns, from pioneers to politicians.
Ruthanne Lum McCunn, *An Illustrated History of the Chinese in America*, 1979
    An illustrated history book which traces the presence of Chinese in America, from the arrival of the Chinese during the California Gold Rush, to contemporary Chinese Americans.

1116

LAURENCE YEP, Editor

American Dragons: Twenty-Five Asian American Voices

(New York: HarperCollins Publishers, 1993)

Subject(s): Multicultural; Identity; Short Stories
Age range(s): Grades 8-Adult
Time period(s): Indeterminate
Locale(s): United States

Summary: A collection of short stories, poetry and play excerpts from both established Asian American writers and new writers about growing up Asian American. Caught between two cultures, the young voices of this collection ask, ''Who am I?'' ''Am I Asian?'' ''Am I American?'' ''Where do I fit in?''

About this book: The ''dragon'' in the title refers to the dragon as the most familiar symbol associated with Asian mythology and art, as well as the inner dragons that Asian immigrants brought with them as they began a new life in the strange and foreign land of America.

Where it's reviewed:
Booklist, March 15, 1994, page 1356
Horn Book Guide, Fall 1993, page 369

Other books by the same author:
Dragon's Gate, 1993
The Star Fisher, 1991
Tongues of Jade, 1991 (folk tales)
The Rainbow People, 1989 (folk tales)
Dragonwings, 1976 (true story)

Other books you might like:
Lori M. Carlson, *American Eyes: New Asian-American Short Stories for Young Adults*, 1994
    A collection of 10 short works about young Asian Americans coming of age and coming to terms with an identity comprised of two very different cultures.
Asian American Coaliton, *Children of Asian America*, 1995
    This collection of original stories about growing up as an Asian American child centers around the diverse ethnic Asian communities of Chicago.
Diane Glancy, *Two Worlds Walking: Short Stories, Essays, and Poetry by Writers with Mixed Heritages*, 1994
    Edited with C.W. Truesdale, this first-of-a-kind anthology brings together the works of 42 writers, each of mixed ancestry, each ''walking in two worlds.''

1117

LAURENCE YEP
JEAN TSENG, Illustrator
MOU-SIEN TSENG, Illustrator

The Boy Who Swallowed Snakes

(New York: Scholastic Inc., 1994)

Subject(s): Folk Tales; Courage; Honesty
Age range(s): Grades 1-4
Major character(s): Little Chou, Child (lives with his widowed mother); Mrs. Chou, Mother (Little Chou's widowed mother)
Time period(s): Indeterminate Past
Locale(s): China (village in southern China)

Summary: Little Chou finds a basket of silver, in which a dangerous *ku* snake is hidden. To prevent evil from spreading, he bravely eats the snake and is not harmed. The greedy, wealthy man, who originally deserted the snake, hears that Little Chou is okay and comes to reclaim his snake, hoping for more riches.

About this book: An original folktale created by Yep, set in ancient China.

Where it's reviewed:
Booklist, December 15, 1993, page 760
Center for Children's Books. Bulletin, February 1994, page 206
Kirkus Reviews, January 1, 1994, page 76
Publishers Weekly, December 13, 1993, page 70
School Library Journal, April 1994, page 123

Other books by the same author:
The City of Dragons, 1995
The Ghost Fox, 1994
The Man Who Tricked a Ghost, 1993
The Shell Woman and the King, 1993
Dragonwings, 1975 (true story)

Other books you might like:
Ed Young, *Little Plum*, 1994
    A childless couple long for a child, even if he were only as small as a plum seed. When such a child is born, he proves that even a man as small as a plum seed can do good deeds if he is brave.
Demi, *The Empty Pot*, 1990
    All the children in China must grow a flower from the Emperor's seeds, but Ping fails. His admission of the fact earns him a reward.

Margaret Chang, *The Cricket Warrior: A Chinese Tale*, 1994
The dutiful son, Wei'nian, takes the form of a cricket and saves his family by becoming the champion of the Emperor's court.

Charlie Chin, *China's Bravest Girl: The Legend of Hua Mu Lan*, 1993
Disguised as a man, Hua Mu Lan takes her elderly father's place in the Emperor's army and becomes a legendary warrior.

1118

LAURENCE YEP

Child of the Owl

(New York: Harper & Row Publishers, 1977)

Subject(s): Multicultural; Fathers and Daughters; Family Relations
Age range(s): Grades 6-12
Major character(s): Casey Young, 12-Year-Old (daughter of itinerant gambler), Chinese American; Barney Young, Father (Casey's unreliable father), Gambler (constantly in debt); Paw-Paw Low, Grandmother (Casey's eccentric grandmother), Chinese American; Mr. Jeh, Friend (Chinatown old-timer), Chinese American; Tallulah Bankhead ''Booger'' Chew, Friend (Casey's classmate and friend)
Time period(s): 1960s (1964-1965)
Locale(s): San Francisco, California (Chinatown)

Summary: When her gambling father is hospitalized, 12-year-old Casey is sent to live with the relatives of her deceased mother whom she never knew. With the help of her loving grandmother, ''Paw-Paw,'' little by little Casey learns great pride in her Chinese American heritage and in the process, discovers her own self.

Where it's reviewed:
Booklist, April 1, 1977, page 1173
Bookwatch, May 1, 1977, page E1
Kirkus Reviews, February 1, 1977, page 99
Publishers Weekly, February 28, 1977, page 123
School Library Journal, April 1977, page 73

Other books by the same author:
American Dragons: Twenty-Five Asian American Voices, 1993 (young adult)
Dragon's Gate, 1993
Tongues of Jade, 1991 (adapted folktales)
The Rainbow People, 1989 (adapted folktales)
Dragonwings, 1975 (true story)

Other books you might like:
Lensey Namioka, *Yang the Third and Her Impossible Family*, 1995
Yingmei tries her best to ''be American'' while her family clings to Chinese customs.

Jean Davies Okimoto, *Molly by Any Other Name*, 1990
At 17, adopted Molly begins to question who she is. Her parents help her find her birth mother and a whole new chapter of Molly's life begins.

Marie G. Lee, *Finding My Voice*, 1992
A senior in high school, Ellen struggles to find her voice

and speak out for what she wants and what she believes in, especially as she faces the racism in her tiny hometown.

Lensey Namioka, *April and the Dragon Lady*, 1994
The only daughter of a traditional Chinese American household, April feels responsible for her grandmother but, leavinhg for college soon, she must make her family aware of their responsibilities.

Kyoko Mori, *One Bird*, 1995
At 15, young Megumi is left behind to live with her cold father and difficult grandmother when her unhappy mother suddenly leaves.

1119

LAURENCE YEP
JEAN TSENG, Illustrator
MOU-SIEN TSENG, Illustrator

The City of Dragons

(New York: Scholastic Inc., 1995)

Subject(s): Identity; Fantasy; Dragons
Age range(s): Grades 1-3
Major character(s): Boy, Child (the saddest face in the world)
Time period(s): Indeterminate Past

Summary: A young boy, who has the saddest face in the world, runs away from home to save his parents further embarrassment. He meets up with a band of friendly giants, who take him to the underwater city of dragons. There, his sad face proves to be a powerful asset, causing the dragons to cry pearls. He is well rewarded and returns to his parents proud and wealthy.

Where it's reviewed:
Booklist, November 15, 1995, page 566
Publishers Weekly, October 2, 1995, page 74

Other books by the same author:
The Ghost Fox, 1994
Dragon's Gate, 1993
Tongues of Jade, 1991 (folk tales)
The Rainbow People, 1989 (folk tales)
Dragonwings, 1976 (true story)

Other books you might like:
Chyng Feng Sun, *Square Beak*, 1993
Square beak is aptly named. She is ostracized because she looks different from the other chickens in the yard and begins to wander outside her small world.

Sandra S. Yamate, *Ashok by Any Other Name*, 1992
Ashok, a young Indian American boy, wishes he had a more ''American'' name, so he tries a new one each day until finally he realizes that ''Ashok'' is the perfect name for him.

Sandra S. Yamate, *Char Siu Bao Boy*, 1991
Charlie's favorite food, *char sui bao*, causes his classmates to tease him until, one day, he brings enough for all of them to taste.

Jeanne M. Lee, *Silent Lotus*, 1991
Beautiful Lotus is unable to hear or speak. When she is ostracized by the local children, her parents take her to see the temple dancers and she begins her training to become one of them.

Amy Tan, *The Chinese Siamese Cat*, 1994
    Ming Mao tells her five kittens about their illustrious Chinese ancestry.

1120

LAURENCE YEP

Dragonwings
(New York: HarperTrophy (HarperCollins), 1975)

Subject(s): Multicultural; Emigration and Immigration; Fathers and Sons
Age range(s): Grades 7-12
Major character(s): Moon Shadow Lee, Immigrant (boy who joins father in U.S.), Chinese; Windrider Lee, Father (Moon Shadow's father), Chinese; Uncle Bright Star Lee, Uncle (distant relative), Businessman (head of the ''The Company''), Aged Person; Miss Whitlaw, Landlord, Friend (of Moon Shadow and Windrider); Robin Whitlaw, Niece (Miss Whitlaw's orphaned niece)
Time period(s): 1900s (1903-1910)
Locale(s): San Francisco, California (Chinatown, then Polk Street); Oakland, California

Summary: Eight-year-old Moon Shadow arrives in California to join his father, a man he has never met. Both work for ''The Company,'' a group of Chinese immigrants who operate a laundry. In the new country, father and son survive the great San Francisco earthquake, separation from family and even robbery to achieve their dream to fly.

About this book: This novel is loosely based on the true story of Chinese immigrant, Fung Joe Guey, who flew a self-built plane in 1909. Yep calls his work a ''historical fantasy'' rather than a ''factual reconstruction.'' Although he made the newspapers with his biplane, Fung remains a shadowy figure about whom little more is known than his aviation achievement.

Where it's reviewed:
Bookwatch, May 10, 1981, page 14
Kirkus Reviews, July 1, 1975, page 719
Kliatt, July 1, 1975, page 719
Publishers Weekly, June 16, 1975, page 82
School Library Journal, September 1975, page 129

Awards the book has won:
Newbery Honor Book, 1976
ALA Notable Children's Book, 1975

Other books by the same author:
American Dragons: Twenty-Five Asian American Voices, 1993 (young adult)
Dragon's Gate, 1993
Tongues of Jade, 1991 (folktales)
The Rainbow People, 1989 (folktales)
Child of the Owl, 1977

Other books you might like:
Lensey Namioka, *Yang the Youngest and His Terrible Ear*, 1992
    Surrounded by a musically talented family, Yingtao struggles to play his violin.
Bette Bao Lord, *In the Year of the Boar and Jackie Robinson*, 1984

Shirley Temple Wong, with her new American name, arrives in Brooklyn. Through new friends and the discovery of baseball, Shirley finds her own special niche in her new home.

1121

LAURENCE YEP
JEAN TSENG, Illustrator
MOU-SIEN TSENG, Illustrator

The Ghost Fox
(New York: Scholastic Inc., 1994)

Subject(s): Multicultural; Folk Tales; Ghosts
Age range(s): Grades 2-6
Major character(s): Little Lee, Child (young son of a bold trader); Big Lee, Father (bold trader along Great River); ''Mama'' Lee, Mother (Little Lee's); Red Robe, Spirit (tries to steal Mama's soul)
Time period(s): 17th century
Locale(s): Hunan, China

Summary: A modern adaptation of a 17th century Chinese ghost story. Big Lee goes on a sea voyage, entrusting the safety of his wife to his young son, Little Lee. Little Lee quickly becomes aware that a vengeful ghost fox is trying to steal his mother's soul. Through ingenuity and perseverance, Little Lee saves his mother.

About this book: The ghost tale was originally collected by 17th-century Chinese scholar, Pu Sung-ling, in the Chinese classic, *Liao-chai chi-yi*.

Where it's reviewed:
Booklist, November 15, 1993, page 626
Kirkus Reviews, December 15, 1993, page 1598
Publishers Weekly, December 13, 1993, page 70

Other books by the same author:
American Dragons: Twenty-Five Asian American Voices, 1993
Dragon's Gate, 1993
Tongues of Jade, 1991 (folk tales)
The Rainbow People, 1989 (folk tales)
Dragonwings, 1976 (true story)

Other books you might like:
Yoshiko Uchida, *The Sea of Gold and Other Tales from Japan*, 1965
    A collection of 12 diverse folktales, including stories about magic monkeys, foolish cats, a talking bowl, mountain gods and vengeful snakes.
Charlie Chin, *China's Bravest Girl: The Legend of Hua Mu Lan*, 1993
    Disguised as a man, Hua Mu Lan takes her father's place in the Emperor's army and becomes a legendary warrior, returning home years later, still undiscovered, a decorated general.
Raymond Chang, *The Cricket Warrior: A Chinese Tale*, 1994
    The Emperor levies a new tax—to be paid in crickets for his cricket matches. When Wei'nian loses his father's promising cricket, the loayl son takes the form of a cricket to save his family.

Demi, *The Magic Tapestry*, 1994

When his mother's heavenly tapestry is stolen by fairies of Sun Mountain, the youngest son must win it back against great odds.

1122

LAURENCE YEP

Hiroshima

(New York: Scholastic Inc., 1995)

Subject(s): World War II; Children and War; Nuclear Warfare
Age range(s): Grades 6 and Up
Major character(s): Riko, 16-Year-Old, Sister (older than Sachi); Sachi, Sister, 12-Year-Old
Time period(s): 1940s (August 6, 1945)
Locale(s): Hiroshima, Japan

Summary: Two sisters, Riko and Sachi, are on their way to school when the B-29 bomber named *Enola Gay* drops the first atom bomb at 8:15 a.m. on the city of Hiroshima. History is changed forever. Yep brings to life the horror of the blast and its tragic aftermath for the survivors, while providing a vivid historical context to the atom bomb tragedy.

About this book: An effective combination of narrative and tragedy that provides a disturbing, necessary, human look at the events of the Hiroshima bombing. Although written for younger audiences, this thin novella is so dense with history that it makes for important reading for adults as well.

Other books by the same author:
American Dragons: Twenty-Five Asian American Voices, 1993
Dragon's Gate, 1993
Tongues of Jade, 1991 (Chinese folktales)
The Rainbow People, 1989 (Chinese folktales)
Child of the Owl, 1977

Other books you might like:
Sheila Hamanaka, *On the Wings of Peace: Writers and Illustrators Speak Out for Peace, in Memory of Hiroshima and Nagasaki*, 1996
Compiled by Hamanaka. A collection of stories, poetry, remembrances and art focusing on the tragedies caused by war, and the hopes for a lasting peace for today's children.
Sheila Hamanaka, *Peace Crane*, 1995
After learning about Sadako, a victim of the Hiroshima bombing, a girl imagines a peaceful world.
Michele Maria Surat, *Angel Child, Dragon Child*, 1983
Young Ut, a recent Vietnamese immigrant, is teased because of her different appearance. Thrown together by the school principal Ut and a once cruel boy develop a new friendship.
Tran Khanh Tuyet, *The Little Weaver of Thai-Yen Village*, 1977
A young Vietnamese refugee arrives in the U.S. and struggles to adjust to her new life. She starts to weave again, as she did in her home country with her late grandmother.

1123

LAURENCE YEP

Later, Gator

(New York: Hyperion Books for Children, 1995)

Subject(s): Brothers; Multicultural; Competition
Age range(s): Grades 5 and Up
Major character(s): Teddy, Child (young boy, very imaginative), Chinese American; Bobby, Brother (Teddy's younger), Chinese American; Oscar, Alligator (baby, Bobby's birthday present)
Time period(s): 1990s (1995)
Locale(s): San Francisco, California (Chinatown)

Summary: Teddy's mother insists he get a special birthday present for his younger brother, Bobby, who everyone already considers perfect. So Teddy comes home with a baby alligator. He figures it's his job as older brother to give Bobby a hard time. But when Oscar the alligator disappears, it's Teddy who comes to Bobby's rescue after all.

Where it's reviewed:
Booklist, May 1, 1995, page 1576
Horn Book Magazine, July 1995, page 463
Library Talk, September 1995, page 36
Publishers Weekly, May 8, 1995, page 296
School Library Journal, July 1995, page 83

Other books by the same author:
American Dragons: Twenty-Five Asian American Voices, 1993 (young adult)
Dragon's Gate, 1993
Tongues of Jade, 1991 (folktales)
Child of the Owl, 1977
Dragonwings, 1975 (true story)

Other books you might like:
Lensey Namioka, *Yang the Youngest and His Terrible Ear*, 1992
Surrounded by a musically talented family, Yingtao struggles to play his violin.
Margaret Chang, *In the Eye of War*, 1990
Shao-shao celebrates his tenth birthday in the final days of the Japanese occupation of China.
Bette Bao Lord, *In the Year of the Boar and Jackie Robinson*, 1984
Shirley Temple Wong, with her new American name, arrives in Brooklyn. Through new friends and the discovery of baseball, Shirley finds her own special niche in her new home.

1124

LAURENCE YEP
ISADORE SELTZER, Illustrator

The Man Who Tricked a Ghost

(New Jersey: Bridgewater Books (Troll Associates), 1993)

Subject(s): Folk Tales; Courage; Ghosts
Age range(s): Grades 1-4
Major character(s): Sung, Young Man (unafraid of anything); Unnamed Character, Spirit (fierce warrior ghost)

Time period(s): Indeterminate Past
Locale(s): China (a distant village)

Summary: One dark night, Sung, a man who is not afraid of anything, meets up with a ghost who happens to be on his way to scare a man named Sung to death. Without revealing his identity, Sung travels with the ghost, learns his secrets, and once home, tricks the ghost at his own game.

About this book: An ancient Chinese folktale, as retold by Yep. The original story was first published in the 3rd century A.D., making it one of the first ghost stories ever printed in China.

Where it's reviewed:
Children's Book Review Service, November 1993, page 33
Children's Bookwatch, November 1993, page 7
Horn Book Guide, Spring 1994, page 112

Other books by the same author:
The City of Dragons, 1995
The Boy Who Swallowed Snakes, 1994
The Ghost Fox, 1994
The Shell Woman and the King, 1993
Dragonwings, 1975 (true story)

Other books you might like:
Ed Young, *Lon Po Po: A Red-Riding Hood Story from China*, 1989
  Three sisters, left home alone and told to keep the door locked, are tricked by a hungry wolf disguised as Grandma.
Lina Mao Wall, *Judge Rabbit and the Tree Spirit: A Folktale from Cambodia*, 1991
  Judge Rabbit helps a young couple trap the tree spirit who has taken the form of the young husband.
Jacquelin Singh, *Fat Gopal*, 1984
  The ruling Nawab wants the Maharajah to do an impossible task: measure the earth, count the stars, the sun's rays and the men on the moon. Fat Gopal will find the answers, for a price.
Suzanne Crowder Han, *The Rabbit's Escape*, 1995
  Turtle volunteers to bring a rabbit from the land kingdom to save the life of the Dragon King of the East Sea. He tricks the rabbit into the underworld, but the rabbit makes his clever escape.
Dianne Snyder, *The Boy of the Three-Year Nap*, 1988
  Lazy Taro hatches a plan to ensure an easy life by convincing a rich merchant that his beautiful daughter must marry Taro.

daughter nightly, dragons trapped in human bodies, a white mouse who helps her pitiful mistress and an old jar that forever provides rice.

About this book: As Yep writes, these stories were a link back to the homeland for many of the early Chinese American immigrants who were struggling to survive and make a new life in the U.S.

Where it's reviewed:
Publishers Weekly, August 17, 1992, page 502
Booklist, April 1, 1989, page 1993
Children's Book Review Service, June 1989, page 128
Kirkus Reviews, May 15, 1989, page 774
School Library Journal, May 1989, page 123

Awards the book has won:
ALA Notable Book, 1989
Boston Globe-Horn Book Honor Book for Nonfiction, 1989

Other books by the same author:
American Dragons: Twenty-Five Asian American Voices, 1993 (young adult)
Dragon's Gate, 1993
Tongues of Jade, 1991 (folktales)
Child of the Owl, 1977
Dragonwings, 1975 (true story)

Other books you might like:
Asian Cultural Centre for Unesco, *Folk Tales From Asia for Children Everywhere*, 1975
  Two volumes of traditional folktales with Asian origins, beautifully illustrated especially for children.
Valorie Slaughter Bejarano, *The Beginning and Other Asian Folktales*, 1995
  Edited by Bejarano, Cecilia Brainard, Susan Montepio and Cecile Ochoa. A delightful collection of adapted folktales of various Asian origin.
Jeannette Faurot, *Asian-Pacific Folktales and Legends*, 1995
  Edited by Faurot. A diverse collection of over 60 folktales from Asia.
Yoshiko Uchida, *The Dancing Kettle and Other Japanese Folk Tales*, 1949
  A collection of 14 folktales, originally from Japan.
Yoshiko Uchida, *The Sea of Gold and Other Tales from Japan*, 1965
  A collection of 12 diverse folktales, including stories about magic monkeys, foolish cats, a talking bowl, mountain gods and vengeful snakes.

1125

LAURENCE YEP, Adaptor
DAVID WIESNER, Illustrator

The Rainbow People

(New York: HarperTrophy (HarperCollins), 1989)

Subject(s): Folk Tales; Multicultural; Short Stories
Age range(s): Grades 6-12
Time period(s): Indeterminate Past

Summary: A collection of 20 folktales, adapted by Yep from age-old Chinese lore, including stories about a gambler turned professor of smells, a dead father who visits his beloved

1126

LAURENCE YEP

Ribbons

(New York: G.P. Putnam's Sons, 1996)

Subject(s): Dancing; Perseverance; Family Life
Age range(s): Grades 7-12
Major character(s): Robin Lee, Dancer (life centers on ballet), Chinese; Gilbert Lee, Father (Robin's), Filmmaker (makes documentary films), Caucasian; Elaine Lee, Mother (Robin's), Lawyer (takes on many pro bono cases), Chinese; Ian Lee, Brother (Robin's younger brother), Chinese;

Asian American Titles

Grandmother Paw-Paw, Grandmother (Robin and Ian's maternal), Chinese (from Hong Kong)
Time period(s): 1990s (1995)
Locale(s): San Francisco, California

Summary: Ballet is the most important thing in Robin Lee's life. But her parents want to bring her grandmother to the U.S. from Hong Kong—an expensive venture. For Robin, that means no more ballet. When her grandmother arrives, Robin is resentful.

Where it's reviewed:
Booklist, January 1, 1996, page 836
Kirkus Reviews, December 15, 1995, page 1778
Publishers Weekly, March 4, 1996, page 66

Other books by the same author:
The Ghost Fox, 1994
Dragon's Gate, 1993
Tongues of Jade, 1991 (folk tales)
The Rainbow People, 1989 (folk tales)
Dragonwings, 1976 (true story)

Other books you might like:
Lauren Lee, *Stella: On the Edge of Popularity*, 1994
   Young Stella must learn who her true friends are, as she defines her own unique place among her classmates at school, and as a first-generation Korean American in the outside world.
Lensey Namioka, *April and the Dragon Lady*, 1994
   The only daughter of a traditional Chinese American household, April feels responsible for her grandmother but, leaving for college soon, she must make her family aware of their responsibilities.
Marie G. Lee, *Finding My Voice*, 1992
   A senior in high school, Ellen struggles to find her voice and speak out for what she wants and what she believes in, especially as she faces the racism in her tiny hometown.
Marie G. Lee, *Saying Goodbye*, 1994
   Ellen has left her small hometown for Harvard where she comes face-to-face with the reality of racial boundaries and racial tensions and must define her own position as an aware Korean American.
Kyoko Mari, *One Bird*, 1995
   At 15, Megumi is left behind to live with her cold father and difficult grandmother when her unhappy mother suddenly leaves.

1127

LAURENCE YEP, Adaptor
YANG MING-YI, Illustrator

The Shell Woman and the King

(New York: Dial Book for Young Readers (Penguin), 1993)

Subject(s): Folk Tales; Greed; Love
Age range(s): Grades 1-5
Major character(s): Uncle Wu, Spouse (of Shell); Shell, Mythical Creature (of the sea); The King, Ruler (cruel)
Time period(s): Indeterminate Past
Locale(s): China (a kingdom in southern China)

Summary: Long ago, Uncle Wu fell in love with and married Shell, a beautiful woman who is able to transform herself into

a seashell. The evil king hears about her powers and summons the couple; he imprisons Wu and demands that Shell bring him three wonders or lose her husband.

Where it's reviewed:
Booklist, July 1993, page 1973
Kirkus Reviews, August 15, 1993, page 1082
Publishers Weekly, July 12, 1993, page 79

Other books by the same author:
The Ghost Fox, 1994
Dragon's Gate, 1993
Tongues of Jade, 1991 (folk tales)
The Rainbow People, 1989 (folk tales)
Dragonwings, 1976 (true story)

Other books you might like:
Ai-Ling Louie, *Yeh-Shen: A Cinderella Story from China*, 1982
   In spite of the wicked machinations of her stepmother, beautiful young Yeh-Shen manages to survive her deprived life, marry the king and live happily ever after.
Nami Rhee, *Magic Spring: A Korean Folktale*, 1993
   A hardworking, childless, elderly couple discover the fountain of youth. Their greedy neighbor rushes to the magic spring and overindulges, leading to a surprise ending.
Oki S. Han, *Sir Whong and the Golden Pig*, 1993
   When a stranger dupes Sir Whong into a loan using a fake golden pig as security, Sir Whong devises a plan to retrieve the money.
Demi, *Liang and the Magic Paintbrush*, 1980
   Young Liang is given a magic paintbrush that brings to life everything he draws.
Jose Aruego, *Rockabye Crocodile*, 1988
   Two elderly boars, a crocodile and her baby teach a lesson about goodness, greed and rewards.

1128

ED YOUNG, Author/Illustrator

Cat and Rat: The Legend of the Chinese Zodiac

(New York: Henry Holt and Company, 1995)

Subject(s): Folk Tales; Astrology; Animals
Age range(s): Grades 1-3
Major character(s): Cat, Cat (best friend of Rat); Rat, Rat (best friend of Cat)
Time period(s): Indeterminate Past
Locale(s): China

Summary: An adaptation of how the 12 animals of the zodiac were selected: the Jade Emperor announced a race in which the first 12 animals who crossed the finish line would represent the 12 animals of the zodiac. Cat and Rat, who were then best friends, devised a plan together, but Rat betrayed Cat and won the race leaving Cat to struggle in at 13th place.

Where it's reviewed:
Booklist, November 1, 1995, page 472
Kirkus Reviews, September 1, 1995, page 1290
School Library Journal, December 1995, page 101
Publishers Weekly, September 11, 1995, page 85

Other books by the same author:
Night Visitors, 1995 (a scholar learns respect for all forms of life, even when they seem insignificant)
Little Plum, 1994
Red Thread, 1993
Seven Blind Mice, 1992
Lon Po Po: A Red-Riding Hood Story from China, 1989 (three children outwit the wolf who appears claiming to be their grandmother)

Other books you might like:
Jose Aruego, *Rockabye Crocodile*, 1988
Edited with Ariane Dewey. Two elderly boars, a crocodile and her baby teach a lesson about goodness, greed and rewards.
Jeanne M. Lee, *Toad is the Uncle of Heaven*, 1985
The Toad asks the King of Heaven for rain. On his journey, he is joined by the Bees, the Rooster and the Tiger. With the help of his friends, Toad convinces the King to provide rain.
Blia Xiong, *Nine-in-One Grr! Grr!*, 1989
Bird comes up with a clever trick to prevent Tiger from having the nine cubs every year as promised by the god Shao, thereby preventing earth from being overpopulated with tigers.
Laurence Yep, *The Ghost Fox*, 1994
A brave boy saves his mother from the evil ghost fox who tries to steal her soul.

1129

ED YOUNG, Author/Illustrator

Little Plum

(New York: Philomel Books (G.P. Putnam's Sons), 1994)

Subject(s): Folk Tales; Courage; Perseverance
Age range(s): Grades 1-4
Major character(s): Little Plum, Child (son of elderly couple), Hero (saves village)
Time period(s): Indeterminate Past
Locale(s): China (a village)

Summary: A childless, elderly couple long for a child, "even if he were only as big as a plum seed." Indeed, the woman bears Little Plum, who never grows larger than his namesake, a plum seed. But he matures into an ingenious, brave young man, eventually saving his entire village from the greedy evil lord.

Where it's reviewed:
Book World, May 7, 1995, page 17
Center for Children's Books. Bulletin, October 1994, page 71

Other books by the same author:
Night Visitors, 1995
Seven Blind Mice, 1992
Lon Po Po: A Red-Riding Hood Story from China, 1989

Other books you might like:
Raymond Chang, *The Cricket Warrior: A Chinese Tale*, 1994
The emperor levies a new tax—to be paid in crickets for his matches. When Wei'nian loses his father's promising cricket, the loyal son takes the form of a cricket to save his family.

Charlie Chin, *China's Bravest Girl: The Legend of Hua Mu Lan*, 1993
Disguised as a man, Hua Mu Lan takes her father's place in the emperor's army and becomes a legendary warrior, returning home years later, a decorated general.
Demi, *Liang and the Magic Paintbrush*, 1980
Young Liang is given a magic paintbrush that brings to life everything he draws.
Laurence Yep, *The Shell Woman and the King*, 1993
The magical shell woman saves her husband and herself from the evil, greedy king.

1130

ED YOUNG, Author/Illustrator

Lon Po Po: A Red-Riding Hood Story from China

(New York: Philomel Books (G.P. Putnam's Sons), 1989)

Subject(s): Folk Tales; Folklore; Survival
Age range(s): Grades 1-4
Major character(s): Shang, Child (daughter); Tao, Child (daughter); Paotze, Child (daughter); Old Wolf, Wolf (disguised as grandmother)
Time period(s): Indeterminate Past
Locale(s): China (in the country)

Summary: A mother makes a birthday visit to her own mother, leaving her three daughters at home with the warning to keep the doors locked. An old wolf, disguised as the birthday grandmother appears late at night, intending to eat the children, but they are finally able to outwit her.

Where it's reviewed:
Booklist, November 1, 1992, page 503
Language Arts, January 1993, page 61

Awards the book has won:
The Caldecott Medal, 1990

Other books by the same author:
Night Visitors, 1995
Little Plum, 1994
Seven Blind Mice, 1992

Other books you might like:
Jeanne M. Lee, *Toad Is the Uncle of Heaven*, 1985
Toad asks the King of Heaven for rain. On his journey, he is joined by the Bees, the Rooster and the Tiger. With the help of his friends, Toad convinces the King to provide rain.
Jose Aruego, *Rockabye Crocodile*, 1988
Two elderly boars, a crocodile and her baby teach a lesson about goodness, greed and rewards.
Suzanne Crowder Han, *The Rabbit's Escape*, 1995
The turtle tricked the rabbit into the underworld, but the clever rabbit makes his escape.
Suzanne Crowder Han, *The Rabbit's Judgment*, 1994
A man is tricke into saving the life of a tiger; a clever rabbit keeps the man from being eaten by the ungrateful, hungry tiger.

1131

ED YOUNG, Author/Illustrator

Night Visitors

(New York: Philomel Books (G.P. Putnam's Sons), 1995)

Subject(s): Folk Tales; Folklore; Animals, Treatment of
Age range(s): Grades 1-4
Major character(s): Ho Kuan, Scholar (gentle and strong young man)
Time period(s): Indeterminate Past
Locale(s): China (a small southern village)

Summary: Ho Kuan is ordered by his father to seal the storehouse or he will flood it to kill the ants who have stolen the grain. That night, Ho's dreams take him on a journey through the ant kingdom, teaching him deep respect for all forms of life. The ants, in turn, lead Ho to a solution.

About this book: This story is based on an ancient Chinese folktale which dates back to the 6th century B.C.

Other books by the same author:
Cat and Rat: The Legend of the Chinese Zodiac, 1995
Little Plum, 1994
Red Thread, 1993
Seven Blind Mice, 1992
Lon Po Po: A Red-Riding Hood Story from China, 1989

Other books you might like:
Margaret Chang, *The Cricket Warrior: A Chinese Tale*, 1994
    Adapted with Raymond Chang. The dutiful son, Wei'nian, takes the form of a cricket and saves his family by becoming the champion of the Emperor's court.
Charlie Chin, *China's Bravest Girl: The Legend of Hua Mu Lan*, 1993
    Adapted by Chin. Disguised as a man, Hua Mu Lan takes her elderly father's place in the Emperor's army and becomes a legendary warrior.
Karen Chinn, *Sam and the Lucky Money*, 1995
    Disappointed that everything he wants to buy with his Chinese New Year gift money costs too much, Sam finally realizes how lucky he is when he sees a lonely stranger without shoes.
Demi, *The Empty Pot*, 1990
    When Ping presents an empty pot to the Emperor, he is rewarded for his honesty.

1132

ED YOUNG, Author/Illustrator

Red Thread

(New York: Philomel Books (G.P. Putnam's Sons), 1993)

Subject(s): Folk Tales; Fate; Marriage
Age range(s): Grades 1-3
Major character(s): Wei Gu, Young Man (wants a family); Matchmaker, Matchmaker (explains the red thread to Wei), Aged Person
Time period(s): Indeterminate Past
Locale(s): China (various villages and provinces throughout ancient China)

Summary: A matchmaker reveals to Wei Gu who his wife will be. The old man explains that at birth, couples are bound together by a red thread that cannot be broken. But Wei's chosen mate, still an infant, is not to his liking. Wei orders a servant to kill the child, but in the end, fate cannot be thwarted.

Where it's reviewed:
Horn Book Guide, Fall 1993, page 330
Language Arts, February 1994, page 134
School Library Journal, April 1994, page 43
Children's Literature in Education, September 1994, page 169

Other books by the same author:
Night Visitors, 1995
Little Plum, 1994
Seven Blind Mice, 1992
Lon Po Po: A Red-Riding Hood Story from China, 1989

Other books you might like:
Laurence Yep, *The Shell Woman and the King*, 1993
    The magical shell woman saves her husband and herself from the greedy, evil king.
Ai-Ling Louie, *Yeh-Shen: A Cinderella Story from China*, 1982
    In spite of the wicked machinations of her stepmother, the beautiful young Yeh-Shen manages to survive her deprived life, marry the king and live happily ever after.
Ellin Greene, *Ling-Li and the Phoenix Fairy: A Chinese Folktale*, 1996
    Ling-Li creates a wedding robe so beautiful that the magpies carry it away. Ling-Li follows the birds to the Phoenix Fairy who returns the robe with her special blessings.

1133

ED YOUNG, Author/Illustrator

Seven Blind Mice

(New York: Philomel Books (G.P. Putnam's Sons), 1992)

Subject(s): Folk Tales; Problem Solving; Blind
Age range(s): Grades 1-2
Major character(s): Mouse, Mouse; Elephant, Elephant
Time period(s): Indeterminate Past

Summary: Six of the seven blind mice identify the parts of an elephant—the leg, the trunk, the tusk, etc.—never realizing that these parts make up a whole. Not until the seventh blind mouse explores the "something" as a whole being do the rest of the mice finally "see" the elephant.

About this book: This was originally an Indian fable with seven blind men identifying the parts of an elephant without realizing the whole animal.

Where it's reviewed:
Booklist, March 15, 1993, page 1329
New Yorker, November 23, 1992, page 76
School Library Journal, December 1992, page 24

Awards the book has won:
A Caldecott Honor Book, 1993

Other books by the same author:
Night Visitors, 1995

Little Plum, 1994
Lon Po Po: A Red-Riding Hood Story from China, 1989
Cat and Rat: The Legend of the Chinese Zodiac, 1995
Red Thread, 1993

Other books you might like:
Jacquelin Singh, *Fat Gopal*, 1984
The Maharajah's servant, Fat Gopal, receives huge sums of money to measure the earth and to count the stars.
Jan Freeman Long, *The Bee and the Dream: A Japanese Tale*, 1996
Shin so believes in the reality of his friend Tasuke's dream of finding gold that he borrows money and sets off to find the treasure.
Margaret Mahy, *The Seven Chinese Brothers*, 1990
Seven identical Chinese brothers, each with an extraordinary power, must call on his special talent to save the others' lives from the cruel emperor.
Demi, *The Empty Pot*, 1990
When Ping presents an empty pot to the emperor, he is rewarded for his honesty.

1134

JUDY YUNG

Chinese Women of America: A Pictorial History

(Seattle: University of Washington Press, 1986)

Subject(s): Multicultural; Emigration and Immigration; Historical
Age range(s): Adult
Time period(s): 1830s; 1980s
Locale(s): United States

Summary: Most likely the first historical text to exclusively examine the experiences of Chinese American women over a 150-year history, utilizing personal interviews, photographs, and long-overlooked documents.

Where it's reviewed:
Booklist, December 15, 1986, page 622
Kliatt, Winter 1987, page 37

Other books by the same author:
Unbound Feet: A Social History of Chinese Women in San Francisco, 1995
Island: Poetry and History of Chinese Immigrants on Angel Island, 1910-1940, 1980 (with Him Mark Lai and Genny Lim.)

Other books you might like:
Ruthanne Lum McCunn, *Chinese American Portraits: Personal Histories 1828-1988*, 1988
Profiles of prominent Chinese Americans, from pioneers to politicians.
Ruthanne Lum McCunn, *An Illustrated History of the Chinese in America*, 1979
An illustrated history book which traces the presence of Chinese in America, from the arrival of Chinese during the California Gold Rush, to contemporary Chinese Americans.

Ruthanne Lum McCunn, *Thousand Pieces of Gold*, 1981
The first biographical novel of Chinese American pioneer woman, Polly Bemis.
Victor G. Nee, *Longtime Californ': A Documentary Study of an American Chinatown*, 1974
Co-author Brett de Bary Nee; history of the Chinese in America told through both personal narratives and extensive interviews, using the backdrop of San Francisco's Chinatown.
Ronald Takaki, *Strangers from a Different Shore*, 1989
Traces the diverse lives of the Japanese, Chinese, Koreans, Filipinos, Asian Indians, Vietnamese, Cambodians and Laotions who have come to the U.S. over the past 150 years.

1135

JUDY YUNG

Unbound Feet: A Social History of Chinese Women in San Francisco

(Berkeley: University of California Press, 1995)

Subject(s): Multicultural; Historical; Emigration and Immigration
Age range(s): Adult
Time period(s): 1900s; 1940s
Locale(s): San Francisco, California

Summary: Using the backdrop of San Francisco, Yung traces the vibrant history of Chinese American women who arrived at the turn of the century as the property of their husbands or even as slaves, and who, through the decades leading up to World War II developed, into active members of American society.

Where it's reviewed:
Library Journal, September 15, 1995, page 83

Other books by the same author:
Chinese Women of America: A Pictorial History, 1986
Island: Poetry and History of Chinese Immigrants on Angel Island, 1910-1940, 1980 (with Him Mark Lai and Genny Lim)

Other books you might like:
Ruthanne Lum McCunn, *Chinese American Portraits: Personal Histories 1828-1988*, 1988
Profiles of prominent Chinese Americans, from pioneers to politicians.
Ruthanne Lum McCunn, *An Illustrated History of the Chinese in America*, 1979
An illustrated history book which traces the presence of Chinese in America, from the arrival of Chinese during the California Gold Rush, to contemporary Chinese Americans.
Ruthanne Lum McCunn, *Thousand Pieces of Gold*, 1981
The first biographical novel of Chinese American pioneer woman, Polly Bemis.
Victor G. Nee, *Longtime Californ': A Documentary Study of an American Chinatown*, 1974
Co-author Brett de Bary Nee; history of the Chinese in America told through both personal narratives and exten-

Asian American Titles

sive interviews, using the backdrop of San Francisco's Chinatown.

Ronald Takaki, *Strangers from a Different Shore*, 1989
Traces the diverse lives of the Japanese, Chinese, Koreans, Filipinos, Asian Indians, Vietnamese, Cambodians and Laotions who have come to the U.S. over the past 150 years.

Native American Literature

Since the first native people of the Caribbean spotted the sails of Columbus' flotilla approaching their Caribbean homeland over five centuries ago, there has been a cataclysmic clash of cultures between the native inhabitants of the Western Hemisphere and the European invaders who "discovered" them. From Columbus' log it is clear that at first he was quite taken by the new people he encountered and named "Indios," but he soon began to look upon the "Indians" as a source of profit. Columbus, taking into account some of the first islanders he came upon said,

> I believe that people from the mainland come here to take them as slaves. They ought to make good and skilled servants, for they repeat very quickly whatever we say to them. I think they can easily be made Christians, for they seem to have no religion (77).

What at first began as a hospitable meeting of cultures rapidly deteriorated as the Spaniards began to enslave the native Arawakan people, forcing them to relentlessly search for gold. Bartoleme de Las Casas, the Catholic priest who journeyed to the New World with Columbus (and who later transcribed Columbus' diary) reported the many injustices that the people of the "Old World" inflicted on the people of the "New." He describes how many of the Europeans who sailed to the New World to find their fortune thought the Indians lacked souls; that they were actually animals who could talk. According to las Casas, the Spaniards "rode the backs of Indians if they were in a hurry," and they "thought nothing of knifing Indians by tens and twenties and of cutting slices off them to test the sharpness of their blades" (de las Casas, *History of the Indies*).

Unfortunately, many of the prejudices that Columbus and his crew carried with them into the "New World" still linger in the Americas today, and acts of genocide against Indian people are far from over. There are still large populations of Indian people who are marginalized, controlled by people of European descent, though Indian people have fought continually for justice. But just as Columbus thought the Indians had no religion, it has often been assumed by other immigrants to the New World that the Indians had no culture either, and that the land itself as well as the native culture consisted of a barren "wilderness." The immigrants often believed they were conquering a land sparsely populated, devoid of humanity, a land without religion, myth, history, story, or song. But nothing could have been further from the truth.

The Western Hemisphere was a place where *millions* of human beings lived. Scholars now believe that at the time of European contact at least 18 million people speaking some two hundred languages and living in 300 distinct cultural groups lived in North America alone. The diversity of culture was staggering. Indian people had invented in the Americas new and varied forms of government in the Americas new and varied forms of government (including democracy), and monumental architecture, and there were hundreds of villages, towns, and even cities (Tenochitilan, the Aztec capital, being larger than any city in Europe at the time). Indian people had also developed a tremendously sophisticated agriculture (few realize that many of the food staples we use every day were developed by Indian farmers: corn, potatoes, tomatoes, beans, squash, chocolate, vanilla, peppers, to name a few). And America was a place where the people, like people everywhere, had reinvented themselves by creating literature—mythology, ritual drama, story, and song.

Of course, the term "Indian" is only meaningful in the context of the European conquest, for the people living in the Americas had never, before the arrival of the Europeans, thought of themselves united as a "race." They were people who belonged to various language and cultural groups: Lakota, Anishinaabe, Taino, Illinois, Omahas, Missouri, Cherokee, Creek, Dine, and the oral literature that first emerged with these peoples developed within the context of their individual languages and cultures. Yet there are unifying themes in the traditional oral literatures that are present throughout the Americas. In virtually all of these cultures there is the idea of respect for the earth, and respect for animal and plant life. Indeed, much of the traditional oral literature takes place in mythic time, a time when animals were actually people. A good deal of Native American oral literature focuses on the idea of harmony, of creating balance within the world at large and within the culture to which one belongs. The notion of man as a spiritual being removed from the natural world is quite alien to Native American people, and much of the oral literature (whether it be from the mythic period or the historical period) reflects the interconnectedness of all things: animate and inanimate.

A number of different genres are represented in Native American oral literatures: song, chant, ritual drama, narrative, and oration. Songs are the most prevalent type of oral literature and can be both sacred and secular. In general, words are seen as having great power in American Indian cultures, and songs are often used as instruments to put the world right, to affect some sort of change in mood, or in the healing of disease, or in nature itself. Songs exist both as part of communal religious ceremonies and as an art of individual expression. In some cases songs are owned by individuals or clans, though in other instances they are communally owned, belonging to the culture at large. Songs are used for a variety of purposes: lullabies were used to rock children to sleep; death songs of Plains men were used by warriors facing their final moments, the song acting as a last affirmation of life and of stoic acceptance of death, which brought power to the singer. Other types of death songs could act as philosophical statements regarding the mystery of life as in this Tlingit song from the Northwest Coast:

> The world is rolling around for all the young
> people, so let's not love our life too much,
> hold ourselves back from dying. (Bierhorst,
> *The Sacred Path*, 143)

Songs could be prayers, or they could be used as magic to make someone fall in love. This Cherokee song titled "For Putting a Woman's Family to Sleep" is humorous in its hopeful determination:

> People, sleep is coming!
> Very quickly all of you are turning over.
> Night is coming.
> Keep on throughout the night: the Dark
> Moon has just come to live in your soul!
> (*Sacred Path*, 54)

Songs could also be used for work—to prepare one for hunting or to pass time in group activities—such as gathering or weaving. There are songs that were traditionally sung at dances, or that people just liked to sing together around the drum (most songs were traditionally accompanied by some kind of percussion instrument, usually a drum). In Eskimo culture dueling songs were even used to settle disagreements between rivals.

Like songs, stories are both religious and secular and are told for a variety of reasons. Stories can both entertain and educate, but it is in the art of storytelling itself that a story becomes alive. Recently, anthropologists and folklorists have begun to pay special attention to the oral nature of storytelling, focusing on the performance event itself, on the subtle yet powerful ways that a storyteller conveys a tale to an audience. Gestures, changes in voice, facial expressions, as well as the context in which the story is being told, are all important elements in the drama of the telling, and Anthropologists (such as Dennis Tedlock) have been experimenting with ways of transcribing these elements to the page (such as changing the font size to emphasize changes in voice, or adding white space or margins around the text so that the reader is aware of shifting rhythms in the original performance).

Traditional oral stories include mythology, legends, and tales. Stories of genesis are found in every culture; in the Southwest these are typically emergence myths: stories in which the ancient ancestors climbed upward through various worlds before getting to this one. In the Northeastern Woodlands, the earth-diver is a common origin story. In this type of tale an animal, usually one good at diving (such as a beaver, muskrat, or loon) goes down into a flooded world to retrieve some earth, and from the mud he brings up, land is created. In most Indian genesis stories animals play a significant part in the creation process, and in general animals are seen as being on an equal spiritual plane as human beings. Hence, there are many hunting prayers, ceremonies, and songs, used to ritually purify the hunter before he took the life of a fellow creature.

Trickster stories, common worldwide, are extremely prevalent in Native American literature, and are probably universal throughout the Americas. The trickster is a character who exists in mythic time and is usually manifested in the form of an animal: Coyote, Raven, Hare, or Spider, yet he has mostly human qualities. He usually expresses infantile behavior, breaking every cultural taboo, and he is obsessed with food and sex, his relentless appetites continually directing his actions. Trickster blunders into one mess after another, and in some cultures (such as the Hopi) he is seen as a worthless beast who is continually getting his comeuppance, for in story after story he ends up pulverized, decimated. Yet, in many other cultures (such as the Winnebago, the Anishinaabe, and the Mesquakie, to name a few) the Trickster actually becomes the Cultural Hero who does good, bringing essential things to mankind: tools, fire, or food, and sometimes even life itself. In many tribes, Trickster stories can only be told in Winter, and historically these tales often acted as relief valves, the humor inherent in the stories relieving the tensions caused by cramped and uncomfortable conditions when people would be forced to spend many months together in close confines. Also, since Trickster can break all the cultural taboos, acting out what is forbidden, he surreptitiously relieves the stress that comes from constantly trying to maintain civil behavior. But the stories educate the children as well, for if trickster is doing something—it is usually wrong—and he usually gets his just desserts (at least for awhile), providing a humorous moral for children (though this is not always obvious). Above all else, however, Trickster is a survivor; for no matter how bad things get, he always rebounds, and this aspect of him is another probable reason he is so popular in the mythology of Native American people, who also had to rebound from continual abuse.

Many other myths and legends also contain cultural heroes who must journey to far away lands in order to do battle with monsters or witches. There is often a twin motif present in these cultural-hero tales. Star-husband, is another prevalent genre of traditional story. In these tales, an earth woman lusts after a star-man (or a star-man comes down and seduces a woman), but the woman's life does not end in a Cinderella story after the mating with the star-man has taken place, as she longs to return to her people. Orpheus tales are another genre, in which someone tries to bring back a loved one from the dead.

For a number of tribes, oratory has been a very important part of traditional life, and many of the anthologies included here include examples of eloquent and moving oration: some spoken for inter-tribal concerns (such as religious ceremonies, that shamans would officiate at), and some directed to an audience outside the tribe (to representatives of the U.S. government, or the white community at large). Bierhorst's *In the Trail of the Wind* gives a good cross-section of traditional tribal orations, while Nabokov's *Native American Testimony* deals primarily with speeches given by Indian people regarding the acculturation process.

Narrated autobiographies are works of collaboration: usually it is an Indian informant recounting his or her life story to a white writer who edits and transcribes the story. The first American Indian autobiography in this As-Told-To format was that of Black Hawk (Sauk), which was told to Antoine Le Claire and later edited by John B. Patterson. The most famous As-Told-To book is *Black Elk Speaks*, which brings out some of the problems inherent in the genre. In this case, Nick Black Elk (Sioux) told his life story to the Nebraskan poet John Neihardt, in Lakota, which was translated into English by Nick's son, Ben. Neihardt's daughter, Hilda, took down the proceedings in short-hand, and from that Neihardt later rewrote ("transformed" is the word he used) those notes into a beautiful literary work, which became *Black Elk Speaks*. The problem is that in the rewriting, Neihardt injected much of his own philosophy, and later scholars (including DeMallie, whose book *The Sixth Grandfather*, contains the original transcriptions of the interviews) have noted that the most often quoted passages of *Black Elk Speaks* come entirely from Neihardt's poetic imagination. Other collaborators, however, have not taken such liberties with the oral material, and no matter the inherent problems, there is much to be gained in reading As-Told-To-Books, for the form allows a speaker foreign to the English language to have his or her story recorded and exposed to a large reading public. David Brumble, in his *American Indian Autobiography*, outlines a number of the disadvantages and advantages that exist in this genre. A number of excellent autobiographies exist, such as Mountain Wolf Woman (Winnebago), Maria Chona (Papago), John Stands in Timber (Cheyenne), James Sewid (Kwakiutl), Left handed (Navajo), and Helen Sekaquaptewa (Hopi).

Personal narratives, which came about as Indian people began to become educated in the written word, consist of works (written primarily in English) by Native Americans. The first known autobiography is by William Apess of the Pequot tribe, *A Son of the Forest*, which was published in 1829. Other important nineteenth century autobiographies are George Copway's (Ojibwa) *The Life, History, and Travels of Kah-ge-ga-gah-bowh* (1847) and Sarah Winnemucca's (Paiute) *Life Among the Piutes* (1883). The very first Native American

author to publish in the English language was Samson Occom (Mogegan, 1723-92). His book, *A Sermon Preached at the Execution of Moses Paul, an Indian* (1772), typifies much of the early writing of Indian people expressing themselves in English. Many of these early literary efforts, obviously aimed at a white audience, were often written to show the dominant American public that Indians could be Christianized and that they were not savages. Yet as self-conscious and apologetic as many of these early personal narratives are, there is often another side that comes through them, as one reads between the lines, a side that is often critical of the way Indian people have been treated by whites and that actually exalts Indian philosophy and culture. In the early twentieth century, Charles Eastman's (Sioux) books, *Indian Boyhood* (1902) and *From the Deep Woods to Civilization* (1926) were very popular. *From the Deep Woods*, which chronicles Eastman's life from traditional tribal life to medical doctor in American society, is fascinating in the way that the tension between his two personas is never quite resolved. Eastman tries to proclaim the benefits of Christian society, yet his other perspective, wholly sympathetic to Native culture and religion keeps breaking through the text. Two other Sioux writers, Luther Standing Bear and Zitkala-Sa, each wrote interesting and important autobiographies in this period that deal with similar themes, as did the Omaha writer, Francis La Flesche. More recent autobiographies have been written by Anna Moore Shaw (Pima), Ted Williams (Tuscarora), James McCarthy (Papago), John Joseph Mathews (Osage) N. Scott Momaday (Kiowa), Gerald Vizenor (Ojibwa), and Joseph Iron Eyes Dudley (Sioux).

Books between autobiography and narrated formats include Chief White Bull's *The Warrior Who Killed Custer* (originally recorded in the DaKota language and later translated into English and published in 1968) and Don Talayesva's (Hopi) book *Sun Chief*, from 1942. Mourning Dove's autobiography, *Mourning Dove: A Salishan Autobiography*, is another important book that falls into this section because it was heavily edited by a white editor, Jay Miller.

The first novel written by a Native American is *The Life and Adventures of Joaquin Muriéta*

(1854) by Rollin Ridge (Cherokee), and his posthumously published *Poems* (1868) is the only Native American volume of poetry published in the 1800s. Sophia Alice Callahan (Creek) was the first Native American woman to write a novel:*Wynema, a Child of the Forest* (1891), which at this time is unavailable in print. The first Indian woman to publish short stories was Pauline Johnson (Mohawk) who wrote *Moccasin Maker* in 1913. She published two volumes of fiction as well as a book of poetry. Johnson was also a performer who interpreted her poems and stories on stages throughout the US, Canada, and Europe.

In the 20th century, many more American Indian people began to write novels of contemporary Indian life, taking up traditional themes and often incorporating traditional tribal mythologies and legends into their work. To help comprehend this literature it is often beneficial to look into the traditional stories that are part of the world-view of each writer, for many authors have subtly woven into their texts important traditional references that to a casual reader would not be apparent. One very important aspect of American Indian literature to emerge with the 20th century Indian novelists is the theme of division: of living between two cultures. Many writers have as a protagonist a person of mixed ancestry. Mourning Dove, one of the first Indian women writers, tells of the pain of racism and alienation in her book *Cogewea, the Half Blood* (1927). Written basically in the form of a romantic Western novel, this book also delves into the difficulties of a "half-breed" woman living in a white man's world. (Mourning Dove's work was heavily edited by Lucullus V. McWhorter, who acted as her collaborator, and one can detect two distinct styles throughout; however, it is Mourning Dove's literary intuition that is superior, and reading this mixed work is fascinating as the text itself is a clash of philosophies and styles). John Joseph Mathews (Osage), a superb literary writer, chronicles in his book *Sundown*, the period of the roaring twenties on the Osage reservation, at a time when the oil boom made many Osage people rich. The novel deals with issues of identity and sovereignty during the period from the allotment through the 1920s oil boom. Challenge Windzer, whose father is one quarter white, finds himself alienated from both cultures and turns to alcohol as a way out. However, the most

sophisticated and literary of the Indian writers of this period was D'Arcy McNickle (Cree & Flathead) whose book *The Surrounded* is an American masterpiece. This novel tells the story of Archilde Leon who is half Flathead and half Spanish. After working in the white world for a short time (as a fiddle player) he returns to the Salish reservation where he gets caught between two worlds: that of his mother (who is basically a traditionalist) and his father (who believes strongly in the white man's work ethic, as well as in the notion of progress). McNickle's book takes the reader into the lives of many of the people who live in and round the reservation—the Catholic priest, the shaman, the owner of the trading post, as well as all of the main characters—and it is marvelous in its balance and perspective.

Satire written by Native Americans include writings by Alexander Posey (Creek) and Will Rogers (Cherokee). Lynn Riggs was the only major American dramatist in the first half of the 1900s, his most popular work being *Green Grow the Lilacs* (1921), which became the musical *Oklahoma!* He also wrote poetry, *Iron Dish* (1930) and other lesser known plays.

In the second half of the 20th century new Indian writers began being published who were trained in the universities. N. Scott Momaday wrote *The House Made of Dawn*, which won the Pulitzer Prize in 1968. This novel, taking up the themes of alienation and mixed ancestry that earlier Indian novelists utilized, tells the story of Abel, an Indian man from the Jemez pueblo who has recently returned from WWII. He eventually leaves his homeland to journey to L.A., where he descends into drinking and trouble. But after being severely beaten, he takes the bus back to Jemez, and in the end is seen struggling to keep up with the traditional runners, suggesting that harmony must be found in the ancient traditions of his people. Momaday has also written other well received books, *Ancient Child*, which chronicles an Indian artist's return to tradition (and Momaday's own mythological spiritual sense of himself as the Bear), as well as *Names*, (an autobiography), and the highly praised mixed genre piece *The Way to Rainy Mountain* which relates Momaday's journey into his ancestral past through a combination of myth, personal remembrance, history, and poetry.

Leslie Marmon Silko's *Ceremony* (1977) takes essentially the same plot as Momaday used in *House Made of Dawn*, but her novel takes place after the Vietnam war and includes a web of ceremonial experiences that the protagonist Tayo must go through to become whole. Tayo, like Momaday's Abel, is also of mixed blood and is an alienated and disturbed survivor of war, but Silko weaves more of the Pueblo culture into her work, and the process of Tayo's healing is what drives the book rather than it being only the final moment. Silko is a superb writer whose prose is always right on target; her richness of detail, superb characterizations, and her delving into the mystery of ritual and its property of making one whole, make this one of the great American novels. Silko has also written a wonderful collection of short stories and poems titled *Storyteller*, which weaves in many traditional myths, updated in wonderful ways (such as Yellow Woman, and Coyote the Trickster). Her latest novel, *Almanac of the Dead* is an ambitious work of nearly eight hundred pages which chronicles Native struggles against European tyranny.

Louise Erdrich (Ojibwa) is one of the most celebrated and successful writers of our time, having won numerous awards and the highest critical praise. She has developed a novel format which consists of interwoven short stories. Her four interconnected novels (here in the chronological order in which they unfold, not in which they were published) are, *Tracks, Love Medicine, Beet Queen,* and *The Bingo Palace.* Erdrich, who co-writes with her husband (the Modoc writer Michael Dorris) has a prose style that is often highly elevated—poetic, lyrical, and romantic (not in the popular sense)—yet she can also incorporate terse vernacular phrasing into her prose, especially her dialogue, which often captures the flavor of reservation English. She deals with the lives of families—Indian, mixed-blood, and white—who live on and off the Ojibwa reservation in North Dakota. Erdrich often incorporates traditional mythology and imagery into her work, which for all of its depth is also highly comic. Many critics have compared her to Faulkner, which is apt. She has also written a number of books of poetry, which like her

prose, often deal with traditional Native American themes. Her most recent work is titled *Tales of Buring Love*, which is about four women, each telling her tale in the first person to the others, all of whom were married to the same man.

Michael Dorris (Modoc) has written a number of books as well, *A Yellow Raft on Blue Water,* which chronicles three generations of women on a Montana reservation, a collection of short stories, and the National Book Award winner in non-fiction, *The Broken Cord,* which is an account of Fetal Alcohol syndrome as it has affected his adopted son, Adam.

James Welch's (Blackfeet-Gros Ventre) first novel *Winter in the Blood* features a nameless protagonist who fights depression and alcoholism, as he tries to uncover his family's background. Welch's book *Fools Crow* is probably the most realistic novel written about Plains Indian life, in which nothing is romanticized. Welch is an expert at his brand of realism, and his works are unflinching in their honesty. His latest work, *The Indian Lawyer*, is a book that deals realistically with the life of a modern day Indian professional who is successful in the white man's world, but is deeply aware, and often affected by, his Indian roots. Welch has also written a number of books of poetry.

Gerald Vizenor (Ojibwa) is one of the most imaginative (and prolific) writers in America today. Vizenor often writes about mixed-bloods and tricksters with a wit that cuts to the core. In his many novels and short stories he satirizes every stripe of political and cultural institution in need of it. He criticizes the pomposity of academia, the gall of anthropologists, ludicrous Indian celebrities, and he pokes at American life in general. At the same time he can write delicate haiku, then go on to write movingly about Ojibway people. Some of his works are exuberant journeys into near surrealism, with the traditional motif of the Trickster almost always present. His novel *Griever: An American Monkey King in China* (the 1987 American Book award in fiction winner) is about an Indian protagonist who goes to China only to meet up with the traditional Chinese trickster. His works are often about liberation, about not allowing the processes of acculturation and prejudice to defeat the individual. His screen-play, *Harold of Orange,* (included in *Shadow Distance: A Gerald Vizenor Reader*, 1994) celebrates a tribal trickster who is able to satirize white society, yet take from it what he needs for his people. This is included in *Shadow Distance: A Gerald Vizenor Reader* (1994). Vizenor's *Earthdivers:Tribal Narratives on Mixed Descent*, is a collection of stories and essays that, in grand Trickster style, lampoon hypocrites of every stripe. *Wordarrows* (1978) is another fine collection of his fiction that tackles similar themes, while *Mainfest Manners* is an important book of Vizenor essays.

Sherman Alexie (Spokane/Coeur d'Alene) is another writer who utilizes humor, tapping into the trickster motif, while dealing with some of the harsh realities of reservation life. While writing in the vernacular, his work also contains brilliant leaps of imagination. In his first novel, *Reservation Blues*, the legendary bluesman—Robert Johnson—appears on the rez, and a new blues band is formed. In Alexie's short story collection, *Tonto and Lone Ranger Fistfight in Heaven*, the reader is taken into the lives of several characters who live on the Spokane reservation. Alexie is also the author of a number of books of poetry.

Another writer who works in the vernacular is Jim Northrup (Ojibwa). His book, *Walking the Rez Road*, which is of mixed genre, both short fiction and poetry, deals with life on a Chippewa reservation. His main character is Luke Warmwater, a veteran of the Vietnam war. His stories are both humorous and tragic, as he walks the thin line between both aspects of the human dilemma.

Ray Young Bear, who is becoming one of the most celebrated poets in the U.S. today, does the same in his book that also utilizes the vernacular prose style: *Black Eagle Child*. Edgar Bearchild is Young Bear's thinly veiled fictional self in this autobiography of life on the Mesquakie reservation in Iowa.

Thomas King (Cherokee) is another Indian author whose work is similar to these writers: his novel *Medicine River* features the protagonist, Will, who comes home to the reservation where he runs into Harlen Bigbear and his tricksteresque plans. *Green Grass, Running Water* is a wonderful, imaginative novel that shifts back and forth between the mythic gods (which include the God of the *Old Testament*, Old Many Coyote, Changing Woman) literary figures (such as The Lone Ranger & Tonto, Robinson Crusoe) and Indian people living on and off a reservation in Canada invloved in the everyday stuggles of life and love.

Diane Glancy is both a poet and fiction writer who has written a number of important works. *Claiming Breath* consists of non-fiction prose that chronicles the writer's life in diary fashion, with clear observations and moving descriptions that often have the feel of prose poems. *Firesticks* is a collection of Glancy's short fiction as is *Monkey Secret,* and *Trigger Dance.* A new novel about the Trail of Tears is titled *Pushing the Bear.*

Some other writers who are gaining prominence are Susan Power (Sioux), whose book *The Grass Dancer* (winner of the Hemingway award for first fiction, and a national best-seller) is structured like Erdrich's novels: individual short stories that tie together as a novel. Her prose style is also highly poetic.

Janet Hale writes of an urban American woman who, while attending law school, deals with the past horrors of her life and her subsequent alcoholism in *The Jailing of Cecilia Capture*. As a writer of realism she is close to Welch in style. Her novel *Owl's Song* is one of the few novels that deal with life both on the reservation and in the city. *Bloodlines: Odyssey of a Native Daughter* is Hale's excellent autobiography.

Another fine novelist, who is primarily known as one of the best Native American poets, is Linda Hogan (Chickasaw) whose novel *Mean Spirit* deals with the murder of an Indian woman in Oklahoma at the time of the oil boom, when Indian communities in the region were often threatened and exploited. She has a superb book of short stories titled *Solar Storms*, as well as a nonfiction work titled

Dwellings: A Spiritual History of the Natural World.

Martin Cruz Smith (Seneca del Sur/Yaqui) is an Indian writer who has written mysteries and popular fiction. Some of his writing is about Native people, such as : *Nightwing* and *Stallion Gate,* while other works of his, such as *Gorky Park, and Solar Star* deal with non-Indian subjects.

Anna Walters (Otoe/Pawnee) is another fine fiction writer who has written mysteries, *Ghost Singer*, as well as literary short stories, *The Sun is Not Merciful* (winner of the 1985 before Columbus association American Book Award).

Though this book is meant to include only prose, I think it is important to bring up some of the excellent Indian poets (who have not been mentioned previously): Roberta Whiteman (Oneida), Paula Gunn Allen (Laguna-Sioux, she is also one of the top scholars on Indian literature), Jim Barnes (Choctaw), Barry Bush (Shawnee), Joy Harjo (Creek), Maurice Kenny (Mohawk), Duane Niatum (Klallam), Simon Ortiz (Acoma), and Wendy Rose (Hope-Miwok).

Works by Native American authors for children, include Michael Dorris's (Modoc), *Morning Girl*, about a young girl and her brother who live in the Caribbean before Columbus, and *Guests*, about a twelve year old boy who is not happy that Pilgrims have been invited to the traditional feast. Both books are appropriate for intermediate grades. Joseph Bruchac (Abenaki) has taken a number of myths and stories from various tribes and rewritten them for children, and they are excellent. Books such as *Flying With the Eagle and Racing with the Great Bear*, *Iroquois Stories: Heroes and Heroines, and Monsters and Magic* , and *The Girl Who Married the Moon* (written in collaboration with Cherokee storyteller Gayle Ross), will keep intermediate readers spellbound, as well as teach them that Native American cultures contain fables and tales equally as great as those of Aesop or Uncle Remus. Simon Ortiz's (Acoma) book, *The People Shall Continue*, tells the story of Indian people and the conquest of them by the Europeans from the Native point of view, and it is written so that second through fourth graders will be able to comprehend this perspective.

Coyote & Little Turtle: Iisaw Niqw Yogosonhoya: A Traditional Hopi Tale, by Hershel Talashoema (Hopi), is the kind of book for young children (first and second grade) that teaches on a number of levels, for the text is in both English and Hopi, which can begin to open up to children the idea that not everyone who lives in America (and whose ancestors lived here for thousands of years) speaks the English language. Virginia Driving Hawk Sneve is a Sioux writer who has written many excellent books for children about Native American people, including a series on various tribal groups. Also, some publishers, are offering special series of books that deal with Native Americans for young people; Lerner Publications, for example, has a superb collection written by Native American writers, such as Sandra King, Monty Roessel, Laura Waterman Wittstock, and Rina Swentzell that show how Indian people are living within their cultures today.

In order to truly understand the American experience, it is important for all Americans to know something about the people who lived here for thousands of years, and it is important to get past the myths and prejudices that so many of us have been indoctrinated with. To deal with the guilt of conquest many have become fascinated with the "fall of the Indian." This take on historical events looks at the conquest of the Americas as the sad but inevitable consequence of Progress. In this sense, the history of the Americas is seen as a kind of historical-literary tragedy, akin to *King Lear* or *Hamlet* , a story line that offers the potent stuff of drama with all its subsequent emotional catharsis. With this philosophy we get the famous paintings of Indians on horseback, broken, heads bowed, vanishing into the sunset: terribly tragic but absolutely necessary. Needless to say, Indian people do not see themselves as "vanishing" or see that the conquest of them and their lands was "necessary."

Since the beginning of contact, the image of "the Indian" has also come to symbolize a host of competing mythologies in European minds: the Savage and the Noble Savage. The Savage represents "the Indian" as beast, devoid of higher intellect and refined emotion (this is the image of the Indian often portrayed in old Westerns), an impediment to the advancement of civilization. Here the Indian is akin to the forests that had to be felled to make way for farms and cities, for Manifest Destiny.

The flip side of this is the concept of the Noble Savage, which is the idea of man living in the Garden of Eden, before the Fall, blissfully unaware of his or her nakedness, primal, close to the earth, near animal, mystical, proud, having instinctual nobility. This is the image that Cooper and many others after him employed. Of course, noble or savage, both Indian types have been seen as necessarily destined to vanish to make way for "civilized man" (just as Cooper's noble Indians do in the end). Many Native American authors have satirized this dual construct (Savage-Noble Savage), showing it to be the farce it is.

Over the years so many other myths have emerged regarding American Indian people that the idea of "Indians" has become a mirror through which we are all often really seeing are our own biases reflected back at us. Roy Harvey Pearce brings this to light in his seminal book, *Savagism and Civilization*. From the white perspective, the notion of who and what Indian people are often changes with the times; Native people have been seen as—stoic, wooden, humorless, devoid of culture, barbarians, or just the opposite—as trickster-like humorists, natural born ecologists, and enlightened democratic socialists. Nowadays, Indian people are portrayed by some as having a genetic disposition to mysticism, as having the ability to communicate with animals, change into other forms ("shape-shift"), and that they are the first real "new agers."

Of course, to Indian people all this is absurd. For Native Americans are human beings, and like human beings everywhere, they are complex; they are *people* with infinite facets to their personalities and their cultures. They are people who love and hate; they are people who care for their children, who feel, who think, and who like all people everywhere, tell jokes, laugh, cry, and are made of neither wood nor crystal. In the past, well meaning people have affectionately called them "Our Indians," while to those who despised their existence they were called "the Indian problem" (not unlike the Nazis' concept of the "Jewish problem"). But Native Americans are not "ours" and never have been. And they are not our problem; we are there's. For far too long it has been the Europeans defining, studying, interpreting,

categorizing. This is one of the most important reasons that literature created by Native Americans be taught and read. For contrary to what the vast majority of history books have told us, Indian people did not ride off into the sunset to disappear from sight. Native Americans are still very much alive, and their cultures and points of view are still very much a part of the fabric of American life today.

Much of American writing can be seen as an attempt to create a literature for the "New World" that would allow the immigrants from Europe to "belong." From Irving, to Twain, to Faulkner, American writers have strived to create a new mythology of this place. But what most have failed to realize is that America has been a place full of literature all along (for 30,000 years anyway). Today, many new Indian writers are telling their stories in voices that are eloquent, moving, and profound. Also, the traditional songs and stories that for far too long were assumed by the dominant culture to have never even existed, are being heard as well. However, this attention is not always welcomed by Native Americans, for many of the traditional songs, stories, myths collected by writers of whatever background are considered by some to be too sacred to be let out into the general population. But for those who are drawn to this literature there is much to be gained, and if those outside the tribe approach the literature with respect, it can only be hoped that those members inside can forgive the intrusion, for by reading these stories and songs one will come away with a much deeper knowledge of who the Native people were and are, and we all come to a much deeper understanding of what it means to live upon this continent that has become the home of many whose ancestral heritage comes from other shores.

NOTE: Most of the material presented in this section has been written by Native American people, and each of the author's tribal affiliations has been listed. However, since it was not the publisher's intent to make this wholly a survey of writing *by* people of Indian ancestry, there are a limited number of fictional works written by people of European ancestry about Native peoples, all of which are noted with each entry. Many of the traditional tales were collected by people of European ancestry as well, which is noted in each instance also. And while this bibliography primarily deals with fiction, I have also included nonfiction texts I thought necessary to the study of American Indian Literature and culture, such as those of Vine DeLoria Jr., Dr. A. LaVonne Ruoff, David Brumble, Roy Harvey Pearce, Arnold Krupat, and Paula Gunn Allen.

In many instances there are two names given for each tribe. This is because historically this has often been the case. Each tribal group has their own name for themselves, which usually would translate as "the people" or "the human beings," as does "Inuit" for the Native Arctic peoples, whom others have called "Eskimo," meaning "eaters of raw meat."

DEDICATION: My portion of this book is dedicated to my friend and teacher, Dr. A. LaVonne Brown Ruoff, who helped me immeasurably in preparing this material.

Native American Titles

1136

SHERMAN ALEXIE, Native American, Spokane and Coeur d'Alene

The Business of Fancydancing: Stories and Poems

(Brooklyn: Hanging Loose, 1992)

Subject(s): Indians of North America; Literature; Poetry
Age range(s): Adult
Time period(s): 1990s
Locale(s): United States

Summary: This short collection of poems and stories reveal more than intimate, family relationships on the Spokane Washington Indian Reservation. They relate the struggle of people to maintain a sense of their culture with an identity outside of the poverty and despair that exist on the reservation. They are at once humorous and full of pain and anger.

Where it's reviewed:
American Poetry Review, July 1995, page 29
Bloomsbury-Review, September 1992, page 7
Kenyon Review, Summer 1993, page 182

Other books by the same author:
The Lone Ranger and Tonto Fist Fight in Heaven, 1993 (short fiction)
First Native American on the Moon, 1993 (poetry)
Old Shirts and New Skins, 1994 (poetry)
Reservation Blues, 1995
Songs from the Film, 1991

Other books you might like:
Ray A. Young Bear, *Black Eagle Child*, 1992
    Life on the Mesquakie Reservation, written in the vernacular, by one of the most exciting Indian poets.
Thomas King, *Green Grass, Running Water*, 1993
    In this wild romp, Coyote, God, Robinson Crusoe, The Lone Ranger and others struggle in the cosmological firmament while on the human plane, Native Americans struggle to make the best of their lives.

Thomas King, *Medicine River*, 1989
    A mixed-blood man, alienated from his people, learns to care about his homeland.
Leslie Marmon Silko, *Storyteller*, 1981
    From Laguna Pueblo where he grew up, Silko weaves traditional mythology into modern stories, recreating old myths and making them relevant for a new generation.
W.P. Kinsella, *Dance Me Outside*, 1977
    These early tales of life on the Ermineskin Reserve in Canada are gems, capturing both the tragic and comedic spirit of reservation life.
W.P. Kinsella, *Moccasin Telegraph*, 1984
    Life on the fictional Ermineskin Reserve in Canada, is full of both comedy and tragedy.
James Northrup, *Walking the Rez Road*, 1993
    Luke Warmwater is a Vietnam vet who is down on his luck, but he, like many of his reservation cohorts, is a survivor in the trickster fashion.
Gerald Vizenor, *Griever: An American Monkey King in China*, 1987
    Vizenor creates a trickster character who leaves his Chippewa home to go to China where he finds himself kin to the Monkey King.
Gerald Vizenor, *Earthdivers: Tribal Narratives on Mixed Descent*, 1981
    In this collection of short stories, Vizenor ceates a conglomeration of trickster figures as he pokes fun, and makes shrewd political commentary, on America and reservation life.
Louise Erdrich, *Love Medicine*, 1984
    Married to Marie, Nector is nevertheless fatefully drawn to Lulu. When his grandson prepares a love medicine to win him back to his grandmother, he uses the wrong ingredients and kills Nector instead.

1137

SHERMAN ALEXIE, Native American, Spokane and Coeur d'Alene

The Lone Ranger and Tonto Fist Fight in Heaven

(New York: Atlantic Monthly, 1993)

Subject(s): Indian Reservations; Cultural Identity; Social Conditions
Age range(s): Adult
Major character(s): Thomas Builds-the-Fire, Storyteller, Native American; Victor Joseph, Native American; Junior Polatkin, Native American
Time period(s): 1980s
Locale(s): United States

Summary: In this brilliantly amusing fiction, exciting new writer, Alexie artfully couples the harsh details of the struggle to survive on the Spokane Indian Reservation with a wry and often wise humour.

Where it's reviewed:
American Poetry Review, July 1995, page 29
Kliatt, January 1995, page 4
New York Times Book Review, October 16, 1994, page 44
Western American Literature, Fall 1994, page 277
Whole Earth Review, Fall 1995, page 57

Other books by the same author:
First Native American on the Moon, 1993 (poetry)
I Would Steal Horses, 1991 (poetry)
Old Shirts and New Skins, 1994 (poetry)
Reservation Blues, 1995
Songs from the Film, 1991

Other books you might like:
Thomas King, *Green Grass, Running Water*, 1993
In this wild romp, Coyote, God, Robinson Crusoe, The Lone Ranger and others struggle in the cosmological firmament, while on the human plane, Native Americans struggle to make the best of their lives.
Thomas King, *Medicine River*, 1989
A mixed-blood man, alienated from his people, learns to care about his homeland.
Leslie Marmon Silko, *Storyteller*, 1981
Ray A. Young Bear, *Black Eagle Child*,
Life on the Mesquakie Reservation, written in the vernacular, by one of the most exciting Indian poets.
W.P. Kinsella, *Dance Me Outside*, 1977
W.P. Kinsella, *Moccasin Telegraph*, 1984
James Northrup, *Walking the Rez Road*, 1993
Luke Warmwater is a Vietnam vet down on his luck, but he, like many of his reservation cohorts, is a survivor in the trickster fashion.
Gerald Vizenor, *Griever: An American Monkey King in China*, 1987
Vizenor creates a trickster character who leaves his Chippewa home to go to China where he finds himself kin to the Monkey King.
Gerald Vizenor, *Earthdivers: Tribal Narratives on Mixed Descent*, 1981
In this collection of short stories, Vizenor creates a con-

glomeration of trickster figures as he pokes fun, and makes shrewd political commentary, on America and reservation life.
Louise Erdrich, *Love Medicine*, 1984
Married to Marie, Nector is nevertheless fatefully drawn to Lulu. When his grandson prepares a love medicine to win him back to his grandmother, he uses the wrong ingredients and kills Nector instead.

1138

SHERMAN ALEXIE, Native American, Spokane and Coeur d'Alene

Reservation Blues

(New York: Atlantic Monthly, 1995)

Subject(s): Humor; Cultural Identity; Indian Reservations
Age range(s): Adult
Major character(s): Robert Johnson, Musician (blues guitarist); Thomas Builds-the-Fire, Storyteller, Musician, Native American
Time period(s): 1990s
Locale(s): United States

Summary: Brilliant novel in which legendary blues musician Robert Johnson comes back from the dead and appears on the Spokane Reservation in eastern Washington, looking for, literally, the woman of his dreams. Thomas Builds-the-Fire suspects he might be looking for "Big Mom" and drives him to the base of the mountain where she lives. But the blues man has left his guitar behind and when Thomas picks it up, the Res begins to rock.

Where it's reviewed:
Booklist, June 1, 1995, page 1726
Kirkus Reviews, March 15, 1995, page 324
Library Journal, June 1, 1995, page 158
Publishers Weekly, May 1, 1995, page 42
Los Angeles Times Book Review, June 18, 1995, page 2

Other books by the same author:
First Native American on the Moon, 1993 (poetry)
I Would Steal Horses, 1991 (poetry)
Old Shirts and New Skins, 1994 (poetry)
Songs from the Film, 1991

Other books you might like:
Thomas King, *Green Grass, Running Water*, 1993
In this wild romp, Coyote, God, Robinson Crusoe, The Lone Ranger and others struggle in the cosmological firmament, while on the human plane, Native American try to make the best of their lives.

1139

PAULA GUNN ALLEN, Editor, Native American, Lakota (Sioux) and Laguna

Grandmothers of the Light

(Boston: Beacon Press, 1991)

Subject(s): Mythology; Folk Tales
Age range(s): Grades 9-Adult
Time period(s): Indeterminate Past

Locale(s): United States

Summary: This collection of myths and legends, edited by the well known writer and scholar Paula Gunn Allen, focuses on the myths of the various Native American goddess traditions. The text is divided into four sections, with an added postscript on cultural dimensions, geological locations, and herstoricalsic circumstances: ''The Living Reality of the Medicine World,'' ''Cosyogyny: The Goddesses, Ritual Magic and Aspects of the Goddesses,'' '' Myth Magic, and Medicine in the Modern World.''

Other books by the same author:
The Sacred Hoop: Recovering the Feminine in American Indian Traditions, 1986 (essays)
Studies in American Indian Literature, 1983 (essays)
Skin and Bones (poetry)
Spider Woman's Granddaughters, 1989

Other books you might like:
John Bierhorst, *The Red Swan: Myths and Tales of the American Indians*, 1976
This book is a compilation of varied stories (creation, trickster, star husband etc.) from forty Indian tribes.
Margot Astrov, *The Winged Serpent*, 1946
This is one of the best collections of oral stories and songs from a large cross-section of Native American cultures.
John Bierhorst, *The Sacred Path*, 1984
This is fine collection of traditional spells, prayers, and power songs from a variety of Native American tribes.
Mourning Dove, *Coyote Stories*, 1933
These are traditional stories about Cayote, the trickster.
John Bierhorst, *The Way of the Earth: Native American and the Environment*, 1994
Bierhorst delves into American Indian philosophies regarding the environment, giving a comprehensive view of native beliefs, myths and practices about nature.
LaVonne Ruoff, *American Indian Literatures: An Introduction, Bibliographic Review, and Selected Bibliography*, 1990
This is the *Bible* of Native American literature, essential to any one who wants to pursue a study of the literature that has been written by American Indian people.
William Bright, *A Coyote Reader*, 1993
This collection includes Coyote stories from a number of North American tribes.

1140

PAULA GUNN ALLEN, Editor, Native American, Lakota (Sioux) and Laguna

Spider Woman's Granddaughters

(Boston: Beacon Press, 1989)

Subject(s): Folk Tales; Mythology
Age range(s): Grades 9-Adult
Time period(s): Indeterminate
Locale(s): United States

Summary: This collection of myths and legends, edited by the well-known writer and scholar Paula Gunn Allen, focuses on the lives of Indian women. It is a compilation of both traditional and contemporary material. Particularly interesting is the commentary by Allen, for she often critiques the old stories in such a way that they become pertinent commentary on the lives of Indian women today. The traditional and contemporary are interwoven in a masterful way; this book is essential to those interested in Native American women's issues.

Where it's reviewed:
New York Times Book Review, May 14, 1989, page 15
Publishers Weekly, April 14, 1989, page 49
Village Voice, September 19, 1989, page 57

Awards the book has won:
American Book Award, 1990

Other books by the same author:
The Sacred Hoop: Recovering the Feminine in American Indian Traditions, 1986 (essays)
Studies in American Indian Literature, 1983 (essays)
Skin and Bones (poetry)
The Woman Who Owned the Shadows, 1983 (fiction)
Voice of the Turtle, 1994 (anthology written by American Indian people from 1900-1970)

Other books you might like:
Beth Brant, *A Gathering of Spirit: A Collection of North American Indian Women*, 1984
This is a collection of stories, letters, essays, and poems from a large cross-section of Native American women writers, such as Linda Hogan, Elizabeth Cook-Lynn, Diana Glancy and others.
Margot Astrov, *The Winged Serpent*, 1946
This is one of the best collections of oral stories and songs from a large cross-section of Indian cultures.
John Bierhorst, *The Sacred Path*, 1984
This is a fine collection of traditional spells, prayers, and power songs from a variety of Indian tribes.
G.M. Mullet, *Spider Woman Stories*,
These are Hopi Indian legends collected from the 1880s.
Zitkala-Sa, *Old Indian Legends Retold by Zitkala-Sa*, 1921
This is a collection of memoirs and essays by an Indian woman who was born into the old buffalo hunting culture of the Sioux.
Robert Franklin Gish, *When Coyote Howls: A Lavaland Fable*, 1994
This is a Coyote novel.
John Bierhorst, *The Red Swan: Myths and Tales of the American Indians*, 1976
This book is a compilation of varied stories (creation, trickster, star husband, etc.) from forty North American Indian tribes.
Frederick Turner, *The Portable North American Indian Reader*, 1973
This anthology of myths, legends, poetry, fiction, and captivity tales contains work by both Native American and non-Native writers.
Mourning Dove, *Coyote Stories*, 1933
These are traditional stories about Coyote, the trickster.
Barry Lopez, *Giving Birth to Thunder, Sleeping with His Daughter: Coyote Builds North America*, 1977
In this book Lopez retells a wide selection of Coyote stories from various North American tribes. As always, Coyote is dynamic, irreverant, wily, paradoxical, mysterious, taboo-breaking and fun.

1141

PAULA GUNN ALLEN, Editor, Native American, Lakota (Sioux) and Laguna

Voice of the Turtle
(New York: Ballantine, 1994)

Subject(s): Literature; Indians of North America
Age range(s): Grades 8-Adult
Time period(s): 20th century
Locale(s): United States

Summary: Edited by the well known writer and scholar Paula Gunn Allen, this book is an anthology of literature written by American Indian people from 1900 to 1970.

Where it's reviewed:
Belles Lettres, Fall 1994, page 5
Library Journal, October 15, 1994, page 73
School Library Journal, May 1995, page 136

Other books by the same author:
The Sacred Hoop: Recovering the Feminine in American Indian Traditions, 1986
Studies in American Indian Literature, 1983 (essays)
Skin and Bones (poetry)
The Woman Who Owned the Shadows, 1983
Spider Woman's Granddaughters, 1989 (traditional tales, contemporary stories)

Other books you might like:
Craig Lesley, *Talking Leaves*, 1991
  This book is an excellent collection of short stories by thirty-five contemporary American Indian writers, such as Louise Erdrich, N. Scott Momaday, Linda Hogan and Roberta Hill Whiteman.
Beth Brant, *A Gathering of Spirit: A Collection of North American Indian Women*, 1984
  Here is a collection of stories, letters, essays, and poems from a large cross-section of Native American women writers, such as Linda Hogan, Elizabeth Cook-Lynn, Diane Glancy, Joy Harjo and W. Rose.
Clifford E. Trafzer, *Blue Dawn, Red Earth: New Native American Storytellers*, 1996
  This is a collection of short stories by 30 new Native American writers: Lorne Simon, Anita Endrezze, Jim Barnes, Annie Hansen, Maurice Kenny, and Patricia Piley, among others.
Brian Swann, *I Tell You Now*, 1989
  This is an excellent collection of autobiographical essays by eighteen contemporary American Indian writers. Co-edited with Arnold Krupat.
Lee Miller, *From the Heart: Voices of the American Indian*, 1995
  This is a collection of orations, speeches, and testimony by more than 250 Indian people that presents a radical alternative to traditionally taught American history.

1142

PAULA GUNN ALLEN, Native American, Lakota (Sioux) and Laguna

The Woman Who Owned the Shadows
(San Francisco: Spinsters/Aunt Lute, 1983)

Subject(s): Women; Historical
Age range(s): Grades 9-Adult
Major character(s): Ephanie Atencio, Native American
Time period(s): 1980s
Locale(s): United States

Summary: Weaving strands of mythology through the pattern of her novel, Allen illustrates the power of myth to transform. Half Indian, Ephanie Atencio struggles unsuccessfully to integrate her two selves and make some sense of her life until she recognizes the symbioses between herself and the stories of her people. Likening the Iroquois Sky Woman myth to her own past helps her to realize her future.

Where it's reviewed:
Journal of Homosexuality, Issue 2, 1993, page 73
Rocky Mountain Review of Language & Literature, Issue 1, 1993, page 61

Other books by the same author:
The Sacred Hoop: Recovering the Feminine in American Indian Traditions, 1986 (essays)
Studies in American Indian Literature, 1983 (essays)
Skin and Bones (poetry)
Spider Woman's Granddaughters, 1989
Voice of the Turtle, 1994

Other books you might like:
Michael Dorris, *A Yellow Raft in Blue Water*, 1987
  This is one of the only novels that deal with "mixed-blood" people who are part African American and part Native American. Dorris has three generations of women tell this story.
John Joseph Mathews, *Sundown*, 1934
  Challenge is educated in White schools, joins the army, and returns to his homeland alienated from his culture. This novel shows the effects of two cultures competing for dominance in an individual.
D'Arcy McNickle, *The Surrounded*, 1936
  A fiddle player returns to his reservation for a visit after years in the White world and finds himself so caught up in its complexities that he knows he can never go back to the White world again.
Louise Erdrich, *Love Medicine*, 1984
  Married to Marie, Nector is nevertheless fatefully drawn to Lulu. When his grandson prepares a love medicine to win him back to his grandmother, he uses the wrong ingredients and kills Nector instead.
Leslie Marmon Silko, *Ceremony*, 1977
  A pueblo man who has returned from the war must realign himself with the traditional ways before becoming whole again.
Maria Campbell, *Halfbreed*,
  This is the moving account of Campbell's life as a Metis, or half-breed, part Indian, part European.

1143

GEORGE APES, Native American, Pequod

A Son of the Forest: The Experience of William Apes, a Native of the Forest, Comprising a Notice of the Pequod Tribe of Indians

(New York: Author, 1831)

Subject(s): Men; Autobiography
Age range(s): Adult
Time period(s): 19th century
Locale(s): United States

Summary: This is the first autobiography written in English by a Native American person. It tells of his conversion to Methodism and his own Christian faith while also relating his sad life as a foster child and the abuses he, and his people have suffered at the hands of Europeans.

Other books by the same author:

The Experience of Five Christian Indians of the Pequod Tribe, 1837 (autobiography)
Eulogy on King Phillip, 1836 (nonfiction)

Other books you might like:

John Joseph Mathews, *Talking to the Moon*, 1945
From his childhood in Oklahoma through his WWI military stint, college, marriage and back again to his homeland, Mathews relates the circle of his life.
Luther Standing Bear, *Stories of the Sioux*, 1988
Standing Bear grows up in the traditional buffalo hunting culture, and he brings to life the stories from his own past.
Ignatia Broker, *Night Flying Woman*, 1983
Oona was of the generation of native people who were ripped away from traditional Ojibway life and forced to live the harsh life of the reservation.
Charles A. Eastman, *From the Deep Woods to Civilization*, 1916
This autobiography is by a Sioux man who grew up in the traditional buffalo hunting culture but leaves it to pursue a ''White'' education and becomes a doctor.
Maude Kegg, *Portage Lake: Memories of an Ojibwe Childhood*, 1991
In these stories, printed in both English and the original Anishinaabe, Maude Kegg relates the cultural wisdom of her many years, detailing important facts of Ojibway life.

1144

MARGOT ASTROV, Editor, Caucasian

The Winged Serpent

(Boston: Beacon Press, 1946, 1974)

Subject(s): Folk Tales; Mythology
Age range(s): Grades 4 and Up
Time period(s): Indeterminate
Locale(s): United States

Summary: This outstanding book examines legends and myths from the oral cultures of North American Indian people, and it is essential reading for those interested in the genre. The book is divided into nine geographical sections, each section featuring a mix of genres: love songs, star husband tales, emergence tales, death songs, chants, trickster tales, etc. The entries are documented as to their sources, making this text an excellent one for use in the classroom.

Where it's reviewed:

Book World, December 16, 1973, page 6
Kliatt, May 1993, page 22
Publishers Weekly, September 28, 1992, page 73

Other books you might like:

Frederick Turner, *The Portable North American Indian Reader*, 1973
Anthology of myths, legends, poetry, fiction, and captivity tales, contains work by both Native American and non-Native writers.
Paula Gunn Allen, *Spider Woman's Granddaughters*, 1989
This is a beautiful collection of traditional tales interwoven with contemporary stories having to do with the lives of Native American women.
Zitkala-Sa, *Old Indian Legends Retold by Zitkala-Sa*, 1921
This is a collection of memoirs and essays by an Indian woman who was born into the old buffalo hunting culture of the Sioux.
Barry Lopez, *Giving Birth to Thunder, Sleeping with His Daughter: Coyote Builds North America*, 1977
In this book, Lopez retells a wide selection of Coyote stories form various North American tribes. As always, Coyote is dynamic, irreverant, wily, paradoxical, mysterious, taboo breaking, and fun.
Paula Gunn Allen, *Voice of the Turtle*, 1994
Edited by the well known writer and scholar Paula Gunn Allen, this book is an anthology of literature written by American Indian people from 1900 to 1970.
William Bright, *A Coyote Reader*, 1993
Traditional Coyote trickster tales from across North America.
Lee Miller, *From the Heart: Voices of the American Indian*, 1995
This is a collection of orations, speeches, and testimony by more than 250 Indian people that presents a radical alternative to traditionally taught American history.
Hasteen Klah, *The Myth and Prayers of the Great Star Chant, and the Myth of the Coyote Chant*, 1988
This exquisite book is a compilation of important Navajp myths, songs, chants, and prayers, that deal with the complex philosophical and religious life of Navajo culture.
Mourning Dove, *Coyote Stories*, 1933
These are traditional stories about Coyote, the trickster.
John Bierhorst, *The Red Swan: Myths and Tales of the American Indians*, 1976
This book is a compilation of varied stories (creation, trickster, star husband, etc.) from forty Indian tribes.

1145

MARILOU AWIAKTA, Native American, Cherokee

Selu: Seeking the Corn-Mother's Wisdom

(Golden: Fulcrum, 1993)

Subject(s): Philosophy; Religion; Social Conditions

Age range(s): Adult
Time period(s): Indeterminate
Locale(s): United States

Summary: To follow the Corn-Mother's wisdom, one must keep things in balance. As a good harvest requires a good balance of sun and rain, so too does contemporary man need to balance modern needs with a respect for the earth and its resources. As harmony is achieved through cooperation and sharing, so too must we learn to share our resources and cooperate in preserving what we have for the generations to come. Through stories, poems and essays, Awiatka applies this wisdom to contemporary issues, like the use of nuclear power, politics and gender issues.

Where it's reviewed:
American Quarterly, March 1995, page 165
Belles Lettres, Fall 1994, page 5
Come-All-Ye, Winter 1994, page 2
Southern Humanities Review, Spring 1995, page 198

Other books you might like:
Robert J. Conley, *Mountain Windsong*, 1992
   This is the love story of two young people who survive the Cherokee's Trail of Tears March.
Wilma Mankiller, *Mankiller: A Chief and Her People*, 1993
   Wilma Mankiller, Chief of the Cherokees, recounts her own life story as well as that of her people.
Yellow Bird, *Life and Adventures of Joaquin Murieta*, 1955
   In this first novel written by a Native American, Murieta, who is a "mixed-Blood," Cherokee and White, becomes a criminal after being driven off his land by greedy Whites.
Leslie Marmon Silko, *Storyteller*, 1981
   This work is a mix of genres; poetry, fiction and mythology.
Paula Gunn Allen, *Spider Woman's Granddaughters*, 1989
   This beautiful collection of traditional tales is interwoven with contemporary short stories about Native American women.

1146

OLAF BAKER, Caucasian
STEPHEN GAMMELL, Illustrator

Where the Buffaloes Begin
(New York: Fredrick Warne, 1981)

Subject(s): Historical; Indians of North America; Pre-Columbian History
Age range(s): Grades 3-5
Major character(s): Little Wolf, 10-Year-Old (boy), Native American (Plains Indian)
Time period(s): Indeterminate Past (pre-Columbian)
Locale(s): United States

Summary: A Plains Indian boy living in pre-Columbian times, sets off to find the place where the buffalo began, a legendary sacred lake.

Other books you might like:
Charles A. Eastman, *From the Deep Woods to Civilization*, 1916
   The autobiography of Charles A. Eastman, who grows up in the traditional buffalo culture of the Lakota (Sioux) but

pursues an education in the White man's world. Introduction by Raymond Wilson.
Zitkala-Sa, *Old Indian Legends Retold by Zitkala-Sa*, 1921
   These stories depict Zitkala-Sa's childhood in the traditional Lakota culture and the difficulties she faced while attending school and college in a world where she was perceived as a "savage."
Luther Standing Bear, *Stories of the Sioux*, 1988
   Standing Bear grew up in the traditional buffalo hunting culture, and he brings to life the stories from his own past.
Virginia Driving Hawk Sneve, *The Chichi Hoohoo Bogeyman*, 1975
   Three young girls discover a strange creature on the prairie of South Dakota, th en later one of the girls disappears.
Charles A. Eastman, *Old Indian Days*, 1907
   Autobiography of a Lakota Sioux man.
Virginia Driving Hawk Sneve, *Jimmy Yellow Hawk*, 1971
   Fiction, award winner of the Council on Interracial Books for Children

1147

VICTOR BARNOUW, Caucasian

Dream of the Blue Heron
(New York: Dell, 1966)

Subject(s): Indians of North America; Cultural Conflict
Age range(s): Grades 5-9
Major character(s): Wallace White Sky, Child (boy), Native American (Anishninaabe)
Time period(s): 1900s (1905)
Locale(s): Wisconsin

Summary: Wallace White Sky, a young Anishinabe (Ojibway) boy growing up in northern Wisconsin at the turn of the century, deals with the conflicts between the old culture and the progressives who want "progress."

Other books you might like:
Sandra King, *Shannon: An Ojibway Dancer*, 1993
   This book follows the life of a young Ojibway girl, Shannon, who lives in the city, yet still participates in tribal ceremonies.
Ignatia Broker, *Night Flying Woman*, 1983
   Oona was of the generation who were ripped away from traditional life and forced to live the harsh life of the reservation. Ignatia Broker tells this moving story of her own grandmother.
Shirley Sterling, *My Name Is Seepeetza*, 1992
   Fictional account based on the life of the author, who as a member of the interior Salish tribe is forced to attend government schools where she is forbidden to reflect anything of her own heritage.
John D. Nichols, *Portage Lake: Memories of an Ojibwe Childhood*, 1991
   In these stories, printed in both English and the original Anishinaabe, Maude Kegg relates the cultural wisdom of her many years, describing important facets of Ojibway life.
Scott O'Dell, *Sing Down the Moon*, 1970
   This chapter book chronicles the life of a fourteen-year-old Navajo girl who lives near Canyon de Chelly. Her life is

happy until she sees the Spanish slave traders invading her homeland in 1864.

Ann Nolan Clark, *Little Navajo Bluebird*, 1943
This chapter book chronicles the day in and day out life of a Navajo girl in the 1940s.

Jean Craighead George, *The Talking Earth*, 1983
A young Seminole girl begins to doubt the beliefs of the elders until she goes into the Everglades, where she begins to understand the importance of her tribal teachings and the world of nature.

Jay Leech, *Moon of the Big-Dog*, 1980
Three young Sioux boys go on a journey to capture the first horses for their tribe, and earn a new name for their Sioux band: Brule. Co-authored by Zane Spencer and illustrated by M. Funai.

Virginia Driving Hawk Sneve, *High Elk's Treasure*, 1972
This novel for middle school readers is about Joe High Elk who longs to bring back the strain of wild mustangs bred by his famous ancestor many years before. Illustrations by Oren Lyons.

Shirley Sterling, *My Name Is Seepeetza*, 1992
Fictional account based on the life of the author, who as a member of the interior Salish tribe is forced to attend government schools where she is forbidden to reflect anything of her own heritage.

1148

GRETCHEN M. BATAILLE, Editor, Caucasian
KATHLEEN M. SAND, Co-Editor, Caucasian

American Indian Women: A Guide to Research

(New York: Harper Perennial, 1990)

Subject(s): Indians of North America; Women
Age range(s): Adult
Time period(s): Indeterminate
Locale(s): United States

Summary: This is a comprehensive bibliography of books and articles having to do with Native American women.

Where it's reviewed:
Booklist, June 1, 1993, page 1879
Journal of Youth Services in Libraries, Spring 1993, page 291
School Library Journal, March 1993, page 123

Other books you might like:
Brian Swann, *I Tell You Now*, 1989
This is an excellent collection of autobiographical essays by eighteen contemporary American Indian writers, co-authored with Arnold Krupat.

Paula Gunn Allen, *The Sacred Hoop: Recovering the Feminine in American Indian Traditions*, 1986
This book is an excellent collection of essays that uncovers the essential role of women in traditional and contemporary Indian life.

Luther Standing Bear, *Stories of the Sioux*, 1988
Standing Bear grew up in the traditional buffalo hunting culture, and he brings to life the stories from his own past.

Paula Gunn Allen, *Spider Woman's Granddaughters*, 1989
This is a beautiful collection of traditional tales interwoven

with contemporary short stories about Native American Women.

Zitkala-Sa, *Old Indian Legends Retold by Zitkala-Sa*, 1921
These stories depict Zitkala-Sa's childhood in the traditional Lakota culture and the difficulties she faces while attending school and college in a world where she is perceived as a "savage."

Joseph Bruchac, *The Girl Who Married the Moon*, 1994
These are mostly traditional tales from a variety of North American tribes about women: initiation ceremonies, shape changing stories, and others.

Mark St. Pierre, *The Spiritual Power and Legacy of American Plains Indian Women*, 1995
This book looks at the lives of Plains Indian women and the myths and culture surrounding them.

1149

PEGGY V. BECK, Editor
ANNA LEE WALTERS, Co-Editor
NIA FRANCISCO, Co-Editor

The Sacred

(Tsaile, NM: Navajo Community College Press, 1995)

Subject(s): Religion
Age range(s): Grades 7 and Up
Time period(s): Indeterminate
Locale(s): United States

Summary: This book is an excellent cross-cultural look at Native American religions that gives the reader a thorough introduction to the sacred ways of a variety of Native American people. For students who are coming to an understanding of Native American religions for the first time, this book is one of the best resources available.

Other books you might like:
Carl Sauer, *Man in Nature*, 1939
This excellent book explores the various Native American cultures that existed in pre-Columbian America and how each interacted with their environment.

William Bright, *A Coyote Reader*, 1993
These are traditional Coyote stories.

John Bierhorst, *The Red Swan: Myths and Tales of the American Indians*, 1976
This book is a compilation of varied stories (creation, trickster, star husband, etc.) from forty Native American tribes.

Frederick Turner, *The Portable North American Indian Reader*, 1973
This anthology of myths, legends, poetry, fiction, and captivity tales, contains work by both Native American and non-Native writers.

Jonathan Broderick, *Stories of Traditional Navajo Life and Culture*, 1977
These are interviews from tape-recorded meetings of the Navajo.

Hasteen Klah, *The Myth and Prayers of the Great Star Chant, and the Myth of the Coyote Chant*, 1988
This exquisite book is a compilation of important Navajo myths, songs, chants, and prayers, portraying the complexity of the philosophical and religious life of Navajo culture.

John Bierhorst, *The Way of the Earth: Native America and the Environment*, 1994

Bierhorst delves into American Indian philosophies regarding the environment, giving a comprehensive view of native beliefs, myths and practices about nature.

1150

SHONTO BEGAY, Native American, Navajo

Ma'ii and Cousin Horned Toad

(New York: Scholastic, 1992)

Subject(s): Trickster Tales; Folklore
Age range(s): Grades 3-6
Major character(s): Ma'ii, Toad; Coyote, Trickster
Time period(s): Indeterminate
Locale(s): Arizona; New Mexico

Summary: Lazy, conniving Ma'ii, the coyote, is hungry and goes to Horny Toad for a free lunch. When he swallows his smaller cousin, Horny Toad teaches Ma'ii a lesson he won't soon forget.

Where it's reviewed:
New Advocate, Spring 1995, page 125
Reading Teacher, March 1995, page 495
Library Talk, March 1993, page 35
Publishers Weekly, December 14, 1992, page 55

Other books you might like:
Mourning Dove, *Coyote Stories*, 1933
    These are traditional Okanagan stories about Coyote, the trickster.
William Bright, *A Coyote Reader*, 1993
    These are traditional Coyote tales from the Karok Indians.
Herschel Talashoema, *Coyote & Little Turtle: Iisaw Niqw Yongosonhoya: A Traditional Hopi Tale*, 1994
    This excellent book for early readers is about Coyote and Little Turtle. It is written in both Hopi and English, with illustrations drawn by Hopi children.
John Bierhorst, *The Red Swan: Myths and Tales of the American Indians*, 1976
    This book is a compilation of varied stories (creation, trickster, star husband, etc.) from forty Native American tribes.
Frederick Turner, *The Portable North American Indian Reader*, 1973
    This anthology of myths, legends, poetry, fiction, and captivity tales, contains work by both Native and non-Native writers.
Hasteen Klah, *The Myth and Prayers of the Great Star Chant, and the Myth of the Coyote Chant*, 1988
    This exquisite book is a compilation of important Navajo myths, songs, chants and prayers portraying the complexity of the philosophical and religious life of the Navajo.

1151

SHONTO BEGAY, Native American, Navajo

Navajo: Visions and Voices Across the Mesa

(New York: Scholastic, 1995)

Subject(s): Cultures and Customs; Indians of North America; Poetry
Age range(s): Grades 3-8
Time period(s): 1990s
Locale(s): New Mexico

Summary: This is a marvelous book for young people about Navajo life by one of the great Indian artists, Shonto Begay, who also writes stories and prose poems about Navajo people and culture.

Other books by the same author:
Ma'ii and Cousin Horned Toad, 1992

Other books you might like:
Hasteen Klah, *The Myth and Prayers of the Great Star Chant, and the Myth of the Coyote Chant*, 1988
    This exquisite book is a compilation of important Navajo myths, songs, chants, and prayers, that deal with the complex philosophical and religious life of Navajo culture.
Mourning Dove, *Coyote Stories*, 1933
    These are traditional Okanagan stories about Coyote, the trickster.
William Bright, *A Coyote Reader*, 1993
    There are traditional coyote stories from across North America.
Marilyne Virginia Mabery, *Right After Sundown: Teaching Stories of the Navajo*, 1991
    These are traditional stories of the world's beginnings as told by the Navajo, with excellent illustrations by Navajo artist Raymond J. Johnson.
Monty Roessel, *Songs from the Loom*, 1995
    This story follows Jaclyn Roessel, a young Navajo girl, as she learns the stories of her family and the cultural wisdom and mythology associated with the art of weaving.
Jonathan Broderick, *Stories of Traditional Navajo Life and Culture*, 1977
    Interviews from tape-recorded meetings of the Navajo.
Broderick H. Johnson, *Navajo Stories of the Long Walk Period*, 1973
    In this intriguing collection, Navajo people recount the stories of the Long Walk period as they have been handed down to them.
Margot Astrov, *The Winged Serpent*, 1946
    One of the best collections of oral stories and songs from a large cross-section of Indian cultures.
Joseph Bruchac, *Flying with the Eagle, Racing with the Bear*, 1993
    These rite-of-passage stories come from various tribal peoples including the Wampanoag, Cherokee, Osage, Lakota and Tlingit.

1152

JASON BETZINEZ, Native American, Apache
WILBUR STURTEVANT NYE, Co-Author, Caucasian

I Fought with Geronimo
(Lincoln: University of Nebraska Press, 1957, 1987)

Subject(s): War; Autobiography; Indian Reservations
Age range(s): Grades 9-Adult
Time period(s): 19th century; 20th century (1850s-1950s)
Locale(s): New Mexico

Summary: Betzinez, who lived to be almost a hundred years old, recounts his life during the great period of change for the Apache: from their traditional life to the life of the reservation system.

About this book: This book was written by Betzinez and edited by Nye, so it is not really an as-told-to book.

Other books you might like:

John Joseph Mathews, *Talking to the Moon*, 1945
    Mathews relates the circle of his life from his childhood in Oklahoma through his World War I military stint, college, married life and back again to his homeland.
Anna Moore Shaw, *A Pima Past*, 1974
    Anna Moore Shaw born in a traditional Pima brush house, and educated in the white world, tells fascinating autobiography of her life.
Refugio Savala, *The Autobiography of a Yaqui Poet*, 1980
    This autobiography by Refugio Savala tells of his family's flight from Mexico to Arizona during the horrible years of torture, and their struggle to make a new home for themselves.
Zitkala-Sa, *Old Indian Legends Retold by Zitkala-Sa*, 1921
    This is a collection of memoirs and essays about the traditional Lakota culture and its adjustments to the real world.
Jane Holden Kelley, *Contemporary Life Histories*, 1978
    This as-told-to book chronicles the lives of four Yaqui women. The author describes many aspects of Yaqui culture in the introduction.
Clinton Rickard, *Fighting Tuscarora: The Autobiography of Chief Clinton Rickard*, 1973
    In this autobiography, Chief Rickard is acquainted with both the Native American and white worlds. He is politically active well into his eighties, when this book was begun.
Angela Sidney, *Life Lived like a Story: Life Stories of Three Yukon Native Elders*, 1990
    This as-told-to-book chronicles the lives of three Yukon women.
Chief John Stands in Timber, *Cheyenne Memories*, 1967
    Stands in Timber was raised in the traditional Cheyenne culture, in the beginning of the reservation period.
Don C. Talayesva, *Sun Chief: The Autobiography of a Hopi Indian*, 1942
    Don C. Talayesva is born in Oraibi, the oldest continually inhabited town in the U.S., in 1890. This is the story of his life and the life of the Hopi people.
John Fire Lame Deer, *Lame Deer, Seeker of Visions*, 1972
    Traditional medicine man Lame Deer tells of his visions

and spiritual quest while relating the philosophy of Lakota religion and culture.

1153

JOHN BIERHORST, Editor, Caucasian

Four Masterworks of American Indian Literature
(Tucson: University of Arizona Press, 1974)

Subject(s): Folk Tales; Mythology; Literature
Age range(s): Grades 9-Adult
Time period(s): Indeterminate
Locale(s): United States

Summary: This books examines four great works of traditional Indian literature: *Quetzalcoatl*, an Aztec hero myth; *The Ritual of Condolence*, an Iroquois Ceremonial that deals with the process of grief; *Cuceb*, a Maya prophecy; and *The Night Chant*, a Navajo healing ceremony.

Where it's reviewed:
Choice, June 1986, page 1504
New York Review of Books, March 26, 1987, page 32

Other books by the same author:
The Sacred Path, 1984 (collection of spells, prayers, and songs)
In the Trail of the Wind, 1971 (collection of orations and poems)
The Red Swan: Myths and Tales of the American Indians, 1976 (collection of orations and poems)

Other books you might like:
Margot Astrov, *The Winged Serpent*, 1946
    This is one of the best collections of oral stories and songs from a large cross-section of Indian cultures.
Paula Gunn Allen, *Spider Woman's Granddaughters*, 1989
    This is a beautiful collection of traditional tales interwoven with contemporary stories having to do with the lives of Native American women.
William Bright, *A Coyote Reader*, 1993
    This is a collection of trickster stories from many North American tribes, the chapters divided by the attributes of Coyote rather than from the origin of the tales.
Zitkala-Sa, *Old Indian Legends Retold by Zitkala-Sa*, 1921
    This is a collection of memoirs and essays by an Indian woman who was born into the old buffalo hunting culture of the Sioux.
Howard Norman, *Northern Tales*, 1990
    This book is a collection of traditional stories that focuses wholly on the Indian and Eskimo people of the far north.
Frederick Turner, *The Portable North American Indian Reader*, 1973
    Anthology of myths, legends, poetry, fiction, and captivity tales, contains work by both Native American and non-Native writers.
Barry Lopez, *Giving Birth to Thunder, Sleeping with His Daughter: Coyote Builds North America*, 1977
    In this book, Lopez retells a wide selection of Coyote stories from various North American tribes. As always, Coyote is dynamic, irreverant, wily, paradoxical, mysterious, taboo breaking, and fun.

Robert Franklin Gish, *When Coyote Howls: A Lavaland Fable*,

This is a Coyote novel.

Paula Gunn Allen, *Voice of the Turtle*, 1994

Edited by the well known writer and scholar Paula Gunn Allen, this book is an anthology of literature written by American Indian people from 1900 to 1970.

Lee Miller, *From the Heart: Voices of the American Indian*, 1995

This collection of orations, speeches, and testimony by more than 250 Indian people that presents a radical alternative to traditionally taught American history.

Mourning Dove, *Coyote Stories*, 1933

These are traditional stories about Coyote, the trickster.

Hasteen Klah, *The Myth and Prayers of the Great Star Chant, and the Myth of the Coyote Chant*, 1988

This exquisite book is a compilation of important Navajo myths, songs, chants, and prayers, that deal with the complex philosophical and religious life of Navajo culture.

1154

JOHN BIERHORST, Editor, Caucasian

The Red Swan: Myths and Tales of the American Indians

(New York: Farrar, 1976)

Subject(s): Mythology; Folklore
Age range(s): Grades 9-Adult
Time period(s): Indeterminate Past
Locale(s): United States

Summary: This book is a compilation of varied stories (creation, trickster, star husband, etc.) from forty Native American tribes.

Where it's reviewed:
Folklore, 1994, page 121

Other books by the same author:
Four Masterworks of American Indian Literature, 1974

Other books you might like:
Frederick Turner, *The Portable North American Indian Reader*, 1973

This anthology of myths, legends, poetry, fiction, and captivity tales, contains work by both Native American and non-Native writers.

Margot Astrov, *The Winged Serpent*, 1946

This mixed genre is one of the best collections of oral stories and songs from a large cross-section of Native American cultures.

G.M. Mullet, *Spider Woman Stories*,

These Hopi Indian legends are collected from the 1880s.

Paula Gunn Allen, *Spider Woman's Granddaughters*, 1989

This is a beautiful collection of traditional tales interwoven with contemporary stories about Native American women.

Zitkala-Sa, *Old Indian Legends Retold by Zitkala-Sa*, 1921

This is a collection of memoirs and essays about the traditional Lakota culture and it's adjustments to European encroachment.

Howard Norman, *Northern Tales*, 1990

This book is a collection of traditional stories that focuses

wholly on the Native American and Ancient people of the far north.

William Bright, *A Coyote Reader*, 1993

These are traditional Coyote stories.

1155

JOHN BIERHORST, Caucasian

The Ring in the Prairie

(New York: Dial Press, 1970)

Subject(s): Folk Tales
Age range(s): Grades 3-4
Major character(s): Waupee, Hunter, Native American
Time period(s): Indeterminate Past (mythic time)
Locale(s): United States

Summary: Waupee is a young warrior who discovers a magic circle where star people come to dance. He captures a star maiden, marries her, but then she leaves him with their son. He is sorrowful, but eventually his bride returns to bring him up to the sky, and eventually they all become white hawks.

About this book: This is a variation of the traditional star husband story.

Other books by the same author:
The Red Swan: Myths and Tales of the American Indians, 1971
The Sacred Path, 1984 (spells, prayers, and songs)
In the Trail of the Wind, 1971 (orations and poems)

Other books you might like:
Joseph Bruchac, *Return of the Sun*, 1990

Traditional tales of the Northeast Woodlands, full of humor and wisdom, equally as enlightening as Aesop's fables, and more fun.

Shonto Begay, *Ma'ii and Cousin Horned Toad*,

Ma'ii is hungry, and he goes to Horny Toad for a free lunch, eventually swallowing his smaller cousin, but that does not fare well for Ma—ii who learns his lesson in the end.

Mourning Dove, *Coyote Stories*, 1933

These are traditional Okanagan stories about Coyote, the trickster.

Herschel Talashoema, *Coyote & Little Turtle: Iisaw Niqw Yongosonhoya: A Traditional Hopi Tale*, 1994

Here is an excellent book for early readers about Coyote and Little Turtle. It is written in both Hopi and English, with illustrations from Hopi children.

John Bierhorst, *The Red Swan: Myths and Tales of the American Indians*, 1976

This book is a compilation of varied stories (creation, trickster, star husband, etc.) from forty Indian tribes.

Frederick Turner, *The Portable North American Indian Reader*, 1973

This anthology of myths, legends, poetry, fiction, and captivity tales, contains work by both Native American and non-Native writers.

1156

JOHN BIERHORST, Editor, Caucasian

The Way of the Earth: Native America and the Environment

(New York: William Morrow, 1994)

Subject(s): Mythology; History; Philosophy
Age range(s): Grades 10-Adult
Time period(s): 1990s
Locale(s): United States

Summary: Bierhorst delves into American Indian philosophies regarding the environment, giving a comprehensive view of native beliefs, myths, and practices about nature. Well researched and documented, this is an excellent book for teachers.

Where it's reviewed:
Horn Book Guide, Fall 1994, page 327
Voice of Youth Advocates, October 1994, page 228
Science Books and Films, October 1994, page 197

Other books by the same author:
Four Masterworks of American Indian Literature, 1974
The Sacred Path, 1984 (spells, prayers, and songs)
In the Trail of the Wind, 1971 (orations and poems)
The Red Swan: Myths and Tales of the American Indians, 1971 (orations and poems)

Other books you might like:
Margot Astrov, *The Winged Serpent*, 1946
    This is one of the best collections of oral stories and songs from a large cross-section of Indian cultures.
Paula Gunn Allen, *Spider Woman's Granddaughters*, 1989
    This is a beautiful collection of traditional tales interwoven with contemporary stories about the lives of Native American women.
Zitkala-Sa, *Old Indian Legends Retold by Zitkala-Sa*, 1921
    This is a collection of memoirs and essays by an Indian woman who was born into the old buffalo hunting culture of the Sioux.
N. Scott Momaday, *The Way to Rainy Mountain*, 1976
    Mixed genre: fiction, poetry, history, mythology, and personal memoir.
John Fire Lame Deer, *Lame Deer, Seeker of Visions*, 1972
    Traditional medicine man Lame Deer tells of his visions and spiritual quest while relating the philosophy of Lakota religion and culture.
Peter Nabokov, *Native American Testimony*, 1991
    This anthology contains oral stories, speeches, prophecies, and essays.
Brian Swann, *I Tell You Now*, 1989
    This is an excellent collection of autobiographical essays by eighteen contemporary American Indian writers.
Arlene Hirschfelder, *Native Heritage*, 1995
    This book is a collection of personal accounts by American Indian people from 1790 through the present.
T.C. McLuhan, *Touch the Earth*, 1971
    This is a collection of speeches and statements from a wide assortment of Indian people.
Frederick Turner, *The Portable North American Indian Reader*, 1973
    This anthology of myths, legends, poetry, fiction, and captivity tales, contains work by both native American and non-Native writers

1157

MOSES NELSON BIG CROW (Eyo Hiktepi)

Hoksila and the Red Buffalo

(Chamberlain, SD: Tipi Press, 1991)

Subject(s): Folk Tales
Age range(s): Grades 3-5
Major character(s): Hoksila, Child (boy), Native American (Lakota (Sioux))
Time period(s): Indeterminate Past (mythic time)
Locale(s): South Dakota

Summary: An ugly red buffalo with black spots has been terrorizing the people for generations. Hoksila (the hero) must find the red buffalo (which killed his father, and mother and fiance) and kill him so that peace is restored.

Other books by the same author:
A Legend from the Crazy Horse Clan, 1987

Other books you might like:
Luther Standing Bear, *Stories of the Sioux*, 1988
    Standing Bear grew up in the traditional buffalo hunting culture, and he brings to life the stories from his own past.
Mourning Dove, *Coyote Stories*, 1933
    These are traditional Okanagan stories about Coyote, the trickster.
Joseph Bruchac, *Iroquois Stories*, 1985
    This book recounts many of the traditional animal, adventure and monster tales of the Iroquois people.
Joseph Bruchac, *The Wind Eagle and Other Abenaki Stories*, 1984
    These are traditional tales of the Abenaki.
Joseph Bruchac, *Return of the Sun*, 1990
    Traditional tales of the Northeast Woodlands, full of humor and wisdom, equally as enlightening as Aesop's fables, and more fun.
Joseph Bruchac, *Flying with the Eagle, Racing with the Bear*, 1993
    These rite-of-passage stories come from various tribal peoples including the Wampanoag, Cherokee, Osage, Lakota and Tlingit.
Charles A. Eastman, *Old Indian Days*, 1907
    Autobiography of a Lakota Sioux man.
Zitkala-Sa, *Old Indian Legends Retold by Zitkala-Sa*, 1921
    These stories depict Zitkala-Sa's childhood in the traditional Lakota culture and the difficulties she faced while attending school and college in a world where she was perceived as a "savage."
John Bierhorst, *The Red Swan: Myths and Tales of the American Indians*, 1976
    This book is a compilation of varied stories (creation, trickster, star husband, etc.) from forty Indian tribes.
Frederick Turner, *The Portable North American Indian Reader*, 1973
    This anthology of myths, legends, poetry, fiction, and captivity tales, contains work by both Native American and non-Native writers.

1158

MOSES NELSON BIG CROW (Eyo Hiktepi)
DANIEL LONG SOLDIER, Illustrator, Native American,
Lakota (Sioux)

A Legend from the Crazy Horse Clan

(Chamberlain, SD: Tipi Press, 1987, 1991)

Subject(s): Folk Tales; Legends
Age range(s): Grades 3-5
Major character(s): Taisha, Child (young girl), Native American (Lakota)
Time period(s): 18th century
Locale(s): South Dakota

Summary: Taisha is five years old when a baby raccoon, Mesu, comes to snuggle up in her buffalo robe. But then a stampede sends the village scattering, all except for Taisha and Mesu, who end up being befriended by the buffalo. Taisha marries a buffalo and lives with the animals for many years until one day a Lakota warrior shows up.

About this book: Well done illustrations by Long Soldier enhance this intriguing tale.

Other books by the same author:
Hoksila and the Red Buffalo, 1991

Other books you might like:
Luther Standing Bear, *Stories of the Sioux*, 1988
    Standing Bear grew up in the traditional buffalo hunting culture, and he brings to life the stories from his own past.
Mourning Dove, *Coyote Stories*, 1933
    These are traditional Okanagan stories about Coyote, the trickster.
Joseph Bruchac, *Iroquois Stories*, 1985
    This book recounts many of the traditional animal, adventure and monster tales of the Iroquois people.
Joseph Bruchac, *The Wind Eagle and Other Abenaki Stories*, 1984
    These are traditional tales of the Abenaki.
Joseph Bruchac, *Return of the Sun*, 1990
    Traditional tales of the Northeast Woodlands, full of humor and wisdom, equally as enlightening as Aesop's fables, and more fun.
Joseph Bruchac, *Flying with the Eagle, Racing with the Bear*, 1993
    These rite-of-passage stories come from various tribal peoples including the Wampanoag, Cherokee, Osage, Lakota and Tlingit.
Zitkala-Sa, *Old Indian Legends Retold by Zitkala-Sa*, 1921
    These stories depict Zitkala-Sa's childhood in the traditional Lakota culture and the difficulties she faced while attending school and college in a world where she was perceived as a ''savage.''
John Bierhorst, *The Red Swan: Myths and Tales of the American Indians*, 1976
    This book is a compilation of varied stories (creation, trickster, star husband, etc.) from forty Indian tribes.
Frederick Turner, *The Portable North American Indian Reader*, 1973
    This anthology of myths, legends, poetry, fiction, and cap-

tivity tales, contains work by both Native American and non-Native writers.

1159

BEN BLACK BEAR, Native American, Lakota (Sioux)
THOMAS E. SIMMS, Illustrator

Otokahekagapi (First Beginnings): Sioux Creation Story

(Chamberlain, SD: Tipi Press, 1987)

Subject(s): Mythology; Creation
Age range(s): Grades 2-4
Major character(s): Inyan, Deity (Creator/God)
Time period(s): Indeterminate Past (mythic time)
Locale(s): South Dakota

Summary: This is the traditional Lakota (Sioux) creation story, written first in Lakota with an English translation at the bottom of each page. Inyan, the creator, longs for someone in the universe other than himself. Then he creates the first word, and follows with the earth (Maka) and the sky (Skan).

About this book: Excellent illustrations by Simms add a wonderful dimension to this book for young people. It is an excellent text to introduce to children (who are not Lakota) the idea that each and every culture has a creation story. The fact that it is told in the Lakota language only teaches cross-cultural lessons.

Other books you might like:
Luther Standing Bear, *Stories of the Sioux*, 1988
    Standing Bear grew up in the traditional buffalo hunting culture, and he brings to life the stories from his own past.
Mourning Dove, *Coyote Stories*, 1933
    These are traditional Okanagan stories about Coyote, the trickster.
Joseph Bruchac, *Iroquois Stories*, 1985
    This book recounts many of the traditional animal, adventure and monster tales of the Iroquois people.
Joseph Bruchac, *The Wind Eagle and Other Abenaki Stories*, 1984
    These are traditional tales of the Abenaki.
Joseph Bruchac, *Return of the Sun*, 1990
    Traditional tales of the Northeast Woodlands, full of humor and wisdom, equally as enlightening as Aesop's fables, and more fun.
Joseph Bruchac, *Flying with the Eagle, Racing with the Bear*, 1993
    These rite-of-passage stories come from various tribal peoples including the Wampanoag, Cherokee, Osage, Lakota and Tlingit.
Zitkala-Sa, *Old Indian Legends Retold by Zitkala-Sa*, 1921
    This collection of essays and memoirs were written by a woman born into the traditional buffalo hunting culture and her adjustment to the white world.
John Bierhorst, *The Red Swan: Myths and Tales of the American Indians*, 1976
    This book is a compilation of varied stories (creation, trickster, star husband, etc.) from forty Indian tribes.
Frederick Turner, *The Portable North American Indian Reader*, 1973

This anthology of myths, legends, poetry, fiction, and captivity tales, contains work by both Native American and non-Native writers.

BLACK ELK, Native American, Lakota (Sioux)
JOHN G. NEIHARDT, Co-Author, Caucasian

Black Elk Speaks

(Lincoln: University of Nebraska Press, 1932)

Subject(s): Biography; Religion
Age range(s): Grades 9-Adult
Time period(s): 19th century; 20th century (1860s-1930s)
Locale(s): South Dakota

Summary: This is the life story of Black Elk as told to John Neihardt. In it, Black Elk recounts his traditional Lakota boyhood, his involvement in the Ghost Dance Movement of the 1880s and his participation in the defeat of Custer at the Battle of the Little Big Horn. But Black Elk was a Holy Man and much of the book details his visions and his spiritual quest. A witness to the massacre at Wounded Knee, he said of it, ''A people's dream died there.''

About this book: *Black Elk Speaks* has had a tremendous impact on both Indians and non-Indians alike and, after its revival in the 1970s, has often been called an Indian *Bible*. It is an as-told-to book, however, and recent criticism has dealt with the ''transformation'' of Black Elk's story through the interpretation of poet John G. Neihardt.

Where it's reviewed:
Choice, June 1986, page 1506
San Francisco Review of Books, Issue 3, 1990, page 32

Other books by the same author:
The Sixth Grandfather, 1984 (interviews)
The Sacred Pipe, 1953 (as-told-to)
The Tree That Flowered

Other books you might like:
Julian Rice, *Black Elk's Story*, 1991
    Rice examines the life of Nick Black Elk, delving into the many areas of Black Elk's life that Neidhart left out.
Michael Steltenkamp, *Black Elk, Holy Man of the Sioux*, 1993
    This is a look at the life of Black Elk which tackles the controversies surrounding *Black Elk Speaks*.
John Fire Lame Deer, *Lame Deer, Seeker of Visions*, 1972
    This is an as-told-to book, Lame Deer telling his story to the writer Richard Erdoes.
Luther Standing Bear, *Stories of the Sioux*, 1988
    Standing Bear grew up in the traditional buffalo hunting culture of the Sioux and he brings to life the stories from his own past.
Ella Cara Deloria, *Waterlily*, 1988
    Waterlily, actually beginning with her mother's story, details the life of the Sioux before European contact, focusing on women's place in the culture and the importance of kinship relationships.
Brian Swann, *I Tell You Now*, 1989
    This is an excellent collection of autobiographical essays by eighteen contemporary American Indian writers.

WALLACE BLACK ELK, Native American, Lakota (Sioux)
WILLIAM S. LYON, Co-Author, Caucasian

Black Elk: The Sacred Ways of a Lakota

(San Francisco: Harper, 1990)

Subject(s): Autobiography; Mythology; Religion
Age range(s): Grades 10-Adult
Time period(s): 20th century
Locale(s): South Dakota

Summary: This is a book about traditional Lakota religion and culture as told to William S. Lyon by the contemporary shaman Wallace Black Elk (who is no relation to Nicholas Black Elk of *Black Elk Speaks* fame.) The book brings together biographical aspects of Wallace Black Elk's life and the traditional religious teachings of Lakota religion and mythology.

Where it's reviewed:
Kirkus Reviews, January 15, 1990, page 84
Publishers Weekly, February 9, 1990, page 54
San Francisco Review of Books, Issue 3, 1990, page 31

Other books you might like:
Black Elk, *Black Elk Speaks*, 1932
    This is the life story of the Holy Man of the Sioux, written with John G. Neihardt.
John Fire Lame Deer, *Lame Deer, Seeker of Visions*, 1972
    This is an as-told-to book, Lame Deer telling his story to the writer Richard Erdoes.
Luther Standing Bear, *Stories of the Sioux*, 1988
    Standing Bear grew up in the traditional buffalo hunting culture of the Sioux and he brings to life the stories from his own past.
Zitkala-Sa, *Old Indian Legends Retold by Zitkala-Sa*, 1921
    This is the life story of Zitkala-Sa, a Lakota who spends her girlhood in the traditional culture but who eventually leaves for the Indian boarding schools out East.
Nicholas Black Elk, *The Sacred Pipe*, 1976
    The Teachings of Black Elk as related to Joseph Epes Brown and edited with a commentary by him.
Mary Crow Dog, *Lakota Woman*, 1990
    This is an as-told-to-book with Richard Erdoes as the author and editor, chronicling the life of a Lakota woman who lives through the hardships of the second Wounded Knee era.
Brian Swann, *I Tell You Now*, 1989
    This is an excellent collection of autobiographical essays by eighteen contemporary American Indian writers. Co-authored with Arnold Krupat.

BLACK HAWK, Native American, Sac and Fox

Black Hawk, an Autobiography

(Urbana: University of Illinois, 1833, 1955)

Subject(s): Government Relations; Resistance Movements; War
Age range(s): Grades 9-Adult

Time period(s): 19th century
Locale(s): Illinois; Iowa

Summary: This is the autobiography of the famous chief who, for awhile, successfully evaded and defeated the U.S. Military in their attempts to subdue the Indians. After several skirmishes, known as Black Hawk's War (1832), the Sauks were defeated on August 3, 1832 when 1300 troops attacked and killed about 300 of Black Hawk's men. After his surrender, he was taken to Washington D.C. to meet President Jackson and became something of a celebrity.

About this book: This was the first narrated autobiography, or as-told-to, by an Indian person.

Other books you might like:
Sarah Winnemucca, *Life Among the Paiutes: Their Wrongs and Claims*, 1883
   Diplomat and outspoken advocate of the rights of native peoples, Winnemucca wrote this book to preserve the history and culture of the Paiute's.
John Fire Lame Deer, *Lame Deer: Seeker of Visions*, 1972
   This is an as-told-to book, Lame Deer telling his story to the writer Richard Erdoes.
Luther Standing Bear, *Stories of the Sioux*, 1988
   Standing Bear grew up in the traditional buffalo hunting culture of the Sioux and he brings to life the stories from his past.
Brian Swann, *I Tell You Now*, 1989
   This is an excellent collection of autobiographical essays by eighteen contemporary Native American writers.
N. Scott Momaday, *The Way to Rainy Mountain*, 1976
   Mixed genre: fiction, poetry, history, mythology and personal memoir.
Francis La Flesche, *The Middle Five: Indian Schoolboys of the Omaha Tribe*, 1900
   This book details the life of La Flesche and his friends in mission school in Oklahoma.

1163

PETER BLUE CLOUD, Native American, Mohawk

Elderberry Flute Song
(Trumansburg, NY: The Crossing Press, 1982)

Subject(s): Trickster Tales; Legends
Age range(s): Grades 10-Adult
Major character(s): Coyote, Trickster
Time period(s): Indeterminate
Locale(s): United States

Summary: These modern day trickster stories deal with the mythological figure, Coyote, who is always getting into trouble, but inadvertently at times does good (like creating the first humans out of his own feces). These often hilarious tales poke fun at everything from Anthropologists to Shamans.

About this book: The mythological trickster figure is one of the most fascinating archetypes in literature, and he plays a prominent role in the stories of Native Americans. He is known as Coyote, Hare, Raven, Rabbit, and Spider, among other names, but he has many similar attributes: a fascination with sexuality, scatology, gluttony, and the breaking of all cultural taboos. Yet in some cultures the trickster is also the Creator.

Other books by the same author:
Turtle, Bear and Wolf, 1976 (poetry)
White Corn Sister, 1977 (poetry)

Other books you might like:
Paul Radin, *The Trickster*, 1956
   This excellent study of the Trickster archetype presents the Winnenago Trickster Cycle of Myths in full, along with the Hare Cycle and summaries of the Assiniboine and Tlingit Trickster Myths.
Barry Lopez, *Giving Birth to Thunder, Sleeping with His Daughter: Coyote Builds North America*, 1977
   In this book, Lopez retells a wide selection of Coyote stories from various North American tribes. As always, Coyote is irreverant, dynamic, wily, paradoxical, mysterious, taboo-breaking and fun.
Thomas King, *Green Grass, Running Water*, 1993
   Coyote, God, Robinson Crusoe, the Lone Ranger and others struggle amongst themselves in the cosmological firmament while on the human plane, various characters struggle with life the best they can.
William Bright, *A Coyote Reader*, 1993
   This is a collection of trickster stories from many North American tribes, divided into chapters by the attributes of Coyote, rather than by their origin.
Gerald Vizenor, *Griever: An American Monkey King in China*, 1987
   Vizenor creates a trickster character who leaves his Chippewa home to go to China where he finds himself to be kin to the Monkey King.
Gerald Vizenor, *Earthdivers: Tribal Narratives on Mixed Descent*, 1981
   In this collection of short stories Vizenor creates trickster figures to poke fun at and make shrewd political commentary on America, reservation life, and just about everything else.
Margot Astrov, *The Winged Serpent*, 1946
   This is one of the best collections of oral stories and songs from a wide cross-section of Indian cultures.
Frederick Turner, *The Portable North American Indian Reader*, 1973
   This anthology of myths, legends, poetry, fiction and captivity tales, contains work by both Native and non-Native writers.
Mourning Dove, *Coyote Stories*, 1933
   These are traditional Okanagan stories about Coyote, the trickster.

1164

SUSAN BRAINE, Native American, Assiniboine

Drumbeat. . .Heartbeat: A Celebration of the Powwow
(Minneapolis: Lerner Publications, 1995)

Series: The We Are Still Here
Subject(s): Indians of North America; Rituals; Cultures and Customs
Age range(s): Grades 3-5
Time period(s): 1990s
Locale(s): Montana

Summary: This is a wonderful introduction to the Powwow for children by a Native American writer and photographer.

Where it's reviewed:
Children's Bookwatch, July 1995, page 1
School Library Journal, September 1995, page 205

Other books you might like:
Herman J. Viola, *Osceola*, 1993
   This is a brief history of the famous Creek leader, Osceola, for younger readers. Illustrated by Yoshi Miyake.
Michael Dorris, *Morning Girl*, 1992
   This short novel about a young girl and her brother takes place in the pre-Columbian Caribbean.
Sandra King, *Shannon: An Ojibway Dancer*, 1993
   This book follows the life of a young Ojibway girl, Shannon, who lives in the city, yet still participates in tribal ceremonies.
Monty Roessel, *Songs from the Loom*, 1995
   This story follows Jaclyn Roessel, a young Navajo girl, as she learns the stories of her family and the cultural wisdom and mythology associated with the art of weaving.
Joseph Bruchac, *Flying with the Eagle, Racing with the Bear*, 1993
   These rite-of-passage stories come from various tribal peoples including the Wampanoag, Cherokee, Osage, Lakota and Tlingit.
Michael Dorris, *A Yellow Raft in Blue Water*, 1987
   This is one of the only novels that deals with ''mixed blood'' people who are part African-American and part Native American.

1165

BETH BRANT (Degonwadonti)

Food & Spirits: Stories
(Ithaca, NY: Firebrand Books, 1991)

Subject(s): Cultures and Customs; Family; Tradition
Age range(s): Adult
Time period(s): 1990s
Locale(s): Michigan; Canada

Summary: This is a collection of short stories about Native American people from Canada and Michigan. They are moving stories, important to Native Americans, that touch on the themes of family, tradition, and myth.

About this book: The author writes in the first person vernacular.

Where it's reviewed:
Canadian Literature, Summer 1995, page 142
Multicultural Review, March 1993, page 57
MS., September 1992, page 62

Other books by the same author:
Mohawk Trail, 1991

Other books you might like:
Craig Lesley, *Talking Leaves*, 1991
   This book is an excellent collection of short stories by thirty-five contemporary Native American writers, including, among others, Erdrich, Dorris, Momaday, Hogan, and Whiteman.

Louise Erdrich, *Love Medicine*, 1984
   Married to Marie, Nector is nevertheless fatefully drawn to Lulu. When his grandson prepares a love medicine to win him back to his grandmother, he uses the wrong ingredients and kills Nector instead.
Paula Gunn Allen, *Spider Woman's Granddaughters*, 1989
   This is a beautiful collection of traditional tales interwoven with contemporary short stories having to do with the lives of Native American women.
Leslie Marmon Silko, *Storyteller*, 1981
   This work is a mixed genre of poetry, fiction, and mythology.
Sherman Alexie, *The Lone Ranger and Tonto Fist Fight in Heaven*, 1993
   This wonderful short fiction is about the ups and downs of reservation life.
James Northrup, *Walking the Rez Road*, 1993
   Luke Warmwater is a Vietnam vet who is down on his luck, but he, like most of his reservation cohorts, is a surviver in the trickster fashion.
Ray A. Young Bear, *Black Eagle Child*, 1992
   This fictional work is about life on a Mesquakie settlement.
Thomas King, *Green Grass, Running Water*, 1993
   Coyote, God, Robinson Crusoe, The Lone Ranger and others struggle amongst themselves in the cosmological firmament. Meanwhile various Native American characters struggle with life the best they can.
Clifford E. Trafzer, *Blue Dawn, Red Earth: New Native American Storytellers*, 1996
   This is a collection of short stories by 30 new Native American writers: Lorne Simon, Anita Endrezze, Jim Barnes, Annie Hansen, Richard Van Camp and Eric L. Gansworth.

1166

BETH BRANT (Degonwadonti)

A Gathering of Spirit: A Collection of North American Indian Women
(Ithaca, NY: Firebrand Books, 1984)

Subject(s): Indians of North America; Women
Age range(s): Grades 10-Adult
Time period(s): 19th century; 20th century (1860s-1930s)
Locale(s): South Dakota

Summary: This collection of stories, letters, essays, and poems is from a large cross-section of Native American women writers, such as Linda Hogan, Elizabeth Cook-Lynn, Diana Glancy, Joy Harjo, Wendy Rose, Doris Seale, Mary Tallmountain, Luci Tapahonso, and Anna Lee Walters, just to name a few of the excellent writers represented here.

Other books by the same author:
Food & Spirits: Stories, 1991
Mohawk Trail, 1991

Other books you might like:
Zitkala-Sa, *Old Indian Legends Retold by Zitkala-Sa*, 1921
   These stories depict Zitkala-Sa's childhood in the traditional Lakota culture and the difficulties she faced while

attending school and college in a world where she was perceived as a "savage."

Brian Swann, *I Tell You Now*, 1989

This is an excellent collection of autobiographical essays by eighteen contemporary American Indian writers, co-edited with Brian Swann.

Paula Gunn Allen, *The Sacred Hoop: Recovering the Feminine in American Indian Traditions*, 1986

This book is an excellent collection of essays that uncovers the essential role of women in traditional and contemporary Indian life.

Paula Gunn Allen, *Spider Woman's Granddaughters*, 1989

This is a beautiful collection of traditional tales interwoven with contemporary short stories having to do with the lives of Native American women.

Joseph Bruchac, *The Girl Who Married the Moon*, 1994

These mostly traditional tales are from a variety of North American tribes and all about women: initiation ceremonies, shape changing stories, and others. Co-edited with Gayle Ross.

Leslie Marmon Silko, *Storyteller*, 1981

A mixed genre anthology of poetry, fiction, and mythology.

Craig Lesley, *Talking Leaves*, 1991

This book is a an excellent collection of short stories by thirty-five contemporary American Indian writers, such as Louise Erdrich, N. Scott Momaday, Linda Hogan and Roberta Hill Whiteman.

Paula Gunn Allen, *Voice of the Turtle*, 1994

Edited by the well known writer and scholar Paula Gunn Allen, this book is an anthology of literature written by American Indian people from 1900 to 1970.

Lee Miller, *From the Heart: Voices of the American Indian*, 1995

This is a collection of orations, speeches, and testimony by more than 250 Indian people that presents a radical alternative to traditionally taught American history.

Clifford E. Trafzer, *Blue Dawn, Red Earth: New Native American Storytellers*,

This is a collection of short stories by 30 new Native American writers: Lorne Simon, Anita Endrezze, Jim Barnes, Annie Hansen, Maurice Kenny, and Patricia Piley, among others.

1167

BETH BRANT, Native American, Mohawk

Mohawk Trail

(Ithaca, NY: Firebrand Books, 1985)

Subject(s): Short Stories
Age range(s): Grades 9-Adult
Time period(s): 1990s
Locale(s): Michigan

Summary: This is a collection of very short stories, vignettes actually, mostly written in the first-person vernacular, about Indians from Canada and Michigan.

Other books by the same author:
Food & Spirits: Stories, 1991

A Gathering of Spirit: A Collection of North American Indian Women, 1988

Other books you might like:

Craig Lesley, *Talking Leaves*, 1991

This book is a an excellent collection of short stories by thirty-five contemporary Native American writers, including, amongst others, Erdrich, Dorris, Momaday, Hogan, and Whiteman.

Louise Erdrich, *Love Medicine*, 1984

Married to Marie, Nector is nevertheless fatefully drawn to Lulu. When his grandson prepares a love medicine to win him back to his grandmother, he uses the wrong ingredients and kills Nector instead.

Paula Gunn Allen, *Spider Woman's Granddaughters*, 1989

This beautiful collection is of traditional tales interwoven with contemporary short stories about Native American women.

Leslie Marmon Silko, *Storyteller*, 1981

This work is a mixed genre of poetry, fiction, and mythology.

Sherman Alexie, *The Lone Ranger and Tonto Fist Fight in Heaven*, 1993

This wonderful short fiction is about the ups and downs of reservation life.

James Northrup, *Walking the Rez Road*, 1993

Luke Warmwater is a Vietnam vet who is down on his luck, but he, like most of his reservation cohorts, is a survivor in the trickster fashion.

Ray A. Young Bear, *Black Eagle Child*, 1992

This fictional work is about life on a Mesquakie settlement.

Thomas King, *Green Grass, Running Water*, 1993

Coyote, God, Robinson Crusoe, the Lone Ranger and others struggle amongst themselves in the cosmological firmament. Meanwhile various Native American characters struggle with life the best they can.

Paula Gunn Allen, *Voice of the Turtle*, 1994

Edited by the well known writer and scholar Paula Gunn Allen, this book is an anthology of literature written by American Indian people from 1900 to 1970.

Lee Miller, *From the Heart: Voices of the American Indian*, 1995

This is a collection of orations, speeches, and testimony by more than 250 Indian people that presents a radical alternative to traditionally taught American history.

Clifford E. Trafzer, *Blue Dawn, Red Earth: New Native American Storytellers*, 1996

This is a collection of short stories by 30 new Native American writers: Lorne Simon, Jim Barnes, Annie Hansen and Richard Van Camp.

1168

BETH BRANT, Native American, Pawnee and Otoe

The Two-Legged Creature

(Flagstaff, AZ: Northland Pub., 1993)

Subject(s): Folk Tales; Animals; Nature
Age range(s): Grades 2-5
Major character(s): Two-Legged, Human
Time period(s): 1980s

Locale(s): United States

Summary: This is a tale about how the Two-Legged creature (man) separated from the other animals.

Other books by the same author:
Mohawk Trail, 1985
A Gathering of Spirit: A Collection of North American Indian Women, 1988 (short stories)

Other books you might like:
Frederick Turner, *The Portable North American Indian Reader*, 1973
 This anthology of myths, legends, poetry, fiction, and captivity tales, contains work by both Native American and non-Native writers.
Mourning Dove, *Coyote Stories*, 1933
 These are traditional Okanagan stories about Coyote, the trickster.
Shonto Begay, *Ma'ii and Cousin Horned Toad*,
 Ma'ii is hungry, and he goes to Horny Toad for a free lunch, eventually swallowing his smaller cousin, but that does not fare well for Ma'ii who learns his lesson in the end.
Hasteen Klah, *The Myth and Prayers of the Great Star Chant, and the Myth of the Coyote Chant*, 1988
 This exquisite book is a compilation of important Navajo myths, songs, chants, and prayers, that deal with the complex philosophical and religious life of Navajo culture.
William Bright, *A Coyote Reader*, 1993
 These are traditional coyote stories.
Herschel Talashoema, *Coyote & Little Turtle: Iisaw Niqw Yongosonhoya: A Traditional Hopi Tale*, 1994
 Here is an excellent book for early readers about Coyote and Little Turtle. It is written in both Hopi and English, with illustrations from Hopi children.
John Bierhorst, *The Red Swan: Myths and Tales of the American Indians*, 1976
 This book is a compilation of varied stories (creation, trickster, star husband, etc.) from forty Indian tribes.
Joseph Bruchac, *Iroquois Stories*, 1985
 This book recounts many of the traditional animal, adventure and monster tales of the Iroquois people.
Joseph Bruchac, *The Wind Eagle and Other Abenaki Stories*, 1984
 These are traditional tales of the Abenaki.
Joseph Bruchac, *Return of the Sun*, 1990
 Traditional tales of the Northeast Woodlands, full of humor and wisdom, equally as enlightening as Aesop's fables, and more fun.
Joseph Bruchac, *Flying with the Eagle, Racing with the Bear*, 1993
 These rite-of-passage stories come from various tribal peoples including the Wampanoag, Cherokee, Osage, Lakota and Tlingit.

`1169`

MARY BRAVE BIRD, Native American, Lakota (Sioux)
RICHARD ERDOES, Co-Author

Ohitika Woman
(New York: Harper Perennial, 1993)

Subject(s): Autobiography; Politics
Age range(s): Grades 9-Adult
Time period(s): 20th century (1970s-1990s)
Locale(s): South Dakota

Summary: This as-told-to book is the sequel to *Lakota Woman* (Mary retook her maiden name after her divorce from Crow Dog). It chronicles the conflicts between feminism and traditional Indian belief, between White and Indian philosophy, and powerfully tells the story of Mary Brave Bird who seeks to define herself, through great hardship, as an Indian woman in the twentieth century.

Where it's reviewed:
Booklist, September 1, 1993, page 10
Library Journal, August 1993, page 112
Publishers Weekly, July 19, 1993, page 243

Awards the book has won:
The National Book Award, 1991

Other books by the same author:
Lakota Woman, 1990 (with Richard Erdoes)

Other books you might like:
Mark St. Pierre, *The Spiritual Power and Legacy of American Plains Indian Women*,
 This book looks at the lives of Plains Indian women and at the myths and culture surrounding them. Written with Tilda Long Soldier.
Paula Gunn Allen, *The Sacred Hoop: Recovering the Feminine in American Indian Traditions*, 1986
 This book is an excellent collection of essays that uncovers the essential role of women in traditional and contemporary Indian life.
Luther Standing Bear, *Stories of the Sioux*, 1988
 Standing Bear grew up in the traditional buffalo hunting culture of the Sioux and he brings to life the stories from his own past.
Paula Gunn Allen, *Spider Woman's Granddaughters*, 1989
 This is a beautiful collection of traditional tales interwoven with contemporary stories having to do with the lives of Native American women.

`1170`

WILLIAM BRIGHT, Caucasian

A Coyote Reader
(Berkeley, CA: U. of California Press, 1993)

Subject(s): Folk Tales; Animals; Trickster Tales
Age range(s): Grades 10-Adult
Major character(s): Coyote, Trickster
Time period(s): Indeterminate Past (mythic time)
Locale(s): United States

Summary: This is a collection of trickster tales from many tribes, the chapters divided according to the various attributes of Coyote, rather than geographically.

Where it's reviewed:
Sierra, November 1993, page 108
American Anthropologist, June 1994, page 443
Studies in Short Fiction, Spring 1994, page 270
Western American Literature, Spring 1994, page 71

Other books you might like:
Mourning Dove, *Coyote Stories*, 1933
These are traditional Okanagan stories about Coyote, the trickster.
Shonto Begay, *Ma'ii and Cousin Horned Toad*,
Ma'ii is hungry, and he goes to Horny Toad for a free lunch, eventually swallowing his smaller cousin, but that does not fare well for Ma—ii who learns his lesson in the end.
Hasteen Klah, *The Myth and Prayers of the Great Star Chant, and the Myth of the Coyote Chant*, 1988
This exquisite book is a compilation of important Navajo myths, songs, chants, and prayers, that deal with the complex philosophical and religious life of Navajo culture.
Herschel Talashoema, *Coyote & Little Turtle: Iisaw Niqw Yongosonhoya: A Traditional Hopi Tale*, 1994
Here is an excellent book for early readers about Coyote and Little Turtle. It is written in both Hopi and English, with illustrations from Hopi children.
John Bierhorst, *The Red Swan: Myths and Tales of the American Indians*, 1976
This book is a compilation of varied stories (creation, trickster, star husband, etc.) from forty Indian tribes.
Paul Radin, *The Trickster*, 1956
This is an excellent study of the Trickster archetype. The Winnebago Trickster Cycle of Myths, the Winnebago Hare Cycle, and summaries of the Assiniboine and Tlingit Trickster Myths are presented.
Barry Lopez, *Giving Birth to Thunder, Sleeping with His Daughter: Coyote Builds North America*, 1977
In this book Lopez retells a wide selection of Coyote stories from various North American tribes. As always, Coyote is dynamic, irreverant, wily, paradoxical, mysterious, taboo breaking and fun.
Frederick Turner, *The Portable North American Indian Reader*, 1973
This anthology of myths, legends, poetry, fiction, and captivity tales, contains work by both Native American and non-Native writers.

1171

CHARLES BRILL, Caucasian

Red Lake Nation: Portraits of Ojibway Life
(Minneapolis: University Of Minnesota Press, 1992)

Subject(s): Indian Reservations; Photography
Age range(s): Grades 9-Adult
Time period(s): 20th century (1974-1992)
Locale(s): Minnesota

Summary: This book is a photographical essay of the Ojibway people of Red Lake, interspersed with observations and por-
tions of interviews with the Red Lake people. The photos are exquisite and give the reader a good look at what life is and has been at Red Lake for the last twenty years.

Other books you might like:
Michael Dorris, *Native Americans: 500 Years After*, 1975
This work contains photos and history of Native Americans across the continent.
Gerald Vizenor, *The People Named the Chippewa: Narrative Histories*, 1984
This mixed genre contains essays, interviews, history, mythology, and stories.
Maude Kegg, *Portage Lake: Memories of an Ojibwe Childhood*, 1991
In these stories, printed in both English and the original Anishinaabe, Maude Kegg relates the cultural wisdom of her many years, describing important facets of Ojibway life.
George Copway, *The Life, History, and Travels, of Kah-ge-ga-bowh*, 1847
Kah-ge-ga-gah-bowh, born in 1818, published this story of his life in 1847 and it contains sections on Ojibway legends, history, wars, and general culture.
Louise Erdrich, *Love Medicine*, 1984
Married to Marie, Nector is nevertheless fatefully drawn to Lulu. When his grandson prepares a love medicine to win him back to his grandmother, he uses the wrong ingredients and kills Nector instead.
James Northrup, *Walking the Rez Road*, 1993
Luke Warmwater is a Vietnam vet who is down on his luck, but he, like most of his reservation cohorts, is a survivor in the trickster fashion.
Ignatia Broker, *Night Flying Woman*, 1983
Oona was of the generation ripped away from the traditional Ojibway life and forced to live the harsh life of the reservation. Ignatia Broker tells this moving story of her own grandmother.

1172

IGNATIA BROKER, Native American, Ojibway (Chippewa)

Night Flying Woman
(St. Paul: Minnesota Historical Society Press, 1983)

Subject(s): Cultures and Customs; History
Age range(s): Grades 7 and Up
Major character(s): Oona Night Flying Woman, Native American, Young Woman
Time period(s): 19th century; 20th century (late 1800s-1900s)
Locale(s): Minnesota

Summary: Oona's life begins just as white influence is beginning to be felt in northern Minnesota. At first her people are forced to move to a land where there are less whites and more resources. Then, as the government begins to implement its policy of forcing Indians onto reservations and boarding their children out to government schools, they are sent to the White Earth Reservation where life is harsh. As an old woman reflecting back on her life, she is sorry for the loss of the old ways and wonders if the younger generation cares at all for them. Broker, an Ojibway storyteller, puts her talents to work relating this important story of her grandmother's life.

Other books you might like:

Maude Kegg, *Portage Lake: Memories of an Ojibwe Childhood*, 1991

> In these stories, written in both English and Anishinaabe, Kegg relates the cultural wisdom of her many years, describing important facets of Ojibway life.

James Northrup, *Walking the Rez Road*, 1993

> Luke Warmwater is a Vietnam vet who is down on his luck, but he, like his reservation cohorts, is a survivor in the trickster fashion.

Gerald Vizenor, *The People Named the Chippewa: Narrative Histories*, 1984

> This collection includes essays, interviews, history, mythology and other stories about Ojibway people.

Angela Sidney, *Life Lived like a Story: Life Stories of Three Yukon Native Elders*, 1990

> This as-told-to-book chronicles the lives of three Yukon women.

Louise Erdrich, *Love Medicine*, 1984

> Married to Marie, Nector is nevertheless fatefully drawn to Lulu. When his grandson prepares a love medicine to win him back to his grandmother, he uses the wrong ingredients and kills Nector instead.

Maria Campbell, *Halfbreed*, 1973

> This is the moving account of Maria Campbell's life as a Metis or halfbreed, part Indian—part European.

Shirley Sterling, *My Name Is Seepeetza*,

> This fictional account, based on the life of the author, recounts her life as a member of the interior Salish tribe. Forced to attend government schools, she is forbidden to reflect her heritage.

1173

JOSEPH BRUCHAC, Native American, Abenaki

Dawn Land

(Golden, CO: Fulcrum, 1993)

Subject(s): Indians of North America; Pre-Columbian History
Age range(s): Grades 8-Adult
Major character(s): Young Hunter, Hunter (boy), Native American
Time period(s): Indeterminate Past (after the last ice age)
Locale(s): United States

Summary: Shortly after the last Ice Age in North America, a band of Abenaki people is struggling to survive against the elements. When Young Hunter is bitten by a snake, it is taken as a spiritual omen by the tribal elders. Young Hunter is believed to be a powerful shaman and protector of his people. Sent to save his tribe from the ''Ancient Ones,'' it is their words he carries with him, their legends and beliefs that sustain him through his many adventures.

Where it's reviewed:
Booklist, March 15, 1994, page 1357
Library Journal, October 1, 1993, page 48
Book Report, November 1993, page 43
World Literature Today, Winter 1994, page 184
Parabola, November 1993, page 106

Other books by the same author:
Return of the Sun, 1990 (traditional tales)

The Wind Eagle and Other Abenaki Stories, 1984 (traditional tales of the Abenaki)
Iroquois Stories, 1985
Keepers of the Earth, 1989
The Road to Black Mountain, 1976
This Earth Is a Drum, 1977

Other books you might like:

James Welch, *Fools Crow*, 1986

> This novel explores White encroachment on the Plains Blackfeet in Montana (1870s). White Man's Dog, who becomes Fools Crow, is a young man vying for a place of respect in his society.

Charles A. Eastman, *From the Deep Woods to Civilization*, 1916

> This is the autobiography of Charles A. Eastman, who grows up in the traditional buffalo culture of the Lakota (Sioux) but pursues an education in the White man's world.

Luther Standing Bear, *Stories of the Sioux*, 1988

> Standing Bear grew up in the traditional buffalo hunting culture, and he brings to life the stories from his own past.

Zitkala-Sa, *Old Indian Legends Retold by Zitkala-Sa*, 1921

> These stories depict Zitkala-Sa's childhood in the traditional Lakota culture and the difficulties she faces while attending school and college in a world where she is perceived as a ''savage.''

Louise Erdrich, *Tracks*, 1988

> Two alternating voices in conflict, one a traditionalist and one the voice of change, reveal the escalating tension between two Chippewa families and their disintegrating culture.

1174

JOSEPH BRUCHAC, Native American, Abenaki

Flying with the Eagle, Racing with the Bear

(Troll Medallion, 1993)

Subject(s): Folk Tales; Animals
Age range(s): Grades 3 and Up
Time period(s): Indeterminate Past
Locale(s): United States

Summary: These sixteen traditional Native American tales from various North American tribes all deal with Rites-of-Passage. They are full of humor and wisdom and show the process of growth and change in the lives of the boys they depict. These stories are wonderful to read aloud.

Where it's reviewed:
Booklist, December 15, 1993, page 749
Book Report, March 1994, page 50
Children's Book Review Service, Winter 1994, page 69
Horn Book Guide, Spring 94, page 105
Learning, Arpil 1994, page 45

Other books by the same author:
The Wind Eagle and Other Abenaki Stories, 1984 (traditional tales)
Iroquois Stories, 1985 (traditional tales)
Keepers of the Earth, 1989

Hoop Snakes, Hide Behinds, and Side Hill Winders, 1991
Keepers of the Animals, 1992

Other books you might like:

Margot Astrov, *The Winged Serpent,* 1946
This mixed genre is one of the best collections of oral stories and songs from a large cross-section of Native American cultures.

Shonto Begay, *Ma'ii and Cousin Horned Toad,*
Ma'ii is hungry, and he goes to Horny Toad for a free lunch eventually swallowing his smaller cousin, but that does not fare well for Ma'ii who learns his lesson in the end.

Herschel Talashoema, *Coyote & Little Turtle: Iisaw Niqw Yongosonhoya: A Traditional Hopi Tale,* 1994
This excellent book for early readers is about Coyote and Little Turtle. It is written in both Hopi and English, with illustrations drawn by Hopi children.

Mourning Dove, *Coyote Stories,* 1933
These traditional stories are about Coyote, the trickster.

1175

JOSEPH BRUCHAC, Native American, Abenaki
GAYLE ROSS, Co-Author, Native American, Cherokee

The Girl Who Married the Moon

(Bridgewater Books, 1994)

Subject(s): Folk Tales; Women
Age range(s): Grades 3 and Up
Time period(s): Indeterminate
Locale(s): United States

Summary: These are mostly traditional tales from a variety of North American tribes about young women coming-of-age. It includes initiation ceremonies, shape changing stories, and other tales.

About this book: Gayle Ross is one of the best known storytellers in the U.S., and Joseph Bruchac is one of the very best writers of traditional Indian tales. Together they do a wonderful job of conveying these intriguing Native tales with elegance and humor.

Where it's reviewed:

Booklist, October 1, 1994, page 315
Horn Book Guide, Spring 1995, page 104
School Library Journal, November 1994, page 112
Voice of Youth Advocates, February 1995, page 354
Social Education, April 1995, page 222

Other books by the same author:

The Wind Eagle and Other Abenaki Stories, 1984
Iroquois Stories, 1985
Keepers of the Earth, 1989
Hoop Snakes, Hide Behinds, and Side Hill Winders, 1991
Keepers of the Animals, 1992

Other books you might like:

Zitkala-Sa, *Old Indian Legends Retold by Zitkala-Sa,* 1921
This is a collection of memoirs and essays about the traditional Lakota culture and the adjustments to the real world.

Shirley Sterling, *My Name Is Seepeetza,* 1992
This fictional account, based on the life of the author,

recounts her life as a member of the interior Salish tribe. Forced to attend government schools, she is forbidden to reflect her own heritage.

Maria Campbell, *Halfbreed,* 1973
This is the moving account of Maria Campbell's life as a Metis or halfbreed, part Indian—part European.

Leslie Marmon Silko, *Storyteller,* 1981
This work is a mixed genre of poetry, fiction, and mythology.

John Bierhorst, *The Red Swan: Myths and Tales of the American Indians,* 1976
This book is a compilation of varied stories (creation, trickster, star husband, etc.) from forty Native American tribes.

Frederick Turner, *The Portable North American Indian Reader,* 1973
This anthology of myths, legends, poetry, fiction, and captivity tales, contains work by both Native American and non-Native writers.

Paula Gunn Allen, *Spider Woman's Granddaughters,* 1989
This is a beautiful collection of traditional tales interwoven with contemporary short stories having to do with the lives of Native American women.

1176

JOSEPH BRUCHAC, Native American, Abenaki

Iroquois Stories

(Freedom, CA: The Crossing Press, 1985)

Subject(s): Folk Tales; Animals
Age range(s): Grades 3 and Up
Time period(s): Indeterminate Past
Locale(s): United States

Summary: These traditional tales of the Iroquois people relate their respect for living things and how they see the world. These are wonderful stories to read aloud and children will be enthralled, charmed and entertained.

Other books you might like:

Margot Astrov, *The Winged Serpent,* 1946
This mixed genre is one of the best collections of oral stories and songs from a large cross-section of Native American cultures.

John Bierhorst, *The Sacred Path,* 1984
This mixed genre is a collection of traditional spells, prayers, and power songs from a variety of Native American tribes.

G.M. Mullet, *Spider Woman Stories,*
These Hopi Indian legends are collected from the 1880s.

Frederick Turner, *The Portable North American Indian Reader,* 1973
This anthology of myths, legends, poetry, fiction, and captivity tales, contains work by both Native American and non-Native writers.

Mourning Dove, *Coyote Stories,* 1933
These traditional stories are about Coyote, the trickster.

John Bierhorst, *The Red Swan: Myths and Tales of the American Indians,* 1976
This is a compilation of varied stories (creation, trickster, star husband, etc.) from forty Native Americn tribes.

1177

JOSEPH BRUCHAC, Native American, Abenaki

Return of the Sun

(Freedom, CA: The Crossing Press, 1990)

Subject(s): Folk Tales; Animals
Age range(s): Grades 3 and Up
Time period(s): Indeterminate Past

Summary: These traditional tales portray the lives of the Northeast Woodlands people and their respect for living things. They are full of humor and wisdom, equally as enlightening as *Aesop's Fables*, and more fun. They are wonderful stories to read aloud.

Other books you might like:
Luther Standing Bear, *Stories of the Sioux*, 1988
  Standing Bear grows up in the traditional buffalo hunting culture, and he brings to life the stories from his own past.
Zitkala-Sa, *Old Indian Legends Retold by Zitkala-Sa*, 1921
  This is a collection of memoirs and essays about the traditional Lakota culture and the adjustments to European encroachment.
Mourning Dove, *Coyote Stories*, 1933
  These traditional stories are about Coyote, the trickster.
Shonto Begay, *Ma'ii and Cousin Horned Toad*,
  Lazy, conniving Mai'i is hungry, and he goes to Horny Toad for a free lunch. He swallows his smaller cousin, but Horny Toad teaches him a lesson he won't forget.
Hasteen Klah, *The Myth and Prayers of the Great Star Chant, and the Myth of the Coyote Chant*, 1988
  This exquisite book is a compilation of important Navajo myths, songs, chants, and prayers, portraying the complexity of the philosophical and religious life of Navajo culture.
William Bright, *A Coyote Reader*, 1993
  These are traditional Coyote stories.
Herschel Talashoema, *Coyote & Little Turtle: Iisaw Niqw Yongosonhoya: A Traditional Hopi Tale*, 1994
  This excellent book for early readers is about Coyote and Little Turtle. It is written in both Hopi and English, with illustrations drawn by Hopi children.
John Bierhorst, *The Red Swan: Myths and Tales of the American Indians*, 1976
  This book is a compilation of varied stories (creation, trickster, star husband, etc.) from forty Native American tribes.
Frederick Turner, *The Portable North American Indian Reader*, 1973
  This anthology of myths, legends, poetry, fiction, and captivity tales, contains work by both Native American and non-Native writers.

1178

MARY BUFF, Caucasian
CONRAD BUFF, Co-Author, Caucasian

Hah-nee of the Cliff Dwellers

(Cambridge: Riverside Press, 1956)

Subject(s): Historical; Pre-Columbian History
Age range(s): Grades 4-6
Major character(s): Hah-nee, Child (young boy), Native American
Time period(s): Indeterminate Past (pre-Columbian history)
Locale(s): United States

Summary: This is a tale about a young boy of a cliff dwelling pueblo at a time of drought.

Other books you might like:
D'Arcy McNickle, *Runner in the Sun: A Story of Indian Maize*, 1954
  This middle school novel is about a young boy who leaves his Pueblo homeland to go south to Mexico to find salt for his tribe.
Frederick Turner, *The Portable North American Indian Reader*, 1973
  This anthology of myths, legends, poetry, fiction, and captivity tales, contains work by both Native American and non-Native writers.
Mourning Dove, *Coyote Stories*, 1933
  These are traditional Okanagan stories about Coyote, the trickster.
Shonto Begay, *Ma'ii and Cousin Horned Toad*,
  Ma'ii is hungry, and he goes to Horny Toad for a free lunch, eventually swallowing his smaller cousin, but that does not fare well for Ma'ii who learns his lesson in the end.
Hasteen Klah, *The Myth and Prayers of the Great Star Chant, and the Myth of the Coyote Chant*, 1988
  This exquisite book is a compilation of important Navajo myths, songs, chants, and prayers, that deal with the complex philosophical and religious life of Navajo culture.
William Bright, *A Coyote Reader*, 1993
  Traditional coyote stories
Herschel Talashoema, *Coyote & Little Turtle: Iisaw Niqw Yongosonhoya: A Traditional Hopi Tale*, 1994
  Here is an excellent book for early readers about Coyote and Little Turtle. It is written in both Hopi and English, with illustrations from Hopi children.
John Bierhorst, *The Red Swan: Myths and Tales of the American Indians*, 1976
  This book is a compilation of varied stories (creation, trickster, star husband, etc.) from forty Indian tribes.
Joseph Bruchac, *Iroquois Stories*, 1985
  This book recounts many of the traditional animal, adventure and monster tales of the Iroquois people.
Joseph Bruchac, *The Wind Eagle and Other Abenaki Stories*, 1984
  These are traditional tales of the Abenaki.
Joseph Bruchac, *Return of the Sun*, 1990
  Traditional tales of the Northeast Woodlands, full of humor and wisdom, equally as enlightening as Aesop's fables, and more fun.
Joseph Bruchac, *Flying with the Eagle, Racing with the Bear*, 1993
  These rite-of-passage stories come from various tribal peoples including the Wampanoag, Cherokee, Osage, Lakota and Tlingit.
Shirley Sterling, *My Name Is Seepeetza*, 1992
  Fictional account based on the life of the author, who as a member of the interior Salish tribe was forced to attend

government schools where she was forbidden to reflect anything of her own heritage.

1179

ANNE CAMERON, Caucasian

Dzelarhons

(Maderia Park: Harbour Publishing, 1986)

Subject(s): Animals; Folk Tales; Mythology
Age range(s): Grades 4-8
Time period(s): Indeterminate Past (mythic time)
Locale(s): British Columbia, Canada

Summary: Traditional stories of the Northwest Coast, retold for children by British Columbia writer, Anne Cameron. Includes ''Raven and Snipe,'' ''Raven Goes Berrypicking,'' ''Orca's Child,'' ''Muddlehead,'' ''The Bearded Woman,'' ''Ta-Naz Finds Happiness,'' ''Lazy Boy'' and ''Dzelarhons.''

Other books you might like:

Joseph Bruchac, *Return of the Sun*, 1990
  Traditional tales of the Northeast Woodlands, full of humor and wisdom, equally as enlightening as Aesop's fables, and more fun.

Joseph Bruchac, *Flying with the Eagle, Racing with the Bear*, 1993
  These rite-of-passage stories come from various tribal peoples including the Wampanoag, Cherokee, Osage, Lakota and Tlingit.

Shonto Begay, *Ma'ii and Cousin Horned Toad*,
  Lazy, conniving, Ma'ii is hungry and goes to Horny Toad for a free lunch. He swallows his smaller cousin, but Horny Toad teaches him a lesson he won't forget.

Mourning Dove, *Coyote Stories*, 1933
  These are traditional Okanagan stories about Coyote, the trickster.

William Bright, *A Coyote Reader*, 1993
  This is a collection of trickster stories from many tribes, with chapters divided according to the various attributes of Coyote, rather than geographically.

Herschel Talashoema, *Coyote & Little Turtle: Iisaw Niqw Yongosonhoya: A Traditional Hopi Tale*, 1994
  This is an excellent book for early readers about Coyote and Little Turtle. It is written in both Hopi and English, with illustrations from Hopi children.

Frederick Turner, *The Portable North American Indian Reader*, 1973
  This anthology of myths, legends, poetry, fiction, and captivity tales, contains work by both Native American and non-Native writers.

Michael Arvaarluk Kusugak, *A Promise Is a Promise*, 1988
  Qallupilluq are Inuit monsters who grab children when they come too near the cracks in the ice. This is the story of Allashua, who comes face to face with these sea monsters.

Joseph Bruchac, *The Girl Who Married the Moon*, 1994
  These are mostly traditional tales from a variety of North American tribes about women: initiation ceremonies, shape changing stories, and others.

Charlie Craigan, *How the Robin Got Its Red Breast*, 1993
  A traditional tale redone for children. Excellent illustra-

tions by Charlie Craigan, in the traditional Northwest Coast style.

Charlie Craigan, *Mayuk: The Grizzly Bear*, 1993
  Children's book of a traditional Northwest Coast tale.

1180

MARIA CAMPBELL, Native American, Cree

Halfbreed

(Lincoln: University of Nebraska Press, 1973)

Subject(s): Autobiography; Racism
Age range(s): Grades 8-Adult
Time period(s): 1940S
Locale(s): Saskatchewan, Canada

Summary: This is the moving account of Maria Campbell's life as a Metis or halfbreed, part Indian—part European. She tells the story of her tremendous struggle for survival and how she and her family endure terrible racist attitudes.

About this book: This is an aspect of North American history to which students are usually not exposed. Yet, the idea of the ''halfbreed,'' of one being caught between two cultures, is one of the dominant themes of Native American Literature.

Other books you might like:

Michael Dorris, *A Yellow Raft in Blue Water*, 1987
  This is one of the few novels that deals with ''mixed blood'' people who are part African-American and part Native American.

Shirley Sterling, *My Name Is Seepeetza*, 1992
  This fictional account, based on the life of the author, recounts her life as a member of the interior Salish tribe. Forced to attend government schools, she is forbidden to reflect her own heritage.

D'Arcy McNickle, *The Surrounded*, 1936
  A fiddle player returns to his reservation for a visit after years in the White world. He is drawn into its complexities so far that he knows he can never go back to the White world.

1181

TOM CHARGING EAGLE, Native American, Lakota (Sioux)
RON ZEILINGER, Illustrator

Black Hills: Sacred Hills

(Chamberlain, SD: Tipi Press, 1992)

Subject(s): Historical; Religion
Age range(s): Grades 4-6
Time period(s): 19th century; 20th century
Locale(s): South Dakota

Summary: Charging Eagle makes the case for the rightful return of the Black Hills to the Indian people in this book geared to children. The author often draws parallels between Lakota Religion and Christianity as a way of explaining the reason many sites in the Black Hills are considered ''sacred.''

About this book: The black and white photos by Zeilinger lend a solemnity to this book, which is a plea for justice.

Other books you might like:

Charles A. Eastman, *Old Indian Days*, 1907
    Autobiography of a Lakota Sioux man.
Luther Standing Bear, *Stories of the Sioux*, 1988
    Standing Bear grew up in the traditional buffalo hunting culture, and he brings to life the stories from his own past.
Zitkala-Sa, *Old Indian Legends Retold by Zitkala-Sa*, 1921
    These stories depict Zitkala-Sa's childhood in the traditional Lakota culture and the difficulties she faced while attending school and college in a world where she was perceived as a ''savage.''

1182

ANN NOLAN CLARK, Caucasian

Little Navajo Bluebird

(New York: Viking, 1943)

Subject(s): Indians of North America; Childhood
Age range(s): Grades 4-6
Major character(s): Doli Wind, Child (girl), Native American (Navajo)
Time period(s): 1940s
Locale(s): New Mexico

Summary: This chapter book chronicles the daily life of a Navajo girl in the 1940's. It is a gentle book, and well-written, weaving in the traditional ceremonies of Navajo Culture with family relationships and everyday life.

Other books by the same author:

In My Mother's House, 1941
Magic Money
Looking-for-Something
Secret of the Andes, 1952
Blue Canyon Horse
Third Monkey

Other books you might like:

Marilyne Virginia Mabery, *Right After Sundown: Teaching Stories of the Navajo*, 1991
    These are traditional Navajo stories of the beginning of the world, with excellent illustrations by Navajo artist Raymond J. Johnson.
Margot Astrov, *The Winged Serpent*, 1946
    This is one of the best collections of oral stories and songs from a large cross-section of Indian cultures.
Broderick H. Johnson, *Stories of Traditional Navajo Life and Culture*, 1977
    Interviews of 22 Navajo men and women from tape-recorded meetings.
Ruth Roessel, *Navajo Stories of the Long Walk Period*, 1973
    In this intriguing collection, Navajo people recount stories of the Long Walk period as they have been handed down to them through their families.
Shonto Begay, *Ma'ii and Cousin Horned Toad*, 1992
    Lazy, conniving Ma'ii is hungry, and he goes to Horny Toad for a free lunch. He swallows his smaller cousin, but Horny Toad teaches him a lesson he won't forget.
Hasteen Klah, *The Myth and Prayers of the Great Star Chant, and the Myth of the Coyote Chant*, 1988
    This exquisite book is a compilation of important Navajo

myths, songs, chants, and prayers, that deal with the complex philosophical and religious life of Navajo culture.
Jean Craighead George, *The Talking Earth*, 1983
    A young Seminole girl begins to doubt the beliefs of the elders until she goes into the Everglades, where she begins to understand the importance of her tribal teachings and the world of nature.
Jay Leech, *Moon of the Big-Dog*, 1980
    Three young Sioux boys go on a journey in which they capture the first horses for their tribe, and earn a new name for their Sioux band: Brule. Co-authored by Zane Spencer and illustrated by M. Funai.
Virginia Driving Hawk Sneve, *The Chichi Hoohoo Bogeyman*, 1975
    Three Sioux Indian girls on a visit to their grandparents' house, encounter a weird creature they're sure is the bogeyman.
Virginia Driving Hawk Sneve, *High Elk's Treasure*, 1972
    This novel for middle school readers is about Joe High Elk who longs to bring back the strain of wild mustangs that his famous ancestor bred many years before. Illustrations by Oren Lyons.
Shirley Sterling, *My Name Is Seepeetza*, 1992
    Fictional account based on the life of the author, who as a member of the interior Salish tribe is forced to attend government schools where she is forbidden to reflect anything of her own heritage.

1183

ROBERT J. CONLEY, Native American, Cherokee

Mountain Windsong

(Norman: Univ. of Oklahoma Press, 1992)

Subject(s): Indians of North America; Historical; Interpersonal Relations
Age range(s): Adult
Major character(s): Oconeechee, Young Woman, Native American (Cherokee); Waguli, Warrior, Native American (Cherokee)
Time period(s): 1830s
Locale(s): United States

Summary: With the backdrop of the Cherokee's Trail of Tears, this tragic story tells of the love of two people, separated by desperation and reunited by their commitment to one another. Forced to leave their homeland by President Jackson's Indian removal policy, Oconeechee escapes to the mountains while Waguli journeys with the others to the new Cherokee reservation land. The two spend years searching for one another before they are finally reunited.

Where it's reviewed:

Western American Literature, November 1993, page 284
Western Historical Quarterly, August 1993, page 443
World Literature Today, Autumn 1993, page 867

Other books you might like:

Yellow Bird, *Life and Adventures of Joaquin Murieta*, 1955
    In this first novel written by a Native American, Murieta, who is ''mixed-blood,'' Cherokee and White, becomes a criminal after being driven off his land by greedy Whites.

Marilou Awiakta, *Selu: Seeking the Corn-Mother's Wisdom*, 1993

    The Cherokee wisdom of sharing and cooperation is here applied to the larger issue of peoples and governments cooperating to share the earth's resources.

Wilma Mankiller, *Mankiller: A Chief and Her People*, 1993

    Wilma Mankiller, Chief of the Cherokees, recounts her life and the history of her people.

1184

ROBERT J. CONLEY, Native American, Cherokee

The Witch of Goingsnake and Other Stories

(Norman: University of Oklahoma Press, 1988)

Subject(s): Traditional Stories
Age range(s): Grades 7 and Up
Time period(s): Indeterminate

Summary: These short stories of the Cherokee are not only remakes of traditional tales, but contain a few new stories as well.

Awards the book has won:
Spur Award for Short Fiction, 1988

Other books by the same author:
The Actor, 1987
Back to Malachi, 1986
Colfax, 1989
Go-Ahead Rider, 1990
Ned Christie's War, 1991

Other books you might like:
Leslie Marmon Silko, *Storyteller*, 1981

    This work is a mixed genre of poetry, fiction, and mythology.

W.P. Kinsella, *Moccasin Telegraph*, 1984

    Life on the Ermineskin Reserve in Canada, as revealed by Silas Ermineskin himself, is full of both comedy and tragedy.

James Northrup, *Walking the Rez Road*, 1993

    Luke Warmwater is a Vietnam vet who is down on his luck, but he, like most of his reservation cohorts, is a survivor in the trickster fashion.

Sherman Alexie, *The Lone Ranger and Tonto Fist Fight in Heaven*, 1993

    This wonderful short fiction is about the ups and downs of reservation life.

Louise Erdrich, *Love Medicine*, 1984

    Married to Marie, Nector is nevertheless fatefully drawn to Lulu. When his grandson prepares a love medicine to win him back to his grandmother, he uses the wrong ingredients and kills Nector instead.

Craig Lesley, *Talking Leaves*, 1991

    This book is an excellent collection of short stories by thirty-five contemporary Native American writers including, among others, Erdrich, Dorris, Momaday, Hogan, and Whiteman.

Paula Gunn Allen, *Spider Woman's Granddaughters*, 1989

    This is a beautiful collection of traditional tales interwoven with contemporary short stories having to do with the lives of Native American women.

Paula Gunn Allen, *Voice of the Turtle*, 1994

    Edited by the well known writer and scholar Paula Gunn Allen, this book is an anthology of literature written by American Indian people from 1900 to 1970.

Lee Miller, *From the Heart: Voices of the American Indian*, 1995

    This is a collection of orations, speeches, and testimony by more than 250 Indian people that presents a radical alternative to traditionally taught American history.

Clifford E. Trafzer, *Blue Dawn, Red Earth: New Native American Storytellers*, 1996

    This is a collection of short stories by 30 new Native American writers, such as Lorne Simon, Jim Barnes, Annie Hansen and Richard Van Camp.

1185

GEORGE COPWAY (Kah-ge-ga-bowh)

The Life, History, and Travels of Kah-ge-ga-bowh

(Albany: Weed & Parsons, 1847)

Subject(s): Men; Autobiography; Cultural Conflict
Age range(s): Grades 10-Adult
Time period(s): 19th century; 20th century (1818-1947)
Locale(s): Minnesota

Summary: Kah-ge-ga-gah-bowh, born in 1818, published this story of his life in 1847 and it contains sections on Ojibway legends, history, wars, and general culture. The book also chronicles the author's ''transformation'' from a person of Ojibway culture to a person schooled in European thought. If one reads between the lines, one can sense the pain of being caught between two cultures and the author's deep feelings for his people and their traditions.

Other books you might like:
Francis La Flesche, *The Middle Five: Indian Schoolboys of the Omaha Tribe*, 1963

    This book details the life of La Flesche and his friends in mission school in Oklahoma.

William Jones, *Ojibway Texts*, 1917

    This work is about the Ojibway.

Gerald Vizenor, *The People Named the Chippewa: Narrative Histories*, 1984

    This mixed genre anthology contains essays, interviews, history, mythology and stories.

John Joseph Mathews, *Talking to the Moon*, 1945

    Mathews relates the cycle of his life from his childhood in Oklahoma through his WWI military stint, college, marriage and his journey back to his homeland.

Maude Kegg, *Portage Lake: Memories of an Ojibwe Childhood*, 1991

    In these stories, printed in both English and Anishinaabe, Kegg relates the cultural wisdom of her many years, describing important facets of Ojibway life.

1186

LEONARD CROW DOG, Native American, Lakota (Sioux)
RICHARD ERDOES, Co-Author

Crow Dog
(New York: Harper Perennial, 1995)

Subject(s): Autobiography; History
Age range(s): Grades 10-Adult
Time period(s): 20th century (1940s-1990s)
Locale(s): South Dakota

Summary: In this as-told-to book, medicine man Leonard Crow Dog tells his story and the story of his people to Richard Erdoes. The book deals with traditional religion and healing practices of the Lakotas as well as issues of politics and social philosophy among the Indians today.

Where it's reviewed:
Kirkus Reviews, March 1, 1995, page 285
Library Journal, April 1, 1995, page 102
Publishers Weekly, March 13, 1995, page 56

Other books you might like:
Charles A. Eastman, *From the Deep Woods to Civilization*, 1916
> This autobiography is about Sioux man who leaves the traditional buffalo hunting culture to become a medical doctor.
Luther Standing Bear, *Stories of the Sioux*, 1988
> These are early life stories of a traditional Lakota (Sioux) man.
Black Elk, *Black Elk Speaks*, 1932
> This is the life story of a Holy man of the Sioux.

1187

MARY CROW DOG, Native American, Lakota (Sioux)
RICHARD ERDOES, Co-Author, Caucasian

Lakota Woman
(New York: Harper Perennial, 1990)

Subject(s): Biography; Indian Reservations; Social Conditions
Age range(s): Grades 10-Adult
Time period(s): 20th century (1970s-1990)
Locale(s): South Dakota

Summary: Mary Crow Dog is the young wife of traditional medicine man, Leonard Crow Dog. This book chronicles her life in the Crow Dog camp as well as her participation, with other AIM members, in the occupation of Wounded Knee in the 1970s.

About this book: The occupation of Wounded Knee in the 1970s was the result of tremendous turmoil between various factions on the Pine Ridge reservation, exacerbated by the U.S. government's aggressive policies with the traditionalists on the Sioux reservations.

Where it's reviewed:
Belles Lettres, Summer 1991, page 5
Kliatt, January 1992, page 28
Village Voice Literary Supplement, November 1991, page 27

Other books by the same author:
Ohitika Woman, 1993

Other books you might like:
Wilma Mankiller, *Mankiller: A Chief and Her People*, 1993
> With Michael Wallis, Chief Mankiller tells her story and the story of her people, the Cherokee.
Mark St. Pierre, *The Spiritual Power and Legacy of American Plains Indian Women*,
> This book looks at the lives of Plains Indian women and the myths and culture surrounding them.
Brian Swann, *I Tell You Now*, 1989
> This is an excellent collection of autobiographical essays by eighteen contemporary American Indian writers co-authored with Arnold Krupat.
Paula Gunn Allen, *The Sacred Hoop: Recovering the Feminine in American Indian Traditions*, 1986
> This book is an excellent collection of essays that uncovers the essential role of women in traditional and contemporary Indian life.
Luther Standing Bear, *Stories of the Sioux*, 1988
> Standing Bear grew up in the traditional buffalo hunting culture of the Sioux, and he brings to life the stories from his own past.
Zitkala-Sa, *Old Indian Legends Retold by Zitkala-Sa*, 1921
> This is the story of Zitkala-Sa, a Loakota woman who spends her childhood in the traditional culture but who eventually leaves for the Indian boarding schools out East.
Black Elk, *Black Elk Speaks*, 1932
> This is the life story of the Holy Man of the Sioux, co-authored with John G. Neihardt.
Paula Gunn Allen, *Spider Woman's Granddaughters*, 1989
> This is a beautiful collection of traditional tales interwoven with contemporary stories having to do with the lives of Native American women.

1188

CHRISTINE CROWL, Author/Illustrator

The Hunter and the Woodpecker: An Indian Legend
(Chamberlain, SD: Tipi Press, 1976)

Subject(s): Folk Tales; Love
Age range(s): Grades 2-4
Major character(s): Two Eagles, Warrior, Native American (Lakota); Wind Dancer, Young Woman, Native American (Lakota)
Time period(s): Indeterminate Past (mythic time)
Locale(s): South Dakota

Summary: The Elk magic is the magic of love, and Two Eagles, wanting to win over Wind Dancer, searches for the medicine that will make the girl fall in love with him.

Other books by the same author:
The White Buffalo Woman: An Indian Legend, 1976 (mythology)

Other books you might like:
Luther Standing Bear, *Stories of the Sioux*, 1988
> Standing Bear grew up in the traditional buffalo hunting culture, and he brings to life the stories from his own past.

Joseph Bruchac, *Return of the Sun*, 1990
 Traditional tales of the Northeast Woodlands, full of humor and wisdom, equally as enlightening as Aesop's fables, and more fun.
Joseph Bruchac, *Flying with the Eagle, Racing with the Bear*, 1993
 These rite-of-passage stories come from various tribal peoples including the Wampanoag, Cherokee, Osage, Lakota and Tlingit.
Zitkala-Sa, *Old Indian Legends Retold by Zitkala-Sa*, 1921
 These stories depict Zitkala-Sa's childhood in the traditional Lakota culture and the difficulties she faced while attending school and college in a world where she was perceived as a ''savage.''
John Bierhorst, *The Red Swan: Myths and Tales of the American Indians*, 1976
 This book is a compilation of varied stories (creation, trickster, star husband, etc.) from forty Indian tribes, edited by Bierhorst.
Frederick Turner, *The Portable North American Indian Reader*, 1973
 This anthology of myths, legends, poetry, fiction, and captivity tales, contains work by both Native American and non-Native writers.

1189

CHRISTINE CROWL, Author/Illustrator

The White Buffalo Woman: An Indian Legend

(Chamberlain, SD: Tipi Press, 1976)

Subject(s): Religion
Age range(s): Grades 2-4
Major character(s): Strong Bow, Warrior, Native American (Lakota); White Buffalo Calf Maiden, Deity (bringer of the sacred pipe), Native American (Lakota)
Time period(s): Indeterminate Past (mythic time)
Locale(s): South Dakota

Summary: The White Buffalo Calf Maiden, one of the important dieties in Lakota culture, comes to the Lakota people in mythic time to bring them the sacred pipe, and this is the story of her appearance on earth.

Other books by the same author:
The Hunter and the Woodpecker: An Indian Legend, 1976

Other books you might like:
Luther Standing Bear, *Stories of the Sioux*, 1988
 Standing Bear grew up in the traditional buffalo hunting culture, and he brings to life the stories from his own past.
Joseph Bruchac, *Return of the Sun*, 1990
 Traditional tales of the Northeast Woodlands, full of humor and wisdom, equally as enlightening as Aesop's fables, and more fun.
Joseph Bruchac, *Flying with the Eagle, Racing with the Bear*, 1993
 These rite-of-passage stories come from various tribal peoples including the Wampanoag, Cherokee, Osage, Lakota and Tlingit.

Zitkala-Sa, *Old Indian Legends Retold by Zitkala-Sa*, 1921
 These stories depict Zitkala-Sa's childhood in the traditinal Lakota culture and the difficulties she faced while attending school and college in a world where she was perceived as a ''savage.''
John Bierhorst, *The Red Swan: Myths and Tales of the American Indians*, 1976
 This book is a compilation of varied stories (creation, trickster, star husband, etc.) from forty Indian tribes.
Frederick Turner, *The Portable North American Indian Reader*, 1973
 This anthology of myths, legends, poetry, fiction, and captivity tales, contains work by both Native American and non-Native writers.

1190

JULIE CRUKSHANK, Caucasian
ANGELA SIDNEY, Co-Author, Native American, Athapaskan and Tlingit
KITTY SMITH, Co-Author, Native American, Athapaskan and Tlingit
ANNIE NED, Co-Author, Native American, Athapaskan and Tlingit

Life Lived like a Story: Life Stories of Three Yukon Native Elders

(Lincoln: University of Nebraska Press, 1990)

Subject(s): Folklore; Women
Age range(s): Grades 11-Adult
Time period(s): 19th century; 20th century (1890s-1990s)
Locale(s): Yukon Territory, Canada

Summary: This as-told-to-book chronicles the lives of three Yukon women whose family relationships and environment shape their stories.

Where it's reviewed:
Journal of American Fiction, Summer 1993, page 365

Other books you might like:
Anna Moore Shaw, *A Pima Past*, 1974
 Anna Moore Shaw, born in a traditional Pima brush house and educated in the white world, tells this fascinating autobiography of her life.
Charles A. Eastman, *From the Deep Woods to Civilization*, 1916
 The autobiography of Eastman who grows up in the traditional buffalo culture of the Lakota but pursues on education in the White man's world.
N. Scott Momaday, *The Names: A Memoir*, 1976
 This is an autobiographical work.
Leslie Marmon Silko, *Storyteller*, 1981
 This work is a mixed genre of poetry, fiction, and mythology.
James Sewid, *Guests Never Leave Hungry: The Autobiography of James Sewid, a Kwakuitl Indian*, 1969
 This is the life story of James Sewid, a Kwakiutl Indian.
Jane Holden Kelley, *Contemporary Life Histories*, 1978
 This as-told-to-book chronicles the lives of four Yaqui women. The author describes many aspects of Yaqui culture in the introduction.

1191

ELLA CARA DELORIA, Native American, Lakota (Sioux)

Waterlily

(Lincoln: University of Nebraska Press, 1988)

Subject(s): Women; Growing Up; Parent and Child
Age range(s): Grades 10-Adult
Major character(s): Waterlily, Native American, Child (young girl)
Time period(s): 19th century
Locale(s): South Dakota

Summary: This novel follows the story of Waterlily from birth, beginning with her mother, Blue Bird's story, and continuing throughout Waterlilly's life.

About this book: This book details the life of the Sioux before contact with Europeans. It is especially interesting in the way it shows a woman's life in the traditional buffalo hunting culture, and in the way it shows the importance of kinship relationships.

Other books you might like:

Charles A. Eastman, *From the Deep Woods to Civilization*, 1916
    The autobiography of Charles A. Eastman, who grows up in the traditional buffalo culture of the Lakota (Sioux) but pursues an education in the White man's world. Introduction by Raymond Wilson.
Charles A. Eastman, *Wigwam Evenings: Sioux Folktales Retold*, 1909
    Folktales, Mythology. Cowritten with Eastmans' wife, Elaine Goodale Eastman
Charles A. Eastman, *Smoky Day's Wigwam Evenings: Indian Stories Retold*, 1910
    Folktales, Mythology. Cowritten with Eastmans' wife, Elaine Goodale Eastman
Charles A. Eastman, *Indian Boyhood*, 1910
    This is the story of Eastman's life as a young boy (until the age of 15) living the traditional Plains Indian life.
Luther Standing Bear, *Stories of the Sioux*, 1988
    Standing Bear grew up in the traditional buffalo hunting culture, and he brings to life the stories from his own past.
Zitkala-Sa, *Old Indian Legends Retold by Zitkala-Sa*, 1921
    These stories depict Zitkala-Sa's childhood in the traditional Lakota culture and the difficulties she faced while attending school and college in a world where she was perceived as a ''savage.''

1192

VINE DELORIA JR., Native American, Lakota (Sioux)

Custer Died for Your Sins: An Indian Manifesto

(Norman, OK: U. of Oklahoma Press, 1969, 1988)

Subject(s): Indians of North America; Politics; History
Age range(s): Grades 10-Adult
Time period(s): 1960s (1969)
Locale(s): United States

Summary: This book rocked the Indian and White worlds when it was first published, for it attacks the stereotypical myths and chronicles the mistreatment and broken treaties that Indian people have lived with for centuries. It is a manifesto that is essential reading for those who want to understand the history that still plagues contemporary Native American people, an issue that is so prevalant in their fiction. It is still relevant—thirty years after its release.

Where it's reviewed:
Wilson Library Bulletin, Issue I, 1992, page 33

Other books by the same author:
We Talk, You Listen: New Tribes, New Turf, 1970 (essays)

Other books you might like:

Gerald Vizenor, *Earthdivers: Tribal Narratives on Mixed Descent*, 1981
    In this collection of short stories Vizenor creates trickster figures to poke fun at and make shrewd political commentary on America, reservation life, and just about everything else.
Robert Allen Warrior, *Tribal Secrets*, 1995
    This Osage writer and philosopher deals with the traditions of American Indian intellectualism.
Arlene Hirschfelder, *Native Heritage*, 1995
    This book is a collection of personal accounts by American Indian people from 1790 through the present.
Peter Nabokov, *Native American Testimony*, 1991
    This is a mixed genre anthology containing oral stories, speeches, prophecies, and essays.
Michael Dorris, *Native Americans: 500 Years After*, 1975
    This work contains photos and history of Native Americans across the continent.
Paula Gunn Allen, *The Sacred Hoop: Recovering the Feminine in American Indian Traditions*, 1986
    This book is an excellent collection of essays that uncovers the essential role of women in traditional and contemporary Indian life.

1193

VINE DELORIA JR., Native American, Lakota (Sioux)

God Is Red

(New York: Delta, 1973)

Subject(s): Religion; Cultures and Customs
Age range(s): Grades 11-Adult
Time period(s): 20th century
Locale(s): United States

Summary: DeLoria tackles religious issues, arguing for Native religious beliefs, while recounting the history of acculturation and missionizing that have plagued Indian people for centuries.

Other books by the same author:
Custer Died for Your Sins: An Indian Manifesto, 1969 (nonfiction)
We Talk, You Listen: New Tribes, New Turf, 1970 (essays)

Other books you might like:
Simon J. Ortiz, *The People Shall Continue*, 1977
    Here is an invaluable history of Native Americans for

younger readers written from their point of view by the highly respected poet and fiction writer, Simon Ortiz.

Gerald Vizenor, *Earthdivers: Tribal Narratives on Mixed Descent*, 1981

In this collection of short stories Vizenor creates trickster figures to poke fun at and make shrewd political commentary on America, reservation life, and just about everything else.

Peter Nabokov, *Native American Testimony*, 1991

Anthology, mixed genre: oral stories, speeches, prophecies, and essays.

Brian Swann, *I Tell You Now*, 1989

This is an excellent collection of autobiographical essays by eighteen contemporary American Indian writers. Edited with Arnold Krupat.

Will Rogers, *"How To Be Funny" & Other Writings of Will Rogers*, 1983

A collection of writings by one of America's best known humorists and political comentators.

T.C. McLuhan, *Touch the Earth*, 1971

This is collection of speeches and statements from a wide assortment of Indian people.

1194

VINE DELORIA JR., Native American, Lakota (Sioux)

Red Earth, White Lies: Native Americans and the Myth of Scientific Fact

(New York: Scribner, 1995)

Subject(s): Politics; History; Philosophy
Age range(s): Adult
Time period(s): 1990s
Locale(s): United States

Summary: DeLoria critiques Western science and argues for the validity of tribal oral histories and sacred traditions. He challenges, among other things, science's interpretation of the evolution and migration of man across the Bering Strait (which places Indians on the continent much later than their oral traditions allow).

Other books by the same author:
We Talk, You Listen: New Tribes, New Turf, 1970 (non fiction)
God Is Red, 1973
Custer Died for Your Sins: An Indian Manifesto, 1969

Other books you might like:
Robert Allen Warrior, *Tribal Secrets*, 1995
This Osage writer and philosopher deals with the traditions of American Indian intellectualism.
Michael Dorris, *Native Americans: 500 Years After*, 1975
Photos and history of Native Americans across the continent, from pre-Columbian times to the present.
Arlene Hirschfelder, *Native Heritage*, 1995
This book is a collection of personal accounts by American Indian people from 1790 through the present.
Peter Nabokov, *Native American Testimony*, 1991
This mixed genre anthology contains oral stories, speeches, prophecies, and essays.

Will Rogers, *"How to be Funny" & Other Writings of Will Rogers*, 1983

A collection of writings by one of America's best known humorists and political commentators.

Gerald Vizenor, *Earthdivers: Tribal Narratives on Mixed Descent*, 1981

In this collection of short stories Vizenor creates trickster figures to poke fun at and make shrewd political commentary on America, reservation life, and just about everything else.

Brian Swann, *I Tell You Now*, 1989

This is an excellent collection of autobiographical essays by eighteen contemporary American Indian writers. Coauthored with Arnold Krupat.

T.C. McLuhan, *Touch the Earth*, 1971

This collection of speeches and statements is from a wide assortment of Indian people.

1195

VINE DELORIA JR., Native American, Lakota (Sioux)

We Talk, You Listen: New Tribes, New Turf

(New York: Macmillan 1970)

Subject(s): Cultures and Customs; Minorities; Cultural Conflict
Age range(s): Grades 11-Adult
Time period(s): 20th century
Locale(s): United States

Summary: DeLoria discusses various gaps in communication, which stem from differing world-views, between Indian people and others in American society.

Other books by the same author:
God Is Red, 1973
Custer Died for Your Sins: An Indian Manifesto, 1969

Other books you might like:
Simon J. Ortiz, *The People Shall Continue*, 1977
Here is an invaluable history of Native Americans for younger readers written from their point of view by the highly respected poet and fiction writer, Simon
Gerald Vizenor, *Earthdivers: Tribal Narratives on Mixed Descent*, 1981
In this collection of short stories Vizenor creates trickster figures to poke fun at and make shrewd political commentary on America, reservation life, and just about everything else.
Peter Nabokov, *Native American Testimony*, 1991
Anthology, mixed genre: oral stories, speeches, prophecies, and essays.
Brian Swann, *I Tell You Now*, 1989
This is an excellent collection of autobiographical essays by eighteen contemporary American Indian writers. Coauthored with Arnold Krupat.
T.C. McLuhan, *Touch the Earth*, 1971
This is collection of speeches and statements from a wide assortment of Indian people.
Will Rogers, *"How To Be Funny" & Other Writings of Will Rogers*, 1983

A collection of writings by one of America's best known humorists and political commentators.

1196

MICHAEL DORRIS, Native American, Modoc

The Broken Cord: A Family's On-Going Struggle with Fetal Alcohol Syndrome
(New York: Harper & Row, 1989)

Subject(s): Adoption; Alcoholism; Family Relations
Age range(s): Adult
Time period(s): 20th century
Locale(s): United States

Summary: Michael Dorris becomes one of the first unmarried men in America to adopt a child, a Sioux boy named Adam, who suffers from Fetal Alcohol Syndrome. This book documents the struggles Adam faces to cope with this affliction.

Where it's reviewed:
Reference Services Review, Issue 2, 1995, page 83
Christian Century, April 27, 1994, page 435
Harvard Journal of Asiatic Studies, Issue 2, 1993, page 59

Other books by the same author:
Morning Girl, 1992
A Yellow Raft in Blue Water, 1987
Paper Trail: Essays, 1994
Rooms in the House of Stone, 1993 (nonfiction)
Working Men, 1993 (short fiction)

Other books you might like:
Brian Maracle, *Crazywater: Native Voices on Addiction and Recovery*, 1994
  In a series of interviews Maracle brings to light the root causes of the alcoholism that has plagued so many Indian people. These stories, told in the first-person, are haunting and frank.
Brian Swann, *I Tell You Now*, 1989
  This is an excellent collection of autobiographical essays by eighteen contemporary American Indian writers, co-edited with Brian Swann.
Janet Campbell Hale, *The Jailing of Cecelia Capture*, 1985
  This novel is about an Indian woman in her thirties, separated from her husband and two kids, attending law school and fighting a terrible battle with alcoholism.
James Welch, *Winter in the Blood*, 1974
  A man is caught in the clutches of alcoholism and tries to discover the truth about his family.

1197

MICHAEL DORRIS, Native American, Modoc

Guests
(New York: Hyperion, 1994)

Subject(s): Indians of North America; Holidays
Age range(s): Grades 3-6
Major character(s): Moss, Child (boy), Native American (Algonquin); Trouble, Child (girl), Native American (Algonquin)
Time period(s): 17th century

Summary: Moss and Trouble, an Alqonquin boy and girl, are not happy that their tribe has asked the Pilgrims to come to their celebration at Thanksgiving time.

About this book: An interesting look from the other side of the Thanksgiving tradition.

Where it's reviewed:
Booklist, October 1, 1994, page 326
Los Angeles Times Book Review, October 30, 1994, page 8
New York Times Book Review, January 29, 1995, page 20
Children's Book Review Service, December 1994, page 45
Horn Book Guide, Spring 1995, page 75

Other books you might like:
Joseph Bruchac, *Iroquois Stories*, 1985
  These are traditional tales of the Iroquois people.
Joseph Bruchac, *The Wind Eagle and Other Abenaki Stories*, 1984
  These are traditional tales of the Abenaki people.
Joseph Bruchac, *Return of the Sun*, 1990
  These are traditional tales of the Northeast Woodlands people.
Joseph Bruchac, *Flying with the Eagle, Racing with the Bear*, 1993
  These are Rite of Passage stories from many tribal people.
Linda Yamane, *When the World Ended, How Hummingbird Got Fire, How People Were Made: Rumsien Ohlone Stories*, 1995
  These three stories of the Rumsien Ohlone people of California deal with creation and how people are made.
Virginia Driving Hawk Sneve, *The Chichi Hoohoo Bogeyman*, 1975
  This fictional work relates three Native American girls encountering a strange creature.

1198

MICHAEL DORRIS, Native American, Modoc

Morning Girl
(New York: Hyperion, 1992)

Subject(s): Indians of the West Indies; Discovery and Exploration
Age range(s): Grades 5-7
Major character(s): Morning Girl, Child (girl), Arawak; Star Boy, Child (boy), Arawak
Time period(s): Indeterminate Past (pre-Columbian)
Locale(s): United States

Summary: A young girl and her brother, alive in the time before Christopher Columbus, must deal with the coming of the Whites to their village. In alternating voices, the two tell of how their close-knit community changes after the coming of the European strangers. This book is an interesting look at the possible lifestyles of Indian people in pre-Columbian America.

Where it's reviewed:
Kliatt, November 1994, page 6
New Advocate, Spring 1995, page 125
New York Times Book Review, November 8, 1992, page 33

Other books you might like:

Shirley Sterling, *My Name Is Seepeetza*, 1992
This fictional account, based on the life of the author, details her life as a member of the interior Salish tribe. Forced to attend government schools, she is forbidden to reflect her own heritage.

Maria Campbell, *Halfbreed*, 1973
This is the moving account of Maria Campbell's life as a Metis or halfbreed, part Indian—part European.

1199

MICHAEL DORRIS, Native American, Modoc
JOSEPH C. FARBER, Illustrator

Native Americans: 500 Years After

(New York: Thomas Y. Crowell Co., 1975)

Subject(s): Photography; History
Age range(s): Grades 6 and Up
Time period(s): 1970s
Locale(s): United States

Summary: This book of photographs documents the lives of Native Americans across North America. The text gives the readers a history from the Native American point of view. The telling black and white photos capture something of the Native American world today.

Other books by the same author:
Working Men, 1993 (short fiction)
A Yellow Raft in Blue Water, 1987
The Broken Cord: A Family's On-Going Struggle with Fetal Alcohol Syndrome, 1989. (nonfiction)
Paper Trail: Essays, 1994
Rooms in the House of Stone, 1993 (nonfiction)

Other books you might like:
Charles Brill, *Red Lake Nation: Portraits of Ojibway Life*, 1992
This book is primarily a photographical essay of the Ojibway people of Red Lake but it is interspersed with observations by Brill and portions of interviews that he conducted with the Red Lake people.

Simon J. Ortiz, *The People Shall Continue*, 1977
Here is an invaluable history of Native Americans for younger readers, written from their point of view, by the highly respected poet and fiction writer, Simon Ortiz.

1200

MICHAEL DORRIS, Native American, Modoc

Working Men

(New York: Henry Holt and Co, 1993)

Subject(s): Indians of North America; Short Stories
Age range(s): Adult
Time period(s): 1990s
Locale(s): United States

Summary: Michael Dorris is a sensitive chronicler of the human condition. These fourteen stories open a window into the everyday lives of working class men and women from all

walks of life. Rich with revealing detail, his observations transform the commonplace into the lyrical.

Where it's reviewed:
American Book Review, December 1994, page 19
Bloomsbury Review, May 1995, page 19
Studies in Short Fiction, Winter 1995, page 99
Times Literary Supplement, December 2, 1994, page 22

Other books by the same author:
The Broken Cord: A Family's On-Going Struggle with Fetal Alcohol Syndrome, 1989 (nonfiction)
Paper Trail: Essays, 1994
Rooms in the House of Stone, 1993 (nonfiction)

Other books you might like:
Beth Brant, *Food & Spirits: Stories*, 1994
This collection of short stories about Indian people from Canada and Michigan, touch on many themes central in the lives of Indian people: family, tradition, myth.

Craig Lesley, *Talking Leaves*, 1991
This book is an excellent collection of short stories by thirty-five contemporary American Indian writers, among them Erdrich, Momaday, Hogan and Whiteman.

Clifford E. Trafzer, *Blue Dawn, Red Earth: New Native American Storytellers*, 1996
This is a collection by 30 new Native American writers: Lorne Simon, Anita Endrezze, Jim Barnes, Annie Hansen, Maurice Kenny and others.

Beth Brant, *A Gathering of Spirit: A Collection of North American Indian Women*, 1984
This is a collection of stories, letters, essays and poems from a large cross-section of Native American women writers: Linda Hogan, Joy Harjo, Doris Seale and Diana Glancy.

Leslie Marmon Silko, *Storyteller*, 1981
This is a mixed genre collection of poetry, fiction and mythology.

W.P. Kinsella, *Moccasin Telegraph*, 1984
Life on the Ermineskin Reserve in Canada, detailed by Silas Ermineskin himself, is full of both comedy and tragedy.

James Northrup, *Walking the Rez Road*, 1993
Luke Warmwater is a Vietnam vet who is down on his luck, but he, like most of his reservation cohorts, is a survivor in the trickster fashion.

Gerald Vizenor, *Earthdivers: Tribal Narratives on Mixed Descent*, 1981
In this collection of short stories Vizenor creates trickster figures to poke fun at and make shrewed political commentary on America, reservation life, and just about everything else.

Louise Erdrich, *Love Medicine*, 1984
Married to Marie, Nector is nevertheless fatefully drawn to Lulu. When his grandson prepares a love medicine to win him back to his grandmother, he uses the wrong ingredients and kills Nector instead.

1201

MICHAEL DORRIS, Native American, Modoc

A Yellow Raft in Blue Water
(New York: Henry Holt and Co, 1987)

Subject(s): Women
Age range(s): Grades 9-Adult
Major character(s): Rayona, Native American (mixed-blood), Young Woman; Christine, Native American, Mother; Ida, Native American, Grandparent (grandmother)
Time period(s): 1980s
Locale(s): United States

Summary: Told from the viewpoints of three generations of women, this novel focuses on the racism mixed-blood Rayona faces on her return to her people's Plains Indian reservation. She is rejected not only for her dark skin and nappy hair, but for her city upbringing as well. This is one of the only novels that deals with "mixed blood" people who are part African American and part Native American.

About this book: Dorris is the husband of the acclaimed writer, Louise Erdrich, and it is well known from interviews that they often work together, collaborating on their manuscripts. If you are a fan of Erdrich, you would do well to read Dorris.

Where it's reviewed:
Times Literary Supplement, December 2, 1994, page 22
Multicultural Review, June 1993, page 33

Other books by the same author:
The Broken Cord: A Family's On-Going Struggle with Fetal Alcohol Syndrome, 1989 (nonfiction)
Paper Trail: Essays, 1994 (essays)
Rooms in the House of Stone, 1993 (nonfiction)
Working Men, 1993 (short fiction)

Other books you might like:
William Loren Katz, *Black Indians: A Hidden Heritage*, 1986
    A study focusing on the history of people who are of both Black and Indian descent.
Paula Gunn Allen, *The Woman Who Owned the Shadows*, 1983
    A "mixed-blood" woman who feels out of place both in the Southwest and San Francisco, begins the process of becoming a shaman on her journey to becoming whole.
D'Arcy McNickle, *The Surrounded*, 1936
    A fiddle player returns to his reservation for a visit after years in the White world and finds himself so caught up in its complexities that he knows he can never go back to the White world again.
Louise Erdrich, *Love Medicine*, 1984
    Married to Marie, Nector is nevertheless fatefully drawn to Lulu. When his grandson prepares a love medicine to win him back to his grandmother, he uses the wrong ingredients and kills Nector instead.
Leslie Marmon Silko, *Ceremony*, 1977
    A pueblo man returned from the war must realign himself with the traditional ways before becoming whole again.
John Joseph Mathews, *Sundown*, 1934
    Challenge is educated in White schools, joins the army and returns to his homeland alienated from his culture. This novel shows the effects of two competing cultures on an individual.
Maria Campbell, *Halfbreed*,
    This is the moving account of Campbell's life as a Metis, or halfbreed, part Indian, part European.
N. Scott Momaday, *House Made of Dawn*, 1968
    Abel leaves his pueblo to fght in the war, only to return alienated from his people. He then begins a long journey towards healing.

1202

TODD DOWNING, Native American, Choctaw

The Mexican Earth
(Norman: University of Oklahoma Press, 1996, 1940)

Subject(s): History; Mythology
Age range(s): Adult
Time period(s): Indeterminate Past
Locale(s): Mexico

Summary: Downing, who is Choctaw, writes about Mexico and Mexican history from an Indian perspective, including the folklore and stories of the people.

Other books by the same author:
The Case of the Unconquered Sisters, 1936 (novel)
The Cat Screams, 1934
Death under the Moonflower, 1938
The Last Trumpet: Murder in a Mexican Bull Ring, 1937 (novel)

Other books you might like:
Louis Owen, *Bone Game*, 1994
    Cole McCurtain, a mixed-blood professor haunted by dreams, becomes involved in a murder mystery that involves ecological crisis.
D'Arcy McNickle, *The Surrounded*, 1936
    A fiddle player returns to his reservation for a visit after years in the White world, finding himself so caught up in its complexities that he knows he can never go back to the White world again.
Leslie Marmon Silko, *Ceremony*, 1977
    Tayo, a pueblo Indian, returns home from the war and finds he must realign himself with his people and the old ways.
James Welch, *Winter in the Blood*, 1974
    An unnamed protagonist who is caught in the web of alcoholism, tries to discover the truth about his family.
Janet Campbell Hale, *The Jailing of Cecelia Capture*, 1985
    An Indian woman in her thirties, separated from her husband and two children, is fighting a terrible battle with alcoholism while attending law school.
Linda Hogan, *Mean Spirit*, 1990
    This novel chronicles the greed and corruption that flows from the Oklahoma oil fields in its boom days.

1203

JOSEPH IRON EYE DUDLEY, Native American, Lakota (Sioux)

Choteau Creek: A Sioux Reminiscence
(Lincoln: University of Nebraska Press, 1992)

Subject(s): Cultures and Customs; Grandparents; Growing Up
Age range(s): Grades 6 and Up
Time period(s): 1990s
Locale(s): South Dakota

Summary: This is the heart-warming story of Dudley's life on the Yankton Sioux Reservation with his grandparents.

Where it's reviewed:
Bloomsbury Review, October 1992, page 12
Christian Century, November 18, 1992, page 1081
New York Times/Book Review, October 11, 1992, page 24
Roundup Quarterly, Winter 1992, page 49
Western Historical Quaterly, May 1993, page 264

Other books you might like:
Charles A. Eastman, *Old Indian Days*, 1907
    This is an autobiographical work.
Shirley Sterling, *My Name Is Seepeetza*, 1992
    This fictional account, based on the life of the author, recounts her life as a member of the interior Salish tribe. Forced to attend government schools, she is forbidden to reflect her own heritage.
Francis La Flesche, *The Middle Five: Indian Schoolboys of the Omaha Tribe*, 1963
    This book deals with the life of La Flesche and his friends in mission school in Oklahoma.
Michael Dorris, *Morning Girl*, 1992
    This short novel is about a young girl in Pre-Columbian America.

1204

ANNE M. DUNN, Native American, Ojibwe (Chippewa)

When Beaver Was Very Great: Stories to Live By
(Mt. Horeb, WI: Midwest Traditions Inc., 1995)

Subject(s): Traditional Stories; Legends
Age range(s): Grades 3 and Up
Time period(s): 20th century
Locale(s): Minnesota

Summary: This collection contains mostly traditional tales with a scattering of poems, memoirs, and personal essays.

Other books you might like:
Frederick Turner, *The Portable North American Indian Reader*, 1973
    This anthology of myths, legends, poetry, fiction, and captivity tales, contains work by both Native American and non-Native writers.
Joseph Bruchac, *Iroquois Stories*, 1985
    These are traditional tales of the Iroquois people.

Joseph Bruchac, *The Wind Eagle and Other Abenaki Stories*, 1984
    These are traditional tales of the Abenaki people.
Joseph Bruchac, *Return of the Sun*, 1990
    These are traditional tales of the Northeast Woodlands people.
Joseph Bruchac, *Flying with the Eagle, Racing with the Bear*, 1993
    These are rite of passage stories from many tribal people.
Margot Astrov, *The Winged Serpent*, 1946
    This mixed genre collection is one of the best, containing oral stories and songs from a large cross-section of Native American cultures.
John Bierhorst, *The Red Swan: Myths and Tales of the American Indians*, 1976
    This book is a compilation of varied stories (creation, trickster, star husband, etc.) from forty North American tribes.

1205

CHARLES A. EASTMAN, Native American, Lakota (Sioux)

From the Deep Woods to Civilization
(Lincoln: University of Nebraska Press, 1977)

Subject(s): Autobiography
Age range(s): Grades 9-Adult
Time period(s): 19th century; 20th century (1850s-1930s)
Locale(s): United States

Summary: This is the life story of Charles A. Eastman, who grows up in the traditional buffalo culture of the Lakota (Sioux), but leaves that life to pursue an education in the White man's world in the East. Eventually he becomes a doctor, in which capacity he returns to his tribe in South Dakota where he witnesses the events of the Wounded Knee massacre and slowly begins to doubt the wisdom of his education and induction into the White man's world. Introduction by Raymond Wilson.

About this book: This is an important book in that it is the first-hand account of a young man who grew up in the traditional Lakota buffalo hunting culture. But this book also chronicles the pain of separation from that culture. Throughout the book there is the obvious conflict of being caught in two worlds, which is a theme that many later Indian writers have dealt with.

Where it's reviewed:
Choice, June 1986, page 1506

Other books by the same author:
Old Indian Days, 1907 (autobiography)
Wigwam Evenings: Sioux Folktales Retold, 1909 (folktales, mythology)
Smoky Day's Wigwam Evenings: Indian Stories Retold, 1910 (folktales, mythology)

Other books you might like:
John Fire Lame Deer, *Lame Deer, Seeker of Visions*, 1972
    This is an as-told-to book, Lame Deer telling his story to the writer Richard Erdoes.

Luther Standing Bear, *Stories of the Sioux*, 1988
  These are early life stories of a traditional Lakota (Sioux) man.

Zitkala-Sa, *Old Indian Legends Retold by Zitkala-Sa*, 1921
  This is the story of Zitkala-Sa, a Lakota who spends her girlhood in the traditional culture but who eventually leaves for the Indian boarding schools out East.

Mary Crow Dog, *Lakota Woman*, 1990
  This as-told-to book, with Richard Erdoes as author/editor, chronicles the life of a Lakota woman who lives through the hardships of the 1973 occupation of Wounded Knee by the AIM.

Black Elk, *Black Elk Speaks*, 1932
  This is the life story of the Holy Man of the Sioux, co-authored with John G. Neihardt.

Brian Swann, *I Tell You Now*, 1989
  This is an excellent collection of autobiographical essays by eighteen contemporary American Indian writers, co-authored by Arnold Krupat.

John Joseph Mathews, *Talking to the Moon*, 1945
  This is a literary biography that deals with nature and man's place in it.

Anna Moore Shaw, *A Pima Past*, 1974
  Born in a traditional Pima brush house and educated in the White world, Shaw recounts her fascinating story.

Francis La Flesche, *The Middle Five: Indian Schoolboys of the Omaha Tribe*, 1900
  This book details the lives of LaFlesche and his friends in mission school in Oklahoma.

Sarah Winnemucca, *Life Among the Paiutes: Their Wrongs and Claims*, 1883
  Diplomat and outspoken advocate of the rights of native peoples, Winnemucca wrote this book to preserve the history and culture of the Paiutes.

N. Scott Momaday, *The Way to Rainy Mountain*, 1976
  Mixed genre: fiction, poetry, history, mythology, and personal memoir.

N. Scott Momaday, *The Names: A Memoir*, 1976
  This is an autobiography of Momaday's life.

`1206`

CHARLES A. EASTMAN, Native American, Lakota (Sioux)

Indian Boyhood
(New York: Fenwyn, 1970)

Subject(s): Autobiography; Growing Up; Assimilation
Age range(s): Grades 5 and Up
Time period(s): 19th century (1850s-1870s)
Locale(s): United States

Summary: This is the story of Eastman's boyhood in the traditional Plains Indian culture before he was taken to live in the White man's world at fifteen.

Other books by the same author:
From the Deep Woods to Civilization, 1916 (autobiography)
Wigwam Evenings: Sioux Folktales Retold, 1909
Smoky Day's Wigwam Evenings: Indian Stories Retold, 1910

Other books you might like:
Luther Standing Bear, *Stories of the Sioux*, 1988
  Standing Bear grows up in the traditional buffalo hunting culture, and he brings to life the stories from his own past.

John Joseph Mathews, *Talking to the Moon*, 1945
  Mathews relates the circle of his life from his childhood in Oklahoma through his World War I military stint, college, married life and back to his homeland.

Anna Moore Shaw, *A Pima Past*, 1974
  Anna Moore Shaw, born in a traditional Pima brush house and educated in the white world, tells this fascinating account of her life.

Francis La Flesche, *The Middle Five: Indian Schoolboys of the Omaha Tribe*, 1900
  Relates the life of ha Tlesche and his friends in mission school in Oklahoma.

N. Scott Momaday, *The Way to Rainy Mountain*, 1976
  This is mixed genre of fiction, poetry, history, mythology, and personal memoir.

N. Scott Momaday, *The Names: A Memoir*, 1976

`1207`

CHARLES A. EASTMAN, Native American, Lakota (Sioux)

Old Indian Days
(Lincoln: University of Nebraska Press, 1907, 1997)

Subject(s): Traditional Stories; Women
Age range(s): Grades 6 and Up
Time period(s): Indeterminate Past (mythic time)
Locale(s): United States

Summary: Traditional stories and stories about Sioux people living in the buffalo hunting culture.

About this book: The book is divided into two chapters: stories about Warriors and stories about Women.

Other books by the same author:
From the Deep Woods to Civilization, 1916 (autobiography)
Wigwam Evenings: Sioux Folktales Retold, 1909 (folktales, mythology)
Smoky Day's Wigwam Evenings: Indian Stories Retold, 1910 (folktales, mythology)

Other books you might like:
Luther Standing Bear, *Stories of the Sioux*, 1988
  Standing Bear grew up in the traditional buffalo hunting culture, and he brings to life the stories from his own past.

Zitkala-Sa, *Old Indian Legends Retold by Zitkala-Sa*, 1921
  These stories depict Zitkala-Sa's childhood in the traditional Lakota culture and the difficulties she faced while attending school and college in a world where she was perceived as a "savage."

Francis La Flesche, *The Middle Five: Indian Schoolboys of the Omaha Tribe*, 1963
  This book deals with the life of La Flesche and his friends in mission school in Oklahoma.

Mary Buff, *Hah-nee of the Cliff Dwellers*,
  This is a tale about a young boy of a cliff dwelling pubelo at a time of drought.

D'Arcy McNickle, *Runner in the Sun: A Story of Indian Maize*, 1954

This middle school novel is about a young boy who leaves his Pueblo homeland to go south to Mexico to find salt for his tribe.

Joseph Iron Eye Dudley, *Choteau Creek: A Sioux Reminiscence*, 1992

This is the heart-warming story of Dudley's life on the Yankton Sioux Reservation with his grandparents.

1208

CHARLES A. EASTMAN, Native American, Lakota (Sioux)

Red Hunters and the Animal People
(New York: AMS 1976, 1904)

Subject(s): Cultures and Customs; Religion
Age range(s): Grades 5 and Up
Time period(s): Indeterminate
Locale(s): North Dakota

Summary: Stories about hunting and Native American spiritual beliefs regarding the sacredness of animal life. As Eastman says in the introduction, "the Indian held the animals to be his brothers . . . He regards the killing of certain of them for his sustenance to be an institution of the Great Mystery' . . . Therefore, he kills them only as necessity and the exigencies of life demand, and not wantonly" (v Forward).

Other books by the same author:
Indian Boyhood, 1970
From the Deep Woods to Civilization, 1916 (autobiography)
Wigwam Evenings: Sioux Folktales Retold, 1909 (folktales, mythology)
Smoky Day's Wigwam Evenings: Indian Stories Retold, 1910 (folktales, mythology)

Other books you might like:
Luther Standing Bear, *Stories of the Sioux*, 1988
  Standing Bear grew up in the traditional buffalo hunting culture, and he brings to life the stories from his own past.
Zitkala-Sa, *Old Indian Legends Retold by Zitkala-Sa*, 1921
  These stories depict Zitkala-Sa's childhood in the traditional Lakota culture and the difficulties she faces while attending school and college in a world where she is perceived as a "savage."
Mourning Dove, *Coyote Stories*, 1933
  These are traditional Okanagan stories about Coyote, the trickster.
Markoosie, *Harpoon of the Hunter*, 1970
  This story chronicles the life of an Eskimo boy who must learn to be a hunter.
Joseph Bruchac, *The Wind Eagle and Other Abenaki Stories*, 1984
  These are traditional tales of the Abenaki.
Joseph Bruchac, *Return of the Sun*, 1990
  Traditional tales of the Northeast Woodlands, full of humor and wisdom, equally as enlightening as Aesop's fables, and more fun.

1209

RICHARD ERDOES, Caucasian
ALFONSO ORTIZ, Co-Author

American Indian Myths and Legends
(New York: Pantheon, 1984)

Subject(s): Mythology; Folk Tales
Age range(s): Grades 5 and Up
Time period(s): Indeterminate
Locale(s): United States

Summary: This is a collection of myths and legends from a great variety of North American Indian tribes. The book is divided into 10 sections, each dealing with a different genre or theme of American Indian tales, such as Emergence tales, Trickster Tales, etc. Some of the tales were collected by anthropologists, some were collected by the editors themselves.

Where it's reviewed:
Booklist, October 1, 1984, page 171
Kirkus Reviews, September 1, 1984, page 844

Other books by the same author:
Lame Deer, Seeker of Visions, 1972 (co-authored with John Fire Lame Deer .)
Lakota Woman, 1990 (co-authored with Mary Crow Dog)
Ohitika Woman, 1993 (co-authored with Mary Brave Bird)
Crow Dog, 1995 (co-authored with Leonard Crow Dog edicine man.)
Gift of Power

Other books you might like:
Margot Astrov, *The Winged Serpent*, 1946
  This is one of the best collections of oral stories and songs from a large cross-section of Indian cultures.
John Bierhorst, *The Sacred Path*, 1984
  This is a fine collection of traditional spells, prayers, and power songs from a variety of Indian tribes.
Frederick Turner, *The Portable North American Indian Reader*, 1973
  Myths, legends, poetry, captivity narratives and fiction are included in this collection.
Mourning Dove, *Coyote Stories*, 1933
  Coyote, the trickster, is the main protagonist in these traditional stories.
Zitkala-Sa, *Old Indian Legends Retold by Zitkala-Sa*, 1921
  This is a collection of memoirs and essays by an Indian woman who was born into the old buffalo hunting culture of the Sioux.
John Bierhorst, *The Red Swan: Myths and Tales of the American Indians*, 1976
  This is a compilation of varied stories (creation, trickster, star husband, etc.) from forty Indian tribes.
Robert Franklin Gish, *When Coyote Howls: A Lavaland Fable*,
  This is a Coyote novel.
Barry Lopez, *Giving Birth to Thunder, Sleeping with His Daughter: Coyote Builds North America*, 1977
  In this book Lopez retells a wide selection of Coyote Stories from various North American tribes. As always,

Coyote is dynamic, irreverant, wily, paradoxical, mysterious, taboo-bracking and fun.

1210

LOUISE ERDRICH, Native American, Ojibwa (Chippewa)

The Beet Queen

(New York: Holt, Rinehard & Winston, 1987)

Subject(s): Indians of North America; Orphans
Age range(s): Adult
Major character(s): Mary Adare, Friend (of Celestine); Celestine James, Friend (of Mary), Native American (mixed-blood)
Time period(s): 20th century (1932-1972)
Locale(s): Argus, North Dakota

Summary: Abandoned by her mother at 11, Mary finds a home with her aunt and uncle in Argus, North Dakota, a town just beyond the borders of the Chippewa Indian reservation. There she befriends a mixed-blood girl, Celestine who, later has a child by Mary's brother. The ''Beet Queen,'' she becomes the spoiled focus of attention at the close of the book.

About this book: Erdrich, who has often been called the best fiction writer of her generation, has a prose style that is lyrical and romantic, yet the exquisitely drawn stories in this collection often deal with harsh realities. But for all of the darkness in her work, a tremendous comic sensibilty runs through most of her stories. Like Faulkner, Erdrich makes a fictional American landscape come alive, bringing to her readers keen insights not only into the reservation world, but into the human heart. In this novel, Erdrich creates characters drawn from the German side of her ancestry.

Where it's reviewed:
American Indian Culture and Research Journal, Issue 3, 1994, page 1
Bloomsbury Review, May 1994, page 3
Instructor, May 1994, page 55

Other books by the same author:
The Bingo Palace, 1994
Love Medicine, 1993 (contains new material not originally included in the first edition)
Tracks, 1988
Tales of Burning Love, 1996
Baptism of Desire, 1989 (poetry)
Jacklight: Poems, 1984

Other books you might like:
D'Arcy McNickle, *The Surrounded*, 1936
 A fiddle player returns to his reservation for a visit after years in the White world, finding himself so caught up in its complexities that he knows he can never go back to the White world again.
N. Scott Momaday, *House Made of Dawn*, 1968
 In this novel a Pueblo man returns from WWII shell-shocked and then must suffer the hardship of alienation from his people.
Gerald Vizenor, *The People Named the Chippewa: Narrative Histories*, 1984
 This mixed genre anthology contains essays, interviews, history, mythology and stories.

Craig Lesley, *Talking Leaves*, 1991
 This is an excellent collection by thirty-five contemporary Native American writers including Louise Erdrich, Michael Dorris, N. Scott Momaday and Linda Hogan.
Leslie Marmon Silko, *Ceremony*, 1977
 Tayo has just returned from WWII, a psychologically traumatized man. Immersing himself in Laguna Pueblo ritual and myth, he learns to enter the world again.
James Northrup, *Walking the Rez Road*, 1993
 Luke Warmwater is a Vietnam vet who is down on his luck, but, he, like most of his reservation cohorts, is a survivor in the trickster fashion.
Janet Campbell Hale, *The Jailing of Cecelia Capture*, 1985
 A thirty-something Indian woman, separated from her husband and two children, fights a terrible battle with alcoholism while attending law school.
Linda Hogan, *Mean Spirit*, 1990
 This novel chronicles the greed and corruption that flows from the Oklahoma oil fields during the boom days.

1211

LOUISE ERDRICH, Native American, Ojibwa (Chippewa)

The Bingo Palace

(New York: Holt, Rinehard & Winston, 1994)

Subject(s): Indians of North America; Gambling
Age range(s): Adult
Major character(s): Shawnee Ray, Mother (of Lyman's illegitimate son), Native American (Chippewa); Lyman Lamartine, Businessman (owns the Bingo Palace), Native American (Chippewa); Lipsha Morissey, Worker (works for Lamartine), Native American (Chippewa)
Time period(s): 1970s
Locale(s): North Dakota

Summary: Lipsha, recently returned to the reservation, and Lyman, a powerful force there, are locked in a struggle to capture the heart of beautiful Shawnee Ray, mother of Lyman's illegitimate son. Shawnee Ray's ambitions extend beyond the reservation and the Bingo Palace to college but she is overwhelmed by Lipsha's unrelenting pursuit.

About this book: This novel is the fourth in Erdrich's continuing saga.

Where it's reviewed:
New York Times Book Review, February 19, 1995, page 36
New York Times Book Review, June 11, 1995, page 58
American Indian Culture and Research Journal, Issue 3, 1994, page 271
Kliatt, May 1995, page 6
Los Angeles Times Book Review, February 19, 1995, page 11

Other books by the same author:
The Beet Queen, 1987
Love Medicine, 1993 (contains new material not included in the first edition)
Tracks, 1988
Jacklight: Poems, 1984 (poetry)
Tales of Burning Love, 1996

Native American Titles

Other books you might like:
D'Arcy McNickle, *The Surrounded*, 1936
A fiddle player returns to his reservation for a visit after years in the White world and finds himself so caught up in its complexities that he knows he can never go back to the White world again.
Paula Gunn Allen, *Spider Woman's Granddaughters*, 1989
This is a beautiful collection of traditional tales interwoven with contemporary stories about Native American women.
James Welch, *Winter in the Blood*, 1974
A man caught in the clutches of alcoholism, tries to discover the truth about his family.
Craig Lesley, *Talking Leaves*, 1991
This is an excellent collection of stories by thirty-five contemporary Native American writers including Louise Erdrich, Michael Dorris, N. Scott Momaday and Linda Hogan.
Leslie Marmon Silko, *Ceremony*, 1977
Tayo has just returned from WWII, a psychology traumatized man. Immersing himself in Laguna Pueblo ritual and myth, he learns to enter the world again.
James Northrup, *Walking the Rez Road*, 1993
Luke Warmwater is a Vietnam vet who is down on his luck, but he, like most of his reservation cohorts, is a survivor in the trickster fashion.
Janet Campbell Hale, *The Jailing of Cecelia Capture*, 1985
A thirty-something Indian woman, separated from her husband and two children, is fighting a terrible battle with alcoholism while attending law school.
Linda Hogan, *Mean Spirit*, 1990
This novel chronicles the greed and corruption that flows from Oklahoma's oil fields during the boom days.
Clifford E. Trafzer, *Blue Dawn, Red Earth: New Native American Storytellers*, 1996
This collection of short stories by 30 new Native American writers includes Lorne Simon, Anita Endrezze, Jim Barnes and others.
Beth Brant, *A Gathering of Spirit: A Collection of North American Indian Women*, 1984
This is a collection of stories, letters, essays, and poems from a large cross-section of Native Ameircan women writers, such as Linda Hogan, Elizabeth Cook-Lynn, Diana Glancy.

1212

LOUISE ERDRICH, Native American, Ojibwa (Chippewa)
MICHAEL DORRIS, Co-Author, Native American, Modoc

The Crown of Columbus
(New York: Harper Collins, 1991)

Subject(s): Indians of North America; History
Age range(s): Grades 10-Adult
Major character(s): Vivian Twostar, Anthropologist; Roger Williams, Professor
Time period(s): 1990s
Locale(s): United States

Summary: When Vivian discovers Columbus' lost diary and the thing intimates the possibility of a hidden relic, she and Williams embark on a journey to the Caribbean. There they struggle to solve the mystery of the truth of Columbus' diary and unveil the truth about their relationship as well.

About this book: This book is written in the style of popular fiction, quite unlike the other books in Erdrich's interrelated opus.

Other books by the same author:
The Beet Queen, 1987
Love Medicine, 1993 (contain new material not in first edition)
Tracks, 1988
Jacklight: Poems, 1984 (poetry)
Tales of Burning Love, 1996

Other books you might like:
Carol LaFavor, *Along the Journey River*, 1996
This is a mystery story about sacred stolen objects that cause the lives of Renee and Salisbury to become intertwined on the Red Earth Reservation of Minnesota.
Martin Cruz Smith, *Nightwing*, 1977
Youngman Duran, an ex-con, returning to his peublo from his stint in the military, becomes a deputy sheriff who must uncover the secret of the plague that threatens the reservation.
Louis Owen, *Bone Game*, 1994
Cole McCurtain is a mixed-blood professor haunted by dreams. He becomes involved in a murder that involves an ecological crisis.
Martin Cruz Smith, *Stallion Gate*, 1986
Joe Pena leaves his pueblo to join the war effort and returns home feeling alienated from his people. He must also confront the power of the atom bomb developed at Los Alamos.
Linda Hogan, *Mean Spirit*, 1990
This murder mystery takes place in Oklahoma's oil boom days.

1213

LOUISE ERDRICH, Native American, Ojibwa (Chippewa)

Love Medicine
(New York: Holt, Rinehard & Winston, 1984)

Subject(s): Indians of North America; Indian Reservations
Age range(s): Adult
Major character(s): Lulu Lamertine, Native American (Chippewa), Mother (many children by many fathers); Marie Lazarre, Native American (Chippewa), Spouse (wife of Nector); Nector Kashpaw, Native American (Chippewa)
Time period(s): 20th century (1934-1983)
Locale(s): North Dakota

Summary: This award winning novel is a collection of stories about the intertwined lives of characters living on a Chippewa reservation in North Dakota. The death of June Kashpaw, in the first story, sets her relatives to reminiscing about the family history which begins with the narrator's grandparents, Marie and Nector. When Nector begins an affair with Lulu Lamertine, his grandson prepares a ''love medicine'' to rekindle the romance between his grandparents. But he has substituted one ingredient for another and Nector chokes to death. Putting the past behind, Marie and Lulu eventually join forces and become tribal elders together.

About this book: A half-a-dozen voices reveal this story, peeling it back layer by layer as they examine their own family history and cultural identity, and concern for the preservation of the old ways. Erdrich's voice is lyrical as she creates the interrelationships among her characters. *Love Medicine* is chronologically the second in a series of interconnected books, though it was the first in the series to have actually been written.

Where it's reviewed:
New Yorker, January 7, 1985, page 76
School Library Journal, November 1984, page 145
Wall Street Journal, October 24, 1984, page 30

Awards the book has won:
National Book Critics Circle Award for Fiction, 1984
Best First Novel, American Academy and Inst. of Arts and Letters, 1985

Other books by the same author:
The Bingo Palace, 1994 (fiction)
Tracks, 1988 (fiction)
The Beet Queen, 1987 (fiction)
Baptism of Desire, 1989 (poetry)
Tales of Burning Love, 1996
Jacklight: Poems, 1984

Other books you might like:
Paula Gunn Allen, *Spider Woman's Granddaughters*, 1989
    This is a beautiful collection of traditional tales interwoven with contemporary stories having to do with the lives of Native American women.
Clifford E. Trafzer, *Blue Dawn, Red Earth: New Native American Storytellers*, 1996
    This is a collection of short stories by 30 new Native American writers: Lorne Simon, Anita Endrezze, Jim Barnes and others.
Charles Kawbawgam, *Ojibwa Narratives*, 1994
    These traditional stories of Ojibwa culture are told by Charles and Charlotte Kawbawgam and Jacques LePique in the late 1800s to Arthur P. Bourgeois.
James Welch, *Winter in the Blood*, 1974
    An unnamed portagonist who is caught in alcoholism tries to discover the truth about his family.
Craig Lesley, *Talking Leaves*, 1991
    This excellent collection by thirty-five contemporary Native American writers includes Louise Erdrich, Michael Dorris, N. Scott Momaday and Linda Hogan.
Leslie Marmon Silko, *Ceremony*, 1977
    Tayo, a puebo Indian, returns home from the war and must realign himself with his people and the old ways.
Beth Brant, *A Gathering of Spirit: A Collection of North American Indian Women*, 1984
    This excellent collection of stories, letters, essays, and poems are from a large cross-section of Native American women writers, such as Linda Hogan, Elizabeth Cook-Lynn, Diana Glancy, and others.
James Northrup, *Walking the Rez Road*, 1993
    Luke Warmwater is a Vietnam vet down on his luck, but, he, like most of his reservation cohorts, is a survivor in the trickster fashion.

Janet Campbell Hale, *The Jailing of Cecelia Capture*, 1985
    This novel is about an Indian woman in her thirties who has two children, who is separated from her husband and kids, going to law school, and fighting a terrible battle with alcoholism.
Linda Hogan, *Mean Spirit*, 1990
    This novel, based in Oklahoma, chronicles the greed and corruption that flows from its oil fields.

1214

LOUISE ERDRICH, Native American, Ojibwa (Chippewa)

Tales of Burning Love
(New York: Harper Collins, 1996)

Subject(s): Women; Divorce; Death
Age range(s): Adult
Major character(s): Jack Mauser, Spouse (husband), Native American; Elanor Mauser, Spouse (wife), Native American; Candice Mauser, Spouse (wife), Native American; Marlis Mauser, Spouse (wife), Native American; Dot Mauser, Spouse (wife), Native American
Time period(s): 1990s
Locale(s): North Dakota

Summary: When Jack Mauser's four former wives are stranded together in a snowstorm, each begins telling the others her outrageous stories.

Other books by the same author:
The Bingo Palace, 1994
Tracks, 1988
The Beet Queen, 1987
Baptism of Desire, 1989 (poetry)
Jacklight: Poems, 1984

Other books you might like:
Paula Gunn Allen, *Spider Woman's Granddaughters*, 1989
    This is a beautiful collection of traditional tales interwoven with contemporary stories about Native American women.
Beth Brant, *A Gathering of Spirit: A Collection of North American Indian Women*, 1984
    This is an excellent collection of stories, letters, essays, and poems from a large cross-section of Native American women writers such as Linda Hogan, Elizabeth Cook-Lynn, Diane Glancy and others.
Paula Gunn Allen, *The Sacred Hoop: Recovering the Feminine in American Indian Traditions*, 1986
    This book is an excellent collection of essays that uncovers the essential role of women in traditional and contemporary Indian life.
Craig Lesley, *Talking Leaves*, 1991
    This book is an excellent collection of short stories by thirty-five contemporary Indian writers including Louise Erdrich, N. Scott Momaday, Linda Hogan and Roberta Hill Whiteman.

1215

LOUISE ERDRICH, Native American, Ojibwa (Chippewa)

Tracks

(New York: Holt, Rinehard & Winston, 1988)

Subject(s): Indians of North America; Indian Reservations; Cultural Identity

Age range(s): Adult

Major character(s): Nanapush, Native American (Chippewa), Aged Person; Pauline Puyat, Native American (mixed-blood), Religious (Catholic nun); Fleur Pillager, Native American (Chippewa)

Time period(s): 1910s (1912-1919)

Locale(s): North Dakota

Summary: This novel is a collection of stories about the intertwined lives of a variety of characters who live on a Chippewa reservation in North Dakota. Though it was written after *Love Medicine*, chronologically it is the first in the series of interlocked stories. Fleur Pillager mysteriously survives drowning in Matchimanito Lake, and much of the book centers on her and her shaman-like characteristics. Telling Fleur's story for the benefit of her daughter is Nanapush, a kind of trickster figure who also manifests some shaman-like characteristics and Pauline, a woman who is caught between the Native American and White worlds. Eventually, she immerses herself in Catholicism, giving up her Native American identity. This leads her down a dangerous path.

About this book: *Tracks* is the first in a series of interconnected books, a family saga about the disintegration of the traditional life on a Chippewa reservation.

Where it's reviewed:
Emergency Librarian, January 1995, page 58
Bloomsbury Review, May 1994, page 3

Other books by the same author:
The Bingo Palace, 1994
Love Medicine, 1993 (contains new material not included in the first edition)
The Beet Queen, 1987
Baptism of Desire, 1989 (poetry)
Jacklight: Poems, 1984 (poetry)
Tales of Burning Love, 1996

Other books you might like:
Paula Gunn Allen, *Spider Woman's Granddaughters*, 1989
 This beautiful collection of traditional tales interwoven with traditional stories touch on the lives of Native American women.
D'Arcy McNickle, *The Surrounded*, 1936
 A fiddle player returns to his reservation for a visit after years in the White world, finding himself so caught up in its complexities that he knows he can never go back to the White world again.
N. Scott Momaday, *House Made of Dawn*, 1968
 In this novel, a Pueblo man returns from WWII shell-shocked and then must suffer the hardship of being alienated from his people.
Craig Lesley, *Talking Leaves*, 1991
 This is an excellent collection of stories by thirty-five contempoarary Native American writers including Louise

Erdrich, Michael Dorris, N. Scott Momaday and Linda Hogan.
Leslie Marmon Silko, *Ceremony*, 1977
 Tayo has just returned from WWII a psychologically traumatized man. Immersing himself in Laguna ritual and myth, he learns to enter the world again.
James Northrup, *Walking the Rez Road*, 1993
 Luke Warmwater is a Vietnam vet down on his luck, but, he, like most of his reservation cohorts, is a survivor in the trickster fashion.
Janet Campbell Hale, *The Jailing of Cecelia Capture*, 1985
 A thirty-something Indian woman, separated from her husband and two children, is fighting a battle with alcoholism while attending law school.
Michael Dorris, *A Yellow Raft in Blue Water*, 1987
 This is one of the few novels that deals with ''mixed blood'' people who are part African-American and part native American.
Linda Hogan, *Mean Spirit*, 1990
 This novel chronicles the greed and corruption that flows from Oklahoma's oil fields during the boom days.
Gerald Vizenor, *The People Named the Chippewa: Narrative Histories*, 1984
 This mixed genre anthology contains essays, interviews, history, mythology and stories.

1216

DAN EVEHEMA, Native American, Hopi
THOMAS E. MAILS, Co-Author, Caucasian

Hotevilla

(New York: Marlowe and Co., 1994)

Subject(s): Autobiography; Cultures and Customs; Indians of North America

Age range(s): Grades 11-Adult

Time period(s): Indeterminate

Locale(s): Arizona

Summary: One of the traditional tribal elders of the Hopi here relates to Thomas E. Mails traditional stories, legends, myths, ceremonies, prophecies, history, and politics regarding the Hopi people.

Other books you might like:
William Bright, *A Coyote Reader*, 1993
 This is a collection of trickster stories from many tribes with chapters divided according to the various attributes of Coyote, rather than geographically.
Herschel Talashoema, *Coyote & Little Turtle: Iisaw Niqw Yongosonhoya: A Traditional Hopi Tale*, 1994
 Here is an excellent book for early readers about Coyote and Little Turtle. It is written in both Hopi and English, with illustrations from Hopi children. Co-authored with John Emory Sekaquaptewqa.
John Bierhorst, *The Red Swan: Myths and Tales of the American Indians*, 1976
 This book is a compilation of varied stories (creation, trickster, star husband, etc.) from forty Indian tribes.
Frederick Turner, *The Portable North American Indian Reader*, 1973
 This anthology of myths, legends, poetry, fiction, and cap-

tivity tales, contains work by both Native American and non-Native writers.

G.M. Mullet, *Spider Woman Stories*, 1979

These Hopi Indian legends are collected from the 1880s.

Don C. Talayesva, *Sun Chief: The Autobiography of a Hopi Indian*, 1942

Don C. Talayesva is born in Oraibi, the oldest continually inhabited town in the U.S., in 1890, and this is the story of his life and the life of the Hopi people.

Martin Cruz Smith, *Nightwing*, 1977

Youngman Duran leaves his pueblo to join the war effort but feels alienated from his people when he returns to the reservation where he must help uncover the secret of a threatening plague.

Albert Yava, *Big Falling Snow: A Tewa-Hopi Indian's Life and Times and the History and Traditions of His People*, 1978

Autobiography

Helen Sekaquaptewa, *Me and Mine: The Life Story of Helen Sekaquaptewa*, 1969

The autobiography of a Hopi woman, written with Louise Udall.

Paula Gunn Allen, *The Sacred Hoop: Recovering the Feminine in American Indian Traditions*, 1986

This book is an excellent collection of essays that uncovers the essential role of women in traditional and contemporary Native American life.

Zitkala-Sa, *Old Indian Legends Retold by Zitkala-Sa*, 1921

This is the story of Zitkala-Sa, a Lakota who spends her girlhood in the traditional culture but who eventually leaves for the Indian boarding schools out East.

Paula Gunn Allen, *Spider Woman's Granddaughters*, 1989

This is a beautiful collection of traditional tales interwoven with contemporary stories having to do with the lives of Native American women.

Anna Moore Shaw, *A Pima Past*, 1974

Born in a traditional Pima brush house and educated in the White world, Shaw recounts her fascinating past.

Francis La Flesche, *The Middle Five: Indian Schoolboys of the Omaha Tribe*, 1900

This book details the lives of LaFlesche and his friends in mission school in Oklahoma.

Sarah Winnemucca, *Life Among the Paiutes: Their Wrongs and Claims*, 1883

1217

RENEE SANSOM FLOOD, Native American, Lakota (Sioux)

Lost Bird of Wounded Knee

(New York: Scribner, 1995)

Subject(s): Cultural Identity; Adoption; Assimilation
Age range(s): Grades 10-Adult
Time period(s): 19th century; 20th century (1890-1920)
Locale(s): South Dakota

Summary: This is the reconstructed life story of Lost Bird, who as an infant survived the Wounded Knee massacre, then was adopted by General Colby, one of the leaders of the attack. Renee Flood traces down the intriguing, sad story of Lost Bird, who was taken from her tribal roots (like many Native American children forced into White adoption), and through Flood's research, is returned to her native land only when her body is discovered in a dilapidated California cemetery without a headstone.

Where it's reviewed:
Booklist, June 1, 1995, page 1722
Booklist, June 1, 1995, page 1748
Library Journal, June 1, 1995, page 134
Publishers Weekly, May 15, 1995, page 62

Other books you might like:
John Fire Lame Deer, *Lame Deer, Seeker of Visions*, 1972

This is an as-told-to book, Lame Deer telling his story to the writer Richard Erdoes.

Mary Brave Bird, *Ohitika Woman*, 1993

This sequel to *Lakota Woman* chronicles the conflicts between feminism and traditional Indian belief, White and Indian philosophy. (Mary retook her maiden name after divorcing Crow Dog.)

Brian Swann, *I Tell You Now*, 1989

This is an excellent collection of autobiographical essays by eighteen contemporary American Indian writers.

1218

JEAN CRAIGHEAD GEORGE, Caucasian

The Talking Earth

(New York: Harper and Row, 1983)

Subject(s): Indians of North America; Ecology
Age range(s): Grades 6-8
Major character(s): Billie Wind, Teenager (girl), Native American (Seminole)
Time period(s): 1980s
Locale(s): Florida

Summary: A young, modern Seminole girl begins to doubt the beliefs of her tribal elders until she goes into the Everglades, where she begins to understand the importance of her tribal teachings, the world of nature and the necessity of preserving the earth.

Where it's reviewed:
Social Studies, July 1992, page 172
Social Studies, January 1993, page 32

Other books by the same author:
Cry of the Crow, 1980 (novel)
The Summer of the Falcon, 1979 (novel)
Julie of the Wolves, 1972 (novel)

Other books you might like:
Jay Leech, *Moon of the Big-Dog*, 1980

Three young Sioux boys go on a journey in which they capture the first horses for their tribe, and earn a new name for their Sioux band: Brule. Co-authored by Zane Spencer and illustrated by M. Funai.

Charles A. Eastman, *From the Deep Woods to Civilization*, 1916

The autobiography of Charles A. Eastman, who grows up in the traditional buffalo culture of the Lakota (Sioux) but pursues an education in the White man's world.

Zitkala-Sa, *Old Indian Legends Retold by Zitkala-Sa*, 1921
These stories recount Zitkala-Sa's childhood in the traditional Lakota culture and the difficulties she faces while attending school and college in a world where she is perceived as a "savage."

Luther Standing Bear, *Stories of the Sioux*, 1988
Standing Bear grew up in the traditional buffalo hunting culture and he brings to life the stories from his own past.

Charles A. Eastman, *Old Indian Days*, 1907
Autobiography of a Lakota Sioux man.

Shirley Sterling, *My Name Is Seepeetza*, 1992
Fictional account based on the life of the author, who, as a member of the interior Salish tribe, is forced to attend government schools where she is forbidden to reflect anything of her own heritage.

Virginia Driving Hawk Sneve, *High Elk's Treasure*, 1972
This novel for middle school readers is about Joe High Elk who longs to bring back the strain of wild mustangs that his famous ancestor bred many years before. Illustrations by Oren Lyons.

1219

ARRELL MORGAN GIBSON, Editor, Caucasian

The American Indian: Prehistory to the Present

(Lexintgon, MA: D.C. Heath and Co., 1980)

Subject(s): History; Indians of North America
Age range(s): Grades 10-Adult
Time period(s): Indeterminate Past
Locale(s): United States

Summary: A comprehensive history of Native American cultures.

Other books you might like:
Sam D. Gill, *Dictionary of Native American Mythology*, 1992
A comprehensive dictionary of Native American mythology.

John Bierhorst, *The Red Swan: Myths and Tales of the American Indians*, 1976
This book is a compilation of varied stories (creation, trickster, star husband, etc.) from forty Indian tribes.

Carl Sauer, *Man in Nature*, 1939
This excellent book explores the Indian cultures that existed in pre-Columbian America, broken down into fourteen geographical areas.

Frederick Turner, *The Portable North American Indian Reader*, 1973
This anthology of myths, legends, poetry, fiction, and captivity tales, contains work by both Native American and non-Native writers.

Margot Astrov, *The Winged Serpent*, 1946
Mixed genre: one of the best collections of oral stories and songs from a large cross-section of Indian cultures.

John Bierhorst, *The Sacred Path*, 1984
Mixed genre: a collection of traditional spells, prayers, and power songs from a variety of Indian tribes.

1220

SAM D. GILL, Editor, Caucasian
IRENE F. SULLIVAN, Co-Editor, Caucasian

Dictionary of Native American Mythology

(Santa Barbara, CA: ABV-CLIO, 1992)

Subject(s): Mythology
Age range(s): Grades 6 and Up
Time period(s): Indeterminate
Locale(s): United States

Summary: A scholarly, comprehensive dictionary of Native American mythology that includes an explanation of themes and concepts as well as rituals and practice.

About this book: An excellent resource for students and teachers.

Where it's reviewed:
Emergency Librarian, September 1994, page 46
American Reference Books Annual, 1994, page 170
Multicultural Review, June 1993, page 88
Parabola, Fall 1994, page 110
School Library Journal, November 1993, page 142

Other books you might like:
Mourning Dove, *Coyote Stories*, 1933
These are traditional Okanagan stories about Coyote, the trickster.

William Bright, *A Coyote Reader*, 1993
Traditional coyote stories

John Bierhorst, *The Red Swan: Myths and Tales of the American Indians*, 1976
This book is a compilation of varied stories (creation, trickster, star husband, etc.) from forty Indian tribes.

Frederick Turner, *The Portable North American Indian Reader*, 1973
This anthology of myths, legends, poetry, fiction, and captivity tales, contains work by both Native American and non-Native writers.

Carl Sauer, *Man in Nature*, 1939
This excellent book explores the Indian cultures that existed in pre-Columbian America, broken down into fourteen geographical areas.

Margot Astrov, *The Winged Serpent*, 1946
Mixed genre: one of the best collections of oral stories and songs from a large cross-section of Indian cultures.

John Bierhorst, *The Sacred Path*, 1984
Mixed genre: a collection of traditional spells, prayers, and power songs from a variety of Indian tribes.

1221

ROBERT FRANKLIN GISH, Native American, Cherokee

When Coyote Howls: A Lavaland Fable

(Albuquerque, NM: University of New Mexico Press, 1994)

Subject(s): Folk Tales; Animals
Age range(s): Grades 10-Adult
Major character(s): Coyote, Trickster
Time period(s): Indeterminate Past (mythic time)
Locale(s): Albuquerque, New Mexico

Summary: In this modern version of a Coyote tale, Coyote slips through space and time on a journey to find his stolen voice.

Where it's reviewed:
Library Journal, October 15, 1994, page 72
Library Journal, August 1994, page 128
Publishers Weekly, July 25, 1994, page 38

Other books by the same author:
First Horses: Stories of the New West, 1993
Song of My Hunter Heart: A Western Kinship, 1994 (nonfiction)

Other books you might like:
William Bright, *A Coyote Reader*, 1993
  This is a collection of trickster stories from many tribes, the chapters divided according to the various attributes of Coyote, rather than geographically.
Mourning Dove, *Coyote Stories*, 1933
  These are traditional Okanagan stories about Coyote, the trickster.
Hasteen Klah, *The Myth and Prayers of the Great Star Chant, and the Myth of the Coyote Chant*, 1988
  This exquisite book is a compilation of important Navajo myths, songs, chants, and prayers, that deal with the complex philosophical and religious life of Navajo culture.
John Bierhorst, *The Red Swan: Myths and Tales of the American Indians*, 1976
  This book is a compilation of varied stories (creation, trickster, star husband, etc.) from forty Indian tribes.
Frederick Turner, *The Portable North American Indian Reader*, 1973
  This anthology of myths, legends, poetry, fiction, and captivity tales, contains work by both Native American and non-Native writers.
Paul Radin, *The Trickster*, 1956
  This is an excellent study of the Trickster archetype. The Winnebago Trickster Cycle of Myths, the Winnebago Hare Cycle, and summaries of the Assiniboine and Tlingit Trickster are presented.
Barry Lopez, *Giving Birth to Thunder, Sleeping with His Daughter: Coyote Builds North America*, 1977
  In this book Lopez retells a wide selection of Coyote stories from various North American tribes. As always, Coyote is dynamic, irreverant, wily, paradoxical, mysterious, taboo breaking and fun.

1222

DIANE GLANCY, Native American, Cherokee

Firesticks
(Norman, OK: U. Of Oklahoma Press, 1993)

Subject(s): Indians of North America; Cultures and Customs
Age range(s): Adult
Time period(s): 20th century
Locale(s): Oklahoma

Summary: The many voices of Glancey's characters harmonize in these stories, essays and poems, creating an anthem for people struggling to use the rhythm of the past to write a song of hope for the future.

Where it's reviewed:
Belles Lettres, Fall 1994, page 4
Studies in Short Fiction, Fall 1994, page 699
Bloomsbury Review, May 1993, page 5
New York Times Book Review, April 11, 1993 page 29

Other books by the same author:
Offering: Poetry and Prose, 1980
One Age in a Dream, 1986 (poetry)
Claiming Breath, 1992 (nonfiction)

Other books you might like:
Linda Hogan, *Red Clay*, 1991
  This is an excellent collection of short stories and poems by one of the best contemporary Native writers.
Leslie Marmon Silko, *Storyteller*, 1981
  A mixed genre anthology of poetry, fiction, and mythology.
Simon J. Ortiz, *Fightin'*, 1969
  This mixed genre anthology contains poetry and short stories.
Craig Lesley, *Talking Leaves*, 1991
  This book is an excellent collection of short stories by thirty-five contemporary American Indian writers, such as Louise Erdrich, N. Scott Momaday, Linda Hogan and Roberta Hill Whiteman.
LaVonne Ruoff, *American Indian Literatures: An Introduction, Bibliographic Review, and Selected Bibliography*, 1990
  This is the *bible* of Native American literature, essential to anyone who wants to pursue a study of the literature that has been written by American Indian people.
Paula Gunn Allen, *Voice of the Turtle*, 1994
  Edited by the well known writer and scholar Paula Gunn Allen, this book is an anthology of literature written by American Indian people from 1900 to 1970.
Lee Miller, *From the Heart: Voices of the American Indian*, 1995
  This is a collection of orations, speeches and testimony by more than 250 Inidan people that presents a radical alternative to traditionally taught American history.
Clifford E. Trafzer, *Blue Dawn, Red Earth: New Native American Storytellers*, 1996
  This is a collection of short stories by 30 new Native American writers: Lorne Simon, Anita Endrezze, Jim Barnes, Annie Hansen, Maurice Kenny, and Patricia Piley, among others.
James Northrup, *Walking the Rez Road*, 1993
  Luke Warmwater is a Vietnam vet down on his luck, but he, like most of his reservation cohorts, is a survivor in the trickster fashion.
Beth Brant, *A Gathering of Spirit: A Collection of North American Indian Women*, 1984
  This anthology of short stories and poetry deals with the lives of contemporary Native American women.
Beth Brant, *Food & Spirits: Stories*, 1991
  This collection of short stories, about Indian people from Canada and Michigan, touch on many themes important to Indian people: family, tradition, myth.

1223

TRUDY GRIFFIN-PERCE, Native American, Catawaban
RONALD HIMLER, Illustrator

The Encyclopedia of Native America
(New York: Viking, 1995)

Subject(s): History; Indians of North America
Age range(s): Grades 4 and Up
Time period(s): Indeterminate
Locale(s): United States

Summary: This is a useful encyclopedia about Native American cultures, written by a Native American writer, divided geographically: an excellent resource for young people in particular.

Where it's reviewed:
Booklist, September 1, 1995, page 106
Children's Book Review Service, August 1995, page 164
Publishers Weekly, June 12, 1995, page 62
School Library Journal, August 1995, page 168

Other books you might like:
John Bierhorst, *The Red Swan: Myths and Tales of the American Indians*, 1976
    This book is a compilation of varied stories (creation, trickster, star husband, etc.) from forty Indian tribes.
Frederick Turner, *The Portable North American Indian Reader*, 1973
    This anthology of myths, legends, poetry, fiction, and captivity tales, contains work by both Native American and non-Native writers.
William C. Sturtevant, *Handbook of North American Indians*, 1990
    A massive multivolume resource, this encyclopedia contains an incredible amount of information about Native North American peoples.
Sam D. Gill, *Dictionary of Native American Mythology*, 1992
    A comprehensive dictionary of Native American mythology. An excellent resource for students and teachers. Written with Irene F. Sullivan.
Margot Astrov, *The Winged Serpent*, 1946
    One of the best collections of oral stories and songs from a large cross-section of Indian cultures.

1224

JANET CAMPBELL HALE, Native American, Coeur d'Alene and Kootenai

The Jailing of Cecelia Capture
(New York: Random House, 1985)

Subject(s): Historical; Alcoholism
Age range(s): Adult
Major character(s): Cecelia Capture, Native American, Alcoholic
Time period(s): 1980s
Locale(s): United States

Summary: This novel examines the life of an Indian woman in her thirties who is separated from her husband and kids while she attends law school and battles her alcoholism. The reader, drawn deeply into her problems, experiences the fragmentation of her self, a fragmentation indicative of the problems that many Indian people face.

Where it's reviewed:
Reference Services Review, Issue 3, 1995, page 25
Rocky Mountain Review of Language & Literature, Issue I, 1993, page 61

Other books by the same author:
Owl's Song, 1976 (fiction)
Custer Lives in Humboldt County, 1978 (poetry)

Other books you might like:
Mary Crow Dog, *Lakota Woman*, 1990
    This as-told-to book, with Richard Erdoes as author/editor, chronicles the life of a Lakota woman who lives through the hardships of the 1973 occupation of Wounded Knee by the AIM.
Mary Brave Bird, *Ohitika Woman*, 1993
    This sequel to *Lakota Woman* chronicles the conflicts between feminism and traditional Indian belief, White and Indian philosophy. (Mary retook her maiden name after divorcing Crow Dog.)
Paula Gunn Allen, *Spider Woman's Granddaughters*, 1989
    This is a beautiful collection of traditional tales interwoven with contemporary stories having to do with the lives of Native American women.
Louise Erdrich, *Love Medicine*, 1984
    Married to Marie, Nector is nevertheless fatefully drawn to Lulu. When his grandson prepares a love medicine to win him back to his grandmother, he uses the wrong ingredients and kills Nector instead.
D'Arcy McNickle, *The Surrounded*, 1936
    A fiddle player returns to his reservation for a visit after years in the White world, finding himself so caught up in its complexities that he knows he can never go back to the White world again.
James Welch, *Winter in the Blood*, 1974
    A man caught in the clutches of alcoholism, tries to discover the truth about his family.
Craig Lesley, *Talking Leaves*, 1991
    This book is an excellent collection by thirty-five contemporary Native American writers including Louise Erdrich, Michael Dorris, N. Scott Momaday, and Linda Hogan.
Leslie Marmon Silko, *Ceremony*, 1977
    A Pueblo man returns from the war and must realign himself with the traditional ways before he can become whole again.
Linda Hogan, *Mean Spirit*, 1990
    This novel chronicles the greed and corruption that flows from Oklahoma's oil fields during the boom days.

1225

JANET CAMPBELL HALE, Native American, Coeur d'Alene and Kootenai

Owl's Song
(New York: Harper, 1974)

Subject(s): Prejudice; Coming of Age
Age range(s): Grades 6-9

Major character(s): Billy White Hawk, Child (adolescent boy), Native American
Time period(s): 1970s
Locale(s): United States

Summary: Billy White Hawk, an adolescent, leaves the Benewah reservation in Idaho and moves to the city with his older half-sister, on his journey to becoming a man.

Where it's reviewed:
Los Angeles Times Book Review, June 18, 1995, page 13

Other books by the same author:
The Jailing of Cecelia Capture, 1985
Custer Lives in Humboldt County, 1978 (poetry)

Other books you might like:
Jean Craighead George, *The Talking Earth*, 1983
A young Seminole girl begins to doubt the beliefs of the elders until she goes into the Everglades and begins to understand the importance of her tribal teachings and the world of nature.
Jay Leech, *Moon of the Big-Dog*, 1980
Three young Sioux boys go on a journey in which they capture the first horses for their tribe and earn a new name for their Sioux band: Brule. Co-authored by Zane Spencer and illustrated by M. Funai.
Virginia Driving Hawk Sneve, *The Chichi Hoohoo Bogeyman*, 1975
Three Sioux Indian girls on a visit to their grandparents' house, encounter a weird creature they're sure is the bogeyman.
Virginia Driving Hawk Sneve, *High Elk's Treasure*, 1972
This novel for middle school readers is about Joe High Elk who longs to bring back the strain of wild mustangs that his famous ancestor bred many years before. Illustrations by Oren Lyons.
Shirley Sterling, *My Name Is Seepeetza*, 1992
Fictional account based on the life of the author, who, as a member of the interior Salish tribe, is forced to attend government schools where she is forbidden to reflect anything of her own heritage.

`1226`

WILLIAM LEAST HEAT MOON (William Lewis Trogdon)

PrairyErth
(New York: Houghton Mifflin, 1991)

Subject(s): Travel
Age range(s): Grades 10-Adult
Time period(s): 1980s
Locale(s): Kansas

Summary: Heat Moon, who wrote the famous *Blue Highways*, takes his readers on a different kind of journey, exploring Chase County, Kansas with great detail, love, and affection. This is a new kind of journey that teaches the reader to see living in one place in a new, deeper way.

Where it's reviewed:
Book World, September 27, 1992, page 12
Kliatt, March 1993, page 41
New York Times Book Review, October 11, 1992, page 36
American Book Review, December 1992, page 10

Christian Science Monitor, December 22, 1992, page 13

Other books you might like:
N. Scott Momaday, *The Way to Rainy Mountain*, 1976
This is mixed genre of fiction, poetry, history, mythology, and personal memoir.
N. Scott Momaday, *The Names: A Memoir*, 1976
This is an autobiographical work.
Leslie Marmon Silko, *Storyteller*, 1981
This work is a mixed genre of poetry, fiction, and mythology.
Brian Swann, *I Tell You Now*, 1989
This is an excellent collection of autobiographical essays by eighteen contemporary Native American writers, co-edited with Brian Swann.

`1227`

TONY HILLERMAN, Caucasian

The Boy Who Made Dragonfly
(New York: Harper and Row, 1972)

Subject(s): Mythology
Age range(s): Grades 4-7
Major character(s): Bow Priest, Zuni Indian; Corn Maiden, Zuni Indian, Deity (goddess)
Time period(s): Indeterminate Past
Locale(s): South Dakota

Summary: When the Bow Priest begins bragging to the other nations about his tribe's abundance of corn, a gigantic food fight ensues. The Corn Maidens, who cannot believe such a thing to be true, disguise themselves as old women and enter the village only to realize their worst fears. The wasting of food has begun.

Where it's reviewed:
Booklist, April 1, 1994, page 1463
Children's Bookwatch, September 1992, page 2

Other books you might like:
Margot Astrov, *The Winged Serpent*, 1946
This mixed genre is one of the best collections of oral stories and songs from a large cross-section of Native American cultures.
Marilyne Virginia Mabery, *Right After Sundown: Teaching Stories of the Navajo*,
These Navajo traditional stories about the beginning of the world are illustrated by Navajo artist Raymond J. Johnson.
Mourning Dove, *Coyote Stories*, 1933
These traditional stories are about Coyote, the trickster.
G.M. Mullet, *Spider Woman Stories*,
These Hopi Indian legends are collected from the 1880s.
Paula Gunn Allen, *Spider Woman's Granddaughters*, 1989
This is a beautiful collection of traditional tales interwoven with contemporary stories having to do with the lives of Native American women.
Zitkala-Sa, *Old Indian Legends Retold by Zitkala-Sa*, 1921
This is a collection of memoirs and essays about the traditional Lakota culture and its adjustments to the real world.

Native American Titles

TONY HILLERMAN, Caucasian

Coyote Waits
(New York: Harper, 1990)

Subject(s): Mystery; Police Procedural; Crime and Criminals
Age range(s): Grades 10-Adult
Major character(s): Jim Chee, Police Officer (tribal police-man), Native American (Navajo); Joe Leaphorn, Police Officer (tribal policeman), Native American (Navajo)
Time period(s): 1990s
Locale(s): New Mexico

Summary: Two Navajo policeman, Joe Leaphorn and Jim Chee, must uncover the murderer of fellow tribal policeman, Delbert Nez. A Navajo shaman, Ashie Pinto, is quickly arrested but refuses to talk. Sifting through the clues means Leaphorn and Chee must sift through the beliefs of the Navajo.

Where it's reviewed:
Western American Literature, Summer 1993, page 99

Other books by the same author:
The Ghostway, 1984 (mystery)
The Blessingway, 1970 (mystery)
Finding Moon, 1995 (mystery)
The Mysterious West, 1994
The Sacred Clowns, 1993
Talking God, 1989
A Thief of Time, 1988
Skinwalkers, 1986

Other books you might like:
Carol LaFavor, *Along the Journey River*, 1996
This is a mystery story about sacred stolen objects, as the lives of Renee and Salisbury become intwined on the red Earth Reservation of Minnesota.
Martin Cruz Smith, *Nightwing*, 1977
Youngman Duran leaves his pueblo to join the war effort but feels alienated from his people when he returns to the reservation where he must help uncover the secret of a threatening plague.
Louis Owen, *Bone Game*, 1994
Cole McCurtain is a mixed-blood professor, haunted by dreams, who becomes embroiled in a murder mystery that involves ecological crisis.
Linda Hogan, *Mean Spirit*, 1990
This murder mystery takes place in the oil boom days of Oklahoma.
Martin Cruz Smith, *Stallion Gate*, 1986
Joe Pena leaves his pueblo to join the war effort but feels alienated when he returns to his people. There he must confront the power of the atom bomb developed at Los Alamos.

ARLENE HIRSCHFELDER, Editor, Caucasian

Native Heritage
(New York: MacMillan, 1995)

Subject(s): Biography
Age range(s): Grades 9-Adult
Time period(s): 18th century; 20th century (1790-present)
Locale(s): United States

Summary: This book is a collection of personal accounts by American Indian people from 1790 through the present. It is divided into eight sections: Family, Land and Its Resources, Language, Native Education, Traditional Storytelling, Traditions, Worship, and Discrimination.

Where it's reviewed:
Los Angeles Times Book Review, August 27, 1995, page 11
Native Peoples, Winter 1996, page 79

Other books by the same author:
American Indian and Eskimo Authors: A Comprehensive Bibliography
American Indian Lives; Artists and Craftspeople
American Indian Stereotypes in the World of Children: A Reader and Bibliography
The Encyclopedia of Native American Religions (co-written with Paulette Moin)

Other books you might like:
Brian Swann, *I Tell You Now*, 1989
This is an excellent collection of autobiographical essays by eighteen contemporary American Indian writers. Co-edited with Arnold Krupat.
Paula Gunn Allen, *Spider Woman's Granddaughters*, 1989
This is a beautiful collection of traditional tales interwoven with contemporary stories having to do with the lives of Native American women.
Paula Gunn Allen, *Voice of the Turtle*, 1994
Edited by the well known writer and scholar Paula Gunn Allen, this book is an anthology of literature written by American Indian people from 1900 to 1970.
Lee Miller, *From the Heart: Voices of the American Indian*, 1995
This is a collection of orations, speeches, and testimony by more than 250 Indian people that presents a radical alternative to traditionally taught American history.
Clifford E. Trafzer, *Blue Dawn, Red Earth: New Native American Storytellers*, 1996
This is a collection of short stories by 30 new Native American writers, such as Lorne Simon, Jim Barnes, Richard Van Camp, and Penny Olson.
Beth Brant, *A Gathering of Spirit: A Collection of North American Indian Women*, 1984
Here is a collection of stories, letters, essays, and poems from a large cross-section of Native American women writers, such as Linda Hogan, Doris Seale, and Ann Lee Walters.

1230

GEARY HOBSON, Editor, Caucasian

The Remembered Earth

(Albuquerque: U. Of New Mexico Press, 1979)

Subject(s): Literature; Indians of North America
Age range(s): Grades 10-Adult
Time period(s): 20th century
Locale(s): United States

Summary: A compilation of stories and poems by contemporary American Indian writers, such as Joy Harjo, Peter Blue Cloud, Luci Ptapahonso, Wendy Rose, Mary Tallmountain, and many more. The book is divided into geographical Sections that represent the writers' origins.

Other books you might like:
Craig Lesley, *Talking Leaves*, 1991
    This book is an excellent collection of short stories by thirty-five contemporary American Indian writers, such as Louise Erdrich, N. Scott Momaday, Linda Hogan and Roberta Hill Whiteman.
Brian Swann, *I Tell You Now*, 1989
    This is an excellent collection of autobiographical essays by eighteen contemporary American Indian writers. Co-edited with Arnold Krupat.
Paula Gunn Allen, *Spider Woman's Granddaughters*, 1989
    This is a beautiful collection of traditional tales interwoven with contemporary stories about Native American women.
Arlene Hirschfelder, *Native Heritage*, 1995
    Personal accounts of Indian people from 1790 to the present.

1231

LINDA HOGAN, Native American, Ojibwa (Chickasaw)

Mean Spirit

(New York: Ivy Books, 1990)

Subject(s): Indians of North America
Age range(s): Adult
Major character(s): Stace Red Hawk, Native American; John Hale, Oil Industry Worker
Time period(s): 1920s
Locale(s): Oklahoma

Summary: When oil is discovered on Indian land, conflict breaks out between the Whites, who want to claim the land, and the Osage, who fight to retain what is their's. Belle and Moses support the Indians—a relative of their's owns the land on which the oil is found—while John Hale, uses corruption and power to drive them off.

Where it's reviewed:
American Poetry Review, July 1995, page 29
MS., September 1992, page 62
Rocky Mountain Review of Language & Literature, Issue 1, 1993, page 61

Other books by the same author:
The Book of Medicines, 1993 (poetry)
Red Clay: Poems and Stories, 1991

Other books you might like:
Leslie Marmon Silko, *Ceremony*, 1977
    A pueblo man, returned from the war, must realign himself with the traditional ways before becoming whole again.
James Welch, *Fools Crow*, 1986
    This novel explores White encroachment on the Plains Blackfeet in Montana (1870s). White Man's Dog, who becomes Fools Crow, is a young man vying for a place of respect in his society.
N. Scott Momaday, *House Made of Dawn*, 1968
    This Pulitzer prize winning novel is about a pueblo man who, having returned from WWII shell-shocked, must figure out who he is and realign himself with his people.
John Joseph Mathews, *Sundown*, 1934
    This novel portrays life in the oil fields in Osage country in the 1920s.
Craig Lesley, *Talking Leaves*, 1991
    This book is an excellent collection of stories by thirty-five contemporary American Indian writers including Louise Erdrich, Michael Dorris, N. Scott Momaday and others.
James Welch, *Winter in the Blood*, 1974
    A man is caught in the clutches of alcoholism and tries to discover the truth about his family.

1232

LINDA HOGAN, Native American, Chickasaw

Red Clay

(Greenfield Center, NY: Greenfield Review Press, 1991)

Subject(s): Indians of North America; Poetry
Age range(s): Adult
Time period(s): 20th century
Locale(s): Oklahoma

Summary: This is an excellent collection of short stories and poems by one of the best contemporary Native writers.

Where it's reviewed:
American Poetry Review, July 1995, page 29
Multicultural Review, July 1992, page 56

Other books by the same author:
Calling Myself Home, 1978 (poetry)
Daughters, I Love You, 1981 (poetry)
Mean Spirit, 1990
Savings, 1988 (poetry)
Seeing through the Sun, 1985 (poetry)

Other books you might like:
Clifford E. Trafzer, *Blue Dawn, Red Earth: New Native American Storytellers*, 1996
    This is a collection of short stories by 30 new Native American writers: Lorne Simon, Anita Endrezze, Jim Barnes, Annie Hansen, Maurice Kenny, and Patricia Piley, among others.
Leslie Marmon Silko, *Storyteller*, 1981
    A mixed genre anthology of poetry, fiction, and mythology.
Janet Campbell Hale, *The Jailing of Cecelia Capture*, 1985
    This novel is about an Indian woman in her thirties who has two children, who is separated from her husband and

kids, going to law school, and fighting a terrible battle with alcoholism.

Simon J. Ortiz, *Fightin'*, 1969

This mixed genre anthology contains poetry and short stories.

John Joseph Mathews, *Sundown*, 1934

Novel about the oil fields in Osage country in the 1920s.

1233

DIANE HOYT-GOLDSMITH, Caucasian
LAWRENCE MIGDALE, Illustrator

Pueblo Storyteller
(New York: Harper Collins, 1996)

Subject(s): Legends; Indians of North America; Storytelling
Age range(s): Grades 3-6
Major character(s): April Trujillo, Storyteller, Child (young girl), Native American (Cochiti)
Time period(s): 1990s
Locale(s): New Mexico

Summary: The story of the famous Cochiti Storyteller clay figurines is here told through a young Cochiti girl, April, who weaves in legends of Cochiti life with this tale of the making of the figurines.

Where it's reviewed:
New Advocate, Spring 1995, page 125
Five Owls, January 1993, page 52
Language Arts, March 1993, pager 220
Reading Teacher, November 1992, page 229

Other books you might like:
Joseph Bruchac, *Return of the Sun*, 1990

Traditional tales of the Northeast Woodlands, full of humor and wisdom, equally as enlightening as Aesop's fables, and more fun.

Joseph Bruchac, *Flying with the Eagle, Racing with the Bear*, 1993

These rite-of-passage stories come from various tribal peoples including the Wampanoag, Cherokee, Osage, Lakota and Tlingit.

Shonto Begay, *Ma'ii and Cousin Horned Toad*,

Lazy, conniving Ma'ii is hungry and goes to Horny Toad for a free lunch. He swallows his smaller cousin, but Horny Toad teaches him a lesson he won't forget.

Herschel Talashoema, *Coyote & Little Turtle: Iisaw Niqw Yongosonhoya: A Traditional Hopi Tale*, 1994

This is an excellent book for early readers about Coyote and Little Turtle. It is written in both Hopi and English, with illustrations from Hopi children. Co-authored by John Emory Sekaquaptewqa.

Joseph Bruchac, *The Girl Who Married the Moon*, 1994

These are mostly traditional tales from a variety of North American tribes about women: initiation ceremonies, shape changing stories, and others.

D'Arcy McNickle, *Runner in the Sun: A Story of Indian Maize*, 1987

This novel for middle school readers is about the cliff dwellers of Chaco Canyon. In this book, Salt must journey from his homeland to find a breed of corn that will save his people.

Monty Roessel, *Songs from the Loom*, 1995

This story follows Jaclyn Roessel, a young Navajo girl, as she learns the stories of her family and the cultural wisdom and mythology associated with the art of weaving.

Sandra King, *Shannon: An Ojibway Dancer*, 1993

This book follows the life of a young Ojibway girl, Shannon, who lives in the city, yet still participates in tribal ceremonies.

Rina Swentzell, *Children of Clay*, 1992

In this book for children, a Santa Clara woman tells the wondrous story of making the famous Santa Clara pottery. Photos by Bill Steen.

1234

VICKIE JENSEN, Caucasian

Carving a Totem Pole
(New York: Henry Holt, 1994)

Subject(s): Artists and Art; Rituals
Age range(s): Grades 3-8
Major character(s): Norman Tait, Artist (totem carver)
Time period(s): 1990s
Locale(s): New Mexico

Summary: Norman Tait is a Nisga'a artist. Carving a totem pole in the traditional fashion, he relates the meaning and importance of the totem pole to the Nisga'a people.

Where it's reviewed:
Junior Bookshelf, February, 1995, page 20
Children's Bookwatch, August 1994, page 2
Quill and Quire, July 1994, page 62

Other books by the same author:
Where the People Gather, 1992

Other books you might like:
Michael Dorris, *Morning Girl*, 1992

This is the story of a young girl in Pre-Columbian Caribbean society.

Sandra King, *Shannon: An Ojibway Dancer*, 1993

This book follows the life of a young Ojibway girl who lives in the city, yet still participates in tribal ceremonies.

Monty Roessel, *Songs from the Loom*, 1995

This story follows Jaclyn Roessel, a young Navajo girl, as she learns the stories of her family and the cultural wisdom and mythology associated with the art of weaving.

Joseph Bruchac, *Flying with the Eagle, Racing with the Bear*, 1993

These rite-of-passage stories come from various tribal peoples including the Wampanoag, Cherokee, Osage, Lakota and Tlingit.

Susan Braine, *Drumbeat. . .Heartbeat: A Celebration of the Powwow*, 1995

This is a wonderful introduction to the Powwow for children by a Native American writer and photographer.

Herman J. Viola, *Osceola*, 1993

This is a brief history of the famous Creek leader, Osceola, for younger readers. Illustrated by Yoshi Miyake.

Albert Marrin, *Plains Warrior: Chief Quanah Parker and the Comanches*, 1996

This book tells the story of Quanah Parker, chief of the Comanches.

Charlie Craigan, *How the Robin Got Its Red Breast*, 1993
  This traditional tale, retold for children, is illustrated in the traditional Northwest Coast style by the author.

Charlie Craigan, *Mayuk: The Grizzly Bear*, 1993

Rina Swentzell, *Children of Clay*, 1992
  In this book for children, a Santa Clara woman tells the wondrous story of making the famous Santa Clara pottery.

1235

BRODERICK H. JOHNSON, Editor, Caucasian

Navajo Stories of the Long Walk Period

(Tsaile, NM: Navajo Community College Press, 1973)

Subject(s): Folklore; History; Indian Removal
Age range(s): Grades 9-Adult
Time period(s): 19th century; 20th century (1800s-1900s)
Locale(s): New Mexico; Arizona

Summary: In this intriguing collection, Navajo people recount the stories told to them of the Long Walk period as handed down in their families through generations. They present history from the Navajo's point of view, a historically overlooked viewpoint.

Other books you might like:

John Bierhorst, *Four Masterworks of American Indian Literature*, 1974
  This book has four great works of traditional Indian literature: *Quetzalcoatl*, *The Ritual of Condolence*, *Cuceb*, and *The Night Chant*.

Hasteen Klah, *The Myth and Prayers of the Great Star Chant, and the Myth of the Coyote Chant*, 1988
  This exquisite book is a compilation of important Navajo myths, songs, chants, and prayers, portraying the complexity of the philosophical and religious life of Navajo culture.

John Bierhorst, *The Red Swan: Myths and Tales of the American Indians*, 1976
  This book is a compilation of varied stories (creation, trickster, star husband, etc.) from forty Native American tribes.

Frederick Turner, *The Portable North American Indian Reader*, 1973
  This anthology of myths, legends, poetry, fiction, and captivity tales, contains work by both Native American and non-Native writers.

Jonathan Broderick, *Stories of Traditional Navajo Life and Culture*, 1977
  These are interviews from tape-recorded meetings of the Navajo.

1236

E. PAULINE JOHNSON, Native American, Mohawk

The Moccasin Maker

(Tucson: U. of Arizona Press, 1913, 1987)

Subject(s): Historical; Indian Reservations; Family Life
Age range(s): Grades 10-Adult

Major character(s): Lydia, Young Woman, English; George Mansion, Native American, Young Man
Time period(s): 19th century (1850-1900)
Locale(s): Canada; United States

Summary: This is a collection of prose pieces, mainly short stories, by one of the first Indian women who wrote poetry and prose and performed her compositions on the stage. Many of the stories are about Johnson's family life on the Mohawk reservation.

About this book: Written in the "romantic" style of the period, Johnson's stories nevertheless show a side of Indian life that avoids the cliched and stereotypical. Johnson, who was of English and Mohawk heritage, was primarily a poet and professional performer who traveled extensively in the U.S. and England, delighting audiences with her portrayals of Indian life.

Other books by the same author:
Canadian Born, 1903 (poetry)
The Shagganappi, 1913
The White Wampum, 1895 (poetry)
Humors and/or Not So Humorous, 1988 (poetry)
Is This Summer Bear, 1985 (poetry)

Other books you might like:

Craig Lesley, *Talking Leaves*, 1991
  This book is a an excellent collection of short stories by thirty-five contemporary American Indian writers, such as Louise Erdrich, N. Scott Momaday, Linda Hogan and Roberta Hill Whiteman.

Paula Gunn Allen, *Voice of the Turtle*, 1994
  Edited by the well known writer and scholar Paula Gunn Allen, this book is an anthology of literature written by American Indian people from 1900 to 1970.

Lee Miller, *From the Heart: Voices of the American Indian*, 1995
  This is a collection of orations, speeches and testimony by more than 250 Inidan people that presents a radical alternative to traditionally taught American history.

Clifford E. Trafzer, *Blue Dawn, Red Earth: New Native American Storytellers*, 1996
  This is a collection of short stories by 30 new Native American writers: Lorne Simon, Anita Endrezze, Jim Barnes, Annie Hansen, Maurice Kenny, and Patricia Piley, among others.

Zitkala-Sa, *Old Indian Legends Retold by Zitkala-Sa*, 1921
  These stories depict Zitkala-Sa's childhood in the traditional Lakota culture and the difficulties she faced while attending school and college in a world where she was perceived as a "savage."

Shirley Sterling, *My Name Is Seepeetza*,
  Fictional account based on the life of the author, who as a member of the interior Salish tribe was forced to attend governmnet schools where she was forbidden to reflect anything of her own heritage.

Maria Campbell, *Halfbreed*,
  This is the moving account of Maria Campbell's life as a Mtis, or halfbreed, part Indian—part European.

Paula Gunn Allen, *Spider Woman's Granddaughters*, 1989
  This is a beautiful collection of traditional tales interwoven with contemporary short stories having to do with the lives of Native American women.

1237

PAMELA GREENHILL KAIZEN, Native American, Lakota (Sioux)
MARK W. MCGINNIS, Illustrator, Caucasian

Lakota & Dakota Animal Wisdom Stories
(Chamberlain, SD: Tipi Press, 1994)

Subject(s): Folk Tales; Traditional Stories
Age range(s): Grades 2-6
Major character(s): Coyote, Trickster; Racoon, Racoon; Beaver, Beaver
Time period(s): Indeterminate Past (mythic time)
Locale(s): South Dakota

Summary: These traditional stories have been retold by the Lakota storyteller Pamela Greenhill Kaizen. The stories in this collection have an Aesop's fables feel about them, as many make direct points about thrift versus excuses, work versus sloth.

About this book: The illustrations by McGinnis are absolutely wonderful. There is also an introduction to this book by Tahunska Tanka (Big Leggings) that helps place these stories in their cultural context.

Other books you might like:
Joseph Bruchac, *Iroquois Stories*, 1985
  This book recounts many of the traditional animal, adventure and monster tales of the Iroquois people.
Joseph Bruchac, *The Wind Eagle and Other Abenaki Stories*, 1984
  These are traditional tales of the Abenaki.
Joseph Bruchac, *Return of the Sun*, 1990
  Traditional tales of the Northeast Woodlands, full of humor and wisdom, equally as enlightening as Aesop's fables, and more fun.
Joseph Bruchac, *Flying with the Eagle, Racing with the Bear*, 1993
  These rite-of-passage stories come from various tribal peoples including the Wampanoag, Cherokee, Osage, Lakota and Tlingit.
John Bierhorst, *The Red Swan: Myths and Tales of the American Indians*, 1976
  This book is a compilation of varied stories (creation, trickster, star husband, etc.) from forty Indian tribes.
Frederick Turner, *The Portable North American Indian Reader*, 1973
  This anthology of myths, legends, poetry, fiction, and captivity tales, contains work by both Native American and non-Native writers.

1238

WILLIAM LOREN KATZ

Black Indians: A Hidden Heritage
(New York: Antheum, 1986)

Subject(s): History; Race Relations; African Americans
Age range(s): Grades 8-Adult
Time period(s): 17th century; 20th century (17th-20th centuries)

Locale(s): United States
Summary: Little has been written about the relations between Native Americans and Black Americans. This book sets the records straight, showing how, from the earliest times, Black and Indian people have married and merged aspects of their cultures.

Other books you might like:
Michael Dorris, *A Yellow Raft in Blue Water*, 1987
  This is one of the few novels that deals with "mixed blood" people who are part African-American and part Native American.

1239

CHARLES KAWBAWGAM, Native American, Ojibwa (Chippewa)
CHARLOTTE KAWBAWGAM, Co-Author, Native American, Ojibwa (Chippewa)
JACQUES LEPIQUE, Co-Author, Native American, Ojibwa (Chippewa)

Ojibwa Narratives
(Detroit: Wayne State Univ. Press, 1994)

Subject(s): Autobiography; Mythology; Traditional Stories
Age range(s): Grades 7-12
Major character(s): Nanabozho, Trickster
Time period(s): Indeterminate Past (mythic time)
Locale(s): Michigan

Summary: Traditional stories of Ojibway culture as told by Charles and Charlotte Kawbawgam and Jacques LePique to Arthur P. Bourgeois.

Other books you might like:
Maude Kegg, *Portage Lake: Memories of an Ojibwe Childhood*, 1991
  In these stories, printed in both English and the original Anishinaabe, Maude Kegg relates the cultural wisdom of her many years, describing important facets of Ojibway life.
George Copway, *The Life, History, and Travels of Kah-ge-ga-bowh*, 1847
  Kah-ge-ga-bowh, born in 1818, published this story of his life in 1847, and it contains sections on Ojibway legends, history, wars, and general culture.
Sandra King, *Shannon: An Ojibway Dancer*, 1993
  This book follows the life of a young Ojibway girl, Shannon, who lives in the city, yet still participates in tribal ceremonies.
Ignatia Broker, *Night Flying Woman*,
  Oona was of the generation who ripped away from the traditional Ojibwa life and forced to live the harsh life of the reservation.
Gerald Vizenor, *Earthdivers: Tribal Narratives on Mixed Descent*, 1981
  In this collection of short stories Vizenor creates trickster figures to poke fun at and make shrewd political commentary on America, reservation life, and just about everything else.
Anne M. Dunn, *When Beaver Was Very Great: Stories to Live By*, 1995

This collection contains mostly traditional tales but with some poems, memoirs, and personal essays scattered throughout.

Gerald Vizenor, *The People Named the Chippewa: Narrative Histories*, 1984

This mixed genre anthology contains essays, interviews, history, mythology, and stories.

1240

MAUDE KEGG, Native American, Ojibwe (Chippewa)
JOHN D. NICHOLS, Co-Author, Caucasian

Portage Lake: Memories of an Ojibwe Childhood

(Minneapolis: University of Minnesota Press, 1991)

Subject(s): Alcoholism; Cultures and Customs
Age range(s): Grades 10-Adult
Time period(s): 19th century; 20th century (1860s-1930s)
Locale(s): Minnesota

Summary: Elder of the Mille Lacs Reservation in Minnesota, Kegg grew up in the late 19th century among Native people who had little contact with Europeans. She has here preserved many of the stories of the daily life of her traditional childhood.

About this book: Having both the English and the Anishinaabe texts makes this a valuable research tool.

Other books by the same author:
Gabekanaansing/At the End of the Trail: Memories of a Chippewa Childhood in Minnesota with Texts in Ojibway and English, 1978
The Little Turtle, in Signs of Spring, 1988 (children's story)
Nookomis Gaa-inaajimotawid/What My Grandmother Told Me, 1990

Other books you might like:
George Copway, *The Life, History, and Travels of Kah-ge-ga-bowh*, 1847
Kah-ge-ga-bowh, born in 1818, published this story of his life in 1847, and it contains sections on Ojibway legends, history, wars, and general culture.
Louise Erdrich, *Love Medicine*, 1984
Married to Marie, Nector is nevertheless fatefully drawn to Lulu. When his grandson prepares a love medicine to win him back to his grandmother, he uses the wrong ingredients and kills Nector instead.
James Northrup, *Walking the Rez Road*, 1993
Luke Warmwater is a Vietnam vet who is down on his luck, but he, like most of his reservation cohorts, is a survivor in the trickster fashion.
Gerald Vizenor, *The People Named the Chippewa: Narrative Histories*, 1984
This mixed genre anthology contains essays, interviews, history, mythology and stories.
Ignatia Broker, *Night Flying Woman*, 1983
Oona was of the generation who were ripped away from traditional Ojibwer life and forced to live the harsh life of the reservation.

1241

JANE HOLDEN KELLEY, Caucasian
DOMINGA TAVA, Co-Author, Native American, Yaqui
CHEPA MORENO, Co-Author, Native American, Yaqui
DOMINGA RAMIREZ, Co-Author, Native American, Yaqui
ANTONIA VALENQUELA, Co-Author, Native American, Yaqui

Contemporary Life Histories

(Lincoln: University of Nebraska Press, 1978)

Subject(s): Autobiography; Women
Age range(s): Grades 11-Adult
Time period(s): 20th century
Locale(s): Arizona

Summary: This as-told-to-book chronicles the lives of four Yaqui women. The author describes many aspects of Yaqui culture in the introduction of the book.

Other books you might like:
Anna Moore Shaw, *A Pima Past*, 1974
Anna Moore Shaw born in a traditional Pima brush house, and educated in the white world, tells this fascinating autobiography of her life.
Zitkala-Sa, *Old Indian Lengends Retold by Zitkala-Sa*, 1921
This is a collection of memoirs and essays about the traditional Lakota culture and the adjustments to the real world.
Angela Sidney, *Life Lived like a Story: Life Stories of Three Yukon Native Elders*, 1990
This as-told-to-book chronicles the lives of three Yukon women.
Mary Crow Dog, *Lakota Woman*, 1990
This as-told-to book, with Richard Erdoes as author/editor, chronicles the life of a Lakota woman who lives through the hardships of the 1973 occupation of Wounded Knee by the AIM.
Mary Brave Bird, *Ohitika Woman*, 1993
This sequel to *Lakota Woman* chronicles the conflicts between feminism and traditional Indian belief, White and Indian philosophy. (Mary retook her maiden name after divorcing Crow Dog.)
Ignatia Broker, *Night Flying Woman*, 1983
Oona was of the generation who ripped away from the traditional life and forced to live the harsh life of the reservation. Ignatia Broker tells this moving story of her own grandmother.
Maude Kegg, *Portage Lake: Memories of an Ojibwe Childhood*, 1991
In these stories, printed in both English and the original Anishinaabe, Maude Kegg relates the cultural wisdom of her many years, describing important facets of Ojibway life.

1242

MATTHEW KING, Native American, Lakota (Sioux)
HARVEY ARDEN, Co-Author

Noble Red Man

(Hillsboro, NY: Beyond Words Publishing Co., 1994)

Subject(s): Autobiography; Religion
Age range(s): Grades 9-Adult
Time period(s): 20th century (1940s-1990s)
Locale(s): South Dakota

Summary: Matthew King, Lakota Wisdomkeeper, is also the interpreter of Lakota Chief, Fools Crow and spokesman for the traditional Lakota chiefs. This book is a collection of his sayings and words of wisdom.

Other books by the same author:
Wisdomkeepers: Meetings with Native American Spiritual Elders (compiled by Harvey Arden)

Other books you might like:
Mary Crow Dog, *Lakota Woman*, 1990
    This as-told-to book, with Richard Erdoes as author/editor, chronicles the life of a Lakota woman who lives through the hardships of the 1973 occupation of Wounded Knee by the AIM.
Luther Standing Bear, *Stories of the Sioux*, 1988
    These are early life stories of a traditional Lakota (Sioux) man.
Charles A. Eastman, *From the Deep Woods to Civilization*, 1916
    This autobiography is by a Sioux man who left the traditional buffalo hunting culture to become a medical doctor.
Black Elk, *Black Elk Speaks*, 1932
    The life story of a Holy Man of the Sioux, as-told-to book.
John Fire Lame Deer, *Lame Deer, Seeker of Visions*, 1972
    In this, as-told-to book, Lame Deer tells his story to the writer Richard Erdoes.

1243

SANDRA KING, Native American, Ojibway (Chippewa)

Shannon: An Ojibway Dancer

(Minneapolis, MN: Lerner Publications, 1993)

Subject(s): Multicultural; Rituals
Age range(s): Grades 3-6
Major character(s): Shannon, Dancer (traditional), Native American
Time period(s): 1990s
Locale(s): Minnesota

Summary: This contemporary book follows the life of a young tribal girl, Shannon, who lives in the city, yet still participates in tribal ceremonies. This accurate portrayal is a refreshing and positive look at a young, contemporary Indian girl's life.

Where it's reviewed:
Reading Teacher, December 1994, page 341
Booklist, January 15, 1994, page 926
School Library Journal, February 1994, page 111
Horn Book Guide, Spring 1994, page 173
Horn Book Magazine, March 1994, page 224

Other books you might like:
Shirley Sterling, *My Name Is Seepeetza*, 1992
    This fictional account, based on the life of the author, recounts her life as a member of the interior Salish tribe. Forced to attend government schools, she is forbidden to reflect her own heritage.
Maria Campbell, *Halfbreed*, 1973
    This is the moving account of Maria Campbell's life as a Metis or halfbreed, part Indian—part European.
Joseph Bruchac, *Flying with the Eagle, Racing with the Bear*, 1993
    These rite-of-passage stories come from many tribal people.

1244

THOMAS KING, Native American, Cherokee
WILLIAM KENT MONKMAN, Illustrator

A Coyote Columbus Story

(Toronto: Douglas and McIntyre, 1992)

Subject(s): Humor; Sports/Baseball
Age range(s): Grades 4-7
Major character(s): Coyote, Coyote
Time period(s): 1990s
Locale(s): Canada

Summary: The traditional Coyote character is brought into the modern world in this comical piece, as a female who wants to play baseball, then Christopher Columbus comes along causing trouble.

Other books by the same author:
Green Grass, Running Water, 1993
Medicine River, 1990
All My Relations: An Anthology of Contemporary Canadian Native Fiction, 1990
The Native in Literature, 1987 (nonfiction)

Other books you might like:
William Bright, *A Coyote Reader*, 1993
    This is a collection of trickster stories from many tribes, the chapters divided according to the various attributes of Coyote, rather than geographically.
Frederick Turner, *The Portable North American Indian Reader*, 1973
    This anthology of myths, legends, poetry, fiction, and captivity tales, contains work by both Native American and non-Native writers.
Mourning Dove, *Coyote Stories*, 1933
    These are traditional Okanagan stories about Coyote, the trickster.
Shonto Begay, *Ma'ii and Cousin Horned Toad*,
    Ma'ii is hungry, and he goes to Horny Toad for a free lunch, eventually swallowing his smaller cousin, but that does not fare well for Ma—ii who learns his lesson in the end.
Hasteen Klah, *The Myth and Prayers of the Great Star Chant, and the Myth of the Coyote Chant*, 1988
    This exquisite book is a compilation of important Navajo myths, songs, chants, and prayers, that deal with the complex philosophical and religious life of Navajo culture.

Herschel Talashoema, *Coyote & Little Turtle: Iisaw Niqw Yongosonhoya: A Traditional Hopi Tale*, 1994
Here is an excellent book for early readers about Coyote and Little Turtle. It is written in both Hopi and English, with illustrations from Hopi children.

John Bierhorst, *The Red Swan: Myths and Tales of the American Indians*, 1976
This book is a compilation of varied stories (creation, trickster, star husband, etc.) from forty Indian tribes.

1245

THOMAS KING, Native American, Cherokee

Green Grass, Running Water
(New York: Houghton Mifflin, 1993)

Subject(s): Indians of North America; Fantasy; Folklore
Age range(s): Adult
Major character(s): Alberta, Professor, Native American; Lionel, Salesman, Native American; Coyote, Trickster
Time period(s): 1990s
Locale(s): Alberta, Canada

Summary: Coyote, God, Robinson Crusoe, The Lone Ranger and others struggle amongst themselves in the cosmological firmament. Meanwhile various Native American characters do their best as they struggle with life. Eventually all head to the Sun Dance on the Blackfoot reservation. This book moves rapidly from place to place, from character to character, and from dimension to dimension. It's a roller coaster ride of great comic proportions.

Where it's reviewed:
New York Times Book Review, July 24, 1994, page 24
Tribune Books (Chicago), August 21, 1994, page 8
Books in Canada, December 1993, page 17
World and I, June 1993, page 285
World Literature Today, Autumn, 1993, page 869

Other books by the same author:
Medicine River, 1990
The Native in Literature, 1987 (nonfiction)
All My Relations: An Anthology of Contemporary Canadian Native Fiction, 1990

Other books you might like:
Gerald Vizenor, *Griever: An American Monkey King in China*, 1987
Vizenor creates a trickster character who leaves his Chippewa home to go to China where he finds himself kin to the Monkey King.

Louise Erdrich, *Love Medicine*, 1984
Married to Marie, Nector is nevertheless fatefully drawn to Lulu. When his grandson prepares a love medicine to win him back to his grandmother, he uses the wrong ingredients and kills Nector instead.

Sherman Alexie, *The Lone Ranger and Tonto Fist Fight in Heaven*, 1993
This wonderful short fiction is about the ups and downs of reservation life.

Sherman Alexie, *Reservation Blues*, 1995
Legendary bluesman Robert Johnson comes to the Rez and things begin to rock.

Ray A. Young Bear, *Black Eagle Child*, 1992
This fictional work is about life on a Mesquakie settlement.

W.P. Kinsella, *Moccasin Telegraph*, 1984
Life on the Ermineskin reserve in Canada, told by Silas Ermineskin himself, is full of both comedy and tragedy.

1246

THOMAS KING, Native American, Cherokee

Medicine River
(New York: Viking, 1989)

Subject(s): Indians of North America
Age range(s): Adult
Major character(s): Will, Photographer, Native American; Harlen Big Bear, Activist (community organizer), Native American
Time period(s): 1980s
Locale(s): Alberta, Canada

Summary: Will has no intention of staying in Medicine River when he returns there for his mother's funeral, but Harlan Bigbear has plans for him. Opening a photography shop in town, he begins to remember growing up in Medicine River and its odd inhabitants.

Where it's reviewed:
Canadian Literature, Winter 1991, page 212

Other books by the same author:
Green Grass, Running Water, 1993
All My Relations: An Anthology of Contemporary Canadian Native Fiction, 1990
A Coyote Columbus Story
The Native in Literature, 1987

Other books you might like:
Gerald Vizenor, *Griever: An American Monkey King in China*, 1987
Vizenor creates a trickster character who leaves his Chippewa home to go to China where he finds himself kin to the monkey king.

Louise Erdrich, *Love Medicine*, 1984
Married to Marie, Nector is fatefully drawn to Lulu. When his grandson prepares a love medicine to get him back for his grandmother, he uses the wrong ingredients and Nector chokes to death.

Louise Erdrich, *Tracks*, 1988
Two alternating voices in conflict, one a traditionalist and one the voice of change, reveal the escelating tension between two Chippewa families and the disintegration of their culture.

Louise Erdrich, *The Beet Queen*, 1987
When Mary Adare is abandoned by her mother for an avaiator she meets at a carnival, Mary finds a home with relatives near a Chippewa reservation.

Louise Erdrich, *The Bingo Palace*, 1994
Lipsha and Lyman are locked in a struggle to capture the heart of Shawnee Ray. But Shawnee Ray's ambitions reach beyond the reservation.

Sherman Alexie, *Reservation Blues*, 1995
This brilliant fiction is about the traits of Native Americans trying to cope in a most difficult world.

Native American Titles

Sherman Alexie, *The Lone Ranger and Tonto Fist Fight in Heaven*, 1993
This wonderful short fiction is about the ups and downs of reservation life.

1247

W.P. KINSELLA, Caucasian

Dance Me Outside
(Boston: David R. Grodine, 1977)

Subject(s): Cultures and Customs
Age range(s): Grades 9-Adult
Major character(s): Silas Ermineskin, Native American; Frank Fencepost, Native American; Mad Etta, Native American
Time period(s): 1970s
Locale(s): Canada

Summary: These seventeen stories are all about life on the fictional Ermineskin Reserve in Canada, as told by the fictional character Silas Ermineskin. These stories are gems, capturing both the comedic and tragic spirit of reservation life, all told in a vernacular voice that rings true.

About this book: Though Kinsella is White, he has a good grasp on the issues that concern Native American people, and is able to show this through a wonderful cast of characters.

Where it's reviewed:
Publishers Weekly, May 2, 1994, page 304

Other books by the same author:
The Moccasin Telegraph, 1984 (stories from the Eremineskin Reserve)
Shoeless Joe (Winner of the Houghton Mifflin Literary Fellowship)

Other books you might like:
Gerald Vizenor, *Earthdivers: Tribal Narratives on Mixed Descent*, 1981
In this collection of short stories Vizenor creates trickster figures to poke fun at and make shrewd politcal commentary on America, reservation life, and just about everything else.
James Northrup, *Walking the Rez Road*, 1993
Luke Warmwater is a Vietnam vet down on his luck, but, he, like most of his reservation cohorts, is a survivor in the trickster fashion.
Louise Erdrich, *Love Medicine*, 1984
Married to Marie, Nector is nevertheless fatefully drawn to Lulu. When his grandson prepares a love medicine to win him back to his grandmother, he uses the wrong ingredients and kills Nector instead.
Leslie Marmon Silko, *Storyteller*, 1981
This work is a mixed genre of poetry, fiction, and mythology.
Simon J. Ortiz, *Fightin'*, 1969
This mixed genre anthology contains poetry and short stories.
Sherman Alexie, *The Lone Ranger and Tonto Fist Fight in Heaven*, 1993
This wonderful short fiction is about the ups and downs of reservation life.

Thomas King, *Green Grass, Running Water*, 1993
Coyote, God, Robinson Crusoe, The Lone Ranger and others struggle amongst themselves in the cosmological firmament while on the human plane, characters struggle with life the best they can.

1248

W.P. KINSELLA, Caucasian

Moccasin Telegraph
(Boston: David R. Grodine, 1984)

Subject(s): Cultures and Customs; Indian Reservations
Age range(s): Grades 9-Adult
Major character(s): Silas Ermineskin, Native American; Frank Fencepost, Native American; Mad Etta, Native American
Time period(s): 1970s
Locale(s): Canada

Summary: These sixteen stories are about life on the fictional Ermineskin Reserve in Canada, as told by the fictional character Silas Ermineskin. These stories are gems, capturing both the comedic and tragic spirit of reservation life, all told in a vernacular voice that rings true.

Where it's reviewed:
Library Journal, August 1994, page 141
New York Times Book Review, September 11, 1994, page 44
Publishers Weekly, May 2, 1994, page 304

Other books by the same author:
Dance Me Outside, 1986 (stories from the Eremineskin Reserve)
Shoeless Joe (Winner of the Houghton Mifflin Literary Fellowship)

Other books you might like:
Louise Erdrich, *Love Medicine*, 1984
Married to Marie, Nector is nevertheless fatefully drawn to Lulu. When his grandson prepares a love medicine to win him back to his grandmother, he uses the wrong ingredients and kills Nector instead.
Craig Lesley, *Talking Leaves*, 1991
This book is an excellent collection of stories by 35 contemporary American Indian writers including Louise Erdrich, Michael Dorris, N. Scott Momaday, Linda Hogan and others.
Clifford E. Trafzer, *Blue Dawn, Red Earth: New Native American Storytellers*, 1996
This is a collection of short stories by 30 new Native American writers including Lorne Simon, Anita Endresse, Jim Barnes, Annie Hansen and others.
Beth Brant, *A Gathering of Spirit: A Collection of North American Indian Women*, 1984
This is a collection of stories, letters, essays and poems from a large cross-section of Native American women writers including Linda Hogan, Elizabeth Cook-Lynn, Diana Glancy and others.
Leslie Marmon Silko, *Storyteller*, 1981
Gerald Vizenor, *Earthdivers: Tribal Narratives on Mixed Descent*, 1981
In this collection of short stories, Vizenor creates a conglomeration of trickster figures as he pokes fun, and makes

shrewd political commentary, on American reservation life.

James Northrup, *Walking the Rez Road*, 1993
These short stories are written in the vernacular about life on an Ojibway reservation.

Sherman Alexie, *The Lone Ranger and Tonto Fist Fight in Heaven*, 1993

Thomas King, *Green Grass, Running Water*, 1993
In this wild romp, Coyote, God, Robinson Crusoe, The Lone Ranger and others struggle in the cosmological firmament while on the human plane, Native Americans struggle to survive as best they can.

1249

HASTEEN KLAH, Native American, Navajo
MARY CABOT WHEELRIGHT, Editor, Caucasian

The Myth and Prayers of the Great Star Chant, and the Myth of the Coyote Chant
(Tsaile, NM: Navajo Community College Press, 1988)

Subject(s): Rituals; Traditional Stories
Age range(s): Grades 9-Adult
Time period(s): Indeterminate
Locale(s): New Mexico; Arizona

Summary: This exquisite book is a compilation of important Navajo myths, songs, chants, and prayers, portraying the complexity of the philosophical and religious life of Navajo culture. Included in this book are many outstanding color plates of Navajo sandpainting.

Other books you might like:

John Bierhorst, *Four Masterworks of American Indian Literature*, 1974
This book has four great works of traditional Indian literature: *Quetzalcoatl, The Ritual of Condolence, Cuceb, The Night Chant.*

Marilyne Virginia Mabery, *Right After Sundown: Teaching Stories of the Navajo*,
These traditional Navajo stories about the beginnings of the world are illustrated by Navajo artist Raymond J. Johnson.

Margot Astrov, *The Winged Serpent*, 1946
This mixed genre collection is one of the best with oral stories and songs from a large cross-section of Native American cultures.

Jonathan Broderick, *Stories of Traditional Navajo Life and Culture*, 1977
These are interviews from tape-recorded meetings of the Navajo.

Broderick H. Johnson, *Navajo Stories of the Long Walk Period*, 1973
In this intruiging collection, Navajo people recount the stories of the Long Walk period as they have been handed down to them in their families.

Frederick Turner, *The Portable North American Indian Reader*, 1973
This anthology of myths, legends, poetry, fiction, and captivity tales, contains work by both Native American and non-Native writers.

John Bierhorst, *The Red Swan: Myths and Tales of the American Indians*, 1976
This book is a compilation of varied stories (creation, trickster, star husband, etc.) from forty Native American tribes.

Mourning Dove, *Coyote Stories*, 1933
These traditional stories are about Coyote, the trickster.

William Bright, *A Coyote Reader*, 1993
These are traditional Coyote stories.

1250

THEODORA KROEBER, Caucasian

Ishi, Last of His Tribe
(New York: Bantam, 1964)

Subject(s): Historical; Survival; Conquest
Age range(s): Grades 6 and Up
Major character(s): Ishi, Native American (Yahi)
Time period(s): 1910s (1911-1914)
Locale(s): California

Summary: This is the amazing story of Ishi, a Yahi Native American whose tribe and family (culturally untouched by civilization) has been destroyed by the White man. Miraculously, Ishi survives totally alone after the death of his last family members, in the wilderness of California, until one day in 1911, unable to stand his solitary existence any longer he goes to a farm where he is "discovered." Anthropologist, Alfred Kroeber, soon discovers that Ishi is the last surviving member of his band, and he takes Ishi to live at the Natural History Museum in San Francisco. While living there, Ishi teaches the Kroebers many things about Yahi life, and this book chronicles Ishi's incredible story in novelized form.

Other books by the same author:

Ishi in Two Worlds: A Biography of the Last Wild Indian in North AmericA, 1961 (biography)

Other books you might like:

Luther Standing Bear, *Stories of the Sioux*, 1988
Standing Bear grew up in the traditional buffalo hunting culture of the Sioux and he brings to life the stories from his past.

Zitkala-Sa, *Old Indian Legends Retold by Zitkala-Sa*, 1921
This book chronicles the life of a Sioux woman who grows up in the traditional buffalo hunting culture but who eventually goes east to Indian boarding school.

Charles A. Eastman, *From the Deep Woods to Civilization*, 1916
Eastman grew up in the Sioux buffalo hunting culture but went East to become a doctor.

Black Elk, *Black Elk Speaks*, 1932
This is the life story of the Sioux Holy Man.

Linda Yamane, *When the World Ended, How Hummingbird Got Fire, How People Were Made: Rumsien Ohlone Stories*, 1995
These three stories are of the Rumsien Ohlone people of California.

Jane Curry, *Back in the Before Time: Tales of the California Indians*, 1987
This collection includes twenty-two tales of the creation of the world from various California Indian tribes.

Sally Russel, *Voices and Dreams*, 1991
In these first-person accounts, 22 people of California Indian descent tell their moving stories about life, culture, racism and survival.

1251

MICHAEL ARVAARLUK KUSUGAK, Native American, Inuit (Eskimo)

Hide and Seek

(North York, ON: Firefly Books, 1992)

Subject(s): Childhood; Folklore; Games
Age range(s): Grades 2-4
Major character(s): Allashua, Child (girl), Inuit
Time period(s): 1990s
Locale(s): Canada

Summary: Allashua wants to play hide-and-seek, but her mother warns her of the Ijiraq; if they hide you—no one will ever find you again!

Where it's reviewed:
CM: Canadian Materials, September 1992, page 208
Emergency Librarian, March 1993, page 13
Bloomsbury Review, September 1992, page 21

Other books by the same author:
Northern Lights: The Soccer Trails, 1995

Other books you might like:
Shonto Begay, *Ma'ii and Cousin Horned Toad*,
Ma'ii is hungry, and he goes to Horny Toad for a free lunch, eventually swallowing his smaller cousin, but Mai'i learns his lesson in the end.

1252

MICHAEL ARVAARLUK KUSUGAK, Inuit (Eskimo)

Northern Lights: The Soccer Trails

(Toronto: Annick Press, 1995)

Subject(s): Childhood; Eskimos; Death
Age range(s): Grades 2-5
Major character(s): Kataujag, Child (girl), Inuit
Time period(s): 1990s
Locale(s): Canada

Summary: Kataujaq's is having some difficulty dealing with her mother's death until her grandmother tells her a story of the Northern Lights and what happens to the ancient people when they die. This book, with excellent illustrations by Vladyana Krykorka, deals with the pain of death, and relates how mythology can give one the strength to go on with life.

Where it's reviewed:
Canadian Children's Literature, Spring 1995, page 55
Canadian Materials, January 1994, page 21
Quill & Quire, September 1993, page 67

Awards the book has won:
Ruth Schwartz Award (Ontario), 1994

Other books by the same author:
Hide and Seek, 1992

Other books you might like:
Shonto Begay, *Ma'ii and Cousin Horned Toad*,
Lazy, conniving Ma'ii is hungry, and he goes to Horny Toad for a free lunch. He swallows his smaller cousin but Horny Toad teaches him a lesson he won't forget.

1253

MICHAEL ARVAARLUK KUSUGAK, Inuit (Eskimo)
ROBERT MUNSCH, Co-Author, Caucasian

A Promise Is a Promise

(Willowdale, ON, Canada: Firefly Books, 1988)

Subject(s): Friendship; Cleanliness; Promises
Age range(s): Grades 2-4
Major character(s): Allashua, Child (girl), Inuit; Qallupilluit, Monster
Time period(s): 1980s
Locale(s): Canada

Summary: Qallupilluq are Inuit monsters who grab children when they come too near the cracks in the ice. In this story, Allashua comes face to face with these sea monsters.

About this book: This is a nice blend of fiction that incorporates traditional Eskimo tales.

Other books you might like:
Herschel Talashoema, *Coyote & Little Turtle: Iisaw Niqw Yongosonhoya: A Traditional Hopi Tale*, 1994
This excellent book for early readers is about Coyote and Little Turtle. It is written in both Hopi and English, with illustrations drawn by Hopi children.
Sandra King, *Shannon: An Ojibway Dancer*, 1993
This book follows the life of a young Ojibway girl, Shannon, who lives in the city, yet still participates in tribal ceremonies.
G.M. Mullet, *Spider Woman Stories*,
These Hopi Indian legends are collected from the 1880s.

1254

FRANCIS LA FLESCHE, Native American, Omaha

The Middle Five: Indian Schoolboys of the Omaha Tribe

(Madison: University of Wisconsin Press, 1963)

Subject(s): Childhood; Autobiography; School Life
Age range(s): Grades 6 and Up
Time period(s): 19th century; 20th century (1860s-1900s)
Locale(s): Nebraska

Summary: This book relates the life of La Flesche and his friends in the Presbyterian mission school in Oklahoma. Boarding close to the Omaha camps, he and his fellow students were able to visit with their people and thus, had a less traumatic experience than most other Indian boarding school students. As La Flesche says, "I have chosen to write the story of my school-fellows rather than that of my other boy friends who knew only the aboriginal life."

Other books you might like:

Charles A. Eastman, *From the Deep Woods to Civilization*, 1916

   The autobiography of Charles Eastman who grows up in the buffalo hunting culture of the Sioux but pursues an education in the White man's world.

Anna Moore Shaw, *A Pima Past*, 1974

   Anna Moore Shaw, born in a traditional Pima brush house and educated in the white world, tells this fascinating autobiography of her life.

Zitkala-Sa, *Old Indian Legends Retold by Zitkala-Sa*, 1921

   This is a collection of memoirs and essays about the traditional Lakota culture and it's adjustments to European encroachment.

John Joseph Mathews, *Talking to the Moon*, 1945

   Mathews relates the full circle of his life from his childhood in Oklahoma, through his WWI military stint, college, marriage and back to his homeland.

Luther Standing Bear, *Stories of the Sioux*, 1988

   Standing Bear grew up in the traditional buffalo hunting culture, and he brings to life the stories from his own past.

1255

CAROL LAFAVOR, Native American, Ojibwa (Chippewa)

Along the Journey River

(Ithaca, NY: Firebrand Press, 1996)

Subject(s): Mystery and Detective Stories; Homosexuality/ Lesbianism

Age range(s): Adult

Major character(s): Renee LaRoche, Native American, Teacher; Samantha Salisbury, Professor

Time period(s): 1990s (1996)

Locale(s): Minnesota

Summary: This is a mystery story about sacred stolen objects, where the lives of Renee and Salisbury become intertwined on the red Earth Reservation of Minnesota.

About this book: This is a first of its kind: a Native American lesbian mystery story.

Other books you might like:

Louise Erdrich, *Love Medicine*, 1984

   Married to Marie, Nector is nevertheless fatefully drawn to Lulu. When his grandson prepares a love medicine to win him back to his grandmother, he uses the wrong ingredients and kills Nector instead.

Louise Erdrich, *Tracks*, 1988

   Two alternating voices in conflict, one a traditionalist and one the voice of change, reveal the escalating tension between two Chippewa families and the disintegration of their culture.

Louise Erdrich, *The Beet Queen*, 1987

   When 11-year-old Mary Adare is abandoned by her mother for an avaiator she meets at a carnival, Mary finds a home with relatives near a Chippewa reservation.

Louise Erdrich, *The Bingo Palace*, 1994

   Lipsha and Lyman are locked in a struggle to capture the heart of beautiful Shawnee Ray. But Shawnee Ray's ambitions reach beyond the reservation.

Craig Lesley, *Talking Leaves*, 1991

   This book is a an excellent collection of short stories by thirty-five contemporary American Indian writers, such as Louise Erdrich, N. Scott Momaday, Linda Hogan and Roberta Hill Whiteman.

LaVonne Ruoff, *American Indian Literatures: An Introduction, Bibliographic Review, and Selected Bibliography*, 1990

   This is the bible of Native American literature, essential to anyone who wants to pursue a study of the literature that has been written by American Indian people.

James Northrup, *Walking the Rez Road*, 1993

   Luke Warmwater is a Vietnam vet down on his luck, but he, like most of his reservation cohorts, is a survivor in the trickster fashion.

Charles Brill, *Red Lake Nation: Portraits of Ojibway Life*, 1992

   This book is primarily a photo essay of the Ojibway people of Red Lake but it is interspersed with observations by Brill and contains portions of interviews with the Red Lake people.

Gerald Vizenor, *Earthdivers: Tribal Narratives on Mixed Descent*, 1981

   In this collection of short stories Vizenor creates trickster figures to poke fun at and make shrewd political commentary on America, reservation life, and just about everything else.

Gerald Vizenor, *The People Named the Chippewa: Narrative Histories*, 1984

   This mixed genre anthology contains essays, interviews, history, mythology, and stories.

1256

JOHN FIRE LAME DEER, Native American, Lakota (Sioux)
RICHARD ERDOES, Co-Author, Caucasian

Lame Deer, Seeker of Visions

(New York: Simon & Schuster, 1972)

Subject(s): Autobiography; Religion

Age range(s): Grades 9-Adult

Time period(s): 20th century (1900-1970s)

Locale(s): South Dakota

Summary: This is the life story of John Fire Lame Deer as told to Richard Erdoes by Lame Deer himself. Lame Deer is a traditional medicine man, and while he tells the story of his life, he also deals with the philosophy of Lakota (Sioux) religion and culture. Much of the book looks at his visions and spiritual quest which often extend to the world at large. Serious on many points, the book is often hilarious, Lame Deer's wit and wisdom shining through on every page.

About this book: This is probably the best as-told-to book on Indian culture in the second half of the 20th century.

Where it's reviewed:

New York Times Book Review, March 18, 1973, page 1657
Publishers Weekly, June 19, 1972, page 55

Other books you might like:

Luther Standing Bear, *Stories of the Sioux*, 1988
These are early life stories of a traditional Lakota (Sioux) man.

Zitkala-Sa, *Old Indian Legends Retold by Zitkala-Sa*, 1921
This is a collection of memoirs and essays by an Indian woman who was born into the old buffalo hunting culture of the Sioux.

Raymond DeMallie, *The Sixth Grandfather*, 1984
These are transcripts of Neihardt's interviews with Black Elk, edited with commentary by DeMallie.

Wallace Black Elk, *Black Elk: The Sacred Ways of a Lakota*, 1990
An as-told-to book about the life story of a contemporary Lakota shaman.

Charles A. Eastman, *From the Deep Woods to Civilization*, 1916
This is an autobiography by a Sioux man who leaves the traditional buffalo hunting culture to become a medical doctor.

Wilma Mankiller, *Mankiller: A Chief and Her People*, 1993
With Michael Wallis, Chief Mankiller tells her story and the story of her people, the Cherokee.

1257

WILLIAM LEAST HEAT MOON (William Lewis Trogdon)

Blue Highways

(Boston: Little, 1982)

Subject(s): Travel
Age range(s): Grades 10-Adult
Time period(s): 1980s
Locale(s): United States

Summary: After losing his job at the college where he taught English, Heat Moon set himself on a path to discover the heart of America, off the beaten path. His travels take him full circle, back to where he began, and, going with him, we are introduced to a wonderful collection of characters, our wisdom accruing by the mile. This has become an American classic of the road.

Other books you might like:

Anna Moore Shaw, *A Pima Past*, 1974
Born in a traditional Pima brush house and educated in the White world, Shaw recounts her fascinating past.

Francis La Flesche, *The Middle Five: Indian Schoolboys of the Omaha Tribe*, 1900
This book details the lives of LaFlesche and his friends in mission school in Oklahoma.

Sarah Winnemucca, *Life Among the Paiutes: Their Wrongs and Claims*, 1883

John Fire Lame Deer, *Lame Deer, Seeker of Visions*, 1972
This is an As-Told-To book, Lame Deer telling his story to the writer Richard Erdoes.

Luther Standing Bear, *Stories of the Sioux*, 1988
Standing Bear grew up in the traditional buffalo hunting culture of the Sioux and he brings to life the stories from his own past.

Brian Swann, *I Tell You Now*, 1989
This is an excellent collection of autobiographical essays by eighteen contemporary American Indian writers.

Paula Gunn Allen, *The Sacred Hoop: Recovering the Feminine in American Indian Traditions*, 1986
This is an excellent collection of essays that uncover the essential role of women in traditional and contemporary Indian life.

N. Scott Momaday, *The Way to Rainy Mountain*, 1976
Mixed genre: fiction, poetry, history, mythology, and personal memoir.

1258

JAY LEECH, Caucasian
MAMORU FUNAI, Illustrator

Moon of the Big-Dog

(New York: Thomas Y. Crowell, 1980)

Subject(s): Indians of North America; Folklore
Age range(s): Grades 5-7
Major character(s): Black Raven, Native American (Sioux), Child (young boy); Strong Bow, Native American (Sioux), Child (young boy); Young Turtle, Native American (Sioux), Child (young boy)
Time period(s): Indeterminate Past
Locale(s): South Dakota

Summary: Three young Sioux boys go a journey in which they capture the first horses for their tribe, and also earn a new name for their Sioux band: Brule.

Other books you might like:

Charles A. Eastman, *From the Deep Woods to Civilization*, 1916
The autobiography of Charles A. Eastman, who grows up in the traditional buffalo culture of the Lakota (Sioux) but pursues an education in the White man's world. Introduction by Raymond Wilson.

Zitkala-Sa, *Old Indian Legends Retold by Zitkala-Sa*, 1921
These stories depict Zitkala-Sa's childhood in the traditional Lakota culture and the difficulties she faced while attending school and college in a world where she was perceived as a ''savage.''

Luther Standing Bear, *Stories of the Sioux*, 1988
Standing Bear grew up in the traditional buffalo hunting culture, and he brings to life the stories from his own past.

Charles A. Eastman, *Old Indian Days*, 1907
Autobiography of a Lakota Sioux man.

Virginia Driving Hawk Sneve, *The Chichi Hoohoo Bogeyman*,
Three Indian girls encounter a weird creature.

Virginia Driving Hawk Sneve, *High Elk's Treasure*, 1972
This novel for middle school readers is about Joe High Elk who longs to bring back the strain of wild mustangs that his famous ancestor had bred many years before. Illustrated by Oren Lyons.

1259

CRAIG LESLEY, Editor, Caucasian

Talking Leaves

(New York: Bantam, Doubleday, Dell, 1991)

Subject(s): Cultures and Customs; Short Stories
Age range(s): Grades 10-Adult
Time period(s): 20th century
Locale(s): United States

Summary: This book is an excellent collection of short stories by thirty-five contemporary Native American writers, among them, Louise Erdrich, Michael Dorris, N. Scott Momaday, Linda Hogan, Roberta Hill Whiteman, James Welch and others.

Where it's reviewed:
Booklist, November 15, 1991, page 603
Library Journal, October 15, 1991, page 126
Publishers Weekly, September 13, 1991, page 72

Awards the book has won:
Pacific Northwest Booksellers Association Award, 1992

Other books by the same author:
Winterkill
River Song

Other books you might like:
Brian Swann, *I Tell You Now*, 1989
  This is an excellent collection of autobiographical essays by 18 contemporary Native American writers.
Paula Gunn Allen, *Spider Woman's Granddaughters*, 1989
  This is a beautiful collection of traditional tales interwoven with contemporary stories about Native American women.
Zitkala-Sa, *Old Indian Legends Retold by Zitkala-Sa*, 1921
  Included are stories of growing up in the traditional culture of the Lakotas, as well as essays and personal memoirs.
Arlene Hirschfelder, *Native Heritage*, 1995
  Personal accounts of Native American people from 1790 to the present.

1260

BARRY LOPEZ, Caucasian

Giving Birth to Thunder, Sleeping with His Daughter: Coyote Builds North America

(New York: Avon Books, 1977)

Subject(s): Mythology; Legends; Trickster Tales
Age range(s): Grades 10-Adult
Major character(s): Coyote, Trickster
Time period(s): Indeterminate Past (mythic time)
Locale(s): United States

Summary: In this book Lopez retells a wide selection of Coyote stories from various North American tribes. As always, Coyote is dynamic, irreverant, wily, paradoxical, mysterious, taboo breaking, and fun.

About this book: This is not a scholarly book, but what Lopez tries to do is recreate these tales for a non-native audience while still retaining some of the magic of the original tellings.

Other books by the same author:
Desert Notes: Reflections in the Eye of a Raven, 1976
River Notes: The Dance of Herons, 1979
Winter Count, 1981

Other books you might like:
Mourning Dove, *Coyote Stories*, 1933
  These are traditional Okanagan stories about Coyote, the trickster.
John Bierhorst, *The Red Swan: Myths and Tales of the American Indians*, 1976
  This book is a compilation of varied stories (creation, trickster, star husband, etc.) from forty Indian tribes.
Frederick Turner, *The Portable North American Indian Reader*, 1973
  This anthology of myths, legends, poetry, fiction, and captivity tales, contains work by both Native American and non-Native writers.
Gerald Vizenor, *Griever: An American Monkey King in China*, 1987
  Vizenor creates a trickster character who leaves his Chippewa home to go to China where he finds himself to be kin to the Monkey King.
Gerald Vizenor, *Earthdivers: Tribal Narratives on Mixed Descent*, 1981
  In this collection of short stories Vizenor creates trickster figures to poke fun at and make shrewd political commentary on America, reservation life, and just about everything else.
Paul Radin, *The Trickster*, 1956
  This is an excellent study of the Trickster archetype. The Winnebago Trickster Cycle of Myths, the Winnebago Hare Cycle, and summaries of the Assiniboine and Tlingit Trickster Myths are presented.

1261

MARILYNE VIRGINIA MABERY, Caucasian
RAYMOND J. JOHNSON, Illustrator

Right After Sundown: Teaching Stories of the Navajo

(Tsaile, AZ: Navajo Community College Press)

Subject(s): Creation; Traditional Stories; Trickster Tales
Age range(s): Grades 3-7
Time period(s): Indeterminate
Locale(s): Arizona; New Mexico

Summary: These are the traditional stories told by the Navajo about creation. They will give children a new understanding of multiculturalism by teaching the Navajo's vision of their genesis and how the world came to be.

Other books you might like:
Hasteen Klah, *The Myth and Prayers of the Great Star Chant, and the Myth of the Coyote Chant*, 1988
  This exquisite book is a compilation of important Navajo myths, songs, chants, and prayers, portraying the complexity of the philosophical and religious life of Navajo culture.
Jonathan Broderick, *Stories of Traditional Navajo Life and Culture*, 1977
  These interviews are from tape-recorded meetings.

Broderick H. Johnson, *Navajo Stories of the Long Walk Period*, 1973

In this intriguing collection, Navajo people recount the stories of the Long Walk period as they have been handed down in their families.

Shonto Begay, *Ma'ii and Cousin Horned Toad*,

Lazy, conniving Ma'ii is hungry, and he goes to Horny Toad for a free lunch. He swallows his smaller cousin, but Horned Toad teaches him a lesson he won't forget.

1262

EKKEHART MALOTKI, Native American, Hopi
MICHAEL LOMATUWAY'MA, Co-Author, Native American, Hopi

Hopi Coyote Tales/Instutuwutsi

(Lincoln: University of Nebraska Press, 1978)

Subject(s): Traditional Stories; Trickster Tales
Age range(s): Grades 9-Adult
Major character(s): Coyote, Trickster
Time period(s): Indeterminate
Locale(s): Arizona

Summary: This is a collection of Hopi Coyote stories, where Coyote, the trickster, gets what's coming to him.

About this book: Since this collection is in both the Hopi and English languages, it makes an excellent teaching tool for children.

Other books by the same author:
Maasaw: Profile of a Hopi God, 1987
Stories of Maasaw, a Hopi God, 1987

Other books you might like:
William Bright, *A Coyote Reader*, 1993
Traditional Coyote trickster tales from across North America.

Gerald Vizenor, *Griever: An American Monkey King in China*, 1987
A novel about the traditional Ojibway trickster who goes to China, and meets the Monkey King, the Chinese trickster.

Gerald Vizenor, *Earthdivers: Tribal Narratives on Mixed Descent*, 1981
In this collection of short stories, Vizenor creates a dearth of trickster figures as he pokes fun (and makes shrewd political commentary) on America, reservation life, and just about everything else.

Hasteen Klah, *The Myth and Prayers of the Great Star Chant, and the Myth of the Coyote Chant*, 1988
This exquisite book is a compilation of importnt Navajo myths, songs, chants, and prayers, that deal with the complex philosophical and religious life of Navajo culture.

Frederick Turner, *The Portable North American Indian Reader*, 1973
These are mixed genre, including myths, legends, poetry, captivity narratives and fiction.

Mourning Dove, *Coyote Stories*, 1933
Traditional stories about Coyote, the trickster.

Paul Radin, *The Trickster*, 1956
An excellent study of the Trickster archetype,this work presents the Winnebago Trickster Cycle of Myths in full.

Barry Lopez, *Giving Birth to Thunder, Sleeping with His Daughter: Coyote Builds North America*, 1977
In this book, Lopez retells a wide selection of Coyote stories from various North American tribes. As always, Coyote is dynamic, irreverant, willy, paradoxical, mysterious, taboo breaking, and fun.

1263

WILMA MANKILLER, Native American, Cherokee
MICHAEL WALLIS, Co-Author, Caucasian

Mankiller: A Chief and Her People

(New York: St. Martin's Press, 1993)

Subject(s): Autobiography; Women
Age range(s): Grades 10-Adult
Time period(s): 1990s
Locale(s): Oklahoma

Summary: Wilma Mankiller is the current Chief of the Cherokees. In this book she recounts her own life story as well as the story of her people.

About this book: Co-author Michael Wallis, an excellent wordsmith, is famous for his book on Route 66.

Where it's reviewed:
Los Angeles Times Book Review, December 11, 1994, page 11
Reference and Research Book News, November 1994, page 12
Book World (Washington Post), September 5, 1993, page 8

Other books you might like:
John Fire Lame Deer, *Lame Deer, Seeker of Visions*, 1972
Traditional medicine man Lame Deer tells of his visions and spiritual guest while relating the philosophy of Lakota religion and culture.

Diane Glancy, *Firesticks*, 1993
A collection of short stories by one of the foremost American Indian poets, dealing with Indian people as its subject.

Zitkala-Sa, *Old Indian Legends Retold by Zitkala-Sa*, 1921
These stories recount Zitkala-Sa's childhood in the traditional Lakota culture and the difficulties she faces while attending school and college in a world where she is perceived as a "savage."

Brian Swann, *I Tell You Now*, 1989
This is an excellent collection of autobiographical essays by eighteen contemporary American Indian writers.

Diane Glancy, *Claiming Breath*, 1992
A collection of observations in diary form, that read like prose poems.

Helen Sekaquaptewa, *Me and Mine: The Life Story of Helen Sekaquaptewa*, 1969
This is the autobiography of a Hopi woman, written with Louise Udall.

Robert J. Conley, *Mountain Windsong*, 1992
Conley weaves stories, songs, and historical documents into this love story about two young Cherokee people who endure the horror of the "Trail of Tears".

Vickie Sears, *Simple Songs*, 1990

This is a collection of short stories by a Cherokee writer.

Mary Crow Dog, *Lakota Woman*, 1990

This as-told-to book chronicles the life of a Lakota woman who struggles through the turbulence of the 1973 occupation of Wounded Knee by the AIM.

Mary Brave Bird, *Ohitika Woman*, 1993

This sequel to *Lakota Woman*, written under her maiden name, tells the story of a woman caught between feminism and traditional Indian belief.

`1264`

BRIAN MARACLE, Caucasian

Crazywater: Native Voices on Addiction and Recovery

(New York: Penguin, 1994)

Subject(s): Alcoholism
Age range(s): Grades 10-Adult
Time period(s): 1990s
Locale(s): Canada

Summary: In interviews with Native Americans, Maracle brings to light the root causes of the alcoholism that has so plagued Indian people. These stories, told in the first-person, are haunting and frank and may help to break down the many stereotypes about Indian people and alcohol promoted for generations.

Where it's reviewed:

Kliatt, July 1994, page 32
Los Angeles Times Book Review, May 8, 1994, page 8

Other books you might like:

Brian Swann, *I Tell You Now*, 1989

This is an excellent collection of autobiographical essays by eighteen contemporary Native American writers, co-edited with Arnold Krupat.

Janet Campbell Hale, *The Jailing of Cecelia Capture*, 1985

An Indian woman in her thirties, separated from her husband and two children, is fighting a terrible battle with alcoholism while attending law school.

Michael Dorris, *The Broken Cord: A Family's On-Going Struggle with Fetal Alcohol Syndrome*, 1989

Dorris is one of the first unmarried men in A merica to adopt a child. He adopts a Sioux named Adam, who suffers from Fetal Alcohol syndrome. This book documents their struggles.

James Welch, *Winter in the Blood*, 1974

A man caught in alcoholism, tries to discover the truth about his family.

`1265`

MARKOOSIE, Inuit (Eskimo)
GERMAINE ARNAKTAUYOK, Illustrator

Harpoon of the Hunter

(Montreal: McGill—Queen's University Press, 1970)

Subject(s): Hunting; Eskimos
Age range(s): Grades 6 and Up

Major character(s): Suluk, Eskimo, Father; Kamik, Eskimo, Son
Time period(s): 19th century; 20th century (1860s-1930s)
Locale(s): Canada (Arctic)

Summary: This story chronicles the life of an Eskimo boy who must learn to be a hunter.

Other books you might like:

Michael Arvaarluk Kusugak, *A Promise Is a Promise*, 1988

Qallupilluq are Inuit monsters who grabs children who come too near the cracks in the ice. This is the story of a young girl, Allashua, who comes face to face with these sea monster.

Frederick Turner, *The Portable North American Indian Reader*, 1973

This anthology of myths, legends, poetry, fiction, and captivity tales, contains work by both Native and non-Native writers.

Michael Arvaarluk Kusugak, *Northern Lights: The Soccer Trails*, 1995

Kataujaq's (who is a young Eskimo girl) mother dies, and Kataujaq feels very sad, until her grandmother tells her a story of the Northern Lights and what happens to the people when they die.

John Bierhorst, *The Red Swan: Myths and Tales of the American Indians*, 1976

This book is a compilation of varied stories (creation, trickster, star husband, etc.) from forty Indian tribes.

`1266`

ALBERT MARRIN, Caucasian

Plains Warrior: Chief Quanah Parker and the Comanches

(New York: Antheum, 1996)

Subject(s): Biography; Cultures and Customs; Indians of North America
Age range(s): Grades 5-8
Time period(s): 19th century
Locale(s): Oklahoma

Summary: This book tells the story of Quanah Parker, chief of the Comanches, whose mother was Cynthia Ann, a white girl kidnapped by the Comanches when she was nine. Quanah became a famous leader of the Quahdi group of Comanches who fought for freedom against the U.S. Cavalry.

Other books by the same author:

1812, the War Nobody Won, 1985
Aztecs and Spaniards: Cortes and the Conquest of Mexico, 1986
Cowboys, Indians, and Gunfighters, 1993
Unconditional Surrender: U.S. Grant and the Civil War, 1994

Other books you might like:

Kathie Billingslea Smith, *Sitting Bull: Tatanka Yotanka*, 1987

This is a brief history of the famous Sioux leader for younger readers. Illustrated by James Seward.

Herman J. Viola, *Osceola*, 1993

This is a brief history of the famous Creek leader for younger readers. Illustrated by Yoshi Mayake.

Michael Dorris, *Morning Girl*, 1992
This is the story of a young girl in pre-Columbian Caribbean society.

Sandra King, *Shannon: An Ojibway Dancer*, 1993
This book follows the life of a young Ojibway girl, Shannon, who lives in the city, yet still participates in tribal ceremonies.

Monty Roessel, *Songs from the Loom*, 1995
This story follows Jaclyn Roessel, a young Navajo girl, as she learns the stories of her family and the cultural wisdom and mythology associated with the art of weaving. For younger readers.

Joseph Bruchac, *Flying with the Eagle, Racing with the Bear*, 1993
These rite-of-passage stories come from various tribal peoples including the Wampanoag, Cherokee, Osage, Lakota and Tlingit.

Susan Braine, *Drumbeat. . .Heartbeat: A Celebration of the Powwow*, 1995
This is a wonderful introduction to the Powwow for children by a Native American writer and photographer.

1267

DAVID MARTINSON

Cheer Up Old Man

(Duluth: School District 709,)

Subject(s): Grandparents
Age range(s): Grades 1-2
Time period(s): 1990s
Locale(s): Minnesota

Summary: This is a first-grade Ojibway reader about the aging process, and a grandfather's relationship with his grandchildren.

Other books by the same author:
Manabozho and the Bullrushes (short Trickster story)
Real Wild Rice, 1975 (rhymed first-grade reader)
Shemay: The Bird in the Sugarbush, 1975 (short story)

Other books you might like:
Shonto Begay, *Ma'ii and Cousin Horned Toad*,
Ma'ii is hungry, and he goes to Horny Toad for a free lunch, eventually swallowing his smaller cousin, an event that does not bode well for Ma'ii who learns his lesson in the end.

1268

DAVID MARTINSON

Manabozho and the Bullrushes

(Duluth: School District 709)

Subject(s): Folk Tales; Trickster Tales
Age range(s): Grades 1-2
Major character(s): Manabozho, Trickster
Time period(s): Indeterminate
Locale(s): Minnesota

Summary: In this short Ojibway tale, Manabozho—Trickster—likes to dance and says he will not let anyone outdance him, but he is fooled.

About this book: This brief book is a good reader for early grades, and a good introduction to the character of Trickster.

Where it's reviewed:
Bookland, March 1993, page 9

Other books by the same author:
Cheer Up Old Man (first-grade reader ng old.)
Shemay: The Bird in the Sugarbush, 1975
Real Wild Rice, 1975 (rymed first-grade reader)

Other books you might like:
Shonto Begay, *Ma'ii and Cousin Horned Toad*,
Ma'ii is hungry, and he goes to Horny Toad for a free lunch, eventually swallowing his smaller cousin, but that does not fare well for Ma'ii who learns his lesson in the end.

1269

DAVID MARTINSON

Real Wild Rice

(Duluth: School District 709, 1975)

Subject(s): Cultures and Customs
Age range(s): Grades K-1
Time period(s): 20th century
Locale(s): Minnesota

Summary: This primary reader is about the Ojibway tradition of collecting wild rice.

Other books by the same author:
Manabozho and the Bullrushes (short Trickster story)
Cheer Up Old Man (Ojibway first-grade reader)

Other books you might like:
Shonto Begay, *Ma'ii and Cousin Horned Toad*,
Lazy, conniving Ma'ii is hungry, and he goes to Horny Toad for a free lunch. When he swallows his smaller cousin, Horny Toad teaches him a lesson he won't forget.

1270

DAVID MARTINSON

Shemay: The Bird in the Sugarbush

(Duluth: School District 709, 1975)

Subject(s): Family; Folklore
Age range(s): Grades 1-2
Major character(s): Liza, Child (girl), Native American
Time period(s): 1990s
Locale(s): Minnesota

Summary: In this short story, Liza, a young girl, goes to collect maple sugar with her family. She learns the story of Shemay the bird, from her Grandmother—who knows the language of birds.

About this book: This short fiction is a good reader for early grades, and a good introduction to Ojibway culture.

Other books by the same author:
Manabozho and the Bullrushes (trickster story)
Real Wild Rice, 1975 (rhymed first-grade reader)
Cheer Up Old Man (Ojibway first-grade reader)

Other books you might like:
Shonto Begay, *Ma'ii and Cousin Horned Toad*,
Lazy, conniving Ma'ii is hungry, and he goes to Horny Toad for a free lunch. He swallows his smaller cousin, but Horny Toad teaches him a lesson he won't forget.

1271

JOHN JOSEPH MATHEWS, Native American, Osage

Sundown

(Norman: University of Oklahoma Press, 1934, 1988)

Subject(s): Historical; Alcoholism; Cultural Identity
Age range(s): Adult
Major character(s): Challenge Windzer, Veteran, Alcoholic, Native American
Time period(s): 1920s
Locale(s): Oklahoma

Summary: This novel about the Osage Indians deals with the conflicts between traditionalists (represented by Challenge's mother) and the assimilationists (represented by Challenge's father). Challenge is educated in White schools, joins the army, but returns to his homeland alienated from his culture. During this period the Osage strike it rich in oil, but Challenge only wastes his money drowning himself in an alcoholic stupor.

About this book: Mathews is adept in creating the complexities of reservation life in the 1920s, a period of great change, and he shows the effect on an individual of two diametrically opposed cultures competing for dominance in the soul.

Where it's reviewed:
Rocky Mountain Review of Language & Literature, Issue 1, 1993, page 61

Other books by the same author:
Life and Death of an Oilman: The Career of E.W. Marland, 1951 (biography)
Talking to the Moon, 1945 (autobiography)
Wah'Kon-Tah: The Osage and the White Man's Road, 1932

Other books you might like:
Paula Gunn Allen, *The Woman Who Owned the Shadows*, 1983
A ''mixed-blood'' woman feels out of place in both the Southwest and San Francisco, begins the process of becoming a shaman, which is her journey towards being whole.
D'Arcy McNickle, *The Surrounded*, 1936
A fiddle player returns to his reservation after years in the White world and finds himself so caught up in its complexities that he knows he can never go back to the White world again.
Louise Erdrich, *Love Medicine*, 1984
Married to Marie, Nector is nevertheless fatefully drawn to Lulu. When his grandson prepares a love medicine to win

him back to his grandmother, he uses the wrong ingredients and kills Nector instead.
Leslie Marmon Silko, *Ceremony*, 1977
A Pueblo man, returned from the war, must reallign himself with the traditional ways before becoming whole again.
Maria Campbell, *Halfbreed*,
This is the moving account of Campbell's life as a Metis, or halfbreed, part Indian, part European.
James Welch, *Winter in the Blood*, 1974
A man caught in the web of alcoholism tries to discover the truth about his family.
N. Scott Momaday, *House Made of Dawn*, 1968
Abel leaves his pueblo to fight in World War I, only to come back alienated from his people and he begins a long effort at healing.

1272

JOHN JOSEPH MATHEWS, Native American, Osage

Talking to the Moon

(Norman: University Of Oklahoma, 1945, 1981)

Subject(s): Autobiography; World War II; Family Life
Age range(s): Grades 10-Adult
Time period(s): 19th century; 20th century (1800s-1940s)
Locale(s): South Dakota

Summary: One of the best, this autobiography covers the author's life from his early years in Oklahoma to his military stint as an aviator in WWI, college, married life in Los Angeles, and full circle to his final return to his homeland. Mathews excels at writing both descriptions of nature and at capturing the spirit of his characters.

Other books by the same author:
Life and Death of an Oilman: The Career of E.W. Marland, 1951 (biography)
Sundown, 1934
Wah'Kon-Tah: The Osage and the White Man's Road, 1932

Other books you might like:
N. Scott Momaday, *The Way to Rainy Mountain*, 1976
This is mixed genre of fiction, poetry, history, mythology, and personal memoir.
N. Scott Momaday, *The Names: A Memoir*, 1976
This is an autobiographical work.
Francis La Flesche, *The Middle Five: Indian Schoolboys of the Omaha Tribe*, 1900
This book details the life of La Flesche and his friends in mission school in Oklahoma.
Sarah Winnemucca, *Life Among the Paiutes: Their Wrongs and Claims*, 1883
This work provides insight into the Paiutes' lives.
John Fire Lame Deer, *Lame Deer, Seeker of Visions*, 1972
Traditional medicine man Lame Deer tells of his visions and spiritual quest while relating the philosophy of Lakota religion and culture.
Luther Standing Bear, *Stories of the Sioux*, 1988
Standing Bear grows up in the traditional buffalo hunting culture and he brings to life the stories from his own past.
Zitkala-Sa, *Old Indian Legends Retold by Zitkala-Sa*, 1921
This is a collection of memoirs and essays about the

traditional Lakota culture and it's adjustments to European encroachment.

Peter Nabokov, *Native American Testimony*, 1991
This anthology is a mixed genre of oral stories, speeches, prophecies, and essays.

Brian Swann, *I Tell You Now*, 1989
This is an excellent collection of autobiographical essays by eighteen contemporary Native American writers, co-edited with Brian Swann.

1273

JOHN JOSEPH MATHEWS, Native American, Osage

Wah'Kon-Tah: The Osage and the White Man's Road

(Norman: University of Oklahoma Press, 1932, 1968)

Subject(s): Indian Reservations; Cultural Conflict
Age range(s): Adult
Major character(s): Major Laban J. Miles, Military Personnel
Time period(s): 19th century; 20th century (1878-1931)
Locale(s): Oklahoma

Summary: Mathews bases this novel on the journal of the historical Major Laban J. Miles, who comes to the Osage reservation in Oklahoma in 1878 with good intentions. Laban believes that the only hope for the Osage is for them to forego the old ways and take up the culture of the White man, but General Miles is stymied in his efforts by the recalcitrant Osage, who always seem determined to hold on to the old ways.

Other books by the same author:
Life and Death of an Oilman: The Career of E.W. Marland, 1951 (biography)
Talking to the Moon, 1945 (autobiography)
Sundown, 1934

Other books you might like:
D'Arcy McNickle, *The Surrounded*, 1936
A fiddle player returns to his reservation for a visit after years in the White world and finds himself so caught up in its complexities that he knows he can never go back to the White world again.

Louise Erdrich, *Love Medicine*, 1984
Married to Marie, Nector is nevertheless fatefully drawn to Lulu. When his grandson prepares a love medicine to win him back to his grandmother, he uses the wrong ingredients and kills Nector instead.

Leslie Marmon Silko, *Ceremony*, 1977
A Pueblo man returned from the war must reallign himself with the traditional ways before becoming whole again.

Maria Campbell, *Halfbreed*, This is t
he moving account of Campbell's life as a Metis, or halfbreed, part Indian, part European.

James Welch, *Winter in the Blood*, 1974
A man caught in the web of alcoholism tries to discover the truth about his family.

N. Scott Momaday, *House Made of Dawn*, 1968
Abel leaves his pueblo to fight in the war, only to return alienated from his people and begins a long effort at healing.

1274

T.C. MCLUHAN, Editor, Caucasian

Touch the Earth

(New York: Outerbridge & Dienstfrey, 1971)

Subject(s): Indians of North America; Cultural Identity
Age range(s): Grades 6 and Up
Time period(s): Indeterminate
Locale(s): United States

Summary: This compilation of statements, speeches, songs, and prayers from a variety of Native American people and tribes, over a large span of time, gives the reader a real insight into the horror Native Americans faced when the European conquest of North America began. Yet, there is also much in this book that deals with the earth-based philosophies of North American tribal people, which is often quite beautiful.

Where it's reviewed:
Instructor, May 1995, page 14

Other books you might like:
Beth Brant, *A Gathering of Spirit: A Collection of North American Indian Women*, 1984
This collection of short stories, letters, essays and poems comes from a wide cross-section of Native American women writers including Linda Hogan, Elizabeth Cook-Lynn, Diana Glancy and others.

John Bierhorst, *The Way of the Earth: Native America and the Environment*, 1994
Bierhorst delves into American Indian philosophies regarding the environment, giving a comprehensive view of native beliefs, myths and practices about nature.

Lee Miller, *From the Heart: Voices of the American Indian*, 1995
This is a collection of orations, speeches, and testimony by more than 250 Indian people that presents a radical alternative to traditionally taught American history.

Paula Gunn Allen, *Voice of the Turtle*, 1994
Edited by the well-known writer and scholar, this book is an anthology of literature written by American Indian people from 1900 to 1970.

Craig Lesley, *Talking Leaves*, 1991
This is an excellent collection of short stories by thirty-five contemporary Native American writers including, among others, Erdrich, Dorris, Momaday, and Hogan.

Peter Nabokov, *Native American Testimony*, 1978
This anthology of mixed genres includes oral stories, speeches, prophecies, and essays.

Clifford E. Trafzer, *Blue Dawn, Red Earth: New Native American Storytellers*, 1996
This collection of short stories by 30 new Native American writers includes Lorne Simon, Anita Endrezze, Jim Barnes and others.

1275

D'ARCY MCNICKLE, Native American, Cree and Salish
BIRGIT HANS, Editor, Caucasian

The Hawk Is Hungry and Other Stories

(Albuquerque: University of New Mexico Press, 1954, 1987)

Series: Suntracks
Subject(s): Indians of North America; Cultures and Customs
Age range(s): Grades 9-Adult
Time period(s): 20th century
Locale(s): United States

Summary: These short stories depict life in the American West, urban life, prejudice, conflicts between whites and Indians, and the accommodations people make to live in the modern world.

About this book: McNickle was one of the most influential of Native American writers.

Where it's reviewed:
Western American Literature, November 1993, page 271
Booklist, January 24, 1993, page 4
Kirkus Reviews, October 1, 1992, page 1209
Western Historical Quarterly, February 1993, page 123

Other books by the same author:
Runner in the Sun: A Story of Indian Maize, 1954
Indian Man: A Biography of Oliver La Farge, 1971
The Surrounded, 1936
Wind from an Enemy Sky, 1978

Other books you might like:
Paula Gunn Allen, *Voice of the Turtle*, 1994
  Edited by the well-known writer and scholar, this book is an anthology of literature written by American Indian people from 1900 to 1970.
Lee Miller, *From the Heart: Voices of the American Indian*, 1995
  This is a collection of orations, speeches and testimony by more than 250 Indian people that presents a radical alternative to traditionally taught American history.
Paula Gunn Allen, *Spider Woman's Granddaughters*, 1989
  This is a beautiful collection of traditional tales interwoven with contemporary short stories having to do with the lives of Native American women.
Leslie Marmon Silko, *Storyteller*, 1981
  This work is a mixed genre of poetry, fiction, and mythology.
Clifford E. Trafzer, *Blue Dawn, Red Earth: New Native American Storytellers*, 1996
  This is a collection of short stories by 30 new Native American writers: Lorne Simon, Anita Endrezze, and Jim Barnes among others.

1276

D'ARCY MCNICKLE, Native American, Cree and Salish

Runner in the Sun: A Story of Indian Maize

(Albuquerque: University of New Mexico Press, 1954, 1987)

Subject(s): Indians of North America; Food; Pre-Columbian History
Age range(s): Grades 6-9
Major character(s): Salt, Child (young boy), Native American
Time period(s): Indeterminate Past (pre-Columbian)
Locale(s): New Mexico

Summary: This middle school novel is about a young boy, one of the cliff dwellers of Chaco Canyon, who leaves his Pueblo homeland and journeys to find a breed of corn that will save his people.

Other books by the same author:
Indian Man: A Biography of Oliver La Farge, 1971
The Surrounded, 1936
Wind from an Enemy Sky, 1978
The Hawk Is Hungry and Other Stories, 1992

Other books you might like:
Maria Campbell, *Halfbreed*, 1973
  This is the moving account of Maria Campbell's life as a Metis or halfbreed, part Indian—part European.
Shirley Sterling, *My Name Is Seepeetza*, 1992
  This fictional account, based on the life of the author, recounts her life as a member of the interior Salish tribe. Forced to attend government schools, she is forbidden to reflect her own heritage.
Michael Dorris, *Morning Girl*, 1992
  This short novel is about a young girl and her brother in Columbian America.

1277

D'ARCY MCNICKLE, Native American, Cree and Salish

The Surrounded

(Albuquerque: University of New Mexico Press, 1936, 1964)

Subject(s): Indians of North America; Historical; Indian Reservations
Age range(s): Grades 9-Adult
Major character(s): Archilde Leon, Musician (fiddle player), Native American (half-blood); Elise, Young Woman
Time period(s): 1930s (1936)
Locale(s): Montana

Summary: Archilde Leon, a young man of Salish and Spanish ancestry, returns to his reservation after spending some time in the white world where he has become a fiddle player. Intending to stay only a short time to visit his mother and reconcile with his father, the reservation life pulls him in, and he finds himself caught in a web of murder and coverup and knows that he can never go back to the White world again.

About this book: This is a brilliant novel that is complex in its vision. Many points of view are represented, without any clear-cut villains or heroes emerging from the background.

Where it's reviewed:
American Book Review, October 1978, page 12
Kliatt, Fall 1978, page 12

Other books by the same author:
Runner in the Sun: A Story of Indian Maize, 1954
Wind from an Enemy Sky, 1978

Other books you might like:
Louise Erdrich, *Love Medicine*, 1984
    Married to Marie, Nector is nevertheless fatefully drawn to
    Lulu. When his grandson prepares a love medicine to win
    him back to his grandmother, he uses the wrong ingredi-
    ents and kills Nector instead.
Louise Erdrich, *Tracks*, 1988
    Two alternating voices in conflict, one a traditionalist and
    one the voice of change, reveal the escalating conflict
    between two Chippewa families and the disintegration of
    their culture.
N. Scott Momaday, *House Made of Dawn*, 1968
    An Indian man, Abel, leaves his pueblo to suffer the
    hardships of fighting in WWII, and returns to suffer the
    hardship of being alienated from his people.
James Welch, *Winter in the Blood*, 1974
    An unnamed protagonist who is caught in alcoholism tries
    to discover the truth about his family.
James Welch, *Fools Crow*, 1986
    As the Blackfeet face White encroachment in Montana,
    White Man's Dog is vying for a place of respect in his
    society. He decides to take the spiritual path and become a
    medicine man.
Craig Lesley, *Talking Leaves*, 1991
    This book is an excellent collection of stories by thirty-five
    contemporary American Indian writers including Louise
    Erdrich, Michael Dorris, N. Scott Momaday and others.
Leslie Marmon Silko, *Ceremony*, 1977
    Tayo, a puebo Indian, returns home from the war and must
    realign himself with his people and the old days.
John Joseph Mathews, *Sundown*, 1934
    This novel portrays life in the oil fields in Osage country in
    the 1920s.
Linda Hogan, *Mean Spirit*, 1990
    This novel, based in Oklahoma, chronicles the greed and
    corruption that flows from its oil field.

1278

MISKA MILES, Caucasian
PETER PARNALL, Illustrator

Annie and the Old One
(New York: Little Brown, 1971)

Subject(s): Grandparents; Death
Age range(s): Grades 3-5
Major character(s): Annie, Child (young girl), Native Ameri-
can (Navajo); Grandmother, Grandmother (tribal elder),
Native American (Navajo)
Time period(s): 1970s
Locale(s): New Mexico

Summary: Annie, a young Navajo girl, must prepare for her
grandmother's death as her grandmother herself is preparing

for it. This is a touching story about acceptance of death and
the affirmation of life.

Other books you might like:
Marilyne Virginia Mabery, *Right After Sundown: Teaching
    Stories of the Navajo*,
    These are the traditional stories of the beginning of this
    world as told by the Navajo, with excellent illustrations by
    Navajo artist Raymond J. Johnson.
Hasteen Klah, *The Myth and Prayers of the Great Star Chant,
    and the Myth of the Coyote Chant*, 1988
    This exquisite book is a compilation of important Navajo
    myths, songs, chants, and prayers, that deal with the com-
    plex philosophical and religious life of Navajo culture.
Jonathan Broderick, *Stories of Traditional Navajo Life and
    Culture*, 1977
    Interviews from tape-recorded meetings
Broderick H. Johnson, *Navajo Stories of the Long Walk Pe-
    riod*, 1973
    In this intriguing collection, Navajo people recount the
    stories told to them of the Long Walk period that have been
    handed down in their families.
Monty Roessel, *Songs from the Loom*, 1995
    This story follows Jaclyn Roessel, a young Navajo girl, as
    she learns the stories of her family and the cultural wisdom
    and mythology that accompanies the art of weaving.

1279

LEE MILLER, Editor, Native American, Eastern Cherokee and
Kaw

*From the Heart: Voices of the American
Indian*
(New York: Random House, 1995)

Subject(s): History; Indians of North America
Age range(s): Grades 10-Adult
Time period(s): Indeterminate
Locale(s): United States

Summary: This collection of orations, speeches, and testimony
by more than 250 Indian people presents a radical alternative
to traditionally taught American history.

Where it's reviewed:
Booklist, May 15, 1995, page 1629
Booklist, May 15, 1995, page 1637
Library Journal, April 1, 1995, page 108
Virginia Quarterly Review, Autumn 1995, page 135

Other books you might like:
Gerald Vizenor, *The People Named the Chippewa: Narrative
    Histories*, 1984
    This mixed genre anthology contains essays, interviews,
    history, mythology, and stories on Ojibway culture.
Peter Nabokov, *Native American Testimony*, 1991
    This anthology contains oral stories, speeches, prophecies,
    and essays.
Brian Swann, *I Tell You Now*, 1989
    This is an excellent collection of autobiographical essays
    by eighteen contemporary American Indian writers. Co-
    edited with Arnold Krupat.

T.C. McLuhan, *Touch the Earth*, 1971
This is a collection of speeches and statements from a wide assortment of Indian people.

Brian Swann, *Coming to Light*, 1994
This book is a comprehensive collection of Native American literature, divided geographically and including many genres of oral literature.

Paula Gunn Allen, *Spider Woman's Granddaughters*, 1989
This is a beautiful collection of traditional tales interwoven with contemporary stories about the lives of Native American women.

Zitkala-Sa, *Old Indian Legends Retold by Zitkala-Sa*, 1921
These stories tell of Zitkala-Sa's childhood in the traditional Lakota culture and the difficulties she faces while attending school and college in a world where she is perceived as a ''savage.''

Arlene Hirschfelder, *Native Heritage*, 1995
Personal accounts of Indian people from 1790 until the present.

Harvey Arden, *Wisdom Keepers: Meetings with Native American Spiritual Elders*,

1280

N. SCOTT MOMADAY, Native American, Kiowa

The Ancient Child
(New York: Doubleday, 1989)

Subject(s): Biography; Dreams and Nightmares; Mythology
Age range(s): Adult
Major character(s): Locke Setman, Artist (painter), Native American (Kiowa); Grey Kope'mah, Young Woman, Native American (Kiowa)
Time period(s): 1980s
Locale(s): New Mexico; San Francisco, California

Summary: This book begins with Grey, a Kiowa woman and native of Oklahoma, who is having mystical visions. At the same time, in San Francisco, a successful painter, Locke (also Kiowa) is troubled by dreams. He makes a pilgrimage to the land of his ancestors where he awakens to the ancient myths. But, interwoven in his dreams of the ancients are some of the Western myths of the White man, for he also dreams of Billy the Kid. When Grey and Locke eventually come together, the power of the Bear overtakes Locke, and he begins to find his place in the ancient mythology of his people.

Where it's reviewed:
Rocky Mountain Review of Language & Literature, Issue 1, 1993, page 61

Other books by the same author:
House Made of Dawn, 1968
The Names: A Memoir, 1976 (autobiography)
The Way to Rainy Mountain, 1969 (poetry, fiction, myth, history)
Angel of Geese and Other Poems, 1974 (poetry)
The Gourd Dancer: Poems, 1976 (poetry)

Other books you might like:
James Welch, *Winter in the Blood*, 1974
A man caught in the clutches of alcoholism, tries to discover the truth about his family.

D'Arcy McNicle, *The Surrounded*, 1936
A fiddle player returns to his reservation for a visit after years in the White world, finding himself so caught up in its complexities that he knows he can never go back to the White world again.

Louise Erdrich, *Love Medicine*, 1984
Married to Marie, Nector is nevertheless fatefully drawn to Lulu. When his grandson prepares a love medicine to win him back to his grandmother, he uses the wrong ingredients and kills Nector instead.

Janet Campbell Hale, *The Jailing of Cecelia Capture*, 1985
A woman law student, trapped in despair and aloholism, separated from her husband and children, tries to make sense of her life.

Linda Hogan, *Mean Spirit*, 1990
This novel chronicles the greed and corruption that flows from Oklahoma's oil fields during the boom days.

Craig Lesley, *Talking Leaves*, 1991
This is an excellent collection of stories by thrity-five contemporary Native American writers including Louise Erdrich, Michael Dorris, N. Scott Momaday and Linda Hogan.

Leslie Marmon Silko, *Ceremony*, 1977
A Pueblo man returns from the war and must realign himself with the traditional ways before he can become whole again.

Clifford E. Trafzer, *Blue Dawn, Red Earth: New Native American Storytellers*, 1996
This is a collection of short stories by 30 new Native American writers: Lorne Simon, Anita Endrezze, Jim Barnes, and others.

Beth Brant, *A Gathering of Spirit: A Collection of North American Indian Women*, 1984
This excellent collection of short stories, letters, essays and poems comes from a wide cross-section of Native American women writers including Linda Hogan, Elizabeth Cook-Lynn, and others.

1281

N. SCOTT MOMADAY, Native American, Kiowa

House Made of Dawn
(New York: Harper & Row, 1968)

Subject(s): Indians of North America; Historical
Age range(s): Adult
Major character(s): Abel, Native American (mixed-blood), Veteran; Father Olguin, Native American; Francisco, Native American
Time period(s): 1960s
Locale(s): New Mexico; Los Angeles, California

Summary: Abel is a troubled mixed-blood young man who finds himself withdrawing from his grandfather and the traditional culture of Jemez Pueblo that he represents after returning home from a foreign war. Abel brings the war home with him and kills an albino Indian before fleeing to Los Angeles, where he meets up with a number of characters, including a charlatan preacher, trickster: J.B.B. Tosamah. Abel is not able to survive the city and ends up beaten, returning home to New

Mexico, barely alive, but he survives and takes his place with his people in the race of the dawn runners.

About this book: This book was the first novel by a Native American writer to win wide critical acclaim.

Where it's reviewed:
Kirkus Reviews, April 1, 1968, page 421
New York Times Book Review, October 9, 1977, page 45
Publishers Weekly, September 22, 1969, page 86

Awards the book has won:
Pulitzer Prize, 1968

Other books by the same author:
The Ancient Child, 1989
The Names: A Memoir, 1976 (autobiography)
The Way to Rainy Mountain, 1969 (poetry, fiction, myth, history)
Angel of Geese and Other Poems, 1974 (poetry)
The Gourd Dancer: Poems, 1976 (poetry)

Other books you might like:
D'Arcy McNickle, *The Surrounded*, 1936
   A fiddle player returns to his reservation for a visit after years in the White world and finds himself so caught up in its complexities that he knows he can never go back to the White world again.
Louise Erdrich, *Love Medicine*, 1984
   Married to Marie, Nector is nevertheless fatefully drawn to Lulu. When his grandson prepares a love medicine to win him back to his grandmother, he uses the wrong ingredients and kills Nector instead.
James Welch, *Winter in the Blood*, 1974
   An unnamed protagonist, who suffers from alcoholism, searches for his family's past on a reservation in Montana.
Craig Lesley, *Talking Leaves*, 1991
   This excellent collection by thirty-five contemporary Native American writers includes Louise Erdrich, Michael Dorris, N. Scott Momaday and Linda Hogan.
Leslie Marmon Silko, *Ceremony*, 1977
   A Pueblo man, returned from the war, must realign himself with the traditional ways before he can become whole again.
Janet Campbell Hale, *The Jailing of Cecelia Capture*, 1985
   A woman law student, trapped in despair and alcoholism, tries to make sense of her life.
Linda Hogan, *Mean Spirit*, 1990
   This novel takes place in the Oklahoma of the oil boom days, and involves corruption and murder.
Susan Scarberry-Garcia, *Landmarks of Healing: A Study of House Made of Dawn*, 1990
   These are critical essays of Momaday's work.
John Joseph Mathews, *Sundown*, 1934
   Challenge is educated in White schools and joins the army, but when he returns to his homeland, is alienated from his culture. This novel shows the effects on an individual of two opposing cultures co

---

1282

N. SCOTT MOMADAY, Native American, Kiowa

The Way to Rainy Mountain
(Albuquerque: U. of New Mexico Press, 1976)

Subject(s): Indians of North America; Folklore
Age range(s): Adult
Time period(s): 1960s
Locale(s): Oklahoma

Summary: This book is the journey Momaday makes to find out about his people, the Kiowa, and to find out about himself. It is a combination of poetry, fiction, mythology, history, and meditation. Much of this fine book takes a close look at the landscape and Momaday's own relationship to it as he weaves in the old Kiowa mythology with the legends and memories of his own family.

Where it's reviewed:
Rocky Mountain Review of Language & Literature, Issue 1, 1993, page 61

Other books by the same author:
The Ancient Child, 1989
House Made of Dawn, 1968
The Names: A Memoir, 1976 (autobiography)
Angel of Geese and Other Poems, 1974 (poetry)
The Gourd Dancer: Poems, 1976 (poetry)

Other books you might like:
Gerald Vizenor, *The People Named the Chippewa: Narrative Histories*, 1984
   This mixed genre anthology contains essays, interviews, history, mythology and stories.
Brian Swann, *I Tell You Now*, 1989
   This is an excellent collection of autobiographical essays by eighteen contemporary American Indian writers. Co-edited with Arnold Krupat.
Paula Gunn Allen, *Spider Woman's Granddaughters*, 1989
   This is a beautiful collection of traditional tales interwoven with contemporary stories having to do with the lives of Native American women.
Leslie Marmon Silko, *Storyteller*, 1981
   This work is a mixed genre of poetry, fiction, and mythology.

1283

MARK MONROE, Native American, Lakota (Sioux) and Cheyenne
CAROLYN REYER, Editor

An Indian in White America
(Philadelphia: Temple Univ. Press, 1994)

Subject(s): Autobiography; Racism; Alcoholism
Age range(s): Grades 11-Adult
Time period(s): 1990s
Locale(s): South Dakota

Summary: Mark Monroe speaks of the various problems he and other Indian people have faced: racism, alcoholism, and poverty. This courageous book tells the story of how he was able to create another kind of life for himself and his family.

About this book: Monroe taped his story and it was edited by Carolyn Reyer.

Where it's reviewed:
Choice, September 1995, page 224
Kirkus Reviews, October 1, 1994, page 1341

Other books you might like:
Wilma Mankiller, *Mankiller: A Chief and Her People*, 1993
    Wilma Mankiller, Chief of the Cherokees, recounts her own life story as well as the story of her people. Written with Michael Wallis.
John Fire Lame Deer, *Lame Deer, Seeker of Visions*, 1972
    Traditional medicine man Lame Deer tells of his visions and spiritual quest while relating the philosophy of Lakota religion and culture.
Luther Standing Bear, *Stories of the Sioux*, 1988
    Standing Bear grew up in the traditional buffalo hunting culture, and he brings to life the stories from his own past.
Zitkala-Sa, *Old Indian Legends Retold by Zitkala-Sa*, 1921
    These stories detail Zitkala-Sa's childhood in the traditional Lakota culture and the difficulties she faces while attending school and college in a world where she is perceived as a "savage."
Brian Swann, *I Tell You Now*, 1989
    This excellent collection of autobiographical essays is by eighteen contemporary American Indian writers. Co-authored with Arnold Krupat.
Albert Yava, *Big Falling Snow: A Tewa-Hopi Indian's Life and Times and the History and Traditions of His People*, 1978
    Autobiography
Helen Sekaquaptewa, *Me and Mine: The Life Story of Helen Sekaquaptewa*, 1969
    This is the autobiography of a Hopi woman, with Louise Udall.
Robert J. Conley, *Mountain Windsong*, 1992
    Conley weaves stories, songs, and historical documents into this love story about two young Cherokee people who have to endure the horror of the Trail of Tears.
Vickie Sears, *Simple Songs*, 1990
    This is a collection of short stories by a Cherokee writer.
Diane Glancy, *Firesticks*, 1993
    This collection of stories, by one of the foremost American Indian poets, deals with Indian people as its subjects.
Mary Crow Dog, *Lakota Woman*, 1990
    This as-told-to book chronicles the life of a Lakota woman who lives through the turbulence of the 1973 occupation of Wounded Knee by the AIM.
Mary Brave Bird, *Ohitika Woman*, 1993
    This sequel to *Lakota Woman*, written under her maiden name, tells the story of a woman caught between feminism and traditional Indian belief.
Diane Glancy, *Claiming Breath*, 1992
    This collection of observations is written in diary form, with entries that read like prose poems.

`1284`

MOURNING DOVE (Hum-ishu-ma and Christine Quintasket)

Cogewea
(Lincoln: University of Nebraska Press, 1981)

Subject(s): Indians of North America; Historical; Cultural Conflict
Age range(s): Grades 9-Adult
Major character(s): Cogewea "The Half Blood", Cowgirl, Native American
Time period(s): 1920s
Locale(s): Washington

Summary: This is the second known novel by an American Indian woman. Cogewea is a young woman growing up caught between the Native American and the White cultures. She lives the life of a cowgirl on a ranch in Eastern Washington and is able to make her way in a man's world. Cogewea falls in love with a no-good Easterner instead of a Native American boy, but eventually she comes to believe that the Native American values are the more worthy.

About this book: Mourning Dove wrote this book while living in unbearably harsh conditions, working as a migrant worker, moving from place to place, barely making enough money to survive. That she was able to complete this novel is itself a kind of miracle. The book deals with popular themes: romance, cowboys, but there is also a good deal of traditional Native American material woven throughout. The editor who worked on the book with Mourning Dove was Lucullus Virgil McWhorter, and his role in creating the text as it stands, was significant. McWorter inserted his own language into the text, and reading the book one can detect two different styles: the simple and direct style of Mourning Dove and the verbose style of McWhorter. Yet for all the difficulties in this book, it is definitely of value.

Where it's reviewed:
Kliatt, Winter 1982, page 12
World Literature Today, Spring 1982, page 388

Other books by the same author:
Mourning Dove: A Salishan Autobiography, 1990 (edited by Jay Miller)

Other books you might like:
Mary Crow Dog, *Lakota Woman*, 1990
    This as-told-to book, with Richard Erdoes as author/editor, chronicles the life of a Lakota woman who lives through the hardships of the 1973 occupation of Wounded Knee by the AIM.
Paula Gunn Allen, *Spider Woman's Granddaughters*, 1989
    This is a beautiful collection of traditional tales interwoven with contemporary stories having to do with the lives of Native American women.
D'Arcy McNickle, *The Surrounded*, 1936
    A fiddle player returns to his reservation for a visit after years in the White world and finds himself so caught up in its complexities that he knows he can never go back to the White world again.
Louise Erdrich, *Love Medicine*, 1984
    Married to Marie, Nector is nevertheless fatefully drawn to Lulu. When his grandson prepares a love medicine to win

him back to his grandmother, he uses the wrong ingredients and kills Nector instead.

Craig Lesley, *Talking Leaves*, 1991

This excellent collection of stories by thirty-five contemporary Native American writers includes Louise Erdrich, Michael Dorris, N. Scott Momaday and Linda Hogan.

Leslie Marmon Silko, *Ceremony*, 1977

A Pueblo man, returning from the war, must realign himself with the traditional ways before he can become whole again.

Janet Campbell Hale, *The Jailing of Cecelia Capture*, 1985

A thirty-something Indian woman, separated from her husband and two children, is fighting a terrible battle with alcoholism while attending law school.

Linda Hogan, *Mean Spirit*, 1990

This novel chronicles the greed and corruption that flows from Oklahoma's oil fields during the boom days.

Leslie Marmon Silko, *Storyteller*, 1981

From Laguna Pueblo where he grew up, Silko weaves traditional mythology into modern stories, recreating old myths and making them relevant for a new generation.

1285

MOURNING DOVE (Hum-ishu-ma and Christine Quintasket)

Coyote Stories

(Lincoln: University of Nebraska Press, 1933, 1990)

Subject(s): Trickster Tales; Mythology; Folklore
Age range(s): Grades 5 and Up
Major character(s): Coyote, Trickster
Time period(s): Indeterminate Past

Summary: Mourning Dove brings to life the traditional Coyote trickster stories about her people, the Okanogans. They are both humorous and insightful.

About this book: Coyote is one of the most fascinating archetypes in Native American literature.

Where it's reviewed:
Legacy, Fall 1993, page 154
Canadian Literature, Spring 1993, page 144

Other books by the same author:
Cogewea, 1981
Mourning Dove: A Salishan Autobiography, 1990

Other books you might like:
William Bright, *A Coyote Reader*, 1993
These are traditional coyote stories.
Hasteen Klah, *The Myth and Prayers of the Great Star Chant, and the Myth of the Coyote Chant*, 1988
This exquisite book is a compilation of important Navajo myths, songs, chants, and prayers, Portraying the complexity of the philosophical and religious life of Navajo culture.

1286

MOURNING DOVE (Hum-ishu-ma and Christine Quintasket)

Mourning Dove: A Salishan Autobiography

(Lincoln: University of Nebraska Press, 1990)

Series: American Indian Lives
Subject(s): Indians of North America; Biography; Cultures and Customs
Age range(s): Grades 9-Adult
Time period(s): Indeterminate Past
Locale(s): Washington

Summary: Mourning Dove leads a life of hardship, working in the fields as a day laborer in the Northwest while fighting for the time and energy to write.

Where it's reviewed:
Kliatt, July 1994, page 27
Legacy, Fall 1993, page 154

Other books you might like:
Mary Crow Dog, *Lakota Woman*, 1990
This as-told-to book, with Richard Erdoes as author/editor, chronicles the life of a Lakota woman who lives through the hardships of the 1973 occupation of Wounded Knee by the AIM.
Mary Brave Bird, *Ohitika Woman*, 1993
This sequel to *Lakota Woman* chronicles the conflicts between feminism and traditional Indian belief, White and Indian philosophy. (Mary retook her maiden name after divorcing Crow Dog.)
Paula Gunn Allen, *The Sacred Hoop: Recovering the Feminine in American Indian Traditions*, 1986
This is a collection of essays that uncover the essential role of women in traditional and contemporary Indian life.
Paula Gunn Allen, *Spider Woman's Granddaughters*, 1989
This is a beautiful collection of traditional tales interwoven with contemporary stories having to do with the lives of Native American women.
Helen Sekaquaptewa, *Me and Mine: The Life Story of Helen Sekaquaptewa*, 1969
This is the autobiography of a Hopi women, written with Louise Udall.
Zitkala-Sa, *Old Indian Legends Retold by Zitkala-Sa*, 1921
This story recounts the life of an Indian woman who spends her childhood in the old Sioux buffalo hunting culture but eventually leaves it for and Indian boarding school in the east.
Wilma Mankiller, *Mankiller: A Chief and Her People*, 1993
With Michael Wallis, Chief Mankiller tells her story and the story of her people, the Cherokee.
Leslie Marmon Silko, *Storyteller*, 1981
This work is a mixed genre of poetry, fiction and mythology

`1287`

PETER NABOKOV, Editor, Caucasian

Native American Testimony
(New York: Viking Penguin, 1978, 1991)

Subject(s): Government Relations; History
Age range(s): Grades 9-Adult
Time period(s): Indeterminate
Locale(s): United States

Summary: This book chronicles the pain of American Indians in dealing with the onslaught of European society. Taking oral statements and speeches from the earliest times of contact, working up through the modern era, mixing in essays from contemporary Native American writers, this book makes a powerful statement about history from the point of view of Native Americans, a point of view seldom given credence until quite recently.

Where it's reviewed:
Bloombury, Review, July 1993, page 17
Kliatt Young Adult Paperback Book Guide, January 1993, page 34
Publishers Weekly, September 28, 1992, page 73
Sierra, November 1992, page 116

Other books by the same author:
The Red Swan: Myths and Tales of the American Indians, 1971 (This is a collection of orations and poems.)

Other books you might like:
Paula Gunn Allen, *Spider Woman's Granddaughters*, 1989
  This is a beautiful collection of traditional tales interwoven with contemporary stories having to do with the lives of Native American women.
Paula Gunn Allen, *Voice of the Turtle*, 1994
  Edited by the well known writer and scholar Paula Gunn Allen, this book is an anthology of literature written by American Indian people from 1900 to 1970.
Brian Swann, *I Tell You Now*, 1987
  Personal life accounts by American Indian writers.
Lee Miller, *From the Heart: Voices of the American Indian*, 1995
  This is a collection of orations, speeches, and testimony by more than 250 Indian people that presents a radical alternative to traditionally taught American history.
Craig Lesley, *Talking Leaves*, 1991
  An excellent collection of short stories by thirty-five contemporary American Indian writers including, among others, Erdrich, Dorris, Momaday, and Hogan.
T.C. McLuhan, *Touch the Earth*, 1971
  This is collection of speeches and statements from a wide assortment of Native American people.
Beth Brant, *A Gathering of Spirit: A Collection of North American Indian Women*, 1984
  Here is a collection of stories, letters, essays, and poems from a large cross-section of Native American women writers, such as Linda Hogan, Diana Glancy, Wendy Rose and Doris Seale.
Clifford E. Trafzer, *Blue Dawn, Red Earth: New Native American Storytellers*, 1996
  This is a collection of short stories by 30 new Native

American writers, such as Lorne Simon, Jim Barnes, Richard Van Camp, and Penny Olson.
LaVonne Ruoff, *American Indian Literatures: An Introduction, Bibliographic Review, and Selected Bibliography*, 1990
  This is the bible of Native American literature, essential to anyone who wants to pursue a study of the literature that has been written *by* American Indian people.

`1288`

JAMES NORTHRUP, Native American, Ojibwa (Chippewa)

Walking the Rez Road
(Stillwater, Minnesota: Voyageur Press, 1993)

Subject(s): Vietnam War; Indian Reservations; Humor
Age range(s): Grades 9-Adult
Major character(s): Luke Warmwater, Native American, Veteran (Vietnam)
Time period(s): 1990s
Locale(s): Minnesota

Summary: This collection of short stories and poems focuses on a cast of characters living on a Chippewa (Ojibway) reservation in Minnesota. Luke Warmwater is a Vietnam vet who is often down on his luck, but he (like most of his other reservation cohorts) is a survivor in the trickster fashion. These stories are almost always hilarious, yet there is often a dark side beneath their comic mask. The stories are told in the vernacular of reservation English, and like the stories of Kinsella, they ring true.

About this book: Northrup creates a world that is blighted by poverty and depression. Yet, from this depressing backdrop shines great humor, insight, and a life lived from the heart that takes the reader in.

Where it's reviewed:
Library Journal, June 1, 1993, page 124
Publishers Weekly, April 26, 1993, page 56

Other books you might like:
Gerald Vizenor, *Earthdivers: Tribal Narratives on Mixed Descent*, 1981
  In this collection of short stories Vizenor creates trickster figures to poke fun at and make shrewd political commentary on America, reservation life, and just about everything else.
Sherman Alexie, *The Lone Ranger and Tonto Fist Fight in Heaven*, 1993
  This wonderful short fiction is about the ups and downs of reservation life.
Gerald Vizenor, *The People Named the Chippewa: Narrative Histories*, 1984
  This mixed genre anthology contains essays, interviews, history, mythology and stories.
Louise Erdrich, *Love Medicine*, 1984
  Married to Marie, Nector is nevertheless fatefully drawn to Lulu. When his grandson prepares a love medicine to win him back to his grandmother, he uses the wrong ingredients and kills Nector instead.
Thomas King, *Green Grass, Running Water*, 1993
  Coyote, God, Robinson Crusoe, The Lone Ranger and

others struggle amongst themselves in the cosmological firmament while on the human plane, various characters struggle with life the best they can.

Leslie Marmon Silko, *Storyteller*, 1981
  This work is a mixed genre of poetry, fiction, and mythology.

Gerald Vizenor, *Griever: An American Monkey King in China*, 1987
  Vizenor creates a trickster character who leaves his Chippewa home to go to China where he finds himself to be kin to the Monkey King.

W.P. Kinsella, *Moccasin Telegraph*, 1984
  Life on the fictional Ermineskin Reserve in Canada, as revealed by Silas Ermineskin himself, is full of both comedy and tragedy.

1289

SCOTT O'DELL, Caucasian

Sing Down the Moon
(New York: Dell, 1970)

Subject(s): Indians of North America; Indian Removal; Conquest

Age range(s): Grades 4-7

Major character(s): Bright Morning, 14-Year-Old (girl), Native American (Navajo)

Time period(s): 17th century

Locale(s): New Mexico

Summary: This chapter book chronicles the life of a fourteen-year-old Navajo girl who lives near Canyon de Chelly. Her life is happy until she sees the Spanish slave traders invading her homeland. Kidnapped by them, she is later saved by a young warrior but faces further upheaval in her life when White soldiers come to remove her people from their canyon land to Fort Sumter.

About this book: Written in first person, from Bright Morning's point of view.

Where it's reviewed:

Children's Literature in Education, December 1992, page 215

Other books by the same author:
Thunder Rolling in the Mountains, 1992
Island of the Blue Dolphins, 1960
My Name Is Not Angelica, 1989

Other books you might like:
Ann Nolan Clark, *Little Navajo Bluebird*, 1943
  This chapter book chronicles the day in and day out life of a Navajo girl in the 1940s.

Marilyne Virginia Mabery, *Right After Sundown: Teaching Stories of the Navajo*, 1991
  These are the traditional stories of the beginning of this world as told by the Navajo, with excellent illustrations by Navajo artist Raymond J. Johnson.

Shirley Sterling, *My Name Is Seepeetza*, 1992
  Fictional account based on the life of the author, who as a member of the interior Salish tribe, is forced to attend government schools where she is forbidden to reflect anything of her own heritage.

Virginia Driving Hawk Sneve, *High Elk's Treasure*, 1972
  This novel for middle school readers is about Joe High Elk who longs to bring back the strain of wild mustangs that his famous ancestor bred many years before. Illustrated by Oren Lyons.

Ruth Roessel, *Navajo Stories of the Long Walk Period*, 1973
  In this intriguing collection, Navajo people recount the stories passed down to them of the Long Walk period.

Hasteen Klah, *The Myth and Prayers of the Great Star Chant, and the Myth of the Coyote Chant*, 1988
  This exquisite book is a compilation of important Navajo myths, songs, chants, and prayers, that deal with the complex philosophical and religious life of Navajo culture.

Jean Craighead George, *The Talking Earth*, 1983
  A young Seminole girl begins to doubt the beliefs of the elders until she goes into the Everglades, where she begins to understand the importance of her tribal teachings and the world of nature.

Jay Leech, *Moon of the Big-Dog*, 1980
  Three young Sioux boys go on a journey in which they capture the first horses for their tribe, and earn a new name for their Sioux band: Brule. Co-authored by Zane Spencer and illustrated by M. Funai.

1290

SIMON J. ORTIZ, Native American, Acoma

Fightin'
(Chicago: Thunder's Mouth Press, 1969)

Subject(s): Indians of North America

Age range(s): Adult

Time period(s): 1980s

Locale(s): United States

Summary: In his fragmented prose style, Ortiz captures the variety of contemporary Native American experience. This short story collection portrays day-to-day life with its marital problems, family and cultural relationships and the evils that afflict the characters from victimization from cultural insensitivity to alcoholism.

Other books by the same author:
Fight Back: For the Sake of the People, for the Sake of the Land, 1980 (poetry and nonfiction)
From Sand Creek, 1981 (poetry)
Going for the Rain, 1976 (poetry)
A Good Journey, 1977 (poetry)
The Howbah Indians, 1978 (short fiction)

Other books you might like:
Ray A. Young Bear, *Black Eagle Child*,
  Life on the Mesquakie Reservation, written in the vernacular, by one of the most exciting Indian poets.

Thomas King, *Green Grass, Running Water*, 1993
  In this wild romp, Coyote, God, Robinson Crusoe, The Lone Ranger and others struggle in the cosmological firmament while on the human plane, Native Americans struggle to make the best of their lives.

Louise Erdrich, *Love Medicine*, 1984
  Married to Marie, Nector is nevertheless fatefully drawn to Lulu. When his grandson prepares a love medicine to win

him back to his grandmother, he uses the wrong ingredients and kills Nector instead.

Leslie Marmon Silko, *Storyteller*, 1981
This work is a mixed genre of poetry, fiction, and mythology.

W.P. Kinsella, *Moccasin Telegraph*, 1984
Life on the Ermineskin Reserve in Canada, is full of both comedy and tragedy.

James Northrup, *Walking the Rez Road*, 1993
Luke Warmwater is a Vietnam vet who is down on his luck, but he, like many of his reservation cohorts, is a survivor in the trickster fashion.

1291

SIMON J. ORTIZ, Native American, Acoma

The Howbah Indians
(Tucson: Blue Moon Press, 1978)

Subject(s): Indians of North America; Short Stories; Indian Reservations
Age range(s): Adult
Time period(s): 1970s
Locale(s): United States

Summary: Short stories, both humorous and moving, of reservation life by one of the best known Native American poets.

Other books by the same author:
Fightin', 1969 (ahort stories)
Fight Back: For the Sake of the People, for the Sake of the Land, 1980 (poetry and nonfiction)
From Sand Creek, 1981 (poetry)
Going for the Rain, 1976 (poetry)
A Good Journey, 1977 (poetry)

Other books you might like:
Leslie Marmon Silko, *Storyteller*, 1981
A mixed genre anthology of poetry, fiction, and mythology.

Craig Lesley, *Talking Leaves*, 1991
This book is an excellent collection of short stories by thirty-five contemporary American Indian writers, such as Louise Erdrich, N. Scott Momaday, Linda Hogan and Roberta Hill Whiteman.

Paula Gunn Allen, *Voice of the Turtle*, 1994
Edited by the well known writer and scholar Paula Gunn Allen, this book is an anthology of literature written by American Indian people from 1900 to 1970.

Lee Miller, *From the Heart: Voices of the American Indian*, 1995
This is a collection of orations, speeches and testimony by more than 250 Inidan people that presents a radical alternative to traditionally taught American history.

James Northrup, *Walking the Rez Road*, 1993
Luke Warmwater is a Vietnam vet down on his luck, but he, like most of his reservation cohorts, is a survivor in the trickster fashion.

Sherman Alexie, *The Lone Ranger and Tonto Fist Fight in Heaven*, 1993
Wonderful short fiction about the ups and downs of reservation life.

Sherman Alexie, *Reservation Blues*, 1995
Brilliant fiction about the trials of Indian people trying to cope in a most difficult world.

Louise Erdrich, *Love Medicine*, 1984
Married to Marie, Nector is nevertheless fatefully drawn to Lulu. When his grandson prepares a love medicine to win him back to his grandmother, he uses the wrong ingredients and kills Nector instead.

W.P. Kinsella, *Moccasin Telegraph*, 1984
Life on the fictional Ermineskin Reserve in Canada, revealed by Silas Ermineskin himself, is full of both comedy and tragedy.

Ray A. Young Bear, *Black Eagle Child*, 1992
This work of fiction is about life on a Mesquakie settlement.

Thomas King, *Green Grass, Running Water*, 1993
Coyote, God, Robinson Crusoe, the Lone Ranger and others struggle amongst themselves in the cosmological firmament while on the human plane, characters struggle with life the best they can.

1292

SIMON J. ORTIZ, Native American, Acoma

The People Shall Continue
(Emeryville, CA: Children's Book Press, 1977)

Subject(s): History; Indians of North America
Age range(s): Grades 9-Adult
Time period(s): Indeterminate Past (1400s-1900s)
Locale(s): United States

Summary: This invaluable history of Native Americans is written for younger readers from their point of view. It recounts the betrayals and broken promises of the Whites as they invade North America from the time of Columbus to the scattering of the People as children are sent to boarding schools far from home. It is well-presented and a source children can learn from.

Where it's reviewed:
Bookbird, March 1993, page 9
Five Owls, January 1993, page 52

Other books by the same author:
Fight Back: For the Sake of the People, for the Sake of the Land, 1980 (poetry and nonfiction)
From Sand Creek, 1981 (poetry)
Going for the Rain, 1976 (poetry)
A Good Journey, 1977 (poetry)
The Howbah Indians, 1978

Other books you might like:
Joseph Bruchac, *The Wind Eagle and Other Abenaki Stories*, 1984
These are traditional tales of the Abenaki people.

Joseph Bruchac, *Iroquois Stories*, 1985
Traditional tales of the Iroquois people.

Joseph Bruchac, *Return of the Sun*, 1990
These are traditional tales of the Northeast Woodlands Indians.

Joseph Bruchac, *Flying with the Eagle, Racing with the Bear*, 1993

These are rite-of-passage stories from many tribal people.

1293

LOUIS OWEN, Native American, Choctaw and Cherokee

Bone Game

(Norman: U. Of Oklahoma, 1994)

Series: American Indian Literature and Critical Studies
Subject(s): Mystery; Ecothriller; Education
Age range(s): Adult
Major character(s): Cole McCurtain, Professor, Native American (mixed-blood)
Time period(s): 1990s
Locale(s): New Mexico

Summary: Cole McCurtain, is a mixed-blood professor haunted by dreams. He becomes involved in a murder mystery that involves ecological crisis.

Where it's reviewed:
Booklist, October 1, 1994, page 243
Los Angeles Times Book Review, February 26, 1995, page 6
New York Times Book Review, October 23, 1994, page 24
World Literature Today, Spring 1995, page 409
Village Voice, November 1, 1994, page 86

Other books by the same author:
The Sharpest Sight, 1992 (American Indian Literature and Critical Studies Series, Vol. 1)

Other books you might like:
Martin Cruz Smith, *Nightwing*, 1977
  Youngman Duran, an ex-con, becomes deputy sheriff and must uncover the secret of the plague that threatens the reservation.
Leslie Marmon Silko, *Ceremony*, 1977
  Tayo, a puebo Indian, returns home from the war and must realign himself with his people and the old ways.
Martin Cruz Smith, *Stallion Gate*, 1986
  Joe Pena, leaves his pueblo to join the war effort but when he returns he feels aliented from his people and must confront the power of the atom bomb developed in his homeland, at Los Alamos.
Linda Hogan, *Mean Spirit*, 1990
  This murder mystery takes place in the Oklahoma oil boom days.
Carol LaFavor, *Along the Journey River*, 1996
  This is a mystery story about sacred stolen objects, as the lives of Renee and Salisbury become intwined on the Red Earth Reservation of Minnesota.

1294

LUCILLE RECHT PENNER, Caucasian

A Native American Feast

(New York: MacMillan, 1994)

Subject(s): Food; History; Indians of North America
Age range(s): Grades 5 and Up
Time period(s): Indeterminate

Locale(s): United States

Summary: This intersting book for both children and adults, looks at the way various Native people eat throughout North America, and includes various customs and myths associated with eating. It also includes many authentic recipes.

Where it's reviewed:
Booklist, November 1, 1994, page 494
Horn Book Guide, Spring 1995, page 165
New Advocate, Spring 1995, page 125
Social Education, April 1995, page 222
School Library Journal, February 1995, page 110

Other books by the same author:
The Honey Book, 1980
The Colonial Cookbook, 1976
The Thanksgiving Book, 1985
Eating the Plates: A Pilgrim Book of Food and Manners, 1991
Celebration: The Story of American Holidays, 1993

Other books you might like:
Trudy Griffin-Perce, *The Encyclopedia of Native America*, 1995
  This is a useful encyclopedia about Native American cultures, written by a Native American writer, divided geographically. An excellent resource for young people in particular.
John Bierhorst, *The Red Swan: Myths and Tales of the American Indians*, 1976
  This book is a compilation of varied stories (creation, trickster, star husband, etc.) from forty Indian tribes.
Frederick Turner, *The Portable North American Indian Reader*, 1973
  This anthology of myths, legends, poetry, fiction, and captivity tales, contains work by both Native American and non-Native writers.
William C. Sturtevant, *Handbook of North American Indians*, 1990
  A massive multivolume resource, this encyclopedia contains an incredible amount of information about Native North American peoples.
Sam D. Gill, *Dictionary of Native American Mythology*, 1992
  A comprehensive dictionary of Native American mythology. An excellent resource for students and teachers. Co-authored by Irene F. Sullivan.
Margot Astrov, *The Winged Serpent*, 1946
  One of the best collections of oral stories and songs from a large cross-section of Indian cultures.
LaVonne Ruoff, *American Indian Literatures: An Introduction, Bibliographic Review, and Selected Bibliography*, 1990
  This is the bible of Native American literature, essential to anyone who wants to pursue a study of the literature that has been written by American Indian people.

1295

SUSAN POWER, Native American, Lakota (Sioux)

The Grass Dancer
(New York: G.P. Putnam's Sons, 1994)

Subject(s): Indians of North America; Historical; Family Relations

Age range(s): Adult

Major character(s): Harley Wind Soldier, Native American, Young Man; Crystal Thunder, Native American, Young Woman; Anna Thunder, Native American, Religious (Medicine Woman)

Time period(s): 20th century (1960s-1980s)

Locale(s): South Dakota

Summary: This is a novel told in a series of interrelated short stories (much in the style of Louise Erdrich). In her exact and mesmerizing prose, Powers weaves a web of stories that cross the boundaries between contemporary and traditional lifestlyes, between harsh realities and magic. The novel begins with Harley's love affair with a girl named Pumpkin at a Pow-wow, where we are also introduced to the reservation witch, Anna (Mercury) Thunder. As the book progresses we flash back and forth through time, meeting a number of characters who make up the intruiging world of this Sioux reservation.

Where it's reviewed:

Bloomsbury Review, May 1995, page 16

Library Journal, March 15, 1995, page 41

Publishers Weekly, November 1, 1994, page 40

School Library Journal, May 1995, page 136

Los Angeles Times Book Review, August 20, 1995, page 10

Other books you might like:

Louise Erdrich, *Love Medicine*, 1984

Married to Marie, Nector is nevertheless fatefully drawn to Lulu. When his grandson prepares a love medicine to win him back to his grandmother, he uses the wrong ingredients and kills Nector instead.

Louise Erdrich, *Tracks*, 1988

Two alternating voices in conflict, one a traditionalist and one the voice of change, reveal the escalating tension between two Chippewa families and the disintegration of their culture.

Louise Erdrich, *The Beet Queen*, 1987

When 11-year-old Mary Adare is abandoned by her mother for an aviator she meets at a carnival, Mary finds a home with relatives near a Chippewa reservation.

Louise Erdrich, *The Bingo Palace*, 1994

Lipsha and Lyman are locked in a struggle to capture the heart of beautiful Shawnee Ray. But Shawnee Ray's ambitions reach beyond the reservation.

Leslie Marmon Silko, *Storyteller*, 1981

A mixed genre anthology of poetry, fiction, and mythology.

Craig Lesley, *Talking Leaves*, 1991

This book is a an excellent collection of short stories by thirty-five contemporary American Indian writers, such as Louise Erdrich, N. Scott Momaday, Linda Hogan and Roberta Hill Whiteman.

Clifford E. Trafzer, *Blue Dawn, Red Earth: New Native American Storytellers*, 1996

This is a collection of short stories by 30 new Native American writers: Lorne Simon, Anita Endrezze, Jim Barnes, Annie Hansen, Maurice Kenny, and Patricia Piley, among others.

James Northrup, *Walking the Rez Road*, 1993

Luke Warmwater is a Vietnam vet down on his luck, but he, like most of his reservation cohorts, is a survivor in the trickster fashion.

Sherman Alexie, *The Lone Ranger and Tonto Fist Fight in Heaven*, 1993

Wonderful short fiction about the ups and downs of reservation life.

1296

CLINTON RICKARD, Native American, Tuscarora

BARBARA GRAYMONT, Editor, Caucasian

Fighting Tuscarora: The Autobiography of Chief Clinton Rickard
(Syracuse: Syracuse University Press, 1973)

Subject(s): Men; Autobiography; Politics

Age range(s): Grades 9-Adult

Time period(s): 19th century; 20th century (1880s-1960s)

Locale(s): New Mexico

Summary: In this autobiography, Chief Rickard is familiar with both the Native American and white worlds. He is politically active well into his eighties, when this book was begun.

About this book: This book was dictated by Rickard to Graymont, who edited the transcript.

Other books you might like:

John Joseph Mathews, *Talking to the Moon*, 1945

Mathews relates the full circle of his life from his childhood in Oklahoma, through his military stint in WWI and back home again.

Jason Betzinez, *I Fought with Geronimo*, 1957

Betzinez lived to be almost a hundred years old, and this autobiography covers the great period of change for the Apache.

N. Scott Momaday, *The Names: A Memoir*, 1976

This is an autobiographical work.

Chief John Stands in Timber, *Cheyenne Memories*, 1967

Stands in Timber was raised in the traditional Cheyenne culture, toward the beginning of the reservation period.

Refugio Savala, *The Autobiography of a Yaqui Poet*, 1980

This autobiography by Refugio Savala tells of his family's flight from Mexico to Arizona during the horrible years of torture, and their struggle to make a new home for themselves.

James Sewid, *Guests Never Leave Hungry: The Autobiography of James Sewid, a Kwakuitl Indian*, 1969

This is the life story of James Sewid, a Kwakiutl Indian.

John Fire Lame Deer, *Lame Deer, Seeker of Visions*, 1972

Traditional medicine man Lame Deer tells of his visions and spiritual quest while relating the philosophy of Lakota religion and culture.

Luther Standing Bear, *Stories of the Sioux*, 1988
   Standing Bear grows up in the traditional buffalo hunting culture, and he brings to life the stories from his own past.
Don C. Talayesva, *Sun Chief: The Autobiography of a Hopi Indian*, 1942
   Don C. Talayesva is born in Oraibi, the oldest continually inhabited town in the U.S., in 1890. This is the story of his life and the life of the Hopi people.

1297

MONTY ROESSEL, Native American, Navajo

Songs from the Loom

(Minneapolis: Lerner Publications, 1995)

Subject(s): Crafts; Cultures and Customs; Folklore
Age range(s): Grades 3-6
Major character(s): Jaclyn Roessel, Artisan (weaver), Native American (Navajo)
Time period(s): 1990s (1995)
Locale(s): Arizona; New Mexico

Summary: This story follows Jaclyn Roessel, a young Navajo girl, as she learns the stories of her family and the cultural wisdom and mythology that accompany the art of weaving. It is a very positive look at Navajo life, the interconnectedness of family with the vibrancy of art.

Where it's reviewed:
Booklist, September 15, 1995, page 156

Other books by the same author:
Kinaalda, 1993

Other books you might like:
Hasteen Klah, *The Myth and Prayers of the Great Star Chant, and the Myth of the Coyote Chant*, 1988
   This exquisite book is a compilation of important Navajo myths, songs, chants, and prayers, portraying the complexity of the philosophical and religious life of Navajo culture.
Sandra King, *Shannon: An Ojibway Dancer*, 1993
   This book follows the life of a young Ojibway girl, Shannon, who lives in the city, yet still participates in tribal ceremonies.
Jonathan Broderick, *Stories of Traditional Navajo Life and Culture*, 1977
   These are interviews from tape-recorded meetings of the Navajo.
Broderick H. Johnson, *Navajo Stories of the Long Walk Period*, 1973
   In this intriguing collection, Navajo people recount the stories of the Long Walk period that as they have been handed down in their families.
Shonto Begay, *Ma'ii and Cousin Horned Toad*,
   Lazy, conniving Ma'ii is hungry, and he goes to Horny Toad for a free lunch. He swallows his smaller cousin, but Horny Toad teaches him a lesson he won't forget.
Rina Swentzell, *Children of Clay*, 1992
   This book tells the wondrous story of making the famous pottery of Santa Clara, told by a Santa Clara woman with photos by Bill Steen.

1298

WILL ROGERS, Native American, Cherokee

"How To Be Funny" & Other Writings of Will Rogers

(Stillwater, OK: U. Of Oklahoma Press, 1983)

Series: The Writings of Will Rogers
Subject(s): Humor; Satire; Politics
Age range(s): Grades 11-Adult
Time period(s): 20th century
Locale(s): Oklahoma

Summary: A collection of writings by one of America's best known humorists and political commentators.

Other books you might like:
Vine DeLoria Jr., *God Is Red*, 1973
   DeLoria tackles issues of religion, arguing for Native religious beliefs, while recounting the history of acculturation and missionizing that have plagued Indian people for centuries.
Gerald Vizenor, *Earthdivers: Tribal Narratives on Mixed Descent*, 1981
   In this collection of short stories Vizenor creates trickster figures to poke fun at and make shrewd political commentary on America, reservation life, and just about everything else.
Peter Nabokov, *Native American Testimony*, 1991
   Anthology, mixed genre: oral stories, speeches, prophecies, and essays.
Brian Swann, *I Tell You Now*, 1989
   This is an excellent collection of autobiographical essays by eighteen contemporary American Indian writers. Coauthored with Arnold Krupat.
Paula Gunn Allen, *Voice of the Turtle*, 1994
   Edited by the well known writer and scholar Paula Gunn Allen, this book is an anthology of literature written by American Indian people from 1900 to 1970.
Lee Miller, *From the Heart: Voices of the American Indian*, 1995
   This is a collection of orations, speeches and testimony by more than 250 Inidan people that presents a radical alternative to traditionally taught American history.

1299

LAVONNE RUOFF, Caucasian

American Indian Literatures: An Introduction, Bibliographic Review, and Selected Bibliography

(New York: The Modern Language Association of America, 1990)

Subject(s): Indians of North America; Literature; History
Age range(s): Grades 10-Adult
Time period(s): Indeterminate
Locale(s): United States

Summary: This is the *bible* of Native American literature, essential to anyone who wants to pursue a study of the literature that has been written by American Indian people.

The introduction is excellent, giving readers an important foundation into the various genres of this literature while explaining the historical record of Indian literature, in both the oral and written forms.

About this book: For any one teaching Native American Literature, at any level, you cannot do without this book.

Where it's reviewed:
Booklist, June 1, 1993, page 1879
Wilson Library Bulletin, December 1992, page 33

Other books you might like:
Beverly Slapin, *Through Indian Eyes: The Native Experience in Books for Children*, 1992
  Essays and poems by Indian writers and an annotated bibliography that focuses on literature about (and mostly by) Native American people that is geared for children.

1300

SALLY RUSSEL, Editor, Caucasian
BRUCE LEVENE, Co-Editor

Voices and Dreams

(Ukiah, CA: Mendocino County Library Press, 1991)

Subject(s): Narrative; Racism; Cultural Conflict
Age range(s): Grades 4 and Up
Time period(s): 20th century
Locale(s): California

Summary: In these first-person accounts, twenty-two people of California Indian descent tell their moving stories about life, culture, racism, and survival.

About this book: This is an excellent resource for teachers.

Other books you might like:
Linda Yamane, *When the World Ended, How Hummingbird Got Fire, How People Were Made: Rumsien Ohlone Stories*, 1995
  These three stories of the Rumsien Ohlone people of California deal with creation and the advent of people on earth.
Jane Curry, *Back in the Before Time: Tales of the California Indians*, 1987
  This collection includes twenty-two tales of the creation of the world from California Indian tribes.

1301

CARL SAUER, Caucasian

Man in Nature

(Berkeley: Turtle Island Foundation, 1939, 1975)

Subject(s): Cultures and Customs
Age range(s): Grades 5 and Up
Time period(s): Indeterminate Past (pre-Columbian)
Locale(s): United States

Summary: This excellent book explores the various Native American cultures that existed in pre-Columbian America, broken down into fourteen geographical areas. Each area discusses how Native American people interacted with their environments in a variety of ways.

About this book: This was originally a junior high textbook, but anthropologists have used it successfully for freshman college classes.

Other books you might like:
Margot Astrov, *The Winged Serpent*, 1946
  This is one of the best collections of oral stories and songs from a large cross-section of Native American cultures.
John Bierhorst, *The Sacred Path*, 1984
  This is fine collection of traditional spells, prayers, and power songs from a variety of Native American tribes.
Paula Gunn Allen, *Spider Woman's Granddaughters*, 1989
  This is a beautiful collection of traditional tales interwoven with contemporary stories having to do with the lives of Native American women.
Zitkala-Sa, *Old Indian Legends Retold by Zitkala-Sa*, 1921
  This is a collection of memoirs and essays by an Native American woman who was born into the old buffalo hunting culture of the Sioux.
Frederick Turner, *The Portable North American Indian Reader*, 1973
  This anthology of myths, legends, poetry, fiction and captivity tales, contains works by both Native and non-Native writers.
Howard Norman, *Northern Tales*, 1990
  This book is a collection of traditional stories that focuses wholly on the Native American and Eskimo people of the far north.

1302

REFUGIO SAVALA, Native American, Yaqui

The Autobiography of a Yaqui Poet

(Tucson: University of Arizona Press, 1980)

Subject(s): Autobiography; Emigration and Immigration
Age range(s): Grades 10-Adult
Time period(s): 20th century (1900-1960s)
Locale(s): Arizona

Summary: Refugio Savala tells the poignant story of his family's flight from Mexico to Arizona during the horrible years of torture, and their struggle to make a new home for themselves.

About this book: This invaluable work details Yaqui culture.

Other books you might like:
John Joseph Mathews, *Talking to the Moon*, 1945
  From his childhood in Oklahoma, tghrough his military stint in WWI, college, marriage and back to his home and, Mathews relates the circle of his life.
Anna Moore Shaw, *A Pima Past*, 1974
  Born in a traditional Pima brush house and educated in the white world, Shaw tells this fascinating autobiography of her life.
Leslie Marmon Silko, *Storyteller*, 1981
  From Laguna Pueblo where he grew up, Silko weaves traditional mythology into modern stories, recreating old myths and making them relevant for a new generation.
Zitkala-Sa, *Old Indian Legends Retold by Zitkala-Sa*, 1921
  This is a collection of memoirs and essays about the

traditional Lakota culture and its adjustments to European encroachment.

Jane Holden Kelley, *Contemporary Life Histories*, 1978
This as-told-to-book chronicles the lives of four Yaqui women. The author describes many aspects of Yaqui culture in the introduction.

John Fire Lame Deer, *Lame Deer, Seeker of Visions*, 1972
Traditional medicine man Lame Deer tells of his visions and spiritual quest while relating the philosophy of Lakota religion and culture.

1303

VICKIE SEARS, Native American, Cherokee

Simple Songs
(Ithaca, NY: Firebrand Books, 1990)

Subject(s): Cultures and Customs; Indians of North America
Age range(s): Grades 9-Adult
Time period(s): 1990s
Locale(s): Arizona

Summary: This is collection of short stories about contemporary Cherokee, many of them young girls, who are coping with the clash of Native philosophy and European ways of thinking.

Where it's reviewed:
Wilson Library Bulletin, December 1992, page 87

Other books you might like:

Craig Lesley, *Talking Leaves*, 1991
This book is a an excellent collection of short stories by thirty-five contemporary Native American writers including, among others, Erdrich, Dorris, Momaday, Hogan, and Whiteman.

Louise Erdrich, *Love Medicine*, 1984
Married to Marie, Nector is nevertheless fatefully drawn to Lulu. When his grandson prepares a love medicine to win him back to his grandmother, he uses the wrong ingredients and kills Nector instead.

Paula Gunn Allen, *Spider Woman's Granddaughters*, 1989
This beautiful collection of traditional tales is interwoven with contemporary short stories about Native American women.

Lee Miller, *From the Heart: Voices of the American Indian*, 1995
This is a collection of orations, speeches, and testimony by more than 250 Indian people that presents a radical alternative to traditionally taught American history.

Clifford E. Trafzer, *Blue Dawn, Red Earth: New Native American Storytellers*, 1996
This is a collection of short stories by 30 new Native American writers, such as Lorne Simon, Jim Barnes, Patricia Piley and Richard Van Camp.

Beth Brant, *A Gathering of Spirit: A Collection of North American Indian Women*, 1984
Here is a collection of stories, letters, essays, and poems from a large cross-section of Native American women writers, such as Linda Hogan, Diana Glancy, Joy Harjo and Wendy Rose.

Anna Lee Walters, *The Sun Is Not Merciful*, 1985
This is a collection of well-crafted and moving stories that deal with the pains and triumphs of Indian life.

1304

JAMES SEWID, Native American, Kwakiutl
JAMES P. SPRADLEY, Editor, Caucasian

Guests Never Leave Hungry: The Autobiography of James Sewid, a Kwakuitl Indian
(New Haven: Yale University Press, 1969)

Subject(s): Autobiography
Age range(s): Grades 11-Adult
Time period(s): 20th century (1913-1960s)
Locale(s): British Columbia, Canada

Summary: This is the life story of James Sewid, as told to James P. Spradley. James Sewid is a Kwakiutl Indian who has spent his life on the coast of British Columbia. In this book he talks about his life as a Kwakiutl person in the twentieth century. He is able to do well in both the Native American and White worlds and it is interesting to note how he can balance the two perspectives in his own life.

Other books you might like:

Anna Moore Shaw, *A Pima Past*, 1974
Anna Moore Shaw born in a traditional Pima brush house, and educated in the white world, tells this fascinating autobiography of her life.

Refugio Savala, *The Autobiography of a Yaqui Poet*, 1980
This autobiography by Refugio Savala tells of his family's flight from Mexico to Arizona during the horrible years of torture, and their struggle to make a new home for themselves.

Zitkala-Sa, *Old Indian Legends Retold by Zitkala-Sa*, 1921
This is a collection of memoirs and essays about the traditional Lakota culture and the adjustments to the real world.

Jason Betzinez, *I Fought with Geronimo*, 1957
Betzinez lived to be almost a hundred years old, and this autobiography covers the great period of change for the Apache.

Jane Holden Kelley, *Contemporary Life Histories*, 1978
This as-told-to-book chronicles the lives of four Yaqui women. The author describes many aspects of Yaqui culture in the introduction of the book.

Clinton Rickard, *Fighting Tuscarora: The Autobiography of Chief Clinton Rickard*, 1973
In this autobiography, Chief Rickard is familiar with both the Indian and white worlds. He is politically active well into his eighties, when this book was begun.

Angela Sidney, *Life Lived like a Story: Life Stories of Three Yukon Native Elders*, 1990
This as-told-to-book chronicles the lives of three Yukon women.

John Fire Lame Deer, *Lame Deer, Seeker of Visions*, 1972
Traditional medicine man Lame Deer tells of his own visions and spiritual quest while relating the philosophy of Lakota religion and culture.

Luther Standing Bear, *Stories of the Sioux*, 1988
  Standing Bear grows up in the traditional hunting culture, and he brings to life the stories from his own past.

1305

ANNA MORE SHAW, Native American, Pima

A Pima Past
(Tucson: University of Arizona Press, 1974)

Subject(s): Women; Autobiography
Age range(s): Grades 9-Adult
Time period(s): 19th century; 20th century (1890s-1970s)
Locale(s): Arizona

Summary: Anna Moore Shaw, born in a traditional Pima brush house and educated in the white world, tells this fascinating autobiography of her life, living between two cultures. This book is particularly valuable for the information about Pima culture it includes.

Other books by the same author:
Pima Indian Legends

Other books you might like:
Refugio Savala, *The Autobiography of a Yaqui Poet*, 1980
  This autobiography by Refugio Savala tells of his family's flight from Mexico to Arizona during the horrible years of torture, and their struggle to make a new home for themselves.
James Sewid, *Guests Never Leave Hungry: The Autobiography of James Sewid, a Kwakuitl Indian*, 1969
  This is the life story of James Sewid, a Kwakiutl Indian.
Luther Standing Bear, *Stories of the Sioux*, 1988
  Standing Bear grew up in the traditional buffalo hunting culture, and he brings to life the stories from his own past.
Zitkala-Sa, *Old Indian Legends Retold by Zitkala-Sa*, 1921
  This is a collection of memoirs and essays about the traditional Lakota culture and its adjustments to White encroachment.
Jane Holden Kelley, *Contemporary Life Histories*, 1978
  This as-told-to-book chronicles the lives of four Yaqui women. The author describes many aspects of Yaqui culture in the introduction.
Angela Sidney, *Life Lived like a Story: Life Stories of Three Yukon Native Elders*, 1990
  This as-told-to-book chronicles the lives of three Yukon women.

1306

LESLIE MARMON SILKO, Native American, Laguna

Almanac of the Dead
(New York: Simon & Schuster, 1991)

Subject(s): Indians of North America; Historical
Age range(s): Adult
Major character(s): Seese, Young Woman, Mother; Lecha, Twin, Aged Person, Psychic; Zeta, Twin, Aged Person
Time period(s): Indeterminate
Locale(s): Southwest

Summary: In this epic novel, Silko presents a cast of characters whose complex and often violent relationships reflect the cultural conflict of 400 years of white encroachment and native accommodation. While Seese searches for her kidnapped son, twins, Lecha and Zeta work to compile the ancient prophetic, history of their people, an indictment of the European conquest of North America that includes a prophecy of their eventual downfall.

Where it's reviewed:
American Book Review, December 1992, page 5
New York Times Book Review, December 20, 1992, page 24
Publishers Weekly, October 12, 1992, page 74

Other books by the same author:
Ceremony, 1977
Laguna Woman, 1974 (poetry)
Storyteller, 1981 (fiction, poetry, myths)

Other books you might like:
James Welch, *Winter in the Blood*, 1974
  An unnamed protagonist, who suffers from alcoholism, searches for his family's past on a reservation in Montana.
Craig Lesley, *Talking Leaves*, 1991
  This is an anthology of short stories.
Janet Campbell Hale, *The Jailing of Cecelia Capture*, 1985
  A woman law student, trapped in despair and alcoholism, tries to make sense of her life.
Linda Hogan, *Mean Spirit*, 1990
  A novel that takes place in Oklahoma of the oil boom days, which deals with corruption and murder.
Clifford E. Trafzer, *Blue Dawn, Red Earth: New Native American Storytellers*, 1996
  This is a collection of short stories by 30 new Native American writers, such as Lorne Simon, Jim Barnes, Richard Van Camp, and Penny Olson.
Beth Brant, *A Gathering of Spirit: A Collection of North American Indian Women*, 1984
  Here is a collection of stories, letters, essays, and poems from a large cross-section of Native American women writers, such as Linda Hogan, Joy Harjo, Wendy Rose, and Doris Seale.
D'Arcy McNickle, *The Surrounded*, 1936
  A fiddle player returns to his reservation for a visit after years in the White world and finds himself so caught up in its complexities that he knows he can never go back to the White world again.
Louise Erdrich, *Love Medicine*, 1984
  Married to Marie, Nector is nevertheless fatefully drawn to Lulu. When his grandson prepares a love medicine to win him back to his grandmother, he uses the wrong ingredients and kills Nector instead.

1307

LESLIE MARMON SILKO, Native American, Laguna

Ceremony
(New York: Viking, 1977)

Subject(s): Indians of North America; Veterans; World War II
Age range(s): Adult
Major character(s): Tayo, Veteran (WWII), Native American (Pueblo)

Time period(s): 1970s
Locale(s): New Mexico

Summary: This novel centers on the character of Tayo, a mixed-blood man from Laguna Pueblo who has just returned from World War II, psychologically damaged. Through the use of ritual and myth, Tayo learns to enter into the world again. This excellent book is full of Native American mythology which sets the stage for Tayo's journey into healing.

About this book: In structure, this book is very similar to Momaday's *House Made of Dawn*, and indeed, Silko wrote it partly in response to the fact that his main character's future is so ambiguous at the end of the novel.

Where it's reviewed:
New Age, Winter 1995, page 30
Western American Literature, Winter 1994, page 301
English Journal, February 1994, page 70

Other books by the same author:
Almanac of the Dead, 1991
Laguna Woman, 1974 (poetry)
Storyteller, 1981 (fiction, poetry, myths)

Other books you might like:
N. Scott Momaday, *House Made of Dawn*, 1968
Story of an Indian man, Abel, who leaves his pueblo to fight in the war, only to come back alienated from his people. He begins a long effort at healing.
Paula Gunn Allen, *Spider Woman's Granddaughters*, 1989
This is a beautiful collection of traditional tales interwoven with contemporary stories having to do with the lives of Native American women.
James Welch, *Winter in the Blood*, 1974
An unnamed protagonist, who suffers from alcoholism, searches for his family's past on a reservation in Montana.
D'Arcy McNickle, *The Surrounded*, 1936
A fiddle player returns to his reservation for a visit after years in the White world and finds himself so caught up in its complexities that he knows he can never go back to the White world again.
Craig Lesley, *Talking Leaves*, 1991
This is an anthology of short stories.
Janet Campbell Hale, *The Jailing of Cecelia Capture*, 1985
A woman law student, trapped in despair and alcoholism, tries to make sense of her life.
Linda Hogan, *Mean Spirit*, 1990
A novel that takes place in Oklahoma of the oil boom days, which deals with corruption and murder.
Clifford E. Trafzer, *Blue Dawn, Red Earth: New Native American Storytellers*, 1996
This is a collection of short stories by 30 new Native American writers, such as Lorne Simon, Jim Barnes, Richard Van Camp, and Penny Olson.
Beth Brant, *A Gathering of Spirit: A Collection of North American Indian Women*, 1984
Here is a collection of stories, letters, essays, and poems from a large cross-section of Native American women writers, such as Linda Hogan, Diana Glancy, and Doris Seale.
James Northrup, *Walking the Rez Road*, 1993
Fiction; humorous short stories that take place on an Ojibway reservation in Minnesota.

LESLIE MARMON SILKO, Native American, Laguna

Storyteller
(New York: Little Brown, 1981)

Subject(s): Indians of North America; Cultures and Customs
Age range(s): Grades 10-Adult
Major character(s): Yellow Woman, Young Woman; Tony Coyote, Trickster
Time period(s): 1980s
Locale(s): New Mexico

Summary: This superb book is a mixed genre of short fiction, poetry, and personal memoirs, with photos of the author's family and Laguna Pueblo, New Mexico, where Silko grew up. Silko recreates the traditional myths by weaving them through her modern stories, thus making them relevant for a new generation. In one story the mythological Yellow Woman comes to life in a modern woman who leaves her family to run off with a Navajo man. In another story, the contemporary reincarnation of the mythological character, Coyote, goes from Laguna to another pueblo to try and seduce a Hopi woman.

Where it's reviewed:
Rocky Mountain Rev. of Language and Literature, Issue 1, 1993, page 61

Other books by the same author:
Almanac of the Dead, 1991
Ceremony, 1977
Laguna Woman, 1974 (poetry)

Other books you might like:
N. Scott Momaday, *The Names: A Memoir*, 1976
This is an autobiography of Momaday's life.
Paula Gunn Allen, *Voice of the Turtle*, 1994
Edited by the well-known writer and scholar, Paula Gunn Allen, this book is an anthology of literature written by American Indian people.
Lee Miller, *From the Heart: Voices of the American Indian*, 1995
This is a collection of orations, speeches and testimony by more than 250 Indian people that presents a radical alternative to traditionally taught American history.
Clifford E. Trafzer, *Blue Dawn, Red Earth: New Native American Storytellers*, 1996
This collection of short stories by 30 new Native American writers includes Lorne Simon, Anita Endrezze, Jim Barnes and others.
Beth Brant, *A Gathering of Spirit: A Collection of North American Indian Women*, 1984
This collection of short stories, letters, essays and poems comes from a wide cross-section of Native American women writers including Linda Hogan, Elizabeth Cook-Lynn, Diana Glancy and others.
Frederick Turner, *The Portable North American Indian Reader*, 1973
This anthology of myths, legends, poetry, fiction, and captivity tales, contains work by both Native and non-Native writers.

John Bierhorst, *The Red Swan: Myths and Tales of the American Indians*, 1976

This book is a compilation of varied stories (creation, trickster, star husband, etc.) from forty Indian tribes.

Paula Gunn Allen, *Spider Woman's Granddaughters*, 1989

This is a beautiful collection of traditional tales interwoven with contemporary stories about Native American women.

John Bierhorst, *The Sacred Path*, 1984

This is a collection of traditional spells, prayers, and power songs from a variety of Native American tribes.

1309

BEVERLY SLAPIN, Caucasian
DORIS SEALE, Co-Author, Native American, Santee and Cree

Through Indian Eyes: The Native Experience in Books for Children

(Philadelphia: New Society Publishers, 1992)

Subject(s): Indians of North America; Literature; History
Age range(s): Adult
Time period(s): Indeterminate
Locale(s): United States

Summary: The first half of this book is a collection of essays and poems by Indian writers such as Dorris, Bruchac, Brant, Durham, Tapahonso, Rose, and others. The second half of the book is an annotated bibliography that focuses on literature about (and mostly by) Native American people that is geared for children. Each book is annotated and reviewed (both positive and negative reviews), and each has a picture of the cover.

About this book: This is a superb resource for discovering books about Indian people (and by Indian people) for children. The authors have done an excellent job of describing why some books (even some classics) that feature Indian people as subjects are far from being either genuine or appropriate.

Where it's reviewed:
Instructor, May 1995, page 14
New Advocate, Spring 1995, page 125

Other books by the same author:
The Sixth Grandfather, 1984 (interviews)
The Sacred Pipe, 1953 (as-told-to)
When the Tree Flowered, 1951

Other books you might like:
LaVonne Ruoff, *American Indian Literatures: An Introduction, Bibliographic Review, and Selected Bibliography*, 1990

This is the *bible* of Native American literature, essential to anyone who wants to pursue a study of the literature that has been written *by* American Indian people.

1310

KATHIE BILLINGSLEA SMITH, Caucasian
JAMES SEWARD, Illustrator

Sitting Bull: Tatanka Yotanka

(New York: Wander Books, 1987)

Series: The Great American
Subject(s): Indians of North America; History
Age range(s): Grades 3-5
Time period(s): 1880s
Locale(s): South Dakota

Summary: This is a brief history of the famous medicine man and leader of the Sioux resistance to White encroachment, culminating in Custer's defeat at the Battle of the Little Big Horn and the Wounded Knee Massacre.

Other books you might like:
Michael Dorris, *Morning Girl*, 1992

This is the story of a young girl in Pre-Columbian Caribbean for younger readers.

Sandra King, *Shannon: An Ojibway Dancer*, 1993

This book follows the life of a young Ojibway girl, Shannon, who lives in the city, yet still participates in tribal ceremonies. For younger readers.

Monty Roessel, *Songs from the Loom*, 1995

This story follows Jaclyn Roessel, a young Navajo girl, as she learns the stories of her family and the cultural wisdom and mythology associated with the art of weaving. For younger readers.

Joseph Bruchac, *Flying with the Eagle, Racing with the Bear*, 1993

These rite-of-passage stories come from various tribal peoples including the Wampanoag, Cherokee, Osage, Lakota and Tlingit.

Susan Braine, *Drumbeat. . .Heartbeat: A Celebration of the Powwow*, 1995

This is a wonderful introduction to the Powwow for children by a Native American writer and photographer.

Herman J. Viola, *Osceola*, 1993

This is a brief history of the famous Creek leader for younger readers. Illustrated by Yoshi Miyake.

Albert Marrin, *Plains Warrior: Chief Quanah Parker and the Comanches*, 1996

This book tells the story of Quanah Parker, chief of the Comanches.

1311

MARTIN CRUZ SMITH, Native American, Seneca del Sur and Yaqui

Nightwing

(New York: W.W. Norton, 1977)

Subject(s): Medicine; Mystery
Age range(s): Adult
Major character(s): Youngman Duran, Police Officer (ex-convict), Native American (Hopi); Hayden Paine, Scientist
Time period(s): 1970s
Locale(s): Arizona

Summary: Youngman Duran, an ex-con, leaves his pueblo to join the war effort. When he returns he feels aliented from his people. He becomes deputy sheriff and must uncover the secret of the plague that threatens the reservation.

Other books by the same author:
Gorky Park, 1981
Gypsy in Amber, 1982
The Indians Won, 1970
Polar Star, 1989
Stallion Gate, 1986

Other books you might like:
Linda Hogan, *Mean Spirit*, 1990
  This is a murder mystery that takes place in the oil boom days of Oklahoma.
Carol LaFavor, *Along the Journey River*, 1996
  This is a mystery story about sacred stolen objects, where the lives of Renee and Salisbury become intwined on the Red Earth Reservation of Minnesota.
Louis Owen, *Bone Game*, 1994
  Cole McCurtain is a mixed-blood professor haunted by dreams. He becomes involved in a murder mystery that involves an ecological crisis.
N. Scott Momaday, *House Made of Dawn*, 1968
  Story of an Indian man, Abel, who leaves his pueblo to fight in the war, only to come back alienated from his people.
James Welch, *Winter in the Blood*, 1974
  A man caught in the web of alcoholism tries to discover the truth about his family.

1312

MARTIN CRUZ SMITH, Native American, Seneca del Sur and Yaqui

Stallion Gate
(New York: Random House, 1986)

Subject(s): Mystery; War; Cultural Identity
Age range(s): Adult
Major character(s): Joe Pena, Military Personnel (soldier), Native American (Pueblo Indian)
Time period(s): 1940s
Locale(s): Arizona

Summary: Joe Pena leaves his pueblo to join the war effort, yet when he returns he feels alienated from his people and he must confront the power of the atom bomb, which has been developed in his homeland, at Los Alamos.

About this book: The book also deals with the conflicts between tribal religion and modern science.

Other books by the same author:
Nightwing, 1977
The Analog Bullet, 1977
Gorky Park, 1981
Gypsy in Amber, 1982
The Indians Won, 1970
Polar Star, 1989

Other books you might like:
N. Scott Momaday, *House Made of Dawn*, 1968
  Story of an Indian man, Abel, who leaves his pueblo to

fight in the war, only to come back alienated from his people.
Leslie Marmon Silko, *Ceremony*, 1977
  Tayo, a puebo Indian, returns home from the war and must realign himself with his people and the old ways.
Linda Hogan, *Mean Spirit*, 1990
  This murder mystery takes place in the Oklahoma oil boom days.
Carol LaFavor, *Along the Journey River*, 1996
  This is a mystery story about sacred stolen objects, where the lives of Renee and Salisbury become intwined on the Red Earth Reservation of Minnesota.
Louis Owen, *Bone Game*, 1994
  Cole McCurtain, is a mixed-blood professor haunted by dreams, who becomes involved in a murder mystery that involves ecological crisis.

1313

VIRGINIA DRIVING HAWK SNEVE, Native American, Lakota (Sioux)

The Chichi Hoohoo Bogeyman
(Lincoln: University of Nebraska Press, 1975)

Subject(s): Legends
Age range(s): Grades 3-5
Major character(s): Mary Jo, Child (girl), Native American; Cindy, Child (girl), Native American; Lori, Child (girl), Native American
Time period(s): 1970s
Locale(s): South Dakota

Summary: Three young cousins, visiting their Sioux grandparents, discover a strange creature on the prairie of South Dakota. Later, one of them disappears.

Other books by the same author:
Jimmy Yellow Hawk, 1971 (Council on Interracial Books for Children award winner)

Other books you might like:
Margot Astrov, *The Winged Serpent*, 1946
  This is one of the best collections of oral stories and songs from a large cross-section of Indian cultures.
Joseph Bruchac, *Flying with the Eagle, Racing with the Bear*, 1993
  These rite-of-passage stories come from many tribal peoples, including the Wampanoag, Cherokee, Osage, Lakota and Tlingit.
Joseph Bruchac, *Iroquois Stories*, 1985
  This book recounts many of the traditional animal, adventure and monster tales of the Iroquois people.
Joseph Bruchac, *The Wind Eagle and Other Abenaki Stories*, 1984
  These are traditional tales of the Abenaki people.
Joseph Bruchac, *Return of the Sun*, 1990
  Traditional tales of the Northeast Woodlands, full of humor and wisdom, equally as enlightening as *Aesop's Fables* and more fun.

1314

VIRGINIA DRIVING HAWK SNEVE, Native American,
Lakota (Sioux)
OREN LYONS, Illustrator

High Elk's Treasure
(New York: Holiday House, 1972)

Subject(s): Indians of North America; Animals/Horses
Age range(s): Grades 6-8
Major character(s): Joe High Elk, Native American, Young Man
Time period(s): 20th century
Locale(s): South Dakota

Summary: This novel for middle school readers is about Joe High Elk who longs to bring back the strain of wild mustangs that his famous ancestor bred many years before.

Where it's reviewed:
Library Talk, November 1994, page 21

Other books by the same author:
Completing the Circle, 1995 (biography)

Other books you might like:
D'Arcy McNickle, *Runner in the Sun: A Story of Indian Maize*, 1954
This novel for middle school readers is about the cliff dwellers of Chaco Canyon. In this book, Salt must journey from his homeland to find a breed of corn that will save his people.
Joseph Bruchac, *Return of the Sun*, 1990
Traditional tales of the Northeast Woodlands, full of humor and wisdom, equally as enlightening as Aesop's fables, and more fun.
Joseph Bruchac, *Flying with the Eagle, Racing with the Bear*, 1993
These rite-of-passage stories come from various tribal peoples including the Wampanoag, Cherokee, Osage, Lakota and Tlingit.
John Bierhorst, *The Red Swan: Myths and Tales of the American Indians*, 1976
This book is a compilation of varied stories (creation, trickster, star husband, etc.) from forty Indian tribes.
Frederick Turner, *The Portable North American Indian Reader*, 1973
This anthology of myths, legends, poetry, fiction, and captivity tales, contains work by both Native American and non-Native writers.
Michael Dorris, *Morning Girl*, 1992
This short novel about a young girl and her brother takes place before Columbus.
Shirley Sterling, *My Name Is Seepeetza*, 1992
Fictional account based on the life of the author, who as a member of the interior Salish tribe was forced to attend governmnet schools where she was forbidden to reflect anything of her own heritage.

1315

VIRGINIA DRIVING HAWK SNEVE, Native American,
Lakota (Sioux)
RONALD HIMLER, Illustrator

The Iroquois
(New York: Holiday House, 1995)

Series: A First Americans Book
Subject(s): Indians of North America; History
Age range(s): Grades 3-5
Time period(s): 1990s
Locale(s): United States

Summary: This concise book details the many facets of Iroquois daily life including creation stories, history, family life, and traditional ceremonies. For young readers.

Where it's reviewed:
Library Talk, November 1994, page 21
School Library Journal, July 1995, page 21

Other books by the same author:
Jimmy Yellow Hawk, 1972 (Council on Interracial Books for Children Award)
When Thunder Spoke, 1974

Other books you might like:
Michael Dorris, *Morning Girl*, 1992
This is the story of a young girl and her brother in pre-Columbian Caribbean society, for younger readers.
Sandra King, *Shannon: An Ojibway Dancer*, 1993
This book follows the life of a young Ojibway girl who lives in the city, yet still participates in tribal ceremonies. For younger readers.
Monty Roessel, *Songs from the Loom*, 1995
This story follows Jaclyn Roessel, a young Navajo girl, as she learns the stories of her family and the cultural wisdom and mythology associated with the art of weaving. For younger readers.
Joseph Bruchac, *Flying with the Eagle, Racing with the Bear*, 1993
These rite-of-passage stories come from various tribal peoples including the Wampanoag, Cherokee, Osage, Lakota and Tlingit.
Susan Braine, *Drumbeat. . .Heartbeat: A Celebration of the Powwow*, 1995
This is a wonderful introduction to the Powwow for children by a Native American writer and photographer.

1316

VIRGINIA DRIVING HAWK SNEVE, Native American,
Lakota (Sioux)

Jimmy Yellow Hawk
(New York: Holiday House, 1972)

Subject(s): Indians of North America; Coming of Age
Age range(s): Grades 4-6
Major character(s): James Henry ''Little Jim'' Yellow Hawk, Native American (Sioux), Child (boy)
Time period(s): 1970s
Locale(s): South Dakota

Summary: A young Sioux boy known as Little Jim, earns an adult name for himself through hard work.

Where it's reviewed:
Library Talk, November 1994, page 21

Other books by the same author:
The Chichi Hoohoo Bogeyman, 1975

Other books you might like:
Charles A. Eastman, *From the Deep Woods to Civilization*, 1916
  The autobiography of Charles A. Eastman, who grows up in the traditional buffalo culture of the Lakota (Sioux) but pursues an education in the White man's world. Introduction by Raymond Wilson.
Zitkala-Sa, *Old Indian Legends Retold by Zitkala-Sa*, 1921
  These stories depict Zitkala-Sa's childhood in the traditional Lakota culture and the difficulties she faced while attending school and college in a world where she was perceived as a ''savage.''
Luther Standing Bear, *Stories of the Sioux*, 1988
  Standing Bear grew up in the traditional buffalo hunting culture, and he brings to life the stories from his own past.
Charles A. Eastman, *Old Indian Days*, 1907
  Autobiography of a Lakota Sioux man.

1317

VIRGINIA DRIVING HAWK SNEVE, Native American, Lakota (Sioux)
RONALD HIMLER, Illustrator

The Navajos
(New York: Holiday House, 1993)

Subject(s): Indians of North America; History
Age range(s): Grades 3-5
Time period(s): 1990s
Locale(s): South Dakota

Summary: This book for young readers tells of the many facets of Najavo life. It includes creation stories, history, family life, and traditional ceremonies.

Where it's reviewed:
Library Talk, November 1994, page 21
Booklist, December 15, 1993, page 759
Horn Book Guide, Spring 1994, page 174
Library Talk, January 1994, page 28
Publishers Weekly, November 8, 1993, page 80

Other books by the same author:
Jimmy Yellow Hawk, 1971 (Council on Interracial Books for Children Award)
When Thunder Spoke

Other books you might like:
Michael Dorris, *Morning Girl*, 1992
  This is the story of a young girl in Pre-Columbian Caribbean society, for younger readers.
Sandra King, *Shannon: An Ojibway Dancer*, 1993
  This book follows the life of a young Ojibway girl who lives in the city, yet still participates in tribal ceremonies. For younger readers.

Monty Roessel, *Songs from the Loom*, 1995
  This story follows Jaclyn Roessel, a young Navajo girl, as she learns the stories of her family and the cultural wisdom and mythology associated with the art of weaving.
Joseph Bruchac, *Flying with the Eagle, Racing with the Bear*, 1993
  These rite-of-passage stories come from various tribal peoples including the Wampanoag, Cherokee, Osage, Lakota and Tlingit.
Susan Braine, *Drumbeat. . .Heartbeat: A Celebration of the Powwow*, 1995
  This is a wonderful introduction to the Powwow for children by a Native American writer and photographer.
Herman J. Viola, *Osceola*, 1993
  This is a brief history of the famous Creek leader, Osceola, for younger readers. Illustrated by Yoshi Miyake.
Albert Marrin, *Plains Warrior: Chief Quanah Parker and the Comanches*, 1996
  This book tells the story of Quanah Parker, chief of the Comanches.

1318

VIRGINIA DRIVING HAWK SNEVE, Native American, Lakota (Sioux)
RONALD HIMLER, Illustrator

The Nez Perce
(New York: Holiday House, 1993)

Series: A First Americans Book
Subject(s): Indians of North America; History
Age range(s): Grades 3-5
Time period(s): 1990s
Locale(s): South Dakota

Summary: This concise book tells of many facets of Nez Perce life for young readers: creation stories, history, family life, and traditional ceremonies.

Where it's reviewed:
Booklist, October 1, 1994, page 331
Horn Book Guide, Spring 1995, page 165
Library Talk, November 1994, page 21
Library Talk, January 1995, page 48
Social Education, April 1995, page 222

Other books by the same author:
Jimmy Yellow Hawk, 1971 (Council on Interracial Books for Children Award.)
When Thunder Spoke

Other books you might like:
Michael Dorris, *Morning Girl*, 1992
  This is the story of a young girl in Pre-Columbian Caribbean society, for younger readers.
Sandra King, *Shannon: An Ojibway Dancer*, 1993
  This book follows the life of a young Ojibway girl who lives in the city, yet still participates in tribal ceremonies.
Monty Roessel, *Songs from the Loom*, 1995
  This story follows Jaclyn Roessel, a young Navajo girl, as she learns the stories of her family and the cultural wisdom and mythology associated with the art of weaving.

Joseph Bruchac, *Flying with the Eagle, Racing with the Bear*, 1993

These rite-of-passage stories come from various tribal peoples including the Wampanoag, Cherokee, Osage, Lakota and Tlingit.

Susan Braine, *Drumbeat. . .Heartbeat: A Celebration of the Powwow*, 1995

This is a wonderful introduction to the Powwow for children by a Native American writer and photographer.

Herman J. Viola, *Osceola*, 1993

This is a brief history of the famous Creek leader, Osceola, for younger readers. Illustrated by Yoshi Miyake.

Albert Marrin, *Plains Warrior: Chief Quanah Parker and the Comanches*, 1996

This book tells the story of Quanah Parker, chief of the Comanches.

1319

VIRGINIA DRIVING HAWK SNEVE, Native American, Lakota (Sioux)
RONALD HIMLER, Illustrator

The Sioux

(New York: Holiday House, 1993)

Subject(s): Indians of North America; History
Age range(s): Grades 3-5
Time period(s): 1990s
Locale(s): South Dakota

Summary: This concise book details the many facets of Sioux (Lakota) life for young readers. It includes creation stories, history, family life, and traditional ceremonies.

Where it's reviewed:
Library Talk, November 1994, page 21
Booklist, December 15, 1993, page 759
Kirkus Reviews, October 15, 1993, page 1337
Publishers Weekly, November 8, 1993, page 80
Horn Book Guide, Spring 1994, page 174

Other books by the same author:
Jimmy Yellow Hawk, 1972 (Council on Interracial Books for Children Award)
When Thunder Spoke, 1974

Other books you might like:
Michael Dorris, *Morning Girl*, 1992
This is the story of a young girl in Pre-Columbian Caribbean society, for younger readers.
Sandra King, *Shannon: An Ojibway Dancer*, 1993
This book follows the life of a young Ojibway girl who lives in the city, yet still participates in tribal ceremonies.
Monty Roessel, *Songs from the Loom*, 1995
This story follows Jaclyn Roessel, a young Navajo girl, as she learns the stories of her family and the cultural wisdom and mythology associated with the art of weaving. For younger readers.
Joseph Bruchac, *Flying with the Eagle, Racing with the Bear*, 1993
These rite-of-passage stories come from various tribal peoples including the Wampanoag, Cherokee, Osage, Lakota and Tlingit.

Susan Braine, *Drumbeat. . .Heartbeat: A Celebration of the Powwow*, 1995

This is a wonderful introduction to the Powwow for children by a Native American writer and photographer.

Herman J. Viola, *Osceola*, 1993

This is a brief history of the famous Creek leader, Osceola, for younger readers. Illustrated by Yoshi Miyake.

Albert Marrin, *Plains Warrior: Chief Quanah Parker and the Comanches*, 1996

This book tells the story of Quanah Parker, chief of the Comanches.

1320

MARK ST. PIERRE, Caucasian
TILDA LONG SOLDIER, Co-Author, Native American, Lakota (Sioux)

The Spiritual Power and Legacy of American Plains Indian Women

(New York; Simon and Schuster, 1995)

Subject(s): History; Women; Indians of North America
Age range(s): Grades 10-Adult
Time period(s): Indeterminate
Locale(s): United States

Summary: Based on first person interviews by the authors, this book looks at the lives of Plains Indian women and at the myths and culture surrounding them.

About this book: Tilda Long Soldier was raised on the Pine Ridge Reservation and is fluent in Lakota.

Other books you might like:
Ella Cara Deloria, *Waterlily*, 1988
Beginning with her mother's story, this novel follows Waterlily's life from her birth in the Sioux buffalo hunting culture before European contact.
Zitkala-Sa, *Old Indian Legends Retold by Zitkala-Sa*, 1921
This is a collection of memoirs and essays by an Indian woman who was born into the old buffalo hunting culture of the Sioux.
Brian Swann, *I Tell You Now*, 1989
This is an excellent collection of autobiographical essays by eighteen contemporary American Indian writers. Co-edited with Arnold Krupat.
Paula Gunn Allen, *The Sacred Hoop: Recovering the Feminine in American Indian Traditions*, 1986
This book is an excellent collection of essays that uncovers the essential role of women in traditional and contemporary Indian life.
Paula Gunn Allen, *Spider Woman's Granddaughters*, 1989
This is a beautiful collection of traditional tales interwoven with contemporary short stories about Native American women.
Joseph Bruchac, *The Girl Who Married the Moon*, 1994
These mostly traditional tales are from a variety of North American tribes and all about women: initiation ceremonies, shape changing stories, and others. Co-authored with Gayle Ross.
Beth Brant, *A Gathering of Spirit: A Collection of North American Indian Women*, 1984

Here is a collection of stories, letters, essays, and poems from a large cross-section of Native American women writers: Linda Hogan, Elizabeth Cook-Lynn, Diana Glancy, Joy Harjo and others.

Mary Crow Dog, *Lakota Woman*, 1991
Mary chronicles the hardships she's lived through, including giving birth to her firstborn during the siege at Wounded Knee in 1973.

Craig Lesley, *Talking Leaves*, 1991
This book is an excellent collection of short stories by thirty-five contemporary American Indian writers, such as Louise Erdrich, N. Scott Momaday, Linda Hogan and Roberta Hill Whiteman.

1321

LUTHER STANDING BEAR (Ota K'te)

My People the Sioux

(Lincoln: University of Nebraska Press, 1928)

Subject(s): Autobiography; Kings, Queens, Rulers, etc.; Assimilation
Age range(s): Grades 9-Adult
Time period(s): 19th century; 20th century (1860s-1930s)
Locale(s): United States

Summary: This is the story of Standing Bear's journey from the old ways to the ways of the White man. There is valuable information about traditional Lakota (Sioux) culture included, as well as valuable insights into the process of assimilation faced by Indian people during this difficult period.

About this book: This life story of Luther Standing Bear is one of the first accounts told from the Indian point of view chronicling the period from the traditional buffalo hunting culture to the institution of the reservation system.

Other books by the same author:
My Indian Boyhood, 1931
Land of the Spotted Eagle, 1933

Other books you might like:
Zitkala-Sa, *Old Indian Legends Retold by Zitkala-Sa*, 1921
This is the life story of Zitkala-Sa, a Lakota who spends her girlhood in the traditional culture but who eventually leaves for the Indian boarding schools out East.

Charles A. Eastman, *From the Deep Woods to Civilization*, 1916
This autobiography is by a Sioux man who leaves the traditional buffalo hunting culture to become a medical doctor.

Black Elk, *Black Elk Speaks*, 1932
This is the life story of the Holy Man of the Sioux, co-authored by John G. Neihardt.

John Joseph Mathews, *Talking to the Moon*, 1945
Mathews relates the circle of his life from his childhood in Oklahoma to his stint as an aviatior in WWI, to college, marriage and back home again to his homeland.

Anna Moore Shaw, *A Pima Past*, 1974
Born in a traditional Pima brush house and educated in the White world, Shaw recounts her fascinating life.

Francis La Flesche, *The Middle Five: Indian Schoolboys of the Omaha Tribe*, 1900

This book details the life of LaFlesche and his friends in mission school in Oklahoma.

Sarah Winnemucca, *Life Among the Paiutes: Their Wrongs and Claims*, 1883
Diplomat and outspoken advocate of the rights of native peoples, Winnemucca wrote this book to preserve the history and culture of the Paiutes.

N. Scott Momaday, *The Names: A Memoir*, 1976
This is an autobiography of Momaday's life.

1322

JOHN STANDS IN TIMBER, Native American, Cheyenne
MARGOT LIBERTY, Editor, Caucasian

Cheyenne Memories

(New Haven: Yale Univ. Press, 1967)

Subject(s): Men; Autobiography
Age range(s): Grades 9-Adult
Time period(s): 19th century; 20th century (1890s-1960s)
Locale(s): New Mexico

Summary: Stands in Timber was raised in the traditional Cheyenne culture, in the beginning of the reservation period. This book has a great deal of valuable information regarding Cheyenne culture and history. This is as-told-to Margot Liberty.

Other books you might like:
John Joseph Mathews, *Talking to the Moon*, 1945
Mathews relates the circle of his life from his childhood in Oklahoma to his WWI military stint, college, marriage and back to his homeland.

Anna Moore Shaw, *A Pima Past*, 1974
Anna Moore Shaw born in a traditional Pima brush house, and educated in the white world, tells this fascinating autobiography of her life.

Refugio Savala, *The Autobiography of a Yaqui Poet*, 1980
This autobiography by Refugio Savala tells of his family's flight from Mexico to Arizona during the horrible years of torture, and their struggle to make a new home for themselves.

Luther Standing Bear, *Stories of the Sioux*, 1988
Standing Bear grows up in the traditional buffalo hunting culture, and he brings to life the stories from his own past.

Zitkala-Sa, *Old Indian Legends Retold by Zitkala-Sa*, 1921
This is a collection of memoirs and essays about the traditional Lakota culture and the adjustments to the real world.

Charles A. Eastman, *From the Deep Woods to Civilization*, 1916
This is the autobiography of a Sioux man who grows up in the tradional buffalo hunting culture but leaves it to pursue a ''White'' education and becomes a doctor.

Jason Betzinez, *I Fought With Geronimo*, 1957
Betzinez lived to be almost a hundred years old, and this autobiography covers the great period of change for the Apache.

Clinton Rickard, *Fighting Tuscarora: The Autobiography of Chief Clinton Rickard*, 1973
In this autobiography, Chief Rickard is familiar with both

the Native American and white worlds. He is politically active well into his eighties, when this book was begun.

Don C. Talayesva, *Sun Chief: The Autobiography of a Hopi Indian*, 1942

Don C. Talayesva is born in Oraibi, the oldest continually inhabited town in the U.S., in 1890. This is the story of his life and the life of the Hopi people.

John Fire Lame Deer, *Lame Deer, Seeker of Visions*, 1972

Traditional medicine man Lame Deer tells of his own visions and spiritual quest while relating the philosophy of Lakota religion and culture.

1323

JOE STARITA, Caucasian

The Dull Knifes of Pine Ridge

(New York: G.P. Putnam's Sons, 1995)

Subject(s): Indians of North America; History; Biography
Age range(s): Grades 10-Adult
Time period(s): 19th century; 20th century (1860-1990s)
Locale(s): United States

Summary: This biography is the story of the remarkable Dull Knife family, beginning with the famous chief of the Northern Cheyenne (he married into the Lakota), who led his people 600 miles in the middle of winter to their homeland, to his descendents: George, Guy, and Guy Junior, of whom Guy and Guy Junior are carrying on the traditions of their people yet today.

Where it's reviewed:
Booklist, March 15, 1995, page 1305
Booklist, March 15, 1995, page 1315
Kirkus Reviews, March 1, 1995, page 311
Library Journal, March 15, 1995, page 80
Publishers Weekly, February 20, 1995, page 185

Other books you might like:
Zitkala-Sa, *Old Indian Legends Retold by Zitkala-Sa*, 1921
These stories depict Zitkala-Sa's childhood in the traditional Lakota culture and the difficulties she faced while attending school and college in a world where she was perceived as a "savage."

Mary Crow Dog, *Lakota Woman*, 1990
This as-told-to book with Richard Erdoes as author/editor, chronicles the life of a Lakota woman who lives through the hardships of the 1973 occupation of Wounded Knee by the AIM.

Wallace Black Elk, *Black Elk: The Sacred Ways of a Lakota*, 1990
This is a book about traditional Lakota religion and culture as told to William S. Lyon, Ph.D by the contemporary shaman Wallace Black Elk (no relation to Ben Black Elk of *Black Elk Speaks*).

Nicholas Black Elk, *Black Elk Speaks*, 1932
The life story of a Holy Man of the Sioux.

John Fire Lame Deer, *Lame Deer, Seeker of Visions*, 1972
This is Lame Deer's story as-told-to the writer Richard Erdoes.

Luther Standing Bear, *Stories of the Sioux*, 1988
Standing Bear grew up in the traditional buffalo hunting culture, and he brings to life the stories from his own past.

Charles A. Eastman, *From the Deep Woods to Civilization*, 1916
The autobiography of Charles A. Eastman, who grows up in the traditional buffalo culture of the Lakota (Sioux) but pursues an education in the White man's world. Introduction by Raymond Wilson.

Leonard Crow Dog, *Crow Dog*, 1995
Contemporary medicine man Leonard Crow Dog recounts his life story to Richard Erdoes.

Mary Brave Bird, *Ohitika Woman*, 1993
This sequel to *Lakota Woman*, written under her maiden name, tells the story of a woman caught between feminism and traditional Indian belief.

1324

SHIRLEY STERLING, Native American, Salish

My Name Is Seepeetza

(Vancouver, Canada: Douglas & McIntyre, 1992)

Subject(s): Childhood; School Life; Assimilation
Age range(s): Grades 6 and Up
Major character(s): Martha Stone, Native American, Student
Time period(s): 1950s (1958-1959)
Locale(s): British Columbia, Canada

Summary: This is a fictional account based on the real life experiences of the author. A member of the interior Salish tribe, she is forced to attend government schools where she is forbidden to speak her language or to reflect her own heritage. It details some of the cruel practices of church and religious institutions that attempted to take the "Indian" out of the native people. It is an important part of North American history usually ignored in history classes.

Where it's reviewed:
Children's Bookwatch, April 1993, page 8
Horn Book Magazine, May 1993, page 365
Quill & Quire, January 1993, page 31

Other books you might like:
Paula Gunn Allen, *Spider Woman's Granddaughters*, 1989
This is a beautiful collection of traditional tales interwoven with contemporary stories about the lives of Native American women.

Zitkala-Sa, *Old Indian Legends Retold by Zitkala-Sa*, 1921
This is a collection of memoirs and essays about the traditional Lakota culture and it's adjustments to the encroachment of the European settlers.

Beth Brant, *A Gathering of Spirit: A Collection of North American Indian Women*, 1984
This excellent collection of stories, letters, essays and poems are from a large cross-section of Native American women writers including Linda Hogan, Elizabeth Cook-Lynn, Diana Glancy and others.

Michael Dorris, *Morning Girl*, 1992
This short novel is about a young girl in pre-Columbian Caribbean.

1325

WILLIAM C. STURTEVANT, Editor, Caucasian

Handbook of North American Indians

(Washington, D.C.: Smithsonian Institution, 1990)

Subject(s): History; Mythology; Anthropology
Age range(s): Grades 10-Adult
Time period(s): Indeterminate
Locale(s): United States

Summary: A massive multivolume resource, this encyclopedia contains an incredible amount of information about Native North American peoples.

Other books you might like:

Carl Waldman, *Timelines: Native American History*, 1994
This is a useful tool for studying Native American history and culture. It includes a twenty page fold out chronological sheet that shows important dates in Native American history.

Arrell Morgan Gibson, *The American Indian: Prehistory to the Present*, 1980
A comprehensive history of Native American cultures.

Sam D. Gill, *Dictionary of Native American Mythology*, 1992
A comprehensive dictionary of Native American mythology.

John Bierhorst, *The Red Swan: Myths and Tales of the American Indians*, 1976
This book is a compilation of varied stories (creation, trickster, star husband, etc.) from forty Indian tribes.

Frederick Turner, *The Portable North American Indian Reader*, 1973
This anthology of myths, legends, poetry, fiction, and captivity tales, contains work by both Native American and non-Native writers.

John Bierhorst, *The Sacred Path*, 1984
This is fine collection of traditional spells, prayers, and power songs from a variety of Indian tribes.

Carl Sauer, *Man in Nature*, 1939
This excellent book explores the Indian cultures that existed in pre-Columbian America, broken down into fourteen geographical areas. (reprinted, 1975)

1326

BRIAN SWANN, Editor, Caucasian

Coming to Light

(New York: Random House, 1994)

Subject(s): Traditional Stories; Mythology; Folk Tales
Age range(s): Grades 10-Adult
Time period(s): Indeterminate
Locale(s): United States

Summary: This book is a comprehensive collection of Native American literature, divided geographically, and including many genres of oral literature. Each selection is presented in context, with extensive notes by the translator.

About this book: This is an excellent resource that restores many of these literary gems to their context within the tribal worldview from which they came.

Where it's reviewed:
Booklist, February 1, 1995, page 986
Kirkus Reviews, December 1, 1994, page 1601
Publishers Weekly, January 9, 1995, page 58
Library Journal, March 15, 1995, page 69
New York Times Book Review, March 19, 1995, page 17

Other books by the same author:
I Tell You Now, 1987 (edited with Arnold Krupat)
Recovering the Word, 1987

Other books you might like:

Paula Gunn Allen, *Spider Woman's Granddaughters*, 1989
This beautiful collection of traditional tales is interwoven with contemporary stories about Native American women.

Arlene Hirschfelder, *Native Heritage*, 1995
Personal accounts of Indian people from 1790 to the present

Frederick Turner, *The Portable North American Indian Reader*, 1973
This anthology of myths, legends, poetry, fiction, and captivity tales contains work by both Native American and non-Native writers.

Margot Astrov, *The Winged Serpent*, 1946
This is one of the best collections of oral stories and songs from a large cross-section of Indian cultures.

John Bierhorst, *The Sacred Path*, 1984
This is a fine collection of traditional spells, prayers, and power songs from a variety of Indian tribes.

1327

BRIAN SWANN, Editor, Caucasian
ARNOLD KRUPAT, Co-Editor, Caucasian

I Tell You Now

(Lincoln: University of Nebraska Press, 1987)

Subject(s): Biography; Cultures and Customs
Age range(s): Grades 10-Adult
Time period(s): 20th century
Locale(s): United States

Summary: This book is an excellent collection of autobiographical accounts by eighteen contemporary American Indian writers. These essays offer many insights into the world of American Indian people today.

Where it's reviewed:
Booklist, January 1, 1988, page 746
Book World, February 7, 1988, page 9
Choice, April 1988, page 1253

Other books by the same author:
Recovering the Word, 1987

Other books you might like:

Paula Gunn Allen, *Spider Woman's Granddaughters*, 1989
This is a beautiful collection of traditional tales interwoven with contemporary stories having to do with the lives of Native American women.

Paula Gunn Allen, *Voice of the Turtle*, 1944
Edited the well-known writer and scholar, this book is an anthology of literature written by American Indian people from 1900 to 1970.

Arlene Hirschfelder, *Native Heritage*, 1995
These personal accounts of Indian people are from 1790 to the present.

Lee Miller, *From the Heart: Voices of the American Indian*, 1995
This is a collection of orations, speechesl, and testimony by more than 250 Indian people that presents a radical alternative to traditionally taught American history.

Clifford E. Trafzer, *Blue Dawn, Red Earth: New Native American Storytellers*, 1996
This collection of short stories by 30 new Native American writers includes Lorne Simon, Anita Endrezze, Jim Barnes and others.

LaVonne Ruoff, *American Indian Literatures: An Introduction, Bibliographic Review, and Selected Bibliography*, 1990
This is the *bible* of Native American literature, essential to anyone who wants to pursue a study of the literature that has been written *by* American Indian people.

Beth Brant, *A Gathering of Spirit: A Collection of North American Indian Women*, 1984
A large cross-section of Native American women writers have contributed to this excellent collection of stories, letters, essays and poems. Among them are Linda Hogan, E. Cook-Lynn and D. Glancy.

Craig Lesley, *Talking Leaves*, 1991
Louise Erdrich, Michael Dorris and N. Scott Momaday are some of the contemporary writers represented in this collection of thirty-five stories.

1328

HERSCHEL TALASHOEMA, Native American, Hopi
JOHN EMORY SEKAQUAPTEWA, Editor
BARBARA PEPPER, Editor

Coyote & Little Turtle: Iisaw Niqw Yongosonhoya: A Traditional Hopi Tale
(Santa Fe: Clear Light Publishers, 1994)

Subject(s): Animals; Folk Tales
Age range(s): Grades 1-3
Major character(s): Coyote, Trickster; Turtle, Animal
Time period(s): Indeterminate Past
Locale(s): Arizona

Summary: This excellent book for early readers is about Coyote and Little Turtle, recounting how Coyote is tricked by his own greed.again. It is written in both Hopi and English, with illustrations drawn by Hopi children.

About this book: This book is a good learning tool for school children unfamiliar with Native American languages.

Where it's reviewed:
Publishers Weekly, February 13, 1995, page 78
School Library Journal, April 1995, page 129

Other books you might like:
G.M. Mullet, *Spider Woman Stories*, 1979
These Hopi Indian legends are collected from the 1880s.

Shonto Begay, *Ma'ii and Cousin Horned Toad*, 1992
Ma'ii is hungry and goes to Horny Toad for a free lunch.

When he swallows his smaller cousin, Toad teaches him a lesson he won't soon forget.

Mourning Dove, *Coyote Stories*, 1933
These traditional tales are about Coyote, the trickster.

1329

DON C. TALAYESVA, Native American, Hopi
LEO W. SIMMONS, Editor, Caucasian

Sun Chief: The Autobiography of a Hopi Indian
(Hew Haven: Yale University Press, 1942)

Subject(s): Men; Cultures and Customs
Age range(s): Grades 9-Adult
Time period(s): 19th century; 20th century (1890s-1940s)
Locale(s): Arizona

Summary: Don C. Talayesva is born in Oraibi, the oldest continually inhabited town in the U.S., in 1890. This is the story of his life and the life of the Hopi people.

Other books you might like:
Anna Moore Shaw, *A Pima Past*, 1974
Anna Moore Shaw, born in a traditional Pima brush house and educated in the white world, tells this fascinating autobiography of her life.

Leslie Marmon Silko, *Storyteller*, 1981
This work is a mixed genre of poetry, fiction, and mythology.

Refugio Savala, *The Autobiography of a Yaqui Poet*, 1980
This autobiography by Refugio Savala tells of his family's flight from Mexico to Arizona during the horrible years of torture, and their struggle to make a new home for themselves.

James Sewid, *Guests Never Leave Hungry: The Autobiography of James Sewid, a Kwakuitl Indian*, 1969
This is the life story of James Sewid, a Kwakiutl Indian.

Luther Standing Bear, *Stories of the Sioux*, 1988
Standing Bear grows up in the traditional buffalo hunting culture, and he brings to life the stories from his own past.

Zitkala-Sa, *Old Indian Legends Retold by Zitkala-Sa*, 1921
This is a collection of memoirs and essays about the traditional Lakota culture and it's adjustments to European encroachment.

Jane Holden Kelley, *Contemporary Life Histories*, 1978
This as-told-to-book chronicles the lives of four Yaqui women. The author describes many aspects of Yaqui culture in the introduction.

1330

STITH THOMPSON, Caucasian

Tales of the North American Indians
(Cambridge: University of Massachusetts Press, 1929)

Subject(s): Mythology; Folk Tales
Age range(s): Grades 9-Adult
Time period(s): Indeterminate
Locale(s): United States

Summary: This book is a collection of folk tales from North America that represents a variety of tribes.

About this book: The notes in the back of the book are particularly helpful. They include the location of other stories similar to these.

Other books you might like:

John Bierhorst, *The Red Swan: Myths and Tales of the American Indians*, 1976
    This book is a compilation of varied stories (creation, trickster, star husband, etc.) from forty Native American tribes.

Frederick Turner, *The Portable North American Indian Reader*, 1973
    This anthology of myths, legends, poetry, fiction, and captivity tales, contains work by both Native American and non-Native writers.

Margot Astrov, *The Winged Serpent*, 1946
    This mixed genre is one of the best collections of oral stories and songs from a large cross-section of Native American cultures.

G.M. Mullet, *Spider Woman Stories*,
    These Hopi Indian legends are collected from the 1880s.

Paula Gunn Allen, *Spider Woman's Granddaughters*, 1989
    This beautiful collection of traditional tales is interwoven with contemporary stories about Native American women.

Zitkala-Sa, *Old Indian Legends Retold by Zitkala-Sa*, 1921
    This is a collection of memoirs and essays about the traditional Lakota culture and it's adjustments to European encroachment.

Howard Norman, *Northern Tales*, 1990
    This book is a collection of traditional stories that focuses wholly on the Native American and Ancient people of the far north.

Donald Bahr, *The Short Swift Time of Gods on Earth: The Hohokam Chronicles*, 1994
    This book is a collection of Pima creation narratives.

William Bright, *A Coyote Reader*, 1993
    These are traditional Coyote stories.

1331

CLIFFORD E. TRAFZER, Caucasian

Blue Dawn, Red Earth: New Native American Storytellers

(New York: Anchor Books, 1996)

Subject(s): Cultures and Customs; Indians of North America; Folklore
Age range(s): Grades 10-Adult
Time period(s): 1990s
Locale(s): United States

Summary: This is a collection of short stories by 30 new Native American writers: Lorne Simon, Anita Endrezze, Jim Barnes, Annie Hansen, Maurice Kenny, Patricia Piley, Richard Van Camp, Penny Olson, Misha, E.K. Caldwell, Eric L. Gansworth, and Chris Fleet, among others.

Other books by the same author:
Earth Song, Sky Spirit, 1993

Other books you might like:

Paula Gunn Allen, *Voice of the Turtle*, 1994
    Edited by the well known writer and scholar, this book is an anthology of literature written by American Indian people from 1900 to 1970.

Peter Nabokov, *Native American Testimony*, 1991
    This anthology contains oral stories, speeches, prophecies, and essays.

Brian Swann, *I Tell You Now*, 1989
    This is an excellent collection of autobiographical essays by eighteen contemporary American Indian writers. Co-edited with Arnold Krupat.

Beth Brant, *A Gathering of Spirit: A Collection of North American Indian Women*, 1984
    Here is a collection of stories, letters, essays, and poems from a large cross-section of Native American women writers, like Linda Hogan, Elizabeth Cook-Lynn, Diane Glancy, Joy Harjo and Wendy Rose.

1332

FREDERICK TURNER, Editor, Caucasian

The Portable North American Indian Reader

(New York: Penguin Books, 1973)

Subject(s): Mythology
Age range(s): Grades 9-Adult
Time period(s): Indeterminate
Locale(s): United States

Summary: This anthology of myths, legends, poetry, fiction, and captivity tales contains work by both Native and non-Native writers and it attempts to span the time of both pre-contact and post-contact of European influence. Hence, the book is divided into the following segments: Myths and Tales, Poetry and Oratory (both of these representing the pre-Columbian epoch), then Culture Contact, and Image and Anti-Image.

Where it's reviewed:
Choice, September 1974, page 946
Library Journal, October 1, 1974, page 2482

Other books you might like:

Clifford E. Trafzer, *Blue Dawn, Red Earth: New Native American Storytellers*, 1996
    This collection of short stories by 30 new Native American writers includes Lorne Simon, Anita Endrezze, Jim Barnes and others.

Paula Gunn Allen, *Spider Woman's Granddaughters*, 1989
    This is a beautiful collection of traditional tales interwoven with contemporary stories having to do with the lives of Native American women.

LaVonne Ruoff, *American Indian Literatures: An Introduction, Bibliographic Review, and Selected Bibliography*, 1990
    This is the bible of Native American literature, essential to anyone who wants to pursue a study of the literature that has been written by American Indian people.

Margot Astrov, *The Winged Serpent*, 1946
  This is one of the best collections of oral stories and songs from a large cross-section of Indian cultures.

John Bierhorst, *The Sacred Path*, 1984
  This is a fine collection of traditional spells prayers, and power songs from a variety of Indian tribes.

Beth Brant, *A Gathering of Spirit: A Collection of North American Indian Women*, 1984
  Here is a collection of stories, letters, essays, and poems from a large cross-section of Native American women writers, such as Linda Hogan, Elizabeth Cook-Lynn, Diana Glancy, and others.

John Bierhorst, *The Red Swan: Myths and Tales of the American Indians*, 1976
  This book is a compilation of varied stories (creation, trickster, star husband, etc.) from forty Indian tribes.

Mourning Dove, *Coyote Stories*, 1933
  These are traditional stories about Coyote, the trickster.

Craig Lesley, *Talking Leaves*, 1991
  Louise Erdrich, Michael Dorris, N. Scott Momaday and Linda Hogan are some of the contemporary Native American writers represented in this collection of thirty-five stories.

1333

ROBERT M. UTLEY, Caucasian

The Lance and the Shield: The Life and Times of Sitting Bull

(New York: Balatine, 1993)

Subject(s): Indians of North America; History
Age range(s): Grades 10-Adult
Time period(s): 19th century
Locale(s): South Dakota

Summary: Devoid of romanticism, this story brings to life many of the memorable events in the life of the great warrior chief and medicine man, among them his victory over Custer at the Little Big Horn, his tour with the Buffalo Bill Cody Wild West Show, his philosophy towards the advance of the White man on Indian territory and his vision of his own death at the hands of an Indian policeman.

Where it's reviewed:
Journal of American History, December 1994, page 1329
New York Times Book Review, December 4, 1994, page 89
Pacific Historical Review, August 1995, page 440

Awards the book has won:
The Spur Award: Best Western Nonfiction Historical Book of, 1993

Other books you might like:
Brian Swann, *I Tell You Now*, 1989
  This excellent collection of autobiographical essays by eighteen contemporary American Indian writers, is co-edited with Brian Swann.

Anna Moore Shaw, *A Pima Past*, 1974
  Born in a traditional Pima brush house, Anna Moore Shaw went on to become educated in the white world, and this fascinating story is of her life, written by herself.

N. Scott Momaday, *The Names: A Memoir*, 1976
  Autobiography

Leslie Marmon Silko, *Storyteller*, 1981
  From Laguna Pueblo where he grew up, Silko weaves traditional mythology into modern stories, recreating old myths and making them relevant for a new generation.

Refugio Savala, *The Autobiography of a Yaqui Poet*, 1980
  This is Refugio Savala's story. His family fled Mexico for Arizona during the horrible years of torture where they struggled to make a new home for themselves.

James Sewid, *Guests Never Leave Hungry: The Autobiography of James Sewid, a Kwakuitl Indian*, 1969
  This is the life story of James Sewid, a Kwakiutl Indian.

Zitkala-Sa, *Old Indian Legends Retold by Zitkala-Sa*, 1921
  These stories depict Zitkala-Sa's childhood in the traditional Lakota culture and the difficulties she faces while attending school and college in a world where she is perceived as a ''savage.''

Jane Holden Kelley, *Contemporary Life Histories*, 1978
  This as-told-to-book chronicles the lives of four Yaqui women, with a long introduction by Jane Kelley that describes many aspects of Yaqui culture.

Don C. Talayesva, *Sun Chief: The Autobiography of a Hopi Indian*, 1942
  Don C. Talayesva is born in Oraibi, the oldest continually inhabited town in the U.S., in 1890, and this is the story of his life and the life of the Hopi people.

John Fire Lame Deer, *Lame Deer, Seeker of Visions*, 1972
  Traditional medicine man Lame Deer tells of his visions and spiritual quest while relating the philosophy of Lakota religion and culture.

1334

NANCY VAN LAAN, Caucasian
BEATRIZ VIDAL, Illustrator

Rainbow Crow

(New York: Alfred A. Knopf, 1989)

Subject(s): Folk Tales; Animals
Age range(s): Grades 2-5
Major character(s): Rainbow Crow, Crow
Time period(s): Indeterminate Past (mythic time)
Locale(s): United States

Summary: This wonderful legend of the Lenape people is about Rainbow Crow, who sacrifices his beautiful colors to help the living things of earth.

Other books you might like:
Mourning Dove, *Coyote Stories*, 1933
  These are traditional Okanagan stories about Coyote, the trickster.

Shonto Begay, *Ma'ii and Cousin Horned Toad*, 1992
  Lazy, conniving Ma'ii is hungry, and he goes to Horny Toad for a free lunch. He swallows his smaller cousin, but Horny Toad teaches him a lesson he won't forget.

Herschel Talashoema, *Coyote & Little Turtle: Iisaw Niqw Yongosonhoya: A Traditional Hopi Tale*, 1994
  This is an excellent book for early readers about Coyote and Little Turtle. It is written in both Hopi and English,

with illustrations from Hopi children. Co-authored with John Emory Sekaquaptewqa.

Joseph Bruchac, *Flying with the Eagle, Racing with the Bear*, 1993

These rite-of-passage stories come from various tribal people including the Wampanoag, Cherokee, Osage, Lakota and Tlingit.

Joseph Bruchac, *Iroquois Stories*, 1985

This book recounts many of the traditional animal, adventure and monster tales of the Iroquois people.

Joseph Bruchac, *The Wind Eagle and Other Abenaki Stories*, 1984

These are traditional tales of the Abenaki.

Joseph Bruchac, *Return of the Sun*, 1990

Traditional tales of the Northeast Woodlands, full of humor and wisdom, equally as enlightening as Aesop's fables, and more fun.

1335

HERMAN J. VIOLA, Caucasian
YOSHI MIYAKE, Illustrator

Osceola

(Austin: Steck-Vaughn, 1993)

Series: The Native American Stories
Subject(s): Indians of North America; Indian Removal
Age range(s): Grades 3-5
Time period(s): 19th century
Locale(s): Alabama

Summary: This is a brief history of the famous Creek leader for younger readers.

Where it's reviewed:
Horn Book Guide, Fall 1993, page 378

Other books you might like:

Michael Dorris, *Morning Girl*, 1992
This short novel is about a young girl in the pre-Columbian Caribbean.

Sandra King, *Shannon: An Ojibway Dancer*, 1993
This book follows the life of a young Ojibway girl, Shannon, who lives in the city, yet still participates in tribal ceremonies.

Monty Roessel, *Songs from the Loom*, 1995
This story follows Jaclyn Roessel, a young Navajo girl, as she learns the stories of her family and the cultural wisdom and mythology associated with the art of weaving.

Joseph Bruchac, *Flying with the Eagle, Racing with the Bear*, 1993
These rite-of-passage stories come from various tribal peoples including the Wampanoag, Cherokee, Osage, Lakota and Tlingit.

Susan Braine, *Drumbeat. . .Heartbeat: A Celebration of the Powwow*, 1995
This is a wonderful introduction to the Powwow for children by a Native American writer and photographer.

1336

GERALD VIZENOR, Native American, Ojibwa (Chippewa)

Earthdivers: Tribal Narratives on Mixed Descent

(Minneapolis: U. of Minnesota Press, 1981)

Subject(s): Historical; Trickster Tales; Indian Reservations
Age range(s): Adult
Major character(s): Naanabozho Wenebojo, Trickster; Captain Shammer, Native American
Time period(s): 1980s
Locale(s): United States

Summary: In this collection of short stories Vizenor creates a plethora of trickster figures as he pokes fun (and makes shrewd political commentary) on America, reservation life, and just about everything else.

About this book: Vizenor's work, noted for its humor, provides the reader with a rolicking ride through the ups and downs of life.

Other books by the same author:

Griever: An American Monkey King in China, 1987
The Everlasting Sky: New Voices From the People Named the Chippewa, 1972 (nonfiction)
Interior Landscapes: Autobiographical Myths and Metaphors, 1990 (autobiography)
Matsushima: Pine Islands, 1984 (poetry)
Tribal Scenes and Ceremonies, 1976 (nonfiction)
The Trickster of Liberty: Tribal Heirs to a Wild Baronage at Petronia, 1988

Other books you might like:

Paul Radin, *The Trickster*, 1956
This excellent study of the Trickster archetype presents the Winnebago Trickster Cycle of Myths in full, along with the Hare Cycle and summaries of the Assiniboine and Tlingit Trickster Myths.

Barry Lopez, *Giving Birth to Thunder, Sleeping with His Daughter: Coyote Builds North America*, 1977
In this book, Lopez retells a wide selection of Coyote stories from various North American tribes. As always, Coyote is dynamic, irreverant, wily, paradoxical, mysterious, taboo-breaking and fun.

William Bright, *A Coyote Reader*, 1993
This is a collection of trickster stories from many North American tribes, the chapters divided by the attributes of Coyote rather than the origin of the tales.

Louise Erdrich, *Love Medicine*, 1984
Married to Marie, Nector is nevertheless fatefully drawn to Lulu. When his grandson prepares a love medicine to win him back to his grandmother, he uses the wrong ingredients and kills Nector instead.

Craig Lesley, *Talking Leaves*, 1991
This is an excellent collection of thirty-five stories by contemporary Native American writers including Louise Erdrich, N. Scott Momaday, and Linda Hogan.

Leslie Marmon Silko, *Storyteller*, 1981
This work is a mixed genre of poetry, fiction, and mythology.

W.P. Kinsella, *Dance Me Outside*, 1977
>These early tales of life on the Ermineskin Reserve in Canada are gems, capturing both the comedic and tragic spirit of reservation life.

W.P. Kinsella, *Moccasin Telegraph*, 1984
>Life on the fictional Ermineskin Reserve in Canada, as revealed by Silas Ermineskin himself, is full of both comedy and tragedy.

James Northrup, *Walking the Rez Road*, 1993
>Luke Warmwater is a Vietnam vet down on his luck, but he, like most of his reservation cohorts, is a survivor in the trickster fashion.

1337

GERALD VIZENOR, Native American, Ojibwa (Chippewa)

Griever: An American Monkey King in China

(Normal, Illinois: Illinois State U., 1987)

Subject(s): Indians of North America; Trickster Tales
Age range(s): Adult
Major character(s): Griever de Hocus, Trickster
Time period(s): 1980s
Locale(s): United States; China

Summary: In this book Vizenor creates a trickster-like, reservation-born, tribal trickster who leaves his Chippewa home to go to China where he takes on the monolithic Chinese structure, which zaps the people of imagination. In this role, Griever finds himself kin to the Monkey King, the trickster from the Chinese Opera, and he sets out to turn the Chinese world upside down, setting the people free.

About this book: Vizenor's work is full of trickster humor, and one must be prepared for a roller-coaster ride in this near-surrealistic adventure novel of liberation.

Where it's reviewed:
Rocky Mountain Review of Language & Literature, Issue I, 1993, page 61

Other books by the same author:
Interior Landscapes: Autobiographical Myths and Metaphors, 1990 (autobiography)
Matsushima: Pine Islands, 1984 (poetry)
Tribal Scenes and Ceremonies, 1976 (nonfiction)
The Trickster of Liberty: Tribal Heirs to a Wild Baronage at Petronia, 1988
Wordarrows: Native Americans and Whites in the New Fur Trade, 1978 (fiction and nonfiction)

Other books you might like:
Paul Radin, *The Trickster*, 1956
>This excellent study of the Trickster archetype presents the Winnebago Trickster Cycle of Myths in full, along with the Hare Cycle and summaries of the Assiniboine and Tlingit Trickster Myths.

Barry Lopez, *Giving Birth to Thunder, Sleeping with His Daughter: Coyote Builds North America*, 1977
>In this book Lopez retells a wide selection of Coyote stories from various North American tribes. As always, Coyote is dynamic, irreverant, wily, paradoxical, mysterious, taboo breaking, and fun.

Thomas King, *Green Grass, Running Water*, 1993
>In this wild romp, Coyote, God, Robinson Crusoe, The Lone Ranger and others struggle in the cosmological firmament while on the human plane, Native Americans try to make the best of their lives.

Mourning Dove, *Coyote Stories*, 1933
>These are traditional stories about Coyote, the trickster.

William Bright, *A Coyote Reader*, 1993
>These are traditional Coyote trickster tales from across North America.

Sherman Alexie, *The Lone Ranger and Tonto Fist Fight in Heaven*, 1993
>Short fiction by one of the best of the young Native writers.

Sherman Alexie, *Reservation Blues*, 1995
>Legendary bluesman, Robert Johnson, comes to the rez and things begin to rock.

Louise Erdrich, *Love Medicine*, 1984
>Married to Marie, Nector is nevertheless fatefully drawn to Lulu. When his grandson prepares a love medicine to win him back to his grandmother, he uses the wrong ingredients and kills Nector instead.

James Northrup, *Walking the Rez Road*, 1993
>Fiction; humorous short stories that take place on an Ojibway reservation in Minnesota.

1338

GERALD VIZENOR, Native American, Ojibwa (Chippewa)

The Heirs of Columbus

(Hanover & London: Wesleyan University Press, 1991)

Subject(s): Trickster Tales; Humor; Television Programs
Age range(s): Adult
Major character(s): Stone Columbus, Trickster
Time period(s): 1990s
Locale(s): United States

Summary: This novel is a trickster romp. Stone Columbus, a cross-blood trickster, takes to the talk shows regarding ''the genetic signature of the heirs that would heal the nation.'' He says Columbus was Mayan and a great trick.

About this book: Vizenor's work is full of trickster humor, and one must be prepared for a roller-coaster ride.

Where it's reviewed:
Rocky Mountain Review of Language & Literature, Issue 1, 1993, page 61

Other books by the same author:
Darkness in Saint Louis Bearheart, 1978
Earthdivers: Tribal Narratives on Mixed Descent, 1981
The Everlasting Sky: New Voices From the People Named the Chippewa, 1972 (nonfiction)
''I Know What You Mean, Erdupps MacChurbbs,'' Growing Up in Minnesota: Ten Writers Remember Their Childhoods, 1976 (autobiography)
Interior Landscapes: Autobiographical Myths and Metaphors, 1990 (autobiography)
Interior Landscapes: Autobiographical Myths and Metaphors, 1990 (autobiography)
Matsushima: Pine Islands, 1984 (poetry)

The People Named the Chippewa: Narrative Histories, 1984 (fiction and nonfiction)

Other books you might like:
Paul Radin, *The Trickster*, 1956
This excellent study of the Trickster archetype presents the Winnebago Trickster Cycle of Myths in full, along with the Hare Cycle and summaries of the Assiniboine and Tlingit Trickster Myths.

1339

GERALD VIZENOR, Native American, Ojibwa (Chippewa)

The People Named the Chippewa: Narrative Histories
(Minneapolis: U. of Minnesota Press, 1981)

Subject(s): Indians of North America; History; Biography
Age range(s): Adult
Major character(s): Naanabozho, Trickster
Time period(s): 1980s
Locale(s): Minnesota

Summary: In this collection of essays, mythological tales, and personal interviews, Vizenor brings to life the people known by three names: the Chippewa, or Ojibwe, and what they call themselves: the Anishinabe.

Other books by the same author:
The Everlasting Sky: New Voices From the People Named the Chippewa, 1972 (nonfiction)
"I Know What You Mean, Erdupps MacChurbbs," Growing Up in Minnesota: Ten Writers Remember Their Childhoods, 1976 (autobiobraphy)
Wordarrows: Native Americans and Whites in the New Fur Trade, 1978 (fiction and nonfiction)

Other books you might like:
Paul Radin, *The Trickster*, 1956
This excellent study of the Trickster archetype presents the Winnebago Trickster Cycle of Myths in full, along with the Hare Cycle and summaries of the Assiniboine and Tlingit Trickster Myths.
Barry Lopez, *Giving Birth to Thunder, Sleeping with His Daughter: Coyote Builds North America*, 1977
In this book, Lopez retells a wide selection of Coyote stories from various North American tribes. As always, Coyote is dynamic, irreverant, wily, paradoxical, mysterious, taboo-breaking and fun.
Charles Kawbawgam, *Ojibwa Narratives*, 1994
Louise Erdrich, *Love Medicine*, 1984
Married to Marie, Nector is nevertheless fatefully drawn to Lulu. When his grandson prepares a love medicine to win him back to his grandmother, he uses the wrong ingredients and kills Nector instead.
Ignatia Broker, *Night Flying Woman*, 1983
Dona was of the generation who was ripped away from traditional life and was forced to live the harsh life of the reservation. This is Broker's grandmother's story.
Maude Kegg, *Portage Lake: Memories of an Ojibwe Childhood*, 1991
In these stories, printed in both English and the original

Anishinaabe, Kegg relates the cultural wisdom of her many years, describing important facets of Ojibwe life.
James Northrup, *Walking the Rez Road*, 1993
Luke Warmwater is a Vietnam vet down on his luck, but he, like most of his reservation cohorts, is a survivor in the trickster fashion.

1340

CARL WALDMAN, Caucasian
MOLLY BRAUN, Illustrator

Timelines: Native American History
(New York: Prentice-Hall, 1994)

Subject(s): Indians of North America; History
Age range(s): Grades 4 and Up
Time period(s): Indeterminate
Locale(s): United States

Summary: This is a useful tool for studying Native American history and culture. It includes an illustrated twenty page fold out chronology that shows important times in Native American history. There is also a dictionary of biographies by and about Native American people.

Other books by the same author:
Atlas of the North American Indian, 1985
Encyclopedia of Native American Tribes, 1988

Other books you might like:
William C. Sturtevant, *Handbook of North American Indians*, 1990
A massive multivolume resource, this encyclopedia contains an incredible amount of information about Native North American peoples.
Arrell Morgan Gibson, *The American Indian: Prehistory to the Present*, 1980
A comprehensive history of Native American cultures.
Sam D. Gill, *Dictionary of Native American Mythology*, 1992
A comprehensive dictionary of Native American mythology.
John Bierhorst, *The Red Swan: Myths and Tales of the American Indians*, 1976
This book is a compilation of varied stories (creation, trickster, star husband, etc.) from forty Indian tribes.
Frederick Turner, *The Portable North American Indian Reader*, 1973
This anthology of myths, legends, poetry, fiction, and captivity tales, contains work by both Native American and non-Native writers.
Margot Astrov, *The Winged Serpent*, 1946
This is one of the best collections of oral stories and songs from a large cross-section of Indian cultures.
John Bierhorst, *The Sacred Path*, 1984
This is a collection of traditional spells, prayers, and power songs from a variety of Indian tribes.
Carl Sauer, *Man in Nature*, 1939
This excellent book explores the Indian cultures that existed in pre-Columbian America, broken down into fourteen geographical areas.

1341

VERLMA WALLIS, Native American, Athabascan

Two Old Women: An Alaskan Legend of Betrayal, Courage, and Survival

(New York: Harper, 1993)

Subject(s): Traditional Stories; Indians of North America; Women
Age range(s): Grades 5 and Up
Major character(s): Ch'idzigyaak, Aged Person (old woman), Native American (Athabascan); Sa', Aged Person (old woman), Native American (Athabascan)
Time period(s): Indeterminate
Locale(s): South Dakota

Summary: During a time of starvation for the Athabascan people of the far north, two old women are abandoned by their tribe.

About this book: This moving story is fascinating for adults and adolescents.

Where it's reviewed:
American Book Review, September 1995, page 12
Belles Lettres, Fall 1994, page 4
Bloomsbury Review, November 1994, page 26
Wilderness, Spring 1995, page 32

Awards the book has won:
Western States Book Award, 1993
Pacific Northwest Booksellers Association Award, 1994

Other books you might like:
Howard Norman, *Northern Tales*, 1990
   This book is a collection of traditional stories that focuses wholly on the Indian and Eskimo people of the far north.
Markoosie, *Harpoon of the Hunter*, 1970
   This story chronicles the life of an Eskimo boy who must learn to be a hunter.
Michael Arvaarluk Kusugak, *A Promise Is a Promise*, 1988
   Qallupilluq are Inuit monsters who grab children who come too near the cracks in the ice. This is the story of a young girl, Allashua, who comes face to face with these sea monsters.
Michael Arvaarluk Kusugak, *Northern Lights: The Soccer Trails*, 1995
   When her mother dies, Kataujaq, a young Eskimo girl, feels very sad until her grandmother tells her a story of the Northern Lights and what happens to people when they die.
Frederick Turner, *The Portable North American Indian Reader*, 1973
   This is an anthology of myths, legends, poetry, fiction, and captivity tales, containing work by both Native American and non-Native writers.

1342

ANNA LEE WALTERS, Native American, Pawnee and Otoe

The Sun Is Not Merciful

(Ithaca, NY: Firebrand, 1985)

Subject(s): Indians of North America
Age range(s): Adult
Time period(s): 1980s
Locale(s): United States

Summary: This is a collection of well-crafted and moving stories that deal with the pains and triumphs of Native American life.

Awards the book has won:
Before Columbus Association American Book Award, 1995

Other books by the same author:
Ghost Singer, 1988 (short stories)
The Two-Legged Creature, 1993 (children's story)

Other books you might like:
Linda Hogan, *Red Clay*, 1991
   This is an excellent collection of short stories and poems by one of the best contemporary Native writers.
Leslie Marmon Silko, *Storyteller*, 1981
   A mixed genre anthology of poetry, fiction, and mythology.
Simon J. Ortiz, *Fightin'*, 1969
   This mixed genre anthology contains poetry and short stories.
Craig Lesley, *Talking Leaves*, 1991
   This book is an excellent collection of short stories by thirty-five contemporary American Indian writers, such as Louise Erdrich, N. Scott Momaday, Linda Hogan and Roberta Hill Whiteman.
LaVonne Ruoff, *American Indian Literatures: An Introduction, Bibliographic Review, and Selected Bibliography*, 1990
   This is the bible of Native American literature, essential to anyone who wants to pursue a study of the literature that has been written by American Indian people.
Paula Gunn Allen, *Voice of the Turtle*, 1994
   Edited by the well known writer and scholar Paula Gunn Allen, this book is an anthology of literature written by American Indian people from 1900 to 1970.
Paula Gunn Allen, *Spider Woman's Granddaughters*, 1989
   This is a beautiful collection of traditional tales interwoven with c
Clifford E. Trafzer, *Blue Dawn, Red Earth: New Native American Storytellers*, 1996
   This is a collection of short stories by 30 new Native American writers: Lorne Simon, Anita Endrezze, Jim Barnes, Annie Hansen, Maurice Kenny, and Patricia Piley, among others.
Beth Brant, *Food & Spirits: Stories*, 1991
   This collection of short stories, about Indian people from Canada and Michigan, touch on many themes important to Indian people: family, tradition, myth.
Beth Brant, *A Gathering of Spirit: A Collection of North American Indian Women*, 1984

This anthology of short stories and poems deals with the lives of Native American women.

1343

ANNA LEE WALTERS, Native American, Pawnee and Otoe

Talking Indian
(Ithaca, NY: Firebrand Books, 1992)

Subject(s): Biography; Tradition
Age range(s): Grades 9-Adult
Time period(s): 1990s
Locale(s): Arizona

Summary: This collection presents a variety of genres: short stories, history, and personal essay on the traditions of the Pawnee. Throughout the book the authors deep feelings for the traditions of her people shine through.

Where it's reviewed:
Belles Lettres, Spring 1993, page 49
Booklist, December 1, 1992, page 644
Library Journal, December 1992, page 150
MS, March 1993, page 63
Publishers Weekly, October 12, 1992, page 72

Other books by the same author:
The Sun Is Not Merciful, 1985

Other books you might like:
Craig Lesley, *Talking Leaves*, 1991
    This book is a an excellent collection of short stories by thirty-five contemporary Native American writers including, among others, Erdrich, Dorris, Momaday, Hogan, and Whiteman.
Louise Erdrich, *Love Medicine*, 1984
    Married to Marie, Nector is nevertheless fatefully drawn to Lulu. When his grandson prepares a love medicine to win him back to his grandmother, he uses the wrong ingredients and kills Nector instead.
Paula Gunn Allen, *Spider Woman's Granddaughters*, 1989
    This beautiful collection of traditional tales is interwoven with contemporary short stories about Native American women.
Leslie Marmon Silko, *Storyteller*, 1981
    This work is a mixed genre of poetry, fiction, and mythology.
Sherman Alexie, *The Lone Ranger and Tonto Fist Fight in Heaven*, 1993
    This wonderful short fiction is about the ups and downs of reservation life.
James Northrup, *Walking the Rez Road*, 1993
    Luke Warmwater is a Vietnam vet who is down on his luck, but he, like most of his reservation cohorts, is a survivor in the trickster fashion.
Ray A. Young Bear, *Black Eagle Child*, 1992
    This fictional work is about life on a Mesquakie settlement.
Thomas King, *Green Grass, Running Water*, 1993
    Coyote, God, Robinson Crusoe, The Lone Ranger and others struggle amongst themselves in the cosmological firmament. Meanwhile various Native American characters struggle with life the best they can.

Paula Gunn Allen, *Voice of the Turtle*, 1994
    Edited by the well known writer and scholar Paula Gunn Allen, this book is an anthology of literature written by American Indian people from 1900 to 1970.
Lee Miller, *From the Heart: Voices of the American Indian*, 1995
    This is a collection of orations, speeches, and testimony by more than 250 Indian people that presents a radical alternative to traditionally taught American history.
Clifford E. Trafzer, *Blue Dawn, Red Earth: New Native American Storytellers*, 1996
    This is a collection of short stories by 30 new Native American writers: Lorne Simon, Jim Barnes, Annie Hansen and Richard Van Camp, among others.
Beth Brant, *A Gathering of Spirit: A Collection of North American Indian Women*, 1984
    Here is a collection of stories, letters, essays, and poems from a large cross-section of Native American women writers, such as Linda Hogan, Joy Harjo, Wendy Rose, and Doris Seale.

1344

JAMES WELCH, Native American, Blackfeet and Gros Ventre

Fools Crow
(New York: Viking, 1986)

Subject(s): Indians of North America; Historical
Age range(s): Adult
Major character(s): Fast Horse, Native American; Fools Crow, Native American, Religious (Shaman)
Time period(s): 1870s
Locale(s): Montana

Summary: During the period of White encroachment on the plains Blackfeet in Montana (the 1870s), White Man's Dog, later known as Fools Crow, is a young man vying for a place of respect in his society. He decides to take the spiritual path and become a medicine man, while another young man, Fast Horse, decides to take the road of revenge against the invading Whites. Weaving in tribal mythology and history, Welch takes the reader into this world in a very believable way as he follows each of the characters down their chosen paths.

About this book: This account of traditional Plains Indian life is one of the best, for Welch takes the reader into the mind-set and world-view of characters who have yet to be influenced by European society. His portrait of this life is realistic, no romanticism here, which is refreshing since so many writers have idealized the Plains culture beyond recognition. The characters here act like real people, not museum stereotypes. One comes away from this book feeling like this Native American world has opened up to let us in.

Where it's reviewed:
Emergency Librarian, September 1995, page 32
Rocky Mountain Review of Language & Literature, Issue 1, 1993, page 71

Awards the book has won:
Los Angeles Times Book Award: Fiction, 1987

Other books by the same author:
Winter in the Blood, 1974

Killing Custer, 1994 (nonfiction, written with Paul Stekler)
The Indian Lawyer, 1990
The Death of Jim Loney, 1979
Riding the Earthboy 40, 1971 (poetry)

Other books you might like:
Ella Cara Deloria, *Waterlily*, 1988
   Waterlily details the life of the Sioux before European contact, focusing on women's place in the culture and the importance of kinship relationships.
Luther Standing Bear, *Stories of the Sioux*, 1988
   Standing Bear grew up in the traditional buffalo hunting culture of the Sioux and he brings to life the stories from his own past.
Black Elk, *Black Elk Speaks*, 1932
   This is the life story of the Sioux Holy Man, as told to John Neihardt.
Zitkala-Sa, *Old Indian Legends Retold by Zitkala-Sa*, 1921
   This is the life story of Zitkala-Sa, a Lakota who spends her girlhood in the traditional culture but who eventually leaves for the Indian boarding schools out East.
Charles A. Eastman, *From the Deep Woods to Civilization*, 1916
   This is the autobiography of a Sioux man who grows up in the traditional buffalo hunting culture but leaves it to pursue a ''White'' education and becomes a doctor.

1345

JAMES WELCH, Native American, Blackfeet and Gros Ventre

The Indian Lawyer
(New York: W.W. Norton, 1990)

Subject(s): Indians of North America
Age range(s): Adult
Major character(s): Sylvester Yellow Calf, Native American, Lawyer; Jack Harwood, Convict
Time period(s): 1990s
Locale(s): Montana

Summary: Sylvester Yellow Calf, a successful lawyer and former Montana basketball star, works for the parole board where he meets Jack Harwood, an inmate for whom parole is denied. Harwood cooks up a scheme involving his wife, Patti Ann. Unaware of her connection to Harwood, Yellow Calf takes Patti Ann as lover, a move which proves to be a terrible mistake as Yellow Calf is running for Congress and, when blackmail is introduced, Yellow Calf (a very decent man) must wrestle with his conscience and deal with these threatening events.

About this book: Welch is a master of realism. His portraits are convincing, and he keeps the reader totally engaged. There is no sentimentality in Welch's characters. There is no hint at Indian mysticism (as in many other writers whose themes are Indian people). Welch tackles the harsh realities unflinchingly, but there is nevertheless a kind of poetry in his realism, poetry of a stark and arresting nature that grabs the reader and won't let go.

Where it's reviewed:
Rocky Mountain Review of Language & Literature, Issue I, 1993, page 61

Other books by the same author:
Winter in the Blood, 1974 (fiction)
Killing Custer, 1994 (nonfiction, written with Paul Stekler)
The Death of Jim Loney, 1979 (fiction)
Riding the Earthboy 40, 1971 (poetry)
Fools Crow, 1986 (fiction)

Other books you might like:
Louise Erdrich, *Love Medicine*, 1984
   Married to Marie, Nector is nevertheless fatefully drawn to Lulu. When his grandson prepares a love medicine to win him back to his grandmother, he uses the wrong ingredients and kills Nector instead.
Clifford E. Trafzer, *Blue Dawn, Red Earth: New Native American Storytellers*, 1996
   This collection of short stories by 30 new Native American writers includes Lorne Simon, Anita Endrezze and Jim Barnes.
N. Scott Momaday, *The Ancient Child*, 1989
   Two Kiowa Indians, one in San Francisco and one in Oklahoma, are troubled by dreams which bring them together and immerses them into the mythology of their people.
Beth Brant, *A Gathering of Spirit: A Collection of North American Indian Women*, 1984
   This collection of short stories, letters, essyas and poems comes from a wide cross-section of Native American women writers including Linda Hogan, Elizabeth Cook-Lynn, Diana Glancy and others.
Leslie Marmon Silko, *Ceremony*, 1977
   A Pueblo man returns from the war and must realign himself with the traditional ways before he can become whole again.
D'Arcy McNickle, *The Surrounded*, 1936
   A fiddle player returns to his reservation for a visit after years in the White world, finding himself so caught up in its complexities that he knows he can never go back to the White world again.
Janet Campbell Hale, *The Jailing of Cecelia Capture*, 1985
   A thirty-something Indian woman, separated from her husband and children, is fighting a terrible battle with alcoholism while attending law school.
Linda Hogan, *Mean Spirit*, 1990
   This novel chronicles the greed and corruption that flows from Oklahoma's oil fields during the boom times.

1346

JAMES WELCH, Native American, Blackfeet and Gros Ventre

Winter in the Blood
(New York: Viking, 1974)

Subject(s): Indians of North America; Historical
Age range(s): Adult
Time period(s): 1970s
Locale(s): Montana

Summary: The main character of this powerful first person novel is nameless, a reflecting of the character's sense of displacement, even in his own homeland. The protagonist is caught in a web of alcohol and violence, and feels tremendous guilt over his twin brother's death (the twin motif is one that a

Native American Titles

number of Native American writers have utilized: Momaday, Silko). This book exposes the grimness of reservation life, yet there is also a good deal of black humor throughout.

Where it's reviewed:
Kirkus Reviews, October 15, 1974, page 1121
Library Journal, December 1, 1974, page 3148
Publishers Weekly, October 27, 1975, page 54

Other books by the same author:
The Indian Lawyer, 1990
The Death of Jim Loney, 1979
Fools Crow, 1986
Riding the Earthboy 40, 1971 (poetry)

Other books you might like:
D'Arcy McNickle, *The Surrounded*, 1936
  A fiddle player returns to his reservation for a visit after years in the White world. He is drawn into its complexities so far that he knows he can never go back to the White world again.
Louise Erdrich, *Love Medicine*, 1984
  Married to Marie, Nector is nevertheless fatefully drawn to Lulu. When his grandson prepares a love medicine to win him back to his grandmother, he uses the wrong ingredients and kills Nector instead.
N. Scott Momaday, *House Made of Dawn*, 1968
  This Pulitzer prize winning novel is about a pueblo man who, having returned from WWII shell-shocked, must figure out who he is and realign himself with his people.
Craig Lesley, *Talking Leaves*, 1991
  This is an excellent collection by thirty-five contemporary Native American writers including Louise Erdrich, Michael Dorris, N. Scott Momaday and Linda Hogan.
Leslie Marmon Silko, *Ceremony*, 1977
  A pueblo man, returned from the war, must realign himself with the traditional ways before becoming whole again.
James Northrup, *Walking the Rez Road*, 1993
  Luke Warmwater is a Vietnam vet down on his luck, but, he, like most of his reservation cohorts, is a survivor in the trickster fashion.
Janet Campbell Hale, *The Jailing of Cecelia Capture*, 1985
  A woman law student, trapped in despair and alcoholism, tries to make sense of her life.
Linda Hogan, *Mean Spirit*, 1990
  This novel chronicles the greed and corruption that flows from Oklahoma's oil fields during the boom days.

1347

TED C. WILLIAMS, Native American, Tuscarora

The Reservation

(Syracuse: Syracuse University Press, 1976)

Age range(s): Adult
Time period(s): 20th century (1930s-1970s)
Locale(s): New York

Summary: In this thinly disguised fiction, Williams tells the story of his life and the life of his Tuscarora family in a way that is often humorous.

Other books you might like:
Louise Erdrich, *Love Medicine*, 1984
  Married to Marie, Nector is nevertheless fatefully drawn to Lulu. When his grandson prepares a love medicine to win him back to his grandmother, he uses the wrong ingredients and kills Nector instead.
Paula Gunn Allen, *Spider Woman's Granddaughters*, 1989
  This beautiful collection of traditional tales is interwoven with contemporary short stories about Native American women.
Leslie Marmon Silko, *Storyteller*, 1981
  This work is a mixed genre of poetry, fiction, and mythology.
Sherman Alexie, *The Lone Ranger and Tonto Fist Fight in Heaven*, 1993
  This wonderful short fiction is about the ups and downs of reservation life.
Sherman Alexie, *Reservation Blues*, 1995
  Legendary bluesman Robert Johnson comes to the rez and things begin to rock.
Ray A. Young Bear, *Black Eagle Child*, 1992
  This fictional work is about life on a Mesquakie settlement.
Thomas King, *Green Grass, Running Water*, 1993
  Coyote, God, Robinson Crusoe, The Lone Ranger and others struggle amongst themselves in the cosmological firmament. Meanwhile various Native American characters struggle with life the best they can.

1348

SARAH WINNEMUCCA, Native American, Paiute

Life Among the Paiutes: Their Wrongs and Claims

(Bishop: Chalfant, 1883, 1969)

Subject(s): Indians of North America; Cultural Conflict
Age range(s): Grades 9-Adult
Time period(s): 19th century; 20th century (1860s-1930s)
Locale(s): United States

Summary: For most of the nineteenth century, Sarah Winnemucca was the only Native American woman to write a personal and tribal history. When she saw that the government was not going to live up to its promises to Native American people, Sarah began lecturing throughout the East to try and raise the consciousness of Americans about the wrongs being done. Her book deals with these wrongs, but it also includes many aspects of her Native American childhood and deals with traditional Paiute society in general.

Where it's reviewed:
Journal of Youth Services in Libraries, Spring 1993, page 291
School Library Journal, March 1993, page 123

Other books you might like:
John Fire Lame Deer, *Lame Deer, Seeker of Visions*, 1972
  This is an as-told-to book, Lame Deer telling his story to the writer Richard Erdoes.
Luther Standing Bear, *Stories of the Sioux*, 1988
  Standing Bear grew up in the traditional buffalo hunting culture of the Sioux and he brings to life the stories from his past.

Zitkala-Sa, *Old Indian Legends Retold by Zitkala-Sa*, 1921
This story chronicles the life of a woman who grows up in the traditional Sioux buffalo hunting culture but eventually goes to Indian boarding school in the east.

Peter Nabokov, *Native American Testimony*, 1991
Anthology, mixed genre: oral stories, speeches, prophecies, and essays.

Brian Swann, *I Tell You Now*, 1989
This is an excellent collection of autobiographical essays by eighteen contemporary American Indian writers.

Mary Crow Dog, *Lakota Woman*, 1990
This as-told-to book, with Richard Erdoes as author/editor, chronicles the life of a Lakota woman who lives through the hardships of the 1973 occupation of Wounded Knee by the AIM.

Mary Brave Bird, *Ohitika Woman*, 1993
This sequel to *Lakota Woman* chronicles the conflicts between feminism and traditional Indian belief, White and Indian philosophy. (Mary retook her maiden name after divorcing Crow Dog.)

Paula Gunn Allen, *The Sacred Hoop: Recovering the Feminine in American Indian Traditions*, 1986
This is an excellent collection of essays that uncover the essential role of women in traditional and contemporary Indian life.

1349

LINDA YAMANE, Author/Illustrator, Native American, Rumsien Ohlone

When the World Ended, How Hummingbird Got Fire, How People Were Made: Rumsien Ohlone Stories
(Berkeley, CA: Oyate, 1995)

Subject(s): Animals; Creation; Mythology
Age range(s): Grades 2-6
Time period(s): Indeterminate Past
Locale(s): California

Summary: These three stories of the Rumsien Ohlone people of California outline the details of creation and the advent of people on earth. Pieced together from a nearly lost oral tradition, it is a beautifully crafted book with superb illustrations by the author.

Other books you might like:
Jane Curry, *Back in the Before Time: Tales of the California Indians*, 1987
This collection includes twenty-two tales of the creation of the world from various California Indian tribes.

Sally Russel, *Voices and Dreams*, 1991
In these first-person accounts, twenty-two people of California Indian descent tell their moving stories about life, culture, racism and survival.

Margot Astrov, *The Winged Serpent*, 1946
This mixed genre collection is one of the best with oral stories and songs from a large cross-section of Native American cultures.

Frederick Turner, *The Portable North American Indian Reader*, 1973

This anthology of myths, legends, poetry, fiction, and captivity tales, contains work by both Native American and non-Native writers.

John Bierhorst, *The Red Swan: Myths and Tales of the American Indians*, 1976
This book is a compilation of varied stories (creation, trickster, star husband, etc.) from forty Native American tribes.

Joseph Bruchac, *Flying with the Eagle, Racing with the Bear*, 1993
These are rite of passage stories come from many tribal people, including the Wampanoag, Cherokee, Osage, Lakota and Tlingit.

1350

YELLOW BIRD (John Ridge)

Life and Adventures of Joaquin Murieta
(Norman: University of Oklahoma Press, 1955, 1986)

Subject(s): Frontier and Pioneer Life; Crime and Criminals
Age range(s): Adult
Major character(s): Joaquin Murieta, Convict, Native American
Time period(s): 1800s
Locale(s): Oklahoma

Summary: Murieta, a "mixed-blood," Cherokee and White, becomes a criminal after being driven off his land by greedy Whites. This is the first novel written by an American Indian and it is the romantic story of a man who seeks justice and revenge against his aggressors.

Other books by the same author:
Poems, 1868

Other books you might like:
Mourning Dove, *Cogewea*, 1981
Cogewea lives the life of a cowgirl on a ranch in Eastern Washington and is able to be successful in a man's world. She falls in love with an Easterner but eventually comes to embrace Indian values.

D'Arcy McNickle, *The Surrounded*, 1936
A fiddle player returns to his reservation for a visit after years in the White world and finds himself so caught up in its complexities that he knows he can never go back to the White world again.

Louise Erdrich, *Love Medicine*, 1984
Married to Marie, Nector is nevertheless fatefully drawn to Lulu. When his grandson prepares a love medicine to win him back to his grandmother, he uses the wrong ingredients and kills Nector instead.

Leslie Marmon Silko, *Ceremony*, 1977
A pueblo man, returning from the war, must align himself with the traditional ways before becoming whole again.

Maria Campbell, *Halfbreed*, 1973
This is the moving account of Campbell's life as a Metis, or halfbreed, part Indian and part European.

James Welch, *Winter in the Blood*, 1974
A man who is caught in the web of alcoholism, tries to discover the truth about his family.

N. Scott Momaday, *House Made of Dawn*, 1968
Story of Abel, who leaves his pueblo to fight in the war,

only to return alienated from his people, beginning long effort at healing.

John Joseph Mathews, *Sundown*, 1934

Challenge is educated in White schools, joins the army and returns to his homeland alienated from his culture. This novel shows the effects of two cultures competing for dominance in a man's life.

1351

RAY A. YOUNG BEAR, Native American, Mesquakie

Black Eagle Child

(Iowa City: University of Iowa Press, 1992)

Subject(s): Biography
Age range(s): Grades 12-Adult
Major character(s): Edgar Bearchild, Native American
Time period(s): 1990s

Summary: In this thinly disguised fiction, Young Bear recreates his own life on the Mesquakie settlement. It is both hilarious and tragic, truly a superb artistic achievement. Young Bear is one of the most gifted and imaginative American poets writing today, and his use of language is always a wonderful surprise. This book resonates.

Where it's reviewed:
Biography, Fall 1993, page 416

Other books by the same author:
The Invisible Musician, 1990 (poetry)
Winter of the Salamander: The Keeper of Importance, 1953 (poetry)

Other books you might like:
Leslie Marmon Silko, *Storyteller*, 1981
From Laguna Pueblo where he grew up, Silko weaves traditional mythology into modern stories, recreating old myths and making them relevant for a new generation.
Lee Miller, *From the Heart: Voices of the American Indian*, 1995
This is a collection of orations, speeches and testimony by more than 250 Indian people that presents a radical alternative to traditionally taught American history.
Sherman Alexie, *The Lone Ranger and Tonto Fist Fight in Heaven*, 1993
This wonderful short fiction is about the ups and downs of reservation life.
Sherman Alexie, *Reservation Blues*, 1995
This brilliant fiction is about the trials of Native Americans trying to cope in a most difficult world.
W.P. Kinsella, *Moccasin Telegraph*, 1984
Life on the Ermineskin Reserve in Canada, told by Silas Ermineskin himself, is full of both tragedy and comedy.

1352

SEVERT YOUNG BEAR, Native American, Lakota (Sioux)
R.D. THEIOSZ, Co-Author, Caucasian

Standing in the Light: A Lakota Way of Seeing

(Lincoln: University of Nebraska Press, 1994)

Subject(s): Autobiography; Rituals; Philosophy
Age range(s): Grades 9-Adult
Time period(s): 1890s
Locale(s): South Dakota

Summary: Well-known educator and traditional singer, Young Bear relates the myths and history of his people on tape, in keeping with the oral traditions. He describes, also, some of the recent historical events in which he participated, like the 1972 occupation of Wounded Knee. In his reflections, he hopes to speak to those who feel most disconnected from their heritage, those at the outer edges of the culture.

About this book: Friend and adopted brother, R.D. Theisz organized and edited the tapes into prose. It is interesting, in the introduction, how much Theisz removes himself from the pattern established by Neihardt of a mystical connection between two minds. Young Bear died in 1994.

Where it's reviewed:
Booklist, November 15, 1994, page 577
Choice, June 1995, page 1639
Library Journal, October 15, 1994, page 73
Whole Earth Review, Summer 1995, page 75
Western Historical Quarterly, Summer 1995, page 262

Other books you might like:
Raymond DeMallie, *The Sixth Grandfather*, 1984
Transcripts of Neihardt's interviews with Black Elk, edited with commentary by DeMallie. These direct transcripts give a much different impression of Black Elk than do Neihardt's creation.
Black Elk, *Black Elk Speaks*, 1932
The life story of Black Elk as told to John Neihardt. Black Elk lives the traditional culture of the Sioux at the time of Custer's Last Stand and is a witness to the Wounded Knee massacre.
John Fire Lame Deer, *Lame Deer, Seeker of Visions*, 1972
Traditional medicine man Lame Deer tells of his visions and spiritual quest while relating the philosophy of Lakota religion and culture.
Zitkala-Sa, *Old Indian Legends Retold by Zitkala-Sa*, 1921
These stories recount Zitkala-Sa's childhood in the traditional Lakota culture and the difficulties she faces while attending school and college in a world where she is perceived as a ''savage.''
Charles A. Eastman, *From the Deep Woods to Civilization*, 1916
This is the autobiography of Charles A. Eastman, who grows up in the traditional buffalo culture of the Lakota (Sioux) but pursues an education in the White man's world.
Luther Standing Bear, *Stories of the Sioux*, 1988
Standing Bear grew up in the traditional buffalo hunting culture, and he brings to life the stories from his own past.

1353

ZITKALA-SA (Gertrude Bonnin)

American Indian Stories

(Lincoln: University of Nebraska Press, 1921)

Subject(s): Biography; Indian Reservations; Social Conditions
Age range(s): Grades 9-Adult
Time period(s): 19th century; 20th century (1870s-1921)
Locale(s): South Dakota

Summary: This is the life story of Zitkala-Sa, a Lakota woman who lives her childhood in the traditional buffalo hunting culture, but who eventually leaves for the Indian boarding schools out East. The book is an important look at the life of traditional Lakota (Sioux) women, yet it also explores the pain of assimilation that many Indian people have experienced as they were forced into the dominant White culture.

Where it's reviewed:
Book World, January 5, 1986, page 12
Choice, June 1986, page 1507
Kliatt, Spring 1986, page 34

Other books you might like:
Sarah Winnemucca, *Life Among the Paiutes: Their Wrongs and Claims*, 1883
   Diplomat and outspoken advocate of the rights of native peoples, Winnemucca wrote this book to preserve the history and culture of the Paiute's.
Black Elk, *Black Elk Speaks*, 1932
   This is the life story of the Holy Man of the Sioux.
John Fire Lame Deer, *Lame Deer, Seeker of Visions*, 1972
   This is an as-told-to book, Lame Deer telling his story to the writer Richard Erdoes.
Luther Standing Bear, *Stories of the Sioux*, 1988
   These are early life stories of a traditional Lakota (Sioux) man.

Mary Crow Dog, *Lakota Woman*, 1990
   This as-told-to book, with Richard Erdoes as author/editor, chronicles the life of a Lakota woman who lives through the hardships of the 1973 occupation of Wounded Knee by the AIM.
Brian Swann, *I Tell You Now*, 1989
   This is an excellent collection of autobiographical essays by eighteen contemporary American Indian writers.
Mourning Dove, *Mourning Dove: A Salishan Autobiography*, 1990
   The autobiography of Mourning Dove, who led a life of hardship in the Northwest, where she worked as a day laborer doing field work while fighting for the time and energy to write.
Ella Cara Deloria, *Waterlily*, 1988
   This novel depicts Waterlily's life story. It shows a woman's life in the traditional buffalo hunting culture and the importance of kinship relationships before the Sioux had contact with Europeans.
Wilma Mankiller, *Mankiller: A Chief and Her People*, 1993
   This is the life story of Wilma Mankiller, current Chief of the Cherokees. In this book she recounts her own story as well as the story of her people.
Mark St. Pierre, *The Spiritual Power and Legacy of American Plains Indian Women*,
   This book looks at the lives of Plains Indian women and at the myths and culture surrounding them.
Paula Gunn Allen, *Spider Woman's Granddaughters*, 1989
   This is a beautiful collection of traditional tales interwoven with contemporary short stories having to do with the lives of Native American women.
Charles A. Eastman, *From the Deep Woods to Civilization*, 1916
   Autobiography by a Sioux man who left the traditional buffalo hunting culture to become a medical doctor.

Native American Titles

Time Period Index

This index chronologically lists the time settings in which the featured books take place. Main headings refer to a century; where no specific time is given, the headings INDETERMINATE PAST, INDETERMINATE FUTURE, and INDETERMINATE are used. The 18th through 21st centuries are broken down into decades when possible. (Note: 1800s, for example, refers to the first decade of the 19th century.) Featured titles are listed alphabetically beneath time headings, with author names, and entry numbers also provided.

21st CENTURY

2050s

2070s

INDETERMINATE FUTURE

INDETERMINATE

Geographic Index

This index provides access to all featured books by geographic settings—such as countries, continents, oceans, and planets. States and provinces are indicated for the United States and Canada. Also interfiled are headings for fictional place names (Spaceships, Imaginary Planets, etc.). Sections are further broken down by city or the specific name of the imaginary locale. Book titles are listed alphabetically under headings, and author names and entry numbers are also provided.

AFRICA

The Captive - Joyce Hansen   *afa*   173
Click Song - John A. Williams   *afa*   459
The Color Purple - Alice Walker   *afa*   426
Echo of Lions - Barbara Chase-Riboud   *afa*   52
Legend of Tarik - Walter Dean Myers   *afa*   312
Monkey-Monkey's Trick - Patricia C. McKissack   *afa*   263
Mufaro's Beautiful Daughters: An African Tale - John Steptoe   *afa*   399
Possessing the Secret of Joy - Alice Walker   *afa*   429
Wild Seed - Octavia Butler   *afa*   38

Egyptica
Captain Africa: The Battle for Egyptica - Dwayne J. Ferguson   *afa*   120

Pandemi
Jacob's Ladder - John A. Williams   *afa*   460

ALTERNATE EARTH

Dustland - Virginia Hamilton   *afa*   160
The Gathering - Virginia Hamilton   *afa*   161

AMERICAN COLONIES

MASSACHUSETTS

Salem
The Captive - Joyce Hansen   *afa*   173

NEW YORK

Wild Seed - Octavia Butler   *afa*   38

ARGENTINA

The Stories of Eva Luna - Isabel Allende   *lat*   500

ASIA

Home Was the Land of Morning Calm: The Saga of a Korean American Family - K. Connie Kang   *asa*   965

AT SEA

Middle Passage - Charles Johnson   *afa*   226

BURMA

The Coffin Tree - Wendy Law-Yone   *asa*   982

CAMBODIA

Judge Rabbit and the Tree Spirit: A Folktale from Cambodia - Lina Mao Wall   *asa*   1095
Silent Lotus - Jeanne M. Lee   *asa*   989

CANADA

A Coyote Columbus Story - Thomas King   *naa*   1244
Crazywater: Native Voices on Addiction and Recovery - Brian Maracle   *naa*   1264
Dance Me Outside - W.P. Kinsella   *naa*   1247
Food & Spirits: Stories - Beth Brant   *naa*   1165
Fresh Girls and Other Stories - Evelyn Lau   *asa*   980
Harpoon of the Hunter - Markoosie   *naa*   1265
Hide and Seek - Michael Arvaarluk Kusugak   *naa*   1251
The Moccasin Maker - E. Pauline Johnson   *naa*   1236
Moccasin Telegraph - W.P. Kinsella   *naa*   1248
Northern Lights: The Soccer Trails - Michael Arvaarluk Kusugak   *naa*   1252
Obasan - Joy Kogawa   *asa*   975
A Promise Is a Promise - Michael Arvaarluk Kusugak   *naa*   1253
Runaway: Diary of a Street Kid - Evelyn Lau   *asa*   981

ALBERTA

Green Grass, Running Water - Thomas King   *naa*   1245
Medicine River - Thomas King   *naa*   1246

Granton
Naomi's Road - Joy Kogawa   *asa*   974

BRITISH COLUMBIA

Disappearing Moon Cafe - Sky Lee   *asa*   998
Dzelarhons - Anne Cameron   *naa*   1179
Guests Never Leave Hungry: The Autobiography of James Sewid, a Kwakuitl Indian - James Sewid   *naa*   1304
My Name Is Seepeetza - Shirley Sterling   *naa*   1324

Slocan
Naomi's Road - Joy Kogawa   *asa*   974

Vancouver
Naomi's Road - Joy Kogawa   *asa*   974
Yellow Fever - R.A. Shiomi   *asa*   1067

ONTARIO

Niagara Falls
Flight to Canada - Ishmael Reed   *afa*   363

Toronto
Coloured Pictures - Himani Bannerji   *asa*   903

SASKATCHEWAN

Halfbreed - Maria Campbell   *naa*   1180

WEST

Tales from Gold Mountain: Stories of the Chinese in the New World - Paul Yee   *asa*   1115

YUKON TERRITORY

Life Lived like a Story: Life Stories of Three Yukon Native Elders - Julie Crukshank   *naa*   1190

CARIBBEAN

Green Cane and Juicy Flotsam: Short Stories by Caribbean Women - Carmen C. Esteves   *lat*   602
Remaking a Lost Harmony: Stories from the Hispanic Caribbean - Margarite Fernandez Olmos   *lat*   606
Tar Baby - Toni Morrison   *afa*   286

Berhama
The Berhama Account - John A. Williams   *afa*   457

Williamson
Junius over Far - Virginia Hamilton   *afa*   162

CENTRAL AMERICA

The Gold Coin - Alma Flor Ada   *lat*   488

CHILE

Happiness: Stories - Marjorie Agosin   *lat*   492
The House of the Spirits - Isabel Allende   *lat*   497
Paula - Isabel Allende   *lat*   499

CHINA

American Visa - Wang Ping   *asa*   1047
Baba: A Return to China upon My Father's Shoulders - Belle Yang   1113
The Boy Who Swallowed Snakes - Laurence Yep   *asa*   1117
Cat and Rat: The Legend of the Chinese Zodiac - Ed Young   *asa*   1128
China Men - Maxine Hong Kingston   *asa*   971
China's Bravest Girl: The Legend of Hua Mu Lan - Charlie Chin   *asa*   920
The Chinese Siamese Cat - Amy Tan   *asa*   1077
The Cricket Warrior: A Chinese Tale - Margaret Chang   *asa*   917
The Empty Pot - Demi   *asa*   934
The Five Chinese Brothers - Claire Huchet Bishop   *asa*   905
Griever: An American Monkey King in China - Gerald Vizenor   *naa*   1337
The Joy Luck Club - Amy Tan   *asa*   1079
Katherine - Anchee Min   *asa*   1019
The Kitchen God's Wife - Amy Tan   *asa*   1080
Liang and the Magic Paintbrush - Demi   *asa*   935
Ling-Li and the Phoenix Fairy: A Chinese Folktale - Ellin Greene   *asa*   940
Little Plum - Ed Young   *asa*   1129
Lon Po Po: A Red-Riding Hood Story from China - Ed Young   *asa*   1130
The Magic Tapestry - Demi   *asa*   936
The Man Who Tricked a Ghost - Laurence Yep   *asa*   1124
The Moon Lady - Amy Tan   *asa*   1081
Night Visitors - Ed Young   *asa*   1131
Red Thread - Ed Young   *asa*   1132
The Seven Chinese Brothers - Margaret Mahy   *asa*   1011
The Shell Woman and the King - Laurence Yep   *asa*   1127
Still Life With Rice: A Young American Woman Discovers the Life and Legacy of Her Korean Grandmother - Helie Lee   *asa*   986
Thousand Pieces of Gold - Ruthanne Lum McCunn   *asa*   1016
The Woman Warrior: Memoirs of a Girlhood Among Ghosts - Maxine Hong Kingston   *asa*   973
Yeh-Shen: A Cinderella Story from China - Ai-Ling Louie   *asa*   1008

Changmian
The Hundred Secret Senses - Amy Tan   *asa*   1078

Dimtao
On Gold Mountain: The One-Hundred-Year Odyssey of a Chinese-American Family - Lisa See   *asa*   1062

Hong Kong
The Hidden Shrine - Walter Dean Myers   *afa*   309

Hunan
The Ghost Fox - Laurence Yep   *asa*   1121

Shanghai
Frontiers of Love - Diana Chang   *asa*   915
In the Eye of War - Margaret Chang   *asa*   918
Red Azalea - Anchee Min   *asa*   1020

COLOMBIA

Saturday Sancocho - Leyla Torres   *lat*   851

CUBA

The Assault - Reinaldo Arenas   *lat*   520
The Autobiography of a Runaway Slave - Esteban Montejo   *lat*   714
The Bossy Gallito - Lucia M. Gonzalez   *lat*   640
Crazy Love - Elias Miguel Munoz   *lat*   729

Exiled Memories: A Cuban Childhood - Pablo Medina   *lat*   699
The Fourteen Sisters of Emilio Montez O'Brien: A Novel - Oscar Hijuelos   *lat*   654
The Gravedigger and Other Stories - Ramon Ferreira   *lat*   611
The Indian Chronicles - Jose Barreiro   *lat*   530
The Marks of Birth - Pablo Medina   *lat*   700
Old Rosa: A Novel in Two Stories - Reinaldo Arenas   *lat*   523
The Palace of the White Skunks - Reinaldo Arenas   *lat*   524
Rabbit Wishes - Linda Shute   *lat*   821
Singing to Cuba - Margarita Engle   *lat*   597
Skywriting - Margarita Engle   *lat*   598
Where the Flame Trees Bloom - Alma Flor Ada   *lat*   491

Havana
Before Night Falls - Reinaldo Arenas   *lat*   521
The Cutter: A Novel - Virgil Suarez   *lat*   842
Rachel's Song: A Novel - Miguel Barnet   *lat*   529

DOMINICAN REPUBLIC

How the Garcia Girls Lost Their Accents - Julia Alvarez   *lat*   502
In the Time of the Butterflies - Julia Alvarez   *lat*   503

EARTH

Adulthood Rites - Octavia E. Butler   *afa*   39
Brainstorm - Walter Dean Myers   *afa*   301
Nine-in-One Grr! Grr! - Blia Xiong   *asa*   1106

EGYPT

Aswan
Tales of a Dead King - Walter Dean Myers   *afa*   325

Morocco
Duel in the Desert - Walter Dean Myers   *afa*   304

EL SALVADOR

A Fire in the Earth - Marcos McPeek Villatoro   *lat*   885
In Search of Bernabe - Graciela Limon   *lat*   679
Magic Dogs of the Volcanoes = Los Perros Magicos de los Volcanes - Manlio Argueta   *lat*   525

ENGLAND

Othello, a Novel - Julius Lester   *afa*   244

EUROPE

Click Song - John A. Williams   *afa*   459
Hanging by Her Teeth - Bonnie Greer   *afa*   153
Hurry Home - John Edgar Wideman   *afa*   448
Our Lady of Babylon - John Rechy   *lat*   770
The Seven League Boots - Albert Murray   *afa*   297
Wild Seed - Octavia Butler   *afa*   38

FICTIONAL COUNTRY

Bellona
Dhalgren - Samuel R. Delany   *afa*   94

Briarsville
Nettie Jo's Friends - Patricia C. McKissack   *afa*   264

Soledad
Sleep of the Innocents - Carole Fernandez   *lat*   603

FRANCE

Paris
Bonjour Lonnie - Faith Ringgold   *afa*   373
City of Light - Cyrus Colter   *afa*   76
Longing - Maria Espinosa   *lat*   601
Night Studies - Cyrus Colter   *afa*   77
The Price You Pay - Barbara Summers   *afa*   402
Sally Hemings - Barbara Chase-Riboud   *afa*   54

GHANA

Too Much Talk - Angela Shelf Medearis   *afa*   273

GREECE

Corinth
For Her Dark Skin - Percival Everett   *afa*   113

GRENADA

Praisesong for the Widow - Paule Marshall   *afa*   255

GUATEMALA

Abuela's Weave - Omar Castaneda   *lat*   563
Among the Volcanoes - Omar Castaneda   *lat*   564
Imagining Isabel - Omar Castaneda   *lat*   565
The Long Night of White Chickens - Francisco Goldman   *lat*   631
Rites: A Guatemalan Boyhood - Victor Perera   *lat*   752

HAITI

If You Please, President Lincoln - Harriette Gillem Robinet   *afa*   375

HELL

The True American: A Folk Fable - Melvin Van Peebles   *afa*   423

INDIA

Aani and the Tree Huggers - Jeannine Atkins   *asa*   900
Arranged Marriage - Chitra Banerjee Divakaruni   *asa*   937
Bombay Talkie - Ameena Meer   *asa*   1017
Buddha - Demi   *asa*   932
Fat Gopal - Jacquelin Singh   *asa*   1068
The Golden Serpent - Walter Dean Myers   *afa*   308
Jasmine - Bharati Mukherjee   *asa*   1030
Love, Stars, and All That - Kirin Narayan   *asa*   1037
Mistaken Identity - Nayantara Sahgal   *asa*   1050
A River Sutra - Gita Mehta   *asa*   1018

Bombay
Wife - Bharati Mukherjee   *asa*   1032

Calcutta
Gay-Neck: The Story of a Pigeon - Dhan Gopal Mukerji   *asa*   1029

Hyderabad
Nampally Road - Meena Alexander   *asa*   896

JAMAICA

Negril
How Stella Got Her Groove Back - Terry McMillan   *afa*   267

Geographic Index

VERMONT

Whitney

Love, Stars, and All That - Kirin Narayan   *asa*   1037

VIRGINIA

Christmas in the Big House, Christmas in the Quarters - Patricia C. McKissack   *afa*   259
Tanya's Reunion - Valerie Flournoy   *afa*   123

Albemarle County

Sally Hemings - Barbara Chase-Riboud   *afa*   54

Monticello

The President's Daughter - Barbara Chase-Riboud   *afa*   53
Sally Hemings - Barbara Chase-Riboud   *afa*   54

Richmond

Flight to Canada - Ishmael Reed   *afa*   363

Turner

1959 - Thulani Davis   *afa*   93

WASHINGTON

Cogewea - Mourning Dove   *naa*   1284
Coyote Stories - Mourning Dove   *naa*   1285
Mourning Dove: A Salishan Autobiography - Mourning Dove   *naa*   1286

Pearl

One Dark Body - Charlotte Sherman   *afa*   389

Seattle

April and the Dragon Lady - Lensey Namioka   *asa*   1034

Cebu - Peter Bacho   *asa*   902
Molly by Any Other Name - Jean Davies Okimoto   *asa*   1043
Nisei Daughter - Monica Sone   *asa*   1070
No-No Boy - John Okada   *asa*   1042
Suder - Percival Everett   *afa*   116
Sushi and Sourdough - Tooru J. Kanazawa   *asa*   964
Touch - Charlotte Sherman   *afa*   390
Yang the Third and Her Impossible Family - Lensey Namioka   *asa*   1035
Yang the Youngest and His Terrible Ear - Lensey Namioka   *asa*   1036

WEST

America Is in the Heart - Carlos Bulosan   *asa*   910
Baseball Saved Us - Ken Mochizuki   *asa*   1023
The Floating World - Cynthia Kadohata   *asa*   962
God's Country - Percival Everett   *afa*   114
Pie-Biter - Ruthanne Lum McCunn   *asa*   1015
Tales from Gold Mountain: Stories of the Chinese in the New World - Paul Yee   *asa*   1115
Thousand Pieces of Gold - Ruthanne Lum McCunn   *asa*   1016
Tripmaster Monkey: His Fake Book - Maxine Hong Kingston   *asa*   972

Buttonhole

An Open Weave - Devorah Major   *afa*   253

WISCONSIN

Dream of the Blue Heron - Victor Barnouw   *naa*   1147

WYOMING

Slut's Hole

Walk Me to the Distance - Percival Everett   *afa*   117

VIETNAM

Captain Blackman - John A. Williams   *afa*   458
Fire and Rain - Oswald Rivera   *lat*   777
The Oddsplayer - Joe Rodriguez   *lat*   787
Silent Lotus - Jeanne M. Lee   *asa*   989
Toad Is the Uncle of Heaven - Jeanne M. Lee   *asa*   990

Chu Lai

Fallen Angels - Walter Dean Myers   *afa*   305

Tam Ky

Fallen Angels - Walter Dean Myers   *afa*   305

Thai-Yen Village

The Little Weaver of Thai-Yen Village - Tran Khanh Tuyet   *asa*   1083

VIETNAM, SOUTH

Shifting Loyalties - Daniel Cano   *lat*   559

WEST INDIES

The Cat's Purr - Ashley Bryan   *afa*   28
Daughters - Paule Marshall   *afa*   254

Subject Index

This index lists subjects which are covered in the featured titles. These can include such things as family life, animals, personal and social problems, historical events, ethnic groups, and story types, e.g. Mystery and Detective Stories. Beneath each subject heading, titles are arranged alphabetically with author names and entry numbers also indicated.

Vanishing Rooms - Melvin Dixon   *afa*   100

Voodoo Dreams: A Novel of Marie Laveau - Jewell Parker Rhodes   *afa*   370

Waiting to Exhale - Terry McMillan   *afa*   269

Walk Me to the Distance - Percival Everett   *afa*   117

Wild Embers - Anita Richmond Bunkley   *afa*   33

Wilhemina Jones, Future Star - Dindga McCannon   *afa*   257

A Woman's Place - Marita Golden   *afa*   140

Women of Brewster Place - Gloria Naylor   *afa*   331

Won't Know Till I Get There - Walter Dean Myers   *afa*   326

Interracial Marriage

The Wedding - Dorothy West   *afa*   445

Jealousy

Othello, a Novel - Julius Lester   *afa*   244

She Come Bringing Me That Little Baby Girl - Eloise Greenfield   *afa*   149

Journalism

Ashes in the Rain: Selected Essays - Al Martinez   *lat*   692

Kidnapping

White Leg - Max Martinez   *lat*   696

Kings, Queens, Rulers, etc.

Chingis Khan - Demi   *asa*   933

The Empty Pot - Demi   *asa*   934

My People the Sioux - Luther Standing Bear   *naa*   1321

Korean War

Echoes of the White Giraffe - Sook Nyul Choi   *asa*   927

Home Was the Land of Morning Calm: The Saga of a Korean American Family - K. Connie Kang   *asa*   965

Still Life With Rice: A Young American Woman Discovers the Life and Legacy of Her Korean Grandmother - Helie Lee   *asa*   986

Year of Impossible Goodbyes - Sook Nyul Choi   *asa*   930

Labor and Labor Classes

All-Bright Court - Connie Porter   *afa*   356

The Brick People - Alejandro Morales   *lat*   724

The Last of the Menu Girls - Denise Chavez   *lat*   575

Language

At the Beach - Huy Voun Lee   *asa*   987

Empire of Dreams - Giannina Braschi   *lat*   547

Hunger of Memory: The Education of Richard Rodriguez, an Autobiography - Richard Rodriguez   *lat*   788

In the Snow - Huy Voun Lee   *asa*   988

Mas Que No Love It: Cuentos/Short Stories - Jim Sagel   *lat*   804

Law

The Autobiography of a Brown Buffalo - Oscar Zeta Acosta   *lat*   485

Learning

At the Beach - Huy Voun Lee   *asa*   987

In the Snow - Huy Voun Lee   *asa*   988

Legends

The Chichi Hoohoo Bogeyman - Virginia Driving Hawk Sneve   *naa*   1313

China's Bravest Girl: The Legend of Hua Mu Lan - Charlie Chin   *asa*   920

Elderberry Flute Song - Peter Blue Cloud   *naa*   1163

Giving Birth to Thunder, Sleeping with His Daughter: Coyote Builds North America - Barry Lopez   *naa*   1260

A Legend from the Crazy Horse Clan - Moses Nelson Big Crow   *naa*   1158

Legend of Tarik - Walter Dean Myers   *afa*   312

Nambe—Year One - Orlando Romero   *lat*   796

Pueblo Storyteller - Diane Hoyt-Goldsmith   *naa*   1233

When Beaver Was Very Great: Stories to Live By - Anne M. Dunn   *naa*   1204

Letters

The Color Purple - Alice Walker   *afa*   426

Dear Peter Rabbit = Querido Pedrin - Alma Flor Ada   *lat*   487

The Mixquiahuala Letters - Ana Castillo   *lat*   568

Literacy

Papa's Stories - Dolores Johnson   *afa*   229

Literature

American Indian Literatures: An Introduction, Bibliographic Review, and Selected Bibliography - LaVonne Ruoff   *naa*   1299

The Business of Fancydancing: Stories and Poems - Sherman Alexie   *naa*   1136

Four Masterworks of American Indian Literature - John Bierhorst   *naa*   1153

Reflex and Bone Structure - Clarence Major   *afa*   251

The Remembered Earth - Geary Hobson   *naa*   1230

Through Indian Eyes: The Native Experience in Books for Children - Beverly Slapin   *naa*   1309

Voice of the Turtle - Paula Gunn Allen   *naa*   1141

Loneliness

The Bluest Eye - Toni Morrison   *afa*   282

Mama - Terry McMillan   *afa*   268

My Brother Fine with Me - Lucille Clifton   *afa*   71

These Same Long Bones - Gwendolyn Parker   *afa*   339

Zulus - Percival Everett   *afa*   119

Love

African Passions and Other Stories - Beatriz Rivera   *lat*   775

American Knees - Shawn Wong   *asa*   1104

Family Resemblances - Lowry Pei   *asa*   1046

The Gift of the Poinsettia = El Regalo de la Flor de Nochebuena - Pat Mora   *lat*   719

Golden Gate: A Novel in Verse - Vikram Seth   *asa*   1064

His Own Where - June Jordan   *afa*   236

How Stella Got Her Groove Back - Terry McMillan   *afa*   267

The Hunter and the Woodpecker: An Indian Legend - Christine Crowl   *naa*   1188

In Search of Snow - Luis Alberto Urrea   *lat*   864

Katherine - Anchee Min   *asa*   1019

Love, Stars, and All That - Kirin Narayan   *asa*   1037

Loverboys, Stories - Ana Castillo   *lat*   567

Ludell's New York Time - Brenda Wilkinson   *afa*   454

Mother Tongue - Demetria Martinez   *lat*   693

Only the Good Times - Bruce-Novoa   *lat*   549

Perez and Martina - Pura Belpre   *lat*   535

Seduction by Light - Al Young   *afa*   481

The Shell Woman and the King - Laurence Yep   *asa*   1127

Lovers

Sapogonia: An Anti-Romance in 3/8 Meter - Ana Castillo   *lat*   569

Loyalty

The Rabbit's Escape - Suzanne Crowder Han   *asa*   948

Magic

The Best of Sabine R. Ulibarri: Selected Stories - Sabine Ulibarri   *lat*   861

The Black Snowman - Phil Mendez   *afa*   274

El Condor and Other Stories - Sabine Ulibarri   *lat*   862

Intaglio: A Novel in Six Stories - Roberta Fernandez   *lat*   605

Jalamanta: A Message from the Desert - Rudolfo Anaya   *lat*   511

Juan Tuza and the Magic Pouch - Francisco X. Mora   *lat*   715

The Magic Tapestry - Demi   *asa*   936

The Magical Adventures of Pretty Pearl - Virginia Hamilton   *afa*   166

Montgomery's Children - Richard Perry   *afa*   344

Mrs. Vargas and the Dead Naturalist - Kathleen Alcala   *lat*   495

My Aunt Otilia's Spirits = Los Espiritus de Mi Tia Otilia - Richard Garcia   *lat*   623

Pig Cookies and Other Stories - Alberto Alvaro Rios   *lat*   774

A Place Where the Sea Remembers - Sandra Benitez   *lat*   539

The Road to Tamazunchale - Ron Arias   *lat*   526

Singing Softly = Cantando Bajito - Carmen de Monteflores   *lat*   589

Singing to Cuba - Margarita Engle   *lat*   597

Song of the Hummingbird - Graciela Limon   *lat*   682

The Stories of Eva Luna - Isabel Allende   *lat*   500

Three Wishes - Lucille Clifton   *afa*   74

Trini - Estela Portillo Trambley   *lat*   854

Walking Stars: Stories of Magic and Power - Victor Villasenor   *lat*   883

Where the Cinnamon Winds Blow = Donde Soplan Los Vientos de Canela - Jim Sagel   *lat*   805

The Woman Who Outshone the Sun - Alejandro Cruz Martinez   *lat*   583

Marriage

The Boy of the Three-Year Nap - Dianne Snyder   *asa*   1069

Chesapeake Song - Brenda Lane Richardson   *afa*   371

Eat a Bowl of Tea - Louis Chu   *asa*   931

The House on the Lagoon - Rosario Ferre   *lat*   608

Jazz - Toni Morrison   *afa*   283

Ling-Li and the Phoenix Fairy: A Chinese Folktale - Ellin Greene   *asa*   940

Longing - Maria Espinosa   *lat*   601

The Old Man and His Door - Gary Soto   *lat*   829

Red Thread - Ed Young   *asa*   1132

Somebody Else's Mama - David Haynes   *afa*   186

Tangled Up in Blue - Larry Duplechan   *afa*   107

The Wedding - Mary Helen Ponce   *lat*   759

Wild Steps of Heaven - Victor Villasenor   *lat*   884

Martial Arts

Pacific Crossing - Gary Soto   *lat*   830

Medicine

Death of an Anglo - Alejandro Morales   *lat*   725

Doctor Magdalena: Novella - Rosa Martha Villarreal   *lat*   880

Nightwing - Martin Cruz Smith   *naa*   1311

Prietita and the Ghost Woman = Prietita y La Llorona - Gloria Anzaldua   *lat*   518

The Rag Doll Plagues - Alejandro Morales   *lat*   726

Men

Cheyenne Memories - John Stands in Timber   *naa*   1322

The Collected Stories of Amado Muro - Amado Muro   *lat*   732

The Dream of Santa Maria de las Piedras - Miguel Mendez   *lat*   701

Fighting Tuscarora: The Autobiography of Chief Clinton Rickard - Clinton Rickard   *naa*   1296

Horse Medicine and Other Stories - Rafael Zepeda   *lat*   895

The Last Known Residence of Mickey Acuna - Dagoberto Gilb   *lat*   629

The Life, History, and Travels of Kah-ge-ga-bowh - George Copway   *naa*   1185

A Son of the Forest: The Experience of William Apes, a Native of the Forest, Comprising a Notice of the Pequod Tribe of Indians - George Apes   *naa*   1143

Murder

Character Name Index

This index alphabetically lists the major characters in each featured title. Each character name is followed by a description of the character. Citations also provide titles of the books featuring the character—listed alphabetically if there is more than one title—author names, and entry numbers.

A

Aani (Young Woman)
Aani and the Tree Huggers - Jeannine Atkins   *asa*   900

Abby (African American; Adoptee; Sister)
Abby - Jeannette Franklin Caines   *afa*   40

Abel (Native American; Veteran)
House Made of Dawn - N. Scott Momaday   *naa*   1281

Abel (Student—College; Brother; Mexican American)
Jesse - Gary Soto   *lat*   827

Achitophel, Alice (Clerk; Outcast; Caucasian)
Zulus - Percival Everett   *afa*   119

Acosta, Oscar Zeta (Lawyer; Chicano)
The Autobiography of a Brown Buffalo - Oscar Zeta Acosta   *lat*   485
The Revolt of the Cockroach People - Oscar Zeta Acosta   *lat*   486

Acuna, Mickey (Streetperson; Chicano)
The Last Known Residence of Mickey Acuna - Dagoberto Gilb   *lat*   629

Ada, Alma Flor (Child; Cuban)
Where the Flame Trees Bloom - Alma Flor Ada   *lat*   491

Adams, Arilla (12-Year-Old; Sister; Interracial)
Arilla Sun Down - Virginia Hamilton   *afa*   156

Adams, Elizabeth "Lisa" (Activist; Secretary; Caucasian)
And All Our Wounds Forgiven - Julius Lester   *afa*   242

Adams, Jack Sun Run (16-Year-Old; Interracial)
Arilla Sun Down - Virginia Hamilton   *afa*   156

Adams, John Quincy (Aged Person; Historical Figure; Caucasian)
Echo of Lions - Barbara Chase-Riboud   *afa*   52

Adams, Thomas Jerrett "T.J." (Teenager; Homosexual; Caucasian)
The Color of Trees - Canaan Parker   *afa*   338

Adare, Mary (Friend)
The Beet Queen - Louise Erdrich   *naa*   1210

Adkins, Mary Dee (Student; Wealthy; African American)
Night Studies - Cyrus Colter   *afa*   77

Adres (Brother)
Happy Days, Uncle Sergio - Magali Garcia Ramis   *lat*   624

Adrianne (Young Woman; Prostitute)
Dark Plums - Maria Espinosa   *lat*   600

Aekyung (Immigrant; Korean American)
Aekyung's Dream - Min Paek   *asa*   1045

Ah Goong (Grandfather)
China Men - Maxine Hong Kingston   *asa*   971

Ah Sing, Wittman (Writer; Chinese)
Tripmaster Monkey: His Fake Book - Maxine Hong Kingston   *asa*   972

Ah Song (Gambler; Rogue; Chinese)
Eat a Bowl of Tea - Louis Chu   *asa*   931

Akin (African American; Child; Genetically Altered Being)
Adulthood Rites - Octavia E. Butler   *afa*   39

Akwara, Artia "El Muerte" (Mercenary; Warrior; Caucasian)
Legend of Tarik - Walter Dean Myers   *afa*   312

Al-Hussain, Adam (Cousin; Indian)
Bombay Talkie - Ameena Meer   *asa*   1017

Al-Hussain, Sabah (Young Woman; Indian American)
Bombay Talkie - Ameena Meer   *asa*   1017

Al-Hussain, Syed Jamal Noor "Jimmy" (Actor; Indian)
Bombay Talkie - Ameena Meer   *asa*   1017

Alamar, Don Mariano (Landowner; Californio)
The Squatter and the Don - Maria Amparo Ruiz de Burton   *lat*   799

Alberta (Professor; Native American)
Green Grass, Running Water - Thomas King   *naa*   1245

Alberto "Beto" (9-Year-Old; Grandson; Meztiso)
La Maravilla - Alfredo Vea Jr.   *lat*   867

Aleluya (Intellectual; Puerto Rican)
Hot Soles in Harlem - Emilio Diaz Valcarcel   *lat*   592

Alex (Friend)
Boys at Work - Gary Soto   *lat*   824

Alex (Child; Niece; African American)
Carousel - Pat Cummings   *afa*   88

Alexander, Marian (Activist; Student—Junior High; African American)
1959 - Thulani Davis   *afa*   93

Ali (Child; African American)
The Girl Who Wore Snakes - Angela Johnson   *afa*   216
The Golden Serpent - Walter Dean Myers   *afa*   308

Alicea, Gil C. (16-Year-Old; Puerto Rican)
The Air Down Here: True Tales from a South Bronx Boyhood - Gil C. Alicea   *lat*   496

Alicia (Artist)
The Mixquiahuala Letters - Ana Castillo   *lat*   568

Alicia (Child; Mexican American)
Treasure Nap - Juanita Havill   *lat*   647

Allashua (Child; Inuit)
Hide and Seek - Michael Arvaarluk Kusugak   *naa*   1251
A Promise Is a Promise - Michael Arvaarluk Kusugak   *naa*   1253

Allende, Isabel (Child; Writer; Chilean)
Paula - Isabel Allende   *lat*   499

Almas, David (Veteran)
Shifting Loyalties - Daniel Cano   *lat*   559

Alston, Derek Andrew (Businessman; Uncle; African American)
The Nubian - Duane Smith   *afa*   393

Alta (Spouse; Mother; Latina)
Naked Ladies - Alma Luz Villanueva   *lat*   877

Amabel (Boar)
Rockabye Crocodile - Jose Aruego   *asa*   897

Amado (Leader; Mexican)
Jalamanta: A Message from the Desert - Rudolfo Anaya   *lat*   511

Amah (Child-Care Giver)
The Moon Lady - Amy Tan   *asa*   1081

Ambrosia (Niece)
Uncle Nacho's Hat = El Sombrero de Tio Nacho - Harriet Rohmer   *lat*   793

Amifika (Child; Cousin; African American)
Amifika - Lucille Clifton   *afa*   62

Amir (12-Year-Old; Foster Child; African American)
The Gift Giver - Joyce Hansen   *afa*   174

Amparo (Mexican)
Cantora: A Novel - Sylvia Lopez-Medina   *lat*   686

Anderson, Everett (Child; African American)
Everett Anderson's 1-2-3 - Lucille Clifton   *afa*   65
Everett Anderson's Christmas Coming - Lucille Clifton   *afa*   66
Everett Anderson's Friend - Lucille Clifton   *afa*   67

Anderson, Everett (African American; Stepson)
Everett Anderson's Nine Month Long - Lucille Clifton   *afa*   68

Anderson, Everett (Child; African American)
Everett Anderson's Year - Lucille Clifton   *afa*   69

Anderson, Everett (6-Year-Old; African American)
Some of the Days of Everett Anderson - Lucille Clifton   *afa*   73

Anderson, Kimako (7-Year-Old; Sister; African American)
Kimako's Story - June Jordan   *afa*   237

Anderson, Kojie (Maintenance Worker; Widow(er); African American)
A Short Walk - Alice Childress   *afa*   57

Andrews, George (Businessman; Spouse; African American)
Mama Day - Gloria Naylor   *afa*   330

Andrews, Ophelia "Cocoa" (Granddaughter; Spouse; African American)
Mama Day - Gloria Naylor   *afa*   330

Angel (Child; Mexican)
Angel's Kite = La Estrella de Angel - Alberto Blanco   *lat*   544

Angel, Miguel (Mexican American)
The Rain God: A Desert Tale - Arturo Islas   *lat*   666

Angel, Miguel Chico (Homosexual; Writer; Mexican American)
Migrant Souls: A Novel - Arturo Islas   *lat*   665

Anibal (Spouse)
Sleep of the Innocents - Carole Fernandez   *lat*   603

Anita (Healer; Mexican)
Across the Great River - Irene Beltran Hernandez   *lat*   648

Anna Marie (Friend)
Halmoni and the Picnic - Sook Nyul Choi   *asa*   929

Annie (Child; Native American)
Annie and the Old One - Miska Miles   *naa*   1278

Antonio (Alcoholic; Chilean)
Longing - Maria Espinosa   *lat*   601

Anyanwu (Immortal; Telepath; Healer)
Wild Seed - Octavia Butler   *afa*   38

Arai, Takashi (Migrant Worker; Immigrant; Japanese)
Face of a Stranger - Yoji Yamaguchi   *asa*   1107

Arenas, Reinaldo (Homosexual; Prisoner; Cuban)
Before Night Falls - Reinaldo Arenas   *lat*   521

Armijo, Nicolas (Brother; Father; Mexican American)
Leonor Park - Nash Candelaria   *lat*   555

Armstrong, Willie (Convict; African American)
Witherspoon - Lance Jeffers   *afa*   213

Arrow, Chris (17-Year-Old; Brother; Caucasian)
Adventure in Granada - Walter Dean Myers   *afa*   299
Ambush in the Amazon - Walter Dean Myers   *afa*   300
Duel in the Desert - Walter Dean Myers   *afa*   304
The Hidden Shrine - Walter Dean Myers   *afa*   309

Arrow, Ken (14-Year-Old; Brother; Caucasian)
Adventure in Granada - Walter Dean Myers   *afa*   299
Ambush in the Amazon - Walter Dean Myers   *afa*   300
Duel in the Desert - Walter Dean Myers   *afa*   304
The Hidden Shrine - Walter Dean Myers   *afa*   309

Arturo (Son; Homosexual; Cuban)
Old Rosa: A Novel in Two Stories - Reinaldo Arenas   *lat*   523

Ashok (Child; Indian American)
Ashok by Any Other Name - Sandra S. Yamate   *asa*   1110

Atariba (Child; Puerto Rican)
Atariba and Niguayona: A Story from the Taino People of Puerto Rico - Harriet Rohmer   *lat*   790

Atencio, Ephanie (Native American)
The Woman Who Owned the Shadows - Paula Gunn Allen   *naa*   1142

Augusta (Aunt; Teacher)
Family Resemblances - Lowry Pei   *asa*   1046

"Aunt Tiger" (Aunt; Korean)
Year of Impossible Goodbyes - Sook Nyul Choi   *asa*   930

Aurelio (Teenager; Italian)
New York City: Too Far from Tampa Blues - T. Ernesto Bethancourt   *lat*   542

Aurelio (Teenager; Student—High School; Italian)
T.H.U.M.B.B. - T. Ernesto Bethancourt   *lat*   543

Autrie (Child; Sister; African American)
Indigo and Moonlight Gold - Jan Spivey Gilchrist   *afa*   137

Avery, Mary Elouise (9-Year-Old; Sister; African American)
Thank You, Dr. Martin Luther King, Jr.! - Eleanora E. Tate   *afa*   406

Avery, Shug (Singer; Bisexual; African American)
The Color Purple - Alice Walker   *afa*   426

Ayam, Isshee (Writer; African American)
Platitudes - Trey Ellis   *afa*   111

Azalea, Arnold (Friend; Classmate)
Donald Duk - Frank Chin   *asa*   924

B

Baba (Father; Immigrant; Chinese American)
China Men - Maxine Hong Kingston   *asa*   971

Baca, Sonny (Detective—Private; Chicano)
Rio Grande Fall - Rudolfo Anaya   *lat*   512
Zia Summer - Rudolfo Anaya   *lat*   515

Baek Hongyang (Grandmother; Korean)
Still Life With Rice: A Young American Woman Discovers the Life and Legacy of Her Korean Grandmother - Helie Lee   *asa*   986

Bailey (Cook; Restauranteur; African American)
Bailey's Cafe - Gloria Naylor   *afa*   328

Bak, Hyunsuk "Mother" (Mother; Korean)
Echoes of the White Giraffe - Sook Nyul Choi   *asa*   927
Year of Impossible Goodbyes - Sook Nyul Choi   *asa*   930

Bak, Inchun (Brother; Korean)
Year of Impossible Goodbyes - Sook Nyul Choi   *asa*   930

Bak, Sookan (15-Year-Old; Korean)
Echoes of the White Giraffe - Sook Nyul Choi   *asa*   927

Bak, Sookan (Student—College; Korean)
Gathering of Pearls - Sook Nyul Choi   *asa*   928

Bak, Sookan (Young Woman; Korean)
Year of Impossible Goodbyes - Sook Nyul Choi   *asa*   930

Baker, Andrew Jackson "Hawk" (12-Year-Old; Caucasian)
Mississippi Chariot - Harriette Gillem Robinet   *afa*   377

Baldwin, Dexter (Homosexual; Writer; African American)
A Hundred Days From Now - Steven Corbin   *afa*   83

Ball, Ian (Writer; African American)
Reckless Eyeballing - Ishmael Reed   *afa*   367

Bang, Joy Clarissa (Entertainer; Neglected Child; African American)
Joy - Marsha Hunt   *afa*   207

Banks, Zora (Epileptic; Singer; African American)
Disappearing Acts - Terri McMillan   *afa*   266

Banzar (Musician; Son; African American)
The Singing Man - Angela Shelf Medearis   *afa*   272

Barbour, Talley (Student—High School; Runner; African American)
A White Romance - Virginia Hamilton   *afa*   171

Barbra (11-Year-Old; Twin; African American)
Whose Side Are You On? - Emily Moore   *afa*   280

Barcia, Pedro (14-Year-Old; Peddler; Gypsy)
Adventure in Granada - Walter Dean Myers   *afa*   299

Barnes, Mae Lee (Aged Person; Divorced Person; African American)
Her Own Place - Dori Sanders   *afa*   380

Barnett, Jonathan (17-Year-Old; Homosexual; Caucasian)
Those Other People - Alice Childress   *afa*   58

Barnett, Nola (Mother; African American)
One Dark Body - Charlotte Sherman   *afa*   389

Barnett, Septeema "Raisin" (Student; African American)
One Dark Body - Charlotte Sherman   *afa*   389

Barraza, Anthony Cemore (Coach)
China Boy - Gus Lee   *asa*   985

Barry, Meshach Coriolanus (Student; Religious; African American)
A Chocolate Soldier - Cyrus Colter   *afa*   75

Bass, Robert Jr. (Racist; Student—College; Caucasian)
Japanese by Spring - Ishmael Reed   *afa*   364

Basu, Amit (Husband; Engineer)
Wife - Bharati Mukherjee   *asa*   1032

Basu, Dimple Dasgupta (Young Woman; Immigrant; Indian)
Wife - Bharati Mukherjee   *asa*   1032

Bearchild, Edgar (Native American)
Black Eagle Child - Ray A. Young Bear   *naa*   1351

Beaufort, Victor (Financier; Oil Industry Worker; African American)
Black Gold - Anita Richmond Bunkley   *afa*   30

Beaver (Beaver)
Lakota & Dakota Animal Wisdom Stories - Pamela Greenhill Kaizen   *naa*   1237

Bechet, Clothilde "Chloe" (Entertainer; African American; Sister)
Colorstruck - Benita Porter   *afa*   352

Bechet, Solomon (Director; African American; Brother)
Colorstruck - Benita Porter   *afa*   352

Beckett, Kelsey (Businesswoman; Lesbian; Caucasian)
In the Game - Nikki Baker   *afa*   5

Bee, Tom (Aged Person; African American)
The Friendship - Mildred D. Taylor   *afa*   407

The Bees (Bee)
Toad Is the Uncle of Heaven - Jeanne M. Lee   *asa*   990

Belen, Maria de (Aged Person; Royalty; Aztec)
Maria Belen: The Autobiography of an Indian Woman: A Novel - Graciela Limon   *lat*   680

Bell, Jason (12-Year-Old; African American)
The Bells of Christmas - Virginia Hamilton   *afa*   157

Beloved (Spirit; 2-Year-Old; African American)
Beloved - Toni Morrison   *afa*   281

Beltran, Hector (7th Grader; Chicano)
Crazy Weekend - Gary Soto   *lat*   826

Bemis, Charlie (Spouse)
Thousand Pieces of Gold - Ruthanne Lum McCunn   *asa*   1016

Bemis, Lalu Nathoy "Polly" (Slave; Chinese American)
Thousand Pieces of Gold - Ruthanne Lum McCunn   *asa*   1016

Ben Loy (Spouse; Chinese)
Eat a Bowl of Tea - Louis Chu   *asa*   931

Benbow, Arden (Professor; Mother; Chicana)
Faultline: A Novel - Sheila Ortiz Taylor   *lat*   848

Benbow, Arden (Professor; Mother)
Southbound: The Sequel to Faultline - Sheila Ortiz Taylor   *lat*   849

Benneck, Faye (12-Year-Old; Student; Caucasian)
Project Wheels - Jacqueline Turner Banks   *afa*   11

Benson, Mattie Mae (12-Year-Old; African American)
Breadsticks and Blessing Places - Candy Dawson Boyd   *afa*   16

Benton, Kyle (Homosexual; African American)
Just as I Am - E. Lynn Harris   *afa*   181

Beppy (Child; Sister; African American)
The Train to LuLu's - Elizabeth Fitzgerald Howard   *afa*   204

Berg, Caroline (13-Year-Old; 8th Grader; Caucasian)
Between Madison & Palmetto - Jacqueline Woodson   *afa*   472

Big Bear, Harlen (Activist; Native American)
Medicine River - Thomas King   *naa*   1246

Big Bird (Drug Dealer; 15-Year-Old; African American)
Children of the Night - Jess Mowry   *afa*   293

Big Lee (Father)
The Ghost Fox - Laurence Yep   *asa*   1121

Bilal, Muhammad (11-Year-Old; Kidnap Victim; African)
Glory Field - Walter Dean Myers   *afa*   307

Bird (Businesswoman; Vampire; Indian)
Gilda Stories - Jewelle Gomez   *afa*   141

Bird (Bird)
Nine-in-One Grr! Grr! - Blia Xiong   *asa*   1106

Bishop, Simon (Spouse; Writer)
The Hundred Secret Senses - Amy Tan   *asa*   1078

Black, Tomsson (Revolutionary; Convict; African American)
Plan B - Chester Himes   *afa*   196

Black Raven (Native American; Child)
Moon of the Big-Dog - Jay Leech   *naa*   1258

Blackman, Abraham (Military Personnel; African American)
Captain Blackman - John A. Williams   *afa*   458

Blake, Alexander (Homosexual; Nobleman; Caucasian)
Free - Marsha Hunt   *afa*   206

Blanca (Young Woman; Puerto Rican)
A Perfect Silence - Alba Ambert   *lat*   505

Bloom (Nurse)
Baby of the Family - Tina McElroy Ansa   *afa*   1

Blue, Gil (Worker; Thief)
White Leg - Max Martinez   *lat*   696

Bobby (Brother; Chinese American)
Later, Gator - Laurence Yep   *asa*   1123

Bodeen, Lucas (Musician; African American)
Another Good Loving Blues - Arthur Flowers   *afa*   124

Boggs, Connie (11-Year-Old; Child of Divorced Parents; African American)
The World of Daughter McGuire - Sharon Dennis Wyeth   *afa*   479

Bokhi (Girlfriend; Student; Refugee)
Echoes of the White Giraffe - Sook Nyul Choi   *asa*   927

Bonillo, Stephanie (15-Year-Old)
Sweet Fifteen - Diane Gonzales Bertrand   *lat*   636

Bonner, Artemis (15-Year-Old; Nephew; African American)
The Righteous Revenge of Artemis Bonner - Walter Dean Myers   *afa*   321

Bonovox (Teacher)
Elaine and the Flying Frog - Heidi Chang   *asa*   916

Booker, Roscoe L. "Dogface" (African American; Worker; Convict)
The True American: A Folk Fable - Melvin Van Peebles   *afa*   423

Bow Priest (Zuni Indian)
The Boy Who Made Dragonfly - Tony Hillerman   *naa*   1227

Boy (Child)
The City of Dragons - Laurence Yep   *asa*   1119

Bradley (Businessman; African American)
Another Present Era - Elaine Perry   *afa*   342

Bradley, Solomon (Lawyer; Convict; African American)
The Road to Memphis - Mildred D. Taylor   *afa*   411

Braithwaite, Cecil Otis (Graduate; Maintenance Worker; Spouse)
Hurry Home - John Edgar Wideman   *afa*   448

Braithwaite, Esther Brown (Abuse Victim; Spouse; Maintenance Worker)
Hurry Home - John Edgar Wideman   *afa*   448

Brandon (7-Year-Old; Brother; African American)
Two and Too Much - Mildred Pitts Walter   *afa*   441

Brazil, Bubbles (Student; Teenager; Caucasian)
Negrophobia: An Urban Parable - Darius James   *afa*   212

Breedlove, Pecola (11-Year-Old; Abuse Victim)
The Bluest Eye - Toni Morrison   *afa*   282

Bright, Elena "Lena" Cecilia (12-Year-Old; Sister; Caucasian)
I Hadn't Meant to Tell You This - Jacqueline Woodson   *afa*   475

Bright Morning (14-Year-Old; Native American)
Sing Down the Moon - Scott O'Dell   *naa*   1289

Brodie, T.J. (11-Year-Old; Tutor; African American)
Whose Side Are You On? - Emily Moore   *afa*   280

Brooks, Louise (Dancer; Sister; African American)
No Easy Place to Be - Steven Corbin   *afa*   84

Brooks, Miriam (Activist; Nurse; African American)
No Easy Place to Be - Steven Corbin   *afa*   84

Brooks, Velma (Sister; Writer; African American)
No Easy Place to Be - Steven Corbin   *afa*   84

Brother (Brother)
Citizen 13660 - Mine Okubo   *asa*   1044

Brown, Adlai (Writer; African American)
South Street - David Bradley   *afa*   20

Brown, "B.J." (13-Year-Old; Runaway; African American)
The Survivors - Kristin Hunter   *afa*   211

Brown, Crystal (16-Year-Old; Model; African American)
Crystal - Walter Dean Myers   *afa*   302

Brown, Elizabeth "Betsey" (13-Year-Old; Sister; African American)
Betsey Brown - Ntozake Shange   *afa*   383

Brown, Frolic D. "Laughing Bear" (12-Year-Old; Orphan; Native American)
The Righteous Revenge of Artemis Bonner - Walter Dean Myers   *afa*   321

Brown, Greer (Doctor; Father; African American)
Betsey Brown - Ntozake Shange   *afa*   383

Brown, Jane (Mother; Social Worker; African American)
Betsey Brown - Ntozake Shange   *afa*   383

Brown, John (Computer Expert)
Golden Gate: A Novel in Verse - Vikram Seth   *asa*   1064

Brown, Junior (13-Year-Old; Musician; African American)
The Planet of Junior Brown - Virginia Hamilton   *afa*   169

Brown, Zambia Renelda (12-Year-Old; Crime Victim; African American)
A Blessing in Disguise - Eleanora E. Tate   *afa*   403

Bruno, Robert (Lover; Caucasian)
Frontiers of Love - Diana Chang *asa* 915

Bubba (Frontiersman; Scout; African American)
God's Country - Percival Everett *afa* 114

Buenrostro, Rafa (Young Man; Veteran; Chicano)
Claros Varones de Belken = Fair Gentlemen of Belken County - Rolando Hinojosa *lat* 658

Buenrostro, Rafe (Young Man; Texas Mexican)
Klail City: A Novel - Rolando Hinojosa *lat* 659

Buenrostro, Rafe (Military Personnel; Veteran; Texas Mexican)
The Useless Servants - Rolando Hinojosa *lat* 660

Builds-the-Fire, Thomas (Storyteller; Native American)
The Lone Ranger and Tonto Fist Fight in Heaven - Sherman Alexie *naa* 1137

Builds-the-Fire, Thomas (Storyteller; Musician; Native American)
Reservation Blues - Sherman Alexie *naa* 1138

Bukay, Noddaman (Patient; Scientist; African American)
Changes - Richard Perry *afa* 343

Bulosan, Carlos (Writer; Immigrant)
America Is in the Heart - Carlos Bulosan *asa* 910

Bulosan, Leon (Brother)
America Is in the Heart - Carlos Bulosan *asa* 910

Bulosan, Macario (Brother)
America Is in the Heart - Carlos Bulosan *asa* 910

Bultron, Sina Rosa (Friend; Widow(er); Healer)
The Red Comb - Fernando Pico *lat* 755

Buni (Friend; Inventor; African American)
Captain Africa: The Battle for Egyptica - Dwayne J. Ferguson *afa* 120

Burke, Kelleen (Classmate)
Elaine and the Flying Frog - Heidi Chang *asa* 916

Butler, Hoyt "Cap'n" (Businessman; Landowner; Caucasian)
The Avenue, Clayton City - C. Eric Lincoln *afa* 245

Butler, William "Beans" (Convict; Student—College; African American)
House of Slammers - Nathan Heard *afa* 192

Bweela (Child; Sister; African American)
Daddy Is a Monster. . .Sometimes - John Steptoe *afa* 397
My Special Best Words - John Steptoe *afa* 400

C

Caballos, Manny (Businessman)
The Devil, Delfina Varela, and the Used Chevy - Louie Garcia Robinson *lat* 783

Cabot, Evan (Model; Father; Caucasian)
Fragments That Remain - Steven Corbin *afa* 82

Cain, Albert (Father; Wealthy; Caucasian)
Black Betty - Walter Mosley *afa* 287

Calderon, Ana (Young Woman; Mexican)
The Memories of Ana Calderon: A Novel - Graciela Limon *lat* 681

Calhoun, Rutherford (Stowaway; Thief; African American)
Middle Passage - Charles Johnson *afa* 226

Cambon-Fournier, Cecile Stephanie (Doctor; Spouse; French)
City of Light - Cyrus Colter *afa* 76

Cammy (Cousin; Granddaughter; African American)
Cousins - Virginia Hamilton *afa* 158

Campos, Julian (Worker; Refugee; Cuban)
The Cutter: A Novel - Virgil Suarez *lat* 842

Capture, Cecelia (Native American; Alcoholic)
The Jailing of Cecelia Capture - Janet Campbell Hale *naa* 1224

Cardenas, Nenita (Young Woman; Mexican American)
Intaglio: A Novel in Six Stories - Roberta Fernandez *lat* 605

Carlos (Child; Mexican)
Carlos and the Cornfield: Story = Carlos y la Milpa de Maiz: Cuento - Jan Romero Stevens *lat* 840
Carlos and the Squash Plant/Carlos y la Planta de Calabaza - Jan Romero Stevens *lat* 841
The Gift of the Poinsettia = El Regalo de la Flor de Nochebuena - Pat Mora *lat* 719

Carlotta (Professor; African American)
The Temple of My Familiar - Alice Walker *afa* 430

Carmello "Mello" (18-Year-Old; Salesman; Latino)
Fast Talk on a Slow Track - Rita Williams-Garcia *afa* 466

Carson, Margie (9-Year-Old; Sister; African American)
Just an Overnight Guest - Eleanora E. Tate *afa* 404

Carson, Tyler (Homosexual; Journalist; Caucasian)
Keeping Secrets - Penny Mickelbury *afa* 276

Carter, Rosalyn (Girlfriend; African American)
Emergency Exit - Clarence Major *afa* 247

Carver, George Abraham "Abe" (Convict; Veteran; African American)
The True American: A Folk Fable - Melvin Van Peebles *afa* 423

Casas, Juani (Lesbian; Cuban American)
Memory Mambo: A Novel - Achy Obejas *lat* 739

Castillo, Cesar (Musician; Brother; Cuban)
The Mambo Kings Play Songs of Love - Oscar Hijuelos *lat* 655

Castillo, Nestor (Musician; Brother; Cuban)
The Mambo Kings Play Songs of Love - Oscar Hijuelos *lat* 655

Castle, Emanuel "Manny" Aaron (Nephew; African American)
The Nubian - Duane Smith *afa* 393

Cat (Cat)
Cat and Rat: The Legend of the Chinese Zodiac - Ed Young *asa* 1128

Cavazos, Heraclio (Immigrant; Mexican)
Rainbow's End - Genaro Gonzalez *lat* 638

Cecilia (Child)
A Birthday Basket for Tia - Pat Mora *lat* 717

Cedar, Encanta "EC" (Lesbian; Student; African American)
From the Notebooks of Melanin Sun - Jacqueline Woodson *afa* 474

Celia (Student; Secretary; African American)
In the Shadow of the Peacock - Grace Edwards-Yearwood *afa* 109

Celia del Pino (Grandmother; Revolutionary; Cuban)
Dreaming in Cuban, A Novel - Cristina Garcia *lat* 617

Celie (Abuse Victim; Lesbian; African American)
The Color Purple - Alice Walker *afa* 426

Chagla (Clerk)
A River Sutra - Gita Mehta *asa* 1018

Chan, Chuck (Lawyer)
Yellow Fever - R.A. Shiomi *asa* 1067

Chan, Rainsford (Orphan; Chinese American)
Homebase - Shawn Wong *asa* 1105

Chan Fong Mei (Spouse)
Disappearing Moon Cafe - Sky Lee *asa* 998

Chang, Carlos Cipriano (Father; Chinese Panamanian)
A Feather on the Breath of God - Sigrid Nunez *asa* 1041

Chang, Helen (Spouse)
Typical American - Gish Jen *asa* 960

Chang, Ralph Yifeng (Student; Businessman)
Typical American - Gish Jen *asa* 960

Chang, Theresa (Sister; Doctor)
Typical American - Gish Jen *asa* 960

Charlie (Child; Chinese American)
Char Siu Bao Boy - Sandra S. Yamate *asa* 1111

Charlie (Child; Brother; African American)
Train Ride - John Steptoe *afa* 401

Chato (Cat)
Chato's Kitchen - Gary Soto *lat* 825

Chee, Jim (Police Officer; Native American)
Coyote Waits - Tony Hillerman *naa* 1228

Chelvaratnam, Arjun "Arjie" (Young Man; Sri Lankan)
Funny Boy - Shyam Selvadurai *asa* 1063

Chelvaratnam, Nalini (Mother)
Funny Boy - Shyam Selvadurai *asa* 1063

Chen, April (Student—High School; Chinese American)
April and the Dragon Lady - Lensey Namioka *asa* 1034

Chen, Gilbert (Father; Son; Chinese American)
April and the Dragon Lady - Lensey Namioka *asa* 1034

Chen, Grandma (Grandmother; Chinese American)
April and the Dragon Lady - Lensey Namioka *asa* 1034

Chen, Harry (Brother; Chinese American)
April and the Dragon Lady - Lensey Namioka *asa* 1034

Chen, Sylvia (Young Woman; Chinese Caucasian)
Frontiers of Love - Diana Chang *asa* 915

Chen Li-sha (Friend; Daughter)
In the Eye of War - Margaret Chang *asa* 918

Chen Liyi (Businessman; Father; Chinese)
Frontiers of Love - Diana Chang *asa* 915

Cheng Ming (Farmer)
The Cricket Warrior: A Chinese Tale - Margaret Chang *asa* 917

Chew, Tallulah Bankhead "Booger" (Friend)
Child of the Owl - Laurence Yep *asa* 1118

Chibi (Duck)
Chibi: A True Story from Japan - Barbara Brenner *asa* 906

Chibi "Crow Boy" (Child)
Crow Boy - Taro Yashima *asa* 1114

Ch'idzigyaak (Aged Person; Native American)
Two Old Women: An Alaskan Legend of Betrayal, Courage, and Survival - Verlma Wallis *naa* 1341

Child (Child)
Peace Crane - Sheila Hamanaka *asa* 946

Chin, Duncan (Child; Chinese American)
Growing Up on Grove Street 1931-1946 - Duncan Chin *asa* 921

Ch'in Shih Huang (Ruler)
The Seven Chinese Brothers - Margaret Mahy *asa* 1011

Chipmunk (13-Year-Old; African American)
Children of the Night - Jess Mowry *afa* 293

Chita (Child; Cousin; African American)
Chita's Christmas Tree - Elizabeth Fitzgerald Howard *afa* 201
Papa Tells Chita a Story - Elizabeth Fitzgerald Howard *afa* 203

Choe, Sok-Won (Mother)
Home Was the Land of Morning Calm: The Saga of a Korean American Family - K. Connie Kang *asa* 965

Chota, John (Police Officer; Puerto Rican)
The Comeback - Ed Vega *lat* 871

Chou (Mother)
The Boy Who Swallowed Snakes - Laurence Yep *asa* 1117

Chow, Elaine (Student—Elementary School; Chinese American)
Elaine and the Flying Frog - Heidi Chang *asa* 916

Chow Yun-lung (Friend)
In the Eye of War - Margaret Chang *asa* 918

Choy, Isabel Pacay (16-Year-Old; Mayan)
Imagining Isabel - Omar Castaneda *lat* 565

Choy, Nona (Aunt)
A Little Too Much Is Enough - Kathleen Tyau *asa* 1086

Christine (Native American; Mother)
A Yellow Raft in Blue Water - Michael Dorris *naa* 1201

Christmas, Moses Lincoln (14-Year-Old; Slave; African American)
If You Please, President Lincoln - Harriette Gillem Robinet *afa* 375

Chun, Faye Inyoung (Daughter)
Clay Walls - Ronyoung Kim *asa* 968

Chun, Haesu (Immigrant; Daughter; Korean)
Clay Walls - Ronyoung Kim *asa* 968

Chun, Youngjune (Immigrant; Husband; Korean)
Clay Walls - Ronyoung Kim *asa* 968

Chung, Eric (Student—College; Businessman)
The Incorporation of Eric Chung - Steven Lo *asa* 1005

Chung, Maibelle (Photographer)
Face - Aimee Liu *asa* 1004

Cindy (Child; Native American)
The Chichi Hoohoo Bogeyman - Virginia Driving Hawk Sneve *naa* 1313

Cipriano, Christa (Mother; German)
A Feather on the Breath of God - Sigrid Nunez *asa* 1041

Clark, Buddy (13-Year-Old; Streetperson; African American)
The Planet of Junior Brown - Virginia Hamilton *afa* 169

Clive (Gang Member; Teenager; African American)
Straight Outta Compton - Ricardo Cortez Cruz *afa* 87

Clora (12-Year-Old; Mother; African American)
Family - J. California Cooper *afa* 79

Coco (Sister; Teenager; African American)
Ten Seconds - Louis Edwards *afa* 108

Cogewea "The Half Blood" (Cowgirl; Native American)
Cogewea - Mourning Dove *naa* 1284

Coile, Weber "Web" (12-Year-Old; Student—Junior High; Caucasian)
Hold Fast to Dreams - Andrea Davis Pinkney *afa* 348

Cole, Burley (Husband; Invalid; African American)
Seduction by Light - Al Young *afa* 481

Cole, Larry (Detective—Homicide; African American)
Chicago Blues - Hugh Holton *afa* 197
Presumed Dead - Hugh Holton *afa* 198

Cole, Larry (Detective—Homicide; Father; African American)
Windy City - Hugh Holton *afa* 199

Coles, Shelby (Young Woman; African American)
The Wedding - Dorothy West *afa* 445

Collins, Angela (12-Year-Old; Student; African American)
Project Wheels - Jacqueline Turner Banks *afa* 11

Collins, Eva (15-Year-Old; Student—High School; African American)
The Girl on the Outside - Mildred Pitts Walter *afa* 433

Collins, Joyce Alicia (15-Year-Old; Bastard Daughter; Dancer)
Blue Tights - Rita Williams-Garcia *afa* 465

Colon, Cristobal (Military Personnel; Explorer; Spanish)
The Aztec Chronicles: The True History of Christopher Columbus, as Narrated by Quilaztli of Texcoco: A Novella - Joseph P. Sanchez *lat* 809

Colon, Diego (Young Man; Taino Indian)
The Indian Chronicles - Jose Barreiro *lat* 530

Colon, Francesca (Single Mother; Police Officer; Puerto Rican)
Streets of Fire - Soledad Santiago *lat* 818

Columbus, Stone (Trickster)
The Heirs of Columbus - Gerald Vizenor *naa* 1338

Conejo, Tio (Rabbit)
Rabbit Wishes - Linda Shute *lat* 821

Conner, Matthew (Friend; Chinese American)
Yang the Youngest and His Terrible Ear - Lensey Namioka *asa* 1036

Connie (Twin)
The Adventures of Connie and Diego = Las Aventuras de Connie y Diego - Maria Garcia *lat* 622

Contreras, Tony (Student—Junior High)
Pacific Crossing - Gary Soto *lat* 830

Contreras, Tony (14-Year-Old; Student—Junior High; Chicano)
Taking Sides - Gary Soto *lat* 836

Contreres, Consuelo (Teenager; Chicana)
Maravilla - Laura Del Fuego *lat* 590

Copeland, Brownfield (Son; Abandoned Child; African American)
The Third Life of Grange Copeland - Alice Walker *afa* 431

Copeland, Grange (Farmer; Father; African American)
The Third Life of Grange Copeland - Alice Walker *afa* 431

Copeland, Mem (Teacher; Wife; African American)
The Third Life of Grange Copeland - Alice Walker *afa* 431

Cordero, Esperanza (Child; Chicana)
The House on Mango Street - Sandra Cisneros *lat* 577

Corn Maiden (Zuni Indian; Deity)
The Boy Who Made Dragonfly - Tony Hillerman *naa* 1227

Coronado, Ricky (Young Man; Mexican American)
A Fabricated Mexican - Rick P. Rivera *lat* 778

Corwul, James (Religious; Terrorist; African American)
Witherspoon - Lance Jeffers *afa* 213

Costanza, Cheryl (Girlfriend; Student; Irish Italian)
Crossover - Dennis Williams *afa* 456

Covington, Paula (Businesswoman; Spouse; African American)
Company Man - Brent Wade *afa* 425

Covington, William "Billy" (Businessman; Spouse; African American)
Company Man - Brent Wade *afa* 425

Cox, Lily (Spouse; Mother; Caucasian)
Your Blues Ain't Like Mine - Bebe Moore Campbell *afa* 48

Coyote (Trickster)
Coyote & Little Turtle: Iisaw Niqw Yongosonhoya: A Traditional Hopi Tale - Herschel Talashoema *naa* 1328

Coyote (Coyote)
A Coyote Columbus Story - Thomas King *naa* 1244

Coyote (Trickster)
A Coyote Reader - William Bright *naa* 1170
Coyote Stories - Mourning Dove *naa* 1285
Elderberry Flute Song - Peter Blue Cloud *naa* 1163
Giving Birth to Thunder, Sleeping with His Daughter: Coyote Builds North America - Barry Lopez *naa* 1260
Green Grass, Running Water - Thomas King *naa* 1245
Hopi Coyote Tales/Instutuwutsi - Ekkehart Malotki *naa* 1262
Lakota & Dakota Animal Wisdom Stories - Pamela Greenhill Kaizen *naa* 1237
Ma'ii and Cousin Horned Toad - Shonto Begay *naa* 1150
When Coyote Howls: A Lavaland Fable - Robert Franklin Gish *naa* 1221

Coyote, Tony (Trickster)
Storyteller - Leslie Marmon Silko *naa* 1308

Crane, Aurora "Ro" (Lover; Photojournalist; Japanese)
American Knees - Shawn Wong *asa* 1104

Crawford, Mitchell "Mitch" Sylvester (Journalist; Homosexual; African American)
B-Boy Blues - Steven Corbin *afa* 81

Craxton, Darryl T. (Government Official; Caucasian)
A Red Death - Walter Mosley *afa* 290

Crews, Donald (Child; Brother; African American)
Bigmama's - Donald Crews *afa* 85
Shortcut - Donald Crews *afa* 86

Crocodile (Crocodile; Mother)
Rockabye Crocodile - Jose Aruego *asa* 897

Cronheim, Sterling (Artist; German American)
Another Present Era - Elaine Perry *afa* 342

Cross, Faith (Crime Victim; Prostitute; African American)
Faith and the Good Thing - Charles Johnson *afa* 225

Crow (Crow; Latino)
La Gran Fiesta - Francisco X. Mora *lat* 716

Crow, Jim (Dancer; Minstrel; Slave)
Darktown Strutters - Wesley Brown *afa* 27

Cruz, Morgana (Teenager)
Heartbeat, Drumbeat - Irene Beltran Hernandez *lat* 649

Cruz, Tito (12-Year-Old; Student—Junior High; Puerto Rican)
Scorpions - Walter Dean Myers *afa* 322

Cudjoe (Divorced Person; Writer; African American)
Philadelphia Fire - John Edgar Wideman *afa* 449

Cummings, Paul (Veteran; Writer; Caucasian)
Click Song - John A. Williams *afa* 459

Cunningham, Giles (Restauranteur; African American)
The Spyglass Tree - Albert Murray *afa* 298

Curtis, DeWayne (Businessman; Divorced Person; African American)
When Death Comes Stealing - Valerie Wilson Wesley *afa* 443

Cypress (Dancer; African American)
Sassafrass, Cypress and Indigo - Ntozake Shange *afa* 385

D

"Dad" (Father)
The Lost Lake - Allen Say *asa* 1058

Dale (Actor; African American)
Reflex and Bone Structure - Clarence Major *afa* 251

Damasco, Gloria (Detective—Private; Widow(er); Chicana)
Cactus Blood: A Mystery Novel - Lucha Corpi *lat* 580

Damasco, Gloria (Wife; Activist; Chicana)
Eulogy for a Brown Angel: A Mystery Novel - Lucha Corpi *lat* 582

Dambridge, Martha Jones (Aged Person; Grandmother; African American)
The Good Negress - A.J. Verdelle *afa* 424

Daniel (Child)
Smoky Night - Eve Bunting *lat* 550

Daniels, Steve (Boyfriend)
April and the Dragon Lady - Lensey Namioka *asa* 1034

Daniels, Vincereta "Viney" (Girlfriend; Mother; African American)
Daughters - Paule Marshall *afa* 254

Darlene (Child; Niece; African American)
Darlene - Eloise Greenfield *afa* 143

Darrow, Pesty (Adoptee; Friend; African American)
The Mystery of Drear House - Virginia Hamilton *afa* 167

Das, Gita (Student—College; Immigrant)
Love, Stars, and All That - Kirin Narayan *asa* 1037

David (Aged Person; Supernatural Being; African American)
Don't Play Us Cheap: A Harlem Party - Melvin Van Peebles *afa* 420

David (Child; Worker)
Radio Man = Don Radio: A Story in English and Spanish - Arthur Dorros *lat* 594

Davis, Charles "Chappie" (Coach; Hotel Worker; African American)
The Junior Bachelor Society - John A. Williams *afa* 461

Davis, Harriet (9-Year-Old; Student; African American)
Addy Learns a Lesson: A School Story - Connie Porter *afa* 353
Addy Saves the Day: A Summer Story - Connie Porter *afa* 354

Davis, Joey (10-Year-Old; Child of Divorced Parents; African American)
Chevrolet Saturdays - Candy Dawson Boyd *afa* 18

Dawkins, Dancer (Young Woman)
Dancer Dawkins and the California Kid - Willyce Kim *asa* 969
Dead Heat - Willyce Kim *asa* 970

Dawson (Military Personnel; Prisoner)
Fire and Rain - Oswald Rivera *lat* 777

Day, Miranda "Mama" (Healer; Aged Person; African American)
Mama Day - Gloria Naylor *afa* 330

de Alvarez, Bernardo (Plantation Owner; Businessman; Peruvian)
The Deaths of Don Bernardo - Barbara Mujica *lat* 728

de Hocus, Griever (Trickster)
Griever: An American Monkey King in China - Gerald Vizenor *naa* 1337

de las Casas, Ramon (Young Man; Dominican American)
Drown, Stories - Junot Diaz *lat* 591

de Mendoza y Soria, Santiago (Rancher; Father; Texas Mexican)
Caballero: A Historical Novel - Jovita Gonzalez Mireles *lat* 705

de Pareja, Juan (Slave; Spanish)
I, Juan de Pareja - Elizabeth Borton de Trevino *lat* 856

De Weese, Tana (Spouse)
Tripmaster Monkey: His Fake Book - Maxine Hong Kingston *asa* 972

Dead, Macon II (Father; Wealthy; African American)
Song of Solomon - Toni Morrison *afa* 284

Dead, Macon "Milkman" III (Son; Traveller; African American)
Song of Solomon - Toni Morrison *afa* 284

Dean, Michael (12-Year-Old; African American)
Mojo and the Russians - Walter Dean Myers *afa* 314

Deek (Drug Dealer; 16-Year-Old; African American)
Way Past Cool - Jess Mowry *afa* 295

Del Campo, Zeferino (Lawyer; Chicano)
The Silver Cloud Cafe - Alfredo Vea Jr. *lat* 868

Delaney, Koya (11-Year-Old; Sister; African American)
Koya Delaney and the Good Girl Blues - Eloise Greenfield *afa* 147

Delcano, Bernabe (Son; Salvadoran)
In Search of Bernabe - Graciela Limon *lat* 679

Delcano, Luz (Mother; Salvadoran)
In Search of Bernabe - Graciela Limon *lat* 679

DeLea, Rosa "Rowena" (18-Year-Old; Model; Caucasian)
Crystal - Walter Dean Myers *afa* 302

DeLisa, Antonio "Tuxedo Tony" (Organized Crime Figure)
Chicago Blues - Hugh Holton *afa* 197

Devadatta (Cousin)
Buddha - Demi *asa* 932

DeWitt, Margo (Businesswoman; Wealthy; Caucasian)
Windy City - Hugh Holton *afa* 199

DeWitt, Neil (Businessman; Wealthy; Caucasian)
Windy City - Hugh Holton *afa* 199

Diablo (Drug Dealer; Criminal; Latino)
Third and Indiana - Steven Lopez *lat* 684

Diane (Mother; African American)
Toning the Sweep - Angela Johnson *afa* 223

Diego (Twin)
The Adventures of Connie and Diego = Las Aventuras de Connie y Diego - Maria Garcia *lat* 622

Diego (Young Man; Deaf Person; Chicano)
Carry Me Like Water - Benjamin Alire Saenz *lat* 801

Diego (Child; Worker; Mexican American)
Radio Man = Don Radio: A Story in English and Spanish - Arthur Dorros *lat* 594

DiMaio, Joan (Activist; Journalist; Caucasian)
Lavender House Murder - Nikki Baker *afa* 6

Ding, Raymond (Administrator; Chinese American)
American Knees - Shawn Wong *asa* 1104

Ding, Woodrow "Wood" (Father)
American Knees - Shawn Wong *asa* 1104

Dingle, Jeffrey (9-Year-Old; Child Of Divorced Parents; African American)
Just My Luck - Emily Moore *afa* 278

Divina, Narcisa "Lola" (Grandmother; Filipino)
Dogeaters - Jessica Hagedorn *asa* 942

Dodd, Christopher Noel (11-Year-Old; Brother; Student)
Have a Happy. . . - Mildred Pitts Walter *afa* 434

Doi, Kogoro (Farmer; Friend)
Face of a Stranger - Yoji Yamaguchi *asa* 1107

Dominic, Frank (Businessman; Political Figure)
Albuquerque - Rudolfo Anaya *lat* 506

Fausto, Don (Aged Person; Traveller; Mexican American)
The Road to Tamazunchale - Ron Arias   *lat*   526

Felita (Child; Puerto Rican)
Felita - Nicholasa Mohr   *lat*   707

Felita (12-Year-Old; Puerto Rican)
Going Home - Nicholasa Mohr   *lat*   708

Fencepost, Frank (Native American)
Dance Me Outside - W.P. Kinsella   *naa*   1247
Moccasin Telegraph - W.P. Kinsella   *naa*   1248

Figueroa, Angela (16-Year-Old; Student; African American)
His Own Where - June Jordan   *afa*   236

Fillis, Norman (Maintenance Worker; Psychic; African American)
Montgomery's Children - Richard Perry   *afa*   344

Finley, Flossie (Child; African American)
Flossie and the Fox - Patricia C. McKissack   *afa*   260

Finney, Marshall Field (Student—High School; African American)
Right by My Side - David Haynes   *afa*   185

Finney, Sam (Father; Maintenance Worker; African American)
Right by My Side - David Haynes   *afa*   185

Firbug (Criminal)
Spidertown - Abraham Rodriguez Jr.   *lat*   785

Fletcher (Librarian)
Ashok by Any Other Name - Sandra S. Yamate   *asa*   1110

Fletcher, Ellie (Mother; Doctor)
Molly by Any Other Name - Jean Davies Okimoto   *asa*   1043

Fletcher, Gerald (Abuse Victim; African American)
Montgomery's Children - Richard Perry   *afa*   344

Fletcher, Molly Jane (Adoptee; Asian; 17-Year-Old)
Molly by Any Other Name - Jean Davies Okimoto   *asa*   1043

Fletcher, Paul (Father; Scientist)
Molly by Any Other Name - Jean Davies Okimoto   *asa*   1043

Flores, Alfredo (17-Year-Old; Mexican American)
The Me Inside of Me - T. Ernesto Bethancourt   *lat*   541

Flores, Maria Elizabeth "Nene" (Child)
Nene and the Horrible Math Monster - Marie Villanueva   *asa*   1094

Fong Yun (Brother; Businessman; Chinese)
On Gold Mountain: The One-Hundred-Year Odyssey of a Chinese-American Family - Lisa See   *asa*   1062

The Foolish Magistrate (Ruler)
The Chinese Siamese Cat - Amy Tan   *asa*   1077

Fools Crow (Native American; Religious)
Fools Crow - James Welch   *naa*   1344

Footman, Annie Moriah "Annie Rye" (10-Year-Old; Sister; African American)
Down in the Piney Woods - Ethel Footman Smothers   *afa*   394
Moriah's Pond - Ethel Footman Smothers   *afa*   395

Footman, Brat (12-Year-Old; Sister; African American)
Moriah's Pond - Ethel Footman Smothers   *afa*   395

Footman, Maybaby (14-Year-Old; Sister; African American)
Moriah's Pond - Ethel Footman Smothers   *afa*   395

Fortunato (Young Man; Revolutionary)
The Palace of the White Skunks - Reinaldo Arenas   *lat*   524

Foster, Jessie (Abuse Victim; Activist; African American)
And Do Remember Me - Marita Golden   *afa*   138

Francie (Young Woman; Niece)
In the Heart of the Valley of Love - Cynthia Kadohata   *asa*   963

Francisco (Native American)
House Made of Dawn - N. Scott Momaday   *naa*   1281

Franklin, Betty (Mother; Sister; African American)
Ten Seconds - Louis Edwards   *afa*   108

Franklin, Dana (Time Traveller; Writer; African American)
Kindred - Octavia Butler   *afa*   36

Franklin, Edward "Eddie" James (Father; Worker; African American)
Ten Seconds - Louis Edwards   *afa*   108

Franklin, Mamie (Maintenance Worker; Psychic; African American)
Seduction by Light - Al Young   *afa*   481

Franklin, Tanya (Child; Sister; African American)
The Patchwork Quilt - Valerie Flournoy   *afa*   122
Tanya's Reunion - Valerie Flournoy   *afa*   123

Freeman, Doretha (13-Year-Old; Sister; African American)
Sister - Eloise Greenfield   *afa*   150

Freeman, Malene (Adoptee; 17-Year-Old; African American)
Not Separate, Not Equal - Brenda Wilkinson   *afa*   455

Freitas, Amy (Daughter)
A Small Obligation and Other Stories of Hilo - Susan Nunes   *asa*   1040

French, Carl (Addict; Veteran; African American)
Sent for You Yesterday - John Edgar Wideman   *afa*   451

Frieda (Mother; Widow(er); African American)
In the Shadow of the Peacock - Grace Edwards-Yearwood   *afa*   109

Fuller, Lance (Military Personnel; Pilot; African American)
Wild Embers - Anita Richmond Bunkley   *afa*   33

Fuse, Joe Toranosuke Thor (Son; Japanese American)
Sushi and Sourdough - Tooru J. Kanazawa   *asa*   964

Fuse, Kennosuke "Ken" (Son; Japanese American)
Sushi and Sourdough - Tooru J. Kanazawa   *asa*   964

Fuse, Matajiro "Mat" (Pioneer; Immigrant; Japanese)
Sushi and Sourdough - Tooru J. Kanazawa   *asa*   964

Fuse, Yaso (Spouse; Japanese)
Sushi and Sourdough - Tooru J. Kanazawa   *asa*   964

G

Gabriel (Store Owner; African American)
Bailey's Cafe - Gloria Naylor   *afa*   328

Gabriel (Prisoner; Uncle; Cuban)
Singing to Cuba - Margarita Engle   *lat*   597

Gabriel, Kenneth (Actor; Homosexual; African American)
Traitor to the Race - Darieck Scott   *afa*   382

Gabriel, LaDonna (Mother; Prisoner; African American)
Heathens - David Haynes   *afa*   183

Gabriel, Marcus (Husband; Teacher; African American)
Heathens - David Haynes   *afa*   183

Gabriel, Verda (Mother; Grandmother; African American)
Heathens - David Haynes   *afa*   183

Galarza, Ernesto (Young Man; Immigrant; Mexican)
Barrio Boy - Ernesto Galarza   *lat*   615

Gallito (Rooster)
The Bossy Gallito - Lucia M. Gonzalez   *lat*   640

Ganifrockwala, Firoze (Student—College)
Love, Stars, and All That - Kirin Narayan   *asa*   1037

Gannon, Marci (Student—College)
Gathering of Pearls - Sook Nyul Choi   *asa*   928

Garboil, Frank (Professor; Puerto Rican Eskimo)
The Comeback - Ed Vega   *lat*   871

Garcia, Bobo (Young Man; Mechanic; Mexican American)
In Search of Snow - Luis Alberto Urrea   *lat*   864

Garcia, Carlos (Father; Doctor; Dominican)
How the Garcia Girls Lost Their Accents - Julia Alvarez   *lat*   502

Garcia, Feliciano (Young Man; Uncle; Mexican American)
George Washington Gomez - Americo Paredes   *lat*   750

Garcia, Laura "Mami" (Mother; Wife; Dominican)
How the Garcia Girls Lost Their Accents - Julia Alvarez   *lat*   502

Garcia, Roberto (17-Year-Old; Immigrant; Mexican Indian)
Macho! - Edmund Villasenor   *lat*   881

Garnett, Vernor (Lawyer; Father; Caucasian)
White Butterfly - Walter Mosley   *afa*   292

Gates, Constance "Cookie" (16-Year-Old; Cousin; Singer)
Like Sisters on the Homefront - Rita Williams-Garcia   *afa*   467

Gay-Neck (Pigeon)
Gay-Neck: The Story of a Pigeon - Dhan Gopal Mukerji   *asa*   1029

Geneia (Sister; Cuban)
Crazy Love - Elias Miguel Munoz   *lat*   729

George (Child; Nephew; African American)
Poppa's New Pants - Angela Shelf Medearis   *afa*   271

Ghond (Teacher; Animal Trainer; Aged Person)
Gay-Neck: The Story of a Pigeon - Dhan Gopal Mukerji   *asa*   1029

Ghosh, Samir (Brother; South Asian Canadian)
Coloured Pictures - Himani Bannerji   *asa*   903

Ghosh, Sujata (Student; South Asian Canadian)
Coloured Pictures - Himani Bannerji   *asa*   903

Gilda (Teenager; Vampire; African American)
Gilda Stories - Jewelle Gomez   *afa*   141

Gilda (Businesswoman; Vampire; Caucasian)
Gilda Stories - Jewelle Gomez   *afa*   141

Givens, Peter Joseph (13-Year-Old; Homosexual; African American)
The Color of Trees - Canaan Parker   *afa*   338

Glasser, Milt (Friend)
Wife - Bharati Mukherjee   *asa*   1032

Goins, Earl (13-Year-Old; Foundling; African American)
Won't Know Till I Get There - Walter Dean Myers   *afa*   326

Gokhale, Durgabai "Little Mother" (Doctor)
Nampally Road - Meena Alexander   *asa*   896

Golden, M'dear (Aged Person; Blind Person; African American)
Happy Birthday, Addy! A Springtime Story - Connie Porter   *afa*   358

Golden Flower (Young Woman)
Ling-Li and the Phoenix Fairy: A Chinese Folktale - Ellin Greene   *asa*   940

Gomez, Amalia (Divorced Person; Mother; Mexican American)
The Miraculous Day of Amalia Gomez: A Novel - John Rechy   *lat*   768

Gomez, George Washington (Young Man; Mexican American)
George Washington Gomez - Americo Paredes   *lat*   750

Gomez, Lupe (Child; Mexican)
Rain of Gold - Victor Villasenor   *lat*   882

Gonzaga, Dolores (Mother; Filipino)
Dogeaters - Jessica Hagedorn   *asa*   942

Gonzaga, Pucha (Cousin; Filipino)
Dogeaters - Jessica Hagedorn   *asa*   942

Gonzaga, Rio (Student; Filipino)
Dogeaters - Jessica Hagedorn   *asa*   942

Gonzalez, Abran (Adoptee; Boxer; Chicano)
Albuquerque - Rudolfo Anaya   *lat*   506

Gonzalez, America (Mother; Housekeeper; Puerto Rican)
America's Dream - Esmeralda Santiago   *lat*   813

Goodman, Absalom (Cancer Patient; Father; African American)
Losing Absalom - Alexs D. Pate   *afa*   341

Goodman, Gwen (Housewife; African American; Spouse)
Losing Absalom - Alexs D. Pate   *afa*   341

Goodman, Sonny (Businessman)
Losing Absalom - Alexs D. Pate   *afa*   341

Gordon (Gang Member; 13-Year-Old; African American)
Way Past Cool - Jess Mowry   *afa*   295

Graetz, Roger (Young Man; Guatemalan)
The Long Night of White Chickens - Francisco Goldman   *lat*   631

Graham, Dalton (Lawyer; Caucasian)
Wild Embers - Anita Richmond Bunkley   *afa*   33

Granados, Tristan (Student—College; Cuban American)
Tristan and the Hispanics - Jose Yglesias   *lat*   890

Grandfather (Grandfather; Immigrant)
Grandfather's Journey - Allen Say   *asa*   1056

Grandmother (Grandmother; Native American)
Annie and the Old One - Miska Miles   *naa*   1278

Grandmother (Grandmother)
Char Siu Bao Boy - Sandra S. Yamate   *asa*   1111

Grandmother (Grandmother; Vietnamese)
The Little Weaver of Thai-Yen Village - Tran Khanh Tuyet   *asa*   1083

Grandmother (Grandmother; Chinese)
The Scent of the Gods - Fiona Cheong   *asa*   919

Grandmother (Grandmother)
Stella: On the Edge of Popularity - Lauren Lee   *asa*   992

Grandmother Paw-Paw (Grandmother; Chinese)
Ribbons - Laurence Yep   *asa*   1126

Grandpa (Grandfather)
Blue Jay in the Desert - Marlene Shigekawa   *asa*   1065

Graves, Griselda (Widow(er); Caucasian)
Night Studies - Cyrus Colter   *afa*   77

Gray, Mercer (Mother; Slave; African American)
The Price of a Child - Lorene Cary   *afa*   51

Gray, Molly (Lawyer)
The Murderer Next Door - Rafael Yglesias   *lat*   893

Great Progenitor (Grandfather)
Baba: A Return to China upon My Father's Shoulders - Belle Yang   *asa*   1113

Green, Angelina (Teacher; African American)
Who Is Angelina? - Al Young   *afa*   484

Green, Cecil (Activist; Father; African American)
A Short Walk - Alice Childress   *afa*   57

Greene, Hermine Rose (Businesswoman; Paralegal; African American)
Crossing over Jordan - Linda Beatrice Brown   *afa*   26

Greene, Story Temple (Principal; Mother; African American)
Crossing over Jordan - Linda Beatrice Brown   *afa*   26

El Guero (Child; Mexican)
El Guero: A True Adventure Story - Elizabeth Borton de Trevino   *lat*   855

Guerrero, Salvador (Child; Mexican American)
Memorias: A West Texas Life - Salvador Guerrero   *lat*   646

Gueye, Aminata (Student; African)
I Get on the Bus - Reginald McKnight   *afa*   265

Gunner, Aaron (Detective—Private; Maintenance Worker; African American)
Fear of the Dark - Gar Anthony Haywood   *afa*   188
Not Long for This World - Gar Anthony Haywood   *afa*   190

Gunner, Aaron (Detective—Private)
You Can Die Trying - Gar Anthony Haywood   *afa*   191

Gusman (Uncle; Puerto Rican)
The Line of the Sun: A Novel - Judith Ortiz Cofer   *lat*   746

Gutherie, Willy "The California Kid" (Young Woman)
Dancer Dawkins and the California Kid - Willyce Kim   *asa*   969

Gutherie, Willy "The California Kid" (Friend; Waiter/Waitress)
Dead Heat - Willyce Kim   *asa*   970

Gutierrez, Lupe (Wife; Immigrant; Mexican)
The Plum Plum Pickers - Raymond Barrio   *lat*   531

Gutierrez, Manuel (Husband; Immigrant; Mexican)
The Plum Plum Pickers - Raymond Barrio   *lat*   531

Gutierrez, Sergio Alberto (Wealthy; Publisher; Mexican)
A Hundred Days From Now - Steven Corbin   *afa*   83

H

Hadley, Sheema (17-Year-Old; Student—High School; African American)
A Little Love - Virginia Hamilton   *afa*   164

Hah-nee (Child; Native American)
Hah-nee of the Cliff Dwellers - Mary Buff   *naa*   1178

Hale, John (Oil Industry Worker)
Mean Spirit - Linda Hogan   *naa*   1231

Half-Chicken (Chicken; Mexican)
Mediopollito = Half-Chicken - Alma Flor Ada   *lat*   489

Hallelujah (11-Year-Old; Orphan; African American)
Children of the Fire - Harriette Gillem Robinet   *afa*   374

Halmoni (Grandmother)
Halmoni and the Picnic - Sook Nyul Choi   *asa*   929

Hamilton, Faith (Sister; Pregnant Teenager; African American)
A Woman's Place - Marita Golden   *afa*   140

Hamilton, Henry Isaiah (Aged Person; Religious; African American)
Gone Quiet - Eleanor Taylor Bland   *afa*   14

Hancock, Everett (Spouse; Caucasian)
Blanche on the Lam - Barbara Neely   *afa*   333

Hanson, Holly (Student)
Yang the Third and Her Impossible Family - Lensey Namioka   *asa*   1035

Hardisen, Ethel (4-Year-Old; Cousin; African American)
Just an Overnight Guest - Eleanora E. Tate   *afa*   404

Harris, Afeni "Feni" (Child of an Alcoholic; Child of Divorced Parents; African American)
The Dear One - Jacqueline Woodson   *afa*   473

Harris, Bernadine (Accountant; Spouse; African American)
Waiting to Exhale - Terry McMillan   *afa*   269

Harwood, Jack (Convict)
The Indian Lawyer - James Welch   *naa*   1345

Hawkins, Andrew (Bastard Son; Slave; African American)
Oxherding Tale - Charles Johnson   *afa*   227

Hawkins, George (Servant; Slave)
Oxherding Tale - Charles Johnson   *afa*   227

Hawkins, Louretta "Lou" (16-Year-Old; Singer; African American)
Lou in the Limelight - Kristin Hunter   *afa*   210

Hawks, Robert (Scientist; African American)
Watershed - Percival Everett   *afa*   118

Hayakawa, Janet "Jan" (Artist; Musician)
Golden Gate: A Novel in Verse - Vikram Seth   *asa*   1064

Hayle, Tamara (Detective—Private; Divorced Person; African American)
Devil's Gonna Get Him - Valerie Wilson Wesley   afa   442

Hayle, Tamara (Divorced Person; Detective—Private; African American)
When Death Comes Stealing - Valerie Wilson Wesley   afa   443

Hector (Teenager; Chicano)
Summer on Wheels - Gary Soto   lat   835

Held, Truman (Activist; Artist; African American)
Meridian - Alice Walker   afa   428

Helen (Friend)
Halmoni and the Picnic - Sook Nyul Choi   asa   929

Helie, Lee (Granddaughter; Korean American; Rebel)
Still Life With Rice: A Young American Woman Discovers the Life and Legacy of Her Korean Grandmother - Helie Lee   asa   986

Helstrom, Bron (Researcher; Human)
Triton - Samuel R. Delany   afa   98

Hemings, Harriet (Daughter; Historical Figure; African American)
The President's Daughter - Barbara Chase-Riboud   afa   53

Hemings, Sally (Historical Figure; Mother; African American)
The President's Daughter - Barbara Chase-Riboud   afa   53
Sally Hemings - Barbara Chase-Riboud   afa   54

Henry, Harriet (Grandmother; African American)
Trouble the Water - Melvin Dixon   afa   99

Henry, Jacob "Jake" (Military Personnel; Diplomat; African American)
Jacob's Ladder - John A. Williams   afa   460

Henry, Jordan (Professor; African American)
Trouble the Water - Melvin Dixon   afa   99

Henry, Velma (Activist; Mother; African American)
The Salt Eaters - Toni Cade Bambara   afa   8

Herbie (African American; Father; Railroad Worker)
Tumbling - Diane McKinney-Whetstone   afa   258

Herman (Spirit)
The Hand I Fan With - Tina McElroy Ansa   afa   2

Hernandez, Chi-Chi (Prisoner; Puerto Rican)
Fire and Rain - Oswald Rivera   lat   777

Herrera, Rudy (Child)
Boys at Work - Gary Soto   lat   824

Herrera, Rudy (5th Grader)
The Pool Party - Gary Soto   lat   832

Hicks, Jamal (12-Year-Old; Student—Junior High; African American)
Scorpions - Walter Dean Myers   afa   322

Hicks, Sassy (8-Year-Old; 3rd Grader; African American)
Scorpions - Walter Dean Myers   afa   322

Hien (Refugee; Child; Vietnamese)
The Little Weaver of Thai-Yen Village - Tran Khanh Tuyet   asa   1083

Higgins, M.C. (Brother; African American)
M.C. Higgins, the Great - Virginia Hamilton   afa   165

High Elk, Joe (Native American; Young Man)
High Elk's Treasure - Virginia Driving Hawk Sneve   naa   1314

HighJohn, Tucept (African American; Occultist; Veteran)
De Mojo Blues - Arthur Flowers   afa   125

Hightower, Hortense (Entertainer; African American)
The Spyglass Tree - Albert Murray   afa   298

Hill, Clover (10-Year-Old; Stepdaughter; African American)
Clover - Dori Sanders   afa   379

Hill, Gaten (Father; Principal; African American)
Clover - Dori Sanders   afa   379

Hill, Holly Rachelle (Sister; Caucasian)
Holly - Albert French   afa   131

Hill, Meridian (Activist; Revolutionary; African American)
Meridian - Alice Walker   afa   428

Hill, Sara Kate Colson (Stepmother; Designer; Caucasian)
Clover - Dori Sanders   afa   379

Hill, Tony (Detective—Police; Spouse; Father)
Cold Medina - Gary Hardwick   afa   178

Hirada, Roland (Friend)
Molly by Any Other Name - Jean Davies Okimoto   asa   1043

Hisae Fujiitano (Grandmother; Immigrant; Japanese)
The Floating World - Cynthia Kadohata   asa   962

Hito, Nomi (Daughter; Japanese American)
A Bridge Between Us - Julie Shigekuni   asa   1066

Hito, Reiko (Grandmother; Japanese American)
A Bridge Between Us - Julie Shigekuni   asa   1066

Hito, Rio (Grandmother; Japanese American; Daughter)
A Bridge Between Us - Julie Shigekuni   asa   1066

Hito, Tomoe Kanemori (Granddaughter; Spouse; Japanese American)
A Bridge Between Us - Julie Shigekuni   asa   1066

Ho Kuan (Scholar)
Night Visitors - Ed Young   asa   1131

Hoi "Pie-Biter" (Immigrant; Railroad Worker)
Pie-Biter - Ruthanne Lum McCunn   asa   1015

Hoksila (Child; Native American)
Hoksila and the Red Buffalo - Moses Nelson Big Crow   naa   1157

Holloday, Deloretto "Imani" (Artist; Single Mother; African American)
Divine Days - Leon Forrest   afa   127

Holton, Roger (Businessman)
The Incorporation of Eric Chung - Steven Lo   asa   1005

Hong, Maxine (Daughter; Chinese American)
The Woman Warrior: Memoirs of a Girlhood Among Ghosts - Maxine Hong Kingston   asa   973

Hong, Mother (Chinese American; Mother)
The Woman Warrior: Memoirs of a Girlhood Among Ghosts - Maxine Hong Kingston   asa   973

Hong, Nancy (Child; Chinese)
Almond Cookies and Dragon Well Tea - Cynthia Chin-Lee   asa   925

Horn, Diane (Nurse; Lesbian; Caucasian)
Coffee Will Make You Black - April Sinclair   afa   392

Howard, Erica (Child; Caucasian)
Almond Cookies and Dragon Well Tea - Cynthia Chin-Lee   asa   925

Howard, Martha (Aged Person; Child-Care Giver; African American)
Rocking the Babies - Linda Raymond   afa   362

Howard, Michelle DuBois (Student—College)
Falling Leaves of Ivy - Yolanda Joe   afa   214

Howell, Brandy (9-Year-Old; 4th Grader; Caucasian)
Thank You, Dr. Martin Luther King, Jr.! - Eleanora E. Tate   afa   406

Hsu, An-Mei (Chinese American; Mother)
The Joy Luck Club - Amy Tan   asa   1079

Hua Mu Lan (Daughter)
China's Bravest Girl: The Legend of Hua Mu Lan - Charlie Chin   asa   920

Huang, Feng (Young Man; Friend)
Frontiers of Love - Diana Chang   asa   915

Huerta, Jorge (Journalist; Mexican)
Cinco de Mayo: An Epic Novel - David Monreal   lat   713

Huitzitzilin (Royalty; Aged Person; Aztec)
Song of the Hummingbird - Graciela Limon   lat   682

Hull, Cora (Actress)
Reflex and Bone Structure - Clarence Major   afa   251

Husband (Spouse)
Judge Rabbit and the Tree Spirit: A Folktale from Cambodia - Lina Mao Wall   asa   1095

Hutchinson, Aubrey (Designer; Homosexual; African American)
Fragments That Remain - Steven Corbin   afa   82

I

Ibarra, Magdalena (Doctor; Daughter; Mexican)
Doctor Magdalena: Novella - Rosa Martha Villarreal   lat   880

Ida (Native American; Grandparent)
A Yellow Raft in Blue Water - Michael Dorris   naa   1201

Imani (17-Year-Old; Psychic; African American)
An Open Weave - Devorah Major   afa   253

Indigo (Musician; African American)
Sassafrass, Cypress and Indigo - Ntozake Shange   afa   385

Ingram, Deborah (Mother; Wife; African American)
Emergency Exit - Clarence Major   afa   247

Ingram, James (Father; Husband; African American)
Emergency Exit - Clarence Major   afa   247

Inyan (Deity)
Otokahekagapi (First Beginnings): Sioux Creation Story - Ben Black Bear   naa   1159

Iree (Epileptic; Psychic; African American)
An Open Weave - Devorah Major   afa   253

Isaac, Elizabeth (Mother; African American)
Crossover - Dennis Williams   afa   456

Isaac, Richard "Ike" (Activist; Student—College; African American)
Crossover - Dennis Williams   afa   456

Ishi (Native American)
Ishi, Last of His Tribe - Theodora Kroeber   naa   1250

Isobe (Teacher)
Crow Boy - Taro Yashima   *asa*   1114

Ives, Edward (Artist; Father)
Mr. Ives' Christmas - Oscar Hijuelos   *lat*   656

Iyapo, Lilith (Captive; Mother; African American)
Dawn - Octavia Butler   *afa*   35

J

Jackson, Abraham Lincoln (12-Year-Old; African American)
Mississippi Chariot - Harriette Gillem Robinet   *afa*   377

Jackson, Abyssinia "Abby" (10-Year-Old; Singer; African American)
Marked by Fire - Joyce Carol Thomas   *afa*   418

Jackson, Andrew "Andy" (Basketball Player; Accident Victim; African American)
Tears of a Tiger - Sharon M. Draper   *afa*   102

Jackson, Billy "Moondance Kid" (Child; Adoptee; African American)
Me, Mop, and the Moondance Kid - Walter Dean Myers   *afa*   313
Mop, Moondance and Nagasaki Knights - Walter Dean Myers   *afa*   315

Jackson, Canada (Revolutionary; Actor; African American)
Reflex and Bone Structure - Clarence Major   *afa*   251

Jackson, Esther (Banker; Businesswoman; African American)
Brothers and Sisters - Bebe Moore Campbell   *afa*   47

Jackson, Lonnie (17-Year-Old; Basketball Player; African American)
Hoops - Walter Dean Myers   *afa*   310

Jackson, Lonnie (Student—College; Basketball Player; African American)
The Outside Shot - Walter Dean Myers   *afa*   320

Jackson, Savannah (Businesswoman; Single Mother; African American)
Waiting to Exhale - Terry McMillan   *afa*   269

Jackson, Tommy "T.J." (11-Year-Old; Adoptee; African American)
Me, Mop, and the Moondance Kid - Walter Dean Myers   *afa*   313
Mop, Moondance and Nagasaki Knights - Walter Dean Myers   *afa*   315

Jackson, Yolanda "Pump" (5th Grader; African American)
Growin' - Nikki Grimes   *afa*   154

Jadine (Model; Student; African American)
Tar Baby - Toni Morrison   *afa*   286

Jake (Child; Caucasian)
God's Country - Percival Everett   *afa*   114

James, Celestine (Friend; Native American)
The Beet Queen - Louise Erdrich   *naa*   1210

James, Cora (Orphan; Mother; African American)
A Short Walk - Alice Childress   *afa*   57

James, Dede (Judge; Spouse; African American)
The Between - Tananarive Due   *afa*   104

James, Genetta "Genny" (Child; African American)
Talk about a Family - Eloise Greenfield   *afa*   151

James, Hilton (Social Worker; Spouse; African American)
The Between - Tananarive Due   *afa*   104

James, Jesse (Husband; Father; African American)
After the Garden - Doris Jean Austin   *afa*   4

Janell (Child; African American)
Me and Neesie - Eloise Greenfield   *afa*   148

Jason (Hero; African American)
For Her Dark Skin - Percival Everett   *afa*   113

Jason (Child; Brother; African American)
My Mama Needs Me - Mildred Pitts Walter   *afa*   439

Jason (8-Year-Old; Slave; African American)
Out from This Place - Joyce Hansen   *afa*   175

Jay (8-Year-Old; Handicapped; Caucasian)
Jay and the Marigold - Harriette Gillem Robinet   *afa*   376

Jay (Child; Baseball Player; African American)
No Trespassing - Ray Prather   *afa*   361

Jdahya (Alien; Father; Teacher)
Dawn - Octavia Butler   *afa*   35

Jefferson (Convict; African American)
A Lesson before Dying - Ernest J. Gaines   *afa*   135

Jefferson, Carlton Lee (12-Year-Old; African American)
The Golden Pasture - Joyce Carol Thomas   *afa*   417

Jefferson, Crystal (Writer; Sister; African American)
A Woman's Place - Marita Golden   *afa*   140

Jefferson, Dorian (13-Year-Old; Healer; African American)
Dustland - Virginia Hamilton   *afa*   160

Jefferson, Dorian (13-Year-Old; Time Traveller; African American)
The Gathering - Virginia Hamilton   *afa*   161

Jefferson, Dorian (13-Year-Old; African American; Twin)
Justice and Her Brothers - Virginia Hamilton   *afa*   163

Jefferson, Grayson (Grandfather; Cowboy; African American)
The Golden Pasture - Joyce Carol Thomas   *afa*   417

Jefferson, Naomi (African American; Activist; Businesswoman)
Big Girls Don't Cry - Connie Briscoe   *afa*   22

Jefferson, Samuel (Father; African American)
The Golden Pasture - Joyce Carol Thomas   *afa*   417

Jefferson, Thomas (Father; Political Figure; Historical Figure)
The President's Daughter - Barbara Chase-Riboud   *afa*   53

Jefferson, Thomas (Father; Historical Figure; Caucasian)
Sally Hemings - Barbara Chase-Riboud   *afa*   54

Jeh (Friend; Chinese American)
Child of the Owl - Laurence Yep   *asa*   1118

Jenkins, Judge (Twin; Dyslexic; African American)
Egg-Drop Blues - Jacqueline Turner Banks   *afa*   9

Jenkins, Judge (12-Year-Old; Twin; African American)
The New One - Jacqueline Turner Banks   *afa*   10

Jenkins, Jury (Twin; Student; African American)
Egg-Drop Blues - Jacqueline Turner Banks   *afa*   9

Jenkins, Jury (12-Year-Old; Twin; African American)
The New One - Jacqueline Turner Banks   *afa*   10
Project Wheels - Jacqueline Turner Banks   *afa*   11

Jennings, Obidiah "Obi" (Slave; Runaway; African American)
Which Way Freedom? - Joyce Hansen   *afa*   176

Jerome (Child; Brother; African American)
Good, Says Jerome - Lucille Clifton   *afa*   70

Jerome "Jerry" (Sidekick)
Wild Meat and the Bully Burgers - Lois-Ann Yamanaka   *asa*   1109

Jesse (Student—College; Brother; Mexican American)
Jesse - Gary Soto   *lat*   827

Jessie (Friend)
Finding My Voice - Marie G. Lee   *asa*   994

Jessie (Sister)
Stranger in the Mirror - Allen Say   *asa*   1060

Jewett, Sherry (Student—College; Runner; African American)
The Outside Shot - Walter Dean Myers   *afa*   320

Jim Jim (5th Grader; African American)
Growin' - Nikki Grimes   *afa*   154

Jim "Ujamaa" (Child; Brother; African American)
All Us Come Cross the Water - Lucille Clifton   *afa*   61

Jive, Billy Jo (Child; Detective—Amateur; African American)
Billy Jo Jive and the Case of the Midnight Voices - John Shearer   *afa*   386
Billy Jo Jive, Super Private Eye: The Case of the Missing Ten Speed Bike - John Shearer   *afa*   387

Joaquin (Child; Immigrant; Mexican)
Friends From the Other Side/Amigos del Otro Lado - Gloria Anzaldua   *lat*   517

Jody (Student—High School; Friend)
The Great Computer Dating Caper - T. Ernesto Bethancourt   *lat*   540

John (Con Artist; Occultist; African American)
Voodoo Dreams: A Novel of Marie Laveau - Jewell Parker Rhodes   *afa*   370

Johnetta (8-Year-Old; Sister; African American)
My Brother Fine with Me - Lucille Clifton   *afa*   71

Johnson, Al (Political Figure; Spouse; African American)
Somebody Else's Mama - David Haynes   *afa*   186

Johnson, Avatara "Avey" (Mother; Widow(er); African American)
Praisesong for the Widow - Paule Marshall   *afa*   255

Johnson, Benjie (13-Year-Old; Addict; African American)
A Hero Ain't Nothin' but a Sandwich - Alice Childress   *afa*   55

Johnson, Beverly "Bev" (Businesswoman; Lesbian; African American)
In the Game - Nikki Baker   *afa*   5

Johnson, DiDi (17-Year-Old; Student—High School; African American)
Motown and Didi: A Love Story - Walter Dean Myers   *afa*   316

Johnson, Esther (Activist; Single Mother; African American)
Long Distance Life - Marita Golden   *afa*   139

Johnson, Jerome (11-Year-Old; Handicapped; African American)
Ride the Red Cycle - Harriette Gillem Robinet   *afa* 378

Johnson, Millicent "Peaches" (Student; 14-Year-Old; African American)
Peaches - Dindga McCannon   *afa* 256

Johnson, Naomi Reeves (Aged Person; Landlord; African American)
Long Distance Life - Marita Golden   *afa* 139

Johnson, Nettie Lee (Aged Person; Child-Care Giver; African American)
Rocking the Babies - Linda Raymond   *afa* 362

Johnson, Paula (Spouse; Teacher; African American)
Somebody Else's Mama - David Haynes   *afa* 186

Johnson, Robert (Musician)
Reservation Blues - Sherman Alexie   *naa* 1138

Johnson, Robert LeRoy "RL" (Musician; African American)
RL's Dream - Walter Mosley   *afa* 291

Johnson, Tashi (Evelyn) (Mentally Ill Person; African American)
Possessing the Secret of Joy - Alice Walker   *afa* 429

Johnson, Yolanda (Addict; Pregnant Teenager; African American)
Rocking the Babies - Linda Raymond   *afa* 362

Jones, Calvin "Spider" F. (Coach; Alcoholic; African American)
Hoops - Walter Dean Myers   *afa* 310

Jones, Claireece Precious (16-Year-Old; Abuse Victim; African American)
Push - Sapphire   *afa* 381

Jones, Clement (Political Figure; African American)
The Terrible Threes - Ishmael Reed   *afa* 368

Jones, Hannibal (Graduate; Veteran; African American)
Shannon - Gordon Parks   *afa* 340

Jones, Jim (11-Year-Old)
Hardscrub - Lionel G. Garcia   *lat* 619

Jones, Joubert Antoine (Stepson; Writer; African American)
Divine Days - Leon Forrest   *afa* 127

Jones, Lewis (Abuse Victim; Divorced Person; Caucasian)
Fish Tales - Nettie Jones   *afa* 234

Jones, Margaret (Mother; Office Worker; African American)
Philadelphia Fire - John Edgar Wideman   *afa* 449

Jones, Nia (15-Year-Old; Student—High School; Orphan)
Where Do I Go From Here? - Valerie Wilson Wesley   *afa* 444

Jones, Ruth Mae (Sister; African American)
In Search of Satisfaction - J. California Cooper   *afa* 80

Jones, Wilhemina Orphelia "Willi" (16-Year-Old; Artist; African American)
Wilhemina Jones, Future Star - Dindga McCannon   *afa* 257

Jong, Lindo (Friend; Mother; Chinese American)
The Joy Luck Club - Amy Tan   *asa* 1079

Jong, Waverly (Daughter; Chinese American)
The Joy Luck Club - Amy Tan   *asa* 1079

Jordan, Beverly (Editor; Sister; African American)
Sisters and Lovers - Connie Briscoe   *afa* 23

Jordan, Rainbow (14-Year-Old; Foster Child; African American)
Rainbow Jordan - Alice Childress   *afa* 56

Jordan, Rose Hsu (Daughter; Chinese American)
The Joy Luck Club - Amy Tan   *asa* 1079

Jose (Friend)
America Is in the Heart - Carlos Bulosan   *asa* 910

Jose (Child; Worker; Mexican American)
Jose's Basket - Karen Papagapitos   *lat* 748

Josefa (Aged Person)
The Gold Coin - Alma Flor Ada   *lat* 488

Joseph, Victor (Native American)
The Lone Ranger and Tonto Fist Fight in Heaven - Sherman Alexie   *naa* 1137

Josephus, Josephus (Father; African American)
In Search of Satisfaction - J. California Cooper   *afa* 80

Josh (Lover; Homosexual)
The Hidden Law - Michael Nava   *lat* 734
How Town: A Novel of Suspense - Michael Nava   *lat* 735

Joyce, Janes Philips (Lover)
Dead Heat - Willyce Kim   *asa* 970

Juan (Refugee; Cuban)
The Doorman - Reinaldo Arenas   *lat* 522

Juan (Thief)
The Gold Coin - Alma Flor Ada   *lat* 488

Juanita (Student—High School; Mexican American)
Juanita Fights the School Board - Gloria Velasquez   *lat* 873

Judge Rabbit (Mythical Creature)
Judge Rabbit and the Tree Spirit: A Folktale from Cambodia - Lina Mao Wall   *asa* 1095

Julian (Brother; Cuban)
Crazy Love - Elias Miguel Munoz   *lat* 729

Junior (Child)
Blue Jay in the Desert - Marlene Shigekawa   *asa* 1065

Justin (10-Year-Old; Brother; African American)
Justin and the Best Biscuits in the World - Mildred Pitts Walter   *afa* 435

K

Kalawati (Aged Person)
Aani and the Tree Huggers - Jeannine Atkins   *asa* 900

Kali (17-Year-Old; Mother; African American)
Her - Cherry Muhanji   *afa* 296

Kamik (Eskimo; Son)
Harpoon of the Hunter - Markoosie   *naa* 1265

Kamiyama, Lance (Friend)
Tripmaster Monkey: His Fake Book - Maxine Hong Kingston   *asa* 972

Kang, Joo-han (Father; Linguist)
Home Was the Land of Morning Calm: The Saga of a Korean American Family - K. Connie Kang   *asa* 965

Kang, K. Connie (Journalist)
Home Was the Land of Morning Calm: The Saga of a Korean American Family - K. Connie Kang   *asa* 965

Kang, Myong-Hwan (Grandfather; Revolutionary)
Home Was the Land of Morning Calm: The Saga of a Korean American Family - K. Connie Kang   *asa* 965

Kannadical, Mira (Professor)
Nampally Road - Meena Alexander   *asa* 896

Kanno, Kenji (Veteran; Friend; Japanese American)
No-No Boy - John Okada   *asa* 1042

Karen (Teenager; 15-Year-Old)
Family Resemblances - Lowry Pei   *asa* 1046

Kari (Child; African American)
Papa's Stories - Dolores Johnson   *afa* 229

Kashpaw, Nector (Native American)
Love Medicine - Louise Erdrich   *naa* 1213

Kat (Composer; Musician; African American)
Muse-Echo Blues - Xam Wilson Cartier   *afa* 50

Kata (Child; Immigrant; Mexican)
Across the Great River - Irene Beltran Hernandez   *lat* 648

Kataujag (Child; Inuit)
Northern Lights: The Soccer Trails - Michael Arvaarluk Kusugak   *naa* 1252

Katherine (Teacher)
Katherine - Anchee Min   *asa* 1019

Kato, Emily "Aunt Emily" (Aunt)
Obasan - Joy Kogawa   *asa* 975

Kato, Kyoshi (Friend)
One Bird - Kyoko Mori   *asa* 1025

Kaweli "James Covey" (Sailor; Linguist; African)
Echo of Lions - Barbara Chase-Riboud   *afa* 52

Kaya (8-Year-Old; Sister)
The Forever Christmas Tree - Yoshiko Uchida   *asa* 1088

Kelly (African American; Dancer; Singer)
The Best Bug to Be - Dolores Johnson   *afa* 228

Kelly, Virginia "Ginny" (Detective—Amateur; Businesswoman; Lesbian)
In the Game - Nikki Baker   *afa* 5
Lavender House Murder - Nikki Baker   *afa* 6
Long Goodbyes - Nikki Baker   *afa* 7

Kenny, Gene (Patient; Young Man; Caucasian)
Dr. Neruda's Cure for Evil - Rafael Yglesias   *lat* 891

Kessey, Paul (Activist; Researcher; African American)
City of Light - Cyrus Colter   *afa* 76

Kessey, Saturn Marie (Mother; Spouse; African American)
City of Light - Cyrus Colter   *afa* 76

Kevin (5-Year-Old)
Chopsticks from America - Elaine Hosozawa-Nagano   *asa* 955

Kevin (Child; Brother; African American)
She Come Bringing Me That Little Baby Girl - Eloise Greenfield   *afa* 149

Kevin (Child; Baseball Player; African American)
What Kind of Baby-Sitter Is This? - Dolores Johnson   *afa* 230

L

Lawson, Tommy (Addict; Thief; African American)
Damballah - John Edgar Wideman *afa* 446

Lawson, Tommy (Fugitive; Cousin; African American)
Hiding Place - John Edgar Wideman *afa* 447

Lazarre, Marie (Native American; Spouse)
Love Medicine - Louise Erdrich *naa* 1213

Lazarus, Robin (Student; African American)
Robin on His Own - Johnniece Marshall Wilson *afa* 470

Lazrus (Teacher; Musician; African American)
Robin on His Own - Johnniece Marshall Wilson *afa* 470

Leaphorn, Joe (Police Officer; Native American)
Coyote Waits - Tony Hillerman *naa* 1228

Lecha (Twin; Aged Person; Psychic)
Almanac of the Dead - Leslie Marmon Silko *naa* 1306

Ledbeder, Clabe (Military Personnel; Caucasian)
Emily, the Yellow Rose - Anita Richmond Bunkley *afa* 31

Lee, Anna (Child)
Anna in Charge - Yoriko Tsutsui *asa* 1085

Lee, Bright Star (Uncle; Businessman; Aged Person)
Dragonwings - Laurence Yep *asa* 1120

Lee, Elaine (Mother; Lawyer; Chinese)
Ribbons - Laurence Yep *asa* 1126

Lee, Gilbert (Father; Filmmaker; Caucasian)
Ribbons - Laurence Yep *asa* 1126

Lee, Hung Man "H.M." (Spouse; Korean American; Immigrant)
Quiet Odyssey: A Pioneer Korean Woman in America - Mary Paik Lee *asa* 997

Lee, Ian (Brother; Chinese)
Ribbons - Laurence Yep *asa* 1126

Lee, Jennifer (Child)
ONE small GIRL - Jennifer L. Chan *asa* 914

Lee, Katy (Sister)
Anna in Charge - Yoriko Tsutsui *asa* 1085

Lee, "Mama" (Mother)
The Ghost Fox - Laurence Yep *asa* 1121

Lee, Mary Kuang Sun Paik (Immigrant; Korean American; Spouse)
Quiet Odyssey: A Pioneer Korean Woman in America - Mary Paik Lee *asa* 997

Lee, Moon Shadow (Immigrant; Chinese)
Dragonwings - Laurence Yep *asa* 1120

Lee, Nanci (Friend; Chinese)
Tripmaster Monkey: His Fake Book - Maxine Hong Kingston *asa* 972

Lee, Robin (Dancer; Chinese)
Ribbons - Laurence Yep *asa* 1126

Lee, Rollo Ezekiel "Cager" (Student; African American)
A Chocolate Soldier - Cyrus Colter *afa* 75

Lee, Windrider (Father; Chinese)
Dragonwings - Laurence Yep *asa* 1120

Lee, Yoon Jun (Immigrant; 7th Grader; Korean)
If It Hadn't Been for Yoon Jun - Marie G. Lee *asa* 995

Lee Mui Lan (Spouse)
Disappearing Moon Cafe - Sky Lee *asa* 998

Leon, Archilde (Musician; Native American)
The Surrounded - D'Arcy McNickle *naa* 1277

Leong, Leon (Father; Chinese American)
Bone - Fae Myenne Ng *asa* 1039

Leong, "Mah" (Mother; Businesswoman; Chinese American)
Bone - Fae Myenne Ng *asa* 1039

Leong, Nina (Daughter; Flight Attendant; Chinese American)
Bone - Fae Myenne Ng *asa* 1039

Letenielle, Rebecca Florice (Healer; African American)
Rainbow Roun' Mah Shoulder - Linda Brown Bragg *afa* 21

Levy, Ellen (Friend; Student)
In the Year of the Boar and Jackie Robinson - Bette Bao Lord *asa* 1007

Lewis, Malcolm (Nephew; Musician; African American)
Glory Field - Walter Dean Myers *afa* 307

Li, Kwan (Sister; Chinese American)
The Hundred Secret Senses - Amy Tan *asa* 1078

Li, Lao "Uncle Li" (Businessman)
Face - Aimee Liu *asa* 1004

Li, Won (16-Year-Old; Chinese)
The Hidden Shrine - Walter Dean Myers *afa* 309

Li Shin (Cousin; Resistance Fighter; Chinese)
The Scent of the Gods - Fiona Cheong *asa* 919

Li Wu-Jiang "Shao-shao" (10-Year-Old; 5th Grader; Chinese)
In the Eye of War - Margaret Chang *asa* 918

Li Yuen (Brother; Chinese)
The Scent of the Gods - Fiona Cheong *asa* 919

Liang (Child; Artist; Chinese)
Liang and the Magic Paintbrush - Demi *asa* 935

Lidea (Child)
Happy Days, Uncle Sergio - Magali Garcia Ramis *lat* 624

Lightfoot, Cassie Louise (Child; Sister; African American)
Aunt Harriet's Underground Railroad in the Sky - Faith Ringgold *afa* 372

Lincoln, Liliane (Artist; Patient; African American)
Liliane: Resurrection of the Daughter - Ntozake Shange *afa* 384

Lindy (Child; African American)
Drylongso - Virginia Hamilton *afa* 159

Ling-Li (Artisan)
Ling-Li and the Phoenix Fairy: A Chinese Folktale - Ellin Greene *asa* 940

Lion (Lion; Puerto Rican)
Dance of the Animals - Pura Belpre *lat* 533
Dance of the Animals - Pura Belpre *lat* 533

Lion Head (Student)
Katherine - Anchee Min *asa* 1019

Lionel (Salesman; Native American)
Green Grass, Running Water - Thomas King *naa* 1245

Lissie (Aged Person; African American)
The Temple of My Familiar - Alice Walker *afa* 430

Lito (Grandfather)
Pablo's Tree - Pat Mora *lat* 721

Little, Cephus "Crab" (Father; Fugitive; African American)
Somewhere in the Darkness - Walter Dean Myers *afa* 323

Little, Jimmy (14-Year-Old; 10th Grader; African American)
Somewhere in the Darkness - Walter Dean Myers *afa* 323

Little Chou (Child)
The Boy Who Swallowed Snakes - Laurence Yep *asa* 1117

Little Lee (Child)
The Ghost Fox - Laurence Yep *asa* 1121

Little Mike (Teenager; Chicano)
Don't Spit on My Corner - Miguel Duran *lat* 596

Little Plum (Child; Hero)
Little Plum - Ed Young *asa* 1129

Little Wolf (10-Year-Old; Native American)
Where the Buffaloes Begin - Olaf Baker *naa* 1146

Liu, Victor (Student—College)
The Incorporation of Eric Chung - Steven Lo *asa* 1005

Livesey, John (Aged Person; Widow(er); Caucasian)
Cutting Lisa - Percival Everett *afa* 112

Liza (Child; Native American)
Shemay: The Bird in the Sugarbush - David Martinson *naa* 1270

Lizzie (Aged Person; Grandmother)
Baby of the Family - Tina McElroy Ansa *afa* 1

Lloyd, Ellen (Student—College; Roommate)
Gathering of Pearls - Sook Nyul Choi *asa* 928

Logan (Doctor; Caucasian)
Death of an Anglo - Alejandro Morales *lat* 725

Logan, Cassie (9-Year-Old; Sister; African American)
The Friendship - Mildred D. Taylor *afa* 407

Logan, Cassie (10-Year-Old; Sister; African American)
Let the Circle Be Unbroken - Mildred D. Taylor *afa* 409

Logan, Cassie (17-Year-Old; Student—High School; African American)
The Road to Memphis - Mildred D. Taylor *afa* 411

Logan, Cassie (9-Year-Old; Sister; African American)
Roll of Thunder, Hear My Cry - Mildred D. Taylor *afa* 412

Logan, Cassie (8-Year-Old; Sister; African American)
Song of the Trees - Mildred D. Taylor *afa* 413

Logan, Christopher-John (7-Year-Old; Brother; African American)
Song of the Trees - Mildred D. Taylor *afa* 413

Logan, David (10-Year-Old; Brother; African American)
The Well: David's Story - Mildred D. Taylor *afa* 414

Logan, Hammer (13-Year-Old; Brother; African American)
The Well: David's Story - Mildred D. Taylor *afa* 414

Logan, Little Man (6-Year-Old; Brother; African American)
Song of the Trees - Mildred D. Taylor *afa* 413

Logan, Stacey (13-Year-Old; Brother; African American)
Let the Circle Be Unbroken - Mildred D. Taylor *afa* 409

Logan, Stacey (10-Year-Old; Brother; African American)
Mississippi Bridge - Mildred D. Taylor *afa* 410

Logan, Stacey (Worker; African American)
The Road to Memphis - Mildred D. Taylor *afa* 411

Logan, Stacey (12-Year-Old; Brother; African American)
Roll of Thunder, Hear My Cry - Mildred D. Taylor *afa* 412

Logan, Stacey (11-Year-Old; Brother; African American)
Song of the Trees - Mildred D. Taylor *afa* 413

Lois (Child; Sister; African American)
The Gold Cadillac - Mildred D. Taylor *afa* 408

Lola (Child; Orphan; Mexican)
Who Would Have Thought It? - Maria Amparo Ruiz de Burton *lat* 800

Long, Ida (Bastard Daughter; Activist; African American)
Your Blues Ain't Like Mine - Bebe Moore Campbell *afa* 48

Lonnie (Child; Orphan; African American)
Bonjour Lonnie - Faith Ringgold *afa* 373

Lonnie (Single Father; Alcoholic; African American)
It Ain't All for Nothing - Walter Dean Myers *afa* 311

Lopez, Arcadia H. (Teacher; Aged Person; Mexican)
Barrio Teacher - Arcadia H. Lopez *lat* 683

Lopez, Ruy (Gardener)
The Devil, Delfina Varela, and the Used Chevy - Louie Garcia Robinson *lat* 783

Lopez-Stafford, Gloria (Child; Mexican)
A Place in El Paso: A Mexican American Childhood - Gloria Lopez-Stafford *lat* 687

Lori (Child; Native American)
The Chichi Hoohoo Bogeyman - Virginia Driving Hawk Sneve *naa* 1313

Lotus (Child; Handicapped)
Silent Lotus - Jeanne M. Lee *asa* 989

Loudermilk, Dottie (Aged Person; Mother; African American)
Bad News Travels Fast - Gar Anthony Haywood *afa* 187
Going Nowhere Fast - Gar Anthony Haywood *afa* 189

Loudermilk, Eddie (Activist; Brother; African American)
Bad News Travels Fast - Gar Anthony Haywood *afa* 187

Loudermilk, Joe (Aged Person; Father; African American)
Bad News Travels Fast - Gar Anthony Haywood *afa* 187
Going Nowhere Fast - Gar Anthony Haywood *afa* 189

Louie, Leila Fu (Daughter; Teacher; Chinese American)
Bone - Fae Myenne Ng *asa* 1039

Louie, Mason (Husband; Mechanic; Chinese American)
Bone - Fae Myenne Ng *asa* 1039

Louie, Pearl (Daughter; Chinese American)
The Kitchen God's Wife - Amy Tan *asa* 1080

Louie, Winnie (Businesswoman; Mother; Chinese American)
The Kitchen God's Wife - Amy Tan *asa* 1080

Lovejoy, Annie Ruth (Sister; Television Personality; African American)
Ugly Ways - Tina McElroy Ansa *afa* 3

Lovejoy, Betty Jean (Businesswoman; Sister; African American)
Ugly Ways - Tina McElroy Ansa *afa* 3

Lovejoy, Emily Mae (Divorced Person; Sister; African American)
Ugly Ways - Tina McElroy Ansa *afa* 3

Lovejoy, Yoruba Evelyn (18-Year-Old; Debutante; African American)
The Cotillion, or, One Good Bull Is Half the Herd - John Oliver Killens *afa* 240

Low, Paw-Paw (Grandmother; Chinese American)
Child of the Owl - Laurence Yep *asa* 1118

Lucero, Ben (Religious; Filipino American)
Cebu - Peter Bacho *asa* 902

Luke (Child)
The Lost Lake - Allen Say *asa* 1058

Lumumba, Ben Ali (Writer; African American)
The Cotillion, or, One Good Bull Is Half the Herd - John Oliver Killens *afa* 240

Luna, Eva (Storyteller)
The Stories of Eva Luna - Isabel Allende *lat* 500

Luna, Lazaro (Baker; Mexican)
Pig Cookies and Other Stories - Alberto Alvaro Rios *lat* 774

Lund, Minna (Friend)
If It Hadn't Been for Yoon Jun - Marie G. Lee *asa* 995

Lupita, Mama (Grandmother)
Face of an Angel - Denise Chavez *lat* 574

Luz (Child; Mexican American)
The Farolitos of Christmas - Rudolfo Anaya *lat* 510

Lydia (Young Woman; English)
The Moccasin Maker - E. Pauline Johnson *naa* 1236

Lynn, Theodora (15-Year-Old; Abuse Victim; Caucasian)
Those Other People - Alice Childress *afa* 58

M

Mabel (Friend; Student; African American)
In the Year of the Boar and Jackie Robinson - Bette Bao Lord *asa* 1007

Mac (9-Year-Old; Brother; African American)
Mac and Marie and the Train Toss Surprise - Elizabeth Fitzgerald Howard *afa* 202

MacAlister, Marti "Big Mac" (Detective—Homicide; Widow(er); African American)
Dead Time - Eleanor Taylor Bland *afa* 12
Done Wrong - Eleanor Taylor Bland *afa* 13
Gone Quiet - Eleanor Taylor Bland *afa* 14

MacAlister, Marti "Big Mac" (Detective—Homicide; Mother; African American)
Slow Burn - Eleanor Taylor Bland *afa* 15

MacKenzie (Teacher)
Nene and the Horrible Math Monster - Marie Villanueva *asa* 1094

MacKenzie (Police Officer; Racist)
Yellow Fever - R.A. Shiomi *asa* 1067

Mackenzie, Primus "PM" (Father; Political Figure; West Indian)
Daughters - Paule Marshall *afa* 254

Mackenzie, Ursa Beatrice (Businesswoman; African American)
Daughters - Paule Marshall *afa* 254

MacTeer, Claudia (9-Year-Old; Sister; African American)
The Bluest Eye - Toni Morrison *afa* 282

MacTeer, Frieda (10-Year-Old; Sister; African American)
The Bluest Eye - Toni Morrison *afa* 282

Mad Etta (Native American)
Dance Me Outside - W.P. Kinsella *naa* 1247
Moccasin Telegraph - W.P. Kinsella *naa* 1248

Madame Bernice (Religious; European)
Our Lady of Babylon - John Rechy *lat* 770

Magalee, Charles (Friend)
House of Waiting - Marina Tamar Budhos *asa* 909

Magalee, Sarita (Spouse)
House of Waiting - Marina Tamar Budhos *asa* 909

Maggie (Child)
Daughter of the Mountain: Un Cuento - Edna Escamill *lat* 599

Maglione, Giovanna "Gianna" (Police Officer; Lesbian; Italian American)
Keeping Secrets - Penny Mickelbury *afa* 276
Night Songs - Penny Mickelbury *afa* 277

Maharajah (Nobleman)
Fat Gopal - Jacquelin Singh *asa* 1068

Ma'ii (Toad)
Ma'ii and Cousin Horned Toad - Shonto Begay *naa* 1150

Malanguezes, Santos (Child; Student; Puerto Rican)
Family Installments: Memories of Growing Up Hispanic - Edward Rivera *lat* 776

Malanguezes, Tego (Brother; Student; Puerto Rican)
Family Installments: Memories of Growing Up Hispanic - Edward Rivera *lat* 776

Maldonado, Loreto (Aged Person; Veteran; Mexican)
Pilgrims in Aztlan - Miguel Mendez *lat* 702

Malinali (Slave; Royalty; Aztec)
Malinche: Slave Princess of Cortez - Gloria Duran *lat* 595

Mama (Mother)
Rise and Shine, Mariko-chan! - Chiyoko Tomioka *asa* 1082

Mama (Mother; Mexican American)
Treasure Nap - Juanita Havill *lat* 647

Mama (Mother)
Tree of Cranes - Allen Say *asa* 1061

Mami (Mother)
When I Was Puerto Rican - Esmeralda Santiago *lat* 814

Manabozho (Trickster)
Manabozho and the Bullrushes - David Martinson *naa* 1268

Manchang (Fiance(e))
Ling-Li and the Phoenix Fairy: A Chinese Folktale -
Ellin Greene *asa* 940

Mandarino, Gary (Businessman; Public Relations;
Italian)
The Berhama Account - John A. Williams *afa* 457

Mando (Teenager; Chicano)
Summer on Wheels - Gary Soto *lat* 835

Manfred, Dorcas (Student; African American)
Jazz - Toni Morrison *afa* 283

Mango, Peter (Sea Captain; Slave; African
American)
Fragments of the Ark - Louise Meriwether *afa* 275

Mango, Rain (Mother; Slave; African American)
Fragments of the Ark - Louise Meriwether *afa* 275

Mansion, George (Native American; Young Man)
The Moccasin Maker - E. Pauline
Johnson *naa* 1236

Manuel (Grandfather; Husband; Yaqui Indian)
La Maravilla - Alfredo Vea Jr. *lat* 867

Manyara (Child; Sister; African American)
Mufaro's Beautiful Daughters: An African Tale - John
Steptoe *afa* 399

Mapes (Lawman; African American)
A Gathering of Old Men - Ernest J. Gaines *afa* 133

March, Carla (Mother; Storyteller; African
American)
No Other Tale to Tell - Richard Perry *afa* 345

March, Phoenix (Mentally Challenged Person;
African American)
No Other Tale to Tell - Richard Perry *afa* 345

Marcialis, Evan (Actor; Homosexual; Caucasian)
Traitor to the Race - Darieck Scott *afa* 382

Marcus, Theophilus J. "Skeeter" (Military
Personnel; Divorced Person; African American)
Wilhemina Jones, Future Star - Dindga
McCannon *afa* 257

Marder, Curt (Rancher; Gambler; Caucasian)
God's Country - Percival Everett *afa* 114

Marez, Antonio (7-Year-Old; Chicano)
Bless Me, Ultima - Rudolfo Anaya *lat* 508

Margot (Student—High School; Girlfriend; African
American)
Understand This - Jervey Tervalon *afa* 415

Maria (Child; Salvadoran)
Journey of the Sparrow - Fran Leeper Buss *lat* 552

Maria (Young Woman; Chicana)
Mother Tongue - Demetria Martinez *lat* 693

Maria (Widow(er); Mother; Mexican American)
To a Widow with Children - Lionel G.
Garcia *lat* 621

Maria (Child)
Too Many Tamales - Gary Soto *lat* 837

Maria Lili (Child)
Saturday Sancocho - Leyla Torres *lat* 851

Marie (Occultist; Healer; African American)
Voodoo Dreams: A Novel of Marie Laveau - Jewell
Parker Rhodes *afa* 370

Marie Victoria (12-Year-Old; 8th Grader)
I Hadn't Meant to Tell You This - Jacqueline
Woodson *afa* 475

Marigold (Singer; Orphan; African American)
When the Nightingale Sings - Joyce Carol
Thomas *afa* 419

Mariko-chan (Child)
Rise and Shine, Mariko-chan! - Chiyoko
Tomioka *asa* 1082

Mario (Young Man; Cuban)
The Greatest Performance - Elias Miguel
Munoz *lat* 730

Marisol (Young Woman; Puerto Rican)
The Line of the Sun: A Novel - Judith Ortiz
Cofer *lat* 746

Marisse, Ann (Young Woman; Student—College)
Only the Good Times - Bruce-Novoa *lat* 549

Marita (Child; Puerto Rican)
Abuelita's Paradise - Carmen Santiago
Nodar *lat* 737

Mark (Child)
A River Dream - Allen Say *asa* 1059

Marr, John (Student—College; African American;
Homosexual)
The Mad Man - Samuel R. Delany *afa* 95

Marroquin, Chayo (Young Woman; Sister; Mexican)
A Place Where the Sea Remembers - Sandra
Benitez *lat* 539

Marshall, Andrea Williams (Activist; Spouse;
African American)
And All Our Wounds Forgiven - Julius
Lester *afa* 242

Marshall, Candy (Landowner; Caucasian)
A Gathering of Old Men - Ernest J. Gaines *afa* 133

Marshall, John Calvin (Activist; Professor; African
American)
And All Our Wounds Forgiven - Julius
Lester *afa* 242

Martens, John (Spy; African American)
The Nicholas Factor - Walter Dean Myers *afa* 319

Martha (14-Year-Old; Granddaughter)
Trouble's Child - Mildred Pitts Walter *afa* 440

Martin, Angela (Wife; Mexican American)
A Shell for Angela - Ofelia Dumas
Lachtman *lat* 676

Martin, Lucas (Student; Teenager; African
American)
Getting Right with God - Lionel Newton *afa* 335

Martin, Phillip (Activist; African American;
Religious)
In My Father's House - Ernest J. Gaines *afa* 134

Martina (Cockroach; Spanish)
Perez and Martina - Pura Belpre *lat* 535

Martinez, Sandy (Psychologist; Latina)
Juanita Fights the School Board - Gloria
Velasquez *lat* 873

Martinez, Santiago (Writer; Young Man;
Columbian)
Latin Moon in Manhattan - Jaime
Manrique *lat* 688

Mary (15-Year-Old; Fiance(e); Religious)
Portrait of Mary - Nikki Grimes *afa* 155

Mary Jo (Child; Native American)
The Chichi Hoohoo Bogeyman - Virginia Driving
Hawk Sneve *naa* 1313

Masaube, Blossom Rose (Blind Person; Healer;
Native American)
Mischief Makers - Nettie Jones *afa* 235

Masaube, Lilly (Femme Fatale; Student; Native
American)
Mischief Makers - Nettie Jones *afa* 235

Masaube, Puma (Mother; Native American)
Mischief Makers - Nettie Jones *afa* 235

Maslin, Blake Jason (Widow(er); Father; Caucasian)
Clay's Ark - Octavia Butler *afa* 34

Mason, Willie (African American; Writer)
Linden Hills - Gloria Naylor *afa* 329

Matchmaker (Matchmaker; Aged Person)
Red Thread - Ed Young *asa* 1132

Mathis, Quinn (Spouse; African American; Stock
Broker)
Invisible Life - E. Lynn Harris *afa* 180

Mathu (Aged Person; Farmer; African American)
A Gathering of Old Men - Ernest J. Gaines *afa* 133

Matsuda, Karen Kumai (Mother; Artist)
Molly by Any Other Name - Jean Davies
Okimoto *asa* 1043

Matsumoto, Aya (Aunt; Japanese)
Shizuko's Daughter - Kyoko Mori *asa* 1026

Matthews, Gloria (Businesswoman; African
American)
Waiting to Exhale - Terry McMillan *afa* 269

Mauser, Candice (Spouse; Native American)
Tales of Burning Love - Louise Erdrich *naa* 1214

Mauser, Dot (Spouse; Native American)
Tales of Burning Love - Louise Erdrich *naa* 1214

Mauser, Elanor (Spouse; Native American)
Tales of Burning Love - Louise Erdrich *naa* 1214

Mauser, Jack (Spouse; Native American)
Tales of Burning Love - Louise Erdrich *naa* 1214

Mauser, Marlis (Spouse; Native American)
Tales of Burning Love - Louise Erdrich *naa* 1214

Max (Child; African American)
Max Found Two Sticks - Brian Pinkney *afa* 349

Maximillian "Max" (Father; Religious; Caucasian)
No Other Tale to Tell - Richard Perry *afa* 345

Maximo (Young Man; Spanish)
Sapogonia: An Anti-Romance in 3/8 Meter - Ana
Castillo *lat* 569

Maya (Child; African American)
Julius - Angela Johnson *afa* 218

Maya (Teenager; Mexican American)
Maya's Divided World - Gloria Velasquez *lat* 874

Maybe, Lorraine (10-Year-Old; Artist; African
American)
Something to Count On - Emily Moore *afa* 279

McCurtain, Cole (Professor; Native American)
Bone Game - Louis Owen *naa* 1293

McDougald, Aileen (Mother; African American)
These Same Long Bones - Gwendolyn
Parker *afa* 339

McDougald, Sirus (Banker; Father; African
American)
These Same Long Bones - Gwendolyn
Parker *afa* 339

McGirk, Mike (Young Man; Worker; Caucasian)
In Search of Snow - Luis Alberto Urrea *lat* 864

McGuire, Daughter (11-Year-Old; Sister; African American)
The World of Daughter McGuire - Sharon Dennis Wyeth *afa* 479

McMann, Mary Ellen "Spike" (Restauranteur; Lesbian; Caucasian)
Long Goodbyes - Nikki Baker *afa* 7

McMillan, Austin (Television Personality; Adoptee; African American)
Home Repairs - Trey Ellis *afa* 110

McNeil, Lute (Businessman; Father; African American)
The Wedding - Dorothy West *afa* 445

McPhee, Ruella "Rooms" (Dancer; Secretary; African American)
Vanishing Rooms - Melvin Dixon *afa* 100

McPherson, Lena (Teenager; African American)
Baby of the Family - Tina McElroy Ansa *afa* 1

McPherson, Lena (Businesswoman; Wealthy; African American)
The Hand I Fan With - Tina McElroy Ansa *afa* 2

McQuillen, Gerald (17-Year-Old; Student—College; Caucasian)
The Nicholas Factor - Walter Dean Myers *afa* 319

Medea (Royalty; Sorceress; African American)
For Her Dark Skin - Percival Everett *afa* 113

Medina, Chato (Teenager)
Famous All over Town - Danny Santiago *lat* 812

Mei-Mei (Child; Chinese American)
Mama Bear - Chyng Feng Sun *asa* 1073

Mei Oi (Spouse; Chinese)
Eat a Bowl of Tea - Louis Chu *asa* 931

Melanin "Mel" Sun (13-Year-Old; Writer; African American)
From the Notebooks of Melanin Sun - Jacqueline Woodson *afa* 474

Melendez, Veronica (Writer; Lesbian; Chicana)
Margins - Terri de la Pena *lat* 588

Menchan, Clea (Businesswoman; Caucasian)
Days Without Weather - Cecil Brown *afa* 24

Mendizabal, Quintin (Spouse; Businessman; Spanish)
The House on the Lagoon - Rosario Ferre *lat* 608

Mendoza, Brian (Student—College; Chicano)
Obsidian Sky: A Novel - Guy Garcia *lat* 618

Mendoza, Ernesto (Storyteller)
Mendoza's Dreams - Ed Vega *lat* 872

Mendoza, Lincoln (Student—Junior High)
Pacific Crossing - Gary Soto *lat* 830

Mendoza, Lincoln (14-Year-Old; Student—Junior High; Chicano)
Taking Sides - Gary Soto *lat* 836

Mendoza, Louie (Musician; Chicano)
La Mollie and the King of Tears - Arturo Islas *lat* 664

Merchant (Businessman)
The Boy of the Three-Year Nap - Dianne Snyder *asa* 1069

Metcalf, Mariah (11-Year-Old; Diver; African American)
Mariah Keeps Cool - Mildred Pitts Walter *afa* 437

Metcalf, Mariah (11-Year-Old; Student; African American)
Mariah Loves Rock - Mildred Pitts Walter *afa* 438

Miata (4th Grader)
The Skirt - Gary Soto *lat* 833

Michael, Mattie (Aged Person; Single Mother; African American)
Women of Brewster Place - Gloria Naylor *afa* 331

Miguel (Student—College; Cuban American)
Shango - James Roberto Curtis *lat* 585

Miguel (16-Year-Old; Gang Member)
Spidertown - Abraham Rodriguez Jr. *lat* 785

Mii (7-Year-Old; Survivor)
Hiroshima No Pika (The Flash of Hiroshima) - Toshi Maruki *asa* 1012

Mike (Child; African American)
A Visit to the Country - Herschel Johnson *afa* 233

Miles (Writer)
What Now My Love - Floyd Salas *lat* 808

Miles, Laban J. (Military Personnel)
Wah'Kon-Tah: The Osage and the White Man's Road - John Joseph Mathews *naa* 1273

Miller, Crockett (Homosexual; Writer; Caucasian)
Tangled Up in Blue - Larry Duplechan *afa* 107

Miller, Jacob (Child; Brother; African American)
The Black Snowman - Phil Mendez *afa* 274

Miller, Mia (Journalist; African American; Alcoholic)
And This Too Shall Pass - E. Lynn Harris *afa* 179

Mills, Willie Bea (12-Year-Old; Sister; African American)
Willie Bea and the Time the Martians Landed - Virginia Hamilton *afa* 172

Min, Anchee (Worker; Actress)
Red Azalea - Anchee Min *asa* 1020

Min, Junho (Friend)
Echoes of the White Giraffe - Sook Nyul Choi *asa* 927

Minatoya, Lydia Yuri (Young Woman; Japanese American)
Talking to High Monks in the Snow: An Asian American Odyssey - Lydia Yuri Minatoya *asa* 1021

Minatoya, Miyeko (Mother; Immigrant; Japanese)
Talking to High Monks in the Snow: An Asian American Odyssey - Lydia Yuri Minatoya *asa* 1021

Ming Miao (Cat)
The Chinese Siamese Cat - Amy Tan *asa* 1077

Mintu, Simba "Simmie" (Child; Survivor; African American)
Philadelphia Fire - John Edgar Wideman *afa* 449

Minty (Seamstress; Slave; African American)
Oxherding Tale - Charles Johnson *afa* 227

Mirabal, Maria Teresa (Young Woman; Activist; Dominican)
In the Time of the Butterflies - Julia Alvarez *lat* 503

Mirabal, Minerva (Young Woman; Activist; Dominican)
In the Time of the Butterflies - Julia Alvarez *lat* 503

Mirabal, Patria (Young Woman; Activist; Dominican)
In the Time of the Butterflies - Julia Alvarez *lat* 503

Miranda, Francisca (Child; Spanish)
Sal y Pimienta: A Culinary Education - Francisca Miranda Schneider *lat* 820

Mirandy (Child; African American)
Mirandy and Brother Wind - Patricia C. McKissack *afa* 262

Mizutani, Kumiko (Friend; Veterinarian)
One Bird - Kyoko Mori *asa* 1025

Monet, Daphne (Abuse Victim; Companion; African American)
Devil in a Blue Dress - Walter Mosley *afa* 288

Monfort, Isabel (Spouse; Writer; Corsican)
The House on the Lagoon - Rosario Ferre *lat* 608

Monk, Ivan (Detective—Private; Brother; African American)
Violent Spring - Gary Phillips *afa* 346

Montejo, Esteban (Slave; Aged Person; African Cuban)
The Autobiography of a Runaway Slave - Esteban Montejo *lat* 714

Montez, Eduardo Ricardo (Young Man; Mexican American)
Stone Horses - Sallie Gallegos *lat* 616

Montez, Luis (Lawyer; Chicano)
The Ballad of Gato Guerrero - Manuel Ramos *lat* 762
The Ballad of Rocky Ruiz: Death of a Martyr - Manuel Ramos *lat* 763
The Last Client of Luis Montez - Manuel Ramos *lat* 764

Montez O'Brien, Emilio (Young Man; Irish Cuban)
The Fourteen Sisters of Emilio Montez O'Brien: A Novel - Oscar Hijuelos *lat* 654

Moon, Harvey (Child; African American)
Clean Your Room, Harvey Moon! - Pat Cummings *afa* 89

Moore, Ernestine (Blind Person; Grandmother; Artisan)
An Open Weave - Devorah Major *afa* 253

Moore, Josephine (Abuse Victim; African American)
Montgomery's Children - Richard Perry *afa* 344

Moore, MC (17-Year-Old; Musician; African American)
Snakes - Al Young *afa* 483

Moore, Sarah (9-Year-Old; Student; African American)
Addy Learns a Lesson: A School Story - Connie Porter *afa* 353

Morissey, Lipsha (Worker; Native American)
The Bingo Palace - Louise Erdrich *naa* 1211

Morning Girl (Child; Arawak)
Morning Girl - Michael Dorris *naa* 1198

Moroni, Petey (Writer; Camper; African American)
Petey Moroni's Camp Runamok Diary - Pat Cummings *afa* 90

Moses, Miranda (14-Year-Old; Student; African American)
Poor Girl, Rich Girl - Johnniece Marshall Wilson *afa* 469

Moss (Child; Native American)
Guests - Michael Dorris *naa* 1197

Mother (Mother)
American Visa - Wang Ping *asa* 1047
At the Beach - Huy Voun Lee *asa* 987

Mother (Mother; Survivor)
Hiroshima No Pika (The Flash of Hiroshima) - Toshi Maruki   *asa*   1012

Mother (Mother)
In the Snow - Huy Voun Lee   *asa*   988

Mother (Mother; Vietnamese)
The Little Weaver of Thai-Yen Village - Tran Khanh Tuyet   *asa*   1083

Mother (Mother; Waiter/Waitress)
Mama Bear - Chyng Feng Sun   *asa*   1073

Mother (Mother)
Silent Lotus - Jeanne M. Lee   *asa*   989

Mothersill, Odell (Social Worker; African American)
Mothersill and the Foxes - John A. Williams   *afa*   462

Mouse (Mouse)
Seven Blind Mice - Ed Young   *asa*   1133

Mullick, Ina (Friend; Immigrant; Indian)
Wife - Bharati Mukherjee   *asa*   1032

Mumsfield (Caucasian)
Blanche on the Lam - Barbara Neely   *afa*   333

Munoz, Blanca (Young Woman; Mexican American)
The Wedding - Mary Helen Ponce   *lat*   759

Murieta, Joaquin (Convict; Native American)
Life and Adventures of Joaquin Murieta - Yellow Bird   *naa*   1350

M'witu, Najee (Adventurer; African; Royalty)
Captain Africa: The Battle for Egyptica - Dwayne J. Ferguson   *afa*   120

N

Naanabozho (Trickster)
The People Named the Chippewa: Narrative Histories - Gerald Vizenor   *naa*   1339

Nacho (Uncle)
Uncle Nacho's Hat = El Sombrero de Tio Nacho - Harriet Rohmer   *lat*   793

Nakane, Ayako "Obasan" (Aunt; Japanese Canadian)
Obasan - Joy Kogawa   *asa*   975

Nakane, Daddy (Father; Musician)
Naomi's Road - Joy Kogawa   *asa*   974

Nakane, Isamu "Uncle" (Uncle; Japanese Canadian)
Obasan - Joy Kogawa   *asa*   975

Nakane, Megumi Naomi (Daughter; Japanese Canadian)
Naomi's Road - Joy Kogawa   *asa*   974

Nakane, Megumi Naomi (Daughter; Teacher; Japanese Canadian)
Obasan - Joy Kogawa   *asa*   975

Nakane, Stephen (Brother; Japanese Canadian)
Naomi's Road - Joy Kogawa   *asa*   974

Nana (Grandmother; Mexican American)
Green Corn Tamales = Tamales de Elote - Gina Macaluso Rodriguez   *lat*   786

Nanabozho (Trickster)
Ojibwa Narratives - Charles Kawbawgam   *naa*   1239

Nanapush (Native American; Aged Person)
Tracks - Louise Erdrich   *naa*   1215

Nariyoshi, Calhoun (Sister)
Wild Meat and the Bully Burgers - Lois-Ann Yamanaka   *asa*   1109

Nariyoshi, Hubert (Father)
Wild Meat and the Bully Burgers - Lois-Ann Yamanaka   *asa*   1109

Nariyoshi, Lovey (Teenager)
Wild Meat and the Bully Burgers - Lois-Ann Yamanaka   *asa*   1109

Narrator (Teenager; Sister; African American)
Autobiography of a Family Photo - Jacqueline Woodson   *afa*   471

Narrator (Researcher; Student—College; Caucasian)
Panther - Melvin Van Peebles   *afa*   422

Narrator (Civil Servant)
A River Sutra - Gita Mehta   *asa*   1018

Natividad, Clara "Aunt Clara" (Friend; Businesswoman)
Cebu - Peter Bacho   *asa*   902

Navarro, Rita (Businesswoman; Seamstress)
Sweet Fifteen - Diane Gonzales Bertrand   *lat*   636

Nawab (Ruler; Indian)
Fat Gopal - Jacquelin Singh   *asa*   1068

Nedeed, Luther (Landowner; Undertaker; African American)
Linden Hills - Gloria Naylor   *afa*   329

Negi (Child)
When I Was Puerto Rican - Esmeralda Santiago   *lat*   814

Nehemiah, Adam (Researcher; Journalist; Caucasian)
Dessa Rose - Sherley Anne Williams   *afa*   463

Neighbor (Neighbor)
Magic Spring: A Korean Folktale - Nami Rhee   *asa*   1049

Neruda, Rafael (Doctor; Cuban American)
Dr. Neruda's Cure for Evil - Rafael Yglesias   *lat*   891

Nettie (Sister; Religious; African American)
The Color Purple - Alice Walker   *afa*   426

Nettie (Boar; Neighbor)
Rockabye Crocodile - Jose Aruego   *asa*   897

Nettie Jo (Child; Cousin; African American)
Nettie Jo's Friends - Patricia C. McKissack   *afa*   264

Nguyen, Betty (Lover; Administrator)
American Knees - Shawn Wong   *asa*   1104

Nguyen, Chi Hai (Sister)
Angel Child, Dragon Child - Michele Maria Surat   *asa*   1075

Nguyen, Hoa "Ut" (Student; Immigrant; Vietnamese)
Angel Child, Dragon Child - Michele Maria Surat   *asa*   1075

Nguyen, Little Quang (Brother; Child)
Angel Child, Dragon Child - Michele Maria Surat   *asa*   1075

Nick (Friend)
America Is in the Heart - Carlos Bulosan   *asa*   910

Nickelson, Elizabeth (Student—College; Businesswoman; Caucasian)
Falling Leaves of Ivy - Yolanda Joe   *afa*   214

Nicole (Mentally Challenged Person; African American)
Humming Whispers - Angela Johnson   *afa*   217

Nieves, Facundo (Businessman; Father; Puerto Rican)
Valentino's Hair - Yvonne V. Sapia   *lat*   819

Nieves, Lupe (Young Man; Son; Puerto Rican)
Valentino's Hair - Yvonne V. Sapia   *lat*   819

Night Flying Woman, Oona (Native American; Young Woman)
Night Flying Woman - Ignatia Broker   *naa*   1172

Niguayona (Child; Puerto Rican)
Atariba and Niguayona: A Story from the Taino People of Puerto Rico - Harriet Rohmer   *lat*   790

Nikanj (Alien; Healer; Student)
Dawn - Octavia Butler   *afa*   35

Nishitani, Brenda (Friend)
American Knees - Shawn Wong   *asa*   1104

Noe (Butcher)
Pig Cookies and Other Stories - Alberto Alvaro Rios   *lat*   774

Nolan (Teacher)
Halmoni and the Picnic - Sook Nyul Choi   *asa*   929

Noon (African American; Wife; Abuse Victim)
Tumbling - Diane McKinney-Whetstone   *afa*   258

Noragua, Timoteo (Adventurer; Mexican)
The Dream of Santa Maria de las Piedras - Miguel Mendez   *lat*   701

Noro Shinpei (Artist; Teacher; Japanese)
The Ink-keeper's Apprentice - Allen Say   *asa*   1057

Norris, Evan (Volunteer; African American)
I Get on the Bus - Reginald McKnight   *afa*   265

North, Adam "Juneboy" (Doctor; Researcher; African American)
Such Was the Season - Clarence Major   *afa*   252

Ntah, Tarik (Captive; Orphan; African)
Legend of Tarik - Walter Dean Myers   *afa*   312

Numa, Tarija (14-Year-Old; Student; Quechuan)
Ambush in the Amazon - Walter Dean Myers   *afa*   300

Nyasha (Child; Sister; African American)
Mufaro's Beautiful Daughters: An African Tale - John Steptoe   *afa*   399

O

Oaks, Johnny (Child; Brother; African American)
Finding the Green Stone - Alice Walker   *afa*   427

Oaks, Katie (Child; Sister; African American)
Finding the Green Stone - Alice Walker   *afa*   427

Oba-san (Grandmother)
Rise and Shine, Mariko-chan! - Chiyoko Tomioka   *asa*   1082

Obaachan (Grandmother)
Thanksgiving at Obaachan's - Janet Mitsui Brown   *asa*   1022

Obasan (Aunt)
Naomi's Road - Joy Kogawa   *asa*   974

Oconeechee (Young Woman; Native American)
Mountain Windsong - Robert J. Conley   *naa*   1183

O'Farrell, Kevin (Engineer; Husband; Irish American)
Shannon - Gordon Parks *afa* 340

Oh (Impostor)
Sir Whong and the Golden Pig - Oki S. Han *asa* 947

Oka, Kunisaburo "Uncle Oka" (Friend; Aged Person; Japanese American)
Journey Home - Yoshiko Uchida *asa* 1089

Okada, Dad (Father; Veteran)
Heroes - Ken Mochizuki *asa* 1024

Okada, Donnie (Child; Japanese American)
Heroes - Ken Mochizuki *asa* 1024

Okada, Yoshi (Uncle; Veteran)
Heroes - Ken Mochizuki *asa* 1024

Okasan (Duck; Mother)
Chibi: A True Story from Japan - Barbara Brenner *asa* 906

Okubo, Mine (Artist; Japanese American)
Citizen 13660 - Mine Okubo *asa* 1044

Okuda, Hanae (Stepmother)
Shizuko's Daughter - Kyoko Mori *asa* 1026

Okuda, Hideki (Father; Japanese)
Shizuko's Daughter - Kyoko Mori *asa* 1026

Okuda, Shizuko Matsumoto (Mother; Japanese)
Shizuko's Daughter - Kyoko Mori *asa* 1026

Okuda, Yuki (Young Woman; Japanese)
Shizuko's Daughter - Kyoko Mori *asa* 1026

Olamina, Lauren Oya (15-Year-Old; Empath; African American)
Parable of the Sower - Octavia Butler *afa* 37

Old Man (Aged Person)
Magic Spring: A Korean Folktale - Nami Rhee *asa* 1049

Old Rosa (Mother; Cuban)
Old Rosa: A Novel in Two Stories - Reinaldo Arenas *lat* 523

Old Wolf (Wolf)
Lon Po Po: A Red-Riding Hood Story from China - Ed Young *asa* 1130

Old Woman (Aged Person; Spouse)
Magic Spring: A Korean Folktale - Nami Rhee *asa* 1049

Olguin (Native American)
House Made of Dawn - N. Scott Momaday *naa* 1281

Olivas, Jesus (Criminal; Murderer; Chicano)
Happy Birthday Jesus - Ronald L. Ruiz *lat* 798

Olivia (9-Year-Old; African American; Detective)
Just My Luck - Emily Moore *afa* 278

O'Meara, Kim (Friend; Student)
Yang the Third and Her Impossible Family - Lensey Namioka *asa* 1035

Orgaz, Ana Magdalena (Young Woman; Prostitute; Peruvian)
The Love Queen of the Amazon - Cecile Pineda *lat* 756

Orgaz y Orgaz, Federico (Writer; Husband; Peruvian)
The Love Queen of the Amazon - Cecile Pineda *lat* 756

Orphelia (Mother; African American)
Wilhemina Jones, Future Star - Dindga McCannon *afa* 257

Osaka, Charles "Charlie-O" (Father; Japanese)
The Floating World - Cynthia Kadohata *asa* 962

Osaka, Mother (Mother; Daughter; Japanese)
The Floating World - Cynthia Kadohata *asa* 962

Osaka, Olivia Ann (Daughter; Japanese)
The Floating World - Cynthia Kadohata *asa* 962

Oscar (Alligator)
Later, Gator - Laurence Yep *asa* 1123

Otake, Anna (11-Year-Old; Japanese American)
The World of Daughter McGuire - Sharon Dennis Wyeth *afa* 479

Ote (Father)
Ote: A Puerto Rican Folk Tale - Pura Belpre *lat* 534

Otero, Inez (Spouse; Artist)
Rituals of Survival: A Woman's Portfolio - Nicholasa Mohr *lat* 711

Othello (Mercenary; Spouse; African)
Othello, a Novel - Julius Lester *afa* 244

Otilia (Puerto Rican)
My Aunt Otilia's Spirits = Los Espiritus de Mi Tia Otilia - Richard Garcia *lat* 623

Outlaw, Lurhetta (Adventurer; Runaway; African American)
M.C. Higgins, the Great - Virginia Hamilton *afa* 165

Owens, Elias Euritides (Composer; Artist; African American)
Holly - Albert French *afa* 131

Oyama, Father (Father; Fisherman)
All I Asking for Is My Body - Milton Murayama *asa* 1033

Oyama, Kiyoshi (Son)
All I Asking for Is My Body - Milton Murayama *asa* 1033

P

Pablo (5-Year-Old)
Pablo's Tree - Pat Mora *lat* 721

Pacay, Isabel (Child; Mayan)
Among the Volcanoes - Omar Castaneda *lat* 564

Paine, Hayden (Scientist)
Nightwing - Martin Cruz Smith *naa* 1311

Painted Turtle (Musician; Singer; Zuni Indian)
Painted Turtle: Woman with Guitar - Clarence Major *afa* 250

Palmer, Willy (14-Year-Old; Handicapped; African American)
Willy's Summer Dream - Kay Brown *afa* 25

Palms, Denise "Neesey" (Sister; Teenager; African American)
The Good Negress - A.J. Verdelle *afa* 424

Paotze (Child)
Lon Po Po: A Red-Riding Hood Story from China - Ed Young *asa* 1130

Pardo, Nelly (Worker)
Holy Radishes - Roberto Fernandez *lat* 607

Pardo, Rudy (Fire Fighter; Widow(er); Cuban American)
Break-In - Jose Yglesias *lat* 889

Park, Henry (Spy)
Native Speaker - Chang-rae Lee *asa* 984

Park, Leila (Spouse; Teacher; Caucasian)
Native Speaker - Chang-rae Lee *asa* 984

Parker, Addie (17-Year-Old; Granddaughter; African American)
Rivers of Eros - Cyrus Colter *afa* 78

Parker, Lester (12-Year-Old; Grandson; African American)
Rivers of Eros - Cyrus Colter *afa* 78

Parrish, Olivia "Mop" (11-Year-Old; Adoptee; Caucasian)
Me, Mop, and the Moondance Kid - Walter Dean Myers *afa* 313
Mop, Moondance and Nagasaki Knights - Walter Dean Myers *afa* 315

Paschen, Rosalee "Rosey" (Lawyer; Abuse Victim; Caucasian)
Long Goodbyes - Nikki Baker *afa* 7

Pasko, Lori (15-Year-Old; Caucasian)
Billy - Albert French *afa* 130

Pastora (Young Woman; Mexican)
Sapogonia: An Anti-Romance in 3/8 Meter - Ana Castillo *lat* 569

Patterson, M. Montgomery "Mimi" (Journalist; Lesbian; African American)
Keeping Secrets - Penny Mickelbury *afa* 276
Night Songs - Penny Mickelbury *afa* 277

Patty Ann (Cousin; African American)
Cousins - Virginia Hamilton *afa* 158

Payne, Quincy (11-Year-Old; Student; African American)
How Stella Got Her Groove Back - Terry McMillan *afa* 267

Payne, Stella (Banker; Divorced Person; African American)
How Stella Got Her Groove Back - Terry McMillan *afa* 267

Peace, Sula (Femme Fatale; Wanderer; African American)
Sula - Toni Morrison *afa* 285

Peacock, Freda (Writer; Alcoholic; African American)
Mama - Terry McMillan *afa* 268

Peacock, Mildred (Housekeeper; Mother; African American)
Mama - Terry McMillan *afa* 268

Pearson, Gloria (Teacher; African American)
The Good Negress - A.J. Verdelle *afa* 424

Pena, Joe (Military Personnel; Native American)
Stallion Gate - Martin Cruz Smith *naa* 1312

Pepita (Child; Mexican)
Pepita Talks Twice = Pepita Habla Dos Veces - Ofelia Dumas Lachtman *lat* 675

Peregrin, Camilo (Young Man; Brother; Cuban)
Skywriting - Margarita Engle *lat* 598

Peregrin, Carmen (Young Woman; Sister; Cuban American)
Skywriting - Margarita Engle *lat* 598

Perera, Victor (Child; Guatemalan)
Rites: A Guatemalan Boyhood - Victor Perera *lat* 752

Perez (Mouse; Spanish)
Perez and Martina - Pura Belpre *lat* 535

Perez, Emma (Lesbian; Chicana)
Gulf Dreams - Emma Perez   *lat*   753

Perkins, Carlene Zenobia "Carla" (Student—High School; Girlfriend; African American)
Coffee Will Make You Black - April Sinclair   *afa*   392

Perkins, Munro (Criminal; Teenager; African American)
Break-In - Jose Yglesias   *lat*   889

Perry, Charmaine (Mother; Secretary; African American)
Sisters and Lovers - Connie Briscoe   *afa*   23

Perry, Pretty Pearl (Child; African American)
The Magical Adventures of Pretty Pearl - Virginia Hamilton   *afa*   166

Perry, Richard "Richie" (17-Year-Old; Military Personnel; African American)
Fallen Angels - Walter Dean Myers   *afa*   305

Perry, Stephen "Steve" Gerard (14-Year-Old; African American)
Won't Know Till I Get There - Walter Dean Myers   *afa*   326

Peter (Child; African American)
Your Dad Was Just Like You - Dolores Johnson   *afa*   232

Peters, Kevin (Guide; Rebel; African American)
Zulus - Percival Everett   *afa*   119

Peterson, Angie (10-Year-Old; Student; African American)
The Shimmershine Queens - Camille Yarbrough   *afa*   480

Pfluggins, Effie (Aged Person; Secretary; African American)
The Secret of Gumbo Grove - Eleanora E. Tate   *afa*   405

Phantom, Flower (Criminal; African American)
Reckless Eyeballing - Ishmael Reed   *afa*   367

Pieh, Sengbe "Joseph Cinque" (Father; Spouse; African)
Echo of Lions - Barbara Chase-Riboud   *afa*   52

Pilar (Granddaughter; Artist; Cuban American)
Dreaming in Cuban, A Novel - Cristina Garcia   *lat*   617

Pilar (Grandmother; Puerto Rican)
Singing Softly = Cantando Bajito - Carmen de Monteflores   *lat*   589

Pilate (Aunt; Sister; African American)
Song of Solomon - Toni Morrison   *afa*   284

Pilgrim, Clotilda (Seamstress; Grandmother; African American)
Rivers of Eros - Cyrus Colter   *afa*   78

Pillager, Fleur (Native American)
Tracks - Louise Erdrich   *naa*   1215

"Pine" (Child; Nephew; African American)
On the Day I Was Born - Debbi Chocolate   *afa*   59

Ping (Child; Gardener; Chinese)
The Empty Pot - Demi   *asa*   934

Pio (Child; Puerto Rican)
The Rainbow-Colored Horse - Pura Belpre   *lat*   536

Pippin, Chartreuse Marie "Charlie" (11-Year-Old; Businesswoman; African American)
Charlie Pippin - Candy Dawson Boyd   *afa*   17

Pittman, Jane (Aged Person; Slave; African American)
The Autobiography of Miss Jane Pittman - Ernest J. Gaines   *afa*   132

Pittman, Joe (African American; Horse Trainer; Husband)
The Autobiography of Miss Jane Pittman - Ernest J. Gaines   *afa*   132

Polatkin, Junior (Native American)
The Lone Ranger and Tonto Fist Fight in Heaven - Sherman Alexie   *naa*   1137

Ponce, Mary Helen (Child; Mexican American)
Hoyt Street: An Autobiography - Mary Helen Ponce   *lat*   758

Pool (Maintenance Worker; Teacher; African American)
The Planet of Junior Brown - Virginia Hamilton   *afa*   169

Post, Mallory (Banker; Businesswoman; Caucasian)
Brothers and Sisters - Bebe Moore Campbell   *afa*   47

Powell, Ernestine Avery (8-Year-Old; Niece; African American)
Back Home - Gloria Jean Pinkney   *afa*   350
The Sunday Outing - Gloria Jean Pinkney   *afa*   351

Powell, Judith (Doctor; Girlfriend; Caucasian)
The Chaneysville Incident - David Bradley   *afa*   19

Pratt, Dabney "Dab" (Mentally Challenged Person; 17-Year-Old; African American)
Sweet Whispers, Brother Rush - Virginia Hamilton   *afa*   170

Pratt, Teresa "Tree" (14-Year-Old; African American)
Sweet Whispers, Brother Rush - Virginia Hamilton   *afa*   170

Prettymon, Sidney "Sitting Pretty" (Divorced Person; Father)
Sitting Pretty - Al Young   *afa*   482

Prietita (8-Year-Old; Mexican American)
Friends From the Other Side/Amigos del Otro Lado - Gloria Anzaldua   *lat*   517
Prietita and the Ghost Woman = Prietita y La Llorona - Gloria Anzaldua   *lat*   518

Pundabi (Aged Person; African American)
The Golden Serpent - Walter Dean Myers   *afa*   308

Puttbutt, Benjamin "Chappie" III (Professor; Administrator; African American)
Japanese by Spring - Ishmael Reed   *afa*   364

Puyat, Pauline (Native American; Religious)
Tracks - Louise Erdrich   *naa*   1215

Q

Qallupilluit (Monster)
A Promise Is a Promise - Michael Arvaarluk Kusugak   *naa*   1253

Quetzalcoatl (Deity)
The Legend of Food Mountain - Harriet Rohmer   *lat*   792

Quickskill, Raven (Runaway; Slave; African American)
Flight to Canada - Ishmael Reed   *afa*   363

Quilaztli (Historian; Aztec)
The Aztec Chronicles: The True History of Christopher Columbus, as Narrated by Quilaztli of Texcoco: A Novella - Joseph P. Sanchez   *lat*   809

Quintana Roo, Andres (Lawyer)
Leona: A Love Story - Elizabeth Borton de Trevino   *lat*   857

Quiro (15-Year-Old; Prisoner; Native American)
Rabid Beasts - Carlos Miralejos   *lat*   704

R

Rabbit (Rabbit)
The Rabbit's Escape - Suzanne Crowder Han   *asa*   948
The Rabbit's Judgment - Suzanne Crowder Han   *asa*   949

Rabinowitz, Lynne (Activist; Wife; Caucasian)
Meridian - Alice Walker   *afa*   428

Rachel (Dancer; Actor; Cuban)
Rachel's Song: A Novel - Miguel Barnet   *lat*   529

Racoon (Racoon)
Lakota & Dakota Animal Wisdom Stories - Pamela Greenhill Kaizen   *naa*   1237

Radja (Friend; 16-Year-Old; Religious)
Gay-Neck: The Story of a Pigeon - Dhan Gopal Mukerji   *asa*   1029

Rafa, Jose Antonio (Grandfather; Mexican)
Inheritance of Strangers - Nash Candelaria   *lat*   554

Rafa, Jose Antonio (Aged Person; Mexican)
Memories of the Alhambra - Nash Candelaria   *lat*   556

Rafa, Jose Antonio (Grandfather; Landowner; Mexican)
Not by the Sword - Nash Candelaria   *lat*   557

Rafa, Tercero (Religious; Landowner; Mexican)
Not by the Sword - Nash Candelaria   *lat*   557

Rahm of Ciron (Human)
They Fly at Ciron - Samuel R. Delany   *afa*   97

Rainbow Crow (Crow)
Rainbow Crow - Nancy Van Laan   *naa*   1334

Ramirez, Eddie (Student—High School)
The Great Computer Dating Caper - T. Ernesto Bethancourt   *lat*   540

Ramirez, Nilda (10-Year-Old; Puerto Rican)
Nilda: A Novel - Nicholasa Mohr   *lat*   710

Ramon (Child; Puerto Rican)
Vejigantes Masquerade - Lucia M. Gonzalez   *lat*   641

Ramos, Alicia Inez (10-Year-Old; Child; Mexican American)
Alicia's Treasures - Diane Gonzales Bertrand   *lat*   635

Ramu (Professor; Lover)
Nampally Road - Meena Alexander   *asa*   896

Rangel, Carmen (Young Woman; Mexican)
Call No Man Master - Tina Juarez   *lat*   667

Rani (Friend; Indian American)
Bombay Talkie - Ameena Meer   *asa*   1017

Rankin, Suzella (15-Year-Old; Cousin; African American)
Let the Circle Be Unbroken - Mildred D. Taylor   *afa*   409

Ransom, Minnie (Healer; Herbalist; African American)
The Salt Eaters - Toni Cade Bambara *afa* 8

Rat (Rat)
Cat and Rat: The Legend of the Chinese Zodiac - Ed Young *asa* 1128

Rawlings, Damius (Businessman; Father; African American)
Junius over Far - Virginia Hamilton *afa* 162

Rawlings, Jackabo (Grandfather; Aged Person; African American)
Junius over Far - Virginia Hamilton *afa* 162

Rawlings, Junius (14-Year-Old; African American)
Junius over Far - Virginia Hamilton *afa* 162

Rawlins, Ezekiel "Easy" (African American; Detective—Private; African American)
Black Betty - Walter Mosley *afa* 287

Rawlins, Ezekiel "Easy" (Worker; Detective—Private; African American)
Devil in a Blue Dress - Walter Mosley *afa* 288

Rawlins, Ezekiel "Easy" (Maintenance Worker; African American; Detective—Private)
A Little Yellow Dog - Walter Mosley *afa* 289

Rawlins, Ezekiel "Easy" (Criminal; Detective—Private; African American)
A Red Death - Walter Mosley *afa* 290

Rawlins, Ezekiel "Easy" (Father; Detective—Private; African American)
White Butterfly - Walter Mosley *afa* 292

Raymond (Classmate)
Angel Child, Dragon Child - Michele Maria Surat *asa* 1075

Rayona (Native American; Young Woman)
A Yellow Raft in Blue Water - Michael Dorris *naa* 1201

Razia (Lover; Young Man)
Mistaken Identity - Nayantara Sahgal *asa* 1050

Rebecca (15-Year-Old; Pregnant Teenager; African American)
The Dear One - Jacqueline Woodson *afa* 473

Red Hawk, Stace (Native American)
Mean Spirit - Linda Hogan *naa* 1231

Red Robe (Spirit)
The Ghost Fox - Laurence Yep *asa* 1121

Reeves, Gregory (Lawyer; Veteran; Caucasian)
The Infinite Plan - Isabel Allende *lat* 498

Remirez, Santiago Antonio "Junior" Jr. (Child; Neighbor; Hispanic)
The Adventures of Sugar and Junior - Angela Shelf Medearis *afa* 270

Rene (17-Year-Old; Gang Member)
Eldorado in East Harlem - Victor Rodriguez *lat* 789

Reuben (Aged Person; Lawyer; African American)
Reuben - John Edgar Wideman *afa* 450

Revueltas, Octavio (Worker; Spouse; Mexican)
The Brick People - Alejandro Morales *lat* 724

Reyes, Gilberto (Young Man; Military Personnel; Mexican American)
A Long Way from Home - Gordon Kahn *lat* 668

Rhondy (Child; African American)
Grandmama's Joy - Eloise Greenfield *afa* 145

Rick (Brother)
A Summer Life - Gary Soto *lat* 834

Ricks, Lena (Businesswoman; Spouse; African American)
The Survivors - Kristin Hunter *afa* 211

Riera, Adan (Child; Puerto Rican)
Yagua Days - Cruz Martel *lat* 689

Riggins, Jessica Nahale (Lover)
Dancer Dawkins and the California Kid - Willyce Kim *asa* 969

Riggs, James J. (Alcoholic; Father; African American)
The Survivors - Kristin Hunter *afa* 211

Rigoletto (Pig)
Holy Radishes - Roberto Fernanez *lat* 607

Riko (16-Year-Old; Sister)
Hiroshima - Laurence Yep *asa* 1122

Rio, Carole (Artist; Lesbian)
Send My Roots Rain - Ibis Gomez-Vega *lat* 634

Rio, Johnny (Chicano; Homosexual)
City of Night - John Rechy *lat* 767

Rio, Johnny (Homosexual; Chicano)
Numbers - John Rechy *lat* 769

Rios, Danny (Veteran)
Shifting Loyalties - Daniel Cano *lat* 559

Rios, Henry (Lawyer; Homosexual; Chicano)
The Death of Friends - Michael Nava *lat* 733
The Hidden Law - Michael Nava *lat* 734
How Town: A Novel of Suspense - Michael Nava *lat* 735

Rios, Pepe (Young Man; Traveller; Mexican)
Pepe Rios - Daniel Cano *lat* 558

Rivers, Buddy (16-Year-Old; Student; African American)
His Own Where - June Jordan *afa* 236

Rivers, Raheim Errol (Courier; Father; Homosexual)
B-Boy Blues - Steven Corbin *afa* 81

Roaney, Ronald P. "Fess" (Veteran; Activist; African American)
The Lakestown Rebellion - Kristin Hunter *afa* 209

Roberts, Cody (Jockey)
Dead Heat - Willyce Kim *asa* 970

Roberts, Eugene "Gene" (Homosexual; Crime Victim; African American)
B-Boy Blues - Steven Corbin *afa* 81

Roberts, Frank (Religious; Doctor; African American)
Things to Be Lost - Lionel Newton *afa* 336

Roberts, Randall (Artist; 12-Year-Old; African American)
Things to Be Lost - Lionel Newton *afa* 336

Robie, John (Teenager; Nephew; Caucasian)
Tales of a Dead King - Walter Dean Myers *afa* 325

Robinson, Dwayne (Critic; Writer; African American)
Urban Romance - Nelson George *afa* 136

Robinson, Zurich (Football Player; African American; Religious)
And This Too Shall Pass - E. Lynn Harris *afa* 179

Rock, Darnell (13-Year-Old; Student—Junior High; African American)
Darnell Rock Reporting - Walter Dean Myers *afa* 303

Rock, Tamika (13-Year-Old; Student—Junior High; African American)
Darnell Rock Reporting - Walter Dean Myers *afa* 303

Rodriguez, Marta (15-Year-Old; Sister; Mexican)
A Place Where the Sea Remembers - Sandra Benitez *lat* 539

Rodriguez, Richard (Child; Mexican American)
Hunger of Memory: The Education of Richard Rodriguez, an Autobiography - Richard Rodriguez *lat* 788

Roessel, Jaclyn (Artisan; Native American)
Songs from the Loom - Monty Roessel *naa* 1297

Roger (Professor)
State of Emergency - Floyd Salas *lat* 807

Rohn (Boyfriend; Businessman)
In the Heart of the Valley of Love - Cynthia Kadohata *asa* 963

Romana (Mother; Puerto Rican)
The Line of the Sun: A Novel - Judith Ortiz Cofer *lat* 746

Romano-V., Octavio I. (Writer; Anthropologist; Mexican American)
Geriatric Fu: My First Sixty-Five Years in the United States - Octavio I. Romano-V, *lat* 794

Romero, Jose Luis (Expatriate; Salvadoran)
Mother Tongue - Demetria Martinez *lat* 693

Romero, Mateo (Young Man; Chicano)
Nambe—Year One - Orlando Romero *lat* 796

Rooster (Gang Member; Teenager; African American)
Straight Outta Compton - Ricardo Cortez Cruz *afa* 87

Rooster (Rooster)
Toad Is the Uncle of Heaven - Jeanne M. Lee *asa* 990

Rosa (Young Woman; Cuban)
The Greatest Performance - Elias Miguel Munoz *lat* 730

Rosa (Spouse; Jewish Chilean)
Longing - Maria Espinosa *lat* 601

Rosalba (Child)
Abuela - Arthur Dorros *lat* 593

Rosario (Grandmother; Mexican)
Cantora: A Novel - Sylvia Lopez-Medina *lat* 686

Rosario (Spouse)
Sleep of the Innocents - Carole Fernandez *lat* 603

Rose, Dessa (Pregnant Teenager; Slave; African American)
Dessa Rose - Sherley Anne Williams *afa* 463

Ross, Baby Palatine (Housewife; Neighbor; African American)
Joy - Marsha Hunt *afa* 207

Rousseau, Johnnie Ray (17-Year-Old; Homosexual; African American)
Blackbird - Larry Duplechan *afa* 105

Rousseau, Johnnie Ray (Singer; Homosexual; African American)
Captain Swing - Larry Duplechan *afa* 106

Rousseau, Lance (Patient; Divorced Person; African American)
Captain Swing - Larry Duplechan *afa* 106

Roy, Janelle (Nurse; Military Personnel; African American)
Wild Embers - Anita Richmond Bunkley *afa* 33

Rubio, Richard (Young Man; Mexican American)
Pocho - Jose Antonio Villarreal *lat* 879

Russo, Lonnie (15-Year-Old; Student—High School; Caucasian)
Vanishing Rooms - Melvin Dixon *afa* 100

Ryo (13-Year-Old; African American)
Children of the Night - Jess Mowry *afa* 293

S

Sa' (Aged Person; Native American)
Two Old Women: An Alaskan Legend of Betrayal, Courage, and Survival - Verlma Wallis *naa* 1341

Saavedra, Miguel (Writer; Cuban)
Fallen Angels Sing - Omar Torres *lat* 852

Sachi (Sister; 12-Year-Old)
Hiroshima - Laurence Yep *asa* 1122

Sachiko (Grandmother)
Sachiko Means Happiness - Kimiko Sakai *asa* 1053

Sachiko (Child)
Sachiko Means Happiness - Kimiko Sakai *asa* 1053

Sagwa of China (Cat; Chinese)
The Chinese Siamese Cat - Amy Tan *asa* 1077

St. Clair, Lena (Daughter; Chinese American)
The Joy Luck Club - Amy Tan *asa* 1079

St. Clair, Ying-ying (Immigrant; Mother; Chinese American)
The Joy Luck Club - Amy Tan *asa* 1079

St. Claire, Geraldine (Journalist; Gambler)
The Thirteenth Apostle - Gloria Gonzalez *lat* 639

St. Cloud (Expatriate; Caucasian)
Mile Zero - Thomas Sanchez *lat* 811

Saiyataca, Baldwin "Baldy" (Musician; Native American)
Painted Turtle: Woman with Guitar - Clarence Major *afa* 250

Sakane, "Father" (Father; Immigrant; Japanese American)
Journey Home - Yoshiko Uchida *asa* 1089

Sakane, Kenichi "Ken" (Brother; Japanese American)
Journey to Topaz: A Story of the Japanese-American Education - Yoshiko Uchida *asa* 1090

Sakane, "Mother" (Mother; Immigrant; Japanese American)
Journey Home - Yoshiko Uchida *asa* 1089

Sakane, "Mother" (Mother; Japanese American)
Journey to Topaz: A Story of the Japanese-American Education - Yoshiko Uchida *asa* 1090

Sakane, Yuki (Young Woman; Japanese American)
Journey Home - Yoshiko Uchida *asa* 1089

Sakane, Yuki (12-Year-Old; Japanese American)
Journey to Topaz: A Story of the Japanese-American Education - Yoshiko Uchida *asa* 1090

Salas, Floyd (Young Man; Boxer; Chicano)
Buffalo Nickel: A Memoir - Floyd Salas *lat* 806

Salazar, Francisco (Young Man; Immigrant; Mexican)
The Dark Side of the Dream - Alejandro Grattan-Dominguez *lat* 645

Salazar, Josie (Divorced Person; Mexican American)
Migrant Souls: A Novel - Arturo Islas *lat* 665

Salazar, Miguel (Veteran; Immigrant; Mexican)
The Dark Side of the Dream - Alejandro Grattan-Dominguez *lat* 645

Salazar Lopez, Maria Isabel (9-Year-Old; 3rd Grader)
My Name Is Maria Isabel - Alma Flor Ada *lat* 490

Salisbury, Samantha (Professor)
Along the Journey River - Carol LaFavor *naa* 1255

Sallis, Nita (Single Mother; Student; African American)
Live at Five - David Haynes *afa* 184

Salt (Child; Native American)
Runner in the Sun: A Story of Indian Maize - D'Arcy McNickle *naa* 1276

Sam (8-Year-Old; African American)
My Friend Jacob - Lucille Clifton *afa* 72

Sam (Child)
Sam and the Lucky Money - Karen Chinn *asa* 926
Stranger in the Mirror - Allen Say *asa* 1060

Sanchez, Gerardo (Immigrant; Puerto Rican)
Hot Soles in Harlem - Emilio Diaz Valcarcel *lat* 592

Sanchez Castillo Soto, Magdalena Armijo (Divorced Person; Aunt; Mexican American)
Leonor Park - Nash Candelaria *lat* 555

Sandel, Tom "Tomper" (Boyfriend)
Finding My Voice - Marie G. Lee *asa* 994

Sandoval, Maria (Young Woman; Chicana)
Chicano - Richard Vasquez *lat* 866

Sandy (Child; Niece; Caucasian)
Chilly Stomach - Jeannette Franklin Caines *afa* 41

Sanjay (Friend; Indian)
Bombay Talkie - Ameena Meer *asa* 1017

Santiago (Child; Puerto Rican)
Santiago - Pura Belpre *lat* 537

Santoro, Gabriel (14-Year-Old; Drug Dealer)
Third and Indiana - Steven Lopez *lat* 684

Sarah (Child; Sister)
Aunt Flossie's Hats (and Crab Cakes Later) - Elizabeth Fitzgerald Howard *afa* 200

Sargent, Rayna (Artist; Social Worker; African American)
Touch - Charlotte Sherman *afa* 390

Sassafrass (Artisan; African American)
Sassafrass, Cypress and Indigo - Ntozake Shange *afa* 385

Sato (Photographer)
Chibi: A True Story from Japan - Barbara Brenner *asa* 906

Saturday, Nance (Driver; Detective—Private; Caucasian)
The Terrible Threes - Ishmael Reed *afa* 368

Saturday, Nance (Criminologist; Spouse; Caucasian)
The Terrible Twos - Ishmael Reed *afa* 369

Saturna (Telepath; Genetically Altered Being; African American)
Saturn's Child - Nichelle Nichols *afa* 337

Schilling, Timothy (Writer)
Love, Stars, and All That - Kirin Narayan *asa* 1037

Scooter (Traveller; Musician; African American)
The Seven League Boots - Albert Murray *afa* 297

Scooter (Student—College; African American)
The Spyglass Tree - Albert Murray *afa* 298

Scott (Uncle)
A River Dream - Allen Say *asa* 1059

Seaweed (Daughter; Immigrant)
American Visa - Wang Ping *asa* 1047

Second Son (Son)
The Magic Tapestry - Demi *asa* 936

See, Florence Jun Oy "Sissee" (Daughter; Chinese)
On Gold Mountain: The One-Hundred-Year Odyssey of a Chinese-American Family - Lisa See *asa* 1062

See, Fong (Immigrant; Businessman; Chinese)
On Gold Mountain: The One-Hundred-Year Odyssey of a Chinese-American Family - Lisa See *asa* 1062

See, Leo Ming Quan "Eddy" (Son; Chinese)
On Gold Mountain: The One-Hundred-Year Odyssey of a Chinese-American Family - Lisa See *asa* 1062

See, Letticie Pruett "Ticie" (Wife; Businesswoman; Caucasian)
On Gold Mountain: The One-Hundred-Year Odyssey of a Chinese-American Family - Lisa See *asa* 1062

Seese (Young Woman; Mother)
Almanac of the Dead - Leslie Marmon Silko *naa* 1306

Sei Koichi (13-Year-Old; Japanese; Apprentice)
The Ink-keeper's Apprentice - Allen Say *asa* 1057

Serena (Social Worker; African American)
A Woman's Place - Marita Golden *afa* 140

Setman, Locke (Artist; Native American)
The Ancient Child - N. Scott Momaday *naa* 1280

Sewa, Adela (Grandmother; Storyteller; Yaqui Indian)
Daughter of the Mountain: Un Cuento - Edna Escamill *lat* 599

Seymour, Vanessa (Businesswoman; Caucasian)
The Price You Pay - Barbara Summers *afa* 402

Shabazz, King (Child; Student; African American)
The Boy Who Didn't Believe in Spring - Lucille Clifton *afa* 63

Shah, Saroj "Aunty" (Aunt)
Love, Stars, and All That - Kirin Narayan *asa* 1037

Shakespeare, Winston (Hotel Worker; Jamaican)
How Stella Got Her Groove Back - Terry McMillan *afa* 267

Shammer (Native American)
Earthdivers: Tribal Narratives on Mixed Descent - Gerald Vizenor *naa* 1336

Shan (Brother)
The Coffin Tree - Wendy Law-Yone *asa* 982

Shang (Child)
Lon Po Po: A Red-Riding Hood Story from China - Ed Young *asa* 1130

Shannon (Dancer; Native American)
Shannon: An Ojibway Dancer - Sandra King *naa* 1243

Stone, Martha (Native American; Student)
My Name Is Seepeetza - Shirley Sterling   *naa*   1324

Storey, Lincoln E. (Businessman; Wealthy; African American)
Devil's Gonna Get Him - Valerie Wilson Wesley   *afa*   442

Stranger (Agent; Cuban)
The Assault - Reinaldo Arenas   *lat*   520

Strong Bow (Native American; Child)
Moon of the Big-Dog - Jay Leech   *naa*   1258

Strong Bow (Warrior; Native American)
The White Buffalo Woman: An Indian Legend - Christine Crowl   *naa*   1189

Stuart, Sophia (17-Year-Old; Student—High School; Caucasian)
The Girl on the Outside - Mildred Pitts Walter   *afa*   433

Sturgis, Lincoln (Activist; Professor; African American)
And Do Remember Me - Marita Golden   *afa*   138

Suder, Craig (Baseball Player; Brother; African American)
Suder - Percival Everett   *afa*   116

Sugar (Child; Neighbor; African American)
The Adventures of Sugar and Junior - Angela Shelf Medearis   *afa*   270

Sugar-Groove (Traveller; African American)
Divine Days - Leon Forrest   *afa*   127

Suggs, Denver (Care Giver; Young Woman; African American)
Beloved - Toni Morrison   *afa*   281

Suggs, Sethe (Mother; Slave; African American)
Beloved - Toni Morrison   *afa*   281

Sullivan, Daniel Christopher Taylor (Spouse; Lawyer; Caucasian)
Tangled Up in Blue - Larry Duplechan   *afa*   107

Sullivan, Maggie Elizabeth Taylor (Spouse; Physical Fitness Expert; Caucasian)
Tangled Up in Blue - Larry Duplechan   *afa*   107

Sullivan, Shannon (Wife; Mother; Irish American)
Shannon - Gordon Parks   *afa*   340

Suluk (Eskimo; Father)
Harpoon of the Hunter - Markoosie   *naa*   1265

Sung (Young Man)
The Man Who Tricked a Ghost - Laurence Yep   *asa*   1124

Sung, Ellen Joyce (Student—High School; Korean American)
Finding My Voice - Marie G. Lee   *asa*   994

Sung, Ellen Joyce (Student—College; Korean American)
Saying Goodbye - Marie G. Lee   *asa*   996

Sung, Michelle (Sister; Student—College; Korean American)
Saying Goodbye - Marie G. Lee   *asa*   996

Sunset, Susie (Child; Detective—Amateur; African American)
Billy Jo Jive and the Case of the Midnight Voices - John Shearer   *afa*   386

Sunset, Susie (Child; African American; Detective—Amateur)
Billy Jo Jive, Super Private Eye: The Case of the Missing Ten Speed Bike - John Shearer   *afa*   387

Supervisor (Filmmaker; Lover)
Red Azalea - Anchee Min   *asa*   1020

Susan (Child; Sister; African American)
Aunt Flossie's Hats (and Crab Cakes Later) - Elizabeth Fitzgerald Howard   *afa*   200

Sutton, Ruth Elizabeth "Rufel" (Southern Belle; Revolutionary; Caucasian)
Dessa Rose - Sherley Anne Williams   *afa*   463

Suwelo (Professor; African American)
The Temple of My Familiar - Alice Walker   *afa*   430

Swift, Franklin (Construction Worker; African American; Alcoholic)
Disappearing Acts - Terri McMillan   *afa*   266

Swille, Arthur (Plantation Owner; Caucasian)
Flight to Canada - Ishmael Reed   *afa*   363

Sylla (Lover)
Mistaken Identity - Nayantara Sahgal   *asa*   1050

T

Ta Fan the Korean (Cook)
Dancer Dawkins and the California Kid - Willyce Kim   *asa*   969

Ta Fan the Korean (Restauranteur)
Dead Heat - Willyce Kim   *asa*   970

Tafolla, Mando (7th Grader; Chicano)
Crazy Weekend - Gary Soto   *lat*   826

Taisha (Child; Native American)
A Legend from the Crazy Horse Clan - Moses Nelson Big Crow   *naa*   1158

Tait, Norman (Artist)
Carving a Totem Pole - Vickie Jensen   *naa*   1234

Tait, Ramona (Housewife; Spouse; African American)
The Avenue, Clayton City - C. Eric Lincoln   *afa*   245

Tait, Walter Pinkney (Doctor; Spouse; African American)
The Avenue, Clayton City - C. Eric Lincoln   *afa*   245

Takashi (Child)
The Forever Christmas Tree - Yoshiko Uchida   *asa*   1088

Tamarindo, Justo (Police Officer; Veteran; Cuban American)
Mile Zero - Thomas Sanchez   *lat*   811

Tamayo, Jessica (Singer; Lesbian)
Latin Satins - Terri de la Pena   *lat*   587

Tamika (Child; African American)
Grandpa's Face - Eloise Greenfield   *afa*   146

Tandy, Rex (Photojournalist; Historian; African American)
Starlight Passage - Anita Richmond Bunkley   *afa*   32

Tanner, Tyrone (10-Year-Old; Brother; African American)
Boss Cat - Kristin Hunter   *afa*   208

Tano (Father; Puerto Rican)
The Rainbow-Colored Horse - Pura Belpre   *lat*   536

Tao (Child)
Lon Po Po: A Red-Riding Hood Story from China - Ed Young   *asa*   1130

Tariq Mia (Teacher; Neighbor)
A River Sutra - Gita Mehta   *asa*   1018

Taro "The Boy of the Three-Year Nap" (Child; Japanese)
The Boy of the Three-Year Nap - Dianne Snyder   *asa*   1069

Tarrant, Dixon (Activist; Professor; African American)
1959 - Thulani Davis   *afa*   93

Tarrant, Katherine "Willie" (Activist; Student—Junior High; African American)
1959 - Thulani Davis   *afa*   93

Tasuke (Friend)
The Bee and the Dream: A Japanese Tale - Jan Freeman Long   *asa*   1006

Tate, Desire Mary (4-Year-Old; Sister; African American)
Don't You Remember? - Lucille Clifton   *afa*   64

Tate, Lucy (Adoptee; Addict; African American)
Sent for You Yesterday - John Edgar Wideman   *afa*   451

Tate, Tyrone (14-Year-Old; Student; African American)
Those Other People - Alice Childress   *afa*   58

Tawfik, Mussa Ahmed (14-Year-Old; Guide; Moroccan)
Duel in the Desert - Walter Dean Myers   *afa*   304

Taylor, Bill (Professor; Husband; African American)
Changes - Richard Perry   *afa*   343

Taylor, Judge (Activist; Veteran; African American)
Panther - Melvin Van Peebles   *afa*   422

Taylor, Mary Kate (Housewife; Mother; African American)
All-Bright Court - Connie Porter   *afa*   356

Taylor, Michael "Mikey" (Child; Student; African American)
All-Bright Court - Connie Porter   *afa*   356

Taylor, Roar (Drug Dealer; Teenager; African American)
Getting Right with God - Lionel Newton   *afa*   335

Taylor, Samuel (Father; Worker; African American)
All-Bright Court - Connie Porter   *afa*   356

Tayo (Veteran; Native American)
Ceremony - Leslie Marmon Silko   *naa*   1307

Teddy (Child; Chinese American)
Later, Gator - Laurence Yep   *asa*   1123

Temple, Sadie Evelyn (Grandmother; African American)
Crossing over Jordan - Linda Beatrice Brown   *afa*   26

Temujin "Chingis Khan" (Child; Artist; Chinese)
Chingis Khan - Demi   *asa*   933

Terasaki, "Dad" (Father)
The Loom and Other Stories - R.A. Sasaki   *asa*   1055

Terasaki, Joanne "Jo" (Daughter)
The Loom and Other Stories - R.A. Sasaki   *asa*   1055

Terasaki, Keiko "Mom" (Mother; Daughter)
The Loom and Other Stories - R.A. Sasaki   *asa*   1055

Terasaki, Linda (Daughter)
The Loom and Other Stories - R.A. Sasaki   *asa*   1055

Uchida, Keiko (Daughter; Japanese American)
Desert Exile: The Uprooting of a Japanese-American Family - Yoshiko Uchida   *asa*   1087

Uchida, Toru (Friend; Teenager)
One Bird - Kyoko Mori   *asa*   1025

Uchida, Yoshiko (Daughter; Japanese American)
Desert Exile: The Uprooting of a Japanese-American Family - Yoshiko Uchida   *asa*   1087

Ulises (Military Personnel; Chicano)
Southern Front - Alejandro Murguia   *lat*   731

Ultima (Healer; Mexican)
Bless Me, Ultima - Rudolfo Anaya   *lat*   508

Unnamed Character (Child; African American)
Africa Dream - Eloise Greenfield   *afa*   142

Unnamed Character (Child; Sister; African American)
Always My Dad - Sharon Dennis Wyeth   *afa*   478

Unnamed Character (Divorced Person; African American; Unemployed)
Be-Bop, Re-Bop - Xam Wilson Cartier   *afa*   49

Unnamed Character (Protagonist; Young Woman)
The Coffin Tree - Wendy Law-Yone   *asa*   982

Unnamed Character (Child; Sister; African American)
Do Like Kyla - Angela Johnson   *afa*   215

Unnamed Character (Narrator; Child; Indian)
Gay-Neck: The Story of a Pigeon - Dhan Gopal Mukerji   *asa*   1029

Unnamed Character (Young Man; Japanese American)
Grandfather's Journey - Allen Say   *asa*   1056

Unnamed Character (Handyman; Secretary; African American)
High Cotton - Darryl Pinckney   *afa*   347

Unnamed Character (Child; African American)
I Love My Family - Wade Hudson   *afa*   205

Unnamed Character (Child; Brother; African American)
I Need a Lunch Box - Jeannette Franklin Caines   *afa*   43

Unnamed Character (Child; African American; Sister)
Just Us Women - Jeannette Franklin Caines   *afa*   44

Unnamed Character (Child; Sister; African American)
The Leaving Morning - Angela Johnson   *afa*   219

Unnamed Character (Spirit)
The Man Who Tricked a Ghost - Laurence Yep   *asa*   1124

Unnamed Character (Young Man)
The Rabbit's Judgment - Suzanne Crowder Han   *asa*   949

Unnamed Character (Child)
Thanksgiving at Obaachan's - Janet Mitsui Brown   *asa*   1022

Uribe, Porfirio (Lawyer; Puerto Rican)
The Labyrinth - Enrique A. Laguerre   *lat*   677

V

Valence, Paul (Young Man; Student—College; Filmmaker)
Only the Good Times - Bruce-Novoa   *lat*   549

Valenzuela de Castillo, Josephina (Grandmother; Healer; Spanish)
La Maravilla - Alfredo Vea Jr.   *lat*   867

Varela, Delfina (Widow(er))
The Devil, Delfina Varela, and the Used Chevy - Louie Garcia Robinson   *lat*   783

Vargas, Carlos (Child; Brother; Mexican)
The Girl from Playa Blanca - Ofelia Dumas Lachtman   *lat*   674

Vargas, Maria Elena (Young Woman; Sister; Mexican)
The Girl from Playa Blanca - Ofelia Dumas Lachtman   *lat*   674

Vasquez, Romilia (Young Woman; Mother)
A Fire in the Earth - Marcos McPeek Villatoro   *lat*   885

Vega, Raul (Journalist; Cuban American)
Room 9 - Soledad Santiago   *lat*   817

Velasquez, Miguel (Professor; Writer; Mexican American)
Voice-Haunted Journey - Eliud Martinez   *lat*   694

Viacom, Ron (14-Year-Old; African American; Space Explorer)
Brainstorm - Walter Dean Myers   *afa*   301

Vicario, Leona (16-Year-Old; Criolla)
Leona: A Love Story - Elizabeth Borton de Trevino   *lat*   857

Villasenor, Juan Jesus (Grandfather; Spanish)
Wild Steps of Heaven - Victor Villasenor   *lat*   884

Villasenor, Margarita (Grandmother; Mexican)
Wild Steps of Heaven - Victor Villasenor   *lat*   884

Villasenor, Salvador (Young Man; Mexican)
Rain of Gold - Victor Villasenor   *lat*   882

Vitita (Child)
The Red Comb - Fernando Pico   *lat*   755

Von Vampton, Hinckle (Aged Person; Librarian; Caucasian)
Mumbo Jumbo - Ishmael Reed   *afa*   366

Vortcir of Hi-Vator (Mythical Creature)
They Fly at Ciron - Samuel R. Delany   *afa*   97

W

Waguli (Warrior; Native American)
Mountain Windsong - Robert J. Conley   *naa*   1183

Wah, Tommy "Tai" (Writer)
Face - Aimee Liu   *asa*   1004

Wah Gay (Father; Chinese)
Eat a Bowl of Tea - Louis Chu   *asa*   931

Wainwright, Corbitt (Student; Runaway; African American)
Six Out Seven - Jess Mowry   *afa*   294

Waipo (Grandmother)
American Visa - Wang Ping   *asa*   1047

Wakatsuki, Jeanne (Daughter; Japanese American)
Farewell to Manzanar - Jeanne Wakatsuki Houston   *asa*   956

Wakatsuki, Ko "Papa" (Father; Fisherman)
Farewell to Manzanar - Jeanne Wakatsuki Houston   *asa*   956

Wakatsuki, Riku "Mama" (Mother)
Farewell to Manzanar - Jeanne Wakatsuki Houston   *asa*   956

Walker, Addy (9-Year-Old; Student; African American)
Addy Learns a Lesson: A School Story - Connie Porter   *afa*   353

Walker, Addy (10-Year-Old; Student; African American)
Addy Saves the Day: A Summer Story - Connie Porter   *afa*   354

Walker, Addy (9-Year-Old; African American)
Addy's Surprise: A Christmas Story - Connie Porter   *afa*   355

Walker, Addy (10-Year-Old; Student; African American)
Changes for Addy: A Winter Story - Connie Porter   *afa*   357

Walker, Addy (9-Year-Old; Student; African American)
Happy Birthday, Addy! A Springtime Story - Connie Porter   *afa*   358

Walker, Addy (9-Year-Old; Slave; African American)
Meet Addy: An American Girl - Connie Porter   *afa*   359

Walker, Alexander (6th Grader; Brother; African American)
Oh, Brother - Johnniece Marshall Wilson   *afa*   468

Walker, Andrew (6th Grader; Brother; African American)
Oh, Brother - Johnniece Marshall Wilson   *afa*   468

Walker, Danny (14-Year-Old; Student; African American)
Marcia - John Steptoe   *afa*   398

Walker, Paul "Pee Wee/Zip" (Friend; Homosexual; African American)
Company Man - Brent Wade   *afa*   425

Wallace, John (Businessman; Caucasian)
The Friendship - Mildred D. Taylor   *afa*   407

Walsh, Emma (Student—High School; 17-Year-Old; African American)
Because We Are - Mildred Pitts Walter   *afa*   432

Wan, Ernie (6-Year-Old; Chinese American)
Lion Dancer: Ernie Wan's Chinese New Year - Kate Waters   *asa*   1099

Wan, Jenny (Sister)
Lion Dancer: Ernie Wan's Chinese New Year - Kate Waters   *asa*   1099

Warmwater, Luke (Native American; Veteran)
Walking the Rez Road - James Northrup   *naa*   1288

Washington, Cornelius (Addict; African American)
Iced - Ray Shell   *afa*   388

Washington, John (Professor; Historian; African American)
The Chaneysville Incident - David Bradley   *afa*   19

Washington, Robert Orlando "Rob" (Basketball Player; Accident Victim; African American)
Tears of a Tiger - Sharon M. Draper   *afa*   102

Waterlily (Native American; Child)
Waterlily - Ella Cara Deloria   *naa*   1191

Waters, Kiki (Abuse Victim; Receptionist; Caucasian)
RL's Dream - Walter Mosley   *afa*   291

Watson, Byron (13-Year-Old; Brother; African American)
The Watsons Go to Birmingham—1963 - Christopher Paul Curtis   afa   91

Watson, Dinizulu "Denzel" (18-Year-Old; Salesman; African American)
Fast Talk on a Slow Track - Rita Williams-Garcia   afa   466

Watson, Joetta (5-Year-Old; Sister; African American)
The Watsons Go to Birmingham—1963 - Christopher Paul Curtis   afa   91

Watson, Kenny (10-Year-Old; Brother; African American)
The Watsons Go to Birmingham—1963 - Christopher Paul Curtis   afa   91

Watson, Kevin "Kayo" (Student—College; Businessman; African American)
Falling Leaves of Ivy - Yolanda Joe   afa   214

Waupee (Hunter; Native American)
The Ring in the Prairie - John Bierhorst   naa   1155

Wayne "Baggy" (5-Year-Old; Brother; African American)
My Brother Fine with Me - Lucille Clifton   afa   71

Weathers, Barbara Ann "Bobby" (8-Year-Old; African American)
A Girl Called Bob and a Horse Called Yoki - Barbara Campbell   afa   46

Webster, Robert (Young Man; Texas Mexican)
Mexican Village - Josephina Niggli   lat   736

Wei Gu (Young Man)
Red Thread - Ed Young   asa   1132

Wei nian (Son)
The Cricket Warrior: A Chinese Tale - Margaret Chang   asa   917

Weinstein, Norvin (Professor)
Love, Stars, and All That - Kirin Narayan   asa   1037

Weintraub, Rachel (Friend)
Stella: On the Edge of Popularity - Lauren Lee   asa   992

Weiss, Philip "Phil" (Activist; Divorced Person)
Golden Gate: A Novel in Verse - Vikram Seth   asa   1064

Wellington, Dewayne (Divorced Person; Writer; African American)
Platitudes - Trey Ellis   afa   111

Wells, Jennifer (16-Year-Old; Student—College; Caucasian)
The Nicholas Factor - Walter Dean Myers   afa   319

Wenebojo, Naanabozho (Trickster)
Earthdivers: Tribal Narratives on Mixed Descent - Gerald Vizenor   naa   1336

Werren, Ola (Aged Person; Cancer Patient; African American)
Toning the Sweep - Angela Johnson   afa   223

West, Emily D. (Servant; Abuse Victim; African American)
Emily, the Yellow Rose - Anita Richmond Bunkley   afa   31

Westby, Moses (Researcher; Husband; African American)
No - Clarence Major   afa   249

Weylin, Rufus (5-Year-Old; Caucasian)
Kindred - Octavia Butler   afa   36

Whitaker, Gayle (14-Year-Old; Mother; Pregnant Teenager)
Like Sisters on the Homefront - Rita Williams-Garcia   467

White, Blanche (Heroine; Housekeeper; African American)
Blanche Among the Talented Tenth - Barbara Neely   afa   332
Blanche on the Lam - Barbara Neely   afa   333

White Buffalo Calf Maiden (Deity; Native American)
The White Buffalo Woman: An Indian Legend - Christine Crowl   naa   1189

White Hawk, Billy (Child; Native American)
Owl's Song - Janet Campbell Hale   naa   1225

White Sky, Wallace (Child; Native American)
Dream of the Blue Heron - Victor Barnouw   naa   1147

Whitlaw (Landlord; Friend)
Dragonwings - Laurence Yep   asa   1120

Whitlaw, Robin (Niece)
Dragonwings - Laurence Yep   asa   1120

Whittman, Ishmael (Military Personnel; Caucasian)
Captain Blackman - John A. Williams   afa   458

Whong (Gentleman; Wealthy)
Sir Whong and the Golden Pig - Oki S. Han   asa   947

Whyte, Skylar Edward (Actor; Homosexual; African American)
Fragments That Remain - Steven Corbin   afa   82

Widow (Mother; Japanese)
The Boy of the Three-Year Nap - Dianne Snyder   asa   1069

Widow (Widow(er); Artisan)
The Magic Tapestry - Demi   asa   936

Wife (Spouse)
Judge Rabbit and the Tree Spirit: A Folktale from Cambodia - Lina Mao Wall   asa   1095

Wiggins, Gloria (15-Year-Old; Landlord; African American)
The Young Landlords - Walter Dean Myers   afa   327

Wiggins, Grant (Professor; African American)
A Lesson before Dying - Ernest J. Gaines   afa   135

Wiggins, Richard "Bubbles" (African American; Worker; Veteran)
The Junior Bachelor Society - John A. Williams   afa   461

Wilbert (Spouse; Father; African American)
The Gold Cadillac - Mildred D. Taylor   afa   408

Wilder, Carey (Bastard Son; Gambler; African American)
Black Gold - Anita Richmond Bunkley   afa   30

Wilder, Leela Brandon Alexander (Niece; Mother; African American)
Black Gold - Anita Richmond Bunkley   afa   30

Will (Photographer; Native American)
Medicine River - Thomas King   naa   1246

William (Child; African American)
The Best Time of Day - Valerie Flournoy   afa   121

William (Child)
William and the Good Old Days - Eloise Greenfield   afa   152

Williams, Charles "Chuckie" (10-Year-Old; African American)
A Girl Called Bob and a Horse Called Yoki - Barbara Campbell   afa   46

Williams, Doris (10-Year-Old; Sister; African American)
The Gift Giver - Joyce Hansen   afa   174

Williams, Doris (6th Grader; Sister; African American)
Yellow Bird and Me - Joyce Hansen   afa   177

Williams, Francis "Stuff" (Teenager; African American)
Fast Sam, Cool Clyde and Stuff - Walter Dean Myers   afa   306

Williams, Francois (Runner; Student—High School; African American)
Understand This - Jervey Tervalon   afa   415

Williams, Frank "Motown" (17-Year-Old; Runaway; African American)
Motown and Didi: A Love Story - Walter Dean Myers   afa   316

Williams, Jake (Father; Maintenance Worker; African American)
Trouble the Water - Melvin Dixon   afa   99

Williams, Josias (Farmer; Passenger; African American)
Mississippi Bridge - Mildred D. Taylor   afa   410

Williams, Lorraine (African American; Traveller)
Hanging by Her Teeth - Bonnie Greer   afa   153

Williams, Marcia (14-Year-Old; Student; African American)
Marcia - John Steptoe   afa   398

Williams, Marcus Garvey (15-Year-Old; Student—High School; Father)
Where Do I Go From Here? - Valerie Wilson Wesley   afa   444

Williams, Paul (15-Year-Old; Landlord; African American)
The Young Landlords - Walter Dean Myers   afa   327

Williams, Roger (Professor)
The Crown of Columbus - Louise Erdrich   naa   1212

Williams, Roxanne (12-Year-Old; Student—Junior High; African American)
Definitely Cool - Brenda Wilkinson   afa   452

Willie (African American; Maintenance Worker)
Mojo and the Russians - Walter Dean Myers   afa   314

Willis, Deirdre "Camera Dee" (Photographer; Student—Junior High; African American)
Hold Fast to Dreams - Andrea Davis Pinkney   afa   348

Willis, Lindsay (Athlete; Student—Junior High; African American)
Hold Fast to Dreams - Andrea Davis Pinkney   afa   348

Wilmanzu, Johari (Royalty; African)
Captain Africa: The Battle for Egyptica - Dwayne J. Ferguson   afa   120

Wilson, Brandon (Television Personality; African American)
Live at Five - David Haynes   afa   184

Wilson, Ida (Stepsister; African American)
Starlight Passage - Anita Richmond Bunkley   afa   32

Wilson, Irene (Teenager; African American)
Rattlebone - Maxine Clair   *afa*   60

Wilson, James "Shorty" (Construction Worker; Father; African American)
Rattlebone - Maxine Clair   *afa*   60

Wilson, Ludell (11-Year-Old; Student; African American)
Ludell - Brenda Wilkinson   *afa*   453

Wilson, Ludell (18-Year-Old; Student—High School)
Ludell's New York Time - Brenda Wilkinson   *afa*   454

Wilson, Pearlean "Pearl" (Mother; Spouse; African American)
Rattlebone - Maxine Clair   *afa*   60

Wind, Billie (Teenager; Native American)
The Talking Earth - Jean Craighead George   *naa*   1218

Wind, Doli (Child; Native American)
Little Navajo Bluebird - Ann Nolan Clark   *naa*   1182

Wind Dancer (Young Woman; Native American)
The Hunter and the Woodpecker: An Indian Legend - Christine Crowl   *naa*   1188

Wind Soldier, Harley (Native American; Young Man)
The Grass Dancer - Susan Power   *naa*   1295

Windy (Child of Divorced Parents; African American)
Daddy - Jeannette Franklin Caines   *afa*   42

Windzer, Challenge (Veteran; Alcoholic; Native American)
Sundown - John Joseph Mathews   *naa*   1271

Wine, Alice (Cook; Friend; African American)
Rainbow Roun' Mah Shoulder - Linda Brown Bragg   *afa*   21

Wing, Big (14-Year-Old; Mentally Challenged Person; African American)
Willie Bea and the Time the Martians Landed - Virginia Hamilton   *afa*   172

Wing, Nancy (Journalist)
Yellow Fever - R.A. Shiomi   *asa*   1067

Winter, Doris (Singer; African American)
Mama, I Want to Sing - Vy Higginsen   *afa*   195

Winter, Geraldine (Mother; Widow(er); African American)
Mama, I Want to Sing - Vy Higginsen   *afa*   195

Wise, Atwater "Soupspoon" (Aged Person; Musician; African American)
RL's Dream - Walter Mosley   *afa*   291

Witherspoon, Jericho (Judge; Lawyer; African American)
Two Wings to Veil My Face - Leon Forrest   *afa*   129

Witherspoon, Lucius (Religious; African American)
Witherspoon - Lance Jeffers   *afa*   213

Witherspoon, Nathaniel Turner (Storyteller; African American)
The Bloodworth Orphans - Leon Forrest   *afa*   126
There Is a Tree More Ancient than Eden - Leon Forrest   *afa*   128

Witherspoon, Nathaniel Turner (Student; Writer; African American)
Two Wings to Veil My Face - Leon Forrest   *afa*   129

Witherspoon, Sweetie Reed (Aged Person; Religious; African American)
Two Wings to Veil My Face - Leon Forrest   *afa*   129

Wolf, Naomi (Lawyer; Lesbian; Caucasian)
Lavender House Murder - Nikki Baker   *afa*   6

Wong (Restauranteur)
Mama Bear - Chyng Feng Sun   *asa*   1073

Wong, Anna Choy (Mother)
A Little Too Much Is Enough - Kathleen Tyau   *asa*   1086

Wong, Daddy (Father; Businessman; Chinese American)
Fifth Chinese Daughter - Jade Snow Wong   *asa*   1102

Wong, Father (Father)
In the Year of the Boar and Jackie Robinson - Bette Bao Lord   *asa*   1007

Wong, Jade Snow (Daughter; Chinese American)
Fifth Chinese Daughter - Jade Snow Wong   *asa*   1102

Wong, Kuhio (Father)
A Little Too Much Is Enough - Kathleen Tyau   *asa*   1086

Wong, Mahealani Suzanne "Mahi" (Young Woman; Chinese Hawaiian)
A Little Too Much Is Enough - Kathleen Tyau   *asa*   1086

Wong, Mother (Mother; Chinese American; Immigrant)
Fifth Chinese Daughter - Jade Snow Wong   *asa*   1102

Wong, Mother (Mother)
In the Year of the Boar and Jackie Robinson - Bette Bao Lord   *asa*   1007

Wong, Shirley Temple "Bandit" (Immigrant; Young Woman; Chinese)
In the Year of the Boar and Jackie Robinson - Bette Bao Lord   *asa*   1007

Wong Choy Fuk (Son)
Disappearing Moon Cafe - Sky Lee   *asa*   998

Wong Gwei Chang (Pioneer)
Disappearing Moon Cafe - Sky Lee   *asa*   998

Woo, Jing-mei "June" (Daughter; Chinese American)
The Joy Luck Club - Amy Tan   *asa*   1079

Woo, Kae Ying (Writer)
Disappearing Moon Cafe - Sky Lee   *asa*   998

Woo, Suyuan (Friend; Mother; Chinese American)
The Joy Luck Club - Amy Tan   *asa*   1079

Wright, Nel (Wife; Mother; African American)
Sula - Toni Morrison   *afa*   285

Wright, Wanda (Psychologist; African American)
I Get on the Bus - Reginald McKnight   *afa*   265

Wu (Spouse)
The Shell Woman and the King - Laurence Yep   *asa*   1127

X

X, Robert (Drifter)
In My Father's House - Ernest J. Gaines   *afa*   134

Xiao Ming (Child)
At the Beach - Huy Voun Lee   *asa*   987

In the Snow - Huy Voun Lee   *asa*   988

Y

Yamada, Ichiro (Political Prisoner; Son; Japanese American)
No-No Boy - John Okada   *asa*   1042

Yamada, Mama (Mother; Businesswoman)
No-No Boy - John Okada   *asa*   1042

Yamada, Pa (Father; Businessman)
No-No Boy - John Okada   *asa*   1042

Yamato (Tutor; Administrator; Japanese)
Japanese by Spring - Ishmael Reed   *afa*   364

Yang, Grandma (Grandmother)
Dumpling Soup - Jama Kim Rattigan   *asa*   1048

Yang, Joseph "Baba" (Son; Grandson)
Baba: A Return to China upon My Father's Shoulders - Belle Yang   *asa*   1113

Yang, Marisa (7-Year-Old; Hawaiian)
Dumpling Soup - Jama Kim Rattigan   *asa*   1048

Yang, Mary "Yang the Third Eldest" (Sister; Musician)
Yang the Youngest and His Terrible Ear - Lensey Namioka   *asa*   1036

Yang, Nainai (Mother)
Baba: A Return to China upon My Father's Shoulders - Belle Yang   *asa*   1113

Yang, Yeye (Father; Son)
Baba: A Return to China upon My Father's Shoulders - Belle Yang   *asa*   1113

Yang, Yingmei "Mary" (Student; Chinese American)
Yang the Third and Her Impossible Family - Lensey Namioka   *asa*   1035

Yang, Yingtao "Yang the Youngest" (Brother; Chinese American)
Yang the Third and Her Impossible Family - Lensey Namioka   *asa*   1035

Yang, Yingtao "Yang the Youngest" (Immigrant; Chinese American)
Yang the Youngest and His Terrible Ear - Lensey Namioka   *asa*   1036

Yang the Eldest (Brother; Musician; Chinese American)
Yang the Youngest and His Terrible Ear - Lensey Namioka   *asa*   1036

Yang the Second Oldest (Sister; Musician; Chinese American)
Yang the Youngest and His Terrible Ear - Lensey Namioka   *asa*   1036

Yeh-Shen (Orphan)
Yeh-Shen: A Cinderella Story from China - Ai-Ling Louie   *asa*   1008

Yellings, Ed (Businessman; African American; Father)
The Last Days of Louisiana Red - Ishmael Reed   *afa*   365

Yellow Calf, Sylvester (Native American; Lawyer)
The Indian Lawyer - James Welch   *naa*   1345

Yellow Hawk, James Henry "Little Jim" (Native American; Child)
Jimmy Yellow Hawk - Virginia Driving Hawk Sneve   *naa*   1316

Yellow Woman (Young Woman)
Storyteller - Leslie Marmon Silko   *naa*   1308

Ying-ying (Grandmother; Chinese)
The Moon Lady - Amy Tan   *asa*   1081

Young, Barney (Father; Gambler)
Child of the Owl - Laurence Yep   *asa*   1118

Young, Casey (12-Year-Old; Chinese American)
Child of the Owl - Laurence Yep   *asa*   1118

Young Boy (Child; Japanese)
Tree of Cranes - Allen Say   *asa*   1061

Young Hunter (Hunter; Native American)
Dawn Land - Joseph Bruchac   *naa*   1173

Young Turtle (Native American; Child)
Moon of the Big-Dog - Jay Leech   *naa*   1258

Young Woman (Young Woman; Chinese
   Panamanian German)
A Feather on the Breath of God - Sigrid
   Nunez   *asa*   1041

Youngest Son (Son)
The Magic Tapestry - Demi   *asa*   936

Yunmi (Child; Korean American)
Halmoni and the Picnic - Sook Nyul Choi   *asa*   929

Z

Zapata, Emiliano (Revolutionary; Zapotec Indian)
Zapata Lives! - Gary D. Keller   *lat*   671

Zapata, Emilio (Revolutionary; Zapotec Indian)
Zapata Rose in 1992 and Other Tales - Gary D.
   Keller   *lat*   672

Zebra (Student)
Katherine - Anchee Min   *asa*   1019

Zenobia "Nobie" (Child; African American)
Three Wishes - Lucille Clifton   *afa*   74

Zenteno, Lucia (Young Woman)
The Woman Who Outshone the Sun - Alejandro Cruz
   Martinez   *lat*   583

Zeta (Twin; Aged Person)
Almanac of the Dead - Leslie Marmon
   Silko   *naa*   1306

Ziggy (10-Year-Old; 5th Grader; African American)
Ziggy and the Black Dinosaurs - Sharon M.
   Draper   *afa*   103

Zumwalt, Oscar (Businessman; Fugitive; Caucasian)
The Terrible Twos - Ishmael Reed   *afa*   369

Character Description Index

This index alphabetically lists descriptions of the major characters in featured titles. The descriptions may be occupations (astronaut, lawyer, etc.), ethnicities, or may describe persona (amnesiac, runaway, teenager, etc.). For each description, character names are listed alphabetically. Also provided are book titles, author names, and entry numbers.

2-YEAR-OLD

Beloved
Beloved - Toni Morrison *afa* 281

4-YEAR-OLD

Hardisen, Ethel
Just an Overnight Guest - Eleanora E. Tate *afa* 404

Tate, Desire Mary
Don't You Remember? - Lucille Clifton *afa* 64

5-YEAR-OLD

Kevin
Chopsticks from America - Elaine Hosozawa-Nagano *asa* 955

Pablo
Pablo's Tree - Pat Mora *lat* 721

Watson, Joetta
The Watsons Go to Birmingham—1963 - Christopher Paul Curtis *afa* 91

Wayne "Baggy"
My Brother Fine with Me - Lucille Clifton *afa* 71

Weylin, Rufus
Kindred - Octavia Butler *afa* 36

6-YEAR-OLD

Anderson, Everett
Some of the Days of Everett Anderson - Lucille Clifton *afa* 73

Logan, Little Man
Song of the Trees - Mildred D. Taylor *afa* 413

Wan, Ernie
Lion Dancer: Ernie Wan's Chinese New Year - Kate Waters *asa* 1099

7-YEAR-OLD

Anderson, Kimako
Kimako's Story - June Jordan *afa* 237

Brandon
Two and Too Much - Mildred Pitts Walter *afa* 441

Logan, Christopher-John
Song of the Trees - Mildred D. Taylor *afa* 413

Marez, Antonio
Bless Me, Ultima - Rudolfo Anaya *lat* 508

Mii
Hiroshima No Pika (The Flash of Hiroshima) - Toshi Maruki *asa* 1012

Yang, Marisa
Dumpling Soup - Jama Kim Rattigan *asa* 1048

8-YEAR-OLD

Hicks, Sassy
Scorpions - Walter Dean Myers *afa* 322

Jason
Out from This Place - Joyce Hansen *afa* 175

Jay
Jay and the Marigold - Harriette Gillem Robinet *afa* 376

Johnetta
My Brother Fine with Me - Lucille Clifton *afa* 71

Kaya
The Forever Christmas Tree - Yoshiko Uchida *asa* 1088

Logan, Cassie
Song of the Trees - Mildred D. Taylor *afa* 413

Powell, Ernestine Avery
Back Home - Gloria Jean Pinkney *afa* 350
The Sunday Outing - Gloria Jean Pinkney *afa* 351

Prietita
Friends From the Other Side/Amigos del Otro Lado - Gloria Anzaldua *lat* 517
Prietita and the Ghost Woman = Prietita y La Llorona - Gloria Anzaldua *lat* 518

Sam
My Friend Jacob - Lucille Clifton *afa* 72

Shatu, Javaka
Birthday - John Steptoe *afa* 396

Socorro
Socorro, Daughter of the Desert - Karen Papagapitos *lat* 749

Weathers, Barbara Ann "Bobby"
A Girl Called Bob and a Horse Called Yoki - Barbara Campbell *afa* 46

9-YEAR-OLD

Alberto "Beto"
La Maravilla - Alfredo Vea Jr. *lat* 867

Avery, Mary Elouise
Thank You, Dr. Martin Luther King, Jr.! - Eleanora E. Tate *afa* 406

Carson, Margie
Just an Overnight Guest - Eleanora E. Tate *afa* 404

Davis, Harriet
Addy Learns a Lesson: A School Story - Connie Porter *afa* 353
Addy Saves the Day: A Summer Story - Connie Porter *afa* 354

Dingle, Jeffrey
Just My Luck - Emily Moore *afa* 278

Durcal, Andrea
First Confession - Montserrat Fontes *lat* 613

Escalante, Victor
First Confession - Montserrat Fontes *lat* 613

Howell, Brandy
Thank You, Dr. Martin Luther King, Jr.! - Eleanora E. Tate *afa* 406

Logan, Cassie
The Friendship - Mildred D. Taylor *afa* 407
Roll of Thunder, Hear My Cry - Mildred D. Taylor *afa* 412

Mac
Mac and Marie and the Train Toss Surprise - Elizabeth Fitzgerald Howard *afa* 202

MacTeer, Claudia
The Bluest Eye - Toni Morrison *afa* 282

Moore, Sarah
Addy Learns a Lesson: A School Story - Connie Porter *afa* 353

Olivia
Just My Luck - Emily Moore *afa* 278

Salazar Lopez, Maria Isabel
My Name Is Maria Isabel - Alma Flor Ada *lat* 490

Turner, Meg
Mayfield Crossing - Vaunda Micheaux Nelson *afa* 334

Walker, Addy
Addy Learns a Lesson: A School Story - Connie Porter *afa* 353
Addy's Surprise: A Christmas Story - Connie Porter *afa* 355

Happy Birthday, Addy! A Springtime Story - Connie
    Porter *afa* 358
Meet Addy: An American Girl - Connie
    Porter *afa* 359

10-YEAR-OLD

Davis, Joey
Chevrolet Saturdays - Candy Dawson Boyd *afa* 18

Footman, Annie Moriah "Annie Rye"
Down in the Piney Woods - Ethel Footman
    Smothers *afa* 394
Moriah's Pond - Ethel Footman Smothers *afa* 395

Hill, Clover
Clover - Dori Sanders *afa* 379

Jackson, Abyssinia "Abby"
Marked by Fire - Joyce Carol Thomas *afa* 418

Justin
Justin and the Best Biscuits in the World - Mildred
    Pitts Walter *afa* 435

Li Wu-Jiang "Shao-shao"
In the Eye of War - Margaret Chang *asa* 918

Logan, Cassie
Let the Circle Be Unbroken - Mildred D.
    Taylor *afa* 409

Logan, David
The Well: David's Story - Mildred D.
    Taylor *afa* 414

Logan, Stacey
Mississippi Bridge - Mildred D. Taylor *afa* 410

MacTeer, Frieda
The Bluest Eye - Toni Morrison *afa* 282

Maybe, Lorraine
Something to Count On - Emily Moore *afa* 279

Peterson, Angie
The Shimmershine Queens - Camille
    Yarbrough *afa* 480

Ramirez, Nilda
Nilda: A Novel - Nicholasa Mohr *lat* 710

Ramos, Alicia Inez
Alicia's Treasures - Diane Gonzales
    Bertrand *lat* 635

Simms, Jeremy
Mississippi Bridge - Mildred D. Taylor *afa* 410

Tanner, Tyrone
Boss Cat - Kristin Hunter *afa* 208

Tomas
*Where the Cinnamon Winds Blow = Donde Soplan
Los Vientos de Canela* - Jim Sagel *lat* 805

Turner, Billy Lee
Billy - Albert French *afa* 130

Walker, Addy
Addy Saves the Day: A Summer Story - Connie
    Porter *afa* 354
Changes for Addy: A Winter Story - Connie
    Porter *afa* 357

Watson, Kenny
The Watsons Go to Birmingham—1963 - Christopher
    Paul Curtis *afa* 91

Williams, Charles "Chuckie"
A Girl Called Bob and a Horse Called Yoki - Barbara
    Campbell *afa* 46

Williams, Doris
The Gift Giver - Joyce Hansen *afa* 174

Ziggy
Ziggy and the Black Dinosaurs - Sharon M.
    Draper *afa* 103

11-YEAR-OLD

Barbra
Whose Side Are You On? - Emily Moore *afa* 280

Bilal, Muhammad
Glory Field - Walter Dean Myers *afa* 307

Boggs, Connie
The World of Daughter McGuire - Sharon Dennis
    Wyeth *afa* 479

Breedlove, Pecola
The Bluest Eye - Toni Morrison *afa* 282

Brodie, T.J.
Whose Side Are You On? - Emily Moore *afa* 280

Delaney, Koya
Koya Delaney and the Good Girl Blues - Eloise
    Greenfield *afa* 147

Dodd, Christopher Noel
Have a Happy. . . - Mildred Pitts Walter *afa* 434

Douglass, Justice
Dustland - Virginia Hamilton *afa* 160
The Gathering - Virginia Hamilton *afa* 161
Justice and Her Brothers - Virginia
    Hamilton *afa* 163

Esha Su Yen "Chief"
The Scent of the Gods - Fiona Cheong *asa* 919

Hallelujah
Children of the Fire - Harriette Gillem
    Robinet *afa* 374

Jackson, Tommy "T.J."
Me, Mop, and the Moondance Kid - Walter Dean
    Myers *afa* 313
Mop, Moondance and Nagasaki Knights - Walter Dean
    Myers *afa* 315

Johnson, Jerome
Ride the Red Cycle - Harriette Gillem
    Robinet *afa* 378

Jones, Jim
Hardscrub - Lionel G. Garcia *lat* 619

Kim, Pauly
Plantation Child and Other Stories - Eve Begley
    Kiehm *asa* 966

Logan, Stacey
Song of the Trees - Mildred D. Taylor *afa* 413

McGuire, Daughter
The World of Daughter McGuire - Sharon Dennis
    Wyeth *afa* 479

Metcalf, Mariah
Mariah Keeps Cool - Mildred Pitts Walter *afa* 437
Mariah Loves Rock - Mildred Pitts Walter *afa* 438

Otake, Anna
The World of Daughter McGuire - Sharon Dennis
    Wyeth *afa* 479

Parrish, Olivia "Mop"
Me, Mop, and the Moondance Kid - Walter Dean
    Myers *afa* 313
Mop, Moondance and Nagasaki Knights - Walter Dean
    Myers *afa* 315

Payne, Quincy
How Stella Got Her Groove Back - Terry
    McMillan *afa* 267

Pippin, Chartreuse Marie "Charlie"
Charlie Pippin - Candy Dawson Boyd *afa* 17

Singh, Maizon
Last Summer with Maizon - Jacqueline
    Woodson *afa* 476
Maizon at Blue Hill - Jacqueline Woodson *afa* 477

Stackhouse, Raisin
The Secret of Gumbo Grove - Eleanora E.
    Tate *afa* 405

Tiffany
Chopsticks from America - Elaine Hosozawa-
    Nagano *asa* 955

Tory, Margaret
Last Summer with Maizon - Jacqueline
    Woodson *afa* 476

Towers, James "Yellow Bird"
Yellow Bird and Me - Joyce Hansen *afa* 177

Wilson, Ludell
Ludell - Brenda Wilkinson *afa* 453

12-YEAR-OLD

Adams, Arilla
Arilla Sun Down - Virginia Hamilton *afa* 156

Amir
The Gift Giver - Joyce Hansen *afa* 174

Baker, Andrew Jackson "Hawk"
Mississippi Chariot - Harriette Gillem
    Robinet *afa* 377

Bell, Jason
The Bells of Christmas - Virginia Hamilton *afa* 157

Benneck, Faye
Project Wheels - Jacqueline Turner Banks *afa* 11

Benson, Mattie Mae
Breadsticks and Blessing Places - Candy Dawson
    Boyd *afa* 16

Bright, Elena "Lena" Cecilia
I Hadn't Meant to Tell You This - Jacqueline
    Woodson *afa* 475

Brown, Frolic D. "Laughing Bear"
The Righteous Revenge of Artemis Bonner - Walter
    Dean Myers *afa* 321

Brown, Zambia Renelda
A Blessing in Disguise - Eleanora E. Tate *afa* 403

Clora
Family - J. California Cooper *afa* 79

Coile, Weber "Web"
Hold Fast to Dreams - Andrea Davis
    Pinkney *afa* 348

Collins, Angela
Project Wheels - Jacqueline Turner Banks *afa* 11

Cruz, Tito
Scorpions - Walter Dean Myers *afa* 322

Dean, Michael
Mojo and the Russians - Walter Dean
    Myers *afa* 314

Douglas, Antoinette Marie "Toni"
Breadsticks and Blessing Places - Candy Dawson
    Boyd *afa* 16

Duk, Donald
Donald Duk - Frank Chin *asa* 924

Felita
Going Home - Nicholasa Mohr *lat* 708

Footman, Brat
Moriah's Pond - Ethel Footman Smothers *afa* 395

Hicks, Jamal
Scorpions - Walter Dean Myers *afa* 322

Jackson, Abraham Lincoln
Mississippi Chariot - Harriette Gillem
    Robinet *afa* 377

Jefferson, Carlton Lee
The Golden Pasture - Joyce Carol Thomas *afa* 417

Jenkins, Judge
The New One - Jacqueline Turner Banks *afa* 10

Jenkins, Jury
The New One - Jacqueline Turner Banks *afa* 10
Project Wheels - Jacqueline Turner Banks *afa* 11

Kofi
The Captive - Joyce Hansen   *afa*   173

Kurihara, Emiko "Emi"
Journey to Topaz: A Story of the Japanese-American Education - Yoshiko Uchida   *asa*   1090

Lawrence, Susan Denise
Breadsticks and Blessing Places - Candy Dawson Boyd   *afa*   16

Logan, Stacey
Roll of Thunder, Hear My Cry - Mildred D. Taylor   *afa*   412

Marie Victoria
I Hadn't Meant to Tell You This - Jacqueline Woodson   *afa*   475

Mills, Willie Bea
Willie Bea and the Time the Martians Landed - Virginia Hamilton   *afa*   172

Parker, Lester
Rivers of Eros - Cyrus Colter   *afa*   78

Roberts, Randall
Things to Be Lost - Lionel Newton   *afa*   336

Sachi
Hiroshima - Laurence Yep   *asa*   1122

Sakane, Yuki
Journey to Topaz: A Story of the Japanese-American Education - Yoshiko Uchida   *asa*   1090

Sims, Buhlaire
Plain City - Virginia Hamilton   *afa*   168

Tippy
It Ain't All For Nothing - Walter Dean Myers   *afa*   311

Williams, Roxanne
Definitely Cool - Brenda Wilkinson   *afa*   452

Young, Casey
Child of the Owl - Laurence Yep   *asa*   1118

13-YEAR-OLD

Berg, Caroline
Between Madison & Palmetto - Jacqueline Woodson   *afa*   472

Brown, "B.J."
The Survivors - Kristin Hunter   *afa*   211

Brown, Elizabeth "Betsey"
Betsey Brown - Ntozake Shange   *afa*   383

Brown, Junior
The Planet of Junior Brown - Virginia Hamilton   *afa*   169

Chipmunk
Children of the Night - Jess Mowry   *afa*   293

Clark, Buddy
The Planet of Junior Brown - Virginia Hamilton   *afa*   169

Douglass, Thomas
Dustland - Virginia Hamilton   *afa*   160
The Gathering - Virginia Hamilton   *afa*   161
Justice and Her Brothers - Virginia Hamilton   *afa*   163

Estrella
Under the Feet of Jesus - Helena Maria Viramontes   *lat*   887

Freeman, Doretha
Sister - Eloise Greenfield   *afa*   150

Givens, Peter Joseph
The Color of Trees - Canaan Parker   *afa*   338

Goins, Earl
Won't Know Till I Get There - Walter Dean Myers   *afa*   326

Gordon
Way Past Cool - Jess Mowry   *afa*   295

Jefferson, Dorian
Dustland - Virginia Hamilton   *afa*   160
The Gathering - Virginia Hamilton   *afa*   161
Justice and Her Brothers - Virginia Hamilton   *afa*   163

Johnson, Benjie
A Hero Ain't Nothin' but a Sandwich - Alice Childress   *afa*   55

Logan, Hammer
The Well: David's Story - Mildred D. Taylor   *afa*   414

Logan, Stacey
Let the Circle Be Unbroken - Mildred D. Taylor   *afa*   409

Melanin "Mel" Sun
From the Notebooks of Melanin Sun - Jacqueline Woodson   *afa*   474

Rock, Darnell
Darnell Rock Reporting - Walter Dean Myers   *afa*   303

Rock, Tamika
Darnell Rock Reporting - Walter Dean Myers   *afa*   303

Ryo
Children of the Night - Jess Mowry   *afa*   293

Sei Koichi
The Ink-keeper's Apprentice - Allen Say   *asa*   1057

Singh, Maizon
Between Madison & Palmetto - Jacqueline Woodson   *afa*   472

Tory, Margaret
Between Madison & Palmetto - Jacqueline Woodson   *afa*   472

Watson, Byron
The Watsons Go to Birmingham—1963 - Christopher Paul Curtis   *afa*   91

14-YEAR-OLD

Arrow, Ken
Adventure in Granada - Walter Dean Myers   *afa*   299
Ambush in the Amazon - Walter Dean Myers   *afa*   300
Duel in the Desert - Walter Dean Myers   *afa*   304
The Hidden Shrine - Walter Dean Myers   *afa*   309

Barcia, Pedro
Adventure in Granada - Walter Dean Myers   *afa*   299

Bright Morning
Sing Down the Moon - Scott O'Dell   *naa*   1289

Christmas, Moses Lincoln
If You Please, President Lincoln - Harriette Gillem Robinet   *afa*   375

Contreras, Tony
Taking Sides - Gary Soto   *lat*   836

Easter
Out from This Place - Joyce Hansen   *afa*   175

Emily
Toning the Sweep - Angela Johnson   *afa*   223

Footman, Maybaby
Moriah's Pond - Ethel Footman Smothers   *afa*   395

Johnson, Millicent "Peaches"
Peaches - Dindga McCannon   *afa*   256

Jordan, Rainbow
Rainbow Jordan - Alice Childress   *afa*   56

Lau, Evelyn
Runaway: Diary of a Street Kid - Evelyn Lau   *asa*   981

Little, Jimmy
Somewhere in the Darkness - Walter Dean Myers   *afa*   323

Martha
Trouble's Child - Mildred Pitts Walter   *afa*   440

Mendoza, Lincoln
Taking Sides - Gary Soto   *lat*   836

Moses, Miranda
Poor Girl, Rich Girl - Johnniece Marshall Wilson   *afa*   469

Numa, Tarija
Ambush in the Amazon - Walter Dean Myers   *afa*   300

Palmer, Willy
Willy's Summer Dream - Kay Brown   *afa*   25

Perry, Stephen "Steve" Gerard
Won't Know Till I Get There - Walter Dean Myers   *afa*   326

Pratt, Teresa "Tree"
Sweet Whispers, Brother Rush - Virginia Hamilton   *afa*   170

Rawlings, Junius
Junius over Far - Virginia Hamilton   *afa*   162

Santoro, Gabriel
Third and Indiana - Steven Lopez   *lat*   684

Simms, Charlie
The Well: David's Story - Mildred D. Taylor   *afa*   414

Sophie
Humming Whispers - Angela Johnson   *afa*   217

Stone, Isaac Jr.
Just Like Martin - Ossie Davis   *afa*   92

Tate, Tyrone
Those Other People - Alice Childress   *afa*   58

Tawfik, Mussa Ahmed
Duel in the Desert - Walter Dean Myers   *afa*   304

Viacom, Ron
Brainstorm - Walter Dean Myers   *afa*   301

Walker, Danny
Marcia - John Steptoe   *afa*   398

Whitaker, Gayle
Like Sisters on the Homefront - Rita Williams-Garcia   *afa*   467

Williams, Marcia
Marcia - John Steptoe   *afa*   398

Wing, Big
Willie Bea and the Time the Martians Landed - Virginia Hamilton   *afa*   172

15-YEAR-OLD

Bak, Sookan
Echoes of the White Giraffe - Sook Nyul Choi   *asa*   927

Big Bird
Children of the Night - Jess Mowry   *afa*   293

Bonillo, Stephanie
Sweet Fifteen - Diane Gonzales Bertrand   *lat*   636

Bonner, Artemis
The Righteous Revenge of Artemis Bonner - Walter Dean Myers   *afa*   321

Collins, Eva
The Girl on the Outside - Mildred Pitts Walter   *afa*   433

Collins, Joyce Alicia
Blue Tights - Rita Williams-Garcia *afa* 465

Jones, Nia
Where Do I Go From Here? - Valerie Wilson
Wesley *afa* 444

Karen
Family Resemblances - Lowry Pei *asa* 1046

Lynn, Theodora
Those Other People - Alice Childress *afa* 58

Mary
Portrait of Mary - Nikki Grimes *afa* 155

Olamina, Lauren Oya
Parable of the Sower - Octavia Butler *afa* 37

Pasko, Lori
Billy - Albert French *afa* 130

Quiro
Rabid Beasts - Carlos Miralejos *lat* 704

Rankin, Suzella
Let the Circle Be Unbroken - Mildred D.
Taylor *afa* 409

Rebecca
The Dear One - Jacqueline Woodson *afa* 473

Rodriguez, Marta
A Place Where the Sea Remembers - Sandra
Benitez *lat* 539

Russo, Lonnie
Vanishing Rooms - Melvin Dixon *afa* 100

Shimizu, Megumi
One Bird - Kyoko Mori *asa* 1025

Wiggins, Gloria
The Young Landlords - Walter Dean
Myers *afa* 327

Williams, Marcus Garvey
Where Do I Go From Here? - Valerie Wilson
Wesley *afa* 444

Williams, Paul
The Young Landlords - Walter Dean
Myers *afa* 327

16-YEAR-OLD

Adams, Jack Sun Run
Arilla Sun Down - Virginia Hamilton *afa* 156

Alicea, Gil C.
*The Air Down Here: True Tales from a South Bronx
Boyhood* - Gil C. Alicea *lat* 496

Brown, Crystal
Crystal - Walter Dean Myers *afa* 302

Choy, Isabel Pacay
Imagining Isabel - Omar Castaneda *lat* 565

Deek
Way Past Cool - Jess Mowry *afa* 295

Figueroa, Angela
His Own Where - June Jordan *afa* 236

Gates, Constance "Cookie"
Like Sisters on the Homefront - Rita Williams-
Garcia *afa* 467

Hawkins, Louretta "Lou"
Lou in the Limelight - Kristin Hunter *afa* 210

Jones, Claireece Precious
Push - Sapphire *afa* 381

Jones, Wilhemina Orphelia "Willi"
Wilhemina Jones, Future Star - Dindga
McCannon *afa* 257

Li, Won
The Hidden Shrine - Walter Dean Myers *afa* 309

Miguel
Spidertown - Abraham Rodriguez Jr. *lat* 785

Radja
Gay-Neck: The Story of a Pigeon - Dhan Gopal
Mukerji *asa* 1029

Riko
Hiroshima - Laurence Yep *asa* 1122

Rivers, Buddy
His Own Where - June Jordan *afa* 236

Vicario, Leona
Leona: A Love Story - Elizabeth Borton de
Trevino *lat* 857

Wells, Jennifer
The Nicholas Factor - Walter Dean Myers *afa* 319

17-YEAR-OLD

Arrow, Chris
Adventure in Granada - Walter Dean
Myers *afa* 299
Ambush in the Amazon - Walter Dean
Myers *afa* 300
Duel in the Desert - Walter Dean Myers *afa* 304
The Hidden Shrine - Walter Dean Myers *afa* 309

Barnett, Jonathan
Those Other People - Alice Childress *afa* 58

Fletcher, Molly Jane
Molly by Any Other Name - Jean Davies
Okimoto *asa* 1043

Flores, Alfredo
The Me Inside of Me - T. Ernesto
Bethancourt *lat* 541

Freeman, Malene
Not Separate, Not Equal - Brenda
Wilkinson *afa* 455

Garcia, Roberto
Macho! - Edmund Villasenor *lat* 881

Hadley, Sheema
A Little Love - Virginia Hamilton *afa* 164

Imani
An Open Weave - Devorah Major *afa* 253

Jackson, Lonnie
Hoops - Walter Dean Myers *afa* 310

Johnson, DiDi
Motown and Didi: A Love Story - Walter Dean
Myers *afa* 316

Kali
Her - Cherry Muhanji *afa* 296

Logan, Cassie
The Road to Memphis - Mildred D. Taylor *afa* 411

McQuillen, Gerald
The Nicholas Factor - Walter Dean Myers *afa* 319

Moore, MC
Snakes - Al Young *afa* 483

Parker, Addie
Rivers of Eros - Cyrus Colter *afa* 78

Perry, Richard "Richie"
Fallen Angels - Walter Dean Myers *afa* 305

Pratt, Dabney "Dab"
Sweet Whispers, Brother Rush - Virginia
Hamilton *afa* 170

Rene
Eldorado in East Harlem - Victor
Rodriguez *lat* 789

Rousseau, Johnnie Ray
Blackbird - Larry Duplechan *afa* 105

Stuart, Sophia
The Girl on the Outside - Mildred Pitts
Walter *afa* 433

Walsh, Emma
Because We Are - Mildred Pitts Walter *afa* 432

Williams, Frank "Motown"
Motown and Didi: A Love Story - Walter Dean
Myers *afa* 316

18-YEAR-OLD

Carmello "Mello"
Fast Talk on a Slow Track - Rita Williams-
Garcia *afa* 466

DeLea, Rosa "Rowena"
Crystal - Walter Dean Myers *afa* 302

Lovejoy, Yoruba Evelyn
The Cotillion, or, One Good Bull Is Half the Herd -
John Oliver Killens *afa* 240

Thibodeaux, Nigel
Captain Swing - Larry Duplechan *afa* 106

Watson, Dinizulu "Denzel"
Fast Talk on a Slow Track - Rita Williams-
Garcia *afa* 466

Wilson, Ludell
Ludell's New York Time - Brenda
Wilkinson *afa* 454

3RD GRADER

Hicks, Sassy
Scorpions - Walter Dean Myers *afa* 322

Salazar Lopez, Maria Isabel
My Name Is Maria Isabel - Alma Flor Ada *lat* 490

4TH GRADER

Howell, Brandy
Thank You, Dr. Martin Luther King, Jr.! - Eleanora E.
Tate *afa* 406

Miata
The Skirt - Gary Soto *lat* 833

5TH GRADER

Herrera, Rudy
The Pool Party - Gary Soto *lat* 832

Jackson, Yolanda "Pump"
Growin' - Nikki Grimes *afa* 154

Jim Jim
Growin' - Nikki Grimes *afa* 154

Li Wu-Jiang "Shao-shao"
In the Eye of War - Margaret Chang *asa* 918

Ziggy
Ziggy and the Black Dinosaurs - Sharon M.
Draper *afa* 103

6TH GRADER

Singh, Maizon
Last Summer with Maizon - Jacqueline
Woodson *afa* 476

Tory, Margaret
Last Summer with Maizon - Jacqueline
Woodson *afa* 476

Towers, James "Yellow Bird"
Yellow Bird and Me - Joyce Hansen *afa* 177

Walker, Alexander
Oh, Brother - Johnniece Marshall Wilson   *afa*   468

Walker, Andrew
Oh, Brother - Johnniece Marshall Wilson   *afa*   468

Williams, Doris
Yellow Bird and Me - Joyce Hansen   *afa*   177

7TH GRADER

Beltran, Hector
Crazy Weekend - Gary Soto   *lat*   826

Kim, Stella Sung Ok
Stella: On the Edge of Popularity - Lauren
  Lee   *asa*   992

Larsen, Alice
If It Hadn't Been for Yoon Jun - Marie G.
  Lee   *asa*   995

Lee, Yoon Jun
If It Hadn't Been for Yoon Jun - Marie G.
  Lee   *asa*   995

Singh, Maizon
Maizon at Blue Hill - Jacqueline Woodson   *afa*   477

Stevens, Lillie
Lillie of Watts Takes a Giant Step - Mildred Pitts
  Walter   *afa*   436

Tafolla, Mando
Crazy Weekend - Gary Soto   *lat*   826

8TH GRADER

Berg, Caroline
Between Madison & Palmetto - Jacqueline
  Woodson   *afa*   472

Marie Victoria
I Hadn't Meant to Tell You This - Jacqueline
  Woodson   *afa*   475

Singh, Maizon
Between Madison & Palmetto - Jacqueline
  Woodson   *afa*   472

Tory, Margaret
Between Madison & Palmetto - Jacqueline
  Woodson   *afa*   472

10TH GRADER

Douglass, Frederick "The Mouse"
Mouse Rap - Walter Dean Myers   *afa*   317

Little, Jimmy
Somewhere in the Darkness - Walter Dean
  Myers   *afa*   323

10-YEAR-OLD

Little Wolf
Where the Buffaloes Begin - Olaf Baker   *naa*   1146

ABANDONED CHILD

Copeland, Brownfield
The Third Life of Grange Copeland - Alice
  Walker   *afa*   431

Singh, Maizon
Last Summer with Maizon - Jacqueline
  Woodson   *afa*   476

ABUSE VICTIM

Braithwaite, Esther Brown
Hurry Home - John Edgar Wideman   *afa*   448

Breedlove, Pecola
The Bluest Eye - Toni Morrison   *afa*   282

Celie
The Color Purple - Alice Walker   *afa*   426

Fletcher, Gerald
Montgomery's Children - Richard Perry   *afa*   344

Foster, Jessie
And Do Remember Me - Marita Golden   *afa*   138

Jones, Claireece Precious
Push - Sapphire   *afa*   381

Jones, Lewis
Fish Tales - Nettie Jones   *afa*   234

Lynn, Theodora
Those Other People - Alice Childress   *afa*   58

Monet, Daphne
Devil in a Blue Dress - Walter Mosley   *afa*   288

Moore, Josephine
Montgomery's Children - Richard Perry   *afa*   344

Noon
Tumbling - Diane McKinney-Whetstone   *afa*   258

Paschen, Rosalee "Rosey"
Long Goodbyes - Nikki Baker   *afa*   7

Snowdon, Patricia
Thereafter Johnnie - Carolivia Herron   *afa*   194

Tippy
It Ain't All for Nothing - Walter Dean
  Myers   *afa*   311

Waters, Kiki
RL's Dream - Walter Mosley   *afa*   291

West, Emily D.
Emily, the Yellow Rose - Anita Richmond
  Bunkley   *afa*   31

ACCIDENT VICTIM

Jackson, Andrew "Andy"
Tears of a Tiger - Sharon M. Draper   *afa*   102

Klein, Max
Fearless: A Novel - Rafael Yglesias   *lat*   892

Lawrence, Susan Denise
Breadsticks and Blessing Places - Candy Dawson
  Boyd   *afa*   16

Washington, Robert Orlando "Rob"
Tears of a Tiger - Sharon M. Draper   *afa*   102

ACCOUNTANT

Harris, Bernadine
Waiting to Exhale - Terry McMillan   *afa*   269

ACTIVIST

Adams, Elizabeth "Lisa"
And All Our Wounds Forgiven - Julius
  Lester   *afa*   242

Alexander, Marian
1959 - Thulani Davis   *afa*   93

Big Bear, Harlen
Medicine River - Thomas King   *naa*   1246

Brooks, Miriam
No Easy Place to Be - Steven Corbin   *afa*   84

Damasco, Gloria
Eulogy for a Brown Angel: A Mystery Novel - Lucha
  Corpi   *lat*   582

DiMaio, Joan
Lavender House Murder - Nikki Baker   *afa*   6

Foster, Jessie
And Do Remember Me - Marita Golden   *afa*   138

Green, Cecil
A Short Walk - Alice Childress   *afa*   57

Held, Truman
Meridian - Alice Walker   *afa*   428

Henry, Velma
The Salt Eaters - Toni Cade Bambara   *afa*   8

Hill, Meridian
Meridian - Alice Walker   *afa*   428

Isaac, Richard "Ike"
Crossover - Dennis Williams   *afa*   456

Jefferson, Naomi
Big Girls Don't Cry - Connie Briscoe   *afa*   22

Johnson, Esther
Long Distance Life - Marita Golden   *afa*   139

Kessey, Paul
City of Light - Cyrus Colter   *afa*   76

Knight, John Calvin
Night Studies - Cyrus Colter   *afa*   77

Long, Ida
Your Blues Ain't Like Mine - Bebe Moore
  Campbell   *afa*   48

Loudermilk, Eddie
Bad News Travels Fast - Gar Anthony
  Haywood   *afa*   187

Marshall, Andrea Williams
And All Our Wounds Forgiven - Julius
  Lester   *afa*   242

Marshall, John Calvin
And All Our Wounds Forgiven - Julius
  Lester   *afa*   242

Martin, Phillip
In My Father's House - Ernest J. Gaines   *afa*   134

Mirabal, Maria Teresa
In the Time of the Butterflies - Julia
  Alvarez   *lat*   503

Mirabal, Minerva
In the Time of the Butterflies - Julia
  Alvarez   *lat*   503

Mirabal, Patria
In the Time of the Butterflies - Julia
  Alvarez   *lat*   503

Rabinowitz, Lynne
Meridian - Alice Walker   *afa*   428

Roaney, Ronald P. "Fess"
The Lakestown Rebellion - Kristin Hunter   *afa*   209

Stone, Isaac Jr.
Just Like Martin - Ossie Davis   *afa*   92

Sturgis, Lincoln
And Do Remember Me - Marita Golden   *afa*   138

Tarrant, Dixon
1959 - Thulani Davis   *afa*   93

Tarrant, Katherine "Willie"
1959 - Thulani Davis   *afa*   93

Taylor, Judge
Panther - Melvin Van Peebles   *afa*   422

Trevino, Delia
Delia's Song - Lucha Corpi   *lat*   581

Weiss, Philip "Phil"
Golden Gate: A Novel in Verse - Vikram
  Seth   *asa*   1064

ACTOR

Al-Hussain, Syed Jamal Noor "Jimmy"
Bombay Talkie - Ameena Meer   *asa*   1017

Dale
Reflex and Bone Structure - Clarence
   Major   *afa*   251

Gabriel, Kenneth
Traitor to the Race - Darieck Scott   *afa*   382

Jackson, Canada
Reflex and Bone Structure - Clarence
   Major   *afa*   251

Marcialis, Evan
Traitor to the Race - Darieck Scott   *afa*   382

Rachel
Rachel's Song: A Novel - Miguel Barnet   *lat*   529

Whyte, Skylar Edward
Fragments That Remain - Steven Corbin   *afa*   82

ACTRESS

Hull, Cora
Reflex and Bone Structure - Clarence
   Major   *afa*   251

King, Virginia
Through the Ivory Gate - Rita Dove   *afa*   101

Min, Anchee
Red Azalea - Anchee Min   *asa*   1020

Springer, Nicole Marie
Invisible Life - E. Lynn Harris   *afa*   180
Just as I Am - E. Lynn Harris   *afa*   181

ADDICT

French, Carl
Sent for You Yesterday - John Edgar
   Wideman   *afa*   451

Johnson, Benjie
A Hero Ain't Nothin' but a Sandwich - Alice
   Childress   *afa*   55

Johnson, Yolanda
Rocking the Babies - Linda Raymond   *afa*   362

Lawson, Tommy
Damballah - John Edgar Wideman   *afa*   446

Tate, Lucy
Sent for You Yesterday - John Edgar
   Wideman   *afa*   451

Thomas, Piri
Down These Mean Streets - Piri Thomas   *lat*   850

Washington, Cornelius
Iced - Ray Shell   *afa*   388

ADMINISTRATOR

Ding, Raymond
American Knees - Shawn Wong   *asa*   1104

Nguyen, Betty
American Knees - Shawn Wong   *asa*   1104

Puttbutt, Benjamin "Chappie" III
Japanese by Spring - Ishmael Reed   *afa*   364

Terranova, Marie
Room 9 - Soledad Santiago   *lat*   817

Yamato
Japanese by Spring - Ishmael Reed   *afa*   364

ADOPTEE

Abby
Abby - Jeannette Franklin Caines   *afa*   40

Darrow, Pesty
The Mystery of Drear House - Virginia
   Hamilton   *afa*   167

Fannie
Tumbling - Diane McKinney-Whetstone   *afa*   258

Fletcher, Molly Jane
Molly by Any Other Name - Jean Davies
   Okimoto   *asa*   1043

Freeman, Malene
Not Separate, Not Equal - Brenda
   Wilkinson   *afa*   455

Gonzalez, Abran
Albuquerque - Rudolfo Anaya   *lat*   506

Jackson, Billy "Moondance Kid"
Me, Mop, and the Moondance Kid - Walter Dean
   Myers   *afa*   313
Mop, Moondance and Nagasaki Knights - Walter Dean
   Myers   *afa*   315

Jackson, Tommy "T.J."
Me, Mop, and the Moondance Kid - Walter Dean
   Myers   *afa*   313
Mop, Moondance and Nagasaki Knights - Walter Dean
   Myers   *afa*   315

Larsen, Alice
If It Hadn't Been for Yoon Jun - Marie G.
   Lee   *asa*   995

McMillan, Austin
Home Repairs - Trey Ellis   *afa*   110

Parrish, Olivia "Mop"
Me, Mop, and the Moondance Kid - Walter Dean
   Myers   *afa*   313
Mop, Moondance and Nagasaki Knights - Walter Dean
   Myers   *afa*   315

Tate, Lucy
Sent for You Yesterday - John Edgar
   Wideman   *afa*   451

ADVENTURER

M'witu, Najee
Captain Africa: The Battle for Egyptica - Dwayne J.
   Ferguson   *afa*   120

Noragua, Timoteo
The Dream of Santa Maria de las Piedras - Miguel
   Mendez   *lat*   701

Outlaw, Lurhetta
M.C. Higgins, the Great - Virginia
   Hamilton   *afa*   165

Smalls, LaRue
The Serpent's Gift - Helen Elaine Lee   *afa*   241

ADVERTISING

Dorati, Ed
Golden Gate: A Novel in Verse - Vikram
   Seth   *asa*   1064

AFRICAN

Bilal, Muhammad
Glory Field - Walter Dean Myers   *afa*   307

Fannie
Tumbling - Diane McKinney-Whetstone   *afa*   258

Fasseke, Chuma
Jacob's Ladder - John A. Williams   *afa*   460

Gueye, Aminata
I Get on the Bus - Reginald McKnight   *afa*   265

Kaweli "James Covey"
Echo of Lions - Barbara Chase-Riboud   *afa*   52

Kofi
The Captive - Joyce Hansen   *afa*   173

Kwesi
The Captive - Joyce Hansen   *afa*   173

M'witu, Najee
Captain Africa: The Battle for Egyptica - Dwayne J.
   Ferguson   *afa*   120

Ntah, Tarik
Legend of Tarik - Walter Dean Myers   *afa*   312

Othello
Othello, a Novel - Julius Lester   *afa*   244

Pieh, Sengbe "Joseph Cinque"
Echo of Lions - Barbara Chase-Riboud   *afa*   52

Wilmanzu, Johari
Captain Africa: The Battle for Egyptica - Dwayne J.
   Ferguson   *afa*   120

AFRICAN AMERICAN

Abby
Abby - Jeannette Franklin Caines   *afa*   40

Adkins, Mary Dee
Night Studies - Cyrus Colter   *afa*   77

Akin
Adulthood Rites - Octavia E. Butler   *afa*   39

Alex
Carousel - Pat Cummings   *afa*   88

Alexander, Marian
1959 - Thulani Davis   *afa*   93

Ali
The Girl Who Wore Snakes - Angela
   Johnson   *afa*   216
The Golden Serpent - Walter Dean Myers   *afa*   308

Alston, Derek Andrew
The Nubian - Duane Smith   *afa*   393

Amifika
Amifika - Lucille Clifton   *afa*   62

Amir
The Gift Giver - Joyce Hansen   *afa*   174

Anderson, Everett
Everett Anderson's 1-2-3 - Lucille Clifton   *afa*   65
Everett Anderson's Christmas Coming - Lucille
   Clifton   *afa*   66
Everett Anderson's Friend - Lucille Clifton   *afa*   67
Everett Anderson's Nine Month Long - Lucille
   Clifton   *afa*   68
Everett Anderson's Year - Lucille Clifton   *afa*   69
Some of the Days of Everett Anderson - Lucille
   Clifton   *afa*   73

Anderson, Kimako
Kimako's Story - June Jordan   *afa*   237

Anderson, Kojie
A Short Walk - Alice Childress   *afa*   57

Andrews, George
Mama Day - Gloria Naylor   *afa*   330

Andrews, Ophelia "Cocoa"
Mama Day - Gloria Naylor   *afa*   330

Armstrong, Willie
Witherspoon - Lance Jeffers   *afa*   213

Autrie
Indigo and Moonlight Gold - Jan Spivey
   Gilchrist   *afa*   137

Greene, Hermine Rose
Crossing over Jordan - Linda Beatrice
Brown *afa* 26

Greene, Story Temple
Crossing over Jordan - Linda Beatrice
Brown *afa* 26

Gunner, Aaron
Fear of the Dark - Gar Anthony Haywood *afa* 188
Not Long for This World - Gar Anthony
Haywood *afa* 190

Hadley, Sheema
A Little Love - Virginia Hamilton *afa* 164

Hallelujah
Children of the Fire - Harriette Gillem
Robinet *afa* 374

Hamilton, Faith
A Woman's Place - Marita Golden *afa* 140

Hamilton, Henry Isaiah
Gone Quiet - Eleanor Taylor Bland *afa* 14

Hardisen, Ethel
Just an Overnight Guest - Eleanora E. Tate *afa* 404

Harris, Afeni "Feni"
The Dear One - Jacqueline Woodson *afa* 473

Harris, Bernadine
Waiting to Exhale - Terry McMillan *afa* 269

Hawkins, Andrew
Oxherding Tale - Charles Johnson *afa* 227

Hawkins, Louretta "Lou"
Lou in the Limelight - Kristin Hunter *afa* 210

Hawks, Robert
Watershed - Percival Everett *afa* 118

Hayle, Tamara
Devil's Gonna Get Him - Valerie Wilson
Wesley *afa* 442
When Death Comes Stealing - Valerie Wilson
Wesley *afa* 443

Held, Truman
Meridian - Alice Walker *afa* 428

Hemings, Harriet
The President's Daughter - Barbara Chase-
Riboud *afa* 53

Hemings, Sally
The President's Daughter - Barbara Chase-
Riboud *afa* 53
Sally Hemings - Barbara Chase-Riboud *afa* 54

Henry, Harriet
Trouble the Water - Melvin Dixon *afa* 99

Henry, Jacob "Jake"
Jacob's Ladder - John A. Williams *afa* 460

Henry, Jordan
Trouble the Water - Melvin Dixon *afa* 99

Henry, Velma
The Salt Eaters - Toni Cade Bambara *afa* 8

Herbie
Tumbling - Diane McKinney-Whetstone *afa* 258

Hicks, Jamal
Scorpions - Walter Dean Myers *afa* 322

Hicks, Sassy
Scorpions - Walter Dean Myers *afa* 322

Higgins, M.C.
M.C. Higgins, the Great - Virginia
Hamilton *afa* 165

HighJohn, Tucept
De Mojo Blues - Arthur Flowers *afa* 125

Hightower, Hortense
The Spyglass Tree - Albert Murray *afa* 298

Hill, Clover
Clover - Dori Sanders *afa* 379

Hill, Gaten
Clover - Dori Sanders *afa* 379

Hill, Meridian
Meridian - Alice Walker *afa* 428

Holloday, Deloretto "Imani"
Divine Days - Leon Forrest *afa* 127

Howard, Martha
Rocking the Babies - Linda Raymond *afa* 362

Hutchinson, Aubrey
Fragments That Remain - Steven Corbin *afa* 82

Imani
An Open Weave - Devorah Major *afa* 253

Indigo
Sassafrass, Cypress and Indigo - Ntozake
Shange *afa* 385

Ingram, Deborah
Emergency Exit - Clarence Major *afa* 247

Ingram, James
Emergency Exit - Clarence Major *afa* 247

Iree
An Open Weave - Devorah Major *afa* 253

Isaac, Elizabeth
Crossover - Dennis Williams *afa* 456

Isaac, Richard "Ike"
Crossover - Dennis Williams *afa* 456

Iyapo, Lilith
Dawn - Octavia Butler *afa* 35

Jackson, Abraham Lincoln
Mississippi Chariot - Harriette Gillem
Robinet *afa* 377

Jackson, Abyssinia "Abby"
Marked by Fire - Joyce Carol Thomas *afa* 418

Jackson, Andrew "Andy"
Tears of a Tiger - Sharon M. Draper *afa* 102

Jackson, Billy "Moondance Kid"
Me, Mop, and the Moondance Kid - Walter Dean
Myers *afa* 313
Mop, Moondance and Nagasaki Knights - Walter Dean
Myers *afa* 315

Jackson, Canada
Reflex and Bone Structure - Clarence
Major *afa* 251

Jackson, Esther
Brothers and Sisters - Bebe Moore
Campbell *afa* 47

Jackson, Lonnie
Hoops - Walter Dean Myers *afa* 310
The Outside Shot - Walter Dean Myers *afa* 320

Jackson, Savannah
Waiting to Exhale - Terry McMillan *afa* 269

Jackson, Tommy "T.J."
Me, Mop, and the Moondance Kid - Walter Dean
Myers *afa* 313
Mop, Moondance and Nagasaki Knights - Walter Dean
Myers *afa* 315

Jackson, Yolanda "Pump"
Growin' - Nikki Grimes *afa* 154

Jadine
Tar Baby - Toni Morrison *afa* 286

James, Cora
A Short Walk - Alice Childress *afa* 57

James, Dede
The Between - Tananarive Due *afa* 104

James, Genetta "Genny"
Talk about a Family - Eloise Greenfield *afa* 151

James, Hilton
The Between - Tananarive Due *afa* 104

James, Jesse
After the Garden - Doris Jean Austin *afa* 4

Janell
Me and Neesie - Eloise Greenfield *afa* 148

Jason
For Her Dark Skin - Percival Everett *afa* 113
My Mama Needs Me - Mildred Pitts
Walter *afa* 439
Out from This Place - Joyce Hansen *afa* 175

Jay
No Trespassing - Ray Prather *afa* 361

Jefferson
A Lesson before Dying - Ernest J. Gaines *afa* 135

Jefferson, Carlton Lee
The Golden Pasture - Joyce Carol Thomas *afa* 417

Jefferson, Crystal
A Woman's Place - Marita Golden *afa* 140

Jefferson, Dorian
Dustland - Virginia Hamilton *afa* 160
The Gathering - Virginia Hamilton *afa* 161
Justice and Her Brothers - Virginia
Hamilton *afa* 163

Jefferson, Grayson
The Golden Pasture - Joyce Carol Thomas *afa* 417

Jefferson, Naomi
Big Girls Don't Cry - Connie Briscoe *afa* 22

Jefferson, Samuel
The Golden Pasture - Joyce Carol Thomas *afa* 417

Jenkins, Judge
Egg-Drop Blues - Jacqueline Turner Banks *afa* 9
The New One - Jacqueline Turner Banks *afa* 10

Jenkins, Jury
Egg-Drop Blues - Jacqueline Turner Banks *afa* 9
The New One - Jacqueline Turner Banks *afa* 10
Project Wheels - Jacqueline Turner Banks *afa* 11

Jennings, Obidiah "Obi"
Which Way Freedom? - Joyce Hansen *afa* 176

Jerome
Good, Says Jerome - Lucille Clifton *afa* 70

Jewett, Sherry
The Outside Shot - Walter Dean Myers *afa* 320

Jim Jim
Growin' - Nikki Grimes *afa* 154

Jim "Ujamaa"
All Us Come Cross the Water - Lucille
Clifton *afa* 61

Jive, Billy Jo
Billy Jo Jive and the Case of the Midnight Voices -
John Shearer *afa* 386
*Billy Jo Jive, Super Private Eye: The Case of the
Missing Ten Speed Bike* - John Shearer *afa* 387

John
Voodoo Dreams: A Novel of Marie Laveau - Jewell
Parker Rhodes *afa* 370

Johnetta
My Brother Fine with Me - Lucille Clifton *afa* 71

Johnson, Al
Somebody Else's Mama - David Haynes *afa* 186

Johnson, Avatara "Avey"
Praisesong for the Widow - Paule Marshall *afa* 255

Johnson, Benjie
A Hero Ain't Nothin' but a Sandwich - Alice
Childress *afa* 55

Johnson, Beverly "Bev"
In the Game - Nikki Baker *afa* 5

Johnson, DiDi
Motown and Didi: A Love Story - Walter Dean
Myers *afa* 316

Johnson, Esther
Long Distance Life - Marita Golden   *afa*   139

Johnson, Jerome
Ride the Red Cycle - Harriette Gillem
     Robinet   *afa*   378

Johnson, Millicent "Peaches"
Peaches - Dindga McCannon   *afa*   256

Johnson, Naomi Reeves
Long Distance Life - Marita Golden   *afa*   139

Johnson, Nettie Lee
Rocking the Babies - Linda Raymond   *afa*   362

Johnson, Paula
Somebody Else's Mama - David Haynes   *afa*   186

Johnson, Robert LeRoy "RL"
RL's Dream - Walter Mosley   *afa*   291

Johnson, Tashi (Evelyn)
Possessing the Secret of Joy - Alice
     Walker   *afa*   429

Johnson, Yolanda
Rocking the Babies - Linda Raymond   *afa*   362

Jones, Calvin "Spider" F.
Hoops - Walter Dean Myers   *afa*   310

Jones, Claireece Precious
Push - Sapphire   *afa*   381

Jones, Clement
The Terrible Threes - Ishmael Reed   *afa*   368

Jones, Hannibal
Shannon - Gordon Parks   *afa*   340

Jones, Joubert Antoine
Divine Days - Leon Forrest   *afa*   127

Jones, Margaret
Philadelphia Fire - John Edgar Wideman   *afa*   449

Jones, Ruth Mae
In Search of Satisfaction - J. California
     Cooper   *afa*   80

Jones, Wilhemina Orphelia "Willi"
Wilhemina Jones, Future Star - Dindga
     McCannon   *afa*   257

Jordan, Beverly
Sisters and Lovers - Connie Briscoe   *afa*   23

Jordan, Rainbow
Rainbow Jordan - Alice Childress   *afa*   56

Josephus, Josephus
In Search of Satisfaction - J. California
     Cooper   *afa*   80

Justin
Justin and the Best Biscuits in the World - Mildred
     Pitts Walter   *afa*   435

Kali
Her - Cherry Muhanji   *afa*   296

Kari
Papa's Stories - Dolores Johnson   *afa*   229

Kat
Muse-Echo Blues - Xam Wilson Cartier   *afa*   50

Kelly
The Best Bug to Be - Dolores Johnson   *afa*   228

Kessey, Paul
City of Light - Cyrus Colter   *afa*   76

Kessey, Saturn Marie
City of Light - Cyrus Colter   *afa*   76

Kevin
She Come Bringing Me That Little Baby Girl - Eloise
     Greenfield   *afa*   149
What Kind of Baby-Sitter Is This? - Dolores
     Johnson   *afa*   230

Kezee, Xenobia Mae
Somebody Else's Mama - David Haynes   *afa*   186

King, Virginia
Through the Ivory Gate - Rita Dove   *afa*   101

Kinney, Joshua
Emily, the Yellow Rose - Anita Richmond
     Bunkley   *afa*   31

Knight, John Calvin
Night Studies - Cyrus Colter   *afa*   77

Knight, Nicole "Nicky"
The Price You Pay - Barbara Summers   *afa*   402

Korga, Rat
Stars in My Pocket Like Grains of Sand - Samuel R.
     Delany   *afa*   96

Krupt, Yingyang
In Search of Satisfaction - J. California
     Cooper   *afa*   80

LaBas, PaPa
The Last Days of Louisiana Red - Ishmael
     Reed   *afa*   365
Mumbo Jumbo - Ishmael Reed   *afa*   366

Lakes, Abraham "Abe"
The Lakestown Rebellion - Kristin Hunter   *afa*   209

Lamont, Josephine "Josie"
Rainbow Jordan - Alice Childress   *afa*   56

Lane, Charles
Chesapeake Song - Brenda Lane
     Richardson   *afa*   371

Lane, Tamra Wells
Chesapeake Song - Brenda Lane
     Richardson   *afa*   371

LaRange, Vernon "Snake"
A Blessing in Disguise - Eleanora E. Tate   *afa*   403

Laveau, Marie
Voodoo Dreams: A Novel of Marie Laveau - Jewell
     Parker Rhodes   *afa*   370

Lawrence, Susan Denise
Breadsticks and Blessing Places - Candy Dawson
     Boyd   *afa*   16

Lawson, "Doot"
Sent for You Yesterday - John Edgar
     Wideman   *afa*   451

Lawson, John
Damballah - John Edgar Wideman   *afa*   446

Lawson, Lizabeth French
Damballah - John Edgar Wideman   *afa*   446

Lawson, Tommy
Damballah - John Edgar Wideman   *afa*   446
Hiding Place - John Edgar Wideman   *afa*   447

Lazarus, Robin
Robin on His Own - Johnniece Marshall
     Wilson   *afa*   470

Lazrus
Robin on His Own - Johnniece Marshall
     Wilson   *afa*   470

Lee, Rollo Ezekiel "Cager"
A Chocolate Soldier - Cyrus Colter   *afa*   75

Letenielle, Rebecca Florice
Rainbow Roun' Mah Shoulder - Linda Brown
     Bragg   *afa*   21

Lewis, Malcolm
Glory Field - Walter Dean Myers   *afa*   307

Lightfoot, Cassie Louise
Aunt Harriet's Underground Railroad in the Sky -
     Faith Ringgold   *afa*   372

Lincoln, Liliane
Liliane: Resurrection of the Daughter - Ntozake
     Shange   *afa*   384

Lindy
Drylongso - Virginia Hamilton   *afa*   159

Lissie
The Temple of My Familiar - Alice Walker   *afa*   430

Little, Cephus "Crab"
Somewhere in the Darkness - Walter Dean
     Myers   *afa*   323

Little, Jimmy
Somewhere in the Darkness - Walter Dean
     Myers   *afa*   323

Logan, Cassie
The Friendship - Mildred D. Taylor   *afa*   407
Let the Circle Be Unbroken - Mildred D.
     Taylor   *afa*   409
The Road to Memphis - Mildred D. Taylor   *afa*   411
Roll of Thunder, Hear My Cry - Mildred D.
     Taylor   *afa*   412
Song of the Trees - Mildred D. Taylor   *afa*   413

Logan, Christopher-John
Song of the Trees - Mildred D. Taylor   *afa*   413

Logan, David
The Well: David's Story - Mildred D.
     Taylor   *afa*   414

Logan, Hammer
The Well: David's Story - Mildred D.
     Taylor   *afa*   414

Logan, Little Man
Song of the Trees - Mildred D. Taylor   *afa*   413

Logan, Stacey
Let the Circle Be Unbroken - Mildred D.
     Taylor   *afa*   409
Mississippi Bridge - Mildred D. Taylor   *afa*   410
The Road to Memphis - Mildred D. Taylor   *afa*   411
Roll of Thunder, Hear My Cry - Mildred D.
     Taylor   *afa*   412
Song of the Trees - Mildred D. Taylor   *afa*   413

Lois
The Gold Cadillac - Mildred D. Taylor   *afa*   408

Long, Ida
Your Blues Ain't Like Mine - Bebe Moore
     Campbell   *afa*   48

Lonnie
Bonjour Lonnie - Faith Ringgold   *afa*   373
It Ain't All for Nothing - Walter Dean
     Myers   *afa*   311

Loudermilk, Dottie
Bad News Travels Fast - Gar Anthony
     Haywood   *afa*   187
Going Nowhere Fast - Gar Anthony
     Haywood   *afa*   189

Loudermilk, Eddie
Bad News Travels Fast - Gar Anthony
     Haywood   *afa*   187

Loudermilk, Joe
Bad News Travels Fast - Gar Anthony
     Haywood   *afa*   187
Going Nowhere Fast - Gar Anthony
     Haywood   *afa*   189

Lovejoy, Annie Ruth
Ugly Ways - Tina McElroy Ansa   *afa*   3

Lovejoy, Betty Jean
Ugly Ways - Tina McElroy Ansa   *afa*   3

Lovejoy, Emily Mae
Ugly Ways - Tina McElroy Ansa   *afa*   3

Lovejoy, Yoruba Evelyn
The Cotillion, or, One Good Bull Is Half the Herd -
     John Oliver Killens   *afa*   240

Lumumba, Ben Ali
The Cotillion, or, One Good Bull Is Half the Herd -
     John Oliver Killens   *afa*   240

Mabel
In the Year of the Boar and Jackie Robinson - Bette Bao Lord   *asa* 1007

Mac
Mac and Marie and the Train Toss Surprise - Elizabeth Fitzgerald Howard *afa* 202

MacAlister, Marti "Big Mac"
Dead Time - Eleanor Taylor Bland *afa* 12
Done Wrong - Eleanor Taylor Bland *afa* 13
Gone Quiet - Eleanor Taylor Bland *afa* 14
Slow Burn - Eleanor Taylor Bland *afa* 15

Mackenzie, Ursa Beatrice
Daughters - Paule Marshall *afa* 254

MacTeer, Claudia
The Bluest Eye - Toni Morrison *afa* 282

MacTeer, Frieda
The Bluest Eye - Toni Morrison *afa* 282

Manfred, Dorcas
Jazz - Toni Morrison *afa* 283

Mango, Peter
Fragments of the Ark - Louise Meriwether *afa* 275

Mango, Rain
Fragments of the Ark - Louise Meriwether *afa* 275

Manyara
Mufaro's Beautiful Daughters: An African Tale - John Steptoe *afa* 399

Mapes
A Gathering of Old Men - Ernest J. Gaines *afa* 133

March, Carla
No Other Tale to Tell - Richard Perry *afa* 345

March, Phoenix
No Other Tale to Tell - Richard Perry *afa* 345

Marcus, Theophilus J. "Skeeter"
Wilhemina Jones, Future Star - Dindga McCannon *afa* 257

Margot
Understand This - Jervey Tervalon *afa* 415

Marie
Voodoo Dreams: A Novel of Marie Laveau - Jewell Parker Rhodes *afa* 370

Marigold
When the Nightingale Sings - Joyce Carol Thomas *afa* 419

Marr, John
The Mad Man - Samuel R. Delany *afa* 95

Marshall, Andrea Williams
And All Our Wounds Forgiven - Julius Lester *afa* 242

Marshall, John Calvin
And All Our Wounds Forgiven - Julius Lester *afa* 242

Martens, John
The Nicholas Factor - Walter Dean Myers *afa* 319

Martin, Lucas
Getting Right with God - Lionel Newton *afa* 335

Martin, Phillip
In My Father's House - Ernest J. Gaines *afa* 134

Mason, Willie
Linden Hills - Gloria Naylor *afa* 329

Mathis, Quinn
Invisible Life - E. Lynn Harris *afa* 180

Mathu
A Gathering of Old Men - Ernest J. Gaines *afa* 133

Matthews, Gloria
Waiting to Exhale - Terry McMillan *afa* 269

Max
Max Found Two Sticks - Brian Pinkney *afa* 349

Maya
Julius - Angela Johnson *afa* 218

Maybe, Lorraine
Something to Count On - Emily Moore *afa* 279

McDougald, Aileen
These Same Long Bones - Gwendolyn Parker *afa* 339

McDougald, Sirus
These Same Long Bones - Gwendolyn Parker *afa* 339

McGuire, Daughter
The World of Daughter McGuire - Sharon Dennis Wyeth *afa* 479

McMillan, Austin
Home Repairs - Trey Ellis *afa* 110

McNeil, Lute
The Wedding - Dorothy West *afa* 445

McPhee, Ruella "Rooms"
Vanishing Rooms - Melvin Dixon *afa* 100

McPherson, Lena
Baby of the Family - Tina McElroy Ansa *afa* 1
The Hand I Fan With - Tina McElroy Ansa *afa* 2

Medea
For Her Dark Skin - Percival Everett *afa* 113

Melanin "Mel" Sun
From the Notebooks of Melanin Sun - Jacqueline Woodson *afa* 474

Metcalf, Mariah
Mariah Keeps Cool - Mildred Pitts Walter *afa* 437
Mariah Loves Rock - Mildred Pitts Walter *afa* 438

Michael, Mattie
Women of Brewster Place - Gloria Naylor *afa* 331

Mike
A Visit to the Country - Herschel Johnson *afa* 233

Miller, Jacob
The Black Snowman - Phil Mendez *afa* 274

Miller, Mia
And This Too Shall Pass - E. Lynn Harris *afa* 179

Mills, Willie Bea
Willie Bea and the Time the Martians Landed - Virginia Hamilton *afa* 172

Mintu, Simba "Simmie"
Philadelphia Fire - John Edgar Wideman *afa* 449

Minty
Oxherding Tale - Charles Johnson *afa* 227

Mirandy
Mirandy and Brother Wind - Patricia C. McKissack *afa* 262

Monet, Daphne
Devil in a Blue Dress - Walter Mosley *afa* 288

Monk, Ivan
Violent Spring - Gary Phillips *afa* 346

Moon, Harvey
Clean Your Room, Harvey Moon! - Pat Cummings *afa* 89

Moore, Josephine
Montgomery's Children - Richard Perry *afa* 344

Moore, MC
Snakes - Al Young *afa* 483

Moore, Sarah
Addy Learns a Lesson: A School Story - Connie Porter *afa* 353

Moroni, Petey
Petey Moroni's Camp Runamok Diary - Pat Cummings *afa* 90

Moses, Miranda
Poor Girl, Rich Girl - Johnniece Marshall Wilson *afa* 469

Mothersill, Odell
Mothersill and the Foxes - John A. Williams *afa* 462

Narrator
Autobiography of a Family Photo - Jacqueline Woodson *afa* 471

Nedeed, Luther
Linden Hills - Gloria Naylor *afa* 329

Nettie
The Color Purple - Alice Walker *afa* 426

Nettie Jo
Nettie Jo's Friends - Patricia C. McKissack *afa* 264

Nicole
Humming Whispers - Angela Johnson *afa* 217

Noon
Tumbling - Diane McKinney-Whetstone *afa* 258

Norris, Evan
I Get on the Bus - Reginald McKnight *afa* 265

North, Adam "Juneboy"
Such Was the Season - Clarence Major *afa* 252

Nyasha
Mufaro's Beautiful Daughters: An African Tale - John Steptoe *afa* 399

Oaks, Johnny
Finding the Green Stone - Alice Walker *afa* 427

Oaks, Katie
Finding the Green Stone - Alice Walker *afa* 427

Olamina, Lauren Oya
Parable of the Sower - Octavia Butler *afa* 37

Olivia
Just My Luck - Emily Moore *afa* 278

Orphelia
Wilhemina Jones, Future Star - Dindga McCannon *afa* 257

Outlaw, Lurhetta
M.C. Higgins, the Great - Virginia Hamilton *afa* 165

Owens, Elias Euritides
Holly - Albert French *afa* 131

Palmer, Willy
Willy's Summer Dream - Kay Brown *afa* 25

Palms, Denise "Neesey"
The Good Negress - A.J. Verdelle *afa* 424

Parker, Addie
Rivers of Eros - Cyrus Colter *afa* 78

Parker, Lester
Rivers of Eros - Cyrus Colter *afa* 78

Patterson, M. Montgomery "Mimi"
Keeping Secrets - Penny Mickelbury *afa* 276
Night Songs - Penny Mickelbury *afa* 277

Patty Ann
Cousins - Virginia Hamilton *afa* 158

Payne, Quincy
How Stella Got Her Groove Back - Terry McMillan *afa* 267

Payne, Stella
How Stella Got Her Groove Back - Terry McMillan *afa* 267

Peace, Sula
Sula - Toni Morrison *afa* 285

Peacock, Freda
Mama - Terry McMillan *afa* 268

Peacock, Mildred
Mama - Terry McMillan *afa* 268

Pearson, Gloria
The Good Negress - A.J. Verdelle *afa* 424

Wiggins, Gloria
The Young Landlords - Walter Dean Myers *afa* 327

Wiggins, Grant
A Lesson before Dying - Ernest J. Gaines *afa* 135

Wiggins, Richard "Bubbles"
The Junior Bachelor Society - John A. Williams *afa* 461

Wilbert
The Gold Cadillac - Mildred D. Taylor *afa* 408

Wilder, Carey
Black Gold - Anita Richmond Bunkley *afa* 30

Wilder, Leela Brandon Alexander
Black Gold - Anita Richmond Bunkley *afa* 30

William
The Best Time of Day - Valerie Flournoy *afa* 121

Williams, Charles "Chuckie"
A Girl Called Bob and a Horse Called Yoki - Barbara Campbell *afa* 46

Williams, Doris
The Gift Giver - Joyce Hansen *afa* 174
Yellow Bird and Me - Joyce Hansen *afa* 177

Williams, Francis "Stuff"
Fast Sam, Cool Clyde and Stuff - Walter Dean Myers *afa* 306

Williams, Francois
Understand This - Jervey Tervalon *afa* 415

Williams, Frank "Motown"
Motown and Didi: A Love Story - Walter Dean Myers *afa* 316

Williams, Jake
Trouble the Water - Melvin Dixon *afa* 99

Williams, Josias
Mississippi Bridge - Mildred D. Taylor *afa* 410

Williams, Lorraine
Hanging by Her Teeth - Bonnie Greer *afa* 153

Williams, Marcia
Marcia - John Steptoe *afa* 398

Williams, Paul
The Young Landlords - Walter Dean Myers *afa* 327

Williams, Roxanne
Definitely Cool - Brenda Wilkinson *afa* 452

Willie
Mojo and the Russians - Walter Dean Myers *afa* 314

Willis, Deirdre "Camera Dee"
Hold Fast to Dreams - Andrea Davis Pinkney *afa* 348

Willis, Lindsay
Hold Fast to Dreams - Andrea Davis Pinkney *afa* 348

Wilson, Brandon
Live at Five - David Haynes *afa* 184

Wilson, Ida
Starlight Passage - Anita Richmond Bunkley *afa* 32

Wilson, Irene
Rattlebone - Maxine Clair *afa* 60

Wilson, James "Shorty"
Rattlebone - Maxine Clair *afa* 60

Wilson, Ludell
Ludell - Brenda Wilkinson *afa* 453

Wilson, Pearlean "Pearl"
Rattlebone - Maxine Clair *afa* 60

Windy
Daddy - Jeannette Franklin Caines *afa* 42

Wine, Alice
Rainbow Roun' Mah Shoulder - Linda Brown Bragg *afa* 21

Wing, Big
Willie Bea and the Time the Martians Landed - Virginia Hamilton *afa* 172

Winter, Doris
Mama, I Want to Sing - Vy Higginsen *afa* 195

Winter, Geraldine
Mama, I Want to Sing - Vy Higginsen *afa* 195

Wise, Atwater "Soupspoon"
RL's Dream - Walter Mosley *afa* 291

Witherspoon, Jericho
Two Wings to Veil My Face - Leon Forrest *afa* 129

Witherspoon, Lucius
Witherspoon - Lance Jeffers *afa* 213

Witherspoon, Nathaniel Turner
The Bloodworth Orphans - Leon Forrest *afa* 126
There Is a Tree More Ancient than Eden - Leon Forrest *afa* 128
Two Wings to Veil My Face - Leon Forrest *afa* 129

Witherspoon, Sweetie Reed
Two Wings to Veil My Face - Leon Forrest *afa* 129

Wright, Nel
Sula - Toni Morrison *afa* 285

Wright, Wanda
I Get on the Bus - Reginald McKnight *afa* 265

Yellings, Ed
The Last Days of Louisiana Red - Ishmael Reed *afa* 365

Zenobia "Nobie"
Three Wishes - Lucille Clifton *afa* 74

Ziggy
Ziggy and the Black Dinosaurs - Sharon M. Draper *afa* 103

AFRICAN CUBAN

Montejo, Esteban
The Autobiography of a Runaway Slave - Esteban Montejo *lat* 714

AGED PERSON

Adams, John Quincy
Echo of Lions - Barbara Chase-Riboud *afa* 52

Barnes, Mae Lee
Her Own Place - Dori Sanders *afa* 380

Bee, Tom
The Friendship - Mildred D. Taylor *afa* 407

Belen, Maria de
Maria Belen: The Autobiography of an Indian Woman: A Novel - Graciela Limon *lat* 680

Ch'idzigyaak
Two Old Women: An Alaskan Legend of Betrayal, Courage, and Survival - Verlma Wallis *naa* 1341

Dambridge, Martha Jones
The Good Negress - A.J. Verdelle *afa* 424

David
Don't Play Us Cheap: A Harlem Party - Melvin Van Peebles *afa* 420

Day, Miranda "Mama"
Mama Day - Gloria Naylor *afa* 330

El Viejo
The Old Man and His Door - Gary Soto *lat* 829

Fausto, Don
The Road to Tamazunchale - Ron Arias *lat* 526

Ghond
Gay-Neck: The Story of a Pigeon - Dhan Gopal Mukerji *asa* 1029

Golden, M'dear
Happy Birthday, Addy! A Springtime Story - Connie Porter *afa* 358

Hamilton, Henry Isaiah
Gone Quiet - Eleanor Taylor Bland *afa* 14

Howard, Martha
Rocking the Babies - Linda Raymond *afa* 362

Huitzitzilin
Song of the Hummingbird - Graciela Limon *lat* 682

Johnson, Naomi Reeves
Long Distance Life - Marita Golden *afa* 139

Johnson, Nettie Lee
Rocking the Babies - Linda Raymond *afa* 362

Josefa
The Gold Coin - Alma Flor Ada *lat* 488

Kalawati
Aani and the Tree Huggers - Jeannine Atkins *asa* 900

Kezee, Xenobia Mae
Somebody Else's Mama - David Haynes *afa* 186

LaBas, PaPa
The Last Days of Louisiana Red - Ishmael Reed *afa* 365
Mumbo Jumbo - Ishmael Reed *afa* 366

Lecha
Almanac of the Dead - Leslie Marmon Silko *naa* 1306

Lee, Bright Star
Dragonwings - Laurence Yep *asa* 1120

Lissie
The Temple of My Familiar - Alice Walker *afa* 430

Livesey, John
Cutting Lisa - Percival Everett *afa* 112

Lizzie
Baby of the Family - Tina McElroy Ansa *afa* 1

Lopez, Arcadia H.
Barrio Teacher - Arcadia H. Lopez *lat* 683

Loudermilk, Dottie
Bad News Travels Fast - Gar Anthony Haywood *afa* 187
Going Nowhere Fast - Gar Anthony Haywood *afa* 189

Loudermilk, Joe
Bad News Travels Fast - Gar Anthony Haywood *afa* 187
Going Nowhere Fast - Gar Anthony Haywood *afa* 189

Maldonado, Loreto
Pilgrims in Aztlan - Miguel Mendez *lat* 702

Matchmaker
Red Thread - Ed Young *asa* 1132

Mathu
A Gathering of Old Men - Ernest J. Gaines *afa* 133

Michael, Mattie
Women of Brewster Place - Gloria Naylor *afa* 331

Montejo, Esteban
The Autobiography of a Runaway Slave - Esteban Montejo *lat* 714

Nanapush
Tracks - Louise Erdrich *naa* 1215

Oka, Kunisaburo "Uncle Oka"
Journey Home - Yoshiko Uchida *asa* 1089

Old Man
Magic Spring: A Korean Folktale - Nami Rhee *asa* 1049

Old Woman
Magic Spring: A Korean Folktale - Nami Rhee   *asa*   1049

Pfluggins, Effie
The Secret of Gumbo Grove - Eleanora E. Tate   *afa*   405

Pittman, Jane
The Autobiography of Miss Jane Pittman - Ernest J. Gaines   *afa*   132

Pundabi
The Golden Serpent - Walter Dean Myers   *afa*   308

Rafa, Jose Antonio
Memories of the Alhambra - Nash Candelaria   *lat*   556

Rawlings, Jackabo
Junius over Far - Virginia Hamilton   *afa*   162

Reuben
Reuben - John Edgar Wideman   *afa*   450

Sa'
Two Old Women: An Alaskan Legend of Betrayal, Courage, and Survival - Verlma Wallis   *naa*   1341

Simpkins, Bess
Hiding Place - John Edgar Wideman   *afa*   447

Sixbury, Chloe
Walk Me to the Distance - Percival Everett   *afa*   117

Smith, Joshua
Do Lord Remember Me - Julius Lester   *afa*   243

Sommer-Hicks, Annie Eliza
Such Was the Season - Clarence Major   *afa*   252

Toda
The Forever Christmas Tree - Yoshiko Uchida   *asa*   1088

Tut
Cousins - Virginia Hamilton   *afa*   158

Von Vampton, Hinckle
Mumbo Jumbo - Ishmael Reed   *afa*   366

Werren, Ola
Toning the Sweep - Angela Johnson   *afa*   223

Wise, Atwater "Soupspoon"
RL's Dream - Walter Mosley   *afa*   291

Witherspoon, Sweetie Reed
Two Wings to Veil My Face - Leon Forrest   *afa*   129

Zeta
Almanac of the Dead - Leslie Marmon Silko   *naa*   1306

AGENT

Stranger
The Assault - Reinaldo Arenas   *lat*   520

ALCOHOLIC

Antonio
Longing - Maria Espinosa   *lat*   601

Capture, Cecelia
The Jailing of Cecelia Capture - Janet Campbell Hale   *naa*   1224

Jones, Calvin "Spider" F.
Hoops - Walter Dean Myers   *afa*   310

Lonnie
It Ain't All for Nothing - Walter Dean Myers   *afa*   311

Miller, Mia
And This Too Shall Pass - E. Lynn Harris   *afa*   179

Peacock, Freda
Mama - Terry McMillan   *afa*   268

Riggs, James J.
The Survivors - Kristin Hunter   *afa*   211

Swift, Franklin
Disappearing Acts - Terri McMillan   *afa*   266

Windzer, Challenge
Sundown - John Joseph Mathews   *naa*   1271

ALIEN

Doyle, Asa Elias "Eli"
Clay's Ark - Octavia Butler   *afa*   34

Jdahya
Dawn - Octavia Butler   *afa*   35

Nikanj
Dawn - Octavia Butler   *afa*   35

ALLIGATOR

Oscar
Later, Gator - Laurence Yep   *asa*   1123

ANIMAL

Turtle
Coyote & Little Turtle: Iisaw Niqw Yongosonhoya: A Traditional Hopi Tale - Herschel Talashoema   *naa*   1328

ANIMAL LOVER

Turner, Idabell
A Little Yellow Dog - Walter Mosley   *afa*   289

ANIMAL TRAINER

Ghond
Gay-Neck: The Story of a Pigeon - Dhan Gopal Mukerji   *asa*   1029

ANTHROPOLOGIST

Romano-V., Octavio I.
Geriatric Fu: My First Sixty-Five Years in the United States - Octavio I. Romano-V,   *lat*   794

Twostar, Vivian
The Crown of Columbus - Louise Erdrich   *naa*   1212

APPRENTICE

Sei Koichi
The Ink-keeper's Apprentice - Allen Say   *asa*   1057

Tokida
The Ink-keeper's Apprentice - Allen Say   *asa*   1057

ARAWAK

Morning Girl
Morning Girl - Michael Dorris   *naa*   1198

Star Boy
Morning Girl - Michael Dorris   *naa*   1198

ARCHITECT

DuBois, Wanda Higgins
Another Present Era - Elaine Perry   *afa*   342

Klein, Max
Fearless: A Novel - Rafael Yglesias   *lat*   892

ARTISAN

Esperanza
Abuela's Weave - Omar Castaneda   *lat*   563

Ling-Li
Ling-Li and the Phoenix Fairy: A Chinese Folktale - Ellin Greene   *asa*   940

Moore, Ernestine
An Open Weave - Devorah Major   *afa*   253

Roessel, Jaclyn
Songs from the Loom - Monty Roessel   *naa*   1297

Sassafrass
Sassafrass, Cypress and Indigo - Ntozake Shange   *afa*   385

Widow
The Magic Tapestry - Demi   *asa*   936

ARTIST

Alicia
The Mixquiahuala Letters - Ana Castillo   *lat*   568

Cronheim, Sterling
Another Present Era - Elaine Perry   *afa*   342

Hayakawa, Janet "Jan"
Golden Gate: A Novel in Verse - Vikram Seth   *asa*   1064

Held, Truman
Meridian - Alice Walker   *afa*   428

Holloday, Deloretto "Imani"
Divine Days - Leon Forrest   *afa*   127

Ives, Edward
Mr. Ives' Christmas - Oscar Hijuelos   *lat*   656

Jones, Wilhemina Orphelia "Willi"
Wilhemina Jones, Future Star - Dindga McCannon   *afa*   257

Liang
Liang and the Magic Paintbrush - Demi   *asa*   935

Lincoln, Liliane
Liliane: Resurrection of the Daughter - Ntozake Shange   *afa*   384

Matsuda, Karen Kumai
Molly by Any Other Name - Jean Davies Okimoto   *asa*   1043

Maybe, Lorraine
Something to Count On - Emily Moore   *afa*   279

Noro Shinpei
The Ink-keeper's Apprentice - Allen Say   *asa*   1057

Okubo, Mine
Citizen 13660 - Mine Okubo   *asa*   1044

Otero, Inez
Rituals of Survival: A Woman's Portfolio - Nicholasa Mohr   *lat*   711

Owens, Elias Euritides
Holly - Albert French   *afa*   131

Pilar
Dreaming in Cuban, A Novel - Cristina Garcia   *lat*   617

Rio, Carole
Send My Roots Rain - Ibis Gomez-Vega   *lat*   634

Roberts, Randall
Things to Be Lost - Lionel Newton   *afa*   336

Sargent, Rayna
Touch - Charlotte Sherman   *afa*   390

Setman, Locke
The Ancient Child - N. Scott Momaday   *naa*   1280

Tait, Norman
Carving a Totem Pole - Vickie Jensen   *naa*   1234

Temujin "Chingis Khan"
Chingis Khan - Demi *asa* 933

ASIAN

Fletcher, Molly Jane
Molly by Any Other Name - Jean Davies
Okimoto *asa* 1043

ASSISTANT

Labrado, Ellen
Cebu - Peter Bacho *asa* 902

ATHLETE

Willis, Lindsay
Hold Fast to Dreams - Andrea Davis
Pinkney *afa* 348

AUNT

Augusta
Family Resemblances - Lowry Pei *asa* 1046

"Aunt Tiger"
Year of Impossible Goodbyes - Sook Nyul
Choi *asa* 930

Choy, Nona
A Little Too Much Is Enough - Kathleen
Tyau *asa* 1086

Kato, Emily "Aunt Emily"
Obasan - Joy Kogawa *asa* 975

Matsumoto, Aya
Shizuko's Daughter - Kyoko Mori *asa* 1026

Nakane, Ayako "Obasan"
Obasan - Joy Kogawa *asa* 975

Obasan
Naomi's Road - Joy Kogawa *asa* 974

Pilate
Song of Solomon - Toni Morrison *afa* 284

Sanchez Castillo Soto, Magdalena Armijo
Leonor Park - Nash Candelaria *lat* 555

Shah, Saroj "Aunty"
Love, Stars, and All That - Kirin Narayan *asa* 1037

Tia
A Birthday Basket for Tia - Pat Mora *lat* 717

Tia Zuelma
*Where the Cinnamon Winds Blow = Donde Soplan
Los Vientos de Canela* - Jim Sagel *lat* 805

AZTEC

Belen, Maria de
*Maria Belen: The Autobiography of an Indian Woman:
A Novel* - Graciela Limon *lat* 680

Huitzitzilin
Song of the Hummingbird - Graciela Limon *lat* 682

Malinali
Malinche: Slave Princess of Cortez - Gloria
Duran *lat* 595

Quilaztli
*The Aztec Chronicles: The True History of Christopher
Columbus, as Narrated by Quilaztli of Texcoco: A
Novella* - Joseph P. Sanchez *lat* 809

BAKER

Luna, Lazaro
Pig Cookies and Other Stories - Alberto Alvaro
Rios *lat* 774

BANKER

Jackson, Esther
Brothers and Sisters - Bebe Moore
Campbell *afa* 47

McDougald, Sirus
These Same Long Bones - Gwendolyn
Parker *afa* 339

Payne, Stella
How Stella Got Her Groove Back - Terry
McMillan *afa* 267

Post, Mallory
Brothers and Sisters - Bebe Moore
Campbell *afa* 47

BASEBALL PLAYER

Jay
No Trespassing - Ray Prather *afa* 361

Kevin
What Kind of Baby-Sitter Is This? - Dolores
Johnson *afa* 230

Suder, Craig
Suder - Percival Everett *afa* 116

Turner, Meg
Mayfield Crossing - Vaunda Micheaux
Nelson *afa* 334

BASKETBALL PLAYER

Douglass, Frederick "The Mouse"
Mouse Rap - Walter Dean Myers *afa* 317

Jackson, Andrew "Andy"
Tears of a Tiger - Sharon M. Draper *afa* 102

Jackson, Lonnie
Hoops - Walter Dean Myers *afa* 310
The Outside Shot - Walter Dean Myers *afa* 320

Washington, Robert Orlando "Rob"
Tears of a Tiger - Sharon M. Draper *afa* 102

BASTARD DAUGHTER

Collins, Joyce Alicia
Blue Tights - Rita Williams-Garcia *afa* 465

Long, Ida
Your Blues Ain't Like Mine - Bebe Moore
Campbell *afa* 48

BASTARD SON

Hawkins, Andrew
Oxherding Tale - Charles Johnson *afa* 227

Spencer, Logan
Long Distance Life - Marita Golden *afa* 139

Turner, Billy Lee
Billy - Albert French *afa* 130

Wilder, Carey
Black Gold - Anita Richmond Bunkley *afa* 30

BEAVER

Beaver
Lakota & Dakota Animal Wisdom Stories - Pamela
Greenhill Kaizen *naa* 1237

BEE

The Bees
Toad Is the Uncle of Heaven - Jeanne M.
Lee *asa* 990

BIRACIAL

Kid
Dhalgren - Samuel R. Delany *afa* 94

BIRD

Bird
Nine-in-One Grr! Grr! - Blia Xiong *asa* 1106

BISEXUAL

Avery, Shug
The Color Purple - Alice Walker *afa* 426

BLIND PERSON

Golden, M'dear
Happy Birthday, Addy! A Springtime Story - Connie
Porter *afa* 358

Masaube, Blossom Rose
Mischief Makers - Nettie Jones *afa* 235

Moore, Ernestine
An Open Weave - Devorah Major *afa* 253

BOAR

Amabel
Rockabye Crocodile - Jose Aruego *asa* 897

Nettie
Rockabye Crocodile - Jose Aruego *asa* 897

BODYGUARD

Stanton, Reggie
Chicago Blues - Hugh Holton *afa* 197

BOXER

Gonzalez, Abran
Albuquerque - Rudolfo Anaya *lat* 506

Salas, Floyd
Buffalo Nickel: A Memoir - Floyd Salas *lat* 806

BOYFRIEND

Daniels, Steve
April and the Dragon Lady - Lensey
Namioka *asa* 1034

Rohn
In the Heart of the Valley of Love - Cynthia
Kadohata *asa* 963

Sandel, Tom "Tomper"
Finding My Voice - Marie G. Lee *asa* 994

BROTHER

Abel
Jesse - Gary Soto   *lat*   827

Adres
Happy Days, Uncle Sergio - Magali Garcia
Ramis   *lat*   624

Armijo, Nicolas
Leonor Park - Nash Candelaria   *lat*   555

Arrow, Chris
Adventure in Granada - Walter Dean
Myers   *afa*   299
Ambush in the Amazon - Walter Dean
Myers   *afa*   300
Duel in the Desert - Walter Dean Myers   *afa*   304
The Hidden Shrine - Walter Dean Myers   *afa*   309

Arrow, Ken
Adventure in Granada - Walter Dean
Myers   *afa*   299
Ambush in the Amazon - Walter Dean
Myers   *afa*   300
Duel in the Desert - Walter Dean Myers   *afa*   304
The Hidden Shrine - Walter Dean Myers   *afa*   309

Bak, Inchun
Year of Impossible Goodbyes - Sook Nyul
Choi   *asa*   930

Bechet, Solomon
Colorstruck - Benita Porter   *afa*   352

Bobby
Later, Gator - Laurence Yep   *asa*   1123

Brandon
Two and Too Much - Mildred Pitts Walter   *afa*   441

Brother
Citizen 13660 - Mine Okubo   *asa*   1044

Bulosan, Leon
America Is in the Heart - Carlos Bulosan   *asa*   910

Bulosan, Macario
America Is in the Heart - Carlos Bulosan   *asa*   910

Castillo, Cesar
The Mambo Kings Play Songs of Love - Oscar
Hijuelos   *lat*   655

Castillo, Nestor
The Mambo Kings Play Songs of Love - Oscar
Hijuelos   *lat*   655

Charlie
Train Ride - John Steptoe   *afa*   401

Chen, Harry
April and the Dragon Lady - Lensey
Namioka   *asa*   1034

Crews, Donald
Bigmama's - Donald Crews   *afa*   85
Shortcut - Donald Crews   *afa*   86

Dodd, Christopher Noel
Have a Happy. . . - Mildred Pitts Walter   *afa*   434

Donny
I Can Do It Myself - Lessie Jones Little   *afa*   246

Dorati, Ed
Golden Gate: A Novel in Verse - Vikram
Seth   *asa*   1064

Douglass, Thomas
Dustland - Virginia Hamilton   *afa*   160

Fong Yun
*On Gold Mountain: The One-Hundred-Year Odyssey
of a Chinese-American Family* - Lisa
See   *asa*   1062

Ghosh, Samir
Coloured Pictures - Himani Bannerji   *asa*   903

Higgins, M.C.
M.C. Higgins, the Great - Virginia
Hamilton   *afa*   165

Jason
My Mama Needs Me - Mildred Pitts
Walter   *afa*   439

Jerome
Good, Says Jerome - Lucille Clifton   *afa*   70

Jesse
Jesse - Gary Soto   *lat*   827

Jim "Ujamaa"
All Us Come Cross the Water - Lucille
Clifton   *afa*   61

Julian
Crazy Love - Elias Miguel Munoz   *lat*   729

Justin
Justin and the Best Biscuits in the World - Mildred
Pitts Walter   *afa*   435

Kevin
She Come Bringing Me That Little Baby Girl - Eloise
Greenfield   *afa*   149

Kim, Joe
Plantation Child and Other Stories - Eve Begley
Kiehm   *asa*   966

Kim, Pauly
Plantation Child and Other Stories - Eve Begley
Kiehm   *asa*   966

Kwesi
The Captive - Joyce Hansen   *afa*   173

Larsen, David
Walk Me to the Distance - Percival Everett   *afa*   117

Lee, Ian
Ribbons - Laurence Yep   *asa*   1126

Li Yuen
The Scent of the Gods - Fiona Cheong   *asa*   919

Logan, Christopher-John
Song of the Trees - Mildred D. Taylor   *afa*   413

Logan, David
The Well: David's Story - Mildred D.
Taylor   *afa*   414

Logan, Hammer
The Well: David's Story - Mildred D.
Taylor   *afa*   414

Logan, Little Man
Song of the Trees - Mildred D. Taylor   *afa*   413

Logan, Stacey
Let the Circle Be Unbroken - Mildred D.
Taylor   *afa*   409
Mississippi Bridge - Mildred D. Taylor   *afa*   410
Roll of Thunder, Hear My Cry - Mildred D.
Taylor   *afa*   412
Song of the Trees - Mildred D. Taylor   *afa*   413

Loudermilk, Eddie
Bad News Travels Fast - Gar Anthony
Haywood   *afa*   187

Mac
Mac and Marie and the Train Toss Surprise -
Elizabeth Fitzgerald Howard   *afa*   202

Malanguezes, Tego
*Family Installments: Memories of Growing Up
Hispanic* - Edward Rivera   *lat*   776

Miller, Jacob
The Black Snowman - Phil Mendez   *afa*   274

Monk, Ivan
Violent Spring - Gary Phillips   *afa*   346

Nakane, Stephen
Naomi's Road - Joy Kogawa   *asa*   974

Nguyen, Little Quang
Angel Child, Dragon Child - Michele Maria
Surat   *asa*   1075

Oaks, Johnny
Finding the Green Stone - Alice Walker   *afa*   427

Peregrin, Camilo
Skywriting - Margarita Engle   *lat*   598

Rick
A Summer Life - Gary Soto   *lat*   834

Sakane, Kenichi "Ken"
*Journey to Topaz: A Story of the Japanese-American
Education* - Yoshiko Uchida   *asa*   1090

Shan
The Coffin Tree - Wendy Law-Yone   *asa*   982

Suder, Craig
Suder - Percival Everett   *afa*   116

Tanner, Tyrone
Boss Cat - Kristin Hunter   *afa*   208

Torres, Beaver
The Secret of Two Brothers - Irene Beltran
Hernandez   *lat*   650

Torres, Cande
The Secret of Two Brothers - Irene Beltran
Hernandez   *lat*   650

Unnamed Character
I Need a Lunch Box - Jeannette Franklin
Caines   *afa*   43

Vargas, Carlos
The Girl from Playa Blanca - Ofelia Dumas
Lachtman   *lat*   674

Walker, Alexander
Oh, Brother - Johnniece Marshall Wilson   *afa*   468

Walker, Andrew
Oh, Brother - Johnniece Marshall Wilson   *afa*   468

Watson, Byron
The Watsons Go to Birmingham—1963 - Christopher
Paul Curtis   *afa*   91

Watson, Kenny
The Watsons Go to Birmingham—1963 - Christopher
Paul Curtis   *afa*   91

Wayne "Baggy"
My Brother Fine with Me - Lucille Clifton   *afa*   71

Yang, Yingtao "Yang the Youngest"
Yang the Third and Her Impossible Family - Lensey
Namioka   *asa*   1035

Yang the Eldest
Yang the Youngest and His Terrible Ear - Lensey
Namioka   *asa*   1036

BUSINESSMAN

Alston, Derek Andrew
The Nubian - Duane Smith   *afa*   393

Andrews, George
Mama Day - Gloria Naylor   *afa*   330

Bradley
Another Present Era - Elaine Perry   *afa*   342

Butler, Hoyt "Cap'n"
The Avenue, Clayton City - C. Eric
Lincoln   *afa*   245

Caballos, Manny
The Devil, Delfina Varela, and the Used Chevy - Louie
Garcia Robinson   *lat*   783

Chang, Ralph Yifeng
Typical American - Gish Jen   *asa*   960

Chen Liyi
Frontiers of Love - Diana Chang   *asa*   915

Chung, Eric
The Incorporation of Eric Chung - Steven Lo   *asa*   1005

Covington, William "Billy"
Company Man - Brent Wade   *afa*   425

Curtis, DeWayne
When Death Comes Stealing - Valerie Wilson Wesley   *afa*   443

de Alvarez, Bernardo
The Deaths of Don Bernardo - Barbara Mujica   *lat*   728

DeWitt, Neil
Windy City - Hugh Holton   *afa*   199

Dominic, Frank
Albuquerque - Rudolfo Anaya   *lat*   506

Eustace
High Cotton - Darryl Pinckney   *afa*   347

Fong Yun
On Gold Mountain: The One-Hundred-Year Odyssey of a Chinese-American Family - Lisa See   *asa*   1062

Goodman, Sonny
Losing Absalom - Alexs D. Pate   *afa*   341

Holton, Roger
The Incorporation of Eric Chung - Steven Lo   *asa*   1005

Lamartine, Lyman
The Bingo Palace - Louise Erdrich   *naa*   1211

Lane, Charles
Chesapeake Song - Brenda Lane Richardson   *afa*   371

LaRange, Vernon "Snake"
A Blessing in Disguise - Eleanora E. Tate   *afa*   403

Lee, Bright Star
Dragonwings - Laurence Yep   *asa*   1120

Li, Lao "Uncle Li"
Face - Aimee Liu   *asa*   1004

Mandarino, Gary
The Berhama Account - John A. Williams   *afa*   457

McNeil, Lute
The Wedding - Dorothy West   *afa*   445

Mendizabal, Quintin
The House on the Lagoon - Rosario Ferre   *lat*   608

Merchant
The Boy of the Three-Year Nap - Dianne Snyder   *asa*   1069

Nieves, Facundo
Valentino's Hair - Yvonne V. Sapia   *lat*   819

Rawlings, Damius
Junius over Far - Virginia Hamilton   *afa*   162

Rohn
In the Heart of the Valley of Love - Cynthia Kadohata   *asa*   963

See, Fong
On Gold Mountain: The One-Hundred-Year Odyssey of a Chinese-American Family - Lisa See   *asa*   1062

Stock, Dave
The True American: A Folk Fable - Melvin Van Peebles   *afa*   423

Storey, Lincoln E.
Devil's Gonna Get Him - Valerie Wilson Wesley   *afa*   442

Uchida, Dwight Takashi
Desert Exile: The Uprooting of a Japanese-American Family - Yoshiko Uchida   *asa*   1087

Wallace, John
The Friendship - Mildred D. Taylor   *afa*   407

Watson, Kevin "Kayo"
Falling Leaves of Ivy - Yolanda Joe   *afa*   214

Wong, Daddy
Fifth Chinese Daughter - Jade Snow Wong   *asa*   1102

Yamada, Pa
No-No Boy - John Okada   *asa*   1042

Yellings, Ed
The Last Days of Louisiana Red - Ishmael Reed   *afa*   365

Zumwalt, Oscar
The Terrible Twos - Ishmael Reed   *afa*   369

BUSINESSWOMAN

Beckett, Kelsey
In the Game - Nikki Baker   *afa*   5

Bird
Gilda Stories - Jewelle Gomez   *afa*   141

Covington, Paula
Company Man - Brent Wade   *afa*   425

DeWitt, Margo
Windy City - Hugh Holton   *afa*   199

Eve
Bailey's Cafe - Gloria Naylor   *afa*   328

Gilda
Gilda Stories - Jewelle Gomez   *afa*   141

Greene, Hermine Rose
Crossing over Jordan - Linda Beatrice Brown   *afa*   26

Jackson, Esther
Brothers and Sisters - Bebe Moore Campbell   *afa*   47

Jackson, Savannah
Waiting to Exhale - Terry McMillan   *afa*   269

Jefferson, Naomi
Big Girls Don't Cry - Connie Briscoe   *afa*   22

Johnson, Beverly "Bev"
In the Game - Nikki Baker   *afa*   5

Kelly, Virginia "Ginny"
In the Game - Nikki Baker   *afa*   5
Lavender House Murder - Nikki Baker   *afa*   6
Long Goodbyes - Nikki Baker   *afa*   7

Kwong, Helen "Auntie Helen"
The Kitchen God's Wife - Amy Tan   *asa*   1080

Leong, "Mah"
Bone - Fae Myenne Ng   *asa*   1039

Louie, Winnie
The Kitchen God's Wife - Amy Tan   *asa*   1080

Lovejoy, Betty Jean
Ugly Ways - Tina McElroy Ansa   *afa*   3

Mackenzie, Ursa Beatrice
Daughters - Paule Marshall   *afa*   254

Matthews, Gloria
Waiting to Exhale - Terry McMillan   *afa*   269

McPherson, Lena
The Hand I Fan With - Tina McElroy Ansa   *afa*   2

Menchan, Clea
Days Without Weather - Cecil Brown   *afa*   24

Natividad, Clara "Aunt Clara"
Cebu - Peter Bacho   *asa*   902

Navarro, Rita
Sweet Fifteen - Diane Gonzales Bertrand   *lat*   636

Nickelson, Elizabeth
Falling Leaves of Ivy - Yolanda Joe   *afa*   214

Pippin, Chartreuse Marie "Charlie"
Charlie Pippin - Candy Dawson Boyd   *afa*   17

Post, Mallory
Brothers and Sisters - Bebe Moore Campbell   *afa*   47

Ricks, Lena
The Survivors - Kristin Hunter   *afa*   211

See, Letticie Pruett "Ticie"
On Gold Mountain: The One-Hundred-Year Odyssey of a Chinese-American Family - Lisa See   *asa*   1062

Seymour, Vanessa
The Price You Pay - Barbara Summers   *afa*   402

Thompson, Christina "Tina"
The Price You Pay - Barbara Summers   *afa*   402

Todd, Delotha
Your Blues Ain't Like Mine - Bebe Moore Campbell   *afa*   48

Trace, Violet
Jazz - Toni Morrison   *afa*   283

Yamada, Mama
No-No Boy - John Okada   *asa*   1042

BUTCHER

Noe
Pig Cookies and Other Stories - Alberto Alvaro Rios   *lat*   774

CALIFORNIO

Alamar, Don Mariano
The Squatter and the Don - Maria Amparo Ruiz de Burton   *lat*   799

CAMPER

Moroni, Petey
Petey Moroni's Camp Runamok Diary - Pat Cummings   *afa*   90

CANCER PATIENT

Goodman, Absalom
Losing Absalom - Alexs D. Pate   *afa*   341

Werren, Ola
Toning the Sweep - Angela Johnson   *afa*   223

CAPTIVE

Iyapo, Lilith
Dawn - Octavia Butler   *afa*   35

Ntah, Tarik
Legend of Tarik - Walter Dean Myers   *afa*   312

CARE GIVER

Smalls, Vesta
The Serpent's Gift - Helen Elaine Lee   *afa*   241

Suggs, Denver
Beloved - Toni Morrison   *afa*   281

CARPENTER

Stone, Isaac Sr.
Just Like Martin - Ossie Davis   *afa*   92

CAT

Cat
Cat and Rat: The Legend of the Chinese Zodiac - Ed Young *asa* 1128

Chato
Chato's Kitchen - Gary Soto *lat* 825

Ming Miao
The Chinese Siamese Cat - Amy Tan *asa* 1077

Sagwa of China
The Chinese Siamese Cat - Amy Tan *asa* 1077

CAUCASIAN

Achitophel, Alice
Zulus - Percival Everett *afa* 119

Adams, Elizabeth "Lisa"
And All Our Wounds Forgiven - Julius Lester *afa* 242

Adams, John Quincy
Echo of Lions - Barbara Chase-Riboud *afa* 52

Adams, Thomas Jerrett "T.J."
The Color of Trees - Canaan Parker *afa* 338

Akwara, Artia "El Muerte"
Legend of Tarik - Walter Dean Myers *afa* 312

Arrow, Chris
Adventure in Granada - Walter Dean Myers *afa* 299
Ambush in the Amazon - Walter Dean Myers *afa* 300
Duel in the Desert - Walter Dean Myers *afa* 304
The Hidden Shrine - Walter Dean Myers *afa* 309

Arrow, Ken
Adventure in Granada - Walter Dean Myers *afa* 299
Ambush in the Amazon - Walter Dean Myers *afa* 300
Duel in the Desert - Walter Dean Myers *afa* 304
The Hidden Shrine - Walter Dean Myers *afa* 309

Baker, Andrew Jackson "Hawk"
Mississippi Chariot - Harriette Gillem Robinet *afa* 377

Barnett, Jonathan
Those Other People - Alice Childress *afa* 58

Bass, Robert Jr.
Japanese by Spring - Ishmael Reed *afa* 364

Beckett, Kelsey
In the Game - Nikki Baker *afa* 5

Benneck, Faye
Project Wheels - Jacqueline Turner Banks *afa* 11

Berg, Caroline
Between Madison & Palmetto - Jacqueline Woodson *afa* 472

Blake, Alexander
Free - Marsha Hunt *afa* 206

Brazil, Bubbles
Negrophobia: An Urban Parable - Darius James *afa* 212

Bright, Elena "Lena" Cecilia
I Hadn't Meant to Tell You This - Jacqueline Woodson *afa* 475

Bruno, Robert
Frontiers of Love - Diana Chang *asa* 915

Butler, Hoyt "Cap'n"
The Avenue, Clayton City - C. Eric Lincoln *afa* 245

Cabot, Evan
Fragments That Remain - Steven Corbin *afa* 82

Cain, Albert
Black Betty - Walter Mosley *afa* 287

Carson, Tyler
Keeping Secrets - Penny Mickelbury *afa* 276

Coile, Weber "Web"
Hold Fast to Dreams - Andrea Davis Pinkney *afa* 348

Cox, Lily
Your Blues Ain't Like Mine - Bebe Moore Campbell *afa* 48

Craxton, Darryl T.
A Red Death - Walter Mosley *afa* 290

Cummings, Paul
Click Song - John A. Williams *afa* 459

DeLea, Rosa "Rowena"
Crystal - Walter Dean Myers *afa* 302

DeWitt, Margo
Windy City - Hugh Holton *afa* 199

DeWitt, Neil
Windy City - Hugh Holton *afa* 199

DiMaio, Joan
Lavender House Murder - Nikki Baker *afa* 6

Garnett, Vernor
White Butterfly - Walter Mosley *afa* 292

Gilda
Gilda Stories - Jewelle Gomez *afa* 141

Graham, Dalton
Wild Embers - Anita Richmond Bunkley *afa* 33

Graves, Griselda
Night Studies - Cyrus Colter *afa* 77

Hancock, Everett
Blanche on the Lam - Barbara Neely *afa* 333

Hill, Holly Rachelle
Holly - Albert French *afa* 131

Hill, Sara Kate Colson
Clover - Dori Sanders *afa* 379

Horn, Diane
Coffee Will Make You Black - April Sinclair *afa* 392

Howard, Erica
Almond Cookies and Dragon Well Tea - Cynthia Chin-Lee *asa* 925

Howell, Brandy
Thank You, Dr. Martin Luther King, Jr.! - Eleanora E. Tate *afa* 406

Jake
God's Country - Percival Everett *afa* 114

Jay
Jay and the Marigold - Harriette Gillem Robinet *afa* 376

Jefferson, Thomas
Sally Hemings - Barbara Chase-Riboud *afa* 54

Jones, Lewis
Fish Tales - Nettie Jones *afa* 234

Kenny, Gene
Dr. Neruda's Cure for Evil - Rafael Yglesias *lat* 891

Klein, Max
Fearless: A Novel - Rafael Yglesias *lat* 892

Kristin
From the Notebooks of Melanin Sun - Jacqueline Woodson *afa* 474

Lacey, Karen
Tales of a Dead King - Walter Dean Myers *afa* 325

Lampkin, Josh
Down in the Piney Woods - Ethel Footman Smothers *afa* 394

Langdon, Nathan
Sally Hemings - Barbara Chase-Riboud *afa* 54

Larsen, David
Walk Me to the Distance - Percival Everett *afa* 117

Lawrence, Reginald Arnold
A Red Death - Walter Mosley *afa* 290

Ledbeder, Clabe
Emily, the Yellow Rose - Anita Richmond Bunkley *afa* 31

Lee, Gilbert
Ribbons - Laurence Yep *asa* 1126

Livesey, John
Cutting Lisa - Percival Everett *afa* 112

Logan
Death of an Anglo - Alejandro Morales *lat* 725

Lynn, Theodora
Those Other People - Alice Childress *afa* 58

Marcialis, Evan
Traitor to the Race - Darieck Scott *afa* 382

Marder, Curt
God's Country - Percival Everett *afa* 114

Marshall, Candy
A Gathering of Old Men - Ernest J. Gaines *afa* 133

Maslin, Blake Jason
Clay's Ark - Octavia Butler *afa* 34

Maximillian "Max"
No Other Tale to Tell - Richard Perry *afa* 345

McGirk, Mike
In Search of Snow - Luis Alberto Urrea *lat* 864

McMann, Mary Ellen "Spike"
Long Goodbyes - Nikki Baker *afa* 7

McQuillen, Gerald
The Nicholas Factor - Walter Dean Myers *afa* 319

Menchan, Clea
Days Without Weather - Cecil Brown *afa* 24

Miller, Crockett
Tangled Up in Blue - Larry Duplechan *afa* 107

Mumsfield
Blanche on the Lam - Barbara Neely *afa* 333

Narrator
Panther - Melvin Van Peebles *afa* 422

Nehemiah, Adam
Dessa Rose - Sherley Anne Williams *afa* 463

Nickelson, Elizabeth
Falling Leaves of Ivy - Yolanda Joe *afa* 214

Park, Leila
Native Speaker - Chang-rae Lee *asa* 984

Parrish, Olivia "Mop"
Me, Mop, and the Moondance Kid - Walter Dean Myers *afa* 313
Mop, Moondance and Nagasaki Knights - Walter Dean Myers *afa* 315

Paschen, Rosalee "Rosey"
Long Goodbyes - Nikki Baker *afa* 7

Pasko, Lori
Billy - Albert French *afa* 130

Post, Mallory
Brothers and Sisters - Bebe Moore Campbell *afa* 47

Powell, Judith
The Chaneysville Incident - David Bradley *afa* 19

Rabinowitz, Lynne
Meridian - Alice Walker *afa* 428

Conner, Matthew
Yang the Youngest and His Terrible Ear - Lensey Namioka *asa* 1036

Ding, Raymond
American Knees - Shawn Wong *asa* 1104

Duk, Donald
Donald Duk - Frank Chin *asa* 924

Hong, Maxine
The Woman Warrior: Memoirs of a Girlhood Among Ghosts - Maxine Hong Kingston *asa* 973

Hong, Mother
The Woman Warrior: Memoirs of a Girlhood Among Ghosts - Maxine Hong Kingston *asa* 973

Hsu, An-Mei
The Joy Luck Club - Amy Tan *asa* 1079

Jeh
Child of the Owl - Laurence Yep *asa* 1118

Jong, Lindo
The Joy Luck Club - Amy Tan *asa* 1079

Jong, Waverly
The Joy Luck Club - Amy Tan *asa* 1079

Jordan, Rose Hsu
The Joy Luck Club - Amy Tan *asa* 1079

Kwong, Helen "Auntie Helen"
The Kitchen God's Wife - Amy Tan *asa* 1080

Leong, Leon
Bone - Fae Myenne Ng *asa* 1039

Leong, "Mah"
Bone - Fae Myenne Ng *asa* 1039

Leong, Nina
Bone - Fae Myenne Ng *asa* 1039

Li, Kwan
The Hundred Secret Senses - Amy Tan *asa* 1078

Louie, Leila Fu
Bone - Fae Myenne Ng *asa* 1039

Louie, Mason
Bone - Fae Myenne Ng *asa* 1039

Louie, Pearl
The Kitchen God's Wife - Amy Tan *asa* 1080

Louie, Winnie
The Kitchen God's Wife - Amy Tan *asa* 1080

Low, Paw-Paw
Child of the Owl - Laurence Yep *asa* 1118

Mei-Mei
Mama Bear - Chyng Feng Sun *asa* 1073

St. Clair, Lena
The Joy Luck Club - Amy Tan *asa* 1079

St. Clair, Ying-ying
The Joy Luck Club - Amy Tan *asa* 1079

Simon, Olivia "Libby-ah"
The Hundred Secret Senses - Amy Tan *asa* 1078

Teddy
Later, Gator - Laurence Yep *asa* 1123

Ting, Kai "China Boy"
China Boy - Gus Lee *asa* 985

Wan, Ernie
Lion Dancer: Ernie Wan's Chinese New Year - Kate Waters *asa* 1099

Wong, Daddy
Fifth Chinese Daughter - Jade Snow Wong *asa* 1102

Wong, Jade Snow
Fifth Chinese Daughter - Jade Snow Wong *asa* 1102

Wong, Mother
Fifth Chinese Daughter - Jade Snow Wong *asa* 1102

Woo, Jing-mei "June"
The Joy Luck Club - Amy Tan *asa* 1079

Woo, Suyuan
The Joy Luck Club - Amy Tan *asa* 1079

Yang, Yingmei "Mary"
Yang the Third and Her Impossible Family - Lensey Namioka *asa* 1035

Yang, Yingtao "Yang the Youngest"
Yang the Third and Her Impossible Family - Lensey Namioka *asa* 1035
Yang the Youngest and His Terrible Ear - Lensey Namioka *asa* 1036

Yang the Eldest
Yang the Youngest and His Terrible Ear - Lensey Namioka *asa* 1036

Yang the Second Oldest
Yang the Youngest and His Terrible Ear - Lensey Namioka *asa* 1036

Young, Casey
Child of the Owl - Laurence Yep *asa* 1118

CHINESE AUSTRALIAN

Lambert, Mimi
Frontiers of Love - Diana Chang *asa* 915

CHINESE CANADIAN

Lau, Evelyn
Runaway: Diary of a Street Kid - Evelyn Lau *asa* 981

CHINESE CAUCASIAN

Chen, Sylvia
Frontiers of Love - Diana Chang *asa* 915

CHINESE HAWAIIAN

Wong, Mahealani Suzanne "Mahi"
A Little Too Much Is Enough - Kathleen Tyau *asa* 1086

CHINESE PANAMANIAN

Chang, Carlos Cipriano
A Feather on the Breath of God - Sigrid Nunez *asa* 1041

CHINESE PANAMANIAN GERMAN

Young Woman
A Feather on the Breath of God - Sigrid Nunez *asa* 1041

CIVIL SERVANT

Narrator
A River Sutra - Gita Mehta *asa* 1018

CLASSMATE

Azalea, Arnold
Donald Duk - Frank Chin *asa* 924

Burke, Kelleen
Elaine and the Flying Frog - Heidi Chang *asa* 916

Raymond
Angel Child, Dragon Child - Michele Maria Surat *asa* 1075

CLERK

Achitophel, Alice
Zulus - Percival Everett *afa* 119

Chagla
A River Sutra - Gita Mehta *asa* 1018

COACH

Barraza, Anthony Cemore
China Boy - Gus Lee *asa* 985

Davis, Charles "Chappie"
The Junior Bachelor Society - John A. Williams *afa* 461

Jones, Calvin "Spider" F.
Hoops - Walter Dean Myers *afa* 310

COCKROACH

Martina
Perez and Martina - Pura Belpre *lat* 535

COLUMBIAN

Martinez, Santiago
Latin Moon in Manhattan - Jaime Manrique *lat* 688

COMPANION

Monet, Daphne
Devil in a Blue Dress - Walter Mosley *afa* 288

COMPOSER

Kat
Muse-Echo Blues - Xam Wilson Cartier *afa* 50

Owens, Elias Euritides
Holly - Albert French *afa* 131

COMPUTER EXPERT

Brown, John
Golden Gate: A Novel in Verse - Vikram Seth *asa* 1064

CON ARTIST

Enos, Bart
To Reach a Dream - Nathan Heard *afa* 193

John
Voodoo Dreams: A Novel of Marie Laveau - Jewell Parker Rhodes *afa* 370

CONSTRUCTION WORKER

Swift, Franklin
Disappearing Acts - Terri McMillan *afa* 266

Wilson, James "Shorty"
Rattlebone - Maxine Clair *afa* 60

CONVICT

Armstrong, Willie
Witherspoon - Lance Jeffers *afa* 213

Black, Tomsson
Plan B - Chester Himes *afa* 196

Booker, Roscoe L. "Dogface"
The True American: A Folk Fable - Melvin Van
Peebles *afa* 423

Bradley, Solomon
The Road to Memphis - Mildred D. Taylor *afa* 411

Butler, William "Beans"
House of Slammers - Nathan Heard *afa* 192

Carver, George Abraham "Abe"
The True American: A Folk Fable - Melvin Van
Peebles *afa* 423

Enos, Bart
To Reach a Dream - Nathan Heard *afa* 193

Harwood, Jack
The Indian Lawyer - James Welch *naa* 1345

Jefferson
A Lesson before Dying - Ernest J. Gaines *afa* 135

Murieta, Joaquin
Life and Adventures of Joaquin Murieta - Yellow
Bird *naa* 1350

COOK

Bailey
Bailey's Cafe - Gloria Naylor *afa* 328

Ta Fan the Korean
Dancer Dawkins and the California Kid - Willyce
Kim *asa* 969

Wine, Alice
Rainbow Roun' Mah Shoulder - Linda Brown
Bragg *afa* 21

CORSICAN

Monfort, Isabel
The House on the Lagoon - Rosario Ferre *lat* 608

COURIER

Rivers, Raheim Errol
B-Boy Blues - Steven Corbin *afa* 81

COUSIN

Al-Hussain, Adam
Bombay Talkie - Ameena Meer *asa* 1017

Amifika
Amifika - Lucille Clifton *afa* 62

Cammy
Cousins - Virginia Hamilton *afa* 158

Chita
Chita's Christmas Tree - Elizabeth Fitzgerald
Howard *afa* 201
Papa Tells Chita a Story - Elizabeth Fitzgerald
Howard *afa* 203

Devadatta
Buddha - Demi *asa* 932

Gates, Constance "Cookie"
Like Sisters on the Homefront - Rita Williams-
Garcia *afa* 467

Gonzaga, Pucha
Dogeaters - Jessica Hagedorn *asa* 942

Hardisen, Ethel
Just an Overnight Guest - Eleanora E. Tate *afa* 404

Kisa
Year of Impossible Goodbyes - Sook Nyul
Choi *asa* 930

Lawson, Tommy
Hiding Place - John Edgar Wideman *afa* 447

Li Shin
The Scent of the Gods - Fiona Cheong *asa* 919

Nettie Jo
Nettie Jo's Friends - Patricia C.
McKissack *afa* 264

Patty Ann
Cousins - Virginia Hamilton *afa* 158

Rankin, Suzella
Let the Circle Be Unbroken - Mildred D.
Taylor *afa* 409

COWBOY

Jefferson, Grayson
The Golden Pasture - Joyce Carol Thomas *afa* 417

COWGIRL

Cogewea "The Half Blood"
Cogewea - Mourning Dove *naa* 1284

COYOTE

Coyote
A Coyote Columbus Story - Thomas
King *naa* 1244

CRIME VICTIM

Brown, Zambia Renelda
A Blessing in Disguise - Eleanora E. Tate *afa* 403

Cross, Faith
Faith and the Good Thing - Charles
Johnson *afa* 225

Knight, John Calvin
Night Studies - Cyrus Colter *afa* 77

Roberts, Eugene "Gene"
B-Boy Blues - Steven Corbin *afa* 81

Smarts, Tremonisha
Reckless Eyeballing - Ishmael Reed *afa* 367

CRIMINAL

Diablo
Third and Indiana - Steven Lopez *lat* 684

Firbug
Spidertown - Abraham Rodriguez Jr. *lat* 785

Olivas, Jesus
Happy Birthday Jesus - Ronald L. Ruiz *lat* 798

Perkins, Munro
Break-In - Jose Yglesias *lat* 889

Phantom, Flower
Reckless Eyeballing - Ishmael Reed *afa* 367

Rawlins, Ezekiel "Easy"
A Red Death - Walter Mosley *afa* 290

CRIMINOLOGIST

Saturday, Nance
The Terrible Twos - Ishmael Reed *afa* 369

CRIOLLA

Vicario, Leona
Leona: A Love Story - Elizabeth Borton de
Trevino *lat* 857

CRITIC

Robinson, Dwayne
Urban Romance - Nelson George *afa* 136

CROCODILE

Crocodile
Rockabye Crocodile - Jose Aruego *asa* 897

CROW

Crow
La Gran Fiesta - Francisco X. Mora *lat* 716

Rainbow Crow
Rainbow Crow - Nancy Van Laan *naa* 1334

CUBAN

Ada, Alma Flor
Where the Flame Trees Bloom - Alma Flor
Ada *lat* 491

Arenas, Reinaldo
Before Night Falls - Reinaldo Arenas *lat* 521

Arturo
Old Rosa: A Novel in Two Stories - Reinaldo
Arenas *lat* 523

Campos, Julian
The Cutter: A Novel - Virgil Suarez *lat* 842

Castillo, Cesar
The Mambo Kings Play Songs of Love - Oscar
Hijuelos *lat* 655

Castillo, Nestor
The Mambo Kings Play Songs of Love - Oscar
Hijuelos *lat* 655

Celia del Pino
Dreaming in Cuban, A Novel - Cristina
Garcia *lat* 617

Esmeralda
Mangos, Bananas, and Coconuts: A Cuban Love Story
- Himilce Novas *lat* 738

Gabriel
Singing to Cuba - Margarita Engle *lat* 597

Geneia
Crazy Love - Elias Miguel Munoz *lat* 729

Juan
The Doorman - Reinaldo Arenas *lat* 522

Julian
Crazy Love - Elias Miguel Munoz *lat* 729

Mario
The Greatest Performance - Elias Miguel
Munoz *lat* 730

Old Rosa
Old Rosa: A Novel in Two Stories - Reinaldo
Arenas *lat* 523

Peregrin, Camilo
Skywriting - Margarita Engle *lat* 598

Rachel
Rachel's Song: A Novel - Miguel Barnet *lat* 529

Rosa
The Greatest Performance - Elias Miguel
Munoz *lat* 730

Saavedra, Miguel
Fallen Angels Sing - Omar Torres *lat* 852

Solano, Guadalupe
Bloody Waters - Carolina Garcia-Aguilera *lat* 625

Stranger
The Assault - Reinaldo Arenas *lat* 520

FOSTER CHILD

Amir
The Gift Giver - Joyce Hansen   *afa*   174

Douglass, Ned
The Autobiography of Miss Jane Pittman - Ernest J. Gaines   *afa*   132

Jordan, Rainbow
Rainbow Jordan - Alice Childress   *afa*   56

FOSTER PARENT

Lamont, Josephine "Josie"
Rainbow Jordan - Alice Childress   *afa*   56

FOUNDLING

Goins, Earl
Won't Know Till I Get There - Walter Dean Myers   *afa*   326

FRENCH

Cambon-Fournier, Cecile Stephanie
City of Light - Cyrus Colter   *afa*   76

FRIEND

Adare, Mary
The Beet Queen - Louise Erdrich   *naa*   1210

Alex
Boys at Work - Gary Soto   *lat*   824

Anna Marie
Halmoni and the Picnic - Sook Nyul Choi   *asa*   929

Azalea, Arnold
Donald Duk - Frank Chin   *asa*   924

Bultron, Sina Rosa
The Red Comb - Fernando Pico   *lat*   755

Buni
Captain Africa: The Battle for Egyptica - Dwayne J. Ferguson   *afa*   120

Chen Li-sha
In the Eye of War - Margaret Chang   *asa*   918

Chew, Tallulah Bankhead "Booger"
Child of the Owl - Laurence Yep   *asa*   1118

Chow Yun-lung
In the Eye of War - Margaret Chang   *asa*   918

Conner, Matthew
Yang the Youngest and His Terrible Ear - Lensey Namioka   *asa*   1036

Darrow, Pesty
The Mystery of Drear House - Virginia Hamilton   *afa*   167

Doi, Kogoro
Face of a Stranger - Yoji Yamaguchi   *asa*   1107

DuBois, Sin-Sin
One Dark Body - Charlotte Sherman   *afa*   389

Englehart, Eileen
Stella: On the Edge of Popularity - Lauren Lee   *asa*   992

Glasser, Milt
Wife - Bharati Mukherjee   *asa*   1032

Gutherie, Willy "The California Kid"
Dead Heat - Willyce Kim   *asa*   970

Helen
Halmoni and the Picnic - Sook Nyul Choi   *asa*   929

Hirada, Roland
Molly by Any Other Name - Jean Davies Okimoto   *asa*   1043

Huang, Feng
Frontiers of Love - Diana Chang   *asa*   915

James, Celestine
The Beet Queen - Louise Erdrich   *naa*   1210

Jeh
Child of the Owl - Laurence Yep   *asa*   1118

Jessie
Finding My Voice - Marie G. Lee   *asa*   994

Jody
The Great Computer Dating Caper - T. Ernesto Bethancourt   *lat*   540

Jong, Lindo
The Joy Luck Club - Amy Tan   *asa*   1079

Jose
America Is in the Heart - Carlos Bulosan   *asa*   910

Kamiyama, Lance
Tripmaster Monkey: His Fake Book - Maxine Hong Kingston   *asa*   972

Kanno, Kenji
No-No Boy - John Okada   *asa*   1042

Kato, Kyoshi
One Bird - Kyoko Mori   *asa*   1025

Kim, Jae-Chun
Saying Goodbye - Marie G. Lee   *asa*   996

Kristiansen, Laura
If It Hadn't Been for Yoon Jun - Marie G. Lee   *asa*   995

Kurihara, Emiko "Emi"
Journey Home - Yoshiko Uchida   *asa*   1089
Journey to Topaz: A Story of the Japanese-American Education - Yoshiko Uchida   *asa*   1090

LaRue, Toussaint
China Boy - Gus Lee   *asa*   985

Lee, Nanci
Tripmaster Monkey: His Fake Book - Maxine Hong Kingston   *asa*   972

Levy, Ellen
In the Year of the Boar and Jackie Robinson - Bette Bao Lord   *asa*   1007

Lund, Minna
If It Hadn't Been for Yoon Jun - Marie G. Lee   *asa*   995

Mabel
In the Year of the Boar and Jackie Robinson - Bette Bao Lord   *asa*   1007

Magalee, Charles
House of Waiting - Marina Tamar Budhos   *asa*   909

Min, Junho
Echoes of the White Giraffe - Sook Nyul Choi   *asa*   927

Mizutani, Kumiko
One Bird - Kyoko Mori   *asa*   1025

Mullick, Ina
Wife - Bharati Mukherjee   *asa*   1032

Natividad, Clara "Aunt Clara"
Cebu - Peter Bacho   *asa*   902

Nick
America Is in the Heart - Carlos Bulosan   *asa*   910

Nishitani, Brenda
American Knees - Shawn Wong   *asa*   1104

Oka, Kunisaburo "Uncle Oka"
Journey Home - Yoshiko Uchida   *asa*   1089

O'Meara, Kim
Yang the Third and Her Impossible Family - Lensey Namioka   *asa*   1035

Radja
Gay-Neck: The Story of a Pigeon - Dhan Gopal Mukerji   *asa*   1029

Rani
Bombay Talkie - Ameena Meer   *asa*   1017

Sanjay
Bombay Talkie - Ameena Meer   *asa*   1017

Shino
Face of a Stranger - Yoji Yamaguchi   *asa*   1107

Short, George
Family Resemblances - Lowry Pei   *asa*   1046

Singh, Surindar
Coloured Pictures - Himani Bannerji   *asa*   903

Tasuke
The Bee and the Dream: A Japanese Tale - Jan Freeman Long   *asa*   1006

Thorp, Mary Lewis
Elaine and the Flying Frog - Heidi Chang   *asa*   916

Uchida, Toru
One Bird - Kyoko Mori   *asa*   1025

Walker, Paul "Pee Wee/Zip"
Company Man - Brent Wade   *afa*   425

Weintraub, Rachel
Stella: On the Edge of Popularity - Lauren Lee   *asa*   992

Whitlaw
Dragonwings - Laurence Yep   *asa*   1120

Wine, Alice
Rainbow Roun' Mah Shoulder - Linda Brown Bragg   *afa*   21

Woo, Suyuan
The Joy Luck Club - Amy Tan   *asa*   1079

FRONTIERSMAN

Bubba
God's Country - Percival Everett   *afa*   114

FUGITIVE

Lawson, Tommy
Hiding Place - John Edgar Wideman   *afa*   447

Little, Cephus "Crab"
Somewhere in the Darkness - Walter Dean Myers   *afa*   323

Zumwalt, Oscar
The Terrible Twos - Ishmael Reed   *afa*   369

GAMBLER

Ah Song
Eat a Bowl of Tea - Louis Chu   *asa*   931

Marder, Curt
God's Country - Percival Everett   *afa*   114

St. Claire, Geraldine
The Thirteenth Apostle - Gloria Gonzalez   *lat*   639

Wilder, Carey
Black Gold - Anita Richmond Bunkley   *afa*   30

Young, Barney
Child of the Owl - Laurence Yep   *asa*   1118

GANG MEMBER

Clive
Straight Outta Compton - Ricardo Cortez Cruz   *afa*   87

Character Description Index

Gordon
Way Past Cool - Jess Mowry   *afa*   295

Miguel
Spidertown - Abraham Rodriguez Jr.   *lat*   785

Rene
Eldorado in East Harlem - Victor
   Rodriguez   *lat*   789

Rooster
Straight Outta Compton - Ricardo Cortez
   Cruz   *afa*   87

GARDENER

Lopez, Ruy
The Devil, Delfina Varela, and the Used Chevy - Louie
   Garcia Robinson   *lat*   783

Ping
The Empty Pot - Demi   *asa*   934

Simms, Theodore "Teenotchy"
Free - Marsha Hunt   *afa*   206

GENEALOGIST

Sheridan, Kiana
Starlight Passage - Anita Richmond
   Bunkley   *afa*   32

GENETICALLY ALTERED BEING

Akin
Adulthood Rites - Octavia E. Butler   *afa*   39

Saturna
Saturn's Child - Nichelle Nichols   *afa*   337

GENTLEMAN

Whong
Sir Whong and the Golden Pig - Oki S.
   Han   *asa*   947

GERMAN

Cipriano, Christa
A Feather on the Breath of God - Sigrid
   Nunez   *asa*   1041

GERMAN AMERICAN

Cronheim, Sterling
Another Present Era - Elaine Perry   *afa*   342

GIRLFRIEND

Bokhi
Echoes of the White Giraffe - Sook Nyul
   Choi   *asa*   927

Carter, Rosalyn
Emergency Exit - Clarence Major   *afa*   247

Costanza, Cheryl
Crossover - Dennis Williams   *afa*   456

Daniels, Vincereta "Viney"
Daughters - Paule Marshall   *afa*   254

Margot
Understand This - Jervey Tervalon   *afa*   415

Perkins, Carlene Zenobia "Carla"
Coffee Will Make You Black - April
   Sinclair   *afa*   392

Powell, Judith
The Chaneysville Incident - David Bradley   *afa*   19

Stevenson, Jean Eloise "Stevie"
Coffee Will Make You Black - April
   Sinclair   *afa*   392

GOVERNMENT OFFICIAL

Craxton, Darryl T.
A Red Death - Walter Mosley   *afa*   290

Lawrence, Reginald Arnold
A Red Death - Walter Mosley   *afa*   290

GRADUATE

Braithwaite, Cecil Otis
Hurry Home - John Edgar Wideman   *afa*   448

Drinkwater, Jonah
Days Without Weather - Cecil Brown   *afa*   24

Jones, Hannibal
Shannon - Gordon Parks   *afa*   340

Stevenson, Jean Eloise "Stevie" -
Ain't Gonna Be the Same Fool Twice - April
   Sinclair   *afa*   391

GRANDDAUGHTER

Andrews, Ophelia "Cocoa"
Mama Day - Gloria Naylor   *afa*   330

Cammy
Cousins - Virginia Hamilton   *afa*   158

Esha Su Yen "Chief"
The Scent of the Gods - Fiona Cheong   *asa*   919

Helie, Lee
*Still Life With Rice: A Young American Woman
   Discovers the Life and Legacy of Her Korean
   Grandmother* - Helie Lee   *asa*   986

Hito, Tomoe Kanemori
A Bridge Between Us - Julie Shigekuni   *asa*   1066

Martha
Trouble's Child - Mildred Pitts Walter   *afa*   440

Parker, Addie
Rivers of Eros - Cyrus Colter   *afa*   78

Pilar
Dreaming in Cuban, A Novel - Cristina
   Garcia   *lat*   617

Tompkins, Elzina
After the Garden - Doris Jean Austin   *afa*   4

Trueba, Alba
The House of the Spirits - Isabel Allende   *lat*   497

GRANDFATHER

Ah Goong
China Men - Maxine Hong Kingston   *asa*   971

Eustace
High Cotton - Darryl Pinckney   *afa*   347

Grandfather
Grandfather's Journey - Allen Say   *asa*   1056

Grandpa
Blue Jay in the Desert - Marlene
   Shigekawa   *asa*   1065

Great Progenitor
Baba: A Return to China upon My Father's Shoulders
   - Belle Yang   *asa*   1113

Jefferson, Grayson
The Golden Pasture - Joyce Carol Thomas   *afa*   417

Kang, Myong-Hwan
*Home Was the Land of Morning Calm: The Saga of a
   Korean American Family* - K. Connie
   Kang   *asa*   965

Lito
Pablo's Tree - Pat Mora   *lat*   721

Manuel
La Maravilla - Alfredo Vea Jr.   *lat*   867

Rafa, Jose Antonio
Inheritance of Strangers - Nash Candelaria   *lat*   554
Not by the Sword - Nash Candelaria   *lat*   557

Rawlings, Jackabo
Junius over Far - Virginia Hamilton   *afa*   162

Villasenor, Juan Jesus
Wild Steps of Heaven - Victor Villasenor   *lat*   884

GRANDMOTHER

Baek Hongyang
*Still Life With Rice: A Young American Woman
   Discovers the Life and Legacy of Her Korean
   Grandmother* - Helie Lee   *asa*   986

Celia del Pino
Dreaming in Cuban, A Novel - Cristina
   Garcia   *lat*   617

Chen, Grandma
April and the Dragon Lady - Lensey
   Namioka   *asa*   1034

Dambridge, Martha Jones
The Good Negress - A.J. Verdelle   *afa*   424

Divina, Narcisa "Lola"
Dogeaters - Jessica Hagedorn   *asa*   942

Gabriel, Verda
Heathens - David Haynes   *afa*   183

Grandmother
Annie and the Old One - Miska Miles   *naa*   1278
Char Siu Bao Boy - Sandra S. Yamate   *asa*   1111
The Little Weaver of Thai-Yen Village - Tran Khanh
   Tuyet   *asa*   1083
The Scent of the Gods - Fiona Cheong   *asa*   919
Stella: On the Edge of Popularity - Lauren
   Lee   *asa*   992

Grandmother Paw-Paw
Ribbons - Laurence Yep   *asa*   1126

Halmoni
Halmoni and the Picnic - Sook Nyul Choi   *asa*   929

Henry, Harriet
Trouble the Water - Melvin Dixon   *afa*   99

Hisae Fujiitano
The Floating World - Cynthia Kadohata   *asa*   962

Hito, Reiko
A Bridge Between Us - Julie Shigekuni   *asa*   1066

Hito, Rio
A Bridge Between Us - Julie Shigekuni   *asa*   1066

Kurihara, Grandma
Journey Home - Yoshiko Uchida   *asa*   1089

Lizzie
Baby of the Family - Tina McElroy Ansa   *afa*   1

Low, Paw-Paw
Child of the Owl - Laurence Yep   *asa*   1118

Lupita, Mama
Face of an Angel - Denise Chavez   *lat*   574

Moore, Ernestine
An Open Weave - Devorah Major   *afa*   253

Nana
Green Corn Tamales = Tamales de Elote - Gina
   Macaluso Rodriguez   *lat*   786

Oba-san
Rise and Shine, Mariko-chan! - Chiyoko Tomioka *asa* 1082

Obaachan
Thanksgiving at Obaachan's - Janet Mitsui Brown *asa* 1022

Pilar
Singing Softly = Cantando Bajito - Carmen de Monteflores *lat* 589

Pilgrim, Clotilda
Rivers of Eros - Cyrus Colter *afa* 78

Rosario
Cantora: A Novel - Sylvia Lopez-Medina *lat* 686

Sachiko
Sachiko Means Happiness - Kimiko Sakai *asa* 1053

Sewa, Adela
Daughter of the Mountain: Un Cuento - Edna Escamill *lat* 599

Shelby, Carolyn "Gram"
The Wedding - Dorothy West *afa* 445

Temple, Sadie Evelyn
Crossing over Jordan - Linda Beatrice Brown *afa* 26

Titay
Trouble's Child - Mildred Pitts Walter *afa* 440

Tompkins, Rosalie
After the Garden - Doris Jean Austin *afa* 4

Tut
Cousins - Virginia Hamilton *afa* 158

Valenzuela de Castillo, Josephina
La Maravilla - Alfredo Vea Jr. *lat* 867

Villasenor, Margarita
Wild Steps of Heaven - Victor Villasenor *lat* 884

Waipo
American Visa - Wang Ping *asa* 1047

Yang, Grandma
Dumpling Soup - Jama Kim Rattigan *asa* 1048

Ying-ying
The Moon Lady - Amy Tan *asa* 1081

GRANDPARENT

Ida
A Yellow Raft in Blue Water - Michael Dorris *naa* 1201

GRANDSON

Alberto "Beto"
La Maravilla - Alfredo Vea Jr. *lat* 867

Parker, Lester
Rivers of Eros - Cyrus Colter *afa* 78

Yang, Joseph "Baba"
Baba: A Return to China upon My Father's Shoulders - Belle Yang *asa* 1113

GUATEMALAN

Esperanza
Abuela's Weave - Omar Castaneda *lat* 563

Graetz, Roger
The Long Night of White Chickens - Francisco Goldman *lat* 631

Perera, Victor
Rites: A Guatemalan Boyhood - Victor Perera *lat* 752

GUIDE

Labrado, Ellen
Cebu - Peter Bacho *asa* 902

Peters, Kevin
Zulus - Percival Everett *afa* 119

Tawfik, Mussa Ahmed
Duel in the Desert - Walter Dean Myers *afa* 304

GYPSY

Barcia, Pedro
Adventure in Granada - Walter Dean Myers *afa* 299

HANDICAPPED

Jay
Jay and the Marigold - Harriette Gillem Robinet *afa* 376

Johnson, Jerome
Ride the Red Cycle - Harriette Gillem Robinet *afa* 378

Lotus
Silent Lotus - Jeanne M. Lee *asa* 989

Palmer, Willy
Willy's Summer Dream - Kay Brown *afa* 25

Staples, Ouida
The Serpent's Gift - Helen Elaine Lee *afa* 241

HANDYMAN

Unnamed Character
High Cotton - Darryl Pinckney *afa* 347

HAWAIIAN

Yang, Marisa
Dumpling Soup - Jama Kim Rattigan *asa* 1048

HEALER

Anita
Across the Great River - Irene Beltran Hernandez *lat* 648

Anyanwu
Wild Seed - Octavia Butler *afa* 38

Bultron, Sina Rosa
The Red Comb - Fernando Pico *lat* 755

Day, Miranda "Mama"
Mama Day - Gloria Naylor *afa* 330

Jefferson, Dorian
Dustland - Virginia Hamilton *afa* 160

Letenielle, Rebecca Florice
Rainbow Roun' Mah Shoulder - Linda Brown Bragg *afa* 21

Marie
Voodoo Dreams: A Novel of Marie Laveau - Jewell Parker Rhodes *afa* 370

Masaube, Blossom Rose
Mischief Makers - Nettie Jones *afa* 235

Nikanj
Dawn - Octavia Butler *afa* 35

Ransom, Minnie
The Salt Eaters - Toni Cade Bambara *afa* 8

Titay
Trouble's Child - Mildred Pitts Walter *afa* 440

Ultima
Bless Me, Ultima - Rudolfo Anaya *lat* 508

Valenzuela de Castillo, Josephina
La Maravilla - Alfredo Vea Jr. *lat* 867

HEALTH CARE PROFESSIONAL

Esquibel, Rocio
The Last of the Menu Girls - Denise Chavez *lat* 575

HEIR

Singh, Bhushan
Mistaken Identity - Nayantara Sahgal *asa* 1050

HERBALIST

Ransom, Minnie
The Salt Eaters - Toni Cade Bambara *afa* 8

HERO

Jason
For Her Dark Skin - Percival Everett *afa* 113

Little Plum
Little Plum - Ed Young *asa* 1129

HEROINE

White, Blanche
Blanche Among the Talented Tenth - Barbara Neely *afa* 332
Blanche on the Lam - Barbara Neely *afa* 333

HISPANIC

Remirez, Santiago Antonio "Junior" Jr.
The Adventures of Sugar and Junior - Angela Shelf Medearis *afa* 270

HISTORIAN

Quilaztli
The Aztec Chronicles: The True History of Christopher Columbus, as Narrated by Quilaztli of Texcoco: A Novella - Joseph P. Sanchez *lat* 809

Small, Walter
The Mystery of Drear House - Virginia Hamilton *afa* 167

Tandy, Rex
Starlight Passage - Anita Richmond Bunkley *afa* 32

Washington, John
The Chaneysville Incident - David Bradley *afa* 19

HISTORICAL FIGURE

Adams, John Quincy
Echo of Lions - Barbara Chase-Riboud *afa* 52

Hemings, Harriet
The President's Daughter - Barbara Chase-Riboud *afa* 53

Hemings, Sally
The President's Daughter - Barbara Chase-Riboud *afa* 53
Sally Hemings - Barbara Chase-Riboud *afa* 54

ITALIAN AMERICAN

Maglione, Giovanna "Gianna"
Keeping Secrets - Penny Mickelbury *afa* 276
Night Songs - Penny Mickelbury *afa* 277

JAMAICAN

Shakespeare, Winston
How Stella Got Her Groove Back - Terry
  McMillan *afa* 267

JAPANESE

Arai, Takashi
Face of a Stranger - Yoji Yamaguchi *asa* 1107

Crane, Aurora "Ro"
American Knees - Shawn Wong *asa* 1104

Fuse, Matajiro "Mat"
Sushi and Sourdough - Tooru J. Kanazawa *asa* 964

Fuse, Yaso
Sushi and Sourdough - Tooru J. Kanazawa *asa* 964

Hisae Fujiitano
The Floating World - Cynthia Kadohata *asa* 962

Kikue
Face of a Stranger - Yoji Yamaguchi *asa* 1107

Matsumoto, Aya
Shizuko's Daughter - Kyoko Mori *asa* 1026

Minatoya, Miyeko
*Talking to High Monks in the Snow: An Asian
  American Odyssey* - Lydia Yuri
  Minatoya *asa* 1021

Noro Shinpei
The Ink-keeper's Apprentice - Allen Say *asa* 1057

Okuda, Hideki
Shizuko's Daughter - Kyoko Mori *asa* 1026

Okuda, Shizuko Matsumoto
Shizuko's Daughter - Kyoko Mori *asa* 1026

Okuda, Yuki
Shizuko's Daughter - Kyoko Mori *asa* 1026

Osaka, Charles "Charlie-O"
The Floating World - Cynthia Kadohata *asa* 962

Osaka, Mother
The Floating World - Cynthia Kadohata *asa* 962

Osaka, Olivia Ann
The Floating World - Cynthia Kadohata *asa* 962

Sei Koichi
The Ink-keeper's Apprentice - Allen Say *asa* 1057

Shimizu, Chie
One Bird - Kyoko Mori *asa* 1025

Shimizu, Megumi
One Bird - Kyoko Mori *asa* 1025

Taro "The Boy of the Three-Year Nap"
The Boy of the Three-Year Nap - Dianne
  Snyder *asa* 1069

Uchida, Dwight Takashi
*Desert Exile: The Uprooting of a Japanese-American
  Family* - Yoshiko Uchida *asa* 1087

Uchida, Iku Umegaki
*Desert Exile: The Uprooting of a Japanese-American
  Family* - Yoshiko Uchida *asa* 1087

Widow
The Boy of the Three-Year Nap - Dianne
  Snyder *asa* 1069

Yamato
Japanese by Spring - Ishmael Reed *afa* 364

Young Boy
Tree of Cranes - Allen Say *asa* 1061

JAPANESE AMERICAN

Fuse, Joe Toranosuke Thor
Sushi and Sourdough - Tooru J. Kanazawa *asa* 964

Fuse, Kennosuke "Ken"
Sushi and Sourdough - Tooru J. Kanazawa *asa* 964

Hito, Nomi
A Bridge Between Us - Julie Shigekuni *asa* 1066

Hito, Reiko
A Bridge Between Us - Julie Shigekuni *asa* 1066

Hito, Rio
A Bridge Between Us - Julie Shigekuni *asa* 1066

Hito, Tomoe Kanemori
A Bridge Between Us - Julie Shigekuni *asa* 1066

Kanno, Kenji
No-No Boy - John Okada *asa* 1042

Kurihara, Emiko "Emi"
Journey Home - Yoshiko Uchida *asa* 1089
*Journey to Topaz: A Story of the Japanese-American
  Education* - Yoshiko Uchida *asa* 1090

Minatoya, Lydia Yuri
*Talking to High Monks in the Snow: An Asian
  American Odyssey* - Lydia Yuri
  Minatoya *asa* 1021

Oka, Kunisaburo "Uncle Oka"
Journey Home - Yoshiko Uchida *asa* 1089

Okada, Donnie
Heroes - Ken Mochizuki *asa* 1024

Okubo, Mine
Citizen 13660 - Mine Okubo *asa* 1044

Otake, Anna
The World of Daughter McGuire - Sharon Dennis
  Wyeth *afa* 479

Sakane, "Father"
Journey Home - Yoshiko Uchida *asa* 1089

Sakane, Kenichi "Ken"
*Journey to Topaz: A Story of the Japanese-American
  Education* - Yoshiko Uchida *asa* 1090

Sakane, "Mother"
Journey Home - Yoshiko Uchida *asa* 1089
*Journey to Topaz: A Story of the Japanese-American
  Education* - Yoshiko Uchida *asa* 1090

Sakane, Yuki
Journey Home - Yoshiko Uchida *asa* 1089
*Journey to Topaz: A Story of the Japanese-American
  Education* - Yoshiko Uchida *asa* 1090

"Shorty"
Baseball Saved Us - Ken Mochizuki *asa* 1023

Sone, Benko
Nisei Daughter - Monica Sone *asa* 1070

Sone, "Father"
Nisei Daughter - Monica Sone *asa* 1070

Sone, Kazuko Monica
Nisei Daughter - Monica Sone *asa* 1070

Uchida, Keiko
*Desert Exile: The Uprooting of a Japanese-American
  Family* - Yoshiko Uchida *asa* 1087

Uchida, Yoshiko
*Desert Exile: The Uprooting of a Japanese-American
  Family* - Yoshiko Uchida *asa* 1087

Unnamed Character
Grandfather's Journey - Allen Say *asa* 1056

Wakatsuki, Jeanne
Farewell to Manzanar - Jeanne Wakatsuki
  Houston *asa* 956

Yamada, Ichiro
No-No Boy - John Okada *asa* 1042

JAPANESE CANADIAN

Nakane, Ayako "Obasan"
Obasan - Joy Kogawa *asa* 975

Nakane, Isamu "Uncle"
Obasan - Joy Kogawa *asa* 975

Nakane, Megumi Naomi
Naomi's Road - Joy Kogawa *asa* 974
Obasan - Joy Kogawa *asa* 975

Nakane, Stephen
Naomi's Road - Joy Kogawa *asa* 974

JEWISH CHILEAN

Rosa
Longing - Maria Espinosa *lat* 601

JOCKEY

Roberts, Cody
Dead Heat - Willyce Kim *asa* 970

JOURNALIST

Carson, Tyler
Keeping Secrets - Penny Mickelbury *afa* 276

Crawford, Mitchell "Mitch" Sylvester
B-Boy Blues - Steven Corbin *afa* 81

DiMaio, Joan
Lavender House Murder - Nikki Baker *afa* 6

Huerta, Jorge
Cinco de Mayo: An Epic Novel - David
  Monreal *lat* 713

Kang, K. Connie
*Home Was the Land of Morning Calm: The Saga of a
  Korean American Family* - K. Connie
  Kang *asa* 965

Miller, Mia
And This Too Shall Pass - E. Lynn Harris *afa* 179

Nehemiah, Adam
Dessa Rose - Sherley Anne Williams *afa* 463

Patterson, M. Montgomery "Mimi"
Keeping Secrets - Penny Mickelbury *afa* 276
Night Songs - Penny Mickelbury *afa* 277

St. Claire, Geraldine
The Thirteenth Apostle - Gloria Gonzalez *lat* 639

Vega, Raul
Room 9 - Soledad Santiago *lat* 817

Wing, Nancy
Yellow Fever - R.A. Shiomi *asa* 1067

JUDGE

James, Dede
The Between - Tananarive Due *afa* 104

Witherspoon, Jericho
Two Wings to Veil My Face - Leon Forrest *afa* 129

KIDNAP VICTIM

Bilal, Muhammad
Glory Field - Walter Dean Myers *afa* 307

KOREAN

"Aunt Tiger"
Year of Impossible Goodbyes - Sook Nyul
  Choi *asa* 930

Baek Hongyang
Still Life With Rice: A Young American Woman Discovers the Life and Legacy of Her Korean Grandmother - Helie Lee   *asa*   986

Bak, Hyunsuk "Mother"
Echoes of the White Giraffe - Sook Nyul Choi   *asa*   927
Year of Impossible Goodbyes - Sook Nyul Choi   *asa*   930

Bak, Inchun
Year of Impossible Goodbyes - Sook Nyul Choi   *asa*   930

Bak, Sookan
Echoes of the White Giraffe - Sook Nyul Choi   *asa*   927
Gathering of Pearls - Sook Nyul Choi   *asa*   928
Year of Impossible Goodbyes - Sook Nyul Choi   *asa*   930

Chun, Haesu
Clay Walls - Ronyoung Kim   *asa*   968

Chun, Youngjune
Clay Walls - Ronyoung Kim   *asa*   968

Lee, Yoon Jun
If It Hadn't Been for Yoon Jun - Marie G. Lee   *asa*   995

KOREAN AMERICAN

Aekyung
Aekyung's Dream - Min Paek   *asa*   1045

Helie, Lee
Still Life With Rice: A Young American Woman Discovers the Life and Legacy of Her Korean Grandmother - Helie Lee   *asa*   986

Kim, Abuji "Father"
Plantation Child and Other Stories - Eve Begley Kiehm   *asa*   966

Kim, Blossom
Plantation Child and Other Stories - Eve Begley Kiehm   *asa*   966

Kim, Jae-Chun
Saying Goodbye - Marie G. Lee   *asa*   996

Kim, Joe
Plantation Child and Other Stories - Eve Begley Kiehm   *asa*   966

Kim, Marita
Plantation Child and Other Stories - Eve Begley Kiehm   *asa*   966

Kim, Pauly
Plantation Child and Other Stories - Eve Begley Kiehm   *asa*   966

Kim, Puni "Little Sister"
Plantation Child and Other Stories - Eve Begley Kiehm   *asa*   966

Kim, Stella Sung Ok
Stella: On the Edge of Popularity - Lauren Lee   *asa*   992

Kwang, John
Native Speaker - Chang-rae Lee   *asa*   984

Larsen, Alice
If It Hadn't Been for Yoon Jun - Marie G. Lee   *asa*   995

Lee, Hung Man "H.M."
Quiet Odyssey: A Pioneer Korean Woman in America - Mary Paik Lee   *asa*   997

Lee, Mary Kuang Sun Paik
Quiet Odyssey: A Pioneer Korean Woman in America - Mary Paik Lee   *asa*   997

Sung, Ellen Joyce
Finding My Voice - Marie G. Lee   *asa*   994

Saying Goodbye - Marie G. Lee   *asa*   996

Sung, Michelle
Saying Goodbye - Marie G. Lee   *asa*   996

Yunmi
Halmoni and the Picnic - Sook Nyul Choi   *asa*   929

LANDLORD

Johnson, Naomi Reeves
Long Distance Life - Marita Golden   *afa*   139

Whitlaw
Dragonwings - Laurence Yep   *asa*   1120

Wiggins, Gloria
The Young Landlords - Walter Dean Myers   *afa*   327

Williams, Paul
The Young Landlords - Walter Dean Myers   *afa*   327

LANDOWNER

Alamar, Don Mariano
The Squatter and the Don - Maria Amparo Ruiz de Burton   *lat*   799

Butler, Hoyt "Cap'n"
The Avenue, Clayton City - C. Eric Lincoln   *afa*   245

Marshall, Candy
A Gathering of Old Men - Ernest J. Gaines   *afa*   133

Nedeed, Luther
Linden Hills - Gloria Naylor   *afa*   329

Rafa, Jose Antonio
Not by the Sword - Nash Candelaria   *lat*   557

Rafa, Tercero
Not by the Sword - Nash Candelaria   *lat*   557

LATINA

Alta
Naked Ladies - Alma Luz Villanueva   *lat*   877

Martinez, Sandy
Juanita Fights the School Board - Gloria Velasquez   *lat*   873

Terranova, Marie
Room 9 - Soledad Santiago   *lat*   817

LATINO

Carmello "Mello"
Fast Talk on a Slow Track - Rita Williams-Garcia   *afa*   466

Crow
La Gran Fiesta - Francisco X. Mora   *lat*   716

Diablo
Third and Indiana - Steven Lopez   *lat*   684

LAWMAN

Mapes
A Gathering of Old Men - Ernest J. Gaines   *afa*   133

LAWYER

Acosta, Oscar Zeta
The Autobiography of a Brown Buffalo - Oscar Zeta Acosta   *lat*   485
The Revolt of the Cockroach People - Oscar Zeta Acosta   *lat*   486

Bradley, Solomon
The Road to Memphis - Mildred D. Taylor   *afa*   411

Chan, Chuck
Yellow Fever - R.A. Shiomi   *asa*   1067

Del Campo, Zeferino
The Silver Cloud Cafe - Alfredo Vea Jr.   *lat*   868

Dorati, Elizabeth "Liz"
Golden Gate: A Novel in Verse - Vikram Seth   *asa*   1064

Eagle Eyes
Heartbeat, Drumbeat - Irene Beltran Hernandez   *lat*   649

Garnett, Vernor
White Butterfly - Walter Mosley   *afa*   292

Graham, Dalton
Wild Embers - Anita Richmond Bunkley   *afa*   33

Gray, Molly
The Murderer Next Door - Rafael Yglesias   *lat*   893

Kristin
From the Notebooks of Melanin Sun - Jacqueline Woodson   *afa*   474

Langdon, Nathan
Sally Hemings - Barbara Chase-Riboud   *afa*   54

Lee, Elaine
Ribbons - Laurence Yep   *asa*   1126

Montez, Luis
The Ballad of Gato Guerrero - Manuel Ramos   *lat*   762
The Ballad of Rocky Ruiz: Death of a Martyr - Manuel Ramos   *lat*   763
The Last Client of Luis Montez - Manuel Ramos   *lat*   764

Paschen, Rosalee "Rosey"
Long Goodbyes - Nikki Baker   *afa*   7

Quintana Roo, Andres
Leona: A Love Story - Elizabeth Borton de Trevino   *lat*   857

Reeves, Gregory
The Infinite Plan - Isabel Allende   *lat*   498

Reuben
Reuben - John Edgar Wideman   *afa*   450

Rios, Henry
The Death of Friends - Michael Nava   *lat*   733
The Hidden Law - Michael Nava   *lat*   734
How Town: A Novel of Suspense - Michael Nava   *lat*   735

Sullivan, Daniel Christopher Taylor
Tangled Up in Blue - Larry Duplechan   *afa*   107

Tyler, Raymond Wilson Jr.
Invisible Life - E. Lynn Harris   *afa*   180
Just as I Am - E. Lynn Harris   *afa*   181

Uribe, Porfirio
The Labyrinth - Enrique A. Laguerre   *lat*   677

Witherspoon, Jericho
Two Wings to Veil My Face - Leon Forrest   *afa*   129

Wolf, Naomi
Lavender House Murder - Nikki Baker   *afa*   6

Yellow Calf, Sylvester
The Indian Lawyer - James Welch   *naa*   1345

LEADER

Amado
Jalamanta: A Message from the Desert - Rudolfo Anaya   *lat*   511

LESBIAN

Beckett, Kelsey
In the Game - Nikki Baker   *afa*   5

Casas, Juani
Memory Mambo: A Novel - Achy Obejas   *lat*   739

Cedar, Encanta "EC"
From the Notebooks of Melanin Sun - Jacqueline
   Woodson   *afa*   474

Celie
The Color Purple - Alice Walker   *afa*   426

Horn, Diane
Coffee Will Make You Black - April
   Sinclair   *afa*   392

Johnson, Beverly "Bev"
In the Game - Nikki Baker   *afa*   5

Kelly, Virginia "Ginny"
In the Game - Nikki Baker   *afa*   5
Lavender House Murder - Nikki Baker   *afa*   6
Long Goodbyes - Nikki Baker   *afa*   7

Kristin
From the Notebooks of Melanin Sun - Jacqueline
   Woodson   *afa*   474

Maglione, Giovanna "Gianna"
Keeping Secrets - Penny Mickelbury   *afa*   276
Night Songs - Penny Mickelbury   *afa*   277

McMann, Mary Ellen "Spike"
Long Goodbyes - Nikki Baker   *afa*   7

Melendez, Veronica
Margins - Terri de la Pena   *lat*   588

Patterson, M. Montgomery "Mimi"
Keeping Secrets - Penny Mickelbury   *afa*   276
Night Songs - Penny Mickelbury   *afa*   277

Perez, Emma
Gulf Dreams - Emma Perez   *lat*   753

Rio, Carole
Send My Roots Rain - Ibis Gomez-Vega   *lat*   634

Staples, Ouida
The Serpent's Gift - Helen Elaine Lee   *afa*   241

Tamayo, Jessica
Latin Satins - Terri de la Pena   *lat*   587

Wolf, Naomi
Lavender House Murder - Nikki Baker   *afa*   6

LIBRARIAN

Fletcher
Ashok by Any Other Name - Sandra S.
   Yamate   *asa*   1110

Von Vampton, Hinckle
Mumbo Jumbo - Ishmael Reed   *afa*   366

LINGUIST

Kang, Joo-han
*Home Was the Land of Morning Calm: The Saga of a
   Korean American Family* - K. Connie
   Kang   *asa*   965

Kaweli "James Covey"
Echo of Lions - Barbara Chase-Riboud   *afa*   52

LION

Lion
Dance of the Animals - Pura Belpre   *lat*   533
Dance of the Animals - Pura Belpre   *lat*   533

LOVER

Bruno, Robert
Frontiers of Love - Diana Chang   *asa*   915

Crane, Aurora "Ro"
American Knees - Shawn Wong   *asa*   1104

Josh
The Hidden Law - Michael Nava   *lat*   734
How Town: A Novel of Suspense - Michael
   Nava   *lat*   735

Joyce, Janes Philips
Dead Heat - Willyce Kim   *asa*   970

Nguyen, Betty
American Knees - Shawn Wong   *asa*   1104

Ramu
Nampally Road - Meena Alexander   *asa*   896

Razia
Mistaken Identity - Nayantara Sahgal   *asa*   1050

Riggins, Jessica Nahale
Dancer Dawkins and the California Kid - Willyce
   Kim   *asa*   969

Sheng, Yan
Red Azalea - Anchee Min   *asa*   1020

Soyza, Shehan
Funny Boy - Shyam Selvadurai   *asa*   1063

Supervisor
Red Azalea - Anchee Min   *asa*   1020

Sylla
Mistaken Identity - Nayantara Sahgal   *asa*   1050

MAGICIAN

Trueba, Clara del Valle
The House of the Spirits - Isabel Allende   *lat*   497

MAINTENANCE WORKER

Anderson, Kojie
A Short Walk - Alice Childress   *afa*   57

Braithwaite, Cecil Otis
Hurry Home - John Edgar Wideman   *afa*   448

Braithwaite, Esther Brown
Hurry Home - John Edgar Wideman   *afa*   448

Fillis, Norman
Montgomery's Children - Richard Perry   *afa*   344

Finney, Sam
Right by My Side - David Haynes   *afa*   185

Franklin, Mamie
Seduction by Light - Al Young   *afa*   481

Gunner, Aaron
Fear of the Dark - Gar Anthony Haywood   *afa*   188
Not Long for This World - Gar Anthony
   Haywood   *afa*   190

Pool
The Planet of Junior Brown - Virginia
   Hamilton   *afa*   169

Rawlins, Ezekiel "Easy"
A Little Yellow Dog - Walter Mosley   *afa*   289

Simmons, Nate
Just an Old Sweet Song - Melvin Van
   Peebles   *afa*   421

Williams, Jake
Trouble the Water - Melvin Dixon   *afa*   99

Willie
Mojo and the Russians - Walter Dean
   Myers   *afa*   314

MATCHMAKER

Matchmaker
Red Thread - Ed Young   *asa*   1132

MAYAN

Choy, Isabel Pacay
Imagining Isabel - Omar Castaneda   *lat*   565

Pacay, Isabel
Among the Volcanoes - Omar Castaneda   *lat*   564

MECHANIC

Garcia, Bobo
In Search of Snow - Luis Alberto Urrea   *lat*   864

Kisa
Year of Impossible Goodbyes - Sook Nyul
   Choi   *asa*   930

Louie, Mason
Bone - Fae Myenne Ng   *asa*   1039

MENTALLY CHALLENGED PERSON

March, Phoenix
No Other Tale to Tell - Richard Perry   *afa*   345

Nicole
Humming Whispers - Angela Johnson   *afa*   217

Pratt, Dabney "Dab"
Sweet Whispers, Brother Rush - Virginia
   Hamilton   *afa*   170

Wing, Big
Willie Bea and the Time the Martians Landed -
   Virginia Hamilton   *afa*   172

MENTALLY ILL PERSON

Johnson, Tashi (Evelyn)
Possessing the Secret of Joy - Alice
   Walker   *afa*   429

Sixbury, Patrick
Walk Me to the Distance - Percival Everett   *afa*   117

MERCENARY

Akwara, Artia "El Muerte"
Legend of Tarik - Walter Dean Myers   *afa*   312

Othello
Othello, a Novel - Julius Lester   *afa*   244

MEXICAN

Amado
Jalamanta: A Message from the Desert - Rudolfo
   Anaya   *lat*   511

Amparo
Cantora: A Novel - Sylvia Lopez-Medina   *lat*   686

Angel
Angel's Kite = La Estrella de Angel - Alberto
   Blanco   *lat*   544

Anita
Across the Great River - Irene Beltran
   Hernandez   *lat*   648

Calderon, Ana
The Memories of Ana Calderon: A Novel - Graciela
   Limon   *lat*   681

Carlos
*Carlos and the Cornfield: Story = Carlos y la Milpa
   de Maiz: Cuento* - Jan Romero Stevens   *lat*   840

Carlos and the Squash Plant/Carlos y la Planta de Calabaza - Jan Romero Stevens   *lat*   841
The Gift of the Poinsettia = El Regalo de la Flor de Nochebuena - Pat Mora   *lat*   719

Cavazos, Heraclio
Rainbow's End - Genaro Gonzalez   *lat*   638

Durcal, Alejo
Dreams of the Centaur - Montserrat Fontes   *lat*   612

Galarza, Ernesto
Barrio Boy - Ernesto Galarza   *lat*   615

Gomez, Lupe
Rain of Gold - Victor Villasenor   *lat*   882

El Guero
El Guero: A True Adventure Story - Elizabeth Borton de Trevino   *lat*   855

Gutierrez, Lupe
The Plum Plum Pickers - Raymond Barrio   *lat*   531

Gutierrez, Manuel
The Plum Plum Pickers - Raymond Barrio   *lat*   531

Gutierrez, Sergio Alberto
A Hundred Days From Now - Steven Corbin   *afa*   83

Half-Chicken
Mediopollito = Half-Chicken - Alma Flor Ada   *lat*   489

Huerta, Jorge
Cinco de Mayo: An Epic Novel - David Monreal   *lat*   713

Ibarra, Magdalena
Doctor Magdalena: Novella - Rosa Martha Villarreal   *lat*   880

Joaquin
Friends From the Other Side/Amigos del Otro Lado - Gloria Anzaldua   *lat*   517

Kata
Across the Great River - Irene Beltran Hernandez   *lat*   648

Lola
Who Would Have Thought It? - Maria Amparo Ruiz de Burton   *lat*   800

Lopez, Arcadia H.
Barrio Teacher - Arcadia H. Lopez   *lat*   683

Lopez-Stafford, Gloria
A Place in El Paso: A Mexican American Childhood - Gloria Lopez-Stafford   *lat*   687

Luna, Lazaro
Pig Cookies and Other Stories - Alberto Alvaro Rios   *lat*   774

Maldonado, Loreto
Pilgrims in Aztlan - Miguel Mendez   *lat*   702

Marroquin, Chayo
A Place Where the Sea Remembers - Sandra Benitez   *lat*   539

Noragua, Timoteo
The Dream of Santa Maria de las Piedras - Miguel Mendez   *lat*   701

Pastora
Sapogonia: An Anti-Romance in 3/8 Meter - Ana Castillo   *lat*   569

Pepita
Pepita Talks Twice = Pepita Habla Dos Veces - Ofelia Dumas Lachtman   *lat*   675

Rafa, Jose Antonio
Inheritance of Strangers - Nash Candelaria   *lat*   554
Memories of the Alhambra - Nash Candelaria   *lat*   556
Not by the Sword - Nash Candelaria   *lat*   557

Rafa, Tercero
Not by the Sword - Nash Candelaria   *lat*   557

Rangel, Carmen
Call No Man Master - Tina Juarez   *lat*   667

Revueltas, Octavio
The Brick People - Alejandro Morales   *lat*   724

Rios, Pepe
Pepe Rios - Daniel Cano   *lat*   558

Rodriguez, Marta
A Place Where the Sea Remembers - Sandra Benitez   *lat*   539

Rosario
Cantora: A Novel - Sylvia Lopez-Medina   *lat*   686

Salazar, Francisco
The Dark Side of the Dream - Alejandro Grattan-Dominguez   *lat*   645

Salazar, Miguel
The Dark Side of the Dream - Alejandro Grattan-Dominguez   *lat*   645

Ultima
Bless Me, Ultima - Rudolfo Anaya   *lat*   508

Vargas, Carlos
The Girl from Playa Blanca - Ofelia Dumas Lachtman   *lat*   674

Vargas, Maria Elena
The Girl from Playa Blanca - Ofelia Dumas Lachtman   *lat*   674

Villasenor, Margarita
Wild Steps of Heaven - Victor Villasenor   *lat*   884

Villasenor, Salvador
Rain of Gold - Victor Villasenor   *lat*   882

MEXICAN AMERICAN

Abel
Jesse - Gary Soto   *lat*   827

Alicia
Treasure Nap - Juanita Havill   *lat*   647

Angel, Miguel
The Rain God: A Desert Tale - Arturo Islas   *lat*   666

Angel, Miguel Chico
Migrant Souls: A Novel - Arturo Islas   *lat*   665

Armijo, Nicolas
Leonor Park - Nash Candelaria   *lat*   555

Cardenas, Nenita
Intaglio: A Novel in Six Stories - Roberta Fernandez   *lat*   605

Coronado, Ricky
A Fabricated Mexican - Rick P. Rivera   *lat*   778

Diego
Radio Man = Don Radio: A Story in English and Spanish - Arthur Dorros   *lat*   594

El Viejo
The Old Man and His Door - Gary Soto   *lat*   829

Estrella
Under the Feet of Jesus - Helena Maria Viramontes   *lat*   887

Eutemio
Death of an Anglo - Alejandro Morales   *lat*   725

Fausto, Don
The Road to Tamazunchale - Ron Arias   *lat*   526

Flores, Alfredo
The Me Inside of Me - T. Ernesto Bethancourt   *lat*   541

Garcia, Bobo
In Search of Snow - Luis Alberto Urrea   *lat*   864

Garcia, Feliciano
George Washington Gomez - Americo Paredes   *lat*   750

Gomez, Amalia
The Miraculous Day of Amalia Gomez: A Novel - John Rechy   *lat*   768

Gomez, George Washington
George Washington Gomez - Americo Paredes   *lat*   750

Guerrero, Salvador
Memorias: A West Texas Life - Salvador Guerrero   *lat*   646

Jesse
Jesse - Gary Soto   *lat*   827

Jose
Jose's Basket - Karen Papagapitos   *lat*   748

Juanita
Juanita Fights the School Board - Gloria Velasquez   *lat*   873

Luz
The Farolitos of Christmas - Rudolfo Anaya   *lat*   510

Mama
Treasure Nap - Juanita Havill   *lat*   647

Maria
To a Widow with Children - Lionel G. Garcia   *lat*   621

Martin, Angela
A Shell for Angela - Ofelia Dumas Lachtman   *lat*   676

Maya
Maya's Divided World - Gloria Velasquez   *lat*   874

Montez, Eduardo Ricardo
Stone Horses - Sallie Gallegos   *lat*   616

Munoz, Blanca
The Wedding - Mary Helen Ponce   *lat*   759

Nana
Green Corn Tamales = Tamales de Elote - Gina Macaluso Rodriguez   *lat*   786

Ponce, Mary Helen
Hoyt Street: An Autobiography - Mary Helen Ponce   *lat*   758

Prietita
Friends From the Other Side/Amigos del Otro Lado - Gloria Anzaldua   *lat*   517
Prietita and the Ghost Woman = Prietita y La Llorona - Gloria Anzaldua   *lat*   518

Ramos, Alicia Inez
Alicia's Treasures - Diane Gonzales Bertrand   *lat*   635

Reyes, Gilberto
A Long Way from Home - Gordon Kahn   *lat*   668

Rodriguez, Richard
Hunger of Memory: The Education of Richard Rodriguez, an Autobiography - Richard Rodriguez   *lat*   788

Romano-V., Octavio I.
Geriatric Fu: My First Sixty-Five Years in the United States - Octavio I. Romano-V,   *lat*   794

Rubio, Richard
Pocho - Jose Antonio Villarreal   *lat*   879

Salazar, Josie
Migrant Souls: A Novel - Arturo Islas   *lat*   665

Sanchez Castillo Soto, Magdalena Armijo
Leonor Park - Nash Candelaria   *lat*   555

Socorro
Socorro, Daughter of the Desert - Karen Papagapitos   *lat*   749

Tia Zuelma
Where the Cinnamon Winds Blow = Donde Soplan Los Vientos de Canela - Jim Sagel   *lat*   805

Tomas
Where the Cinnamon Winds Blow = Donde Soplan Los Vientos de Canela - Jim Sagel *lat* 805

Velasquez, Miguel
Voice-Haunted Journey - Eliud Martinez *lat* 694

MEXICAN INDIAN

Garcia, Roberto
Macho! - Edmund Villasenor *lat* 881

MEZTISO

Alberto "Beto"
La Maravilla - Alfredo Vea Jr. *lat* 867

MIDWIFE

Titay
Trouble's Child - Mildred Pitts Walter *afa* 440

MIGRANT WORKER

Arai, Takashi
Face of a Stranger - Yoji Yamaguchi *asa* 1107

Estrella
Under the Feet of Jesus - Helena Maria Viramontes *lat* 887

MILITARY PERSONNEL

Blackman, Abraham
Captain Blackman - John A. Williams *afa* 458

Buenrostro, Rafe
The Useless Servants - Rolando Hinojosa *lat* 660

Colon, Cristobal
The Aztec Chronicles: The True History of Christopher Columbus, as Narrated by Quilaztli of Texcoco: A Novella - Joseph P. Sanchez *lat* 809

Dawson
Fire and Rain - Oswald Rivera *lat* 777

Fuller, Lance
Wild Embers - Anita Richmond Bunkley *afa* 33

Henry, Jacob "Jake"
Jacob's Ladder - John A. Williams *afa* 460

Kire of Myetra
They Fly at Ciron - Samuel R. Delany *afa* 97

Ledbeder, Clabe
Emily, the Yellow Rose - Anita Richmond Bunkley *afa* 31

Marcus, Theophilus J. "Skeeter"
Wilhemina Jones, Future Star - Dindga McCannon *afa* 257

Miles, Laban J.
Wah'Kon-Tah: The Osage and the White Man's Road - John Joseph Mathews *naa* 1273

Pena, Joe
Stallion Gate - Martin Cruz Smith *naa* 1312

Perry, Richard "Richie"
Fallen Angels - Walter Dean Myers *afa* 305

Reyes, Gilberto
A Long Way from Home - Gordon Kahn *lat* 668

Roy, Janelle
Wild Embers - Anita Richmond Bunkley *afa* 33

Ulises
Southern Front - Alejandro Murguia *lat* 731

Whittman, Ishmael
Captain Blackman - John A. Williams *afa* 458

MINSTREL

Crow, Jim
Darktown Strutters - Wesley Brown *afa* 27

MODEL

Brown, Crystal
Crystal - Walter Dean Myers *afa* 302

Cabot, Evan
Fragments That Remain - Steven Corbin *afa* 82

DeLea, Rosa "Rowena"
Crystal - Walter Dean Myers *afa* 302

Jadine
Tar Baby - Toni Morrison *afa* 286

Knight, Nicole "Nicky"
The Price You Pay - Barbara Summers *afa* 402

MONSTER

Qallupilluit
A Promise Is a Promise - Michael Arvaarluk Kusugak *naa* 1253

MOROCCAN

Tawfik, Mussa Ahmed
Duel in the Desert - Walter Dean Myers *afa* 304

MOTHER

Alta
Naked Ladies - Alma Luz Villanueva *lat* 877

Bak, Hyunsuk "Mother"
Echoes of the White Giraffe - Sook Nyul Choi *asa* 927
Year of Impossible Goodbyes - Sook Nyul Choi *asa* 930

Barnett, Nola
One Dark Body - Charlotte Sherman *afa* 389

Benbow, Arden
Faultline: A Novel - Sheila Ortiz Taylor *lat* 848
Southbound: The Sequel to Faultline - Sheila Ortiz Taylor *lat* 849

Brown, Jane
Betsey Brown - Ntozake Shange *afa* 383

Chelvaratnam, Nalini
Funny Boy - Shyam Selvadurai *asa* 1063

Choe, Sok-Won
Home Was the Land of Morning Calm: The Saga of a Korean American Family - K. Connie Kang *asa* 965

Chou
The Boy Who Swallowed Snakes - Laurence Yep *asa* 1117

Christine
A Yellow Raft in Blue Water - Michael Dorris *naa* 1201

Cipriano, Christa
A Feather on the Breath of God - Sigrid Nunez *asa* 1041

Clora
Family - J. California Cooper *afa* 79

Cox, Lily
Your Blues Ain't Like Mine - Bebe Moore Campbell *afa* 48

Crocodile
Rockabye Crocodile - Jose Aruego *asa* 897

Daniels, Vincereta "Viney"
Daughters - Paule Marshall *afa* 254

Delcano, Luz
In Search of Bernabe - Graciela Limon *lat* 679

Diane
Toning the Sweep - Angela Johnson *afa* 223

Duk, Daisy
Donald Duk - Frank Chin *asa* 924

DuMont, Evelyn
Sisters and Lovers - Connie Briscoe *afa* 23

Dupree, Effie
Another Good Loving Blues - Arthur Flowers *afa* 124

Durcal, Felipa
Dreams of the Centaur - Montserrat Fontes *lat* 612

Eady, Elizabeth "Black Betty"
Black Betty - Walter Mosley *afa* 287

Fletcher, Ellie
Molly by Any Other Name - Jean Davies Okimoto *asa* 1043

Franklin, Betty
Ten Seconds - Louis Edwards *afa* 108

Frieda
In the Shadow of the Peacock - Grace Edwards-Yearwood *afa* 109

Gabriel, LaDonna
Heathens - David Haynes *afa* 183

Gabriel, Verda
Heathens - David Haynes *afa* 183

Garcia, Laura "Mami"
How the Garcia Girls Lost Their Accents - Julia Alvarez *lat* 502

Gomez, Amalia
The Miraculous Day of Amalia Gomez: A Novel - John Rechy *lat* 768

Gonzaga, Dolores
Dogeaters - Jessica Hagedorn *asa* 942

Gonzalez, America
America's Dream - Esmeralda Santiago *lat* 813

Gray, Mercer
The Price of a Child - Lorene Cary *afa* 51

Greene, Story Temple
Crossing over Jordan - Linda Beatrice Brown *afa* 26

Hemings, Sally
The President's Daughter - Barbara Chase-Riboud *afa* 53
Sally Hemings - Barbara Chase-Riboud *afa* 54

Henry, Velma
The Salt Eaters - Toni Cade Bambara *afa* 8

Hong, Mother
The Woman Warrior: Memoirs of a Girlhood Among Ghosts - Maxine Hong Kingston *asa* 973

Hsu, An-Mei
The Joy Luck Club - Amy Tan *asa* 1079

Ingram, Deborah
Emergency Exit - Clarence Major *afa* 247

Isaac, Elizabeth
Crossover - Dennis Williams *afa* 456

Iyapo, Lilith
Dawn - Octavia Butler *afa* 35

James, Cora
A Short Walk - Alice Childress *afa* 57

Johnson, Avatara "Avey"
Praisesong for the Widow - Paule Marshall *afa* 255

Jones, Margaret
Philadelphia Fire - John Edgar Wideman *afa* 449

Jong, Lindo
The Joy Luck Club - Amy Tan   *asa*   1079

Kali
Her - Cherry Muhanji   *afa*   296

Kessey, Saturn Marie
City of Light - Cyrus Colter   *afa*   76

Kezee, Xenobia Mae
Somebody Else's Mama - David Haynes   *afa*   186

Lamertine, Lulu
Love Medicine - Louise Erdrich   *naa*   1213

Lane, Tamra Wells
Chesapeake Song - Brenda Lane
    Richardson   *afa*   371

Lau, Marie
Cultural Revolution - Norman Wong   *asa*   1103

Lawson, Lizabeth French
Damballah - John Edgar Wideman   *afa*   446

Lee, Elaine
Ribbons - Laurence Yep   *asa*   1126

Lee, "Mama"
The Ghost Fox - Laurence Yep   *asa*   1121

Leong, "Mah"
Bone - Fae Myenne Ng   *asa*   1039

Loudermilk, Dottie
Bad News Travels Fast - Gar Anthony
    Haywood   *afa*   187
Going Nowhere Fast - Gar Anthony
    Haywood   *afa*   189

Louie, Winnie
The Kitchen God's Wife - Amy Tan   *asa*   1080

MacAlister, Marti "Big Mac"
Slow Burn - Eleanor Taylor Bland   *afa*   15

Mama
Rise and Shine, Mariko-chan! - Chiyoko
    Tomioka   *asa*   1082
Treasure Nap - Juanita Havill   *lat*   647
Tree of Cranes - Allen Say   *asa*   1061

Mami
When I Was Puerto Rican - Esmeralda
    Santiago   *lat*   814

Mango, Rain
Fragments of the Ark - Louise Meriwether   *afa*   275

March, Carla
No Other Tale to Tell - Richard Perry   *afa*   345

Maria
To a Widow with Children - Lionel G.
    Garcia   *lat*   621

Masaube, Puma
Mischief Makers - Nettie Jones   *afa*   235

Matsuda, Karen Kumai
Molly by Any Other Name - Jean Davies
    Okimoto   *asa*   1043

McDougald, Aileen
These Same Long Bones - Gwendolyn
    Parker   *afa*   339

Minatoya, Miyeko
*Talking to High Monks in the Snow: An Asian
    American Odyssey* - Lydia Yuri
    Minatoya   *asa*   1021

Mother
American Visa - Wang Ping   *asa*   1047
At the Beach - Huy Voun Lee   *asa*   987
Hiroshima No Pika (The Flash of Hiroshima) - Toshi
    Maruki   *asa*   1012
In the Snow - Huy Voun Lee   *asa*   988
The Little Weaver of Thai-Yen Village - Tran Khanh
    Tuyet   *asa*   1083
Mama Bear - Chyng Feng Sun   *asa*   1073
Silent Lotus - Jeanne M. Lee   *asa*   989

Okasan
Chibi: A True Story from Japan - Barbara
    Brenner   *asa*   906

Okuda, Shizuko Matsumoto
Shizuko's Daughter - Kyoko Mori   *asa*   1026

Old Rosa
Old Rosa: A Novel in Two Stories - Reinaldo
    Arenas   *lat*   523

Orphelia
Wilhemina Jones, Future Star - Dindga
    McCannon   *afa*   257

Osaka, Mother
The Floating World - Cynthia Kadohata   *asa*   962

Peacock, Mildred
Mama - Terry McMillan   *afa*   268

Perry, Charmaine
Sisters and Lovers - Connie Briscoe   *afa*   23

Romana
The Line of the Sun: A Novel - Judith Ortiz
    Cofer   *lat*   746

St. Clair, Ying-ying
The Joy Luck Club - Amy Tan   *asa*   1079

Sakane, "Mother"
Journey Home - Yoshiko Uchida   *asa*   1089
*Journey to Topaz: A Story of the Japanese-American
    Education* - Yoshiko Uchida   *asa*   1090

Seese
Almanac of the Dead - Leslie Marmon
    Silko   *naa*   1306

Shawnee Ray
The Bingo Palace - Louise Erdrich   *naa*   1211

Shimizu, Chie
One Bird - Kyoko Mori   *asa*   1025

Simmons, Priscilla
Just an Old Sweet Song - Melvin Van
    Peebles   *afa*   421

Sixbury, Chloe
Walk Me to the Distance - Percival Everett   *afa*   117

Snowdon, Patricia
Thereafter Johnnie - Carolivia Herron   *afa*   194

Sofia
So Far from God: A Novel - Ana Castillo   *lat*   570

Sone, Benko
Nisei Daughter - Monica Sone   *asa*   1070

Suggs, Sethe
Beloved - Toni Morrison   *afa*   281

Sullivan, Shannon
Shannon - Gordon Parks   *afa*   340

Taylor, Mary Kate
All-Bright Court - Connie Porter   *afa*   356

Terasaki, Keiko "Mom"
The Loom and Other Stories - R.A.
    Sasaki   *asa*   1055

Ting, Dai-li Mar
China Boy - Gus Lee   *asa*   985

Todd, Delotha
Your Blues Ain't Like Mine - Bebe Moore
    Campbell   *afa*   48

Tompkins, Elzina
After the Garden - Doris Jean Austin   *afa*   4

Trini
Trini - Estela Portillo Trambley   *lat*   854

Uchida, Iku Umegaki
*Desert Exile: The Uprooting of a Japanese-American
    Family* - Yoshiko Uchida   *asa*   1087

Vasquez, Romilia
A Fire in the Earth - Marcos McPeek
    Villatoro   *lat*   885

Wakatsuki, Riku "Mama"
Farewell to Manzanar - Jeanne Wakatsuki
    Houston   *asa*   956

Whitaker, Gayle
Like Sisters on the Homefront - Rita Williams-
    Garcia   *afa*   467

Widow
The Boy of the Three-Year Nap - Dianne
    Snyder   *asa*   1069

Wilder, Leela Brandon Alexander
Black Gold - Anita Richmond Bunkley   *afa*   30

Wilson, Pearlean "Pearl"
Rattlebone - Maxine Clair   *afa*   60

Winter, Geraldine
Mama, I Want to Sing - Vy Higginsen   *afa*   195

Wong, Anna Choy
A Little Too Much Is Enough - Kathleen
    Tyau   *asa*   1086

Wong, Mother
Fifth Chinese Daughter - Jade Snow
    Wong   *asa*   1102
In the Year of the Boar and Jackie Robinson - Bette
    Bao Lord   *asa*   1007

Woo, Suyuan
The Joy Luck Club - Amy Tan   *asa*   1079

Wright, Nel
Sula - Toni Morrison   *afa*   285

Yamada, Mama
No-No Boy - John Okada   *asa*   1042

Yang, Nainai
Baba: A Return to China upon My Father's Shoulders
    - Belle Yang   *asa*   1113

MOUSE

Mouse
Seven Blind Mice - Ed Young   *asa*   1133

Perez
Perez and Martina - Pura Belpre   *lat*   535

MURDERER

Olivas, Jesus
Happy Birthday Jesus - Ronald L. Ruiz   *lat*   798

MUSICIAN

Banzar
The Singing Man - Angela Shelf Medearis   *afa*   272

Bodeen, Lucas
Another Good Loving Blues - Arthur
    Flowers   *afa*   124

Brown, Junior
The Planet of Junior Brown - Virginia
    Hamilton   *afa*   169

Builds-the-Fire, Thomas
Reservation Blues - Sherman Alexie   *naa*   1138

Castillo, Cesar
The Mambo Kings Play Songs of Love - Oscar
    Hijuelos   *lat*   655

Castillo, Nestor
The Mambo Kings Play Songs of Love - Oscar
    Hijuelos   *lat*   655

Hayakawa, Janet "Jan"
Golden Gate: A Novel in Verse - Vikram
    Seth   *asa*   1064

Maglione, Giovanna "Gianna"
Keeping Secrets - Penny Mickelbury *afa* 276
Night Songs - Penny Mickelbury *afa* 277

Tamarindo, Justo
Mile Zero - Thomas Sanchez *lat* 811

POLITICAL FIGURE

Dominic, Frank
Albuquerque - Rudolfo Anaya *lat* 506

Fasseke, Chuma
Jacob's Ladder - John A. Williams *afa* 460

Jefferson, Thomas
The President's Daughter - Barbara Chase-
   Riboud *afa* 53

Johnson, Al
Somebody Else's Mama - David Haynes *afa* 186

Jones, Clement
The Terrible Threes - Ishmael Reed *afa* 368

Kwang, John
Native Speaker - Chang-rae Lee *asa* 984

Lakes, Abraham "Abe"
The Lakestown Rebellion - Kristin Hunter *afa* 209

Mackenzie, Primus "PM"
Daughters - Paule Marshall *afa* 254

Trueba, Esteban
The House of the Spirits - Isabel Allende *lat* 497

POLITICAL PRISONER

Singh, Bhushan
Mistaken Identity - Nayantara Sahgal *asa* 1050

Yamada, Ichiro
No-No Boy - John Okada *asa* 1042

PREGNANT TEENAGER

Hamilton, Faith
A Woman's Place - Marita Golden *afa* 140

Johnson, Yolanda
Rocking the Babies - Linda Raymond *afa* 362

Rebecca
The Dear One - Jacqueline Woodson *afa* 473

Rose, Dessa
Dessa Rose - Sherley Anne Williams *afa* 463

Whitaker, Gayle
Like Sisters on the Homefront - Rita Williams-
   Garcia *afa* 467

PRINCIPAL

Greene, Story Temple
Crossing over Jordan - Linda Beatrice
   Brown *afa* 26

Hill, Gaten
Clover - Dori Sanders *afa* 379

PRISONER

Arenas, Reinaldo
Before Night Falls - Reinaldo Arenas *lat* 521

Dawson
Fire and Rain - Oswald Rivera *lat* 777

Durcal, Alejo
Dreams of the Centaur - Montserrat Fontes *lat* 612

Gabriel
Singing to Cuba - Margarita Engle *lat* 597

Gabriel, LaDonna
Heathens - David Haynes *afa* 183

Hernandez, Chi-Chi
Fire and Rain - Oswald Rivera *lat* 777

Quiro
Rabid Beasts - Carlos Miralejos *lat* 704

Torres, Beaver
The Secret of Two Brothers - Irene Beltran
   Hernandez *lat* 650

PROFESSOR

Alberta
Green Grass, Running Water - Thomas
   King *naa* 1245

Benbow, Arden
Faultline: A Novel - Sheila Ortiz Taylor *lat* 848
Southbound: The Sequel to Faultline - Sheila Ortiz
   Taylor *lat* 849

Carlotta
The Temple of My Familiar - Alice Walker *afa* 430

Garboil, Frank
The Comeback - Ed Vega *lat* 871

Henry, Jordan
Trouble the Water - Melvin Dixon *afa* 99

Kannadical, Mira
Nampally Road - Meena Alexander *asa* 896

Marshall, John Calvin
And All Our Wounds Forgiven - Julius
   Lester *afa* 242

McCurtain, Cole
Bone Game - Louis Owen *naa* 1293

Puttbutt, Benjamin "Chappie" III
Japanese by Spring - Ishmael Reed *afa* 364

Ramu
Nampally Road - Meena Alexander *asa* 896

Roger
State of Emergency - Floyd Salas *lat* 807

Salisbury, Samantha
Along the Journey River - Carol LaFavor *naa* 1255

Sturgis, Lincoln
And Do Remember Me - Marita Golden *afa* 138

Suwelo
The Temple of My Familiar - Alice Walker *afa* 430

Tarrant, Dixon
1959 - Thulani Davis *afa* 93

Taylor, Bill
Changes - Richard Perry *afa* 343

Velasquez, Miguel
Voice-Haunted Journey - Eliud Martinez *lat* 694

Washington, John
The Chaneysville Incident - David Bradley *afa* 19

Weinstein, Norvin
Love, Stars, and All That - Kirin Narayan *asa* 1037

Wiggins, Grant
A Lesson before Dying - Ernest J. Gaines *afa* 135

Williams, Roger
The Crown of Columbus - Louise
   Erdrich *naa* 1212

PROSTITUTE

Adrianne
Dark Plums - Maria Espinosa *lat* 600

Cross, Faith
Faith and the Good Thing - Charles
   Johnson *afa* 225

Kikue
Face of a Stranger - Yoji Yamaguchi *asa* 1107

Orgaz, Ana Magdelena
The Love Queen of the Amazon - Cecile
   Pineda *lat* 756

Shino
Face of a Stranger - Yoji Yamaguchi *asa* 1107

PROTAGONIST

Unnamed Character
The Coffin Tree - Wendy Law-Yone *asa* 982

PSYCHIC

Fannie
Tumbling - Diane McKinney-Whetstone *afa* 258

Fillis, Norman
Montgomery's Children - Richard Perry *afa* 344

Franklin, Mamie
Seduction by Light - Al Young *afa* 481

Imani
An Open Weave - Devorah Major *afa* 253

Iree
An Open Weave - Devorah Major *afa* 253

Lecha
Almanac of the Dead - Leslie Marmon
   Silko *naa* 1306

PSYCHOLOGIST

DuMont, Evelyn
Sisters and Lovers - Connie Briscoe *afa* 23

Martinez, Sandy
Juanita Fights the School Board - Gloria
   Velasquez *lat* 873

Wright, Wanda
I Get on the Bus - Reginald McKnight *afa* 265

PUBLIC RELATIONS

Mandarino, Gary
The Berhama Account - John A. Williams *afa* 457

PUBLISHER

Gutierrez, Sergio Alberto
A Hundred Days From Now - Steven
   Corbin *afa* 83

PUERTO RICAN

Aleluya
Hot Soles in Harlem - Emilio Diaz
   Valcarcel *lat* 592

Alicea, Gil C.
*The Air Down Here: True Tales from a South Bronx
   Boyhood* - Gil C. Alicea *lat* 496

Atariba
*Atariba and Niguayona: A Story from the Taino
   People of Puerto Rico* - Harriet Rohmer *lat* 790

Blanca
A Perfect Silence - Alba Ambert *lat* 505

Chota, John
The Comeback - Ed Vega *lat* 871

Colon, Francesca
Streets of Fire - Soledad Santiago *lat* 818

Cruz, Tito
Scorpions - Walter Dean Myers   *afa*   322

Felita
Felita - Nicholasa Mohr   *lat*   707
Going Home - Nicholasa Mohr   *lat*   708

Gonzalez, America
America's Dream - Esmeralda Santiago   *lat*   813

Gusman
The Line of the Sun: A Novel - Judith Ortiz
 Cofer   *lat*   746

Hernandez, Chi-Chi
Fire and Rain - Oswald Rivera   *lat*   777

Lion
Dance of the Animals - Pura Belpre   *lat*   533
Dance of the Animals - Pura Belpre   *lat*   533

Malanguezes, Santos
*Family Installments: Memories of Growing Up
 Hispanic* - Edward Rivera   *lat*   776

Malanguezes, Tego
*Family Installments: Memories of Growing Up
 Hispanic* - Edward Rivera   *lat*   776

Marisol
The Line of the Sun: A Novel - Judith Ortiz
 Cofer   *lat*   746

Marita
Abuelita's Paradise - Carmen Santiago
 Nodar   *lat*   737

Nieves, Facundo
Valentino's Hair - Yvonne V. Sapia   *lat*   819

Nieves, Lupe
Valentino's Hair - Yvonne V. Sapia   *lat*   819

Niguayona
*Atariba and Niguayona: A Story from the Taino
 People of Puerto Rico* - Harriet Rohmer   *lat*   790

Otilia
*My Aunt Otilia's Spirits = Los Espiritus de Mi Tia
 Otilia* - Richard Garcia   *lat*   623

Pilar
Singing Softly = Cantando Bajito - Carmen de
 Monteflores   *lat*   589

Pio
The Rainbow-Colored Horse - Pura Belpre   *lat*   536

Ramirez, Nilda
Nilda: A Novel - Nicholasa Mohr   *lat*   710

Ramon
Vejigantes Masquerade - Lucia M.
 Gonzalez   *lat*   641

Riera, Adan
Yagua Days - Cruz Martel   *lat*   689

Romana
The Line of the Sun: A Novel - Judith Ortiz
 Cofer   *lat*   746

Sanchez, Gerardo
Hot Soles in Harlem - Emilio Diaz
 Valcarcel   *lat*   592

Santiago
Santiago - Pura Belpre   *lat*   537

Tano
The Rainbow-Colored Horse - Pura Belpre   *lat*   536

Thomas, Piri
Down These Mean Streets - Piri Thomas   *lat*   850

Uribe, Porfirio
The Labyrinth - Enrique A. Laguerre   *lat*   677

PUERTO RICAN ESKIMO

Garboil, Frank
The Comeback - Ed Vega   *lat*   871

QUECHUAN

Numa, Tarija
Ambush in the Amazon - Walter Dean
 Myers   *afa*   300

RABBIT

Conejo, Tio
Rabbit Wishes - Linda Shute   *lat*   821

Rabbit
The Rabbit's Escape - Suzanne Crowder
 Han   *asa*   948
The Rabbit's Judgment - Suzanne Crowder
 Han   *asa*   949

RACIST

Bass, Robert Jr.
Japanese by Spring - Ishmael Reed   *afa*   364

MacKenzie
Yellow Fever - R.A. Shiomi   *asa*   1067

RACOON

Racoon
Lakota & Dakota Animal Wisdom Stories - Pamela
 Greenhill Kaizen   *naa*   1237

RAILROAD WORKER

Herbie
Tumbling - Diane McKinney-Whetstone   *afa*   258

Hoi "Pie-Biter"
Pie-Biter - Ruthanne Lum McCunn   *asa*   1015

RANCHER

de Mendoza y Soria, Santiago
Caballero: A Historical Novel - Jovita Gonzalez
 Mireles   *lat*   705

Marder, Curt
God's Country - Percival Everett   *afa*   114

RAT

Rat
Cat and Rat: The Legend of the Chinese Zodiac - Ed
 Young   *asa*   1128

REBEL

Helie, Lee
*Still Life With Rice: A Young American Woman
 Discovers the Life and Legacy of Her Korean
 Grandmother* - Helie Lee   *asa*   986

Peters, Kevin
Zulus - Percival Everett   *afa*   119

RECEPTIONIST

Stevenson, Jean Eloise "Stevie"
Ain't Gonna Be the Same Fool Twice - April
 Sinclair   *afa*   391

Turner, July
When Death Comes Stealing - Valerie Wilson
 Wesley   *afa*   443

Waters, Kiki
RL's Dream - Walter Mosley   *afa*   291

RECLUSE

Simpkins, Bess
Hiding Place - John Edgar Wideman   *afa*   447

REFUGEE

Bokhi
Echoes of the White Giraffe - Sook Nyul
 Choi   *asa*   927

Campos, Julian
The Cutter: A Novel - Virgil Suarez   *lat*   842

Hien
The Little Weaver of Thai-Yen Village - Tran Khanh
 Tuyet   *asa*   1083

Juan
The Doorman - Reinaldo Arenas   *lat*   522

RELIGIOUS

Barry, Meshach Coriolanus
A Chocolate Soldier - Cyrus Colter   *afa*   75

Corwul, James
Witherspoon - Lance Jeffers   *afa*   213

Fools Crow
Fools Crow - James Welch   *naa*   1344

Hamilton, Henry Isaiah
Gone Quiet - Eleanor Taylor Bland   *afa*   14

Lawson, Lizabeth French
Damballah - John Edgar Wideman   *afa*   446

Lucero, Ben
Cebu - Peter Bacho   *asa*   902

Madame Bernice
Our Lady of Babylon - John Rechy   *lat*   770

Martin, Phillip
In My Father's House - Ernest J. Gaines   *afa*   134

Mary
Portrait of Mary - Nikki Grimes   *afa*   155

Maximillian "Max"
No Other Tale to Tell - Richard Perry   *afa*   345

Nettie
The Color Purple - Alice Walker   *afa*   426

Puyat, Pauline
Tracks - Louise Erdrich   *naa*   1215

Radja
Gay-Neck: The Story of a Pigeon - Dhan Gopal
 Mukerji   *asa*   1029

Rafa, Tercero
Not by the Sword - Nash Candelaria   *lat*   557

Roberts, Frank
Things to Be Lost - Lionel Newton   *afa*   336

Robinson, Zurich
And This Too Shall Pass - E. Lynn Harris   *afa*   179

Smith, Joshua
Do Lord Remember Me - Julius Lester   *afa*   243

Thunder, Anna
The Grass Dancer - Susan Power   *naa*   1295

Tompkins, Rosalie
After the Garden - Doris Jean Austin   *afa*   4

Witherspoon, Lucius
Witherspoon - Lance Jeffers   *afa*   213

Witherspoon, Sweetie Reed
Two Wings to Veil My Face - Leon Forrest   *afa*   129

Character Description Index

RESEARCHER

Helstrom, Bron
Triton - Samuel R. Delany   *afa* 98

Kessey, Paul
City of Light - Cyrus Colter   *afa* 76

Narrator
Panther - Melvin Van Peebles   *afa* 422

Nehemiah, Adam
Dessa Rose - Sherley Anne Williams   *afa* 463

North, Adam "Juneboy"
Such Was the Season - Clarence Major   *afa* 252

Westby, Moses
No - Clarence Major   *afa* 249

RESISTANCE FIGHTER

Li Shin
The Scent of the Gods - Fiona Cheong   *asa* 919

RESTAURANTEUR

Bailey
Bailey's Cafe - Gloria Naylor   *afa* 328

Cunningham, Giles
The Spyglass Tree - Albert Murray   *afa* 298

Duk, King
Donald Duk - Frank Chin   *asa* 924

McMann, Mary Ellen "Spike"
Long Goodbyes - Nikki Baker   *afa* 7

Ta Fan the Korean
Dead Heat - Willyce Kim   *asa* 970

Wong
Mama Bear - Chyng Feng Sun   *asa* 1073

REVOLUTIONARY

Black, Tomsson
Plan B - Chester Himes   *afa* 196

Celia del Pino
Dreaming in Cuban, A Novel - Cristina
  Garcia   *lat* 617

Father
The Coffin Tree - Wendy Law-Yone   *asa* 982

Fortunato
The Palace of the White Skunks - Reinaldo
  Arenas   *lat* 524

Hill, Meridian
Meridian - Alice Walker   *afa* 428

Jackson, Canada
Reflex and Bone Structure - Clarence
  Major   *afa* 251

Kang, Myong-Hwan
*Home Was the Land of Morning Calm: The Saga of a
  Korean American Family* - K. Connie
  Kang   *asa* 965

Sutton, Ruth Elizabeth "Rufel"
Dessa Rose - Sherley Anne Williams   *afa* 463

Zapata, Emiliano
Zapata Lives! - Gary D. Keller   *lat* 671

Zapata, Emilio
Zapata Rose in 1992 and Other Tales - Gary D.
  Keller   *lat* 672

ROGUE

Ah Song
Eat a Bowl of Tea - Louis Chu   *asa* 931

ROOMMATE

Lloyd, Ellen
Gathering of Pearls - Sook Nyul Choi   *asa* 928

Thomas, Leecia
Saying Goodbye - Marie G. Lee   *asa* 996

ROOSTER

Gallito
The Bossy Gallito - Lucia M. Gonzalez   *lat* 640

Rooster
Toad Is the Uncle of Heaven - Jeanne M.
  Lee   *asa* 990

ROYALTY

Belen, Maria de
*Maria Belen: The Autobiography of an Indian Woman:
  A Novel* - Graciela Limon   *lat* 680

Huitzitzilin
Song of the Hummingbird - Graciela Limon   *lat* 682

Kofi
The Captive - Joyce Hansen   *afa* 173

Malinali
Malinche: Slave Princess of Cortez - Gloria
  Duran   *lat* 595

Medea
For Her Dark Skin - Percival Everett   *afa* 113

M'witu, Najee
Captain Africa: The Battle for Egyptica - Dwayne J.
  Ferguson   *afa* 120

Siddhartha
Buddha - Demi   *asa* 932

Tetrok
Saturn's Child - Nichelle Nichols   *afa* 337

Wilmanzu, Johari
Captain Africa: The Battle for Egyptica - Dwayne J.
  Ferguson   *afa* 120

RULER

Ch'in Shih Huang
The Seven Chinese Brothers - Margaret
  Mahy   *asa* 1011

Dragon King of the East Sea
The Rabbit's Escape - Suzanne Crowder
  Han   *asa* 948

The Emperor
The Empty Pot - Demi   *asa* 934

The Foolish Magistrate
The Chinese Siamese Cat - Amy Tan   *asa* 1077

The King
The Shell Woman and the King - Laurence
  Yep   *asa* 1127

King
Yeh-Shen: A Cinderella Story from China - Ai-Ling
  Louie   *asa* 1008

King of Heaven
Toad Is the Uncle of Heaven - Jeanne M.
  Lee   *asa* 990

Nawab
Fat Gopal - Jacquelin Singh   *asa* 1068

RUNAWAY

Brown, "B.J."
The Survivors - Kristin Hunter   *afa* 211

Jennings, Obidiah "Obi"
Which Way Freedom? - Joyce Hansen   *afa* 176

Lau, Evelyn
Runaway: Diary of a Street Kid - Evelyn
  Lau   *asa* 981

Outlaw, Lurhetta
M.C. Higgins, the Great - Virginia
  Hamilton   *afa* 165

Quickskill, Raven
Flight to Canada - Ishmael Reed   *afa* 363

Wainwright, Corbitt
Six Out Seven - Jess Mowry   *afa* 294

Williams, Frank "Motown"
Motown and Didi: A Love Story - Walter Dean
  Myers   *afa* 316

RUNNER

Barbour, Talley
A White Romance - Virginia Hamilton   *afa* 171

Jewett, Sherry
The Outside Shot - Walter Dean Myers   *afa* 320

Williams, Francois
Understand This - Jervey Tervalon   *afa* 415

SAILOR

Kaweli "James Covey"
Echo of Lions - Barbara Chase-Riboud   *afa* 52

Son
Tar Baby - Toni Morrison   *afa* 286

SALESMAN

Carmello "Mello"
Fast Talk on a Slow Track - Rita Williams-
  Garcia   *afa* 466

Lionel
Green Grass, Running Water - Thomas
  King   *naa* 1245

Trace, Joe
Jazz - Toni Morrison   *afa* 283

Watson, Dinizulu "Denzel"
Fast Talk on a Slow Track - Rita Williams-
  Garcia   *afa* 466

SALOON KEEPER/OWNER

King, Hong
Thousand Pieces of Gold - Ruthanne Lum
  McCunn   *asa* 1016

SALVADORAN

Delcano, Bernabe
In Search of Bernabe - Graciela Limon   *lat* 679

Delcano, Luz
In Search of Bernabe - Graciela Limon   *lat* 679

Maria
Journey of the Sparrow - Fran Leeper Buss   *lat* 552

Romero, Jose Luis
Mother Tongue - Demetria Martinez   *lat* 693

Tonio, Don
*Magic Dogs of the Volcanoes = Los Perros Magicos
  de los Volcanes* - Manlio Argueta   *lat* 525

SCHOLAR

Ho Kuan
Night Visitors - Ed Young   *asa*   1131

SCIENTIST

Bukay, Noddaman
Changes - Richard Perry   *afa*   343

Domonique, Nyota
Saturn's Child - Nichelle Nichols   *afa*   337

Doyle, Asa Elias "Eli"
Clay's Ark - Octavia Butler   *afa*   34

Fletcher, Paul
Molly by Any Other Name - Jean Davies
   Okimoto   *asa*   1043

Hawks, Robert
Watershed - Percival Everett   *afa*   118

Lane, Tamra Wells
Chesapeake Song - Brenda Lane
   Richardson   *afa*   371

Paine, Hayden
Nightwing - Martin Cruz Smith   *naa*   1311

Tetrok
Saturn's Child - Nichelle Nichols   *afa*   337

SCOUT

Bubba
God's Country - Percival Everett   *afa*   114

Stock, Dave
The True American: A Folk Fable - Melvin Van
   Peebles   *afa*   423

SEA CAPTAIN

Mango, Peter
Fragments of the Ark - Louise Meriwether   *afa*   275

SEAMSTRESS

Minty
Oxherding Tale - Charles Johnson   *afa*   227

Navarro, Rita
Sweet Fifteen - Diane Gonzales Bertrand   *lat*   636

Pilgrim, Clotilda
Rivers of Eros - Cyrus Colter   *afa*   78

SECRETARY

Adams, Elizabeth "Lisa"
And All Our Wounds Forgiven - Julius
   Lester   *afa*   242

Celia
In the Shadow of the Peacock - Grace Edwards-
   Yearwood   *afa*   109

McPhee, Ruella "Rooms"
Vanishing Rooms - Melvin Dixon   *afa*   100

Perry, Charmaine
Sisters and Lovers - Connie Briscoe   *afa*   23

Pfluggins, Effie
The Secret of Gumbo Grove - Eleanora E.
   Tate   *afa*   405

Unnamed Character
High Cotton - Darryl Pinckney   *afa*   347

SERVANT

Fat Gopal
Fat Gopal - Jacquelin Singh   *asa*   1068

Hawkins, George
Oxherding Tale - Charles Johnson   *afa*   227

West, Emily D.
Emily, the Yellow Rose - Anita Richmond
   Bunkley   *afa*   31

SIDEKICK

Jerome "Jerry"
Wild Meat and the Bully Burgers - Lois-Ann
   Yamanaka   *asa*   1109

SINGER

Avery, Shug
The Color Purple - Alice Walker   *afa*   426

Banks, Zora
Disappearing Acts - Terri McMillan   *afa*   266

Gates, Constance "Cookie"
Like Sisters on the Homefront - Rita Williams-
   Garcia   *afa*   467

Hawkins, Louretta "Lou"
Lou in the Limelight - Kristin Hunter   *afa*   210

Jackson, Abyssinia "Abby"
Marked by Fire - Joyce Carol Thomas   *afa*   418

Kelly
The Best Bug to Be - Dolores Johnson   *afa*   228

Marigold
When the Nightingale Sings - Joyce Carol
   Thomas   *afa*   419

Painted Turtle
Painted Turtle: Woman with Guitar - Clarence
   Major   *afa*   250

Rousseau, Johnnie Ray
Captain Swing - Larry Duplechan   *afa*   106

Springer, Nicole Marie
Invisible Life - E. Lynn Harris   *afa*   180
Just as I Am - E. Lynn Harris   *afa*   181

Tamayo, Jessica
Latin Satins - Terri de la Pena   *lat*   587

Winter, Doris
Mama, I Want to Sing - Vy Higginsen   *afa*   195

SINGLE FATHER

Lonnie
It Ain't All for Nothing - Walter Dean
   Myers   *afa*   311

SINGLE MOTHER

Colon, Francesca
Streets of Fire - Soledad Santiago   *lat*   818

Holloday, Deloretto "Imani"
Divine Days - Leon Forrest   *afa*   127

Jackson, Savannah
Waiting to Exhale - Terry McMillan   *afa*   269

Johnson, Esther
Long Distance Life - Marita Golden   *afa*   139

Michael, Mattie
Women of Brewster Place - Gloria Naylor   *afa*   331

Sallis, Nita
Live at Five - David Haynes   *afa*   184

Turner, Cinder
Billy - Albert French   *afa*   130

SISTER

Abby
Abby - Jeannette Franklin Caines   *afa*   40

Adams, Arilla
Arilla Sun Down - Virginia Hamilton   *afa*   156

Anderson, Kimako
Kimako's Story - June Jordan   *afa*   237

Autrie
Indigo and Moonlight Gold - Jan Spivey
   Gilchrist   *afa*   137

Avery, Mary Elouise
Thank You, Dr. Martin Luther King, Jr.! - Eleanora E.
   Tate   *afa*   406

Bechet, Clothilde "Chloe"
Colorstruck - Benita Porter   *afa*   352

Beppy
The Train to LuLu's - Elizabeth Fitzgerald
   Howard   *afa*   204

Bright, Elena "Lena" Cecilia
I Hadn't Meant to Tell You This - Jacqueline
   Woodson   *afa*   475

Brooks, Louise
No Easy Place to Be - Steven Corbin   *afa*   84

Brooks, Velma
No Easy Place to Be - Steven Corbin   *afa*   84

Brown, Elizabeth "Betsey"
Betsey Brown - Ntozake Shange   *afa*   383

Bweela
Daddy Is a Monster. . .Sometimes - John
   Steptoe   *afa*   397
My Special Best Words - John Steptoe   *afa*   400

Carson, Margie
Just an Overnight Guest - Eleanora E. Tate   *afa*   404

Chang, Theresa
Typical American - Gish Jen   *asa*   960

Coco
Ten Seconds - Louis Edwards   *afa*   108

Delaney, Koya
Koya Delaney and the Good Girl Blues - Eloise
   Greenfield   *afa*   147

Douglas, Antoinette Marie "Toni"
Breadsticks and Blessing Places - Candy Dawson
   Boyd   *afa*   16

Footman, Annie Moriah "Annie Rye"
Down in the Piney Woods - Ethel Footman
   Smothers   394
Moriah's Pond - Ethel Footman Smothers   *afa*   395

Footman, Brat
Moriah's Pond - Ethel Footman Smothers   *afa*   395

Footman, Maybaby
Moriah's Pond - Ethel Footman Smothers   *afa*   395

Franklin, Betty
Ten Seconds - Louis Edwards   *afa*   108

Franklin, Tanya
The Patchwork Quilt - Valerie Flournoy   *afa*   122
Tanya's Reunion - Valerie Flournoy   *afa*   123

Freeman, Doretha
Sister - Eloise Greenfield   *afa*   150

Geneia
Crazy Love - Elias Miguel Munoz   *lat*   729

Hamilton, Faith
A Woman's Place - Marita Golden   *afa*   140

Hill, Holly Rachelle
Holly - Albert French   *afa*   131

SON

Arturo
Old Rosa: A Novel in Two Stories - Reinaldo
   Arenas   *lat*   523

Banzar
The Singing Man - Angela Shelf Medearis   *afa*   272

Chen, Gilbert
April and the Dragon Lady - Lensey
   Namioka   *asa*   1034

Copeland, Brownfield
The Third Life of Grange Copeland - Alice
   Walker   *afa*   431

Dead, Macon "Milkman" III
Song of Solomon - Toni Morrison   *afa*   284

Delcano, Bernabe
In Search of Bernabe - Graciela Limon   *lat*   679

Eldest Son
The Magic Tapestry - Demi   *asa*   936

Fuse, Joe Toranosuke Thor
Sushi and Sourdough - Tooru J. Kanazawa   *asa*   964

Fuse, Kennosuke "Ken"
Sushi and Sourdough - Tooru J. Kanazawa   *asa*   964

Kamik
Harpoon of the Hunter - Markoosie   *naa*   1265

Lau, Michael
Cultural Revolution - Norman Wong   *asa*   1103

Nieves, Lupe
Valentino's Hair - Yvonne V. Sapia   *lat*   819

Oyama, Kiyoshi
All I Asking for Is My Body - Milton
   Murayama   *asa*   1033

Second Son
The Magic Tapestry - Demi   *asa*   936

See, Leo Ming Quan "Eddy"
*On Gold Mountain: The One-Hundred-Year Odyssey
   of a Chinese-American Family* - Lisa
   See   *asa*   1062

Ting, Kai "China Boy"
China Boy - Gus Lee   *asa*   985

Toshio, Oyama
All I Asking for Is My Body - Milton
   Murayama   *asa*   1033

Wei nian
The Cricket Warrior: A Chinese Tale - Margaret
   Chang   *asa*   917

Wong Choy Fuk
Disappearing Moon Cafe - Sky Lee   *asa*   998

Yamada, Ichiro
No-No Boy - John Okada   *asa*   1042

Yang, Joseph "Baba"
Baba: A Return to China upon My Father's Shoulders
   - Belle Yang   *asa*   1113

Yang, Yeye
Baba: A Return to China upon My Father's Shoulders
   - Belle Yang   *asa*   1113

Youngest Son
The Magic Tapestry - Demi   *asa*   936

SORCERESS

Medea
For Her Dark Skin - Percival Everett   *afa*   113

SOUTH ASIAN CANADIAN

Ghosh, Samir
Coloured Pictures - Himani Bannerji   *asa*   903

Ghosh, Sujata
Coloured Pictures - Himani Bannerji   *asa*   903

SOUTHERN BELLE

Sutton, Ruth Elizabeth "Rufel"
Dessa Rose - Sherley Anne Williams   *afa*   463

SPACE EXPLORER

Viacom, Ron
Brainstorm - Walter Dean Myers   *afa*   301

SPANISH

Colon, Cristobal
*The Aztec Chronicles: The True History of Christopher
   Columbus, as Narrated by Quilaztli of Texcoco: A
   Novella* - Joseph P. Sanchez   *lat*   809

de Pareja, Juan
I, Juan de Pareja - Elizabeth Borton de
   Trevino   *lat*   856

Martina
Perez and Martina - Pura Belpre   *lat*   535

Maximo
Sapogonia: An Anti-Romance in 3/8 Meter - Ana
   Castillo   *lat*   569

Mendizabal, Quintin
The House on the Lagoon - Rosario Ferre   *lat*   608

Miranda, Francisca
Sal y Pimienta: A Culinary Education - Francisca
   Miranda Schneider   *lat*   820

Perez
Perez and Martina - Pura Belpre   *lat*   535

Valenzuela de Castillo, Josephina
La Maravilla - Alfredo Vea Jr.   *lat*   867

Villasenor, Juan Jesus
Wild Steps of Heaven - Victor Villasenor   *lat*   884

SPINSTER

Smalls, Vesta
The Serpent's Gift - Helen Elaine Lee   *afa*   241

SPIRIT

Beloved
Beloved - Toni Morrison   *afa*   281

Herman
The Hand I Fan With - Tina McElroy Ansa   *afa*   2

Red Robe
The Ghost Fox - Laurence Yep   *asa*   1121

Tree Spirit
*Judge Rabbit and the Tree Spirit: A Folktale from
   Cambodia* - Lina Mao Wall   *asa*   1095

Unnamed Character
The Man Who Tricked a Ghost - Laurence
   Yep   *asa*   1124

SPORTSWRITER

Elliott, Sean
And This Too Shall Pass - E. Lynn Harris   *afa*   179

SPOUSE

Alta
Naked Ladies - Alma Luz Villanueva   *lat*   877

Andrews, George
Mama Day - Gloria Naylor   *afa*   330

Andrews, Ophelia "Cocoa"
Mama Day - Gloria Naylor   *afa*   330

Anibal
Sleep of the Innocents - Carole Fernandez   *lat*   603

Bemis, Charlie
Thousand Pieces of Gold - Ruthanne Lum
   McCunn   *asa*   1016

Ben Loy
Eat a Bowl of Tea - Louis Chu   *asa*   931

Bishop, Simon
The Hundred Secret Senses - Amy Tan   *asa*   1078

Braithwaite, Cecil Otis
Hurry Home - John Edgar Wideman   *afa*   448

Braithwaite, Esther Brown
Hurry Home - John Edgar Wideman   *afa*   448

Cambon-Fournier, Cecile Stephanie
City of Light - Cyrus Colter   *afa*   76

Chan Fong Mei
Disappearing Moon Cafe - Sky Lee   *asa*   998

Chang, Helen
Typical American - Gish Jen   *asa*   960

Covington, Paula
Company Man - Brent Wade   *afa*   425

Covington, William "Billy"
Company Man - Brent Wade   *afa*   425

Cox, Lily
Your Blues Ain't Like Mine - Bebe Moore
   Campbell   *afa*   48

De Weese, Tana
Tripmaster Monkey: His Fake Book - Maxine Hong
   Kingston   *asa*   972

Doyle, Asa Elias "Eli"
Clay's Ark - Octavia Butler   *afa*   34

Fasseke, Chuma
Jacob's Ladder - John A. Williams   *afa*   460

Fuse, Yaso
Sushi and Sourdough - Tooru J. Kanazawa   *asa*   964

Goodman, Gwen
Losing Absalom - Alexs D. Pate   *afa*   341

Hancock, Everett
Blanche on the Lam - Barbara Neely   *afa*   333

Harris, Bernadine
Waiting to Exhale - Terry McMillan   *afa*   269

Hill, Tony
Cold Medina - Gary Hardwick   *afa*   178

Hito, Tomoe Kanemori
A Bridge Between Us - Julie Shigekuni   *asa*   1066

Husband
*Judge Rabbit and the Tree Spirit: A Folktale from
   Cambodia* - Lina Mao Wall   *asa*   1095

James, Dede
The Between - Tananarive Due   *afa*   104

James, Hilton
The Between - Tananarive Due   *afa*   104

Johnson, Al
Somebody Else's Mama - David Haynes   *afa*   186

Johnson, Paula
Somebody Else's Mama - David Haynes   *afa*   186

Kessey, Saturn Marie
City of Light - Cyrus Colter   *afa*   76

Lakes, Abraham "Abe"
The Lakestown Rebellion - Kristin Hunter   *afa*   209

Lazarre, Marie
Love Medicine - Louise Erdrich   *naa*   1213

Collins, Angela
Project Wheels - Jacqueline Turner Banks   *afa*   11

Costanza, Cheryl
Crossover - Dennis Williams   *afa*   456

Davis, Harriet
Addy Learns a Lesson: A School Story - Connie Porter   *afa*   353
Addy Saves the Day: A Summer Story - Connie Porter   *afa*   354

Dodd, Christopher Noel
Have a Happy. . . . - Mildred Pitts Walter   *afa*   434

DuBois, Sin-Sin
One Dark Body - Charlotte Sherman   *afa*   389

Figueroa, Angela
His Own Where - June Jordan   *afa*   236

Ghosh, Sujata
Coloured Pictures - Himani Bannerji   *asa*   903

Gonzaga, Rio
Dogeaters - Jessica Hagedorn   *asa*   942

Gueye, Aminata
I Get on the Bus - Reginald McKnight   *afa*   265

Hanson, Holly
Yang the Third and Her Impossible Family - Lensey Namioka   *asa*   1035

Jadine
Tar Baby - Toni Morrison   *afa*   286

Jenkins, Jury
Egg-Drop Blues - Jacqueline Turner Banks   *afa*   9

Johnson, Millicent "Peaches"
Peaches - Dindga McCannon   *afa*   256

Lazarus, Robin
Robin on His Own - Johnniece Marshall Wilson   *afa*   470

Lee, Rollo Ezekiel "Cager"
A Chocolate Soldier - Cyrus Colter   *afa*   75

Levy, Ellen
In the Year of the Boar and Jackie Robinson - Bette Bao Lord   *asa*   1007

Lion Head
Katherine - Anchee Min   *asa*   1019

Mabel
In the Year of the Boar and Jackie Robinson - Bette Bao Lord   *asa*   1007

Malanguezes, Santos
Family Installments: Memories of Growing Up Hispanic - Edward Rivera   *lat*   776

Malanguezes, Tego
Family Installments: Memories of Growing Up Hispanic - Edward Rivera   *lat*   776

Manfred, Dorcas
Jazz - Toni Morrison   *afa*   283

Martin, Lucas
Getting Right with God - Lionel Newton   *afa*   335

Masaube, Lilly
Mischief Makers - Nettie Jones   *afa*   235

Metcalf, Mariah
Mariah Loves Rock - Mildred Pitts Walter   *afa*   438

Moore, Sarah
Addy Learns a Lesson: A School Story - Connie Porter   *afa*   353

Moses, Miranda
Poor Girl, Rich Girl - Johnniece Marshall Wilson   *afa*   469

Nguyen, Hoa "Ut"
Angel Child, Dragon Child - Michele Maria Surat   *asa*   1075

Nikanj
Dawn - Octavia Butler   *afa*   35

Numa, Tarija
Ambush in the Amazon - Walter Dean Myers   *afa*   300

O'Meara, Kim
Yang the Third and Her Impossible Family - Lensey Namioka   *asa*   1035

Payne, Quincy
How Stella Got Her Groove Back - Terry McMillan   *afa*   267

Peterson, Angie
The Shimmershine Queens - Camille Yarbrough   *afa*   480

Rivers, Buddy
His Own Where - June Jordan   *afa*   236

Sallis, Nita
Live at Five - David Haynes   *afa*   184

Shabazz, King
The Boy Who Didn't Believe in Spring - Lucille Clifton   *afa*   63

Sims, Buhlaire
Plain City - Virginia Hamilton   *afa*   168

Stevens, Lillie
Lillie of Watts Takes a Giant Step - Mildred Pitts Walter   *afa*   436

Stone, Martha
My Name Is Seepeetza - Shirley Sterling   *naa*   1324

Tate, Tyrone
Those Other People - Alice Childress   *afa*   58

Taylor, Michael "Mikey"
All-Bright Court - Connie Porter   *afa*   356

Wainwright, Corbitt
Six Out Seven - Jess Mowry   *afa*   294

Walker, Addy
Addy Learns a Lesson: A School Story - Connie Porter   *afa*   353
Addy Saves the Day: A Summer Story - Connie Porter   *afa*   354
Changes for Addy: A Winter Story - Connie Porter   *afa*   357
Happy Birthday, Addy! A Springtime Story - Connie Porter   *afa*   358

Walker, Danny
Marcia - John Steptoe   *afa*   398

Williams, Marcia
Marcia - John Steptoe   *afa*   398

Wilson, Ludell
Ludell - Brenda Wilkinson   *afa*   453

Witherspoon, Nathaniel Turner
Two Wings to Veil My Face - Leon Forrest   *afa*   129

Yang, Yingmei "Mary"
Yang the Third and Her Impossible Family - Lensey Namioka   *asa*   1035

Zebra
Katherine - Anchee Min   *asa*   1019

STUDENT—COLLEGE

Abel
Jesse - Gary Soto   *lat*   827

Bak, Sookan
Gathering of Pearls - Sook Nyul Choi   *asa*   928

Bass, Robert Jr.
Japanese by Spring - Ishmael Reed   *afa*   364

Butler, William "Beans"
House of Slammers - Nathan Heard   *afa*   192

Chung, Eric
The Incorporation of Eric Chung - Steven Lo   *asa*   1005

Das, Gita
Love, Stars, and All That - Kirin Narayan   *asa*   1037

Ganifrockwala, Firoze
Love, Stars, and All That - Kirin Narayan   *asa*   1037

Gannon, Marci
Gathering of Pearls - Sook Nyul Choi   *asa*   928

Granados, Tristan
Tristan and the Hispanics - Jose Yglesias   *lat*   890

Howard, Michelle DuBois
Falling Leaves of Ivy - Yolanda Joe   *afa*   214

Isaac, Richard "Ike"
Crossover - Dennis Williams   *afa*   456

Jackson, Lonnie
The Outside Shot - Walter Dean Myers   *afa*   320

Jesse
Jesse - Gary Soto   *lat*   827

Jewett, Sherry
The Outside Shot - Walter Dean Myers   *afa*   320

Kim, Jae-Chun
Saying Goodbye - Marie G. Lee   *asa*   996

Knight, Nicole "Nicky"
The Price You Pay - Barbara Summers   *afa*   402

Lawson, "Doot"
Sent for You Yesterday - John Edgar Wideman   *afa*   451

Lawson, John
Damballah - John Edgar Wideman   *afa*   446

Liu, Victor
The Incorporation of Eric Chung - Steven Lo   *asa*   1005

Lloyd, Ellen
Gathering of Pearls - Sook Nyul Choi   *asa*   928

Marisse, Ann
Only the Good Times - Bruce-Novoa   *lat*   549

Marr, John
The Mad Man - Samuel R. Delany   *afa*   95

McQuillen, Gerald
The Nicholas Factor - Walter Dean Myers   *afa*   319

Mendoza, Brian
Obsidian Sky: A Novel - Guy Garcia   *lat*   618

Miguel
Shango - James Roberto Curtis   *lat*   585

Narrator
Panther - Melvin Van Peebles   *afa*   422

Nickelson, Elizabeth
Falling Leaves of Ivy - Yolanda Joe   *afa*   214

Scooter
The Spyglass Tree - Albert Murray   *afa*   298

Starr, Cyndi "White Butterfly"
White Butterfly - Walter Mosley   *afa*   292

Sung, Ellen Joyce
Saying Goodbye - Marie G. Lee   *asa*   996

Sung, Michelle
Saying Goodbye - Marie G. Lee   *asa*   996

Thomas, Leecia
Saying Goodbye - Marie G. Lee   *asa*   996

Valence, Paul
Only the Good Times - Bruce-Novoa   *lat*   549

Watson, Kevin "Kayo"
Falling Leaves of Ivy - Yolanda Joe   *afa*   214

Wells, Jennifer
The Nicholas Factor - Walter Dean Myers   *afa*   319

STUDENT—ELEMENTARY SCHOOL

Chow, Elaine
Elaine and the Flying Frog - Heidi Chang   *asa*   916

STUDENT—HIGH SCHOOL

Aurelio
T.H.U.M.B.B. - T. Ernesto Bethancourt   *lat*   543

Barbour, Talley
A White Romance - Virginia Hamilton   *afa*   171

Chen, April
April and the Dragon Lady - Lensey
  Namioka   *asa*   1034

Collins, Eva
The Girl on the Outside - Mildred Pitts
  Walter   *afa*   433

Finney, Marshall Field
Right by My Side - David Haynes   *afa*   185

Hadley, Sheema
A Little Love - Virginia Hamilton   *afa*   164

Jody
The Great Computer Dating Caper - T. Ernesto
  Bethancourt   *lat*   540

Johnson, DiDi
Motown and Didi: A Love Story - Walter Dean
  Myers   *afa*   316

Jones, Nia
Where Do I Go From Here? - Valerie Wilson
  Wesley   *afa*   444

Juanita
Juanita Fights the School Board - Gloria
  Velasquez   *lat*   873

Lacey, Karen
Tales of a Dead King - Walter Dean
  Myers   *afa*   325

Logan, Cassie
The Road to Memphis - Mildred D. Taylor   *afa*   411

Margot
Understand This - Jervey Tervalon   *afa*   415

Perkins, Carlene Zenobia "Carla"
Coffee Will Make You Black - April
  Sinclair   *afa*   392

Ramirez, Eddie
The Great Computer Dating Caper - T. Ernesto
  Bethancourt   *lat*   540

Russo, Lonnie
Vanishing Rooms - Melvin Dixon   *afa*   100

Stevenson, Jean Eloise "Stevie"
Coffee Will Make You Black - April
  Sinclair   *afa*   392

Stuart, Sophia
The Girl on the Outside - Mildred Pitts
  Walter   *afa*   433

Sung, Ellen Joyce
Finding My Voice - Marie G. Lee   *asa*   994

Tom
T.H.U.M.B.B. - T. Ernesto Bethancourt   *lat*   543

Walsh, Emma
Because We Are - Mildred Pitts Walter   *afa*   432

Williams, Francois
Understand This - Jervey Tervalon   *afa*   415

Williams, Marcus Garvey
Where Do I Go From Here? - Valerie Wilson
  Wesley   *afa*   444

Wilson, Ludell
Ludell's New York Time - Brenda
  Wilkinson   *afa*   454

STUDENT—JUNIOR HIGH

Alexander, Marian
1959 - Thulani Davis   *afa*   93

Coile, Weber "Web"
Hold Fast to Dreams - Andrea Davis
  Pinkney   *afa*   348

Contreras, Tony
Pacific Crossing - Gary Soto   *lat*   830
Taking Sides - Gary Soto   *lat*   836

Cruz, Tito
Scorpions - Walter Dean Myers   *afa*   322

Hicks, Jamal
Scorpions - Walter Dean Myers   *afa*   322

Mendoza, Lincoln
Pacific Crossing - Gary Soto   *lat*   830
Taking Sides - Gary Soto   *lat*   836

Rock, Darnell
Darnell Rock Reporting - Walter Dean
  Myers   *afa*   303

Rock, Tamika
Darnell Rock Reporting - Walter Dean
  Myers   *afa*   303

Stackhouse, Raisin
The Secret of Gumbo Grove - Eleanora E.
  Tate   *afa*   405

Tarrant, Katherine "Willie"
1959 - Thulani Davis   *afa*   93

Williams, Roxanne
Definitely Cool - Brenda Wilkinson   *afa*   452

Willis, Deirdre "Camera Dee"
Hold Fast to Dreams - Andrea Davis
  Pinkney   *afa*   348

Willis, Lindsay
Hold Fast to Dreams - Andrea Davis
  Pinkney   *afa*   348

SUPERNATURAL BEING

David
Don't Play Us Cheap: A Harlem Party - Melvin Van
  Peebles   *afa*   420

Trinity
Don't Play Us Cheap: A Harlem Party - Melvin Van
  Peebles   *afa*   420

SURVIVOR

Father
Hiroshima No Pika (The Flash of Hiroshima) - Toshi
  Maruki   *asa*   1012

Korga, Rat
Stars in My Pocket Like Grains of Sand - Samuel R.
  Delany   *afa*   96

Mii
Hiroshima No Pika (The Flash of Hiroshima) - Toshi
  Maruki   *asa*   1012

Mintu, Simba "Simmie"
Philadelphia Fire - John Edgar Wideman   *afa*   449

Mother
Hiroshima No Pika (The Flash of Hiroshima) - Toshi
  Maruki   *asa*   1012

TAINO INDIAN

Colon, Diego
The Indian Chronicles - Jose Barreiro   *lat*   530

TEACHER

Augusta
Family Resemblances - Lowry Pei   *asa*   1046

Bonovox
Elaine and the Flying Frog - Heidi Chang   *asa*   916

Copeland, Mem
The Third Life of Grange Copeland - Alice
  Walker   *afa*   431

Gabriel, Marcus
Heathens - David Haynes   *afa*   183

Ghond
Gay-Neck: The Story of a Pigeon - Dhan Gopal
  Mukerji   *asa*   1029

Green, Angelina
Who Is Angelina? - Al Young   *afa*   484

Isobe
Crow Boy - Taro Yashima   *asa*   1114

Jdahya
Dawn - Octavia Butler   *afa*   35

Johnson, Paula
Somebody Else's Mama - David Haynes   *afa*   186

Katherine
Katherine - Anchee Min   *asa*   1019

LaRoche, Renee
Along the Journey River - Carol LaFavor   *naa*   1255

Lazrus
Robin on His Own - Johnniece Marshall
  Wilson   *afa*   470

Lopez, Arcadia H.
Barrio Teacher - Arcadia H. Lopez   *lat*   683

Louie, Leila Fu
Bone - Fae Myenne Ng   *asa*   1039

MacKenzie
Nene and the Horrible Math Monster - Marie
  Villanueva   *asa*   1094

Nakane, Megumi Naomi
Obasan - Joy Kogawa   *asa*   975

Nolan
Halmoni and the Picnic - Sook Nyul Choi   *asa*   929

Noro Shinpei
The Ink-keeper's Apprentice - Allen Say   *asa*   1057

Park, Leila
Native Speaker - Chang-rae Lee   *asa*   984

Pearson, Gloria
The Good Negress - A.J. Verdelle   *afa*   424

Pool
The Planet of Junior Brown - Virginia
  Hamilton   *afa*   169

Sheridan, Kiana
Starlight Passage - Anita Richmond
  Bunkley   *afa*   32

Stephenson, Stephen "Big Steve"
Coloured Pictures - Himani Bannerji   *asa*   903

Tariq Mia
A River Sutra - Gita Mehta   *asa*   1018

Turner, Idabell
A Little Yellow Dog - Walter Mosley   *afa*   289

TEENAGER

Adams, Thomas Jerrett "T.J."
The Color of Trees - Canaan Parker   *afa*   338

Aurelio
New York City: Too Far from Tampa Blues - T.
  Ernesto Bethancourt   *lat*   542
T.H.U.M.B.B. - T. Ernesto Bethancourt   *lat*   543

Wei Gu
Red Thread - Ed Young   *asa*   1132

Wind Soldier, Harley
The Grass Dancer - Susan Power   *naa*   1295

YOUNG WOMAN

Aani
Aani and the Tree Huggers - Jeannine
Atkins   *asa*   900

Adrianne
Dark Plums - Maria Espinosa   *lat*   600

Al-Hussain, Sabah
Bombay Talkie - Ameena Meer   *asa*   1017

Bak, Sookan
Year of Impossible Goodbyes - Sook Nyul
Choi   *asa*   930

Basu, Dimple Dasgupta
Wife - Bharati Mukherjee   *asa*   1032

Blanca
A Perfect Silence - Alba Ambert   *lat*   505

Calderon, Ana
The Memories of Ana Calderon: A Novel - Graciela
Limon   *lat*   681

Cardenas, Nenita
Intaglio: A Novel in Six Stories - Roberta
Fernandez   *lat*   605

Chen, Sylvia
Frontiers of Love - Diana Chang   *asa*   915

Coles, Shelby
The Wedding - Dorothy West   *afa*   445

Dawkins, Dancer
Dancer Dawkins and the California Kid - Willyce
Kim   *asa*   969
Dead Heat - Willyce Kim   *asa*   970

Elise
The Surrounded - D'Arcy McNickle   *naa*   1277

Eltern, Anna
Nightside - Soledad Santiago   *lat*   816

Escobar, Becky
Becky and Her Friends - Rolando Hinojosa   *lat*   657

Esmeralda
Mangos, Bananas, and Coconuts: A Cuban Love Story
- Himilce Novas   *lat*   738

Esquibel, Rocio
The Last of the Menu Girls - Denise
Chavez   *lat*   575

Francie
In the Heart of the Valley of Love - Cynthia
Kadohata   *asa*   963

Golden Flower
Ling-Li and the Phoenix Fairy: A Chinese Folktale -
Ellin Greene   *asa*   940

Gutherie, Willy "The California Kid"
Dancer Dawkins and the California Kid - Willyce
Kim   *asa*   969

Kope'mah, Grey
The Ancient Child - N. Scott Momaday   *naa*   1280

Kurihara, Emiko "Emi"
Journey Home - Yoshiko Uchida   *asa*   1089

Lambert, Mimi
Frontiers of Love - Diana Chang   *asa*   915

Lydia
The Moccasin Maker - E. Pauline
Johnson   *naa*   1236

Maria
Mother Tongue - Demetria Martinez   *lat*   693

Marisol
The Line of the Sun: A Novel - Judith Ortiz
Cofer   *lat*   746

Marisse, Ann
Only the Good Times - Bruce-Novoa   *lat*   549

Marroquin, Chayo
A Place Where the Sea Remembers - Sandra
Benitez   *lat*   539

Minatoya, Lydia Yuri
*Talking to High Monks in the Snow: An Asian
American Odyssey* - Lydia Yuri
Minatoya   *asa*   1021

Mirabal, Maria Teresa
In the Time of the Butterflies - Julia
Alvarez   *lat*   503

Mirabal, Minerva
In the Time of the Butterflies - Julia
Alvarez   *lat*   503

Mirabal, Patria
In the Time of the Butterflies - Julia
Alvarez   *lat*   503

Munoz, Blanca
The Wedding - Mary Helen Ponce   *lat*   759

Night Flying Woman, Oona
Night Flying Woman - Ignatia Broker   *naa*   1172

Oconeechee
Mountain Windsong - Robert J. Conley   *naa*   1183

Okuda, Yuki
Shizuko's Daughter - Kyoko Mori   *asa*   1026

Orgaz, Ana Magdelena
The Love Queen of the Amazon - Cecile
Pineda   *lat*   756

Pastora
Sapogonia: An Anti-Romance in 3/8 Meter - Ana
Castillo   *lat*   569

Peregrin, Carmen
Skywriting - Margarita Engle   *lat*   598

Rangel, Carmen
Call No Man Master - Tina Juarez   *lat*   667

Rayona
A Yellow Raft in Blue Water - Michael
Dorris   *naa*   1201

Rosa
The Greatest Performance - Elias Miguel
Munoz   *lat*   730

Sakane, Yuki
Journey Home - Yoshiko Uchida   *asa*   1089

Sandoval, Maria
Chicano - Richard Vasquez   *lat*   866

Seese
Almanac of the Dead - Leslie Marmon
Silko   *naa*   1306

Singh, Sarah Weissberg
House of Waiting - Marina Tamar Budhos   *asa*   909

Suggs, Denver
Beloved - Toni Morrison   *afa*   281

Thunder, Crystal
The Grass Dancer - Susan Power   *naa*   1295

Trevino, Delia
Delia's Song - Lucha Corpi   *lat*   581

Unnamed Character
The Coffin Tree - Wendy Law-Yone   *asa*   982

Vargas, Maria Elena
The Girl from Playa Blanca - Ofelia Dumas
Lachtman   *lat*   674

Vasquez, Romilia
A Fire in the Earth - Marcos McPeek
Villatoro   *lat*   885

Wind Dancer
The Hunter and the Woodpecker: An Indian Legend -
Christine Crowl   *naa*   1188

Wong, Mahealani Suzanne "Mahi"
A Little Too Much Is Enough - Kathleen
Tyau   *asa*   1086

Wong, Shirley Temple "Bandit"
In the Year of the Boar and Jackie Robinson - Bette
Bao Lord   *asa*   1007

Yellow Woman
Storyteller - Leslie Marmon Silko   *naa*   1308

Young Woman
A Feather on the Breath of God - Sigrid
Nunez   *asa*   1041

Zenteno, Lucia
The Woman Who Outshone the Sun - Alejandro Cruz
Martinez   *lat*   583

ZAPOTEC INDIAN

Zapata, Emiliano
Zapata Lives! - Gary D. Keller   *lat*   671

Zapata, Emilio
Zapata Rose in 1992 and Other Tales - Gary D.
Keller   *lat*   672

ZUNI INDIAN

Bow Priest
The Boy Who Made Dragonfly - Tony
Hillerman   *naa*   1227

Corn Maiden
The Boy Who Made Dragonfly - Tony
Hillerman   *naa*   1227

Painted Turtle
Painted Turtle: Woman with Guitar - Clarence
Major   *afa*   250

Age Index

This index groups books for children and young adults according to the grade levels for which they are most appropriate. Adult books are also included under the heading, Adult. Beneath each heading book titles are listed alphabetically, followed by the author's name and entry number.

GRADES K-1

Listen to the Desert/Oye al Desierto - Pat Mora *lat* 720
Pablo's Tree - Pat Mora *lat* 721
The Rainbow-Colored Horse - Pura Belpre *lat* 536
Real Wild Rice - David Martinson *naa* 1269

GRADES K-2

The Adventures of Connie and Diego = Las Aventuras de Connie y Diego - Maria Garcia *lat* 622
Angel's Kite = La Estrella de Angel - Alberto Blanco *lat* 544
Calling the Doves = El Canto de las Palomas - Juan Felipe Herrera *lat* 651
Carlos and the Cornfield: Story = Carlos y la Milpa de Maiz: Cuento - Jan Romero Stevens *lat* 840
Dear Peter Rabbit = Querido Pedrin - Alma Flor Ada *lat* 487
The Desert Is My Mother = El Desierto Es Mi Madre - Pat Mora *lat* 718
The Desert Mermaid = La Sirena Del Desierto - Alberto Blanco *lat* 545
The Gift of the Poinsettia = El Regalo de la Flor de Nochebuena - Pat Mora *lat* 719
The Gold Coin - Alma Flor Ada *lat* 488
La Gran Fiesta - Francisco X. Mora *lat* 716
Green Corn Tamales = Tamales de Elote - Gina Macaluso Rodriguez *lat* 786
Jose's Basket - Karen Papagapitos *lat* 748
Juan Tuza and the Magic Pouch - Francisco X. Mora *lat* 715
The Little Ant = La Hormiga Chiquita - Michael Rose Ramirez *lat* 760
Mediopollito = Half-Chicken - Alma Flor Ada *lat* 489
The Old Man and His Door - Gary Soto *lat* 829
Pepita Talks Twice = Pepita Habla Dos Veces - Ofelia Dumas Lachtman *lat* 675
The Race of Toad and Deer - Pat Mora *lat* 722
Saturday Sancocho - Leyla Torres *lat* 851
The Song of el Coqui and Other Tales of Puerto Rico - Nicholasa Mohr *lat* 712
Treasure Nap - Juanita Havill *lat* 647
Yagua Days - Cruz Martel *lat* 689

GRADES K-3

Chato's Kitchen - Gary Soto *lat* 825
Hair = Pelitos - Sandra Cisneros *lat* 576
In My Family = En Mi Familia - Carmen Lomas Garza *lat* 627

Ote: A Puerto Rican Folk Tale - Pura Belpre *lat* 534
Rabbit Wishes - Linda Shute *lat* 821
Uncle Nacho's Hat = El Sombrero de Tio Nacho - Harriet Rohmer *lat* 793
Vejigantes Masquerade - Lucia M. Gonzalez *lat* 641

GRADES 1-2

Abby - Jeannette Franklin Caines *afa* 40
The Adventures of Sugar and Junior - Angela Shelf Medearis *afa* 270
Africa Dream - Eloise Greenfield *afa* 142
At the Beach - Huy Voun Lee *asa* 987
Atariba and Niguayona: A Story from the Taino People of Puerto Rico - Harriet Rohmer *lat* 790
The Best Bug to Be - Dolores Johnson *afa* 228
The Best Time of Day - Valerie Flournoy *afa* 121
Birthday - John Steptoe *afa* 396
A Birthday Basket for Tia - Pat Mora *lat* 717
Carlos and the Squash Plant/Carlos y la Planta de Calabaza - Jan Romero Stevens *lat* 841
Cheer Up Old Man - David Martinson *naa* 1267
Chilly Stomach - Jeannette Franklin Caines *afa* 41
Clean Your Room, Harvey Moon! - Pat Cummings *afa* 89
Daddy - Jeannette Franklin Caines *afa* 42
Dance of the Animals - Pura Belpre *lat* 533
Darlene - Eloise Greenfield *afa* 143
Do Like Kyla - Angela Johnson *afa* 215
Don't You Remember? - Lucille Clifton *afa* 64
Double Dog Dare - Ray Prather *afa* 360
Everett Anderson's 1-2-3 - Lucille Clifton *afa* 65
Everett Anderson's Christmas Coming - Lucille Clifton *afa* 66
Everett Anderson's Friend - Lucille Clifton *afa* 67
Everett Anderson's Nine Month Long - Lucille Clifton *afa* 68
Everett Anderson's Year - Lucille Clifton *afa* 69
The Girl Who Wore Snakes - Angela Johnson *afa* 216
Good, Says Jerome - Lucille Clifton *afa* 70
I Love My Family - Wade Hudson *afa* 205
I Need a Lunch Box - Jeannette Franklin Caines *afa* 43
In the Snow - Huy Voun Lee *asa* 988
Indigo and Moonlight Gold - Jan Spivey Gilchrist *afa* 137
Jay and the Marigold - Harriette Gillem Robinet *afa* 376
Julius - Angela Johnson *afa* 218
Just Us Women - Jeannette Franklin Caines *afa* 44

The Leaving Morning - Angela Johnson *afa* 219
Manabozho and the Bullrushes - David Martinson *naa* 1268
Max Found Two Sticks - Brian Pinkney *afa* 349
My Special Best Words - John Steptoe *afa* 400
No Trespassing - Ray Prather *afa* 361
On the Day I Was Born - Debbi Chocolate *afa* 59
One of Three - Angela Johnson *afa* 220
ONE small GIRL - Jennifer L. Chan *asa* 914
The One That Got Away - Percival Everett *afa* 115
Rise and Shine, Mariko-chan! - Chiyoko Tomioka *asa* 1082
Seven Blind Mice - Ed Young *asa* 1133
She Come Bringing Me That Little Baby Girl - Eloise Greenfield *afa* 149
Shemay: The Bird in the Sugarbush - David Martinson *naa* 1270
Shoes Like Miss Alice's - Angela Johnson *afa* 221
Shortcut - Donald Crews *afa* 86
Smoky Night - Eve Bunting *lat* 550
Some of the Days of Everett Anderson - Lucille Clifton *afa* 73
The Story of the Three Kingdoms - Walter Dean Myers *afa* 324
Tell Me a Story, Mama - Angela Johnson *afa* 222
Things I Like about Grandma - Francine Haskins *afa* 182
Three Wishes - Lucille Clifton *afa* 74
Too Many Tamales - Gary Soto *lat* 837
Too Much Talk - Angela Shelf Medearis *afa* 273
The Train to LuLu's - Elizabeth Fitzgerald Howard *afa* 204
Two and Too Much - Mildred Pitts Walter *afa* 441
What Kind of Baby-Sitter Is This? - Dolores Johnson *afa* 230
What Will Mommy Do When I'm at School? - Dolores Johnson *afa* 231
When I Am Old with You - Angela Johnson *afa* 224
Willie Blows a Mean Horn - Ianthe Thomas *afa* 416
Window Wishing - Jeannette Franklin Caines *afa* 45

GRADES 1-3

Abuela - Arthur Dorros *lat* 593
Abuela's Weave - Omar Castaneda *lat* 563
All the Colors of the Earth - Sheila Hamanaka *asa* 944
Almond Cookies and Dragon Well Tea - Cynthia Chin-Lee *asa* 925
Always My Dad - Sharon Dennis Wyeth *afa* 478
Anna in Charge - Yoriko Tsutsui *asa* 1085

Illustrator Index

This index lists the illustrators of the featured titles. Illustrators are listed alphabetically, followed by the title, author, and entry number of the book or books in which the artist's work appears.

A

Arai, Tomie
China's Bravest Girl: The Legend of Hua Mu Lan - Charlie Chin 920
Sachiko Means Happiness - Kimiko Sakai 1053

Arnaktauyok, Germaine
Harpoon of the Hunter - Markoosie 1265

Arnold, Jeanne
Carlos and the Cornfield: Story = Carlos y la Milpa de Maiz: Cuento - Jan Romero Stevens 840
Carlos and the Squash Plant/Carlos y la Planta de Calabaza - Jan Romero Stevens 841

Artzybasheff, Boris
Gay-Neck: The Story of a Pigeon - Dhan Gopal Mukerji 1029

B

Barnett, Moneta
First Pink Light - Eloise Greenfield 144
Me and Neesie - Eloise Greenfield 148
My Brother Fine with Me - Lucille Clifton 71

Bearden, Romare
A Visit to the Country - Herschel Johnson 233

Braun, Molly
Timelines: Native American History - Carl Waldman 1340

Brooks, Kevin
Window Wishing - Jeannette Franklin Caines 45

Brooks, Maya Itzna
The Race of Toad and Deer - Pat Mora 722

Brown, Bradford
Addy Saves the Day: A Summer Story - Connie Porter 354

Changes for Addy: A Winter Story - Connie Porter 357
Happy Birthday, Addy! A Springtime Story - Connie Porter 358

Brown, David
Ride the Red Cycle - Harriette Gillem Robinet 378

Bryan, Ashley
The Cat's Purr - Ashley Bryan 28
The Story of Lightning & Thunder - Ashley Bryan 29
The Story of the Three Kingdoms - Walter Dean Myers 324

Burford, Kay
Kimako's Story - June Jordan 237

Byard, Carole
Africa Dream - Eloise Greenfield 142
The Black Snowman - Phil Mendez 274
Grandmama's Joy - Eloise Greenfield 145
Have a Happy. . . - Mildred Pitts Walter 434
I Can Do It Myself - Lessie Jones Little 246
Working Cotton - Sherley Anne Williams 464

C

Calvin, James
Talk about a Family - Eloise Greenfield 151

Carrillo, Graciela
How We Came to the Fifth World: A Creation Story from Ancient Mexico - Harriet Rohmer 791
The Legend of Food Mountain - Harriet Rohmer 792

Carter, Gail Gordon
Mac and Marie and the Train Toss Surprise - Elizabeth Fitzgerald Howard 202

Casilla, Robert
Boys at Work - Gary Soto 824
The Pool Party - Gary Soto 832

The Train to LuLu's - Elizabeth Fitzgerald Howard 204

Cepeda, Joe
The Old Man and His Door - Gary Soto 829

Chang, Heidi
Elaine and the Flying Frog - Heidi Chang 916

Chen, Chihsien
Square Beak - Chyng Feng Sun 1074

Cherin, Robin
My Aunt Otilia's Spirits = Los Espiritus de Mi Tia Otilia - Richard Garcia 623

Chin, Duncan
Growing Up on Grove Street 1931-1946 - Duncan Chin 921

Collette, Rondi
Socorro, Daughter of the Desert - Karen Papagapitos 749

Colon, Raul
Always My Dad - Sharon Dennis Wyeth 478

Cook, Scott
Nettie Jo's Friends - Patricia C. McKissack 264

Cooper, Floyd
Chita's Christmas Tree - Elizabeth Fitzgerald Howard 201
Grandpa's Face - Eloise Greenfield 146
Papa Tells Chita a Story - Elizabeth Fitzgerald Howard 203

Cooper, Martha
Lion Dancer: Ernie Wan's Chinese New Year - Kate Waters 1099

Crews, Donald
Bigmama's - Donald Crews 85
Shortcut - Donald Crews 86

Crowl, Christine
The Hunter and the Woodpecker: An Indian Legend - Christine Crowl 1188
The White Buffalo Woman: An Indian Legend - Christine Crowl 1189

Cruz, Ray
New Life: New Room - June Jordan 238

Cummings, Pat
Carousel - Pat Cummings 88
Chilly Stomach - Jeannette Franklin Caines 41
Clean Your Room, Harvey Moon! - Pat Cummings 89
I Need a Lunch Box - Jeannette Franklin Caines 43
Just Us Women - Jeannette Franklin Caines 44
Mariah Keeps Cool - Mildred Pitts Walter 437
Mariah Loves Rock - Mildred Pitts Walter 438
My Mama Needs Me - Mildred Pitts Walter 439
Petey Moroni's Camp Runamok Diary - Pat Cummings 90
Two and Too Much - Mildred Pitts Walter 441

D

Davis, Lambert
The Bells of Christmas - Virginia Hamilton 157

de Kiefte, Kees
Yang the Third and Her Impossible Family - Lensey Namioka 1035
Yang the Youngest and His Terrible Ear - Lensey Namioka 1036

de Paola, Tomie
The Tiger and the Rabbit and Other Tales - Pura Belpre 538

Deeter, Catherine
Finding the Green Stone - Alice Walker 427

Delacre, Lulu
The Bossy Gallito - Lucia M. Gonzalez 640

Demi
Buddha - Demi 932
Chingis Khan - Demi 933
The Empty Pot - Demi 934

Illustrator Index

Author Index

This index is an alphabetical listing of the authors of books featured in entries and those listed under "Other books by the author" and "Other books you might like." For each author, the titles of books written and entry numbers are also provided. Editors, co-authors, and adaptors are interfiled with Author names. Bold numbers indicate a featured main entry; other numbers refer to books recommended for further reading.

Mitsui Brown, Janet
Thanksgiving at Obaachan's 926, **1022**, 1048, 1053, 1073, 1099

Mochizuki, Ken
Baseball Saved Us **1023**, 1024, 1065
Heroes 1023, **1024**, 1065, 1074, 1110, 1111

Mohr, Nicholasa
El Bronx Remembered: A Novella and Stories 493, 496, 542, **706**, 707, 708, 709, 710, 711, 712, 845
Felita 490, 537, **707**, 708, 712, 748, 833
Going Home **708**
In Nueva York 706, 707, 708, **709**, 710, 711, 712, 845
Nilda: A Novel 564, 565, 577, 648, 649, 706, 707, 708, 709, **710**, 711, 712, 850
Nilda; A Novel 609
Rituals of Survival: A Woman's Portfolio 706, 707, 708, 709, 710, **711**, 712, 744, 745, 747, 784
The Song of el Coqui and Other Tales of Puerto Rico 487, 489, 535, 538, 545, 711, **712**, 715

Momaday, N. Scott
The Ancient Child **1280**, 1281, 1282, 1345
Angel of Geese and Other Poems 1280, 1281, 1282
The Gourd Dancer: Poems 1280, 1281, 1282
House Made of Dawn 1201, 1210, 1215, 1231, 1271, 1273, 1277, 1280, **1281**, 1282, 1307, 1311, 1312, 1346, 1350
The Names: A Memoir 1190, 1205, 1206, 1226, 1272, 1280, 1281, 1282, 1296, 1308, 1321, 1333
The Way to Rainy Mountain 1156, 1162, 1205, 1206, 1226, 1257, 1272, 1280, 1281, **1282**

Monreal, David
Cellmates 713
Cinco de Mayo: An Epic Novel 554, 557, 705, **713**, 726
The New Neighbor and Other Stories 713

Monroe, Mark
An Indian in White America **1283**

Montejo, Esteban
The Autobiography of a Runaway Slave 530, **714**, 809

Moore, Emily
Just My Luck 46, **278**, 279, 280, 387
Something to Count On 278, **279**, 280, 480
Whose Side Are You On? 169, 278, 279, **280**, 300, 304, 309, 398

Mora, Francisco X.
The Coyote Rings the Wrong Bell 715, 716
La Gran Fiesta 641, 715, **716**, 719, 786
Juan Tuza and the Magic Pouch 525, **715**, 716
The Legend of the Two Moons 715, 716
The Tiger and the Rabbit: A Puerto Rican Folk Tale 715, 716

Mora, Pat
Agua Santa = Holy Water 718, 719, 722

A Birthday Basket for Tia 550, 563, 593, 647, **717**, 718, 719, 720, 721, 737, 793, 825, 837, 840, 841
Borders 718
Communion 722
The Desert Is My Mother = El Desierto Es Mi Madre 545, 717, **718**, 719, 720, 721, 722, 790, 791
The Gift of the Poinsettia = El Regalo de la Flor de Nochebuena 510, 716, **719**, 837
Listen to the Desert/Oye al Desierto 536, 545, 717, 718, 719, **720**, 721, 722, 840, 841
Pablo's Tree 576, 594, 717, 718, 719, 720, **721**, 722
The Race of Toad and Deer 489, 640, **722**, 760, 792

Moraga, Cherrie
Cuentos: Stories by Latinas **632**
The Last Generation **723**, 859
Loving in the War Years: Lo que Nunca Paso por sus Labios 516, 587, 588, 634, 723, 730, 740, 753, 761, 859
The Sexuality of Latinas **494**

Morales, Alejandro
The Brick People 554, 555, 557, 686, 705, **724**, 725, 726, 750, 799, 800, 882
Death of an Anglo 498, 656, 724, **725**, 726, 801
Old Faces and New Wine 724, 725, 726
The Rag Doll Plagues 595, 618, 704, 713, 724, 725, **726**, 880
Reto en el Paraiso 724

Morales, Aurora Levins
Getting Home Alive **727**

Morales, Rosario
Getting Home Alive **727**

Moreno, Chepa
Contemporary Life Histories **1241**

Mori, Kyoko
The Dream of Water 1025, 1026
One Bird 992, 994, **1025**, 1026, 1029, 1057, 1118, 1126
Shizuko's Daughter 1025, **1026**, 1057

Mori, Toshio
The Chauvinist and Other Stories **1027**, 1028, 1051, 1112
Woman from Hiroshima 1027, 1028
Yokohama, California 1027, **1028**, 1051, 1112

Morrison, Toni
Beloved 2, 8, 51, 53, 54, 79, 124, 129, 207, 227, **281**, 282, 283, 284, 285, 286, 370, 430, 463
The Bluest Eye 78, 281, **282**, 283, 284, 285, 286, 431
Jazz 133, 245, 281, 282, **283**, 284, 285, 286, 345, 450, 451
Song of Solomon 32, 281, 282, 283, **284**, 285, 286, 297
Sula 267, 281, 282, 283, 284, **285**, 286, 296
Tar Baby 77, 111, 131, 281, 282, 283, 284, 285, **286**

Mosley, Walter
Black Betty **287**, 288, 289, 290, 291, 292

Devil in a Blue Dress 12, 13, 178, 188, 189, 190, 191, 197, 199, 277, 287, **288**, 289, 290, 291, 292, 346, 442
A Little Yellow Dog **289**
A Red Death 197, 287, 288, 289, **290**, 291, 292
RL's Dream 50, 127, 138, 194, 243, 287, 288, 289, 290, **291**, 292
White Butterfly 198, 287, 288. 289, 290, 291, **292**

Mourning Dove
Cogewea **1284**, 1285, 1350
Coyote Stories 1139, 1140, 1144, 1150, 1151, 1153, 1155, 1157, 1158, 1159, 1163, 1168, 1170, 1174, 1176, 1177, 1178, 1179, 1208, 1209, 1220, 1221, 1227, 1244, 1249, 1260, 1262, **1285**, 1328, 1332, 1334, 1337
Mourning Dove: A Salishan Autobiography 1284, 1285, **1286**, 1353

Mowry, Jess
Children of the Night **293**, 294, 295, 322
Six Out Seven 293, **294**, 295, 335, 336
Way Past Cool 55, 87, 293, 294, **295**, 322

Muhanji, Cherry
Her 4, 20, 109, 235, 267, 285, **296**, 391, 484

Mujica, Barbara
Antologia de la Literatura Espanola: Edad Media 728
Calderon's Characters: An Existential Point of View 728
The Deaths of Don Bernardo 530, 680, 682, **728**
Readings in Spanish Literature 728
Texto y Vida: Introduccion a la Literatura Hispanoamericana 728

Mukerji, Dhan Gopal
Gay-Neck: The Story of a Pigeon **1029**
Kari the Elephant 1029

Mukherjee, Bharati
Darkness 1030, 1031, 1032
The Holder of the World 1030, 1031, 1032
Jasmine 896, 909, 937, 962, 1017, 1018, **1030**, 1031, 1032, 1037, 1041
The Middleman and Other Stories 909, 1017, 1030, **1031**, 1032
The Tiger's Daughter 1030, 1031, 1032
Wife 937, 1005, 1030, 1031, **1032**, 1037

Mullet, G.M.
Spider Woman Stories 1140, 1154, 1176, 1216, 1227, 1253, 1328, 1330

Munoz, Elias Miguel
Crazy Love 522, 673, 700, **729**, 730, 844
En Estas Tierras = In This Land 729, 730
The Greatest Performance 520, 521, 523, 588, 688, 729, **730**, 848, 849

Munsch, Robert
A Promise Is a Promise **1253**

Murayama, Milton
All I Asking for Is My Body 924, 969, 975, 1003, 1010, **1033**, 1086, 1103, 1109

Murguia, Alejandro
Farewell to the Coast 731
Southern Front 559, 660, **731**, 787

Muro, Amado
The Collected Stories of Amado Muro **732**, 772

Murray, Albert
The Seven League Boots **297**
The Spyglass Tree 111, 297, **298**, 347, 456
Train Whistle Guitar 297, 298

Myers, Walter Dean
Adventure in Granada **299**
Ambush in the Amazon **300**
Brainstorm **301**, 327
Crystal 195, 210, 257, **302**, 305, 310, 316, 419, 444, 454, 465, 466, 471
Darnell Rock Reporting 9, 17, 156, 168, 177, **303**, 315, 317, 321, 325, 348, 405
Duel in the Desert **304**
Fallen Angels 102, 164, **305**, 307, 310, 316, 320, 322, 326, 474
Fast Sam, Cool Clyde and Stuff 25, 299, 300, 301, 302, 303, 304, 305, **306**, 307, 309, 310, 311, 312, 313, 314, 315, 316, 317, 319, 320, 321, 322, 323, 325, 326, 327
Glory Field 175, 176, **307**, 310, 312, 316, 320, 322, 326, 409, 412
The Golden Serpent 272, 273, **308**, 318, 324, 399
The Hidden Shrine **309**
Hoops 102, 301, 302, 306, **310**, 466, 474
It Ain't All for Nothing **311**
Legend of Tarik 244, 299, 301, 302, 306, **312**, 327
Me, Mop, and the Moondance Kid 177, 208, 303, **313**, 315, 334, 414
Mojo and the Russians 120, 278, 280, 299, 300, 304, 309, **314**
Mop, Moondance and Nagasaki Knights 9, 313, **315**, 334
Motown and Didi: A Love Story 195, 223, 236, 244, 302, 305, 306, 307, 312, **316**, 320, 322, 327, 415, 444, 466
Mouse Rap 18, 103, 162, 167, 303, 311, 313, 314, **317**, 319, 321, 323, 325
Mr. Monkey and the Gotcha Bird: An Original Tale 28, 260, 263, 308, **318**, 324
The Nicholas Factor 120, 160, 161, 167, 299, 300, 303, 304, 309, 313, 314, **319**, 323, 325
The Outside Shot 305, 307, 312, 316, **320**, 322, 326
The Righteous Revenge of Artemis Bonner 161, 173, 300, 304, 309, 311, 313, 314, 317, 319, **321**, 323, 377, 417, 435
Scorpions 55, 87, 293, 294, 295, 305, 307, 310, 312, 320, **322**, 326, 474
Somewhere in the Darkness 17, 311, 315, 317, 319, 321, **323**, 325, 377, 403
The Story of the Three Kingdoms 29, 115, 308, 318, **324**

Title Index

This index alphabetically lists all titles featured in entries and those listed under "Other books by the author" and "Other books you might like." Each title is followed by the author's name and the number of the entry of that title. Bold numbers indicate featured main entries; other numbers refer to books recommended for further reading.

B

Title Index

E

Title Index